Giving those who offend the opportunity, the resources, and the support to become better people has always seemed the most ethical of penal aims, but in insecure and turbulent times it has invariably been the hardest to defend and sustain. Historically, not all that has been done in rehabilitation's name has been wise, kind, or effective and it has long needed the sort of critical friends it finds here to ensure that in both theory and practice it is aligned with human rights and goes beyond merely meeting criminogenic needs. Never before have the philosophical, political, and empirical arguments in its favour – and the numerous unresolved tensions in debate about them – been brought together as comprehensibly as they are in this welcome collection. It sets out all the models of good practice and identifies the contexts and cultures in which they are likely to thrive. It faces up squarely to the moral and practical challenges that champions of rehabilitation will always face, including the new technological ones. It makes a better world possible.

Mike Nellis, *Emeritus Professor of Criminal and Community Justice, University of Strathclyde, UK*

Providing effective rehabilitation is a critically important function of the criminal justice system. Significant advances have been made but are hard won, and require careful attention to matching interventions to needs. At the same time, reforms are often compromised by political considerations and resource constraints. This admirable collection by a range of leading scholars and practitioners provides the reader with an up-to-date map and assessment of contemporary theories and practices to help them navigate this complex area, and understand how to choose or implement effective solutions.

Stuart Ross, *Professor of Criminology, School of Social and Political Sciences, University of Melbourne, Australia*

This collection of essays brings together an impressive group of authors to push forward knowledge and thinking on processes of desistance and rehabilitation.

Stephen Farrall, *Research Professor in Criminology, College of Business, Law and the Social Sciences, University of Derby, UK*

The history of punishing crime is intimately tied to the concept of rehabilitation – or the process and potential of reforming people who break the law into law-abiding citizens. Across time and place, academics and practitioners have debated if rehabilitation through criminal justice interventions is possible and whether it ought to be one of the core goals of punishment. *The Routledge Companion to Rehabilitative Work in Criminal Justice* provides a fresh international and cross-disciplinary look at these questions, considering rehabilitation and desistance from the perspective of researchers, practitioners, and people experiencing criminal justice contact.

Michelle Phelps, *Assistant Professor of Sociology, University of Minnesota (Twin Cities), USA*

The Routledge Companion to Rehabilitative Work in Criminal Justice

All the world's criminal justice systems need to undertake direct work with people who have come into their care or are under their supervision as a result of criminal offences. Typically, this is organized in penal and correctional services – in custody in prisons, or in the community, supervised by services such as probation. Bringing together international experts, this book is the go-to source for students, researchers, and practitioners in criminal justice looking for a comprehensive and authoritative summary of available knowledge in the field.

Covering a variety of contexts, settings, needs, and approaches, and drawing on theory and practice, this Companion brings together over 90 entries, offering readers concise and definitive overviews of a range of key contemporary issues on working with offenders. The book is split into thematic sections and includes coverage of:

- Theories and models for working with offenders
- Policy contexts of offender supervision and rehabilitation
- Direct work with offenders
- Control, surveillance, and practice
- Resettlement
- Application to specific groups, including female offenders, young offenders, families, and ethnic minorities
- Application to specific needs and contexts, such as substance misuse, mental health, violence, and risk assessment
- Practitioner and offender perspectives
- The development of an evidence base

This book is an essential and flexible resource for researchers and practitioners alike and is an authoritative guide for students taking courses on working with offenders, criminal justice policy, probation, prisons, penology, and community corrections.

Pamela Ugwudike is Associate Professor of Criminology at the University of Southampton, UK. She is also affiliated with the Alan Turing Institute as a Turing Fellow. Her research interests include studying advances in critical criminological theory and analyzing criminal justice policy and practice. She is particularly interested in theoretical and empirical studies of interactions between digital technology and criminal justice, and the implications for social justice. Her recent publications include *An Introduction to Critical Criminology* (2015) and *Evidence-Based Skills in Criminal Justice: International Research on Supporting Rehabilitation and Desistance* (2018, co-edited with Peter Raynor and Jill Annison).

Hannah Graham is Senior Lecturer in Criminology in the Scottish Centre for Crime and Justice Research (SCCJR) in the Faculty of Social Sciences,

University of Stirling, UK. As a criminologist and social scientist, Hannah works with governments and parliaments, practitioners, citizens, communities, and civic society to help inform real-world change and collaboratively build more just societies. She has made contributions in Scottish, European, and Australasian contexts. Also, Hannah is developing a growing research agenda on innovation and justice, on which she has researched, written, and spoken in different countries. Her publications include *Rehabilitation Work: Supporting Desistance and Recovery* (2016), *Innovative Justice* (2015), and *Working with Offenders: A Guide to Concepts and Practices* (2010), all published internationally by Routledge.

Fergus McNeill is Professor of Criminology and Social Work at the University of Glasgow, UK, where he works in the Scottish Centre for Crime and Justice Research (SCCJR). He has published extensively on institutions, cultures, and practices of punishment – and on how they might be best reformed in the light of evidence about desistance from crime. This work has led to a series of engagements with policy, practice, and people with lived experience of punishment in numerous jurisdictions.

Peter Raynor is Emeritus Research Professor of Criminology at Swansea University, UK, and has been carrying out and publishing research on criminal justice and offender management for more than 40 years. Over 200 publications include jointly edited collections on offender supervision (with McNeill and Trotter), compliance (with Ugwudike), social work with offenders (with McIvor), and race and probation (with Lewis, Smith, and Wardak). He is a member of the Correctional Services Accreditation and Advisory Panel for England and Wales, and a Fellow of the Academy of Social Sciences.

Faye S. Taxman is University Professor in the Criminology, Law and Society Department and Director of the Center for Advancing Correctional Excellence at George Mason University, USA. Her work covers the breadth of the correctional system from jails and prisons to community corrections and adult and juvenile offenders, including all types of interventions and system improvement factors. Dr Taxman has published over 125 articles. She is the author (with Steve Belenkos) of *Implementing Evidence-Based Community Corrections* and *Addiction Treatment* (2011). She is also on the Editorial Boards of the *Journal of Experimental Criminology, Criminology and Public Policy* and *Journal of Offender Rehabilitation*.

Chris Trotter is Emeritus Professor in the Social Work Department at Monash University, Australia, and Director, Monash Criminal Justice Research Consortium. Prior to his university appointment he worked for many years in adult corrections, child protection, and youth justice. He has undertaken more than 30 funded research projects and has more than 100 publications, including eight books. His book *Working with Involuntary Clients*, now in its third edition, is published in English, Chinese, Japanese, French, and German. He has a strong international reputation, particularly for his work on pro-social modelling, and has been invited to more than 15 different countries to present conference plenary sessions and workshops for probation officers and others who work with offenders.

The Routledge Companion to Rehabilitative Work in Criminal Justice

Edited by Pamela Ugwudike, Hannah Graham, Fergus McNeill, Peter Raynor, Faye S. Taxman and Chris Trotter

Routledge
Taylor & Francis Group

LONDON AND NEW YORK

First published 2020
by Routledge
2 Park Square, Milton Park, Abingdon, Oxon OX14 4RN

and by Routledge
52 Vanderbilt Avenue, New York, NY 10017

Routledge is an imprint of the Taylor & Francis Group, an informa business

British Library Cataloguing-in-Publication Data
A catalogue record for this book is available from the British Library

Library of Congress Cataloging-in-Publication Data
Names: Ugwudike, Pamela, 1969– editor.
Title: The Routledge companion to rehabilitative work in criminal justice/edited by Pamela Ugwudike [and five others].
Description: Abingdon, Oxon ; New York, NY : Routledge, 2019. | Includes bibliographical references and index.
Identifiers: LCCN 2019013051 | ISBN 9781138102057 (hardback) | ISBN 9781138103320 (pbk.)
Subjects: LCSH: Criminals—Rehabilitation. | Ex-convicts—Rehabilitation.
Classification: LCC HV9275 .R68 2019 | DDC 365/.661—dc23
LC record available at https://lccn.loc.gov/2019013051

ISBN: 978-1-138-10205-7 (hbk)
ISBN: 978-1-138-10332-0 (pbk)
ISBN: 978-1-315-10283-2 (ebk)

Typeset in Stone Serif and Rockwell
by Apex CoVantage, LLC

Contents

Preface

This book is a team effort, with six editors and over 90 chapters, and it feels appropriate to say something at the beginning about how it came into being and about the kind of book we have tried to produce. There are many books about criminal justice and about the rehabilitation of people who have found themselves in trouble with the law. Why would we need another one? The explanation lies partly in its history and in the particular role we hope it will play in promoting effective rehabilitative work in the criminal justice system.

The initial idea came from Tom Sutton of Routledge who has been an invaluable collaborator throughout the long process from first idea to finished book. He saw that there was room for a book like this within Routledge's series of 'Companions' and approached Peter Raynor with the idea of re-forming the editorial team of Fergus McNeill, Peter Raynor, and Chris Trotter from an earlier successful edited compilation, *Offender Supervision* (McNeill, Raynor, and Trotter 2010). It was quickly obvious to all three that the proposed publication was on a much larger scale, and that a larger editorial team would be needed. Pamela Ugwudike, Faye S. Taxman, and Hannah Graham responded to invitations to join, which greatly increased the effectiveness of the team as well as reducing its average age. Early discussions linked three continents by Skype, a proposal was produced and accepted, and Pamela took on the heroic task of coordinating our efforts.

What we have tried to produce is a 'go-to' introduction to as broad a range of rehabilitative work as we could manage. We have also tried to cover established schools of thought, some of which are in disagreement (which is not unusual in theories and research on rehabilitative work). Our aim has been to ensure that the Companion reflects accurately the breadth of scholarship in this field. Contributors have been recruited internationally, and this also helps to reflect the diversity of environments and approaches.

There are already a number of specialist publications covering particular topics within rehabilitation and criminal justice at some depth and at quite a specialist level, many of them involving members of the current editorial team: examples are compilations on evidence-based skills (Ugwudike, Raynor, and Annison 2018), risk assessment (Trotter, McIvor, and McNeill 2016), penal practice (Durnescu and McNeill 2014), compliance with supervision (Ugwudike and Raynor 2013), and several based on European collaborations (for example, Robinson and McNeill 2016; Boone and Maguire 2018). All these books owe something to the work of two research networks: CREDOS (the Collaboration of Researchers for the Effective Development of Offender Supervision), which was set up in 2007 as an international network for researchers and practitioners, and the European Society of Criminology's Working Group on Community Sanctions, both of which have generated productive international collaboration. In addition, there are collections focusing in detail on psychological methods and research (such as McGuire 2002). What was missing was a broad introductory collection to introduce students, practitioners, and researchers to a full range of rehabilitative activities and issues, and showing them where they can find out more.

With these aims in mind, and drawing partly on contacts established through CREDOS and the European group, we asked contributors for chapters which are short by academic standards but still substantive chapters rather than encyclopaedia entries, introducing key issues and research around each topic and citing key sources where readers could go for more depth and detail. For example, where we discuss specific skills and techniques, reading a chapter in this book will probably not equip a beginning practitioner to apply them immediately and effectively, but it should show them where they can find out more. Similarly, readers will not find here a summary of all relevant research but they should be able to find out where to go to obtain it. We debated whether we should include only methods and approaches which had a strong evidence-base demonstrating effectiveness, but decided that this would be too restrictive, excluding a number of newer developments which are interesting but not yet fully researched. This means that the chapters cover a mixture of the proven and the promising, and we hope they are both useful and interesting to readers who will start their investigations here.

The Editors
December 2018

References

Boone, M. and Maguire, N. (Eds.) (2018) *The Enforcement of Offender Supervision in Europe. Understanding Breach Processes*. Abingdon: Routledge.

Durnescu, I. and McNeill, F. (Eds.) (2014) *Understanding Penal Practice*. Abingdon: Routledge.

McGuire, J. (2002) Integrating findings from research reviews. In J. McGuire (Ed.), *Offender Rehabilitation and Treatment*. Chichester: Wiley, pp. 3–38.

McNeill, F., Raynor, P. and Trotter, C. (Eds.) (2010) *Offender Supervision: New Directions in Theory, Research and Practice*. Abingdon: Willan.

Robinson, G. and McNeill, F. (Eds.) (2016) *Community Punishment: European Perspectives.* Abingdon: Routledge.

Trotter, C., McIvor, G. and McNeill, F. (Eds.) (2016) *Beyond the Risk Paradigm in Criminal Justice: Beyond the Risk Paradigm.* Basingstoke: Palgrave Macmillan.

Ugwudike, P., Annison, J. and Raynor, P. (Eds.) (2018) *Evidence-Based Skills in Criminal Justice: International Research on Supporting Rehabilitation and Desistance.* Bristol: Policy Press.

Ugwudike, P., Raynor, P. and Annison, J. (Eds.) (2013) *What Works in Offender Compliance: International Perspectives and Evidence-Based Practice.* Basingstoke: Palgrave Macmillan.

Figures

Tables

Contributors

Katherine Albertson is Senior Lecturer in Criminology at the Department of Law and Criminology at Sheffield Hallam University, UK. Katherine began working with the Armed Forces community through leading on an evaluation of a veteran-specific recovery project. Katherine has also conducted a British Academy/Leverhulme Trust grant-funded Life History research project, undertaken with ex-forces with contact in the criminal justice system, focusing on exploring identity transitions. She has most recently been leading on the South Yorkshire Armed Forces Covenant Project. Her work with the Armed Forces community is widely published in international books, academic journals, and institutional blogs.

Katherine M. Auty is Postdoctoral Research Associate in the Prisons Research Centre at the Institute of Criminology, University of Cambridge, UK. She completed her PhD at the Forensic Psychiatry Research Unit, Barts and the London School of Medicine, examining the intergenerational transmission of criminal offending, psychopathy, and other personality disorders using data from the Cambridge Study in Delinquent Development. Her current research focuses on measuring prison culture and its relationship to outcomes for prisoners.

Susan Baidawi is Senior Research Fellow in the Department of Social Work at Monash University, Australia.

Sherah L. Basham is Adjunct Instructor in the Department of Criminal Justice at the University of Central Florida, USA. Her research interests include policing, campus law enforcement, and use of force.

Tim Bateman is Reader in Youth Justice at the University of Bedfordshire, UK, and he has written and researched widely in the area of youth crime and responses to it. He is co-editor of *Safer Communities* and contributes the 'youth justice news' section for *Youth Justice* journal. Tim is Deputy Chair of the National Association for Youth Justice.

Cormac Behan teaches criminology at the Centre for Criminological Research, University of Sheffield, UK. His research interests include penal history, prisoners' rights, comparative penology, and prison education. Prior to taking up this position, he taught politics and history in Irish prisons for 14 years.

Kristel Beyens is Full Professor of Criminology and Penology and Head of the Criminology Department of the Vrije Universiteit Brussel, Belgium. She leads the Research Group Crime & Society (CRiS) and more in particular the research line Penality & Society, which focuses on research on penal decision-making, imprisonment, community punishment, and migration detention.

Philip Birch is Senior Lecturer in Criminology at Charles Sturt University (Port Macquarie), Australia. He is a Fellow of the Higher Education Academy and holds an honorary research fellowship in the School of Psychology (Forensic Centre), University of Central Lancashire, UK, as well as a Senior Research Associate in the Ashworth Research Centre, Ashworth High Secure Forensic Mental Health Hospital, as part of the National Health Services, UK. Philip was the Co-Founder and Editor-in-Chief of the *Journal of Criminological Research, Policy and Practice* (2014–2017). Currently he is the Editor-in-Chief of *Salus: An International Journal for Law Enforcement and Public Safety* as well as an editorial board member of the *Journal of Aggression, Conflict and Peace Research*.

Brandy L. Blasko is Assistant Professor at Sam Houston State University, USA. Previously, Brandy had been a Postdoctoral Research Fellow with a joint appointment at ACE! and the Human Emotions Research Laboratory (Department of Psychology). A common theme reflected in each of her research interests is discretion in criminal justice decision-making and how these processes influence the equity of outcome. Before joining George Mason University, Brandy worked as a clinician for several years within the Pennsylvania Department of Corrections. She received her BS in Psychology and BA in Administration of Justice from the University of Pittsburgh and her MA in Forensic Psychology from John Jay College of Criminal Justice.

Barbara E. Bloom, PhD, is Professor Emerita of Criminology and Criminal Justice Studies at Sonoma State University, USA. She is Co-Director of the Center for Gender and Justice. Dr. Bloom has directed a range of research projects focused on gender-responsive and trauma-informed interventions and services for justice-involved women and girls. For over 30 years, she has provided professional services to federal, state, and local criminal justice agencies including the National Institute of Corrections, the California Department of Corrections and Rehabilitation, various sheriff's and probation departments, and community-based organizations throughout the US. Dr. Bloom is a Past President of the Western Society of Criminology (WSC) and a recipient of the 2003 WSC Fellow Award for important contributions to the field of criminology. She is a recipient (with Dr. Barbara Owen and Dr. Stephanie S. Covington) of the American Probation and Parole Association 2003 University of Cincinnati Award for the publication *Gender Responsive Strategies: Research Practice and Guiding Principles for Women Offenders*. She was also honored (with Owen) by the American Society of Criminology Division on Women and Crime with the 2006 Saltzman Award and by the Western Society of Criminology with the 2014 Meda Chesney-Lind Award for significant contributions to the fields of gender, crime, and justice.

Gillian Buck is Senior Lecturer in Social Work at the University of Chester, UK. Her teaching interests include social work theory and methods and approaches to research. Her research interests include (peer) mentoring, user-led approaches, and voluntary sector practice more broadly. She is currently an Associate Director of CRIMVOL, the international research network for the penal voluntary sector.

Lol Burke is Professor in Criminal Justice at Liverpool John Moore's University, UK, and specializes in the areas of probation research, policy, and practice. He has an extensive publication record in CJ/Probation. These include co-authored monographs *Delivering Rehabilitation* (Routledge 2014) and *Redemption, Rehabilitation and Risk Management* (Routledge 2011), chapters in seven edited collections, and over 30 published outputs in refereed journals and professional publications.

Christina Burton is a PhD student at the University of Central Florida, USA. Her research interests include the use of technology in police agencies, environmental criminology, and the application of situational crime prevention to wildlife law enforcement.

James Byrne is Associate Chair and Professor in the School of Criminology and Justice Studies at the University of Massachusetts, Lowell, USA. He is the author of several publications on a wide range of criminal and juvenile justice policy and programme evaluation issues. Since 2008, Dr Byrne has served as the Editor-in-Chief of the journal *Victims and Offenders: An International Journal of Evidence-based Research, Policy, and Practice* (Routledge, Taylor and Francis Group). Dr Byrne also serves on the editorial boards of several professional journals, including *Criminology and Public Policy, Health and Justice, Federal Probation*, and the *European Journal of Probation*.

Kelli E. Canada is Associate Professor and Associate Director for Research, School of Social Work, University of Missouri, USA. She is a Robert Wood Johnson Fellow and recipient of the Hazel M. Hatcher HES Research Scholar Award. In addition to her research on vulnerable populations within the criminal justice system, Dr Canada works to increase access to quality mental health treatment for vulnerable populations in the community. In September of 2014, she and Co-Director Rebekah Freese opened the Integrative Behavioral Health Clinic (IBHC), a free clinic for uninsured mid-Missourians in need of comprehensive mental healthcare, provided by faculty and graduate students in the MU School of Social Work.

Rob Canton is Professor in Community and Criminal Justice at De Montfort University, Leicester, UK. A former probation officer, he has worked with the Council of Europe to develop human rights standards for probation practice. His recent books include *Probation* (2018, with Jane Dominey) and *Why Punish? An Introduction to the Philosophy of Punishment* (2017).

Nicola Carr is Associate Professor in Criminology at the University of Nottingham, UK, where she is Co-Director of the Criminal Justice Research Centre. She is the Editor of the *Probation Journal* and an Editorial Board member of the *Irish Probation Journal*. She is Co-Convenor of the European Society of Criminology's Working Group on Community Sanctions and Measures.

Stephen Case is Professor of Criminology and Head of the Social and Policy Studies Unit at Loughborough University, UK. His research interests focus on the pursuit of child first, positive and socially inclusive understandings of and responses to offending by children.

Laura Caulfield, PhD, is Chair of the Institute for Community Research and Development at the University of Wolverhampton, UK. She is an expert in the evaluation of creative programmes within the criminal justice system. She has designed and conducted numerous research evaluations and has received funding from the Home Office, Economic and Social Research Council, the National Criminal Justice Arts Alliance, the NHS, and several third-sector organizations. In November 2016 she was invited to speak at the House of Lords about her work on the arts in criminal justice. She is an expert in research design and methodology, and is the author of *Criminological Research for Beginners* (Routledge, 2014, 2018).

Nick Chadwick is a PhD student in Forensic Psychology at Carleton University, Canada. He has contributed to research on the use and implementation of evidence-based practices in community supervision, the utility of assessing dynamic risk and protective factors in the prediction of recidivism, and effective correctional programming.

Tim Chapman is Visiting Lecturer in Restorative Practices at Ulster University, Northern Ireland. His teaching and research is focused primarily on restorative justice. He is active in promoting restorative justice in Europe and beyond through the European Forum for Restorative Justice.

Helen Codd is Professor of Law & Social Justice at the University of Central Lancashire, UK. She has an extensive international record of research and publications in relation to prisons, prisoners, and prisoners' families. Her work has been cited with approval by the Grand Chamber of the European Court of Human Rights and she has been an invited speaker at the UN. Questions of diversity, especially in relation to gender and ageing, have underpinned her research throughout her career. She has a strong record of collaboration and consultancy with third sector voluntary organizations and NGOs, and is currently a Lay Adviser to the Lancashire MAPPA Strategic Management Board, appointed by the Ministry of Justice.

Bankole Cole is Reader in Criminology and Human Rights in the Helena Kennedy Centre for International Justice (Department of Law and Criminology), Sheffield Hallam University, UK. His areas of expertise include 'race' and diversity issues in criminal justice, policing, and youth justice. His publications include, with A. Calverley, G. Kaur, S. Lewis, P. Raynor, S. Sadeghi, D. Smith, M. Vanstone, and A. Wardak, *Black and Asian Offenders on Probation* (Home Office, 2004); 'Working with Ethnic Diversity' in S. Green, E. Lancaster, and S. Feasey (eds.), *Addressing Offending Behaviour: Content, Practice and Values* (2008); and 'Young People, 'Race' and Criminal Justice' in S. Chattoo, K. Atkin, G. Craig, and R. Flynn (eds.), *Understanding 'Race' and Ethnicity* 2nd Edition (2019). Bankole is a member of the Ministry of Justice Advisory Groups for statistics on 'Race' and Women in the CJS (Section 95 of the Criminal Justice Act 1991). He is also a member of the National Police Chiefs' Council's (NPCC) Strategic Group on Race, Religion and Belief.

Ronald P. Corbett, Jr, former Acting Commissioner of the Massachusetts Probation Department, is Project Advisor for the Robina Institute of Criminal Law and Criminal Justice's Community Sanctions and Revocations Project, USA, on nationwide practice in the area of parole and probation revocations. Corbett has published widely, including articles in *Federal Probation, Corrections Today*, and *Justice Quarterly*. His publications include *Transforming Probation through Leadership: The 'Broken Windows' Model*, published by the Manhattan Institute. He served as Editor of *Perspectives*, the journal of the American

Probation and Parole Association, and Co-Editor of the 'Up to Speed' column in *Federal Probation*.

Stephanie S. Covington, PhD, LCSW, is an internationally recognized clinician, author, lecturer, and organizational consultant and is a pioneer in the field of women's issues, addiction, trauma, and recovery. With over 35 years of experience, she is noted for her work in the design and implementation of gender-responsive and trauma-informed treatment services in public, private, and institutional settings. She is the author of numerous books, as well as ten research-based, manualized treatment curricula. For the past 25 years, Dr. Covington has worked to help institutions and programs in the criminal justice system develop effective gender-responsive services. She has provided training and consulting services to the United Nations Office on Drugs and Crime; the Ministries of Justice in England, Scotland, and Switzerland; the Correctional Service of Canada; and, in the US, the Federal Bureau of Prisons, the National Institute of Corrections, the Center for Substance Abuse Treatment, the California Department of Corrections and Rehabilitation, and many other state and local jurisdictions. In addition, she helped to design women's services at the Betty Ford Treatment Center and was the featured therapist on the Oprah Winfrey Network (OWN) TV show entitled *Breaking Down the Bars*. Dr. Covington has served on the faculties of the University of Southern California, San Diego State University, and the California School of Professional Psychology. She is co-director of the Institute for Relational Development and the Center for Gender and Justice in La Jolla, California.

Craig Cumming is a Research Fellow, currently undertaking a PhD at the School of Population and Global Health at the University of Western Australia. Originally coming from a law and criminology background, he has been involved in research focusing on the health of people who have had contact with the justice system since 2011. He has spent several years attending police lockups and prisons to interview detainees and prisoners in person. His work focuses on health outcomes associated with drug and alcohol use and mental illness in this population.

John Deering is Associate Professor of Criminology and Criminal Justice at the University of South Wales, UK. He previously worked as a probation officer. His research interests include the probation service, youth justice, and the criminal justice system.

Matthew DeMichele is Senior Research Sociologist in Research Triangle Institute's Division for Applied Justice Research, USA. He has conducted criminal justice research for nearly 20 years with a focus on correctional population trends, community corrections, risk prediction, terrorism/

extremism prevention, and programme evaluation. He is currently leading research for local, federal, and foundation partners to assess criminal justice reforms, judicial decision-making, and disengagement from extremist organizations. His research has recently been published in *Crime & Delinquency*, *American Sociological Review*, and the *Probation Journal*.

Ioan Durnescu is Professor in the Faculty of Sociology and Social Work at the University of Bucharest, Romania. He teaches and conducts research in the area of probation and prison. His special interest is comparative probation. Ioan is also Co-Editor of the *European Journal of Probation*. He is also a member of prestigious organizations such as the Confederation of European Probation and the European Society of Criminology.

Phillipa Evans has over 18 years' experience as a social worker in clinical, policy, and academic roles across a variety of contexts including juvenile justice, child protection, and mental health. These positions include counsellor, senior project officer, research fellow, and currently Lecturer in Social Work at the University of New South Wales, Australia. Dr Evans successfully obtained her PhD from Monash University examining effective methods of challenging pro-criminal attitudes and behaviours of juvenile offenders.

Flora Fitzalan Howard is a forensic psychologist and Researcher at Her Majesty's Prison and Probation Service (HMPPS), UK.

Theo Gavrielides is an international expert in restorative justice and human rights. He is the Founder and Director of the IARS International Institute, a user-led NGO, and he has also founded and directs Restorative Justice for All (RJ4All), an international NGO. He is Adjunct Professor at the School of Criminology of Simon Fraser University (Canada) as well as a Visiting Professor at Buckinghamshire New University (UK). His publications include the monograph 'Restorative Justice Theory and Practice', and the co-edited publications *Rights and Restoration within Youth Justice*, *Reconstructing Restorative Justice Philosophy*, and *The Routledge International Handbook of Restorative Justice*.

Loraine Gelsthorpe is Professor of Criminology and Criminal Justice and Director of the Institute of Criminology at the Institute of Criminology, University of Cambridge, UK. She has worked at the Institute of Criminology since 1991, after research posts at the Centre for Youth, Crime and Community at the University of Lancaster, University College of North Wales UCNW (Bangor), and at the London School of Economics (LSE). She completed her PhD at the University of Cambridge in 1985. Loraine has conducted a wide range of empirical studies, many of them relating to women, crime, and criminal justice. She has published extensively on topics ranging from psychoanalytical dimensions of criminology, pre-sentence reports, community crime prevention, government policy on youth justice, the criminalization of migrant women, deaths under criminal justice system supervision in the community, the challenges of ethics in criminology and criminal justice, to women, crime, and criminal justice.

Martin Glynn is Lecturer in Criminology at Birmingham City University, UK. He is an internationally renowned criminologist, critical race scholar, theatre director, and dramatist. His research focuses on race and crime, black masculinities, and performance-driven research dissemination. His publications include *Black Men, Invisibility and Crime: Towards a Critical Race Theory of Desistance (International Series on Desistance and Rehabilitation)*, published by Routledge.

Kate Gooch is Associate Professor at Leicester Law School, University of Leicester, UK. She joined the Law School in January 2017, having previously worked at the University of Birmingham. Her primary research and teaching interests lie in the areas of criminal law, child law (including youth justice), and criminology (particularly prisons research).

Hannah Graham is Senior Lecturer in Criminology in the Scottish Centre for Crime and Justice Research (SCCJR) in the Faculty of Social Sciences, University of Stirling, UK. As a criminologist and social scientist, Hannah works with governments and parliaments, practitioners, citizens, communities, and civic society to help inform real-world change and collaboratively build more just societies. She has made contributions in Scottish, European, and Australasian contexts. Also, Hannah is developing a growing research agenda on innovation and justice, on which she has researched, written, and spoken in different countries. Her publications include *Rehabilitation Work: Supporting Desistance and Recovery* (2016), *Innovative Justice* (2015), and *Working with Offenders: A Guide to Concepts and Practices* (2010), all published internationally by Routledge.

Patricia Gray is Reader in Criminology and Criminal Justice in the School of Law, Criminology and Government at the University of Plymouth, UK. Her research and publications focus on penal governance, youth justice, and social justice.

Simon Green is Reader in Criminology and Associate Dean for Research at the University of Hull, UK. He researches in the areas of victimology, community justice, and reducing reoffending. His most recent book is *Crime, Community and Morality* (Routledge, 2015).

Stephen M. Haas is Fellow and Technical Director for Research and Evaluation in the Justice and Community Development department at ICF. His education and career have centred on the study of corrections and criminological theory, with emphasis in community-based supervision and treatment, risk assessment and classification, and correctional rehabilitation. His peer-reviewed works include studies published in peer-reviewed journals. He recently served as guest editor for a special issue of the *Justice Research and Policy* journal titled 'Toward Evidence-Based Decision Making in Community Corrections: Research and Strategies for Successful Implementation'.

Kevin Haines is Professor of Criminology and Public Safety at the Institute of Criminology and Public Safety, University of Trinidad and Tobago. His research has focused on critical issues in the response of criminal justice agencies to the behaviour of children. In particular his work has included debunking the myth of the effectiveness of the risk factor prevention paradigm and evidencing the effectiveness of a children first, offenders second approach.

Lauren Hall is Lecturer in Criminology at the University of Lincoln, UK, and is in the writing up stages of her PhD with Sheffield Hallam University, which explores the social components of recovery from addiction and desistance from crime. Lauren worked as a research assistant on a veteran-specific recovery project evaluation. Lauren has also supported further projects which work with people from a strengths-based perspective to examine the relational aspects of recovery and desistance and to help create meaningful links to the community for marginalized groups.

John Halushka is Assistant Professor of Justice Studies at San Jose State University, USA. He is an ethnographer whose research explores prisoner re-entry, urban poverty, and social welfare. His research has appeared in *Ethnography* and *Punishment & Society*.

Kelly Hannah-Moffat is Professor of Criminology and Sociolegal Studies at the University of Toronto, Canada. She studies risk, gender, and diversity in penal and court systems. Her research has traced the historical antecedents of the internationally acclaimed 'women-centred' model of penal governance employed in Canadian federal women's prisons. Most recently, Professor Hannah-Moffat and Professor Paula Maurutto have teamed up for a project titled Customized Knowledges: Risk, Diversity and Gender in Specialized Courts, which examines how non-actuarial risk knowledges shape bail and sentencing practices in four distinct specialized courts across Canada. This project is supported by SSHRC.

Ines Hasselberg completed a PhD in Anthropology at the University of Sussex, UK, after which she worked at the Centre for Criminology, University of Oxford, and later at the Centre for Research in Anthropology (CRIA), University of Minho, as a Postdoctoral Research Fellow. Her work has focused on the intersections between border control and criminal justice, with particular attention devoted to how policies are translated into the everyday lives of foreign nationals.

David Hayes is Lecturer in Law at the University of Sheffield, UK. He researches penal theory and the pains of punishment and is the author of *Confronting Penal Excess: Retribution and the Politics of Penal Minimalism*, due to be published in late 2019.

Martine Herzog-Evans is Professor of Law, teaching Criminal Law and Criminology at Reims University, France. Her majors are criminal law, sentences, Therapeutic Jurisprudence, probation, prisons and re-entry, and legitimacy of justice. She has published extensively, and her latest publications include *Offender Release and Supervision: The Role of Courts and the Use of Discretion* (2015) and *Sentences Implementation Law* (*Droit de l'exécution des peines*), Dalloz.

Clive R. Hollin is Emeritus Professor of Criminological Psychology at the University of Leicester, UK. He is the author or editor of 25 books, mainly on topics relating to violence and criminal behaviour.

Ueli Hostettler is a social anthropologist (PhD, University of Bern, Switzerland; postdoc at the University of Florida, Gainesville, USA, and the University of Texas at Austin). He is Senior Researcher at the Institute for Penal Law and Criminology at the University of Bern, Switzerland, and Professor at the PHBern – University of Teacher Education (Bern, Switzerland). Since 2003, he has been engaged in research in the field of prison studies and has established the Prison Research Group at the University of Fribourg and, since 2015, at the University of Bern (www.prisonresearch.ch).

Jane L. Ireland is Professor of Forensic Psychology at the School of Psychology at the University of Central Lancashire, UK. Her research interests concern aggression and violence, in particular bullying in secure settings; treatment of aggression and anger; self-harm; violence risk assessment; psychopathy, personality disorder and violence; indirect aggression; sex differences in aggression; and sleeping difficulties and aggression. Jane was Co-Editor for the British Psychological Society publication *Forensic Update* from 2000 to 2005 and is Consulting Editor for the international journal *Aggressive Behaviour*. She has acted as an independent expert reviewer for NHS, LREC, and MREC committees for forensic research proposals, and reviewed grant proposals for NHS forensic grant programmes. She also represents the University of Central

Lancashire as the Academic Research Lead for the Ashworth Research Centre, Mersey Care NHS Trust.

Keir Irwin-Rogers is Lecturer in Criminology at the Open University, UK. His research interests include post-release supervision, sentencing, and alternatives to imprisonment. Keir's most recent research explores the harms associated with young people's involvement in illicit drug markets.

Yvonne Jewkes is Professor of Criminology at the University of Bath, UK. She is an expert on prison architecture and design and their potential to rehabilitate. She recently held two ESRC grants to study these topics and has worked as a consultant to prison architects and senior prison service personnel around the world.

Karen Johnson is a British Psychological Society Chartered and HCPC Registered Forensic Psychologist employed within HM Prison Service as a cluster Lead Psychologist. Karen is also completing a PhD at Queen's University Belfast titled 'Developing a Measure of Desistance Self-Narrative for a UK Prison Sample', which is supervised by Professor Shadd Maruna.

Hazel Kemshall is currently Professor of Community and Criminal Justice at De Montfort University, Leicester, UK. She has research interests in risk assessment and management and the community management of sexual and violent offenders.

Bridget Kerr is Visiting Research Associate at the Centre for Criminal Justice and Criminology, Swansea University, Wales, UK. A former probation officer, her research interests include service evaluation and practitioner skills development in probation settings.

Anna Kotova is Lecturer in Criminology at the University of Birmingham, UK, Department of Social Policy, Sociology and Criminology. She read for a BA in Law, MSc in Criminology and Criminal Justice, and D.Phil in Criminology at the University of Oxford. Her research interests are broadly within the area of prison sociology, focusing on the pains of imprisonment as experienced by people in prison and their families.

Kimberly R. Kras is Assistant Professor in the School of Criminology and Justice Studies at the University of Massachusetts, Lowell, USA. Dr Kras earned her PhD in Criminology and Criminal Justice from the University of Missouri-St. Louis in 2014, following a career with the Missouri Department of Corrections. Her work centres on the study of community corrections, re-entry, and desistance from offending behaviour, and utilizes both quantitative and qualitative methodologies. Dr Kras's research considers how offender behaviour change occurs from both the offenders' and community corrections agents' perspectives by examining re-entry-related experiences, collateral consequences of convictions, and evidence-based practices.

Pamela K. Lattimore is Senior Director for Research Development for Research Triangle Institute's Division for Applied Justice Research, USA. She has led several evaluations, including the NIJ-funded evaluation of the Honest Opportunity Probation with Enforcement Demonstration Field Experiment. She has published extensively, has served on the editorial boards of multiple academic journals, and is Co-Editor of the annual series *Handbook on Corrections and Sentencing*, which is published by Routledge. Before joining RTI in 1998, Dr Lattimore worked for ten years at the National Institute of Justice, most recently as Director of the Criminal Justice and Criminal Behavior Division, Office of Research and Evaluation.

Thomas P. LeBel is Associate Professor of Criminal Justice and Criminology at the University of Wisconsin-Milwaukee, USA. Dr LeBel is the author or co-author of numerous articles and book chapters about prisoner re-entry, desistance from crime, the stigma of incarceration, and interventions for criminal justice-involved women with drug and alcohol problems.

Jill S. Levenson is Professor of Social Work at Barry University in Miami, USA. She is a SAMHSA-trained internationally recognized expert in trauma-informed care. She has published over 100 articles and has been invited to speak about trauma-informed care in the US, Canada, Australia, and New Zealand. She has been a practicing clinical social worker for nearly 30 years, using a scientist-practitioner model to inform her research and her forensic work.

Alison Liebling is Professor of Criminology and Criminal Justice at the University of Cambridge, UK, and the Director of the Institute of Criminology's Prisons Research Centre. Her main interests lie in the changing shape and effects of imprisonment; the role of values in criminal justice; and in the role of safety, trust, and fairness in shaping the prison experience.

Caleb D. Lloyd is Senior Lecturer at the Centre for Forensic Behavioural Science at Swinburne University of Technology, Australia. He directs a programme of research on offender change in corrections and the community and collaborates on projects within multiple countries (New Zealand, US, Australia, and Canada).

Shannon Magnuson is a doctoral student in Criminology, Law and Society and a Graduate Research Assistant at the Center for Advancing Correctional Excellence (ACE!) at George Mason University, USA. She is an aspiring mixed-methods researcher with current projects using qualitative in-depth interviews and observations as well as survey data with prison and probation/parole agencies. Currently, her main projects involve translation and implementation of research evidence in practice. Her research interests include organizational change, corrections, process evaluation, and translational criminology.

Mike Maguire is Emeritus Professor of Criminology and Criminal Justice at the School of Social Sciences, University of Cardiff, UK. He spent most of his early career (1975–1989) at the Oxford University Centre for Criminological Research, latterly as a Senior Research Fellow. He was employed full-time at Cardiff University from 1989 to 2005, being promoted to Professor in 1995. From 2005 he worked part-time at both Cardiff University and the University of Glamorgan, before becoming Emeritus at Cardiff in 2010.

Niamh Maguire is Lecturer in Criminal Law and Criminology at Waterford Institute of Technology (WIT), Ireland. She was a member of the management committee of the COST Action Exploring Offender Supervision in Europe (IS1106) and was Co-Chair of its Working Group on Decision Making. Arising from that work is a book she recently co-edited with Professor Miranda Boone, titled *The Enforcement of Offender Supervision: Understanding Breach Processes*, published by Routledge. Niamh is also a co-founding member of the European Society of Criminology's (ESC) Working Group on Sentencing and Penal Decision Making and a member of the ESC's Working Group on Community Sanctions.

Lina Marmolejo is a doctoral student in the Criminology, Law and Society Department at George Mason University, USA. Prior to starting the doctoral programme, she worked as a Citizen Security Specialist at the Inter-American Development Bank (IDB). She has more than a decade of experience managing and designing development projects, with an emphasis on crime prevention in Latin America and the Caribbean. Before working at the IDB, she worked at the Organization of American States (OAS) as a specialist in topics related to the use of information and communication technologies and the modernization process of public institutions. She holds a Master's degree in Public Administration from the Institute of Political Studies, Paris (Sciences Po) and a Bachelor of Finance and International Relations from Universidad Externado de Colombia, Bogota.

Irene Marti studied social anthropology and sociology at the Universities of Basel and Neuchâtel in Switzerland. Since 2013 she has been a member of the

Prison Research Group (PRG) at the University of Bern, Switzerland (http://prisonresearch.ch/). Currently, she is a PhD candidate at the University of Neuchâtel and a Research Assistant at the Institute of Penal Law and Criminology at the University of Bern.

Shadd Maruna, PhD, is Professor of Criminology at Queen's University Belfast, Northern Ireland. Previously he worked at the University of Cambridge, Rutgers University, and the University of Manchester. His research focuses on desistance from crime, rehabilitation, and parole and personality. In 2004, he was named the Distinguished New Scholar in Corrections and Sentencing by the American Society of Criminology.

Rob Mawby has been a criminal justice researcher and teacher for over 25 years, working since 2009 in the University of Leicester's Criminology Department, UK, where he now retains an academic home as a University Fellow. He has researched and written widely on police-media relations and criminal justice occupational cultures.

Trish McCulloch is Reader and Social Work Lead at the University of Dundee, UK. Prior to joining the university, Trish worked as a social worker within youth and adult justice settings. Recent research and knowledge exchange activity straddles criminal and community justice and professional learning, with a particular interest in participatory approaches.

Paula McLean is a PhD student in Criminology at Sheffield Hallam University, UK. Her research is focused on the experiences of black women in the criminal justice system with a focus on resettlement. Paula's area of interest for research is around race, gender, and crime. Paula is also a probation officer and has worked extensively across most parts of the Probation Service including Offender Management, Approved Premises, Programmes, and Unpaid Work as well as within the Prison Service for almost six years.

Fergus McNeill is Professor of Criminology and Social Work at the University of Glasgow, UK, where he works in the Scottish Centre for Crime and Justice Research (SCCJR). He has published extensively on institutions, cultures, and practices of punishment – and on how they might be best reformed in the light of evidence about desistance from crime. This work has led to a series of engagements with policy, practice, and people with lived experience of punishment in numerous jurisdictions.

Rosie Meek is Professor of Psychology and Criminology and was founding Head of the School of Law at Royal Holloway University of London, UK. Her research is broadly focused on the development and evaluation of prison-based initiatives, with a particular focus on the role of voluntary and community organizations in criminal justice and the use of sport in prisons and other criminal justice settings.

Nena P. Messina, PhD, is a criminologist at UCLA Integrated Substance Abuse Programs, USA, and has been involved in substance abuse research for over 20 years. Dr. Messina's areas of expertise include the specialized treatment needs of drug-dependent women offenders and the association between crime, mental health, and substance abuse. Dr. Messina was appointed as a Special Consultant to act as a Governor's Rehabilitation Strike Team Member to create a strategic plan to reform the California prison system in response to Legislative Bill AB 900 – The Public Safety & Offender Rehabilitation Services Act of 2007. Dr. Messina has a successful history as the Principal Investigator of several NIDA-funded grants and California state contracts assessing the effectiveness of gender-responsive treatment for women offenders (on parole, in prison, or under community supervision such as re-entry programs, drug court, and Prop 36). Recently, Dr. Messina was awarded a large grant from the California Department of Corrections to determine the impact of several prison-based gender responsive programs to reduce violence and consequences of childhood trauma. Dr. Messina has collaborated on numerous publications on the psychosocial correlates of substance abuse treatment outcomes and has contributed a great deal to the understanding of co-occurring disorders, trauma and abuse, and treatment responsivity for women offenders.

Kimberly S. Meyer is Assistant Professor of Criminology/Criminal Justice at Central Connecticut State University, USA. She enjoys partnering with agencies to help advance the use of evidence-based practices and promote effective implementation among street-level workers such as probation officers. Agency partnerships to date have examined the disproportionate use of probation violations with black and Hispanic juvenile probationers and the effect of probation violations on continued delinquency for teenaged juvenile probationers.

Matthew Millings is Senior Lecturer in Criminal Justice. His time is split between Criminal Justice and supporting the development of practitioner-led research in the Liverpool Centre for Advanced Policing Studies, UK (where he is Course Leader for the PG Dip in Evidence-Informed Practice).

Alice Mills is Senior Lecturer in Criminology at the University of Auckland, New Zealand. Her research has examined the role and position of third-sector organizations in the UK (with Rosie Meek) and New Zealand. She is currently leading a three-year study examining the importance of housing for people leaving prison.

Kelly Struthers Montford is Assistant Professor of Sociology at the University of British Columbia Okanagan, Canada. Her research appears in *Radical Philosophy Review*, the *New Criminal Law Review*, *PhiloSophia*, the *Canadian Journal of Women and the Law*, and *Societies*, among other venues.

Christine Morgenstern is Senior Research Fellow at Trinity College Dublin, Ireland. Before, she had been working as Lecturer and Research Fellow for Criminology and Criminal Law at the University Greifswald and as a Visiting Professor at the Free University Berlin and the University Göttingen. Her research interests lie in the intersection between penal law, human rights, and criminology.

Jason Morris joined Her Majesty's Prisons and Probation Service (HMPPS; UK) in 2001. He qualified as a chartered psychologist in 2008. In 2010, he joined HMPPS Interventions Services where he later became a National Specialist Lead for Intimate Partner Violence programmes. He is a co-author of a few peer-reviewed journal articles on using technology in prisons and probation contexts.

Sheena Norton is a probation officer in the Probation Service, Ireland. She is a professionally qualified social worker, registered with CORU, Ireland. She holds a degree in Social Science, University College Dublin, and a Masters in Social Work, Trinity College Dublin.

Emma J. Palmer is Reader in Forensic Psychology at the University of Leicester, UK. Her research focuses on the development of antisocial behaviour, aggression, and offending, with specific references to social cognition, victimization, risk and needs assessment of offenders, and the design and evaluation of interventions with offenders. She is also a member of the University of Leicester Prisons Research Network.

Nicholas Pamment is Principal Lecturer and Associate Head (Students) at the Institute of Criminal Justice Studies, University of Portsmouth, UK. Following a BSc (Hons) and MSc, he completed his doctorate within the area of community reparation and restorative justice for young offenders. He has published studies within the fields of policing, multi-agency working, research methodology, community sentences, and wildlife crime.

Dominic A. S. Pearson is Senior Lecturer in Forensic Psychology and member of the International Centre for Research in Forensic Psychology at the University of Portsmouth, UK. He has research and practitioner experience with high-risk offenders managed by prisons, probation, and the police. Dominic is a registered practitioner psychologist and a Chartered Fellow of the British Psychological Society.

Charlene Pereria works as a Research Assistant with the Monash University Criminal Justice Research Consortium, Australia, and holds the position of Clinical Supervisor with the Professional Supervision and Coaching Centre in Victoria. She provides clinical supervision to practitioners working with adult and young offenders and family violence practitioners within the Department of Justice and Court Services Victoria. Her research interests include training, staff supervision, evidence-based practice skills, and case management interventions with offenders. She is currently completing her PhD examining the relationship between the style of professional supervision on the development and implementation of core effective practice skills by practitioners working with offenders.

Jake Phillips is Reader in Criminology at Sheffield Hallam University, UK. He teaches and researches in the field of probation and community sanctions with a particular focus on the intersection between policy and practice. He is currently undertaking research on the deaths of offenders in the community, the emotional labour of probation practice, and the impact of inspection on probation policy and practice.

Mayumi Purvis is a criminologist and private consultant/researcher; she is also an Honorary Fellow at the University of Melbourne, Australia, School of Social and Political Science (Criminology). She has worked in mixed government and academic roles such as managing the policy and projects arm of the Sex Offender Management Branch (Corrections Victoria), offender case management, and teaching and researching positions at several Australian universities.

Peter Raynor is Emeritus Research Professor of Criminology at Swansea University, UK, and has been carrying out and publishing research on criminal justice and offender management for more than 40 years. Over 200 publications include jointly edited collections on offender supervision (with McNeill and Trotter), compliance (with Ugwudike), social work with offenders (with McIvor), and race and probation (with Lewis, Smith, and Wardak). He is a member of the Correctional Services Accreditation and Advisory Panel for England and Wales, and a Fellow of the Academy of Social Sciences.

Carla Reeves is Subject Leader in Criminology and Policing at the University of Huddersfield, UK. Her research interests are primarily in sex offender management, desistance, and the work of Probation Approved Premises and Prisons to achieve these aims.

Nicole Renehan is an ESRC-funded PhD candidate at the University of Manchester, UK. She worked for many years in the domestic abuse arena within a multi-agency setting and her research interests include domestic abuse, domestic violence interventions, gender, and masculinities. She is currently researching the statutory domestic violence perpetrator programme 'Building Better Relationships' using previously untested evaluation methods.

Edward E. Rhine directs the Parole Release and Revocation Project under the Robina Institute of Criminal Law and Criminal Justice, University of Minnesota Law School, USA. He has written and edited numerous publications addressing the work of paroling authorities, the impact of judicial intervention on prison discipline, change issues in probation and parole, the emergence of offender re-entry, and correctional best practices. His most recent publications include a co-authored article (with Professor Anthony Thompson) on 'The Reentry Movement in Corrections: Resiliency, Fragility and Prospects' in the *Criminal Law Bulletin*, and a chapter on 'The Present Status and Future Prospects of Parole Boards and Parole Supervision' in *The Oxford Handbook of Sentencing and Corrections*.

Marina Richter is a geographer and sociologist who has worked extensively in the field of prison research, including on topics such as health and dying, education and work, and issues related to questions of prisons as organizations. She presently is Senior Researcher at the Prison Research Group of the University of Bern (Switzerland) and Assistant Professor for Social Space at the School for Social Work in Sierre (Switzerland).

John Rico is currently completing a PhD programme at Middlesex University, UK, and is also the Research Manager for MTCNovo, which operates the London Community Rehabilitation Company (London CRC), Thames Community Rehabilitation Company (TV-CRC), and Rainsbrook Secure Training Centre (STC).

Anne Robinson started work as probation officer in Bristol, UK, in 1993 and subsequently pursued a career in youth justice from practitioner through to youth offending team manager. She joined Sheffield Hallam University in 2005 and has since taken a key role in leading and managing programmes for probation officer training across the north of England. Alongside online teaching, she has developed undergraduate modules on young people, youth justice, gender, and desistance from crime. She is author of *Foundations for Youth Justice: Positive Approaches to Practice* and co-editor and contributor to *Moving on from Crime and Substance Use: Transforming Identities* (both published by Polity Press).

Gwen Robinson is Reader in Criminal Justice at the University of Sheffield, UK. She has published widely in the fields of probation practice, rehabilitation, and restorative justice.

Marijke Roosen holds a PhD in Criminology that focuses on electronic monitoring officers. She is a member of the Research Group Crime & Society (CRiS), Belgium, where she joins the research line Penality & Society.

Danielle S. Rudes is Associate Professor of Criminology, Law and Society and the Deputy Director of ACE!, George Mason University, USA. She serves as Associate Editor of the journal *Victims & Offenders* and publishes regularly in journals such as *Criminal Justice and Behavior, Federal Probation, Law & Policy*, and *Justice Quarterly*. She is also the 2012 winner of the Teaching Excellence Award and the 2015 Mentoring Excellence Award at George Mason University.

Ralph C. Serin is Professor at Carleton University, Canada, where he is Director of the Criminal Justice Decision Making Laboratory and member of the Forensic Psychology Research Center. From 1975 to 2003 he worked for Correctional Service of Canada in various clinical and research capacities. His current research relates to dynamic risk assessment, offender change, and crime desistance within the context of correctional decision-making.

Mairead Seymour is Senior Lecturer at the School of Languages, Law and Social Sciences in the Technological University Dublin, Ireland. Her research interests encompass youth justice, probation, community supervision, offender compliance, prisoner reintegration, desistance, procedural justice, and comparative criminal justice.

Gilly Sharpe is Lecturer in Criminology at the University of Sheffield, UK. Her research focuses on two areas. The first of these is youth justice policy and practice – in particular the assessment, criminalization, and penal governance of young women – and the second concerns (ex-)offenders' experiences of life after punishment and their transitions into adulthood. Her first monograph, *Offending Girls: Young Women and Youth Justice*, was published by Routledge in 2012. She also co-authored *Criminal Careers in Transition: The Social Context of Desistance from Crime.*

Ella Simpson is Lecturer in Criminology and PhD researcher at Bath Spa University, UK. Ella's PhD research is concerned with the role of creative arts interventions in prisons, with a particular focus on the role of the practitioner in engaging prisoners. Ella is an established creative arts facilitator with several years of experience in designing and delivering creative arts interventions in prisons and other custodial settings. Ella has recently completed work on an evaluation of a music programme run by Birmingham Youth Offending Service and an evaluation of Making for Change at HMP Downview.

Jaclyn Smith is Research and Evaluation Manager at ICF. She has spent more than 15 years working with local, state, and national organizations as well as government agencies to integrate data-informed decision-making with trauma-informed and survivor-centred principles to improve services for victims of crime. Her current research and evaluation projects include two National Institute of Justice-funded evaluations of a wraparound legal model to address the legal needs of victims of crime and of human trafficking services provided to American Indian women and children. She has also recently received funding from the Office for Victims of Crime (OVC) to evaluate financial training and technical assistance provided to Tribal Grantees.

Karen A. Souza is a PhD student in the Department of Psychology at City, University of London, UK. Karen is also Visiting Scholar at the Institute of Criminology, University of Cambridge. She achieved her MA and BA (with distinction) in Psychology from the University of Victoria, Canada.

Faye S. Taxman is University Professor in the Criminology, Law and Society Department and Director of the Center for Advancing Correctional Excellence at George Mason University, USA. Her work covers the breadth of the correctional system from jails and prisons to community corrections and adult and juvenile offenders, including all types of interventions and system improvement factors. Dr Taxman has published over 125 articles. She is the author (with Steve Belenkos) of *Implementing Evidence-Based Community Corrections* and *Addiction Treatment* (2011). She is also on the Editorial Boards of the *Journal of Experimental Criminology, Criminology and Public Policy* and *Journal of Offender Rehabilitation*.

Susan Thomas is Head of Oversight and Support at the Youth Justice Board in Wales (YJB CYMRU).

John Todd-Kvam is a PhD candidate at the University of Oslo, Norway. His ongoing PhD project focuses on understanding desistance from crime in Norway. In addition to desistance, John has researched populism and

Euroscepticism. He has previously worked in a number of civil service policy roles in Belfast and London.

Heather Toronjo is Research Assistant at ACE! and a graduate student in the Department of Criminology, Law and Society at George Mason University, USA. She received her BA in Anthropology from Texas A&M University in College Station, Texas, and her Masters of Public Policy from George Mason's Schar School of Policy and Government. Her research interests include corrections workforce professional development, desistance and narrative criminology, and social learning theory. Her current work centres around curriculum development for criminal justice workers and partnering with practitioners to implement evidence-based supervision models.

Chris Trotter is Professor in the Department of Social Work at Monash University in Australia. Prior to his appointment to Monash he worked for many years as a social worker and manager in child protection, juvenile justice, and adult probation and parole. He has undertaken many research projects and published more than 50 articles and book chapters during the past decade. He is internationally recognized for his work on pro-social modelling, has assisted probation services around the world in the implementation of the programme, and has provided advice and consultancy on effective practice in offender supervision. He has authored two books – *Working with Involuntary Clients*, now in its second edition and translated into German, Japanese, and Chinese, and *Helping Abused Children and Their Families*. Additionally, in 2011, Dr Trotter co-edited, with Fergus McNeill and Peter Raynor, the book *Offender Supervision: New Directions in Theory, Research, and Practice*.

Sarah Turnbull is Lecturer in Criminology in the School of Law, Birkbeck, University of London, UK. She is currently completing a research project examining immigration detention and deportation in the UK, with specific focus on the experiences of confinement and removal in relation to affective issues of home, belonging, and identity in contemporary Britain.

Thomas Ugelvik is Professor of Criminology at the University of Oslo, Norway. His work is published in journals such as *British Journal of Criminology*; *Crime, Media, Culture*; *European Journal of Criminology*; and *Punishment & Society*. He is series co-editor of the book series *Palgrave Studies in Prisons and Penology*.

Pamela Ugwudike is Associate Professor of Criminology at the University of Southampton, UK. Her research interests include studying advances in critical criminological theory and analyzing criminal justice policy and practice. She is particularly interested in theoretical and empirical studies of interactions between digital technology and criminal justice, and the implications for social justice. Her recent publications include *An Introduction to Critical Criminology* (2015) and *Evidence-Based Skills in Criminal Justice: International Research on Supporting Rehabilitation and Desistance* (2018) (co-edited with Peter Raynor and Jill Annison).

Maurice Vanstone is Emeritus Professor of Criminology, College of Law, Swansea University, UK. He has written extensively on criminal justice-related subjects. His latest book (with Philip Priestley) is *Probation and Politics* (2016).

Brittney Via is a Research Specialist in the Office of Research and Strategic Planning (ORSP) at the West Virginia Division of Justice and Community Services (DJCS), USA. She has a Master's in Criminology, Law and Society from George Mason University with a BA in Sociology from Randolph College.

Jill Viglione is Assistant Professor in the Department of Criminal Justice at the University of Central Florida, USA. Her research focuses on the implementation of evidence-based practices, decision-making within criminal justice agencies, and the use of risk and needs assessments.

Tony Ward is a clinical psychologist by training and has been working in the clinical and forensic field since 1987. He was formerly Director of the Kia Marama Sexual Offenders' Unit at Rolleston Prison in New Zealand and has taught both Clinical and Forensic Psychology at Victoria, Deakin, Canterbury, and Melbourne Universities. He is currently Professor of Forensic Clinical Psychology at Victoria University of Wellington, New Zealand. He is also the developer of the Good Lives Model for the rehabilitation of offenders.

Tim Warton is a senior practice officer with NSW Youth Justice, Australia, and has a private practice working with adults who have sexually offended or are concerned about sexually offending and young people with sexualized behavioural problems. He is completing a PhD on the development of a criminal identity among young offenders and has a passion for effective direct practice skills in offender treatment and integrating notions of pro-social identities into practice. Tim has over 15 years' experience in direct practice with juvenile and adult offenders and hopes to maintain face-to-face work.

Megan Welsh is Assistant Professor of Criminal Justice and Public Administration in the School of Public Affairs at San Diego State University, USA. She is an ethnographer who seeks to understand how people experience, navigate, and at times subvert social welfare and criminal justice institutions.

Anne Worrall is Emerita Professor of Criminology at Keele University, UK. A former probation officer, she has researched and written widely on two related areas – women and criminal justice, and probation work. She currently edits *Probation Quarterly*, the professional magazine of the Probation Institute in the UK.

Jessica J. Wyse is Research Assistant Professor, School of Public Health, Oregon Health Science University-Portland State University and a Research Assistant Professor for the VA Portland Health Care System, USA. Dr. Wyse's research focuses on vulnerable populations, particularly treatment of substance use disorders among vulnerable populations, and the ways in which evidence-based treatments for these disorders can be made more available to those who need them.

Ronen Ziv is a Fellow of the University of Cincinnati Corrections Institute and a Teaching Fellow in the Department of Socials Sciences, School of Criminology at the University of Haifa, Israel. He works as a criminal defence lawyer and teaches graduate students' courses in correctional theory and policy and conducts a practicum in correctional rehabilitation. His current research interests are in developing and testing the evidence-based approach to correctional rehabilitation, the integration of motivational theories in correctional intervention, and the capacity of correctional agencies to implement a promising correctional framework that aims to rehabilitate offenders.

An introduction to *The Routledge Companion to Rehabilitative Work in Criminal Justice*

Pamela Ugwudike and Peter Raynor

All the world's criminal justice systems need to undertake direct rehabilitative work with people who have come under their supervision as a result of criminal offences. Typically, this is organized in penal and correctional services – in custody in prisons, or in the community supervised by services such as probation. Over time, a large corpus of theory and research has emerged to inform the delivery of humane and effective rehabilitative work in these settings. Contemporary models of rehabilitative work such as the Risk-Need-Responsivity model (Bonta and Andrews 2017) and the desistance model (Maruna 2001, 2004) represent key examples. Other models exist alongside these, and the relative utility or suitability of each model is hotly contested within criminological and criminal justice scholarship. For instance, criminology scholars and others interested in rehabilitative work will be familiar with oppositional discourses targeted at the RNR model. An example is the claim that the model is a deficit-based model which focuses on individual deficiencies (or criminogenic needs) and ignores the strengths and capabilities that should be reinforced to achieve rehabilitative goals (Ward and Fortune 2013). The desistance model has also been criticized for lacking robust empirical basis and being primarily essayist (Andrews 2011). It is, however, worth noting that despite their limitations, the models have several strengths and share a similar aim, which is to inform humane and effective rehabilitative work in criminal justice systems. Proponents of the models have therefore continued to refine them in the light of emerging criticisms, evidence, and policy changes.

This Companion captures the developmental trajectory of the key rehabilitation models and approaches. It contains chapters which variously address their origins; empirical and theoretical bases; key strengths; and main limitations (and criticisms). It also comprises chapters which provide examples of interventions based on the models in adult criminal justice settings and youth justice contexts. Furthermore, the Companion explores other aspects of rehabilitative work including the impact of: diverse policy and organizational contexts; specific settings (prison, hospital, community); and the automatization of rehabilitative work in the digital age. The text also explores approaches to working with diverse groups including women, ethnic minorities, and young people.

Work with people who have offended is often but not always about reducing further offending through rehabilitation, and this perspective is particularly well represented in the book. A variety of other aims can include education, health, deterrence, restorative justice, safety, resettlement, and more. Contributions in this Companion give some attention to these. As the detailed outline below makes clear, we organized the Companion into sections reflecting different contexts, settings, needs, and approaches. Each section starts with a brief overview of key issues by members of the editorial team, and contributors to each section deliver a concise chapter of approximately 4,000 words covering key themes, summarizing relevant research and/or arguments, and identifying further sources which allow the reader to follow up the subject in greater depth.

The Companion comprises ten sections. It begins with Section 1, which sets the scene by discussing the theories and models underpinning rehabilitative work in criminal justice systems. The section explores historical developments in rehabilitative work. It also critically examines justifications for rehabilitative work and introduces readers to models of rehabilitation such as the RNR model, desistance models, and therapeutic justice approaches.

The next section moves away from the theoretical underpinnings of rehabilitative work and focuses on its policy contexts. Contemporary policy transformations such as the Transforming Rehabilitation agenda in England and Wales are explored. The chapters in Section 3 extend the focus on policy developments by exploring the emergence and implementation of risk assessment policy, which is a key policy development in criminal justice systems across several Western and non-Western jurisdictions.

Section 4 focuses on frontline practice. It explores several dimensions of real-world rehabilitative work, from applying supervision skills and innovative interventions, to working with violent offenders, sex offenders, and victims. Section 5 assesses the dynamics of resettlement policy and practice whilst Section 6 examines the impact of rehabilitative work on diverse groups such as women, ethnic minorities, young people, older people, and foreign nationals. The section also explores the experiences of families affected by imprisonment. Section 7 has as its main theme the application of control and surveillance mechanisms during rehabilitative work. Electronic monitoring practices represent examples and the chapters in Section 7 discuss these and other practices such as enforcement and multi-agency practices. In Section 8, the book's focus turns to practitioners' perspectives and practice cultures. Section 9 continues the discussion about the perspectives of key stakeholders in the penal system by bringing to the fore the views of people involved in the system, under the supervision of prison and probation services. The final section of the Companion explores evidence-based rehabilitative approaches and emphasizes the importance of evaluating real-world practice to strengthen its evidence base.

In sum, the Companion aims to be the primary go-to source for practitioners, managers, and researchers in criminal justice who need a comprehensive and authoritative summary of available knowledge in the field. To this end we have established an exceptionally well-qualified and experienced international editorial team which is well equipped to identify and work with contributors from different countries and jurisdictions and different parts of the penal system. As no other publication in this field aims at such comprehensive coverage over such a wide range of topics, we hope to make a key contribution to informed, effective, and ethical work with offenders.

References

Andrews, D. (2011) The impact of nonprogrammatic factors on criminal-justice interventions. *Legal and Criminological Psychology*, 16(1), 1–23.

Bonta, J. and Andrews, D. A. (2017) *The Psychology of Criminal Conduct*, 6th edition. New York: Routledge.

Maruna, S. (2001) *Making Good: How Ex-Convicts Reform and Rebuild Their Lives.* Washington, DC: American Psychological Association Books.

Maruna, S. (2004) Pygmalion in the reintegration process: Desistance from crime through the looking glass. *Psychology, Crime and Law*, 10(3), 271–281.

Ward, T. and Fortune, C. (2013) The good lives model: Aligning risk reduction with promoting offenders' personal goals. *European Journal of Probation*, 5(2), 29–46.

Section 1

Theories and models for working with offenders

Section 1 Introduction

The first section of the Companion extends and develops the work of Fergus McNeill and Hannah Graham (see Chapter 2), putting more flesh on the bones of rehabilitation both as a concept and as a set of practices. As such, this section provides crucial context for the rest of the Companion. Just as with the previous chapter, the various contributions to this section raise questions and discuss frameworks that will recur throughout the collection.

In Chapter 3, Maurice Vanstone looks at the recent history of rehabilitation in England and Wales, particularly within the context of probation work. His analysis reveals the importance of the shifting policy contexts within which rehabilitation is perennially reconstructed and often distorted and undermined. In particular, he laments current developments which, in his assessment, will make it difficult for practitioners in England and Wales to deliver the 'humanitarian, socially conscious, vocationally based' services central to the pursuit of rehabilitation.

Rob Canton's contribution (in Chapter 4) perhaps offers us a conceptual road map back from this predicament by developing the case for a human rights-based approach to rehabilitation. Responding to powerful critiques of conceptualizations and practices of rehabilitation that have sometimes ridden roughshod over the autonomy and liberty of citizens caught up in criminal justice, and drawing on the work of Rotman (1986) and others, Canton (in Chapter 4) and Morgenstern (in Chapter 5) show both why rehabilitation must be constrained by respect for human rights – of 'offenders', victims, and communities – and how this can realized in policy and practice.

In Chapter 6, David Hayes provides a similarly compelling and important contribution; insisting that, instead of treating retribution and rehabilitation as alternative approaches to offending, we should see them as connected and, at least to some extent, compatible. Just as retributivists must take rehabilitation seriously (as a necessary component of punishment that censures and communicates), so rehabilitationists must take seriously the pains that it entails. The latter recognition is key to sustaining a commitment to parsimony in our recourse to punishment of any form, especially when we think it is somehow doing good to or for or through its subjects.

Tim Chapman (in Chapter 7) outlines the key tenets of restorative justice (RJ). He defines RJ as an approach that is concerned with 'restoring justice' in the relations between the people involved in and affected by crime and their communities. While RJ is often cast as an alternative to traditional criminal justice (and 'offender'-centred rehabilitation), Chapman focuses on an example of the mainstreaming of restorative practice within the statutory youth justice system of Northern Ireland, before going on to provide a concise review of research into the effectiveness of RJ. He concludes that, in its focus on enabling people to take responsibility for offending, on repairing relationships and on developing self-respect within and mutual respect between those involved, RJ aligns with key aspects of desistance theory linked to maturation, social bonds, and identity transformation.

While Chapters 2–7 focus primarily on developing our conceptualizations and models of rehabilitation by exploring normative questions and principles, Chapters 8–12 are more focused on research evidence and its implications for our approaches to policy and practice.

In Chapter 8, Ronen Ziv introduces the Risk-Need-Responsivity model, and presents an account of its developments and of its strengths and limitations. While noting the importance of the RNR model in powerfully rebutting the once-prevailing 'nothing works' doctrine (Martinson 1974) and in restoring rehabilitation's legitimacy, ultimately he focuses on what he considers to be the main limitation of the model, its understanding of 'offenders'' motivations as being primarily linked to 'the impact of external incentives on their cognitive situation'. Ziv argues that this is an inadequate account of motivation – and one which hinders the development of the concept and the model.

Mayumi Purvis and Tony Ward, in Chapter 9, outline the theory and evidence behind the Good Lives Model of offender rehabilitation – a model which, through its focus on the pursuit of human flourishing, seeks to attend to both the interests of those who have offended and of the community. By helping people navigate the path towards a 'good life', the GLM provides a framework for practice that is, according to Purvis and Ward, 'deeply respectful' of the rights and interests of people engaged in rehabilitation, while also being 'highly targeted and meaningful'.

In Chapters 10 and 11, Fergus McNeill and Hannah Graham and Karen John-son and Shadd Maruna introduce another way of thinking about rehabilitation, not through the lens of treatment or practice, but through seeking to under-stand and support the processes of human development within social contexts involved in desistance from crime. McNeill and Graham very briefly summa-rize the burgeoning literature on desistance before focusing on the extent to which issues and questions of diversity have been adequately addressed within it. They suggest that while much important work has been done to diversify our understandings of desistance, much more work needs to be done – and that work will likely require the 'decentring of the hegemony of traditional penal institutions, policies, and practices' in the framing of our enquiries into desistance and rehabilitation. Johnson and Maruna focus their chapter on the importance of narratives (and their re-development) in desistance processes, and provide a fascinating account of how psychologists have begun to seek to understand and measure narrative changes; but they also acknowledge the importance of the social contexts within which human lives and personal and social identities evolve.

In the last chapter in this section, Herzog-Evans introduces one final frame-work for thinking about rehabilitative processes: Therapeutic Jurisprudence (TJ). Drawing on the pioneering work of David Wexler and others (Winick and Wexler 2003; Wexler 2016), she argues that TJ shifts the business of the courts (and specifically judges) from dispute settlement to conflict resolution, ulti-mately in pursuit of the well-being of the protagonists involved in crime-related conflicts. TJ's problem-solving orientation requires it to function at 'the cross-roads of mental health, law, criminology, and other theoretical and treatment models'. Like many developments in the history of rehabilitation, TJ emerged bottom-up as a pragmatic adaptation to everyday problems that judges face in responding to the business of criminal courts. While this may represent a practical strength, it also poses some challenges both in relation to theoret-ical coherence and evaluation. That said, Herzog-Evans sees 'extraordinary potential' in TJ, and in judges playing an active role in delivering 'legitimate and humane justice'.

As such, this first section both begins and ends with questions of justice – and that is fitting. In discussing rehabilitation – and especially its effectiveness in reducing reoffending – it is perhaps too easy to forget that the rehabilitation of 'offenders' is or should be, first and foremost, part of a system of justice; and that how we conceptualize and pursue justice must be at the heart of how we think about, develop, practice, and evaluate rehabilitation (McNeill 2009).

References

McNeill, F. (2009) What works and what's right. *European Journal of Probation*, 1(1), 21–40.

Martinson, R. (1974) What works? Questions and answers about prison reform. *The Public Interest*, 35, 22–54.

Rotman, E. (1986) Do criminal offenders have a constitutional right to rehabilitation? *The Journal of Criminal Law and Criminology*, 77(4), 1023–1068.

Wexler, D. (2016) Getting started with the mainstreaming of therapeutic jurisprudence in criminal cases: Tips on how and where to begin. *Revista Española de Investigación Criminológica*, 14(Monografía 1), 1–12.

Winick, B. and Wexler, D. (Eds.). (2003) *Judging in a Therapeutic Key: Therapeutic Jurisprudence and the Courts*. Durham: Carolina Academic Press.

2

Conceptualizing rehabilitation

Four forms, two models, one process, and a plethora of challenges

Fergus McNeill and Hannah Graham

Introduction

Within the complex and contested context of criminal justice, rehabilitation still manages to stand out as a particularly complex and contested concept. Its resultant ambiguity is a problem both for its advocates and its critics; it is hard to debate a concept that is so slippery. Since we cannot hope to resolve these complexities in this brief introductory chapter, we settle instead for clarifying them, expecting that the rest of this Companion will add substance to the initial frameworks we offer here.

Before we can turn to the meanings and forms of rehabilitation, it is necessary to set the scene with respect to punishment itself. The justification, nature, and proper role of punishment within criminal justice in democratic states is also endlessly contested, but many legal philosophers agree on three key features: (1) Punishment communicates censure of offending. (2) It involves 'hard treatment' of some sort. (3) It is administered on behalf of the state by a legitimate, lawful authority. Intriguingly, du Bois-Pedain (2017) has recently argued that there is a fourth feature of punishment that is often neglected, despite being central to punishment's social function:

> As a general social practice, punishment does not merely mark out the punishee's actions as wrong and blames him for engaging in this wrongful act. It also defines how both punishee and punisher will move forward from here. The penal agent lays down the terms of his or her future co-existence with the offender in a shared social world. Because this is punishment's central social function, *there is reintegrative momentum inherent in punishment* that gives the offender himself an interest in being punished. Far from threatening or challenging an offender's membership in the community, punishment reasserts or reinforces it.
>
> (du Bois-Pedain 2017: 203, emphasis added)

Whether or not we accept this particular line of philosophical argument, and even if it is also easily sidelined by the punitive impulses that offending often provokes, the importance of 'reintegrative momentum' is undeniable. Unless we intend to kill, disable, exile, or permanently imprison people who have offended, we *must* be concerned with the question of their social reintegration. Whether as a matter of self-interest (linked to our future safety) or as a matter of principle (linked to a concern to ensure that we do not punish excessively and therefore unfairly), when we ask whether, how and how much we should punish, the impact of our answers on reintegrative momentum should be a central concern.

In one sense, the question of how to generate and sustain reintegrative momentum is the practical question that binds this Companion together. Perhaps a little simplistically, as a starting point, we can understand rehabilitation broadly as referring to those processes and practices that aim at the successful reintegration of those who have offended. This is very often hard, slow, and painful work. Reintegrative momentum is exceptionally hard to generate and it is easily lost. And yet this is crucial work that, at its best, both reasserts and reconstructs the common humanity of all those involved.

In the remainder of this short chapter, we aim to further articulate four interrelated forms of rehabilitation and reintegration, to very briefly introduce three different models of rehabilitative processes, and to provide some examples of how these forms and models relate to the plethora of challenges that face rehabilitation in its different sites, in its various practices, and with its diverse populations.

Four forms of rehabilitation and reintegration

Confusingly, the term 'rehabilitation' can be applied to both processes and outcomes within criminal justice; we sometimes talk of people undergoing rehabilitation and we sometimes talk of people having achieved rehabilitation. To avoid this confusion, and following on from the argument of the preceding section, we will distinguish here between four forms of *rehabilitative processes* that aim at four forms of *reintegration*. In a recent book, Burke et al. (2018), set out to explore and reimagine these four forms of rehabilitation (refining and elaborating an earlier taxonomy developed by McNeill [2012, 2014]). Importantly, they insist that although the four forms need to be 'de-fankled' (or disentangled) in order to be more clearly understood, it is crucial to recognize their interdependencies.

Personal rehabilitation includes but extends far beyond what Raynor and Robinson (2009) had previously referred to as 'correctional rehabilitation'. It refers to any rehabilitative effort that seeks to somehow change, improve, or develop the person who has offended. This is perhaps the most commonly understood form of rehabilitation (at least in Anglophone countries) and, as we will see in the next section, it is the form of rehabilitation pursued in the most influential models of rehabilitative practice. Personal rehabilitation is commonly pursued through 'offending behaviour programmes' but it also includes a much wider range of broadly educational work with people in penal systems. It involves and encompasses work to develop new attitudes, skills, or abilities, or to address and resolve personal limitations or problems. The intended outcome of this form of rehabilitation is the development of a person who has integrated new capacities for leading a law-abiding life. In sum, s/he is equipped and ready for integration.

The second form of rehabilitation is **judicial or legal rehabilitation**. Rather than being concerned with the intrinsic development of the individual who has offended, this form encompasses processes and practices which work to restore their civil or human rights. It addresses questions of when, how, and to what extent a person is to be *formally* and legally reintegrated into the full, free, and equal citizenship that they (notionally) enjoyed before the offence and its punishment. Related forms of rehabilitative practice include processes and measures that address the issue of criminal records and whether, how, and when the formal stigma that they represent can be set aside, sealed, or surpassed. No amount of personal rehabilitation – no amount of supporting people to change themselves – can be sufficient to the tasks and challenges of reintegration if formal, legal barriers to integration are left in place. To do so is simply to make a person ready for a situation that they are not entitled to occupy. As Burke et al. (2018) argue, the idea of judicial and legal rehabilitation can also be useful in helping us to explore the ways in which judges impose, supervise, and terminate punishment, and whether and how these practices aim at and achieve reintegration (see Herzog-Evans 2011 and in this volume).

However, there are moral barriers to reintegration as well as personal and legal ones and these require careful attention to processes of **moral rehabilitation**. Neither personal nor legal conceptions of rehabilitation are adequate to addressing the moral offence that crime represents. In and of themselves, neither personal nor legal rehabilitation offer moral redress to victims and communities; they may involve some kinds of moral interaction between the state (via its 'penal agents' in courts, prisons, or probation services) and the individual 'offender', but they do not directly address the conflict that the crime may have created between the 'offender', the victim, and/or the community (Zedner 1994). In Duff's (2005) terms, because these forms of rehabilitation fail to mediate this conflict, they leave the relational breach between 'offenders', victims, and communities unrepaired and that makes social reintegration unlikely or, at worst, impossible. These are, of course, the relationships that restorative justice often seeks to address and repair (see Chapman, this volume).

However, that conflict may have another, antecedent, dimension that complicates moral responsibility for the offence if an unjust society has permitted criminogenic social inequalities to go unaddressed, creating barriers to the achievement of integration and citizenship for people at the hard end of the enduring and entrenched inequalities suffered by certain groups in post-colonial, patriarchal, and/or capitalist societies (see McNeill and Graham, this volume). In this case, there may be debts that the state and the community owe the 'offender' (and, indirectly, the victim) – and these debts must also be settled in and through the support for integration that it makes available. Indeed, in its broadest sense, moral rehabilitation requires forms of dialogue that mediate the terms of integration or reintegration for all concerned. Contrary to du Bois-Pedain's (2017: 203) formulation above, we would suggest that the penal agent does not 'lay down the terms of his or her future co-existence with the offender in a shared social world'; rather, if there is any *collective* responsibility for the offending at all, then s/he must *mediate and negotiate* those terms (see Canton, this volume). Here, the moral dialogue involved in rehabilitation also becomes a political dialogue (see Behan, this volume).

It may seem that we have already complicated the meanings or forms of rehabilitation enough, but perhaps the greatest challenges relate to the fourth form. Even where personal development is secured, where legal requalification is confirmed, and where moral debts are settled, the question of **social rehabilitation** remains. In European jurisprudence, the concept of 'social rehabilitation' refers both to working for the restoration of the citizen's formal social status and to making available the personal and social means to do so (Van Zyl Smit and Snacken 2009). But here, we mean instead something that is broader, deeper, and more subjective; specifically, we refer to working for the informal social recognition and acceptance of the returning citizen.

This informal recognition and acceptance is important because ultimately social reintegration is not something that the state itself can order or provide. None of us can be meaningfully integrated by the state or at its command; rather, it is in our families, friendships, employment, civic associations, and social networks that we *feel and find ourselves integrated* – or in which we feel or find ourselves disintegrated. In other words, the processes by which a returning citizen finds affinity and becomes socially reintegrated depend largely on the dispositions of other citizens and of civil society. The state may have a duty to cultivate, underwrite, and support the development of such integrative civic dispositions, but ultimately the state cannot be the author and agent of integration. Rather it falls to us to integrate ourselves with one another – or not – and that is why rehabilitation and reintegration are or should be everyone's concerns.

We noted at the outset and have illustrated in this short account how these four forms are interrelated. We know from criminological research that, even when people have been deeply invested in the hard work of personal transformation, efforts to desist from offending are very difficult to sustain in the face, for example, of labour market exclusion and stigmatization within one's community (Schinkel 2014; Nugent and Schinkel 2016). This is an important observation at the start of a collection such as this Companion: it highlights the inadequacy – perhaps even the futility – of taking a simplistic or partial approach to rehabilitation and reintegration. The resources that we invest in any one of these four forms will be wasted unless we can align our efforts in the other three areas; we can spend millions, for example, on offending behaviour programmes, while undermining their potential effectiveness by doing nothing about the social contexts within which newly acquired attitudes or skills might be reinforced and exercised. But equally, if we legally rehabilitate without due regard to supporting and sustaining the personal development of people in our penal systems, we may expose communities to certain risks.

Two models of and for rehabilitative practice

Perhaps unsurprisingly, the most influential models of rehabilitation that have been developed through and for correctional or forensic practice tend to be focused on delivering personal rehabilitation. Yet even within this single form of rehabilitative activity, there has been plenty of room for debate about what forms of personal change to support and how best to do so. The relevant chapters that follow in the first section of this Companion can do more justice to these important debates; here, we merely suggest where and how these two models might fit within the broader approach to rehabilitation and reintegration that we have just outlined.

The pre-eminent model of rehabilitative practice in many Western countries – the Risk-Need-Responsivity (or RNR) model (see Ziv, this volume) – rests upon a certain kind of scientific approach to studying and changing 'criminal conduct'. The RNR model, first developed by psychologists Don Andrews and Jim Bonta (1994), rests on an empirically derived theory about the causes and/ or correlates of criminal behaviour, using this to suggest a framework for correctional intervention. As Ziv (this volume) outlines, this framework offers specific guidance about *who* should be 'treated' (i.e. which 'offenders'), *what* should be 'treated' (i.e. which sorts of factors, flaws, issues, or problems associated with their offending), and *how* to intervene. In very broad-brush terms, the answers to these questions are that we should treat those at significant risk of reoffending, that we should treat (only) their 'criminogenic needs' (or crime-related needs), and that we should use mainly cognitive behavioural methods.

RNR therefore is, in the terms we have outlined above, a very specific and quite narrow form of personal rehabilitation. Indeed, it can reasonably be described as belonging to that subset of personal rehabilitation which, following Raynor and Robinson (2009), we defined as 'correctional rehabilitation' above. The RNR model confines itself to addressing a specific set of crime-related needs mainly by developing 'pro-social' attitudes, skills, and behaviours (see Polaschek 2012). This narrow focus can be defended ethically – in that it limits the intrusions of rehabilitation to those factors that can be demonstrably associated with offending – and practically – in that the model's proponents claim that this narrow focus has been shown to be effective in terms of reducing reconviction. RNR's narrow focus may also suit the field of corrections, in that it provides correctional administrators and practitioners with a method and means for doing rehabilitation that do not require complex partnerships beyond prisons and probation. RNR locates the problem within the offender and the solution within the prison or probation 'treatment' room. Since RNR's goal is to promote public safety by reducing the risk of reoffending, it also offers a simple measure of success: reduced reconviction. Indeed, in contradistinction to the broader framework offered above, RNR does not aim ultimately at reintegration; rather, it settles for securing behavioural compliance with the law.

The second influential model of rehabilitative practice is more expansive both in its aims and in its approach, as might be expected of a model influenced both by Aristotelian philosophy and by evolutionary psychology. As its name suggests, the Good Lives Model (GLM) (see Purvis and Ward, this volume) rests on the assumption that interventions should aim to promote a person's 'goods' as well as to manage or reduce risk. A major aim of rehabilitative work under the GLM is to help a person develop a life plan that involves ways of effectively securing 'primary human goods' without harming others. These 'primary human goods' include, for example, life, knowledge, excellence in play and work, agency or autonomy, inner peace, friendship, community, spirituality, happiness, and creativity (Ward and Maruna 2007). Clearly, this is not just about tackling 'criminogenic needs' or risk factors; it entails a much broader project of personal rehabilitation involving the holistic reconstruction of the self, and – though focused on the individual – it requires practitioners to also consider and address relational and contextual factors. Interestingly, the GLM approach necessarily requires an explicit focus on exploring and conceptualizing what a 'good life' is for and with each person, taking account of individual strengths and priorities, and encouraging and respecting people's capacities to make choices for themselves. Though this does not necessarily entail the kinds of mediation and reparation that might be required for moral rehabilitation (as defined above), it certainly means that the practitioner and person should be engaged in moral and philosophical dialogue about the terms and nature of reintegration.

We will leave it to other contributors to assess the merits of these two models and of the accumulating evidence about their effectiveness in practice, turning instead not to a model of rehabilitative practice, but rather to an altogether different way of thinking about the processes involved.

One process, many paths: desistance

Though we can speak of *the* 'desistance' process, in fact there are many and varied pathways away from offending. The relationship between theories of desistance from crime and rehabilitation are far from straightforward but, in simple terms, whereas models of rehabilitation tend to start with the question of how best to intervene to 'produce' change, desistance theories start with trying to describe and understand the process of change in and of itself. The distinction is important, not least because there is plenty of evidence that *most* desistance happens *without* rehabilitative intervention. Just as criminologists recognize that some involvement in offending is normative in adolescence (i.e. most of us do it), so they have come to recognize that 'spontaneous' desistance (or at least desistance without rehabilitative intervention) is also normative (i.e. most people stop offending without someone directly attempting to help them stop).

We might therefore think of desistance theories as accounts of a kind of 'natural' or 'spontaneous' rehabilitation, if by that we mean an unassisted, un-engineered movement away from offending and towards social integration. But, of course, like everything else in this field, it is not quite so simple. As Graham and McNeill (2017, and in this volume) explain and as Johnson and Maruna (this volume) illustrate, to say that the process of desistance need not be engineered by the state's penal agents is not necessarily to say that it is unassisted. Indeed, many of the most common explanations of desistance, on closer examination, do imply some form of assistance. For example, if desistance is the result of maturation, we should understand this not as a spontaneous and inevitable physiological and psychological process associated with ageing, but rather as a social process which can be enabled or impeded by a person's associates and environments. Similarly, if desistance is often linked to the development of new social bonds like those associated with intimate relationships, parenthood, or employment, for example, it should be obvious that we find our ways into these important connections not entirely by accident. More often, they reflect supported changes in our social positions. Similarly, if desistance is often about a re-conceptualization of oneself (away from a deviant and towards a more positive identity), that is a process which, for most of us, requires a receptive audience for the reformed (or evolved) self. In other words, in each of these cases, while rehabilitation is not being engineered by a *penal* agent, it is being supported by social actors, relationships, and contexts – and it can be just as easily undermined by them.

Moreover, for at least 20 years now (see, for example, Rex 1999), many scholars have been exploring whether and how penal agents *can* work to actively sponsor, support, and sustain desistance, without necessarily imposing an over-engineered model of correctional rehabilitation on the process. Indeed, though there is no single model of desistance-based rehabilitation, as one of us argued some time ago,

> building an understanding of the human processes and social contexts in and through which desistance occurs is a necessary precursor to developing practice paradigms; put another way, constructions of practice should be embedded in understandings of desistance. . . . Put simply, the implication is that offender management services need to think of themselves less as providers of correctional treatment (that belongs to the expert) and more as supporters of desistance processes (that belong to the desister).
>
> (McNeill 2006: 46)

Desistance research therefore is an exceptionally important evidence base to consider in debates about rehabilitation, and in the development of related policies and practices. Indeed, the original articulation of the four forms of rehabilitation discussed above was driven as much by desistance research as by work in the philosophy of punishment (see McNeill 2012).

Perhaps most importantly, in returning to the question of reintegration, it is desistance research that has helped us to understand that changes in offending behaviour are insecure at best until and unless they are sustained by social reintegration – and this insight makes a key link between the philosophical arguments about reintegrative momentum with which we began and (Anglophone) rehabilitation's more prosaic and immediate concern with reoffending. It turns out that the latter depends to a large extent on the former, explaining why a narrow approach to rehabilitation is as insufficient to the pragmatic challenge of reducing reoffending as it is to the moral purposes of punishment.

Conclusion: a plethora of challenges

While section one of this Companion continues to offer an elaboration of theories of and models for rehabilitation, the complex relationships between the four forms of rehabilitation will recur in the plethora of policy and practice challenges that the book explores. When we look to the different settings in which rehabilitation is attempted or supported – in prisons or halfway houses or approved hostels; through parole and probation and community service; in the public, private or third sector; in communities, in clubs, in places of worship, in families, in friendships, etc. – we should ask what form of rehabilitation is being attempted here, to what end, and with what effects? Similar questions should recur when exploring specific practices of risk assessment or different approaches to intervention, as well as paying attention perhaps to which forms of rehabilitation are being neglected and why. When we look at different populations involved in rehabilitation, we should consider whether the meaning and nature of the process differs for them and for those attempting to support them; and whether any such differences represent appropriate responses to diversity or illegitimate discrimination. And when we examine specific responses to other problems disproportionately affecting people involved in offending (like substance use, homelessness, or mental health), we should ask whether and how recovery from these difficulties relates to desistance from crime, and which goal should be prioritized (see Graham 2016; Graham and McNeill, this volume). Crucially, if we really want to understand what rehabilitation is in practice – and not just what it is *intended* to be – we should pay close attention to the perspectives of participants in the process, whether as people going through rehabilitation or as practitioners of it.

The final section of the Companion explores the development of the evidence base for rehabilitative work in criminal justice. We hope that this brief chapter makes obvious why responding to the plethora of challenges that rehabilitation poses requires the development of a much more expansive conception of the evidence base than has hitherto been accepted. Rehabilitation is about much, much more than 'what works' in reducing reconviction rates. If reintegration matters as much as we have argued that it does, then evaluating whether and to what extent our criminal justice systems can minimize and mitigate the disintegration that punishment typically entails becomes imperative – and that requires a very careful assessment of the practices we employ for better or worse in relation to all four forms of rehabilitation, as well as a much clearer articulation of what we mean by integration and a willingness to confront what we see when we look in that evaluative mirror.

References

Andrews, D. A. and Bonta, J. (1994) *The Psychology of Criminal Conduct*. Cincinnati, OH: Anderson.

Burke, L., Collett, S. and McNeill, F. (2018) *Reimagining Rehabilitation: Beyond the Individual*. London: Routledge.

du Bois-Pedain, A. (2017) Punishment as an inclusionary practice: Sentencing in a liberal constitutional state. In A. du Bois-Pedain, M. Ulväng and P. Asp (Eds.), *Criminal Law and the Authority of the State*. Oxford: Hart, Bloomsbury.

Duff, A. (2005) Punishment and rehabilitation – or rehabilitation as punishment. *Criminal Justice Matters*, 60(1), 18–19.

Graham, H. (2016) *Rehabilitation Work: Supporting Desistance and Recovery*. London: Routledge.

Graham, H. and McNeill, F. (2017) Desistance: Envisioning futures. In P. Carlen and L. A. França (Eds.), *Alternative Criminologies*. London: Routledge, pp. 433–451.

Herzog-Evans, M. (2011) Judicial rehabilitation in France: Helping with the desisting process and acknowledging achieved desistance. *European Journal of Probation*, 3(1), 4–19.

McNeill, F. (2006) A desistance paradigm for offender management. *Criminology and Criminal Justice*, 6(1), 39–62.

McNeill, F. (2012) Four forms of 'offender' rehabilitation: Towards an interdisciplinary perspective. *Legal and Criminological Psychology*, 17(1), 18–36.

McNeill, F. (2014) Punishment as rehabilitation. In G. Bruinsma and D. Weisburd (Eds.), *Encyclopedia of Criminology and Criminal Justice*. New York: Springer Science and Business Media.

Nugent, B. and Schinkel, M. (2016) The pains of desistance. *Criminology and Criminal Justice*, 16(5), 568–584.

Polaschek, D. (2012) An appraisal of the Risk-Need-Responsivity (RNR) model of offender rehabilitation and its application in correctional treatment. *Legal and Criminological Psychology*, 17(1), 1–17.

Raynor, P. and Robinson, G. (2009) *Rehabilitation, Crime and Justice*. Houndmills: Palgrave Macmillan.

Rex, S. (1999) Desistance from offending: Experiences of probation. *Howard Journal of Criminal Justice*, 36(4), 366–383.

Schinkel, M. (2014) *Being Imprisoned: Punishment, Adaptation and Desistance*. Basingstoke: Palgrave Macmillan.

Van Zyl Smit, D. and Snacken, S. (2009) *Principles of European Prison Law and Policy*. Oxford: Oxford University Press.

Ward, T. and Maruna, S. (2007) *Rehabilitation: Beyond the Risk Paradigm*. London: Routledge.

Zedner, L. (1994) Reparation and retribution: Are they reconcilable? *The Modern Law Review*, 57, 228–250.

3

Promoting inclusion and citizenship?

Selective reflections on the recent history of the policy and practice of rehabilitation in England and Wales

Maurice Vanstone

Introduction

In what seems a valedictory piece, Burke and Collett (2016) contend that in England and Wales the neo-liberal project, Transforming Rehabilitation, has resulted in the probation service being apportioned the task of supervising and managing highly troubled and, to use the current label, high-risk people while its traditional rehabilitative role has been privatized and fragmented. Somewhat cautiously they proffer the hope that sense 'will return to the organisational delivery of rehabilitative endeavour' (p. 132).[1] Suffused with similar hope, but tempered with a realistic assessment of the recent unprecedented change in a criminal justice landscape that has been shaped by the politicization of crime, the rise of populism, the punitive ideal, and political governance, this chapter will examine the theoretical and practical anatomy of rehabilitation and the often fraught relationship between policy and practice. While respectfully heeding relevant international milestones in the evolution of rehabilitation, the primary focus of the chapter will be on some important, interesting, and, in some cases, forgotten efforts to assist the rehabilitation of those people with a history of offending in England and Wales. Where relevant, account will be taken of the influence of research findings, but because of the uncertainties surrounding the newly created privatized world of CRCs (Community Rehabilitation Companies), it begins with an examination of four (if not unremarkable certainly unoriginal) propositions: first, that identity is as problematic and complex as the individual it is ascribed to; second, that the number of causal theories of crime is only equalled by the number of attendant uncertainties; third, that invariably personal change is only partial, often indiscernible, and always slow and incremental; and finally, that rehabilitation, partly because of the preceding factors, is a contentious concept both in definition and in substance.

Identity

The word 'offender', ubiquitous in criminological writings (including, I confess, my own), consigns the individual to the role of outsider distinct from law-abiding insiders, and encourages an 'us' and 'them' construct. Referring to Shakespearean drama in a text of this kind may seem unusual, but in an interesting (in some respects contestable) attempt to unravel the criminological pedigree of Shakespeare, Wilson, an American criminologist, argues that within Shakespearean characterization the person who offends can be both a villain and a victim (2014: 99–100). Whether we need Shakespeare to tell us that is a moot point, for there are many other claimants in the literary canon; however, Wilson provides a useful reminder via Shakespeare's work that current challenges to the use of the word 'offender' are by no means new. As he explains, in contemporary popular culture 'the word "criminal" refers to an identity – a criminal is a kind of person, one who is always guilty, always caught, and always punished – but in a Shakespearean model, the word "criminal" describes an action, not identity' (Wilson 2014: 100). What seems to be stating the obvious is worth repeating not only because of the current dominance of condemnatory populism and its impact on political thought and action but also because it alludes to a fundamental problem in much of mainstream rehabilitative work on which Erving Goffman throws some penetrating light. Although aspects of his treatise on stigma (Goffman 1968), such as his focus on the stigmatized rather than those who stigmatize and a less-than-curious concern about what factors in society lead to stigmatization, have not worn well, his differentiation between what he describes as 'virtual social identity' based on assumptions and judgement made about the individual and 'actual social identity' (who the person is) still provides a useful starting point and stimulus for exploring the concept of rehabilitation. In the light of this insight, it seems reasonable to argue that thinking and writing about people as 'offenders' has contributed significantly to rehabilitative endeavour being focused on virtual social identity rather than actual identity and all its complexity, as captured by Tony Parker (1962: 15) in his description of his collaborator, Robert Allerton:

> [l]ike any other man he is a diamond of different facets which, as it turned out, alternatively catch the light [and] depend much on the observer's point of view and even more on the diamond's movements.

The aetiology of crime

Customarily, attention has been drawn more to the sparkle of the diamond than the light surrounding it. In other words, the process of rehabilitation has been premised on the idea that the individual requires changing or 'curing' with the result that the treatment or medical model has been predominant. Confirmation of this hegemony is manifest in attempts to formulate models more fitting to contemporary theory: for example, Bottoms and McWilliams's (1979) non-treatment paradigm of help, shared assessment, and collaborative effort and Raynor and Vanstone's (1994) update adjusting for harm reduction, criminogenic need, and effectiveness. While it is arguable that these models influenced practice, the medical model lives on, if only symbolically, in the organizational description of some staff as *treatment managers*. Demonstrably, the resilience of the notion of the treatable 'offender' is remarkable when juxtaposed to an age-old recognition of the impact of social and economic deprivation on criminal behaviour: for example, in an assertion that could have referred to the financial crisis of 2008 and its consequences, the 14th-century philosopher Nicholas of Oresme (1956: 34) identified one source of deprivation, alienation, and exclusion:

> money-changers, bankers and dealers in bullion . . . take a great part of the profit or gain arising from changes in coinage and by guile or good luck, draw wealth from them [but] others, who are the best sections of the community, are impoverished by it.[2]

Moreover, in Shakespeare's plays crime itself is deemed to be 'a complex web of competing assumptions, motives, and commitments; as the unfortunate outcome of too many people competing for too few resources' (Wilson 2014: 99–100). Several centuries later such sentiments found an echo when Charles Darrow (1919), in his address to men in Chicago prison, argued that crime can be eliminated by making society fairer and abolishing prison. So, modern theorizing about what contributes to offending and its cessation is not new (Farrall 2002; Laub and Sampson 2001): the point here is not to score points or place explanations of crime in one basket or another, but rather to stress how the contested nature of causality sets traps for anyone engaged in rehabilitative work.

Change

A cynical perspective might lead to the conclusion that the persistence of the treatment model is attributable to the assumption that changing the individual is easier than changing the environment. Alluring though that explanation might be, it fails to take into account the part played by theories, moral assumptions, and religious and cultural discourse, and it underestimates the challenge of changing the individual. Where it *is* appropriate (and a pluralistic approach to rehabilitation underlies this chapter), engaging people in a process of change – whether this is about acquiring new skills, developing different problem-solving and thinking strategies, or resolving feelings – should be informed by a realistic assessment of what is being asked of them. In this respect, the 'us' and 'them' construct plays a part because it discourages self-reflection by 'us', self-reflection that might threaten the authenticity of our own personal experience of change, and raise questions about why, how, and if we have changed. Unpalatable though they may be, the answers are likely to reveal that change for 'us' is slow, often imperceptible, difficult to explain, and incremental, and that 'we' spend more time resisting change, clinging to the 'stable state' (Schon 1973), and honing the art of cognitive dissonance, only actually changing when it suits. Why, therefore, should it be different for 'them'? Further layers are added to this argument by Prochaska and DiClemente's (1986) five-stage model of change and by Phillips's (2017: 101–102) recent assertion that the change associated with desistance from crime 'involves multiple becomings [and is] a non-linear and non-ending process'.

Rehabilitation

Currently, the idea of rehabilitation hangs by a fragile humanistic thread over a largely unchallenged prison system and a criminal justice system saturated, even in its community sentencing functions, by the philosophy of punishment and retribution (Garland 2001; Young 1999). As if such fragility is not enough, it is burdened with moral assumptions about normality, acceptability, deviance, and what is best for people, is unclear in definition, and has a perennial association with the imposition of power and discipline. Nowhere is this more apparent than in the development of the penitentiary and the inauguration of institutions designed to reform young people in the 19th century. To take one example, the French opened Mettray as an agricultural colony in 1840, basing it on the theory that reform might accrue from contact with nature and decontamination from the effects of the city. White (1994), in his biography of the writer Jean Genet, states that the reforming ideal had all but disappeared by the time Genet arrived in Mettray in the 1920s but, according to Foucault (1977) that ideal was tarnished from the beginning as discipline had always underpinned the regime. Indeed, Foucault heralds the opening of Mettray as the moment the carceral system was completed because it constituted the 'model in which are concentrated all the coercive technologies of behaviour' (p. 293) and ushered in a new form of 'supervision – both knowledge and power – over individuals who resisted disciplinary normalization' (p. 296). Provocatively, perhaps, Foucault argues that the 'carceral archipelago' spread beyond the prison to 'all the disciplinary mechanisms that function throughout society' (p. 298). Even though his argument displays some of the flaws of macro-theorizing – at the micro level of practice and human interaction the picture is invariably more complex and varied – it is difficult to rebut the view that, in England and Wales at least, the development of probation work was bound up with state control and power (Vanstone 2004; Young 1976).

Definition is problematical and contentious too. Raynor and Robinson (2005), referring firstly to the OED definition of rehabilitation as 'the action of restoring something to a previous (proper) condition or status', identify three criminological definitions or models: first, effecting positive change in individuals, and associated with the orthodox treatment model; second, reintegration into the community, associated with restoration, social inclusion, and resettlement with an emphasis on social and economic causes of crime; and third, deletion of criminal records as in the Rehabilitation of Offenders Act 1974, and associated with the restoration of citizenship (and in Goffman's terms, the transformation of virtual social identity). Crow (2001: 5), on the other hand, describes rehabilitation as 'any form of intervention that is designed to alter the way that offenders think, feel or behave [while] involving the active participation of all parties'. Helpful though these definitions are, the waters are muddied by doubts about ideas of reintegration or restoration that depend for their legitimacy on the pre-eminence of 'virtual social identity'. It is as if the task of professional helpers is to convert people from virtual to actual identity when on the ground the communities within which people on probation, on community payback schemes, or on post-release licence live, or return to, usually (unless the exceptional nature of the offence determines otherwise) respond to actual identity, and so displacement or severance cannot be assumed (Foster 1990). Accepting also that natural processes lead people out of crime as they develop social bonds through employment, family relationships, educational advancement, in how they perceive themselves and others, rehabilitation can be seen as a process incorporating these complexities. This chapter, therefore, settles on a collaborative model of rehabilitation focused on social and contextual issues as well as on the individual in terms of their social capital, well-being, maturation, and self-image (Farrall 2002; Farrall and Calverley 2006; Maruna 2001; McNeill 2006; Ward and Brown 2004).

Illustrations from history

It is not within the ambit of this chapter to detail the search for rehabilitative effectiveness,[3] but the need for context demands a summary. Pinpointing a specific starting point for this search is difficult: it could be argued that an interest in effectiveness has always been embedded haphazardly in the unfettered inquisitiveness of practitioners about how to guide people away from criminal solutions to their problems. However, the largely but not totally negative findings of IMPACT in the United Kingdom (Folkard et al. 1976) and the 'nothing works' moment in America (Martinson 1974) begin most accounts, followed by rehabilitation's gradual redemption; first through the Reasoning and Rehabilitation work of Ross and his colleagues in Canada (Ross et al. 1988), then in the STOP experiment that it inspired (Raynor and Vanstone 1997), in the development of pro-social modelling in Australia (Trotter 1993), and in the rediscovery of the vital role played by the skilled, committed, and empathic practitioner in effective rehabilitative effort and practice (Farrall 2002; Raynor et al. 2014). As for the practice of rehabilitation itself, there is extensive coverage in the literature, so this chapter will be confined to some reminders of innovative, promising work and projects, some of which have been thrown on a bonfire of political vanities during a period of unprecedented transformation.

Unsurprisingly, the individual has been the focus of mainstream rehabilitative work in the latter part of the 20th century, but such work has been influenced by the concept of non-treatment and collaborative change effort referred to above. Of course, this does not render rehabilitative work immune to the criticism of some commentators who argue that it has perpetuated the idea of looking to the individual rather than external factors for the causes of crime. Any attempt to trace the lineage of rehabilitative work in England and Wales demands reference to the influence of pioneering work and research particularly in Canada and America. For example, the social skills and problem-solving approach (Priestley et al. 1978) built on the ideas in the Saskatchewan Newstart Life Skills Coaching Manual and the STOP programme in Mid Glamorgan (Raynor and Vanstone 1997) was an adaption of the Canadian Reasoning and Rehabilitation programme (Ross et al. 1988). Moreover, the Risk-Need-Responsivity model has been highly influential (Andrews et al. 1990) both theoretically and practically.[4] What developments in the United Kingdom also those elsewhere was that theyere harnessed to the need and desire to discover effective practice, and that was not solely the result of international influence. The experimental status of the Day Training Centres placed demands on staff to justify their existence (Vanstone 1993), and although the increase in governance exemplified by the publication of the Statement of National Objectives and Priorities (Home Office 1984) is often justifiably cast in a pejorative light, the subsequent scrutiny of the work of policy and practice heightened awareness of accountability and increased motivation to be effective. Certainly, the curiosity and experimental inclinations of both practitioners and managers is evidenced in research frameworks built around early work with men convicted of sexual crime (Shaw and Crook 1977; Weaver and Fox 1984), offending behaviour groups (Linscott and Crossland 1989), alcohol dependence intervention (Singer 1991), the Geese Theatre Group in Hereford and Worcester (Hereford and Worcester Probation Service 1989), and psychodrama in the Afan Alternative (Raynor 1988).

Pioneering though much of the above work was, a focus on the individual as a target of change is, as Barkley and Collett (2000: 235) have made clear, 'counter-productive if probation and other service providers cannot respond to the more general needs of offenders'. Admittedly, intervention in the environment of probationers has always been a fringe activity, nevertheless it too has been driven by enthusiasm and ingenuity, and has embraced actions aimed at addressing discrimination and socio-economic problems; for example, the community-based work in Bristol that followed unrest in the early 1980s (Lawson 1984) and the Llamau Housing Project in South Glamorgan (Drakeford and Vanstone 1996). However, engagement in such work was not always straightforward, nor was it necessarily greeted with enthusiasm within the Service. Green (1987) relates the cautionary tale of how the City and Handsworth Alternative Scheme, which arose out of concern within the Service about the number of people from minority ethnic groups going to prison, was hampered by the reluctance of probation officers to make referrals with the result that the organizers placed their own worker in the courts. That said, the emergence of Inner London's Black Group Initiative, which among other things aimed to 'help black clients develop their potential and consider a more constructive and empowerment lifestyle', suggests that some did listen to Green's plea for a different response from the Service (Jenkins and Lawrence 1993: 83). This is also true of the Greater Manchester Area whose Black Offender Groupwork Programme shifted emphasis to the social environments in which minority ethnic people lived. Although in his description of the programme Williams (2006: 149) offers the caveat that there is 'little the probation service can do to change the social environments within which offenders live', he accentuates that it can empower and increase opportunities. Designed to do exactly that, the programme, which was run by black tutors and supplemented by black community-based mentors, focused on analyzing racism and its impact, exploring the historical context of black people's lives, enhancing self-perception, and developing survival strategies. It closed in 2004 following the restructuring of the Home Office research programme. With an eye on accelerating political interference, Lewis (2009) voiced concern that the creation of NOMS and the resultant fragmentation would have an adverse effect on both the traditional culture of the probation service and its ability to deal with the problems of minority ethnic people. Unfortunately, that concern seems justified because, as Williams and Durrance (2018: 382) confirm, while in 2001 there were four specific programmes for minority ethnic people, now there are none. They attribute this to 'the ascendency of risk [transcending] the previously held ideals and assumptions of the NPS (and CRCs)' thereby diminishing the manoeuvrability of practitioners to address the problems of ethnic minority people. Awareness of risk is, of course, important, but, as they imply, the first casualty of that ascendency is the risk-taking that is necessary for innovation and experimentation to flourish.

On reflection, initiatives to address the particular needs of women perhaps stimulated some of the most imaginative practice in the probation service's recent history, but seem to have suffered the same fate. In London, the Women's Probation Centre, a response to the uniqueness of the needs of women who offend, delivered a programme not only designed to address offending but also to concentrate on personal development, health, fitness, and addiction, while attempting to widen opportunity in relation to employment, training, and education (Durrance and Ablitt 2001). Evaluation of the programme highlighted the holistic approach and empowerment as significant factors in the positive impact it had on those women who completed the programme. West Mercia (formerly Hereford and Worcester) generated another women-centred programme that was designed by looking through the 'women's window' rather than trying to extract content from existing programmes designed for men (Roberts 2002). The model of change adopted was based on the view that offending was the outcome of inability to manage external demands, limited resources and opportunities, and functioning impaired by disadvantage. It included raising awareness about how external demands are constructed, developing strategies to meet them, enhancing self-esteem, problem-solving skills, and ability to access resources. Organizers eschewed the treatment model in favour of the empowerment of normal, capable people: moreover, in a nod to systems intervention, attempts were made to influence the attitudes of relevant agencies.[5]

Although examples are not so easily found, the Service has also tried to ameliorate the problem of poverty and its attendant problems by appointing fuel debt workers (Ward 1979) and developing the welfare benefits expertise of staff (Broadbent 1989). Concern with the same problems stimulated the setting up of the New Careers project in Bristol in 1973. An enterprising example of reintegration, it was inspired by federal government–sponsored social and community projects in America that addressed problems of poverty through improved services and professional training and job opportunities in America. It offered a combination of probation supervision, hostel accommodation, and training for a career in social work (Caddick 1994; Priestley 1975).[6]

Conclusion

In concluding it would be remiss not to mention probation-related efforts to help prisoners during and after their sentence. Ryan and Sim (2007: 710) remind us that successful programmes such as those in the Barlinnie Special Unit and Grendon Underwood 'have been mercilessly attacked, closed down or remain on the periphery of the prison estate, constructed as idealistic "experiments" while prisons get on with the "real" business of punishing offenders'. Grendon, which opened in 1962, provides an enduringly vibrant example of empowerment through the use of the therapeutic community model in which the therapeutic role is shared among all members of the group who have joint involvement in decision-making and feedback. More recently, the Resettlement Pathfinders piloted the For a Change programme that prepared prisoners for release by attempting to increase motivation to resolve resettlement problems (Clancy et al. 2006).

Despite the recent 'revelation' that the practitioners most likely to be effective are empathic, skilled communicators and helpers, the first robot officer may already be on the production line in some secret Home Office factory![7] Meanwhile, the desire to assist the rehabilitation of people who offend still survives in the minds of some politicians and in the commitment and values of some managers and practitioners in what is left of the newly established CRCs and the National Probation Service (NPS). That is not the problem; rather, it is the capacity to support the delivery of such effort that has been brought into doubt. In reflecting on the current state of rehabilitation it is important not to replicate the ideological rigidity displayed in the political decision-making that has led to the current position: the CRCs and the truncated probation service may be able to provide the services that people need to re-order their lives and avoid further offending. However, a situation in which a much-reduced state sector organization is too weighed down by the needs of risk management and public protection to take on experimentation, and private companies governed by market are pressured to turn to the rehabilitative equivalent of the local take-away, does not augur well for the future. CRCs may yet confound the pessimistic tone of this chapter, but it is hard to resist the view that the privatization of the probation service was just another act in the government's ideological agenda to further reduce the public sector, and that the failure to bolster a humanitarian, socially conscious, vocationally based probation service committed to accountable and evidence-based rehabilitative endeavour will be a matter for great regret in future years. To many of us (and now, perhaps, some members of the government), it already is.

Notes

1 At the time of reviewing the final draft of this chapter sense may well have prevailed because the Secretary of State for Justice, David Gauke, has announced the government's

intention to re-nationalise the probation service. What shape the new service will take is, however, still a matter for speculation.
2   I am indebted to Professor John Drakakis for drawing my attention to the work of Nicholas of Oresme.
3   For a typically forensic analysis see Raynor (2018).
4   Arguably less influential but nevertheless important is the Good Lives Model (Ward and Brown 2004).
5   For another interesting example see the Women in Focus project in Scotland involving mentoring support services in partnership with Barnardo's (Malloch et al. 2014).
6   I worked with New Careerists in Gloucester in the early 1970s and was witness to the unique and valuable contribution they made.
7   For a sensible use of technology, see McGreavy (2017).

References

Andrews, D. A., Bonta, J. and Hoge, R. E. (1990) Classification for effective rehabilitation. *Criminal Justice and Behaviour*, 17(1), 19–51.

Barkley, D. and Collett, S. (2000) Back to the future: Housing and support for offenders. *Probation Journal*, 47(4), 235–242.

Bottoms, A. E. and McWilliams, W. (1979) A non-treatment paradigm for probation practice. *British Journal of Social Work*, 9(2), 159–202.

Broadbent, A. (1989) Poor clients: What can I do? *Probation Journal*, 36(4), 151–154.

Burke, L. and Collett, S. (2016) Transforming Rehabilitation: Organisational bifurcation and the end of probation as we know it? *Probation Journal*, 63(2), 120–135.

Caddick, B. (1994) The "new careers" experiment in rehabilitating offenders: Last messages from a fading star. *British Journal of Social Work*, 24(4), 449–460.

Clancy, A., Hudson, K., Maguire, M., Peake, R., Raynor, P., Vanstone, M. and Kynch, J. (2006) *Getting Out and Staying Out: Results of the Prisoner Resettlement Pathfinders. Researching Criminal Justice Series*. Bristol: Policy Press.

Crow, I. (2001) *The Treatment and Rehabilitation of Offenders*. London: Sage Publications.

Darrow, C. (1919) *Address to the Prisoners in the Chicago Jail*. Chicago: Charles Kerr.

Drakeford, M. and Vanstone, M. (Eds.). (1996) *Beyond Offending Behaviour*. Aldershot: Arena.

Durrance, P. and Ablitt, F. (2001) "Creative solutions" to women's offending: An evaluation of the women's probation centre. *Probation Journal*, 48(4), 247–259.

Farrall, S. (2002) *Rethinking What Works with Offenders*. Cullompton: Willan Publishing.

Farrall, S. and Calverley, A. (2006) *Understanding Desistance from Crime. Theoretical Directions in Resettlement and Rehabilitation*. Maidenhead: Open University Press.

Folkard, M. S., Smith, D. E. and Smith, D. D. (1976) *IMPACT Volume 11: The Results of the Experiment*. Home Office Research Study 36. London: HMSO.

Foster, J. (1990) *Villains: Crime and Community in the Inner City*. London: Routledge.

Foucault, M. (1977) *Discipline and Punish: The Birth of the Prison*. Harmondsworth: Penguin Books.

Garland, D. (2001) *The Culture of Control*. Oxford: Oxford University Press.

Goffman, E. (1968) *Stigma: Notes on the Management of Spoiled Identity*. Harmondsworth: Penguin Books.

Green, R. (1987) Racism and the offender: A probation response. In J. Harding (Ed.), *Probation and the Community Response: A Practice and Policy Reader*. London: Tavistock Publications.

Hereford and Worcester Probation Service. (1989) *Programme for Achievement and Challenge*. Worcester: Hereford and Worcester Probation Service.

Home Office. (1984) *Statement of National Objectives and Priorities*. London: Home Office.

Jenkins, J. and Lawrence, D. (1993) Inner London's black group initiative. *Probation Journal*, 40(2), 82–84.

Laub, J. H. and Sampson, R. J. (2001) Understanding desistance from crime. In M. Tonry (Ed.), *Crime and Justice: A Review of Research*, Vol. 28. Chicago: University of Chicago Press.

Lawson, J. (1984) Probation in St. Pauls. Teamwork in a multi-racial, inner city area. *Probation Journal*, 31(3), 93–95.

Lewis, S. (2009) The probation service and race equality. In H. Singh Bhui (Ed.), *Race and Criminal Justice*. London: Sage Publications.

Linscott, C. J. and Crossland, R. S. (1989) *Offending Behaviour Group Programme*. Exeter: Devon Probation Service.

Malloch, M., McIvor, G. and Burgess, C. (2014) 'Holistic' community punishment and criminal justice interventions for women. *Howard Journal of Criminal Justice*, 53(4), 395–410.

Maruna, S. (2001) *Making Good: How Ex-Convicts Reform and Rebuild Their Lives*. Washington, DC: American Psychological Association.

Martinson, R. (1974) What works? Questions and answers about prison reform. *The Public Interest*, 35, 22–54.

McGreavy, G. (2017) "Changing lives" using technology to promote desistance. *Probation Journal*, 64(3), 276–281.

McNeill, F. (2006) A desistance paradigm for offender management. *Criminology and Criminal Justice*, 6(1), 39–63.

Oresme, N. (1956) *The De Moneta of Nicholas Oresme and English Mint Documents*. Translated from the Latin with Introduction and Notes by Charles Johnson. London: Thomas Nelson & Sons Ltd.

Parker, T. (1962) *The Courage of His Convictions*. New York: W. W. Norton & Company.

Phillips, J. (2017) Towards a rhizomatic understanding of the desistance journey. *Howard Journal of Criminal Justice*, 56(1), 92–104.

Priestley, P. (1975) New careers: Power sharing in social work. In H. Jones (Ed.), *Towards a New Social Work*. London: Routledge & Kegan Paul.

Priestley, P., McGuire, J., Flegg, D., Hemsley, V. and Welham, D. (1978) *Social Skills and Personal Problem Solving: A Handbook of Methods*. London: Tavistock.

Prochaska, J. O. and DiClemente, C. C. (1986) Towards a comprehensive model of change. In W. R. Miller and N. Heather (Eds.), *Treating Addictive Behaviors: Processes of Change*. New York: Plenum Press.

Raynor, P. (1988) *Probation as an Alternative to Custody*. Aldershot: Avebury.

Raynor, P. (2018) The search for impact in British probation: From programmes to skills and implementation. In P. Ugwudike, P. Raynor and J. Annison (Eds.), *Evidence-Based Skills in Criminal Justice: International Research on Supporting Rehabilitation and Desistance*. Bristol: Policy Press.

Raynor, P. and Robinson, G. (2005) *Rehabilitation, Crime and Justice*. Basingstoke: Palgrave Macmillan.

Raynor, P., Ugwudike, P. and Vanstone, M. (2014) The impact of skills in probation work: A reconviction study. *Criminology and Criminal Justice*, 14(2), 235–249.

Raynor, P. and Vanstone, M. (1994) Probation practice, effectiveness and the non-treatment paradigm. *British Journal of Social Work*, 24(4), 387–404.

Raynor, P. and Vanstone, M. (1997) *Straight Thinking on Probation (STOP): The Mid-Glamorgan Experiment*. Probation Studies Unit. Oxford: Oxford University Press.

Roberts, J. (2002) Women-centred: The West Mercia community-based programme for women offenders. In P. Carlen (Ed.), *Women and Punishment: The Struggle for Justice*. Collumpton: Willan Publishing.

Ross, R. R., Fabiano, E. A. and Elwes, C. D. (1988) Reasoning and rehabilitation. *International Journal of Offender Therapy and Comparative Criminology*, 32(1), 29–35.

Ryan, M. and Sim, J. (2007) Campaigning for and campaigning against prisons: Excavating and reaffirming the case for prison abolition. In Y. Jewkes (Ed.), *Handbook of Prisons*. Cullompton: Willan Publishing.

Schon, D. A. (1973) *Beyond the Stable State*. New York: W. W. Norton & Company.

Shaw, R. and Crook, H. (1977) Group techniques. *Probation*, 24(2), 61–65.

Singer, L. R. (1991) A non-punitive paradigm for probation practice: Some sobering thoughts. *British Journal of Social Work*, 21, 611–626.

Trotter, C. (1993) *The Supervision of Offenders – What Works? A Study Undertaken in Community-Based Corrections*. Victoria, Melbourne: Social Work Department, Monash University, and the Victoria Department of Justice.

Vanstone, M. (1993) A missed opportunity re-assessed: The influence of the day training centre experiment on the criminal justice system and probation practice. *British Journal of Social Work*, 23(1), 213–229.

Vanstone, M. (2004) *Supervising Offenders in the Community: A History of Probation Theory and Practice*. Aldershot: Ashgate.

Ward, K. (1979) Fuel debts and the probation service. *Probation Journal*, 26(4), 110–114.

Ward, T. and Brown, M. (2004) The good lives model and conceptual issues in offender rehabilitation. *Psychology, Crime and Law*, 10(3), 243–257.

Weaver, C. and Fox, C. (1984) Berkeley sex offenders group: A seven year evaluation. *Probation Journal*, 31(4), 143–146.

White, E. (1994) *Genet: A Biography*. New York: Vintage Books.

Williams, P. (2006) Designing and delivering programmes for minority ethnic offenders. In S. Lewis, P. Raynor, D. Smith and A. Wardak (Eds.), *Race and Probation*. Cullompton: Willan Publishing.

Williams, P. and Durrance, P. (2018) Resisting effective approaches for BAME offenders in England and Wales: The triumph of inertia. In P. Ugwudike, P. Raynor and J. Annison (Eds.), *Evidence-Based Skills in Criminal Justice: International Research on Supporting Rehabilitation and Desistance*. Bristol: Policy Press.

Wilson, J. R. (2014) Shakespeare and criminology. *Crime, Media and Culture*, 10(2), 97–114.

Young, J. (1999) *The Exclusive Society*. London: Sage Publications.

Young, P. (1976) A sociological analysis of the early history of probation. *British Journal of Law and Society*, 3(1), 44–58.

4 Should there be a right to rehabilitation?

Rob Canton

Human rights

Human rights are those rights that we have in virtue of our humanity. They represent a particular set of fundamental interests that set them apart from other rights (Clapham 2007). They do not have to be earned and they do not depend on people's acceptance of their responsibilities, which is not to deny that we have such obligations towards one another. There is a need for a special and compelling justification for these rights to be forfeit and some may never be forfeit at all. Griffin grounds human rights in 'the values of personhood' (Griffin 2008: 34). To be a person is to be a responsible moral agent and this entails rights of:

- Autonomy (to decide on one's pathways and projects for oneself)
- Choice (and genuine choice requires adequate information)
- Ability to act (which requires a minimum provision of resources and capabilities)
- Liberty (against anyone blocking this) (Griffin 2008)

Some have found the idea of such rights to be obscure. Rights, it could be thought, imply a 'right-giver' and while the law may bestow (or refuse to or take away) rights, the idea of human or natural rights was notoriously dismissed by Bentham as 'nonsense on stilts'. Yet we need an ethical basis from which to challenge and criticize government. Indeed, the growth of international instruments, like the United Nations Universal Declaration of Human Rights or the European Convention on Human Rights, begins with a recognition that states can be over-mighty and intrusive, as well as self-serving and negligent of their duties towards their citizens. The matter of the rights that we have remains open, indeterminate, and inherently contested. But these are first and foremost moral questions that cannot be resolved by scrutiny of any legal code or by judicial interpretation of the law. Rights can be established in law and are deployed in political and institutional arrangements, but their foundation is ethical (Nagel 1995; Sen 2009).

A good way to understand rights is to regard them not as 'things', but as imperatives – 'strong ethical pronouncements as to what *should* be done' (Sen 2009: 357, emphasis in original). So understood, rights are no more (or less) obscure or contestable than any other moral imperative. While human rights do not exhaust the field of ethics, a great many moral concerns can be expressed in this way. Sen (2009) also argues that while it may be beyond most of us to frame an adequate theory of justice, we all think we can recognize an *injustice* when we see one. Appeal to rights is often a powerful and politically resonant way of articulating demands and protests against injustice. The injustice that is being done to them, you, or us is declared to be a special case of a violation of a more general entitlement – a right.

Historically, rights have been invoked to take a stand against cruelty and injustice, to remind governments of their limits, that ends may not be assumed to justify means, that individuals and minorities may not simply be disregarded in the relentless pursuit of any conception of the general welfare. But they have also been asserted to articulate claims about the social and economic conditions that governments should develop in order that people may thrive and prosper. These are positive obligations of the state. The United Nations Universal Declaration of Human Rights accordingly begins by setting out articles that prohibit oppression and cruelty, but then goes on to affirm claims for human flourishing – a structure mirrored by the European Convention.

Conor Gearty writes of these two dimensions to human rights: one, a rejection of oppression and insistence on 'the moral wrongness of cruelty and humiliation'; the other, a commitment to human flourishing (2006: 140). This corresponds to a philosophical distinction between *liberties* and *claims*. As governments pursue the general welfare, liberty rights may challenge and sometimes constrain their projects. Proclaimed liberty rights include a right to life (not to be killed); a right not to be tortured or subjected to inhuman and degrading treatment and punishment; a right not to be enslaved. These are liberties that the state may not take away. And this is a moral 'may not' because in practice and in law they can indeed be vulnerable.

For people to have real chances to pursue their interests and projects, however, calls not only for forbearance from interference by others, but also for propitious circumstances and meaningful opportunities. This imposes positive obligations (Mowbray 2004). Claims asserting these obligations may include: the right to education, the right to social security, the right to an adequate standard of living, the right to employment and to fair remuneration. For these rights to be respected, it will not be enough for the state to refrain from intrusion; rather it must take positive action to give them effect. Rights can conflict and how such tensions are to be resolved is the very stuff of politics. Some liberties may have to be restrained in order to safeguard others. Again, since the resources of the state are finite, not all claims can be readily met and there is always political debate about priority. Liberties and claims too may be in conflict: for example, in relation to taxation, it can be argued that the state should respect the liberty of citizens to dispose of their resources as they choose, yet the state needs sufficient revenue to meet its positive obligations.

Human rights is an international discourse. Among the reasons why this is politically so important is that rights – both claims and liberties – are commonly invoked against the state. The governments of democratic states will argue that their policies are designed to advance the common good. Yet Dworkin described rights as trump cards that may be played successfully against other considerations like the collective welfare (Dworkin 1984), while Nozick asserted: 'Individuals have rights, and there are things that no person or group may do to them (without violating their rights)' (1974: ix). In those circumstances where a government's judgement about the common good is in conflict with an affirmation of rights, it can be very difficult for the state to be an even-handed judge in its own cause. The discipline of international agreements and accountability to other nations whose fundamental values are held in common can be an essential corrective and safeguard against abuses. When international courts like the European Court of Human Rights uphold the complaints of individuals against their state, politicians sometimes react defensively. This is understandable, perhaps, but these judgements should rather be welcomed as an opportunity for the government to learn and to do (morally) better in future.

Rights and criminal justice

Human rights have an especial salience in the area of criminal justice. When people are reduced to the status of 'offender' or 'prisoner', human rights stand as a reminder of their essential humanity. They also have considerable potential to oppose the unfair discrimination which so often mars criminal justice processes (Canton 2017) since, as we have seen, they depend on nothing other than being a person and cannot be compromised on the grounds of race, gender, sexuality, (dis)ability, age, or any other dimension of difference.

The powers of the state are at their most stark when the criminal law is being enforced. Enforcement commonly involves arrest, detention, and punishment and is consequently at risk of trespassing upon the most fundamental human rights. It is for this reason that international conventions typically include several articles that bear upon these practices. Rights to life and protection from torture and cruelty are usually the very first to be asserted in a declaration and it is in the processes of law enforcement that these are most vulnerable. Procedural rights are therefore affirmed: for example, rights when someone is arrested and/or under investigation, the presumption of innocence, the right to a fair trial. Rights regulating punishment are especially important. Punishment usually involves 'hard treatment' – some form of hardship, imposition, restriction, or deprivation. Here, the withdrawal or compromising of rights is not a regrettable side effect of policy, but is deliberate: it *constitutes* the punishment. Foucault at one point defines punishment as 'an economy of suspended rights' (Foucault 1977: 11), while in a very different philosophical tradition, Rawls includes being 'deprived of some of the normal rights of a citizen' as part of his formal definition of punishment (Rawls 1967: 150). How is this to be managed in a principled manner?

Respect for rights requires a more precise account of which rights are intentionally forfeit as (all or part of) the punishment and which ought to be retained and protected. Important attempts have been made to specify these limits, but while the law may be clarified, the moral entitlements are still contested. One telling example concerns the rights of serving prisoners. The principle of Raymond v. Honey is that 'under English law, a convicted prisoner, in spite of his imprisonment, retains all civil rights which are not taken away expressly or by necessary implication' (quoted van Zyl Smit 2007: 569). Yet in some respects the idea of necessary implication cannot resolve disputes, since it is precisely the question of which implications are necessary that is at issue. For example, is losing the right to vote a necessary implication of imprisonment? While the law may be clarified and perhaps improved, this remains at root a moral question: whether or not prisoners *ought* to have the vote is not a matter that can be resolved by reference to the law. Even if the law is clear, it may be morally exceptionable and liable to challenge (European Court of Human Rights 2005).

Having considered what might be understood by human rights and noted their singular importance in criminal justice and punishment, we turn next to rights and rehabilitation.

A rights-based critique of rehabilitation

In contrast to responses to crime that emphasize punitive hard treatment, at first sight rehabilitation looks like a promising way of protecting and enhancing human rights. Proponents of rehabilitation, after all, have typically presented their projects as decent and humane, reflecting a recognition of the adverse personal and social circumstances that have marked the lives of so many offenders, which may be associated with their offending behaviour and which often frustrate their efforts at desistance. Opposition to rehabilitation from those who favour stern punishment may take the form of dismissing such adversity as mere excuse, pointing to the many people whose lives have been quite as troubled but who nevertheless have not been convicted of crimes.

Yet the emergence of the justice model in the final quarter of the 20th century was based on a very different kind of critique. Rehabilitation that involved 'enforced therapy' imperilled the 'right to be different' (Kittrie 1971). Founded on an untenable understanding of crime as disease (Flew 1973), 'the medical model' was accused of offending against justice by urging interventions of a nature and duration that would be determined by 'treatment' needs rather than by desert and would therefore be likely to be disproportionate (von Hirsch 1976). It was said to collude with social injustice by interpreting as mere personal weakness criminal behaviour which was strongly associated with structural injustices (American Friends Service Committee 1971; Bean 1976).

At an earlier time, C. S. Lewis powerfully objected that 'the humanitarian theory of punishment' countenances dabbling with the mind in ways which violate personal autonomy (Lewis 1949). Arguing that it is *desert* that links justice and punishment, Lewis protested:

> when we cease to consider what the criminal deserves and consider only what will cure him or deter others, we have tacitly removed him from the sphere of justice altogether; instead of a person, *a subject of rights*, we now have a mere object, a patient, a 'case'.
>
> (Lewis 1949: 7, emphasis added)

The reference to 'a mere object' anticipates the argument of Peter Strawson (Strawson 1960). Holding people accountable for what they do, entailing such responses as resentment, blame, gratitude, forgiveness, and anger – the 'reactive attitudes' – is part of the very fabric of human exchange and reciprocity. We may sometimes adopt 'an objective attitude' – perhaps when people did not know what they were doing or in some sense could not help themselves – but this is exceptional: this is not and could not be sustained as the usual basis on which people relate to each other. Developing Strawson's argument, Christopher Bennett (2008) argues that to fail to censure people who have violated the norms of society, as set out in the criminal law, would be to fail to accord them respect as persons. Respect for moral agency requires punishment because and just to the extent that it is deserved. The personhood on which Griffin (2008) insists (see above) entails *a right to be punished* which is compromised and perhaps violated by rehabilitation.

While the language of rights is not always used, rights – prominently liberty rights – are immanent in these critiques. There are ways in which people may not be treated, because it violates their rights and inherent dignity, and rehabilitation threatens those rights. While expressing his own misgivings about some approaches to rehabilitation, however, Bennett (2010) rightly insists that rehabilitative interventions can take many forms and sets out some criteria by which their ethical propriety might be appraised. These include the objectives of rehabilitation, the reasons for attempting to influence people, the means by which this is to be achieved, whether rehabilitation is offered or required and whether rehabilitation is meant to replace or to accompany due retributive punishment.

Trying to change people's attitudes and behaviour for the sake of a wider public good – alone and without regard to the individual's own interests and participation in this process – is morally questionable. Deceitful, manipulative or excessively intrusive techniques will also fail to satisfy Bennett's criteria. Consent is an especially difficult matter. Few if any criminal justice responses to crime are optional, as it were, and imprisonment (notably) is not usually ruled out for that reason. Sometimes critics of rehabilitation come close to supposing that offenders have a settled commitment to different values with which the state has no right to interfere – as if they have a course of behaviour to which they are committed and which it would be a violation of their integrity to try to change. But (almost all) offenders are not 'moral strangers' (Ward and Maruna 2007: 125): their aspirations are most often for the same human goods as others', though the means they choose are often wrong. Working with offenders typically involves helping them to develop legitimate means of achievement, rather than oppressive attempts to interfere with their value commitments. Their motivation to change is often variable, as all practitioners know. However this may be, whether or not formal consent is expressed in court (which is required in some countries, though not in others), practitioners should and very often do attempt to secure the individual's understanding of and cooperation with any treatment endeavour (Canton 2014).

Bennett's attempt to set out the ethical parameters of principled rehabilitation could be the basis of a reply to the rights-based critique. Perhaps we should go further and argue that there is a right to rehabilitation. It is to this that discussion now turns.

Rights to rehabilitation?

A powerful case for a right to rehabilitation was mounted by Edgardo Rotman (1986). Rotman was well aware of the hazards of the misapplication of a medical or treatment model. He argues, however, that a right to rehabilitation can be inferred from US Constitutional principles as well as from international conventions and from a great deal of case law. Much of his account discusses prison conditions and he argues that unless prisons can provide a decent and humane rehabilitative environment, marked by educational and socialization opportunities as well as 'treatment', there must be a compelling presumption against imprisonment. Rotman also discusses the idea of rehabilitative effectiveness, arguing that rehabilitation should be regarded both as a right of the individual and as a governmental interest (in terms of reducing offending). Yet while the right does not depend upon effectiveness, dealing with people in ways that demonstrate respect for their rights and interests is a precondition of legitimacy and there is a great deal of evidence that compliance is improved and effectiveness enhanced by working in this way (Ugwudike and Raynor 2013; Tankebe and Liebling 2013). So, an emphasis on rights and on ethical practice may turn out to be effective – indeed perhaps more effective than approaches that are preoccupied with effectiveness and then stumble over rights as impediments to their achievement (Canton 2013).

Like Rotman, Fergus McNeill (2012) avoids reducing rehabilitation to 'treatment' and calls for other and wider understandings of what rehabilitation should involve. Setting out 'four forms' of rehabilitation, in addition to the sorts of psychological rehabilitation implied in treatment, McNeill distinguishes legal, social, and moral rehabilitation. These are conceptually separate, although related to one another in interesting ways. Legal rehabilitation restores the individual to their civil rights once a punishment has been served. (The *Rehabilitation of Offenders Act* bears this sense of the word, setting out individuals' rights in relation to their record of past offending. These rights in no way depend on any personal reform, other than refraining from further offending.) Social and moral rehabilitation are distinct again. These relate to an individual's opportunities to have fair access to the resources available to others – one definition of social inclusion – and a chance to earn redemption, perhaps through reparation, and of gaining reacceptance into the community whose values were violated by the offence. There is very much more to be said about these forms of rehabilitation, but the points to emphasize here are, first, that none of them is vulnerable to what we have been calling the rights-based critique of rehabilitation; second, that, far from being incompatible with desert-based punishment, they are required by it; and, third, they require active measures by the state, not merely forbearance. They involve, in other words, *claims* as well as *liberties*.

Nigel Walker (1991) drew attention to what he called the 'incidental' impacts of many punishments. By this he meant those aspects of the punishment that are not intrinsic and intended, but side effects. For instance, a sentence of imprisonment often leads to a loss of employment or accommodation even though this is not part of the intended punishment. Walker (1980) also considered the stigma that is associated not only with crime but with punishment. The stigma and mistrust of ex-offenders – especially the stigma of having been in prison – persist, even long after the completion of the punishment, and are directly relevant to 'moral rehabilitation' and a significant impediment to 'social rehabilitation'. Walker argues that all such incidental effects ought either to be taken into account as part of the burden of the punishment matched to desert or that active steps should be taken to minimize them. Justice – desert-based retributive justice – insists that the sentence should be proportionate. To the extent that courts are entrusted to determine this, any additional hardship or imposition, however 'incidental', is excessive and therefore unjust (Rotman 1986).

The profile of prison populations always and everywhere is marked by profound social disadvantage (for example, Muller and Wildeman 2013; Reiman and Leighton 2013). Indeed, Barbara Hudson (1998) argued that in some circumstances poverty and disadvantage have so troubled the lives of offenders as to entitle them to mitigation at the point of sentence. Whether or not this is persuasive, it is widely recognized that personal and social adversity make it much harder to achieve desistance (for a useful review of the evidence, McNeill and Weaver 2010). And punishment can frustrate the process – in particular, imprisonment blocks opportunities for social inclusion, often leads to homelessness and makes it very much harder for people to find work on release (Henley 2015). It also unavoidably disrupts and often wrecks relationships with family and friends.

Much of this was acknowledged in an influential policy paper in 2004 where a number of 'pathways' out of crime were recognized (Home Office 2004). These pathways were said to be:

- Accommodation
- Education, training, and employment
- Mental and physical health
- Drug and alcohol treatment
- Finance, benefit, and debt
- Children and families
- Attitudes, thinking, and behaviour

While that paper focused on the effectiveness of enabling people to follow these pathways in terms of reducing reoffending, the support of the Universal Declaration of Human Rights could also be invoked to affirm associated moral rights. Article 25.1 asserts, 'Everyone has the right to a standard of living adequate for the health and well-being of himself and of his family, including food, clothing, housing and medical care'. This implies an entitlement to access the pathways of accommodation, healthcare (including, it may be argued, treatment for misuse of drugs and alcohol) and safeguards against poverty. Article 26.1 sets out that 'Everyone has the right to education. . . . Technical and professional education shall be made generally available and higher education shall be equally accessible to all on the basis of merit'. Article 23.1 declares that 'Everyone has the right to work, to free choice of employment, to just and favourable conditions of work and to protection against unemployment'. There is a further declaration that 'The family is the natural and fundamental group unit of society and is entitled to protection by society and the State' (Article 16.3) and while this is not elaborated upon, a right to enjoy a family life may be inferred.

These are not only liberties (so that the state may not deny people the relevant opportunities), but claims – claims for the provision of social services and resources that are a precondition of a full and flourishing life that the state should foster for everyone. There is no suggestion that people who have offended, and in particular those leaving prison, should have privileged opportunities for services and resources that in reality are not available to many other people. But they should enjoy the same entitlement. More than this, perhaps, since it is the actions of the state in imposing its punishments that have led to the worsening of so many of their difficulties, there is a corresponding duty on the state to redress this (Rotman 1986). This again is a matter of justice: the punishment may have been deserved, but the incidental detrimental consequences are beyond desert. A 'capabilities approach' (Sen 2005; Nussbaum 2011), moreover, emphasizes the importance of making opportunities genuine and recognizing that 'two persons can have very different substantial opportunities even when they have exactly the same set of means' (Sen 2005: 154). In other words, there may be obstacles to accessing resources that confront offenders that do not affect other people. This too calls for active steps to make these opportunities real. Claims as well as liberties are involved in affirming these rights.

What, however, of the 'attitudes, thinking, and behaviour' pathway? This represents the insights and practices of cognitive behavioural psychology which has been the theoretical underpinning of the dominant contemporary approach to (psychological) rehabilitation. Rejecting medicalized conceptions of rehabilitation, Rotman proposes a 'humanistic rehabilitation' that presumes that

> significant change can result only from the individual's own insight and uses dialogue to encourage the process of self-discovery. This model does not rely on idealistic preaching to reintegrate offenders to a hostile society. Instead, humanistic rehabilitation offers inmates a sound and trustworthy opportunity to remake their lives. Thus, this model seeks to awaken in inmates a deep awareness of their relationships with the rest of society, resulting in a genuine sense of social responsibility.
>
> (Rotman 1986: 1026)

A central test of ethical propriety is the 'transparency' of the intervention (Duff 2001; Bennett 2010). The practitioner's methods and purposes are made clear and explicit, while deceit, coercion, and manipulation are rejected. Transparent persuasion involves an attempt 'to persuade the offender to accept that offending behaviour is wrong by offering him good and relevant reasons against acting in this way' (Bennett 2010: 62). This fully respects the person's capacity for moral agency and honours the idea of their membership of a community that holds many of its most fundamental values in common.

The argument here has been that McNeill's four forms of rehabilitation, properly implemented, respect some of people's most fundamental rights, while neglecting these dimensions of rehabilitation would amount to a violation. The history of psychological rehabilitation should encourage us to set out criteria to safeguard rights, as Bennett (2010) has done, but within those parameters it is not only permissible but offenders' entitlement that society do all it can to enable them to 'remake their lives' (Rotman 1986: 1026). Principles of legal, social, and moral rehabilitation involve liberties (the state must not frustrate these processes), but also claims: the state must do all that it can to set the legal framework, offer fair chances for social inclusion, and enable people to make amends in suitable cases. There must also be an encouragement of attitudes that do not discriminate or reduce people to the worst they have ever done. Without this, persistent stigma will amount to an unjust continuation of punishment.

Putting rights into practice

How is this to be realized in practice? Many rights are established in international conventions and in domestic law. They are, however, often and unavoidably, framed in general and abstract terms. It may be agreed, for example, that there is a right not to be tortured or subjected to 'inhuman or degrading treatment or punishment' (European Convention Article 3). But at what point do the degrading and squalid conditions in so many prisons amount to inhuman or degrading treatment or punishment? It is true that the substance of these rights can be clarified progressively through the case law of the European Court, associated with violations, infringements, oppressions, and loss of liberties. This, however, can be a slow process. The Court, moreover, has a very large backlog of cases with some 80,000 outstanding at the end of 2016 (with some signs of increase after a period of successful reduction – European Court of Human Rights 2017) and can of course only adjudicate on applications received. If the determination of precisely what some rights mean in practice depends upon the Court, the wait could be a long one.

It is here that the work of the Council of Europe can be invaluable. The Council promulgates Rules which, once adopted by the Committee of Ministers (the Council's decision-making body) as Recommendations, carry considerable authority. Essentially the Rules point to the possibility of a relatively detailed and specific working out of the liberties – and often the rights claims – required by the Convention. In this way, Rules can respond to the potential limitation in the form of the rights in the Convention, their remoteness and abstraction. The Rules draw out what it will mean in practice to respect the rights of offenders, victims, criminal justice staff, and the community – and how to resolve conflicts of rights in a principled way. Rights may then become the beginning and the focus of policy (Canton 2010).

There will, in the nature of the case, always be disputes and difficult decisions to be made and this will be so whether or not the debate is conducted in the language of rights. For example, how far can a right to family life be honoured for serving prisoners and for their families (who ought not to be subject to punishment)? What are the boundaries of rights to privacy for people who may pose a risk of serious harm to others? For while completion of the lawful sanction ought normally to restore people to their full rights, the continuing risk posed by some people means that their rights may have to continue to be circumscribed. Few rights are absolute and there will be times when some rights must give way to other rights or to a compelling public interest. But an established right denotes a moral entitlement and when this cannot be met there should be a sense of regret and a resolve to look for ways in which the right can be better respected. Asserting rights to rehabilitation is an important part of that process and must always be part of debates about the ethics of punishment.

References

American Friends Service Committee. (1971) *Struggle for Justice: A Report on Crime and Punishment in America, Prepared for the American Friends Service Committee*, New York: Hill & Wang.

Bean, P. (1976) *Rehabilitation and Deviance*. London: Routledge.

Bennett, C. (2008) *The Apology Ritual: A Philosophical Theory of Punishment*. Cambridge: Cambridge University Press.

Bennett, C. (2010) Punishment and rehabilitation. In J. Ryberg and J. Angelo Corlett (Eds.), *Punishment and Ethics: New Perspectives*. Basingstoke: Palgrave Macmillan.

Canton, R. (2010) European Probation Rules: What they are, why they matter. *EuroVista* 1(2), 62–71.

Canton, R. (2013) The point of probation: On effectiveness, human rights and the virtues of obliquity. *Criminology & Criminal Justice*, 13(5), 577–593.

Canton, R. (2014) Yes, no, possibly, maybe: Community sanctions, consent and cooperation. *European Probation Journal*, 6(3), 209–224.

Canton, R. (2017) *Why Punish? An Introduction to the Philosophy of Punishment*. London: Palgrave Macmillan.

Clapham, A. (2007) *Human Rights: A Very Short Introduction*. Oxford: Oxford University Press.

Duff, R. A. (2001) *Punishment, Communication and Community*. Oxford: Oxford University Press.

Dworkin, R. (1984) Rights as trumps. In J. Waldron (Ed.), *Theories of Ethics*. Oxford: Oxford University Press.

European Court of Human Rights. (2005) *Hirst v. The United Kingdom (No. 2)* (Application no. 74025/01). Available at: http://www.bailii.org/eu/cases/ECHR/2005/681.html (Accessed May 2019).

European Court of Human Rights. (2017) *The Court in 2016: Overview*. Available at: http://echrblog.blogspot.co.uk/2017/01/the-court-in-2016-overview.html (Accessed October 2017).

Flew, A. (1973) *Crime or Disease*. Basingstoke: Palgrave Macmillan.

Foucault, M. (1977) *Discipline and Punish: The Birth of the Prison*. Harmondsworth: Penguin.

Gearty, C. (2006) *Can Human Rights Survive?* Cambridge: Cambridge University Press.

Griffin, J. (2008) *On Human Rights*. Oxford: Oxford University Press.

Henley, A. (2015) Abolishing the stigma of punishments served. *Criminal Justice Matters*, 102(1), 57–58.

Home Office. (2004) Reducing re-offending: National action plan. Available at: www.i-hop.org.uk/ci/fattach/get/51/0/filename/Reducing+Reoffending+Delivery (Accessed October 2017).

Hudson, B. (1998) Mitigation for socially deprived offenders. In A. von Hirsch and A. Ashworth (Eds.), *Principled Sentencing: Readings on Theory and Policy*, 2nd edition. Oxford: Hart.

Kittrie, N. (1971) *The Right to be Different: Deviance and Enforced Therapy*. Harmondsworth: Penguin.

Lewis, C. S. (1949) The humanitarian theory of punishment. *The Twentieth Century: An Australian Quarterly Review*, 3(3), 5–12. Available at: http://archive.churchsociety. org/churchman/documents/Cman_073_2_Lewis.pdf (Accessed October 2017).

McNeill, F. (2012) Four forms of "offender" rehabilitation: Towards an interdisciplinary perspective. *Legal and Criminological Psychology*, 17(1), 18–36.

McNeill, F. and Weaver, B. (2010) *Changing Lives? Desistance Research and Offender Management, Scottish Centre for Crime and Justice Research Report No. 3/2010*. Available at: www.sccjr.ac.uk/publications/changing-lives-desistance-research-and-offender-management/ (Accessed October 2017).

Mowbray, A. (2004) *The Development of Positive Obligations Under the European Convention on Human Rights by the European Court of Human Rights*. Oxford: Hart.

Muller, C. and Wildeman, C. (2013) Punishment and inequality. In Jonathan Simon and Richard Sparks (Eds.), *The Sage Handbook of Punishment & Society*. London: Sage Publications.

Nagel, T. (1995) Personal rights and public space. *Philosophy & Public Affairs*, 24(2), 83–107.

Nozick, R. (1974) *Anarchy, State and Utopia*. Oxford: Blackwell.

Nussbaum, M. (2011) *Creating Capabilities: The Human Development Approach*. Cambridge, MA: Harvard University Press.

Rawls, J. (1967) Two concepts of rules. In P. Foot (Ed.), *Theories of Ethics*. Oxford: Oxford University Press.

Reiman, J. and Leighton, P. (2013) *The Rich Get Richer and the Poor Get Prison: Ideology, Class and Criminal Justice*, 10th edition. New York: Pearson, Longman.

Rotman, E. (1986) Do criminal offenders have a constitutional right to rehabilitation? *The Journal of Criminal Law and Criminology*, 77(4), 1023–1068.

Sen, A. (2005) Human rights and capabilities. *Journal of Human Development*, 6(2), 151–166.

Sen, A. (2009) *The Idea of Justice*. London: Allen Lane.

Strawson, P. (1960) *Freedom and Resentment*. Reproduced in a Number of Anthologies. Available online at http://people.brandeis.edu/~teuber/P._F._Strawson_Freedom_&_Resentment.pdf (Accessed October 2017).

Tankebe, J. and Liebling, A. (Eds.). (2013) *Legitimacy and Criminal Justice: An International Exploration*. Oxford: Oxford University Press.

Ugwudike, P. and Raynor, P. (Eds.). (2013) *What Works in Offender Compliance*. Basingstoke: Palgrave Macmillan.

Van Zyl Smit, D. (2007) Prisoners' rights. In Y. Jewkes (Ed.), *Handbook on Prisons*. Cullompton: Willan Publishing.

Von Hirsch, A. (1976) *Doing Justice: The Choice of Punishments*. New York: Hill and Wang.

Walker, N. (1980) *Punishment, Danger and Stigma: The Morality of Criminal Justice*. Oxford: Blackwell.

Walker, N. (1991) *Why Punish?* Oxford: Oxford University Press.

Ward, T. and Maruna, S. (2007) *Rehabilitation*. London: Routledge.

Human rights and rehabilitative work in criminal justice

Christine Morgenstern

Introduction

This chapter explores the relevance of human rights concepts (for example, fairness and respect for human dignity) to rehabilitative work within the criminal justice system. It will focus on specific European human rights standards such as the European Convention on Human Rights (ECHR).

The ECHR prohibits inhuman or degrading treatment or punishment, guarantees the right to liberty, and the right to a fair procedure. The 47 Member States of the Council of Europe are parties to the ECHR, including all Member States of the European Union. The convention rights and the decisions of its judicial body, the European Court of Human Rights (ECtHR), are binding for the parties. This means that the state party to the convention must abide by the final judgement of the Court, if necessary, compensate the victim of a human rights violation, and sometimes alter its practice or legislation when a case is lost and the Court has ordered such consequences.

Beyond the ECHR, the Council of Europe has over a period of time been actively developing more specific instruments and standards with regard to the treatment of offenders – these 'recommendations' set more specific standards for their human rights position. First, the Council of Europe has been mainly concerned with prisoner's rights – the European Prison Rules are well known[1] – but with regard to offender supervision and rehabilitative work in the community, the crucial standards are the European Rules on Community Sanctions and Measures (ERCSM) and the Council of Europe's Probation Rules (EProbR) of 2010.

As mere recommendations, these instruments are not legally binding. A certain authority might be deduced, however, from the fact that government representatives adopted them unanimously. Additionally, they have been endorsed by several NGOs active in the field of offender supervision, for example the European Confederation of Probation (CEP), and by independent experts, partly academics. Similar to their more famous sibling, the European Prison Rules, the two standards (will) gain authority with their use and acknowledgement by practitioners and scholars. Over time, they have gradually attracted some academic attention (Morgenstern 2002, 2009; Canton 2014; van Zyl Smit et al. 2015; Herzog-Evans 2016). They now also sometimes serve to inform and instruct European bodies including the European Union that are dealing with cross-border and pan-European problems of offender supervision (Morgenstern and Larrauri 2013).

Human rights violations may be less likely when imposing or enforcing sanctions outside a prison than within, and they may be more difficult to identify. On the other hand it was predicted that in a modern, punitive society the discipline and control that characterizes prison life may be reproduced within the community when sanctions are enforced there (Foucault 1977; Cohen 1985). Additionally, community sanctions are sometimes seen as a benefit or privilege for offenders because they do not have to serve 'inside'; hence their potential risks, for the rights of offenders may be underestimated and safeguards need to be developed.

This chapter will adopt the Council of Europe's definition of community sanctions and these comprise all non-custodial sanctions (before, instead of, or after a trial) which have a penal content or penal value. The term therefore also applies to diversion, compensation, reparation, or even mediation as long as those concepts are backed by any type of control by law enforcement agencies (in the widest sense). As the latter are technically not always penal sanctions following a judicial decision, the term 'measures' is added. For the purpose of this chapter, the shorter term of 'community sanctions' will be used; sometimes 'offender supervision' is applied synonymously.

These community sanctions are not always truly 'rehabilitative' – punitive and rehabilitative purposes often cannot neatly be separated. From the human rights point of view, it is important to note that as soon as the sanctions are imposed within the criminal context, and independently from a potential supportive (and rehabilitative) character, they restrict personal freedom, and may inflict pain on the person affected.

Rights at risk: safeguarding human rights in the context of community sanctions

Human dignity and the prohibition of inhuman or degrading punishment

Offenders' human rights may be infringed by the *nature* of a measure, in particular when it is incompatible with human dignity. Aspects of human dignity are the ability to reflect, to exercise choice, and to exercise social responsibilities. Unlike many domestic constitutions or human rights bills that expressly and prominently protect human dignity,[2] the ECHR does not contain such a provision. Article 3 of the ECHR, however, protects the individual not only from torture but also from 'inhuman' or degrading treatment or punishment. Therefore, no community sanction may (intentionally) humiliate the offender; otherwise it will be deemed an inhuman punishment. An example would be a sanction that forces the offender to publicly express sentiments that s/he does not hold or a supervisory sanction that leaves no privacy and makes the offender a mere object of state control.

Human rights violations, however, occur more frequently when a – generally acceptable – community sanction or measure is *implemented*. Particularly if its legal prerequisites are not entirely clear and much discretion is left to judges and enforcing agencies, the restrictions may well go beyond what is acceptable from the human rights point of view. Here again, human dignity may be at risk, for example when a community service order is enforced in a way that exposes the offender or contains dangerous, unhealthy, or otherwise unacceptable tasks. The ECtHR has, however, only applied Article 3 of the ECHR reluctantly even with regard to imprisonment – it was only from the 1990s onwards that the Court acknowledged that miserable prison conditions could lead to the inhuman treatment of those detained. This acknowledgement has so far never been applied to community sanctions.

Liberty

Article 5 of the ECHR protects the 'right to liberty and security of person'. 'Liberty' in this case means the physical liberty of the person, which is part of 'the first rank of the fundamental rights that protect the physical security of an individual'.[3] This right is of paramount importance to freedom in a democratic society and closely connected to the principle of legal certainty and the rule of law – altogether Article 5 should ensure that no one is deprived of his or her liberty in an arbitrary fashion. However, deprivation of liberty is justified by Article 5 in a closed list of six modalities; two of them have some relevance with regard to offender supervision: lit. a) a prison sentence following a conviction and lit. c) remand custody. Both modalities can play a role in the context of non-compliance by an offender (suspect or convict) who does not comply with the conditions and obligations of his or her sanction or in the pre-trial context with bail conditions.

Article 5(1) lit. a) requires that a person is only imprisoned 'after a conviction' meaning that there has to be a direct causal link between the imprisonment and the initial conviction by a court or judge. However, only very few cases exist in which the ECtHR has applied Article 5 in relation to community sanctions or measures. One example is the British case of *Weeks*,[4] a relatively complicated case involving an indeterminate sentence with custodial and non-custodial parts for a person deemed to be dangerous that entailed all sorts of conditions. The Court spelled out that, with the passage of time, the causal link between the original conviction and later consequences – recalls to prison for the breach of licence conditions – gradually became less strong. It could eventually have been broken when decisions to re-detain were based on grounds unconnected to the objectives of the law and the original conviction and sentencing. In those circumstances, a detention that is lawful at the outset is transformed into a deprivation of liberty that is arbitrary and, hence, incompatible with Article 5. In the *Weeks* case, however, the Court was satisfied that a recall to prison was sufficiently connected to the original conviction.

Nevertheless, the procedural leg of the right to liberty, the entitlement to 'take proceedings by which the lawfulness of his detention shall be decided speedily by a court and his release ordered if the detention is not lawful' (Art. 5(4) ECHR) was not fulfilled. The term 'court' describes a body that is independent of the executive and of the parties to the case (usually therefore not a parole board). The person affected is entitled to a judicial procedure in which the lawfulness of a recall to prison is examined. In addition, the decision-making body must not have merely advisory functions but must have the competence to decide the lawfulness of the detention and to order release if the detention is found to be unlawful (see also Herzog-Evans 2016).

The case shows that procedural guarantees are important to fully implement the material guarantees of Article 5. It also shows, however, that the ECtHR is quite reserved in making ample use of material guarantees – one reason being the subsidiary function of international bodies and respect for domestic provisions and procedures. Indeed, a closer look reveals that the Court in the case of Weeks could have gone further to protect of the appellant's right to liberty because the decision to re-detain referred to a technical violation and not to continued dangerousness of the appellant.[5] From this point of view, the decision to re-detain was based on an unreasonable assessment of the objectives of the sentencing judge, which were of a preventive nature. Article 5 (1) lit. a) ECHR could thus have been used in this specific case and probably could be used in other cases of recalls to prison for technical violations, too.

The ECtHR, however, claims a right to interpret 'detention' or 'deprivation of liberty' autonomously from national understandings, and the Court adopts a flexible interpretation. In modern penal law, the lines between custodial and non-custodial forms of sanctions are increasingly blurred – open prisons, house arrest, or semi-open therapeutic institutions for mentally ill offenders are examples for this phenomenon. Nevertheless, the ECtHR does not use a single definition but conceives of a continuum of restrictions of liberties in different intensities that at a certain tipping point turn from restriction to deprivation. Objective criteria are, among others, the degree of isolation of the community, the possibility to have social contacts, and the duration of the restriction; they could cumulatively amount to such a restriction of personal liberty that they must be seen as actually depriving it. The aim of this flexible approach is to provide greater scope for the guarantees spelled out in Article 5 ECHR. As a result, intensive forms of house arrest that allow only for very limited time outside the house have been labelled deprivations of liberty and have to be measured against Article 5.[6] This can be relevant to questions of breach procedures especially when they result in an intensified supervision measure, leaving the offender with fewer possibilities to move freely. The Court has, however, not yet decided upon electronically monitored house arrest – the question of whether it can be in the scope of Article 5 depends on the concrete arrangements.

Fairness

The third human rights guarantee that merits attention is the right to a fair trial (Article 6 ECHR). It encompasses the principle of the rule of law and underlines the paramount role of the independent judiciary in the administration of justice, guaranteeing due process and procedural rights of the defendant (accused or suspect) in criminal proceedings. Even if the Court has stressed that the right is of such importance 'that there can be no justification for interpreting Article 6 (1) of the Convention restrictively',[7] its wording seems to restrict its scope to the original criminal *charge* and therefore only to the trial that leads to conviction (or not). It is not, however, used with regard to the process of enforcement of a sentence (van Zyl Smit and Snacken 2009; Herzog-Evans 2016).[8] Guarantees are thus missing for example in breach proceedings.

Even though the ECtHR has not broadly applied fair trial principles to the enforcement stage of a sentence yet, it may use the above-mentioned concept of autonomous interpretation if necessary to overcome the strict meaning of 'charge' as in Article 6 ECHR: at least when a breach procedure may result in an additional burden for the offender (for example because he or she has not just to serve the remainder of a sentence, but the full sentence despite having been under probation and obligations for some time already), the breach allegation equals a new 'charge' in the sense of a new imposition or encumbrance, based on a new incident. It is therefore necessary to provide fairness guarantees in the same way as for the original charge, including a transparent procedure and judicial oversight.

The recommendations by the Council of Europe

The need for additional instruments

The scarce involvement of the ECtHR with regard to community sanctions can rightly be criticized. On the other hand it also took the Court a long while before it used the potential of the convention to monitor the human rights of prisoners more effectively; most of the relevant jurisprudence dates from the 1990s onwards. This development needed facilitators; in this case it was the work of the Committee for the Prevention of Torture (CPT) as well as the other work done by the Council of Europe, namely developing European Prison Rules. To explore whether such a development and impact of the relevant instruments can be expected also in the field of community sanctions, a closer look at the ERCSM and the EProbR is required. The potential impact will be exemplified by highlighting questions of compliance and breach.

The European rules on community sanctions and measures

The ERCSM, initially adopted in 1992[9] and updated in 2017,[10] are a principled approach towards the human rights based on the use of community sanctions. The principal aims of the 1992 version was to safeguard the rights of the offender and to supply guidelines for good practice – so basically they promoted the approach that only what is just is working well. They underlined the need for legal safeguards for every sanction or measure that has a penal content, stressing that the idea of alternative or community sanctions being soft options or privileges for the offender in comparison with a custodial sentence is wrong.

Already in 2000, the rules had been amended with a new recommendation to guide Member States to achieve a more effective use of community sanctions and measures.[11] Two rules were amended, explicitly advocating for electronic monitoring in suitable cases and allowing for indeterminate measures in exceptional cases, subtly shifting emphasis from justice to effectiveness. In 2017 an update – de facto a completely new version – of the ERCSM was adopted with the aim of bringing together the substance of these two earlier recommendations and taking into account criminal justice changes that have taken place since 2000.

Modern penal policies have not left the updated ERCSM untouched: in particular, with the very first part on the scope and purpose of the rules, which express the need for 'maintenance of legal order' in the first place. While this can be seen as the symbolic tribute that has to be paid to some Member States' governments, the 2017 version keeps a lot of the human rights spirit of the original version, stressing – in second place – that 'the fundamental rights of all concerned' must be protected. In the chapter on 'Basic Principles' the function of community sanctions to 'enhance the prospects of social inclusion on which desistance from crime usually depends' is highlighted. Reference to human dignity as umbrella principle is made, but it is also connected more concretely to the right to privacy of persons affected (including offender's families). An interesting 'modern' amendment has been made to the proportionality provision – while the old version foresaw that 'the nature and the duration of community sanctions and measures shall both be in proportion to the *seriousness of the offence* for which an offender has been sentenced or of which a person is accused and *take into account his personal circumstances*', the new version complements this relatively strict requirement of seriousness with 'the *harm done to victims*' and, more importantly, requires to take into account '*any risks assessed as well as the individual's needs and circumstances*' (more on risks below).

New regulations demanding a fair application of community sanctions for all types of offenders, including foreign offenders who are often given a prison sentence instead of a community option, and serious or repeat offenders who are sometimes excluded from all non-custodial options. Both provisions are positive developments from a human rights point of view.

Another laudable new and clear rule is No. 11:

> Community sanctions and measures shall be implemented in a way that does not aggravate their afflictive character. Rights shall not be restricted in the implementation of any community sanction or measure to a greater extent than necessary follows from the decision imposing it.

This has implications for the consequences of non-compliance: where the modification or revocation of a sanction puts additional burden upon the offender that is not justified by the fact of non-compliance but must be understood as extra sanction for his or her disobedience or is clearly disproportionate, this rule may be violated. The old version of the ERCSM, however, included an explicit provision that non-compliance with conditions shall not in itself constitute an offence. This unfortunately has been deleted.[12]

Generally, the importance of adequate compliance and breach procedures is acknowledged: the ERCSM request clear and explicit provisions for defining conditions and obligations attached to the community sanctions and measures and for consequences of non-compliance; in the latter case automatic conversions to imprisonment are prohibited. Fairness and proportionality aspects play a role in the requirement for the breach decisions to take into account achievements already made.

Judicial guarantees as foreseen by the old version of the ERCSM, however, were significantly watered down: for example any 'authority defined by law' is now entitled to decide on revocations. While the possibility of appeal to a judicial authority against a decision *subjecting* a person to a community sanction is still required, judicial appeal with regard to *implementation decisions* (for example breach) no longer exists. In the relevant chapter on 'Complaints Procedures, Inspection, Monitoring', judicial oversight plays no role at all. A 'fair, simple and impartial complaints procedure' shall be available; whether this is an adequate replacement for judicial oversight that represents an independent and neutral procedure is doubtful. In any case this means that the current minimum standards for revocation procedures in Art. 5 ECHR will not be expanded via the ERCSM – it must be emphasized, however, that these standards remain valid with regard to recall to prison along the lines of the case law discussed above.

Two new provisions regulate the involvement of 'legal assistance' in breach procedures and 'if necessary' in complaints procedures against implementation decisions. They may strengthen the position of the offender supervised but depends on apt lawyers and their availability.

The European Probation Rules

The European Probation Rules (EProbR), adopted in 2010,[13] are a practice-oriented addition to the existing ERCSM, taking into account that probation agencies are among the key agencies of justice and it is their practice that is crucial for a fair and just enforcement of community sanctions. The EProbR were not part of the update, although it would be sensible to have a single instrument that includes all aspects of safeguarding human rights, good policy and practice, and instructions for actual probation work. The EProbR also aim to shape the way community penalties are implemented including the context in which non-compliance is interpreted and constructed by the different decision makers involved. They emphasize that staff should not rely solely on the prospect of sanctions for non-compliance to ensure the compliance of the offender. This means that breach procedure should not be instrumentalized as a 'sword of Damocles' but that motivational skills must be used and proactive work is needed to avoid breach, for example by discussing obstacles to compliance and how they could be overcome.

The EProbR repeat the principle that the offender has a right to full information on what is expected from him or her, on the consequences of non-compliance but also of the duties and responsibilities of probation staff; indicating that both sides are responsible for the outcome of a sentence. In case of failure, active and prompt response is needed, taking 'full account of the circumstances' allowing for some discretion of the supervisor in case of less significant transgressions. As mentioned above, 'risk' is considered as a criterion to assess the significance of non-compliance, assuming that the failure to comply may at the same time indicate a greater risk of reoffending. While 'risk' in that way is linked to non-compliance, the commentary to the EProbR at the same time argues that failures to comply could also point to changing needs of the supervised person who changes his or her lifestyle and clearly relies on the Risk-Need- Responsivity model (e.g. Andrews et al. 2011). The commentary to the Rules explains that the supervisor must investigate the reasons for non-compliance, for example how far it was a 'wilful disregard of the sanction' or perhaps 'confusion about what is required of them' played a role (in which case a negative consequence may be regarded as unfair). 'A disorganised personal life' and even the 'despair about the possibility of change' should be taken into account. These provisions suggest that fairness requires on the one hand a clarification and validation of what is expected (and that non-compliance is unacceptable), but also a dynamic approach that leaves room for compliance in the future.

Human rights standards and criminological research

The instruments discussed in this chapter are relevant in different ways. They not only set a standard of rights for those under supervision, but also establish some procedural provisions which are embedded in the compliance and effectiveness research. It has been argued recently that policy and practice should be 'grounded on human rights rather than on direct endeavours for effectiveness', rejecting the idea that the firsts are obstacles to the second (Canton 2013; Herzog-Evans 2016).

The requirement of information, warnings, and transparent procedures in the implementation phase could be dismissed as purely formal arrangements – handing out leaflets – to give the procedure a legitimate character. Indeed some have argued that the human rights debate bears a certain risk of 'proceduralization' if the procedural rules do not convey material value and truly respect human dignity (Snacken 2015).[14] These procedural guarantees, however, correspond to material content: transparency and information are necessary elements of a procedure that treats the offender as a subject (and not as an object) of supervision, as an actor who has a say on his or her fate. They are also necessary to satisfy the human need to know why and to 'make sense of an event'. This again, as criminological research on compliance (Bottoms 2001; Robinson and McNeill 2008) and procedural justice (Tyler 1990/2006) as well as the psychosocial research on the sense of coherence (Antonovsky 1979) has shown, is necessary to provide for a constructive outcome of what can be called a 'crisis'.

Reflecting the breach procedure this means that the right to have an incident as potential failure objectively examined, as well as the right to be heard, is necessary not only as a matter of fairness, but also for (further) compliance. It is also necessary for the legitimacy and acceptance of the criminal justice system as such. Procedural justice research (Tyler 1990/2006) shows that certain elements are crucial here – the right to be heard and to present one's own view ('voice'); the impartiality and independence of the deciding body ('neutrality'); consistency, decision quality, and correctability ('trustworthiness'); and the respect for general ethical values (in particular respect for human dignity and privacy of the offender) – usually tangible as being treated politely and with respect ('respect'). As Bottoms (2001) has elaborated, a relevant sub-type of normative compliance is the one that emerges from legitimacy – only when the supervised person perceives that the supervisors exercise their formal authority properly, he or she will accept it. Transparent and coherent procedures as in the European instruments described above can encourage compliance, as they can undermine it when such standards are not met. As for the instrumental kind of compliance, information, and transparency seems crucial, because the supervised person needs to know exactly the negative consequences of non-compliance and the positive outcomes of compliant behaviour (for example an early termination for good progress).

Human rights thinking can impact on the question of proportionate reactions – they are part of distributive justice requirements that emphasize the need for a *fair outcome* of a procedure. In modern penal practice, however, risk assessments seem to play a greater role than the seriousness of the failure. It is therefore important to take into account both the nature and seriousness of the violation of rules, the circumstances of non-compliance, including the motivation of the offender as subjective element of the violation (and their significance for risk). Overstating risk elements can violate the proportionality requirement but also aggravate the initial sentence to a degree that comes close to a second punishment. It is therefore important that the ERCSM underline the need to take into account any achievements reached by the supervisee so far.

The European instruments also stress the need for a general reductionist criminal policy (Morgenstern 2002; van Zyl Smit et al. 2015): continuously prison is considered as last resort, but also the burden laid on those subject to community sanctions and measures (and their specific conditions) must be restricted to the necessary. For Europe we can now speak of a mass supervision phenomenon (McNeill and Beyens 2013), moreover, a net widening effect actually has been found in a longitudinal study using comparative European data (Aebi et al. 2015). When we do reflect upon these findings, we should not forget that breach procedures with a disproportionate recourse to prison are drivers of such a development. The recommendations therefore rightly insist on avoiding prison: first this reductionist approach has to be taken at the sentencing stage, both when choosing a non-custodial sanction and when determining the obligations and conditions that need to be proportionate and manageable. Second, this approach must be followed at the enforcement stage, requiring flexible and modest reactions to breach.

Conclusion: the European touch

Human rights requirements can be found in national legislation and practice and often shape them without support or European influences. Nevertheless, the ECHR in particular, and the jurisprudence of the ECtHR, have impacted on national practice in criminal justice matters and many national systems would have weaker human rights records without them.

European 'added value' for community justice matters can be seen in the promotion of human rights ideas on the European level as such. While an offender's legal protection becomes weaker once he or she is 'properly' convicted and a sentence is enforced, the ECtHR has increasingly departed from this position with regard to prison sentences and has sought to strengthen the offender's rights. There is (modest) potential that this can happen also with regard to offender supervision in the community: the relevant Council of Europe's recommendations interpret the basic human rights concepts in the penal field and implement them in the practice of offender supervision – the process of breach here being a crucial aspect. They benefit from different legal and legal-cultural backgrounds of their authors. In that way they can serve as a reservoir of human rights concepts, a reliable yardstick and encouragement for national practice.

Secondly there is a more practical use: within Europe, at least in the European Union, we increasingly have to deal with cross-border cases (see also Morgenstern and Larrauri 2013). Such intensified cooperation needs mutual knowledge and trust – here, a common normative basis provided by the Recommendations by the Council of Europe is a helpful starting point.

Notes

1 All recommendations in the area of prison and probation can be found on the Council of Europe's website: www.coe.int/t/dghl/standardsetting/prisons/Recommendations_en.asp (accessed 4 February 2018).
2 For example in the preamble of the Irish constitution; Article 1 of the German constitution or as first of the 'Fundamental Rights' in Art. 10 of the Spanish constitution.
3 The European Court of Human Rights (ECtHR) has spelled this out on various occasions, for example in McKay v. UK (2006). The reader may easily find all decisions under the appellant's name or initials in the Court's databank (HUDOC), www.echr.coe.int/.
4 Weeks v. The United Kingdom (1987); a second similar case is van Droogenbroeck v. Belgium (1982).
5 See for details Morgenstern/Murillo/Ravagnani (2017: 23).
6 Mancini v. Italy (2001), Lavents v. Latvia (2002), Pekov v. Bulgaria (2006).
7 Perez v. France (2004).
8 See for some rare exceptions in special cases Morgenstern et al. (2017: 25).
9 European rules on community sanctions and measures: Recommendation no. R (92) 16 with explanatory memorandum.
10 Recommendation CM/Rec (2017) 3 on the European Rules on community sanctions and measures accompanied by its commentary.
11 'Improving the implementation of the European rules on community sanctions and measures' Rec (2000) 22.
12 This probably is a concession to contradicting practices in Member States where disobedience is penalized separately, for example for the breach of bail conditions (England/Wales) or for the breach of special supervision conditions for certain types of dangerous offenders (Germany).
13 Recommendation CM/Rec (2010)1 of the Committee of Ministers to Member States on the Council of Europe Probation Rules.
14 Snacken (2015).

References

Aebi, M. F., Delgrande, N. and Marguet, Y. (2015) Have community sanctions and measures widened the net of the European criminal justice systems? *Punishment & Society*, 17, 575–597.

Andrews, D. A., Bonta, J. and Wormith, J. S. (2011) The Risk-Need-Responsivity model (RNR). Does adding the good lives model contribute to effective crime prevention? *Criminal Justice and Behavior*, 38, 735–755.

Antonovsky, A. (1979) *Health, Stress and Coping*. San Francisco: Jossey-Bass.

Bottoms, A. (2001) Compliance and community penalties. In A. Bottoms, L. Gelsthorpe and S. Rex (Eds.), *Community Penalties: Change and Challenges*. London: Willan Publishing.

Canton, R. (2013) The point of probation: On effectiveness, human rights and the virtues of obliquity. *Criminology and Criminal Justice*, 13, 577–593.

Canton, R. (2014) Yes, no, possibly, maybe: Community sanctions, consent and cooperation. *European Journal of Probation*, 6, 209–224.

Cohen, S. (1985) *Visions of Social Control: Crime, Punishment and Classification*. Cambridge: Polity Press.

Foucault, M. (1975) *Surveillir et punir. La naissance de la prison*. Paris: Gallimard (English version: Discipline and Punish: The Birth of the Prison, 1977, Harmondsworth: Pantheon).

Herzog-Evans, M. (2016) Law as an extrinsic responsivity factor. *European Journal of Probation*, 8, 146–169.

McNeill, F. and Beyens, K. (2013) Studying mass supervision. In F. McNeill and K. Beyens (Eds.), *Offender Supervision in Europe*. London: Palgrave Macmillan.

Morgenstern, C. (2002) *Internationale Mindeststandards für Ambulante Strafen und Maßnahmen*. Mönchengladbach: Forum Verlag.

Morgenstern, C. (2009) European initiatives for harmonisation and minimum standards in the field of community sanctions and measures. *European Journal of Probation*, 1, 128–141.

Morgenstern, C. and Larrauri, E. (2013) European norms, policy and practice. In F. McNeill and K. Beyens (Eds.), *Offender Supervision in Europe*. Hampshire and New York: Palgrave Macmillan.

Morgenstern, C., Murillo, C. and Ravagnani, L. (2017) Fairness and offender's rights in the breach process: European perspectives. In M. Boone and N. Maguire (Eds.), *The Enforcement of Offender Supervision in Europe*. Understanding Breach Processes. London: Routledge, pp. 19–38.

Robinson, G. and McNeill, F. (2008) Exploring the dynamics of compliance with community penalties. *Theoretical Criminology*, 12, 431–449.

Snacken, S. (2015) Punishment, legitimate policies and values: Penal moderation, dignity and human rights. *Punishment & Society*, 17, 397–423.

Tyler, T. (1990/2006) *Why People Obey the Law*, 2nd edition with new afterword. Princeton, NJ: Princeton University Press.

Van Zyl Smit, D. and Snacken, S. (2009) *Principles of European Prison Law and Policy: Penology and Human Rights*. Oxford and New York: Oxford University Press.

Van Zyl Smit, D., Snacken, S. and Hayes, D. (2015) "One cannot legislate kindness": Ambiguities in European legal instruments on non-custodial sanctions. *Punishment & Society*, 17, 3–26.

6 Retribution and rehabilitation

Taking punishment seriously in a humane society

David Hayes

Introduction: penal theory and the practice of working with offenders

Any criminal justice institution that works with (and indeed, 'on' or 'against') offenders is intimately concerned with *punishment* in at least some sense. But punishment intrudes upon the freedoms of citizens in ways that look profoundly authoritarian, creating a range of tensions with modern liberal-democratic values (Boonin 2008). These tensions do not (necessarily) make criminal punishment unjustifiable, but they do require a justification, and penal theorists have attempted to provide many such justifications for punishment over the years (ibid.: 1–36; Canton 2017). Two groups of theories are particularly prevalent: *retributive* approaches, which view punishment as something deserved in proportion to the degree of criminal wrongdoing; and *rehabilitative* theories, which stress the value of punishment as a way of resolving the cause of an offender's criminality, usually in order to reduce future crime rates.

Since retribution is about imposing unpleasantness on offenders, seemingly as an end in itself, and rehabilitation is focused in some sense on changing them for the better, these two theories are often seen as being mutually exclusive, at least to the extent that we must choose between them when thinking through how we should structure and operate criminal justice systems. Starting from that view, there is a tendency amongst criminologists to dismiss retribution as either an indefensible sop to barbaric punitiveness, and/or as a failure to live up to the aspirations of liberal-democratic states, which cannot be reconciled with effective and humane rehabilitative work (Cohen 1985: 245–254; Hudson 1987; Lacey and Pickard 2015b; and compare McNeill's [2014] critique). This chapter critically examines that tendency, arguing that not only are rehabilitation and retribution compatible on at least some level, but also that rehabilitation in a criminal justice context has an inevitably retributive character. Firstly, however, the core features of retributive and rehabilitative theories need defining more fully.

Retribution

A theory of punishment can be described as retributive if it claims: firstly, that punishment is *inherently good* because it delivers *deserved censure* of the offender; secondly, that punishment is primarily concerned with the offender's *responsibility* for their conduct; and thirdly, that punishment is just if and only if it is *proportionate* to the wrongness of the offender's conduct (von Hirsch 2017). In short, retributivism is retrospective, act-focused, and bounded by a conception of justice as getting one's 'just deserts'. Those deserts are typically derived from retributivists' treatment of offenders as *responsible moral actors*, who deserve punishment because they chose to break the law, to at least some extent (Duff 2007; see also Lacey 2016a; Tadros 2005). This does not mean that retributivists are committed to treating offenders as *wholly* rational actors, or as ignoring the influence of their upbringing and circumstances. It is only necessary that offenders retain enough autonomous control over their actions to be said to have made a moral choice, however constrained, and therefore to be responsible for the consequences of that choice (Moore 2010; Duff 2007: 43–56; compare Hudson 1987; Seelmann 2014).

However, what response one's wrongdoing deserves is contested (Kleinig 2011). Most contemporary theories only go so far as to claim that it is *censure* (that is, a formal expression of disapproval) that is deserved, and not suffering as such (von Hirsch 1993; Duff 1998: 50; Kleinig 2011). On these accounts, however, the unpleasantness of criminal punishment is presented as the best way to properly censure offending, because crimes represent serious violations of publicly agreed values, for which not even the strongest reprimand could properly express the level of social disapproval (Glasgow 2015). On these accounts, punishment communicates specific levels of censure, expressed through the mode of punishment (Duff 2001: 143–155) and by the overall onerousness of the sentence (von Hirsch 2017: 67–70). So, it is not quite true that retributivists see the offender's suffering as inherently good – the suffering is only a means to an end, part of a culturally agreed, symbolic vocabulary of censure.

Retributive theories also argue that only *proportionate* sentences are justifiable: that is, the severity of the sentence must in some sense 'fit' the seriousness of the crime. To judge whether or not this 'fit' is achieved, one must understand: firstly, how serious the crime is, relative to all possible crimes; secondly, how severe sanctions are, relative to one another; and thirdly, the relative severity of sanction necessary to match the relative seriousness of the offence (von Hirsch and Ashworth 2005). Offence seriousness is generally calculated with reference to the harm caused by the offence, and the offender's culpability for it (von Hirsch and Jareborg 1991). The severity of punishment is also related to the harm imposed upon the offender, but usually only indirectly, using a more-or-less abstract understanding of the deprivations of liberty we would normally *expect* to result (von Hirsch 2017: 17–28, 67–69; compare Hayes 2016). Modern retributivist accounts generally do not require a mathematically exact equivalence between punishment and crime, considering it to be enough that the punishment is *more-or-less* in proportion (or 'not disproportionate') to the crime (Duff 2001: 132–143; Ashworth and van Zyl Smit 2004).

Proportionality provides an additional, instrumental benefit by imposing strict limits on punishment when sentencing individuals – and therefore on the overall size of the penal state (Ashworth 2017; von Hirsch 2017: 107–126; compare Hart 2008; Frase 2013). This claim was especially made in the context of a backlash against lengthy and indeterminate sentencing in the name of psycho-medical rehabilitation (Cohen 1985; Hudson 1987), but that backlash has undoubtedly failed to secure a longer-term reduction in prison or probation populations more generally (Lacey and Pickard 2015a; Lacey 2016b; compare Cohen 1985: 245–249). Retributivists tend to argue that this is the result of other factors overriding proportionate sentencing imperatives in particular contexts (e.g. Ashworth 2017; von Hirsch 2017: 125–126). However, this argument neglects the strong retributive trappings that remain in practice in Anglo-American sentencing (Dingwall 2008), which has maintained a high penal population. The claimed limiting role of proportionality is by no means empirically self-evident, and is certainly not immune to wider socio-political factors in any event.

Rehabilitation

As with retributivism, there is considerable variation in specific theories of rehabilitation, and the perspectives they take on the offender's capacities, culpability, and agency (Raynor and Robinson 2005; McNeill 2006; Ward et al. 2007). Despite this, modern rehabilitative justifications of criminal punishment share three fundamental characteristics which differ in key respects to the features of retributivism considered above. Specifically, rehabilitative punishment is: a *prospective* and preventative intervention; to be judged not as a response to the offence, but by the extent to which it is *effective* at changing the offender or their social circumstances in some way; and an *instrumental* intervention – a means to an end that is only therefore justifiable if and to the extent that it actually achieves those ends (Raynor and Robinson 2005).

Rehabilitative accounts treat criminal justice as being about doing some practical good after a crime, rather than seeking normative justice (Cohen 1985: 245–254). In particular, rehabilitative interventions essentially aim to change the offender for the better (generally from the state's perspective, but also potentially from the offender's, too: Bennett 2010). However, most contemporary accounts of rehabilitation attempt to justify themselves as means to the end of making society safer by reducing the future risk of crime (Raynor and Robinson 2005; but importantly, compare Rotman 1987). Despite the benevolent language, in other words, instrumentalist accounts of rehabilitation care less (if at all) about improving the offender's situation than they do about tackling the offender as a source of social harm (Carlen 2013). Although movements towards more agency-focused approaches to rehabilitation are motivated by precisely this seeming lack of concern about offenders as human beings (Ward and Fortune 2013), even these approaches ultimately justify themselves by the claim that treating offenders as individual agents is a good idea *because* it makes rehabilitative interventions more effective, and not (only) because doing so is intrinsically right (Ward et al. 2007, 2011). In part, they do so because they have to, given that policymaking is increasingly dominated by concerns about public protection and risk-management (Robinson 2008; compare McNeill 2006). Nevertheless, it remains the case that these more individualistic approaches accommodate the dehumanizing instrumentalist accounts as much as they challenge them, at least at the level of public policymaking.

Indeed, rehabilitative policies are remarkably susceptible to supporting authoritarian interventions in the increasing insecurity, populism, and risk-aversion characteristic of 'late modernity' (Robinson 2008; compare Schept 2015). These conditions enable an approach to rehabilitation that retains its liberal, humanitarian language, and which genuinely pursues benevolent intentions, but which is open to more illiberal consequences in pursuit of reducing reoffending in practice (Robinson 2008; Carlen 2013). It is very easy to use rehabilitative sentiments to excuse the excesses of criminal justice processes, and to sacrifice strong commitments to both criminal and social justice as a result, as less stigmatizing, social welfare systems of order-maintenance break down and are replaced with criminal justice alternatives (Garland 2001; Wacquant 2009). The euphemistic language of rehabilitation can conceal the painfulness of punishment's intrusive interventions, and obscure authoritarian behaviour behind a benevolent, humane mask (Christie 1982: 13–19; Cohen 1985: 276–278; Schept 2015; compare Lewis 1953). For this reason, numerous scholars have attempted some degree of reconciliation between the benevolence and prospective constructive focus of rehabilitation with the retributivist's limiting proportionality and normative focus on justice.

Reconciling retribution and rehabilitation: sentencing, practice, and pluralism

Table 6.1 summarizes the main features of these two ideal types, and suggests a number of fundamental oppositions between retributivism and rehabilitation. Nevertheless, there are three reasons why we can still accommodate both approaches alongside one another, at least to some extent.

Firstly, sentencing regimes typically accommodate multiple penal goals in practice, notwithstanding their theoretical oppositions (e.g. Criminal Justice Act 2003, s. 142). These approaches may invite conceptual inconsistency, but that does not mean that they are doomed to fail (compare Dingwall 2008). Table 6.1 certainly records *tensions* between the pursuit of retributive and rehabilitative aims, but it does not necessarily follow that these differences are insurmountable (McNeill 2011).

Indeed, secondly, a number of 'hybrid' theories have been proposed to attempt to move beyond these tensions to a greater or lesser extent, by fixing the relationship between retribution and rehabilitation in a way that attempts to maximize the benefits of both (e.g. Duff 2001, 2003; Hart 2008; Frase 2013;

Table 6.1 Key differences between retributive and rehabilitative theories

	Focus	Justification for specific sanctions	Fundamental aim
Retribution	Retrospective: The offender's acts determine the punishment.	Proportionality: The sanction will fit the offender's crime.	Justice: Proportionate sanctions are inherently good, because they express deserved censure.
Rehabilitation	Prospective: The offender's needs determine the punishment.	Reform: The sanction will change the offender's behaviour.	Effectiveness: Sanctions are only good if they achieve wider aims (such as reducing reoffending).

Morris 1974). These theories essentially attempt to balance pragmatism and pluralism, recognizing that democratic penal politics will inevitably be subject to multiple, equally legitimate pressures, which must all be harmonized as much as possible within criminal justice institutions, processes, and policy. However, these approaches are inevitably compromises that may not satisfy everyone, and there is no guarantee that mixing theories will always eliminate their weaknesses whilst retaining their strengths. Hybrid models are not magic bullets, in other words, but they at least suggest that rehabilitative and retributive theories can sometimes accommodate one another.

Thirdly, tensions between rehabilitative and retributive accounts can be overcome by recognizing these theories' differing concerns with and relevance to *sentencing*, as against *penal practice*. There are particular differences between the purely instrumental approaches to rehabilitation discussed thus far, and the predominant approach of the practitioners (especially probation officers) who actually 'do' rehabilitative work. Here, there is a tendency to maintain a benevolent conception of rehabilitation as an end in itself, because it gives support to fellow human beings who need it – in other words, as something that is intrinsically *as well as* instrumentally valuable (Robinson and McNeill 2004; Robinson and Svensson 2013; compare Rotman 1987 and see generally Durnescu and McNeill [eds.] 2014). This conception survives in spite of the dominant, purely instrumental approach to rehabilitation described above, and reveals key differences between the concerns of *sentencing* and of the *implementation of individual sentences* (Hart 2008: 9–13).

Indeed, there is nothing to stop macro-level retributive policies from co-existing with micro-level rehabilitative practices. Indeed, doing so is an important step forward, because it recognizes the inherently punitive nature of (penal) rehabilitation (Bennett 2010; McNeill 2011, 2014). Recall that retributivists are fundamentally concerned with questions of *distribution*: the severity of punishment X ought not to be ought of proportion with the seriousness of crime Y, which it punishes (von Hirsch and Ashworth 2005). To a retributivist, sentencing is a matter of balancing crime and punishment on a set of scales, and it is only the overall 'weight' of the punishment relative to the offence that matters – not, necessarily, what materials that weight is composed of (compare Hart 2008: 11–13). Therefore, for the pursuit of penal rehabilitation to satisfy the needs of retributive policy, two further questions arise: firstly, does rehabilitation work communicate censure; and secondly, is it capable of providing sufficient hard treatment to be a proportionate response to particular offences? If so, then rehabilitative work *can* be retributive in principle. In practice, of course, whether it is or not depends upon how proportionate specific interventions are to the offence in question.

In the first instance, the imposition of a rehabilitative sanction represents censure, in and of itself. It is censorious in that it is the result of a censorious trial procedure, in which the offender is labelled as guilty of a criminal wrong (Feeley 1979; Duff 2007), but also in that rehabilitative practices tend to emphasize the need to confront the crime *as* something wrongful, which the offender bears responsibility for avoiding in future, and which they must therefore recognize *as* wrongful in order to meaningfully reform (e.g. McNeill 2006; Canton 2011: 80–83, 115–128; Robinson et al. 2013: 329–332). All of this confronts the offender with the wrong they have done, *as* something wrong, something disapproved of. In other words, all of this *is* censure – even if censure is not the primary or end goal of the probation officer, who may well pursue more reintegrative goals (compare Braithwaite 1989), and may not seek to focus on the offender's blameworthiness in the longer term.

Secondly, is probation hard treatment? Rehabilitation workers may be resistant to the idea that they are actively 'doing' punishment: they usually intend to work *with* offenders, not *against* them. But even the most successful probation practice, providing the most wonderful improvements in the offender's life, is invested with pain. Some of these pains are the result of the processes and contexts within which probation work is undertaken (Durnescu 2011: 536–538; Hayes 2015: 96–98), but others were intimately associated with rehabilitation itself. After all, rehabilitation is essentially an extrinsically required change and, even when one is willing, meaningfully changing one's behaviour is always difficult. Indeed, those most willing to engage in rehabilitation – to recognize what they have done and to try to reconcile the person they want to be with the wrongs that they have done in the past – are exposed to uniquely painful experiences, that more resistant offenders may avoid (Hayes 2015: 91–94; compare Nugent and Schinkel 2016). This pain – especially when required by state processes – is perfectly capable of amounting to retributive hard treatment (Duff 2001: 99–106; von Hirsch 2017: 87–96), especially if we conceive of a punishment's severity as being at least partly determined by the offender's subjective experience (Hayes 2016). We can, in short, be retributive about the *distribution* of punishment, whilst also being rehabilitative in the *imposition* of that punishment upon (with, against) particular offenders.

Conclusion: humane but honest punishment

It is therefore wrong to assume that rehabilitative work can never contribute to punishment – it is capable of satisfying a retributive agenda in at least some cases, depending upon the specific 'pains of rehabilitation' associated with the sanction in question (Hayes 2015: 91; Nugent and Schinkel 2016). Retributivist theorists must therefore take the value of rehabilitative work seriously as a component of the punishment that is demanded in retributive sentencing systems. But by the same token, advocates of and actors undertaking rehabilitative work with offenders must recognize the unpleasantness inherent within it. They must move beyond an assumption that punishment takes place elsewhere, and recognize that rehabilitation workers have at least some power to shape the pains of probation (Durnescu 2011: 539–543). The painfulness of punishment does not mean that it cannot benefit offenders. But neither do those benefits cancel out the pains they bring with them.

Fundamentally, the strength of retributive theories is that they confront us with the painfulness of punishment, to an extent that rehabilitative accounts do not (Christie 1982: 100–103). The need for rehabilitation is always a sign of societal failure (compare Koch 2017), because the central tenet of rehabilitative intervention is that crime is at least partially caused by social and other factors in the offender's life, which we can change. But if they can be changed, then the crime could have been avoided in the first place, with the right state (or civil society) intervention (Carlen 2013). By all means, criminal justice systems should take the opportunity to rehabilitate those persons who end up under penal control, but that does not excuse those persons ending up there in the first place (Cohen 1985: 236–237). Given the pains (and wider harms) accompanying any criminal justice intervention, penal rehabilitation is a poor alternative to social 'habilitation' in a society predicated on freedom and respect for human dignity, and cannot adequately replace a dwindling welfare state (Carlen 2013; compare Garland 2001; Wacquant 2009). Too much trust in rehabilitation ultimately obscures the wider socio-political context of criminal justice (Christie 1982: 100–103; Hudson 1993). We must take punishment seriously, as something that hurts, even if (and even as) it does good, and therefore as something which we ought to use only as a last resort, if at all.

References

Ashworth, A. (2017) Prisons, proportionality, and recent penal history. *Modern Law Review* 80(3), 473–488.

Ashworth, A. and van Zyl Smit, D. (2004) Disproportionate sentences as human rights violations. *Modern Law Review*, 67(4), 541–560.

Bennett, C. (2010) Punishment and rehabilitation. In Jesper Ryberg and J. Angelo Corlett (Eds.), *Punishment and Ethics: New Perspectives*. Palgrave Macmillan.

Boonin, D. (2008) *The Problem of Punishment: A Critical Introduction*. Cambridge University Press.

Braithwaite, J. (1989) *Crime, Shame and Reintegration*. Cambridge University Press.

Canton, R. (2011) *Probation: Working with Offenders*. Routledge.

Canton, R. (2017) *Why Punish? An Introduction to the Philosophy of Punishment*. Palgrave Macmillan.

Carlen, P. (2013) Against rehabilitation, for reparative justice. In Kerry Carrington, Matthew Ball, Erin O'Brien and Juan Tauri (Eds.), *Crime, Justice and Social Democracy: International Perspectives*. Palgrave Macmillan, 89–104.

Christie, N. (1982) *Limits to Pain*. Oxford: Martin Robinson.

Cohen, S. (1985) *Visions of Social Control: Crime, Punishment, and Classification*. Polity Press.

Dingwall, G. (2008) Deserting desert? Locating the present role for retribution in the sentencing of adult offenders. *The Howard Journal*, 47(4), 400–410.

Duff, R. A. (1998) Punishment, communication and community. In Matt Matravers (Ed.), *Punishment and Political Theory*. Hart, pp. 48–68.

Duff, R. A. (2001) *Punishment, Communication, and Community*. Oxford University Press.

Duff, R. A. (2003) Probation, punishment and restorative justice: Should Al Truism be engaged in punishment? *The Howard Journal*, 49(2), 181–197.

Duff, R. A. (2007) *Answering for Crime: Responsibility and Liability in the Criminal Law*. Hart.

Durnescu, I. (2011) Pains of probation: Effective practice and human rights. *International Journal of Offender Therapy and Comparative Criminology*, 55(4), 530–545.

Durnescu, I. and McNeill, F. (Eds.). (2014) *Understanding Penal Practice*. Routledge.

Feeley, M. (1979) *The Process is the Punishment: Handling Cases in a Lower Criminal Court*. Russell Sage Foundation.

Frase, R. (2013) *Just Sentencing: Principles and Procedures for a Workable System*. Oxford University Press.

Garland, D. (2001) *The Culture of Control: Crime and Social Order in Contemporary Society*. Oxford University Press.

Glasgow, J. (2015) The expressivist theory of punishment defended. *Law and Philosophy*, 34(6), 601–631.

Hart, H. L. A. (2008) Prolegomenon to the principles of punishment. In H. L. A. Hart (Ed.), *Punishment and Responsibility: Essays in the Philosophy of Law*, 2nd edition. Oxford University Press.

Hayes, D. (2015) The impact of supervision on the pains of community penalties in England and Wales: An exploratory study. *European Journal of Probation*, 7(2), 85–102.

Hayes, D. (2016) Penal impact: Towards a more intersubjective measurement of penal severity. *Oxford Journal of Legal Studies*, 36(4), 724–750.

Hudson, B. (1987) *Justice Through Punishment: A Critique of the 'Justice' Model of Corrections*. Macmillan Education.

Hudson, B. (1993) *Penal Policy and Social Justice*. Macmillan Education.

Kleinig, J. (2011) What does wrongdoing deserve? In Michael Tonry (Ed.), *Retributivism Has a Past: Has It A Future?* Oxford University Press, pp. 46–62.

Koch, I. (2017) Moving beyond punitivism: Punishment, state failure, and democracy on the margins. *Punishment & Society*, 19(2), 203–220.

Lacey, N. (2016a) *In Search of Criminal Responsibility: Ideas, Interests, and Institutions*. Oxford University Press.

Lacey, N. (2016b) The metaphor of proportionality. *Journal of Law and Society*, 43(1), 27–44.

Lacey, N. and Pickard, H. (2015a) The chimera of proportionality: Institutionalising limits on punishment in contemporary social and political systems. *Modern Law Review*, 78(2), 216–240.

Lacey, N. and Pickard, H. (2015b) To blame or to forgive? Reconciling punishment and forgiveness in criminal justice. *Oxford Journal of Legal Studies*, 35(4), 665–696.

Lewis, C. S. (1953) The humanitarian theory of punishment. *Res Judicatae*, 6(2), 224–230.

Mair, G. (2016) "A difficult trip, I think": The end days of the probation service in England and Wales? *European Journal of Probation*, 8(1), 3–15.

McNeill, F. (2006) A desistance paradigm for offender management. *Criminology and Criminal Justice*, 6(1), 39–62.

McNeill, F. (2011) Probation, credibility and justice. *Probation Journal*, 58(1), 9–22.

McNeill, F. (2014) Punishment as rehabilitation. In Gerben Bruinsma and David Weisburd (Eds.), *Encyclopedia of Criminology and Criminal Justice*. Springer, pp. 4195–4206.

Moore, M. (2010) *Placing Blame: A Theory of the Criminal Law*. Oxford University Press.

Morris, N. (1974) *The Future of Imprisonment*. University of Chicago Press.

Nugent, B. and Schinkel, M. (2016) The pains of desistance. *Criminology and Criminal Justice*, 16(5), 568–584.

Raynor, P. and Robinson, G. (2005) *Rehabilitation, Crime and Justice*. Palgrave Macmillan.

Robinson, G. (2008) Late-modern rehabilitation: The evolution of a penal strategy. *Punishment & Society*, 10(4), 429–445.

Robinson, G. and McNeill, F. (2004) Purposes matter: Examining the "ends" of probation. In George Mair (Ed.), *What Matters in Probation?* Willan Publishing, pp. 277–304.

Robinson, G., McNeill, F. and Maruna, S. (2013) Punishment in society: The improbable persistence of probation and other community sanctions and measures. In Jonathan Simon and Richard Sparks (Eds.), *The SAGE Handbook of Punishment & Society*. SAGE, pp. 321–340.

Robinson, G. and Svensson, K. (2013) Practising offender supervision. In Fergus McNeill and Kristel Beyens (Eds.), *Offender Supervision in Europe*. Palgrave Macmillan, pp. 97–124.

Rotman, E. (1987) Do criminal offenders have a constitutional right to rehabilitation? *Journal of Criminal Law and Criminology*, 77(4), 1023–1068.

Schept, J. (2015) *Progressive Punishment: Job Loss, Jail Growth, and the Neoliberal Logic of Carceral Expansion*. New York University Press.

Seelmann, K. (2014) Does punishment honour the offender? In A. P. Simester, Antje du Bois-Pedain and Ulfrid Neumann (Eds.), Antje du Bois-Pedain (Trans.), *Liberal Criminal Theory: Essays for Andreas von Hirsch*. Hart, pp. 111–122.

Tadros, V. (2005) *Criminal Responsibility*. Oxford University Press.

von Hirsch, A. (2017) *Deserved Criminal Sentences: An Overview*. Hart.

von Hirsch, A. (1993) *Censure and Sanctions*. Oxford University Press.

von Hirsch, A. and Ashworth, A. (2005) *Proportionate Sentencing: Exploring the Principles*. Oxford University Press.

von Hirsch, A. and Jareborg, N. (1991) Gauging criminal harm: A living-standard analysis. *Oxford Journal of Legal Studies*, 11(1), 1–38.

Wacquant, L. (2009) *Punishing the Poor: The Neoliberal Government of Social Insecurity*. Duke University Press.

Ward, T. and Fortune, C. A. (2013) The good lives model: Aligning risk reduction with promoting offenders' personal goals. *European Journal of Probation*, 5(2), 29–46.

Ward, T., Melser, J. and Yates, P. (2007) Reconstructing the Risk-Needs-Responsivity model: A theoretical elaboration and evaluation. *Aggression and Violent Behavior*, 12, 208–228.

Ward, T., Yates, P. and Willis, G. (2011) The Good Lives Model and the Risk Needs Responsivity model: A reply to Andrews, Bonta, and Wormith. *Criminal Justice and Behavior*, 39(1), 94–110.

7

Restorative justice

A different approach to working with offenders and with those whom they have harmed

Tim Chapman

Introduction

Restorative justice is not primarily a method of working with or supervising offenders. It is a means of engaging people affected by harm in determining how the harm should be repaired. Yet I want to argue for its relevance to and effectiveness in this field. I will briefly outline what restorative justice is and the principles upon which its processes are based. I describe the only restorative justice approach that is fully integrated into the statutory supervision of offenders in Britain and Ireland, the youth conference order in Northern Ireland. This is followed by a concise review of the research into restorative justice in the criminal justice system. Finally, I want to identify distinctive qualities of restorative justice, which could contribute to more effective and credible methods of working with offenders generally.

What is restorative justice?

In the context of criminal justice, restorative justice engages those most affected by the harm caused by criminal behaviour in a process that restores what has been lost, damaged, and violated by the harm. In this way it is designed to undo an injustice and to restore justice. Restoring justice is based upon a set of core premises:

- Crime causes harm to people and to the quality of relationships required for them to flourish in society.
- People suffer harm in ways that are specific to them.
- Justice requires that those responsible for the harm should make themselves accountable for it and be obliged to put things right and to repair as far as they are able the damage they have caused.
- Fulfilling these obligations makes it more likely that perpetrators will gain access to the resources and relationships that they need for a good life without recourse to harming others.

Restorative justice is distinguished from the formal processes of the criminal justice system by the inclusion and active participation of victims, perpetrators, and their communities in dialogue to reach a mutual understanding of the harm and to agree on action on how to address the needs arising from it.

Victims and offenders are connected by their relationship to the harmful incident and consequently they may need each other to disconnect themselves from this relationship. To recover the victim may have questions that only the perpetrator can answer. The perpetrator may need a release from stigma and a pathway to reintegrate in the community. If the communication between the parties is effective, both will experience a quality of justice in which the consequences of the harm no longer dominate their lives and which enables them to move on.

There are different processes for implementing restorative justice. Victim offender mediation involves the victim and perpetrator of the harm engaged with a mediator to agree on some form of reparation. Restorative conferences and circles engage a wider range of participants including the victim, the offender, and people they invite to support them. It can also include members of the community affected by the harm and professionals such as police officers, probation officers, and psychologists who can offer to support any plan for offender reintegration or victim recovery. Restorative principles and practices can also be used in informal conversations and daily interactions to strengthen pro-social relationships and to build a culture of respect, for example in prisons.

The integration of restorative justice with the supervision of people subject to court orders: youth conferences in Northern Ireland

Northern Ireland is one of the few jurisdictions in the world that has put restorative justice at the core of working with young offenders (Zinsstag and Chapman 2012). The Justice (Northern Ireland) Act 2002 empowers the Public Prosecution Service to arrange restorative youth conferences for virtually every young person who admits to a criminal offence in Northern Ireland. Young people responsible for less serious offences will be cautioned restoratively by the police, in collaboration with Youth Justice Agency staff, through a process known as Youth Engagement cautions. Those who continue to offend will be referred for a diversionary youth conference, thus avoiding prosecution. If they do not comply with the agreement made at the conference, they may be prosecuted in court for the original offence. Young people who have committed serious offences or have developed a persistent pattern of offending will be prosecuted in the Youth Court. In all cases, except for those criminal offences, which attract mandatory sentences (e.g. murder), the District Judge must offer the young person a youth conference.

Participation in a youth conference is voluntary. A conference can be arranged if there is no victim present, though every effort is made to enable the person or community who has been harmed to participate. The young person responsible for the harm can bring a lawyer to ensure that rights are protected. The objectives of the youth conference are to engage young people who have offended in making amends to their victims and to commit to actions, which will prevent further offending. Youth conferences are facilitated by full-time trained youth conference coordinators employed by the Youth Justice Agency. There is a process of engagement and each party is prepared for the process of dialogue, which is critical to the conference. The Northern Irish model does not employ a 'scripted' approach (Chapman 2012).

Actions specified in a plan may include a verbal or written apology, direct reparation to the victim or indirectly to the community in the form of unpaid work, financial compensation, supervision by an adult, participation in activities or programmes to address offending, restrictions on actions (these may include curfews, prohibitions from entering certain places, e.g. a shop, electronic monitoring, and custody), and treatment for a mental health condition or for alcohol or drugs.

The conference agreement is authorized by the Public Prosecution Service or the Youth Court. Both can amend the agreement on the grounds of proportionality. Once an agreement has been endorsed by the Youth Court, it becomes an enforceable youth conference order. This order is supervised by the Youth Justice Agency (YJA).

YJA staff support the young person to complete the agreed plan in full and hold the young person accountable if he or she does not comply with the agreed actions. The commitments that the young person has entered into as a result of the conference must be honoured to the letter. This is of critical importance to the victim's sense of justice, to the young person's sense of responsibility, and to the community's confidence in restorative justice.

Since 2003, when youth conferencing began in Northern Ireland, there have been over 22,000 conferences. This is a substantial number in a population of approximately 1.8 million. In Northern Ireland the previous system of court disposals informed by pre-sentence reports continues, in a relatively limited way, to operate in parallel with the new restorative system because some young people who have admitted to an offence will not consent to a youth conference. This offers a comparison group to assess the effectiveness of restorative conference compared to community supervision orders and custody.

It is important to bear in mind that the youth conference system in Northern Ireland addresses the full range of offences. Furthermore, no matter how many conferences a young person has participated in, the court must offer him or her the opportunity of another conference. This means that youth conferences are addressing many very serious offences and that they are engaging persistent and prolific offenders.[1]

Personal victims, defined as those directly affected by the offence, were present in half of all youth conferences in 2010 (see also Campbell et al. 2005). This is a significant level of victim participation given that many offences committed by young people do not have direct victims (e.g. retail theft, vandalism, drug offences, disorderly behaviour). In 2009–2010, 84% of victims were satisfied with their conference experience.

The fact that the conference plan has been endorsed by a victim and sometimes by community representatives, as well as freely entered into by the young person and his or her parents or carers, has made it a popular order with most district judges in Northern Ireland. Another benefit is that the court can see exactly what the young person has committed to doing to make amends and to stay out of trouble. Its specificity increases transparency and accountability and also offers the opportunity for achievement in the young person's life.

Perhaps for these reasons there is a very high completion rate of conference plans. The Criminal Justice Inspection Northern Ireland report (2008) found that 52% of almost 800 conference plans arising from referrals in 2006 had been completed as of June 2007, while 46% were ongoing. Just 2% of the plans had been revoked by the courts or returned to the PPS for non-compliance. It may be that these factors have encouraged courts to sentence very few young people to the Juvenile Justice Centre, the custodial institution for young people in Northern Ireland.

Official reoffending rates are calculated over a one-year follow-up period. They are measured through both convictions and out of court sanctions such as cautions or diversionary youth conferences. The latest figures were published in 2011 (Lyness and Tate 2011). The reoffending rate for custody was 68%. The rate for the range of community supervision orders (probation orders, community service orders, etc.) was 54%. The reoffending rate for the (court ordered) youth conference order was 45%. The rate for diversionary youth conferences was at 29%. Given that a significant proportion of young people who participate in court referred youth conferences are serious or persistent offenders, there is a clear trend that restorative responses to youth offending have generally been more effective in reducing reoffending than the long-established court orders.

The Northern Irish conference model has been endorsed by a succession of reports within the UK – The Centre for Social Justice (2012) *Rules of Engagement: Changing the Heart of Youth Justice*, Department of Justice NI (2011) *A Review of the Youth Justice System in Northern Ireland*, Independent Commission on Youth Crime and Anti-social Behaviour (2010) *Time for a Fresh Start*, Prison Reform Trust (Jacobson and Gibbs 2009) *Making Amends: Restorative Youth Justice in Northern Ireland*. This model has also become an exemplar of good practice in Europe (European Forum for Restorative Justice (2011) *Conferencing: A Way Forward for Restorative Justice in Europe*).

What are the research findings on the effectiveness of restorative justice?

There is no evidence that any types of offences or groups of offenders are more or less suitable for restorative justice processes (Shapland et al. 2012). There may be certain individuals who might be assessed as not ready or not competent to participate or too high risk of further harming the victim to participate.

In relation to the restorative process, research studies are consistent in reporting that at least 85% of victims express satisfaction (Shapland et al. 2012; Beckett et al. 2004; Strang 2002; Strang et al. 2006; Umbreit 1993). For the people responsible for harming others, the positive aspects of the process are the opportunities to express remorse, to meet the victim, and to actively participate (Shapland et al. 2012). They also appreciated not being made to feel that they were a bad person (Morris and Maxwell 2001).

Perpetrators tend to have a very high rate of compliance to commitments made through restorative processes. A comparative study found that 81% of youth participating in victim offender mediation (VOM) completed their agreements, as opposed to 57% of youth who were not in the VOM programme (Umbreit et al. 2001).

Offenders in restorative programmes are more likely to complete the programmes and less likely to reoffend compared to a control group (De Beus and Rodgriguez 2007). A meta-analysis of victim offender mediation and family group conferencing studies found that family group conferencing was shown to have twice the effect as traditional justice programmes, and victim offender mediation had an even larger effect on recidivism (Bradshaw and Roseborough 2005). Bouffard et al. (2016) found that young people who engaged in a range of restorative processes reoffended at a significantly lower level than those processed through the juvenile court. Another meta-analysis in 2005 found that restorative processes were associated with reduced recidivism for both youth and adults (Latimer et al. 2005). A rigorous study (Shapland et al. 2012) in England found that significantly fewer (14%) offences were committed by those who participated in restorative processes over two years than those in a control group. This research also demonstrated that £9 expenditure in the criminal justice was saved for every £1 spent on restorative justice.

A meta-analysis found that both victims and offenders associated restorative processes with being treated fairly (Latimer et al. 2005). The same meta-analysis of both youth and adult studies also demonstrated restorative processes to be associated with greater victim satisfaction over the payment of restitution. People who had been harmed appreciated receiving information on the completion of the agreed action (Morris and Maxwell 2001).

After a restorative process people who have been harmed say that they are less afraid that the offender would commit further crimes against them (Strang 2002). Victims also reported lower levels of post-traumatic stress symptoms and were less likely to express feelings of revenge (Angel 2005; Strang et al. 2013). They are far more likely to forgive their offenders after they heard their story (Sherman and Strang 2007). Personal victims of young and older adult robbers and burglars in London, and of youth offenders in Canberra, were much more likely to think any apologies they received were sincere than those whose case had been dealt with in courts (Strang 2002; Angel 2005).

Having participated in a restorative process, people who have harmed others tend to have more positive attitudes towards police, law, and justice than those who were prosecuted through the courts. They also tend to appreciate how much harm they have caused and feel remorse (McGarrell et al. 2000). Offenders tend to feel they have been treated more fairly and to be more satisfied with restorative justice than with conventional justice (Strang et al. 1999).

Restorative justice has been greatly influenced by Christie's perception of conflict as property (1977) that has been appropriated by the state system of justice. He criticized criminal justice professionals for excluding those most affected by the conflict caused by criminal behaviour. These positive results require victims and perpetrators to experience real inclusion and participation in the restorative process.

There is a growing body of evidence that as restorative justice becomes a mainstream rather than marginal practice in criminal justice, it tends to operate within the strategic priorities, structures, culture, systems, and constraints of the system (Zernova 2009). The research by Bolívar et al. (2015) into mediation in Europe found that a closer relationship between the restorative justice process and the criminal justice system meant that it was more likely that the victim would have an unsatisfactory experience.

Statutory agencies introduce standards to monitor professionals' performance and to assure the quality and consistency of practice (Johnstone 2012). This can result in limiting the autonomy of those most affected by the harm, victims, and perpetrators, to participate freely in the decision-making. Barnes (2015) observed that at youth conferences in Northern Ireland there seemed to be a tariff, which determined the degree of reparation. This was justified by the principle of proportionality of punishment according to the seriousness of the offence, thus introducing legalistic thinking into a restorative process.

Suzuki and Wood (2017) and Barnes (2015) reported that the principle of voluntary participation can be compromised by the awareness of the young person responsible for the harm that restorative justice is offered as a diversion from prosecution. Barnes (2015) observed that sitting in a room full of adults resulted in some young people saying very little and having little or no influence on the agreed-upon plan.

In an English police-led scheme, Young and Hoyle (2003) assessed only two out of 23 observed restorative processes as genuinely restorative in that the process was dominated by the facilitator. Similarly youth offender panels were also controlled by the youth offending team worker whose assessment report drove the proceedings (Rosenblatt 2015).

In spite of this wish to meet the expectations of the system, in many countries restorative justice struggles to attract referrals from the police, prosecutors, or courts (Laxminarayan 2014; Shapland et al. 2012). When referrals are made, many schemes struggle to engage the active participation of victims (Hoyle 2002), often due to paying insufficient attention to their perspective. Research by Hoyle et al. (2002) found that victim attendance at restorative meetings was 14%. Rosenblatt observed 39 youth offender panel meetings. In only one was there a victim present and in only two were victim statements available.

The absence of victims results in practitioners attempting to represent the harm caused. This can lead to hyperbole (Hoyle et al. 2002) in an attempt to shock the individual into empathy. These attempts are unlikely to appear authentic to the perpetrator (Rosenblatt 2015).

When victims participate in a restorative meeting with a perpetrator, they are often inadequately prepared (Hoyle et al. 2002) and not actively facilitated to participate in the decision-making process. This has the inevitable effect of marginalizing victims' needs (Bolívar 2015; Choi et al. 2013; Zernova 2007). When victims express dissatisfaction with their experience of restorative processes, they tend to stress a lack of attention to their needs and care in preparing them to participate in the process (Choi and Gilbert 2010; Umbreit et al. 2005), often due to greater attention given to offenders (Hoyle et al. 2002; Strang 2002).

Over time restorative justice processes within the criminal justice system have become more concerned with the goals of compliance, risk management, reducing reoffending, and rehabilitation than addressing the needs of victims arising from the harm that they have suffered. (Pavlich 2005; Choi et al. 2013; Suzuki and Wood 2017). Hoyle et al. (2002) found that most reparation was symbolic, usually a direct or written apology. Their research into a police-led scheme in England observed apologies that were often extracted by putting the perpetrator under pressure. Barnes (2015) also observed that in restorative conferences apologies seemed rehearsed and prompted by the facilitator.

The form that the reparation takes is more often determined by the facilitator than the victim or perpetrator (Hoyle et al. 2002; Barnes 2015). Research into youth offender panels in England (Hoyle and Rosenblatt 2016) found that activities directed at reducing reoffending took precedence over reparation. There seemed to be a limited menu of available reparation opportunities rather than activities that had some connection with the harm or the victim's wishes (confirmed by Barnes 2015). In some cases, where reparation was agreed, it was not undertaken or completed. Apology letters were seen as part of the rehabilitation plan rather than reparation to victims who rarely received them.

It should be noted that these research findings do not apply to every case. Yet there is evidence that institutionalization generally results in the assimilation of restorative justice into the prevailing culture of the criminal justice system. It becomes bureaucratized, dominated by the professionals, and instrumentalized as a tool to reduce risk of reoffending. In doing so the key elements of restorative justice that add so much value to people's experience of justice are so substantially diluted that one would question whether they are indeed restorative processes.

What is it about restorative justice that is distinctive?

1. The meaning of crime

Crime viewed through a restorative lens (Zehr 2005) is an unjust act causing harm to a person, organization, or social group. This viewpoint shifts the focus from the offender to the victim. In restorative justice, the primary question is: how can this injustice be undone through addressing the victims' needs, questions, and requests?

In relation to the offender, the question is: what obligations arise from having perpetrated the harm? These obligations include the reparation of the harm and a commitment to avoid causing further harm.

It is acknowledged that some perpetrators may need support to meet these obligations due to current adverse circumstances or past events. However, rather than framing these as risk factors or criminogenic needs, they are often seen in a restorative process as harms in need of restoration if he or she is to desist from harming others.

2. The aim of restorative justice is to restore justice

The value of safety dominates public discourse on crime. The aims of those working in the criminal justice system are above all to reduce offending and to protect the public. Restorative justice puts the value of justice at the core of working with offenders.

This means having perpetrators make *themselves* accountable to the victim, of enabling the victim to express their feelings, and to describe their suffering, and to seek both reparation and assurance that this harm will not be repeated. The perpetrator of the harm acknowledges that what they did was wrong and puts it right. The restorative process also frees the concept of justice from its strong association with punishment.

3. Restorative justice focuses on the actions of the perpetrator rather than the practices of the professional

Other than a sensible assessment of risk to any party involved in a restorative process, the key is not to assess the perpetrator or victim but to enable *them* to understand what happened and its impact so that they can make themselves understood to the others. The participants' understanding, communication skills, and ability to come up with a viable plan to address the harm are what drive the process, not the practitioner's knowledge or skill (though they are important in facilitating the process).

People's relationship to harm and the stories they tell about it and the relationships that need to be strengthened are critical to the restorative process. The relationship with the facilitator is important but temporary. The opportunity to repair social bonds and to extend bridging social capital is critical to the recovery of the victim and the reintegration of the perpetrator. Restorative justice changes the focus from the individual to the ecosystem on which the individuals depend.

The lived reality of being a victim or perpetrator of crime is often highly emotional, chaotic, idiosyncratic, and unpredictable, not only because there are so many variables but because these variables are in a constant state of interaction. The restorative process enables these variables to be articulated in the form of narratives and dialogue rather than breaking down a contextualized harmful act into factors. In a (ideally face to face) restorative process the victim and the perpetrator are present, whereas when engaging offenders in offending programmes, the victim can only be represented in an imagined form. In restorative justice mutual understanding and agreed-upon action emerges often with unpredictable results from the dynamic complexity of a communicative process rather than the detailed complexity of assessment and intervention planning (Senge 1990: 70–71).

4. The nature of commitment

There is a high level of compliance by perpetrators to the commitments made at restorative processes. The restorative process enrols (Senge 1990) perpetrators into a commitment to repair the harm. It does so by inviting them to *make themselves* accountable directly to the people whom they have harmed, and through offering the perpetrator the opportunity to understand fully the harm caused, to contribute to an action plan that addresses the needs of both parties and to make promises to the victim often witnessed by people significant to him or her. As O'Mahony and Doak (2017) state, agency and accountability are critical to the quality and effectiveness of restorative justice. The supervision of the agreed-upon plan derives its authority from the agreement and is focused upon supporting the perpetrator's accountability to his or her word. This form of commitment seems closest to what Bottoms (2001) defines as normative compliance, which he believes supports desistance.

5. Restorative justice enables people to move on from harmful events

The restorative process enables people who have been harmed to have their suffering recognized and to have their needs for justice met. Through this they can put the incident, which interrupted and disrupted their lives, behind them and move on.

For perpetrators a restorative process is an opportunity to 'make good' (Maruna 2001) and not only to change the way they see themselves but also to signal (Bushway et al. 2012) to others that they are making efforts to change their identity and behaviour. They earn redemption (Bazemore 1998) by being seen to make amends and, thus, release themselves from the stigma of having offended. This redemption can repair significant relationships and open up the possibilities of other relationships, which may support their efforts to move away from harming others. Circles of Support and Accountability (Chapman and Murray 2015) are practical examples of this.

Conclusions

In relation to working with offenders the evidence demonstrates that restorative justice is generally effective in engaging offenders in keeping to their commitments to repair the harm that they have caused. This effort to make amends also delivers positive results in relation to reoffending. The restorative process of inviting perpetrators to take responsibility for their behaviour, to repair relationships and to gain both self-respect and the respect of others by doing so has much in common with the key desistance processes of maturation, strengthening social bonds, and transformation of identity. The restorative process may be the solution to the problem that Porporino (2010) poses when he states that desistance theory lacks any sort of organized practice framework. Restorative justice offers a glimpse of what might be possible if there was shift from a preoccupation with reducing offending towards a commitment to undoing the injustice that victims experience (Pemberton and Letschert 2016).

Tyler (2003) argues that people comply with the law when they perceive legal authorities to be legitimate and deserving of compliance. It may be that a criminal justice system whose priority is to restore justice will actually make us all feel safer.

Note

1   Twenty-six percent serious or very serious offences, 53% intermediate offences, 21% minor offences (YJA statistics).

References

Angel, C. (2005) *Crime Victims Meet Their Offenders: Testing the Impact of Restorative Justice Conferences on Victims' Post-Traumatic Stress Symptoms*. PhD. Dissertation, University of Pennsylvania.

Barnes, O. M. (2015) *Restorative Justice in the Criminal Justice System: The McDonaldization of Diversionary Youth Conferencing*. PhD Thesis, Ulster University, Belfast.

Bazemore, G. (1998) Restorative justice and earned redemption: communities, victims, and offender reintegration. *American Behavioral Scientist*, 41(6), 768–813.

Beckett, H., Campbell, C., O'Mahony, D., Jackson, J. and Doak, J. (2004) *Interim Evaluation of the Northern Ireland Youth Conferencing Scheme: Research and Statistical Bulletin 1/2005*. Belfast: Northern Ireland Statistics and Research Agency.

Bolívar, D. (2015) The local practice of restorative justice: Are victims sufficiently involved? In I. Vanfraechem, D. Bolívar and I. Aertsen (Eds.), *Victims and Restorative Justice*. Oxon: Routledge, pp. 203–238.

Bolívar, D., Pelikan, C. and Lemonne, A. (2015) Victims and restorative justice: Towards a comparison. In I. Vanfraechem, D. Bolívar and I. Aertsen (Eds.), *Victims and Restorative Justice*. Oxon: Routledge, pp. 172–200.

Bottoms, A. (2001) Compliance and community penalties. In A. Bottoms, L. Gelsthorpe and S. Rex (Eds.), *Community Penalties: Change and Challenges*. Cullompton: Willan Publishing.

Bouffard, J., Cooper, M. and Bergseth, K. (2016) The effectiveness of various restorative justice interventions on recidivism outcomes among juvenile offenders. *Youth Violence and Juvenile Justice*, 15(4), 1–16.

Bradshaw, W. and Roseborough, D. (2005) Restorative justice dialogue: The impact of mediation and conferencing on juvenile recidivism. *Federal Probation*, 69(2), 15–21.

Bushway, Shawn D. and Apel, R. (2012) A signaling perspective on employment-based reentry programming: Training completion as a desistance signal. *Criminology and Public Policy*, 11(1), 73–86.

Campbell, C., Devlin, R., O'Mahony, D., Doak, J., Jackson, J., Corrigan, T., et al. (2005) *Evaluation of the Northern Ireland Youth Conference Service*. Belfast: Northern Ireland Statistics and Research Agency.

Chapman, T. (2012) Facilitating restorative conferences in Northern Ireland. In E. Zinsstag and I. Vanfraechem (Eds.), *Conferencing and Restorative Justice: Challenges, Developments and Debates*. Oxford: Oxford University Press.

Chapman, T. and Murray, D. (2015) Restorative justice, social capital and desistance from offending. *Revista de Asistenţ Social*, XIV(4), 47–60.

Christie, N. (1977) Conflicts as property. *British Journal of Criminology*, 17(1), 1–15.

Choi, J. J. and Gilbert, M. J. (2010) 'Joe everyday, people off the street': A qualitative study on mediators' roles and skills in victim – offender mediation. *Contemporary Justice Review*, 13(2), 207–227.

Choi, J. J., Gilbert, M. J. and Green, D. L. (2013) Patterns of victim marginalization in victim-offender mediation: Some lessons learned. *Crime, Law and Social Change*, 59(1), 113–132.

Criminal Justice Inspection Northern Ireland. (2008) *Inspection of the Youth Conference Service in Northern Ireland*. Belfast: Criminal Justice Inspection Northern Ireland.

De Beus, K. and Rodgriguez, N. (2007) Restorative justice practice: An examination of program completion and recidivism. *Journal of Criminal Justice*, 35(3), 337–347.

Hoyle, C., Young, R. and Hill, R. (2002) *Proceed with Caution: An Evaluation of the Thames Valley Police Initiative in Restorative Cautioning*. Oxford: Joseph Rowntree Foundation.

Hoyle, C. and Rosenblatt, F. F. (2016) Looking back to the future: Threats to the success of restorative justice in the United Kingdom. *Victims & Offenders*, 11(1), 30–49.

Jacobson, J. and Gibbs, P. (2009) *Out of Trouble: Making Amends: Restorative Youth Justice in Northern Ireland*. London: Prison Reform Trust.

Johnstone, G. (2012) The standardization of restorative justice. In T. Gavriliedes (Eds.), *Rights and Restoration Within Youth Justice*. London, IARS Publications.

Latimer, J., Dowden, C. and Muise, D. (2005) The effectiveness of restorative justice practices: A meta-analysis. *Prison Journal*, 85(2), 127–144.

Laxminarayan, M. (2014) *Accessibility and Initiation of Restorative Justice*. Leuven: European Form for Restorative Justice.

Lyness, D. and Tate, S. (2011) *Northern Ireland Youth Reoffending: Results from the 2007 Cohort*. Statistical Bulletin 2/2011. Belfast: Youth Justice Agency.

Maruna, S. (2001) *Making Good: How Ex-Convicts Reform and Rebuild Their Lives*. Washington, DC: American Psychological Association Books.

McGarrell, E. E., Olivares, K., Crawford, K. and Kroovand, N. (2000) *Returning Justice to the Community: The Indianapolis Juvenile Restorative Justice Experiment*. Indianapolis: Hudson Institute.

Morris, A. and Maxwell, G. (2001) *Restorative Justice for Juveniles*. Oxford: Hart Publishing.

O'Mahony, D. and Doak, J. (2017) *Reimagining Restorative Justice: Agency and Accountability in the Criminal Process*. London: Hart.

Pavlich, G. C. (2005) *Governing Paradoxes of Restorative Justice*. London: Glasshouse Press.

Pemberton, A. and Letschert, R. M. (2016) Justice as the art of muddling through. The importance of nyaya in the aftermath of international crimes. In C. Brants and S. Karstedt (Eds.), *Engagement, Legitimacy, Contestation: Transitional Justice and Its Public Spheres*. Oxford: Hart Publishers.

Porporino, F. (2010) Bringing sense and sensitivity to corrections: From programmes to "x" offenders to services to support desistance. In J. Brayford, F. Cowe and J. Deering (Eds.), *What Else Works? Creative Work with Offenders*. Cullompton: Willan Publishing.

Rosenblatt, F. F. (2015) *The Role of Community in Restorative Justice*. Abingdon: Routledge.

Senge, P. (1990) *The Fifth Discipline: The Art and Practice of the Learning Organisation*. London: Random House.

Shapland, J., Robinson, G. and Sorsby, A. (2012) *Restorative Justice in Practice: Evaluating What Works for Victims and Offenders*. Abingdon, Oxon: Routledge.

Sherman, L. W. and Strang, H. (2007) *Restorative Justice: The Evidence*. London: The Adam Smith Institute.

Strang, H. (2002) *Repair or Revenge: Victims and Restorative Justice*. Oxford: Clarendon Press.

Strang, H., Barnes, G. C., Braithwaite, J. and Sherman, L. (1999) *Experiments in Restorative Policing: A Progress Report on the Canberra Reintegrative Shaming Experiments (RISE)*. Canberra: Australian National University. Available at www.aic.gov.au/rjustice/rise/progress/1999.html

Strang, H., Sherman, L., Angel, C. M., Woods, D. J., Bennett, S., New- bury-Birch, D. and Inkpen, N. (2006) Victim evaluations of face-to-face restorative justice experiences: A quasi-experimental analysis. *Journal of Social Issues*, 62, 281–306.

Strang, H., Sherman, L. W., Mayo-Wilson, E., Woods, D. and Ariel, B. (2013) *Restorative Justice Conferencing (RJC) Using Face-to-Face Meetings of Offenders and Victims: Effects on Offender Recidivism and Victim Satisfaction. A Systematic Review*. Campbell: Systematic Reviews.

Suzuki, M. and Wood, W. R. (2017) Co-option, coercion and compromise: Challenges of restorative justice in Victoria, Australia. *Contemporary Justice Review*, 20(2), 274–292.

Tyler, T. R. (2003) Procedural justice, legitimacy, and the effective rule of law. *Crime and Justice*, 30, 283–357.

Umbreit, M. S. and Coates, R. (1993) Cross-site analysis of victim offender mediation in four states. *Crime and Delinquency*, 39(4), 565–585.

Umbreit, M. S., Coates, R. B. and Vos, B. (2001) The impact of victim-offender mediation: Two decades of research. *Federal Probation*, 65(3), 29–35.

Umbreit, M. S., Vos, B. and Coates, R. B. (2005) Restorative justice dialogue: A review of evidence-based practice. *Offender Programs Report*, 9(4), 49–64.

Young, R. and Hoyle, C. (2003) New improve restorative justice? Action research and the Thames valley initiative in restorative cautioning. In A. V. Hirsch, J. Roberts, A. E. Bottoms, K. Roach and M. Schiff (Eds.), *Restorative Justice and Criminal Justice: Competing or Complementary Paradigms*. Oxford: Hart Publishing.

Zehr, H. (2005) *Changing Lenses: A New Focus for Crime and Justice*, 3rd edition. Scottdale, PA: Herald Press.

Zernova, M. (2007) Aspirations of restorative justice proponents and experiences of participants in family group conferences. *British Journal of Criminology*, 47(3), 491–509.

Zernova, M. (2009) Integrating the restorative and rehabilitative models: Lessons from one family group conferencing project. *Contemporary Justice Review*, 12(1), 59–75.

Zinsstag, E. and Chapman, T. (2012) *Restorative Youth Conferencing in Northern Ireland*. In E. Zinsstag and I. Vanfraechem (Eds.), *Conferencing and Restorative Justice: Challenges, Developments and Debates*. Oxford: Oxford University Press.

8

The evidence-based approach to correctional rehabilitation

Current status of the Risk-Need-Responsivity (RNR) model of offender rehabilitation

Ronen Ziv

Introduction

In the aftermath of the Martinson's (1974) 'nothing works doctrine', the futility of correctional rehabilitation was echoed within academia and the criminal justice system as a criminological fact (Cullen and Gilbert 2013). Within this hostile environment, advocates of rehabilitation identified only one way to rebuild the legitimacy of rehabilitation: showing empirical evidence that correctional interventions can reduce reoffending (Gendreau and Ross 1979). Back then, Donald Andrews joined with a number of psychologist colleagues to pursue a more effective approach to correctional treatment. This group included in particular James Bonta and Paul Gendreau who would work closely with Andrews across subsequent decades (other colleagues were Jerry Kiessling, Robert Hog, Robert Ross, and Stephen Wormith). During the last four decades, their work enabled them to advance the discussion around correctional rehabilitation from 'nothing works', to 'what works', to 'best practice'. Within the field of corrections, it seems that this group of scholars saved the notion of offender rehabilitation from death row (Cullen 2005; Ward and Maruna 2007).

This chapter presents the current status of the Risk-Need-Responsivity (RNR) model of offender rehabilitation. Andrews and his colleagues developed this model to reflect their evidence-based approach to correctional rehabilitation. In brief, since the mid-1970s, they have worked on a coherent treatment paradigm that explains the observed variation in criminal behaviour of individuals. Their research endeavours consisted of describing, predicting, and influencing this variation. In the early 1990s, they accumulated sufficient theoretical and empirical knowledge to articulate a unique comprehensive framework to undertake rehabilitation – the RNR model (Andrews and Bonta 1994; Andrews, Bonta, and Hoge 1990; Gendreau 1996).

By the early 21st century, the scientific approach to corrections enabled the reaffirmation of rehabilitation as a guiding correctional philosophy, and the issue of how to rehabilitate offenders effectively has since become a central challenge in corrections. In this new era of rehabilitation, policymakers tend to prefer correctional interventions that can demonstrate success, or at least employ promising rehabilitative aspects that can be tested scientifically (Cullen and Gendreau 2000). Moreover, they tend to prefer interventions that focus on reducing reoffending (enhancement of crime control) over increasing offenders' well-being (enhancement of individual welfare) (Garland 2001). Based on these priorities, the RNR model's scientific approach to recidivism has become the dominant theory of offender treatment (Ogloff and Davis 2004).

The next three sections discuss the essence of the RNR model. The first section introduces the model's theoretical framework. Andrews and his colleagues developed an empirically defensible theoretical perspective of criminal behaviour that aims to explain criminal behaviour, future offending, and changes in criminality. The second section introduces the RNR model's correctional framework. This framework distils the scientific information into a package of principles that guide practitioners on how to conduct effective intervention. These principles offer guidance that cover three clinical key concerns: (1) *who* should be treated; (2) *what* should be treated; (3) *how* to intervene. The current version of the RNR model consists of 15 principles of correctional assessment and treatment (Bonta and Andrews 2017). The third section discusses the impact of the model's evidence-based approach on a core issue of offender rehabilitation: offenders' motivation. This section demonstrates how the RNR model's empirical and practical orientation hinders the model's future development.

The RNR model's theoretical framework: a scientific perspective of criminal conduct

Long before Andrews and his colleagues introduced the Risk-Need-Responsivity model, they started to develop their theoretical perspective. In the 1970s, they realized that practitioners conducted treatment programs that were often 'based on incomplete theory and woeful lack of descriptive data or demonstrated poor integration of theory with treatment methods' (Gendreau and Ross 1979: 466). Thus, they aimed to bridge the gap between theory and practice by emphasizing the importance of using scientific knowledge for serving practical purposes.

Essentially, Andrews and his colleagues used systematic programme evaluations to test their theoretical ideas on the variation in criminal behaviour of individuals (Andrews 1980; Andrews, Zinger et al. 1990). In this regard, they underscored the normative aspects of rehabilitation and asserted that 'what makes the correctional system unique is its focus upon the management of a court-imposed sentence and the public mandate to reduce the likelihood of recidivism during the period of sentence' (Andrews 1982: 9). Indeed, this emphasis on recidivism reframed the evolution of the RNR model as an attempt to construct 'a theory of recidivism' (Cullen 2013: 342).

As psychologists who worked in the Canadian correctional system, Andrews and his collaborators were strongly influenced by the social psychology approach to human behaviour and, in particular, by social learning theory. This theoretical and practical influence led them to develop a unique perspective of criminal behaviour – the General Personality Cognitive Social Learning (GPCSL) perspective. According to the GPCSL perspective, biological factors at the base of behaviour and the cognitions of the individual are the causes of behaviour. It posits that all human beings share the same constellation of personality dimensions and the same way of behavioural learning. In that sense, offenders and nonoffenders are the same. Where they differ, however, is in where they lie on these personality dimensions and in their basic cognitive capabilities. According to this perspective, the way in which offenders perceive situations and respond to them influence where they stand on these personality and cognitive spectrums.

An essential aspect of the RNR model's theoretical framework is the role of criminology in the GPCSL perspective. This framework emphasizes general personality and social psychology perspective in criminological theories and research. Specifically, Andrews and his colleagues uncovered how the 'psycho-dynamic, social bonding, differential association, and strain theoretical perspectives are converging on general personality and cognitive social learning perspective' (Andrews and Bonta 2010a: 129). They analyzed which aspects of these theories had empirical support and provided explicit explanation of criminality in the immediate situation of action.

This theoretical analysis that integrates criminology and correctional rehabilitation led Andrews and his colleagues to propose four key factors that explain the occurrence and reoccurrence of criminal behaviour. These 'Big Four' variables are (1) pro-criminal attitudes that support the behaviour; (2) history of engaging in criminal behaviour; (3) pro-criminal associates who approve the behaviour; (4) antisocial personality pattern that predisposes the behaviour (Andrews and Bonta 2010a). They concluded that 'the most empirical defensible theories will be those that assign causal significance to at least two of the four' (p. 132).

In addition to the Big Four factors, empirical findings revealed four other risk factors that are correlated with criminal behaviour – the Moderate Four: family/marital, school/work, substance use, and leisure/recreation. Within the GPCSL perspective, these four risk/need factors are 'environmental factors that influence recidivism rates directly by providing opportunities for criminal behavior and indirectly by interacting with the Big Four' (Grieger and Hosser 2014). That is, (1) family/marital factor represents the 'quality of relationships' and 'behavioural expectations' within offenders' family of origins and marital circumstances; (2) school/work factor represents social achievement and 'interpersonal relationships' within school and/or work; (3) substance use factor represents problems that flow from consuming alcohol and/or drugs; and (4) leisure/recreation factor represents offenders' level 'of involvement and satisfaction in prosocial leisure pursuits' (Bonta and Andrews 2017: 45–46). Recently, Bonta and Andrews (2017) argue that new empirical studies justify the exclusion of this distinction between the Big Four and Moderate Four. They have concluded that it might be more appropriate to use the more omnibus term of the 'Central Eight Risk/Need Factors' of offender rehabilitation (pp. 44–45).

The RNR model's theoretical framework also provides explanation of how a therapeutic process can maximize its influence on offenders' reoffending. Andrews and his colleagues assert that correctional intervention should focus on rewarding alternative pro-social behaviours because it serves two proposes: it reduces offenders' motivation for crime and increases the potential cost of participating in crime. They expect that such practice will modify offenders' cognitive processes that favour pro-social behaviour over antisocial behaviour. Overall, during the 1980s, these Canadian scholars continued their scientific journey to demarcate the theoretical, empirical, and practical bases for intervening effectively with offenders. Thus, when they first presented the RNR model, the model's theoretical foundation was an empirically defensible perspective of criminal conduct.

The RNR model's correctional framework: the principles of effective correctional treatment

In the early 1990s, Andrews and his colleagues relied on ample empirical research to propose a general correctional framework – a set of principles for correctional interventions designed to reduce reoffending (Andrews 1995; Andrews, Bonta, and Hoge 1990). Essentially, they designed these principles in a form that provides both testable hypotheses for researchers and clear guidance for practitioners (Cullen 2005). Since first presented, this correctional framework has been developed through six editions of Andrews and Bonta's book (*The Psychology of Criminal Conduct*) and in a series of articles (e.g. Andrews et al. 2011).

Although the current version of the RNR model's correctional framework includes 15 principles, this model is often known because its three Risk-Need-Responsivity core principles for best practice. In a nutshell, the *risk principle* – the first 'R' in the RNR model – guides correctional interventions to deliver high level of service for high-risk cases and minimal level of service to low-risk cases. According to this principle, high-risk offenders need more service simply because there is more to change about them. In addition, this principle guides correctional intervention to separate high-risk offenders from low-risk offenders. That is either because high-risk offenders may become anti-social role models, or low-risk offenders may suffer from intensive treatment that deteriorates the ability to maintain conventional aspects in their life.

The need principle – the 'N' in the RNR model – proposes that correctional interventions should focus on a particular subset of dynamic risk factors as intermediate targets. Specifically, these risk factors should be 'dynamic attributes of offenders and their circumstances that, when changed, are associated with changes in the chances of recidivism' (i.e. criminogenic needs) (Andrews, Bonta, and Hoge 1990). Within the RNR model's correctional framework, there are seven criminogenic needs (the Central Eight risk/need factors minus the static 'criminal history' factor). Essentially, the need principle distinguishes between 'criminogenic needs' and 'non-criminogenic needs'. As opposed to criminogenic needs, non-criminogenic needs represent dynamic and changeable attributes of offenders that 'have a very minor or no causal relationship to criminal behavior' (Andrews and Bonta 2010b: 45).

In addition to the 'who' and 'what' should be treated, the responsivity principle – the last 'R' in the RNR model – involves aspects that address 'how' to do treatment. According to Bonta and Andrews (2017), the *general responsivity principle* is 'quite straightforward: Offenders are human beings, and the most powerful influence strategies available are cognitive-behavioral and cognitive social learning strategies' (pp. 180–182). They argue that empirical evidence support the general capability of these strategies to influence offenders' criminogenic needs. Based on their GPCSL perspective of criminal behaviour, they specified the strategies that provide the most effective way to teach new pro-social behaviours: 'modeling, reinforcement, role-playing, skill building, modification of thoughts and emotions through cognitive restructuring, and practicing new, low-risk alternative behaviors over and over again in a variety of high-risk situations until one gets very good at it' (p. 182).

Another aspect of the responsivity principle guides practitioners to modify rehabilitative strategies in accordance with the offender's specific learning style and characteristics – the *specific responsivity principle*. These specific considerations include factors such as verbal skills, motivation to engage in treatment, level of anxiety, level of impulsiveness, psychiatric problems, level of interpersonal sensitivity, level of interpersonal and cognitive maturity, intelligence, gender, age, and ethnicity (Andrews and Bonta 2010a). According to this principle, it is important to address these factors in correctional intervention because they may hinder or enhance the process of learning.

In addition to these core principles, the RNR model's correctional framework consists of several clinical principles that aim to improve its implementation. One of these principles guides practitioners to target more criminogenic needs than non-criminogenic needs (the Breadth principle). The second clinical principle emphasizes the potential of assessing offenders' strength factors for predicting reoffending or removing barriers to full participation in service (the Strength principle). Another clinical principle guides practitioners to employ structured and validated assessment tools and integrate the findings into a treatment plan (the Structured Assessment principle). The last clinical principle stresses the importance of adhering to the principle of the RNR model (the Professional Discretion principle).

The last group of the RNR model's principles consists of organizational guidance for effective intervention. First, the RNR model underscores community-based services as the preferable setting to intervene with offenders (the Community-based principle). Second, advocates of this model assert that correctional therapists and staff should have high-quality relationship skills (for creating interpersonal influent) in combination with high-quality structuring skills (for shifting offenders' behavioural expressions from pro-criminal to pro-social) (the GPCSL-Based Staff Practice principle). The last principle in the RNR model's correctional framework guides programme managers. It suggests that managers should be responsible for implementing the core RNR principles, maintaining integrity, and promoting the intervention outside the agency (the Management principle). Overall, with these 15 principles, the RNR model provides a comprehensive approach to rehabilitation that is theoretically informed, evidence-based, and practical.

Current status and core controversial issue: the role of motivation in the RNR model

Andrews and his colleagues encourage the development of the model's theoretical and correctional frameworks in accordance to the accumulated empirical knowledge. They described the RNR model as 'a work-in-progress' – a model that allows future developments to 'enhance the multiple contributions of psychology to the understanding and management of criminal offending' (Andrews and Bonta 2010b: 51). As mentioned above, this practical evidence-based approach to rehabilitation has proven to be an effective strategy for reducing recidivism and has bolstered the dominancy of the RNR model in correctional rehabilitation.

However, some aspects of the RNR model remain controversial (Ziv 2018). In general, scholars criticized the RNR model's strict evidence-based orientation to rehabilitation. They argued that such orientation may improve assessments, treatment integrity, or programme implementation, but will not enrich rehabilitation with a new theoretical breakthrough (Porporino 2010). They also criticized the model's narrow perspective of offenders' needs and motivation. According to this argument, the RNR model's empirical and practical orientation focuses on achieving 'treatment needs' for reducing participant's tendency to reoffend and neglects the achievement of 'offender needs' for promoting personal goals in a socially appropriate manner. That is, the model guides practitioners to provide psychological services that pay very little attention to offenders' inner motivation to achieve personal goals that maximize their psychological well-being (Ward and Maruna 2007). In the light of these criticism, this section discusses how the RNR model's empirical and practical orientation to offender rehabilitation limits the future development of the model's motivational strategies.

Since first presented, motivational issues have remained an undeveloped aspect of the RNR model. In a nutshell, this model understands offenders' motivation to commit criminal acts through the impact of external incentives on their cognitive situation. That is, the way people perceive reward and cost contingencies motivates them to act, and the interaction between this motivation and the Central Eight risk/need factors explains the variation in criminal behaviour. Accordingly, they guide interventions to motivate offenders by helping them to understand the incentives that lead to offending, teaching them new pro-social behaviours, and rewarding pro-social behavioural responses to those incentives. They follow the findings from empirical studies and assert that this approach to addressing offenders' criminogenic needs is the most efficient way to make offenders choose pro-social over antisocial behavioural responses and, therefore, to reduce their future offending.

Although successful in reducing recidivism, this evidence-based approach to rehabilitation limits the potential role of motivation in correctional interventions. Specifically, this approach has led the RNR model to exclude theoretical concepts that explain motivation through offenders' innate motivation to attain basic human needs (e.g. the need of autonomy, competence, and relatedness; see Deci and Ryan 2000), or rehabilitative strategies that build on such human needs to enhance offenders' psychological well-being (e.g. how to attain their 'primary human good'; see Ward and Maruna 2007). Advocates of the RNR model are aware of this limitation but consistently insist on adhering their evidence-based approach to motivation. They assert that any theoretical idea about the impact of inner sources on human behaviour must be operation-alized and tested 'within the context of understanding *criminal* behavior' before it can be integrated within the RNR model (Andrews et al. 2011: 740, emphasis in original). In addition, they argue that the role of such motivational concepts should be determined by its potential impact on recidivism. Overall, they con-tend that the role of offender motivation is limited because there are insuffi-cient scientific studies that have evaluated whether such motivational concepts or strategies have incremental value for improving offender rehabilitation.

Within the RNR model's correctional framework, the integration of moti-vational interviewing (MI) demonstrates the limited role the model ascribes to offenders' intrinsic motivation to change their life. In brief, MI emerged from practical experience as 'a directive, client-centered counseling style for eliciting behavior change by helping clients to expose and resolve ambivalence' (Roll-nick and Miller 1995: 325). This is a rehabilitative method that helps people to 'find their intrinsic motivation to improve themselves, have better lives, and make decisions that they value' (Stinson and Clark 2017: 4). Studies have found a positive effect of MI model in treatment for nonoffenders (medical patients, gamblers, addictions), but only slim reduction of recidivism in treatment for offenders (Alexander et al. 2012). Thus, from an evidence-based perspective of offender rehabilitation, MI is a non-theoretical, unstructured method that is unlikely to have an significant independent impact on criminal recidivism.

Despite its weak evidence base, MI is the only rehabilitative method that advocates of the RNR model consistently recommend for enhancing offend-ers' motivation (Bonta and Andrews 2017). However, they limit the role of the MI in the model's correctional framework. Specifically, they integrated the MI as a technique to facilitate changes in offenders' criminogenic needs (an aspect of specific responsivity principle), rather than as a general strat-egy to influence criminal behaviour (general responsivity principle). That is, within this framework, the goal of MI is 'to increase motivation to attend and adhere to treatment', rather than reducing recidivism (Andrews and Bonta 2010a: 291). Thus, the model evaluates a successful integration of MI by the achievement of treatment goals (e.g. minimum attrition), rather than social goals (e.g. reducing future offending, social reintegration) or personal goals (e.g. optimal psychological functioning). Accordingly, they recommend cor-rectional interventions to use the MI method in two ways. One way is to use the MI as 'a preparatory first step to more formal, structured treatment and relapse prevention treatment' (Bonta and Andrews 2017: 168). The second way is use the MI as a counselling technique that builds strong therapeutic relationships with offenders (Bonta and Andrews 2017).

Conclusions

This chapter presented the current status of the RNR model through its com-prehensive theoretical and correctional frameworks. As described above,

Andrews and his colleagues developed a coherent theoretical framework that bridges the gap between criminology and behavioural science. The framework aims to explain variation in criminal behaviour and identify the factors that give rise to criminal involvement generally, and specifically, to recidivism (Central Eight risk/need factors). In addition, advocates of the RNR model have developed a correctional framework that bridges the gap between the scientific research and human service. They have advanced a set of principles, with the three RNR principles at its core, for effectively rehabilitating offenders in correctional settings. Taken together, the RNR model's theoretical and correctional frameworks have emerged in the correctional system as the dominant approach to undertaking rehabilitation.

Yet, the closing section of this chapter has shown that the RNR model's empirical and practical orientation to rehabilitation limits the model's theoretical development. Such limitation is demonstrated through the impact of the model's position on offenders' motivation. That section has shown that the RNR model's empirical and practical orientation to offender motivation hinders the development of this concept. The model emphasizes external sources of motivation to change, and guides correctional interventions to use motivation for facilitating rehabilitative processes that address criminogenic needs and achieve reduction in recidivism. However, due to a lack of scientific evidence of alternative sources of motivation that result in decrease in recidivism, advocates of the RNR model remain reluctant to expand the role of offender motivation. That is, they ignore the possibility that the internal drive to achieve basic human needs may be another source of motivation to change criminal behaviour. They are also reluctant to guide correctional intervention in using motivation for the attainment of offenders' personal goals, which may enhance their well-being.

This limited role of offender motivation was demonstrated by the integration of motivational interviewing (MI) in the RNR model. While MI is a method that elicits offenders' intrinsic motivation to improve their life, the RNR model uses it as a technique to motivate them to achieve treatment goals (e.g. minimum attrition and maximum therapeutic relationship). Overall, future initiatives that aim to develop the role of motivation in the RNR model depend on scientific evidence that show the capacity of internal sources of motivation to reduce recidivism – the gold standard of any RNR-based correctional intervention that aims to secure and promote the legitimacy of offender rehabilitation.

References

Alexander, M., Lowenkamp, C. T. and Robinson, C. R. (2012) A tale of two innovations: Motivational interviewing and core correctional practices in United States probation. In P. Ugwudike and P. Raynor (Eds.), *What Works in Offender Compliance*. New York: Palgrave Macmillan, pp. 242–255.

Andrews, D. A. (1980) Some experimental investigations of the principles of differential association through deliberate manipulations of the structure of service systems. *American Sociological Review*, 45, 448–462.

Andrews, D. A. (1982) *The Supervision of Offenders: Identifying and Gaining Control Over the Factors That Make a Difference*. Program Branch User Report. Ottawa, ON: Solicitor General of Canada.

Andrews, D. A. (1995) The psychology of criminal conduct and effective treatment. In J. McGuire (Ed.), *What Works: Reducing Reoffending – Guidelines from Research and Practice* (pp. 35–62). New York: John Wiley.

Andrews, D. A. and Bonta, J. (1994) *The Psychology of Criminal Conduct*. Cincinnati, OH: Anderson.

Andrews, D. A. and Bonta, J. (2010a) *The Psychology of Criminal Conduct*, 5th edition. New Providence, NJ: Anderson, LexisNexis.

Andrews, D. A. and Bonta, J. (2010b) Rehabilitating criminal justice policy and practice. *Psychology, Public Policy, and Law*, 16, 39–55.

Andrews, D. A., Bonta, J. and Hoge, R. D. (1990) Classification for effective rehabilitation: Rediscovering psychology. *Criminal Justice and Behavior*, 17, 19–52.

Andrews, D. A., Bonta, J. and Wormith, J. S. (2011) The Risk-Need-Responsivity (RNR) model: Does adding the good lives model contribute to effective crime prevention? *Criminal Justice and Behavior*, 38, 735–755.

Andrews, D. A., Zinger, I., Hoge, R. D., Bonta, J., Gendreau, P. and Cullen, F. T. (1990) Does correctional treatment work? A clinically relevant and psychologically informed meta-analysis. *Criminology*, 28, 369–404.

Bonta, J. and Andrews, D. A. (2017) *The Psychology of Criminal Conduct*, 6th edition. New York: Routledge.

Cullen, F. T. (2005) The twelve people who saved rehabilitation: How the science of criminology made a difference. *Criminology*, 43, 1–42.

Cullen, F. T. (2013) Rehabilitation: Beyond nothing works. In M. Tonry (Ed.), *Crime and Justice in America, 1975 to 2025 – Crime and Justice: A Review of Research*, Vol. 42. Chicago: University of Chicago Press, pp. 299–376.

Cullen, F. T. and Gendreau, P. (2000) Assessing correctional rehabilitation: Policy, practice, and prospects. In J. Horney (Ed.), *Policies, Processes, and Decisions of the Criminal Justice System: Criminal Justice*, Vol. 3. Washington, DC: US Department of Justice, National Institute of Justice, pp. 109–175.

Cullen, F. T. and Gilbert, K. E. (2013) *Reaffirming Rehabilitation*, 2nd edition, 30th anniversary edition. Waltham, MA: Anderson, Elsevier.

Deci, E. L. and Ryan, R. M. (2000) The "what" and "why" of goal pursuits: Human needs and the self-determination of behavior. *Psychological Inquiry*, 11, 227–268.

Garland, D. (2001) *The Culture of Control: Crime and Social Order in Contemporary Society*. Chicago: University of Chicago Press.

Gendreau, P. (1996) The principles of effective intervention with offenders. In A. T. Harland (Ed.), *Choosing Correctional Interventions That Work: Defining the Demand and Evaluating the Supply*. Thousand Oaks, CA: Sage Publications, pp. 117–130.

Gendreau, P. and Ross, B. (1979) Effective correctional treatment: Bibliotherapy for cynics. *Crime and Delinquency*, 25, 463–489.

Grieger, L. and Hosser, D. (2014) Which risk factors are really predictive? An analysis of Andrews and Bonta's "Central Eight" risk factors for recidivism in German youth correctional facility inmates. *Criminal Justice and Behavior*, 41, 613–634.

Martinson, R. (1974) What works? – questions and answers about prison reform. *Public Interest*, 35(2), 22–54.

Ogloff, J. R. P. and Davis, M. R. (2004) Advances in offender assessment and rehabilitation: Contributions of the Risk-Needs-Responsivity approach. *Psychology, Crime and Law*, 10, 229–242.

Porporino, F. J. (2010) Bringing sense and sensitivity to corrections: From programmes to 'fix' offenders to services to support desistence. In J. Brayford, F. Cowe and J. Deering (Eds.), *What Else Works? Creative Work with Offenders*. Cullompton, Devon: Willan Publishing, pp. 61–85.

Rollnick, S. and Miller, W. R. (1995) What is motivational interviewing? *Behavioural and Cognitive Psychotherapy*, 23, 325–334.

Stinson, J. D. and Clark, M. D. (2017) *Motivational Interviewing with Offenders*. New York: The Guilford Press.

Ward, T. and Maruna, S. (2007) *Rehabilitation: Beyond the Risk Paradigm*. New York: Routledge.

Ziv, R. (2018) *The Future of Correctional Rehabilitation: Moving Beyond the RNR Model and Good Lives Model Debate*. New York: Routledge.

9 An overview of the Good Lives Model

Theory and evidence

Mayumi Purvis and Tony Ward

Introduction

In 2002, the first paper on a new framework for the management and treatment of sexual offenders emerged, referred to as the Good Lives Model (GLM) of offender rehabilitation (Ward 2002a, 2002b). What ensued in the following decade were in excess of 200 more GLM publications, including published theoretical refinement, practice papers, empirical research, and papers outlining the GLM's diverse application to a range of client groups, and the research and application of the GLM is ongoing and strong.

In 2010, not long after the GLM was first outlined, the findings of a Canadian survey of sex offender treatment programs were revealed, which spoke to the popularity of the GLM with practitioners (McGrath et al. 2010). Respondents selected from a list of 13 theories, the three that best described their preferred treatment approaches. The GLM was the newest framework on the list, and yet, 75% of all female programs and 50% of all adult male programs identified the GLM as their preferred framework. Clearly, the GLM's central premise, that rehabilitation must also focus on enhancing positive capabilities rather than just suppressing dysfunctional ones (Ward and Maruna 2007; Ward and Willis 2016), is an appealing approach for practitioners.

The Good Lives Model represents a strengths-based approach to working with offenders and is premised on the idea that, in order for long-term change to be achievable, offenders need the opportunity for better lives: lives that are both personally meaningful and socially responsible (Ward and Fortune 2016). Furthermore, the best way to achieve these long-term prospects is via capability building. Simply put, if offenders are to have any real chance at giving up their harmful behaviours, in lieu of living healthy, pro-social, meaningful lives, then they need to be equipped to live differently. Merely teaching them how to identify their own risk factors and avoid those scenarios where they are likely to engage in antisocial behaviours is at best a bandaid for the 'successful' completion of a correctional order.

Whilst the central aim of the GLM is to build psychological and social capacities, it is also important to understand that it pays equally detailed attention to risk reduction. In fact, the GLM advocates for a dual emphasis on *risk management* and *goods promotion* (Barnao et al. 2016; Ward and Willis 2016). Put another way, application of the GLM in offender management has two associated goals, being:

1 *Monitor the offender*: manage the risk posed by an offender to the community (risk management); and
2 *Engage the offender*: enhance offender well-being by increasing the offender's strengths and capability so that they are better equipped to live a pro-social and personally meaningful life (goods promotion).

The core premise of the GLM is that rehabilitation is an evaluative and capability-building process, whereby change requires not just the targeting of isolated 'factors', but also the holistic reconstruction of the self (Ward 2010; Ward and Heffernan 2017).

It is important to understand that the GLM is not a theory of offending behaviour or a treatment model. It does not explain the offence process and it is also not an aetiological theory, although it has aetiological assumptions concerning offending behaviour embedded within it (Ward and Maruna 2007). The GLM is, in actuality, a model of healthy human functioning. In line with positive psychology, it provides practitioners with an objective reference to what constitutes a healthy, pro-social adult life, characterized by optimal levels of well-being (see Fortune et al. 2015). The framework can therefore be used to assist individuals to develop the competencies needed to subjectively pursue a healthier, happier, and more pro-social life.

Before briefly setting out the theoretical components of the model, there are three key comprehension points we wish to articulate. First is an explanation of how the GLM conceptualizes offending behaviour. Second is to outline the GLM's aetiological position, and third is to identify how understanding the first and second points helps us to work more meaningfully with offenders.

GLM's conceptualization of offending behaviour

The GLM conceptualizes offending behaviour in completely natural and humanistic terms (see Barnao et al. 2015; Ward and Fortune 2016). Human beings are goal directed, and human behaviour, therefore, is meaningful and purposeful and is directed by one or more legitimate goals. As such, the GLM explains that all meaningful human actions represent attempts to secure Primary Human Goods (PHGs). PHGs are explained later, but for now it is helpful to know that they essentially represent overarching life pursuits or ultimate concerns and are expressed in the many and varied goals that we set for ourselves (see Emmons 1999). PHGs are such powerful human motivators that human beings are naturally predisposed to seek them for the sake of their overall psychological, physical, and social well-being. Therefore, the seeking of primary human goods is inherently natural and valuable (Ward and Heffernan 2017).

Even offending behaviour has an underlying legitimate goal and as such, it can be viewed in terms of the (albeit problematic) pursuit of PHGs. Take for example a young man drinking in a bar. He is pushed from behind and spills his drink and is superficially injured in the process. He turns and confronts his perceived aggressor, and whilst it is clear it was an accident, the person responsible is unapologetic and unsympathetic and tersely tells the young man to 'get over it' and insults him by engaging in some name-calling. The young man feels enraged by this injustice, and due to an absence of adaptive coping skills, and an inability to control his impulsivity, poor consequential thinking, and social supports for violence as a means for resolution, he physically assaults the other party, leaving them seriously injured. This results in criminal charges and formal sanctions. So, one might ask, what was the legitimate goal? Some might say that his goal was to hurt another person, and this is surely not okay. In fact, the causing of physical harm to another was actually a dysfunctional means or strategy for achieving an otherwise legitimate end. The actual goal is likely to be the need for control or agency, to regain some perceived loss of power, and/or perhaps to feel respected and admired by others. These are normal states for adults to pursue; however, in the above example, it is the *way* in which these goals are achieved which is problematic. Therefore, it is the strategy or means that is the target for intervention, not the goal itself.

GLM's aetiological position

In explaining why people offend, that is, why people use a problematic means for an otherwise legitimate goal, the GLM identifies capabilities, or specifically, the lack thereof, as the primary source of dysfunction. An absence of capabilities typically indicates that the person has a collection of deficits or problematic characteristics in place of adaptive ones. These deficits or weaknesses can be internal or external (Purvis et al. 2014). *Internal factors* refer to the person's skills, attitudes, beliefs, psychological characteristics, physical health, educational background, and so on, whereas *external factors* refer to environmental, social, cultural, and interpersonal opportunities and circumstances. As clients often lack the strengths and positive attributes and environments to overcome their life's challenges pro-socially, they act in problematic, harmful, or antisocial ways, symptomatic and reflective of their unique profile of deficits and obstacles. Remembering that PHGs are such powerful human motivators that all human beings are naturally inclined to seek them, the GLM argues that people offend in the pursuit of PHGs, but do so in harmful ways due to their individual set of internal and external deficits and obstacles. Those internal and external deficits that drive offending behaviour in the pursuit of PHGs, arguably represent an individual's unique set of dynamic risk factors.

Using the GLM to promote offender collaboration with workers

If we understand what the client was or is seeking, in terms of PHGs, when they offended, then we understand something key about what motivates this person and what they value and desire for themselves. Deciphering the legitimate goal in offending behaviour enables us to link this to, and understand, the PHG that the offender was seeking, meaning we can tailor our intervention and rehabilitative efforts at helping the offender to build capacity in precisely those areas that are under-resourced. By helping offenders to build the necessary conditions (i.e. internal and external capacities) for fulfilling their needs and pursuing their PHGs in adaptive, pro-social ways, the associated effect is that they will be less likely to harm others and themselves. Furthermore, motivation is more likely to arise in those offenders who are working on goals or life domains that are prized and highly weighted. This in turn is more likely to foster ongoing engagement and a collaborative approach to rehabilitation. As such, the enhancement of offender well-being (in a goods promotion sense) directly functions to reduce risk and protect the community. It does so in two ways: (1) the acquisition of certain capacities involved in successfully implementing the Good Lives plan will reduce risk (e.g. emotional control) and (2) individuals are likely to be more motivated to engage in programmes because they view them as a means to achieve valued goals (Ward and Fortune 2016).

GLM core concepts: primary human goods

Primary human goods are actions, states of affairs, characteristics, experiences, and states of mind that are intrinsically beneficial to human beings and are sought for their own sake rather than as a means to a more fundamental end (Ward 2002b; Ward and Marshall 2004). They represent the ultimate concerns of human beings, which sit across multiple life domains. This means that they have intrinsic value (are meaningful and valuable in and of themselves) and in addition, they represent fundamental purposes and ultimate ends of human behaviour.

The generation of the PHGs draws from research findings and theories identified in a range of disciplines, including psychological research (Cummins 1996; Emmons 1999), evolutionary theory (Arnhart 1998; Durrant and Ward 2015), practical ethics (Murphy 2001), philosophical anthropology (Nussbaum 2000; Rescher 1990), and philosophy (Becker 1992). Based on past and current cross-cultural and cross-discipline research, there are 11 PHGs (see Purvis et al. 2014). It should be noted that these PHGs have emerged from thorough analysis of research findings related to personal strivings and the pursuit of healthy lives characterized by high levels of well-being. Given this, the GLM and its account of PHGs may be considered an evolving theory, always open to adaptation, refinement, and development, based on the ever-evolving nature of world knowledge and empirical research. Finally, there is no 'right' order to these PHGs; they can only be subjectively ordered according to priority and value. These PHGs form the foundation of human beings' ultimate pursuits. Each of our personal, professional, and life goals can be linked to one or a combination of these PHGs. The active and successful pursuit of PHGs brings about overall life satisfaction, happiness, contentedness, and well-being across the three domains of human functioning, being physical, psychological, and social. The definition for each PHGs is provided below, along with some examples of pro-social seeking and problematic seeking. These examples refer to the functional or dysfunctional ways in which people may attempt to secure the PHG in their lives, that is the means by which they seek the PHG, not the form the PHG takes necessarily.

Life

The primary good of Life essentially incorporates all the physical needs and factors that are important for healthy living and physical functioning: food, water, shelter, a physically healthy body, and so on. Essentially, fulfilment of this good requires not only that the individual's basic needs for survival are met, but that beyond this, his/her physical health is determined to be sound. The good of Life also requires that the person's living circumstances are adequate and suited to their needs. Ideal fulfilment of this good would mean that the person presents as a physically healthy person whose physical functioning and living circumstances are optimal. Examples of pro-social seeking would include securing stable accommodation, exercise, financial management to meet basic needs, and properly managing health problems. Examples of problematic seeking might include squatting, couch surfing, self-medicating, and theft.

Knowledge

This primary human good is based on the notion that people are inherently curious beings that possess the desire to understand aspects of themselves, their natural environments, and other people. The good of Knowledge satisfies this need and includes acquiring wisdom or information such as facts, theories, ideas, which we can use to answer a number of questions: what does this mean? What is valuable? Why did this happen? How do things work? And so on. This good is not concerned with IQ or how smart someone is; instead, Knowledge acquisition should be assessed according to how well informed an individual feels about things that are important to them. Examples of pro-social seeking could include studying, taking lessons, and asking questions. Examples of problematic seeking might be extortion and stand-over tactics.

Excellence in Play

Human beings seek to enjoy and be good at a range of recreational tasks that may or may not be structured into games or events. This good refers to the desire to engage in leisure or fun activities, which provide the person with a sense of pride, achievement, satisfaction, or skill development. The underlying idea of this good involves both engaging in activities for the purpose of enjoyment, as well as to achieve mastery in the area. This good is likely to have both an intrinsic value (accomplishment for the sake of it, i.e. for personal enjoyment) and an instrumental value (accomplishment for a specific purpose, i.e. to win a competition, move up to the next grade/level, or to achieve greater physical fitness) and must be matched to an individual's personal set of skills, interests, preferences, and desires. Examples of pro-social seeking could be participating in team sports or competitive online gaming. Examples of problematic seeking could include acts like cheating and sabotaging others in order to get ahead.

Excellence in Work

This good refers to one's need to be meaningfully employed in a role that provides mastery experiences and challenges that are matched to the person's level of functioning. This good refers to the desire to engage in work, which provides the person with a sense of pride, achievement, satisfaction, and/or skill development. Meaningful employment will have both an intrinsic value (accomplishment for the sake of it, i.e. for personal fulfilment) and an instrumental value (accomplishment for a specific purpose, i.e. a promotion, greater responsibility, or salary increase) and must be matched to an individual's personal set of skills, interests, preferences, and desires. Examples of pro-social seeking would be paid or volunteer work, self-employment, and apprenticeships. Examples of problematic seeking could be organized crime, white-collar crime, and taking credit for other people's work and achievements.

Excellence in Agency

This good refers to the desire human beings have to formulate their own goals and seek ways to realize them in actions and activities of their own choice and accommodates an adult's need for autonomy, self-directedness, personal power, control, and mastery. It concerns the individual's ability to act in a way that produces a specific and desired outcome. Excellence in Agency also refers to the desire to make up one's own mind and to function as an independent being to at least some minimal degree without interference from others (moderated by cultural and social norms of course). The good encompasses the desire to stand on one's own two feet, to be able to pursue the things an individual values most and to shape their lives in ways that are consistent with their deepest values and concerns. Examples of pro-social seeking would be acting assertively, up-skilling, and achieving financial independence. Examples of problematic seeking could include aggression, violence, and manipulation in order to dominate others.

Inner Peace

The primary human good of Inner Peace refers to emotional self-regulation and one's ability to achieve a state of emotional balance. It also refers to the need for emotional competence. Emotional competence is basically the application of self-regulation processes to the emotional domain and therefore consists of a number of skills, such as awareness and understanding of one's own emotional state, the ability to express how we feel, the capacity to identify other peoples' emotions, the capacity to respond empathically to other people, and the ability to manage aversive emotions through a range of adaptive strategies. Examples of pro-social seeking might include meditation, counselling, and exercise. Examples of problematic seeking could be self-harm, avoidance, and use of drugs or alcohol to manage aversive emotions.

Relatedness

The good of Relatedness is based upon the natural desire of human beings to establish warm affectionate bonds with other people, ranging from romantic relationships to intimate family relationships and platonic yet close friendships. As such, this PHG refers to the close, caring, mutual relationships that adults establish with an intimate partner, family members, and close friends. The activities that constitute the good of Relatedness include disclosure, support, sexual activity, physical contact, honesty, spending time together, sharing interests, mutual emotional caring, equality, and so on. Examples of pro-social seeking could be adult romantic relationships, close family relationships, and very close friends. Examples of problematic seeking are promiscuity, and stalking.

Community

The primary good of Community refers to the desire human beings have to belong to social groups, to feel connected to (sometimes a variety of) groups that reflect their interests, concerns, and values. It is the sense of being part of a wider social and/or cultural network, to feel you are contributing to a larger social unit and to be able to rely on this larger group to meet one's own needs. Examples of pro-social seeking could include volunteer work, membership in special interest groups, and religious affiliation. Examples of problematic seeking could be cult association, membership with antisocial/hate groups, and criminal gangs.

Spirituality

The primary good of Spirituality refers to the desire people have to discover a sense of meaning and purpose in life and achieve the overall experience of being content and satisfied with one's life. This could involve seeking religious truths and involvement, a spiritual connection with a transcendent being or reality, or simply the experience of being part of a wider whole. In short, this good refers to a variety of activities in which participation provides a broad sense of purpose and direction in an individual's life and relates to the overall feeling of happiness and contentedness that emerges from understanding one's involvement with the world around them. Examples of pro-social seeking include belonging to a church or religious group, living one's life according to a spiritual belief system, having connection to land and an environmental association. An example of problematic seeking could be cult association or living life according to fanatical religious ideology.

Pleasure

The primary human good of Pleasure refers to a state of being (feeling good in the here and now), and refers to hedonic pleasure seeking, which is essentially healthy self-indulgence and gratification. It is often implicated in activities that bring about feelings of enjoyment, deep satisfaction, and excitement. Examples of pro-social seeking could include massage, food, sex, and thrill-seeking activities. Examples of problematic seeking might include drug taking, over-eating, self-harm, and risky sexual encounters.

Creativity

The primary human good of Creativity refers to a desire for novelty, innovation, and individuality in one's life. It may be reflected in the experience of doing things differently, being engaged in a specific type of activity that results in an artistic output, or perhaps producing a novel product of some kind. Creativity does not require that an individual be artistic in a traditional sense, as it may be implicated in a range of everyday activities; Creativity is essentially the expression of oneself through alternative forms. Examples of pro-social seeking could be gardening, solving problems, playing a musical instrument, and interior decorating. An example of problematic seeking is illegal graffiti art.

Primary human goods compared to goals

Often, PHGs are mistakenly referred to as life goals, and whilst it is true that people inherently aspire to acquire PHGs for the sake of their overall well-being, PHGs are fundamentally different to goals. Goals are a way of achieving PHGs, which are ultimate ends, and essentially underpin the goods. A comparison can be drawn to assist in the differentiation as set out in Table 9.1.

Table 9.1 Comparison table of primary human goods (PHGs) and goals

Primary human goods	Goals
Objective	**Subjective**
PHGs are objectively defined and are not bound by age, class, culture, or gender.	Goals are the subjective means by which people pursue PHGs and are shaped by age, class, gender, culture, personal preference, and all other human attributes.
Finite	**Infinite**
There are 11 PHGs and the number of PHGs is representative of and bound by research and discoveries about human strivings.	The number and type of goals that people can set for themselves in reference to any one PHG is only bound by social and cultural norms (at best) and is potentially unlimited.
Static	**Dynamic**
Although PHGs have the potential to evolve on the basis of research and discovery, they are essentially unchanging due to their objective nature.	The potential for goals to change and develop is ongoing. Goals will change as a result of achievements, failures, financial status, age, religion, relationship status, education, and a wide range of other factors.
Universal	**Individual**
Due to their objective nature and wide research base, PHGs are said to be universally relevant to human beings.	Goals are constructed in an entirely individual way and essentially represent a person's unique identity.

Four key problems that diminish human well-being

According to Ward (Barnao et al. 2015; Ward 2002a, 2002b; Ward and Fisher 2005), there are four primary types of problems that undermine human well-being and lead to unhappy, disconnected lives. These have been identified as capacity, means, conflict, and scope, and each of these factors link together in an ongoing way. Although each of these concepts have been set out in detail elsewhere (e.g. see Purvis et al. 2013), the following summary and linkages is provided.

Poor capacity refers to a lack (or under-representation) of the internal and external resources required by a person to enable their successful pursuit of PHGs in pro-social and personally meaningful ways. When internal and external resources are ample and available, the person is considered to have good capacity and therefore is able to engage in behaviours and strategies (means) that are enabling and productive (thus promoting the attainment of PHGs). However, when capacity is lacking, the individual is likely to have a range of internal and external obstacles (deficits and weaknesses) that hinder the pro-social and healthy pursuit of PHGs. As a result the person engages in behaviours and strategies (means) to pursue PHGs in a way that is problematic, harmful, or illegal. This is referred to as problematic or inappropriate means. The earlier example of the young man in the bar who seeks to gain respect or justice via violence and aggression is an example of how poor capacity (internal: poor emotional coping, impulsivity, lack of consequential thinking; and external: social supports for violence as a means for resolution) drives problematic means (behaviour). As such, in order to intervene with behaviour, we must first understand its purpose (the goal/s and PHG/s) and then understand the capacity issues that fuel the strategies chosen, with the aim of bolstering capacity in order to promote alternative means.

When PHGs are sought via problematic means (which are driven by capacity issues) they cause conflict in other areas of functioning. For example, someone who seeks freedom from emotional distress (PHG *Inner Peace*) by abusing drugs or alcohol (problematic means) due to poor emotional regulation skills (problems in internal capacity) and a lack of social supports (problems with external capacity) is going to experience problems and dysfunction in other areas of their life due to the problematic means used; this is referred to as conflict. Specifically, seeking *Inner Peace* via substance misuse might undermine (conflict with) the person's health (PHG *Life*); produce relationship strain (PHG *Relatedness*); and incite poor work performance or job loss (PHG *Excellence in Work*), which in turn will only function to increase the person's psychological turmoil (compounding problems with PHG *Inner Peace*).

The final problem is referred to as a lack of scope. Within the GLM, healthy functioning and optimal well-being is considered to be achieved when all 11 PHGs are accounted for to varying degrees in a person's life (full scope).

However, when not all PHGs are present (poor scope), this may lead to a neglect or absence of one or more of the three components of human well-being: social, physical, and psychological. A neglect of one such cluster could lead to either physiological dysfunction, psychological distress leading to mental health problems, or social maladjustment (Ward 2002b), all of which will invariably lead to poor overall life satisfaction and therefore emotional distress.

In sum, we can see how problems with internal and external resources (lack of capacity) cause problematic behaviours (inappropriate means) for otherwise legitimate goals, which leads to a thwarting of (conflict with) other PHGs, which in turn, disables full access of all 11 PHGs (lack of scope). Each of these problems build on one another in a linear way, but also create circular traps that hold the person in a perpetual cycle of an endless lack of fulfilment and resultant problem behaviours. The aim of rehabilitation, therefore, is to build and add to individuals' social and psychological resources. In this way, we increase and improve the person's capacity, choice, opportunity, well-being, and outcomes. This building up of the person then allows the individual to access goods in pro-social ways that are also intrinsically beneficial and meaningful.

GLM empirical research

The GLM has been developed based on an extensive and ongoing review of interdisciplinary theory and research; therefore its construction emerges from strong, established, and widely accepted theoretical and empirical foundations. Yet, it is important that the GLM has its own research base, and as a result, empirical studies on the GLM are beginning to build, as are the associated positive findings. A number of studies, for example, have been published which highlight the positive implications associated with implementing GLM-consistent ideas into treatment programs (e.g. Chu and Ward 2015; Fortune 2018; Leaming and Willis 2016; Lorito et al. in press; Loney and Harkins in press; Mann et al. 2004; Martin et al. 2010; Taylor in press; Van Damme et al. 2016, 2017; Ware and Bright 2008; Willis and Ward 2013).

We will briefly describe two studies that illustrate this work. Simons et al. (2006) conducted one of the pivotal empirical studies into the application of the GLM and essentially compared the outcomes of those participants who received GLM consistent management and treatment, to those who received the traditional relapse prevention approach. The study found that GLM participants were more motivated and more likely to complete treatment. Furthermore, those who did not complete treatment stayed in treatment longer than the comparison group. In addition, GLM participants were identified as being more likely to have a social support group in place upon completion of treatment. More recently, Harkins et al. (2012) noted that the GLM improved client and therapist satisfaction with treatment experiences (also see Loney and Harkins in press), and Gannon et al. (2011) found that a group of mentally disordered offenders were able to engage well in a GLM treatment programme, despite their complex mental health needs. Despite emerging positive findings, the GLM's empirical research base is still in its early stages and there is ongoing need for further evaluation of GLM-oriented programs and services.

Concluding remarks

Services and practitioners who are serious about promoting the rehabilitation of clients will know that punitive responses not only trap individuals in feelings of helplessness and cycles of offending behaviour, but they also undermine the health and well-being of communities as a whole. Given this awareness, the GLM has experienced notable popularity in offender rehabilitation programs and has undergone continued theoretical development. For example, a number of recent papers and books have started to systematically explore the theoretical status of dynamic risk factors (e.g. Ward and Fortune 2016) and the degree to which the RNR and GLM can be coherently integrated (e.g. Ziv 2017). Even in light of its limited but growing empirical research base, the GLM's humanistic and logical approach to problem behaviours make it a useful and comprehensive rehabilitation framework for working with people. It advocates for a practice that is deeply respectful and yet highly targeted and meaningful (Ward and Gannon 2006). Within GLM-consistent programs, clients are able to realize a genuinely attainable alternative to their previous way of living; that is, a life that is not just pro-social, but personally meaningful and deservedly fulfilling.

References

Arnhart, L. (1998) *Darwinian Natural Right: The Biological Ethics of Human Nature*. Albany: State University of New York Press.

Barnao, M., Ward, T. and Casey, S. (2015) Looking beyond the illness: Forensic service users perceptions of rehabilitation. *Journal of Interpersonal Violence*, 30, 1025–1045.

Barnao, M., Ward, T. and Robertson, P. (2016) The good lives model: A new paradigm for forensic mental health. *Psychiatry, Psychology, & Law*, 23, 288–301.

Becker, L. C. (1992) Good lives: Prolegomena. *Social Philosophy and Policy*, 9, 15–37.

Chu, C. M. and Ward, T. (2015) The Good Lives Model of offender rehabilitation: Working positively with sex offenders. In N. Ronel and D. Segev (Eds.), *Positive Criminology*. Abingdon: Routledge.

Cummins, R. A. (1996) The domains of life satisfaction: An attempt to order chaos. *Social Indicators Research*, 38, 303–328.

Durrant, R. and Ward, T. (2015) *Evolutionary Criminology: Towards a Comprehensive Explanation of Crime and its Management*. New York: Academic Press.

Fortune, C. A., Ward, T. and Mann, R. (2015) Good lives & the rehabilitation of sex offenders: A positive treatment approach. In A. Linley and S. Joseph (Eds.), *Positive Psychology in Practice*, 2nd edition. Chichester: John Wiley & Sons.

Lorito, C., Vollm, B. and Dening, T. (in press) The individual experience of ageing prisoners: Systematic review and meta-synthesis through a good lives model framework. *International Journal of Geriatric Psychiatry*.

Emmons, R. A. (1999) *The Psychology of Ultimate Concerns*. New York: The Guilford Press.

Fortune, C. (2018) The good-lives-model: A strength-based approach for youth offenders. *Aggression and Violent Behavior*, 38, 21–30.

Gannon, T. A., King, T., Miles, H., Lockerbie, L. and Willis, G. M. (2011) Good lives sexual offender treatment for mentally disordered offenders. *British Journal of Forensic Practice*, 13, 153–168.

Harkins, L., Flak, V. E., Beech, A. and Woodhams, J. (2012) Evaluation of a community-based sex offender treatment program using a good lives model approach. *Sexual Abuse: A Journal of Research and Treatment*, 24, 519–543.

Leaming, N. and Willis, G. M. (2016) The good lives model: New avenues for Maori rehabilitation? *Sexual Abuse in Australia and New Zealand*, 7, 59–69.

Loney, D. M. and Harkins, L. (in press) Examining the good lives model and antisocial behavior. *Psychology, Crime & Law*.

Mann, R. E., Webster, S. D., Schofield, D. and Marshall, W. L. (2004) Approach versus avoidance goals in relapse prevention with sexual offenders. *Sexual Abuse: A Journal of Research and treatment*, 16, 65–76.

Martin, A. M., Hernandez, B., Hernandez-Fernaud, E., Arregui, J. L. and Hernandez, J. A. (2010) The enhancement effect of social and employment integration on the delay of recidivism of released offenders trained with the R & R programme. *Psychology, Crime & Law*, 16, 401–413.

McGrath, R., Cumming, G., Burchard, B., Zeoli, S. and Ellerby, L. (2010) *Current Practices and Emerging Trends in Sexual Abuser Management: The Safer Society 2009 North American Survey*. Brandon, VT: Safer Society Press.

Murphy, M. C. (2001) *Natural Law and Practical Rationality*. New York: Cambridge University Press.

Nussbaum, M. C. (2000) *Women and Human Development: The Capabilities Approach*. New York: Cambridge University Press.

Purvis, M., Ward, T. and Shaw, S. (2013) *Applying the Good Lives Model to the Case Management of Sexual Offenders: A Practical Guide for Probation Officers, Parole Officers, and Case Workers*. Brandon, VT: Safer Society Press.

Purvis, M., Ward, T. and Willis, G. (2014) The Good Lives Model of offender rehabilitation. In M. Carich and S. Mussack (Eds.), *The Safer Society Handbook of Adult Sexual Offense Assessment and Treatment*. Brandon, VT: Safer Society Press, pp. 193–220.

Rescher, N. (1990) *Human Interests: Reflections on Philosophical Anthropology*. Stanford, CA: Stanford University Press.

Simons, D. A., McCullar, B. and Tyler, C. (2006) *Evaluation of the Good Lives Model Approach to Treatment Planning*. Paper presented at the 25th Annual Association for the Treatment of Sexual Abusers Research and Treatment Conference, Chicago, IL, September.

Taylor, E. (in press). 'I should have been a security consultant': The good lives model and residential burglars. *European Journal of Criminology*.

Van Damme, L., Fortune, C., Vandevelde, S. and Vanderplasschen, W. (2017) The good lives model among detained female adolescents. *Aggression and Violent Behavior*, 37, 179–189.

Van Damme, L., Hoeve, M., Vermeiren, R., Vanderplasschen, W. and Colins, O. F. (2016) Quality of life in relation to future mental health problems and offending: Testing the good lives model among detained girls. *Law and Human Behavior*, 40, 285–294.

Ward, T. (2002a) Good lives and the rehabilitation of sexual offenders: Promises and problems. *Aggression and Violent Behavior*, 7, 513–528.

Ward, T. (2002b) The management of risk and the design of good lives. *Australian Psychologist*, 37, 172–179.

Ward, T. (2010) The Good Lives Model of offender rehabilitation: Basic assumptions, aetiological commitments, and practice implications. In F. McNeill, P. Raynor and C. Trotter (Eds.), *Offender Supervision: New Directions in Theory, Research and Practice*. Devon: Willan Publishing.

Ward, T. and Fisher, D. D. (2005) New ideas in the treatment of sexual offenders. In W. L. Marshall, Y. Fernandez, L. Marshall and G. A. Serran (Eds.), *Sexual Offender Treatment: Issues and Controversies*. Chichester: John Wiley and Sons Ltd.

Ward, T. and Fortune, C. (2016) The role of dynamic risk factors in the explanation of offending. *Aggression and Violent Behavior*, 29, 79–88.

Ward, T. and Gannon, T. (2006) Rehabilitation, etiology, and self-regulation: The good lives model of sexual offender treatment. *Aggression and Violent Behavior*, 11, 77–94.

Ward, T. and Heffernan, R. (2017) The role of values in forensic and correctional rehabilitation. *Aggression and Violent Behavior*, 37, 42–51.

Ward, T. and Marshall, W. L. (2004) Good lives, etiology and the rehabilitation of sex offenders: A bridging theory. *Journal of Sexual Aggression*, 10, 153–169.

Ward, T. and Maruna, S. (2007) *Rehabilitation: Beyond the Risk Assessment Paradigm*. London: Routledge.

Ward, T. and Willis, G. (2016) Dynamic risk factors and offender rehabilitation: A comparison of the good lives model and the risk-need responsivity model. In D. R. Laws and W. O'Donohue (Eds.), *Treatment of Sex Offenders: Strengths and Weaknesses in Assessment and Intervention*. New York: Springer, pp. 175–190.

Ware, J. and Bright, D. A. (2008) Evolution of a treatment programme for sex offenders: Changes to the NSW Custody-Based Intensive Treatment (CUBIT). *Psychiatry, Psychology and Law*, 15, 340–349.

Willis, G. and Ward, T. (2013) The good lives model: Evidence that it works. In L. Craig, L. Dixon and T. A. Gannon (Eds.), *What Works in Offender Rehabilitation: An Evidence Based Approach to Assessment and Treatment*. Chichester: John Wiley & Sons, pp. 305–318.

Ziv, R. (2017) *The Future of Correctional Rehabilitation: Moving Beyond the RNR Model and Good Lives Model Debate*. London: Routledge.

10

Diversifying desistance research

Hannah Graham and Fergus McNeill

Introduction

With the proliferation of desistance scholarship in the last two decades, some might argue that a saturation point has been reached. We beg to differ. More diverse research is needed to generate more detailed and wide-ranging understandings of desistance. In this chapter, we pinpoint several areas for further development. We have chosen to highlight diverse international studies and authors in the sections which follow, providing an alternative reading list of desistance scholarship to be celebrated alongside the landmark studies of (already) highly cited authors.

Why critically analyze the state of desistance research and make future recommendations in a collection on rehabilitative work? Because, as demonstrated in various chapters in this volume (McNeill and Graham; Johnson and Maruna; Morris and Graham), desistance and rehabilitation are relevant to one another in important ways. Improving knowledge of desistance can aid the development of desistance-oriented policies and practices, especially in working with specific groups of people (for example, women, LGBTQ+ people, migrants and foreign nationals, people who use drugs, etc.). It can also help to warn against things done in the name of supporting desistance, however benevolently intended, which may have the capacity to hinder or harm desistance. Even in contexts where desistance and rehabilitation have been invoked as lodestars of criminal justice policymaking and institutional practices, mixed legacies linger.

This chapter builds upon some key analyses of the state of desistance research, theory, policy, and practice. Over a decade ago, one of us conceptualized the development of the desistance paradigm (McNeill 2006) and Lila Kazemian (2007) reviewed extant knowledge at that point, raising a series of theoretical, empirical, methodological, and policy considerations for the future. Kazemian's (2007) analysis was apt. However, with the exception of discussing comparative research, this chapter does not consider the methodological points she raised, as these have been well analyzed and addressed by others in the interim. Her analysis tended to focus on developing research and knowledge at the level of the individual, whereas social-structural influences have become considerably more prominent in international desistance literatures since then (see Shapland et al. 2016; Segev 2018). More than ten years later, following a period of considerable growth in research, reflexive accounts of desistance have also emerged, such as those in Hart and van Ginneken (2017); Shapland and colleagues (2016); Graham and McNeill (2017); and McNeill and Graham (2018). The sections that follow here build on these contributions to champion the need for more diversity in desistance research in several areas.

The final section of this chapter considers solidarities and social movements, and calls for some repositioning and decentring of institutions, policies, sanctions, and practices in understandings of desistance. This is *not* to say that the latter don't matter. Rather, it is to contend that desistance should not necessarily be chiefly understood and framed by them. New desistance research increasingly indicates that the forms of social problems, harms, and inequalities from which people are trying to move on – which include but are rarely limited to crime – are often intertwined and simultaneous, not separate (Graham 2016; van Ginneken and Hart 2017). Over time, forms of penal supervision and experiences of criminal justice, among other state systems and interventions, can blur and become indistinct for those who are more criminalized and institutionalized (see McNeill 2018). Desistance is not often the language of people in such processes; indeed, some uses of the term may be the self-justifying rhetoric of the criminal justice institutions that ensnare them. Critically and ironically, words like rehabilitation and desistance may be used as a resistance strategy to make sense of processes of leaving behind the harms, losses, criminogenic risks, and negative identities produced by *criminalization, punishment,* and *penal policy*, not just those arising from crime and leaving behind crime (see Armstrong and Lam 2017; Schinkel et al. 2018). In light of this, seeing people and processes predominantly through the lens of their current sentence is a blinkered view to take if their hope and goal is living in community, independent of sanctions and institutions.

Desistance theories show that an individual's normative development of stopping offending might be the result of processes of ageing and maturation, and associated transitions and opportunities (often called 'ontogenic' desistance theories), or of changing social bonds ('sociogenic' desistance theories). Desistance processes may influence and be influenced by a combination of personal and social factors, including people reshaping their sense of themselves and their priorities (identity-related and structuration desistance theories) (for a detailed explanation of desistance theories and synthesized review of international literatures, see Weaver 2015; Graham and McNeill 2017).

Desistance is characterized here as dynamic and developmental, where individual processes are situated in communities and profoundly affected by social structures (McNeill 2016). Bottoms and Shapland (2011) have noted that neither the dispositions (or 'potential') of individuals, nor their social positions and resources (or 'capital') are static. Rather, they are dynamic and can change over time, producing interaction effects in the broader process of change. In this chapter, understanding and supporting desistance is framed in such a way as to implicate *both* normative personal development *and* political and social-structural change. Desistance *might* sometimes involve working through rehabilitative programmes and interventions in the context of penal institutions, but they may not always be a necessary component of it and they are never sufficient for it (Burke et al. 2018). As we have said elsewhere (McNeill and Graham this volume), while rehabilitation and desistance processes are not being engineered by a *penal* agent, they are being supported by social actors, relationships, and social-structural contexts – and they can be just as easily undermined by them.

Decolonizing and culturally diversifying desistance research

A critique of desistance scholarship is that its theoretical formulations and empirical findings have been predominantly derived from studies and scholars in the United Kingdom and United States. This has held true in the past, and it is raised here as an ongoing area for development. Yet, some of what needs to develop is awareness and citation of *existing* desistance research from beyond the UK and US among British and American desistance scholars. Better attention might be paid to contributions to knowledge of continental European desistance research, for example, from the Netherlands, Belgium, Spain, Denmark, Finland, Sweden, and Norway (see Blokland and Nieuwbeerta 2005; Bersani et al. 2009; Savolainen 2009; Carlsson 2013; Søgaard et al. 2015; Lauwaert and Aertsen 2015; Skardhamar and Savolainen 2014, 2016; Rodermond et al. 2016; Colman and Vander Laenen 2012, 2017; Cid and Martí 2012, 2016; Sivertsson 2018). In a Norwegian study of the role of employment and desistance with a sample of 783 male offenders, Skardhamar and Savolainen's (2014) findings challenge theorizations of employment as a positive 'turning point' for desistance. Instead, their findings are coherent with maturation theories of desistance, finding that the vast majority of participants desisted prior to employment and becoming employed was not associated with further reductions in crime.

Importantly, there is a need to decolonize desistance research and pay more attention to knowledge and ways of knowing from the Global South, what Carrington (2017) calls 'southern epistemologies' in criminology. This means further efforts to contextualize, nuance, and diversify knowledge about desistance, rather than continuing to singularly privilege knowledge and a few studies and voices from English-speaking 'Western' countries like the United Kingdom and United States, as though they have universal and global application. There is much to be learned from desistance research in, for example, Chile (see Villagra 2015; Droppelmann 2017), Brazil (Bugnon 2015), and Mexico (Campbell and Hansen 2012). In Chile, the longitudinal 'Trajectories Study' uses mixed methods and a multifaceted dataset from a panel of 334 Chilean young offenders to explore persistence and desistance from crime: This study:

> brings new evidence to show that the binary oppositional categories of the completely reformed desister and the categorically antisocial and non-virtuous persister are hardly found, and that individuals can be better identified as half-way desisters/persisters who oscillate between crime and conformity. . . . [Interviewees discuss matters] in a social context in which ambivalence, attachment, consumerism and masculinity emerge as key transversal issues in regards to the desistance process, both as factors that pull individuals away from crime and also push them back towards it.
>
> (Droppelmann 2017: 214)

Droppelmann's (2017) analysis of participants' emotional attachments to crime and emotional dynamics of desistance is compelling. In explaining a notion she calls 'crime grief', she charts how participants express emotion in transitioning, ambivalently, through stages of grieving in leaving crime behind, mourning it as a loss, with some fantasising about a 'farewell episode', committing their last crime. This Chilean desistance study serves as just one example of nuanced insights from which those in Anglophone countries in the Global North might learn and further research.

Beyond studies in any one country, positive international collaborations – of which there should be more – include the open access Special Issue on desistance of the *EuroVista* journal of the Confederation of European Probation. Guest edited by Beth Weaver (2013a, 2013b), this Issue features a series of articles and life stories written by people with lived experiences of desistance, from different countries. In his autoethnographic contribution about imprisonment, desistance, and education, going on to get a PhD in the social sciences, Tietjen (2013: 5) observes how '"insider" experiences allow me to shed light on perspectives and issues that many relatively sheltered criminologists may not otherwise recognize'. Co-producing open access resources and using approaches such as autobiography, autoethnography, stories, and narrative criminology are positive examples of diversifying knowledge of desistance across cultural, national, and disciplinary borders.

Comparative desistance research

In her review, Kazemian (2007) observed the lack of cross-national comparative research on desistance and questioned the generalizability of empirical findings from the United States, for example, to other countries. Recently, comparative desistance research has started to come to the fore, fostering insights across national, cultural, and linguistic borders. A few pioneering comparative studies are worth highlighting here.

Linnea Österman (2017) used qualitative feminist methods to research women's experiences of desistance and penal cultures in Sweden and England. She offers nuanced insights into notions of Nordic exceptionalism and Anglophone excess by considering how participants in both countries face and overcome internal barriers (e.g. mental health, trauma) and external barriers to change (e.g. lack of social housing, liveable income). The most contrasting comparison is that the women's narratives in Sweden entail examples of being offered 'ladders' as infrastructures for change, that is, opportunities and supports to overcome these internal and external barriers, whereas accounts of such opportunities and supports for change are rare in the women's narratives in England (Österman 2017).

Dana Segev's (2018) PhD research was a comparative study of desistance in Israel and England, involving a sample of male participants and using a range of mixed methods. In presenting her data and findings, she charts how 'contextual factors structured the pathways out of crime in each country; interacted with identity and agency; and gave rise to variances in the dynamics of desistance' (Segev 2018: 6). For example, her study demonstrates how understandings of labels and identities are situated in Israeli and English cultures and societies, illustrating variances in stigmatization and culturally shaped ideas about what people 'should and should not' be or do.

In a similar vein, Monica Barry (2017) explored cultural influences on similarities and differences in young offenders' perspectives of desistance in Japan and Scotland. The most common similarity was their emphasis on relational factors as a motivation or reason for wanting to leave crime behind. However, the Japanese young people emphasized relational factors in more social or collective terms, whereas Scottish young people emphasized relational factors in more personal and individual terms, to some extent influenced by cultural and societal factors (Barry 2017). Comparative studies such as these are currently few and far between; much more comparative desistance research is needed.

Diversity and social differences in desistance research

For a body of scholarship which has yielded rich theoretical and empirical knowledge about the influences of identity, social bonds, and belonging in desistance processes, it seems somewhat ironic that some identities and social groups are under-researched. To an extent, this may be due to some identities and groups being minorities in the general population and/or under-represented in criminal justice populations. Historically, a key critique of desistance research has been that some influential studies paid insufficient attention to issues of diversity as they focused on men's experiences of desistance (for an overview of such critiques and ripostes, see Graham and McNeill 2017). Conversely, in the last decade, there has been significant growth in international research on gendered differences for women and men in desistance processes, including insights on gender, relationships, and parenthood (see McIvor et al. 2009; Leverentz 2014; Carlsson 2013; Rodermond et al. 2016; Österman 2017; Bax and Han 2018). In developing future desistance research agendas, more diversity and social differentiation is needed; in this section, we outline five key areas, of equal importance and in no particular order.

Firstly, building on previous sections, more needs to be understood about race and ethnicity and desistance. The contributions of Calverley (2013), Glynn (2013, and in this volume) and Fader and Traylor (2015) are apt examples of the type of rich insights to be gained in this area. Researching race and ethnicity further implicates some related issues. More needs to be understood about aboriginality and indigeneity, particularly in countries where Indigenous, Aboriginal, and First Nation people are disproportionately criminalized and punished, and may have personal and intergenerational experiences of injustice and institutional intervention. In Australia, Marchetti and Daly (2017) illuminate some of the issues involved in their article about Indigenous partner violence, Indigenous sentencing initiatives and desistance, including appreciation of differences in how family relationships and social bonds (and the harms caused to them by violence) are understood and responded to in Indigenous communities. Another cognate area warranting more research is that of migration and integration, including consideration of disproportionate rates at which foreign nationals are criminalized and punished, for example, in many European countries, including Nordic countries otherwise lauded for their penal exceptionalism (Ugelvik 2014).

Secondly, while a modest amount of progress has been made in researching the influences of religion and faith-based groups, this mainly relates to Christianity and finding faith and being supported by Christian communities, churches, and organizations in desistance processes (see Armstrong 2014). More research needs to be done among other religions and faith groups in different countries and cultures. How might the influences of religion and faith be understood in instances where religion and faith (or distortions of them) are implicated in offending? Diverse examples might include: terrorism and violent extremism; sectarian crimes; religious hate crimes; religiously influenced 'honour'-based violence, abuse, or coercive control; civil disobedience; or clergy child sexual abuse within religious organizations.

Third, better understanding is needed of sexuality and gender diversity and the lived experiences of desistance for people who identify as lesbian, gay, bisexual, transgender, and queer (LGBTQ). Queer criminology offers valuable perspectives to draw upon in developing desistance scholarship (see Ball et al. 2016). Australian criminologists Asquith et al. (2017) use queer criminology to offer excellent critical insights to advocate better understanding of criminal careers and desistance processes of young queer people, and the intersectionality and complexity involved. They note how desistance theories have traditionally focused on the importance of parenthood and intimate partner relationships, especially marriage, neglecting the reality that, in many countries, same-sex marriage and adoption rights are not legal and LGBTQ people live with what they call 'partial social citizenship' (Asquith et al. 2017: 175). Asquith and colleagues consider the centrality of social bonds and social capital in age and maturation desistance theories, discussing how family ties and peer friendships may be affected by coming out, in some cases leading to homelessness, social exclusion, and employment barriers – problems that can occur in the same age or life stage as criminal offending and desistance processes. Finally, they cogently critique the heteronormative and cisnormative assumptions of what is considered 'pro-social' and what is risky in rehabilitative work in criminal justice, calling for more sexuality and gender diverse understandings of *resistance and desistance* strategies in penal contexts. These contributions and the insights of people who are LGBTQ+ warrant considerable empirical and theoretical exploration.

Fourth, with few exceptions, class and privilege have been neglected in desistance research. How do people in positions of power and privilege leave crime behind? How and why is this similar or different to desistance processes of people who have less power and limited access to opportunities and resources? People who are upper or middle class, with histories of 'white collar' crime or involvement in crimes of the powerful, are largely missing in desistance literatures. Ben Hunter's (2016) research on white collar offenders and desistance from crime is relatively unparalleled in this area to date. Desistance from state crime has been, as far as we aware, entirely unexamined.

Fifth, intersecting issues in health and justice warrant more exploration. Recent research on concurrent processes of desistance and recovery illustrate the importance of this, and why more is needed (see McSweeney 2014; Graham 2016; Best et al. 2016; Colman and Vander Laenen 2017; Kay and Monaghan 2018). Yet, relative to the hefty amount of existing interdisciplinary research on the drugs-crime nexus, interactions and divergences in recovery and desistance processes are only partially understood. In turn, this may affect the development of more recovery-oriented and desistance-oriented supports. Other intersections of health and justice warranting further exploration include the influences of victimization and trauma on desistance processes, and the lack of research on victims with convictions, as well as the influences of adversity, grief, and loss on desistance processes. Anderson's (2016, 2019) work on the value of bearing witness to desistance underscores how justice practitioners can be attendant to the humanity, values, and experiences of people in such processes. She explains how bearing witness may be as much a response to structural violence and systemically induced issues as it is to victimization, trauma, and individual adverse experiences (Anderson 2016, 2019). Such things are relevant considerations for researchers, albeit in a different role to practitioners.

Developing solidarities and social movements

In this final section, desistance is considered in terms of collectives and collective action, situated in communities. Both Weaver (2013b) and Maruna (2017) conceptualize desistance as a social movement, as accessible, participatory, and civic. Maruna's ideas resonate with the focus of this chapter:

> Reframing the understanding of desistance as not just an individual process or journey, but rather a social movement, in this way better highlights the structural obstacles inherent in the desistance process and the macro-social changes necessary to successfully create a 'desistance-informed' future.
>
> (Maruna 2017: 6)

Maruna (2017) considers how the future of desistance might be similar to the solidarities, struggles, and achievements of the Civil Rights movement in the United States; the LGBTQ movement in support of same sex marriage in the Republic of Ireland; the 'ban the box' movement to end employment-related discrimination for people with convictions; and user advocacy groups, recovery movements, and communities for substance misuse and mental health around the world. Deinstitutionalization of desistance research is implied in Maruna's (2017: 11) vision of 'desistance as a social movement', contending that the 'next step' is for desistance as a concept to move 'from the Ivory Tower to the professional world of probation and prisons, back to the communities where desistance takes place'.

One of the proud strengths of desistance scholarship is the egalitarian sense of whose knowledge is recognized and counted. Desistance scholars commonly argue (or assume) that people with experience of desistance processes and those who support them have important knowledge about the process, and about how to enable and encourage it. This foundational argument or assumption lends itself to developing future research agendas exploring solidarities, collective action, cooperation, and social movements. Raewyn Connell's (2015a: 14) notion that knowledge production can be 'a radically social process' is apt. Her calls for 'solidarity-based epistemology', rather than hierarchical notions of whose knowledge is privileged, are echoed here (see Connell 2015a, 2015b) as ways of emboldening more diversity and epistemic emancipation. Engaging and mobilizing citizens and communities in supporting desistance as a social movement means being able to communicate about it, in different voices, formats, and forums. This means knowledge production 'with', not simply 'for' or 'about' people at the centre of desistance processes and those affected by them. It requires humility and solidarity in the prospect of academic research being repositioned, as only one factor or element, of the bigger picture of what may be achieved through collective action and social movements (Maruna 2017). It also serves as a reminder that researching and responding to desistance may implicate 'us' as scholars, students, practitioners, and fellow citizens, but it is not 'ours'. Exceptions to this rule are academics and 'pracademics' with convictions and their own experiences of desistance (see Weaver and Weaver 2013; Honeywell 2013; Hart and Healy 2018).

Conclusion

In this chapter, we have argued that more desistance research needs to be done with people in areas that are of quintessential importance to criminologists, sociologists, and psychologists: sexualities and gender; class and power; religion and faith-based groups; health and recovery; race, ethnicity, and migration; decolonization, cross-national and cross-cultural knowledges; and solidarities and social movements. Developing these areas of research will likely necessitate some repositioning and decentring of the hegemony of traditional penal institutions, policies, and practices as a dominant framing of research design and understandings of desistance. Clearly, criminal justice policies and practices will continue to need tenacious evaluation and development, or abandonment for better non-penal options – not least to ameliorate some of the known pains of and barriers to desistance (see Nugent and Schinkel 2016; Halsey et al. 2017). When it comes to understanding and supporting desistance therefore, far from the field being over-saturated, there is much yet to know and do together, to pursue change in the hope of better futures.

References

Anderson, S. (2016) The value of 'bearing witness' to desistance. *Probation Journal*, 63(4), 408–424. DOI:10.1177/0264550516664146.

Anderson, S. (2019) *Punishing Trauma: Narratives, Desistance and Recovery*. PhD thesis, College of Social Sciences, University of Glasgow.

Armstrong, R. (2014) Trusting the untrustworthy: The theology, practice and implications of faith-based volunteers' work with ex-prisoners. *Studies in Christian Ethics*, 27(3), 299–309.

Armstrong, S. and Lam, A. (2017) Policy as crime scene. In S. Armstrong, J. Blaustein and A. Henry (Eds.), *Reflexivity and Criminal Justice: Intersections of Policy, Practice and Research*. Basingstoke: Palgrave Macmillan, pp. 101–122.

Asquith, N., Dwyer, A. and Simpson, P. (2017) A queer criminal career. *Current Issues in Criminal Justice*, 29(2), 167–180.

Ball, M., Crofts, T. and Dwyer, A. (Eds.). (2016) *Queering Criminology*. Basingstoke: Palgrave Macmillan.

Barry, M. (2017) Young offenders' views of desistance in Japan: A comparison with Scotland. In J. Liu, M. Travers and L. Chang (Eds.), *Comparative Criminology in Asia*. New York: Springer, pp. 119–129.

Bax, T. and Han, Y. (2018) Desistance from and persistence in male offending: The case of South Korea. *International Journal of Law, Crime and Justice*, 54, 53–65.

Bersani, B., Laub, J. and Nieuwbeerta, P. (2009) Marriage and desistance from crime in the Netherlands: Do gender and socio-historical context matter? *Journal of Quantitative Criminology*, 25(1), 3–24.

Best, D., Irving, J. and Albertson, K. (2016) Recovery and desistance: What the emerging recovery movement in the alcohol and drug area can learn from models of desistance from offending. *Addiction Research and Theory*, 25(1), 1–10.

Blokland, A. and Nieuwbeerta, P. (2005) The effects of life circumstances on longitudinal trajectories of offending. *Criminology*, 43(4), 1203–1240.

Bottoms, A. and Shapland, J. (2011) Steps towards desistance among young adult recidivists. In S. Farrall, M. Hough, S. Maruna and R. Sparks (Eds.), *Escape Routes: Contemporary Perspectives on Life After Punishment*. London: Routledge.

Bugnon, G. (2015) Desistance from crime in Brazil: The impact of experience with the world of crime and juvenile justice. *Penal Issues*, July bulletin. Available at: www.cesdip.fr/wp-content/uploads/2014/02/PI_2015_07.pdf (Accessed 19 November 2018).

Burke, L., Collett, S. and McNeill, F. (2018) *Reimagining Rehabilitation: Beyond the Individual*. London: Routledge.

Calverley, A. (2013) *Cultures of Desistance: Rehabilitation, Reintegration and Ethnic Minorities*. London: Routledge.

Campbell, H. and Hansen, T. (2012) Getting out of the game: Desistance from drug trafficking. *International Journal of Drug Policy*, 23(6), 481–487.

Carrington, K. (2017) Asian criminology and Southern epistemologies. In J. Liu, M. Travers and L. Chang (Eds.), *Comparative Criminology in Asia*. New York: Springer, pp. 61–69.

Carlsson, C. (2013) Masculinities, persistence and desistance. *Criminology*, 51(3), 661–693.

Cid, J. and Martí, J. (2012) Turning points and returning points: Understanding the role of family ties in the process of desistance. *European Journal of Criminology*, 9(6), 603–620.

Cid, J. and Martí, J. (2016) Structural context and pathways to desistance. In J. Shapland, S. Farrall and T. Bottoms (Eds.), *Global Perspectives on Desistance: Reviewing What We Know and Looking to the Future*. London: Routledge.

Colman, C. and Vander Laenen, F. (2012) "Recovery came first": Desistance versus recovery in the criminal careers of drug-using offenders. *The Scientific World Journal*, 1–10.

Colman, C. and Vander Laenen, F. (2017) The desistance process of offenders who misuse drugs. In E. Hart and E. van Ginneken (Eds.), *New Perspectives on Desistance: Theoretical and Empirical Developments*. Basingstoke: Palgrave Macmillan, pp. 61–84.

Connell, R. (2015a) Social science on a world scale: Connecting the pages. *Journal of the Brazilian Sociological Society/Revista da Sociodade Brasileira de Sociologica*, 1(1), 1–16.

Connell, R. (2015b) Meeting at the edge of fear: Theory on a world scale. *Feminist Theory*, 16(1), 49–66. DOI:10.1177/1464700114562531.

Droppelmann, C. (2017) Leaving behind the deviant other in desistance-persistence explanations. In E. Hart and E. van Ginneken (Eds.), *New Perspectives on Desistance: Theoretical and Empirical Developments*. Basingstoke: Palgrave Macmillan, pp. 213–240.

Fader, J. and Traylor, L. (2015) Dealing with difference in desistance theory: The promise of intersectionality for new avenues of inquiry. *Sociology Compass*, 9(4), 427–460.

Glynn, M. (2013) *Black Men, Invisibility and Crime: Towards a Critical Race Theory of Desistance*. London: Routledge.

Graham, H. (2016) *Rehabilitation Work: Supporting Desistance and Recovery*. London: Routledge.

Graham, H. and McNeill, F. (2017) Desistance: Envisioning futures. In P. Carlen and L. A. França (Eds.), *Alternative Criminologies*. London: Routledge, pp. 433–451.

Halsey, M., Armstrong, R. and Wright, S. (2017) 'F*ck it!' matza and the mood of fatalism in the desistance processes. *British Journal of Criminology*, 57(5), 1041–1060. DOI:10.1093/bjc/azw041.

Hart, W. and Healy, D. (2018) 'An inside job': An autobiographical account of desistance. *European Journal of Probation*, 10(2), 103–119. DOI:10.1177/2066220318783426.

Hart, E. and van Ginneken, E. (Eds.). (2017) *New Perspectives on Desistance: Theoretical and Empirical Developments*. Basingstoke: Palgrave Macmillan.

Honeywell, D. (2013) Desistance from crime. *EuroVista*, 3(1), 1–5. Available at: www.euro-vista.org/wp-content/uploads/2015/01/EuroVista-vol3-no1-32-Honeywell.pdf (Accessed 19 November 2018).

Hunter, B. (2016) *White-Collar Offenders and Desistance from Crime: Future Selves and the Constancy of Change*. London: Routledge.

Kay, C. and Monaghan, M. (2018) Rethinking recovery and desistance processes: Developing a social identity model of transition. *Addiction Research and Theory* [Advance Access Online].

Kazemian, L. (2007) Desistance from crime: Theoretical, empirical, methodological and policy considerations. *Journal of Contemporary Criminal Justice*, 23(1), 5–27.

Lauwaert, K. and Aertsen, I. (Eds.). (2015) *Desistance and Restorative Justice: Mechanisms for Desisting from Crime Within Restorative Justice Practices*. Leuven: European Forum for Restorative Justice.

Leverentz, A. (2014) *The Ex-Prisoner's Dilemma: How Women Negotiate Competing Narratives of Reentry and Desistance*. New Brunswick: Rutgers University Press.

Marchetti, E. and Daly, K. (2017) Indigenous partner violence, indigenous sentencing courts, and pathways to desistance. *Violence Against Women*, 23(12), 1513–1535. DOI:10.1177/1077801216662341.

Maruna, S. (2017) Desistance as a social movement. *Irish Probation Journal*, 14, 5–20.

McIvor, G., Trotter, C. and Sheehan, R. (2009) Women, resettlement and desistance. *Probation Journal*, 56(4), 347–361. DOI:10.1177/0264550509346515.

McNeill, F. (2006) A desistance paradigm for offender management. *Criminology & Criminal Justice*, 6(1), 39–62.

McNeill, F. (2016) Desistance and criminal justice in Scotland. In H. Croall, G. Mooney and M. Munro (Eds.), *Crime, Justice and Society in Scotland*. London: Routledge.

McNeill, F. (2018) *Pervasive Punishment: Making Sense of Mass Supervision*. Bingley: Emerald Publishing.

McNeill, F. and Graham, H. (2018) Resettlement, reintegration and desistance in Europe. In F. Dünkel, I. Pruin, A. Storgaard and J. Weber (Eds.), *Prisoner Resettlement in Europe*. London: Routledge.

McSweeney, T. (2014) *Promoting Compliance, Recovery and Desistance: Comparative Case Studies of Pre-Sentence Diversion Schemes for Drug Misusing Arestees in Australia and England*. PhD thesis, University of New South Wales.

Nugent, B. and Schinkel, M. (2016) The pains of desistance. *Criminology & Criminal Justice*, 16(5), 568–584.

Österman, L. (2017) *Penal Cultures and Female Desistance.* London: Routledge.

Rodermond, E., Kruttschnitt, C., Slotboom, A. and Bijleveld, C. (2016) Female desistance: A review of the literature. *European Journal of Criminology*, 13(1), 3–28. https://doi.org/10.1177/1477370815597251.

Savolainen, J. (2009) Work, family and criminal desistance: Adult social bonds in a Nordic welfare state. *British Journal of Criminology*, 49(3), 285–304.

Schinkel, M., Atkinson, C. and Anderson, S. (2018) 'Well-kent faces': Policing persistent offenders and the possibilities for desistance. *British Journal of Criminology*, advance access online. DOI:10.1093/bjc/azy050 (Accessed 19 December 2018).

Segev, D. (2018) *Societies and Desistance: Exploring the Dynamics of Desistance in England and Israel.* PhD thesis, School of Law, University of Sheffield. Available at: http://etheses.whiterose.ac.uk/20949/1/Thesis_Segev_Final.pdf (Accessed 19 November 2018).

Shapland, J., Farrall, S. and Bottoms, T. (Eds.). (2016) *Global Perspectives on Desistance: Reviewing What We Know and Looking to the Future.* London: Routledge.

Sivertsson, F. (2018) Adult-limited offending: How much is there to explain? *Journal of Criminal Justice*, 55, 58–70.

Skardhamar, T. and Savolainen, J. (2014) Changes in criminal offending around the time of job entry: A study of employment and desistance. *Criminology*, 52(2), 263–291.

Skardhamar, T. and Savolainen, J. (2016) Timing of change: Are life course transitions causes or consequences of desistance? In J. Shapland, S. Farrall and T. Bottoms (Eds.), *Global Perspectives on Desistance: Reviewing What We Know and Looking to the Future.* London: Routledge.

Søgaard, T., Kolind, T., Thylstrup, B. and Deuchar, R. (2015) Desistance and the micro-narrative reconstruction of reformed masculinities in a Danish rehabilitation centre. *Criminology & Criminal Justice*, 16(1), 99–118.

Tietjen, G. (2013) Auto-ethnography on desistance from crime. *EuroVista*, 3(1), 1–7. Available at: www.euro-vista.org/wp-content/uploads/2015/01/EuroVista-vol3-no1-39-Tietjen.pdf (Accessed 19 November 2018).

Ugelvik, T. (2014) The incarceration of foreigners in European prisons. In S. Pickering and J. Ham (Eds.), *The Routledge Handbook on Crime and International Migration.* London: Routledge, pp. 107–120.

Van Ginneken, E. and Hart, E. (2017) New perspectives and the future of desistance: An afterword. In E. Hart and E. van Ginneken (Eds.), *New Perspectives on Desistance: Theoretical and Empirical Developments.* Basingstoke: Palgrave Macmillan.

Villagra, C. (2015) *Socio-Historical Contexts, Identity and Change: A Study of Desistance from Crime in Chile.* PhD thesis, University of Leicester. Available at: https://lra.le.ac.uk/bitstream/2381/37817/1/2016VILLAGRACPhD.pdf (Accessed 19 November 2018).

Weaver, A. and Weaver, B. (2013) Autobiography, empirical research and critical theory in desistance: A view from the inside out. *Probation Journal*, 60(3), 259–277. DOI:10.1177/0264550513489763.

Weaver, B. (2013a) The realities of crime, punishment and desistance: First hand perspectives. *EuroVista*, 3(1). Available at: www.euro-vista.org/wp-content/uploads/2015/01/EuroVista-vol3-no1-complete1.pdf (Accessed 19 November 2018).

Weaver, B. (2013b) Epilogue. *EuroVista*, 3(1). Available at: www.euro-vista.org/wp-content/uploads/2015/01/EuroVista-vol3-no1-complete1.pdf (Accessed 19 November 2018).

Weaver, B. (2015) *Offending and Desistance: The Importance of Social Relations.* London: Routledge.

11

Doing justice to desistance narratives

Karen Johnson and Shadd Maruna

Introduction

In the past two decades, the concept of the self-narrative has become closely linked to desistance from crime. With its deep overtones of personal redemption, desistance is, of course, a great story. Indeed, it may be *the* great story – at least in some cultures (see McAdams 2006). Desistance researchers are interested in the content of these stories and what they can teach us about the desistance process. Yet, researchers are equally interested in the *function* of desistance narratives – that is, what they are doing for their tellers (see e.g. Denver and Ewald 2018). In a process he labels 'making good', Maruna (2001: 7) argues that desistance is fundamentally a narrative process, involving a reworking of a person's self-understanding or re-biographing. Individuals trying to desist from crime 'need a coherent and credible self-story to explain (to themselves and others) how their chequered pasts could have led to their new, reformed identities'. Desistance narratives therefore are not only useful accounts of how people change, but also are themselves a key aspect of sustaining that change in a new life path.

In subsequent developments of desistance theory and research, transformation of self-narrative has been a recurring theme (see e.g. Aresti et al. 2010; Healy 2010; King 2013; Hart and Healy 2018; Stone 2015; Weaver and Weaver 2013). However, the concept of a desistance narrative has received relatively little by way of in-depth empirical or theoretical scrutiny (Harding et al. 2017), and remains somewhat 'veiled' in mystery (Serin and Lloyd 2009) for those interested primarily in informing applied practice. Part of the problem in this regard is that, to date, the vast majority of research on desistance narratives has been, for obvious reasons, qualitative and exploratory in nature. As such this research does not sit naturally in a field dominated by quantitative risk factor research.

In this chapter we briefly define the concepts of desistance and self-narrative before reviewing what subsequent research has uncovered about this narrative process of 'making good'. In particular, we focus on efforts to use quantitative research to approximate the distinctly qualitative concept of the desistance narrative, providing examples of new scales and measures being developed. We conclude with a discussion about the potential relevance of the desistance narrative concept to justice practice and policy.

What is desistance?

Desisting from crime involves not just ceasing criminal behaviour but also actively refraining from future offending, as such desistance is not about a single event or turning point, but rather a long-term developmental process of behaviour change (see McNeill et al. 2012). In another chapter, McNeill and Graham (this volume) characterize desistance processes as dynamic and developmental, where individual processes are situated in communities and profoundly affected by social structures. The pathway to desistance can be messy and multiplicitous, therefore, involving the 'to-ing' and 'fro-ing', progress and setbacks as described in Glaser's (1964) 'zig-zag path' to rehabilitation and Phillips's (2017) theorization of desistance processes as rhizomatic. Similar to overcoming sustained patterns of any type of potentially harmful or 'addictive' behaviours, the road from crime can involve an array of personal and social-structural obstacles, temptations, and setbacks, especially in those whose lives have been more heavily criminalized and institutionalized (see Nugent and Schinkel 2016, on the 'pains' of desistance). Desistance narratives have the potential to offer insight on how these are overcome and navigated.

Maruna et al. (2004) have further differentiated between what they label 'primary desistance', meaning a lull or gap in criminal behaviours, and 'secondary desistance', involving a change in the way that an individual sees themselves and is recognized by others. Essentially, secondary desistance involves ceasing to see oneself as an offender and establishing a more positive identity. Of course, these two aspects of desistance (behaviour and identity) work together in a complementary fashion, and despite the language of primary/secondary, it is not clear that behaviour change necessarily precedes changes in identity (Harding et al. 2017). The two, likely, develop together with identity shaping behaviour and behaviour shaping identity.

What is a self-narrative?

Self-narrative refers to the personal story an individual develops to make sense of the links between their past, present, and future (McAdams 1996). The so-called 'narrative turn' in the social sciences begins with Sartre's argument that the human being is fundamentally a story-telling creature – or 'homo narrativus' (Ferrand and Weil 2001). Sartre (1938/1965: 61) writes:

> A [person] is always a teller of tales, he lives surrounded by his stories and the stories of others, he sees everything that happens to him through them; and he tries to live his life as if he were recounting it.

Theorists like McAdams (1996) have argued that the development of this internal story is, itself, the process of identity construction. Over the last two decades, this notion that identity is an internal narrative has achieved a privileged place in the social sciences and humanities, with adherents like Paul Ricoeur and Charles Taylor. For instance, the distinguished Harvard psychologist Jerome Bruner (1987: 15) argues:

> Eventually the culturally shaped cognitive and linguistic processes that guide the self-telling of life narratives achieve the power to structure perceptual experience, to organise memory, to segment and purpose-build the very 'events' of a life. In the end, we become the autobiographical narratives by which we 'tell about' our lives.

The sociologist Anthony Giddens (1991: 54) agrees, arguing that in modernity, 'A person's identity is not to be found in behaviour, nor – important though this is – in the reactions of others, but in the capacity to keep a particular narrative going'. In the field of criminology, Stone (2015) has observed how narrative identity theory is consistent with the emerging paradigm of narrative criminology, an interdisciplinary approach that examines the relationship between crime and narratives or stories about crime (see Dollinger 2018; Presser and Sandberg 2015), and similarly offers a useful overarching framework for examining the relationship between desistance processes and narratives about desistance.

Theories of desistance self-narratives

Maruna (2001) was among the first to link this narrative sense-making project with the process of desistance from crime. In his research, he explored the self-narratives of both persisting and desisting offenders in a series of interviews with individuals in the community. He identified two types of self-narrative: condemnation scripts (reflecting the narrative of 'persisters') and redemption scripts (the narrative of 'desisters'). Condemnation scripts were typified by a sense of being 'condemned' to lives of crime and disrepute, limited future goals, and a belief that change was unachievable. They saw their lives as having been written for them and thought the blame for their offending was on society. In contrast, redemption narratives sought to separate the person's 'true self' from his or her past offending. Like with condemnation scripts, the narratives portrayed offending as something that happened to the person, but the stories involved a shift in agency in which the person has regained control over his or her life and destiny. Redemption scripts were therefore characterized by hope, self-efficacy, and a desire to give something back to their communities and families as a way of redeeming their past mistakes.

Similarly in their own identity theory of desistance, Paternoster and Bushway (2009) argue that desistance from crime is more cognitive than had previously been considered. They suggest that at a certain point, individuals become tired of their criminal lifestyle and identity, and actively seek to change who they are. Rather than a change in identity resulting from changes in social attachments (Laub and Sampson 2004), Paternoster and Bushway argue that life failures or dissatisfactions culminate in a 'crystallisation of discontent' whereby an individual begins to imagine a new, entirely possible, conformist self (2009: 1121; see also e.g. Giordano et al. 2002; Healy 2010).

Measuring desistance self-narratives

Research on self-narratives of desistance has been almost entirely qualitative to date, which makes perfect sense as presumably the best way to access a person's internalized story of themselves is to conduct lengthy life story interviews (McAdams 1993). The audio-recorded and transcribed narratives produced through such research methods are not thought to be, themselves, perfect approximations for the individuals internalized self-narrative, but rather are thought to 'hold the outlines' (McAdams 1993: 20). Yet, such in-depth qualitative methodology is not well suited to surveying large samples or to hypothesis testing through quantitative analysis. As such, to further examine the role of self-narrative and their relationship to behaviour, a variety of studies have begun to explore more streamlined measures that can reliably measure the same dynamics that are captured in qualitative interview data.

Lloyd and Serin (2012) were among the first to develop and administer a series of measures attempting to capture the individual features of desistance such as agency and self-efficacy. The ten-item Personal Agency for Desistance Questionnaire was developed by the authors to assess perceived sense of agency for desistance. Items were developed through reviewing the international desistance literature. Their results provide an initial step in developing self-report scales that measure desistance-supportive beliefs.

Rocque et al. (2016) have also developed a measure of 'pro-social identity' drawing on desistance literatures and the notion of secondary desistance in particular. The scale asks participants to identify how often (on a five-point scale, ranging from never to always) they feel they are a 'good person', think of themselves 'as a delinquent', feel they are 'mean', and feel that they are 'dishonest and cannot be trusted'. The results provided support for identity theories of desistance, indicating that pro-social identity increased over time and was a robust predictor of criminal behaviour over the life course. The authors argued that future work should seek to examine the factors related to these changes in pro-social identity beyond simple biological maturation or the passage of time.

O'Sullivan and colleagues (2017) developed a 'Belief in Redemption' (BIR) Scale designed to measure belonging, agency, and optimism in self-narratives as identified in Maruna (2001) and elsewhere (e.g. Vaughan 2007). The authors found a significant negative correlation between BIR scores and standardized measures of risk, although this work found only a small, non-significant correlation between BIR scores and failure on supervision.

Desistance narratives in practice

Much of the interest in quantifying desistance narratives has emerged from the practice community. That is, if a link between self-narrative and sustained desistance could be empirically established, the concept would represent an important 'intermediate outcome' for those working with prisoners and probationers. For this reason, HM Prison and Probation Services (HMPPS) in England and Wales have developed the 'Redemption and Condemnation Self-Narrative (RCSN) Scale' with the aim of providing a reliable and valid measure of desistance self-narratives that can be used as an assessment tool in prison and probation work (Baker and McCathie 2012). Drawing on the findings of Maruna's (2001) study, Baker and McCathie (2012) first sought to identify whether redemption and condemnation self-narratives existed within a prisoner population (in comparison to Maruna's community sample) and could be measured using a questionnaire design. They identified 18 statements indicative of either a redemption self-narrative (e.g. 'I know I have done some bad stuff in the past, but I am a good person') or a condemnation self-narrative (e.g. 'I often feel powerless to change my behaviour'). They hypothesized that the Redemption Self-Narrative subscale would show convergent validity with measures of Hope (Snyder 1995) and General Self-Efficacy (Schwarzer and Jerusalem 1995) and that the Condemnation Self-Narrative subscale would show discriminate convergent validity with both measures. Outcomes from administration to 168 male prisoners indicated that the Condemnation Self-Narrative subscale had good internal reliability and a moderate negative correlation with measures of hope and self-efficacy. The Redemption Self-Narrative scale had lower internal reliability and non-significant positive correlation with hope and self-efficacy, and the authors concluded the scale needed further development.

Todd and Bowers (2015) tested the use of the RCSN scales with individuals convicted of sexual offences and examined the association between self-narrative and take up of rehabilitative services in prison. Principle Components Analysis identified that the RCSN scale measured three components: *Condemned*; *Purposeful Recovery*; *Defined by the System*. Results indicated that participants who had positive views of and had taken up rehabilitative services in prison had a self-narrative focused on maintaining a positive self-identity and a sense of hope and purpose.

Johnson and colleagues administered the RCSN scale as part of an overall evaluation of a rehabilitative regime designed to help prisoners progress from higher security prisons into open prison conditions within HMPPS (Johnson and McCathie 2015; Woulfe and Johnson 2016). This research explored whether successful engagement in the rehabilitative regime resulted in a change in participants' self-evaluation regarding desistance. A significant reduction in condemnation self-narrative was found between induction and progress within the regime, indicating a positive shift away from self-beliefs that might hinder desistance. No change was found with regard to the redemption self-narrative.

Finally, the RCSN was recently included in a recent research project examining the psychological characteristics of short sentenced prisoners, including comparison with longer sentenced prisoners, exploration of their experience in custody and analysis of characteristics predictive of reoffending (Falgate 2018). The study found that a condemnation self-narrative as measured by the RCSN was significantly correlated with reoffending as were measures of social capital and perception of problems. However, following a regression analysis, only the condemnation self-narrative was a significant predictor of reoffending. Recommendations were made for practical application of findings (see Falgate 2018), particularly in terms of supporting identity change with short-term sentenced prisoners, and that further development of the scale may include consideration of hope and intention to desist.

Conclusion

The idea of the desistance narrative has developed considerably in a short amount of time. Initially explored through qualitative research on how people desist from crime, the concept has recently attracted the attention of applied researchers and practitioners in justice contexts, seeking to establish its value in assessing therapeutic progress in treatment interventions. It is important, however, that self-narratives do not become yet another 'risk factor' or 'treatment target' for psychologists. Narratives of desistance 'say as much about subcultural and societal pressures facing ex-deviants . . . as they do about individual competencies and inclinations' (Maruna 2001: 9). In other words, offenders do not exist in a vacuum but rather in a social network and social-structural conditions that may powerfully help or hinder their efforts to stop offending (Hart and Healy 2018; Weaver and Weaver 2013). These stories need to be understood, therefore, as both sociological and psychological artefacts and explored accordingly (Harding et al. 2017).

For those deeply entrenched in criminal networks and living in disadvantaged circumstances, desistance from crime requires a tremendous amount of self-belief, and is made highly difficult, if not impossible, if opportunities and resources are limited and those around the person believe they will fail (see Nugent and Schinkel 2016). An understanding of culture – described as the 'therapeutic landscapes of recovery' (Wilton and DeVerteuil 2006) in the recovery literature – is particularly significant when considering the implications of desistance narratives. If individuals find themselves in a culture with a set of norms that precludes the telling of a story of desistance, or regards desistance and rehabilitation as impossible, what effect will that have on an individual's efforts to stop offending? This appears particularly relevant when considering prisons, rarely places characterized by an abundance of hope and generativity, but for which the issue of creating 'rehabilitative cultures' has recently risen to the fore (O'Brien et al. 2014).

Future research in this area might therefore usefully examine *how* self-narratives transform. Remarkably little is known in this regard (see Porporino 2010). Maruna (2011) has argued that more attention needs to be paid to 'rites of passage' in the shaping of identity. Others have focused on role changes and opportunities for the development of new social networks (Laub and Sampson 2004; LeBel et al. 2008). At times these approaches are pitted against one another to see, for instance, whether changes in social bonds (e.g. marriage or employment) explain more of the variance in the desistance process than changes at the level of cognition or self-narrative. However, what is needed is research that combines both types of research, recognizing that human lives have both social and psychological aspects and the two are meaningless alone.

In terms of applied research in the justice system, psychologists need to recognize that individuals create and revise their own narratives, but they do so in dialogue with the world around them. The 'good news' for those seeking to help individuals re-write their own stories is that extant theory and research suggests that the best tools in this regard might be the sharing of stories. After all, a considerable amount of therapeutic work inside and outside of criminal justice contexts – from group therapy in therapeutic communities to the mutual aid of Alcoholics Anonymous – already involves working with self-narratives through the exploration of life histories, listening to the personal testimonies of others, and various forms of talk therapy (see Marsh 2011). The more that individuals are exposed to other stories – from people like them, who have walked similar paths, who have overcome similar obstacles and 'made good' – the more likely they may be to imagine such hopeful narratives for themselves. Without such narrative role models, this sort of unlikely transformation would seem logically impossible.

References

Aresti, A., Eatough, V. and Brooks-Gordon, B. (2010) Doing time after time: An interpretative phenomenological analysis of reformed ex-prisoners' experiences of self-change, identity and career opportunities. *Psychology, Crime & Law*, 16(3), 169–190.

Baker, L. and McCathie, G. (2012) *Making Good' in Prison. Developing a Measure of Self-Narrative Amongst Prisoners as an Indicator of Desistance.* Unpublished manuscript.

Bruner, J. S. (1987) Life as narrative. *Social Research*, 54, 11–32.

Denver, M. and Ewald, A. (2018) Credentialing decisions and criminal records: A approach. *Criminology*, 56(4), 715–749.

Dollinger, B. (2018) Subjects in criminality discourse: On the narrative positioning of young defendants. *Punishment & Society*, 20(4), 477–497.

Falgate, C. (2018) *A Prospective Longitudinal Study of Short Sentenced Prisoners'.* Unpublished Doctoral Dissertation.

Ferrand, N. and Weil, M. (Eds.). (2001) *Homo narrativus, recherches sur la topique romanesque dans les fictions de langue française 1800.* Montpellier: Presses de l'Université Paul-Valéry.

Giddens, A. (1991) *Modernity and Self-Identity: Self and Society in the Late Modern Age.* Stanford, CA: Stanford University Press.

Giordano, P. C., Cernkovich, S. A. and Rudolph, J. L. (2002) Gender, crime, and desistance: Toward a theory of cognitive transformation. *American Journal of Sociology*, 107(4), 990–1064.Glaser, D. (1964) *Effectiveness of a Prison and Parole System.* Indianapolis, IN: Bobbs-Merrill.

Harding, D. J., Dobson, C. C., Wyse, J. J. B. and Morenoff, J. D. (2017) Narrative change, narrative stability, and structural constraint: The case of prisoner reentry narratives. *American Journal of Cultural Sociology*, 5(1), 261–304. DOI:10.1057/s41290-016-0004-8.

Hart, W. and Healy, D. (2018) 'An inside job': An autobiographical account of desistance. *European Journal of Probation*, 10(2), 103–119. DOI:10.1177/2066220318783426.

Healy, D. (2010) Betwixt and between: The role of psychosocial factors in the early stages of desistance. *Journal of Research in Crime and Delinquency*, 47(4), 419–438. DOI:10.1177/0022427810375574.

Johnson, K. and McCathie, G. (2015) *Establishing a Baseline Measure to Explore the Relationship Between Attendance in a Progression Regime and Attitudes Towards Desistence Using the Redemption and Condemnation Self-Narrative Scale* (RCSN, Baker & McCathie, 2011). Unpublished manuscript.

King, S. (2013) Assisted desistance and experiences of probation supervision. *Probation Journal*, 60(2), 136–151. DOI:10.1177/0264550513478320.

Laub, J. H. and Sampson, R. J. (2004) Strategies for bridging the quantitative and qualitative divide: Studying crime over the life course. *Research in Human Development*, 1(1–2), 81–99.

LeBel, T. P., Burnett, R., Maruna, S. and Bushway, S. (2008) The 'chicken and egg' of subjective and social factors in desistance from crime. *European Journal of Criminology*, 5(2), 131–159. DOI:10.1177/1477370807087640.

Lloyd, C. D. and Serin, R. C. (2012) Agency and outcome expectancies for crime desistance: Measuring offenders' personal beliefs about change. *Psychology, Crime & Law*, 18(6), 543–565.

Marsh, B. (2011) Narrating desistance: Identity change and the 12 step script. *Irish Probation Journal*, 8, 49–68.

Maruna, S. (2001) *Making Good How Ex-Convicts Reform and Rebuild Their Lives.* Washington, DC: American Psychological Association.

Maruna, S. (2011) Reentry as a rite of passage. *Punishment & Society*, 13(1), 3–28.

Maruna, S., Immarigeon, R. and LeBel, T. (2004) Ex-offender reintegration: Theory and practice. In S. Maruna and R. Immarigeon (Eds.), *After Crime and Punishment: Pathways to Ex-Offender Reintegration*. Cullompton: Willan Books, pp. 1–25.

McAdams, D. P. (1993) *The Stories We Live By: Personal Myths and the Making of the Self*. New York: Guilford Press.

McAdams, D. P. (1996) Personality, modernity, and the storied self: A contemporary framework for studying persons. *Psychological Inquiry*, 7(4), 295–321.

McAdams, D. P. (2006) *The Redemptive Self: Stories Americans Live by*. New York: Oxford University Press.

McNeill, F., Farrall, S., Lightowler, C. and Maruna, S. (2012) How and why people stop offending: Discovering desistance. In *Insights Evidence Summary to Support Social Services in Scotland*. Glasgow: IRISS.

Nugent, B. and Schinkel, M. (2016) The pains of desistance. *Criminology & Criminal Justice*, 16(5), 568–584.

O'Brien, R., Marshall, J. and Karthaus, R. (2014) *Building a Rehabilitation Culture*. London: RSA. Available at: www.thersa.org/globalassets/pdfs/reports/rsa_building_a_rehabilitation_culture_11_06_14.pdf.

O'Sullivan, K., Holderness, D., Hong, X. Y., Bright, D. and Kemp, R. (2017) Public attitudes in Australia to the reintegration of ex-offenders: Testing a Belief in Redeemability (BiR) Scale. *European Journal on Criminal Policy and Research*, 23(3), 409–424.

Paternoster, R. A. Y. and Bushway, S. (2009) Desistance and the "feared self": Toward and identity theory of criminal desistance. *The Journal of Criminal Law and Criminology*, 99(4), 1103–1156.

Phillips, J. (2017) Towards a rhizomatic understanding of the desistance journey. *The Howard Journal of Criminal Justice*, 56(1), 92–104.

Porporino, F. J. (2010) Bringing sense and sensitivity to corrections: From programmes to 'fix' offenders to services to support desistance. *What Else Works? Creative Work with Offenders*, 61–85.

Presser, L. and Sandberg, S. (Eds.). (2015) *Narrative Criminology: Understanding Stories of Crime*. New York: New York University Press.

Rocque, M., Posick, C. and Paternoster, R. (2016) Identities through time: An exploration of identity change as a cause of desistance. *Justice Quarterly*, 33(1), 45–72.

Sartre, J. P. (1938/1965) *Nausea* (Translated by Robert Baldick). Harmandsworth: Penguin.

Schwarzer, R. and Jerusalem, M. (1995) Generalized self-efficacy scale. Measures in health psychology: A user's portfolio. *Causal and Control Beliefs*, 1(1), 35–37.

Serin, R. C. and Lloyd, C. D. (2009) Examining the process of offender change: The transition to crime desistance. *Psychology, Crime & Law*, 15(4), 347–364.

Snyder, C. R. (1995) Conceptualizing, measuring, and nurturing hope. *Journal of Counseling & Development*, 73(3), 355–360.

Stone, R. (2015) Desistance narratives and identity repair: Redemption narratives as resistance to stigma. *British Journal of Criminology*, 56(5), 956–975.

Todd, R. and Bowers, L. (2015) *Evaluating a Measure of Desistance Self-Narrative*. Unpublished manuscript.

Vaughan, B. (2007) The internal narrative of desistance. *British Journal of Criminology*, 47, 390–404.

Weaver, A. and Weaver, B. (2013) Autobiography, empirical research and critical theory in desistance: A view from the inside out. *Probation Journal*, 60(3), 259–277. DOI:10.1177/0264550513489763.

Wilton, R. and DeVerteuil, G. (2006) Spaces of sobriety/sites of power: Examining social model alcohol recovery programs as therapeutic landscapes. *Social Science & Medicine*, 63(3), 649–661.

Woulfe, T. and Johnson, K. (2016) *An Exploration of Attitudes Toward Desistance Amongst Prisoners in a Progression Regime*. Unpublished manuscript.

Therapeutic justice and rehabilitation

12

Martine Herzog-Evans

Introduction

Therapeutic Jurisprudence (TJ) is a lens and a focus, which tends to perceive the law not only as the solution to a dispute, nor as the strong arm of the state, but also as a humane and holistic way of solving conflicts. It also aims to attend to and solve human and social difficulties, with the ultimate goal of generating the well-being and appeasement amongst individuals, families, the community, and society as a whole. However, it does not shy away from addressing and dealing with emotions and pain. TJ exists at the crossroads of mental health, law, criminology, and other theoretical and treatment models. It focuses on the entirety of the legal system (e.g. family law, constitutional law, etc.), and its practitioners (e.g. judges, psychologists, probation officers, etc.). However, in this chapter, I focus exclusively on the penal continuum.

Therapeutic Jurisprudence is a revolutionary way of practicing law, doing rehabilitation with humanity, and caring for fellow human beings and their well-being at its core (Winick and Wexler 2003). It is not only a theory but also a problem-solving method, which courts tend to heavily draw upon. However, because it is rather flexible and goal-oriented, and lacks theoretical construct validity in the scientific sense (Nolan 2009; Kaiser and Holtfreter 2015), it is at risk of remaining in a parallel altruist universe. Therefore, mainstreaming TJ is a main challenge (Wexler 2016). Clearly, then, there is a need for integrating TJ into empirically validated models of doing justice, supervision, and treatment, which is what this chapter tries to initiate.

The genesis of Therapeutic Jurisprudence

The term and concept of TJ were first formulated in 1987 by David Wexler, during a conference at the US's National Institute of Mental Health. At the time, Wexler met strong opposition from mental health practitioners (Backhouse 2016). TJ was further elaborated, thanks to Wexler's association with Winick (Wexler and Winick 1991, 1996). It later became an international movement thanks to, on the one hand, intense legal doctrine and scientific production, and, on the other hand, TJ's theoretical contribution to the understanding of the problem-solving court movement (see below). Problem-solving courts (PSCs), that is due process courts with a focus on solving specific issues, such as substance abuse, domestic violence, mental health, or veterans' trauma, on the basis of multi-agency integrative partnerships, shall be discussed below. Importantly at this point, whilst TJ was later adopted to offer PSCs a legal and theoretical framework (Hora et al. 1999), PSCs did reciprocally offer TJ an operational showcase.

Therapeutic Jurisprudence: a vessel for fairness

TJ translates humanity, respect, and care into intelligible legal terms and practical guidelines. With its focus on fair processes and end results, such as well-being, healing, and desistance (Birgden 2015), it also provides purpose.

However, selling humanity and procedural fairness in punitive and managerial 'move the docket' contexts is challenging. Conversely, those who are strong partisans of due process – but often confuse it with adversarialism (Freiberg 2011; Stobbs 2013), in spite of its nocebo effects (Fan 2014) against what the TJ movement actually built (Stobbs 2011) – criticize PSCs and TJ, claiming they are controlling (Miller 2004) or representing a threat to due process (Brakel 2007).

For all these reasons, TJ requires both a renewed theoretical reformulation (Stobbs 2017; Stobbs et al. 2019) and empirical validation (Herzog-Evans 2017, 2018, 2019).

Empirical Therapeutic Jurisprudence

Currently, there is no such thing as a measurable TJ theory, in the empirical sense (Kaiser and Holtfreter 2015). To be fair, a legal theory provides structures to a legal field (e.g. criminal law) or a concept (e.g. presumption of innocence), and it is able to justify how substantive and procedural norms are articulated; however, it is not meant to be empirically measured, nor is it meant to measure or validate programmes.

We know, however, that problem-solving courts – and, therefore, TJ – work, thanks to six meta-analyses (Latimer et al. 2006; Gutierrez and Bourgon 2009; Shaffer 2011; Mitchell et al. 2012; Gutierrez et al. 2017). More contrasted results have been found in Mental Health Courts (Lowder et al. 2017). Most importantly, though, Lowder and colleagues' review found vast differences between courts.

It has, therefore, become imperative to uncover which TJ and other variables make PSCs work (Kaiser and Holtfreter 2015). As we shall see in this chapter, several of the key variables pertain to due process. However, due process is typically limited to courts, and to a certain degree, to policing; whereas, probation and forensic treatment are mostly governed by psycho-criminological treatment models with little attention to the exact content of ethics (Herzog-Evans 2016), beyond general statements (Canton and Eadie 2008; Bonta and Andrews 2017). Reciprocally, dosage, intensity levels, and breadth treatment principles (Bonta and Andrews 2017) cannot be enforced without compatible legal systems and mandates (Herzog-Evans 2018). It follows that a renewed TJ model would have to fit in the current offender rehabilitation models and the PSC's main principles.

Therapeutic Jurisprudence theory

PSCs work, as research into their key components have shown, and TJ has proven that it is a powerful theory. However, TJ is a legal theory which, for this reason, does not truly explain why PSCs and, more generally, legitimacy of justice work (Kaiser and Holtfreter 2015). There is, therefore, a need for an integrative theory.

Reformulating TJ within already-validated models can be done in three different steps:

1   By linking, on the one hand, Legitimacy of Justice-Procedural Justice (LJ-PJ), an empirical psychology research domain that focuses on penal processes and has shown that humans first and foremost need respect and due process, that is they are more interested in how they are treated as opposed to what the outcome of the process itself is, with, on the other hand, TJ, whilst integrating both these domains into legal theory;

2   By linking LJ-PJ-TJ to a decluttered and reconstructed definition of the Risk-Needs-Responsivity offender rehabilitation model (Bonta and Andrews 2017) and other treatment models with a common reinsertion goal (McNeill 2012, 2015); and

3   By merging this model into the empirically validated PSCs' key components also uncovered by research.

Legitimacy of Justice-Procedural Justice (LJ-PJ) provides empirical support for many TJ core principles, such as, inter alia, care, and respect for criminal justice service users. However, it is in TJ literature that one will find practical and legal explanatory details related to LJ-PJ's components (Casey et al. 2013; Richardson et al. 2016).

LJ-PJ studies were first initiated by Thibaut and Walker (1975), who found that litigants could be unsatisfied with their trial even though they had won the case, a finding which was later consistently repeated across contexts. Tyler's (2006, 2013) model, as augmented by De Mesmaecker (2014), is in my own presentation, which includes TJ (i.e. the 'LJ-PJ-TJ paradigm') (Herzog-Evans 2017, 2019), divided into four legal-behavioural principles and two strictly behavioural principles.

The first legal-behavioural principle is *VOICE*, i.e. a 'a forum in which [people] can tell their story' (Tyler 2013: 21). In legal terms, voice refers to due process principles, such as parties' ability to express their opinion, and their ability to actively participate in the procedure. Moreover, it requires a hearing, appearance of the parties, right to counsel, and, when relevant, a translator. In behavioural terms, voice means that practitioners must truly and ostensibly listen to the parties.

The second legal-behavioural principle is *NEUTRALITY*. In procedural terms, neutrality translates into impartiality, which must be both apparent and objective (EHRCt, Morel v. Belgium, 6 June 2000, n° 34130/96). Neutrality also refers to parties having equal rights, which in behavioural terms, requires that they are ostensibly treated identically. Neutrality, furthermore, refers to the fact that the decision-making authority must not have, or appear to have, already formed an opinion or reached a decision before the case is heard.

De Mesmaecker (2014) has later added *FACT-FINDING*, which refers to several fundamental legal principles: (1) the burden of proof; (2) the presumption of innocence and its cousin principle *in dubio pro reo*; and (3) the rigorous study of the evidence. As with voice and neutrality, fact-finding is both about reality and ostensible appearances; for instance, being seen as checking facts and taking enough time to collect and analyze them.

Leventhal (1980) and Tyler (1988) also referred to *CORRECTABILITY*, which is linked to due process (see e.g. Art. 13 of the European Human Rights Convention – ECHR) and represents a second chance for the decision to be amended (i.e. an appeal, or access to an administrative review). In behavioural terms, correctability requests that the remedy be effective and not meaningless. Thus, the appellate authority must also abide by all the other LJ-PJ principles.

The first behavioural LJ-PJ principle, *RESPECT*, is essential, because it refers to the fundamental human need for relatedness (Ryan and Deci 2017). Disrespect is perceived as ostracising fellow human beings, which, in turn, activates their brain alarm system (Eisenberger et al. 2003). Respect is often linked in LJ-PJ literature to the principle of dignity. However, nowhere, other than in the TJ doctrine, is the principle of dignity made clearer or more concrete in the context of real judicial and other criminal justice settings (Perlin 2017).

A second behavioural principle, CARE, has also been labelled as representing an 'ethic of care' (Stolle et al. 2000) and has been better formulated in TJ literature (Wexler and Winick 1996). Concretely, it means, amongst other things, that it must be made apparent to the person that his or her circumstances and well-being are worth one's attention and preoccupation. In research I conducted, pertaining to the release of short-term prisoners in the French context (Herzog-Evans 2017), I unfortunately encountered numerous cases where both judges and probation officers ostensibly showed prisoners that they did not care.

In conclusion on this first point, TJ is what gives practical substance to Legitimacy of Justice-Procedural Justice empirically validated components. It also helps link the LJ-PJ-TJ paradigm to fundamental legal principles. However, LJ-PJ-TJ cannot be subsumed into legal principles, because it requires practitioners, institutions, and processes to be behaviourally virtuous and humane (Herzog-Evans 2015a).

The LJ-PJ-TJ paradigm also has empirical value, since it produces less reoffending (Kaiser and Reisig 2017), less attrition, and more compliance (Colquitt et al. 2013); but it is more efficient when it is linked to the RNR model of offender rehabilitation.

Currently, the Risk-Need-Responsivity (RNR) model (Bonta and Andrews 2017; Ziv this volume), albeit criticized, is the most validated offender rehabilitation model. Even its strongest detractors have included their own models within its framework (Yates et al. 2010). However, RNR is multi-layered, which comes with its hosts of overlapping and sometimes under-theorized satellites, such as overreaching principles and non-programmatic factors. RNR is also linked to Core Correctional Practices (CCPs), which actually represent two models – Andrews and Kiessling's (1980) model and Trotter's (2015) model.

A theoretical model's internal validity requires each component not only to be empirically validated but also logically classified. I have, therefore, suggested (Herzog-Evans 2018): (1) that the superfluous 'non-programmatic-factors' construct be eliminated, and some of its non-overlapping factors included in RNR's main principles; (2) that Andrews and Kiessling's and Trotter's CCPs be merged; and (3) that the concept of general responsivity be repealed, since it does not truly pertain to responsivity, but to treatment principles. Then, I followed in the footsteps of Birgden (2004), who suggested responsivity be divided into external and internal categories; thus, I proposed it be divided into intrinsic (i.e. individual, offender-related) and extrinsic (i.e. institutional, legal) responsivity. I then argued that the LJ-PJ-TJ paradigm constitute a fundamental dimension of extrinsic responsivity, since it has a validated and decisive impact on offender compliance, retention in treatment programmes, and reoffending rates.

Principles and features of problem-solving courts

Problem-solving courts (PSCs), the international therapeutic jurisprudential (TJ) showcase, come with ten principles of their own. Because they represent potentially additional operant variables, and are often referred to in the TJ literature, they must be integrated into the LJ-PJ-TJ-RNR framework. Several attempts have been made at listing PSC's main components, notably in the TJ literature (NADCP 1997; King 2009; Hora 2011). In this chapter, I propose my own formulation (Herzog-Evans 2015b, 2019).

One of the main PSC principles is *judicial decision-making and contribution to offender supervision*. Traditionally, common law legal systems consider that criminal law's province ends when the sentence is passed, and consequently, that judicial contribution is no longer required. Conversely, in other European jurisdictions such as France, Italy, Spain, Germany, or in Latin American states, a specialized court has oversight over the probation and rehabilitation process, thus allowing for due process to extend its bearing. It is this model that PSCs have emulated. Importantly, judicial intervention has been empirically validated as contributing to the positive outcomes of PSCs (Rossman et al. 2011), and it is supported by offenders (Gallagher et al. 2015).

A second principle is that of fair and *public hearing*. Publicity is expected to extend the efficacy of the model to all the offenders or problem-solving court participants who sit in the audience. It is also part of a general due process principle enshrined in Article 6 of the ECHR. However, publicity has yet to be empirically validated as a key variable. Tellingly, the LJ-PJ literature has not included publicity in its model.

A third principle is *specialization*, which is also a key TJ principle (Rottman 2000). Specialization can refer to a specific legal field and the issues raised within its specific boundaries; for instance, in the French context, juvenile judges. In the context of PSCs' specialization, it refers to the issue at stake (e.g. substance abuse, mental health, or domestic violence) and implies that judges and other practitioners are knowledgeable in these domains. In itself, specialization has not been empirically validated; although, being knowledgeable in a given subject probably increases the chances of implementing evidence-based treatment methods.

A fourth principle, *problem-solving*, can mean four different things. It can first take us back to pre-Martinson social work (Martinson 1974; McCord 1978, 2003); secondly, it can refer to the treatment of criminogenic needs (Bonta and Andrews 2017); thirdly, it can refer to problem-solving social work in the CCPs (Trotter 2015) or evidence-based (EBP) social work (Hepworth et al. 2013) sense; fourthly, it can also refer to cognitive behavioural treatment models (Beck 2011). Ideally, the second, third, and fourth understanding of problem-solving should be preferred, since they are empirically validated. Importantly, though, social support is also linked to professional duty of care

(Canton and Eadie 2008) and is a human right (Office of the United Nations High Commissioner for Human Rights 2008).

A fifth principle, *swift intermediary sanctions* and *rewards*, or accountability, refers to non-eliminatory and gradual sanctions. Gottfredson et al. (2007) found this principle to be strongly linked to positive outcomes, in accordance with operant conditioning (Bandura 1977) and social learning theory (Akers 2009). Drug treatment models routinely use tangible rewards (e.g. vouchers), and the efficacy of this approach has been supported (Schumacher et al. 2007). However, self-determination theory has empirically shown time and again that one can be 'punished by [tangible] rewards', since they only support extrinsic motivation that is short-lived (Ryan and Deci 2017). A conclusion on this point is perhaps that if encouragement and praise are efficient (Trotter 2015), tangible rewards only serve instrumental compliance (Robinson and McNeill 2008).

Related to accountability is the *administration of regular drug tests* where PSC participants' offending is drug-related, which, again, is further supported by cognitive behavioural drug treatment models, notably the development of insight (Beck et al. 1993). It has recently been recommended by the American Society of Addiction Medicine (2017).

A seventh key principle, *interagency collaborative works* is central to the PSC model (Berman and Feinblatt 2015). Evidence-based practice (EBP) collaborative models (Sullivan and Skelcher 2002; Pycroft and Gough 2010; Graham 2016) are egalitarian and include LJ-PJ-TJ governance principles; notably, voice and respect.

An eighth principle, *community embeddedness*, is in its minimal form, also present in the RNR overreaching principle of community partner availability. However, in the PSC model, local embeddedness more substantially signifies that the court or treatment agency has strong ties with the community and is focused on its well-being.

One of the greatest strengths of PSCs is that they usually operate within a *one-stop shop* setting. This essential factor explains their success, regarding attrition rates and their negative consequences (Hatcher et al. 2012). For indeed, attrition is often related to issue of access and distance, and to a form of burnout experience by offenders who have to travel back and forth from one place to another to obtain support with their multiple needs. A one-stop-shop system eliminates this particular obstacle to compliance.

The last PSC component is the existence of *desistance rituals*, as advocated by Maruna (2001, 2011) and in the TJ literature (Walker and Kobayashi 2015), which celebrate successful programme termination and seem to be important in the desistance process of leaving crime behind.

Conclusion

Therapeutic Jurisprudence specialists tend to be resistant to theorization. This chapter has argued that, in order for TJ to become a mainstream model of ethical and humane justice, and to be measurable and replicable, such theorizing ought to happen (Stobbs 2013) and be linked to other empirically validated models. The potential consequences of TJ becoming mainstream – not only in courts but also in offender supervision, treatment, release, and sanction – are extraordinary, because, inter alia, it produces less reoffending (Kaiser and Reisig 2017).

TJ implies that more due process decision-making occurs, and it also suggests that judges participate actively in supervision and do not limit themselves to the definition of the judicial mandate. TJ requires that 'good' practitioners are recruited and adequately trained (Paparozzi and Guy 2009) and that institutions are effectively and ethically operated. It makes for more engaging practitioners and institutions and, thus, increases the efficacy of treatment models.

Thus, the exact role played by TJ, in itself, is two-fold. First, TJ is a lawyer-friendly model of legitimacy and humane justice. Second, TJ gives legal and practical substance to the respect and care dimensions of LJ-PJ.

References

Akers, R. (2009) *Social Learning and Social Structure: A General Theory of Crime and Deviance*. New Brunswick: Transaction Publishers.

American Society of Addiction Medicine (ASAM). (2017) Appropriate use of drug testing in clinical addiction. *Journal of Addiction Medicine*. [Online] 11(Supplement 1), 1–56. http://dx.doi.org/10.1097/ADM.0000000000000322.

Andrews, D. and Kiessling, J. (1980) Program structure and effective correctional practices: A summary of the CaVIC research. In R. Ross and P. Gendreau (Eds.), *Effective Correctional Treatment*. Toronto: Butterworth, pp. 441–463.

Backhouse, C. (2016) An introduction to David Wexler, the person behind therapeutic jurisprudence. *International Journal of Therapeutic Jurisprudence*, 1(1), 1–21.

Bandura, A. (1977) Self-efficacy: Toward a unifying theory of behavioral change. *Psychological Review*, 84(2), 191–215.

Beck, A., Wright, F., Newman, C. and Liese, B. (1993) *Cognitive Therapy of Substance Abuse*. New York: The Guilford Press.

Beck, J. (2011) *Cognitive-Behavioral Therapy: Basics and Beyond*. New York: The Guilford Press.

Berman, G. and Feinblatt, J. (2015) *Good Courts: The Case for Problem-Solving Justice*, 2nd edition. [Online] New Orleans: Quid Pro Books. Available at Quid Pro Books: http://quidprolaw.com/ (Accessed 15 December 2017).

Birgden, A. (2004) Therapeutic jurisprudence and responsivity: Finding the will and the way in offender rehabilitation. *Psychology, Crime & Law*, 10(3), 283–295.

Birgden, A. (2015) Maximizing desistance: Adding therapeutic jurisprudence and human rights to the mix. *Criminal Justice and Behavior*, 42(1), 19–31.

Bonta, J. and Andrews, D. (2017) *The Psychology of Criminal Conduct*, 6th edition. New York: Routledge.

Brakel, S. (2007) Searching for the therapy in therapeutic jurisprudence. *New England Journal on Criminal and Civil Confinement*, 33, 455–499.

Canton, R. and Eadie, T. (2008) Accountability, legitimacy, and discretion: Applying criminology in professional practice. In B. Stout, J. Yates and B. Williams (Eds.), *Applied Criminology*. London: Sage Publications, pp. 86–102.

Casey, P., Burke, K. and Leben, S. (2013) Minding the court: Enhancing the decision-making process. *International Journal for Court Administration*. [Online] 5(1), 45–54. http://doi.org/10.18352/ijca.8.

Colquitt, J., Scott, B., Rodell, J., Long, D., Zapata, C., Colon, D. and Wesson, M. (2013) Justice at the millennium, a decade later: A meta-analytic test of social exchange and affect-based perspectives. *Journal of Applied Psychology*, 98(2), 199–236.

De Mesmaecker, V. (2014) *Perceptions of Criminal Justice*. Abingdon: Routledge.

Eisenberger, N., Lieberman, M. and Williams, K. (2003) Does rejection hurt? An fMRI study of social exclusion. *Science*, 302(5643), 290–292.

Fan, M. (2014) The adversarial justice's casualties: Defending victim-witness protection. *Boston College Law Review*, 55(3), 755–820.

Freiberg, A. (2011) Post-adversarial and post-inquisitorial justice: Transcending traditional penological paradigms. *European Journal of Criminology*, 8(1), 82–101.

Gallagher, J., Nordberg, A. and Kennard, T. (2015) A qualitative study assessing the effectiveness of the key components of a drug court. *Alcoholism Treatment Quarterly*, 33(1), 64–81.

Gottfredson, D., Kearley, B., Najaka, S. and Rocha, C. (2007) How drug treatment courts work: An analysis of mediators. *Journal of Research in Crime & Delinquency*, 44(1), 3–35.

Graham, H. (2016) *Rehabilitation Work: Supporting Desistance and Recovery*. London: Routledge.

Gutierrez, L., Blais, J. and Bourgon, G. (2017) Do domestic violent courts work? A meta-analytic review examining treatment and study quality. *Justice Research and Policy*. [Online] 17(2), 75–99. https://doi.org/10.1177/1525107117725012.

Gutierrez, L. and Bourgon, G. (2009) *Drug Treatment Courts: A Quantitative Review of Study and Treatment Quality 2009–04*. Ottawa: Public Safety Canada.

Hatcher, R., McGuire, J., Bilby, C., Palmer, E. and Hollin, C. (2012) Methodological considerations in the evaluation of offender intervention: The problem of attrition. *International Journal of Offender Therapy and Comparative Criminology*, 56(3), 447–464.

Hepworth, D., Rooney, R., Dewberry-Rooney, G. and Strom-Gottfried, K. (2013) *Direct Social Work Practice: Theory and Skills*, 9th edition. Belmont: Brooks, Cole.

Herzog-Evans, M. (Ed.). (2015a) *Offender Release and Supervision: The Role of Courts and the Use of Discretion*. Nijmegen: Wolf Legal Publishers.

Herzog-Evans, M. (2015b) A 70 year old French re-entry court. Is the French Juge de l'application des peines a Problem-Solving Court? In M. Herzog-Evans (Ed.), *Offender Release and Supervision: The Role of Courts and the Use of Discretion*. Nijmegen: Wolf Legal Publishers, pp. 409–445.

Herzog-Evans, M. (2016) Law as an extrinsic responsivity factor: What's just is what works! *European Journal of Probation*, 8(3), 146–169.

Herzog-Evans, M. (2017) *La mise en France de la libération sous contrainte dans le Nord-Est de la France*. Report to the Mission Droit et Justice.

Herzog-Evans, M. (2019). Towards an evidence-based legitimacy of justice-procedural justice model in offender release and supervision. In N. Stobbs, L. Bartels and M. Vols (Eds.), *The Methodology and Practice of Therapeutic Jurisprudence*. Durham: Carolina Academic Press, pp. 197–225.

Herzog-Evans, M. (2018) RNR, evidence diversity and integrative theory. In P. Ugwudike, P. Raynor and J. Annison (Eds.), *International Research on Supporting Rehabilitation and Desistance*. Bristol: Policy Press, pp. 99–126.

Hora, P. (2011) Courting new solutions using problem-solving justice: Key components, guiding principles, strategies, responses, models, approaches, blueprints and tool kits. *Chapman Journal of Criminal Justice*, 2(1), 7–52.

Hora, P., Schma, W. and Rosenthal, J. (1999) Therapeutic jurisprudence and the drug treatment court movement: Revolutionizing the criminal justice system's response to drug abuse and crime in America. *Notre Dame Law Review*, 74, 439–537.

Kaiser, K. and Holtfreter, K. (2015) An integrated theory of specialized court programs: Using procedural justice and therapeutic jurisprudence to promote offender compliance and rehabilitation. *Criminal Justice and Behavior*, 43(1), 45–62.

Kaiser, K. and Reisig, M. (2017) Legal socialization and self-reported criminal offending: The role of procedural justice and legal orientations. *Journal of Quantitative Criminology*. [Online], 1–20. https://doi.org/10.1007/s10940-017-9375-4.

King, M. (2009) *Solution-Focused Judging Bench Book*. Melbourne: Australasian Institute of Judicial Administration.

Latimer, J., Morton-Bourgon, K. and Chrétien, J. A. (2006) *A Meta-Analytic Examination of Drug Treatment Courts: Do They Reduce Recidivism?* Department of Justice Canada. Available at https://www.justice.gc.ca/eng/rp-pr/csj-sjc/jsp-sjp/rr06_7/rr06_7.pdf.

Leventhal, G. (1980) What should be done with equity theory? New approaches to the study of fairness in social relationships. In K. Gergen, M. Greenberg and R. Willis (Eds.), *Social Exchange: Advances in Theory and Research*. New York: Plenum Press, pp. 27–55.

Lowder, E., Rade, C. and Desmarais, S. (2017) Effectiveness of mental health courts in reducing recidivism: A meta-analysis. *Psychiatric Services*. [Online]. https://doi.org/10.1176/appi.ps.201700107.

Martinson, R. (1974) What works? Questions and answers about prison reform. *The Public Interest*, 35, 22–34.

Maruna, S. (2001) *Making Good: How Ex-Convicts Reform and Rebuild Their Lives*. Washington, DC: American Psychological Association.

Maruna, S. (2011) Reentry as a rite of passage. *Punishment & Society*, 13(1), 3–28.

McCord, J. (1978) A thirty-year follow-up of treatment effects. *American Psychologist*, 33(3), 284–289.

McCord, J. (2003) Cures that harm: Unanticipated outcomes of crime prevention programs. *The ANNALS of the American Academy of Political and Social Science*, 587(1), 16–30.

McNeill, F. (2012) Four forms of 'offender' rehabilitation: Towards an interdisciplinary perspective. *Legal and Criminological Psychology*, 17(1), 18–36.

McNeill, F. (2015) Rethinking what helps? Beyond probation and desistance. *The Howard Journal of Crime and Justice*, 54(3), 311–312.

Miller, R. (2004) Embracing addiction: Drug courts and the false promise of judicial interventionism. *Ohio State Law Journal*, 65, 1479–1576.

Mitchell, O., Wilson, D., Eggers, A. and MacKenzie, D. (2012) Assessing the effectiveness of drug courts on recidivism: A meta-analytic review of traditional and non-traditional drug courts. *Journal of Criminal Justice*, 40(1), 60–71.

National Association of Drug Court Professionals (NADCP). (1997) *Defining Drug Courts: The Key Components*. Washington, DC: Bureau of Justice Assistance, pp. 1–32.

Nolan J. (2009) *Legal Accents, Legal Borrowing: The International Problem-Solving Court Movement*. Princeton, NJ: Princeton University Press.

Office of the United Nations High Commissioner for Human Rights. (2008) *Frequently Asked Questions on Economic, Social, and Cultural Rights* [Fact Sheet No. 33]. Geneva: Office of the United Nations High Commissioner for Human Rights, pp. 1–53.

Paparozzi, M. and Guy, R. (2009) The giant that never woke: Parole authorities as the lynchpin to evidence-based practices and prisoner reentry. *Journal of Contemporary Criminal Justice*, 25(4), 397–411.

Perlin, M. (2017) *'Have You Seen Dignity?': The Story of the Development of the Therapeutic Jurisprudence*. Available at SSRN: https://ssrn.com/abstract=2932149 (Accessed 14 December 2017).

Pycroft, A. and Gough, D. (Eds.). (2010) *Multi-Agency Working in Criminal Justice: Control and Care in Contemporary Correctional Practice*. Bristol: The Policy Press.

Richardson, E., Spencer, P. and Wexler, D. (2016) The international framework for court excellence and therapeutic jurisprudence: Creating excellent court and enhancing wellbeing. *Journal of Judicial Administration*, 25, 148–166.

Robinson, G. and McNeill, F. (2008) Exploring the dynamics of compliance with community penalties. *Theoretical Criminology*, 12(4), 431–449.

Rossman, S., Roman, J., Zweig, J., Rempel, M. and Lindquist, C. (2011) *The Multi-Site Adult Drug Court Evaluation: Executive Summary*. Washington, DC: Urban Institute.

Rottman, D. (2000) Does effective therapeutic jurisprudence require specialized courts (and do specialized courts imply specialized judges)? *Court Review*, 22–27, Spring.

Ryan, R. and Deci, E. L. (2017) *Self-Determination Theory: Basic Psychological Needs in Motivation, Development, and Wellness*. New York: The Guilford Press.

Shaffer, D. (2011) Looking inside the black box of drug courts: A meta-analytic review. Justice *Quarterly*, 28(3), 493–521.

Schumacher, J., Milby, J., Wallace, D., Meehan, D. C., Kertesz, S., Vuchinich, R., Dunning, J. and Usdan, S. (2007) Meta-analysis of day treatment and contingency-management dismantling research: Birmingham homeless cocaine studies (1990–2006). *Journal of Consulting and Clinical Psychology*, 75(5), 823–828.

Stobbs, N. (2011) The nature of juristic paradigms exploring the theoretical and conceptual relationship between adversarialism and therapeutic jurisprudence. *Washington University Jurisprudence Review*, 4(1), 97–149.

Stobbs, N. (2013) *Mainstreaming Therapeutic Jurisprudence and the Adversarial Paradigm – Incommensurability and the Possibility of a Shared Disciplinary Matrix*. PhD. Bond University.

Stobbs, N. (2017) Therapeutic jurisprudence and due process – Consistent in principle and in practice. *Journal of Judicial Administration*, 26(4), 248–264.

Stobbs, N., Bartels, L. and Vols, M. (Eds.). (2019) *The Method and Practice of Therapeutic Jurisprudence*. Durham: Carolina Academic Press.

Stolle, D., Wexler, D. and Winick, B. (Eds.). (2000) *Practising Therapeutic Jurisprudence: Law as a Helping Profession*. Durham: Carolina Academic Press.

Sullivan, H. and Skelcher, C. (2002) *Working Across Boundaries: Collaboration in Public Services*. Basingstoke: Palgrave Macmillan.

Thibaut, J. and Walker, L. (1975) *Procedural Justice: A Psychological Analysis*. Hillsdale: Erlbaum.

Trotter, C. (2015) *Working with Involuntary Clients: A Guide to Practice*, 3rd edition. Abingdon: Routledge.

Tyler, T. (1988) What is procedural justice? Criteria used by citizens to assess the fairness of legal procedures. *Law and Society Review*, 22(1), 103–136.

Tyler, T. (2006) *Why People Obey the Law*. Princeton, NJ: Princeton University Press.

Tyler, T. (2013) Legitimacy and compliance: The virtues of self-regulation. In A. Crawford and A. Hucklesby (Eds.), *Legitimacy and Compliance in Criminal Justice*. Abingdon: Routledge, pp. 8–28.

Walker, L. and Kobayashi, L. (2015) Rituals: Restorative and therapeutic reentry rituals. In M. Herzog-Evans (Ed.), *Offender Release and Supervision: The Role of Courts and the Use of Discretion*. Nijmegen: Wolf Legal Publishers, pp. 351–372.

Wexler, D. (2016) Getting started with the mainstreaming of therapeutic jurisprudence in criminal cases: Tips on how and where to begin. *Revista Española de Investigación Criminológica*, 14(Monografía 1), 1–12.

Wexler, D. and Winick, B. (1991) *Essays in Therapeutic Jurisprudence*. Durham: Carolina Academic Press.

Wexler, D. and Winick, B. (Eds.). (1996) *Law in a Therapeutic Key: Developments in Therapeutic Jurisprudence*. Durham: Carolina Academic Press.

Winick, B. and Wexler, D. (Eds.). (2003) *Judging in a Therapeutic Key: Therapeutic Jurisprudence and the Courts*. Durham: Carolina Academic Press.

Yates, P., Prescott D. and Ward, T. (2010) *Applying the Good Lives and Self-Regulation Models to Sex Offender Treatment: A Practical Guide for Clinicians*. Brendon: Safer Society Press.

Section 2

Policy contexts and cultures

Section 2 Introduction

This section considers the policy contexts and cultures in which penal supervision and rehabilitative work take place. Penal welfarism is a theme interwoven throughout this section, with fascinating contrasts and synergies apparent within and between chapters which feature Nordic examples and Anglophone examples from England and Wales. John Todd-Kvam and Thomas Ugelvik (Chapter 15) explore the Scandinavian penal-welfare model, charting some distinctive features and revealing a surprising lack of research about release and reintegration processes in Nordic countries. Their chapter is a reflexive account of re-entry and 'through-the-gate' supports in principle and in practice. Scandinavian penal-welfarist examples feature alongside Anglo-Welsh and Scottish examples in Yvonne Jewkes and Kate Gooch's excellent chapter (Chapter 14) on prison architectures and penal cultures. Drawing upon their own research, they analyze whether the 'rehabilitative prison' is an oxymoron or an opportunity to drastically reconfigure how prisons are designed and used, without losing sight of the need for diversion and decarceration.

Three chapters in this section raise cogent issues and questions about recent policy reforms and penal cultures in the context of England and Wales. An emerging theme here is one of researching and undertaking rehabilitative work in the midst of crises, rapid change, and adverse conditions. Informed by a long and deep history of prisons research in England and Wales, Alison Liebling (Chapter 17) raises profoundly important questions about the relationships between austerity, moral climates, and imprisonment. She frames rehabilitation work as a moral enterprise, aligning with cognate conceptualizations by others (see Burke et al. 2018; Graham 2016), to accentuate differences in how penal systems can damage and how penal systems can support or repair (resonating with the theme of penal welfarism). In their chapter, Matthew Millings, Lol Burke, and Gwen Robinson (Chapter 13) use a research case study to explain the emerging consequences of Transforming Rehabilitation reforms involving the part-privatization of probation services in England and Wales. They skilfully attest to the impact on occupational and organizational working cultures in probation, including the difficulties and uncertainties faced by probation practitioners who may perceive differences between their values and *modus operandi* of working, and what is expected of them in the midst of rapid policy and systemic changes in their field of work. In their chapter, Jason Morris and Hannah Graham (Chapter 16) explore cutting-edge bespoke technologies being developed for use in prisons and probation services in England and Wales. Their chapter discusses how apps, digital toolkits and animation, and other technologies can be used in rehabilitation and desistance-oriented ways, giving practice examples to illustrate, which can be clearly differentiated from punitive surveillant uses. Technology can be used constructively in response to acute issues and systemic crises (e.g. the digital toolkit for violence reduction in prisons described by Morris and Graham, with violence a pronounced issue in numerous prisons in England and Wales at the time of writing), while not being bound or wholly defined by them.

Each of the chapters in this section explore the dynamics of context and cultures and how these interact with individual processes and institutional infra-structures. Overall, the importance of the chapters in this section and their place in this book can be illustrated using the analogy of weather forecasting and meteorology.

Trying to understand the complex social problem of crime, those who commit it (individually and collectively), and how they leave crime behind predominantly based on criminogenic risk instruments and recidivism rates is like trying to understand complex weather conditions and events predominantly based on the use of a thermometer. Such instruments and metrics have their uses. However, to accurately gauge the temperature (or criminogenic risk or recidivism rates) is not the same as knowing the seasons and conditions which influence weather patterns and events (that is, the relational, socio-political, spatial, and temporal conditions and generative structures in which crime, punishment, and rehabilitation exist) (Graham 2015).

Chapters in this section transcend a tendency to narrow the empirical focus almost exclusively to that which is easily measurable and knowable about individuals, discrete tools, and interventions in rehabilitative work. As necessary and valuable as this type of precise and focused knowledge is, on its own it does not yield sufficient depth and breadth of insight about the policies, actors, cultures, and conditions of criminal justice, in which rehabilitation processes and rehabilitative work take place. Macro- or structural issues can have very real consequences, for better or worse, affecting lives and life chances. Liebling's (Chapter 17) discussions of austerity and imprisonment and Todd-Kvam and Ugelvik's (Chapter 15) discussions of Scandinavian penal welfarism and resettlement processes are good examples of why such things matter. An edited book with a title about this given field of work would be incomplete without attending to policy contexts and cultures – the chapters in this section do precisely this, in interesting and timely ways.

References

Burke, L., Collett, S. and McNeill, F. (2018) *Reimagining Rehabilitation: Beyond the Individual*. London: Routledge.

Graham, H. (2015) 'Seasons, senses, spaces: Discerning the social choreography of the penal field' blog post on the COST action. *Offender Supervision in Europe Blog*, 18 June. Available at: www.offendersupervision.eu/blog-post/seasons-senses-spaces-discerning-the-social-choreography-of-the-penal-field.

Graham, H. (2016) *Rehabilitation Work: Supporting Desistance and Recovery*. London: Routledge.

13

The 'Transforming Rehabilitation' agenda in England and Wales

Implications of privatization

Matthew Millings, Lol Burke, and Gwen Robinson

Introduction

This chapter considers the initial impact of the part-privatization of probation provision in England and Wales through the creation of Community Rehabilitation Companies (CRC) in the context of the Coalition Government's Transforming Rehabilitation (TR) reform programme. We will consider the drivers behind the transfer of probation from public to private ownership and explore, in three distinct phases, how change was implemented in one case study area. We will focus on the *creation of the CRC*, outlining the process involved in splitting the staff group(s) and reflecting on attempts by management to establish a new organizational identity. The second phase, *mobilization*, examines the challenges facing the CRC as it established itself in the local criminal justice landscape. The third phase considers the hopes and fears of the staff at *the point of transition into new ownership*. By way of conclusion we consider what lessons can be learnt in examining the experiences of implementing and adapting to profound change in the way that rehabilitation is imagined, organized, and delivered.

Context

In 2010, the newly assembled Coalition (Conservative/Liberal Democrat) Government, stated that a key strand of the administration's criminal justice policy would 'involve paying independent organisations by results' (Clarke 2010) in order to reduce reoffending. By May 2013, these ambitions had been operationalized in a set of reforms (collectively known as 'Transforming Rehabilitation') that would open up probation services to the 'best of the public, voluntary and private sectors' in a new operating environment where the stimulus for innovation would be competition. The Transforming Rehabilitation (TR) agenda represented the most wide-ranging manifestation of a broader ideological and political project to redefine the state's role in the delivery of rehabilitation through the transfer of risk to the private sector (Burke and Collett 2015, 2016; Teague 2016). The programme of reform outlined the establishment of payment by results mechanisms where a proportion of a service provider's payment was to be determined by the reductions in reoffending they achieved. The proposals also included a network of local resettlement prisons, and the extension of post-sentence supervision to those sentenced to less than a year. The most profound changes concerned the part-privatization of probation services. The Ministry of Justice oversaw the splitting of probation services with the creation of a new public sector probation service (the National Probation Service) with direct responsibility for high-risk offenders only, and then outlined plans to contract directly with private, voluntary, and community sector organizations across 21 geographical contract package areas in England and Wales. Having been successful in a tendering process the contracted providers – Community Rehabilitation Companies (CRC) – would be responsible for all low- and medium-risk offenders (Ministry of Justice 2013a, 2013c).

By October 2017, however, three years on from the implementation of the reforms, the Chief Executive of the National Offender Management Service declared that the new system of offender supervision 'wasn't working' as it should (BBC News, 13 October 2017). Similarly, in her assessment of probation services, the Chief Inspector of Probation commented that 'we are in a very unsettling position' and expressed concern that 'rather than seeing a large amount of activity . . . we are seeing less happening than any of us would be comfortable with' (Stacey 2017). Later that same month the House of Commons Justice Select Committee, having questioned a range of stakeholders about the reasons for the challenges with the implementation of the programme, launched an enquiry into TR. What became apparent was that the new owners of privatized probation services were facing financial challenges as the number of service users they were engaging was smaller than anticipated. The complexity of the new working arrangements had proved challenging to operate within, and there was no evidence of significant impact on reoffending rates. In her submission to the Justice committee Dame Stacey identified the challenges of forcing organizational, and occupational, change on the sector:

> [the reforms were] a very significant cultural challenge and change for probation. It is a caring profession . . . yet this wholesale move to fragment the service and to give it a commercial edge has been enormously difficult.
>
> (Justice Committee 2017)[1]

In this chapter, we capture the perspectives of probation staff experiencing this change from the inside, and report on 16-months of fieldwork within one case study area that covered a period starting with the splitting of probation services through to the subsequent creation and transferring into private ownership of a CRC. This presentation of the experiences of implementing and adapting to change, we suggest, captures and illustrates the challenges alluded to by the Justice Select Committee and others. Devolving probation services has followed a unique transitional journey where, rather than seeing a complete transfer of public provision into private ownership, the state's retention of responsibility for the National Probation Service (NPS) and a role in the governance of the CRCs through a loosely defined transitional period determines that this been 'privatisation by stealth' (Kirton and Guillaume 2015: 5). There is much, we contend, that examining staff experiences here can illustrate about the tangible impacts on the individual and collective esteem and operational capacity of those involved in profound organizational change.

We undertook observational, interview, and focus group research into the implementation of the reforms in one of the 'contract package areas' between March 2014 and June 2015.[2] Capitalizing on a unique opportunity to observe change from the practitioner's perspective, the semi-ethnographic fieldwork involved the observation of management and decision-making processes and routine attendance at staff forums and team meetings. A total of 120 interviews were undertaken with members of the Senior Management Team (n = 8); Middle Managers (n = 21); Probation Practitioners (n = 30); and other support/operational staff (n = 11), with a number of our participants interviewed on multiple occasions. We have chosen to highlight certain events and responses in order to illuminate the key moments in this transition (see Burke et al. 2017a; Millings et al. 2019) for a fuller analysis of the diverse range of personal 'journeys' that profound organizational change induced). We do not claim that our observations can be generalized across all of the 21 CRCs as our case study area was somewhat 'atypical' in that it was not required to merge with other probation area(s). Our account of the implementation of reform is also incomplete in that we did not canvas the views of those working in the newly formed NPS, as our primary focus concerned the impact of those workers moving from the public sector towards private ownership.

From creation to mobilization: the assignment process

The process of reallocating Probation Trust staff took place during the early part of 2014 in advance of the operationalization of the CRC in June 2014. Staff had initially been invited to express a preference for working in either the NPS or CRC. The decision to locate individuals in the respective organizations was ultimately based on an evaluation of their role and the number of high-risk cases held by them on a single day in November 2013, in line with guidelines produced by the Ministry of Justice.[3] As a process, the involuntary and clinical nature of the split had a profound impact upon all those involved in our study. The consultation process on the proposals drew almost unanimous opposition from the main probation stakeholders (Ministry of Justice 2013b) and NAPO had conducted a sustained campaign to 'Keep Probation public' which had culminated in industrial action. Many of the objections centred upon the threat of 'fragmentation, loss of expertise, conflicts of interest, inconsistent practices and the danger to public safety' (Senior 2013: 1) and, in our locale, the act of splitting the Trust was regretted by all:

> In very few areas in life splitting something in two works. It's like a divorce, you know, two houses to pay for. You don't often get splits which don't have immediate fallout; financial fallout as well as emotional fallout.
>
> (Probation Practitioner)

Kirton and Guillaume's (2015) survey of probation staff found that those placed in the CRCs were far less likely to agree with their allocation (52%) compared with those placed in the NPS (87%) and that this was a consistent finding across all grades. In our study, we found people who felt they'd been given insufficient information to make an informed choice about their stated preference. In other cases, individuals felt disadvantaged in that, despite opting to work in the NPS, they had been automatically assigned to the CRC because they were newly qualified or had recently changed posts and hadn't built up their caseload of high-risk cases.[4] The emotional costs were evident in the tone of the majority of our interviews where respondents described strong feelings centring on 'hurt', 'anger', 'confusion', and 'uncertainty' (see Robinson et al. 2016). Staff also generally believed that the timescales for implementing the split were unrealistic and the failure to develop and test changes saw them report 'an indecent rush to prepare ourselves for these two almost arbitrary organisations' (Probation Practitioner).

Linked to this were perceptions around the form and future directions of the respective probation organizations. In terms of the NPS, there were those who saw demand to attend to high-risk cases exclusively as being more likely to utilize valued probation skills. Others however feared that the NPS, organizationally, would become too centrally controlled and too focused on management and surveillance. In respect of the CRC, there were deep concerns for many that they would no longer be required to utilize skills which they had been trained to use, such as report writing and supervising high-risk cases. Others, however, were more pragmatic:

> My reason for joining probation was about rehabilitation, not about the other processes that go on, in probation. I've gone to CRC with that intention that I want to continue doing that rehabilitative work.
>
> (Probation Practitioner)

The sense of loss that staff were experiencing underpinned many interviews, and this was experienced in different ways. In real terms, there was the loss of relationships with colleagues who were now working in the NPS or in separate offices. For some there was a loss of certainty and security that came with working for an established public sector organization with highly developed working practices. For others, there was the feared loss of professional identity where working for the CRC was perceived as a sign of 'professional failure' (Kirton and Guillaume 2015: 22) in contrast to the status secured by NPS colleagues working with high-risk individuals. Associated with this perceived loss of certainty was, for some, the threat to professional identity of reconciling the notion of a public service ethos with the values of the private sector.

In the period leading up to the operationalization of the CRC, the challenge for managers was to establish the legitimacy of the new arrangements, both in terms of how it was seen by its external stakeholders and its own staff. The challenge of translating a nationally driven policy locally was difficult and was made harder by what was experienced as a shifting, unsettling, and contradictory political landscape. Senior managers talked of their duty 'to steward the organisation. . . [to] carry through the values that we want into the next iteration' and to manage the process 'not just in the best way to get the programme delivered, but in the best way for staff and trying to take them along'. The Senior Management Group adopted a purposefully corporate approach to providing information, consulting staff, and promoting the organizational identity through communication champions and hosting events to launch the CRC.

A key strategy deployed was the formulation of an agreed-upon set of organizational values that staff were encouraged to sign up to. In this respect the promotion of values was recognized as a powerful feature of the change process and of trying to establish a CRC working identity, yet the authenticity and meaning of the messages was not always clearly communicated. Engagement events to identify and sign up to collectively authored values didn't always generate commensurate investment with some staff refusing to sign up to the values:

> They were discussing what our values are, the way forward as if we walked into that room with no values at all. We've belonged to an organisation for hundreds of years that has values. . . . I bring those values with me. It's not a new set of values, it's the same.
>
> (Probation Practitioner)

The apparent vacuum between the well thought-through and considered values of senior managers and the consumption of these messages throughout the wider staff group emphasizes the challenge(s) of information sharing and communication during a period of rapid change and uncertainty (see Millings et al. 2019). In the short term the pace and scope of change was creating real concerns in terms of the working practice of probation service delivery, whilst, in the longer term, the uncertainty surrounding the identity and credibility of future owners concerned staff. After the transition period ended, from February 2015 onwards, there was a period when the bidders to assume ownership of the CRCs were mobilizing with a reported 800 organizations, including 399 from the voluntary sector, expressing an interest in providing probation services, either as lead providers or at some other stage in the supply chain (Ministry of Justice 2013d).

Changing relationships and issues at the interface

For senior managers, the creation of the CRC on 1 June 2014 was characterized by holding the new organization together and managing staff expectations. There were ongoing practical issues arising from the split – such as transferring service users between organizations – and the need to replace the governance arrangements of the former Trust. The tight implementation schedule timelines and the increasingly evident demands of contract management made it a relentlessly pressurized environment. This required a level of resilience in what for some members of the management team was still a steep learning curve and was, on a personal level, having a significant emotional impact. Members of the group were working long hours and expressed feelings of being simultaneously energized and exhausted by the demands of creating a new organization with the additional responsibilities this entailed.

What emerged through interviews at this point and would characterize later phases also, was the very different experiences managers and groups of staff were reporting. Managers, being more involved in decision-making processes and more exposed to the evolving demands placed on CRCs, were routinely concerned with future planning and setting organizational goals. Conversely, practitioners and administrative staff were concerned with real-time challenges of operating within an evolving and occasionally disjointed environment. Amongst a now leaner management group there was evidence of a growing confidence to embrace what was perceived to be an opportunity to build a new organizational culture that was distinct from, but true to, the traditions of probation and one that engaged all grades of staff. Having been through the personally and professionally challenging administration of the allocation process, leaders sought collectively to 'create the best CRC we can so that any new owners will be inclined to leave us be' (Senior Manager). This involved attempts to capitalize on the relaxation of national standards for probation work to create new roles, to creatively consider income generation activities, and by building new partnerships in addition to, and distinct from, those with former NPS colleagues.

For many others, however, it was challenging to engage in such forward thinking. The speed of change and continuing conjecture over the future – a future they felt less certain about determining than managers – meant feelings of unease endured. New working and organizational structures were taking time to embed; there had been problems with accessing and using IT systems; and uncertainty surrounding who would assume ownership of the organization remained. There were staff who viewed the new beginning as an opportunity to 'reboot' probation services that some felt had 'got lost into this tranche of missives and directives' (Probation Practitioner). The apparent freedom from nationally determined standards and priorities was seen positively by some who felt it offered scope for CRCs to empower themselves and anchor their working culture(s) in rehabilitation. But these more optimistic tones were evident only in a minority and whilst staff would report that at the point of transition 'not as much had changed as was expected' (Support/Operational Staff), what many referred to as the distracting 'noise of TR' (Support/Operational Staff) was slowly being replaced by complications in operational practice.

The perceived loss of identity and the authority of being a public sector organization continued to be articulated. Respondents reported that local sentencers had expressed reservations about dealing with the CRC. There was a growing realization that the CRC was 'not the only game in town anymore' (Senior Manager) and no longer held a near-monopoly position in the delivery of community-based rehabilitative interventions. Staff at all levels reported how their relationships with existing partners were continually being reframed, and the confusion around the respective roles of the CRC and NPS was linked not simply to the practical arrangements around delivering services and representation in multi-agency settings, but also was seen as indicative of a deeper ambivalence towards the CRC's status and authority as a privately financed provider.

Where relationships were at their most fraught concerned the CRC's engagement with the NPS. At a practical level this involved the transfer of cases, but more fundamentally it revolved around changes in the working relationship(s) between the two organizations. At the time of the fieldwork, most probation offices still housed both NPS and CRC staff, although workplaces had been physically divided or partitioned and it was apparent that there were signs of increasing tensions, resentment, and other negative emotions towards former colleagues. The findings of Kirton and Guillaume's (2015: 24) national survey resonate with our study in that whilst the trivial 'everyday signs of the split' included separate fridges and teabag supplies, they actually capture the 'serious consequences of the separation of function/tasks for service delivery and for their own professional ethics'. Both probation services were feeling the strain with the insecurities of CRC staff mirrored by the frustrations reported by NPS staff working within what they considered the bureaucratic and inflexible culture of the Civil Service and the relentless demands of supervising an exclusively high-risk caseload (see also Phillips et al. 2016). As Dame Stacey's submission to the Justice Committee in 2017 captured, the values of a caring profession were being threatened and nowhere was this more apparent than in how the two organizations – largely comprised of former colleagues – were reshaping their professional exchanges. The intent to make the new working environment operationally viable was being eclipsed by the CRC feeling the need to assert itself in a more business-like manner, where, in the words of one senior manager 'the days of motherhood and apple pie are over' (Senior Manager). Allied to this was the growing appreciation that they were now working in an environment that was governed by their contractual obligations as a provider rather than a public sector organization.

The transition to new ownership

HM Treasury announced the preferred bidders for the 21 CRCs in October 2014 and the contracts were awarded in December 2014. The National Audit Office (2016: 16) identified how challenging the procurement process had been, both because changes in legislation and sentencing practices had made future business volumes hard to predict and because CRCs had only existed as separate entities for several months, and so had short track records. The seven-year contracts were almost exclusively awarded to large for-profit organizations despite the Government rhetoric around promoting voluntary and not-for-profit providers. Two outsourcing companies, Sodexo and Interserve, won the contracts to deliver more than half of probation services with voluntary sector organizations' involvement mostly as minor partners or subcontractors to large private 'prime' providers – Durham Tees Valley is the only CRC where no major private company is involved. A report by Clinks (2015) concluded that voluntary sector involvement in TR was undermined by funding cuts, a lack of transparency and clarity regarding what services would be funded by commissioners under the new arrangements.

Though the successful bidders signed contracts in December 2014, full ownership of the CRCs did not formally commence until February 2015. Rules of commercial confidentiality restricting what they could disclose meant that all involved had to contend with an additional layer of uncertainty. The CRC found itself within the liminal state of being betwixt and between public and private ownership and models of working and organizational changes were implicitly tied up with new ownership (Robinson et al. 2016). There was conjecture surrounding how much decision-making and leadership capacity would be retained locally as the new owners had secured a number of contracts nationally and because delivering probation services was but one part of a wider portfolio of activities the consortium were engaged in. This saw staff having to formulate their assessment of their new owner's aspirations and credibility for working in the sector using very little information.

The initial communications from the new owners were viewed positively, stressing as they did their commitment to deliver a public service and not force through immediate change. The emphasis on a slow and methodical transition was seen as positively contrasting with some of the other owners of the CRC contract package areas and there was recognition that shifting dates in the bidding process, uncertainty over how many contract areas consortia would acquire, and the precariousness of investing in rehabilitation services meant TR was a challenging experience for new owners in the sector too. As a consequence, and despite elements of positivity locally, there remained more broadly 'an impending sense of doom' (Middle Manager) if not in the short term then certainly into the future. The bidding process, its opaqueness, and the failure of the announcement of new owners to lift the uncertainty added to the insecurity as concerns lingered upon the exact mechanisms for funding and the extent to which market principles could be applied to the work of the CRC. The optimism of 'working smarter' was tempered with what was seen as the financial imperative to promote more efficient working practices that threatened the desire to retain a focus on the individual service user. The promise of more flexible and mobile working, of building a 'supply chain' of support agencies, and of implementing new IT systems did galvanize many to consider how positively change could impact upon their practice. This optimism was however compromised by the caveat that most of these ideas and messages were largely that – ideas and messages as opposed to clear examples of exported best practice. These concerns were often informed by a deeper anxiety about the commodification of service users and probation work per se.

Conclusion

This chapter has sought to capture and explore the experiences of staff within one CRC from the period of its creation until the point of its transition into new ownership. Whilst it would be disingenuous to state that TR has been the cause of all the problems currently facing probation,[5] there is certainly little doubt that it has exacerbated many of them and has led to new sites of potential conflict. As an example of penal policymaking, it was clear that implementing the organizational changes required by the reforms was extremely challenging and four years on from implementation this is being recognized by policymakers.

The scale and speed of the changes that the reform agenda ushered in was a source of anxiety and unease for staff at all levels. Throughout the fieldwork, there remained an overwhelming sense of struggling to maintain business as usual whilst also contemplating a longer-term future under new ownership. Even at the conclusion of the fieldwork, it was still painfully obvious that staff, in the main, continued to feel unsettled by a process of transition that had been neither smooth nor straightforward. The reviews and assessments of the TR reforms that have followed its implementation illustrate how these tensions have endured and how the new arrangements still aren't fully embedded. On a practical level, it has been very difficult for probation practitioners to deliver unrelentingly demanding front-line services in a working environment that is coming to terms with what had been lost, and with ongoing uncertainties about what would happen in both the medium and longer terms. On another level, the impact on the organizational and occupational working culture(s) of probation as professionals in the field has left staff feeling that their professional imperatives have become compromised and manipulated by others.

In both respects the conceptualization of rehabilitation became both a problem and solution. Practitioners in our CRC area had to adapt to models of working that demanded they reconcile increased caseloads of service users with the encouragement to be more discretionary in terms of how frequently and directly they engaged individuals. The prospect of operating supervisory relationships differently, of being imaginative in how and where to engage service users, and of utilizing the input of partners from an expanded CRC 'supply chain' clearly did stimulate some of the practitioners in our case study area (see Burke et al. 2017b). Many others, in contrast, expressed deep concern for how the quality of rehabilitative work would be diluted as responsibility for supervision was devolved to other partners and a particular concern was that probation officers would increasingly assume a more distant role in respect of clients they would rarely encounter in person.

Conversely, for leaders, the scope to anchor the work of the CRC in rehabilitation provided the organization with the opportunity to stimulate a distinctive approach to operational practice, one that would start to distinguish the CRC from the NPS. Here the 'shift in gear' was informed by a belief that emphasis would fall on the role of 'offender manager [rather than] probation officer' (Senior Manager) where a focus on rehabilitation would surpass the attention to monitoring and supervision. Having been involved in the development of a set of values to shape the organizational character of the CRC, some managers felt that the organization provided them with the 'best opportunity to engage in the rehabilitative work that first attracted me to probation' (Senior Manager). The optimism of these leaders in the early days of the CRC centred upon the building of new partnership arrangements and engaging with models that promoted the personalization of service provision (Burke et al. 2017b; Millings et al. 2019). In time however, these same leaders – in line with findings reported across the sector more generally (see National Audit Office 2016) – would record their concern with how the attention to developing and delivering meaningful rehabilitative work had to contend with the pressures to meet the terms of the CRC contract and the routine negotiation and management of new partnership and working arrangements. As a manager at the start of our research remarked, 'we are all on a personal journey in a situation not of our making', and this continues to capture the predicaments of probation staff in England and Wales today.

Notes

1 Justice Select Committee, *Transforming Rehabilitation* (HC 1018) Q2 para 6 available at: http://data.parliament.uk/writtenevidence/committeeevidence.svc/evidencedocument/justice-committee/transforming-rehabilitation/oral/49239.html (accessed 28 November 2017).
2 This work was supported by the Economic and Social Research Council (Grant Number ES/M280000/1).
3 This was in common with most Probation Trusts although there were reports that some areas were randomly drawing workers names out of a hat (Simons 2014).
4 Some probation officers we engaged who had very recently qualified were equally frustrated and upset, having (in their view) now been relegated to probation service officer roles they had previously occupied prior to putting themselves through a training regime in order to experience a fuller range of functions – including work in courts and prisons and with high-risk offenders.
5 Robinson and Burnett (2007) found that an earlier succession of organizational changes in probation stimulated 'initiative confusion' and 'change fatigue'.

References

Burke, L. and Collett, S. (2015) *Delivering Rehabilitation: The Politics, Governance and Control of Probation*. Routledge.

Burke, L. and Collett, S. (2016) Organisational bifurcation and the end of probation as we knew it. *Probation Journal*, 63(2), 120–136.

Burke, L., Millings, M. and Robinson, G. (2017a) Probation migration(s), Examining occupational culture in a turbulent field. *Criminology and Criminal Justice*, 17(2), 192–208.

Burke, L., Millings, M. and Robinson, G. (2017b) Is constructive practice still possible in a competitive environment? Findings from a case study of a community rehabilitation company in England and Wales. In P. Ugwudike, P. Raynor and J. Annison (Eds.), *Evidence-Based Skills in Criminal Justice: International Research on Supporting Rehabilitation and Desistance*. Policy Press.

Clarke, K. (2010) *The Government's Vision for Criminal Justice Reform*. London: Speech on Criminal Justice Reform at the Centre for Crime and Justice Studies, 30 June. Available at: http://webarchive.nationalarchives.gov.uk/+/www.justice.gov.uk/news/sp300610a.htm (Accessed 28 November 2017).

Clinks. (2015) *Early Doors: The Voluntary Sector's Role in Transforming Rehabilitation.* London: Clinks. Available at: www.clinks.org/trackTR (Accessed 14 November 2017).

Justice Committee. (2017) *Oral Evidence: Transforming Rehabilitation,* 21 March 2017, HC 1018, Qq1–2. Available at: http://data.parliament.uk/writtenevidence/committee evidence.svc/evidencedocument/justice-committee/transforming-rehabilitation/ oral/49239.html (Accessed 28 November 2017).

Kirton, G. and Guillaume, C. (2015) *Employment Relations and Working Conditions in Probation After Transforming Rehabilitation.* London: NAPO.

Millings, M., Burke, L. and Robinson, G. (2019) Lost in transition? The personl and professional challenges for probation leaders engaged in delivering public sector reform. *Probation Journal,* 66(1), 60–76.

Ministry of Justice. (2013a) *Transforming Rehabilitation: A Revolution in the Way We Manage Offenders.* London: Ministry of Justice.

Ministry of Justice. (2013b) *Transforming Rehabilitation: Summary of Responses.* London: Ministry of Justice.

Ministry of Justice. (2013c) *Transforming Rehabilitation: A Strategy for Reform.* London: Ministry of Justice.

Ministry of Justice. (2013d) Search begins to find best organisations to tackle high reoffending rates. *Press Release,* 19 September. Available at: www.gov.uk/government/ news/search-begins-to-find-best-organisations-to-tackle-high-reoffending-rates (Accessed 28 November 2017).

National Audit Office. (2016) *Transforming Rehabilitation: Report by the Comptroller and Auditor General.* London: NAO.

Phillips, J., Westaby, C. and Fowler, A. (2016) It's relentless': The impact of working primarily with high-risk offenders. *Probation Journal,* 63(2), 182–193.

Robinson, G., Burke, L. and Millings, M. (2016) Criminal justice identities in transition: The case of devolved probation services in England and Wales. *British Journal of Criminology,* 56(1), 161–178.

Robinson, G. and Burnett, R. (2007) Experiencing modernization: Frontline probation perspectives on the transition to a national offender management service. *Probation Journal,* 54(4), 318–337.

Senior, P. (2013) Probation peering through the uncertainty. *British Journal of Community Justice,* 11(2–3), 1–8.

Simons, N. (2014) Probation service accused of randomly outsourcing jobs by 'picking names out of a hat'. *Huffingtonpost.co.uk.* Available at: www.huffingtonpost. co.uk/2014/07/03/chris-grayling-probation-drawn-from-a-hat_n_5554340.html (Accessed 28 November 2017).

Stacey, G. (2017) *Can Probation Services Deliver What We All Want and Expect?* Keynote Speech of the Criminal Justice Management Conference 2017, 19 September. Available at: www.justiceinspectorates.gov.uk/hmiprobation/wp-content/uploads/ sites/5/2016/10/Dame-Glenys-Stacey-Keynote-Address-Sept-17-Westminster.pdf (Accessed 28 November 2017).

Teague, M. (2016) Probation, people and profits: The impact of neoliberalism. *British Journal of Community Justice,* 14(1), 99–111.

The rehabilitative prison

14

An oxymoron, or an opportunity to radically reform the way we do punishment?

Yvonne Jewkes and Kate Gooch

Introduction

At first glance, the rehabilitation of those in custody might appear to be a laudable and desirable goal, but ultimately an unachievable one. Reoffending rates for those released from prison remain stubbornly high, with evidence suggesting that a custodial sentence might, in and of itself, have a crimino-genic effect, increasing the likelihood of future offending behaviour (Bales and Piquero 2012). For some individuals in prison – especially women – who have a history of trauma, mental health problems and have suffered poverty, homelessness, and domestic abuse, prison may be a place of refuge and respite, rather than rehabilitation (Cain 2016). At the other end of the spectrum, there is an emerging trend in male offenders deliberately returning to prison on 'licence recall'[1] to earn vast sums of money from the sale of contraband items such as drugs and mobile telephones within prison (Gooch and Treadwell forthcoming). Meanwhile, for those who succeed in desisting from crime, it is not clear how and to what extent this success is a product of their experiences in prison, if at all. Moreover, it would appear that the coercive nature of confinement, the risk-laden prison environment and the government, media, and general public's insistence that prisons should be places of punishment, all mitigate against the implementation of rehabilitative ideals at a micro level.

However, in England and Wales, and against a backdrop of ongoing operational challenges, successive Lord Chancellors, Secretary of States for Justice, and Prisons Ministers have reinforced the centrality of, and a commitment to, rehabilitation and reform. In addition, the concept of 'rehabilitative culture' has rapidly gained currency across Her Majesty's Prisons and Probation Service (HMPPS) (Mann et al. 2018), with prison governors developing local initiatives to implement and develop a rehabilitative approach. Perhaps the most noteworthy recent example of an attempt to radically reimagine imprisonment in line with this rehabilitative vision – the outcomes of which are not yet quantifiable – is the commitment by HMP Berwyn's senior management to operate a 2,106 bed facility with the overarching aim of being a 'rehabilitative prison' (Ministry of Justice [MoJ] 2017).

This chapter will discuss the efforts made across a small number of prisons in the UK and Europe to rehabilitate, rather than punitively punish, those in custody. It will explore whether prisons can be architecturally designed with an explicit mission to rehabilitate offenders, and whether they can succeed in this goal even when (as in the example of Berwyn) rehabilitation is not an underpinning philosophy in their planning and design. Finally, the chapter will consider whether the aspiration to transform thought and behaviour in order to improve recidivism rates is even morally acceptable. Does rehabilitation have a place and purpose in the modern penal landscape or does it simply amount to a kind of 'coerced correction' (McNeill 2014) that becomes meaningless when offenders are released back into the community and to the structural inequalities they faced prior to conviction, together with new disadvantages in the form of parole restrictions and a criminal record? In short, is the 'rehabilitation prison' an oxymoron, or is it an opportunity to radically reform the way we do punishment?

'Trauma-informed' and 'normalization': the new lexicon of rehabilitation

These are complex, contested times in the history of imprisonment with criminologists, penologists, prison reform groups, and criminal justice professionals divided on what prisons can realistically hope to achieve, and whether they should even exist. Few would argue that the bloated prison systems in the UK – and especially England and Wales – have become dangerous places that have little hope of rehabilitating offenders. During 2015, over 20,000 assaults were recorded in prisons (a 27% increase on the previous year), with 'serious' assaults rising by almost a third in the same period (HMIP 2016). In the 12 months to March 2016 there were 290 deaths in prison custody, an increase of 51 compared to the 12 months ending March 2015. One hundred of these were self-inflicted (up from 79 in the previous 12-month period), and a further escalation in suicides in prisons occurred in 2017, accounting for 113 deaths between April 2016 and March 2017 (Ministry of Justice [MoJ] 2017). In Scotland, deaths in custody have been rising steadily over the last decade and numbered 28 deaths in 2016, while attempted suicides rose by 50% (SPS 2017). Across the island of Ireland there was a spike in deaths in custody in 2015, when 22 prisoners died (Smyth 2016). The prisons Inspectorates in all jurisdictions have highlighted the pressing problems facing the penal systems and Peter Clarke, Her Majesty's Chief Inspector of Prisons in England and Wales, summed up the crisis when he said that the 'simple and unpalatable truth' about prisons is that they have become 'unacceptably violent and dangerous places' characterized by poor mental health, drug use, and the 'perennial problems of overcrowding, poor physical environments in ageing prisons, and inadequate staffing' (HMIP 2016: 8–9).

Against this backdrop, the re-emergence of 'rehabilitation' as a goal of imprisonment arguably seems like a well-meaning but fruitless endeavour. As we shall discuss further, a new lexicon of 'improvement' in corrections has emerged to highlight the rehabilitative mission underpinning matters as diverse as the planning design, management, operationalization, and culture of prisons. At the same time, however, the UK government has pledged to provide 10,000 new prison places by 2020–2021 in England and Wales, and has reneged on its 2017 election pledge to continue closing very old prisons that are deemed to be no longer fit for purpose. The news that prisons previously slated for closure are to remain open for at least five years was greeted with dismay by many, not least because Michael Spurr, the then Director General of Her Majesty's Prison and Probation Service, who was left to make the announcement, was unable to explain how the situation has become so bad that pressure of prison numbers (approximately 86,000 in total, double what it was in 1993), has resulted in the retention of establishments that former Secretary of State for Justice, Michael Gove, said contain the 'dark corners' which facilitate violence and drug-taking (along with a host of other serious negative behaviours) (Jewkes and Moran 2014).

Nonetheless, there has been a noticeable and concerted effort by many individual prison managers to do what they can to improve their prison environments, both physically and culturally. Many have embraced social media platforms such as Twitter to publicize their efforts, which include community-orientated music and performing arts projects, hosting TEDx events, creating new sporting opportunities (such as 'Park Run'), charitable giving, and 'bottom up' penal reform projects. In addition, several prison governors have commissioned research, employed academic advisors, invited scholars like us to their establishments to give lectures and present our research findings to managers, staff, and prisoners, or have themselves registered for higher degrees during which they have undertaken empirical research for their theses, and then taken to speaking at conferences to share the evidence-based 'good practices' they have implemented. Commonly, they present examples of how they are attempting to deinstitutionalize their prisons, to treat the men and women held there with greater decency and humanity, and to foster greater feelings of trust and respect between prisoners and staff.

Amid this wave of good intention, two new buzzwords have gained rapid traction – 'trauma-informed' and 'normalization' – both of which are already ubiquitous in discussions of prison reform and are frequently conflated with 'rehabilitation'. 'Trauma Informed Care and Practice' (TICP) is an approach that originated in prison healthcare services and delivery in the United States, but it has since been employed more broadly. Although it has had some notable success in juvenile facilities there, in the UK TICP has thus far been focused almost exclusively on women's prisons. One of the key pioneers of TICP in the US, clinical psychologist Stephanie S. Covington, undertook a lecture tour of the UK in 2017 ('One Small Thing', co-facilitated by prison philanthropist and reformer Lady Edwina Grosvenor), as a result of which 'trauma-informed training' has been rolled out to HMPPS staff across the female prison estate in England and Wales. At New Hall Prison in Wakefield, for example, 100% of staff have already been trained in TICP and at the other female prisons in England and Wales, at least 75% of staff have been TICP trained (Hardwick 2017). The extent to which TICP can be described as 'rehabilitative' is debatable (and it remains empirically untested) but, as a model of care, TICP aims to understand the individual within her own social context, and to increase feelings of safety and hope for recovery by (re)building a sense of control and empowerment. These principles can also inform the design of the physical environment, acknowledging its impact on mental health and well-being. For example, Elliott et al. (2005: 467) note that trauma-informed services should strive to create an atmosphere 'respectful of survivors' need for safety, respect, and acceptance'. Central to this is a 'welcoming environment', which includes sufficient personal space for comfort and privacy, absence of exposure to violent/sexual material, and sufficient staffing to monitor behaviour of others 'that may be perceived as intrusive or harassing' (ibid.).

Key to creating a healthy prison atmosphere is what many commentators have described as 'normalcy' or 'normalization'. At the annual meeting of the International Corrections and Prisons Association (ICPA) in October 2017 – a conference attended largely by academic prison researchers, serving and retired prison managers from the private and public sectors, prison planners, architects, and (on this occasion, as it was held in London) senior personnel from HMPPS – it seemed that hardly a paper was presented without claims being made about custodial environments becoming more 'normalized' and therefore, it was said, more likely to rehabilitate offenders. Usually summed up by the aphorism that people get sent to prison as punishment, not for punishment, the Mandela rules (United Nations 2016) state that the prison regime should 'seek to minimise any differences between prison life and life at liberty that tend to lessen the responsibility of prisoners or the respect due to their dignity' (Rule 5).

Within the academy, 'normalization' is usually thought to have three components. Firstly, on an individual level, it recognizes the prisoner as a social being with many facets to their identity, not just a 'prisoner'. This aspect of normalization was highlighted in the prison reform agenda announced by then Prime Minister David Cameron in his 'prisons speech' at the Policy Exchange, on 8 February 2016, which might help to explain why the term has become so well used among prison service professionals in the UK. Announcing radical prison estate transformation proposals that included plans for nine new prisons in England and Wales, a Prime Minister who had formerly said that giving prisoners the vote made him feel 'physically ill', on this occasion said: 'we need a prison system that doesn't see prisoners as simply liabilities to be managed, but instead as potential assets to be harnessed'.

Second, on a collective level, normalization is concerned with offering services as similar as possible to the collective services and community agencies provided on the outside. In many prisons this is already achieved. In healthcare, for example, medical, psychiatric, and dental services in prisons are frequently as good, if not better, than those in the free community. In some prisons, education and library provision often goes well beyond what adults might reasonably expect to have access to in the community, and it is not unusual to find excellent computer technologies, art resources, and music recording facilities within newer facilities, although the best examples we have seen have been in countries such as Norway and Denmark, rather than in the UK, where political antipathy and austerity measures have compromised the provision of even basic educational and recreational activities.

The third aspect of normalization concerns the drive to make prison conditions approximate 'normal' living and working conditions in society as far as possible. Here, the aim is to deinstitutionalize prisons by reducing or eliminating overt situational security paraphernalia and by 'softening' the environment with fixtures and fittings that are more domestic in feel than the robust, vandal-resistant type more usually found in custodial settings. Cells are increasingly designed along similar lines to bedrooms in student halls of residence, and spaces that are 'social' (association rooms, visiting halls, etc.) are borrowing design cues from shopping malls and airports (Jewkes 2018). A great deal of attention has also been paid to the 'greening' of outdoor spaces, with, for example: grass replacing concrete exercise yards; planting of trees and shrubs; introduction of 'therapeutic' and sensory gardens; reduction of razor wire around trees and buildings; and horticulture, beekeeping, and animal husbandry now present in several prisons across the UK. While some of these initiatives are simply aesthetic or recreational, others are explicitly designed to reduce trauma in prisoners and improve working environments for staff, while others still have an unambiguous rehabilitative agenda and are classed as 'green-collar' training, leading to qualifications and potential future work opportunities.

Nordic 'normalization'

The ambition to make prisons less institutional – and by inference, prisoners less institutionalized – is one that few of us would disagree with. But to what extent is 'normalization' synonymous with 'rehabilitation'? Can an aesthetically pleasing environment nurture feelings of self-worth and a hopeful, future-oriented outlook? Can access to nature change thoughts and behaviour in ways that cognitive programmes fail to? Can friendly, personal interactions between a prisoner and prison officer be a catalyst for the formation of meaningful relationships going forward? In short, can prisons be places that encourage long-term flourishing, rather than breaking, of human spirits (Jewkes 2018; Liebling 2016)?

The prison most commonly cited as the 'model prison' for both its architecture and the regime that the design facilitates – both of which are said to be manifestations of the principle of normalization – is Halden Fengsel, a high-security prison in southern Norway. This famous establishment – the 'world's most humane prison', as *Time* magazine described it – is actually intended to go further than emulating the normal living and working conditions that prisoners might experience in ordinary life; the ambition here is to 'inspire prisoners and motivate them to lead better lives' (said in an interview with one of the lead architects from Eric Møller Architects; see Jewkes 2018). Among Halden's unusual (from an Anglophone perspective) design features are: the forest that encroaches into the prison grounds; the large bar-less windows throughout the entire prison (including segregation); the sophisticated lighting system that mimics natural daylight; the open-plan living/cooking/dining areas that (to these observers, at least) resemble something from the pages of an IKEA catalogue; the comfortable Family House, where prisoners can invite their partners and children to stay overnight; a sophisticated music recording studio; and a tranquil and visually imaginative multi-faith room which encourages calm reflection as well as more formal religious devotion.

Since it opened in 2010, many other architects have sought to emulate Halden's vision including, most recently, C. F. Møller, who designed the 250-bed high-security Storstrøm Fængsel in Falster, Denmark, which opened in September 2017. C. F. Møller suggests that Storstrøm is a physical manifestation of the Danish post-war welfare model – 'the dream of a society where everyone has access to the same social infrastructure, along with healthy homes and common recreational facilities' (C.F. Møller 2017). It is, they say, the social responsibility of architects to support a 'political vision of a society where everyone has access to the same democratic architecture'. Like Halden, then, Storstrøm is intended to be both familiar and also aspirational. The prison, according to lead architect Mads Mandrup Hansen, 'stimulates the urge and ability to rejoin society after serving a prison sentence' (ibid.), suggesting it is the very model of a rehabilitative prison design.

Storstrøm's living accommodation is also arguably very 'normal' in being not unlike a bedroom in a budget hotel. Each cell receives daylight from two sides with a small window on one wall and a very large window (full cell height, and bar-less, naturally), with views of the surrounding countryside, on the other side. The cells measure a relatively generous 13 m² and have been designed with a curved wall, in contrast to the usual boxiness of conventional prison accommodation. Clusters of four to seven cells form social communities and prisoners have access to a sitting room and communal kitchen in which they can cook for themselves or with others. Throughout the site, green open spaces have been incorporated for activity with an 'urban touch', where prisoners can 'commune with nature, or take part in sport and other communal activities' (ibid.). In short, while references to imprisonment being like living in a submarine are common in the Anglophone prisons literature, being in Halden or Storstrøm is not like being submerged at all. These are light, bright, aesthetically stimulating environments and, if any prison might be described as 'rehabilitative', then, Halden and Storstrøm surely fit the bill. They are also pleasantly normal environments for prison staff, for whom creating a relatively relaxed environment may lessen the preoccupation with personal safety and security, allowing them to find purpose and fulfilment in their work.

How 'normal' can UK prisons be?

In England and Wales, there has been a growing recognition within HMPPS of the importance of the 'principle of normality' (United Nations 2016) in creating a 'rehabilitative culture' (Mann et al. 2018) and, despite the Government's apparently unshakeable faith in the effectiveness and efficiencies of very large 'mega-prisons', attention at a local level has somewhat counter-intuitively become focused on how their physical design might be 'softened'. For example, there has been a growing trend to redesign and refurbish family visits rooms, moving away from drab, highly regimented, and security-focused facilities to ones that offer soft furnishings (rather than bolted down tables and chairs), children's play areas, and café- and bistro-style facilities often staffed by prisoners themselves. In some instances, university students have been enlisted in these design projects, reinforcing a commitment to be 'outward facing' and community focused.

Perhaps the most concerted attempt to experiment with the principle of normality in England and Wales is evidenced at the newly opened HMP Berwyn, a medium-security Category C prison in North Wales. Despite the relatively standard, 'future-proofed', and 'value-engineered' Category B (high-security) prison design imposed upon them, attempts have been made by the senior management team to improve the physical environment by, for example: using large-scale photographic imagery to fill the available wall space; introducing a wide colour palette; placing inspirational quotes on the walls; and using soft, colourful furniture in areas of the prison not usually associated with 'soft' or 'comfortable', including the prisoner reception holding cells (Gooch 2017). The outdoor spaces have been enhanced by the introduction of seating areas, trees, flower beds, and bird boxes.

Innovation at Berwyn has extended to local, as opposed to central, recruitment and training of prison officers (and recruiting staff on the basis of personal 'values', as well as qualifications and experience). They have also implemented a wide programme of cultural change focusing on the new lexicon of the rehabilitative prison. Here, the prison's occupants are 'men', not 'prisoners', who are housed in 'communities', rather than in 'houseblocks' or on 'landings', and in 'rooms' not 'cells'. In-cell telephony and laptops have been introduced, the latter allowing men to connect to a 'digital hub', access educational resources, arrange family visits, and complete basic administrative processes, such as making a complaint and 'shopping' for personal items. In short, Berwyn's senior management team have taken principles of 'normality' more usually associated with the small prisons of Scandinavian penal systems (average capacity 83) and implemented them in a 'Titan' prison that can accommodate 2,106 men. Seeking to moderate the possible problems of scale, the management is committed to 'making big feel small', using the physical layout to create discreet communities of 88 men, several of which have a dedicated function tailored to particular groups of prisoners. The implementation of a rehabilitative vision is not without its challenges: 'rehabilitation is hard not easy', both for prison officers who need to remain resilient in the face of challenge and confrontation from those in custody, and for men who, for example, are learning new habits and changing established 'coping strategies' (such as substance misuse) and patterns of behaviour.

Moving in the opposite direction to England and Wales, with small-scale, community-based custodial facilities that promote the idea that architecture and design may play a part in prisoner rehabilitation, Scotland has led the way in the UK (and looked to their Scandinavian neighbours, rather than south of the border, for design inspiration; Armstrong 2014). A Scottish prison that was to be both normalized and trauma-informed was HMP Inverclyde, the plans for which were shelved following recommendations by the Angiolini Commission of 2012, which was convened to look at ways of improving the way women are treated by the criminal justice system. There was also a sustained campaign by academics, activists, and reform groups, who were opposed to a national facility that would house up to three-quarters of Scotland's female prison population (entailing issues of remoteness to own communities, families, etc.), combined with a fundamental belief that Scotland should be pursuing a policy of decarceration for women.

Instead, the Scottish Prison Service (SPS) is now planning a new 80-bed national prison to stand on the site currently occupied by HMP Cornton Vale, plus an additional five community-based prisons, each with 20 places; all of which will incorporate many of the design cues of the original plans for Inverclyde. Among the aesthetic and architectural characteristics prioritized in Scotland's new women's estate are: maximum exploitation of natural daylight including through large, bar-less windows; gender-responsive colour palettes; bedrooms (not cells) that emulate student hall-of-residence rooms with sofa beds and study areas; association areas that feel like 'normal' social spaces; and well-planned landscapes. Although ultimately it did not get beyond the architect's drawing board, Inverclyde was one of the prisons that inspired the team responsible for the commissioning and planning of a new women's prison in Limerick. In this project, a requirement for design innovation has been heavily emphasized and the Irish Prison Service (IPS) has put out the Design & Build to competitive tender in a competition of the type more usually found in northern Europe (Jewkes 2018).

Indigenous factors that mitigate against rehabilitation

A 'normal', aesthetically pleasing, design-led, and deinstitutionalized custodial environment that fosters feelings of safety and empowerment is undoubtedly desirable compared to one that is the opposite of all these things. However, its ability to rehabilitate remains a moot point. Although we noted at the beginning of this chapter that prison can function as a refuge, respite, or even lucrative business opportunity for some prisoners, one of the risks in advancing a penal agenda focused on normalization is not that more people might be willing to go to prison, but that the language and rhetoric will have an anaesthetic quality, overlooking the real and continued 'pains of imprisonment' (Sykes 1958). Losing one's liberty, being incarcerated against one's will and having one's movement, behaviour, and even thinking coercively controlled is not 'normal', and nothing can make it so. Moreover, what is 'normal', and whose 'normal' should we aspire to recreate in custodial settings? The architects of Storstrøm in Denmark may have designed green spaces with an 'urban touch', but we find it difficult to endorse the view put to us by several prison planning and design consultants in England and Wales (frequently ex-prison security managers) that there is no point in planting trees or including gardens and horticulture in prison settings, because most prisoners come from inner cities and simply won't know how to respond to beautiful natural environments!

Perhaps, then, we are using the wrong language. Rather than trying to make prisons 'normalized' in the sense of preparing prisoners for their re-entry into society, we should aim to make them humanizing, healing, and nurturing – 'trauma-informed' but in a non-clinical, intuitive sense. One prison that succeeded in this regard was Norgerhaven, the prison in the Netherlands that has been leased to Norway since 2015, but has recently (as of 31 August 2018) had its contract terminated by the Norwegian Ministry of Justice because they have now reduced the 'waiting list' of people awaiting a place in prison from 1,200 to zero. With no 'treatment' of any kind on offer (no behavioural or cognitive programmes, no therapy, no education even, beyond basic numeracy and literacy), Norgerhaven certainly could not be accused of engaging in coercive correction. But what it does have is an interior landscape known as The Park, with picnic tables, benches, racquet sports and – most importantly of all – 54 mature trees. The environment encourages prisoners to hang out in small groups, chat, smoke, chill. It is, then, assuredly normal.

'Proving' a causal link between nature and well-being is, however, notoriously difficult. Such studies as there are tend to be found in the realms of health studies and environmental psychology, where views of, and contact with, nature have been found to reduce stress, enhance concentration, and hasten recovery times in patients (Jewkes 2018).Yet, the designers and landscape architects responsible for prisons in the Nordic countries take for granted that the two are inextricably linked, and even asking the question of how they know this to be true tends to elicit a shrug of the shoulders and a response of 'It's obvious, isn't it . . . it's just common sense' (ibid.). Moreover, the prisoners (of many nationalities) and (mostly Dutch) staff at Norgerhaven all intimated that the landscape there heals and inspires. As more than one prisoner commented in research undertaken by one of this chapter's authors,[2] 'these trees are powerful'. Questioning a Norwegian prisoner about whether it was actually rehabilitative, he expressed refreshing candour, saying that he didn't know if it was enough to stop him from reoffending in future, but he did know that he had been a serial criminal all his life and had served many sentences in more conventional prisons, none of which had rehabilitated him. Norgerhaven, however, stood a chance, he said, because the focus was not on his past, on what he had done, and how he could be 'fixed'. Here he could be contemplative and tranquil:

> My parents like that I've grown myself again. *This* is rehabilitation. No drugs courses. No behaviour courses. Just looking at the trees. I'm better because of the trees.
>
> (interview at Norgerhaven, August 2017)

In decoupling 'offending behaviour programmes' and interventions from the concept of rehabilitation, this Norwegian prisoner brings into sharp focus the ongoing debate about 'what works' in prison, and who decides. As Sykes notes (1958: 17):

> When we turn to the idea of imprisonment as reform, it is clear that there are few who will quarrel with such a desirable goal – the disputes centre on how it will be achieved. . . . Unfortunately, the advocates of confinement

as a method of achieving rehabilitation of the criminal have often found themselves in the position of calling for an operation where the target of the scalpel remains unknown.

Sykes goes as far as to say that of all the tasks that the prison is called to perform, 'none is more ambiguous' than rehabilitation (1958: 17). Thus, it is not the principle of rehabilitation itself, but the *implementation* of it that produces the most anxiety and confusion. All too often, this slippery concept signifies an intention to do good rather than harm, but with almost scant regard for the short- and long-term outcomes of whatever new idea has been implemented (and we all know that the road to Hell is paved with good intentions).

It is perhaps for these reasons that many scholars (see McNeill 2014, for an overview) have argued that the notion of rehabilitation is meaningless unless historic, pervasive, deeply embedded social inequalities are addressed – inequalities of power between prison staff and inmates, and inequalities including of wealth, life choices, and future opportunities between individuals who have been to prison and those who have not, in society at large. For McNeill (2012, 2014) and others, rehabilitation is a social contract between individual and the state, and the moral legitimacy of the state's demand that people refrain from offending is valid only if, as a minimum, the state offers each offender an opportunity to reintegrate into society as a useful human being. Given that this social contract implies willingness from the community (as well as from the individual ex-prisoner) to achieve successful reintegration, and given also that it rests on the questionable assumption that rehabilitation can overcome the numerous harms done by imprisonment and from wider, lifelong forms of social exclusion, any opportunities offered to individuals while in prison may count for little when they are returned to the community with the stigma of a criminal record to further diminish their life chances.[3]

In the Nordic countries which, as the press release for Storstrøm noted, tend to be more welfarist in orientation, it is not the case that ex-prisoners are not burdened by the shame of having a criminal record – they are. But in Norway, for example, most types of employer would not be able to get hold of a criminal records transcript for any reason; it is only sex offenders and very violent offenders who keep their criminal records for life, and even then it is only certain employers (e.g. schools and preschools) that can gain access to information about their criminal pasts that pertains to the job they have applied for (so, for example, a school would not be granted access to records about a motoring offence or white-collar crime). Very few agencies (the armed forces, prison service, and the police) can gain a full transcript of past criminal convictions with no time limit (this also applies in child adoption procedures). To reiterate, then, most employers and other agencies and institutions in Norway have no right to gain access to an individual's criminal records transcript for any reason, which many scholars of punishment and desistance would regard as an important component of the social contract between individual and state, and a vital element of rehabilitation.

Concluding thoughts

Throughout UK history, prisons – and the post-prison experience of being 'on licence' and carrying a criminal record – have been designed to inflict punishment and retribution, rather than to encourage rehabilitation and reform. In very recent years, rehabilitation has reappeared as a goal of HMPPS, but the broader political landscape has changed little, with the result that successive Secretaries of State for Justice have pursued the arguably mutually exclusive goals of punishment and reform. This chapter has set out to discuss the limits of rehabilitation, particularly in the context of it being achieved by imprisonment. The chapter has also discussed its conflation with concepts and practices that are labelled 'normalized' and 'trauma-informed' which, we have argued, may give an impression of good intent, but are difficult to evaluate and, in any case, do little to challenge the fundamental deprivations and structural disadvantages experienced by people who come to prison and the harms that may be inflicted upon them while subject to the coercive controls that are indigenous to incarceration.

Our tentative conclusion, then, is that prisons can probably succeed in treating people with kindness, respect, trust, and decency in a spatial and cultural environment conducive to nurturing self-esteem and well-being. They may even instil a long-term appreciation and aspiration for good design. Prisons can, and must, also offer meaningful education, work, and training that will better equip ex-offenders for life post-release. But even an enlightened approach does not inevitably counteract the pains of imprisonment or mitigate against poor choices and flawed decision-making by damaged individuals. Future research might usefully empirically test these hypotheses.

In countries such as Norway, rehabilitation might be a more realistic goal – the Norwegian Department of Corrections certainly claims a recidivism rate of about half of that found in England and Wales (that is, 20–25% as opposed to 44%). But even if Scandi-style prisons were introduced in the UK (and, as already indicated, Scotland is already leading the way in this respect), individuals leaving prisons in the UK arguably face much greater challenges in resettling. Stigma and discrimination often lead to difficulties in finding suitable, long-term accommodation and work, on top of which ex-prisoners must navigate the complexities of post-release control and supervision and return to relationships which may be strained, broken, or changed by enforced separation. For those who have served long sentences, adjusting to a fast-paced, technologically advanced and digital online world can also represent a huge challenge (Jewkes and Reisdorf 2016). The 'rehabilitative prison' may thus be, at best, an oxymoron and, at worst, a dangerous smokescreen, camouflaging the multiple harms that imprisonment, pathways to prison, and post-prison experience inflict.

Notes

1 When individuals are released from prison, they may do so under parole and/or under licence conditions. If those conditions are breached, the individual may be returned to custody either to serve out the remainder of their fixed-term sentence or until the parole board authorizes their release.

2 Yvonne Jewkes visited Norgerhaven with Alison Liebling in the summer of 2016, and returned a year later with a research team funded by the Norwegian Department of Corrections to carry out an MQPL (Measuring the Quality of Prison Life) survey.

3 The rules about criminal records, when they are spent, and who has a right to access them are complicated in most countries. In simple terms, in the UK, a criminal conviction resulting in a sentence of up to six months is spent after two years; a sentence of 6–30 months carries a criminal record for four years; 30 months–three years ensures a criminal record for seven years; and a sentence of four years or more means that the criminal record is never spent. In theory, only certain employers for certain types of role can access someone's record. However, most employers and many other agencies (including housing agencies and universities) require applicants to declare whether they carry any unspent criminal convictions.

References

Armstrong, S. (2014) Scotland's newest prison is another nod to Scandinavia. *The Conversation*. Available at: https://theconversation.com/scotlands-newest-prison-is-another-nod-to-scandinavia-24145

Bales, D. B. and Piquero, A. R. (2012) Assessing the impact of imprisonment on recidivism. *Journal of Experimental Criminology*, 8(1), 71–101.

Cain, C. (2016) Women shouldn't be forced to seek refuge inside a prison. *Politics.co.uk*. Available at: www.politics.co.uk/comment-analysis/2016/05/20/women-s-only-refuge-shouldn-t-be-inside-a-prison.

C.F. Møller. (2017) *Storstrøm Prison North Falster*. Copenhagen: Architects' Press Pack.

Elliott, D., Bjelajac, P. Fallot, R., Markoff, L. and Reed, B. (2005) Trauma-informed or trauma-denied: Principles and implementation of trauma-informed services for women. *Journal of Community Psychology*, 33, 461–477.

Gooch, K. (2017) *Building Berwyn – Interim Report*. Leicester: University of Leicester.

Gooch, K. and Treadwell, J. (forthcoming) *Transforming the Violent Prison*. Basingstoke: Palgrave Macmillan.

Hardwick, C. (2017) *Developing trauma-informed awareness for staff and prisoners across the women's estate*. Conference of the International Corrections and Prisons Association (ICPA), London 25 October 2017.

HM Inspectorate of Prisons for England and Wales (HMIP). (2016) *Annual Report 2015–16*. London: HMSO.

Jewkes, Y. (2018) Just design: Healthy prisons and the architecture of hope. *Australian & New Zealand Journal of Criminology*, 51(3), 319–338.

Jewkes, Y. and Moran, M. (2014) Bad design breeds violence in sterile megaprisons. *The Conversation*. Available at: https://theconversation.com/bad-design-breeds-violence-in-sterile-megaprisons-22424

Jewkes, Y. and Reisdorf, B. (2016) A brave new world: The problems and opportunities presented by new media technologies in prisons. *Criminology & Criminal Justice*, 16(5), 534–551.

Liebling, A. (2016) The Dalai Lama, prisons, and prisons research: A call for trust, a 'proper sense of fear', dialogue, curiosity and love. *Prison Service Journal*, 225, 58–63.

Mann, et al. (2018) What is a rehabilitative culture? *Prison Service Journal*, 235, 3–9.

McNeill, F. (2012) Four forms of 'offender' rehabilitation: Towards an interdisciplinary perspective. *Legal and Criminological Psychology*, 17(1), 18–36.

McNeill, F. (2014) Punishment as rehabilitation. In G. Bruinsma and D. Weisburd (Eds.), *Encyclopedia of Criminology & Criminal Justice*. New York: Springer, pp. 4195–4206.

Ministry of Justice (MoJ). (2017) *Safety in Custody Quarterly*. London: Ministry of Justice.

Scottish Prison Service (SPS). (2017) *Prisoner Deaths*. Available at: www.sps.gov.uk/Corporate/Information/PrisonerDeaths.aspx.

Smyth, C. (2016) Spike in prison inmate deaths last year with 22 fatalities. *The Irish Times*. Available at: www.irishtimes.com/news/crime-and-law/spike-in-prison-inmate-deaths-last-year-with-22-fatalities-1.2910359.

Sykes, G. (1958) *The Society of Captives: A Study of a Maximum-Security Prison*. Princeton, NJ: Princeton University Press.

United Nations. (2016) *United Nations Standard Minimum Rules for the Treatment of Prisoners (the Nelson Mandela Rules)*. UN-Doc A/Res/70/175.

Rehabilitation and re-entry in Scandinavia

15

John Todd-Kvam and Thomas Ugelvik

Introduction

The Scandinavian penal-welfare model has been held up by many as an ideal. Much research has been done on the exceptional nature of imprisonment in the Nordic[1] countries, both in terms of sentence length and prison conditions. Scandinavian prisons have been described as more humane, constructive, and welfare oriented than prisons elsewhere. Given the fervent research activity of recent years, it is striking how little is known about the rehabilitation and resettlement journey from prison to the community in Scandinavia. This chapter accounts for the limited research on the subject that does exist. We examine how the ideal resettlement pathway *should* work in Norway before examining the challenges of providing seamless 'through the gate' provision even in the context of a strong Scandinavian welfare state. We also discuss possible reasons for the surprising lack of research-based knowledge about the release and re-entry process in Scandinavia.

Scandinavian exceptionalism

The Scandinavian social democratic welfare state is often highlighted in discussions of penal policy. The Scandinavian countries are seen as counterweights to an increasingly repressive control climate globally, apparently able to resist the international 'punitive turn'. The Scandinavian criminal justice systems manage to retain relatively low rates of imprisonment (the Swedish imprisonment rate has even decreased in recent years) and short average sentences. Several authors have argued that the Scandinavian countries and their prisons are somehow special cases; that they are exceptional compared with similar institutions elsewhere (see inter alia Cavadino and Dignan 2006; Pratt 2008a, 2008b; Pratt and Eriksson 2011a, 2011b, 2012). Others have criticized such claims, arguing that there is no reason to put the Scandinavian prison systems on a pedestal (Mathiesen 2012; Smith 2012; Shammas 2017).

The Scandinavian welfare states are often seen as one. There are a number of similarities between the Scandinavian countries, but there are also significant differences that are often lost in comparative analyses (Smith and Ugelvik 2017a). In some cases, what looks like similarities on paper may in fact mask fundamental differences in practice. The format of this chapter does not allow us to give comprehensive accounts of all three Scandinavian countries (not to mention the monumental task of explaining the myriad differences between the eight Nordics). Therefore, this chapter will take Norway as its main example. We will, however, draw on research from the other Scandinavian countries where relevant.

The Norwegian prison and probation system

The Norwegian prison and probation system is small, with a relatively low imprisonment rate of 74 per 100,000 inhabitants (World Prisons Brief 2017). According to the *Correctional Service Year Statistics 2016* (Kriminalomsorgen 2017), the prison system had a total capacity of 4,122 prisoners – sentenced and remand combined – spread out across 40 different institutions. On an average day, 997 prisoners were imprisoned pre-trial. Of the sentences passed on to the Correctional Service from the court system that year, 14% were for drug offences, 55% for 'offences for profit' (mainly theft and robbery) and 15% for violent offences. Approximately 34% of prisoners were foreign nationals. Six percent were women. Norwegian prison sentences are often short, with 87% of sentenced prisoners released within a year of imprisonment. The average time spent in prison for convicted prisoners has, however, increased in recent years though. It is currently 173 days.

In addition to the prisons, the Correctional Service system includes 16 probation offices. For prisoners with sentences of 74 days or more, it is possible to apply to be released from prison on licence after having served two-thirds of a sentence. In 2016, 2,135 individuals were released on licence. A minority of licensees, 760 individuals in 2016, have to meet regularly with the probation service for a period following their conditional release, but most former prisoners will have no contact with the prisons and probation system post-release. The probation offices are also responsible for the implementation of community sanctions, a programme for intoxicated drivers, home detention with or without electronic monitoring, and for the writing of pre-sentence reports.

Despite their extensive and far-reaching public sectors, third-sector organizations are by no means insignificant in the Scandinavian countries. Several voluntary organizations fill an important role in the re-entry process, helping newly released prisoners find suitable accommodation, work, and a pro-social network. In Norway, the three largest are Network after Imprisonment (a Red Cross initiative that have recently opened 'Norway's first re-entry centre'), the Norwegian Church's City Mission, and the ex-prisoner run WayBack. In Sweden, KRIS (Criminals Return Into Society) is a major contributor.

The ideal re-entry pathway

Re-entry is a complex process that can be studied and understood on different levels. Successful re-entry is the result of individual transitions, but in many cases, it is also the result of cooperation and interaction with others (Laub and Sampson 2001; Weaver 2015). Re-entry may also be seen as the result of government policies and practices – perhaps especially in the strong-state context of Scandinavia. This section outlines the ideal rehabilitation and re-entry pathway from prison to the community in Norway from the perspective of the prisons and probation system, before examining some of the challenges to its realization in practice. The distance between ambitions and plans set out in policy documents and what actually happens in practice is often, after all, significant.

In overall terms, the framework for punishment, rehabilitation, and resettlement is set out in a report to the Norwegian parliament entitled *Punishment That Works – Less Crime – a Safer Society* (Det Kongelige Justis- og Politidepartementet 2007; Norwegian Ministry of Justice and the Police 2007). Even though this report is over a decade old, it remains – formally at least – the guiding document that sets the strategic context for rehabilitation and re-entry work in the Norwegian Correctional Service. The report was developed and published by a left-of-centre coalition led by the Labour Party and, despite this government losing power to a minority coalition of the centre-right Conservative Party and populist Progress Party in 2013, it has yet to be replaced. That being said, concerns have been raised about the commitment of the Progress Party (who hold the office of Justice Minister) to the Norwegian Correctional Service's emphasis on rehabilitation and resettlement (Todd-Kvam 2018).

The report highlights that the Norwegian Correctional Service are committed to upholding what is known as 'the principle of normality' or 'the principle of normalization'. Indeed, this principle is described as a 'lodestar' for effective penal policy and practice. According to Engbo (2017), there are two versions of this principle. The defensive version takes as its starting point that prisoners should retain all legal rights that they would be entitled to in their normal lives outside the prison, with the obvious exception of the interference into their freedom of movement and the crime prevention and security measures necessary in a prison setting. The proactive version of the principle goes further; here, the prison system should actively try to create 'normal living conditions' (whatever they may be) in their institutions, and try to motivate prisoners to want to live 'normal lives'. The smaller the difference between life inside and outside prison, the easier the transition from incarceration to freedom will be (Norwegian Ministry of Justice and the Police 2007). In this version, normalization is seen less as a rights-based principle, but more as a means to an end: rehabilitation and reintegration through 'normal' living conditions.

Linked to the normality principle is the importation model, whereby welfare state services are imported into prisons. The prison education department is part of the Norwegian public school system, the prison libraries part of the system of municipal libraries. Prison doctors and nurses are hired by the national healthcare system, not the Correctional Service. The criminologist Nils Christie (1993), the inventor of the importation model, argued that greater transparency would be an important by-product of giving these professional groups regular access to the prisons. Today, all major welfare agencies have a permanent presence in all prisons (Fridhov 2013). Bourdieu (2000) talks about a left and a right hand of government, where the right hand is composed of the 'harder' control organs of the state and the left the 'softer' welfare services. The idea behind the importation model is to get these two hands to work together, introducing the 'softer', more welfare-oriented services into the 'harder' prisons sphere.

In addition to the normality principle and import model, an emphasis is placed on rehabilitation and reducing recidivism. In doing so, it is recognized that this work must be done both in prison and as an inmate is released back into society.

In prison

So, the ideal re-entry pathway begins with a prison experience that is as 'normal' as possible. At the same time, the needs and resources of inmates are assessed via a standardized assessment tool[2] with appropriate initiatives and programmes identified and delivered. Rehabilitation work in prison may include education, training, and work experience, addressing physical and mental health needs, dealing with addiction and programmes on familiar themes like motivation and change, domestic violence and sex offending (Det Kongelige Justis- og Politidepartementet 2007).

Another important element of the ideal pathway whilst in prison is *progression*. In general, sentenced prisoners progress from a high-security prison to a lower security prison over the course of their sentence. Progression also involves achieving a greater degree of freedom via leave and day-release. In addition to compassionate leave, inmates on a sentence over 120 days may be granted leave for up to 18 days per year (30 in some special circumstances) in order to maintain contact with family and to attend meetings with public services. These periods of leave are seen as critical in preparing inmates for freedom and in assisting reintegration (Det Kongelige Justis- og Politideparte- mentet 2007: 122). Day-release to school, work, or 'other crime-preventative measures' is also seen as an important tool for resettlement (ibid.: 123–124). The final element of progression is transfer to a halfway house.

On release

In terms of the ideal re-entry pathway, nearly all the hard work should have been done before an inmate reaches the prison gate. As mentioned above, this reintegration work begins with identifying needs and resources and extends to ensuring that relevant external agencies are brought in to deliver their services in good time prior to release. So-called *return coordinators* have been employed in the prisons to coordinate this cooperation between the relevant government agencies (Sverdrup 2013; Fridhov 2013). The report *Punishment That Works* (Det Kongelige Justis- og Politidepartementet 2007, p. 176) sets out six key elements of helping prisoners return to society:

1   Satisfactory housing;
2   Opportunity for education or training;
3   Work, benefits, and government support in finding employment;
4   Social services, including an individual action plan (in the Norwegian context this means government assistance with economic and social problems);
5   Health services including treatment for mental health problems and addiction;
6   Financial advice including assistance with debt settlement.

This idea behind this work is to ensure that inmates can have their pre-existing rights as Norwegian citizens fulfilled. As mentioned above, inmates may apply for conditional release after having served two-thirds of their sentence. If it is deemed necessary by the prison authorities, those on probation may be required to meet regularly with a caseworker. The goal of this compulsory attendance at probation is to prevent reoffending via 'promoting offenders' ability to counteract criminal behaviour patterns through control measures' (Kriminalomsorgen n.d.).

Overall then, the ideal pathway towards resettlement starts at the beginning of the prison sentence with mapping of needs and resources. Relevant programmes are identified and delivered, with the inmate progressing through the system, achieving more freedom and lower levels of control and security. Periods of leave and day-release help prepare the inmate for life on the outside. Perhaps a period in one of Norway's open prisons like Bastøy may pave the way for transfer to a halfway house or release on probation. In theory, all relevant public agencies will have been brought to bear in order to arrange housing, employment, and other relevant support for the inmate as he or she transitions from the prison back to the community. Of course, how an ex-prisoner and potential desister is met by this local community is also important, with the report to parliament noting that the chances of someone keeping themselves out of criminal contexts is small if they are not accepted in other contexts (Det Kongelige Justis- og Politidepartementet 2007). The following section addresses some further challenges to how this ideal pathway is realized in practice, after which we conclude by identifying some of the key gaps in knowledge of what happens post-release.

Challenges for rehabilitation and re-entry

It has long been established that former prisoners face significant problems upon release (inter alia Petersilia 2004; Decarpes and Durnescu 2014) and Scandinavian prisoners are no exception (Nilsson 2003; Skardhamar and Telle 2012; Revold 2015). That being said, there are no large-scale studies of the entire release and re-entry process in Norway. What we do have are several studies of various parts of the process that can be woven into something like an account of the process as a whole. The problems identified in these studies are often directly connected to the living conditions of the prison population as a whole, as discussed by Skardhamar (2002) and Friestad and Hansen (2004). The latter study shows that the prisoner populations' living conditions are characterized by an accumulation of problems that often begin in childhood: the more problems they experience while growing up, the worse their living conditions are likely to be as adults. The report concludes that successful reintegration cannot be achieved through isolated measures. Instead it must be based on a comprehensive understanding of the wide-ranging marginalization of this group. There are a number of important difficulties and challenges in addressing these issues of multiple marginalization. Some of these challenges have been addressed in existing research and some we have identified in our ongoing fieldwork and interviews with potential desisters and probation workers.

Regarding the normality principle, it is undoubtedly a laudable idea. However, we must ask ourselves how close to 'normal' can prison life really be? And whose normal are we using as a point of comparison? Engbo (2017) has claimed that any effort to create 'normal' living conditions in prison and motivate prisoners to live 'normal' lives risks becoming over-involved paternalism. In terms of *ab*normality, Scandinavian jurisdictions including Norway have been criticized for highly restrictive and isolating remand conditions (Smith 2006). Uses of isolation in high-security prisons has also been criticized, with the Parliamentary Ombudsman recently criticizing the long-term isolation of those with mental health problems in the high-security Ila prison (Sivilombudsmannen 2017). Even Norway's open prisons can be experienced as abnormal, painful places (Neumann 2011; Shammas 2014).

In terms of rehabilitation in prison, the number of short prison sentences and increasing budgetary constraints limit what can be achieved. The challenges of delivering well-planned rehabilitation and re-entry work when dealing with short sentences is well recognized (see, for example, Johnston and Godfrey 2013). In terms of government funding, the Correctional Service budget has been cut in recent years whilst prison capacity has been increased: this means a dramatically reduced focus on programme delivery (for an analysis of how these resource constraints play out in one particular Norwegian prison, see Anderson and Gröning 2017). Even from within Correctional Service leadership, public concerns have been raised that the cuts are 'virtually unmanageable' (Fredriksen et al. 2017). In addition, the current government's relative lack of emphasis on work to reduce reoffending has been described as a passive erosion of Norway's penal welfare model (Shammas 2017; Todd-Kvam 2018). This lack of political emphasis on rehabilitation has also been mentioned in our interviews with probation workers and informal conversations with those working in the criminal care system.

The technocratic challenge of achieving joined-up working between the various parts of the Norwegian welfare state machine is also not to be underestimated. The importation model has in many ways contributed to the success of the Norwegian system. However, it has also meant that less desirable aspects of the welfare system have been imported into prisons, including communication and cooperation problems. Inmates often slip between the fingers as they are juggled back and forth between the giving left and controlling right hands of the Scandinavian welfare state. Probation officers have for example described to us the difficulty of getting NAV, the work and welfare agency, to engage constructively with some of their clients. The move away from face-to-face contact to online services is also a challenge for those re-entering society after a long period behind bars – not least for those with literacy and numeracy problems.

This challenge of joined-up working has been acknowledged by the government, with relevant ministers recently signing a pledge to work together to reduce reoffending (Departementene 2017). This pledge is set out in a strategy document that also highlights some further important issues with current rehabilitation and reintegration practices in Norway. It notes that only just over half those released from prison move into accommodation they own or rent, with 20% planning to live with family, in a hostel or other low-threshold accommodation and 24% having no plan at all for where they will live. An estimated 60% of released prisoners are neither in education nor employment and many have problems with debt and insufficient income. Nearly 65% of those released had problems with substance and/or alcohol use, whilst 92% 'indicated a personality disorder or other mental illness' (ibid.: 4). So we can see that the re-entry experience for many prisoners is very different from the ideal pathway set out above (see Revold 2015 for more on the often difficult living conditions of inmates in Norway). Seamless 'through the gate' provision remains an ambition rather than a reality for many.

Despite the relatively strong welfare safety net, the re-entry literature depicts a succession of obstacles for newly released prisoners entering the housing market. Indeed, in articles on housing problems in Norway, a 'typical' homeless person is often described as a man with a criminal record and a lack of social network (Ludvigsen et al. 2008; Karagøz 2010; Snertingdal and Bakkeli 2013). The majority of prisoners interviewed by Dyb et al. (2006) said they needed help to obtain housing, but less than half believed that the social services in prison and outside would be able to help them efficiently, and the majority believed that private landlords would not be interested in letting to former prisoners. Olesen (2013) addresses debt problems in one of the most thorough and extensive study of parole and related problems in the Scandinavian literature. Based on interviews with repeat offenders in Denmark, Olesen studies the economic impact of multiple prison sentences and how debt hinders integration back into society (including access to housing). Inspired by Bourdieu, she introduces the concept 'underground legal capital' to describe the 'insider' knowledge of institutions and legal awareness obtained through experiences in a criminal milieu. See also Todd-Kvam (2019) for an analysis of how debt impacts resettlement and reintegration in Norway.

Employment is often seen as a key factor for former prisoners if they are going to be able to desist from crime. Using Norwegian data, Skardhamar and Savolainen (2014) found that for an overwhelming majority of offenders, a decline in criminal activity *precedes* job entry; the typical path to employment seems to be a period of criminal inactivity of around two years (ibid.: 22). The results contradict the view of employment as a turning point, instead highlighting the need for change prior to job entry. The authors, however, do suggest that these results may be unique to the Nordic welfare state context. Here, the presence of a strong social safety net makes possible a prolonged disengagement from the labour market without an active engagement with the illegal economy. In addition, little has been done to examine whether the various vocational training programmes delivered in prison actually increase prisoners' job prospects or reduce recidivism. One report by Schafft (2004) concludes though that one of the major problems with these programmes is that clients have a complex set of problems that need to be addressed *before* they can be expected to hold a job, including addiction and lack of accommodation.

The probation service has historically played a part in helping to ease the re-entry process for newly released prisoners. Currently in Norway, however, most prisoners are released after serving their full sentence and therefore never come into contact with the probation service. Only 7% of those released from prison in 2016 met with probation at all (Kriminalomsorgen 2017; see also Falck 2015). Probation officers have been given new control functions that impact the more welfare-/social work-oriented aspects of their job. That being said, whilst many of our probation informants are concerned about resourcing and budget cuts, most consider that the control and support aspects of their role still work reasonably well together.

Conclusion: much still to be discovered about re-entry in Scandinavia

The results of re-entry work are hard to measure (Sverdrup 2013). Research highlights the importance of hope, agency, and motivation (Maruna 2001; Maruna and Ramsden 2004; LeBel et al. 2008; McMurran and Ward 2010). Hope is also emphasized by the former prisoners in contact with third-sector organizations in Norway (Aarvold and Solvang 2008). Moreover, the literature is replete with evidence that social structures such as employment, accommodation, family, and so on play a crucial role in desistance (McCulloch and McNeill 2007; Farrall 2013). In the Norwegian context, some quantitative studies examine the link between crime cessation/desistance and employment (Skardhamar and Savolainen 2014), marriage (Lyngstad and Skardhamar 2013), and family formation (Skardhamar and Lyngstad 2009). Whilst these factors are important in some cases, the majority of those who desist from crime in Norway do so for other, as yet undefined, reasons (Skardhamar and Aase 2014).

Overall then, when it comes to prison release and reintegration, paternalistic, or, perhaps more accurately, maternalistic (Smith and Ugelvik 2017b), interventions do not seem to be a big issue. Very few former prisoners come into contact with the probation service at all. Together with a lack of (government funded) research in the area, critical voices might argue that this suggests that the government prefers not to know and as a result many issues remain unaddressed in the Norwegian and wider Scandinavian literature. This lack of knowledge might seem surprising given the amount of both academic and journalistic interest in the Norwegian criminal care system, but both Norwegian-based and international researchers have focused almost exclusively on prisons. The historic emphasis on abolitionism helps explain this focus on prisons for Norwegian researchers, whilst international interest has focused on the 'exceptional' nature of Scandinavian prisons and imprisonment rates, often visiting certain 'celebrity' prisons like Halden and Bastøy. There is therefore a relative paucity of research on post-release practices and experiences and as such the release process and the work of the probation system is still very much research *terra incognita*.

Notes

1 For those not well versed in the terminology, Scandinavia refers to Norway, Sweden, and Denmark, whilst the Nordic countries are Denmark, Finland, Iceland, Norway,

and Sweden (plus their associated territories the Åland Islands, Greenland, and the Faroe Islands).

2   For an overview of BRIK and its non risk-based approach, see Tallving (2017: 15).

References

Aarvold, R. and Solvang, I. (2008) *Fra innsatt til utsatt*. Oslo: Røde Kors.

Anderson, Y. A. and Gröning, L. (2017) Rehabilitation in principle and practice: Perspectives of inmates and officers. *Bergen Journal of Criminal Law & Criminal Justice*, 4(2), 220–246.

Bourdieu, P. (2000) *Acts of Resistance: Against the New Myths of Our Time*. Cambridge: Polity Press.

Cavadino, M. and Dignan, J. (2006) *Penal Systems: A Comparative Approach*. London: Sage Publications.

Christie, N. (1993) *Kriminalitetskontroll som industri: Mot Gulag, vestlig type?* Oslo: Universitetsforlaget.

Decarpes, P. R. and Durnescu, I. (2014) Where are we in resettlement research? *EuroVista*, 3(2), 47–67.

Departementene. (2017) *Redusert tilbakefall til ny kriminalitet: Nasjonal strategi for samordnet tilbakeføring etter gjennomført straff 2017–2021*. Oslo: Justis- og beredskapsdepartementet.

Det Kongelige Justis-og Politidepartementet. (2007) *St.meld. nr. 37: Straff som virker – mindre kriminalitet – tryggere samfunn*. Oslo: Justis- og politidepartementet.

Dyb, E., et al. (2006) *Løslatt og hjemløs*. Oslo: Norsk institutt for by-og regionforskning. ISBN: 8270716243.

Engbo, H. J. (2017) Normalisation in Nordic prisons: From a prison governor's perspective. In P. S. Smith and T. Ugelvik (Eds.), *Scandinavian Penal History, Culture and Penal Practice: Embraced By the Welfare State?* London: Palgrave Macmillan.

Falck, S. (2015) *Tilbakeføringsgarantien som smuldret bort: Mellom kriminalomsorg og kommunale tjenester. Tiltaksbro, systematikk eller tilfeldighet?* Oslo: Statens institutt for rusmiddelforskning. ISBN: 8271714287.

Farrall, S. (2013) *Rethinking What Works with Offenders*. London: Routledge.

Fredriksen, I., Aarøy, T. A. and Tjeldflåt, G. M. (2017) Slår alarm om norske fengsler: – Situasjonen nærmest uhåndterlig. *Bergens Tidende*, 4 December.

Fridhov, I. (2013) Norge: Tilbakeføringsgarantien og forvaltningssamarbeid. In A. Storgaard (Ed.), *Løsladelse: Planlægning og samarbeid I Danmark, Norge og Sverige*. Aarhus: Nordisk Samarbeidsråd for kriminologi, pp. 26–33.

Friestad, C. and Hansen, I. S. (2004) *Levekår Blant Innsatte*. Oslo: FAFO.

Johnston, H. and Godfrey, B. (2013) Counterblast: The perennial problem of short prison sentences. *The Howard Journal of Criminal Justice*, 52(4), 433–437.

Karagøz, E. M. N. (2010) "Hvor lenge skal han bo på TEDD?": Forståelse av bostedsløshet – kontra retten til en varig bolig, et hjem. *Tidsskrift for psykisk helsearbeid*, 7(1), 16–25.

Kriminalomsorgen. (2017) *Kriminalomsorgens årsstatistikk – 2016*. Oslo: Kriminalomsorgen.

Kriminalomsorgen. (n.d.) *Prøveløslatelse*. [Online]. Available at: www.kriminalomsorgen. no/proeveloeslatelse.244620.no.html (Accessed 19 November 2017).

Laub, J. H. and Sampson, R. J. (2001) Understanding desistance from crime. *Crime and Justice*, 28, 1–69.

LeBel, T. P., Burnett, R., Maruna, S. and Bushway, S. (2008) The 'chicken and egg' of subjective and social factors in desistance from crime. *European Journal of Criminology*, 5, 131–159.

Ludvigsen, K., Taksdal, A. and Ravneberg, B. (2008) Respektabel hjemløshet? Kjønnede erfaringer fra samfunnets randsone. *Tidsskrift for psykisk helsearbeid*, 5(3), 237–246.

Lyngstad, T. H. and Skardhamar, T. (2013) Changes in criminal offending around the time of marriage. *Journal of Research in Crime and Delinquency*, 50(4), 608–615.

Maruna, S. (2001) *Making Good: How Ex-Convicts Reform and Rebuild Their Lives.* Washington, DC: American Psychological Association.

Maruna, S. and Ramsden, D. (2004) Living to tell the tale: Redemption narratives, shame management, and offender rehabilitation. In A. Lieblich, D. McAdams. And R. Josselson (Eds.), *Healing Plots: The Narrative Basis of Psychotherapy*. Washington, DC: American Psychological Association.

Mathiesen, T. (2012) Scandinavian exceptionalism in penal matters: Reality or wishful thinking? In T. Ugelvik and J. Dullum (Eds.), *Penal Exceptionalism? Nordic Prison Policy and Practice*. London: Routledge.

McCulloch, T. and McNeill, F. (2007) Consumer society, commodification and offender management. *Criminology & Criminal Justice*, 7(3), 223–242.

McMurran, M. and Ward, T. (2010) Treatment readiness, treatment engagement and behaviour change. *Criminal Behaviour and Mental Health*, 20(2), 75–85.

Neumann, C. B. (2011) Imprisoning the soul. In T. Ugelvik and J. Dullum (Eds.), *Penal Exceptionalism? Nordic Prison Policy and Practice*. London: Routledge.

Nilsson, A. (2003) Living conditions, social exclusion and recidivism among prison inmates. *Journal of Scandinavian Studies in Criminology and Crime Prevention*, 4(1), 57–83.

Norwegian Ministry of Justice and the Police. (2007) *Punishment that Works – Less Crime – a Safer Society*. Oslo: Norwegian Ministry of Justice and the Police.

Olesen, A. (2013) Eftergivelse af gæld vedrørende sagsomkostninger I straffesager. *Juridiske emner ved Syddansk Universitet*, 327–344.

Petersilia, J. (2004) What works in prisoner reentry-reviewing and questioning the evidence. *Federal Probation*, 68, 4–8.

Pratt, J. (2008a) Scandinavian exceptionalism in an era of penal excess: Part I: The nature and roots of Scandinavian exceptionalism. *The British Journal of Criminology*, 48(2), 119–137.

Pratt, J. (2008b) Scandinavian exceptionalism in an era of penal excess: Part II: Does Scandinavian exceptionalism have a future? *The British Journal of Criminology*, 48(3), 275–292.

Pratt, J. and Eriksson, A. (2011a) In defence of Scandinavian exceptionalism. In T. Ugelvik and J. Dullum (Eds.), *Penal Exceptionalism? Nordic Prison Policy and Practice*. Abingdon: Routledge.

Pratt, J. and Eriksson, A. (2011b) 'Mr. Larsson is walking out again': The origins and development of Scandinavian prison systems. *Australian and New Zealand Journal of Criminology*, 44(1), 7–23.

Pratt, J. and Eriksson, A. (2012) *Contrasts in Punishment: An Explanation of Anglophone Excess and Nordic Exceptionalism*. London: Routledge.

Revold, M. K. (2015) *Innsattes levekår 2014: Før, under og etter soning*. Oslo, Kongsvinger: Statistisk Sentralbyrå.

Schafft, A. (2004) *Ny start i arbeidslivet. Evaluering av et samarbeidsprosjekt mellom aetat og kriminalomsorgen*, Oslo: Arbeidsforskningsinstituttet/Work Research Institute.

Shammas, V. L. (2014) The pains of freedom: Assessing the ambiguity of Scandinavian penal exceptionalism on Norway's Prison Island. *Punishment & Society*, 16(1), 104–123.

Shammas, V. L. (2017) Prisons of labor: Social democracy and the triple transformation of the politics of punishment in Norway, 1900–2014. In P. S. Smith and T. Ugelvik (Eds.), *Scandinavian Penal History, Culture and Prison Practice: Embraced By the Welfare State?* London: Palgrave Macmillan.

Sivilombudsmannen. (2017) *Besøksrapport: Ila fengsel og forvaringsanstalt 6.-9- mars 2017*. Oslo: Sivilombudsmannen.

Skardhamar, T. (2002) *Levekår og livssituasjon blant innsatte I norske fengsler*. Oslo: Universitetet i Oslo.

Skardhamar, T. and Aase, K. N. (2014) *Desistance from Crime: How Much Can Be Explained by Life Course Transitions?* Norway: Statistics Norway.

Skardhamar, T. and Lyngstad, T. H. (2009) *Family Formation, Fatherhood and Crime: An Invitation to a Broader Perspectives on Crime and Family Transitions*. Norway: Statistics Norway. ISSN: 0809-733X.

Skardhamar, T. and Savolainen, J. (2014) Changes in criminal offending around the time of job entry: A study of employment and desistance. *Criminology*, 52(2), 263–291.

Skardhamar, T. and Telle, K. (2012) Post-release employment and recidivism in Norway. *Journal of Quantitative Criminology*, 28(4), 629–649.

Smith, P. S. (2006) The effects of solitary confinement on prison inmates: A brief history and review of the literature. *Crime and Justice*, 34(1), 441–528.

Smith, P. S. (2012) A critical look at Scandinavian exceptionalism: Welfare state theories, penal populism, and prison conditions in Denmark and Scandinavia. In T. Ugelvik and J. Dullum (Eds.), *Penal Exceptionalism? Nordic Prison Policy and Practice*. London: Routledge.

Smith, P. S. and Ugelvik, T. (2017a) Introduction: Punishment, welfare and prison history in Scandinavia. In Peter Scharff Smith and Thomas Ugelvik (Eds.), *Scandinavian Penal History, Culture and Prison Practice*. London: Palgrave Macmillan.

Smith, P. S. and Ugelvik, T. (2017b) Punishment and welfare in Scandinavia. In Peter Scharff Smith and Thomas Ugelvik (Eds.), *Scandinavian Penal History, Culture and Penal Practice: Embraced By the Welfare State?* London: Palgrave Macmillan.

Snertingdal, M. and Bakkeli, V. (2013) Tre sårbare overganger til bolig. En kunnskapsopp-summering. *FAFO Rapport*.

Sverdrup, S. (2013) *Evaluering av tilbakeføringskoordinatorene. Analyse av implementering-sprosessen*. Oslo: Diakonhjemmet Høgskole. ISBN: 8280481354.

Tallving, G. (2017) *Report: Risk and Needs Assessment Workshop 12–13 October 2017*. The Hague: The European Organisation of Prisons and Correctional Services.

Todd-Kvam, J. (2018) Bordered penal populism: When populism and Scandinavian exceptionalism meet. *Punishment & Society*. https://doi.org/10.1177/1462474518 757093

Todd-Kvam, J. (2019) An unpaid debt to society: How 'punishment debt' affects reintegration and desistance from crime in Norway. *The British Journal of Criminology*. https://doi.org/10.1093/bjc/azz024

Weaver, B. (2015) *Offending and Desistance: The Importance of Social Relations*. London: Routledge.

World Prisons Brief. (2017) *Norway*. [Online]. Available at: www.prisonstudies.org/country/norway (Accessed 8 December 2017).

Using technology and digitally enabled approaches to support desistance

Jason Morris and Hannah Graham

Introduction

This chapter provides an overview of rehabilitation and desistance-orientated uses of digital tools and approaches in prison and probation settings. Considerable attention is often given to 'what' established and emerging technologies can do in criminal justice. Yet 'how' and 'why' such technologies are used and advanced, by whom and for whom remain indispensably important. 'Digital justice' and digitally enabled supports for rehabilitation are explored here, reflecting on their potential, alongside considerations of purposes and practicalities of implementing them. Monitoring and reporting technologies can be differentiated from technologies which are more therapeutic and rehabilitation orientated in their uses; this chapter concentrates on the latter. International literature and practices are incorporated throughout; however, the chapter purposely focuses on applied examples from England and Wales.

This chapter has been co-produced from two complementary perspectives: the first author works as a psychologist involved in practice development in prison and probation service settings* in England and Wales, with expertise in developing digitally enabled tools and frameworks with different groups of people with convictions (see Morris and Knight 2018; Morris and Bans 2018; Morris et al. in press). The second author is a criminologist based in Scotland and working internationally to research rehabilitation and criminal justice work, practices and policies, and uses of technology in criminal justice (see Graham 2016; Graham and White 2015; Hucklesby et al. 2016; Graham 2018a, 2018b). Language differs across the interdisciplinary literatures and areas in which we work, and co-writing this chapter offers an occasion to reflect and grapple with some of the nuances in terms. 'Service users', 'participants', 'residents', and 'people with convictions' are used here to describe people in prison and probation services. Terms such as 'therapeutic', 'forensic', and 'offending behaviour programmes' (OBPs) regularly feature in interdisciplinary literature and practice. Where we use them, it is done with reflexive acknowledgement of their clinical origins and implicit emphasis on professional intervention, while recognizing that rehabilitation and desistance processes are simultaneously influenced by people, interpersonal and social-structural factors beyond the scope of professional practices and institutions. The ethos underpinning the main case examples featured in this chapter is that of co-production, where professionals work together with participants in egalitarian ways, in the recognition that rehabilitation and desistance can be co-produced with individuals and groups (see Weaver 2013) and digital tools and approaches, where used ethically, can support such processes. This chapter concludes by raising a few key considerations for advancing rehabilitative uses of technology in criminal justice in the future.

Digital justice and using technology in desistance-orientated work

Digital service design and efforts to digitalize existing approaches are increasingly featuring in criminal justice institutions and work, with such reforms often referred to under the remit of 'digital justice'. Increased interconnection or integration between services and systems usually features in digital justice agendas. Van de Steene and Knight (2017: 256) contend that 'the inevitability of digital transformation is set to shape the way justice is done and experienced'.

Among criminal justice practitioners and service users, increasing digitalization can induce different responses (for discussions relating to probation work, see Phillips 2017, and rehabilitation and resettlement, see Champion and Edgar 2013). For some, the prospect of technology increasingly featuring in how a justice system is run has a longstanding relationship with the notion of dystopia, with surveillance, dehumanized and distant practices set in Orwellian visions of the future (see Nellis 2018; McNeill 2018). For others, increasing uses of technology and digitalization may evoke the notion of retrotopia (Bauman 2017), a retrospective nostalgic yearning for (perceivably) less complicated and more human, benevolent rehabilitative practices past. It is helpful to temper ideas about digital innovation in criminal justice with the recognition that such innovation is not morally or politically neutral – just because something is new does not necessarily mean it is ethical or effective (Graham and White 2016; Graham 2017).

A growing number of technologies and digital approaches are being used in criminal justice systems internationally. In prison and probation service contexts, particularly in Europe, Australasia, and North America, examples include: electronic monitoring technologies (e.g. tags); apps for mobiles and other digital devices; kiosks; in-cell technologies; animation, digital story-telling, digital toolkits, and information communication technologies; virtual reality; Skype and video conferencing; gaming; artificial intelligence and machine learning; social media, websites, and online portals. A positive example is the award-winning 'Changing Lives' mobile phone app, developed by the Probation Board for Northern Ireland. This free app includes a contacts and diary function for appointments, a journal section where text and emojis can be used (and later discussed in conversation with a probation officer, if the individual wants to), detailed information about probation supervision and the victim information scheme, and addictions and mental health information and referral options (McGreevy 2017).

These technologies and digital approaches may be designed and used for diverse purposes and goals in criminal justice, which can span personal, professional, systemic, and public or societal domains. Are digital justice agendas within prisons, probation, and community corrections services clearly oriented towards goals of supporting rehabilitation and desistance? They can be, but are not necessarily or intrinsically so. Technology can be used proportionately and responsively, or punitively and disproportionately in criminal justice, underscoring the need to discern purposes and goals of use. According to Graham (2018a, 2018b), purposes and goals for using technology in criminal justice include:

- Punishment: retribution, restriction of liberty and/or privacy
- Decarceration and diversion: reducing the use of custody by using technology as/within a community sanction or measure
- Surveillance and monitoring
- Motivating compliance
- Crime control and reducing reoffending
- Risk management, victim protection, community safety, and public protection
- Digital innovation and staff 'intrapreneurship' in their work

- Responsivity and personalization to the individual and their circumstances, respecting a person's agency and self-efficacy
- Supporting (or being less harmful to and inhibitive of) desistance, recovery, and re/integration processes
- Involving service user voices and expertise in co-production of digital approaches and tools, peer relationships, and input
- Instrumental and systemic purposes: trying to reduce time, money, workload, and resource inefficiencies; information sharing and communication; digitizing or digitally enabling traditional interventions or services; efforts to overcome inertia in large risk-averse organizations and public services

(Graham 2018a, 2018b)

Uses are influenced by context, cultures, and implementation, raising a variety of questions – how and why are digital justice 'transformations' and activities being pursued? What else is happening concurrently to this? To what extent should 'digital rehabilitation' (Reisdorf and Rikard 2018) be a focus for prisons, parole and resettlement support services, within or alongside other forms of rehabilitation (see McNeill 2012; Burke et al. 2018)? Nellis (2006, 2018) has called for those involved in advancing uses of digital technology to make a 'conscious educative effort' to ensure this does not reinforce punitive values in such processes.

Desistance-orientated uses of technology in criminal justice

While the type and range of available technologies to meet the needs of people with convictions continues to grow internationally, empirical evidence about their effectiveness is nascent but modest. Some research has evaluated uses of technology for rehabilitative purposes from the perspectives of 'e-health' and the forensic psy-disciplines. Kip et al. (2018) conducted a systematic review of 50 studies of e-health services delivered to people with convictions who (for the most part) experienced mental health difficulties or substance misuse. The technologies featured in these studies were diverse, including: communication technologies (e.g. video conferencing), interactive language-based digital interventions (e.g. online courses accessible through various devices), virtual reality and visual simulation of offence-related realistic situations, gaming, user-generated platforms, and social media. Many of these studies featured psychosocial approaches commonly used in rehabilitative work in criminal justice, including psycho-education, cognitive behavioural therapy, motivational interviewing, mindfulness, relapse prevention, violence reduction, and approaches focused on developing recovery capital, social capital, positive change and self-efficacy, including self-help and peer support approaches.

Kip and colleagues (2018) identified that digital approaches falling into the 'Interactive, Predominantly Language-Based Interventions' category are often based on existing evidence-informed rehabilitative approaches. Like offending behaviour programmes (OBPs), these digital services aim to change offence-related thinking and/or behaviour, using psycho-educational presentations, assignments, or exercises. More than one modality tends to be used in this type of approach, for example, written text, videos, and audio. One example of this approach is the Breaking Free Online health and justice digital interventions (see Elison et al. 2016; Elison-Davies et al. 2018).

Kip and colleagues' (2018) systematic review identified strengths and advantages, as well as disadvantages and complexities of these digitally enabled tools and approaches, taking into account the perspectives of service users, professionals, and service providers. In some (but not all) cases, the advantages of using these technologies included:

- Increasing access and engagement
- Personalization and responsivity to individuals
- Positive opinions of service users (e.g. finding it helpful, or fun to use)
- Enhancing rapport and relationships with professional staff
- Helping in eliciting or communicating sensitive information
- Receiving care in highly secure settings
- Consistency and standardization of service delivery
- Reductions in time and costs of interventions

It is noteworthy that parallels exist between the 'active ingredients' of e-health approaches (as identified by Kip et al. 2018) and the literature on desistance-orientated approaches, which are often strengths-based in nature (e.g. McNeill 2012). These approaches are designed to be educative and responsive to participant learning preferences (Andrews and Bonta 2003) and tend to emphasize the importance of participants forming meaningful relationships with practitioners (see Ross et al. 2008), having positive peer relationships, and developing useful skills that enable them to lead a better life (Looman and Abracen 2013).

Notwithstanding, in the review by Kip and colleagues (2018), as well as in discussions raised by Yardley and colleagues (2016), Ross (2018), and Graham (2018b), a series of coherent themes emerge which show the potential disadvantages and challenges of using technology with people with convictions, even where these uses seek to be rehabilitative. These themes are synthesized and summarized here, with the caveat that this is an illustrative, not exhaustive list. Firstly, it is widely acknowledged that the empirical evidence of effectiveness is limited or still emerging for some technologies and for uses in certain contexts or with certain groups in criminal justice. Secondly, a point well made by Ross (2018) is to note that a large proportion of what is known about existing technologies such as mobile apps for people with convictions comes from a health perspective, and important differences may be apparent in how they are applied by authorities and used by participants in statutory or mandated services in criminal justice. Furthermore, several practical challenges of using technology and digital approaches persist, including issues like battery life, lack of or slow/lost connection or signal, faulty technology and safeguarding against misuses/unintended uses of technology. Where technologies can increasingly be integrated in their use in criminal justice (e.g. apps, devices, and tags), privacy and data protection considerations remain paramount. Also, Hollis and colleagues (2018) highlight the need to do further research on the safety and efficacy of digital technology interventions compared to face-to-face interventions.

Co-producing digital content to promote desistance

The second part of this chapter explores an applied case example of a recent innovation, Complementary Digital Media (CDM). It is one of a range of digitally enabled approaches being used in England and Wales, where Her Majesty's Prison and Probation Service (HMPPS) Digital Studio leads the development of an ecosystem of interconnected technologies which operate in accordance with the Government Digital Service (GDS) design principles, first and foremost of which is the principle of 'user needs, not government needs' (see Bracken 2015).

Complementary Digital Media (CDM) is a technology-based approach that harnesses the stories and voices of people with convictions and lived experiences of criminal justice within engaging media clips to enhance desistance-orientated services (see Morris and Knight 2018). CDM combines pictures, audio, text, and meaningful stories which service providers can use in coaching and supporting participants to help them develop skills and make positive choices in processes of desistance from crime.

Practitioners are encouraged to use CDM clips interactively (e.g. by pausing, rewinding, and replaying clips) during sessions. The clips explicitly complement existing OBP session learning outcomes by prompting participants to discuss the personal relevance of these messages during one-to-one or group discussions. Structured therapeutic discussions that CDM clips instigate are intended to lead into further exercises, skills practices, and coaching to help participants to integrate skills into their day-to-day lives. CDM focuses on explaining and building *skills* (e.g. for managing thoughts, emotions, and behaviours), reflecting a key therapeutic ingredient of OBPs emphasized by Clarke et al. (2004).

Yardley and colleagues (2016) and Hodge and colleagues (2015) emphasize the iterative nature of co-producing digital content and approaches, where service design and provision is intentionally user-centred. Morris and Knight (2018) describe the CDM co-production process where people from a prospective target group in prison or probation services are recruited to a Service

User Reference Group (SURG) that meets regularly to develop therapeutic digital content, in collaboration with and facilitated by staff. SURG volunteers draw on their lived experiences of issues likely to be experienced by the target group. Morris and Knight (2018) describe how members of one peer support group (self-titled: 'The Innovators') co-produced CDM to assist their peers in managing challenges of prison life that can lead to violence. This involved co-creating scenarios for CDM clips and providing voiceovers in a style that was relatable for their peers who would access the service. For example, the Innovators co-produced one CDM clip that modelled different styles of self-talk used by a character to self-manage his aggressive thinking about his medication being confiscated.

Service user reference groups create a forum in which they can explore the nature of situations where they are likely to encounter challenges in desistance processes, incorporating discussions of risks that are relevant to specific cohorts or groups. To date, CDM projects have co-developed digital content focused on self-management and violence reduction in prisons, intimate partner violence (IPV), and group-affiliated offending.

Morris et al. (in press) describe the co-production process undertaken with men with intimate partner violence (IPV) or domestic abuse convictions. This project yielded two series of CDM clips: one for men with male partners and one for men with female partners. Each series (or variant) of clips was based around the experiences of a central character, who – across the course of the series – adopts skills to self-manage a range of challenges associated with his IPV risk. For each variant, volunteers co-created semi-autobiographical scripts and delivered voiceovers to produce clips (usually around three minutes in length). The SURG process enabled us to tap into lived experiences that have largely been neglected in offending behaviour programmes. This led to the development of digital content such as the 'Change, Accept, Let Go' clip where the central character uses a self-talk skill to resolve rumination linked to his behaviour of checking his ex-partner's social media posts.

As illustrated in the focus group extract below, initial indications are that SURG participants can become highly invested in the SURG process and find it to be rewarding (described in Morris and Knight 2018; Morris et al. in press).

Facilitator:	'What is the best way to put content across to people on probation?'
Participant 1:	'Make it real life'.
Participant 2:	' . . . with these [clips], the images and the words flashing up. It gets your appeal straight away. That's why I've taken so much interest in this . . . you can hear it in his voice when he is talking about a scenario, you can hear that this is real. . . . It's coming from a real person, with real experience'.

Facilitator:	'It sounds like the visuals and having the words incorporated into. . .'.
Participant 2:	'Seeing the pictorial cartoon characters did a lot more for me than seeing real people . . . and the fact of having the voiceovers you can hear the story, you can hear the true voices. It's coming from someone who has actually done it'.
Participant 1:	'It is coming from someone who has either actually done it, or been through it themselves. It is real life. It's not like *EastEnders* or *Coronation Street*. It's not written for you. What we are both saying is coming from our head, our heart and our voice, so it is real, it is true . . . it's the realness'.

Implementing digitally enabled desistance-orientated approaches

Ross (2018) argues that a key benefit of explicitly therapeutic digital services in criminal justice is that they have the potential to provide a cost-effective means to extend periods of service engagement and provide service to participants who may be out of the scope of mainstream OBPs. Whilst Complementary Digital Media was originally conceived as a method to complement conventional OBP sessions, it soon became apparent that the discrete micro-learning experiences created by CDM can also lend themselves to more flexible delivery models for people who may be unsuitable for conventional OBPs. For example, the two variants of digital content about intimate partner violence highlighted in this chapter are now being piloted in a variety of delivery contexts in England and Wales: within OBP sessions, as a short programme, and as a toolkit delivered flexibly by Offender Managers during one-to-one supervision sessions.

Another example of CDM in England and Wales is the 'Timewise Channel' (see Morris and Bans 2018), which provides a useful prototype to exemplify a flexible digital toolkit approach. This service is available to all residents at a 'digital prison' and exists as a series of clips in a digital content store (developed by the HMPPS Digital Studio) accessed via in-cell computers. Launched in February 2017, the Timewise Channel has been iterated in conjunction with The Innovators (who also peer-supported Timewise participants, with the coordination of the prison's psychology department). In the 12-month period between 1 September 2017 and 31 August 2018, they assisted 163 participants to complete a comprehensive workbook that evidenced participant goals, understanding and use of skills depicted on the Timewise Channel. One of the Innovators (a SURG volunteer) produced an article for the prison newspaper, which describes this digital service as follows:

Why is Timewise so popular?

Because of two things: Simplicity and Flexibility

Timewise is a simplified OBP that breaks down all psychological jargon in simple, user friendly terms. While Timewise is a simplified OBP, it is not accredited and it does not replace any other programme.

Timewise is so flexible that users can do it anytime by watching the 20+ video clips on their laptop and answering the booklet. There is no time limit to complete the booklet. It is a self-directed programme, that means no assessment, no group sessions and no individual interviews. Anyone can do Timewise any time.

If it is not accredited, then why bother?

Well, Timewise surely is designed to help develop new strengths and skills to do our time wisely, but most of all, when our time for Cat D progression comes up, if the question 'what have you done off your own back?' is asked, we can say 'I have done Timewise'.

Source: *Berwyn Times* (June 2018)

As well as having the capacity to host CDM, a range of devices (e.g. interactive televisions, in-room computers, and tablet-based software solutions) also have the technical potential to change the way that therapeutic services like Timewise are coordinated and delivered by enabling remote communication between prison residents and practitioners. In the case of the Timewise Channel, the 'Unilink' system (evaluated by McDougall et al. 2017) has a messaging feature that enables the psychology staff to provide specific instructions to peer mentors about who they should support, how, and when. This has significantly increased the capability of the prison to integrate Timewise as a fluid component of an overarching care framework.

Following its original inception, the CDM content comprising the Timewise Channel was subsequently re-purposed as the 'Timewise Toolkit' (and deployed via DVD players, laptops, or paper storyboards) at 14 further pilot sites in England and Wales. Preliminary reactions of staff and participants to the Timewise Toolkit provide promising indications that it shares some of the active ingredients of desistance-orientated approaches described earlier. A key strength according to practitioners is its potential to let them tailor their approach to the needs and preferences of participants, in keeping with the responsivity principle of rehabilitation (see Andrews and Bonta 2010):

> [T]he use of animation clips is supportive and I like the flexibility of the Timewise conversations and how they can be tailored to individual's needs.

> [I]t is tailor made/one to one and the onus is on [the] candidate to complete the work . . . the process gives more ownership to the individual.

The Timewise Toolkit has facilitated meaningful engagement opportunities for people in some of the most restrictive personal circumstances in criminal justice. For example, one participant with complex needs at a high-security prison used his engagement with Timewise as part of a successful (albeit temporary) attempt to progress from the segregation unit: 'I was really believing – appreciating, and understanding the course. I was gradually feeling much better about myself, and I was beginning to feel really hopeful'. Participant feedback indicates that Timewise appears to have helped them form more meaningful relationships with practitioners and other staff: 'by the end of the Timewise toolkit he was regularly engaging in discussions with staff on his unit as well evidencing good communication skills with his key worker'. Timewise can also provide a context in which peer supporters can develop important working alliances with residents who are in crisis:

> When I go into the cell and there is someone there who is ringing wet and they've caused chaos. It works. It 100% works. Some of them will say 'hang on, you're a screw boy'. I'll say 'whoa, don't ever call me that, I'm here to try and help you'. And once you break that ice, it really does work. Peer led work is the way forward [Timewise Peer Supporter].

With regard to implementation, Timewise Toolkit pilot sites have encountered some difficulties embedding this new digitally enabled one-to-one service within existing violence reduction efforts. While staff with OBP facilitation experience have successfully engaged highly challenging participants, pressure on resources has restricted wider rollout to staff who do not have OBP experience. This has prevented the Timewise Toolkit being delivered at scale when compared to the Timewise Channel available at a digital prison. While this underlines the potential of digital platforms to create reach for digitally enabled courses, questions remain around the extent to which this reach creates workload pressures for supporters and may compromise quality of learning experiences.

One challenge for digitally enabled desistance-orientated approaches is navigating the tension that exists between the reach and the quality of delivery of these new services. This challenge can be met through the expedient use of existing expertise and infrastructure. CDM delivered as part of a blended learning approach within high volume OBPs, accredited by the Correctional Services Advisory & Accreditation Panel (CSAAP), offers some assurance that it will be used as intended. The same Complementary Digital Media can also then be used as an auxiliary 'wrap around' service that involves front-line staff and peer supporters in the process of extending the engagement period for OBPs, with pre- and post-OBP support outside of the group that both prepares participants to learn and supports skills generalization in the day-to-day lives of participants.

Emerging horizons

More technologically sophisticated and inventive digital approaches are emerging and being trialled in some forensic settings, and we wish to briefly acknowledge them here. The level of immersion and automaticity provided by new e-health technologies and applications represent two important dimensions in advancing reach and effectiveness in supporting recovery, change, and desistance processes. For example, Van Rijn et al. (2017) describe an avatar-based therapy system that uses simulated environments to enable participants to develop insight into interpersonal dynamics, take perspective, and practice pro-social skills. Services like this have the potential to offer qualitatively distinct, immersive experiences that can either be self-directed, guided by in-person support, or guided via two-way telephony with a trained supporter in a remote location. There is also the potential to integrate with artificially intelligent therapeutic approaches to help service users reframe negative thinking and track mood states, which can be raised, if they want to, in conversation with staff. Economic, ethical, safeguarding, and regulatory issues remain, and these will temper whether more innovative uses of technology are 'the right thing to do'. First, key questions need to be addressed around the purposes of their use, and how such services map onto existing care and management frameworks in criminal justice service settings.

Conclusion

The empirical literature and reflective practice summarized within this chapter indicate the value in championing digital services that: explicitly draw on desistance theories, research, and principles; focus on the development of participants' strengths, knowledge, and skills; and are co-produced, placing service users as close to the centre of their design and implementation as possible. Extending rehabilitative and therapeutic service engagement beyond the scope of mainstream OBPs is an opportunity for using digitally enabled tools and services. Such services can be tailored to different criminogenic needs, delivered flexibly within routine contacts between practitioners and services users, and accessed by service users outside of face-to-face contacts.

Digitally enabled content accessed via approved digital platforms has the potential to change the way change-orientated interventions and desistance-orientated conversations take place in criminal justice services. The complex blend of flexibility and fidelity of delivery offered by some digital services means they can be delivered consistently across a range of settings. Platforms offered by providers (such as Core Systems, Breaking Free Online,

Virtual Campus/Meganexus, and Socrates Software) have the potential to ensure the dependable continuity required for providing through-the-gate services for people leaving prison and re/integrating within communities, where they can continue to use the same digital tools and approaches.

Some digitally enabled desistance-orientated approaches have evolved directly out of traditional OBP frameworks. Digital services, such as Breaking Free Online and Complementary Digital Media toolkits, are aligned to existing commissioning and sentencing approaches and, as such, fit with existing prisons and probation service structures in England and Wales. While more sophisticated digital approaches are on the horizon (see Kip et al. 2018), simple digital services offer the potential to create immediate reach across a range of platforms and, importantly, capitalize on the existing expertise of current practitioners.

Designing digitally enabled services with service users – ensuring that their voices are at the heart of designing digital content – represents an important advancement on existing OBP content, which has typically been professionally led. Co-producing innovative digital tools and approaches has the potential to give service users more of 'a voice' and a role in ensuring that digital services meet the needs of their peers and, importantly, do no harm (Morris and Knight 2018). Their involvement matters if new uses of technology are to be innovative and ethical:

> Innovation is a multi-faceted topic that has the capacity to be researched and celebrated in inclusive and emancipatory ways, making the knowledge base more epistemologically open and co-produced by hearing voices, experiences and expertise that may not have been included or valued as much in the past.
>
> (Graham 2017: 206)

We believe that some rehabilitative uses of technology can add capacity within desistance-orientated approaches, for mainstream and for marginalized groups in criminal justice. Opportunities exist to use readily accessible platforms to extend the reach of existing rehabilitative approaches and content, while building in and bearing witness to the voices and lived experiences of service users. It may help in processes of delivering through-the-gate services using digital tools that work across prison and probation service settings to support rehabilitation and desistance processes (Champion and Edgar 2013; HMIP 2017). In essence, this chapter emphasizes the importance of purposes, ethics, and the 'how' and 'why' behind 'what' technology can do, while keeping a firm eye on the real-world challenges that exist in technologically innovating in this area.

Note

*   This chapter comprises the authors' views on technologies in criminal justice and digitally enabled services supporting desistance. It is not intended to set out Her

Majesty's Prison and Probation Service (HMPPS) policy on digital justice and criminal justice. We acknowledge and thank HMPPS for giving permission for examples from practice in England and Wales to be included in this chapter.

References

Andrews, D. and Bonta, J. (2003) *The Psychology of Criminal Conduct*, 3rd edition. Cincinnati, OH: Anderson Publishing Co.

Andrews, D. and Bonta, J. (2010) *The Psychology of Criminal Conduct*, 5th edition. New Providence, NJ: Matthew Bender & Company, Inc., LexisNexis Group.

Bauman, Z (2017) *Retrotopia*. Cambridge: Polity Press.

Berwyn Times (2018) June Edition. Wrexham.

Bracken, M. (2015) *Mapping New Ideas for the Digital Justice System*. Available at: https://gds.blog.gov.uk/2015/08/18/mapping-new-ideas-for-the-digital-justice-system-2/ (Accessed 20 November 2018).

Burke, L., Collett, S. and McNeill, F. (2018) *Reimagining Rehabilitation: Beyond the Individual*. London: Routledge.

Champion, E. and Edgar, K. (2013) *Through the Gateway: How Computers Can Transform Rehabilitation*. London: The Prison Reform Trust.

Clarke, A., Simmonds, R. and Wydall, S. (2004) *Delivering Cognitive Skills Programmes in Prison: A Qualitative Study* (Home Office Online Report 27/04). London: Home Office.

Elison-Davies, S., Davies, G., Ward, J., Dugdale, S. and Weekes, J. (2018) The role of technology in offender rehabilitation. *Advancing Corrections*, 5, 107–119.

Elison, S., Weston, S., Dugdale, S., Ward, J. and Davies, G. (2016) A qualitative exploration of UK prisoners' experiences of substance misuse and mental health difficulties, and the Breaking Free Health and Justice interventions. *Journal of Drug Issues*, 46(3), 198–215.

Graham, H. (2016) *Rehabilitation Work: Supporting Desistance and Recovery*. London: Routledge.

Graham, H. (2017) Innovation and criminal justice: Editorial introduction to the special issue on 'innovation. December 2017'. *European Journal of Probation*, 9(3), 203–209. http://journals.sagepub.com/doi/full/10.1177/2066220317747058.

Graham, H. (2018a) Apps, tags, tracks: Ten questions about uses of technology in probation. *Confederation of European Probation (CEP) Website*. Available at: www.cep-probation.org/apps-tags-tracks-ten-questions-about-uses-of-technology-in-probation/ (Accessed 19 November 2018).

Graham, H. (2018b) *Using Technology in Probation: Reflections on the Evidence and Questions for Probation Work*. Presentation at the Confederation of European Probation (CEP) Technology in Probation Expert Group, Helsinki, 3–4 September.

Graham, H. and White, R. (2015) *Innovative Justice*. London: Routledge.

Hodge, P., Davis, J., Maiden, N., Mann, B., Nidsjo, A., Simpson, A., et al. (2015) StreetWise: A valid ecology for a serious game in a secure forensic mental health setting. *Procedia Computer Science*, 63, 252–259.

HM Inspectorate of Prisons & Probation (HMIP). (2017) *An Inspection of Through the Gate Resettlement Services for Prisoners Serving 12 Months or More A Joint Inspection by HM Inspectorate of Probation and HM Inspectorate of Prisons*. London: Her Majesty's Inspectorate of Prisons.

Hollis, C., Sampson, S., Simons, L., Davies, E. B., Churchill, R., Betton, V., Butler, D., Chapman, K., Easton, K., Gronlund, T. A., Kabir, T., Rawsthorne, M., Rye, E. and Tomlin, A. (2018) Identifying research priorities for digital technology in mental health care: Results of the James Lind alliance priority setting partnership. *Lancet Psychiatry*, 5(10), 845–854.

Hucklesby, A., Beyens, K., Boone, M., Dünkel, F., McIvor, G. and Graham, H. (2016) *Creativity and Effectiveness in the Use of Electronic Monitoring: A Case Study of Five Jurisdictions*. Leeds: University of Leeds and Criminal Justice Programme of the European Commission.

Kip, H., Bouman, Y., Kelders, S. and van Gemert-Pijnen, L. (2018) eHealth in treatment of offenders in forensic mental health: A review of the current state. *Frontiers in Psychiatry*, 9(42), 1–19.

Looman, J. and Abracen, J. (2013) The Risk-Need-Responsivity model of offender rehabilitation: Is there really a need for a paradigm shift? *International Journal of Behavior and Consultation Therapy*, 8(3), 30–36.

McDougall, C., Pearson, D., Torgerson, D. and Garcia-Reyes, M. (2017) The effect of digital technology on prisoner behavior and reoffending: A natural stepped wedge design. *Journal of Experimental Criminology*. DOI:10.1007/s11292-017-9303-5.

McGreevy, G. (2017) 'Changing lives': Using technology to promote desistance. *Probation Journal*, 64(3), 276–281.

McNeill, F. (2012) Four forms of 'offender' rehabilitation: Towards an interdisciplinary perspective. *Legal and Criminological Psychology*, 17(1), 18–36.

McNeill, F. (2018) *Pervasive Punishment: Making Sense of Mass Supervision*. Bingley: Emerald Publishing.

Morris, J. and Bans, M. K. (2018) Developing digitally enabled interventions for prison and probation settings: A review. *Journal of Forensic Practice*, 20(2), 134–140.

Morris, J., Gibbs, C., Jonah, O., Bloomfield, S. et al. (in press). Developing content to promote desistance in men who have used violence against a male intimate partner.

Morris, J. and Knight, V. (2018) Co-producing digitally-enabled courses that promote desistance in prison and probation setting. *Journal of Criminological Research, Policy and Practice*, 4(4), 269–279.

Nellis, M. (2006) Future punishment in American science fiction films. In Mason P. (Ed.), *Captured by the Media: Prison Discourse and Popular Culture*. Cullompton: Willan.

Nellis, M. (2018) Clean and dirty electronic monitoring. *Justice Trends* (3), 14–18.

Phillips, J. (2017) Probation practice in the information age. *Probation Journal*, 64(3), 209–225.

Reisdorf, B. and Rikard, R. (2018) Digital rehabilitation: A model of reentry into the digital age. *American Behavioral Scientist*. [Advance Access Online].

Ross, E. C., Polaschek, D. L. L. and Ward, T. (2008) The therapeutic alliance: A theoretical revision for offender rehabilitation. *Aggression and Violent Behavior*, 13, 462–480.

Ross, S. (2018) Policy, practice and regulatory issues in mobile technology treatment for forensic clients. *European Journal of Probation*, 10(1), 44–58.

Van De Steene, S. and Knight, V. (2017) Digital transformation for prisons: Developing a needs-based strategy. *Probation Journal*, 64(3), 256–268.

Van Rijn, B., Cooper, M., Jackson, A. and Wild, C. (2017) Avatar-based therapy within prison settings: Pilot evaluation. *British Journal of Guidance & Counselling*, 45(3), 268–283.

Weaver, B. (2013) Co-producing desistance: Who works to support desistance? In I. Durnescu and F. McNeill (Eds.), *Understanding Penal Practice*. London: Routledge.

Yardley, L., Spring, B. J., Riper, H., Morrison, L. G., Crane, D., Curtis, K. E., Merchant, G., Fulton, E. A. and Blandford, A. (2016) Understanding and promoting effective engagement with digital behavior change interventions. *American Journal of Preventive Medicine*, 51(5), 833–842.

Prisons, personal development, and austerity

17

Alison Liebling

Introduction

What we know about the effects of imprisonment and what goes on in prison is rapidly growing. The gap between what we know and 'what goes on', however, is increasing, perhaps especially in England and Wales. There is a relationship between the material resources of prisons and their moral quality, in the sense that low resource prisons tend to squeeze out order, humanity, and personal development. Staff in low resource prisons either share power with prisoners, in ways that can be dangerous, or they withdraw from the task of intervening in life on the landings, which results in chaos and violence. Cheap prisons are not a good policy option.

Rehabilitation work is essentially a *moral* enterprise, and we now know quite a lot collectively about what supports or undermines it. There are good reasons to trust the principle that 'values grow virtues'. This principle is not restricted either in its derivation or applicability to prisons but is central in our understanding of them. It has been evidenced in many different research projects. 'Growing values in prison', or establishing a normative order, requires a minimum level of prison officer presence and professional training, as well as a high standard of professional expertise among prison governors.

The key problem is that the prison has been found to be, on balance, criminogenic (Nagin et al. 2009) or negative in its effects. Policymakers tend to avoid this inescapable fact, and critical penal scholars resist moving beyond it. In my view, it is important, whatever our overall attitude towards imprisonment, to understand the differences between prisons and penal systems that damage, and prisons or penal systems that support or repair.

My original interest in prisons arose as a result of my engagement as a Research Assistant on a Home Office-funded project on young offender through-care in the 1980s. This project was intended to explore the experience of young people in prison and, in particular, to investigate joint working between the prison and probation services and the extent to which initiatives intended to support rehabilitation in prison were followed through on release into the community (McAllister et al. 1992). Despite the obvious sense this policy makes, and the shift in language from the then familiar concept of aftercare to the more integrated term 'through-care', the overriding impression I developed of prison life was of separation and cultural antagonism between the prison and probation services, of the sadness and tragedy of many young offenders' lives, and of the often damaging effects of custody on them (Liebling 1989). I ended up specializing in the study of suicides and suicide attempts in prison and have devoted many years of my professional life to this topic (e.g. Liebling 1992, 1999). This trajectory is important because it helpfully connects several sets of related questions:

- What makes a prison survivable?
- What explains the difference between hopelessness and hope in prison?
- How do human beings flourish and develop in prison? What facilitates this? What gets in the way?
- Under what circumstances is it possible for prisons to heal and repair rather than damage?
- What kinds of programmes, courses, regimes, and activities support this process?

These questions should be set in the context of a larger question:

- How do prisons uphold rather than undermine social order?

That aspiration is a tall order for a dense and complex institution that is inherently depriving, politically constrained, and full of power. Where we see models of good practice with desirable outcomes, we learn not just about how prisons function but how order, authority, and human flourishing work in communities in general. This is important territory.

Yvonne Jewkes recently completed a three-year study on prison architecture, design, and technology and the lived experience of imprisonment (see www.prisonspaces.com). Inspired by Maggie's Centres for the treatment of terminally ill cancer patients, she argues, following Wener, that the design of a prison is critically related to the philosophy of the institution, or maybe even of the entire criminal justice system. It is the physical manifestation of a society's goals and approaches for dealing with . . . convicted men and women, and it is a stage for acting out plans and programs for addressing their future.

(Wener 2012: 7)

As Jewkes writes, the first Maggie's Centre opened in Edinburgh in 1986, and was designed by a cancer sufferer, Maggie Jencks. It was grounded in a belief that joy could be found even in the process of dying, and that the physical and emotional well-being of both sufferers and their families could be strengthened in an uplifting and supportive environment. The work that goes on in these centres starts with the principle that they should be warm, welcoming, stimulating, and intriguing places that encourage social interaction and a sense of community (see Jewkes and Moran 2017; Jewkes 2018). There are now 18 of these centres, with more being built, and a rapidly developing evidence base about their impact. They show how clear aims and a determined ethos can come to life physically, creating a kind of 'holding frame' for living and working.

Applying this model to prisons, Jewkes's concept of the *architecture of hope* is hugely relevant to prison life, work, and experience. The politics and financing of 'hope-filled' prisons is less straightforward. Some of the questions she asks in her study include, what is the level of humanity and hope a prison architect can incorporate into a prison? Is good design necessarily more expensive than bad design? Can architecture and design help to deliver rehabilitation, or in the end, are buildings 'trumped' by other aspects of prison life?

I have found myself inspired by some of the new designs, and the thinking that goes into them, but I also have two caveats. The first is that design *can* be a framework, when it is thought about in that way, but it is not everything – some of the best prisons I have studied over time happen to be in rather bad, old, and inefficient buildings. This tells us that there is more to prison life than design, and that outstanding practices can go on in poorly designed prisons (and vice versa). Prisoners often tell us that relationships with staff both *vary* more, and are more *important*, in their day-to-day experience, than material conditions. Secondly, we are tending to see larger and cheaper buildings appear on the international landscape in practice, even in traditionally imaginative, non-punitive, and liberal countries, like Norway and the Netherlands, because of the appeal of economies of scale. As I noted at the outset, there are relationships between the material and the moral, but these links are complex. Buildings and day-to-day resources, like staffing levels, matter. But so does the ethos or purpose of the prison. This chapter, then, focuses mainly on the relational side of prison life and the way in which a recent decline in prison staffing levels and experience has undermined some of the 'relational and moral glue' that has made some prisons 'work'.

The moral qualities of prisons and of prison staff

Drawing mainly on work carried out at the Cambridge Prisons Research Centre, we have learned a great deal over many years about how prisons function, differences between them, and the relationship between the 'moral qualities' of prisons and outcomes. I will highlight some of the more important lessons learned, briefly, below.

First, 'what matters' most to prisoners and, as it happens, to staff, is the moral climate: interpersonal relationships and treatment. An important characteristic of a good moral climate is the way it finely balances 'security' with 'harmony', or clarity and organization, and the policing of boundaries and behaviour, with care and opportunities for personal development. It is a climate in which authority flows but has *moral meaning*. This understanding of prison life tells us that prison officers are critical in the overall accomplishment of rehabilitative regimes. The work of prison staff at its best, 'jailcraft', models the *good use of authority* (see e.g. Liebling, Price et al. 2011; Crewe et al. 2014).

Prison officers matter far more than they realize. They constitute 80% of the costs of running a prison, but they also make up 80% of the quality, as experienced by prisoners. They are not 'turnkeys' but 'gatekeepers' – to goods, services, opportunities, and other people, and they are 'peacekeepers': figures with both *moral* and *instrumental* power. Their most important skills are 'talk' and 'presence', of a certain kind.

Prisoners, and other officers, know exactly who the best prison officers are in an establishment. They are sometimes 'hidden' from senior managers on the quieter wings. They take many forms and have different styles. But they share certain qualities. They are neither lax nor overly rule bound. They use their discretion well: that is, *for* rather than *against* legitimacy.

Outstanding officers think what they are doing is common sense but it is not. When outstanding officers take the temperature down, reduce tension, avert a potential conflict, or persuade an angry prisoner to go to work and resolve his or her problem the quiet way, they are using the same kind of refined, experience-laden skills that outstanding footballers use when they score goals. Neither are especially good at describing their highly skilled practices in words. The outstanding outcome for a prison officer, however, is that nothing happens. The day ends peacefully. At the end of a successful day, a lot of very hard work has had to go in to repairing challenges to order, reducing tensions, and soothing frustrations: making the regime 'flow smoothly', sometimes against the odds (Liebling et al. 1999). This best kind of work is largely invisible and is precisely what gets overlooked in most accounts of their work. Prison officers doing this kind of work well are *accomplishers* rather than keepers of the peace – or of order – in prison. They don't just 'keep' it, they 'create' it. Much 'very hard, barely visible work', goes into ending each day peacefully. The way in which this kind of work is carried out is an important piece of the overall jigsaw in a prison that is more rather than less rehabilitative.

In the best prison climates, prison officers are 'moral dualists': that is, they are neither exclusively 'security' nor 'harmony' oriented. Most *people* are one or the other – conservative or liberal, self-protecting or egalitarian. To be both is unusual and uncomfortable. The best officers manage the tensions between conflicting priorities and values: suicide or escapes, security or order, risk or trust, safety or liberty, rehabilitation or discipline. Prisoners, like good prison officers, are moral dualists. What they want, and need, if they are to grow in new directions, is stability, clarity, protection and support, decent treatment, *and* freedoms and opportunities (Liebling and Arnold 2004).

As I argued in *Prisons and Their Moral Performance*, 'What matters to those who live and work . . . in prison is a set of concepts that are all about relationships, fairness, and order, and the quality of their respective treatment by those above them' (Liebling and Arnold 2004: 458). The nature and quality of this interpersonal environment can impact either negatively or positively on prisoners. Prisoners often describe dismissive encounters with prison officers, some arguing that these experiences of disrespect and denial of recognition 'seem minor' but can 'turn you into a different person'.

Measuring and modelling moral quality

This argument is supported empirically. The Cambridge Prisons Research Centre team have spent long periods of time talking with staff and prisoners about what matters to them most, using the methodology 'appreciative inquiry'. Appreciative inquiry starts with questions like, 'tell me about the best day you have ever had as a prison officer', or for prisoners, 'tell me something about yourself or your life that you are most proud of', and 'about the best encounter you have had with a prison officer', 'when you have felt most human, in here'. With their help, we turned these creative conversations into a set of 'dimensions that matter', and then into a quality-of-life survey. We call this approach 'ethnography-led measurement' (Liebling 2015a). Each dimension is defined and operationalized using a set of key items or statements which together measure the moral climate of a prison.

We have found that prisoners develop in ways that lead to longer-term change, and better outcomes, where staff professionalism, humanity, help and assistance, and clarity and organization are higher (see Figure 17.1). Figure 17.1 is an empirical or research-based figure based on extensive research in seven prisons (some of which were private). The outcome of a good moral climate, which is humane, helpful, and well-policed, is higher levels of personal development among prisoners. Personal development is defined as the experience of being in 'an environment that helps prisoners with offending behaviour, preparation for release and the development of their potential'.

The 'big five' dimensions of prison quality contributing to personal development[1]

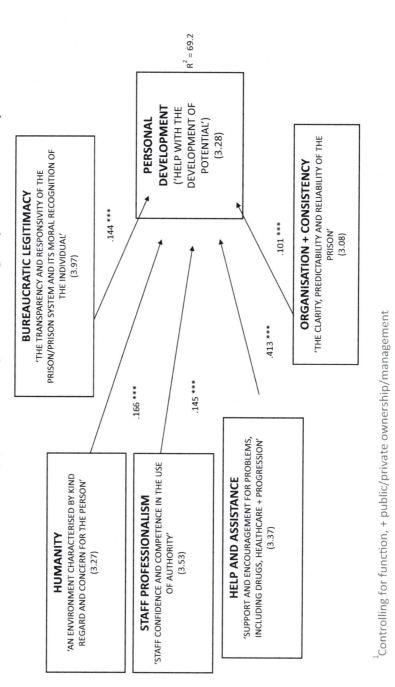

BUREAUCRATIC LEGITIMACY
'THE TRANSPARENCY AND RESPONSIVITY OF THE PRISON/PRISON SYSTEM AND ITS MORAL RECOGNITION OF THE INDIVIDUAL'
(3.97)

.144 ***

PERSONAL DEVELOPMENT
('HELP WITH THE DEVELOPMENT OF POTENTIAL')
(3.28)

R^2 = 69.2

ORGANISATION + CONSISTENCY
'THE CLARITY, PREDICTABILITY AND RELIABILITY OF THE PRISON'
(3.08)

.101 ***

HUMANITY
'AN ENVIRONMENT CHARACTERISED BY KIND REGARD AND CONCERN FOR THE PERSON'
(3.27)

.166 ***

STAFF PROFESSIONALISM
'STAFF CONFIDENCE AND COMPETENCE IN THE USE OF AUTHORITY'
(3.53)

.145 ***

HELP AND ASSISTANCE
'SUPPORT AND ENCOURAGEMENT FOR PROBLEMS, INCLUDING DRUGS, HEALTHCARE + PROGRESSION'
(3.37)

.413 ***

[1] Controlling for function, + public/private ownership/management

Figure 17.1 The 'big five' dimensions of prison quality contributing to personal development

Personal development consists of 'generative' or 'capability' items, to do with growth and development, as well as offending behaviour work.

Only once a prison has accomplished respect, humanity, safety, good staff-prisoner relationships, professionalism, and organization and clarity, does it become a place in which personal development – or engagement with the self – can take place. This is quite rare, and only takes place in the very best prisons. Where it happens, well-being is also higher. A prison has to be good at the basic custodial task of achieving order, providing help and assistance, and using authority professionally, before it becomes a place in which prisoners can grow and develop.

The key message is that 'the whole' prison environment can at best provide, let's say, the right kind of 'containment'. Just as in childhood, autonomy and personal development are an outcome of safety, trust, reliability, and 'holding' without coercion: of being in a facilitating environment. This is not 'freedom', laxity, or anarchy, but neither is it tyranny or repression. It is a finely balanced synthesis of power with fairness and humanity.

Good order – which has a very specific meaning here incorporating humanity and care as well as clarity and organization – is good for our well-being, our mood, and our personal development or capacity to flourish. As Frank Porporino argued:

> [P]ositive emotions broaden one's awareness and encourage novel, varied and exploratory thoughts and actions (which build skills over time). Negative emotions, on the other hand, mostly prompt narrow survival-oriented behaviours. When we go out of our way to make offenders miserable, both they and we suffer the consequences.
>
> (Porporino 2010: 80)

As Geoff Mulgan, a political theorist, put it:

> [O]rder and safety are essential not just for life to carry on but also for people to live well. The available data suggest that political stability and order, the rule of law and justice, are decisive to happiness. . . . It is hard to overestimate the value of strong, stable, protective and legitimate governance to human well-being.
>
> (Mulgan 2007: 45)

One of the questions I began this chapter with was what explains the difference between hopelessness and hope, in prison? Hope requires trust in others, confidence in our environment, and a sense of real possibilities for the future. It is precarious in prison, and depends on having a supportive, approachable staff group who treat prisoners with respect, as well as offering meaningful activities. We found our way to this model via the study of suicides in prison, which showed a clear relationship between distress (which is linked to institutional suicide rates) and poor moral climates, or more positively stated, between good order and well-being (Liebling and Tait 2005). We found strong relationships between feelings of safety, experienced as a kind of trust in the environment, and well-being. Safety is created out of relationships, care for the vulnerable, good and consistent drug control, family contact, and engagement in offending behaviour and personal development programmes. A survivable prison, in other words, is a prison which feels safe, well organized, and interpersonally decent.

Knowing that our moral climate measures are linked to better internal outcomes, we started to work more directly on the complex question of whether improvements to moral climates in prison are linked to outcomes on release using larger datasets. We have found two promising trends. First, we see a relationship between higher scores on the key dimensions of a prison's moral quality and lower than expected reconviction outcomes (Auty and Liebling 2019). In more legitimate social environments, characterized by orderliness and normative engagement, safety and some freedom to make choices, the possibility of avoiding drugs and the consequences of a drugs trade, it is possible for prisoners to develop their potential.

When we control for all the relevant variables that might explain these variations, we still see a core group of dimensions emerge from the analysis. These dimensions are related to safety, autonomy, and decency. As we learned in the suicide studies, safety is grown out of interpersonal interactions: approachable and responsive staff. This is a highly plausible, specific, and subtle combination of dimensions supporting our developing understanding of the need for discipline (a framework), right and supportive relationships between staff and prisoners, and some autonomy in the process of rehabilitation or desistance.

The second trend is that in our analysis, the impact of programmes only showed up when these programmes were delivered in a better moral climate. In other words, prison climate, specifically understood, acts as a *moderator variable*. What happens *between* people matters a great deal in relation to what happens *within* them, as Fergus McNeill has argued. There is a fit between these empirical findings and theories of social and political life more broadly which suggest that 'the virtues' encourage a kind of 'moral literacy' (Sacks 2000; Sandel 1996). An underlying model linking fairness, safety, and hope is beginning to emerge from our various analyses over time.

Building trust and supporting change

In this section, I want to add to this developing model, briefly, by outlining a recent empirical study of the location and building of trust in high-security prisons (see Liebling et al. 2015). We carried out this research in light of some worrying observations about the decline of trust and the quality of staff-prisoner relationships in prison life as sentences lengthen, population demographics change, and staff feel less 'at home' with an increasingly diverse prisoner population (Liebling, Arnold et al. 2011).

We found the highest moral climate scores in therapeutic or 'enabling' environments, which are psychologically supported and planned, and values-driven, and in which staff receive additional training and support in understanding and managing challenging behaviour. Among these kinds of units are PIPES, or Psychologically Informed and Planned Environments, in which prisoners are viewed as 'emergent' or 'on a journey', and in need of both practical and interpersonal support on that journey. We rarely see almost wholly positive moral climates, but these wings, or occasionally whole prisons, have the highest scores on 'moral climate' measures that we have seen (see, for example, Liebling et al. 2019).

Conversely, we found that in the poorer prisons, feelings of outrage and indignation were generated by the rejection of deeply felt claims to respect and recognition, to lower levels of humanity and fairness, and to the lack of any possibility of progression or development. So, in an attempt to consider life in high-security prisons, for example, we found that high levels of 'political charge', or anger and alienation among prisoners, were being generated by an *I-It* (a narrowed or reduced) rather than an *I-Thou* approach to prisoners (Buber 1937; Liebling 2015b): where a real meeting or encounter takes place between whole, unique persons. In *I-It* encounters, those belonging to 'suspect groups' – gang members, those who converted to Islam, minority groups, and those regarded as dangerous or high risk – are regarded as 'experienced objects' rather than 'experiencing subjects'. This orientation is essentially cynical.

As I suggested in the introduction, one way of synthesizing these findings is to propose, as moral philosophers have for many hundreds of years, that *values grow virtues*, and that relationships and good order are required for our capacity to flourish. Axel Honneth argues that human flourishing is dependent on the existence of well-established, 'ethical relations' – in particular, relations of love, law, and the 'ethical life' (Honneth 1995). Drawing on his argument, we have found that 'the conditions for self-realisation' turn out to be dependent on the establishment of 'relationships of recognition' (Honneth 1995: 172–174). This is the deepest form of respect, and requires the ascription of some positive status, and the combining of harmony or care with security, power, or rules. In this kind of climate (positive) identity formation is possible.

Rehabilitation, emergence, and austerity

Social theorist Christian Smith, amongst others, has also argued that human persons have depth and complexity, are irreducibly socially constituted, and are emergent (see also, e.g., Sandel 2009). They 'exist in a state of dynamic tension between power and limits, action and reflection, capacity and finitude' (Smith 2010: 197). Smith used the idea of 'emergent personhood' to argue that our relationship to ourself (our *identity*) is not a matter of a solitary ego appraising itself, but is an intersubjective process, in which one's attitude towards oneself emerges in encounters with another's attitude toward oneself.

These ideas make good sense of our empirical findings and of the maxim that 'staff-prisoner relationships' matter most in prison. We claim that higher quality prison environments are 'enabling' of emergent personhood, or that in these prisons staff are oriented towards prisoners in a distinctive way. Smith argues that realizing our personhood is an innate drive: we have emergent properties, such as emotional experience, language use, and imagination. To realize these properties, we require relationships with others, as well as structures of social relations. If our core purpose, as he argues, is 'pursuing and realising our personhood' (ibid.), then we will use any available means to do this. If one avenue is blocked, we will find another. Some prison environments offer these opportunities (are 'generative') and others do not. Human capacities can all be negatively or positively charged, so those that are responsible for many of the best aspects of being human (like self-awareness) also underlie our most serious deficiencies and problems. The capacity for self-reflection, for example, can become either a capacity for moral reflection or for egotism.

We emerge and develop as persons both proactively and reactively. When we are proactive, we are the agents of our own growth; *responsive* emergence is caused by other agents, in which case we are the objects of this process. This process of 'being the object' of others' doing never works so well.

Smith's question is, what would a form of social order look like that fosters human growth or emergence? What opportunities exist that build up personhood? He is not talking about prisons, but this is an important insight that resonates with our findings, and with phenomenological accounts given by prisoners of their experience. Some combination of *I-Thou* encounters, which approach whole people as they are (as people and not, for example, as a prisoner, a terrorist, or 'a danger') as an experiencing subject, not an experienced object, and a sense of the importance of emergent personhood, seems to characterize prison environments that enable rather than frustrate and damage.

The problem, then, for contemporary prisons is how to make them 'relational' when the financial template on which they have been remodelled is skeletal and 'task driven'. The aspiration to keep the same staff on a wing in order to get to know their prisoners has been replaced by a 'more efficient' model of pooling larger numbers of staff, in order to deploy them where they are most 'needed', to deliver the bare bones of a regime. Prisoners and staff are adamant that this model cannot work. Everything that outstanding staff are good at (the skilled use of discretion, the use of talk, persuasion, and encouragement, the reading of a prisoner's mood and circumstances, the prediction and handling of danger) is rooted in knowledge. Relationships provide information and insight. Power is deployed most legitimately and effectively through relationships. The recent cuts to prison budgets, whilst retaining high levels of imprisonment, have contributed to some very damaging developments in prison life and quality, including in particular drastic reductions in staffing levels, experience, and longevity in the job. Even highly skilled staff have found it increasingly difficult to use their skills, as getting though the day has become an urgent priority. The model of order has shifted from 'present' to 'absent', making it exceptionally difficult for staff to deploy their authority, or for officers to become 'professionals' (Crewe and Liebling 2017). These changes to the cost and quality of prison life have, however indirectly, been facilitated by the introduction of private sector competition. Public prisons increasingly resemble lean private sector prisons. There is, at least at the time of writing, a kind of physical, emotional, and moral exhaustion among staff in the least well-resourced prisons which produces the opposite of hope (Solnit 2016). The price being paid by both staff and prisoners is high. Promises of a return to more manageable staffing levels are yet to be realized.

Conclusion

The philosopher Bernard Williams said that the 'first political question' for any society is 'how that society can establish and maintain "order, protection, safety, trust, and the conditions of cooperation"' (Williams 2005; Bottoms and Tankebe 2017). In other words, 'how can I live safely, and what is the price of giving you power, so that I can do so?' This question – of finding the right balance between safety and discipline, on the one hand, and personal autonomy and growth on the other – lies at the heart of the question, what is the difference between 'enabling' and 'disabling' environments? Fairness and professionalism bind safety, autonomy, and growth together. This question is relevant to us all, but it can be explored with particular acuteness in the prison. 'Disabling environments' undo human capacities and make the world a more dangerous place. 'Enabling environments' facilitate the fullest expression of human personhood. There is a material price at the heart of this question too: a cost threshold can be crossed below which prisons become simply ungovernable and therefore disabling to all.

There are some promising developments taking place in prisons, including the (educational) use of technology, the reframing of disciplinary practices using restorative justice, and the development of psychologically informed environments (which receive additional resources and training from National Health Service sources). Many of the most inspirational 'enabling' practices in criminal justice are developing outside of prisons, using arts, music, peer mentoring, families, and the building of 'cultural capital' to encourage young people away from drugs, gangs, and knife crime. There are untapped resources inside and outside prisons keen to contribute to the larger task of building our collective human potential. Our knowledge base is increasing. But there are also new risks – of using technology to depersonalize prisons, of reducing costs below a minimum threshold, of expansion, of degrading the role of the prison officer, reducing staffing levels below a safe minimum, and of narrow thinking about the processes of change. Prison officers should be professionally developed and should form an important part of the rehabilitative effort.

There are things we know with increasing confidence about what does *not* work in prison rehabilitation. Stigmatization and labelling don't work; policies and practices that construct people as damaged, diminished or deficient and in need of 'expert' correctional intervention diminish agency. 'Doing to' rather than 'doing with' creates resistance. Punitive or deterrence-based regimes generate hostility and negative affective states. Misplaced faith in managerialism as a mechanism for prison reform can have counterproductive effects; a preoccupation with risk and information-gathering, or 'closed questions' (alone) distracts from our curiosity about what might work with this person, in this situation. Chaos, laxity, or radical liberalism don't work: prisoners need order and organization if they are to learn self-control. As one prisoner recently put it, 'if the wing is chaotic, I am chaotic'. Too much 'corrections technology' is counterproductive: commodification and commercialization, or 'turning people into units to be efficiently processed in pursuit of profit or fashion' (McNeill 2017) brings risks. Ideologically driven, hasty, and 'evidence-lite' policy and practice often (perhaps increasingly) takes us in the wrong direction.

There are many things we know about 'what can work'. Legitimate sentencing (Liebling 2014) has to be part of the process. If prisoners cannot accept the basic premise of their sentence, or its length, they will reject attempts to engage them productively during it. Getting the moral climate right is critical. The key ingredients here are humanity, staff professionalism; clarity and organization; help and assistance; and bureaucratic legitimacy. Staff professionalism means confidence and competence in the use of authority. Staff should be provided with the intellectual and moral as well as financial resources to do the job well (Liebling, Crew et al. 2011; Liebling, Arnold et al. 2011; Liebling 2014). Education is fundamental, and there are many promising initiatives, including Inside Out, Learning Together, and Philosophy for Prisoners courses, which inspire and support prisoners with very promising outcomes (see e.g. Armstrong and Ludlow 2016; Szifris 2017). There is increasing empirical support for, as well as theoretical understanding of, mentoring and peer support programmes. We know that contact with families and formal or practical resettlement initiatives are valuable. Facilitating 'diachronic self-control', or the capacity to self-limit or develop one's own moral agency, is an important part of the desistance pathway (Shapland and Bottoms 2017). Yoga, meditation, and mindfulness are found to improve several relevant outcomes (Auty et al. 2017). In general, a strengths-based, 'good lives', 'recovery', or 'enabling' model (Ward and Maruna 2007) seems to provide the best kind of framework for rehabilitative efforts.

Above all, seeing and working with the prisoner as an 'emergent person' seems to be transformational. We see this *I-Thou* or emergent personhood phenomenon in many of the processes and activities I have referred to above – in philosophy classes in which prisoners discuss stoicism, justice, what is society, what are our moral foundations, and what are their implications for our own lives and behaviour? These kinds of mutual explorations, grounded in a certain vision of personhood, are transformative because they work with the naturally emergent nature of the self. We should make the prison a minor, and therefore properly affordable, but morally intelligible and 'enabling' part of the rehabilitation effort.

References

Armstrong, R. and Ludlow, A. (2016) Educational partnerships between universities and prisons: How learning together can be individually, socially and institutionally transformative. *Prison Service Journal*, 225, 9–17.

Auty, K., Cope, A. and Liebling, A. (2017) A systematic review and meta-analysis of yoga and mindfulness meditation in prison. Effects on psychological well-being and behavioural functioning. *International Journal of Offender Therapy and Comparative Criminology*, 61(6), 689–710.

Auty, K. M. and Liebling, A. (2019) Exploring the relationship between prison social climate and reoffending. *Justice Quarterly*, 1–24. DOI:10.1080/07418825.2018.1538421.

Bottoms, A. E. and Tankebe, J. (2017) Police legitimacy and the authority of the state. In A. du Bois-Pedain, M. Ulväng and P. Asp (Eds.), *Criminal Law and the Authority of the State*. Oxford: Hart Publishing.

Buber, M. (1937) *I and Thou*. New York: T & T Clark.

Crewe, B. and Liebling, A. (2017) Reconfiguring penal power. In A. Liebling, S. Maruna and L. McArra (Eds.), *The Oxford Handbook of Criminology*. Oxford: Oxford University Press, pp. 889–913.

Crewe, B., Liebling, A. and Hulley, S. (2014) Staff-prisoner relationships, staff professionalism and the use of authority in public and private sector prisons. *Law and Social Inquiry*, 40(2), 305–344.

Honneth, A. (1995) *The Struggle for Recognition: The Moral Grammar of Social Conflicts*. Cambridge, MA: The MIT Press.

Jewkes, Y. (2018) Just design: Healthy prisons and the architecture of hope. *Australian and New Zealand Journal of Criminology*, 44(1), 94–115.

Jewkes, Y. and Moran, D. (2017) Prison architecture and design: Perspectives from criminology and carceral geography. In A. Liebling, S. Maruna and L. McCara (Eds.), *The Oxford Handbook of Criminology*, 6th edition. Oxford: Oxford University Press.

Liebling, A. (1989) Temporary release: Getting embroiled with prisons. *Howard Journal of Criminal Justice*, 28(1), 51–55.

Liebling, A. (1992) *Suicides in Prison*. London: Routledge, p. 273.

Liebling, A. (1999) Prison suicide and prisoner coping. In M. Tonry and J. Petersilia (Eds.), *Crime and Justice: An Annual Review of Research*, Vol. 26. Chicago: The University of Chicago Press, pp. 283–359.

Liebling, A. (2014) Moral and philosophical problems of long-term imprisonment. *Studies in Christian Ethics*, 27(3), 258–269.

Liebling, A. (2015a) Appreciative inquiry, generative theory, and the 'failed state' prison. In J. Miller and W. Palacios (Eds). *Advances in Criminological Theory*. New Jersey: Routledge Publishers, pp. 251–270.

Liebling, A. (2015b) Description at the edge? *I-It/I-Thou* relations and action in prisons research. *International Journal for Crime, Justice and Social Democracy*, 4(1), 18–32.

Liebling, A., Armstrong, R., Williams, R. J. and Bramwell, R. (2015) *Locating Trust in a Climate of Fear: Religion, Moral Status, Prisoner Leadership, and Risk in Maximum Security Prisons – Key Findings from an Innovative Study*. Prisons Research Centre, Institute of Criminology: University of Cambridge. Available at: www.prc.crim.cam.ac.uk/publications/trust-report.

Liebling, A. and Arnold, H. (2004) *Prisons and Their Moral Performance: A Study of Values, Quality and Prison Life*. Oxford: Clarendon Studies in Criminology, Oxford University Press, p. 588.

Liebling, A., Arnold, H. and Straub, C. (2011) *An Exploration of Staff-Prisoner Relationships at HMP Whitemoor: Twelve Years On*. London: National Offender Management Service.

Liebling, A., Crewe, B. and Hulley, S. (2011) Staff culture, the use of authority, and prisoner outcomes in public and private prisons. *Australia and New Zealand Journal of Criminology*, 44(1), 94–115.

Liebling, A., Elliot, C. and Price, D. (1999) Appreciative inquiry and relationships in prison. *Punishment & Society: The International Journal of Penology*, 1(1), 71–98.

Liebling, A., Laws, B., Lieber, E., Auty, K., Schmidt, B.E., Crewe, B., Gardom, J., Kant, D. and Morey, M. (2019) Are hope and possibility achievable in prison? *The Howard Journal of Crime and Justice*, 58(1), 104–126.

Liebling, A., Price, D. and Shefer, G. (2011) *The Prison Officer*, 2nd edition. Cullompton, Devon: Willan Publishing, p. 256.

Liebling, A. and Tait, S. (2005) Revisiting prison suicide: The role of fairness and distress. In A. Liebling and S. Maruna (Eds.), *The Effects of Imprisonment*. Cullompton, Devon: Willan Publishing.

McAllister, D., Bottomley, K. and Liebling, A. (1992) *From Custody to Community: Throughcare for Young Offenders*. Aldershot: Avebury.

McNeill, F. (2017) *Supervisible: Experiences of Criminal Justice in Scotland*. London: The Howard League for Penal Reform. Available at: http://howardleague.org/publications/supervisible-experiences-of-criminal-justice-supervision-in-scotland/.

Mulgan, G. (2007) *Good and Bad Power: The Ideals and Betrayals of Government*. London: Allen Lane.

Nagin, D. S., Cullen, F. T. and Jonson, C. L. (2009) Imprisonment and reoffending. In M. Tonry (Ed.), *Crime and Justice: An Annual Review of Research*, Vol. 38. Chicago: Chicago University Press, pp. 115–200.

Porporino, F. (2010) Bringing sense and sensitivity to corrections: From programmes to "fix" offenders to services to support desistance. In J. Brayford, F. Cowe and J. Deering (Eds.), *What Else Works? Creative Work with Offenders*. Cullompton: Willan Publishing.

Sacks, J. (2000) *The Politics of Hope*. New York: Vintage (Rand).

Sandel, M. (1996) *Democracy's Discontent: America in Search of a Public Philosophy*. Cambridge, MA: Belknap Press.

Sandel, M. (2009) *Justice: What's the Right Thing to Do?* London: Penguin Group.

Shapland, J. and Bottoms, A. (2017) Desistance from crime and implications for offender rehabilitation. In A. Liebling, L. McAra and S. Maruna (Eds.), *The Oxford Handbook of Criminology*, 6th edition. Oxford: Oxford University Press.

Smith, C. (2010) *What Is a Person? Rethinking Humanity, Social Life, and the Moral Good from the Person Up*. Chicago: University of Chicago Press.

Solnit, R. (2016) *Hope in the Dark*. Edinburgh: Canongate Books.

Szifris, K. (2017) Socrates and Aristotle: The role of ancient philosophers in the self-understanding of desisting offenders. *Howard League for Penal Reform Journal*, 56(4), 419–436.

Ward, T. and Maruna, S. (2007) *Rehabilitation: Beyond the Risk Paradigm*. New York: Routledge.

Wener, R. (2012) *The Environmental Psychology of Prisons & Jails: Creating Humane Spaces in Secure Settings*. Cambridge: Cambridge University Press.

Williams, B. (2005) *In the Beginning Was the Deed: Realism and Moralism in Political Argument*. Princeton, NJ: Princeton University Press.

Section 3

Assessment practice

Section 3 Introduction

This third section of the Companion engages with the crucial practice of assessment. Evidently the success of any rehabilitative effort is likely to be significantly undermined by a faulty or partial view either of the causes of offending, or of the issues that are central to the processes of desistance and reintegration. To relapse into decidedly old-fashioned language, which, as we noted in Section 1, is highly problematic in this context; appropriate 'treatment' rarely stems from faulty 'diagnosis'. Even setting aside the flaws of a medical or therapeutic model of rehabilitation, the principle holds good.

It is telling that four of the five chapters in this section engage – even if critically – with risk assessment. As the discussion of the policy and organizational contexts in the last section revealed, risk has become a dominant logic within criminal justice and, especially, we would suggest, in the fields of prisons, probation, and parole. Indeed, the logic and discourse of risk has become so dominant that it sounds almost odd to discuss 'assessment' with the prefix 'risk' (see Trotter et al. 2016). Yet, the chapters in this section suggest three key conclusions about the importance of disentangling 'risk' and 'assessment'.

Firstly, the concept of risk itself is complex and contested and can mean many things to and for different people. It can refer both to the probability of an adverse event (as in risk of reoffending) and/or to the severity an event's consequences (as in risk of harm). It can also refer to different subjects or targets of risk; the risk of self-harm, or the risk to specific individuals in a particular relationship with the risk-bearer (like children or partners), or the risk to the general public, for example. In criminal justice contexts, 'riskiness' is often treated as an attribute of individuals who come to be seen as the bearers of risk; but it might also be seen as an attribute of environments and situations; or of the interaction between individual characteristics, environments, and situations. These vagaries suggest the need, discussed in these chapters, for clarity and precision in processes and outcomes of risk assessment.

Secondly, these chapters make clear that risk assessment is not sufficient to the challenge of assessment for rehabilitation more generally. It is also crucial to understand people's environments and contexts, their hopes, aspirations, and strengths, and their social needs – including material needs likely generated by structural inequalities. Absent this kind of social contextualization of offending behaviour, risk assessment can easily refract and intensify pre-existing social inequalities associated, for example, with gender, ethnicity, and poverty. And it will lead to rehabilitative practices which, even if well-intentioned, are also likely to exacerbate social inequalities.

If this second set of observations hints at the links between assessment, rehabilitation, and social in/justice (on which see Burke et al. 2018), then the last of the five chapters in this section (by Niamh Maguire) also reminds us crucially that the assessment for rehabilitation takes place within the context of criminal *justice*. In the practical challenge of providing assessments and (sometimes) sentencing recommendations for courts, probation officers and/ or social workers find themselves at a very complex and challenging intersection between the pursuit of individual and social welfare and the demands of justice; often including retributive justice. Ultimately, probation and social work assessments at the sentencing stage exist to bridge between these two forms of discourse and sets of issues. But that bridge might be more like a pontoon that floats between two marshy and murky islands, neither of which has well-defined edges, and neither of which seems solid enough on which to stand.

In these challenging circumstances, the best we can do here is to clarify the challenges and to chart the complexity as far as we are able – and we think our contributors have done an excellent job in these respects.

References

Burke, L., Collett, S. and McNeill, F. (2018) *Reimagining Rehabilitation: Beyond the Individual.* London: Routledge.

Trotter, C., McIvor, G. and McNeill, F. (Eds.). (2016) *Beyond the Risk Paradigm in Criminal Justice.* Basingstoke: Palgrave Macmillan.

18

Risk and need assessment

Development, critics, and a realist approach

Peter Raynor

Introduction: background and context

One of the most important, widespread, and continuing developments of the last 20 years in offender management has been the adoption in many jurisdictions of standardized instruments for risk assessment, and for risk and need or risk-need assessment. This chapter traces these developments and some of the controversies that have arisen as a result. It ends by proposing a realistic approach to what risk-need assessment can and cannot do, and by recognizing the importance and influence of the policy context in which it is located.

The attempt to predict who was likely to offend and to identify special characteristics of potential offenders goes back much further than the recent past, and many writers point to the work of Cesare Lombroso (Lombroso 1876) as an early version of risk assessment. Lombroso believed that it was possible to identify characteristics of imperfect or degenerated human beings which pointed to a constitutional inferiority; this then made them more likely to resort to a criminal lifestyle, or to commit violent crimes. He identified physical defects which are in fact largely irrelevant to criminal behaviour and are more often consequences of poverty or disease or random variation. However, such ideas have been remarkably persistent and were still current, for example, in Spanish prisons during the 1960s: during his imprisonment in Spain the Scottish anarchist Stuart Christie was referred to a prison 'anthropometry' department and was found, to the delight of the anthropometrists, to have no ear lobes, which was one of Lombroso's supposed indicators of atavistic criminality (Christie 2004).

More recently social theorists such as Ulrich Beck and David Garland have argued that a concern about risk is pervasive in modern societies as social and technological change have undermined traditional sources of security and a sense of belonging. Beck argues that 'risks, as opposed to older dangers, are consequences which relate to the threatening force of modernisation and to its globalisation of doubt' (Beck 1992: 21). Criminologists have also commented on this: the late Jock Young wrote about the 'vertigo of late modernity' (2007), others point to ontological insecurity and lack of trust in traditional sources of authority, and Garland describes how a sense of threat helps to produce a punitive 'culture of control' (2001). Criminologists, then, should not be surprised at the emergence of new risk-related concerns and practices in criminal justice (Kemshall 2003). In many jurisdictions we have seen the emergence in criminal justice of a general concern about risk, the progressive modification of sentencing practice to reflect perceptions of risk, and the development of complex evidence-based risk assessment techniques which increasingly shape and even dominate the practice of criminal justice agencies.

Because of the central role played in many countries by the Probation Service (or equivalent 'offender management' services) in the assessment of offenders, both prior to sentence and after imprisonment through the provision of risk assessments in relation to the discretionary release of prisoners, this chapter particularly reflects the risk-related practice of probation officers and is particularly concerned with developments since the 1990s. By then, criminologists on both sides of the Atlantic were commenting on the impact of risk-related practices on criminal justice: Feeley and Simon (1992, 1994) in the US produced their theory of 'actuarial justice', in which they saw measures of coercive control being applied to whole sections of society on the basis of perceived or measured risk, with little regard for traditional notions of justice or even guilt. What mattered was belonging to a risky group rather than having actually been convicted of offences. In Britain, Kemshall was beginning to work on a series of studies of the management of dangerous people by the criminal justice system (Kemshall 1998), in which the probation officer was beginning to take over the risk assessment role formerly occupied by the psychiatrist or the psychologist.

At this early stage two major problems were already evident. The first was that in most jurisdictions probation officers had no reliable methods available for assessing risk, beyond their own individual and subjective judgement. The second was that they were really being asked, under the heading of 'risk', to address two rather different problems. One was the risk of reoffending presented by the ordinary recidivist offender, responsible for his or her share of the high volume property crimes (mainly thefts and burglaries) which make up most of the crime figures. The other was what is often described as 'risk of harm' or 'dangerousness', which relates to those offenders (far fewer in number) who may commit serious violent or sexual offences resulting in major personal trauma or even death. These are relatively rare events but cause severe harm and are the focus of much public anxiety, and also of public anger at the criminal justice authorities if they are committed by people who are under supervision or have recently been released from prison. However, in the early 1990s most probation officers lacked evidence-based methods for approaching either of these problems.

Three generations of risk assessment

The Canadian criminologist and psychologist James Bonta, who has been a leading figure in the international development of risk assessment methods for criminal justice, has described 'three generations' of risk assessment (Bonta and Wormith 2007). The 'first generation' is individual professional judgement, which tends to be subjective, non-standardized, and unreliable in predicting reoffending: some individual professionals will obtain good results from using this approach to risk assessment, but others will not, and overall it is the least reliable approach. The 'second generation' refers to actuarial instruments developed by identifying correlates of reconviction in large samples of offenders' criminal records, usually using statistical techniques of logistic regression to generate lists of weighted risk factors which can be used to estimate the probability of reoffending (or, more accurately, reconviction) for individual offenders. Typically these will produce a probability score indicating the percentage risk of reconviction in a specific follow-up period such as two years. Such methods have the practical advantage that they can use criminal history data stored in central databases and do not require personal contact with the offender, so that risk assessments can be carried out quickly using computer programmes. They can also achieve useful levels of reliability (around 70% correct prediction of reconviction is regarded as a fairly good performance in this field: see, for example, Raynor et al. 2000). A good example of a second-generation instrument is the Offender Group Reconviction Scale developed by the Home Office in London and widely used to assign offenders to risk categories in England and Wales (Home Office 1996). However, because second-generation instruments are based only on 'static' risk factors (such as sex, age, and previous criminal history) that cannot be changed by intervention, they do not point to social and personal circumstances which can be changed through effective offender management or supervision in order to reduce the risk. They also fail to take into account other changes which can make a substantial difference to the prospect of reconviction, such as the start of a stable relationship with a non-criminal partner, the acquisition of a rewarding job, or the arrival of children.

These disadvantages led to the development of 'third generation' risk assessment methods, also known as 'risk-need' assessments, which use a range of information about the offender, including personal interviews, to identify social or personal needs which are known from research to be associated with a higher risk of offending. These are usually 'dynamic' risk factors, meaning that they can in principle be modified (examples are educational achievement, employment status, attitudes, and beliefs). These dynamic factors, also known as 'criminogenic needs', are combined with static factors to produce overall risk scores, but in addition they can point to targets for change: in other words, to rehabilitative intervention which can lower the risk of reconviction by reducing dynamic risk factors. Several such instruments are now in use in various countries, including the LSI-R (Level of Service Inventory-Revised) developed by Bonta with Don Andrews in Canada (Andrews and Bonta 1995). A 'fourth generation' has recently emerged with various enhancements, including specific case management guidance based on the risk and need assessment (for example, the LS/CMI [Andrews et al. 2004] currently in use in Scotland and elsewhere), but this has yet to impact on practice to the same extent as the widely used third-generation instruments. The use of these instruments and the data they provide about the relationship between risk factors and recidivism has also produced significant contributions to risk factor research: for example, Bonta and Andrews (2017) identify the 'big four' risk factors which consistently emerge from research (namely criminal history, pro-criminal attitudes, pro-criminal associates, and antisocial personality pattern) and another four which carry significant but lesser weight (family or marital problems, unsatisfactory involvement in school or work, substance abuse, and absence of pro-social leisure or recreational activity). Together these make up the 'central eight'. There is also clear evidence that changes in assessed risk-need levels during supervision are associated with reductions in reconviction (see, for example, Raynor 2007).

In Britain, different jurisdictions have taken different routes towards comprehensive risk-need assessment. Scotland uses LS-CMI; so do some neighbouring jurisdictions such as Jersey in the Channel islands and the Republic of Ireland. England and Wales, after a brief experiment with LSI-R and a locally developed instrument ACE (Raynor et al. 2000), went on to develop an unusually elaborate and comprehensive instrument known as OASys (the Offender Assessment System), but also continued to use OGRS (the Offender Group Reconviction Scale), which is a second-generation instrument providing no needs assessment. Both OGRS and several derivatives of OASys are currently in use as well as the full OASys itself.

Critics of risk-need

The widespread adoption of these methods has also led to a number of criticisms. A long-standing theme in sentencing theory has been proportionality, i.e. the sentence should reflect the seriousness of the crime, but sentencing is also concerned with the prevention of future crimes, leading to concern that people may be sentenced more severely because they are believed likely to offend in the future. Many scholars have argued that this can lead to injustice and to disproportionate sentencing (for example Von Hirsch 1976; Hood 1974), and in sentencing systems which are prone to drift in this direction, risk assessments and risk-need assessments can provide an evidence base for more coercive sentencing. Although there is evidence that risk-need methods can contribute to reductions in custodial sentencing (for example Raynor and Miles 2007; van Wingerden and Moerings 2014), its increasing use has clearly coincided with growth in custodial sentencing in other penal systems, including large ones such as England and Wales.

Other critics have argued that risk assessment techniques derived from research on white male offenders could have limitations when uncritically applied to minority ethnic groups or to women (Shaw and Hannah-Moffatt 2000; Hudson 2002). One study pointed to possible over-prediction of risk among minority ethnic groups (Hudson and Bramhall 2005), and there were also concerns that if sentencers took likely future offending into account, this could result in more severe sentencing for women who committed minor offences. Certainly the rate of imprisonment of women increased steadily in England and Wales as risk assessment came into general use, but there were also other pressures towards more punitive sentencing, and it is not clear how far risk assessment methods might have contributed to this trend. There is some evidence of possible overestimation of risk for women offenders from at least one jurisdiction outside England and Wales (Raynor 2007), and evidence that although the relationship between risk factors and offending is *broadly* similar for men and women (Andrews et al. 2012) there are also important differences in motivation, opportunity, onset, and desistance (Gelsthorpe et al. 2007). As the forensic psychologist Caroline Logan pointed out at a recent international workshop: 'Women are not funny-shaped men' (Logan 2017). However, all these criticisms, although seen as arguments against risk assessment, could equally be seen as arguments for more thoroughly researched and better implemented risk-need assessment, as advocated by some of the key developers of the risk-need approach (Andrews et al. 2006). Critics of risk factor research and risk assessment in youth justice (Case and Haines 2016) have argued that these approaches are too deterministic; that they concentrate too much on deficits rather than strengths, protective factors or resilience; that they can lead to over-intervention, and that they underestimate the capacity of young people to develop and change. However, these problems could also be attributable to drawing the wrong practical conclusions from assessments, rather than being necessary consequences of the theory and practice of assessment.

One recent study of risk-need assessment and sentencing of minority ethnic groups in Britain suggests that disparities in sentencing are much more important than any variations in risk-need assessment, to the extent that risk assessments can actually contribute to evidence of sentencing disparity when minority ethnic offenders are shown to be sentenced more severely than white offenders with similar risk-need assessment scores (Raynor and Lewis 2011).

A balanced view of risk-need assessment

It can certainly be argued that the routine practice of risk assessment has improved the management of dangerous offenders in the community in England and Wales. These are now subject to regular assessment and supervision by multi-agency panels as part of Multi-Agency Public Protection Arrangements (MAPPA), and some high-risk violent or sexual offenders, including paedophiles, may be in contact with probation and/or police several times per week. They may also be subject to restrictions about where they can live and where they can go, and to such measures as electronic tagging and supervised accommodation (Kemshall 2008). Good practice in these arrangements is based on thorough planning and careful decision-making, in which the risk assessment is only one element. While it is difficult to demonstrate conclusively that the public is safer as a result, it certainly seems likely that this is the case, in spite of some high-profile exceptions. In general it could reasonably be argued that improvement in MAPPA arrangements has been a beneficial consequence of the focus on risk in England and Wales.

Overall, it is clear that risk-need assessment has been one of the central components of the international move towards evidence-based offender management and has contributed to the development of effectively targeted practice. It provides a method of assessment to underpin implementation of the risk principle (which advises the provision of more intensive services to higher-risk offenders), and the use of risk-need assessment forms one of the key indicators of effectiveness in comprehensive approaches to service evaluation such as the Correctional Program Assessment Inventory (Gendreau et al. 2010). However, it does not guarantee effectiveness: as a technique, it can support rehabilitation but it can also support 'new penology' approaches in which it is simply used to determine the appropriate degree of coercion in individual cases. This is a particular concern when engaging with groups of offenders for whom the use of risk-need assessment is still controversial. As with all the techniques and methods of effective practice, we need to ask 'effective for what?'. We cannot determine its fitness for purpose until we are clear about what the purposes are. Experience to date suggests that the rehabilitative potential of risk-need assessment is real, but quite easily eroded by unfavourable contexts of policy and practice.

Those countries identified by research on European sentencing as being both committed to rehabilitation and parsimonious in their use of both prison and community punishments (Aebi et al. 2015) tend to be systematic users of risk-need assessment, in some cases strongly influenced by established instruments such as OASys. In other jurisdictions an emphasis on other aims of criminal justice has tended to blunt the rehabilitative edge in spite of quite extensive use of assessment instruments derived from the risk-need tradition. For example, the growth in imprisonment in Britain since the early 1990s has largely coincided with the general adoption of risk-need assessment, suggesting that when populist punitiveness is a dominant narrative and encouraged by politicians engaging in a competitive display of toughness, risk-need assessment becomes subservient to policy rather than a source of more humane alternatives (Raynor 2016). Similarly, a preoccupation with speed of delivery can reduce the time available for assessment (Robinson 2017). One response to this environment is to simplify assessment: for example, pre-sentence reports in England and Wales now mainly depend on stripped-down assessments, usually derived from parts of OASys, which provide information for limited purposes within the sentencing process. There is a cost to this: faster assessment tools tend to rely more on static risk factors which do not require any input from the defendant.

Estimation of the risk of future offences in England and Wales is now usually based, at the point of sentence, on an updated form of the second-generation instrument OGRS, and such heavy reliance on static factors, in the pursuit of speed, means that the assessment of need can be crowded out of the decision-making process at the point of sentence. Recent research on the National Probation Service's work in courts in England (Robinson 2018) shows that the time actually spent in discussion with the defendant before producing a report can be as little as 15 minutes. This limits the information on which a rehabilitative approach could be based, and it is tempting to see this as connected to the recent well-documented decline in the use of community sentences by English and Welsh courts. There are indications of a loss of confidence by sentences, and very clear evidence of a lack of knowledge about community sentences (du Mont and Redgrave 2017), both of which might be addressed if reasoned and detailed proposals for community sentences were a familiar feature of court proceedings (Gelsthorpe and Raynor 1995). In earlier decades, more time was available to develop these: the author recalls standard practice in the 1970s when a two- or three-week adjournment would usually allow two interviews with the defendant and often an opportunity to develop and discuss a proposal for a non-custodial sentence, to be put forward in a reasoned written report. Other priorities, and in particular the aim of delivering accelerated justice, now work against this kind of practice. Of course detailed assessment can be carried out later when a prison sentence or period of community supervision requires a more detailed assessment to be undertaken, but by then the important sentencing decision has been taken. Punitiveness and haste between them can drastically reduce the scope for rehabilitative thinking. In fairness, as Robinson (2017) points out, the service provided to courts through stand-down reports and rapidly delivered assessments is often impressively skilled and efficient, but the quest for speed has changed priorities and tasks.

Other recent developments retain more of the original rehabilitative aims of risk-need assessment. Some assessments focus more on public protection and the risk of harm rather than simply on the probability of a further offence (Kemshall 2008). A variety of evidence-based instruments or assessment processes are now available for a range of purposes, including assessing the risk of serious recidivism (e.g. the quick RSR assessment currently used in England and Wales), the risk of serious harm (RoSH, currently part of the Case Allocation System which determines whether cases in England and Wales will be allocated to the National Probation Service or to a Community Rehabilitation Company), violent offending (e.g. the OASys Violence Predictor OVP), sexual recidivism (e.g. Risk Matrix 2000), and most recently terrorism (Herzog-Evans 2018). The Scottish Risk Management Authority publishes a very useful guide to available evidence-based instruments and their uses (Risk Management Authority 2017).

Some of these instruments (for example risk assessments for sex offenders or violent extremists) are used by specialists who are likely to have some responsibility for management or treatment of the offenders concerned, and therefore usually have an interest in helping them to change as well as managing the risks they present. Such difficult and complex cases sometimes point to further limitations of statistically based instruments: derived from aggregated data in the interests of statistical validity, they often need supplementing in individual cases by closer study of exactly how, where, when, why and to whom risks might manifest themselves. In some cases knowing the exact probability of a problematic event is less important than knowing the circumstances in which it might occur and how to prevent these circumstances arising, or how to prevent them triggering a dangerous response. This detailed and descriptive approach to case formulation is increasingly advocated by psychologists dealing with dangerous people. Predicting high-volume crime rests on a degree of similarity among the quite large group of people who commit it, but for people who are less typical of the offending population a more individualized approach has strong support. This is not surprising: all risk-need instruments require individual application, and the development of supervision plans is ideally a process of dialogue, since knowing that a risk factor is present is not always the same as knowing how it influences attitudes, decisions, and behaviour in particular cases and circumstances. This also helps to explain some of the reported weaknesses of risk management approaches in relation to young people and to women: risk-need assessment methods were developed to *support* rehabilitative human services, not to do practitioners' work for them. Often additional work is needed to identify strengths, and also other needs which may be deemed non-criminogenic but which need to be addressed as part of the process of establishing a helpful relationship. However, the clearest evidence of the efficacy and potential of risk-need assessment comes from what is by now a large number of research studies which show that targeting by risk, i.e. providing more services to people at greater risk of reoffending, is consistently a feature of effective practice. Risk assessment has come a long way since Lombroso, and mostly in the right direction. For a thorough, committed, empirically supported explanation of risk-need assessment and the theories behind it, see Bonta and Andrews (2017); for a more critical review, see Trotter et al. (2016).

References

Aebi, M., Delgrande, N. and Marguet, Y. (2015) Have community sanctions and measures widened the net of European criminal justice systems? *Punishment & Society*, 17(5), 575–597.

Andrews, D. A. and Bonta, J. (1995) *The Level of Service Inventory-Revised Manual*. Toronto: Multi-Health Systems.

Andrews, D. A., Bonta, J. and Wormith, J. S. (2004) *LS/CMI Level of Service/Case Management Inventory*. Toronto: Multi-Health Systems.

Andrews, D. A., Bonta, J. and Wormith, J. S. (2006) The recent past and near future of risk assessment. *Crime and Delinquency*, 52(1), 7–27.

Andrews, D. A., Guzzo, L., Raynor, P., Rowe, R. C., Rettinger, L. J., Brews, A. and Wormith, J. S. (2012) Are the major risk/need factors predictive of both female and male reoffending? *International Journal of Offender Therapy and Comparative Criminology*, 56(1), 113–133.

Beck, U. (1992) *Risk Society: Towards a New Modernity*. London: Sage Publications.

Bonta, J. and Andrews, D. (2017) *The Psychology of Criminal Conduct*, 6th edition. Abingdon: Routledge.

Bonta, J. and Wormith, S. (2007) Risk and need assessment. In G. McIvor and P. Raynor (Eds.), *Developments in Social Work with Offenders*. London: Jessica Kingsley.

Case, C. and Haines, K. (2016) Taking the Risk Out of Youth Justice. In C. Trotter, G. McIvor and F. McNeill (Eds.), *Beyond the Risk Paradigm in Criminal Justice*. London: Palgrave Macmillan, pp. 61–75.

Christie, S. (2004) *Granny Made Me an Anarchist*. London: Simon and Schuster.

Du Mont, S. and Redgrave, H. (2017) *Where Did It All Go Wrong? A Study into the Use of Community Sentences in England and Wales*. London: Crest Advisory.

Feeley, M. and Simon, J. (1992) The new penology: Notes on the emerging strategy of corrections and its implications. *Criminology*, 30, 449–474.

Feeley, M. and Simon, J. (1994) Actuarial justice: The emerging new criminal law. In D. Nelken (Ed.), *The Futures of Criminology*. London: Sage Publications.

Garland, D. (2001) *The Culture of Control*. Oxford: Oxford University Press.

Gelsthorpe, L. and Raynor, P. (1995) Quality and effectiveness in probation officers' reports to sentencers. *British Journal of Criminology*, 35(2), 188–200.

Gelsthorpe, L., Sharpe, G. and Roberts, J. (2007) *Provision for Women Offenders in the Community*. London: The Fawcett Society.

Gendreau, P., Andrews, D. and Thériault, Y. (2010) *Correctional Program Assessment Inventory – 2010*. Saint John: University of New Brunswick.

Herzog-Evans, M. (2018) A comparison of two structured professional judgment tools for violent extremism and their relevance in the French context. *European Journal of Probation*. Online advance publication, 11 February.

Home Office. (1996) *Guidance for the Probation Service on the Offender Group Reconviction Scale*. Probation Circular 63/1996. London: Home Office.

Hood, R. (1974) *Tolerance and the Tariff*. London: NACRO.

Hudson, B. (2002) Gender issues in penal policy and penal theory. In P. Carlen (Ed.), *Women and Punishment.* Cullompton: Willan Publishing.

Hudson, B. and Bramhall, G. (2005) Assessing the "other": Constructions of "Asianness" in risk assessments by probation officers. *British Journal of Criminology,* 45, 721–740.

Kemshall, H. (1998) *Risk in Probation Practice.* Aldershot: Ashgate.

Kemshall, H. (2003) *Understanding Risk in Criminal Justice.* Maidenhead: Open University Press.

Kemshall, H. (2008) *Understanding the Community Management of High Risk Offenders.* Maidenhead: Open University Press.

Logan, C. (2017) *The Clinical Risk Assessment and Management of Women.* Presentation to Europris Workshop on Risk and Needs Assessment, Brussels, 13 October 2017.

Lombroso, C. (1876) *L'Uomo delinquente studiato in rapporto alla antropologia, alla medicina legale ed alle discipline carceriare.* Milan: Ulrico Hoepli.

Raynor, P. (2007) Risk and need assessment in British probation: The contribution of LSI-R. *Psychology, Crime and Law,* 13(2), 125–138.

Raynor, P. (2016) Three narratives of risk: corrections, critique and context. In C. Trotter, G. McIvor F. and McNeill (Eds.), *Beyond the Risk Paradigm in Criminal Justice.* London: Palgrave Macmillan, pp. 24–45.

Raynor, P. and Lewis, S. (2011) Risk-need assessment, sentencing and minority ethnic offenders in Britain. *British Journal of Social Work,* 41(7), 1357–1371.

Raynor, P. and Miles, H. (2007) Evidence-based probation in a microstate: The British Channel Island of Jersey. *European Journal of Criminology,* 4(3), 299–313.

Raynor, P., Kynch, J., Roberts, C. and Merrington, M. (2000) *Risk and Need Assessment in Probation Services: An Evaluation.* Research Study 211. London: Home Office.

Risk Management Authority. (2017) *Risk Assessment Tools Evaluation Directory (RATED).* Paisley: RMA Scotland, published online at rated.rmascotland.gov.uk (Accessed 21 March 2018).

Robinson, G. (2017) Stand-down and deliver: Pre-sentence reports, quality and the new culture of speed. *Probation Journal,* 64(4), 337–353.

Robinson, G. (2018) Transforming probation services in magistrates' courts. *Probation Journal,* 65(3), 316–334.

Shaw, M. and Hannah-Moffatt, K. (2000) Gender, diversity and risk assessment in Canadian corrections. *Probation Journal,* 47, 163–172.

Trotter, C., McIvor, G. and McNeill, F. (Eds.). (2016) *Beyond the Risk Paradigm in Criminal Justice.* London: Palgrave Macmillan.

Van Wingerden, S., van Wilsem, J. and Moerings, M. (2014) Pre-sentence reports and punishment: A quasi-experiment assessing the effects of risk-based pre-sentence reports on sentencing. *European Journal of Criminology,* 11(6), 723–744.

von Hirsch, A. (1976) *Doing Justice: The Choice of Punishments.* Report of the Committee for the Study of Incarceration. New York: Hill and Wang.

Young, J. (2007) *The Vertigo of Late Modernity.* London: Sage Publications.

19

A critical review of risk assessment policy and practice since the 1990s, and the contribution of risk practice to contemporary rehabilitation of offenders

Hazel Kemshall

Introduction

Since the 1990s, risk assessment policy and practice with offenders has become a sizeable industry. The key drivers for this development have been correctional, financial, and to a lesser extent rehabilitative (see Kemshall 2003, 2008 for a full review). These, at times competing, drivers have taken place within a wider discourse of public protection and penal populism (Ericson 2007; Garland 2001; Robinson 2002) often serving to replace rehabilitative efforts with surveillance and control (McNeill 2009). This trend has been particularly acute in the Anglophone jurisdictions, most notably the UK and US, and to a lesser degree in Australia and Canada (see Kemshall 2008).

In England and Wales, the late 1990s and early 2000s saw increased central control of risk practice via various national guidance, probation circulars, and legislation (UK Home Office 1996; Home Office 2002, 2007; NPS 2005). This period saw the development of formal risk assessment tools accelerate with input from academics in Canada, the US, and the UK dominating both risk of recidivism and risk of harm tools (Andrews and Bonta 2010; Bonta and Andrews 2010; Bonta and Wormith 2007). Early risk assessment tools were concerned with aggregated probabilities of recidivism (Copas et al. 1996), and from the late 1990s onwards tools also focused on the assessment of risk of harm. Over time limits with probability-based actuarial tools were increasingly recognized (Bonta and Andrews 2010; Fitzgibbon 2009; Tully et al. 2009). By the 2000s, tools attempted to blend actuarial and clinical assessments within structured risk assessment tools that focused on producing individualized and more holistic assessments. Such tools aimed at assisting practitioners to better match interventions to risk factors (see Bonta and Andrews 2010 for a review). More recent approaches have seen a focus on strengths-based assessments and those factors most likely to assist desistance from offending. In this latter approach risk management is seen as more likely to be effective when offenders are given routes out of crime.

The early years

Risk assessment in the 1990s was largely characterized by actuarial techniques, that is, statistical calculations of risk probability based on aggregated populations. For much of the 20th century such techniques had been deployed within criminal justice. One of the earliest examples of actuarial techniques for risk prediction was Burgess's parole predictor, in which data on factors associated with success or failure on parole were collected and aggregated, applied retrospectively to a sample for validation, and subsequently formalized into a risk assessment tool to calculate parole failure probabilities (Burgess 1928, 1929, 1936). This technique has been used to calculate risk of reoffending and translated into prediction tools, for example, the *Offender Group Reconviction Score* (OGRS) used as the basis for the England and Wales reconviction predictor the *Offender Assessment System* (OASys) (Copas et al. 1994). This approach to risk objectively frames risk as knowable and measurable through formalized risk assessment methods. Accurately measuring risk is seen as a matter of appropriate tool design and appropriate use by practitioners (Bonta and Wormith

2007). Across the Anglophone jurisdictions in particular, actuarial risk assessment tools were adopted, with the Level of Service Case Management Inventory (LSCMI) taking root in Canada, and later in Scotland (see Kemshall 2003 for a full discussion); and the adoption of risk/needs tools in Canada, UK, and US (Andrews and Bonta 2010); and the launch of the Offender Assessment System (OASys) in England (Home Office 2002; Moore 2015).

However, they were increasingly critiqued on the grounds of low predictive accuracy (Cole 2015) and generating too many false positives (Harcourt 2007; Netter 2007), and on the grounds of discrimination against certain groups (Fitzgibbon 2007; Hannah-Moffat 2004a, 2006). Practitioners also saw such tools as something of a blunt instrument, de-individualizing offenders, and divorcing them from their social context (Deering 2011; Wandall 2006). Where needs were identified these were transformed into risks, with the offender objectified into a repository of risk requiring transformation into a non-risky subject, and when offenders did not change then long-term custodial warehousing of risk was justified (Hannah-Moffat 2004b). Interventions followed a correctional approach in order to promote 'straight thinking', targeting behaviours and cognitions, focused on how to make 'positive choices' and engage in rational choices to avoid crime.

This decade also saw an increasing conflation of risk of reoffending and risk of harm resulting in the misuse of generic risk of reoffending tools when assessing offenders who posed a risk of committing seriously harmful offences (Kemshall 2008). The risk management plans generated by actuarial tools were also critiqued on the grounds that they lacked individual fit with the individual offender, and tended towards over-controlling interventions and an over-dependence on surveillance and 'managing offenders in place' rather than rehabilitating them (Kemshall 2003, 2008).

Out of balance

By 2010 in England and Wales, Her Majesty's Inspectorate of Probation recognized that practice with offenders was out of balance, and that 'Getting the Right Mix' was essential (HMI Probation and HMI Constabulary 2010). The report argued for a shift towards 'constructive interventions' rather than an over-reliance on 'restrictive interventions'. The inspection concluded that:

> Successful work with sexual offenders requires the right mix of restrictive interventions to control the offender and help prevent reoffending and constructive interventions to change their behaviour and contribute to their safe rehabilitation into the community.
>
> (HMI Probation and HMI Constabulary 2010: 8)

The inspection report was arguably the culmination of various critiques of controlling interventions and the beginning of policy and practice recognition of the need to focus on mixed interventions that effectively promoted and enhanced rehabilitative efforts (see Kemshall 2010).

Rediscovering rehabilitation

By the mid-2000s two key developments had taken place. First was a research and practice focus on desistance – prompted in large part by the work of Maruna (2001; Ward and Maruna 2007). The 2000s saw a growing focus on enabling offenders to desist from offending, and a recognition that control and containment had limited long-term impact (Weaver 2014). Research into the process of desistance grew (see the seminal work by Maruna 2001), with attention to those factors most likely to assist desistance, and in particular on how probation work could aid the offender towards a nonoffending lifestyle (Farrall and Calverley 2006). Arrigio and Ward (2015) provide a helpful introduction to the concept.

Empirical research (for example by Farrall 2002), found that critical to desistance is the role of social relations (and more broadly social capital) in enabling and sustaining desistance. Such relationships not only enable offenders to reflect on their offending lives, choices, and identities (Vaughan 2007), but importantly aid offenders in making the transition to a nonoffending identity, lifestyle, and choices (Weaver 2016). The desistance research whilst initially largely theoretical, qualitative, and small scale, now benefits from larger-scale empirical studies. For example, Skardhamar and Savolainen (2014) on the role and timing of job entry and its impact on desistance amongst a Norwegian sample; the role of 'salient life events' such as marriage on desistance (Bersani et al. (2009; McGlorin et al. 2011); and the role of adult social bonds on desistance (Savolainen 2009). Such studies, whilst empirically illuminating the complexity of the process of desistance (see Skardhamar and Savolainen 2014 in particular), they also illustrate that practical focus on social relationships, social bonds, and social capital can be helpful to the process of desistance.

The second development was a focus on effective supervision of offenders (Burnett et al. 2007), and the critical ingredients that enhance the efficacy of supervision (McNeill et al. 2005; McIvor and Raynor 2007). This saw a renewed focus on the therapeutic relationship, and the use of pro-social modelling to enhance rehabilitation (Trotter 2009; see also Robinson and Crow 2009).

Both these developments underpinned a renewed focus on rehabilitation, emphasizing that 'something can work' and that rehabilitation efforts are just, moral, and effective (Farrow et al. 2007). Risk assessment in this period began to focus on protective factors as well as risk factors, attempting to identify those factors most likely to mitigate risk and aid desistance (Burnett 2010), although risk management, particularly for high-risk offenders remained largely controlling and restrictive (Kemshall 2008). 'Needs' were certainly a focus of probation interventions, although most were reframed as sources of risk (Kemshall 2010), and probation continued to be enmeshed in:

> a vast architecture of risk literally boxing them into programmes, particu-lar methods based on cognitive behavioural treatments, and a sense that one size fits all.
>
> (Kemshall 2010: 159)

By the mid-2000s, both practice and research placed a greater emphasis upon holistic approaches to assessment and interventions, focusing less on individ-ual deficits requiring correction, and more on the contextual and social fac-tors requiring attention if offenders were to be assisted towards living a 'Good Life' (Ward and Maruna 2007). The 'Good Lives Model' promotes attention to the skills and resources required by offenders to satisfy primary goods, or basic human values, in personally meaningful and socially acceptable ways. Its tailored and holistic approach arguably addresses some of the limitations of Risk-Needs-Responsivity (RNR) including influencing levels of treatment attrition (Ward and Willis 2016; Willis and Ward 2011). Fortune et al. for example, helpfully outline a 'positive treatment' approach to sex offenders (2015). Importantly it should be recognized that GLM is not offered as an alternative for risk reduction approaches, but rather: 'The GLM was designed to augment the RNR and incorporates the dual aims of risk reduction and well-being enhancement' (Willis et al. 2014: 60). As Ward puts it:

> The aim of rehabilitation is to assist offenders to re-enter society and ulti-mately to become productive and accepted citizens; a critical piece of the rehabilitation puzzle is to enable offenders to live fulfilling and happy lives.
>
> (Ward 2010: 44)

This approach has gained much traction in recent years, and key introductions to both conceptual underpinnings and practice implications can be found in Ward (2010; see also Maruna and LeBel 2010; Yates et al. 2010; Willis and Ward 2011; Purvis and Ward this volume). There is now an extensive website with numerous publications and a range of researchers testing and critically evaluating the approach (Good Lives Model). Evaluations of the effectiveness of GLM are less prevalent than theoretical expositions, and those which have been undertaken emphasize the appropriate operationalization of GLM (see Willis et al. 2013 for a useful example).

Rehabilitative risk assessment

During the 2000s improvements in risk assessment tools also took place, partly to address issues of diversity (Hannah-Moffat and O'Malley 2007), but also as a response to critiques that risk assessment pathologized offending and ignored social factors (Farrall et al. 2010). Researchers and practitioners began to promote a holistic approach which took into account protective factors, 'needs', and the situation of the offender with a view to better matching interventions to individual risks and needs (Bonta and Wormith 2007). Most notably amongst these 'fourth generation' risk assessment tools was the Level of Service/Case Management Inventory (LS/CMI), a Canadian based tool focused on strengthening individual assessments and aligning interventions and case management with risks and needs (Andrews et al. 2008, 2011). Whilst earlier risk assessment tools had been concerned with tiering risk (low, medium, high), LS/CMI was concerned with overall case management of the individual and appropriate alignment of interventions. This attention to case management also resulted in practice attention to risk reduction, and assessment became one part of a larger overall emphasis on offence and harm reduction. Assessing to reduce risk rather than to merely contain it became the aim (Gordon et al. 2015).

This decade also saw the development of specialized risk assessment tools, ranging from those for domestic violence, violence, and various types of sexual offending. Tools aimed to be both individualized to both offender and offence type, and also holistic in terms of providing a comprehensive understanding of the offender, including motivations to offend as well as to desist. This has resulted in an 'industry' of tool production and training, but also challenges for policymakers and practitioners in choosing risk assessment tools. The Risk Management Authority in Scotland responded to this challenge by adopting criteria for selecting tools from McIvor et al. (2002):

- Empirical grounding
- Inter-rater reliability
- Validation history

and then literally rating tools against the criteria (Risk Management Authority 2016). The Risk Assessment Tools Evaluation Directory (RATED) enables policymakers and practitioners to make well-informed choices about tool adoption and use.

Desistance, pro-social supervision, and holistic risk assessment have also permeated assessment with high-risk offenders where an integrated approach that balances control with rehabilitation known as 'blended public protection' has been promulgated (Kemshall 2008, 2014). The two strategies for managing high-risk offenders – the protection strategy which aims to protect through control of risks; and the reintegration strategy which aims to reduce risk and protect through resettlement, rehabilitation, and reintegration, are often presented as opposing management strategies. However, they are not mutually exclusive and can be combined to provide both safety and reintegration to the benefit of both public and offender (Kemshall 2008).

The approach recognizes the limits of the 'community protection model', particularly in a climate of low resources, and where never-ending community control and surveillance cannot be provided. The approach emphasizes offender self-assessment, motivational work, rehabilitative interventions, promoting protective factors alongside risk mitigation, and appropriate controls and limits on negative behaviours (see Kemshall 2008, 2014; Weaver 2014). The focus is on a greater balance between the 'pursuit of control and the promotion of change' (Weaver and Barry 2014a: 153; Weaver and Barry 2014b).

Risk in the 21st century

The 'risk' industry from the 1990s onwards has grown at great pace, particularly within the criminal justice arena. There have been numerous changes, from formal actuarial tools, to structured clinical tools, assessment tools combining protective and risk factors, and those aimed at providing holistic yet individualistic assessments to aid interventions and service delivery. Critiques of 'risk factorology', that is an exclusive focus on risk factors, have paved the way for both research and practice attention to the process and journey of desistance, and how best to conduct assessments that can contribute to this process. This has resulted in more recent attention on motivational assessment as well as risk assessment, looking at motivations to offend as well as motivations to desist. This has seen the production of motivational tools alongside risk tools (Miller and Rollnick 2002; McMurran 2009), and emphasis on the journey into and out of risk (Weaver 2016; Weaver and Weaver 2016). Self-risk management and the acquisition or skills by offenders to enhance their transition out of crime are now emphasized, with strengths-based work focusing on enhancing strengths and protective factors. The latter can be understood as factors such as: education, employment, constructive use of leisure time, mixing with pro-social peers, developing coping strategies and improving resilience, pursuing realistic goals, using interventions, and genuinely engaging with treatment (Weaver 2014). This has become the foundation of an alternative paradigm rooted in the 'Good Lives Model' with a focus on building strengths and assisting offenders to achieve legitimate goals and transition out of crime (Trotter et al. 2016a)

Whilst such developments have refined risk assessment, and resulted in more holistic, balanced, and individualized assessments, claims that we are 'beyond the risk paradigm' may be overstated (Trotter et al. 2016b). Risk continues to play a key role in resource allocation, for example in the recent split of the National Probation Service in England and Wales, placing low- to medium-risk offenders with private Community Rehabilitation Companies and leaving a residual 'lump' of high-risk offenders with the National Probation Service (Mythen et al. 2012). This presents challenges and risks for the NPS, particularly in terms of potential risk failures, media criticism, and political blamism (Kemshall 2016).

In addition, police are now playing a central role, both in the assessment and management of persistent offenders, but also offenders who pose a high risk of harm to others particularly through Integrated Offender Management schemes, and Multi Agency Public Protection Arrangements where police are often the lead agency (see Kemshall 2016). With powers of arrest and capacity to offer surveillance 24/7, police risk management has a number of advantages over an overstretched probation service with less powers. The blurring of roles and colonization of risk by police foreseen by Nash in 1999 has come to fruition in the intervening years. This of itself has created a burgeoning risk caseload for police, now with offender managers of their own, and an increasing focus on the community management of 'risky offenders'. This trend is well established across the UK as a whole, and may 'creep' across the Anglophone jurisdictions particularly where probation resources and therefore capacity to manage offenders are reduced. The continued strains of austerity and public sector cuts within the UK, and for much of the European Union, also present challenges to the ever-increasing preoccupation with crime risk. Ironically, whilst much of the 1990s discourse on risk was concerned with rationing resources towards the most risky, what has actually occurred in the intervening years is an ever-increasing and ever-expanding risk agenda. In effect, a rationing mechanism has become a beast requiring ever more resources, and demand is never satisfied. In this climate it will be interesting to see if alternative approaches can gain traction, and if a sufficiently robust evidence base can be amassed to support alternative paradigms as more effective, efficient, and cheaper. Perhaps the ultimate paradigm shift will occur when rehabilitation is seen as the most cost-effective route to effective risk management.

References

Arrigo, B. and Ward, T. (Eds.). (2015) Response, rehabilitation, and reconciliation: The normative dimension of offenders desistance journey. *Criminal Justice and Behavior*, 42, 5–124. DOI:10.1177/0093854814550022.

Andrews, D. and Bonta, J. (2010) *The Psychology of Criminal Conduct*, 5th edition. New Providence, NJ: Matthew Bender.

Andrews, D., Bonta, J. and Wormith, S. (2008) *LS/CMI Supplement: A Gender-Informed Risk/Need/Responsivity Assessment*. Toronto: Multi-Health Systems Inc.

Andrews, D., Bonta, J. and Wormith, S. (2011) The Risk-Need-Responsivity (RNR) Model: does adding the good lives model contribute to effective crime prevention? *Criminal Justice and Behavior*, 38(7), 735–755, https://doi.org/10.1177/0093854811406356

Bersani, B., Laub, J. H. and Nieuwbeerta, P. (2009) Marriage and desistance from crime in the Netherlands: Do gender and socio-historical context matter? *Journal of Quantitative Criminology*, 25, 3–24. DOI:10.1007/s10940-008-9056-4.

Bonta, J. and Andrews, D. (2010) Viewing offender assessment and rehabilitation through the lens of the Risk-Need-Responsivity model. In F. McNeil, P. Raynor and C. Trotter (Eds.), *Offender Supervision: New Directions in Theory, Research and Practice*. New York: Willan Publishing, pp. 19–40.

Bonta, J. and Wormith, S. (2007) Risk and need assessment. In G. McIvor and P. Raynor (Eds.), *Developments in Social Work with Offenders*. Research Highlights 48. London: Jessica Kingsley.

Burgess, E. W. (1928) Factors making for success or failure on parole. *Journal of Criminal Law and Criminology*, 19(2), 239–306.

Burgess, E. W. (1929) Is prediction feasible in social work? *Social Forces*, 7, 535–545.

Burgess, E. W. (1936) Protecting the public by parole and parole prediction. *Journal of Criminal Law and Criminology*, 27, 491–502.

Burnett, R. (2010) The will and ways of becoming an ex-offender. *The International Journal of Comparative Offender Therapy*, 54, 663.

Burnett, R., Baker, K. and Roberts, C. (2007) Assessment, supervision and intervention: Fundamental practice in probation. In L. Gelsthorpe and R. Morgan (Eds.), *Handbook of Probation*. Cullompton: Willan Publishing.

Cole, D. (2015) The difference prevention makes: Regulating preventive justice. *Criminal Law and Philosophy*, 9(3), 501–519.

Copas, J., Ditchfield, J. and Marshall, P. (1994) *Development of a New Reconviction Score*. Research Bulletin, Vol. 36. London: HMSO.

Copas, J., Marshall, P. and Tarling, R. (1996) *Predicting Reoffending for Discretionary Release*. Home Office Research Study 150. London: HMSO.

Deering, J. (2011) *Probation Practice and the New Penology: Practitioner Reflections*. London: Routledge.

Ericson, R. (2007) *Crime in an Insecure World*. Cambridge: Policy Press.

Farrall, S. (2002) *Rethinking What Works with Offenders: Probation, Social Context and Desistance from Crime*. Cullompton, Devon: Willan Publishing.

Farrall, S., Bottoms, A. and Shapland, J. (2010) Social structures and desistance from crime. *European Journal of Criminology*, 7(6), 546–570. DOI:10.1177/1477370810376574.

Farrall, S. and Calverley, A. (2006) *Understanding Desistance from Crime: Theoretical Directions in Resettlement and Rehabilitation*, Crime and Justice Series. Maidenhead and New York: Open University Press.

Farrow, K., Kelly, G. and Wilkinson, B. (2007) *Offenders in Focus: Risk, Responsivity and Diversity*. Bristol: Policy Press.

Fitzgibbon, D. W. (2007) Institutional racism, pre-emptive criminalization and risk analysis. *Howard Journal of Crime and Justice*, 46(2), 128–144.

Fitzgibbon, D. W. (2009) Risk analysis and the new practitioner: Myth or reality? *Punishment & Society*, 9(1), 87–97. https://doi.org/10.1177/1462474507070554 (Accessed 21 November 2017).

Fortune, C. A., Ward, T. and Mann, R. (2015) Good lives & the rehabilitation of sex offenders: A positive treatment approach. In A. Linley and S. Joseph (Eds.), *Positive Psychology in Practice*, 2nd edition. Chichester: John Wiley & Sons.

Garland, D. (2001) *The Culture of Crime Control: Crime and Social Order in Contemporary Society*. Oxford: Clarendon. Good Lives at: www.goodlivesmodel.com/publications (Accessed 4 December 2017).

Gordon, H., Kelty, S. F. and Julian, R. (2015) Psychometric evaluation of the level of service/case management inventory among Australian offenders completing community-based sentences. *Criminal Justice and Behavior*, 42(11), 1089–1109. https://doi.org/10.1177/0093854815596419.

Hannah-Moffat, K. (2004a) Losing ground: Gender, responsibility and parole risk. *Social Politics*, 11(3), 363–385. Available at: http://sp.oxfordjournals.org/content/11/3/363.abstract?sid=df1aa746-0859-46f3-b0be-2b63ba5da3cc.

Hannah-Moffat, K. (2004b) Criminogenic need and the transformative risk subject: Hybridizations of risk/need in penality. *Punishment & Society*, 7(1), 29–51. Available at: http://pun.sagepub.com/content/7/1/29.abstract.

Hannah-Moffat, K. (2006) Pandora's box: Risk/need and gender-responsive corrections. *Criminology and Public Policy*, 5(1), 1301–1311.

Hannah-Moffat, K. and O'Malley, P. (2007) *Gendered Risks*. London: Routledge Cavendish.

Harcourt, B. (2007) *Against Prediction: Profiling, Policing and Punishment in the Actuarial Age*. Chicago: University of Chicago Press.

Her Majesty's Inspectorate of Probation and Her Majesty's Inspectorate of Constabulary. (2010) *Restriction and Rehabilitation: Getting the Right Mix*. London: Criminal Justice Joint Inspection. Available at: www.justiceinspectorates.gov.uk/hmiprobation/inspections/restriction-and-rehabilitation-getting-the-right-mix-an-inspection-of-the-management-of-sexual-offenders-in-the-community/ (Accessed 11 December 2017).

Home Office. (1996) *Guidance for the Probation Service on the Offender Group Reconviction Scale*. London: Home Office.

Home Office. (2002) *Offender Assessment System: OASys User Manual, V2*. London: Home Office.

Home Office. (2007) *OASys Handbook*. London: Home Office.

Kemshall, H. (2003) *Understanding Risk in Criminal Justice*. Maidenhead: Open University, McGraw-Hill.

Kemshall, H. (2008) *Understanding the Community Management of High Risk Offenders*. Maidenhead: Open University, McGraw-Hill.

Kemshall, H. (2010) The role of risk, needs and strengths assessment in improving the supervision of offenders. In F. McNeill, P. Raynor and C. Trotter (Eds.), *Offender Supervision: New Directions in Theory, Research and Practice*. Abingdon: Willan Publishing. Pp. 155–171.

Kemshall, H. (2014) Public protection: What works in the safe management of sexual offenders. *Irish Probation Journal*, 11, 103–112, October.

Kemshall, H. (2016) The rise of risk in probation work: Historical reflections and future speculations. In M. Vanstone and P. Priestley (Eds.), *Probation and Politics: Academic Reflections from Former Practitioners*. London: Palgrave Macmillan, pp. 195–213. https://doi.org/10.1057/978-1-137-59557-7_11.

Maruna, S. (2001) *Making Good: How Ex-Convicts Reform and Rebuild Their Lives*. Washington, DC: American Psychological Association.

Maruna, S. and LeBel, T. P. (2010) The desistance paradigm in correctional practice: From programmes to lives. In F. McNeill, P. Raynor and C. Trotter (Eds.), *Offender Supervision: New Directions in Theory, Research and Practice*. Cullompton: Willan, pp. 65–89.

McGloin, J. M., Sullivan, C. J., Piquero, A R., Blokland, A. and Nieuwbeerta, P. (2011) Marriage and offending specialization: Expanding the impact of turning points and the process of desistance. *European Journal of Criminology*, 8(5), 361–376. DOI:10.1177/1477370811414103.

McIvor, G., Levy, G. and Kemshall, H. (2002) *Serious Violent and Sexual Offenders: The Use of Risk Assessment Tools in Scotland*. Scottish Executive: Crime and Criminal Justice. Available at: www.gov.scot/Publications/2002/11/15734/12646.

McIvor, G. and Raynor, P. (Eds.). (2007) *Developments in Social Work with Offenders*. Research Highlights 48. London: Jessica Kingsley.

McMurran, M. (2009) Motivational interviewing with offenders: A systematic review. *Legal and Criminological Psychology*, 14, 83–100. DOI:10.1348/135532508X278326.

McNeill, F. (2009) *Towards Effective Practice in Offender Supervision*. Report 01/09. Scottish Centre for Crime and Justice Research. Available at: www.sccjr.ac.uk/wp-content/uploads/2012/10/McNeil_Towards.pdf (Accessed 21 November 2017).

McNeill, F. Batchelor S., Burnett, R. and Knox, J. (2005) *21st Century Social Work Reducing Reoffending: Key Skills*. Edinburgh: Scottish Executive. Available at: https://strathprints.strath.ac.uk/38070/1/21st_c.pdf (Accessed 21 November 2017).

Miller, W. R. and Rollnick, S. (2002) *Motivational Interviewing*, 2nd edition. New York: The Guilford Press.

Moore, R. (2015) *A Compendium of Research and Analysis of the Offender Assessment System (OASys) 2009–2013*. London: National Offender Management Service.

Mythen, G., Walklate, S. and Kemshall, H. (2012) Decentralizing risk: The role of the voluntary and community sector in the management of offenders. *Criminology and Criminal Justice Online 26/9/12*. Available at: http://crj.sagepub.com/content/early/2012/09/24/1748895812458295 (Accessed 4 December 2017).

Nash, M. (1999) Enter the 'polibation officer'. *International Journal of Police Science and Management* 1(4), 360–368.

Netter, B. (2007) Using groups' statistics to sentence individual criminals: An ethical and statistical critique of the Virginia risk assessment program. *Journal of Criminal Law and Criminology*, 97(3), 699–730.

National Probation Service (NPS). (2005) *Offender Assessment System (OASys) Quality Management Plan*. Probation Circular 48/2005. London: Home Office.

Risk Management Authority. (2016) *Risk Assessment Tool Evaluation Directory (RATED)*. Available at: http://rated.rmascotland.gov.uk/ (Accessed 4 December 2017).

Robinson, G. (2002) A rationality of risk in the Probation Service: Its evolution and contemporary profile. *Punishment & Society*, 4(1), 5–25.

Robinson, G. and Crow, I. (2009) *Offender Rehabilitation: Theory, Research and Practice*. London: Sage Publications.

Savolainen, J. (2009) Work, family and criminal desistance. Adult social bonds in a ordic welfare state. *British Journal of Criminology*, 49, 285–304. DOI:10.1093/bjc/azn084.

Skardhamar, T. and Savolinen, J. (2014) Changes in criminal offending around the time of job entry: A study of employment and desistance. *Criminology*, 52(2), 263–291. DOI:10.1111/1745-9125.12037.

Trotter, C. (2009) Pro-social modelling. *European Journal of Probation*, 1(2), 142–152. https://doi.org/10.1177/206622030900100206.

Trotter, C., McIvor, G. and McNeill, G. (2016a) Changing risks, risking change. In C. Trotter, G. McIvor and F. McNeill (Eds.), *Beyond the Risk Paradigm in Criminal Justice*. Basingstoke: Palgrave Macmillan.

Trotter, C., McIvor, G. and McNeill, G. (Eds.). (2016b) *Beyond the Risk Paradigm in Criminal Justice*. Basingstoke: Palgrave Macmillan.

Tully, R. J, Chou, S. and Browne, K. D. (2009) A systematic review on the effectiveness of sex offender risk assessment tools in predicting sexual recidivism of adult male offenders. *Clinical Psychology Review*, 33(2), 287–316. https://doi.org/10.1016/j.cpr.2012.12.002 (Accessed 21 November 2017).

Vaughan, B. (2007) The internal narrative of desistance. *British Journal of Criminology*, 47, 390–404.

Wandall, R. (2006) Actuarial risk assessment. The loss of recognition of the individual offender. *Law, Probability and Risk*, 5, 175–200.

Ward, T. and Maruna, S. (2007) *Rehabilitation: Beyond the Risk Paradigm*. London: Routledge.

Ward, T. (2010) The good lives model of offender rehabilitation: Basic assumptions, etiological commitments, and practice implications. In McNeill, F., Raynor, P. and Trotter, C. (Eds.), *Offender Supervision: New Directions in Theory, Research and Practice*. Devon: Willan Publishing, pp. 41–64.

Ward, T. and Willis, G. (2016) Dynamic risk factors and offender rehabilitation: A comparison of the good lives model and the risk-need responsivity model. In D. R. Laws and W. O'Donohue (Eds.), *Treatment of Sex Offenders: Strengths and Weaknesses in Assessment and Intervention*. New York: Springer, pp. 175–190.

Weaver, B. (2014) Change or control? Developing dialogues between desistance research and public protection practice. *Probation Journal*, 61(1), 8–26 Available at: https://doi.org/10.1177%2F0264550513512890 (Accessed 21 November 2017).

Weaver, B. (2016) *Offending and Desistance*. London: Routledge.

Weaver, B. and Barry, M. (2014a) Risky business? Supporting desistance from sexual offending. In K. McCartan (Ed.), *Responding to Sexual Offending: Perceptions, Risk Management and Public Protection*. Basingstoke: Palgrave Macmillan.

Weaver, B. and Barry, M. (2014b) Managing high risk offenders in the community: Compliance, cooperation and consent in a climate of concern. *European Journal of Probation*, 6, 278–295.

Weaver, B. and Weaver, A. (2016) An unfinished alternative: Towards a relational paradigm. In C. Trotter, G. McIvor and F. McNeill (Eds.), *Beyond the Risk Paradigm in Criminal Justice*. Basingstoke: Palgrave Macmillan.

Willis, G. M. and Ward, T. (2011) Striving for a good life: The good lives model applied to released child molesters. *Journal of Sexual Aggression*, 17, 290–303. http://dx.doi.org/10.1080/13552600.2010.505349.

Willis, G. M., Ward, T. and Levenson, G. (2013) The Good Lives Model (GLM): An evaluation of GLM operationalization in North American treatment programs. *Sexual Abuse: A Journal of Research and Treatment*, 26(1), 58–81. https://doi.org/10.1177/1079063213478202.

Willis, G., Ward. T. and Levenson, J. (2014) The Good Lives Model (GLM), An evaluation of GLM operationalization in North American treatment programs. *Sexual Abuse: A Journal of Research and Treatment*, 26, 58–81. Available at: http://journals.sagepub.com/doi/pdf/10.1177/1079063213478202 (Accessed 11 December 2017).

Yates, P. M., Prescott, D. S. and Ward, T. (2010) *Applying the Good Lives and Self Regulation Models to Sex Offender Treatment: A Practical Guide for Clinicians*. Brandon, VT: Safer Society Press.

20

The promises and perils of gender-responsivity

Risk, incarceration, and rehabilitation

Kelly Struthers Montford and
Kelly Hannah-Moffat

Introduction

Risk structures how criminal justice systems assess, manage, and imprison offenders. Concerns about an individual's threat to public safety in the form of reoffending are central to policing, pre-trial detention, sentencing, correctional programming, and release decisions (O'Malley 2010). Despite its foundational aspect to CJS decisions, risk and how it is measured is fluid and shifting. Since the 1970s, a science of risk premised on the prediction of recidivism, referred to as actuarial risk, has dominated and continues to inform how individuals are assessed and consequently managed. Actuarial approaches continue to be upheld as evidence-based and objective in comparison to professional judgement (see Bonta 2007), regardless of the fact that unstructured clinical assessments continue to be used in many settings (Hannah-Moffat et al. 2009). Proponents of prediction-based risk assessments claim that the likelihood of an individual's recidivism can be measured against an aggregate population. An individual's 'risk' is then calculated using assessment tools containing variables shown to be statically correlated to recidivism in the (male) population upon which the tools were designed (see Hannah-Moffat 2013).

Initial actuarial assessment tools are assigned a risk score based on an individual's static factors such as age, gender, and amount and type of past convictions (Hannah-Moffat 2013). In the 1980s, dynamic risk variables were added to existing static assessments as a way to better identify interventions that 'work' to solve crime and offending (Andrews 1989). Dynamic variables are understood as 'criminogenic needs' that if identified and addressed through targeted programming can change over time. Factors such as lifestyle and leisure activities, antisocial attitudes, family and relationships, substance use, as well as education and employment are common dynamic risk factors. This approach to risk works to translate need into risk. Responsibility for change is then placed in individuals who are to be provided with appropriate interventions designed to support their rehabilitation. In the 1990s, psychologists such as Andrews et al. (1990) argued for the inclusion of responsivity factors into risk assessment tools and practices (RNR: Risk-Needs-Responsivity). The responsivity principle is premised on the idea that assessing and matching services based on an individual's needs, learning style, available interventions, as well as their inhibiting and motivating/protective factors is the most effective form of rehabilitation. Uniting these evidence-based approaches to risk assessment is the idea that risk can be predicted, and in the case of dynamic and RNR approaches, remedied by the individual despite structures of social marginalization and inequality.

Feminist criminologists, prison advocates, and civil liberties associations have repeatedly expressed concern over the use of risk tools – normed on male populations – for women (see CHRC 2003; Hannah-Moffat 2009; Hannah-Moffat 2004; Salisbury et al. 2009; Van Voorhis 2012; Van Voorhis et al. 2010). Given that women and men vary in their past experiences and reasons for offending as a function of gender, which also impacts histories of trauma, poverty, victimization, education, employment, and substance use (see, for example, Salisbury et al. 2016), critics charge that assessment tools designed on statistical correlations between male demographics, past behaviour, and recidivism will be inappropriate when applied to women. However, with the emergence of the responsivity principle and gender-responsive penal initiatives, gender-specific risk assessment tools, such as the Security Reclassification Scale for Women, Women's Pretrial Inventory of Need (ION), the Women's Risk/Needs Assessment standalone (WRNA), and the WRNA-trailer (for use with the Level of Service Inventory-Revised [LSI-R], or COMPAS, for example), were developed in an effort to have relevant and appropriate methods of determining women's risk (Salisbury et al. 2016). In this chapter, we provide an overview of gender-specific corrections and risk assessment, to ultimately focus on how risk and security interact with rehabilitation efforts. We caution that the elision between risk and needs functions to translate issues of social inequality into dynamic needs that are to be remedied by incarcerated women. Because risk/needs and security are often linked in carceral settings, the reduction of dynamic needs from that related to broader structures of social inequality to an individual deficit can impede rehabilitative efforts, in contrast to the rationale supporting this form of risk assessment.

Addressing and assessing women's needs

Feminist criminologists, reformers, and prison advocates have long argued that it is inappropriate to manage criminalized and imprisoned women in systems designed for men (see, for example, Hayman 2006). The construction of women-specific institutions and correctional initiatives was the subject of the Canadian Task Force on Federally Sentenced Women (1990), whose recommendations catalyzed the closure of the notoriously punitive Prison for Women, and saw it replaced by six regional centres for women. Not only were these new institutions meant to better serve the unique needs of women, but the design and the regime of corrections therein would be based on a women-specific penal philosophy that provided opportunities for criminalized women to heal and become empowered.[1] Underpinning women-centred penalty is the notion that gender mediates offending, imprisonment, and rehabilitation. As such, institutions and practices premised on male populations will fail to achieve similar outcomes when applied to criminalized women. It then follows that substantive equality can only be achieved by taking seriously women's circumstances surrounding their offending and their past experiences in relation to broader social and political contexts.

A key issue for feminist-inspired scholars, prisoners-rights advocates, and policymakers has been the development of gender-relevant classification schemes. Classification is an essential feature of effective correctional management and 'evidence-based' programming. To ensure women have access to appropriate programs, advocates of a gender-responsive approach have argued that women prisoners need to be appropriately classified. A 2003 report of the Canadian Human Rights Commission (CHRC) recommended that CSC develop gender-specific classification and assessment tools to remedy the problem of gender discrimination in women's prisons. The United Nations, correctional jurisdictions, and feminist researchers have also supported and initiated the development of risk-need classification/assessment instruments that can identify and programme for women's needs (Blanchette and Brown 2006; Bloom et al. 2003; CSC 2017; Salisbury et al. 2016; UN General Assembly 2011; Van Voorhis et al. 2010). The core premises of gender-responsivity challenges male normativity and builds on women's 'differences'. Such an approach produces gender-informed norms that can serve as an organizing principle for women's penal policy, programs, and research.

Gender-responsive tools

Critics of the use of actuarial risk technologies for women have argued that the tools are ineffective and over-classify women because risk scores are derived using tools developed and normed on male populations (Hannah-Moffat 2009). The emergence of gender-responsive assessment tools in the 2000s has been positioned by proponents as an appropriate and reliable remedy to concerns around gender bias (Blanchette and Brown 2006; Salisbury et al. 2016; Van Voorhis et al. 2010). During this time, prison services, academics, and practitioners in Canada and the United States, for example, have turned their attention to the development, validation, and implementation of 'gender-responsive' risk assessment tools. Such research is premised on feminist pathways literature that shows women's offending is qualitatively and quantitatively different in comparison to that of men, regardless of whether they are charged with the same type of offence. The pathways literature suggests that victimization and trauma, circumstances, relationships, substance use, mental health, and social marginalization factor into women's reasons for offending in ways that are not significant for criminalized men in the same way (see, for example, Salisbury et al. 2016). This has led proponents of actuarial risk to argue that gender-responsive risk assessment tools should be designed and normed on aggregate populations of women, in lieu of modifying existing androcentric tools. Such an approach has been called a ground-up or 'women-up' framework for doing actuarial risk science. Factors included in a 'women-up' approach include mental health issues, self-esteem, victimization as a child and adult, parenting difficulties, as well as poverty (Blanchette and Brown 2006; Salisbury et al. 2009).

The CSC, for example, has developed a Security Reclassification Scale for Women (SRSW) as a measure to 'ensure the use of gender-informed tools within women's facilities across Canada' (Thompson and McConnell 2013: 3). However, it is important to note that this tool is used to *reclassify* women (over the course of their sentence), who have been initially classified using the Custody Rating Scale (CRS). The CRS is not gender specific. Designed 25 years ago, it is normed on male populations (Office of the Editor General of Canada 2017). Broadly, classification weighs the prisoner's (1) degree of supervision and restrictions required in the penitentiary (institutional adjustment), (2) likelihood of escape (including the risk to public safety should they escape), (3) criminal history/risk of violence. Offenders are then assigned a security classification of minimum, medium, or maximum.

While these metrics could appear to be gender neutral, women's circumstances, experiences of imprisonment, and needs are not adequately captured or responded to when these criteria are applied. For example, not only does the CSC use the CRS for women's initial classification, but it also uses the tool to match women to programming – a purpose for which the tool was not designed or tested (Office of the Editor General of Canada 2017). Others have analyzed CSC's own data to show that aspects of the CRS have '*no* predictive power for Aboriginal women' meaning that their classification will be inaccurate (Webster and Doob 2004: 402). Only institutional adjustment has been shown to be correlated to women's risk, and validation samples have not included a large enough population to measure risk of escape or risk of violence (Webster and Doob 2004). As well, a study on the SRSW indicates that the reliability of the scale improved when 'ever being unlawfully at large' was removed (Thompson and McConnell 2013). Given that there are too few women offenders who escape for this to be a reliable or validated item on the scale, this measure is not appropriate when classifying women. Despite this, the measure remains in use (Blanchette and Taylor 2005; Thompson and McConnell 2013). A recent study on a reweighted CRS scale for women (2014) noted that this had little effect on the disproportionate classification of Indigenous women as requiring medium and maximum security levels. As the reweighted CRS showed little improvement in predicting institutional misconducts, as well as only a slight improvement in the classification of Indigenous women in comparison to the CRS, its implementation was not recommended (Rubenfeld 2014).

Concerns about gender-responsive classification persist despite the fact that various tools have been validated using women's populations. The current approach to classification in Canadian federal penitentiaries uses tools that take gender to be a binary concept. Such tools thus fail to take into consideration gender fluidity, gender non-conforming persons, and/or transgender prisoners. The CRS, for example, is not gender responsive, nor does it allow for the meaningful consideration of intersecting axes of identity such as disability, Indigeneity, or race. The SRSW, while designed based on a population of women prisoners, was primarily comprised of white women, with Indigenous women comprising 25% of the sample (Blanchette and Taylor 2005). As such, its appropriateness for Indigenous women remains contested. Overall, the current tools used by CSC fail to capture and respond to women's multiple subjectivities, as well as the ways in which aspects of their identities interact with their experience of imprisonment and prison adaptation. This can have a negative impact for women's correctional programming, rehabilitation, and reintegration.

Gender and racial neutrality: discriminatory impact

In 2017, the Office of the Auditor General of Canada stated that because the CRS is designed and normed on male populations, it does not have 'appropriate program referral tools for women offenders' (122). The result of which is that CSC has not 'provided women offenders with correctional programs . . . in a manner that adequately supported their timely and successful reintegration into the community' (2017: 122). Indigenous women represent approximately 5% of the Canadian population, but are 38% of the federal prison population (Office of the Correctional Investigator Canada 2017). While 11% of federally sentenced women are classified as maximum security, 50% of maximum security women are Indigenous (Vecchio 2018). These statistics require context. Indigenous women's lived experiences, including high rates of intergenerational trauma, victimization, under-education, under-employment, histories of depression, suicide attempts, and mental illness result in their being assessed as higher risk. In addition, Indigenous women are often classified as maximum not because of their threat to public safety, but due to issues surrounding institutional adjustment.

Institutional adjustment for Indigenous women must also be contextual-ized. Given that Indigenous persons are more likely than their white coun-terparts to have experienced over-policing (police contact for the purposes of criminalization) and under-policing (police ignoring their calls for help, or not intervening in violent situations), and to have had negative experi-ences with child welfare services, they are more likely to enter penitentiaries with a mistrust of state representatives, including staff (Rudin 2016; Vecchio 2018). Critics have also noted that correctional staff often view Indigenous women as 'uncooperative, unmanageable, risky, [and] challenging' (Mangat as cited in Vecchio 2018: 85). The current approach is therefore flawed in that it does not take into consideration that the 'high levels of risk' and 'poorer institutional adjustment' attributed to Indigenous women can be reflective of their unique cultural experiences, and does not necessarily mean they require increased security. Indigenous women are disadvantaged due to their cultural context and are punished more severely because actuarial instruments do not consider the ways in which the items on the scale interact with being Indige-nous, thus creating a systemic bias.

A maximum-security designation not only entails increased restrictive con-ditions of confinement, but has tangible effects on access to programming and reintegration. For example, women designated as requiring maximum security are housed in secure units. The operational realities in these units mean that women are limited in their access to programming, including programs designed to be culturally responsive. Women with maximum secu-rity designations are also prevented from accessing the Indigenous Healing Lodges (minimum security facilities designed to respond to the unique needs of Indigenous prisoners). Because maximum security women do not have access to programs or facilities as do those who are classified as medium and minimum security, they are less likely to be granted parole – this is especially pronounced for Indigenous women (Office of the Correctional Investigator Canada 2017; Vecchio 2018). As such, actuarial risk assessments continue to be limited in terms of meaningfully identifying and responding to wom-en's needs – limits that are compounded by intersections of racialization and trauma.

Predicting recidivism: gender-responsive RNR tools

In 2013 the research branch of the CSC released their findings on the development and testing of a women-specific dynamic risk assessment tool (Zakaria et al. 2013). Researchers had intended to construct a tool to identify dynamic treatment needs and assess a woman's progress both during and after incarceration (p. 38). Theoretically informed by the pathways literature and designed and tested on an aggregate population of federally sentenced women released during the fiscal year of 2002–2003 (the construction sample), the tool included the following eight static variables found to be statistically correlated with recidivism within two years of release:

> previous adult convictions (5+), termination/revocation of conditional release prior to current release, average number of major institutional misconducts, history of unstable employment, break and enter offence prior to current sentence, contraband charge during current sentence, assault offence prior to current sentence, and previous youth convictions (2+).
>
> (Zakaria et al. 2013: 21)

While dynamic risk factors such as 'self-esteem, associates with criminalized peers, motivation, drug/alcohol use' were analyzed in terms of correlation with recidivism, such factors were not statistically significant (p. 39) and were not included in the final model. The gender-specific factors identified in the literature base, including histories of victimization, mental health, and parenting were not found to be better predictors of recidivism than were variables such as criminal history and employment contained in current assessment tools. A focus on *prediction and recidivism* in this sense, detracts from questions of gender appropriateness. Focus is constrained to an evaluation on whether the tools better predict recidivism, instead of whether the tools appropriately refer individuals to programming that would support their subsequent transition to the community. Questions of construct validity are annexed in favour of questions of predictive validity.

The final model was tested on a population of federally sentenced women released on day parole, full parole, statutory release, or upon warrant expiry during the 2003–2004 fiscal year. Both the construction and validation sample were similar in their demographic characteristics: women were approximately 33 years of age, were single (62%), did not have a high school diploma (68%), and were not Indigenous (75%) (pp. 11–12). When applied to the validation sample, the tool in question was not found to be significantly associated with recidivism. Zakaria et al. (2013) found that the variables included in the model were static in nature and that gender-specific inputs such as self-esteem or victimization did not improve the tool's predictive capacity (p. iii). Given these results the authors concluded that static factors were likely better predictors of recidivism, with gender-specific factors better able to identify needs. Ultimately a women-specific risk assessment tool was not validated. These researchers suggested that a gender-informed (albeit not gender-specific, as their tool does not better predict recidivism in women than do tools designed for men) *static* tool could be of use in the Canadian federal service, while an appropriate dynamic tool has not been implemented. While dynamic factors can identify needs that might curb future criminalization, the population was approached with a specific view to predicting their recidivism within two years following release. As such, need remains narrowly configured as related to recidivism rather than as symptomatic of larger social structures of gender and racial inequality. When viewed through male-centric actuarial tools, women's high needs are translated to produce them as risky subjects. This is especially the case for Indigenous women and those with disabilities (see, for example, Hannah-Moffat 2016a).

US-based researchers such as Patricia Van Voorhis, Emily Wright, Emily Salisbury, and Ashley Bauman have developed gender-specific tools for women held in pre-trial detention, sentenced custody, and those released into the community (Salisbury et al. 2016, 2009; Van Voorhis 2016; Van Voorhis et al. 2010). These researchers have drawn on feminist research addressing women's criminalization including pathways, trauma, relational theory, holistic addiction, and social capital theories to build 'women-up' standalone and trailer tools. The Women's Risk/Needs Assessment (WRNA) standalone and trailer,[2] as well as the Women's Pretrial Inventory of Need (ION) have been developed and compared to tools normed on male populations. Based on their analyses, they have identified gender-specific factors statistically correlated with recidivism. The WRNA is now used by more than 30 US jurisdictions, and the ION has been implemented as a pilot project in others (Van Voorhis 2016).

In their development and testing of the WRNA, Van Voorhis et al (2010) argued that while the LSI-R was in fact accurate in its prediction of women's recidivism, its shortcoming lay in its inability to appropriately match women's needs to treatment priorities. For example, while the LSI-R often identifies 'criminal thinking' including attitudes and associates as a main treatment need for men, this is not the case for women. Instead, Van Voorhis et al. (2010: 281) state that

> substance abuse, economic, educational, parental and mental health needs appear to be the needs most associated with future offending. Additionally, trauma, dysfunctional relationships, and mental health concerns are key to prison adjustment and ought to be viewed as essential to the maintenance of safe prisons.

Their research also revealed specific protective factors that would function to prevent recidivism, including self-esteem, self-efficacy, family supports, and educational assets. Protective factors are considered strengths that will reduce an individual's risk score (Salisbury et al. 2016; Van Voorhis et al.

2010). However, tension remains between the evidenced-based construction of a high-risk, high-needs woman, who might benefit from a high level of intervention, and how this is operationalized within a punishment-oriented criminal justice system. In a context of penal austerity and limited resources, some remain concerned that while the risk of under-classifying women poses a low public safety threat, it will result in women not receiving appropriate interventions (Salisbury et al. 2016). Given that race, disability, education, and employment are linked in a multitude of ways, we are concerned that tool inputs contain a built-in bias, in addition to the possibility that notions of benevolence might cause scores to be overridden by some who see risk assessments as a way to provide services with disproportionate ramifications for racialized and disabled women. We note that with increased attention on gender-specific variables, a new penal subject has emerged. She is now both high risk and high needs based on gender-specific variables, rather than the low-risk/high-needs woman prisoner of the past (Salisbury et al. 2016). Here risk is less about a threat to public safety, because when men are removed as the norm, how risk is conceptualized changes. The elision between risk and need, as well as between causation and correlation, warrants attention.

Risk and need are no longer not easily distinguishable in many correctional contexts. With the adoption and advent of the third generation of risk assessments, the terms dynamic risk and criminogenic need are used interchangeably to refer to a subset of offender 'needs' that are statistically related to recidivism. Within this framework, needs are considered alterable. This common correctional framing of need deprioritizes needs that are self-identified. The emphasis on statistical relationships between need variables and recidivism in programme development and assessment is also misinterpreted and causally linked to criminality or an undesirable behaviour (escape). In this instance, the need variables shown to be correlated with recidivism on an aggregate level are erroneously ascribed to a decontextualized individual. This conceptual framing of dynamic risk tends to minimize the complexities of offender personalities and socio-structural factors (Heffernan and Ward 2015). The core criminogenic logic requires that these risk factors be rooted in individual, alterable, and robust statistical predictors of recidivism. Consequently, current conceptualizations of dynamic risk are unavoidably disconnected from wider social processes and contexts and ensure that an offender's needs are distinct (Hannah-Moffat 2016b). Categorical definitions of risk/need discredit, exclude, and co-opt alternative interpretations of offender needs, and dissociate understandings of needs from broader social and political contexts. Individuals are positioned as potential recipients of predefined services, rather than as active agents involved in processes of self-identifying and self-managing needs.

The overlay of risk-based concerns onto existing correctional structures has produced new concerns about women's needs as promising targets for correctional intervention. However, when needs are targeted in this way, additional and/or intensified interventions into the life or psyche of a woman are justified in the name of prevention or reformation. Correctional programme narratives contain a focus on interventions that 'target criminogenic needs' and stratify service delivery, rather than focus on the empowerment of women or responding to their self-identified needs. Moreover, the current emphasis on criminogenic need may in fact disadvantage some women. Before the integration of risk/need logics in women's correctional management, self-injurious behaviour was not typically considered a risk/need factor. Instead it was viewed a reaction to past trauma and a means of coping with pain and controlling one's environment (Heney 2003). More recently, however, self-injurious behaviour has become more overtly identified as behaviour that is 'difficult to manage', symptomatic of an underlying mental health problem and undifferentiated from assaultive behaviour directed at another that requires some form of 'behavioural management and basic skills building' (ODCW 2003: 20). Recent evidence suggests that needs associated with female offenders, such as those related to children, self-injury, past abuse, and trauma, are reconfigured as criminogenic needs (dynamic risk factors) because they are statistically linked to recidivism and can be addressed through available correctional programming. Furthermore, should women choose not to engage in programming associated with their 'needs', they are often categorized as untreatable or un-empowerable, and thus deserving of high-security levels and more interventions because of their 'poor choices' and propensity for violence (Hannah-Moffat 2001).

Conclusion

Feminist critiques of gender neutrality and penal inequities are producing new knowledge, lines of criminological enquiry, and penal practices. The male norm is no longer defensible as an organizing principle of penal research, policy, or programming, and gender-responsivity is producing new knowledges about the gendered subject, as well as new criteria through which women are managed. In many cases, gender-based knowledge is legitimated and considered superior to traditional male-derived knowledges by virtue of being either feminist-inspired, or in some cases simply resulting from the study of women. While gender-responsivity relies on a female norm to measure women, underlying assumptions about women, disability, socio-economic status, Indigeneity, and race require closer examination.

Relationships, children, past victimizations, mental health, self-injury, and self-esteem have all become correctional targets in the pursuit of normative femininity and gender conformity. Critical feminist scholarship has empirically documented how an emphasis on these factors in penal settings leads to increased levels of security and scrutiny. Gendered therapeutic approaches (see, for example, Kendall and Pollack 2005) may be based on a decontextualized understanding of women as lacking self-esteem, emotionally fragile, dependent, and psychologically unstable. The logical extension of these characterizations is the development of correctional programs designed to address these 'needs', which if left unmet become 'risks'. While this characterization of gender-responsive penalty is relatively benign, other feminist scholars have indicated that women prisoners are pathologized through seemingly progressive gendered understandings of their needs, and that treatment strategies for women fail to account for power relations or structural concerns (McCorkel 2003). Inasmuch as gender-responsive tools are meant to be rooted in feminist research methodologies and theories that understand women's inequality and criminal offending as political, the focus on individual needs and recidivism in risk assessment absents this political critique. Criminalized individuals are tasked with remedying various aspects and effects of social inequality (such as colonialism, racism, sexism, and ableism), rather than responsibility being placed on broader political and social institutions. Rehabilitation efforts will therefore remain constrained by the prison's foundational focus on security, and through the conceptualization of rehabilitation as accomplished solely by individuals.

Notes

1 The CSC has not implemented *Creating Choices* in a manner consistent with the women-centered philosophy upon which its recommendations were based (Hannah-Moffat 2000; Hayman 2006; Struthers Montford 2015).
2 Although developed and normed on women's populations, the trailer is meant to be applied to gender-neutral or men's tools in an effort to promote gender responsivity through actuarial risk assessment (Salisbury et al. 2016).

References

Andrews, D. A. (1989) Recidivism is predictable and can be influenced: Using risk assessments to reduce recidivism. *Forum on Corrections Research*, 1(2), 11–18.

Andrews, D. A., Bonta, J. and Hoge, R. D. (1990) Classification for effective rehabilitation: Rediscovering psychology. *Criminal Justice Behaviour*, 17, 19–52.

Blanchette, K. and Brown, S. L. (2006) *The Assessment and Treatment of Women Offenders: An Integrative Perspective*. Chichester: John Wiley & Sons.

Blanchette, K. and Taylor, K. (2005) *Development and Field-Test of a Gender-Informed Security Reclassification Scale for Women Offenders*. Ottawa, ON: Research Branch, Correctional Service of Canada Ottawa.

Bloom, B., Covington, S. and Raeder, M. (2003) *National Institute of Corrections: Gender-Responsive Strategies – Research, Practice, and Guiding Principles for Women Offenders [WWW Document]*. Available at: https://s3.amazonaws.com/static.nicic.gov/Library/018017.pdf (Accessed 16 October 2018).

Bonta, J. (2007) Offender risk assessment and sentencing. *Canadian Journal of Criminology and Criminal Justice*, 49, 519–529.

Canadian Human Rights Commission. (2003) Protecting Their Rights: A Systemic Review of Human Rights in Correctional Services for Federally Sentenced Women. Canadian Human Rights Commission, Ottawa, Ontario, Canada. Available at: https://www.chrc-ccdp.gc.ca/eng/content/protecting-their-rights-systemic-review-human-rights-correctional-services-federally

Correctional Service of Canada. (2017) *Gender Responsive Corrections for Women in Canada: The Road to Successful Reintegration [WWW Document]*. Available at: www.csc-scc.gc.ca/women/002002-0005-en.shtml#t10 (Accessed 16 October 2018).

Hannah-Moffat, K. (2000) Prisons that empower. *British Journal of Criminology*, 40, 510–531.

Hannah-Moffat, K. (2001) *Punishment in Disguise: Penal Governance and Federal Imprisonment of Women in Canada*. Toronto: University of Toronto Press, Scholarly Publishing Division.

Hannah-Moffat, K. (2004) Losing ground: Gendered knowledges, parole risk, and responsibility. *Social Politics: International Studies in Gender, State & Society*, 11, 363–385.

Hannah-Moffat, K. (2009) Gridlock or mutability: Reconsidering "gender" and risk assessment. *Criminology & Public Policy*, 8, 209–219.

Hannah-Moffat, K. (2013) Punishment and risk. In J. Simon and R. Sparks (Eds.), *The Sage Handbook of Punishment & Society*. London: Sage Publications, pp. 129–151.

Hannah-Moffat, K. (2016a) A conceptual kaleidoscope: Contemplating 'dynamic structural risk' and an uncoupling of risk from need. *Psychology, Crime & Law*, 22, 33–46.

Hannah-Moffat, K. (2016b) Purpose and context matters: Creating a space for meaningful dialogues about risk and need. In *Handbook on Risk and Need Assessment: Theory and Practice*. Abingdon, Oxon: Routledge, pp. 431–446.

Hannah-Moffat, K., Maurutto, P. and Turnbull, S. (2009) Negotiated risk: Actuarial illusions and discretion in probation. *Canadian Journal of Law and Society*, 24, 391–409.

Hayman, S. (2006) *Imprisoning Our Sisters*. Montréal and Kingston: McGill-Queen's University Press.

Heffernan, R. and Ward, T. (2015) The conceptualization of dynamic risk factors in child sex offenders: An agency model. *Aggression and Violent Behaviour*, 24, 250–260.

Heney, J. (2003) Report on, *Self-Injurious Behaviour in the Kingston Prison for Women*.

Kendall, K. and Pollack, S. (2005) Taming the shrew: Regulating prisoners through women-centered mental health programming. *Critical Criminology*, 13, 71–87.

McCorkel, J. A. (2003) Embodied surveillance and the gendering of punishment. *Journal of Contemporary Ethnography*, 32, 41–76.

Office of the Auditor General of Canada. (2017) Report 5, *Preparing Women Offenders for Release – Correctional Service Canada* (Independent Auditor's Report). Available at: http://www.oag-bvg.gc.ca/internet/English/parl_oag_201711_05_e_42670.html

Office of the Correctional Investigator Canada. (2017) Annual Report of the Office of the Correctional Investigator. Available at: https://www.oci-bec.gc.ca/cnt/rpt/pdf/annrpt/annrpt20162017-eng.pdf

Office of the Deputy Commissioner for Women. (2003) *Secure Unit Operational Plan: Intensive Intervention in a Secure Environment*. Ottawa: Correctional Service of Canada.

O'Malley, P. (2010) *Crime and Risk*. London: Sage Publications.

Rubenfeld, S. (2014) *An Examination of a Reweighted Custody Rating Scale for Women*. Ottawa, ON: Correctional Service of Canada, Research Branch.

Rudin, J. (2016) *Aboriginal Peoples and the Criminal Justice System*. Available in: https://www.publicsafety.gc.ca/cnt/rsrcs/lbrr/ctlg/dtls-en.aspx?d=PS&i=26919486

Salisbury, E. J., Boppre, B. and Bridget, K. (2016) Gender-responsive risk and need assessment: Implications for the treatment of justice-involved women. In Taxman, F. S. (Ed.), *Handbook on Risk and Need Assessment: Theory and Practice*. New York: Taylor & Francis, pp. 220–243.

Salisbury, E. J., Van Voorhis, P. and Spiropoulos, G. V. (2009) The predictive validity of a gender-responsive needs assessment: An exploratory study. *Crime & Delinquency*, 55, 550–585.

Struthers Montford, K. (2015) Transforming choices: The marginalization of gender-specific policy making in Canadian approaches to women's federal imprisonment. *Canadian Journal of Women and the Law*, 27(2), 284–310.

Task Force on Federally Sentenced Women. (1990) *Creating Choices: The Report of the Task Force on Federally Sentenced Women*. Ottawa, ON: Task Force on Federally Sentenced Women.

Thompson, J. and McConnell, A. (2013) *A Re-Validation of the Security Reclassification Scale (SRSW) Among Federal Women Offenders for a Period of at Least Six Months*. Ottawa, ON: Correctional Service of Canada, Research Branch.

UN General Assembly. (2011) *United Nations Rules for the Treatment of Women Prisoners and Non-Custodial Measures for Women Offenders (the Bangkok Rules): Note by the Secretariat, 6 October 2010*. A/C.3/65/L.5. Available at: https://www.refworld.org/docid/4dcbb0ae2.html (Accessed 8 July 2019).

Van Voorhis, P. (2012) On behalf of women offenders. *Criminology & Public Policy*, 11, 111–145.

Van Voorhis, P. (2016) Jail Tip #5: Use Gender Responsive Assessment Tools. National Resource Centre on Justice Involved Women. Available at: https://cjinvolvedwomen.org/wp-content/uploads/2016/03/Jail-Tip-Sheet-5.pdf

Van Voorhis, P., Wright, E. M., Salisbury, E. and Bauman, A. (2010) Women's risk factors and their contributions to existing risk/needs assessment: The current status of a gender-responsive supplement. *Criminal Justice & Behaviour*, 37, 261–288.

Vecchio, K. (2018) *A Call to Action: Reconciliation with Indigenous Women in the Federal Justice and Correctional Systems: Report of the Standing Committee on the Status of Women (42nd Parliament, 1st Session)*. Ottawa, ON: Standing Committee on the Status of Women.

Webster, C. and Doob, A. (2004) Classification without validity or equity: An empirical examination of the custody rating scale for federally sentenced women offenders in Canada. *Canadian Journal of Criminology and Criminal Justice*, 46, 395–421.

Zakaria, D., Allenby, K., Derkzen, D. M. and Jones, N. (2013) *Preliminary Development of a Dynamic Risk Assessment Tool for Women Offenders: An Examination of Gender Neutral and Gender Specific Variables*. Ottawa, ON: Correctional Service of Canada, Research Branch.

Assessing risks and needs in youth justice

21

Key challenges

Stephen Case and Kevin Haines

Introduction

When we set out to write *Understanding Youth Offending: Risk Factor Research, Policy and Practice* (Case and Haines 2009), the original concept behind the book was to bridge the gulf between proponents and critics of risk factor research. Risk factor research (RFR), it seemed to us, was proliferating as an explanatory paradigm and was becoming increasingly influential in youth justice policy and practice, but it was not advancing. Rarely, if ever, did an exponent of RFR cite (or even show an awareness of) the growing body of scholarship that presented critiques of the paradigm, conduct, and conclusions of said research,[1] especially in its pseudo-psychological, quantified, 'artefactual' form – despite the cogency and power of many of these critiques. Our aim, therefore, was to bring proponent and critic together in order to draw out any such conclusions concerning our understanding of offending by children and its treatment that, we believed, retained some degree of validity.

We began our journey in the scholarly tradition, by researching the international corpus of published RFR. The deeper we delved into this body of research, however, the more we realized that we were not going to be able to deliver the original concept of the book for two main reasons:

1   The mainly positivist attitudes and approaches of risk factor researchers evidenced a very poor understanding of (the lives of) children;
2   Despite claims that RFR was the 'appliance of science' (Porteus 2007) to the understanding of offending by children and its treatment, the quality of the science (methodology) was very poor.

Reflecting on the conclusions reached by risk factor researchers, we were compelled to conclude that they were either (1) overstated or (2) simply wrong. Consequently, our book (Case and Haines 2009) became one focused on a comprehensive and international critique of RFR and, to a certain extent, risk factor researchers.

It would be gratifying if, nearly ten years after the publication of *Understanding Youth Offending*, our work had made some impact upon risk factor researchers and research. Sadly, it has not. RFR endures (mostly, it has to be recognized in the United States), unaltered by our critique or that of any other critic, and the worst examples of RFR continue to be published in peer-reviewed academic journals. In slight contrast, our work and that of others has made some impact in England and Wales to the extent that the Youth Justice Board for England and Wales has moved away from an over-reliance on the assessment of risk and risk-based offence and offender-focused interventions. In their place has been the development and roll out of AssetPlus: a revised assessment tool that de-emphasizes risk (although it retains an element of risk assessment) in favour of more holistic, whole child assessments and a focus on achieving, through varied interventions, positive outcomes for children that include, but are not limited to, reductions in offending (see Haines and Case 2015). In making this move, however, the YJB retains, in AssetPlus, a proforma approach to the assessment of risk (ticking boxes and using rating scales), whereas the majority of AssetPlus (where the more child-centric assessments take place) are unstructured and rely on practitioner's professional assessments and judgements. It is, perhaps, not too surprising, therefore, that recent research (e.g. Goddard and Myers 2017; Armitage et al. 2016; Dunkel 2014) has found that (too) many youth justice practitioners continue to (over) rely on assessments of risk to the neglect of a more rounded and wholistic child-centred assessment (and consequent intervention).[2]

The challenge for youth justice managers and practitioners (and, indeed, policymakers), and the challenge for us in this chapter is, therefore, to better understand a situation where RFR continues unabated and unaltered – despite its lacking in veracity, the influence of RFR continues to be felt on policy and practice – and although diminished, it is not extinguished and a greater emphasis on child centric assessments and interventions remains nascent – there are glimmers of hope but they remain quite dim. Approaches to assessment and intervention in youth justice systems globally face significant challenges in their journey towards offering more complete understandings of, and appropriate responses to, children who offend. The key challenges identified to structure chapter discussions are:

1   *Evidence* – it is imperative that assessment-intervention practice with children who offend is informed by a comprehensive, valid (meaningful, accurate, representative), and ethical evidence base;
2   *Extrication* – contemporary youth justice policy and practice must extricate itself from an obsession with actuarial risk management based on a partial evidence base, which has led to problems of invalidity, reductionism, negativity, practice prescription, and adult centrism – bad science (mis)informing bad practice;
3   *Evolution* – progressive alternative approaches must be developed to address embedded problems with practice and to evolve assessment-intervention in evidenced, ethical, and child-centred ways.

Taking into account the foregoing contextualization, this chapter juxtaposes our personal academic, critical, and evidence-based journey towards evolving youth justice assessment-intervention with the contemporaneous, slower, and more complex journey of policy and practice in addressing the challenges facing the contemporary assessment-intervention that progresses understandings of children who offend.

The risk factor research 'evidence' base

Criminological RFR originated in the United States in the 1930s through the work of the Gluecks (Glueck and Glueck 1930), who 'factorised' (converted to quantified factors) a wide range of individualized, psychosocial (psychological and immediate social) risk factors in their attempt to understand and explain offending by children. Notably, the factor that they found to be most influential on reductions in and cessations of offending was *maturation* – growing up and growing out of crime. Notwithstanding this cogent argument for minimum necessary/radical non-intervention, the Gluecks' RFR was soon consolidated and extrapolated by the seminal criminological study of the efficacy of risk-focused intervention, the Cambridge-Sommerville Youth Study (Cabot 1940). Notably, the study concluded that there were no significant effects of risk-based intervention on crime prevention or reduction and that such intervention could even be harmful due to labelling processes and encouraging system contact (McCord 1978).

Methods and findings of RFR (those that did not contradict the central thesis that predictive risk factors can be identified and targeted through crime prevention activity) were subsequently driven forward in the UK by the influential 'Cambridge Study in Delinquent Development' (West and Farrington 1973). The only so-called risk factor not adopted in what now constitutes nearly 90 years of RFR was maturation! Thus was born a research paradigm that came to dominate youth justice policy and practice in England and Wales, indeed, internationally (Case in press; Goddard and Myers 2017; Dunkel 2014). Since West and Farrington's 'Cambridge Study' (which persists to this day) published its initial results, a vast movement of artefactual RFR (converting risks into artefacts or factors) has proliferated across the United Kingdom, North America, and Australasia – research based on the relentless replication of a restricted group of needs, problems, and experiences in psychosocial domains of children's lives that have been reconstructed as 'risk factors' and understood as predictive of an increased likelihood of future offending (Case and Haines 2009). Consequently, preventative interventions with and the treatment of children identified as 'offenders' or identified (through assessment) as 'at risk' of offending should target and seek to ameliorate these risk factors. This is the 'Risk Factor Prevention Paradigm' (Hawkins and Catalano 1992) that dominates the policy and practice of contemporary youth justice systems across the Western world (Case and Haines 2015; Goddard 2014; Briggs 2013).

The Risk Factor Prevention Paradigm (RFPP) has provided governments with a vast and reliable (widely replicated) evidence base to underpin policy formation, resource allocation, and practice prescriptions for risk-based assessment and intervention; an evidence base that has been (mis)interpreted as illustrating an effective, efficient, and economical method of responding to children who offend (Case 2016; Stephenson et al. 2011). However, this is an evidence base largely ignorant of the realities of the lives of the children it purported to understand for a number of crucial reasons, all of which implicate the through-going conceptual and methodological *invalidity* of the RFPP and question its influence over policy and practice. The scope and breadth of scholarship that is critical of RFR and its influence over policy and practice is far too extensive to even summarize cogently in this chapter (but see Goddard and Myers 2017; Case and Haines 2015, 2009; Muncie 2014; Bateman 2011; O'Mahony 2009). Accordingly, we will limit ourselves to an overview of some of the main criticisms. Table 21.1 sets out the invalidating elements of the RFPP as a paradigm for understanding and responding to offending by children, juxtaposed with the marginalized and neglected challenges to/ criticisms of these limitations.

The inevitable outcome of this burgeoning evidence base and practice paradigm founded on adult-centric reductionism, partiality, and methodological invalidity has been the proliferation of psychosocial risk assessments and individualized risk-, offence-, and offender-focused interventions, to the detriment of needs-led, whole-child and future-oriented responses. However, the application of the RFPP in practice has been underpinned by an evidence base of extensively replicated limitations and weaknesses that cohere to invalidate understandings of and responses to children who offend. Bad science begets bad practice. The initial challenge for youth justice when assessing

Table 21.1 Exploring the invalidities of the RFPP

Invalidity	Challenge/criticism
Adult-centrism	
The RFPP has been developed by adults – academic researchers (typically developmental and life-course criminologists) doing research *to* children and animated by policymakers with a limited understanding of the methods, findings, practice realities, and associated limitations of RFR. The methods of RFR have been chosen and applied by adults (e.g. the content of risk assessment tools), the findings have been analyzed and interpreted by adults (e.g. as most influential in children's lives) and recommendations for preventative interventions and broader youth justice policy have been made by adults on this basis.	The RFPP was not developed through research consultation or practice *with* the people who possess the deepest and most meaningful understanding of the target behaviour: children! We could also add youth justice practitioners as a neglected key stakeholder group – the very adults tasked to make sense of and mobilize the RFPP on a daily basis. Developing a practice paradigm without the full participation of the two most important stakeholder groups – those who commit the behaviour and those who respond to it inherently invalidates the explanations produced and responses recommended.
Negative perceptions of children who offend	
'The basic idea [of the RFPP] . . . is very simple: Identify the key risk factors for offending and implement prevention methods designed to counteract them. There is often a related attempt to identify key protective factors against offending and to implement prevention methods designed to enhance them' (Farrington, in Maguire et al. 2007: 606). As such, a series of psychosocial risk factors have been identified and widely replicated across international RFR as predictive of future offending and thus appropriate targets for ameliorative intervention and treatment.	The RFPP has reinforced a prevention agenda for youth justice systems and practitioners, prioritizing the prevention of negative behaviours (e.g. offending, reoffending, substance use) and negative outcomes (e.g. exposure to risk factors, reconviction). However, this agenda promotes negative perceptions (and treatment) of children who offend as bundles of individualized risks and deficits to be corrected and controlled by adults. Understandings through the lens of 'risk' portray children as dangerous, threatening, and flawed, yet also passive recipients of damaging risk factors, rather than as children experiencing problems and unmet needs or as agentic negotiators of their own lives.
Reductionism	
The RFPP actively facilitates the reduction/simplification of important experiences, relationships, behaviours, and attitudes in children's lives into quantifiable 'risk factors' that can be statistically related to offending behaviour and targeted by subsequent intervention. The result is a common-sense, practical paradigm that 'is easy to understand and to communicate, and it is readily accepted by policymakers, practitioners, and the general public. Both risk factors and interventions are based on empirical research rather than theories' (Farrington 2000: 7).	Whilst the RFPP may offer a common-sense, readily understandable and practical response model, its essential reduction of different elements of children's lives to quantifiable, generalized factors serves to oversimplify and invalidate its findings and recommendations. The concept of the 'risk factor' washes away the multifaceted, complex, dynamic, nuanced, and negotiated nature of the lives of different children in different places at different times. The lived experience is reduced to a single risk score or series of meaningless statistics that are interpreted and extrapolated by adults (adult-centrism) detached from the realities of the child's life.

(Continued)

Table 21.1 Continued

Invalidity	Challenge/criticism
Partiality	
The RFR evidence base that underpins the RFPP has been championed as comprehensive and robust, largely due to its durability (90 years and counting) and extensive replication of a growing number of psychosocial risk factors across demographic groups and different countries (Farrington et al. 2019). In other words, the same risk factors have been consistently identified as linked to offending by children over time and place. Consequently, the RFPP forms the backbone of the 'evidence-based practice' and 'effective practice' tenets of the Youth Justice System of England and Wales (Stephenson et al. 2011).	The evidence base is partial and thus limited in scope and validity. It has been partial (biased) towards psychosocial explanations of offending to the neglect of considering the influence of factors that may be socio-structural (e.g. unemployment, poverty, neighbourhood destabilization, cultural and political context), interpersonal/interactional (e.g. relationships and interactions with key adults and peers, public opinion, and treatment), and systemic (e.g. harmful contact with the youth justice systems and its agents). It has been partial (limited) in its understanding of the nature of the risk factor-offending relationship – ambiguous as to whether risk factors operate as causes, predictors, indicators, correlates, or even symptoms of offending. As such, we have little conclusive understanding of exactly how risk factors may influence offending (if at all), or why, how, and if they should be targeted.
Methodological inadequacy	
Much of the claim to the validity and superiority of RFR as providing and explanation of offending by children and proscriptions for interventions that reduce future offending rest on RFR's self-proclamation that it is the 'appliance of science'. That RFR has, as a body of research, utilized a scientific and hence robust and globally applicable methodology that is beyond question is at the centre of its assertions to its practical utility. These claims, however, are simply not sustainable.	Far from embodying the 'appliance of science', RFR has embodied the misapplication of poor quality science (see Case and Haines 2009 for a more detailed methodological analysis and critique of RFR). Despite claims to global consistency and replicability, RFR has actually comprised a very disparate body of research with more difference than commonality. All too often cross-sectional research designs have been utilized in RFR, from which causal linkages between risk factors and offending have been asserted or, more accurately, imputed. Cross-sectional research cannot determine causality. Compounding these issues, statistical tests of association have been consistently misapplied in RFR to determine linear and causal relationships between variables. The inappropriate application and interpretation of these statistical tests invalidates the conclusions of RFR.

children's risks and needs is to extricate itself from a misguided loyalty to the methods and findings of the RFPP. The challenge then becomes to evolve policy and practice into more valid, wholistic forms that respond to more valid, wholistic understandings of the lives and experiences of children who offend. A nascent model of child-centric assessment is emerging that offers the potential for such extrication and evolution of the ways in which youth justice responds to the challenges of assessing risks and needs.

Child-centric assessment

It is clear that a different form of assessment-intervention framework is required following the political and academic rejection of the RFR evidence base, which necessitates extrication from the RFPP and exploration of alternative approaches. This necessity is even more urgent as a response to the contemporary phenomena (most notably evidenced in England and Wales) of fewer children being dealt with by youth justice systems and as first-time entrants, offenders, and reoffenders (Bateman 2017), necessitating less intervention/ism and more appropriate assessment-intervention, along with the associated higher proportion of children with multiple complex needs remaining in youth justice systems (Taylor 2016), necessitating more appropriate, wholistic assessment-intervention. Accordingly, new child-centric assessment methods are developing across Westernized youth justice systems for application in the contemporary youth justice context to augment, challenge, and even replace traditional frameworks grounded in the RFPP. The revised assessment methods have presented as more wholistic (whole child/family/system), child-friendly, child-appropriate, relationship-based, and promotional of positive behaviours/outcomes than those pursued through the RFPP.

By way of example, the risk-based 'Scaled Approach' assessment and intervention framework in the Youth Justice System (YJS) of England and Wales was replaced in 2015 by 'AssetPlus', a significantly revised practice paradigm that sought to address several of the commonly identified limitations of the RFPP (YJB 2013, 2012). The AssetPlus 'Core Record' instrument consists of three sections, beginning with the four-part 'Information Gathering' (assessment) component, which covers personal, family, and social factors; offending and antisocial behaviour; foundations for change; and self-assessment by the child. The information collected informs an 'Explanations and Conclusions' section linking these different influences to the child's offending behaviour, which in turn informs the 'Pathways and Planning' (intervention) element of the tool. Whilst the quadrants within the Information Gathering/Assessment section measure the influences of different 'factors' on offending, they do not quantify them, nor do they explore them through the lens of risk. A more wholistic and valid assessment of the child's life is facilitated by understanding the influences-offending relationship as more dynamic, contextualized, interactive, and qualitative than was permitted through the Scaled Approach. Furthermore, wholistic and valid assessment is supported by more focus on factors linked to positive behaviour, the child's motivations to change and the role of personal strengths and capacities – each of which is assessed and interpreted by accessing the much-neglected voices of the child (through self-assessment) and the youth justice practitioner (though enabling discretion) and by making space for relationship-based practice/assessment between these two key stakeholders (see Johns et al. 2017; Drake et al. 2014; Creaney and Smith 2014).

A more localized and developed example of child-centric assessment has evolved in Surrey, England. The 'Youth Support Service' integrates a range of services for children (e.g. social care, health, education, youth justice) to offer a whole child/family, rights-based, needs-led, safeguarding, and restorative response to all children demonstrating vulnerability, need, and problematic behaviour. The Youth Support Service (YSS) is, therefore, a needs-led, not risk-based, 'one-stop shop' for all local children identified as vulnerable due to their circumstances and/or behaviour. In order to service this child-centric, positive-facing response framework, the YSS has eschewed AssetPlus (youth justice-focused) assessment in favour of a comprehensive (needs-led), wholistic assessment (the 'Common Assessment Framework') and broad intervention plan prioritizing relationship-based, jointly determined response (rejecting siloed, adult-centric youth justice interventions) for all children (Byrne and Case 2016; Brooks and Byrne 2015). Outcomes for local children who have offended have been promising, with Surrey evidencing the lowest level of first-time entrants in to the YJS throughout England and Wales, along with one of the lowest per capita levels of custody for children (Ministry of Justice/Youth Justice Board 2016). Indeed, the recent Government review of the YJS identified Surrey as an exemplar of a progressive, positive, child-centric approach and a viable alternative to the RFPP (Taylor 2016).

Then nascent AssetPlus framework and the Surrey YSS model indicate the potential for child-centric, relationship-based, positive, and wholistic alternative approaches to assessment with children who offend and the potential for such assessment to shape equivalent forms of intervention. A clear challenge to the child-centric progression of youth justice assessment, however, is the need to re-educate a significant number of existing youth justice staff who have become wedded to risk-based working due to their training and experience with RFPP-centric 'evidence-based' and 'effective' practice methods. It is highly likely that a proportion of youth justice staff, especially less experienced staff from the 21st-century risk management era, will require support to extricate themselves from their practical and philosophical ties to the RFPP and its partial and invalid methodologies and evidence base (Morris 2015; Drake et al. 2014; Case and Hester 2010).

Conclusion: where next?

Assessment is crucial in youth justice. However, assessment is not just about assessing things. Either explicitly or (all too often) implicitly, the type, form, and content of assessment modalities and tools contains a model for understanding behaviour (e.g. offending) and proscriptions for responding to (treating) the behaviour. In this way, assessments of risk lead quite naturally to interventions targeted on those same risks – this is good 'common sense'. The problem is that common sense is quite dangerous and potentially harmful to children – particularly when it comes to areas of professional practice.

Therefore, we need more than common sense. We need thorough-going and expertly informed academic analysis to properly understand complex social phenomena. Such expert academic analysis has clearly and consistently shown that RFR is deeply flawed and wholly unreliable as an evidence base for assessment and intervention planning with children who have offended. The time has come (in fact it is long overdue) to abandon risk as the animator of assessment in youth justice and to abandon its sinister relation: risk-focused interventions. In fact, many academics, politicians, policymakers, managers, and practitioners have already moved on from risk to new and, as yet, emerging forms of assessment that have been developed with children (not on them), that are sensitive to the special period in our lives known as childhood and to the personal and social characteristics that go with it, and that hold out a positive vision and enabled future for all children. This journey is nascent, but it is one that we must all pursue with vigour. This is the challenge that we now face.

Notes

1   We found this state of affairs quite troubling. One of the claims to the veracity of risk factor research was that it was the 'appliance of science' to the study of offending by children (too frequently referred to as 'offenders') and its treatment. Yet a central premise of science is that it advances through critique. For us, it is not possible to sustain claims to be scientific when one eschews a central tenet of the paradigm.
2   There is a notable perversity in practice here. Recent developments in youth justice in England and Wales have seen significant developments and growth in the numbers of children being diverted away from the Youth Justice System (Bateman 2017. Those children who do become embroiled in the formal Youth Justice System, therefore, tend to have committed more serious offences (or a greater number of offences) and they tend to be those who present the most serious personal problems as well as experiencing the worst social conditions (Johns et al. 2017; Taylor 2016; Yates 2012). The perversity is that it is these children who are still exposed to predominantly risk-focused assessments and interventions – despite the severity of their social circumstances and the very real need to enhance their social capital.

References

Armitage, V., Kelly, L. and Phoenix, J. (2016) Janus-faced youth justice work and the transformation of accountability. *Howard Journal of Crime and Justice*, 55(4), 478–495.

Bateman, T. (2011) Punishing poverty: The 'scaled approach' and youth justice practice. *Howard Journal of Penal Reform*, 50(2), 171–183.

Bateman, T. (2017) *The State of Youth Justice 2017: An Overview of Trends and Developments*. London: NAYJ.

Briggs, D. (2013) Conceptualising risk and need: The rise of actuarialism and the death of welfare? Practitioner assessment and intervention in the youth offending service. *Youth Justice*, 13(1), 17–30.

Brooks, K. and Byrne, K. (2015) *Post-YOT Youth Justice: Howard League What Is Justice? Working Papers*. London: Howard League.

Byrne, B. and Case, S. P. (2016) Towards a positive youth justice. *Safer Communities*, 15(2), 69–81.

Cabot, R. (1940) A long-term study of children: The Cambridge-Somerville youth study. *Child Development*, 11(2), 143–151.

Case, S. P. (in press) *Contemporary Youth Justice*. Abingdon: Routledge.

Case, S. P. (2016) Communicating risk in youth justice: A numbers game. In J. Crichton, C. Candlin and A. Firkins (Eds.), *Communicating Risk*. Basingstoke: Palgrave Macmillan.

Case, S. P. and Haines, K. R. (2009) *Understanding Youth Offending: Risk Factor Research Policy and Practice*. Cullompton: Willan Publishing.

Case, S. P. and Haines, K. R. (2015) Children first, offenders second positive promotion: Reframing the prevention debate. *Youth Justice Journal*, 15(3), 226–239.

Case, S. P. and Hester, R. (2010) Professional education in youth justice. Mirror or motor? *British Journal of Community Justice*, 8(2), 45–56.

Creaney, S. and Smith. R. (2014) Youth justice back at the crossroads. *Safer Communities*, 13(2), 83–87.

Drake, D. H., Fergusson, R. and Briggs, D. B. (2014) Hearing new voices: Re-viewing youth justice policy through practitioners' relationships with young people. Youth *Justice*, 14(1), 22–39.

Dunkel, F. (2014) Juvenile justice systems in Europe – reform developments between justice, welfare and 'new punitiveness'. *Criminological Studies*, 1.

Farrington, D. P. (2000) Explaining and preventing crime: The globalization of Knowledge. *Criminology*, 38(1), 1–24.

Farrington, D. P., Kazemian, L. and Piquero, A. R. (Eds.). (2019) *The Oxford Handbook of Developmental and Life-Course Criminology*. New York: Oxford University Press.

Glueck, S. and Glueck, E. (1930) *500 Criminal Careers*. New York: Alfred Knopf.

Goddard, T. (2014) The indeterminacy of the risk factor prevention paradigm: A case study of community partnerships implementing youth and gang violence prevention policy. *Youth Justice*, 14(1), 3–21.

Goddard, T. and Myers, R. (2017) Against evidence-based oppression: Marginalized youth and the politics of risk-based assessment and intervention. *Theoretical Criminology*, 21(2), 151–167.

Haines, K. R. and Case, S. P. (2015) *Positive Youth Justice: Children First, Offenders Second*. Bristol: Policy Press.

Hawkins, J. D. and Catalano, R. F. (1992) *Communities That Care*. San Francisco: Jossey-Bass.

Johns, D., Williams, K. and Haines, K. R. (2017) Ecological youth justice: Understanding the social ecology of young people's prolific offending. *Youth Justice*, 17(1), 3–21.

Maguire, M., Morgan, R. and Reiner, R. (2007) *Oxford Handbook of Criminology*. Oxford: Oxford University Press.

McCord, J. (1978) A thirty-year follow-up of treatment effects. *American Psychologist*, 284–289, March.

Ministry of Justice/Youth Justice Board. (2016) *Youth Justice Annual Statistics*. London: MOJ/YJB.

Morris, R. (2015) Youth justice practice is Just Messy' youth offending team practitioners: Culture and identity. *British Journal of Community Justice*, 2(13), 45–57.

Muncie, J. (2014) *Youth and Crime*. London: Sage Publications.

O'Mahony, P. (2009) The risk factors paradigm and the causes of youth crime: A deceptively useful analysis? *Youth Justice*, 9(2), 99–115.

Porteus, D. (2007) The prevention of youth crime: A risky business? In B. Stephenson, H. Giller and S. Brown (Eds.), *Effective Practice in Youth Justice*. Cullompton: Willan Publishing.

Taylor, C. (2016) *Review of the Youth Justice System in England and Wales*. London: Ministry of Justice.

West, D. and Farrington, D. (1973) *Who Becomes Delinquent?* London: Heinemann.

Yates, J. (2012) What prospects youth justice? Children in trouble in the age of austerity. *Journal of Social Policy and Administration*, 46(4), 432–447.

Youth Justice Board. (2012) *AssetPlus Rationale*. London: YJB.

Youth Justice Board. (2013) *Assessment and Planning Interventions Framework – AssetPlus. Model Document*. London: YJB.

22

Pre-sentence reports

Constructing the subject of punishment and rehabilitation

Niamh Maguire

Introduction

Pre-sentence reports provide information to the court about the offender and the offence and usually include a sentencing proposal or recommendation. In most jurisdictions, their main formal purpose is to inform sentencing decisions by providing background information on the offender and offence that helps to contextualize the offence and individualize the offender. Pre-sentence reports (PSRs) are known by various names depending on the jurisdiction, time, and place of use including a social enquiry report, a probation report, a pre-investigation report, a pre-disposition report, an advisory report, and a pre-sanction report. Pre-sentence reports are typically prepared by probation officers and represent a core task of probation services in most European countries (Val Kalmthout and Durnescu 2008) and in many other jurisdictions including Australia, New Zealand, Canada, and the US (Hannah-Moffat and Maurutto 2010). While reports are generally prepared after conviction and in advance of the sentencing hearing, some variation exists around the world in terms of the point in the process at which reports are prepared and the types of reports prepared (Boone and Herzog-Evans 2013; Val Kalmthout and Durnescu 2008).

In the late 20th century most jurisdictions experienced a distinct increase in the number of PSRs generated and used in sentencing (Durnescu et al. 2013). Despite this overall growth, PSRs are a finite resource and are thus only available in a small proportion of all criminal cases that come before the courts. In the Canadian province of Ontario for instance they were provided in about 10% of cases in 2006–2007 (Hannah-Moffat and Maurutto 2010: 266). In Ireland, while the District and Circuit Criminal Courts resolved 310,220 cases in 2015 (Court Service 2015), only 5,072 PSRs were requested by these courts in the same year (Probation Service 2016). The realization that PSRs are only available in a small proportion of all cases sentenced in any jurisdiction underscores the importance of understanding their use.

Origins and early development

Although very little is written about the historical origins of reports, the collection of personal and social data about the defendant as a means of informing sentencing has been a common practice in most legal systems for some time (Boone and Herzog-Evans 2013). In England and Wales, references to officers making enquiries about offenders and reporting back to court has been found in late 19th-century court records (McWilliams 1986). This early practice was based on verbal enquiries aimed at identifying cases that deserved greater leniency (McWilliams 1986) and verbal reports continued up until the 1960s after which point written reports emerged as the dominant practice. In recent years the verbal tradition has returned in England and Wales where the dominant type of PSR prepared by probation officers is now a short report presented orally in court (Robinson 2017). In Sweden, PSRs were first written in 1918 when suspended sentences were introduced and the first report writers were usually court clerks (Persson and Svennson 2012). In Denmark pre-sentence reports emerged as an important practice as early as the 1930s (Wandall 2010).

In most countries PSRs are discretionary although they are mandatory in some jurisdictions in certain circumstances. Normally, PSRs are requested by judges and written by probation officers but there is some variation. Prosecutors may request PSRs in Sweden and Denmark (Persson and Svensson 2012; Wandall 2010). In Canada, PSRs are generally prepared by probation officers but may be contracted out to a partner organization in particularly complex cases and *Gladue* reports prepared for Aboriginal offenders are written by specially trained Aboriginal court report writers (Hannah-Moffat and Maurutto 2010). Lay investigators (often university students) prepare PSRs in Denmark where a summary of the report is typically read aloud in court by the defence lawyer (Wandall 2010). In some jurisdictions in the US private investigation companies provide pre-sentence investigations (PSIs) and like PSRs, they have been associated with the imposition of less severe sentences (Teague 2011).

Based on interviews with the defendant, in which they are asked about family background, education and work, health and substance misuse, housing, and attitudes to crime, the information in PSRs is often not externally validated (Maguire and Carr 2017). Research on the practice of writing reports before the introduction of actuarial risk assessment tools (and in some cases even since its introduction) suggests that reports in most jurisdictions were written by probation officers who used social work skills and primarily focused on identifying and addressing the social problems facing defendants and contextualizing the offending within its broader social and structural contexts. Probation officers drew upon their professional social work skills and clinical experience when making assessments of the offender's risk of reoffending and such assessments were expressed in narrative terms. PSRs are thus traditionally associated with penal-welfarism and rehabilitation orientations and practices.

Purpose of reports

While the formal purpose of PSRs is usually to assist and inform sentencer decision-making by providing accurate and relevant information about the offence and the offender, a cursory exploration of the available literature shows that PSRs serve a range of latent purposes aside from their more obvious, formal ones. Carr and Maguire's (2017) study on pre-sentence reports found that both probation officers and judges perceived the report-writing process as providing an opportunity for a momentary pause in a larger process during which the person can make a choice about whether or not they wish to engage by demonstrating a willingness and capacity to change. The functionality of reports went beyond the formal purpose of providing assistance to judges in some instances by acting as a form of intervention in itself as clients were linked up with various services that would otherwise be difficult for them to access (Maguire and Carr 2017).

Reports contribute to the process of individualizing the offender (Tata et al. 2008; Maguire and Carr 2017) by proactively constructing the identity and defining the character of the offender (Johansen 2017). This is achieved by choosing the type of information that is communicated to the court and by deciding how to frame or present that information (Johansen 2017). As Hannah-Moffat and Maurutto (2010: 263) observe, PSRs 'frame legal subjectivities for the court'. Reports put forward a social construction of the offender to the court. Therefore, how they are structured, the types of information they contain, and the analyses they are informed by are thus crucially important.

Tata (2017) highlights how reports facilitate 'ritual individualisation'. In the lower courts in adversarial systems, especially where guilty pleas are common, courts rarely hear about the life of the offender because there is no trial. Reports provide the opportunity for the defendant to participate and have a voice (Tata 2010). Reports 'perform the display of individualisation for the court' thus helping to fortify 'legal identities, norms and court communities' by allowing punishment to be perceived as legitimate by court actors (Tata 2018: 21).

Reports provide an opportunity for knowledge from other 'institutional settings and epistemologies' to influence the work of the courts (Field and Tata 2010; Johansen 2017) and act as a vehicle for a form of inter-professional communication (Carr and Maguire 2017). Indeed, as pre-sentence reports occupy a central position in the work of probation services in most jurisdictions, how they are perceived and valued may both reflect on and echo the way that probation work itself is perceived and valued. Reports are also vital for allowing legal actors to process cases in good conscience (Tata 2010). They make legal actors feel better about processing large numbers of cases as they allow a momentary pause in which to consider individual cases in some depth, thus putatively enhancing justice (Tata 2010; Carr and Maguire 2017).

Policy imperatives: increasing reliance on alternatives to prison

In many contexts pre-sentence reports have been associated with the specific policy imperative of reducing reliance on imprisonment by increasing the use of non-custodial and, more specifically, community sanctions. This policy imperative is explicit in certain countries such as Scotland (Tata et al. 2008) and England and Wales (Gelsthorpe and Raynor 1995) and more implicit in countries such as Ireland and Belgium (Carr and Maguire 2017; Beyens and Scheirs 2010). In Denmark, pre-sentence reports are associated with a rehabilitative framework that emphasizes the use of treatment and community sanctions; PSRs are typically requested in minor offences where a community sentence is likely (Wandall 2010; Johansen 2017). Additionally, the Probation Service in Denmark operates an unofficial stance that, where possible, defendants are to be assessed as suitable for community service. In Sweden, a key purpose of PSRs involves assessing the suitability for a community sanction (Persson and Svensson 2012). In some countries PSRs also operate as a form of sentence planning where the appropriate form of supervision, including specific programming elements such as training and education, and relevant conditions, are identified (Wandall 2010; Persson and Svensson 2012; Hannah-Moffat and Maurutto 2010).

The instrumental purposes of pre-sentence reports (as a means to a particular policy end) are most pronounced in the UK where successive governments have sought to use them to influence judges to reduce the use of imprisonment and increase the use of community sentences (Tata 2018). In the early 1990s, shortly after the introduction of the Criminal Justice Act 1991 in England and Wales, which made the use of PSRs mandatory in certain cases, Bredar (1992: 2) observed a 'British tendency to regard sentencing reports as only relevant to the question of whether custody should or should not be imposed, and not relevant to other considerations such as how lengthy a term should be imposed, or how the defendant should be supervised upon release from custody'.

In the intervening period, it is clear that these instrumental purposes have not been achieved. Tata (2018) argues that the persuasive approach to reducing the use of custody through reports has not been successful; reductions in prison use remain as elusive as ever and recent evidence (Aebi et al. 2015) shows a rise in *both* custodial and community penalties. In Scotland and in England and Wales, Tata (2018) argues that governments have failed to confront the assumption of judicial ownership of sentencing (Ashworth 2015), instead preferring to take the indirect route by adopting a policy of persuasion. Policymakers, in light of this failure, have redoubled their efforts to persuade judges by focusing on enhancing the quality of PSRs (Tata 2018). Drawing on theories of consumption as a cultural practice, he argues that attempts to satisfy judicial demands will not succeed but will instead continue to impel their dissatisfaction. Beyens and Scheirs (2010) draw similar conclusions from their study of pre-sentence reports in Belgium. They found that the relatively marginal use of social reports was related to judicial ownership of sentencing decision-making and the fact that judges adhered to their own penal culture, which prioritized neo-classical theories of crime over rehabilitation.

Two of the most recurrent issues highlighted in the PSR literature are (1) the relationship between the 'quality' of reports and their ability to influence the sentencing decision and (2) the impact that the introduction of actuarial risk assessment has had on the traditional probation welfare emphasis on offenders' background and needs.

Quality and influence of reports

The issue of 'quality' in pre-sentence reports is a recurrent and dominant theme in the research literature on pre-sentence reports. While it appears to be widely accepted that pre-sentence reports do influence sentencing, relatively little is known about the actual processes involved. Although the majority of research on the issue of quality relates to the UK, and more specifically to England and Wales, quality issues also feature in other jurisdictions. Before examining some of the research findings on quality, we need to disentangle the various meanings of 'quality' in the literature.

Quality as it relates to reports has at least three meanings. The first relates to actual internal quality of a report in terms of how well written it is, how informative, comprehensive, and logical it is, its relationship to empirical evidence and how realistic the recommendation is (Gelsthorpe and Raynor 1995; Downing and Lynch 1997; Tata 2018). Presumably internal quality also refers to the extent to which the report has followed any prescribed or practitioner guidelines for writing reports in terms of including all the relevant information. Second, what might be termed external quality relates to the extent to which the report has been effective in influencing or persuading a judge to pass a particular sentence, usually a community sanction (Gelsthorpe and Raynor 1995; Downing and Lynch 1997; Tata 2018). The third sense in which quality has been addressed in the literature is in the context of diversity issues and anti-discriminatory practice (Gelsthorpe 1992; NAPO 1991; Downing and Lynch 1997).

In much of the research literature the issue of the quality of PSRs is often conflated with the issue of the effectiveness of reports in terms of their ability to influence sentencing outcomes. Downing and Lynch (1997) observe that the concept of 'quality assurance' arose out of the desire of the Probation Service in England and Wales in the 1980s to increase the potential for influencing judges by assuring that the best possible quality report went to court. This melded with the managerialism discourse that emerged in the late 1980s. At about the same time, evidence of discriminatory practices embedded within the pre-sentence reports (Gelsthorpe 1992; NAPO 1991) meant that professional and academic interests in 'quality' as an expression of anti-oppressive practice overlapped with managers' concerns to ensure the effectiveness of reports (Downing and Lynch 1997). With the introduction of National Standards for PSRs in England and Wales, the issue of quality became more 'strongly associated with compliance' so that a 'good' report was 'seen as one which most closely complie[d] with national standards' (Downing and Lynch 1997: 176). However, they note that it is possible for PSRs to tick all the boxes of the requirements of National Standards and still fail on other 'quality' grounds.

Critics of the conflation of quality and effectiveness argue that quality in the context of reports should be 'related not to instrumental objectives but rather the expressive good of fulfilling offender needs, reducing harm to the individual and society and excellence in practice' (Downing and Lynch 1997: 188). They argue that the concept of quality assurance which involves monitoring the 'quality' and 'effectiveness' of reports emerged from the considerable body of research into the value and effectiveness of PSRs and that it is responsible for the assumption that high quality reports were those that had high levels of concordance between recommendations and sentencing outcomes.

But how can influence be evaluated? Previous studies across various jurisdictions that have explored the issue of influence have relied upon the concept of concordance between recommendations in reports and sentencing outcomes as a way of evaluating influence. High levels of concordance between recommendations in PSRs and sentencing outcomes have been found in many countries: between 63% (Stanley and Murphy 1984) and 78% (Thorpe and Pease 1976) in England and Wales; 69% in Scotland (Curran and Chambers 1982); 80% in New Zealand (Deane 2000); and 92% in the United States (Norman and Wadman 2000).

The idea that concordance between sentencing decisions recommended in reports and sentences passed is a reliable way of measuring influence is, however, contested (Gelsthorpe and Raynor 1995; Tata et al. 2008). 'Concordance', 'concurrence', or 'agreement' suggests a causal relationship that may simply not exist. High levels of concordance between recommendations in PSRs and sentencing outcomes do not, in themselves, prove impact and may simply involve correlational rather than causal evidence. High agreement levels may also reflect the fact that in many cases probation officers, when writing their recommendation, will often anticipate the sentence the court will impose (Gelsthorpe and Raynor 1995). While the conflation of concordance with influence suggests a mechanistic model, other research has highlighted how reports are a project of and 'infused by inter-professional power dynamics' (Tata et al. 2008; Tata 2018). Indeed, research in Scotland has shown that the meaning of reports is contingent on these power relations and their interpretation may differ from the meaning originally intended by those who write them (Tata et al. 2008; Halliday et al. 2008).

A number of studies have evaluated the 'effectiveness' of PSRs in terms of both internal and external quality by first examining the quality of reports and then relating the quality of reports to the imposition of custodial and community sentences. Gelsthorpe and Raynor's (1995: 195) study based in the Crown Court in England and Wales found that higher quality reports were more likely to result in the passing of a community rather than a custodial sentence and assume that this is because 'these reports were more successful in enabling sentencers to pass community sentences with confidence and to rely correspondingly less on imprisonment'.

Using a similar methodology, Downing and Lynch (1997) examined the relationship between the quality of PSRs and the concordance rates of probation sentencing proposals and outcomes in the Magistrates courts. They found that while there was little or no relationship between quality and concordance for all reports there was some relationship between the two for reports proposing community sentences. They argue that their finding does not undermine earlier research, which suggests that reports have only a limited capacity to divert offenders from custody (Moxon 1988; Parker et al. 1989) and that any report of whatever quality may have a marginal influence in terms of diverting sentencers away from (and sometimes into) custody (Bottoms and McWilliams 1986). The idea that reports do have some effect on sentencing is supported by research from the Netherlands which adopted a quasi-experimental methodology to examine the effects of risk-based PSRs on sentencing outcomes (van Wingerden et al. 2014). They found that, contrary to expectations, persons who were sentenced with risk-based PSRs were not more likely to be sentenced severely than those without such reports. Moreover, they found that overall persons sentenced with such reports were more likely to be given a less punitive and more rehabilitative sentence (van Wingerden et al. 2014).

Perhaps somewhat counter-intuitively, research on short reports found that their quality 'did not differ significantly from the average quality of reports for which longer preparation times had been allowed' (Gelsthorpe and Raynor

1995: 193). However, Gelsthorpe and Raynor (1995) did find that short reports contained less discussion of offending behaviour, were mainly based on information from the offender, and were less likely to suggest 'packages' involving additional requirements and facilities when discussing the possibility of a probation. Robinson's (2017) recent study found significant changes to the required structure, format, and timeframe within which PSRs must be delivered in England and Wales. Reports are now much more likely to be presented orally in court than written and much less likely to contain detailed risk assessments and sentence plans. Robinson (2017) reminds us that quality is always socially constructed and what was appropriate or acceptable two decades ago may not be so today. As such, she argues for a reconsideration of what we mean by quality in relation to PSRs; one that considers the cultural and structural changes that have impacted the production of PSRs, particularly the different modes of delivery (oral and written) and one that is responsive to the needs and expectations of different stakeholders.

The rise and fall of risk in PSRs

From about the 1990s a major shift in emphasis occurred in probation practice from one based on welfare and needs to one based on risk and actuarial assessment in many countries where probation was well established (Hannah Moffat 2004; Robinson 2003). The rise in emphasis on risk in PSRs is associated with several broader shifts in penalty that have impacted probation practice more generally including: the emergence of penal managerialism with its focus on effectiveness and efficiency; the emergence of actuarial assessment tools; and the reframing of offender management and rehabilitation around public protection (Hannah-Moffat 2004; Ward and Maruna 2007). Following the rise of the 'new penology' (Feeley and Simon 1992, 1994) and more actuarial approaches to punishment which resulted in the adoption of risk assessment tools at a policy level in many Western countries, many feared that risk assessment would supplant traditional welfare-oriented probation practice (Hannah-Moffat and Maurutto 2010)

As a result, a considerable number of recent studies on the practice of pre-sentence reports have focused on the extent to which risk approaches to offender management have overtaken more traditional approaches based on the welfare model of using professional discretion and social work skills to identify and respond to offenders' needs. As a result of the introduction of risk tools it was widely expected that actuarial risk assessment would change the nature of reports to focus more narrowly on criminogenic risks to the exclusion of the needs of the offender and thus result in more severe sentencing outcomes. However, research shows that this has not happened in many cases. Instead several studies have found that report writers, while influenced to some extent by actuarial justice, continue to approach reports from within rehabilitative, welfare-oriented frames of reference and, drawing on their social work professional ideology, continue to focus on the needs of offenders as opposed to (or as well as) prioritizing their risk of reoffending (Robinson 2003; Fitzgibbon et al. 2010; McNeill et al. 2009; Beyens and Scheirs 2010; Persson and Svensson 2012; Wandall 2010; Maguire and Carr 2017).

Hannah-Moffat (2005) uses the concept of the 'transformative risk subject' to describe the idea that risk is compatible with a range of different approaches and does not necessarily cancel out approaches based on needs. Instead, the incorporation of actuarial risk logic and approaches into PSRs 'reframes rehabilitative concerns, social histories and sentencing recommendations' (Hannah-Moffat and Maurutto 2010: 263). Although not eclipsing the focus on criminogenic needs and rehabilitation, the emphasis on risk logic changes how legal subjects are characterized and alters the type of information presented about them to the court (ibid.).

In some countries, however, this reframing effect may not have occurred at all. For instance, Persson and Svensson's (2012) research shows that despite the introduction of Risk-Needs-Responsivity principles in 2009, standardized tools were only used in a minority of reports in 2008 and in 2010. Instead, pre-sentence reports continue to resemble 'more of a social investigation than a risk assessment focusing on re-offending' (Persson and Svensson 2012: 185). According to McNeill et al. (2009), evidence of only partial change in penal practices and discourses does not represent a counter-example of penal trans- formation but instead reflects the fact that our analysis of how actuarial justice has altered the penal landscape is still incomplete. However, as discussed earlier, full risk assessments are being omitted in increasingly prevalent oral reports in England and Wales (Robinson 2017) and so we may yet see the fall of actuarial risk assessment before we fully appreciate the penal transformation it embodied.

Race, gender, and discriminatory practices in pre-sentence reports

Concerns about the role PSRs play in reproducing discrimination and bias which are an inherent part of the criminal justice system are longstanding. Moxon (1988) found that black Crown Court offenders were less likely to be selected for a pre-trial report than comparable white defendants as black defendants were more likely to plead not guilty and thus less likely to be cho- sen for a pre-trial report. Gelsthorpe's (1992) study of social enquiry reports between 1989 and 1991 focused on the issue of disparity in content and eth- nic and gender bias. She concluded that gender bias was much more evident than bias on the grounds of race or ethnicity. Women were much more likely to be portrayed in reports as suffering from stress and psychological difficul- ties than men, and explanations for their offending were more likely to draw upon accounts of depression and emotional distress. Gelsthorpe (1992) found neither overt racist language nor stereotyping according to ethnicity. Simi- larly, Deane's (2000) study in New Zealand examined a sample of pre-sentence reports for racial and gender bias. She found no significant differences on the grounds of ethnicity but did find that gender differences were obvious in the choice of community-based sanction. Horn and Evans's (2000) analysis of 6,792 PSRs also found considerable gender-related differences both in the allocation of cases and in the explanation for criminal behaviour.

In contrast to these findings, other studies have found evidence that racial discrimination in PSRs typically impacts on ethnic minority groups that are over-represented in the criminal justice system. For example, Hudson and Bramhall's (2005) study shows that the alchemy of 'risk' and 'race' contained in pre-sentence reports contributes to construction of Pakistani/Muslim as criminalized 'Other', which in turn leads to unintended but demonstrable disadvantages for this group of offenders. Similarly, Power's (2003) examination of the over-representation of Irish Travellers in the criminal justice system pointed to overt and embedded racism and prejudice in the construction and language of PSRs. Hannah-Moffat and Maurutto (2010) compared the treatment of racial issues in *Gladue* reports used specifically for Aboriginals in the Canadian province of Ontario with risk-based PSRs. Whereas *Gladue* reports examine the unique systematic race, cultural, and historical factors specific to Aboriginal offenders and typically recommend alternatives to incarceration, racial issues tend to take second place in risk-based PSRs which provide a 'decontextualized and limited understanding of the impact of racial histories of offending, sentencing and treatment options' (Hannah-Moffat and Maurutto 2010: 264).

Reliance on actuarial risk assessment tools that cannot contextualize the social, cultural, and historical factors underpinning the over-representation of certain marginalized ethnic groups in the criminal justice system means that the character, family, and community background of ethnic minorities are more likely to be interpreted as risky thus leading to more punitive treatment.

Conclusion

Pre-sentence reports construct the identity of individuals in a way that is meaningful to sentencers and to other court actors. The preponderance of evidence currently available suggests that they are still associated with welfare-oriented and rehabilitative approaches to punishment. Nevertheless, their potential to lead to enhanced punishment, particularly for certain marginalized groups, should not be underestimated. As such, it is important that we fully understand their use and impact. While a considerable body of research now exists from which to begin this analysis, important gaps still remain. For instance, while we know that PSRs are only requested in a small proportion of cases, we still know very little about why reports are requested in some cases and not in others, and we have even less understanding of how courtroom dynamics might influence this decision. Perhaps more importantly we know almost nothing about defendants' perspectives on PRSs that ostensibly describe them.

References

Aebi, M. F., Delgrande, N. and Marguet, Y. (2015) Have community sanctions and measures widened the net of the European criminal justice systems? *Punishment & Society*, 17(5), 575–597.

Ashworth, A. (2015) *Sentencing and Criminal Justice*, 6th edition. Cambridge: Cambridge University Press.

Beyens, K. and Scheirs, V. (2010) Encounters of a different kind – social enquiry and sentencing in Belgium. *Punishment & Society*, 12(3), 309–328.

Boone, M. and Herzog-Evans, M. (2013) Offender supervision and decision-making in Europe. In F. McNeill and K. Beyens (Eds.), *Offender Supervision in Europe*. Basingstoke: Palgrave Macmillan.

Bottoms, A. E. and McWilliams, W. (1986) Social enquiry reports: Twenty-five years after the Streatfield Report. In Bean, P. and Whynes, D. (Eds.), *Barbara Wootton – Social Science and Public Policy, Essays in Her Honour*, London: Tavistock, pp. 245–276.

Bredar, J. K. (1992) *Justice Informed: The Pre-Sentence Report Trials in the Crown Court*. London: HMSO.

Carr, N. and Maguire, N. (2017) Pre-sentence reports and individualised justice: Consistency, temporality and contingency. *Irish Probation Journal*, 14, 52–71.

Court Service. (2015) *Annual Report*. Dublin: Stationary Office.

Curran, J. and Chambers, G. (1982) *Social Enquiry Reports in Scotland*. Edinburgh: HMSO.

Deane, H. (2000) The influence of pre-sentence reports on sentencing in a district court in New Zealand. *Australian and New Zealand Journal of Criminology*, 33(1), 91–106.

Downing, K. and Lynch, R. (1997) Pre-sentence reports: Does quality matter? *Social Policy and Administration*, 31(2), 173–190.

Durnescu, I., Enengl, C. and Grafl, G. (2013) Experiencing Supervision. In McNeill, F. and Beyens, K. (Eds.), *Offender Supervision in Europe*. Basingstoke: Palgrave, pp. 19–50.

Feeley, M. and Simon, J. (1992) The new penology: Notes on the emerging strategy for corrections. *Criminology*, 30(4), 449–474.

Feeley, M. and Simon, J. (1994) Actuarial justice: The emerging new criminal law. In D. Nelken (Ed.), *The Futures of Criminology*. London: Sage Publications, pp. 173–201.

Field, S. and Tata, C. (2010) Connecting legal and social justice in the neo-liberal world? The construction, interpretation and use of pre-sentence reports. *Punishment & Society*, 12(3), 235–238.

Fitzgibbon, W., Hamilton, C. and Richardson, M. (2010) A risky business: An examination of Irish Probation Officers' attitudes towards risk assessment. *Probation Journal*, 56(1), 72–91.

Gelsthorpe, L. (1992) Social Inquiry Reports: Race and gender considerations. *Home Office Research and Statistics Department Research Bulletin*, 21.

Gelsthorpe, L. and Raynor, P. (1995) Quality and effectiveness in probation officers' reports to sentencers. *British Journal of Criminology*, 35(2), 188–200.

Hannah-Moffat, K. (2004) 'Criminogenic needs and the transformative risk subject: Hybridizations of risk/need in penality'. *Punishment & Society*, 7(1), 29–51.

Hannah-Moffat, K. and Maurutto, P. (2010) Re-contextualizing pre-sentence reports. Risk and race. *Punishment & Society*, 12(3), 262–286.

Halliday, S. Burns, N. Hutton, N., McNeill, F. and Tata, C. (2008) Shadow-writing and participant observation. *Journal of Law and Society*, 35(2), 189–213.

Horn, R. and Evans, M. (2000) The effect of gender on pre-sentence reports. *Howard Journal of Criminal Justice*, 39(2), 184–197.

Hudson, B. and Bramhall, G. (2005) Assessing the 'other' – constructions of 'Asianness' in risk assessments by probation officers. *British Journal of Criminology*, 45(5), 721–740.

Johansen, L. V. (2017) Between standard, silence and exception: How texts construct defendants as *persons* in Danish pre-sentence reports. *Discourse & Society*, 29, 1–19.

Maguire, N. and Carr, N. (2017) *Individualising Justice: Pre-Sentence Reports in the Irish Criminal Justice System*. Dublin: Probation Service.

McNeill, F., Burns, N., Halliday, S., Hutton, N. and Tata, C. (2009) Risk, responsibility and reconfiguration: Penal adaptation and misadaptation. *Punishment & Society*, 11(4), 419–442.

McWilliams, W. (1986) *The English Social Enquiry Report: Development and Practice*. Unpublished Ph.D. dissertation submitted to the University of Sheffield.

Moxon, D. (1988) *Sentencing in the Crown Court*. Home Office Research Study 103. London: HMSO.

NAPO (1991) *Pilot Trials on Pre-Sentence Reports in Selected Crown Courts*. London: NAPO Professional Committee.

Norman, M. D. and Wadman, R. C. (2000) Utah presentence investigation reports: User group perceptions of quality and effectiveness. *Federal Probation*, 64(1), 7–12.

Parker, H., Sumner, M. and Jarvis, G. (1989) *Unmasking the Magistrates*. Milton Keynes: Open University Press.

Persson, A. and Svensson, K. (2012) Shades of professionalism: Risk assessment in pre-sentence reports in Sweden. *European Journal of Criminology*, 9(2), 172–190.

Power, C. (2003) Irish Travellers: Ethnicity, racism and pre-sentence reports. *Probation Journal*, 50(3), 252–266.

Probation Service. (2016) *Annual Report*. Dublin: Probation Service.

Robinson, G. (2003) Risk and risk assessment. In: W. H. Chui and M. Nellis (Eds.), *Moving Probation Forward: Evidence, Arguments and Practice*. Harlow: Pearson.

Robinson, G. (2017) Stand-down and deliver: Pre-sentence reports, quality and the new culture of speed. *The Probation Journal*, XX(X), 1–17.

Stanley, S. and Murphy, S. (1984) *Inner London Probation Service: Survey of Social Enquiry Reports*. London: Inner London Probation Service.

Tata, C. (2010) A sense of justice: The role of pre-sentence reports in the production (and disruption) of guilt and guilty pleas. *Punishment & Society*, 12(3), 239–261.

Tata, C. (2017) *Ritual Individualisation at Sentencing, Mitigation and Conviction*. Paper Presented to the Socio-Legal Studies Association Annual Conference.

Tata, C. (2018) Reducing prison sentencing through pre-sentence reports? Why the quasi-market logic of 'selling alternatives to custody' fails. *The Howard Journal of Criminal Justice*, 57(4), 472–494.

Tata, C., Burns, N., Halliday, S., Hutton, N. and McNeill, F. (2008) Assisting and advising the sentencing decision process: The pursuit of 'quality' in pre-sentence reports. *British Journal of Criminology*, 48(6), 835–855.

Teague, M. (2011) Probation in America: Armed, private and affordable? *Probation Journal*, 58(4), 317–332.

Thorpe, J. and Pease, K. (1976) The relationship between recommendations made to the court and sentences passed. *British Journal of Criminology*, 16(4), 393–394.

Val Kalmthout, A. M. and Durnescu, I. (Eds.). (2008) *Probation in Europe*. Nijemgen: Wolf Publishers.

Van Wingerden, S., van Wilsem, J. and Moerings, M. (2014) Pre-sentence reports and punishment: A quasi-experiment assessing the effects of risk-based pre-sentence reports on sentencing. *European Journal of Criminology*, 11(6), 723–744.

Wandall, R. H. (2010) Resisting risk assessment? Pre-sentence reports and individualized sentencing in Denmark. *Punishment & Society*, 12(3), 329–347.

Ward, T. and Maruna, S. (2007) *Key Ideas in Criminology. Rehabilitation: Beyond the Risk Paradigm*. New York: Routledge.

Section 4

Direct work with offenders

Section 4 Introduction

The chapters in this section of the Companion bring together theoretical and empirical insights into effective real-world practice in a range of settings. In particular, the chapters address a much-ignored aspect of practice which is the actual content or 'black box' of front-line practice. Two broad dimensions of rehabilitative work are explored: the nature and impact of supervision skills, and the application of specific interventions such as arts-based and mentoring programmes.

There is a paucity of research on the content of rehabilitative work in penal settings. In the context of probation supervision, this can be traced to several developments in the recent history of probation services. A key historical development pertains to the decline of rehabilitation as the fundamental penal ideal from the 1970s onwards. This decline occurred amidst claims that nothing works effectively to rehabilitate criminalized people (Martinson 1974) and in the context of the punitive 'law and order' politics of the late 1970s onwards. By the 1980s and 1990s however, researchers on both sides of the Atlantic started to collate evidence of effective rehabilitative work (see, for example, Andrews et al. 1990, and for British examples Raynor 1988; McIvor 1990). Several studies including large scale meta-analytic studies emerged, indicating that several principles of practice were associated with rehabilitative outcomes such as reductions in reconviction rates (see generally Andrews et al. 1990; McGuire 1995). Heralded as the 'what works'[1] approach, the principles known as 'Risk-Need-Responsivity' went on to inform policy and practice development in several Western jurisdictions including the UK, Australia, Canada, and the US. Following the advent of the 'what works' approach, much of the research on rehabilitative work began to focus mainly on evaluating the impact of the approach on outcomes. Not much attention was paid to the processes leading to the outcomes. In other words, the actual content or black box of rehabilitative work was overlooked in the focus on outcomes (typically operationalized as reconviction rates). That said, it is worth noting that since the 1990s, researchers based in jurisdictions such as Australia and Canada have been studying the nature and impact of skills during one-to-one supervision and some of the earliest studies in this field were conducted by Chris Trotter in Australia (Trotter 1996, 2006).

Chris Trotter and others such as Andrews and Kiessling (1980) and Dowden and Andrews (2004) have since shed some light on the content of rehabilitative work, particularly the skills employed by practitioners in one-to-one supervision contexts. Although there are some differences in their articulation of these skills,[2] it is clear from their research that the skills tend to coalesce around several areas. These are known as Core Correctional Practices (CCPs) and they include the following: interpersonal and relationship-building skills; pro-social modelling; effective reinforcements and disapproval; pro-social skills building; problem-solving; cognitive restructuring; advocacy and brokerage practices; effective use of authority; and motivational interviewing (Andrews and Kiessling 1980; Dowden and Andrews 2004; Herzog-Evans 2018; Raynor et al. 2014; Raynor and Vanstone 2018; Trotter 2013, 2018; Trotter et al. 2015).

Recent international research on supervision skills has found that service users supervised by practitioners who apply the CCPs during routine supervision tend to achieve reduced rates of reconviction (see, for example, Chadwick et al. 2015; Raynor et al. 2014; Trotter 2018). Several chapters in this section of the Companion explore the use of these and other supervision skills.

Other chapters similarly explore the content of rehabilitative work and provide examples of such work. Thus, the chapters in this section address the following themes: trauma-informed work with young people; approaches to working with veterans; the impact of experiential knowledge on rehabilitative work; and approaches to working with domestic violence perpetrators. This section also includes chapters on the following innovative approaches to rehabilitative work: arts-based and sports-based interventions; approaches to working with violent offenders and sex offenders; interventions based on conversations with offenders; mindfulness approaches; mentoring; co-productive work; and victim-focused interventions. Collectively, the chapters in this section help illuminate a much-neglected aspect of rehabilitative work which is its content or black box.

Notes

1   It is beyond the scope of this section to engage a detailed description of the 'what works' model, also known as the Risk-Need-Responsivity model. Readers interested in finding out more about the model may consult Bonta and Andrews (2017).
2   See Herzog-Evans (2018) for a detailed analysis of the different theoretical and empirical orientations underpinning recent research on supervision skills.

References

Andrews, D. A., Bonta, J. and Hoge, R. D. (1990) Classification for effective rehabilitation: Rediscovering psychology. *Criminal Justice and Behavior*, 17(1), 19–52.

Andrews, D. A. and Kiessling, J. (1980) Program structure and effective correctional practices: A summary of the CaVIC research. In R. Ross and P. Gendreau (Eds.), *Effective Correctional Treatment*. Toronto: Butterworth, pp. 441–463.

Andrews, D. A., Zinger, I., Hoge, R. D., Bonta, J., Gendreau, P. and Cullen, F. T. (1990) Does correctional treatment work? A clinically relevant and psychologically informed meta-analysis. *Criminology*, 28(3), 369–404.

Bonta, J. and Andrews, D. (2017) *The Psychology of Criminal Conduct*, 6th edition. Abingdon: Routledge.

Chadwick, N., Dewolf, A. and Serin, R. (2015) Effectively training community supervision officers: A meta-analytic review of the impact on offender outcome. *Criminal Justice and Behaviour*, 42(10), 977–989.

Dowden, C. and Andrews, D. A. (2004) The importance of staff practice in delivering effective correctional treatment: A meta-analytic review of the literature. *International Journal of Offender Therapy and Comparative Criminology*, 48, 203–214.

Herzog-Evans, M. (2018) The Risk-Need-Responsivity model: Evidence diversity and integrative theory. In Ugwudike P., Raynor P. and Annison J. (Eds.), *Evidence-Based Skills in Criminal Justice: International Research on Supporting Rehabilitation and Desistance*. Bristol: Policy Press.

Martinson, R. (1974) What works? Questions and answers about prison reform. *The Public Interest*, 35, 22–34.

McGuire, J. (Ed.). (1995) *What Works: Reducing Re-Offending*. Chichester: Wiley.

McIvor, G. (1990) *Sanctions for Serious or Persistent Offenders*. Stirling: Social Work Research Centre.

Raynor, P. (1988) *Probation as an Alternative to Custody*. Aldershot: Avebury.

Raynor, P., Ugwudike, P. and Vanstone, M. (2014) The impact of skills in probation work: A reconviction study. *Criminology and Criminal Justice*, 14(2), 235–249.

Raynor, P. and Vanstone, M. (2018) What matters is what you do: The rediscovery of skills in probation practice. *European Journal of Probation*. Online First. https://doi.org/10.1177/2066220318820199.

Trotter, C. (1996) The impact of different supervision practices in community corrections. *Australian and New Zealand Journal of Criminology*, 28(2), 29–46.

Trotter, C. (2006) *Working With Involuntary Clients: A Guide to Practice*, 2nd edition. London and Thousand Oaks, CA: Sage Publications.

Trotter, C. (2013) Effective supervision of young offenders. In P. Ugwudike and P. Raynor (Eds.), *What Works in Offender Compliance: International Perspectives and Evidence-Based Practices*. Hampshire: Palgrave Macmillan, pp. 227–241.

Trotter, C. (2018) The impact of training and coaching on the development of practice skills in youth justice: Findings from Australia. In P. Ugwudike, P. Raynor and J. Annison (Eds.), *Evidence-Based Skills in Criminal Justice: International Research on Supporting Rehabilitation and Desistance*. Bristol and Chicago: Policy Press.

Trotter, C., Evans, P. and Baidawi, S. (2015) The effectiveness of challenging skills in work with young offenders. *International Journal of Offender Therapy and Comparative Criminology*, 61(4), 397–412.

23

Examining community supervision officers' skills and behaviours

A review of strategies for identifying the inner workings of face-to-face supervision sessions

Nick Chadwick, Ralph C. Serin, and Caleb D. Lloyd

Introduction

Many correctional systems rely heavily on community supervision orders to facilitate the administration of a sentence. The majority of offenders are either sentenced directly to probation or will be conditionally released from custody onto parole or some variant of community supervision. In Canada, approximately 80% of the offender population was serving a sentence in the community, on any given day in 2015–2016 (Reitano 2017). A similar proportion is observed in the United States, with approximately 69% of the adult correctional population being supervised on either probation or parole, in 2015 (Kaeble and Glaze 2016). Relying on community supervision is appealing in that it is substantially cheaper (72% less expensive for federal offenders in Canada; Public Safety Canada, 2017) and can either reinforce existing pro-social behaviour in the community (e.g. employment) or can facilitate reintegration of the offender to the community (Abadinsky 2009; Gibbons and Rosecrance 2005). Compared to release without supervision, supervising offenders in the community tends to be associated with reductions in recidivism, but effects are small, suggesting that there is room for improvement (Bonta et al. 2008). Additionally, revocation and breach rates continue to be high, underscoring a need to improve the way that community supervision is conducted.

To understand why community supervision is not achieving the expected reductions in recidivism, a comprehensive assessment of supervision practices and officer skills is required. Early research on supervision practice began in the late 1970s, when Kiessling and Andrews (1979; Andrews and Kiessling 1980) explored the effectiveness of community supervision by examining community supervision officer behaviour and their interactions with clients. This study established a foundation of effective skills associated with supervision. Briefly, this framework for effective supervision includes adhering to the principles of effective correctional treatment, known as the Risk-Need-Responsivity (RNR) principles (Andrews et al. 1990). Additionally, officers are often taught specific intervention skills that have a foundation in cognitive behavioural techniques. Specific intervention skills are encompassed in the concepts of evidence-based practices (EBPs), often referred to Core Correctional Practices (CCPs) in community corrections (Dowden and Andrews 2004). There are five dimensions of effective correctional practice that are included within this framework and encompass the following skills: (1) Effective use of authority, (2) pro-social modelling, (3) effective problem-solving strategies, (4) the use of community resources, and (5) interpersonal relationship factors (Andrews and Kiessling 1980; Dowden and Andrews 2004). Briefly, models of community supervision that adhere to evidence-based practices attempt to move away from surveillance-based and brokerage of services activities toward a model where officers serve as an active participant in the delivery of rehabilitative services. This emphasis on officer involvement in rehabilitative work has often been referred to as being a change agent (Bourgon et al. 2011).

As evidence emerged surrounding the skills and practices associated with effective community supervision, supplemental training programmes tailored to these skills began to be developed and implemented. Given that jurisdictions often invest substantial resources in implementing such programmes, it is understandable that the primary interest surrounding these programmes tends to be whether they reduce recidivism. Although this is an important metric of performance, the tendency to focus on long-term outcomes of clients supervised by trained officers overlooks the importance of first assessing whether training has had the desired effect on officer behaviours. Nevertheless, evaluations of EBP programs tend to examine the extent of reductions in recidivism compared to the status quo training provided to community supervision officers. A recent meta-analysis of training programs aimed at enhancing the use of evidence-based practices in community supervision found that clients supervised by trained officers demonstrated an approximately 13% reduction in recidivism, compared to clients supervised by officers who did not receive the supplemental training (Chadwick et al. 2015).

To enhance understanding regarding how the training programmes may be contributing to reductions in recidivism, an examination of activities conducted during a one-on-one supervision session is critical. Without focusing on what is occurring during these meetings, we tend to assume that any observed treatment effects are due to the training received, but cannot confirm that behavioural change has occurred among trained officers, compared to officers who did not receive additional training. Several strategies for examining the inner workings of supervision strategies have been developed, including conducting file reviews or examinations of case notes, audiotaping or videotaping supervision sessions, and directly observing supervision sessions. A review of information gleaned from each approach follows, with an emphasis on the relative strengths and weaknesses.

File review

Examining officer case notes or file reviews has been a common technique for understanding how supervising officers are conducting their sessions with clients (Finn et al. 2017; Paparozzi and Gendreau 2005; Taxman 2008; Trotter 1996; Trotter 2000; Wodahl et al. 2011). File notes have the advantage of being the least intrusive data collection method, removing the potential concern that officers may be performing differently as a result of knowing they are being monitored. In addition to limiting the disruption, examining a client's file in conjunction with case notes would allow researchers to link the case notes and file to other information potentially collected by the jurisdiction (e.g. risk assessments, referrals to programming). From a research perspective, conducting a review of file notes is also an efficient process, particularly when specific situations are of interest (e.g. sessions where officers discussed risk assessments with clients). Depending on the organization of case notes in a particular jurisdiction, researchers can conduct a simple keyword search to reveal those sessions that warrant further examination.

However, given that officers are responsible for entering the information into the file, there is the potential that the officers may not be entering the information as accurately as possible. Additionally, how diligent the officer is in their notes will also dictate the quality of the information available to researchers. The quality of the information will influence the researchers' ability to sufficiently code the presence, quality, and duration of particular skills. If an officer merely indicates that they conducted a cognitive behavioural intervention throughout a supervision session, a coder would be restricted to indicating that the given intervention took place, without being able to ascertain the quality of the intervention. Differentiating between frequency of a skill and overall quality is important for informing the expected effect on client outcome. If officers are consistently demonstrating a particular skill (e.g. cognitive behavioural intervention), but it is very poorly done or does not match the client's needs at the time in the session, the expected effect on improving client outcome would be diminished relative to high quality interventions.

An organization's policy may also dictate what appears in case notes, with some jurisdictions relying on monitoring case notes as a supervision strategy for probation officers. As a result, cross jurisdiction comparisons can become problematic if one organization expects their officers to focus their case notes primarily on surveillance-based activities, while others may place more of an emphasis on rehabilitative work. Although identifying these differences at the organization level is informative, it is possible that the differences are an artefact of the organization's expectations around information management, rather than true differences in the activities of supervising officers. Given this potential for inconsistency between an officer's practice and what is reported in a case note, a more rigorous strategy would include corroborating what is mentioned in case notes with documented activities on an offender's file (e.g. collateral contacts made, referrals to additional services, assessments conducted).

Audiotaping

The most common method for examining the supervision practices with clients is utilizing audiotapes submitted by officers (Alexander et al. 2013; Andrews and Kiessling 1980; Bonta et al. 2008; Bonta et al. 2011; Clodfelter et al. 2016; Eno Louden et al. 2012; Kiessling and Andrews 1979; Labrecque et al. 2013; Labrecque and Smith 2017; Labrecque et al. 2015; Lowenkamp et al. 2014; Robinson et al. 2012; Smith et al. 2012). Audiotaping has the advantage of providing an exact record of the activities conducted within the supervision context, while still maintaining a relatively naturalistic environment. Although officers may be anxious about recording their supervision sessions (e.g. Alexander et al. 2013), a tape recorder is less conspicuous than having an observer present in a supervision session, but still provides access to almost the same rich contextual information (except non-verbal cues). One aspect where utilizing audiotapes is an improvement over file review and questionnaires is the ability to assess quality and duration of a given skill. Having the clear record of a supervision session facilitates forming an independent conclusion about the officer's use of a particular skill and allows for consideration of whether particular components were present. This additional layer of information allows researchers to more readily examine the relationship between specific skills and outcome. However, relying on audio recordings also limits the ability to assess engagement by both parties in the conversation, in addition to other potentially relevant non-verbal cues. This is a distinct advantage that video recording or direct observation offers.

Video recording

Although video recording has been used infrequently to evaluate the behaviours of officers in supervision sessions (Durnescu et al. 2013; Raynor and Ugwudike 2013; Raynor et al. 2014), there are some unique advantages that may warrant more frequent use. Video recording makes assessing non-verbal cues and environmental factors possible. Considering the office environment might be relevant for assessing how conducive it is for active learning. For example, examining the extent to which there are easily accessible learning aids or if the setting was organized and situated to stimulate engaging conversation (e.g. proximity between officer and client). Non-verbal cues can also be assessed to determine the extent that the officer and client are engaged in their conversation (e.g. eye contact, posture, distracted by electronics). It's possible that considering client engagement will affect the relationship between supervision officer skills and client outcome; effective supervision skills would not be expected to have as strong as an effect if the client is not actively engaged in learning. Although research on the utility of non-verbal cues within the context of community supervision is limited, Raynor and colleagues (2014) found higher scores on non-verbal communication skills by officers were related to clients remaining crime free in the community at two years. Similar to audio recordings, preserving the record of supervision sessions allows researchers to examine detailed qualitative information and revisit the recordings for additional research questions, if necessary. Additionally, video recordings of natural supervision sessions could be useful for training efforts, allowing other supervision officers to observe how effective skills are utilized in real supervision sessions. This may be particularly useful for demonstrating how officers can secure buy-in from clients, especially if officers are reluctant to engage in a supervision model that is drastically different from their previous experience.

Since video recordings are more intrusive (i.e. officers and clients know they are being monitored), there is a greater potential that officers will filter their behaviour. This limitation can be mitigated by corroborating observations with case notes or measures assessing relevant constructs. For example, it may be beneficial to have officers and clients independently assess their perceived relationship with each other (e.g. Dual-Role Relationship Inventory [DRI-R]; Skeem et al. 2007; Kennealy et al. 2012) and consider this information alongside the recordings to evaluate the consistency with the video observations. In addition, the point of view of the video camera has the potential to substantially alter the observer's interpretation of the session, such that sole focus on the officer may not provide sufficient context to assess how the officer responds to cues from the client, whereas sole focus on the client may lead to perceptions that the client is taking a greater role in leading the direction of the session.

Direct observation

Direct observation of supervision sessions provides access to the highest level of qualitative information. Although this technique has only occasionally been utilized in community supervision research (e.g. Maass et al. 2013; Trotter 2013; Trotter 2017; Trotter and Evans 2012; Viglione et al. 2015; Viglione et al. 2017), there are distinct advantages that make considering this approach worthwhile. The primary advantage is that by observing the session in an unfiltered setting, researchers can corroborate what is said to have occurred, as made apparent in case notes, for example. One example of this issue was demonstrated by Viglione et al. (2015) who examined risk/need assessment practices among community corrections. Although results derived from case notes and officer questionnaires suggested that risk/need tools were frequently administered, direct observation of practices suggested that the application of the assessment results was rarely associated with key case management or supervision decisions. Similar to video recordings, directly observing the interaction between an officer and client permits examining non-verbal cues and overall engagement, concepts that are relevant to assessing the working relationship.

The primary drawback associated with direct observation is the time commitment and logistical considerations for researchers. Firstly, travel to and from supervision offices, time directly observing, and then the time required to make detailed notes are all activities that are otherwise removed from the previously discussed approaches. Additionally, given constant schedule changes (e.g. a client not showing up on time for their session), researchers might be unable to control what client and officer session is observed to ensure that a sufficient number of representative sessions are assessed. Although not inherently problematic, this prevents examining the use of particular skills with a given client throughout their supervision period.

Common considerations

A discussion of the relevant considerations and potential issues common to utilizing recordings (i.e. audio and video) or direct observation of supervision practices follows. It is important to be aware of these issues when considering the types of conclusions that are intended to be able to be made as a result of the examination of officer behaviour.

Creating officer skill score

Given that the information obtained through audio/video recording and direct observation is so rich, it is not practical to examine all possible supervision sessions and code them for the presence and quality of skills. Instead, researchers are left to develop strategies to sample segments of a supervision period to develop a rating of a given supervisor's use of skills. Inherent in this approach is the assumption that the behaviours apparent during recorded sessions are generalizable to the remainder of supervision.

To develop a proxy for overall officer skill, researchers have previously tended to aggregate across all clients and sessions examined for a given officer. This approach allows researchers to examine skills used across a variety of sessions, often at different periods of supervision (e.g. initial interaction, three months into supervision, then six months into supervision), to create an overall skill level. This skill level is then used to differentiate groups of officers (e.g. above and below average) to examine the relationship between overall competency and client outcome. Developing these aggregated skills also depends on the coding procedure that is used by the researchers. One approach is to examine each session for the presence and quality of a skill and then aggregate across all recordings submitted from a given officer to derive their score (e.g. Bonta et al. 2011; Robinson et al. 2012). Another approach considers whether there was an opportunity for a skill to be used, and whether the skill or intervention included all major steps when it was delivered (e.g. Labrecque and Smith 2017; Smith et al. 2012). The latter approach acknowledges that certain skills or interventions are more likely to be delivered at specific periods of supervision. Additionally, the proportion of sessions where a skill was used when presented with an opportunity to do so can be compared to all total sessions examined, to get a ratio of skill use. For example, an officer may perform a role clarification within the first few sessions of supervision, but this skill is unlikely to be used in sessions after the client has been supervised for six months. If the former strategy is applied to a collection of observations that is balanced across officers (e.g. two observations per period of supervision per officer), then the aggregate scores would be comparable across officers. It would become problematic if some officers had more observations from different periods of supervision, and therefore would be more likely to demonstrate some skills over others, contributing to their aggregate score relative to other officers. Similarly, if a researcher was interested in developing the ratio of sessions where a skill was used to total sessions recorded, the ratio could be artificially decreased without considering opportunity for using a skill. However, determining whether there was sufficient opportunity to use a skill in a given situation is a subjective decision that will largely depend on the complexity of the skill or intervention, as well as the phase of supervision. When the skills being assessed are less concrete and clinical in nature (e.g. effective disapproval), it is substantially more arbitrary to rely on an outside observer to determine whether there was an appropriate opportunity for an officer to utilize a skill. This is especially true given the limited information (i.e. one recorded supervision session) that an observer has available to form their judgement. It is possible that the officer used their judgement to decide not to use an intervention based on previous experience with their client, but an observer would not be aware of this and would likely conclude an opportunity for an intervention was missed.

Discussion content

Examining supervision sessions through recordings or observation also provides the opportunity to assess the content and duration of discussion topics. This improves over an analysis of case notes as researchers are able to determine the depth of conversation as well as the length, compared to relying on a description of the conversation that would be indicated in a case note. Examining the topic and the duration of conversation has been demonstrated to be related to client outcome, with clients supervised by officers who spend a substantial portion of their sessions on either non-criminogenic needs or conditions of supervision more likely to have poorer outcomes (Bonta et al. 2011).

Access to conversation also provides the ability to develop a proxy for the working relationship between officer and client. Research suggests that when a relationship between an officer and client is characterized as caring, warm, and enthusiastic, combined with respect, fairness, and trust, the relationship can reduce the likelihood of recidivism (Dowden and Andrews 2004; Kennealy et al. 2012). In a sample of offenders that rated the quality of their relationship with their supervising officer, results indicated that the higher the quality of the relationship, the greater the reduction in recidivism (Kennealy et al. 2012). However, relying on a small sample of sessions between an officer and a given client is a crude proxy for their working relationship, so it is likely advantageous to supplement these estimates with structured assessments. Nonetheless, creating an aggregate score for an officer's use and quality of relationship skills across all clients and sessions is informative and could provide an estimate of the quality of the working relationship that the officer typically establishes with their clients.

Measurement schedule for sessions

Despite providing access to very rich qualitative information, there are drawbacks that are associated with utilizing these methods (audio/video and observation) to assess supervision practices. As mentioned previously, the type and quality of information is dependent on the frequency of observation that is built into a research protocol. Recording or observing numerous sessions per officer and client results in a more stable estimate of their skills and use for a given client, but the trade-off is that significant resources need to be invested to code this information. Additionally, it can be challenging to maintain a schedule or quota for the number of recordings an officer submits. Even if a data collection protocol specifies that a certain number of recordings are requested over a given time period, it is unlikely that all recordings will be submitted. This incomplete information then makes it challenging to make comparisons between officers who have adhered to the protocol compared to those who have inconsistently participated. However, the alternative of relying on only a few recordings per officer and client requires making larger extrapolations about how reflective the observed skills are of the officer's overall skill level and the type of supervision to which the client was exposed. This issue has largely prevented an examination of the impact of exposure to specific skills and interventions throughout a supervision period. Even though this information could be gleaned from observations, the initial questions about supervision activity have generally focused on the frequency of skills. The sample sizes would need to be large with sufficient variation within each skill to be able to examine potential differences on client outcome. Similarly, as mentioned previously, relying on aggregated skill scores, derived from all observations for the officer, ignores the potential for variation in the application of those skills across clients. This limits the ability to understand potential officer-by-client interaction effects, whereas the aggregated score is likely to offer a better estimate of overall skill level at the level of the officer (e.g. Epstein 1983).

Selecting clients for analysis

The selection procedure for identifying clients and the number or type of sessions (e.g. introductory session, working sessions/interventions) will influence the conclusions that can be made from the methods described above. In some instances, officers may be asked to participate in a training programme or research project and then are expected to recruit clients to allow the session to be recorded or have an observer present. A selection bias is present in these cases, which limits the generalizability of the findings from these observations. It is likely that officers are approaching clients with whom they have already established a working relationship, or selecting those that they anticipate will be cooperative, to ensure that they have the ability to utilize their skills in a manner that would reflect positively on them. Therefore, it is likely that results obtained from strategies utilizing this selection technique are an overestimation of the skill frequency or quality. Ideally, clients would be randomly selected to remove this potential bias and provide a more representative portrayal of the use and quality of skills in typical supervision sessions. This potential bias also speaks to the issue of field studies often having weaker effect sizes than research studies (Edens and Boccaccini 2017).

Research stocktake and future directions

Increasingly, fairly consistent findings across different research methodologies suggest that specific officer skills can be effective at reducing client recidivism (alternatively, confrontational officer characteristics and authoritarian skills can exacerbate client recidivism). Nonetheless, the studies to date reflect only a microcosm of the practice of community supervision. Hence, these small, selective samples of predominantly volunteer officers and clients may provide undue optimism for practitioners.

This suggests future research might focus on: (1) further replication with non-volunteers to develop a more precise estimate of the effect of officer skill on client outcome in the field, (2) greater consideration of the phase of supervision and specific skills might yield refinements that differentially influence skill presentation and client response, (3) development and validation of a measure of interpersonal and behavioural skill competencies might augment existing coding efforts and inform a multimethod assessment protocol, (4) greater utilization of random assignment designs would strengthen generalizability of findings, (5) examining potential covariates or moderators, such as case load size, client risk level, officer age and experience, and dosage of training would further refine critical aspects of CCP training.

Is there an optimal strategy?

The motive for developing an understanding of the inner workings of supervision sessions will largely dictate the optimal measurement strategy. For example, direct observation may be preferable when piloting a new approach, as it will facilitate an in-depth examination of the officers' use of the techniques and skills. Once it is determined that the individual has the capacity to deliver the skills as intended, it may be appropriate to rely on audio or video recordings to obtain a more naturalistic assessment of the interaction during supervision sessions. Determining the preferred unit of analysis will also assist with selecting an appropriate method. If a researcher is interested in examining the experience on supervision for a sample of clients, and expects to generalize the findings to a larger population, utilizing direct observation is likely impractical, given the requirement that multiple supervision sessions will need to be examined. In this case, relying on case notes might sufficiently indicate the topics of conversation and the interventions administered throughout the duration of supervision. However, if an organization is interested in monitoring the use and quality of skills by their employees for quality assurance purposes, relying on case notes may not be appropriate as they may not permit access to the necessary qualitative information pertaining to how an intervention was delivered.

Ideally, a multimethod approach would be employed to corroborate the information available from any single approach. Further developing our understanding of the inner workings of community supervision sessions is critical to identifying strengths and weaknesses associated with a given supervision model and specific skills or interventions. There are considerable resources invested in training officers in Core Correctional Practices, and the strategies reviewed throughout this chapter present viable mechanisms to examine whether community supervision officers are employing skills and interventions that are expected to be related to improved client outcome.

Further work is needed to determine how to capitalize on the limitations of the approaches highlighted throughout this chapter. For example, research to date has largely been unable to examine how officers' skills develop over time (e.g. considering time since training). There has been an emphasis on the importance of continuous development or learning through the use of peer coaches (e.g. Alexander et al. 2013; Labrecque and Smith 2017), but an individual's level of experience with a skill when examining its effectiveness has not been investigated. It is expected that this would affect how effective a particular intervention would be. For example, an officer with limited experience with an intervention may be less likely to effectively deliver it to the client. Future research may want to investigate whether the effectiveness of a given skill or intervention depends on the officer's overall competency or experience (possibly measured as time since training), in addition to their level of engagement in continuous learning. Recognizing the importance of client characteristics in examining the inner workings of supervision practices is also essential for understanding the role of specific skills and interventions. Incorporating information on the client's motivation to change and engagement in learning will facilitate a more direct test of whether the skills of the officer are contributing to more effective supervision practices, or if it is simply that the characteristics of clients involved in these examinations are already more likely to have positive supervision outcomes. Given that community supervision serves the vast majority of individuals involved in the criminal justice system, efforts to refine the examination of officer behaviour during supervision sessions and its contribution to client outcomes are worthwhile. Doing so will continue to inform how to enhance and maintain the supervision practices that have the potential to lead to substantial improvements to the efficiency and effectiveness of community corrections.

References

Abadinsky, H. (2009) *Probation and Parole: Theory and Practice*. Upper Saddle River, NJ: Pearson Prentice Hall.

Alexander, M., Palombo, L., Cameron, E., Wooten, E., White, M., Casey, M. and Bersch, C. (2013) Coaching: The true path to proficiency, from an officer's perspective. *Federal Probation*, 77(2), 64–68.

Andrews, D. A. and Kiessling, J. J. (1980) Program structure and effective correctional practices: A summary of the CaVIC research. In R. R. Ross and P. Gendreau (Eds.), *Effective Correctional Treatment*. Toronto: Butterworth, pp. 439–463.

Andrews, D. A., Zinger, I., Hoge, R. D., Bonta, J., Gendreau, P. and Cullen, F. T. (1990) Does correctional treatment work? A clinically relevant and psychologically informed meta-analysis. *Criminology*, 28, 369-404. DOI:10.1111/j.1745-9125.1990.tb01330.x.

Bonta, J., Bourgon, G., Rugge, T., Scott, T-L., Yessine, A., Gutierrez, L. and Li, J. (2011) An experimental demonstration of training probation officers in evidence based community supervision. *Criminal Justice and Behavior*, 38, 1127–1148. DOI:10.1177/0093854811420678.

Bonta, J., Rugge, T., Scott, T., Bourgon, G. and Yessine, A. (2008) Exploring the black box of community supervision. *Journal of Offender Rehabilitation*, 47, 248–270. DOI:10.1080/10509670802134085.

Bourgon, G., Gutierrez, L. and Ashton, J. (2011) The evolution of community supervision practice: The transformation from case manager to change agent. *Irish Probation Journal*, 8, 28–48.

Chadwick, N., Dewolf, A. and Serin, R. (2015) Effectively training community supervision officers: A meta-analytic review of the impact on offender outcome. *Criminal Justice and Behavior*, 42, 977–989. DOI:10.1177/0093854815595661.

Clodfelter, T. A., Holcomb, J. E., Alexander, M. A., Marcum, C. D. and Richards, T. N. (2016) A case study of the implementation of Staff Training Aimed at Reducing Rearrest (STARR). *Federal Probation*, 80, 30–38.

Dowden, C. and Andrews, D. A. (2004) The importance of staff practice in delivering effective correctional treatment: A meta-analytic review of core correctional practices. *International Journal of Offender Therapy and Comparative Criminology*, 48, 203–214. DOI:10.1177/0306624X03257765.

Durnescu, I., Grigoras, V., Lazar, F. and Witec, S. (2013) Who works in the probation service in Romania? In I. Durnescu and F. McNeill (Eds.), *Understanding Penal Practice*. New York: Routledge, pp. 46–62.

Edens, J. F. and Boccaccini, M. T. (2017) Taking forensic mental health assessment "out of the lab" and into "the real world": Introduction to the special issue on the field utility of forensic assessment instruments and procedures. *Psychological Assessment*, 29, 599–610. DOI:10.1037/pas0000475.

Eno Louden, J., Skeem, J. L., Camp, J., Vidal, S. and Peterson, J. (2012) Supervision practices in specialty mental health probation: What happens in officer – probationer meetings? *Law and Human Behavior*, 36, 109–119. DOI:10.1037/h0093961.

Epstein, S. (1983) Aggregation and beyond: Some basic issues on the prediction of behavior. *Journal of Personality*, 51, 360–392. DOI:10.1111/j.1467-6494.1983.tb00338.x.

Finn, M. A., Prevost, J. P., Braucht, G. S., Hawk, S., Meredith, T. and Johnson, S. (2017) Home visits in community supervision: A qualitative analysis of theme and tone. *Criminal Justice and Behavior*, 44, 1300–1316. DOI:10.1177/0093854817711209.

Gibbons, S. G. and Rosecrance, J. D. (2005) *Probation, Parole, and Community Corrections in the United States*. Boston, MA: Pearson, Allyn and Bacon.

Kaeble, D. and Glaze, L. (2016) *Correctional Populations in the United States, 2015*. Washington, DC: Department of Justice.

Kennealy, P. J., Skeem, J. L., Eno Louden, J. and Manchak, S. M. (2012) Firm, fair, and caring officer-offender relationships protect against supervision failure. *Law and Human Behavior*, 36, 496–505. DOI:10.1037/h0093935.

Kiessling, J. J. and Andrews, D. A. (1979) *Volunteers and the One-to-One Supervision of Adult Probationers: An Experimental Comparison with Professionals and a Field-Description of Process and Outcome*. Toronto: Ministry of Correctional Services.

Labrecque, R. M., Schweitzer, M. and Smith, P. (2013) Probation and parole officer adherence to the core correctional practices: An evaluation of 755 offender-officer interactions. *Advancing Practices*, 3, 20–23.

Labrecque, R. M. and Smith, P. (2017) Does training and coaching matter? An 18-month evaluation of a community supervision model. *Victims and Offenders*, 12, 233–252. DOI:10.1080/15564886.2015.1013234.

Labrecque, R. M., Smith, P. and Luther, J. D. (2015) A Quasi-experimental evaluation of a model of community supervision. *Federal Probation*, 79(3), 14–19.

Lowenkamp, C. T., Holsinger, A. M., Robinson, C. R. and Alexander, M. (2014) Diminishing or durable treatment of STARR? A research note on 24-month re-arrest rates. *Journal of Crime and Justice*, 37, 275–283. DOI:10.1080/0735648X.2012.753849.

Maass, S. A., Taxman, F. S., Serin, R., Crites, E., Watson, C. A. and Lloyd, C. (2013) *SOARING 2: An eLearning Training Program to Improve Knowledge of EBPs*. Paper Presented at the American Society of Criminology Annual Conference, Atlanta, GA, November.

Paparozzi, M. A. and Gendreau, P. (2005) An intensive supervision program that worked: Service delivery, professional orientation, and organizational supportiveness. *The Prison Journal*, 85, 445–466. DOI:10.1177/0032885505281529.

Public Safety Canada. (2017) *Corrections and Conditional Release Statistical Overview, 2016 Annual Report*. Ottawa: Public Safety Canada.

Raynor, P. and Ugwudike, P. (2013) Skills and training in British Probation: A tale of neglect and possible revival. *Federal Probation*, 77(2), 49–53.

Raynor, P., Ugwudike, P. and Vanstone, M. (2014) The impact of skills in probation work: A reconviction study. *Criminology and Criminal Justice*, 14, 235–249. DOI:10.1177/1748895-813494869.

Reitano, J. (2017) *Adult Correctional Statistics in Canada, 2015/2016*. Ottawa, ON: Statistics Canada.

Robinson, C. R., Lowenkamp, C. T., Holsinger, A. M., VanBenschoten, S. W., Alexander, M. and Oleson, J. C. (2012) A random study of Staff Training Aimed at Reducing Re-arrest (STARR): Using core correctional practices in probation interactions. *Journal of Crime and Justice*, 35, 167–188. DOI:10.1080/0735648X.2012.674823.

Skeem, J. L., Eno Louden, J., Camp, J. and Polaschek, D. (2007) Assessing relationship quality in mandated community treatment: Blending care with control. *Psychological Assessment*, 19(4), 397–410. DOI:10.1037/1040-3590.19.4.397.

Smith, P., Schweitzer, M., Labreque, R. M. and Latessa, E. J. (2012) Improving probation officers' supervision skills: An evaluation of the EPICS model. *Journal of Crime and Justice*, 35, 189–199. DOI:10.1080/0735648X.2012.674826.

Taxman, F. S. (2008) No illusions: Offender and organizational change in Maryland's proactive community supervision efforts. *Criminology and Public Policy*, 7, 275–302. DOI:10.1111/j.1745-9133.2008.00508.x.

Trotter, C. (1996) The impact of different supervision practices in community corrections: Cause for optimism. *Australian and New Zealand Journal of Criminology*, 29(1), 29–46. DOI:10.1177/000486589602900103.

Trotter, C. (2000) Social work education, pro-social orientation and effective probation practice. *Probation Journal*, 47, 256–261. DOI:10.1177/026455050004700405.

Trotter, C. (2013) Effective supervision of young offenders. In P. Ugwudike and P. Raynor (Eds.), *What Works in Offender Compliance: International Perspectives and Evidence-Based Practices*. Hampshire: Palgrave Macmillan, pp. 227–241.

Trotter, C. and Evans, P. (2012) An analysis of supervision skills in youth probation. *Australian and New Zealand Journal of Criminology*, 45, 255–273. DOI:10.1177/0004865812443678.

Trotter, C., Evans, P. and Baidawi, S. (2017) The effectiveness of challenging skills in work with young offenders. *International Journal of Offender Therapy and Comparative Criminology*, 61, 397–412. DOI:10.1177/0306624X15596728.

Viglione, J., Rudes, D. S. and Taxman, F. S. (2015) Misalignment in supervision: Implementing risk/needs assessment instruments in probation. *Criminal Justice and Behavior*, 42, 263–285. DOI:10.1177/0093854814548447.

Viglione, J., Rudes, D. S. and Taxman, F. S. (2017) Probation officer use of client-centered communication strategies in adult probation setting. *Journal of Offender Rehabilitation*, 56, 38–60. DOI:10.1080/10509674.2016.1257534.

Wodahl, E. J., Garland, B., Culhane, S. E. and McCarty, W. P. (2011) Utilizing behavioral interventions to improve supervision outcomes in community-based corrections. *Criminal Justice and Behavior*, 38, 386–405. DOI:10.1177/0093854810397866.

24

Motivational interviewing

Application to practice in a probation context

Sheena Norton

Introduction

Motivational interviewing is a practice approach in probation work allowing for improved outcomes for non-voluntary clients and rehabilitation goals. It can be employed as a practical, respectful, effective, and guiding intervention tool for practitioners to evoke client self-motivation to change at various stages of probation engagement, including assessment, case management planning, and supervision. The essence of probation work is motivating offenders to change, providing opportunities to change, and facilitating change. Motivational interviewing equips the worker with effective skills to foster non-directive, nonjudgemental, respectful relationship building with clients, allowing them to take ownership of addiction issues and collaboratively engage them in a process of changing behaviours.

Motivational interviewing approaches offer opportunities for interventions 'Probation staff can examine how to impose sanctions and build helpful relationships, and with training, agents can build the skills to supervise for compliance and increase the offender's readiness for change' (Clark et al. 2006: 25). Stinson and Clark (2017) detail the effectiveness of motivational interviewing as an appropriate intervention tool in probation work with offenders, facilitating the change that is required from those engaged in offending behaviours in a 'positive, pro-social direction' (p. 2). Hart and Healy (2018) highlight the role of probation supervision as a catalyst for change and outline how desistance-focused practice models promote approaches that 'take account of the complex and gradual nature of change; offer individualised supports, foster agency, hope and motivation' (2018: 13).

Confrontational approaches can inhibit change and serve to encourage the person to continue with their addiction (Clark et al. 2006). 'Locking horns creates a downward spiral that satisfies neither. Research finds that when we push for change, the typical offender response is to defend the problem behaviour' (Clark et al. 2006: 39). Motivational interviewing can provide an alternative, 'It allows offenders to reconsider the positive and negative consequences of their behaviour more thoroughly and to relate their behaviour to their value system' (Mann et al. 2002: 91). Motivational interviewing can also be effective in dealing with client resistance (Clark et al. 2006; Mann et al. 2002). Through highlighting and emphasizing the person's own ambivalence and discomfort about their situation, it can effectively stimulate the person's personal desire for change.

Theoretical underpinnings

Motivational Interviewing is a collaborative conversation style for strengthening a person's own motivation and commitment to change.

(Millner and Rollnick 2013)

The essence of the approach is one of guiding the person whilst also endeavouring to provide direction. Acceptance and recognition that ambivalence is a normal part of preparing for change is fundamental. Trying to impose change is counterproductive, and arguments for change merely serve to encourage opposing arguments when ambivalence is apparent. Fundamental is recognition that people are more likely to be persuaded by what they hear themselves say. Motivational interviewing is client centred and holds the person at the fore of the approach. It is a directive means of communication, with the focus to elicit the person's intrinsic motivation for change primarily through exploring and resolving internal ambivalence. The client is respected as the expert of their own situation and motivational interviewing seeks to activate the client's own motivation and ability for change.

There are five broad principles in motivational interviewing (Rollnick 1996; Miller and Rollnick 2002: 36):

1   **Roll with resistance:** confrontation is not considered beneficial as it can create resistance to change, the opposite to what is desired from the person. The client is respected as the expert of their situation and must be engaged in a process of developing solutions to their own problems. Reframing the issue to stimulate the client's self-examination of their situation is considered to be more productive than challenging. New perspectives cannot be imposed upon the client but the client must be actively involved in the process of problem-solving.

2   **Expressing empathy:** the task of the worker is to convey to the client that they comprehend their thoughts, feelings, values, and meaning. The worker must not just understand their client's feelings and perspectives, or sympathize with their problems. The worker must seek to objectively identify with the affective state of the client and not just their experiences. The worker must actively practice empathic responses and convey this to the client in a manner which does not present as judgemental, critical, or apportioning blame. Mirroring the clients experience back to them may allow them to really see and experience their situation.

3   **Avoiding argumentation:** arguments are considered counterproductive and damaging, leading to defensiveness. Arguing forces the client to defend their own behaviour and merely reinforces the reasons to stay the same. Resistance from the client is a signal to change strategies to avoid further difficulties. A directive and argumentative approach for change with a person who is ambivalent will merely serve to draw out opposing arguments.

4   **Supporting self-efficacy:** an inherent belief in client individualization and the unique capacity to change is paramount in motivational interviewing. The client is responsible for their own personal change and this must be relayed to them. The development and support of self-efficacy builds confidence in the client and their ability to cope with challenges.

5   **Developing discrepancies:** building discrepancies between client's actual behaviour and goals which are important to them can motivate change. If discrepancies between current behaviours and a core value can be established, this can serve as a powerful motivator for change when explored in a safe and encouraging environment. In the field of psychology, it may be understood as cognitive dissonance, 'a situation involving conflicting attitudes, beliefs or behaviours. This produces a feeling of discomfort leading to an alteration in one of the attitudes, beliefs or behaviours to reduce the discomfort and restore balance'.

(McLeod 2018)

Applying the five principles outlined above requires the probation officer to explore ambivalence displayed by the client, identifying and elaborating discrepancies between what the client says, believes, and does, enabling the client to view the reality of their situation in a non-threatening manner, and examining the causes and consequences of the client's drug use on their significant others.

Probation officers can employ skills in the motivational interviewing process to facilitate clients in taking ownership of their addiction issues and collaboratively engage them in a process of problem behaviour exploration, recognition, ownership, and motivation to change. OARS (open-ended questions, affirmations, reflective listening, summaries), is a widely used acronym for four communication techniques to build rapport and understanding. These basic interaction skills facilitate client engagement to guide motivational interviewing interventions.

- **Open-ended questions:** facilitates conversation, encouraging the client to do most of the talking. They allow for exploration of the client's situation and their thoughts and feelings. Open-ended questions are a valuable communication tool in counselling approaches. E.g. 'Tell me about your cannabis use, the things you enjoy about it? The things which may not be so good?'; 'How would you like things to be different than they currently are?'; 'Have you ever tried to make a change before and what was that?' Closed questions may also be employed at times in an appropriate manner.
- **Affirmations:** affirming and supporting the client and their strengths and efforts can build rapport between client and worker. It also serves to build self-confidence in the ability to change by acknowledging positive behaviours, no matter how small. Affirmations must be positive and congruent in line with Rogerian principles (Rogers 1951). For example, 'Thank you for coming on time today, I know that that can sometimes be difficult'; 'It sounds like despite some difficulties from your alcohol use, you can manage well at other times'; 'I have enjoyed meeting with you today and look forward to meeting again next week'; 'You have worked hard today in exploring some tough issues and that will stand to you in making the changes you want to'.
- **Reflective listening:** more than just listening skills, this requires the worker to reflect back to the client an accurate account of what was said. This involves the worker listening and making statements back to client reflecting what was heard, summarizing statements of the meaning, feelings, thoughts articulated by the client. Paraphrasing allows for clarification and further exploration. Reflections may be simple, amplified, double-sided, shift the focus, agreement with a twist, at all times reframing to emphasize personal choice and control. E.g. 'It sounds like you. . .'; 'Am I right in saying you feel. . .'; 'You don't think that drugs are that much of a problem for you, yet your partner expresses concerns. . .'.
- **Summaries:** periodic summaries throughout interviews allows the client to again hear what they said, aids clear communication between worker and client, demonstrates that the worker has been listening well and encourages the client to elaborate further on the topic. It also allows

for recap of what has been covered so far and highlights areas requiring further exploration. It is particularly useful to summarize at the end of sessions and commence new sessions with an overview of previous discussions, e.g. 'So let's sum up what we talked about today so far. . .' . 'Last week you talked about the effects of alcohol on your relationships with family . . . this week let's focus on how it impacts on your work'.

Change-talk

Change-talk is client language that indicates consideration for changing behaviour, an expression of the client's desire to change, in their own words. Change-talk or self-motivational statements (Miller and Rollnick 1991) indicate client ambivalence, the diminishing of resistance and that the desire for change is being fostered, not imposed. The worker must facilitate this process where the client recognizes how their life may be better in making a change and select to do so themselves. The aim is to have the client express their own concern about their situation (Rollnick and Allison 2004). It is a process which 'reinforces movement towards change: your questions evoke change-talk, the offender responds with positive statements, you reflect and reinforce such statements, and the client continues to elaborate and solidify his or her commitments' (Stinson and Clark 2017: 11). The MINT trainers manual (Motivational Interviewing Network of Trainers) recommends the following ten strategies to evoke change talk (MINT: 128):

1 Ask evocative questions using open-ended questions to stimulate change talk. 'Why would you want to make this change?'; 'How might you go about it?'; 'What are the best reasons for you to do it?'; How important is it for you to make this change?'
2 Explore the decisional balance, the good things of the current situation as opposed to the negative aspects.
3 Seek elaboration of any change-talk that emerges.
4 Seek specific examples from the areas that emerge. 'When do you think you will start?'; 'What would be a first step?'; 'What do you need to do to begin?'
5 Look back – how were things better, worse, or different.
6 Look forward – how would things be if they continue the way they are. The miracle question is effective here, exploration of how life would be different and better if client woke up one morning and the problem had simply disappeared overnight (see Berg and Dolan 2001).
7 Query extremes – the worst and best case outcomes for making or not making a change.
8 Use of change rulers or sliding scales in relation to the level of commitment to change. Self-evaluation techniques and visual tools allow the

client to identify on a continuum between making a change or not. E.g. 'on a scale of 0–10 how important is the change to you?'

9   Explore goals and values of the individual – 'What do you want for your future?'

10   Come alongside: explicitly side with the negative side of the ambivalence. 'It sounds like you do not want to stop drinking, no matter what the negative consequences are for you and your family'.

Motivational interviewing is especially useful in work with those with low or no motivation to change and can be employed successfully at different stages of treatment (Mann et al. 2002). Studies have found that when heroin users attending a methadone clinic were also treated using motivational interviewing techniques, they showed more commitment to treatment goals, more compliance with treatment requirements, fewer heroin-related problems and fewer relapses than a control group who did not receive the benefits of such approaches alongside methadone maintenance (Gossop 2009). Rodriguez et al. (2017) detail that motivational interviewing is appropriate within criminal justice systems to both improve outcomes for substance-misusing clients and for public safety issues. Whilst the criminal justice system may focus on offenders' problems or deficits, motivational interviewing provides opportunities to instead focus on offenders' strengths and stimulate internal motivations to make a change (Walters et al. 2013). McMurran (2009) concluded from a review of 19 studies that motivational interviewing leads to improved retention in treatment, enhanced client motivation to change and reduced offending rates. Miller and Rollnick (2013) acknowledge that ethical issues arise within the processes of motivational interviewing which should be considered in its application and propose guidelines for practice.

Case study

Tom, a drug user is referred to the Probation Service, under threat of prison if he does not stop using drugs (cannabis) but does not present as self-motivated to address his substance use. The task of the probation officer is to raise doubts by eliciting the gains and losses of either staying the same or changing his behaviour, e.g. the worker attempts to develop discrepancies between short-term gains of drug use and long-term goals for Tom. The challenge for the probation officer is 'to first identify and increase [this] ambivalence, and then try to resolve it by creating discrepancy between the actual present and the desired future' (Clark et al. 2006: 40). The probation officer should seek to facilitate a process where Tom presents his own reasons for change and to elicit from him self-motivational statements. The following motivational interviewing approaches can be employed to initiate change:

1   Explore the decisional balance (pros and cons) of making or not making a change (both options can be explored from both perspectives, employing simple visual tools). So, elicit from Tom what he perceives are the positive experiences of using cannabis, e.g. the pro list as outlined by Tom, the benefits he perceives to derive from his drug use. This begins the process as non-confrontational while also serving to engage Tom and build rapport. Collaborative engagement at this point will allow Tom to feel comfortable regarding talking about change. Tom may be employing denial techniques to allow him to remain in a situation that is damaging or he may never have acknowledged the difficulties from drug use. Allowing him the freedom to identify what he perceives are the benefits is an opening to the process of moving him forward from these stances.

2   Explore Tom's negative experiences of drugs, e.g. the con list, the negative effects that Tom can identify for himself. By doing so, the aim is to identify the types of problems or difficulties Tom has experienced from using cannabis. By Tom identifying adverse consequences himself, his internal ambivalence may become apparent. It may be appropriate to use prompts from the 4 L's tool (Roizen and Weisner 1979). This model aids examination of the impact of drug use upon four key areas of a person's life. Liver: the health of Tom, his physical, psychological, emotional well-being; Lover: the relationships Tom has with his partner, children, family, friends and how his drug use may have impacted upon these; Lifestyle/Livelihood: problems Tom may have encountered relating to employment, finances, education, leisure activities, accommodation; Legal: encounters with the law.

3   Identify Tom's goals for the future, what it is he wants and how does his drug use fit with his life goals and values. If Tom can identify discrepancies between where he is in life and where he actually wants to be, and engages in problem recognition from his current behaviour, this will motivate his desire for change. In reality, someone like Tom is likely to develop motivation to change to eliminate the risk of a custodial sanction; nonetheless this is a valid starting point for Tom and from this he identifies the goal of retaining his employment and relationship with his partner and children, all of which would be severely affected were he to serve a prison sentence. E.g. 'If things were different for you, how might that be?

What do you want to achieve? How does your use of drugs fit with what you want in life?'

4   Encourage Tom to reach his own decision to change – emphasize and highlight Tom's dilemmas and ambivalence, then prompt decision-making from him, e.g. 'Have you made a decision about what you want to do?' 'Have you decided to continue as you are or to stop using drugs?'

5   Set goals with Tom in order for him to commence the change process. Goals should be SMART (specific, meaningful, assessable, realistic, timely), e.g. 'What will your first step be?' 'When would you think you could stop using drugs?' 'Who can help and support you through this?'

The cycle of change

A guide for the worker and client alike may be the Wheel of Change model, which was developed by Prochaska and DiClemente (1983). It is a model of behaviour change and it was developed to explain how people change undesirable behaviour as well as develop and maintain new behaviours. Motivational interviewing complements the Wheel of Change and allows for facilitating change in the early stages, even with clients who are resistant or not yet ready to change. Clients in each stage of the cycle respond to different skills and strategies and the worker needs awareness of this. This model provides a structure for understanding where each client is at in relation to the change process.

Using the Wheel of Change, the probation officer can match each intervention appropriately. The task of the probation officer is to assess the client's readiness to change and to enhance the client's motivation through a series of techniques, depending on where the client is at. It is important for probation officers to understand that clients vary in the time it takes them to go around the Wheel of Change and in the time they spend at each stage of the change process. Some clients can be quickly motivated and moved along. Others will be resistant and slower.

> Though it can occur by sudden insight or dramatic shifts (i.e. epiphanies, 'wake up calls', the vast majority of changes take place slowly and incrementally.
>
> (Clark 2005: 24)

Many clients go through the process several times. Clients need to know that they will not be judged but will be supported. Use of motivational interviewing techniques, employing the Wheel of Change as a frame of reference, guides the worker in their intervention. The model allows change to be viewed as a progression through five stages (Prochaska and DiClemente 1983).

The stages of change:

1   **Pre-contemplation:** the person is not aware, denies, or refuses to acknowledge that there is in fact a problem. The person does not identify the negative consequences as outweighing the positive consequences in their circumstances. The person continues to remain in a situation which is damaging and does not consider change. Self-talk at this point may include statements such as 'I haven't got a problem, it is just others who disapprove'.

2   **Contemplation:** the person acknowledges that they have a problem and begins to seriously consider dealing with it. It may be acknowledging the negative aspects drugs have caused in their life through exploration of the 'Four L's'. Clients can spend varying lengths of time in this stage before actually making a decision to change.

3   **Preparation/decision:** the person reaches the decision themselves to make a change. Something finally tips the balance to awareness that there are more negative consequences than positive and a window of opportunity can be opened. The person needs to plan for how they will make the changes.

4   **Action:** the person begins to take the relevant action to change their behaviour. It is still early in the change process. Immense effort is required to maintain the changes following initial action. Essential to the process is changes in attitude and thinking. It is the first steps of change, to actually doing something about their situations, as opposed to denying it or merely considering it.

5   **Maintenance:** the person maintains the change over a significant period, often dealing with challenges and difficulties. The 'honeymoon' period may pass, elation may not always accompany the benefits, and yearning for the past may have to be overcome. It requires determination, hard work, and support to stay on track. The client needs to develop new skills and coping mechanisms to avoid a return to habitual behaviours. The long-haul requires planning, commitment, vigilance, and supports.

A sixth stage, **Relapse**, has been incorporated into the 'Wheel of Change' (Prochaska and DiClemente 1983). This recognizes that relapse is part of the cycle and that people may go around the wheel more than once in their efforts to sustain long-term changes. Relapse should not be considered as a failure, but as a learning experience. Relapse should be addressed quickly and the person returned to action as a soon as possible. Relapse can enhance the possibilities of success in future attempts to change.

Conclusion

This chapter aims to explain how motivational interviewing 'fits' with probation work and can be applied to rehabilitation of offenders and in particular improved outcomes for non-voluntary clients of the judicial system. Motivational interviewing is a practical, respectful, and effective intervention tool for practitioners to evoke client self-motivation to change at various stages of probation engagement, including assessment, case management planning, and supervision. Clients of probation services are typically court mandated and present with addiction issues. They may be required to address addiction issues and change behaviours, which up until the point of court requirements they had not themselves considered particularly problematic. Motivational interviewing is an effective tool for handling such client resistance, by seeking to highlight the client's own ambivalence and discomfort about their situation, thus stimulating their own desire to change. Probation work with offenders requires skills in balancing the care and control responsibilities of the worker and motivational interviewing assists in this balancing. Such skills allows the worker to set the scene in relation to facilitating non-directive, nonjudgemental, respectful relationship building with clients, encouraging them to take ownership of their addiction issues and for the worker and client to collaboratively engage in a process of problem behaviour exploration, recognition, ownership, and motivation to change. It will assist practitioners to recognize and engage in 'change-talk' with clients to elicit intrinsic motivation for change. The core value of probation interventions to bring about positive change in the behaviour of offenders, reduce recidivism, make communities safer and repair the harm done by offending is certainly enhanced when motivational interviewing is incorporated by practitioners.

References

Berg, I. K. and Dolan, Y. (2001) *Tales of Solutions: A Collection of Hope-Inspiring Stories.* New York: W. W. Norton & Company.

Clark, M. (2005) Motivational interviewing for probation staff: Increasing the readiness to change. *Federal Probation*, 69, 2.

Clark, M., Walters, S., Gingerich, R. and Meltzer, M. (2006) Motivational interviewing for probation officers: tipping the balance toward change. *Federal Probation*, 70(1).

Gossop, M. (2009) *Treating Drug Misuse Problems: Evidence of Effectiveness.* Available at: www.nta.nhs.uk/publications/documents/nta.pdf.

Hart, W. and Healy, D. (2018) An inside job: An autobiographical account of desistance. *European Journal of Probation*, 1–17.

Mann, R., Ginsburg, J. and Weekes, J. (2002) Motivational interviewing with offenders. In M. McMurran (Ed.), *Motivating Offenders to Change: A Guide to Enhancing Engagement in Therapy*. Chichester: John Wiley & Sons, Ltd.

McLeod, S. A. (2018) *Cognitive Dissonance*. Available at: www.simplypsychology.org/cognitive-dissonance.html.

McMurran, M. (2009) Motivational interviewing with offenders: A systemic review. *Legal & Criminological Psychology*, 14(1), 83–100.

MINT Trainers Manual Motivational Interviewing Network of Trainers. Available at: www.motivationalinterviewing.org/sites/default/files/tnt_manual_2014_d10_2015 0205.pdf.

Miller, W. and Rollnick, S. (1991) *Motivational Interviewing: Preparing People to Change Addictive Behaviour*. New York: The Guilford Press.

Miller, W. and Rollnick, S. (2002) *Motivational Interviewing: Preparing People for Change*. New York: The Guilford Press.

Miller, W. and Rollnick, S. (2013) *Motivational Interviewing: Helping People Change*. New York: The Guilford Press.

Prochaska, J. and DiClemente, C. (1983) Stages and processes of self-change in smoking: Towards an integrative model of change. *Journal of Consulting & Clinical Psychology*, 51, 390–395.

Rodriguez, M., Walters, S., Houck, J., Alexis Ortiz, J. and Taxman, F. (2017) The language of change among criminal justice clients: Counselor language, client language, and substance use outcomes. *Journal of Clinical Psychology*, 74, 626–636.

Rogers, C. R (1951) *Client-Centered Therapy*. Boston, MA: Houghton Mifflin.

Roizen, R. and Weisner, C. (1979) *Fragmentation in Alcoholism Treatment Services: An Exploratory Analysis*. Berkley, CA: Alcohol Research Group, University of California.

Rollnick, M. W. (1996) *Motivational Interviewing*. London: The Guilford Press.

Rollnick, S. and Allison, J. (2004) Motivational interviewing. In N. Heather and T. Stockwell (Eds.), *The Essential Handbook of Treatment and Prevention of Alcohol Problems*. Chichester: John Wiley & Sons Ltd.

Stinson, J. and Clark, M. (2017) *Motivational Interviewing with Offenders: Engagement, Rehabilitation and Re-Entry*. New York: The Guilford Press.

Walters, S. T., Ressler, E., Douglas, L. and Taxman, F. S. (2013) Motivational interviewing in criminal justice: A new approach to addressing treatment motivation and related behaviours. *Counselor: The Magazine for Addiction Profession*, 5, 48–53.

Trauma-informed practices with youth in criminal justice settings

25

Jill S. Levenson

Trauma-informed practices with youth in criminal justice settings

There are many factors that contribute to delinquent behaviour, but a primary research finding is that youth in the juvenile justice system have often been victims of child maltreatment (Baglivio et al. 2014). Research findings are consistent that justice-involved youth are more likely than youth in the general population to have experienced child abuse and neglect, family dysfunction, polyvictimization, and other traumas (Abram et al. 2004; Baglivio and Epps 2016; Dierkhising et al. 2013). Juveniles involved in the justice system are likely to have lived in chaotic home environments with parents or caregivers who may not have offered effective parenting or protection from harm. Furthermore, these youngsters are more likely to have been involved with child protection and foster care systems, aggravating traumagenic factors that contribute to delinquent behaviour (Barrett et al. 2013).

Adverse childhood experiences (ACEs) place children at higher risk for poor health, mental health, and behavioural outcomes across the lifespan (Felitti et al. 1998). Chronic exposure to adverse conditions generates a persistent 'fight or flight' response in children, increasing the production of stress hormones in the body and altering the neurochemistry of the brain (van der Kolk 2006). Chronic toxic stress can lead to emotional and behavioural self-regulation deficits, paving the way for disciplinary problems in school and in the community – ultimately shifting a child's trajectory toward the 'pipeline to prison' (Wald and Losen 2003).

Correctional youth services are often focused exclusively on offence behaviours and might be confrontational, disregarding the principles of effective correctional rehabilitation and trauma-informed care (TIC) (Kubiak et al. 2017; Levenson et al. 2017). For example, behavioural interventions like level systems are designed to change the contingencies of reinforcement, but may not address underlying self-regulation problems or secondary gain. As well, challenging offence-related thinking errors might ignore underlying core schemas about self, others, and the world. TIC is not intended to excuse criminal behaviour or dismiss the suffering of crime victims. It is a way of conceptualizing and responding to delinquent behaviour through the lens of trauma by understanding that behavioural and emotional dysregulation are often trauma symptoms.

Many juvenile justice practitioners have heard of TIC, and some are familiar with its basic principles, but much remains unknown about how its principles are embedded into service delivery and translated into practice (Berliner and Kolko 2016). Delinquency services pose unique challenges to applying trauma-informed practices that engage youngsters in healing relationships that model and encourage positive change (Donisch et al. 2016). Some of these dilemmas reflect the dual roles of juvenile justice: how can we help troubled youth while also holding them accountable? How do we provide a nurturing service environment that doesn't compromise safety and security of residents and staff? There is a need to help juvenile justice administrators and case managers translate TIC concepts into practice based on the guiding principles published by SAMHSA.

TIC is a framework for delivering services in a way that assimilates evidence about the neurobiological, social, and psychological effects of trauma into policies, procedures, and practices that foster a safe, compassionate, respectful service delivery environment (Bloom and Farragher 2013; Brown et al. 2012; Fallot and Harris 2009; Lang et al. 2016; Levenson et al. 2017; SAMHSA 2014). Trauma-informed juvenile justice practitioners hold the perspective that problematic behaviours are best understood in the context of a youth's past experiences. Counsellors and supervision officers can transform their interventions to be more collaborative, empowering, and client-centred, which facilitates a corrective experience for youngsters who have lacked nurturing, positive role models, and support systems.

Core principles of TIC

The United States Substance Abuse and Mental Health Services Administration (SAMHSA 2014) describes four guiding principles for trauma-informed service delivery. They include: (1) realizing that trauma is extremely prevalent and can create lifelong impacts in many areas of functioning; (2) recognizing that many presenting problems are best conceptualized as symptoms of trauma; (3) incorporating knowledge about trauma into system-wide policies, procedures, and practices; and (4) avoiding the repetition of re-traumatizing and disempowering dynamics in the service delivery setting. The final principle is crucial in working with troubled youth, since nurturing interactions with warm, trustworthy, and responsible adults can help alter the learned helplessness of chaotic home environments (Skinner-Osei and Levenson 2018).

Trauma is defined as an experience that threatens a person's sense of physical or psychological safety, and generates feelings of fear or helplessness (American Psychiatric Association 2013). Traumatic experiences take many forms, but ACEs are a specific set of traumagenic conditions including five types of child maltreatment (physical, emotional and sexual abuse, and physical and emotional neglect) and five types of common household dysfunction (domestic violence, mental illness, substance abuse, criminal behaviour, and an absent parent). Youth in the justice system have often grown up in households where multiple ACEs are present (Baglivio et al. 2014).

Research is somewhat limited in the area of trauma and offending but scholars advise that attention must be paid to the legacy of early relational trauma in the development of antisocial behaviour (Ardino 2012; Miller and Najavits 2012). Attachment theorists (Bowlby 1977) suggest that early relationships with caregivers can be determinative, and when a small child does not have a responsive and consistent parent, subsequent relationships may be fraught with anxiety and resentment. Ansbro (2008) cautioned that the distorted thinking and emotional or behavioural dysregulation that characterizes criminality may be deeply rooted in poor attachments; therefore, rather than focusing simply on cognitive reframing or behavioural reconditioning, workers should attempt to 'provide a taste of a secure base' (p. 15). This is accomplished through a strong therapeutic alliance with professional helpers.

For children exposed to chronic abuse or neglect, daily survival skills become prioritized while other areas of the brain, including executive functioning (decision-making and self-regulation), remain underdeveloped. From a social learning perspective, a child who grows up with a lack of role modelling for responsible behaviour and healthy relationships may develop negative expectations of others. This means that ACEs can contribute to a cascade of psychosocial consequences, including the development of behavioural and personality disorders (Anda et al. 2006; Grady et al. 2016; Masten and Cicchetti 2010). Obviously not all abused children become engaged in criminal behaviour, but the biological, social, and psychological impacts of early mistreatment increase the risk for involvement in crime (Baglivio et al. 2014; Topitzes et al. 2012).

TIC is different from trauma-specific interventions (Levenson 2017). There are many evidence-based, cognitive behavioural treatments designed to help clients resolve trauma and reduce PTSD symptoms. TIC relies more on the process of interaction between helper and client, however, and is a way of providing a sense of safety, empowerment, trust, and respect in the service environment (SAMHSA 2014). TIC is based on a foundation of research documenting the pervasive nature and enduring impacts of chronic childhood adversity (Anda et al. 2006; Felitti et al. 1998). It is not a treatment model or a structured programme per se, but rather it is a framework adjusted on a continuous basis to the context of the client's history, current needs, and rehabilitation goals (Levenson et al. 2017).

Trauma-informed practice skills

For workers in juvenile justice care systems, there are two primary goals of TIC (Levenson et al. 2017): (1) view maladaptive, problematic behaviour and presenting problems through the lens of trauma (case conceptualization), and (2) avoid re-traumatizing clients or replicating disempowering dynamics in the helping relationship (trauma-informed responding).

Case conceptualization through the lens of trauma

TIC emphasizes a holistic understanding of the individual in the context of his or her collective life experiences. As discussed earlier, ACEs can disrupt neurobiological and social development, alter one's sense of self and identity, and reinforce unhealthy interaction styles. Developmental psychopathologists suggest that we process thoughts and emotions in a way that allows us to attach meaning to our experiences. By integrating past experiences into our expectations of the world, we 'establish a coherence of functioning as a thinking, feeling human being' (Rutter and Sroufe 2000: 265). In a constant reciprocal process, our experiences inform our expectations, and our expectations are projected onto new experiences. A pathogenic childhood environment, with relationships characterized by betrayal or invalidation, deprives children of the types of role-modelling and relational skills that promote healthy functioning across the lifespan – often creating what they expect.

ACEs contribute to criminogenic risk factors such as substance abuse, associations with non-conforming peers, and a sense of entitlement or resentment that predisposes one to criminal thinking (Finkelhor 1995; Masten and Cicchetti 2010; Patterson et al. 1990; Rutter and Sroufe 2000). Polyvictimization is not uncommon in troubled households, and violent or deprivational environments can promote development of PTSD and personality disorders

(Baglivio and Epps 2016; Finkelhor 1995; Finkelhor and Kendall-Tackett 1997; Finkelhor et al. 2011). Some children may endorse a sense of learned help-lessness, while others become angry and combative. Survival skills show up in different ways, such as aggressive behaviour (fight response), avoidance of relationships or tendency to self-medicate (flight response), or passivity and difficulties setting boundaries (freeze response).

By understanding the dynamics of a youth's early family relationships, workers can conceptualize presenting problems as coping styles that were once adaptive in the dysfunctional environment (Levenson and Willis 2017). Crim-inality, substance abuse, or aggression are used to cope with distress because they provide a sense of personal power, relief from emotional pain, self-efficacy, group inclusion, or acceptance that might be missing elsewhere in a youth's life. These behaviours are thus reframed as survival skills that were programmed by painful life experiences, have been well rehearsed, and have become ingrained. Maladaptive coping was once necessary to survive in a traumagenic environment but now interferes with the capacity to establish healthy relationships and boundaries. By using a strengths-based approach to post-traumatic growth, we can help youth decrease conduct problems, engage in healthy relationships, regulate emotions, and cope with crises more effectively. Ultimately, we hope to help them someday parent and protect their own children in a more nurturing and responsive manner – thereby disrupting the intergenerational cycle of trauma and victimization (Harris and Fallot 2001).

Trauma-informed responding

The acronym SHARE (safety, hope, autonomy, respect, empathy) can help juvenile justice practitioners translate trauma-informed concepts into service delivery (Levenson and Willis 2017). Historically, our approaches to delin-quent behaviour have involved external controls, moving the locus of con-trol away from the youth. However, this undermines personal ownership of change, and often reinforces the very disempowering experiences that brought them into the system. Instead, TIC replaces control with collabora-tion, denouncing the belief that we must actively restrict troubled children's behaviour at all times in order to manage risk.

Above all, rehabilitative services should feel *Safe*. Children need physical and psychological safety in their environment and in relationships with oth-ers, especially those on whom they are dependent. *Hope* is instilled through encouraging belief that change is possible. Many troubled youths have expe-rienced hopelessness and helplessness for so long that there is no expectation that things can ever be different. Through collaborative approaches that allow clients to identify their problems and goals, clients can participate in devis-ing strategies by which, together with a caring professional, they can make the self-improvements they desire. *Autonomy* helps youngsters to learn and practice skills that enable them to take control of their own destiny, explore options and alternatives, and engage in a deliberate decision-making process rather than impulsive and reactive behaviour. *Respect* is important, because they may have been treated at home or in the community with disdain, contempt, or disempowerment. By making each individual feel valued, special, and important, they can recognize their own strengths and internalize a new sense of self. *Empathy* plays a huge role in helping clients to appreciate the perspectives of others. Healing relationships with caring adults foster human connections – a deterrent to harming others (Levenson and Willis 2017).

Trauma-informed responses as a corrective experience

Entry into delinquency services is typically precipitated by disciplinary problems at school or in the community, and minority youth are at higher risk for police referrals (Wald and Losen 2003). Parents, teachers, and other adults often respond in ways that are punitive rather than trauma-informed, potentially re-traumatizing children. Though limit-setting and consequences reflect good intentions designed to foster self-management and a sense of right and wrong, these responses alone seldom lead to long-lasting behavioural change. When practitioners use stigmatizing or pathologizing labels, we can reinforce a youth's feelings of mistrust and vulnerability. Traumatic re-enactment occurs through repetition of disempowering dynamics and can confirm negative expectations of adults while strengthening a troubled youth's anger, depression, or maladaptive coping (Levenson and Willis 2017; Skinner-Osei and Levenson 2018).

Trauma-informed responding attempts to understand *why* a youngster is acting in a certain way. Adult helpers can provide a corrective experience by engaging with youth in a respectful and caring encounter that is different from what the child expects. When children grow up in adverse conditions, they become accustomed to scanning for environmental threats in order to respond quickly to avoid danger or protect themselves. Knowledge of trauma can help juvenile justice practitioners reframe troublesome behaviours as adaptive survival mechanisms. Trauma-informed interventions are designed to coach youngsters in better reality testing and self-correction, so they can develop improved strategies for distress tolerance, healthy coping, self-regulation, and implementing a range of problem-solving skills (Levenson and Willis 2017; Skinner-Osei and Levenson 2018).

The TIC paradigm approaches youth behaviour problems by asking 'what happened to you?' rather than 'what's wrong with you?' (SAMHSA 2014). Early relational trauma shapes the way children think about themselves and others, which often translates into an expectation that the world is not a safe place (Levenson and Willis 2017; Skinner-Osei and Levenson 2018). Traumatized youth with conduct problems are often predisposed to mistrust and may use anger and rebellion toward authority figures to compensate for feelings of vulnerability. They may have poor collaboration and intimacy skills, engage in self-destructive behaviour, or relieve distress through substance abuse. Chaotic home environments can make stability unfamiliar and elusive. There are many evidence-based CBT interventions delivered in rehabilitative criminal justice programs; however, the neurobiological changes that result from chronic toxic stress can make it more difficult for traumatized individuals to process and successfully utilize interventions (Levenson et al. 2017).

Maslow's hierarchy of needs (Maslow 1943) proposed that all humans require survival essentials, a sense of safety, acceptance and belonging, and self-efficacy to reach one's potential. Troubled youth may seek to meet these basic needs using maladaptive methods. In the absence of safe and nurturing environments, youngsters are vulnerable to the promise of belonging and empowerment attained through delinquency or gang activity (Levenson and Willis 2017; Skinner-Osei and Levenson 2018). ACEs are associated with early sexual behaviour and unintended pregnancies, perhaps due to teens seeking unconditional love that has been lacking in their lives. Substance abuse can be a way of numbing painful feelings. However, psychoeducation about birth control and the dangers of gangs or drugs may be ineffective unless we help youngsters understand and overcome painful experiences that have shaped their beliefs about self, others, and the world. Because the origins of troubled conduct have roots in childhood trauma (Halldorsdottir 2007), a positive, corrective, and healing relationship with an adult mentor can enable youth to bond and attach with others, pursue meaningful life goals, and feel a sense of self-efficacy and self-sufficiency (Skinner-Osei and Levenson 2018).

Troubled youth need to encounter adults who validate their experiences and feelings while also modelling and coaching new problem-solving skills. This promotes personal accountability, empathy, an internal locus of control, and enhanced emotional and behavioural self-management. Risk for re-traumatization can occur when punitive consequences are prioritized as the only way to re-condition behaviour. When adult helpers respond to antagonistic or combative youngsters in a rejecting or dismissive way, this can confirm negative expectations, disrupt the therapeutic alliance, and lead to treatment failures (Binder and Strupp 1997). Ironically, those who seem most resistant to intervention are often those most in need of trauma-informed responses (Levenson and Willis 2017; Skinner-Osei and Levenson 2018). In summary, rehabilitative juvenile justice systems must attend to youth well-being as a crucial element of risk management and recidivism reduction.

Implications for practice

There are some 'take-home messages' for practitioners who work with youth in correctional settings to keep in mind (Levenson and Willis 2017; Skinner-Osei and Levenson 2018). First, remember that child maltreatment, family dysfunction, poverty, and community violence are frequently found in the histories of children involved with the justice system. Next, these youths have often experienced polyvictimization and their behaviours may be indicative of complex trauma syndrome. For instance, the DSM-5 criteria for PTSD includes irritable behaviour and angry outbursts, reckless or self-destructive behaviour, hypervigilance and exaggerated startle response, concentration problems, avoidance of stimuli associated with traumatic events, and negative cognition and mood (American Psychiatric Association 2013). These post-traumatic stress indicators are often displayed as self-management deficits and lead to disciplinary action in schools and in the community. Thus, in many juvenile justice cases, the emotional and behavioural self-regulation problems seen in troubled children should be viewed in the context of neurobiological impacts of traumagenic conditions throughout a youngster's life (Levenson and Willis 2017; Skinner-Osei and Levenson 2018).

Children in juvenile justice systems need workers who can engage them with compassion and respect, and who can become positive role models (Skinner-Osei and Levenson 2018). Helping children develop healthy boundaries and self-management skills is important, and these goals can be furthered with strategies that contextualize disciplinary actions with trauma-informed care. Limit-setting and decision-making strategies can be coached in a positive and respectful way, so that children have a chance to develop and practice self-correction skills that may have been lacking in chaotic households or communities. Expecting youth with a history of conduct problems to be able to deal effectively with crisis, or resolve conflict in rational and appropriate ways, may be unrealistic until those skills are modelled, learned, and rehearsed. Trauma can compromise executive functioning, and these youths may not know how to engage in successful problem-solving and effective coping skills until someone teaches them. Punitive consequences alone are not an antidote for 'bad' behaviour if the underlying trauma is not recognized, understood, and addressed.

Finally, and importantly, troubled youth may have had negative experiences with help-seeking in their homes or communities, and formal services can be perceived as oppressive and disempowering (Levenson and Willis 2017; Skinner-Osei and Levenson 2018). Asking for help can activate shame or fear, which can be reinforced when adults respond to youngsters with harsh criticism or disdain. Authority figures are commonly perceived as rigid, threatening, or judgemental by marginalized groups, so it is important for helping professionals to avoid disempowering dynamics. By modelling respectful, shared decision-making, we can help troubled youth achieve positive self-determination, self-advocacy, and self-efficacy skills.

When working with delinquent youth in justice settings, the helping relationship becomes a chance to offer safe and nurturing interactions, facilitate human connections and exposure to corrective and empowering relationships. New patterns are shaped as these youngsters have a chance to develop new healthy interpersonal skills with adults who listen to them with kindness, interest, and respect. Attachment difficulties and conduct problems often reflect early adversity, and therefore trauma-informed interventions are crucial to cultivating self-regulation skills for troubled youth. Trauma-informed interventions rely on a corrective experiential process, which might mitigate risk for future offending, ultimately benefitting public safety.

References

Abram, K. M., Teplin, L. A., Charles, D. R., Longworth, S. L., McClelland, G. M. and Dulcan, M. K. (2004) Posttraumatic stress disorder and trauma in youth in juvenile detention. *Archives of General Psychiatry*, 61(4), 403–410. DOI:10.1001/archpsyc.61.4.403.

American Psychiatric Association. (2013) *Diagnostic and Statistical Manual of Mental Disorders*, 5th edition. Washington, DC: Author.

Anda, R. F., Felitti, V. J., Bremner, J. D., Walker, J. D., Whitfield, C., Perry, B. D., et al. (2006) The enduring effects of abuse and related adverse experiences in childhood. *European Archives of Psychiatry and Clinical Neuroscience*, 256, 174–186.

Ansbro, M. (2008). Using attachment theory with offenders. *Probation Journal*, 55(3), 231–244.

Ardino, V. (2012) Offending: The role of trauma and PTSD. *European Journal of Psychotraumatology*, 3(1), 18968. DOI:10.3402/ejpt.v3i0.18968.

Baglivio, M. T. and Epps, N. (2016) The interrelatedness of adverse childhood experiences among high-risk juvenile offenders. *Youth Violence and Juvenile Justice*, 14(3), 179–198. DOI:10.1177/1541204014566286.

Baglivio, M. T., Epps, N., Swartz, K., Huq, M. S., Sheer, A. and Hardt, N. S. (2014) The prevalence of Adverse Childhood Experiences (ACE) in the lives of juvenile offenders. *Journal of Juvenile Justice*, 3(2), 1–23.

Barrett, D. E., Katsiyannis, A., Zhang, D. and Zhang, D. (2013) Delinquency and recidivism: A multicohort, matched-control study of the role of early adverse experiences, mental health problems, and disabilities. *Journal of Emotional and Behavioral Disorders*. DOI:10.1177/1063426612470514.

Berliner, L. and Kolko, D. J. (2016) Trauma informed care. *Child Maltreatment*, 21(2), 168–172. DOI:10.1177/1077559516643785.

Binder, J. and Strupp, H. (1997) Negative process: A recurrently discovered and underestimated facet of therapeutic process and outcome in the individual psychotherapy of adults. *Clinical Psychology: Science and Practice*, 4, 121–139.

Bloom, S. L. and Farragher, B. (2013) *Restoring Sanctuary: A New Operating System for Trauma-Informed Systems of Care*. New York: Oxford University Press.

Bowlby, J. (1977) The making and breaking of affectional bonds. I. Aetiology and psychopathology in the light of attachment theory. An expanded version of the fiftieth lecture, delivered before the Royal college of psychiatrists, 19 November 1976. *The British Journal of Psychiatry*, 130(3), 201–210.

Brown, S. M., Baker, C. N. and Wilcox, P. (2012) Risking connection trauma training: A pathway toward trauma-informed care in child congregate care settings. *Psychological Trauma: Theory, Research, Practice, and Policy*, 4(5), 507–515.

Dierkhising, C. B., Ko, S. J., Woods-Jaeger, B., Briggs, E. C., Lee, R. and Pynoos, R. S. (2013) Trauma histories among justice-involved youth: Findings from the national child traumatic stress network. *European Journal of Psychotraumatology*, 4. http://dx.doi.org/10.3402/ejpt.v4i0.20274.

Donisch, K., Bray, C. and Gewirtz, A. (2016) Child welfare, juvenile justice, mental health, and education providers' conceptualizations of trauma-informed practice. *Child Maltreatment*, 21(2), 125–134. DOI:10.1177/1077559516633304.

Fallot, R. and Harris, M. (2009) Creating cultures of trauma-informed care (CCTIC): A self-assessment and planning protocol. *University of Iowa: Community Connections.* Available at: www.healthcare.uiowa.edu/icmh/documents/CCTICSelf-Assessmentan dPlanningProtocol0709.pdf.

Felitti, V. J., Anda, R. F., Nordenberg, D., Williamson, D. F., Spitz, A. M., Edwards, V., et al. (1998) Relationship of childhood abuse and household dysfunction to many of the leading causes of death in adults: The Adverse Childhood Experiences (ACE) study. *American Journal of Preventive Medicine*, 14(4), 245–258.

Finkelhor, D. (1995) The victimization of children: A developmental perspective. *American Journal of Orthopsychiatry*, 65, 177–193.

Finkelhor, D. and Kendall-Tackett, K. (1997) A developmental perspective on the childhood impact of crime, abuse, and violent victimization. In D. Cicchetti and S. Toth (Eds.), *Rochester Symposium on Developmental Psychopathology: Developmental Perspectives on Trauma: Theory, Research, and Intervention*, Vol. 8. Rochester: University of Rochester Press, pp. 1–32.

Finkelhor, D., Turner, H. A., Hamby, S. L. and Ormrod, R. (2011) *Polyvictimization: Children's Exposure to Multiple Types of Violence, Crime, and Abuse.* Washington, DC: US Department of Justice, Office of Justice Programs, Office of Juvenile Justice and Delinquency Prevention.

Grady, M. D., Levenson, J. S. and Bolder, T. (2016) Linking adverse childhood effects and attachment a theory of etiology for sexual offending. *Trauma, Violence, & Abuse.* DOI:1524838015627147.

Halldorsdottir, S. (2007) A psychoneuroimmunological view of the healing potential of professional caring in the face of human suffering. *International Journal for Human Caring*, 11(2), 32.

Harris, M. E. and Fallot, R. D. (2001) *Using Trauma Theory to Design Service Systems.* San Fransisco, CA: Jossey-Bass.

Kubiak, S., Covington, S. and Hillier, C. (2017) Trauma-informed corrections. In D. Springer and A. Roberts (Eds.), *Social Work in Juvenile and Criminal Justice System*, 4th edition. Springfield, IL: Charles C. Thomas.

Lang, J. M., Campbell, K., Shanley, P., Crusto, C. A. and Connell, C. M. (2016) Building capacity for trauma-informed care in the child welfare system. *Child maltreatment*, 21(2), 113–124. DOI:10.1177/1077559516635273.

Levenson, J. S. (2017) Trauma-informed social work practice. *Social Work*, 62(2), 105–113.

Levenson, J. S. and Willis, G. (2017) Implementing trauma-informed care in correctional treatment and supervision. *Journal of Aggression, Maltreatment & Trauma*, 28(4), 481–501. doi:10.1080/10926771.2018.1531959

Levenson, J. S., Willis, G. and Prescott, D. (2017) *Trauma-Informed Care: Transforming Treatment for People Who Sexually Abuse.* Brandon, VT: Safer Society Press.

Maslow, A. S. (1943) A theory of human motivation. *Psychological review*, 50(4), 370–396.

Masten, A. S. and Cicchetti, D. (2010) Developmental cascades. *Development and psychopathology*, 22(3), 491–495.

Miller, N. A. and Najavits, L. M. (2012) Creating trauma-informed correctional care: A balance of goals and environment. *European Journal of Psychotraumatology*, 3, 1–8.

Patterson, G. R., DeBaryshe, B. D. and Ramsey, E. (1990) A developmental perspective on antisocial behavior. *American Psychologist*, 44(2), 329–335.

Rutter, M. and Sroufe, L. (2000) Developmental psychopathology: Concepts and challenges. *Development and Psychopathology*, 12(3), 265–296.

SAMHSA. (2014) *SAMHSA's Concept of Trauma and Guidance for a Trauma-Informed Approach.* Available at: http://store.samhsa.gov/shin/content//SMA14-4884/SMA14-4884.pdf: Substance Abuse and Mental Health Services Administration.

Skinner-Osei, P. and Levenson, J. S. (2018) Trauma-informed services for children with incarcerated parents. *Journal of Family Social* Work, 21(4–5), 421–437.

Topitzes, J., Mersky, J. P. and Reynolds, A. J. (2012) From child maltreatment to violent offending: An examination of mixed-gender and gender-specific models. *Journal of Interpersonal Violence*, 27(12), 2322–2347.

Van der Kolk, B. (2006) Clinical implications of neuroscience research in PTSD. *Annals of the New York Academy of Sciences*, 1071(1), 277–293.

Wald, J. and Losen, D. J. (2003) Defining and redirecting a school to prison pipeline. *New Directions for Youth Development* (99), 9–15.

26

Building social capital to encourage desistance

Lessons from a veteran-specific project

Katherine Albertson and
Lauren Hall

Introduction

The concept of social capital has expanded in intellectual currency as a way of understanding the importance and value of family, community, and civic relationships. Social capital remains a complex term to define and is vigorously contested in some quarters (Schuller et al. 2000; Navarro 2002; Daly and Silver 2008; Fine 2010). Within the discipline of criminology and criminal justice, social capital has been theoretically linked to aiding desistance (Laub and Sampson 1993; Laub et al. 1995). The significance of the role of wider relational factors in supporting the desistance process is increasingly being called for in the practitioner literature (Farrall 2004; McNeill 2006). The first half of this chapter introduces the origins and development of the concept of social capital, providing an overview of the two main approaches, before moving into a critical engagement with the usefulness of the term with regard to the desistance process. The remainder of this chapter presents six key social capital building components identified in the delivery of a veteran-specific community-based addictions recovery project. This chapter concludes that while the concept of social capital is useful as a framework through which practitioners can work to co-construct strategies to increase offenders social interaction, social capital building strategies to aid desistance are best served when made deferential to the broader and more holistic understandings of the tertiary desistance process.

Origins, levels, and dimensions of social capital

The essential idea regarding the significance of social capital is that if one has a diverse range of relationships with family members, friends, work colleagues, and wider social acquaintances, these relationships can constitute significant assets when an individual, group, or community faces changes, difficulties, or transitions. Originating from mainstream economics, social capital is defined as 'networks together with shared norms, values and understandings that facilitate co-operation within or among groups' (OECD 2017: 41). However, the concept is understood theoretically, empirically, and explanatorily in different ways across and indeed between disciplines.

There are two main approaches to social capital, the network perspective – focusing on describing the levels and dimensions of social capital – and the social structural perspective – prioritizing the features and characteristics of social capital. While both approaches are overviewed separately here for clarity, they are commonly used interchangeably. From a network approach, key distinctions are made between three different levels of social capital. First, bonding social capital refers to more intimate horizontal ties between similar individuals within the same family, social group, or local community, as being the source of a sense of belonging and solidarity (Putnam 2000). Second, bridging social capital refers to the ties between different social groupings within a community, which enable access into more vertical social network resources and provide opportunities for cross-group reciprocity (Szreter and Woolcock 2004). Finally, linking social capital describes connections made through the sharing of social norms such as respect and trust which interact across more formal, civic, and institutionalized authority in wider society (Gitell and Vidal 1998). It is posited that the more homogeneous the community, the more bonding social capital is exhibited and less bridging and linking social capital (Lin 2001; Costa and Kahn 2003). A key point here is that if social capital building is based on exclusive ties (e.g. gender, race or in this case ex-forces) as a way of empowering disadvantaged groups, this may unintentionally reinforce group boundaries, thereby making it more difficult for groups to develop other forms of social capital (see Pahl and Spencer 2004).

Likewise, from a more social structural approach to social capital, three similar dimensions are highlighted, describing the range of the manifestations of social capital. First, fulfilment of structural social capital involves attainment of established social roles, which enhance access to the social networks and the rights and responsibilities that are associated with them (Hitt et al. 2002). Second, achieving cognitive social capital involves being exposed to social settings where shared norms, values, attitudes, and beliefs which predispose people towards mutually beneficial collective action are promoted (Krishna and Uphoff 2002; Uphoff 1999). Finally, realizing relational social capital is said to be based on investment in intimate social relationships – commonly described as a source of trustworthiness and hope – which are considered key to facilitating unfamiliar or more creative, innovative tasks (Moran 2005). Therein prioritizing the quality or strength of social ties, this approach draws on the distinction made between 'strong' and 'weak' social ties (Granovetter 1973; Hawkins and Maurer 2009; Chapman and Murray 2015). Generally, the strength and/or quality of these bonds are considered to reduce the further away from those similar to oneself these social ties reach. This conclusion however is not dissimilar from the network perspective position regarding the issues of dissimilar levels of the different types of social capital in homogeneous communities outlined in the section above.

Social capital and desistance

Within the desistance literature, the term social capital has been largely, if not uncritically, used to define resources that reside in social networks and social relationships (Weaver and McNeil 2010). Approaches to building social capital to aid desistance have mirrored the advances in the wider social capital literature as described above. These studies range from exploring opportunities to mobilize the social capital of families within criminal justice practitioner work (Wright et al. 2001; Mills and Codd 2008), to tapping into the social capital securing employment can provide (Farrall 2004), and assessing the community-level social capital inherent in faith and volunteer groups (O'Connor and Bogue 2010; Fox 2016). Further work is ongoing around the potential of mobilizing community capacity via the civic engagement route (Bazemore and Erbe 2003; Uggen et al. 2006) and opportunities afforded by mentoring roles (Brown and Ross 2010). Social capital building initiatives designed to support community self-regulation around crime and subsequent challenges around community capacity building are also a growing area of interest (e.g. Braithwaite 1989; Van Ness and Strong 2014; Kruttschnitt et al. 2000). Broader strategies designed to address the negative impact of enduring structural inequalities on access to realistic opportunities to build social capital have also been considered (Bracken et al. 2009; Cattell 2001).

The social capital building potential of innovative cooperative community projects are just beginning to be demonstrated (e.g. Ruiu 2016: Weaver 2016). Likewise, national initiatives such as the National Criminal Justice Mentoring scheme (Ministry of Justice 2013; Aiken 2016), the Prison Reform Trust's Active Citizen's pilot (Prison Reform Trust 2017), and civic governance-related innovations such as User Voice initiatives (Schmidt 2013), Debating for a Change (Fleming-Williams and Gordon 2011), and A Fair Response (Edgar et al. 2011) can all be described as responding to the broad range of different levels of social capital-related issues within the criminal justice setting.

While approaches to building social capital to support desistance may differ in terms of focusing on the main relational source of this capital, to paraphrase Rose and Clear (1998: 471), they all prioritize retaining offenders in the community, as treating offenders as having a valuable contribution to make and insist that utilizing local resources can assist transformational journeys for offenders. However, the authors of this chapter assert that it is essential for future work conducted on the development of theoretical approaches to fostering this broad range of social relationships is both securely embedded and more closely aligned to our understandings of the desistance process, specifically tertiary desistance stages.

Recognized as a three-stage process, desistance trajectories involve movement from a state of primary desistance or a cessation in offending, to a more permanent underlying change in self-identity no longer associated with offending behaviour, or secondary desistance (Maruna et al. 2004). The importance of wider relational factors in the cementing of these desistance processes are encapsulated within the third stage of the desistance processes, that of tertiary desistance (McNeill 2014). This is a broad concept based on the importance of recognition and validation of fledgling desister identities by others. Significantly, this third stage of the desistance process is distinct from the first two through its near complete disassociation with offending behaviour per se. Importantly, the tertiary desistance narrative prioritizes opportunities to gain a sense of social inclusion, acceptance, belonging, and participation, ideally both within one's own community and wider society, embodying concepts of citizenship, social justice, integration, and solidarity (Maruna 2012; McNeil 2014; Fox 2015).

The social capital building continuum

This section presents findings from the evaluation of an explicitly social capital building project designed for ex-forces personnel accessing a community-based addictions recovery service in the North of England.[1] For full details of the study see Albertson et al. (2017a) and for practice implications of this approach for practitioners working with the Armed Forces community in prison, see Albertson et al. (2017b). Testing the potential of a social capital building approach as both an individual and community-level concept prefaced the evaluation of this post-Transforming Rehabilitation initiative (Albertson et al. 2015). Themes of social capital building, agency, identity, and transition are identified as feeding into the development of a positive outward facing community participation-based identity, captured in the concept of 'military veteran citizenship' role played out for this cohort (Albertson et al. 2017a: 68).

Three key elements pre-empted the group membership criteria: attendance is voluntary; members all have similar life experience; the project activities are tailored by the group members. The evaluation identified six key social capital building components or strategies incorporated by this project, which ensured opportunities to develop positive relationships throughout the continuum of bonding through to bridging and linking social capital:

1   **Regular association with peers:** regular association with peers occurs with weekly group meetings with other veterans, based on the mutual aid group model,[2] providing structured opportunities for reflection on past, present, and future goals and behaviours are provided. Mutual commitment motivates continued attendance (O'Connor and Bogue 2010), creating a sense of belonging, assisting 'personal healing through the reacquisition of cultural traditions' as 'one way to overcome structural constraints while at the same time supporting an individual decision to desist from crime' (Bracken et al. 2009: 61). Members both receive and reciprocate reinforcement of motivation and hope, providing a forum where members begin to construct a story to redeem themselves of their past behaviours and assert a meaningful future, as encapsulated by the term redemption scripts (Maruna 2001).

2   **Involvement in group-based discussion settings:** external agency attendance raises awareness of citizenship-based rights, i.e. the duties and responsibilities which 'include respecting the rights and legitimate expectations of others' (Faulkner 2003: 289), whilst establishing pathways into advice services (e.g. benefits; housing). Q and A or discussion format is utilized to raise awareness of, reinforce, and legitimize the rights and responsibilities of the group 'as matters of social and civic responsibility' (Faulkner 2003: 295). These activities enable the group to have a sense of informed knowledge about the services available and their appropriateness for the veteran cohort, thus raising members' sense of self-determination and confidence in decision-making, alongside enhancing their sense of authority with regard to recommending services as veteran-friendly.

3   **Participation in social events, group tasks, and activities:** group members select events, tasks, and activities to foster positive networks (e.g. walking groups; allotment garden). Group residential opportunities prove particularly effective and link into wider regional and national organizations events and social activities. This kind of active civic engagement facilitates the transmission of community morals, expressing

'the values of inclusion, citizenship, fundamental human rights, and for-giveness' (Fox 2015: 86). Devolution of responsibilities for negotiating external social connections occurs; involving increasingly civic engage-ment provides group members with a sense of authority, based on their effective community representation to external bodies.

4   **Engaging in acts of reciprocity and generative activities:** train-ing for Veteran Recovery Champion roles, delivered by other local support agencies as providing pathways into voluntary work that is enjoyable, rewarding, and in some way supportive of one's own community (Baze-more and Erbe 2004) is identified as indicative of desistance signalling (Maruna 2012). Over time members take up volunteering roles in other non-veteran and non-recovery specific agencies. A key distinction here is that engagement with generative activities needs to be based on reciproc-ity, not self-interest (Forrest and Kearns 2001: 2141).

5   **Participation in wider non-veteran community events:** veter-ans are encouraged to contribute knowledge and experience to represent their group, thereby supporting positive and affirming social interaction in the wider community (e.g. local fetes/fairs; charity fundraisers). This increases sense of ability and confidence of individuals' to make a valu-able contribution on behalf of their group in the wider community. The veterans' cohort narrative is infused with a sense of pride and an embed-ded forward-facing 'military veteran citizenship' role (Albertson et al. 2017a: 68), which is 'accompanied by an alteration to the individual's sense of moral agency' (King 2013: 161).

6   **Formal civic, governance/decision-influencing settings:** mem-bers attend formal meetings (e.g. conferences; seminars; Westmin-ster-briefings). Veterans described these opportunities within a narrative sense of restoration as a citizen, with both rights and obligations, thus increasing the potential for cooperative action and political change. The groups' collective response to the stigma around veterans in addiction services and prison motivates them to contribute to national debates on the subject (see LeBel 2013). This illustrates this delivery models' success in providing the community the context in which the rights and responsibilities of citizenship are given practical expression (Faulkner 2003).

Utilizing notions of social capital to aid desistance

The practical building social capital model outlined above is in essence predi-cated on developing effective strategies to draw individuals 'beyond a narrow preoccupation with themselves and their own problems' (Burnett and Maruna 2006: 94) and into an increasing concern for others. This 'other centring' afforded by social capital opportunities facilitates strong generative concerns that 'come to the forefront, concerns intended to satisfy both personal aspirations for new meaning and the desire to gain pro-social legitimacy' (Porporino 2010: 73). More broadly, this building social capital model facilitates a process of the 'recommunalization of the disenfranchised' (Arrigo and Takahashi 2006: 313). Illustrating the potential of social capital building activities to assist the move from the 'I', of stigmatized socially excluded individual status, to the 'we', required by 'full democratic participation' as a stakeholder (Uggen et al. 2006: 283).

In the context of supporting desistance, this chapter asserts that the process of building social capital is most usefully viewed as enhancing opportunities to assist individuals to move through the social capital continuum informed by the framework of tertiary desistance. The role communities can play in creating and reinforcing the non-criminal identity is increasingly being highlighted as anchoring desistance moments (Arrigo and Takahashi 2006; Day and Ward 2010; Fox 2016). The required shift from prioritizing criminal justice services to prioritizing communities that support desistance 'means engaging much more directly and meaningfully with communities than has hitherto been the case' (McNeill 2009: 52). When thinking about the potential for social capital building opportunities to aid desistance, this chapter illustrates there are key common areas we can focus on. These areas can be effectively mapped out along with those we work with, by getting to know them and their social world. Becoming aware of the world views, areas of interest, relationships, and passions of these individuals and their social networks means we can begin to co-identify opportunities for social capital building to support desistance trajectories.

Notes

1 Addaction is one of the UK's largest specialist community drug and alcohol treatment charities. For more details see the web page: www.addaction.org.uk/. For more details about the Right Turn project, see the web page: www.addaction.org.uk/help-and-support/adult-drug-and-alcohol-services/right-turn. The evaluation was funded by the Forces in Mind Trust: See web page: www.fim-trust.org/.
2 Mutual aid group models operate on an ethos of egalitarianism and self-help.

References

Aiken, J. (2016) *Centre for Social Justice Meaningful Mentoring Report*. Available at: www.centreforsocialjustice.org.uk/core/wp-content/uploads/2016/08/mm.pdf.

Albertson, K., Banks. J. and Murray, E. (2017b) Military veteran-offenders: Making sense of developments in the debate to inform service delivery. *The Prison Service Journal*, 234, 23–30.

Albertson, K., Best, D., Pinkney, A., Murphy, T., Irving, J. and Stevenson, J. (2017a) *"It's Not Just About Recovery": The Right Turn Veteran-Specific Recovery Service Evaluation*. Final report, Sheffield Hallam University: Helena Kennedy Centre for International Justice. ISBN: 978-1-5272-0919-0.

Albertson, K., Irving, J. and Best, D. (2015) A social capital approach to assisting veterans through recovery and desistance transitions in civilian life. *The Howard Journal of Crime and Justice*, 54(4), 384–396.

Arrigo, B. A. and Takahashi, Y. (2006) Recommunalization of the disenfranchised: A theoretical and critical criminological inquiry. *Theoretical Criminology*, 10(3), 307–336.

Bazemore, G. and Erbe, C. (2003) Operationalizing the community variable in offender reintegration: Theory and practice for developing intervention social capital. *Youth Violence and Juvenile Justice*, 1(3), 246–275.

Bazemore, G. and Erbe, C. (2004) Reintegration and restorative justice: Towards a theory and practice of informal social control and support. In S. Maruna and R. Immarigeon (Eds.), *After Crime and Punishment: Pathways to Offender Reintegration*. Devon: Willan Publishing.

Bracken, D. C., Deane, L. and Morrissette, L. (2009) Desistance and social marginalization: The case of Canadian Aboriginal offenders. *Theoretical Criminology*, 13(1), 61–78.

Braithwaite, J. (1989) *Crime, Shame and Reintegration*. Cambridge: Cambridge University Press.

Brown, M. and Ross, S. (2010) Mentoring, social capital and desistance: A study of women released from prison. *Australian and New Zealand Journal of Criminology*, 43(1), 31–50.

Burnett, R. and Maruna, S. (2006) The kindness of prisoners: Strengths-based resettlement in theory and in action. *Criminology and Criminal Justice*, 6(1), 83–106.

Cattell, V. (2001) Poor people, poor places, and poor health: The mediating role of social networks and social capital. *Social Science and Medicine*, 52, 1501–1516.

Chapman, T. and Murray, D. (2015) Restorative justice, social capital and desistance from offending. *Revista de Asistena Sociala*, 47–60.

Costa, D. and Kahn, M. (2003) Understanding the American decline in social capital, 1952–1998. *KYKLOS International Review for Social Sciences*, 56(1), 17–46.

Daly, M. and Silver, H. (2008) Social exclusion and social capital: A comparison and critique. *Theoretical Sociology*, 37, 537–566.

Day, A. and Ward, T. (2010) Offender rehabilitation as a value-laden process. *International Journal of Offender Therapy and Comparative Criminology*, 54, 289–306.

Edgar, K., Jacobson, J. and Biggar, K. (2011) *Time Well Spent: A Practical Guide to Active Citizenship and Volunteering in Prison*. London: Prison Reform Trust. Available at: www.prisonreformtrust.org.uk/Portals/0/Documents/Time%20Well%20Spent%20report%20lo.pdf.

Farrall, S. (2004) Social capital and offender reintegration: Making probation desistance. In S. Maruna and R. Immarigeon (Eds.), *After Crime and Punishment: Pathways to Offender Reintegration*. Devon: Willan Publishing.

Faulkner, D. (2003) Taking citizenship seriously: Social capital and criminal justice in a changing world. *Criminal Justice*, 3(3), 287–315.

Fine, B. (2010) *Theories of Social Capital: Researchers Behaving Badly*. London: Pluto Press.

Fleming-Williams, A. and Gordon, A. (2011) *Debating for a Change: Improving Prison Life Through Prisoner/Staff Working Groups*. Available at: www.prisonreformtrust.org.uk/Portals/0/Documents/DebatingforaChange.PDF.

Forrest, R. and Kearns, A. (2001) Social cohesion, social capital and the neighbourhood. *Urban Studies*, 38(12), 2125–2143.

Fox, K. J. (2015) Theorizing community integration as desistance-promotion. *Criminal Justice and Behavior*, 42(1), 82–94.

Fox, K. J. (2016) Civic commitment: Promoting desistance through community integration. *Punishment & Society*, 18(1), 68–94.

Gitell, R. V. and Vidal, A. (1998) *Community Organizing: Building Social Capital as a Development Strategy*. Newbury: Park Sage Publications.

Granovetter, M. S. (1973) The strength of weak ties. *American Journal of Sociology*, 78(6), 1360–1380.

Hawkins, R. L. and Maurer, K. (2009) Bonding, bridging and linking: How social capital operated in New Orleans following Hurricane Katrina. *British Journal of Social Work*, 40(6), 1777–1793.

Hitt, M. A., Ho-UK, L. and Yucel. E. (2002) The importance of social capital to the management of multinational enterprises: Relational networks among Asian and Western firms. *Asia Pacific Journal of Management*, 19, 353.

Krishna, A. and Uphoff, N. (2002) Mapping and measuring social capital through assessment of collective action to conserve and develop watersheds in Rajasthan, India. In T. Van Bastelaer (Ed.), *The Role of Social Capital in Development*. Melbourne: Cambridge University Press.

King, S. (2013) Early desistance narratives: A qualitative analysis of probationers' transitions towards desistance. *Punishment & Society*, 15(2), 147–165.

Kruttschnitt, C., Uggen, C. and Shelton, K. (2000) Predictors of desistance among sex offenders: The interaction of formal and informal social controls. *Justice Quarterly*, 17(1), 61–87.

Laub, J. H. and Sampson, R. J. (1993) Turning points in the life course: Why change matters to the study of crime. *Criminology*, 31(3), 301–325.

Laub, J. H., Sampson, R. J., Corbett, R. P. and Smith, J. S. (1995) The public policy implications of a life-course perspective on crime. *Crime and Public Policy: Putting Theory to Work*, 91–106.

LeBel, T. P. (2013) Formerly incarcerated persons' use of advocacy/activism as a coping orientation in the reintegration process. In *How Offenders Transform Their Lives*. Milton: Willan Publishing, pp. 178–200.

Lin, N. (2001) *Social Capital: A Theory of Social Structure and Action*. New York: Cambridge University Press.

Maruna, S. (2001) *Making Good*. Washington, DC: American Psychological Association.

Maruna, S. (2012) Elements of successful desistance signaling. *Criminology and Public Policy*, 11(1), 73–86.

Maruna, S., LeBel, T. P., Mitchell, N. and Naples, M. (2004) Pygmalion in the reintegration process: Desistance from crime through the looking glass. *Psychology, Crime and Law*, 10(3), 271–281.

McNeill, F. (2006) A desistance paradigm for offender management. *Criminology and Criminal Justice*, 6(1), 39–62.

McNeill, F. (2009) *Towards Effective Practice in Offender Supervision Report 01/09*. Available at: www.sccjr.ac.uk/wp-content/uploads/2012/10/McNeil_Towards.pdf.

McNeill, F. (2014) *Three Aspects of Desistance? Discovering Desistance*. Available at: http://blogs.iriss.org.uk/discoveringdesistance/2014/05/23/three-aspects-of-desistance/.

Mills, A. and Codd, H. (2008) Prisoners' families and offender management: Mobilizing social capital. *Probation Journal*, 55(1), 9–24.

Ministry of Justice. (2013) Mentoring reduces re-offending. Available at: www.gov.uk/government/news/mentoring-scheme-reduces-reoffending; www.gov.uk/government/news/offender-mentor-hub-launched.

Moran, P. (2005) Structural vs. relational embeddedness: Social capital and managerial performance. *Strategic Management Journal*, 26(12), 1129–1151.

Navarro, V. (2002) A critique of social capital. *International Journal of Health Services*, 32(3), 423–432.

O'Connor, T. P. and Bogue, B. (2010) Collaborating with the community, trained volunteers and faith traditions: Building social capacity and making meaning to support desistance. Offender supervision. *New Directions in Theory, Research and Practice*, 301–319.

Organization for Economic Cooperation and Development. (2017) *OECD Insights*. Available at: www.oecd.org/insights/37966934.pdf.

Pahl, R. and Spencer, L. (2004) Personal communities: Not simply families of 'fate' or 'choice'. *Current Sociology*, 52(2), 199–221.

Prison Reform Trust. (2017) *A Different Lens: Report on a Pilot Programme of Active Citizen Forums in Prison*. Available at: www.prisonreformtrust.org.uk/Portals/0/Documents/A%20Different%20Lens.pdf.

Porporino, F. J. (2010) Bringing sense and sensitivity to corrections: From programmes to 'fix' offenders to services to support desistance. *What Else Works? Creative Work with Offenders*, 61–85.

Putnam, R. (2000) *Bowling Alone: The Collapse and Revival of American Community*. New York: Simon and Schuster.

Rose, D. R. and Clear, T. R. (1998) Incarceration, social capital, and crime: Implications for social disorganization theory. *Criminology*, 36(3), 441–480.

Ruiu, M. L. (2016) The social capital of cohousing communities. *Sociology*, 50(2), 400–415.

Schmidt, B. (2013) User voice and the prison council model. *Prison Service Journal*, 209, 12–17.

Schuller, T. Baron, S. and Field, J. (2000) *Social Capital a Review and Critique, in Social Capital: Critical Perspectives*. Oxford: Oxford University Press.

Szreter, S. and Woolcock, M. (2004) Health by association? Social capital, social theory, and the political economy of public health. *International Journal of Epidemiology*, 33(4), 650–667.

Uggen, C., Manza, J. and Thompson, M. (2006) Citizenship, democracy, and the civic reintegration of criminal offenders. *The Annals of the American Academy of Political and Social Science*, 605(1), 281–310.

Uphoff, N. (1999) Understanding social capital: Learning from the analysis and experience of participation. In I. Serageldin (Ed.), *Social Capital: A Multifaceted Perspective*. Washington, DC: World Bank.

Van Ness, D. W. and Strong, K. H. (2014) *Restoring Justice: An Introduction to Restorative Justice*. Abingdon-on-Thames: Routledge.

Weaver, B. (2016) Co-producing desistance from crime: The role of social cooperative structures of employment. *ECAN Bulletin* (28), 12–24 February. Available at: https://howardleague.org/wp-content/uploads/2016/09/ECAN-Bulletin-Issue-28-February-2016.pdf.

Weaver, B. and McNeill, F. (2010) *Travelling Hopefully: Desistance Theory and Probation Practice*. Cullompton: Willan Publishing, pp. 36–60.

Wright, J. P., Cullen, F. T. and Miller, J. T. (2001) Family social capital and delinquent involvement. *Journal of criminal Justice*, 29(1), 1–9.

27 Working with veterans and addressing PTSD

Kelli E. Canada

Justice-involved veterans: an overview

Most people who serve in the military will never enter the criminal justice system. However, for those veterans who do have contact with the criminal justice system, it is important to identify, assess, and intervene when appropriate to address the unique needs of justice-involved veterans (i.e. a term commonly used in the United States to refer to veterans who have contact with the criminal justice system), particularly when they have been exposed to trauma. Since the early 2000s, studies consistently identify between 8 and 10% of the United States jail and prison population as veterans (Berzofsky et al. 2015). National estimates of the number of veterans in other facets of the criminal justice system, for example number of people arrested, awaiting trial, or involved in court programming, is difficult to obtain due to inconsistent practices of documenting veteran status and varying approaches to data collection.

Veterans and trauma exposure

When taking a close look at justice-involved veterans, many experience symptoms of post-traumatic stress disorder (PTSD) or traumatic brain injury

(TBI), struggle with substance use problems, or have co-occurring disorders. Although PTSD affects people regardless of their military experience, studies find that veterans who have been incarcerated have high rates of trauma exposure during the military, before and after the military, and during childhood. In a sample of male veterans who participated in a jail diversion programme, 93% reported trauma exposure during their lifetimes, with most experiencing trauma before the age of 18 (Hartwell et al. 2014). Another study estimated 42% of veterans in their sample who served in Iraq and Afghan conflicts were exposed to four or more adverse childhood events (ACEs) and that for every additional exposure to ACEs, suicide attempts increased by 24% (Carroll et al. 2017).

Significant research now recognizes the long-term impact that ACEs have on physical health, mental health, substance use, and quality of life (read more about ACEs here: www.cdc.gov/violenceprevention/acestudy/index. html). Rehabilitation is particularly important for people who enter the military with exposure to trauma in childhood. Not all people who are exposed to trauma will develop PTSD; however, repeated or extended exposure to trauma can increase the likelihood of developing symptoms. Overall, incarcerated veterans are twice as likely to be diagnosed with PTSD compared to the general prison population and nearly 70% of justice-involved veterans meet criteria for substance use disorders. Having any one of these disorders can alter the way people assess potential risks to their safety and thoughts about actions and ways to address problems.

The larger literature on veterans suggests that rates of PTSD, TBI, and other service-related injuries may be higher than in the past. Advances in medicine contribute to survival rates being much higher for veterans from recent conflicts in comparison to those from conflicts more than 20 years ago (Ling et al. 2009). Veterans are surviving more serious injury and the path to recovery for some can be quite challenging. It is common for people to experience changes in mental health alongside adjustment to major life changes, particularly when physical abilities are permanently changed. Nearly one-fifth of veterans from the most recent conflicts have symptoms of PTSD, major depression, or TBI (RAND Corporation 2008). Thus, many veterans are returning home with readjustment-related challenges for both their physical and mental health.

Across populations, having PTSD increases the risk of developing a co-occurring substance use problem. Some studies suggest there is also an increased risk of anger or aggression (Taft et al. 2007). When one problem area puts a person at risk of other problem areas, it does not mean the conditions always co-occur. It simply means that having PTSD symptoms puts people at a slightly higher risk than before they were having these symptoms. Substance use and aggression or difficulties controlling anger can lead people to have contact with the criminal justice system. In fact, over half (57%) of justice-involved veterans are serving a sentence for a crime considered to be violent, which is higher than their non-veteran counterparts (47%; Noonan and Mumola 2007). Having PTSD alone does not cause a person to become involved in the criminal justice system. However, mixed with other risk factors like substance use or difficulty adjusting, untreated PTSD can increase the risk of police contact.

Preventing criminal justice involvement through the identification of risks, needs, and appropriate intervention is important. Once veterans become involved in the criminal justice system, they face high risk of negative outcomes including a heightened risk of suicide (Frisman and Griffin-Fennell 2009; Wortzel et al. 2009) and exacerbation of symptoms while in custody (Sigafoos 1994). Incarceration can be stressful and common practices (e.g. command and control strategies) may trigger PTSD symptoms due to the prison environment, interrupted treatment if people were connected with services, and poor treatment while in custody. Prisons were not created as treatment facilities and thus are not equipped to provide the same level of care that community- or hospital-based facilities can provide. Once released, felony convictions can interfere with finding and securing employment and may impact benefits for veterans and families (Addlestone and Chaset 2008). Economic vulnerability contributes to high rates of homelessness and poverty among justice-involved veterans (Greenberg and Rosehheck 2008).

Effectively preventing criminal justice involvement and intervening with justice-involved veterans requires some understanding of how and why veterans enter the criminal justice system. Existing research does attempt to identify the factors that cause offending among veterans, but across studies, findings are mixed and inconclusive. Some scholars argue that military experience is related to criminal justice involvement while others suggest veterans are no different than their non-veteran counterparts who enter the criminal justice system. That is, risk factors for criminal justice involvement are consistent across populations and include, for example, antisocial personality, antisocial family and friends, and substance use (see Taylor et al. 2012). Additional research is needed to further understand the similarities and differences between veterans and civilians who have criminal justice contact.

Although it remains unclear why veterans are encountering the law, there is sufficient evidence to suggest that veterans are at risk of mental health problems and difficulty in adjusting post-deployment. When comparing justice-involved veterans to veterans with no criminal justice contact, justice-involved veterans have higher rates of depression, psychosis, and substance use. The likelihood of being diagnosed with bipolar disorder is also higher for justice-involved veterans but there are no major differences in physical health diagnoses except hepatitis and HIV. Justice-involved veterans are three times more likely to be diagnosed with hepatitis and 64% more likely to have HIV compared to veterans without arrests.

In addition, justice-involved veterans are twice as likely to be hospitalized (medical or psychiatric) and twice as likely to have died during the study timeframe (LePage et al. 2016). Given the unique health and mental health needs of justice-involved veterans, it is essential to tailor targeted interventions for this population in the community and within correctional institutions.

Treatment, services, and programming for rehabilitation of justice-involved veterans

Specialized interventions and services for justice-involved veterans are available at multiple points throughout the criminal justice system including jail-diversion, court-based, jail- and prison-based, and re-entry programming. The programmes aim to rehabilitate and reduce the risk of recidivism. Preventing criminal justice contact altogether is ideal; however, there are no evidence-based interventions specifically designed to prevent criminal justice involvement for veterans. Although specific preventative programming is not available, there are myriad services that could reduce the risks of criminal justice involvement. For example, the Veterans Administration offers a programme to prevent homelessness called HUD-Veterans Administration Supportive housing programme (HUD-VASH). Housing vouchers coupled with case management and other clinical services are provided to keep people housed and to address complex and co-occurring needs. In addition, given substance use increases the risk of criminal justice contact, intervening to treat substance use problems may prevent some people from being arrested. Dual diagnosis programming treats substance use issues while also addressing mental health problems.

Diversion programs

Some veterans regardless of prevention efforts will have police contact. Crisis Intervention Teams (CIT) and alternative sentencing courts are two examples of programs that aim to keep people out of jail and prison. Although CIT was not designed specifically for veterans, it is relevant to the needs of justice-involved veterans. CIT includes a specialized 40-hour training for police and a model for effective community partnerships. CIT provides police officers with additional skills and knowledge on the best response strategies for people having mental health crises. Officers learn about mental health through lecture, discussion, skill building, role play scenarios, site visits to providers, and exercises to simulate the impact symptoms can have on daily living. CIT also creates clear pathways for successful community partnerships which offer additional resources to assist with crisis responses, referrals, and other options besides arrest. Veteran Justice Outreach coordinators (VJOs) are employed through the Veterans Administration and engage with veterans and their families to prevent and intervene when they contact the criminal justice system. VJOs can play an important role in CIT through contribution to the training where information about the unique needs of veterans is shared and through thoughtful partnerships with police. VJOs may also provide more specialized trainings for police officers on core issues that justice-involved veterans may face (e.g. PTSD, TBI).

Despite CIT, some veterans may be arrested. For some veterans, alternative sentencing or treatment courts may be an option rather than serving a sentence in jail or prison. Many communities have drug treatment or mental health courts. Although fewer have veterans treatment courts (VTCs), VTCs are based on the same model as drug treatment courts and are growing across the United States. VTCs have a specific docket for veterans, are typically voluntary programs, and may last for one to two years. The aim of the courts is to rehabilitate veterans using treatment and services to improve mental health, reduce substance misuse, and reduce future criminal recidivism. They do vary based on community need and resources, but most require participants to engage in intensive, community-based treatment and have a mental health or substance use need. VTC participants have regular status hearings with the VTC judge, random drug testing, clinical treatments, peer support, job readiness training, and peer mentoring. The VTC team (i.e. judge, administrators, probation, VJOs, other treatment providers, mentor coordinator) provides intensive oversight throughout programme participation with the use of rewards and sanctions. Participants move through five phases until the participant ultimately graduates from VTC, is terminated by the VTC team, or decides to withdraw from the programme.

VTCs are similar to drug treatment and mental health courts, but they are different in that VTCs facilitate bonding and camaraderie between participants by identifying and celebrating participants' shared histories of military experience and culture. In addition, VTCs work closely with the Veterans Administration so service access is often not a barrier for court participants. Research on VTCs is sparse. Early research does show improvements in psychiatric symptoms and substance use during and following court. It is unclear if VTCs are reducing participants' criminal offending (see Knudsen and Wingenfeld 2015). In addition to VTCs, other alternative sentencing models include a track for veterans within a drug treatment or mental health court, a docket dedicated to veterans within a criminal court, and other hybrid programs with both court and treatment professionals.

Some communities also have MISSION DIRECT VET (MDV), which is court based. It differs from VTC because participants do not attend regular court hearings. Supervision is conducted by the treatment team. MDV is a 12-month, post-adjudication programme. Following sentencing, eligible participants can engage in treatment in the community rather than being sentenced to jail or prison. All services provided through MDV are trauma-informed and include case management, peer support, dual recovery therapy, and care coordination. Research on the effectiveness of MDV found it increased community functioning and reduced PTSD symptoms in the 12 months following participation (Hartwell et al. 2014).

Jail- and prison-based programmes

Jail- and prison-based programming for justice-involved veterans is expanding and changing. Most recently, veterans' dorms or pods within jails and prisons are proliferating within the United States. These dorms are only open to veterans. They offer camaraderie, support, and predictable routines that many veterans take comfort in during an otherwise chaotic and stressful time. Although the dorms differ across institutions, some allow the veterans to conduct flag ceremonies and drills or other military-inspired activities. For veterans with PTSD, having the opportunity to build trust in this capacity can help control their symptoms.

Treatment for PTSD within corrections can be limited to medication only. Some facilities do have the resources to offer more therapy and rehabilitative treatment options like group therapy, vocational training, education, and skill-building groups. Most prisons offer some kind of structured mental health assessment to identify people with mental health conditions. If a new inmate identifies as a veteran, VJOs may work with prison staff to exchange medical records to improve cohesiveness of care. Communication across these systems, however, can be challenging.

When a veteran is identified in jails, VJOs are able to work with the veteran during jail including completing needs assessments for the individual and their family but the same treatment provided in the community is often not an option for incarcerated veterans. VJOs may start building rapport if the veterans are new to the Veterans Administration and planning for the treatment and services needed when they release.

Jail stays are generally considerably shorter compared to prisons, so the types of services needed when people exit jail and prison may vary. Veterans may need assistance in securing housing, finding treatment or services, maintaining sobriety, and finding work. VJOs play a critical role in assisting veterans and families to plan prior to release. The Veterans Administration also offers Health Care for Re-entry Veterans Program (HCRV). The HCRV addresses the needs of veterans exiting in prison. VJOs and HCRVs may collaborate but HCRVs are primarily responsible for assisting veterans with needs identification during prison to help prepare a plan for when they exit. HCRV may provide referral to health and mental health services, HUD-VASH programs, and employment services. When available, HCRVs can assist with transportation from prison and provide assistance to ensure veterans are linked with services. All people, including veterans, are especially vulnerable in the weeks following exit of prison. There are higher risks of death including suicide, overdose, homelessness, and victimization so connecting with HCRVs is especially important during this period of vulnerability to ensure safety and connection with needed services.

Regardless of the type of programme, justice-involved veterans, as a population, are exposed to high rates of childhood and adult trauma. The use of trauma-informed care models and other interventions designed to address trauma are critical for addressing the complex needs of justice-involved veterans. Trauma-informed care recognizes the multifaceted impact of trauma on thinking, feeling, relating, and behaving. Using a trauma-informed care lens requires organizations and programmes to engage people with practice and policy that does not re-traumatize them (SAMHSA 2015). Trauma impacts treatment in many ways including help-seeking, engagement (both verbal and non-verbal), and trust and rapport building. Power differentials can impact people negatively and in the criminal justice system, these differentials are hard to ignore. It is important that staff and providers be sensitive to questions about trauma and to be aware of how their physical positioning and forceful touch can negatively impact someone with a history of trauma. There are simple strategies that staff can employ to build trust and rapport including (1) collaborate as often as possible; (2) be respectful; (3) provide options; (4) de-escalate when possible rather than using command and control or physical constraints; (5) utilize strengths-based assessments; and (6) recognize and acknowledge successes and gains.

The criminal justice system was not designed to be a community mental health provider; however, people with serious mental health needs are coming into contact with police officers, living in institutions, reporting to probation officers, and appearing before judges in court. Engaging veterans in interventions designed specifically for their needs in mind is a critical strategy for interrupting the cycle of recidivism so often seen in vulnerable populations.

References

Addlestone, D. F. and Chaset, A. (2008) Veterans in the criminal justice system. In *The American Veterans and Service Members Survival Guide: How to Cut Through the Bureaucracy and Get What You Need and Are Entitled to.* Available at: www.veteransforamerica.org/.

Berzofsky, M., Bronson, J., Carson, E. A. and Noonan, M. (2015) *Veterans in Prison and Jail, Bureau of Justice Statistics Special Report*. Washington, DC: US Dept. of Justice.

Carroll, T. D., Currier, J. M., McCormick, W. H. and Drescher, K. D. (2017) Adverse childhood experiences and risk for suicidal behavior in male Iraq and Afghanistan veterans seeking PTSD treatment. *Psychological Trauma: Theory, Research, Practice, & Policy*, 9(5), 583–586.

Frisman, L. K. and Griffin-Fennell, F. (2009) Commentary: Suicide and incarcerated veterans – Don't wait for the numbers. *Journal of the American Academy of Psychiatry & Law*, 37, 92–94.

Greenberg, G. and Rosehheck, R. (2008) Jail incarceration, homelessness, and mental health: A national study. *Psychiatric Services*, 59, 170–177.

Hartwell, S. W., James, A., Chen, J., Pinals, D. A., Marin, M. C. and Smelson, D. (2014) Trauma among justice-involved veterans. *Professional Psychology: Research & Practice*, 45(6), 425–432.

Knudsen, K. J. and Wingenfeld, S. (2015) A specialized treatment court for veterans with trauma exposure: Implications for the field. *Community Mental Health Journal*, 52(2), 127–135.

Kromer, B. and Holder, K. (2015) *Taking a Look at Veterans Across America*. United States Census Bureau. Available at: http://blogs.census.gov/2015/11/10/taking-a-look-at-veterans-across-america/.

LePage, J. P., Bradshaw, L. D., Cipher, D. J., Crawford, A. M. and Parish-Johnson, J. A. (2016) The association between recent incarceration and inpatient resource use and death rates: Evaluation of a US veteran sample. *Public Health*, 134, 109–113.

Ling, G. I., Bandak, F., Armonda, R., Grant, G. and Ecklund, J. (2009) Explosive blast neurotrauma. *Journal of Neurotrauma*, 26(6), 815–825.

Noonan, M. E. and Mumola, C. J. (2007) Veterans in state and federal prison, 2004. In *Bureau of Justice* Statistics *Special Report*. Washington, DC: US Department of Justice.

RAND Corporation. (2008) *One in Five Iraq and Afghanistan Veterans Suffer from PTSD or Major Depression*. Available at: www.rand.org/news/press/2008/04/17.html.

SAMHSA. (2015) *Trauma-Informed Approach and Trauma-Specific Interventions*. Available at: www.samhsa.gov/nctic/trauma-interventions.

Sigafoos, C. E. (1994) A PTSD treatment program for combat (Vietnam) veterans in prison. International *Journal of Offender Therapy & Comparative Criminology*, 38(2), 117–130.

Stiner, M. (2012) Veterans treatment courts and the U.S. Department of Labor. *Dispatch From the Front Lines*. Available at: www.justiceforvets.org.

Taft, C. T., Kaloupek, D. G., Schumm, J., Marshall, A. D., Panuzio, J., King, D. W. and Keane, T. M. (2007) Posttraumatic stress disorder symptoms, physiological reactivity, alcohol problems, and aggression among military veterans. *Journal of Abnormal Psychology*, 116, 498–507.

Taylor, J., Parkes, T., Haw, S. and Jepson, R. (2012) Military veterans with mental health problems: A protocol for systematic review to identify whether they have an additional risk of contact with the criminal justice systems compared with other veteran groups. *Systematic Reviews*, 1, 53–61.

Wortzel, H. S., Binswanger, I. A., Anderson, C. A. and Adler, L. E. (2009) Suicide among incarcerated veterans. *Journal of the American Academy of Psychiatry & Law*, 37, 82–91.

Resources

1   Justice for Vets: www.justiceforvets.org/what-is-a-veterans-treatment-court
2   US Department of Veterans Affairs: www.va.gov/homeless/vjo.asp
3   National Center on Domestic and Sexual Violence: www.ncdsv.org/images/va_structured-evidence-review-to-identify-treatment-needs-of-justice-involved-veterans_2013.pdf
4   National Institute of Corrections: https://info.nicic.gov/jiv/
5   Institute for Veteran Policy (2011). *Veterans and criminal justice: A review of the literature*. Swords to Plowshares: San Francisco.

Pro-social modelling[1]

Chris Trotter

Introduction

The term pro-social modelling in its most limited sense refers to the way in which probation officers, or others who work with involuntary clients, model pro-social values and behaviours in their interactions with clients. The term is, however, often interpreted more broadly to include a group of skills which include supervisors' modelling pro-social values, reinforcing clients' pro-social expressions and actions and challenging their pro-criminal actions and expressions of those clients. Sometimes the term is interpreted even more broadly to also include other skills including role clarification, problem-solving, and relationship skills as they are set out in my book *Working with Involuntary Clients* (Trotter 2015). The definition of pro-social modelling that is used in this chapter includes modelling, positive reinforcement, and challenging.

Research on pro-social modelling

The importance of pro-social modelling in the supervision of offenders has been shown in studies as early as 1967. Schwitzgebel (1967) found improved outcomes among young offenders who were given positive reinforcement for successful accomplishments, compared to a matched control. Subsequent studies using pro-social modelling and reinforcement found similar outcomes (e.g. Sarason and Ganger 1973; Fo and O'Donnell 1974, 1975).

Don Andrews and his colleagues (1979) examined tape recordings of interviews between Canadian probation officers and their clients and found that probation officers who modelled and reinforced pro-social values and who also made use of reflective listening practices had clients with lower recidivism rates in comparison to other probation officers. Probation officers who scored above the mean on a socialization scale (a measure of pro-social orientation) and an empathy scale (a measure of workers' understanding of others' points of view) also had clients with lower recidivism. The value of pro-social modelling in the supervision of offenders has been further demonstrated in meta-analyses undertaken by Don Andrews and James Bonta (Andrews 2000; Andrews and Bonta 2003).

A study undertaken in Australia (Trotter 1990) found that volunteer probation officers had clients with lower recidivism if they scored above the median on the socialization scale regardless of the levels of empathy of the clients. In other words, pro-social officers did better. A later study (Trotter 1996) which again replicated aspects of the Andrews et al. (1979) study found that professional probation officers also did better when they had high levels of socialization and when their file notes indicated that they reinforced pro-social expressions and actions of their clients. This again was regardless of empathy levels.

A similar study (Trotter 2004) found that child protection workers, who in many cases work with young people and families who are involved in the criminal justice system, did better on a range of outcome measures, including client and worker satisfaction and early case closure, if they used pro-social modelling skills.

How do workers model pro-social values?

The Gough socialization scale which was used in the Andrews et al. study (1979) and in Trotter (1990, 1996) places individuals on a continuum from pro-social to pro-criminal behaviours and forecasts the likelihood that they will transgress mores accepted by their particular culture (Megargee 1972). The scale was originally developed as a delinquency scale. It reflects a person's 'social maturity, integrity and rectitude' (p. 328). It reflects family cohesiveness, social sensitivity, empathy, optimism, and self-confidence (Megargee 1972).

In both the Canadian and Australian studies those who scored high on the scale were more likely to model and to express views which support the value of a law-abiding lifestyle. Some examples of the practice of pro-social modelling, based on studies in corrections and child protection, are set out below (Andrews et al. 1979; Trotter 1996, 2004, 2015).

Pro-social modelling involves the worker keeping appointments, being punctual, honest, and reliable, following up on tasks, respecting other people's feelings, expressing views about the negative effects of criminal behaviour, expressing views about the value of social pursuits such as non-criminal friends, good family relations, and the value of work. It involves interpreting people's motives positively and being optimistic about the rewards which can be obtained by living within the law.

One finding from the child protection study referred to earlier (Trotter 2004) which clearly illustrates the importance of simple modelling processes, was that when the clients reported that their workers were in the habit of responding to phone calls and keeping appointments, both the clients and the workers were almost twice as likely to be satisfied with the outcome of the intervention. The cases were also likely to be closed earlier. This was independent of client risk levels.

The following comments illustrate the differences between the kind of things more pro-social probation officers say in comparison to the things which less pro-social officers say. I have constructed these examples; however they are consistent with the comments which have been made in the research studies and with the views expressed by practitioners in workshops. More detail is provided about the kinds of conversations conducted by pro-social workers in Trotter (2004, 2015).

The following comments are not pro-social:

I know you are doing well and complying with the conditions but I need to see you more often anyway because you have still got problems.

The police seem to be having a go at a lot of my clients lately. They never leave you alone, do they?

It is good that you went for the interview – but with the unemployment situation the way it is you can't expect too much, can you?

The first comment effectively punishes a pro-social action, the second is not supportive of a law abiding perspective, and the third is pessimistic. The following comments are more pro-social.

Because you have been keeping your appointments and doing your community work, you will have to report monthly from now on.

It must be frustrating if you feel that the police are really out to get you. I think most police are really just doing their job. Is there some way that you can change what you are doing so that they are less interested in you?

That is great that you went for the employment interview and that you have kept the appointment with me today. I can see that you are really making an effort.

The first comment rewards pro-social behaviour, the second responds to the issue of police harassment with a more pro-social perspective, and the third is more optimistic and acknowledges the pro-social actions of the client.

Pro-social reinforcement

It was evident in both the Canadian study (Andrews et al. 1979) and the Australian studies (Trotter 2004, 2015) that more pro-social workers were inclined to reinforce pro-social comments and actions by their clients. Some examples of pro-social actions and comments include those related to compliance with the order such as keeping appointments, being punctual, completing community work, not offending, and complying with special conditions such as attending drug treatment. Other client pro-social actions include working through problem-solving processes with the worker, accepting responsibility for offences, making comments about the harm that crime can do to others and yourself, having empathy for the victim, and stating that crime is wrong. Pro-social workers are also inclined to reinforce comments and actions which value non-criminal activities and associations including family, sport, non-criminal friends, hobbies, and attending school or work. Pro-social workers are likely to reinforce expressions which are fair, non-sexist, and non-racist. They also reinforce optimistic attitudes, for example expressing a belief that life without crime is achievable, that goals can be achieved, that workers can help, and that clients can change.

How do the workers reinforce these things? The first and most obvious method of providing reinforcement is through body language (e.g. smiling, attentive listening, leaning forward) and the use of praise. Rewards can also be provided by the worker giving time to the client, attending court with the client and providing positive evidence, reducing the frequency of contact, helping the client find a job or accommodation, doing home visits or meeting a client outside the office, compiling a positive report for a court or parole board, speaking to other agencies/professionals such as social security or the police about the client's needs, and making positive comments in file notes.

The idea of pro-social reinforcement is that the rewards should be contingent on the behaviour. The reinforcement should be offered clearly in response to the pro-social behaviour. The clients need to clearly see the link. The clients should understand that the reduction in visits, the praise used by the supervisor, or a visit to court is directly linked to their pro-social behaviour, for example the fact they have kept appointments, been punctual, been attending job interviews, and not reoffended.

One of the most powerful rewards available to the probation officer in his/her day-to-day work is the capacity to reduce the frequency of contact. It is important in using this model to make the link between reduced frequency of contact and the pro-social activities of the client. It should not be seen simply as usual procedure; rather, it should be seen as a reward for good progress. In this way the client gains a sense that his or her goals can be achieved through pro-social behaviour.

The other aspect of pro-social modelling as I have defined it in this chapter is challenging offenders' pro-criminal comments and actions. There is very little research that can inform practitioners about which forms of challenging most effectively engage young people. We found (Trotter and Evans 2017) based on examination of 116 audiotaped interviews between youth justice workers and their clients that clients were more positively engaged by, and responsive to, challenging that was exploratory, non-blaming, and accompanied by positive reinforcement of their pro-social comments and actions.

Empathy, pro-social modelling, and legitimacy

The concept of pro-social modelling and legitimacy has been raised by Bottoms and Rex (1998) referring to the moral authority of the worker. It seems clear that the pro-social orientation of supervisors relates to the ongoing recidivism of those under supervision. Is this influence greater, however, if the client identifies with the worker, if the worker is young or old or if the worker understands the client's point of view? Are supervisors effective if they have a pro-social orientation but at the same time have little understanding or empathy for the client's perspective?

Some of the work which has been done on this issue is contradictory. I referred earlier to the Canadian study (Andrews et al. 1979) which found that probation officers who had high levels of empathy and high levels of socialization had clients with lower recidivism. On the other hand, probation officers with high levels of socialization and low levels of empathy had clients with higher recidivism rates than other clients. It seems that a pro-social disposition accompanied by a lack of understanding of the clients' perspective was counterproductive. Whilst both of my Australian studies in corrections (Trotter 1991, 1996) found that high scores on the socialization scale were related to lower recidivism, regardless of levels of empathy, it was also apparent that judgemental comments in file notes (e.g. no hoper, lazy) were related to higher recidivism even after taking risk levels into account.

It does seem therefore that a pro-social disposition needs to be accompanied at least by a willingness to be reasonably nonjudgemental. Further research on the notion of pro-social modelling and legitimacy might shed further light on the situations in which pro-social modelling is most effective.

Peer group association

Modelling pro-social values by workers appears to influence the reoffence rates of their clients. There is also some evidence that modelling by other offenders also influences reoffence rates. An Australian study (Trotter 1995) found that clients placed on community worksites with other offenders had higher reoffence rates than clients placed on community worksites with community volunteers or by themselves. This was particularly so with young offenders (aged 17 to 21) and was evident after risk levels had been taken into account. This is certainly consistent with theories of differential association and a range of research studies pointing to the influence of peer group association (see Trotter 1995 for more detail on this issue).

Strengths and weaknesses of pro-social modelling

The greatest strength of pro-social modelling is that the research evidence suggests that it works. It does seem to be related to client outcomes with offenders and with a range of involuntary clients. The evidence from my studies (Trotter 1996, 2004) found also that the use of the approach was significantly correlated with a number of client satisfaction measures. The success of this approach can also be explained theoretically by reference to learning theory.

The pro-social approach seems to work because it provides a method for discouraging and challenging antisocial comments and behaviours within a positive framework. It puts into practice the idea that people learn best by encouragement rather than discouragement. The approach also helps workers to take control of a reinforcement process which occurs anyway. Whether they are aware of it or not, workers with involuntary clients make judgements about the things they wish to encourage in their clients and they in turn influence their clients' behaviour. By understanding the process and using this approach, workers are able to take some control over this process.

Criticisms of pro-social modelling

The concept of pro-social modelling has nevertheless received some criticism. Outlined below are some of these criticisms and my responses to them. The issues are addressed in more detail in *Working with Involuntary Clients* (Trotter 2015).

Some workers feel that the pro-social approach merely describes a process which they already use unconsciously. However there is evidence that those who work with involuntary clients do not routinely use these skills. Two Canadian studies (Andrews et al. 1979; Bonta and Rugge 2004) and the Australian studies (Trotter 1996, 2004, 2018) found that workers used the pro-social approach very erratically. Some workers use it and some don't. The qualitative study referred to earlier found that many probation officers inadvertently reinforced the very behaviour they were hoping to change, often through use of smiling and body language as much as direct comment or actions (Burns 1994).

There seems little doubt that whilst pro-social skills might come naturally to some workers, they do not come naturally to everyone. One of the strongest arguments in favour of this approach relates to the notion that the modelling process occurs anyway. It seems that whether they are conscious of it or not, to one degree or another, workers reinforce different behaviours in their clients. As I mentioned earlier it is preferable that they are explicit about this process both with themselves and their clients and that they take some control over it.

It might be argued that the approach is superficial and symptom focused and it is therefore unlikely to address the complex long-term issues which have led offenders into the criminal justice system, for example peer group influence, unemployment, family breakdown, drug use, homelessness, and school failure. It is certainly true that pro-social modelling will not address all the problems faced by clients of the criminal justice system. It is, however, one skill which will address some issues, it relates to client outcomes, and it can be used along with a range of other skills.

It can be argued that the pro-social approach is manipulative – it attempts to change the behaviour of the client often without the client's knowledge, in directions set by the worker. On the other hand, the reinforcement and modelling process inevitably occurs in worker/client relationships and the process is less likely to be manipulative if it is explicit and if the worker understands and attempts to take some control of the process.

Pro-social modelling may also be criticized as being judgemental. It is based on value judgements. The term pro-social has connotations of social control, of there being a right way of doing things. It suggests that what is socially acceptable is best. Again probation officers and others who work with offenders inevitably make judgements about what are acceptable and unacceptable standards in relation to such issues as drug use, reporting patterns, or minor offending. A number of studies (Andrews et al. 1979; Trotter 2012) suggest that workers reinforce different expressions and behaviours regardless of whether they have any awareness of doing so. Again it is better that they take some control over this process.

It is important nevertheless that pro-social behaviour is defined in explicit and limited terms. It should not be interpreted as meaning having values consistent with the worker. As discussed earlier, the Canadian study in corrections (Andrews et al. 1979) found that supervisors who practiced the pro-social approach were only effective if they also practiced reflective listening and had high levels of empathy. It does seem that if this approach is in any way used as an excuse for moralizing on the part of the worker it is not going to work. Perhaps one of the strongest arguments for focusing on clients' pro-social actions and comments rather than their pro-criminal or antisocial actions and comments is that it is likely to avoid the possibility that the pro-social approach will come across as moralistic and disapproving.

Ethical issues relating to pro-social modelling have been addressed elsewhere (Trotter and Ward 2012); suffice to say that challenging should be limited to factors which relate to the mandate for the worker's involvement with the client. For the most part this relates to illegal behaviour, for example offending, domestic violence, truancy, or failure to comply with the court order. Other 'desirable' behaviours which the worker may wish to encourage, such as seeking employment, mixing with pro-social peers or returning to study, should be encouraged if the worker believes they are pro-social. Care should however be taken in challenging in relation to these issues.

It could be argued that pro-social modelling may by inappropriate with clients with particular cultural backgrounds. Definitions of pro-social are inevitably entrenched in social and cultural mores. Punctuality, work ethic, domestic violence, child neglect may mean different things in different cultures. Workers and clients are influenced by their racial, social, religious, and economic milieu. It is important therefore that workers attempt to understand the views and actions of their clients in terms of their cultural context. In forming views about what is pro-social in any given situation, the worker should take the client's cultural background into account. This involves talking to the client about cultural differences. Pro-social modelling aims to help make explicit the cultural issues in the supervision of offenders and in turn to contribute to culturally sensitive practice.

Pro-social modelling may also be criticized because of the difficulties involved in judging the genuineness of clients. Clients may make pro-social comments; however, their behaviour may not be consistent with those comments. This is certainly part of the challenge in using this approach. The aim of pro-social modelling is to reward pro-social behaviour and comments, that is comments and behaviour which are honest and genuine. A dishonest or frivolous array of comments about how a client may have changed for example should not be defined as pro-social and should not be rewarded.

At the same time it can be difficult to determine whether someone is genuine or not. The worker clearly needs to avoid being 'conned' and should avoid reinforcing behaviour which attempts to do this. Nonetheless, if in doubt, it seems that the most appropriate approach is to accept the client's word – at least until the worker has information that what the client is saying is incorrect.

One final criticism which is sometimes made about pro-social modelling is that it is very difficult to carry out because many clients do not say or do anything pro-social. How do you identify pro-social comments and actions when a client has a severe drug addiction, no work, no personal or family supports, and is resistant to supervision? However, the challenge in these situations is for the worker to search for the pro-social actions and comments. There is no evidence that the client will be helped by a focus on things that he or she has done wrong. The worker should instead search for pro-social comments and actions as they occur (for example keeping an appointment and talking to the worker).

Training

Can pro-social modelling be taught? Personality traits and beliefs such as optimism, fairness, punctuality, reliability, and honesty are hard to develop or change. Is effective use of the skills of pro-social modelling limited to workers with these personality traits? A number of studies have suggested that while the general use of pro-social modelling and other skills is low, workers make more use of good practice skills, including pro-social modelling, following training and coaching (e.g. Bonta et al. 2011; Trotter 2018).

Conclusion/summary

In this chapter I have acknowledged the difficulties of defining pro-social modelling. I have, nevertheless, defined it in this chapter as an approach to the supervision of offenders which involves workers modelling pro-social values, comments, and actions; reinforcing pro-social values, comments, and actions of offenders; and appropriately challenging pro-criminal values, actions, and expressions. The research consistently points to the value of pro-social modelling in work with offenders. In fact research in Australia and elsewhere suggests that it can make considerable difference to the reoffence rates of those under supervision.

The chapter has outlined the specific ways in which pro-social modelling is undertaken and discusses and responds to some criticisms of pro-social modelling. The research to date suggest that pro-social modelling and other skills are minimally used by probation officers although training and coaching may influence the development of these skills. Nevertheless the challenge today is how to help probation services implement these practices and how to encourage individual workers to participate in training and make use of the principles with their clients.

Note

1 Adapted from Trotter, C. (2009). Pro-social modelling. *European Probation Journal*, 1(2), 124–134.

References

Andrews, D. A. (2000) Effective practice future directions. In D. Andrews, C. Hollin, P. Raynor, C. Trotter and B. Armstrong (Eds.), *Sustaining Effectiveness in Working with Offenders*. Cardiff: Cognitive Centre Foundation.

Andrews, D. A. and Bonta, J. (2003) *The Psychology of Criminal Conduct*. Cincinnati: Anderson Publishing Coy.

Andrews, D. A., Keissling, J. J., Russell, R. J. and Grant, B. A. (1979) *Volunteers and the One to One Supervision of Adult Probationers*. Toronto: Ontario Ministry of Correctional Services.

Bonta, J., Bourgon, G., Rugge, T., Scott, T. L., Yessine, A. K., Gutierrez, L. and Li, J. (2011) Community supervision: An experimental demonstration of training probation officers in evidence-based practice. *Criminal Justice and Behavior*, 38(11), 1127–1148.

Bonta, J. and Rugge, T. (2004) *Case Management in Manitoba Probation*. Ottawa, ON: Solicitor General.

Burns, P. (1994) *Pro-Social Practices in Community Corrections Honours Thesis*. Melbourne: Monash University, Department of Social Work.

Bottoms A. and Rex S. (1998) Pro-social modelling and legitimacy: Their potential contribution to effective probation practice. In Rex S. and Maltravers A. (Eds.), *Pro-social Modelling and Legitimacy: The Clark Hall Day Conference*. Cambridge: Cambridge University Press, pp. 11–27.

Fo Walter, S. and O'Donnell, Clifford. (1974) The buddy system: Relationship and contingency conditions in a community prevention program for youth with non professionals as change agents. *Journal of Counselling and Clinical Psychology*, 163–169, April.

Fo Walter, S. and O'Donnell, Clifford. (1975) The buddy system, effect of community intervention on delinquent offences. *Behaviour Therapy*, 6, 522–524.

Megargee, E. I. (1972) *The California Psychological Inventory Handbook*. London: Jossey Bass Inc.

Sarason, I. G. and Ganzer, V. J. (1973) Modelling and group discussion in the rehabilitation of juvenile delinquents. *Journal of Consulting Psychology*, 20(5), 442–449.

Schwitzgebel, R. L. (1967) Short-term operant conditioning of adolescent offenders on socially relevant variables. *Journal of Abnormal Psychology*, 72(2), 134–142.

Trotter, C. J. (1990) Probation can work, a research study using volunteers. *Australian Journal of Social Work*, 43(2), 13–18.

Trotter, C. J. (1995) Contamination theory and unpaid community work. *Australian and New Zealand Journal of Criminology*, 28(2), 163–177.

Trotter, C. J. (1996) The impact of different supervision practices in community corrections. *Australian and New Zealand Journal of Criminology*, 29(1), 29–46.

Trotter, C. J. (2004) *Helping Abused Children and Their Families*. Sydney: Allen and Unwin.

Trotter, C. J. (2015) *Working with Involuntary Clients A Guide to Practice*. Sydney: Allen & Unwin.

Trotter, C. J. (2018) The impact of training and coaching on the development of practice skills in youth justice In P. Ugwedike, P. Raynor and J. Annison (Eds.), *Evidence Based Skills In Criminal Justice*. Bristol: Policy Press.

Trotter, C., Evans, P. and Baidawi, S. (2017) The effectiveness of challenging skills in work with young offenders. *International Journal of Offender Therapy and Comparative Criminology*, 61(4), 397–412.

Trotter C. and Ward T. (2012) Involuntary clients, pro-social modelling and ethics. *Ethics and Social Welfare*, 7(1), 74–90.

Core Correctional Practice

29

The role of the working alliance in offender rehabilitation

Stephen M. Haas and Jaclyn Smith

Introduction

Rates of recidivism for individuals under correctional supervision continue to be a major concern for policymakers and correctional administrators in the United States. According to the latest figures from the Bureau of Justice Statistics (BJS), 67.8% of prisoners released in 2005 in 30 states were arrested within three years of release, and 76.6% were arrested within five years of release. More than one-third (36.8%) of these individuals were arrested within the first six months of release, with more than half of the 404,638 state prisoners arrested by the end of their first year of release (Markman et al. 2016). Individuals sentenced directly to federal probation or a term of supervised release tend to fare better, with studies reporting five-year rates of recidivism ranging from 27.7% to 43.0%, depending on the study design (Johnson 2017).

Nonetheless, these statistics indicate that there is much room for improvement in how correctional personnel go about supervising and delivering services to individuals who come into contact with the criminal justice system.

Research evidence on what works in the rehabilitation of offenders has continued to grow over the past several decades. This has led to the discovery of many evidence-based practices and principles of effective correctional intervention that – when properly adhered to – have been shown to improve reductions in recidivism (Andrews and Bonta 2010; Bonta et al. 2013; Duwe 2017; Haas 2013). Scholars and students of correctional rehabilitation know these principles well and often recite them with little effort. The Risk-Need-Responsivity model or 'RNR principles' have become a mainstay in correctional practice. These principles offer guidance for best correctional practice by articulating 'who' (i.e. risk principle) should be the target of intensive interventions, 'what' to address (i.e. need principle), and 'how' to go about the delivery of services (i.e. responsivity principle). It is the latter principle where special attention is given to the manner in which services are provided to clients.

The responsivity principle seeks to 'maximize the offender's ability to learn from a rehabilitative intervention by providing cognitive behavioural treatment and tailoring the intervention to the learning style, motivation, abilities and strengths of the offender' (Bonta and Andrews 2007: 1). This principle states that interventions should be based on theoretically relevant models best for teaching people new behaviours, and that cognitive behavioural interventions and approaches are the most empirically supported models for accomplishing this task. Interventions that employ techniques that target both thinking and behaviour have been shown to be most effective with offender populations (Bonta and Andrews 2017). Rooted in a cognitive social learning approach, general responsivity operates on the *relationship principle* (i.e. the establishment of warm, respectful, and collaborative working alliance with the client) and the *structuring principle* which seeks to change behaviour through appropriate modelling, reinforcement, problem-solving, and other skill-building modes of intervention. Consistent with the specific responsivity principle, these approaches should be tailored to the unique learning style, motivation, abilities, and strengths of the offender. Such cognitive social learning approaches have come to be known as Core Correctional Practices.

Core Correctional Practices (CCPs) are designed to 'increase the therapeutic potential of rehabilitation programs for offenders' (Dowden and Andrews 2004: 204). They recognize that an offender is both more apt to engage in treatment, and services are more likely to be effective, if a good therapeutic alliance is created. This is evidenced by positive relationship factors such as an officers' appropriate use of authority, use of effective reinforcement and disapproval techniques, and a conscientious effort on the part of staff to create an open, caring, genuine, and respectful relationship with the client (Kennedy 2000). They underscore the importance of *how* services should be delivered and offer strategies for effective delivery of correctional treatment. The rationale for employing CCPs is that offenders learn 'pro-social and anticriminal attitudinal, cognitive, and behavioural patterns from their regular interactions with front-line staff' (Dowden and Andrews 2004: 205). As a result, they are applicable to corrections officers, probation, and parole officers, as well as counsellors and case managers alike. Correctional staff are expected to create a 'working alliance' with clients and structure the delivery of services to promote skill-building. This requires correctional staff to develop new, specialized skills in communication and interaction with offenders to enhance the therapeutic potential of their relationships with clients.

The role of staff-client relationship in behaviour change

Several decades of research on offender populations have centred on the importance of the relationship, or 'working alliance' between both juvenile and adult clients and staff (Paparozzi and Gendreau 2005; Skeem et al. 2007). A 'working alliance', often referred to as a therapeutic alliance in the psychological literature, is built on collaboration. It is the collaboration between the staff member and the client that sets the stage for positive behaviour change. This involves active role clarification between the officer and the client as well as the creation of collaborative, agreed-upon goals (i.e. goal setting) for the period of supervision and treatment. The working relationship results in mutual trust between the correctional staff member and the client and provides the foundation for the delivery of effective, skill development-based interventions. It is important that the working alliance be established prior to the establishment of case supervision plans and the delivery of interventions (Bordin 1979).

Traditionally, the role of many corrections staff such as community supervision officers has largely been that of a case manager with emphasis on managing their clients and the services they receive (Bourgon et al. 2011). Oftentimes case management styles were dictated by officers' personal view of their job and duties. In 1972, Klockars's theoretical work called attention to the potential for probation officers themselves to impact case outcomes. He posited that officers' attitudes or 'working philosophy' may impact how they manage their cases and that officers differ in how they view their job and duties. Some officers stress the law enforcement aspects of the job while others see themselves as 'therapeutic agents' (Klockars 1972: 555). Over the years empirical research has confirmed the impact of officers' attitudes on client behaviour and outcomes, noting the importance of a 'hybrid approach' (i.e. a balance between law enforcement and human services supervision styles) in the supervision of individuals in the community (Aos et al. 2006). It is this approach that has been associated with the greatest reduction in recidivism. Paparozzi and Gendreau (2005) found that only 6% of offenders supervised by officers with a hybrid approach were convicted of a new crime compared to 32% and 16% of offenders supervised by treatment-oriented and law enforcement-oriented officers, respectively. Such research underscores the importance of proper role clarification for officers and the need to hold clients accountable for their behaviour, while also offering support, guidance, and interventions that encourage behaviour change.

Today, the expectations for staff have changed as knowledge of 'what works' in correctional rehabilitation has grown. In recognizing the value of a balanced community supervision and the importance of a 'working alliance' in producing behaviour change, correctional staff are increasingly expected to become 'change agents' as opposed to case managers (Bourgon and Guiterrez 2013). Changing behaviour requires the development of problem-solving skills on the part of the offender, and officers are increasingly expected to play a pivotal role in the offenders' pursuit to develop these new ways of thinking. As a result, research has pointed to need for correctional staff to identify and counter clients' pro-criminal ways of thinking (i.e. attitudes), teach new skills (i.e. problem-solving, coping strategies, social skills, etc.) as well as motivate offenders toward change (Bogue and Nandi 2012; Bogue et al. 2013; Bourgon and Gutierrez 2012; Simourd et al. 2016). As change agents, correctional staff are expected to engage in strategies designed to enhance the intrinsic motivation of clients, offer appropriate pro-social models, and increase the use of reinforcements in supervision and treatment. Additionally, they are expected to hold clients accountable for their behaviour with the use of effective disapproval techniques, while purposefully engaging clients in a manner that promotes the development of new ways of thinking.

Core Correctional Practice and the working alliance

Core Correctional Practices detail the specific skills that represent a cognitive social learning approach. They lay emphasis on the officer-client relationship and the specific skills correctional staff need (e.g. pro-social modelling, the appropriate use of reinforcement and disapproval, and problem-solving) to promote behaviour change in their clients (Haas and Spence 2016). In effective correctional treatment, Andrews and Kiessling (1980) identified a set of Core Correctional Practices (CCP) that enhance the impact of rehabilitation programs and ensure that interactions between staff and offenders are appropriate and beneficial. These practices are organized into five dimensions of effective treatment: (1) the appropriate use of authority; (2) the modelling and reinforcement of appropriate behaviours; (3) skill-building and problem-solving strategies; (4) the effective use of community resources; and, (5) the quality of staff-offender relationships. In combination, these five dimensions describe a variety of staff characteristics and skills known to enhance the therapeutic potential of staff-offender interactions and the context in which services are delivered. Table 29.1 provides a summary description of each dimension.

Table 29.1 Summary of Core Correctional Practices (CCPs)

Appropriate use of authority may be described as staff adopting a 'firm but fair' approach with offenders. Staff are direct and specific concerning their demands, and rules are clear. Staff monitor progress and reward compliance with rules, give encouraging messages, and support their words with action. Staff respectfully guide offenders toward compliance and refrain from controlling and shaming disciplinary practices. Staff members keep the focus of the message on the behaviour and not the prisoner performing it.

Appropriate modelling and reinforcement entails staff engaging in pro-social modelling and role playing and employing positive reinforcement and effective disapproval techniques when interacting with offenders. Staff consistently demonstrate and reinforce appropriate alternatives to pro-criminal styles of thinking, feeling, and acting. Includes structured learning procedures such as the use of role playing/rehearsal, modelling, and providing appropriate feedback on offender performance.

Skill-building and problem-solving strategies refer to the use of structured learning and cognitive behavioural techniques to foster skill development and improve the problem-solving ability of offenders. Staff members seek to identify offender problems, help offenders generate alternatives, and develop an implementation plan.

Effective use of community resources, also referred to as advocacy and brokerage, involves staff connecting the offender to other helping agencies that provide supportive or intervention-based services such as substance abuse treatment or employment services.

Relationship factors refer to the quality of staff-offender relationships. Staff relate to offenders in open, genuine, respectful, caring, and enthusiastic ways. Staff members are empathic, competent, and committed to helping the offender.

Source: Adapted from Andrews 2000; Dowden and Andrews 2004

The use of these practices have extensive empirical support for enhancing the effectiveness of correctional interventions (Dowden and Andrews 2004; Lipsey and Cullen 2007). Several studies have examined the principal components of CCP and their impact on offender outcomes. In a large-scale meta-analysis of 273 primary studies of correctional programs, Dowden and Andrews (2004) found that correctional programs which implemented CCP produced greater reductions in recidivism (i.e. larger effect sizes) than those that did not. Additionally, several recent studies have investigated the impact of CCP officer training on the commission of new offences and community supervision revocations. This research shows that when community supervision officers have been trained in CCP-informed approaches, officers are more likely to apply the newly developed skills and offenders are less likely to commit new offences or experience parole or probation revocations (Bonta et al. 2011; Chadwick et al. 2015; Labrecque et al. 2013; Latessa et al. 2013; Lowenkamp et al. 2014; Robinson et al. 2012; Robinson et al. 2011; Smith et al. 2012).

A large body of research also demonstrates the singular impact of each of the five dimensions. Recent studies in the area of procedural justice have found that prisoners are less likely to engage in misconduct and other disruptive behaviours when they believe that they have been treated with fairness and respect by correctional staff (Beijersbergen et al. 2014; Beijersbergen et al. 2015). In a similar manner, research has found positive post-release outcomes to be associated with the appropriate use of authority among correctional staff (Howells 2000).

Lastly, research has shown that the development of high quality staff-offender relationships can promote a better prison environment, thereby leading to improved offender outcomes (Paparozzi and Gendreau 2005; Skeem et al. 2007). For example, studies illustrate that the quality of staff-offender relationships can have important effects on prison operations, including reducing the level of interpersonal violence (Bottoms 1999) and decreasing the likelihood of riots and other catastrophic outcomes (Useem and Goldstone 2002). Haas and Spence (2016) found that inmates that perceived correctional staff delivery services in a manner consistent with Core Correctional Practices felt more prepared for release from prison. Meanwhile, in the context of community corrections, the adoption of a supportive rather than a punitive relationship style by supervision officers has been shown to reduce levels of anxiety and reactance by parolees and probationers (Morash et al. 2015). The findings highlight the importance of utilizing CCPs to improve correctional service delivery and offender outcomes.

Application of CCP in corrections

The effectiveness of correctional interventions on reducing recidivism is largely contingent on the quality of service delivery. Services designed to reduce recidivism among correctional populations must have 'treatment integrity' or fidelity (Rhine et al. 2006). That is, interventions and services implemented as they were designed. In contemporary correctional practice, this means that services should adhere to the RNR principles and employ cognitive behavioural strategies to counter pro-criminal attitudes and styles of thinking. They should also be applied in a collaborative manner that fosters client motivation and engagement. Yet, research has shown that adherence to the RNR principles and other evidence-based practices is more of the exception than the rule (Lowenkamp et al. 2006).

Plausible explanations for this poor adherence may in part be related to the training correctional staff and officers receive. Most trainings of correctional staff tend to focus heavily on aspects of the law, safety concerns, the administration of risk assessments, and the writing pre-sentence investigation or social inquiry reports (i.e. reports prepared on request by the court which summarizes an offenders' history to assist in determining an appropriate sentence) (Annison et al. 2008). Far less attention is paid to the proper application of the RNR principles and how to interact with offenders on a one-on-one basis (Birgden 2004). As a result, Bonta and his colleagues (2008) found only modest adherence to the RNR principles when exploring the 'black box' of community supervision. Using case file and audiotaped supervision sessions of 62 probation officers with 154 clients, they found that the frequency of officer-client contact was minimally related to the offender's risk level and criminogenic needs were often not addressed. Perhaps even more of a concern was the almost non-existent cognitive behavioural techniques (e.g. role playing, rehearsal, homework, etc.) and the lack of effort on the part of officers to create a collaborative, working alliance with clients to promote an environment best suited for learning new skills.

Findings such as these have ushered in a new area of corrections research focused on achieving fidelity in the application of evidence-based practices (Haas 2013). The lack of fidelity in the application of the responsivity principle has led to the development of a variety of curricula or trainings (e.g. Strategic Training Initiative in Community Supervision or STICS; Effective Practices in Community Supervision or EPICS; Staff Training Aimed at Reducing Re-arrest or STARR)[1] designed to teach officers a core set of skills rooted in cognitive social learning theory (i.e. Core Correctional Practices) (Bonta et al. 2018; Toronjo and Taxman 2018). In turn, these skills are taught to clients/offenders in one-on-one supervision sessions in an effort to have them learn each skill and apply them on their own. Officers are trained to teach clients new pro-social ways of thinking and problem-solving. It is hoped that clients will utilize the new skills to better manage their lives and navigate situations that may lead to criminal conduct. These newly developed skills centre on the practical application of Core Correctional Practices.

Methods for assessing the use of Core Correctional Cractices

Demonstrating that EBPs (including CCPs) can be implemented with fidelity in large-scale correctional settings remains a challenge for the field. As briefly noted above, the capacity for evidence-based approaches such as Core Correctional Practices to reduce recidivism are substantially diminished when they are not applied with fidelity. It is not entirely clear whether effect sizes seen in smaller RNR demonstration projects can be consistently achieved in correctional organizations characterized by multiple layers of bureaucracy and limited resources (Haas 2013). As Bonta and colleagues (2013) have pointed out, many of the treatment interventions commonly included in meta-analytic studies that offer support for the RNR principles and other evidence-based approaches are based upon small, group-based treatment programs led by highly qualified researchers and professionals. These small-scale demonstration projects tend to yield more robust effect sizes than larger interventions in the real world. Therefore, the reasons for this may have to do more with quality implementation issues rather than with the treatment itself.

This conclusion highlights the importance of both quality implementation as well as the need to develop sound methods for monitoring the actual use of evidence-based practices in the field. Such monitoring efforts need to be coupled with routine coaching and feedback sessions to improve correctional staff adherence to the RNR principles and other associated evidence-based practices. Over the past couple of decades there have been a series of tools developed to inform correctional practitioners about their programs and how closely they adhere to the known principles of effective intervention. Two noteworthy examples include the Correctional Program Assessment Inventory (CPAI; Gendreau and Andrews 2001) and the Correctional Program Checklist (CPC; Latessa 2013). Both tools rely on data gathered from structured interviews with programme staff and participants, and observation of groups and services. Other sources of information include policy and procedure manuals, schedules, treatment materials and curriculums, a review of case files. Once the information is gathered and reviewed, the programme is scored with areas of strength and need for improvement highlighted. While not designed to solely measure the use of Core Correctional Practices among staff, both of these instruments provide a valid approach for measuring the 'content' and 'capacity' of programmes to adhere to the principle of effective correctional intervention (Duriez et al. 2017; Lowenkamp et al. 2006; Nesovic (2003).

There has also been recent efforts to more closely measure the 'working relationship' between officers and client. Based on the work of Trotter (1996) and Dowden and Andrews (2004), Skeem and her colleagues (2007) developed the Dual Role Relationship Inventory-Revised (DRI-R). The DRI-R sought to assess officer-client relationship quality unique to the context of community supervision. The tool was designed to capture the dual roles of officers as agents of support and control, and assess domains of affiliation (e.g. trust, caring) as well as officer's use of authority (e.g. firm but fair practices). Versions of the instrument capture separate input from the perspectives of the 'probationer', 'officer', and 'observer'. Subsequent studies applying the DRI-R has demonstrated that good relationship quality is a critical element in the success of offenders on community supervision (Kennealy et al. 2012; Manchak et al. 2014). Other efforts have focused on measuring the use of Core Correctional Practices in the context of institutions.

Haas and Spence (2016) applied a newly developed survey-based tool, the Core Correctional Practice (CCPSR), to examine staff-inmate relationships in the context of state prison facilities. The CCPSR closely measures Core Correctional Practices as first described by Andrews and Kiessling (1980) and later operationalized by Dowden and Andrews (2004). The tool is unique in that it relies upon the input of inmates and their perceptions of how services are delivered to them. The authors argue that inmates, as the primary consumers of correctional services in prisons, are uniquely positioned to provide meaningful input on the quality of services and their delivery. Using the CCPSR, Haas and Spence (2016) found that prisoners indicated they were more prepared for release when they perceived the delivery of re-entry services to be consistent with CCPs. Other research on the CCPSR indicates that it varies predictably across facilities with different security levels and treatment orientations (Haas and Bauer-Leffler 2010) and is predictive of inmate misconduct (Haas and Spence 2017). These findings suggests the CPPSR to be a valid and internally consistent measure of CCPs.

Conclusion

In this era of evidence-based practices the measure of RNR adherence and Core Correctional Practices is no longer a luxury for corrections professionals. Research has shown the importance of staff adherence to evidence-based practices to maximize reductions in offender recidivism. Additionally, a growing body of literature underscores the importance of continuous training, coaching, and feedback for the development of officer and staff skills. To achieve a meaningful working alliance between correctional staff and clients, it is essential that the proper relationship and structuring skills be developed and adhered to by staff. Additionally, research shows that the application of evidence-based practices is largely dependent on the ability of correctional staff to establish collaborative, purposive professional relationships with their clients. Thus, it has become increasingly important to train correctional personnel on how to create and maintain relationships with clients that are conducive to producing behaviour change. This chapter described the core skills necessary to foster such relationships and support cognitive behavioural approaches aimed at reducing recidivism. Future research should seek develop innovative methods for measuring staff adherence to the responsivity principle, along with other evidence-based practices, and provide routine coaching and feedback to corrections professionals. Only in this way will meaningful reductions in recidivism be achieved and public safety be maximized.

Note

1 STICS was the first full-scale curriculum to be developed to assist community supervision officers in structuring client contact sessions and infusing cognitive behavioural interventions. STICS was developed by Jim Bonta et al. (2010) and supported by Leticia Gutierrez, Jennifer Ashton, Jobina Li, Kyle Simpson, Leslie Helmus, and Julie Blais. EPICS was developed at the University of Cincinnati, Center for Criminal Justice Research, Corrections Institute by Paula Smith, Myrinda Schweitzer, Ryan Labrecque, and Edward Latessa. STARR was developed by Charles Robinson, Scott VanBenschoten, Christopher Lowenkamp, and Melissa Alexander, Administrative Office of the US Courts, Office of Probation and Pretrial Services.

References

Andrews, D. A. (2000) Principles of effective correctional programs. In L. Motiuk and R. C. Serin (Eds.), *Compendium2000 on Effective Correctional Programming: Contributing to Effective Correctional Programs*. Ottawa, ON: Correctional Service Canada.

Andrews, D. A. and Bonta, J. (2010) *Psychology of Criminal Conduct*, 5th edition. New Providence, NJ: Matthew Bender.

Andrews, D. A. and Kiessling, J. J. (1980) Program structure and effective correctional practices: A summary of the CaVic research. In R. R. Ross and P. Gendreau (Eds.), *Effective Correctional Treatment* (pp. 441–463). Toronto, Canada: Butterworths.

Annison, J., Eadie, T. and Knight, C. (2008) People first: Probation officer perspectives on probation work. *The Probation Journal*, 55(3), 259–271.

Aos, S., Miller, M. and Drake, E. (2006) *Evidence-Based Public Policy Options to Reduce Future Prison Construction, Criminal Justice Costs, and Crime Rates* (Document 06 – 10–1201). Olympia, WA: Washington State Institute for Public Policy.

Beijersbergen, K. A., Dirkzwager, A. J. E., Eichelsheim, V. I., Laan, P. H. and van der Nieuwbeerta, P. (2014) Procedural justice and prisoners' mental health problems: A longitudinal study. *Criminal Behaviour and Mental Health*, 24(2), 100–112.

Beijersbergen, K. A., Dirkzwager, A. J., Eichelsheim, V. I., Van der Laan, P. H. and Nieuwbeerta, P. (2015) Procedural justice, anger and prisoners' misconduct: A longitudinal study. *Criminal Justice and Behavior*, 42, 196–218.

Birgden, A. (2004) Therapeutic jurisprudence and responsivity: Finding the will and the way in offender rehabilitation. *Psychology, Crime, & Law*, 10, 283–295.

Bonta, J. and Andrews, D. A. (2007) *Risk-Need-Responsivity Model for Offender Assessment and Treatment* (User Report No. 2007–06). Ottawa, ON: Public Safety Canada.

Bonta, J. and Andrews, D. A. (2017) *Psychology of Criminal Conduct*, 6th edition. New Providence, NJ: Matthew Bender.

Bonta, J., Bourgon, G. and Rugge, T. (2018) From evidence-informed to evidence-based: The Strategic Training Initiative in Community Supervision (STICS). In P. Ugwudike, P. Raynor and J. Annison (Eds.), *Evidence-Based Skills in Criminal Justice: International Research on Supporting Rehabilitation and Desistance*. Bristol: Policy Press.

Bonta, J., Bourgon, G., Rugge, T., Gress, C. and Gutierrez, L. (2013) Taking a leap: From pilot project to wide-scale implementation of the strategic training initiative in community supervision (STICS). *Justice Research and Policy*, 15(1), 17–35.

Bonta, J., Bourgon, G., Rugge, T., Scott, T. L., Yessine, A. K., Gutierrez, L. and Li, J. (2010) *The Strategic Training Initiative in Community Supervision: Risk-Need-Responsivity in the Real World*. Ottawa, ON: Public Safety Canada.

Bonta, J., Bourgon, G., Rugge, T., Scott, T-L., Yessine, A., Gutierrez, L. and Li, J. (2011) An experimental demonstration of training probation officers in evidence based community supervision. *Criminal Justice and Behavior*, 38, 1127–1148. DOI:10.1177/0093854811420678.

Bonta, J., Rugge, T., Scott, T., Bourgon, G. and Yessine, A. (2008) Exploring the black box of community supervision. *Journal of Offender Rehabilitation*, 47, 248–270. DOI:10.1080/10509670802213408510.

Bordin, E. S. (1979) The generalizability of the psychoanalytic concept of the working alliance. *Psychotherapy: Theory, Research & Practice*, 16(3), 252–260.

Bourgon, G. and Gutierrez, L. (2012) The general responsivity principle in community supervision: The importance of probation officers using cognitive intervention techniques and its influence on recidivism. *Journal of Crime and Justice*, 35(2), 149–166.

Bourgon, G. and Guiterrez, L. (2013) The importance of building good relationships in community corrections: Evidence, theory, and practice of the therapeutic alliance. In P. Ugwudike and P. Raynor (Eds.), *What Works in Offender Compliance: International Perspectives and Evidence-Based Practice*. Basingstoke: Palgrave Macmillan.

Bourgon, G., Gutierrez, L. and Ashton, J. (2011) The evolution of community supervision practice: The transformation from case manager to change agent. *Irish Probation Journal*, 8, 28–48.

Bogue, B. and Nandi, A. (2012) *Motivational Interviewing in Corrections: A Comprehensive Guide to Implementing MI in Corrections*. Washington, DC: National Institute of Corrections.

Bogue, B., Pampel, F. and Pasini-Hill, D. (2013) Progress toward motivational interviewing proficiency in corrections: Results of a staff development program. *Justice Research and Policy*, 15(1), 37–66.

Bottoms, A. (1999) Interpersonal violence and social order in prisons. In M. Tonry and J. Petersilia (Eds.), *Crime and Justice: A Review of Research*, Vol. 26. Chicago: University of Chicago Press, pp. 205–281.

Chadwick, N., Dewolf, A. and Serin, R. (2015) Effectively training community supervision officers: A meta-analytic review of the impact on offender outcome. *Criminal Justice and Behavior*, 42(10), 977–989. DOI:10.1177/0093854815595661.

Dowden, C. and Andrews, D. A. (2004) The importance of staff practice in delivering effective correctional treatment: A meta-analytic review of core correctional practice. *International Journal of Offender Therapy and Comparative Criminology*, 48(2), 203–214.

Duriez, S. A., Sullivan, C., Latessa, E. J. and Brusman-Lovins, L. (2017) The evolution of correctional program assessment in the age of evidence-based practices. *Corrections: Policy, Practice, and Research*, 1–18, Published online, 11 October.

Duwe, G. (2017) *The Use and Impact of Correctional Programming for Inmates on Pre-and Post-Release Outcomes*. Washington, DC: National Institute of Corrections.

Gendreau, P. and Andrews, D. A. (2001) *The Correctional Program Assessment Inventory – 2000*. Saint John, New Brunswick: University of New Brunswick.

Haas, S. M. (2013) Current practice and challenges in evidence-based community corrections. *Justice Research and Policy*, 15(1), 1–15.

Haas, S. M. and Bauer-Leffler, S. (2010) *Core Correctional Practice in Offender Reentry: An Examination of Service Delivery Across Settings*. Paper Presented at the Annual Conference of the Bureau of Justice Statistics/Justice Research and Statistics Association in Portland, ME. Available at: www.jrsa.org/events/conference/presentations-10/Stephen_Haas.pdf (Accessed 12 May 2016).

Haas, S. M. and Spence, D. H. (2016) Use of core correctional practice and inmate preparedness for release. *International Journal of Offender Therapy and Comparative Criminology*, 1–24. DOI:10.1177/0306624X15625992.

Haas, S. M. and Spence, D. H. (2017) *The Impact of Staff-Inmate Relationships on Inmate Misconduct: A Partial Test of a Self-Report Measure of Core Correctional Practice*. Unpublished manuscript.

Howells, K. (2000) *Psycho-Social Environment (PSE) of Prisons and Its Relationship to Recidivism*. Canberra: Criminology Research Council of Australia Australian Institute of Criminology.

Johnson, J. L. (2017) Comparison of recidivism studies: AOUSC, USSC, and BJS. *Federal Probation*, 75(2), 57–63.

Kennealy, P. J., Skeem, J. L., Manchak, S. M. and Eno Louden, J. (2012) Firm, fair, and caring officer-offender relationships protect against supervision failure. *Law and Human Behavior*, 36, 496–505.

Kennedy, S. M. (2000) Treatment responsivity: Reducing recidivism by enhancing treatment effectiveness. In L. Motiuk and R. C. Serin (Eds.), *Compendium 2000 on Effective Correctional Programming: Contributing to Effective Correctional Programs*. Ottawa, ON: Correctional Service Canada.

Klockars, C. (1972) A theory of probation supervision. *Journal of Criminal Law, Criminology, and Police Science*, 64(4), 549–557.

Labrecque, R. M., Schweitzer, M. and Smith, P. (2013) Probation and parole officer adherence to the core correctional practices: An evaluation of 755 offender-officer interactions. *Advancing Practices*, 3, 20–23.

Latessa, E. J. (2013) *Evaluating Correctional Programs: 151st International Training Course, Visiting Expert's Papers*. New York: United Nations Publications.

Latessa, E. J., Smith, P., Schweitzer, M. and Labreque, R. M. (2013) *Evaluation of the Effective Practices in Community Supervision Model (EPICS) in Ohio*. Unpublished manuscript.

Lipsey, M. W. and Cullen, F. T. (2007) The effectiveness of correctional rehabilitation: A review of systematic reviews. *Annual Review of Law and Social Science*, 3, 297–320.

Lowenkamp, C. T., Holsinger, A. M., Robinson, C. R. and Alexander, M. (2014) Diminishing or durable treatment of STARR? A research note on 24-month re-arrest rates. *Journal of Crime & Justice*, 37, 275–283.

Lowenkamp, C. T., Latessa, E. J. and Smith, P. (2006) Does correction program quality really matter? The impact of adhering to the principles of effective intervention. *Criminology and Public Policy*, 5(3), 575–594.

Manchak, S. M., Skeem, J. L., Kennealy, P. J. and Louden, J. E. (2014) High-fidelity specialty mental health probation improves officer practices, treatment access, and rule compliance. *Law and Human Behavior*, 38(5), 450–461.

Markman, J. A., Durose, M. R., Rantala, R. R. and Tiedt, A. D. (2016) *Recidivism of Offenders Placed on Federal Community Supervision in 2005: Patterns from 2005 to 2010*. Bureau of Justice Statistics, Washington DC: US Department of Justice, June. NCF 249743.

Morash, M., Kashy, D. A., Smith, S. W. and Cobbina, J. E. (2015) The effects of probation or parole agent relationship style and female offenders' criminogenic needs on offenders' responses to supervision interactions. *Criminal Justice and Behavior*, 42, 412–434. DOI: 10.1177/0093854814551602.

Nesovick, A. (2003) Psychometric evaluation of the correctional program assessment inventory. *Dissertation Abstracts International*, 64(9), 4674B. (UMI No. AAT NQ83525).

Paparozzi, M. A. and Gendreau, P. (2005) An intensive supervision program that worked: Service delivery, professional orientation, and organizational supportiveness. *The Prison Journal*, 85(4), 445–466.DOI: 10.1177/0032885505281529.

Rhine, E. E., Mawhorr, T. L. and Parks, E. C. (2006) Implementation: The bane of effective correctional programs. *Criminology and Public Policy*, 5(2), 347–358.

Robinson, C. R., Lowenkamp, C. T., Holsinger, A. M., VanBenschoten, S., Alexander, M. and Oleson, J. C. (2012) A random study of staff training aimed at reducing rearrest (STARR): Using core correctional practices in probation interactions. *Journal of Crime and Justice*, 35(2), 167–188.

Robinson, C. R., VanBenschoten, S. W., Alexander, M. and Lowenkamp, C. T. (2011) A random (Almost) Study of Staff Training Aimed at Reducing Rearrest (STARR): Reducing recidivism through intentional design. *Federal Probation*, 75(2), 57–63.

Simourd, D. J., Olver, M. E. and Brandenburg, B. (2016) Changing criminal attitudes among incarcerated offenders: Initial examination of a structured treatment program. *International Journal of Offender Therapy and Comparative Criminology*, 60(12), 1425–1445. DOI:10.1177/0306624X15 579257.

Skeem, J. L., Eno Louden, J., Polaschek, D. and Camp, J. (2007) Assessing relationship quality in mandated treatment: Blending care with control. *Psychological Assessment*, 19(4), 397–410.

Skeem, J. L., Louden, J. E., Polaschek, D. and Camp, J. (2007) Assessing relationship quality in mandated community treatment: Blending care with control. *Psychological Assessment*, 19, 397–410. DOI:10.1037/1040-3590.19.4.397.

Smith, P., Schweitzer, M., Labrecque, R. M. and Latessa, E. J. (2012) Improving probation officers' supervision skills: An evaluation of the EPICS model. *Journal of Crime and Justice*, 35(2), 189–199.

Toronjo, H. and Taxman, F. S. (2018) Supervision face-to-face contacts: The emergence of an intervention. In P. Ugwudike, P. Raynor and J. Annison (Eds.), *Evidence-Based Skills in Criminal Justice: International Research on Supporting Rehabilitation and Desistance*. Bristol: Policy Press.

Trotter, C. (1996) The impact of different supervision practices in community corrections: Cause for optimism. *Australia & New Zealand Journal of Criminology*, 29(1), 1–19.

Useem, B. and Goldstone, J. A. (2002) Forging social order and its breakdown: Riot and reform in US prisons. *American Sociological Review*, 67(4), 499–525.

30

Gut check

Turning experience into knowledge

Heather Toronjo

> Learning is the process whereby knowledge is created through the transformation of experience.
>
> David Kolb (1984)

The aspiration of the evidence-based practices movement in corrections is finding 'what works' to stop criminal behaviour, typically measured by a rearrest, a return to prison or jail, or a reconviction. However, the scientific rationalism of the evidence-based supervision movement cannot hope to capture completely the complexity of everyday work within community supervision agencies – work that involves interacting with myriad people with complex lives situated within all types of local communities and working within organizations, each of which have their own particular histories and cultures. While not a diminishment of the contribution of the evidence-based movement to understanding effective correctional practices, this is a recognition that too often the label of EBP is accepted as a definitive answer both to what correctional workers can do and what they should do. This is problematic for several reasons. First, the outcomes observed in empirical testing of supervision strategies used within supervision settings rely heavily on researcher involvement in implementing the practices, and current studies suggest feasibility issues. Second, the complex nature of social reality assures that correctional professionals will need to use an incredible amount of discretion in situating EBPs within unlimited variations of context-dependent situations. Which leads to the third issue, behavioural outcomes are not the only factor in a supervision officer's decision-making process and EBPs in and of themselves cannot guide correctional workers on what they should do in specific situations. All of this suggests the importance of the experience of correctional workers, and specifically, the need to incorporate practical knowledge or craft with scientific knowledge and to improve what Aristotle termed phronesis, or practical wisdom. Practical wisdom is the ability to know the right thing to do in a specific situation. In other words, it is the ability to reflect on possibly competing values and decide what is the most ethical course of action. Evidence-based practices on their own cannot prescribe the most effective and appropriate way to act in every particular situation.

Fortunately, however, the current dominant model of effective community supervision, the Risk-Need-Responsivity model, and specifically its Management principle, provides a foundation for addressing the problems inherent with integrating empirical science with craft and improving practical wisdom. The 15th principle of the RNR model advises agencies to promote the 'selection, training, and clinical supervision of staff according to RNR' and notes the importance of having 'monitoring, feedback, and adjustment systems' (Bonta and Andrews 2016: 177). This 'clinical supervision' with 'monitoring, feedback, and adjustment systems' is, as this chapter argues, an ideal vehicle for improving both officer adherence to EBPs but also decision-making generally. To that end, this chapter examines the structure of clinical supervision in current evidence-based supervision models, and proposes a specific form of clinical supervision referred to here as coaching. While the call for coaching in evidence-based supervision practices is not new, many researchers have noted the necessity of maintaining adequate and ongoing staff training and clinical supervision (Bonta and Andrews 2016; Fixsen et al. 2005; Landenberger and Lipsey 2005; Taxman 2018), this chapter goes further by (1) providing a theoretical foundation for a new coaching model, (2) specifying the practices that comprise quality coaching, and (3) proposing a research agenda for studying coaching efforts as part and parcel of EBP implementation in community supervision.

Overview of the RNR model

The RNR model as articulated by Bonta and Andrews (2016) comprises 15 principles in three categories: (1) overarching principles, (2) core RNR principles and key clinical issues, and (3) organizational principles. Overwhelmingly, it is the core RNR principles of risk, need, and responsivity that are most familiar to correctional staff as these have become the basis for the various risk/need assessments used by the field.[1] The risk principle advises us to spend the most time with those people with higher risk scores. The risk score is measured by a person's criminal history, as well as eight other dynamic risk factors. The need principle tells us to focus our efforts on those eight dynamic risk factors, and the responsivity principle tells us to use a cognitive behavioural approach and to take other individual issues into account that may affect a person's ability to engage in supervision. Another important principle in the RNR model relates to specific staff practices. These suggested practices, termed Core Correctional Practices (CCP), have become increasingly popular with the advent of several CCP-based training models, most notably STICS, STARR, EPICS, and SOARING2. An examination of these existing models informs this chapter's main thesis that current 'technology transfer' models focus on transferring from lab to the front lines with insufficient attention given to integrating science with craft and helping officers know the right thing to do in specific situations. This chapter focuses on the clinical supervision principle as a vehicle for improving both the use of evidence-based practices and decision-making generally.[2]

The science of changing behaviour

The Core Correctional Practices (CCP) embody the scientific evidence on behaviour change. These practices stem from social learning theory and its specific application to criminal behaviour, differential association theory. CCPs leverage the understanding that all human behaviour is learned to provide guidance to correctional workers on changing client behaviour (Toronjo and Taxman 2017). Canadian clinical psychologists, Andrews and Kiessling, first introduced the practices in 1980 when they developed a programme for volunteers working with a Canadian probation population (Andrews and Kiessling 1980). CCPs include the following as laid out in Dowden and Andrews (2004): (1) effective use of authority, which is characterized by a firm but fair approach; (2) appropriate modelling and reinforcement. Reinforcement is broken down into effective reinforcement wherein the client is immediately told why the officer approves of a specific behaviour or encourages the client to think about why the behaviour is desirable, and effective disapproval wherein the client is immediately told why the officer disapproves of a specific behaviour and encourages the client to consider why the behaviour is undesirable. The modelling component includes structured learning procedures where officers define a skill, model the skill, role play, provide progressively difficult role-playing scenarios, or provide feedback regarding the client's performance; (3) problem-solving, which involves helping clients identify a problem, think through and evaluate options and alternatives, craft a plan of action, and then evaluate that plan after the client tries it out; and (4) quality interpersonal relationships which includes being 'warm, genuine, humorous, enthusiastic, self-confident, empathic, respectful, flexible, committed to help-ing the client, engaging, mature, or intelligent' (p. 208), and using directive, solution-focused, structured, non-blaming, or contingency-based forms of communication with individuals under supervision. The important take away is that these skills and the RNR model position the front-line correctional offi-cer as a 'change agent' who uses clinical skills rooted in cognitive behavioural therapy to address problem behaviour (Taxman 2008; Bourgon et al. 2012).

Different training models exist for helping officers learn the skills related to the RNR model. These are referred to as STICS (see Bonta et al. 2011), STARR (see Robinson et al. 2011), EPICS (see Labrecque and Smith 2017), and SOAR-ING2 (see Donohoe 2017; Maass 2017).[3] STICS, STARR, and EPICS all cen-tre around changing a person's thoughts and include a specific set of skills with specific skill steps that officers are expected to learn and use in practice. These skills include active listening, feedback, role clarification, effective use of disapproval, effective use of reinforcement, effective use of authority, prob-lem-solving, and the cognitive model. The STICS, STARR, and EPICS models differ in small ways in how skills steps are broken down and each model may include an intervention or skill not included in the other but generally they are very similar, particularly in operationalizing correctional practices (Bonta et al. 2017). SOARING2 was different in that the skills did not align as closely with the CCPs. The skills officers and coaches focused on in SOAR-ING2 included working relationship, engagement and motivation, risk man-agement, and problem-solving skills. In each model, officers are expected to learn skills and then integrate them into their regular supervision sessions with high fidelity, meaning they use them appropriately (i.e. timing and style) and with all steps completed in the correct order. To accomplish this, STICS, STARR, and EPICS include in-person trainings for staff combined with some sort of additional post-training support, referred to in various instances as clinical supervision, clinical support, or coaching. The post-training compo-nent includes the use of videotapes or audiotapes to examine how individuals use the skills (similar to clinical practice). SOARING2 substitutes a self-paced eLearning course in place of an initial in-person training. SOARING2 facilita-tors also train agency supervisors on observing and scoring the SUSTAIN skills via a two-day in-person training. It is worth examining these coaching models in greater detail including empirical knowledge to date on the coaching com-ponent of these supervision models and the methods by which they attempt to affect officer behaviour.

Clinical supervision/coaching in EBP supervision

Clinical supervision has a long history in human service fields, particularly social work, psychology, nursing, and teaching, but virtually no history in corrections in the United States (Joyce and Showers 2002; Kadushin and

Harkness 2014; Milne and James 2000; Schoenwald et al. 2009). One of the few places coaching shows up in corrections is the current evidence-based supervision models. Published studies on the effectiveness of Core Correctional Practice models do shed some light on current coaching practices within existing evidence-based supervision models. As summarized in Table 30.1, using experimental and quasi-experimental designs, empirical studies on PCS (Proactive Community Supervision was an experimental project implemented in Maryland Department of Probation and Parole), STICS, STARR, EPICS, and SOARING2 models show generally positive effects on both officer use of skills and client outcomes (e.g. recidivism) for those agents trained in the models versus those not trained (Bonta et al. 2011; Chadwick et al. 2015; Hiller 2017; Labrecque and Smith 2017; Latessa et al. 2013; Maass et al. 2013; Robinson et al. 2012; Maass 2017; Robinson et al. 2011; Trotter 2015).

Each supervision model uses some form of coaching as the key mechanism by which agents improve their use of skills. Some studies have attempted to isolate the effect of coaching on the outcomes as shown in Table 30.2. Coaching is considered so key that STICS, STARR, and EPICS developers have universally advised that agencies develop their own internal coaches for the

Table 30.1 Summary of findings in studies of PCS, STICS, STARR, EPICS, and SOARING2

Model	Unit	Training method	Officer outcomes	Client outcomes
PCS (Taxman 2008)	548 clients	2 day/4 boosters 2 day/4 boosters on-site learning sessions	Completed LSI-R Categorized client Identified triggers Developed case plan Assigned responsibilities	Rearrest 30% v. 42% Violation 34.7% v. 40.1% Positive drug test – no effect
STICS (Bonta et al. 2011)	52 officers 143 clients	3 day 12 boosters 1 refresher training	➢ Crim needs discussed ➢ Use of CBT techniques	Reconviction 25.3% v. 40.5%
STARR (Robinson et al. 2011)	59 officers 462 clients	3.5 day 4 boosters	➢ Use of CCPs ➢ Longer contact sessions	Supervision Failure (mod) 16% v. 30% Supervision Failure (high) – No effect
EPICS (Labrecque and Smith 2017)	43 officers	3 day 24 coaching sessions	➢ Use of CCPs	–
SOARING2 (Maass 2017)	139 officers	eLearning quarterly observations	Motivation to learn and Pre-train know => EBP knowledge Pre-train know and pre-train use of skills => SR use of skills	–

Table 30.2 Summary of findings on coaching in EBP-supervision models

Model	Unit of analysis	Coaching measure	Outcome	Findings
STICS (Bonta et al. 2011)	23 officers	Degree of officer participation in coaching	Officer use of skills	−.455 (noncrim needs) .464 (cog intervention)
EPICS (Labrecque and Smith 2017)	43 officers	Number of coaching sessions	Use of skills over time	Improved over time
STARR (Alexander et al. 2013)	13 officers	Survey items on perceptions of audiotaping and coaching	Officer perceptions of coaching	Useful and helpful
STARR (Lowenkamp et al. 2012)	90 officers	Survey items on perception of value and usefulness of coaching	Officer perception of coaching	Helpful and likely to increase use of skill
SOARING2 (Maass 2017)	170 officers	Survey items on perception of general utility of coaching	Officer perception of coaching	Favourable perceptions

models to have a chance of success. The consensus seems to be that without internal coaching, an agency should not expect much change in front-line staff supervision methods.

A close look at the coaching methods included in each model reveal that the strategies used to foster officer skill use mirror the principles on which the skills themselves are founded – that behaviour is learned. The models use the same structured learning techniques to train officers as officers are expected to use with clients.

The clinical supervision (also referred to as clinical support) in STICS includes monthly meetings, individual feedback, and refresher courses. Monthly meetings include various types of exercises such as reviewing small samples of audiotaped sessions between officers and clients. Officers were also encouraged to submit audiotapes to the trainers (researchers) for individual clinical feedback. This feedback was provided orally and/or in written format. As noted by Bonta et al (2010), 'The feedback focused on the officer's use of STICS concepts, skills and techniques with an emphasis on rewarding and encouraging their use' (p. 8). To better understand the impact of officer participation in clinical support on the officers' use of skills, STICS researchers created a Global On-going Supervision to capture the degree of officer participation. The index was the summation of three scored aspects of participation: (1) points for attendance and participation in monthly meetings, (2) points for receiving feedback on audiotapes, and (3) 1 point for attending a refresher course (one-year post-training).[4] Officers with scores of 3 or less were categorized as the 'low-participation' group and officers with scores of 4 or more were categorized as the 'high-participation' group. The researchers then ran correlations to examine the relationship between participation in clinical supervision and officer's use of skills starting nine months post-initial training. There were no statistically significant relationships. But, the authors note that each of the three clinical support items and the Global On-Going Supervision score were positively correlated with all CCPs except Relationship Skills, which appeared to have a minimal and negative association with participation in the clinical support activities. They also ran correlations between participation in clinical supervision and the content of discussion between officers and clients; with the idea being that those who engaged in more clinical supervision should be discussing the major criminogenic need of pro-social attitude. They found a positive but statistically insignificant relationship between participation in clinical supervision and increased discussions with clients on pro-criminal attitudes. Officers spent less time on non-criminogenic needs.

The initial study on STARR did not attempt to parse out the effect of additional coaching or support after the initial STARR training. But subsequently, the Administrative Office of the Courts attempted to implement STARR throughout its agencies nationwide on a voluntary basis (Clodfelter et al. 2016). STARR creators trained in-house coaches within US federal probation to help officers improve their use of STARR skills. Coaches were trained in a two-day training focusing on coaching STARR. It is unclear what coaching skills were taught. They also received mentoring from the expert trainer but it is unclear what the mentoring consisted of. The STARR coaches' responsibilities included listening to audiotapes and giving individual feedback, as well as running group coaching sessions with their assigned officers. Group coaching sessions lasted 1–1.5 hours and included didactic review of skills, discussion of problems/issues encountered, tips for using the skills, listening of audiotapes and peer feedback, and role play of skills with immediate peer and coach feedback. While the coaching aspect of STARR has not been studied explicitly, Alexander et al. (2013) report the results of a survey of 13 US federal probation officers on the use of coaching. Officers reported that they found the coaching helpful and they believed that it enhanced their skills.

In perhaps the most targeted study of coaching in evidence-based supervision, Labrecque and Smith (2015) randomly assigned probation officers to be either trained and coached in the use of EPICS skills (n = 28) or not trained or coached (n = 15). The treatment group received a three-day in-person training followed by 24 monthly group coaching sessions. These coaching sessions were designed to 'refresh officers on the EPICS model' (p. 239). The coaching session structure modelled was a supervision contact session. Each session began with a check-in to discuss any outstanding questions or concerns. Next, the group discussed the topic of the previous session 'until everyone felt comfortable using the specific skill/technique' (p. 239). Then, a different topic from the initial training was reviewed and modelled, and officers were given feedback on their performance. As they left each session, officers were tasked with using the skill discussed during a contact session with one of their clients. Officers also received feedback from researchers based on audiotapes of their contact sessions. The feedback focused on the components of the skills that were completed satisfactorily and components that needed improvement. To test the effectiveness of the training and coaching sessions, the researchers coded audiotapes from treatment and control over 18 months. The study had several notable findings. First, audiotape submission declined precipitously after the first six months from 108 recordings in months 1–3 down to 20 recordings in months 16–18. Second, despite the study ending early, the researchers were able to see that over time the trained group increased their use of skills over time while the control group did not. And finally, over time the percentage of audiotapes submitted by the treatment group rated as high-fidelity increased. While the authors attribute this trend to the coaching that the trained group received, it is unclear given that the study was terminated and the officers did not produce a steady flow of tapes.

An implementation evaluation of the SOARING2 model in one large urban probation agency provides interesting insight on the feasibility of coaching with observations and feedback to assess and improve officer use of skills. Using data from n = 4,345 observations entered by SOARING2 coaches into an online database, Donohoe et al. (2017, June) conducted psychometric testing on the SOARING2 observation rating form. A Principle Axis Factor analysis verified the four domains representing Risk Assessment and Risk Management Skills; Engagement Skills; Problem Solving Skills; and Working Relationship Skills. Alphas ranged from 0.79 to 0.86 and the Principal Axis Factor analysis showed each had a single underlying latent variable. While the psychometric analysis of the observation rating form is encouraging, the implementation measures showed mixed results. Captured via focus groups, Donohoe et al. (2017, June) found that while supervisors felt that the SOARING2 skills observations were acceptable and desirable in order to identify and correct POs with difficulty using evidence-based practices, they also felt that the frequency (i.e. three–four observations per PO each quarter) was unreasonable once the PO had demonstrated mastery of skills, and only targeted or periodic check-ins would be necessary. And a consistent complaint from both supervisors and line officers was the lack of organizational support for the SOARING2 skills. In particular, staff felt that agency leaders focused on quantity over quality. For example, leadership focused on the number of individuals an officer could see in a day while not recognizing or appreciating what goes into ensuring those interactions are quality.

The studies on training in evidence-based supervision models highlight two noteworthy features about coaching. First, despite study samples being comprised of volunteers, each published study saw a precipitous drop in the number of audiotapes officers turned in over the course of the study, which suggests some feasibility issues. Some officers did not turn in a single tape, and in fact the EPICS study had to be cut short due to the dearth of audiotape submissions after 18 months. EPICS creators ultimately concluded that, 'external coaches need to develop the skills of supervisors to both deliver the EPICS model and coach others on the model' (Smith et al. 2012: 196). STARR also ran into its fair share of issues with attempts at creating peer coaches noting that, 'it was not anticipated how cumbersome it would be to balance their new STARR responsibility with existing job requirements' (Clodfelter et al. 2016: 37).

A second important take away is the definition of the coaching role in each of these efforts. In the studies discussed, the coaching role has been conceptualized as relatively one-way. The coaches have something to teach, and the officers have something to learn (although officers are also encouraged to learn from each other via group coaching). While the coaching sessions typically included officers sharing their experiences with using a skill, it is unclear to what degree the models incorporate officers' experiences (e.g. helping an officer reflect on action) or focus on concerns outside of RNR practices (e.g. balancing competing values or making a decision on how to handle a particularly tough case).

Finally, while the researchers have a prominent role in crafting and implementing the models, it is not always clear whether or how participant feedback was included in the process of implementation. In their case study of implementing STARR, Clodfelter et al. (2016) note the use of an organizational survey that asked participants about the 'necessity, relevance, and value' of changes to current officer practice, and Alexander et al. (2013) also anonymously surveyed 13 offices about their thoughts on audiotaping and coaching. An early evaluation of an EPICS pilot notes the need for supervisors and peer coaches to be 'systematically engaged in the process in order to develop the infrastructure to support continued use of the model' (Smith et al. 2012: 190). The pilot study notes that researchers designated a time post-coaching session in which external coaches and supervisors discussed the coaching session to identify barriers to implementation, possible solutions, and next steps, as well as a pre-coaching session in which external coaches and supervisors discussed the upcoming coaching session to enhance supervisor buy-in. In an example of learning from practitioners, Bonta et al. (2017) explain how the wide scale roll-out of STICS was paused when it was evident that participation was not adequate. Researchers then conducted structured interviews with probation officers, managers, and senior officials at headquarters (as well as administered questionnaires and analyzed post-training audio recordings). The results led to modifications in the training and coaching.

It is these lessons learned that inform the recommendations for a new coaches' model that seeks to address feasibility issues by including a mechanism for continuous participant feedback, and, puts officer experience at the heart of the coaching effort. The next section focuses on the role of officer experience in coaching for continuous professional development. By examining the role of discretion, values of community corrections, and the processes by which professionals learn, we can more clearly see the role that coaches must play to effectively contribute officers' professional development.

Challenges to implementation of the RNR model: discretion in a dynamic world

The RNR model centres around the ability to identify and quantify several risk factors that to varying degrees can predict criminal behaviour. It requires officers to balance the individual risks presented by those on their caseload with the mission and goals of the agency. And, it requires officers to understand the tensions among facilitating behavioural change with being an officer of the court.

Discretion: risk v. survival issues. Dynamic risks include antisocial peers, antisocial personality pattern, antisocial cognitions, experiences with education or employment, family/marital issues, substance use, and unstructured leisure time.[5] The presence and severity of these risk factors are measured by a risk/need assessment instrument. Officers are trained to score these different domains via a structured interview with the individual under supervision. Supervision science scholars have noted the many challenges with implementing the RNR model with its use of a risk/need assessment and Core Correctional Practices (Rhine et al. 2006; Viglione et al. 2015; Viglione 2017). Problems in using risk/need assessments range from relying on professional judgement (Bosker et al. 2013), to not focusing on criminogenic needs (Oleson et al. 2012), to an inappropriate focus on risk-related supervision techniques (Viglione et al. 2015). In their own work, Bonta and Andrews (2016) 'confirmed the fear that although empirically based offender assessments were being *administered*, they were not being *used*' (p. 198, emphasis in original). The implications distilled from studies on the use of risk/need assessments in practice generally centre around the need for additional translational tools, for example, adding a case planning function to the tool, or attention to various implementation issues, such as improving staff buy-in and training (VanBenschoten 2008). Not surprisingly, the past decade has seen a rise in implementation science as applied to correctional settings.

A less talked about aspect is the complexity of the needs themselves.[6] In their qualitative study of officer use of risk/need assessments Viglione et al. (2015) note the top four areas of discussion among probation officers and individuals under supervision was employment, housing, fines, and physical health. They compare this with the four topics of conversation offices were taught in training to address – criminal personality, criminal thinking, criminal associates, and criminal history. This comparison illustrates an important reality in community supervision work – officers steer away from the tougher, murkier needs like thoughts and personality to focus on more concrete and actionable needs like employment and housing, or issues that affect stability in the community. This makes sense in light of the fact that in areas of thoughts, personality, and peers, the science itself is considered more difficult and murkier. This concession is not meant as a form of knowledge destruction but rather an acknowledgement of the complexity of the research topic. A brief look at personality research illustrates this point.

The dominant model of personality is the Five-Factor Model (FFM) (Costa and McCrae 1992), but it is not the only model. Other models, for example the Big Seven Model, conceptualize personality traits somewhat differently. For the purposes of this illustration let us assume officers are taught about personality based on the FFM. Even accepting the five general dimensions of personality captured by the popular FFM we must then contend with the link between personality and criminal behaviour. Of the five general personality factors, four have been shown to have a link with criminal behaviour (agreeableness, conscientiousness, neuroticism, and extraversion); only one has not been indicated (openness to experience) (Jones et al. 2011). These personality factors are comprised of facets. These facets are dimensions of a normal personality meaning any of them may be found in any one of us; however, the facets themselves are also dimensional, meaning a person may fall anywhere along a continuum of having more or less of a particular facet. For example, the facets in neuroticism include anxious, angry hostility, and impulsivity. Most people have some degree of these personality traits but some people are characterized by more anger hostility than others. So, officers are advised that particular personality traits are related to criminal behaviour. Exactly what those traits are differs by risk assessment. But, typically traits related to criminal behaviour include self-control, impulsivity, low contentiousness, anger hostility, and callous disregard for others (Bonta and Andrews 2016: 90). So, accepting this, one must then be able to measure personality facets of an individual under supervision and that is where the last hurdle comes into place. The degree to which personality traits are stable is also debatable (Costa and McCrea 2010; Mischel 1969). Personality traits exist in tandem with other psychological processes (sometimes referred to as cognitive-affective processes) which themselves act to interpret various situations (Mischel and Shoda 2008). Andrews and Bonta (2017) note, 'Personality is no longer just the study of stable personality traits but also the study of the dynamic psychological processes that are mediators between traits and the situation of action' (p. 92). So, what is a supervision officer to do with a person who scores high on the antisocial personality pattern domain? Must they understand the individual's cognitive-affective process too? Even if applied researchers distilled this area of research into something digestible for practitioners or crafted tools for practitioners to use in practice, it still remains that the underlying construct is a complicated idea that when manifested in a real human being presents officers with innumerable situations for which they must be prepared to make a judgement and do something.

Similar issues surface when attempting to understand any of the dynamic risk factors. Drilling down into the dynamic risks reveals their complexity and leads naturally to a second problem which is the dynamic, interlocking, and very particular nature of how these risk factors work within an individual's life. For example, regarding antisocial cognitions, it is not hard to imagine how thoughts can morph and fluctuate with changing situations. A situation that might fill us with righteous rage in one instance may spur a completely different emotion with the addition of a few small details. Situational triggers for thoughts could be things like the people you are with, or emotions stemming from something else going in your life, or any number of details of that particular situation. We see this dynamic, interrelated nature in all of the risk domains captured on a risk/need assessment. Substance use, for example, presents many forms of the chicken/egg problem. For example, was the person a sensation-seeker (an antisocial personality trait according to RNR) which led to their substance use problem, or is the substance a coping mechanism for other problems? Correctional workers must decide what to talk to people about, and when to focus on one problem versus another. They must also decide how to focus on a particular problem (e.g. is it time for an intervention, skill building, or a sanction?). In other words, officers must use discretion. Erik Erickson captures the complexity of human problems best in his description of therapy patients as each being 'a universe of one' who must be understood in terms of the unique experiences of his or her life (Schön 1983: 16). The RNR model acknowledges this too in principle 12, which notes the need to maintain professional discretion to deviate from the prescribed list of criminogenic needs when there is reason to believe that a particular person has a risk factor not included in the eight major risk factors defined by empirical measurement. While the wording of the principle limits this practice to exceptional cases, it is an acknowledgement of the limits of statistical probabilities in understanding individual human behaviour. Despite the complexity of understanding and managing dynamic risk, EBP supervision models tend to conceptualized coaching mainly as a component of fidelity, a way of ensuring that officers use the skills appropriately and with high quality. It seems clear that coaching must involve more than quality assurance or fidelity monitoring. Coaching must not only seek to improve officer's competence but also their capability to adapt.

Implementation challenges. Challenges of using the RNR model are typically cast as failures of implementation due to staff resistance, lack of organizational support, poor implementation planning, or poor organizational readiness for change (Taxman and Belenko 2012). As organizations and researchers attempt to put research into practice all aspects of implementation have been segmented, studied, and tested, from levels of 'adoption' to staff perceptions of 'appropriateness', 'acceptability', and 'feasibility', to 'fidelity' to the model, implementation cost, and the degree to which changes have penetrated the organization and are sustainable (Proctor et al. 2011). While organizational development scholars have produced profound insights into the organizational change process, the models developed around how to implement EBPs within an organization have been criticized for being too one-way. With too much focus on getting research into practice with not much effort to get practice into research (Green 2008; Willis and Mastrofski 2018).

Balancing Values. We now turn to another layer of complexity – managing values. In other words, how does a supervision officer know the right thing to do? The Executive Session on Community Corrections included members from all over the community corrections spectrum such as practitioners, academics, advocates, and others. Together, this Executive Session published a consensus document calling for a new punishment paradigm. The consensus document laid out five guiding values and their associated paradigm shifts. The goal of the document is to re-orient community corrections to its responsibilities as a democratic institution and all of the normative values that it entails. To that end, the document lays out the following core values of community corrections agencies: first, the number one mission of community corrections is the 'well-being and safety of American communities'. While at first blush this may seem like the same public safety rhetoric dominating the justice system for the past several decades, the Committee goes on to describe that community well-being entails, 'stability in everyday life, rooted in the social bonds of neighborhoods and families that allow individuals to flourish' (p. 2). This broad view of community deviates from the hyper-focus on the individual person that has dominated corrections for decades. Second, the Committee notes the need to use state power to arrest, discipline, and incarcerate 'parsimoniously and justly'. Officers must balance promoting public safety, holding individuals accountable, and giving justice to those affected by crime with 'the possibility of harm to the individuals, their families, communities, and the foundational principles of our democracy' (p. 2). After all, part of the fundamental goal of community corrections is strengthening the social bonds of neighbourhoods and families. Third, community corrections should recognize the worth of justice-involved individuals. In doing so, officers should facilitate individuals' success, integration into community life, and repairing harm they may have caused. They note that doing these things, 'restores human agency and dignity, a sense of control over one's destiny, and helps individuals promote the sustained well-being of their families and communities, over time and across generations' (p. 2). Fourth, community supervision agencies must hold themselves to a high standard of democratic excellence, meaning they follow the rule of law, respect human dignity, and treat individuals under supervision as citizens in a democratic society. This means they do not impose arbitrary treatment, treat people with disrespect, or abuse their power. The Committee also emphasizes the need to build community trust and be viewed as fair and legitimate. To do this the Committee advocates for agencies to mobilize and engage community residents as 'co-producers of justice'. And finally, the Committee expands the commonly espoused goals of community supervision (i.e. harm reduction, order maintenance, and shrinking the size of the justice system) to establish that the aspiration of community corrections should be to infuse justice and fairness into the broader criminal justice system. One overarching theme of the consensus document is that the criminal justice system, and community corrections specifically, does not and should not exist outside of American communities but rather part and parcel of them.

What does this mean for supervision, and specifically for officers? As stated earlier, this means that officers must balance strengthening communities and families with individual-level public safety concerns along and with other ideals such as accountability and justice. They must prioritize an individual's agency while also aspiring to help people become better 'parents, siblings, neighbors and citizens' (p. 2). They must facilitate success and integration into community life with an involuntary population while steering clear of arbitrary treatment, disrespect, and abuses of power. Officers must make decisions about what to do with individuals on their caseload and that involves managing conflicting values. For example, how do you balance restoring individual agency with the need for unwanted treatment? Or, what if a decision to uphold accountability destabilizes a family? Additionally, while the Committee lays out these core values of community supervision, this document remains aspirational. Each agency will have its own mission and values meant to guide correctional practice, and each officer will come to their jobs with their own set of values and beliefs (many of which may remain latent or unexplored). These dilemmas can also be part of the coaching conversation.

Coaching the (reflective) practitioner

The preceding discussion suggests the need for officers to engage in 'sense-making' as a routine part of their job (Weick et al. 2005). With or without a risk/need assessment, officers encounter on a day-to-day basis all of the issues with which clients present. They hear the faulty logic and risky thinking of clients even if they do not have a name for it. They see the patterns of drug use and family drama even if they do not have a substance use screener to measure severity of use. They also see the role larger social issues play in the concentrated disadvantage of certain populations or areas. Every day, officers experience small and large successes and failures that start accumulating in their mind as data to be drawn from in future uncertain situations. All of this is to say that experience is important. But, experience alone is insufficient. Experiences are filtered by the individual officers' pre-existing mental models which consist of their values, goals, purposes, interests, and tacit knowledge (Argyis and Schön 1974; Edmondson and Moingeon 1998; Senge 1998). And as Schön (1983) explains, experience is contingent on a person's ability or opportunity to reflect-in-action.

In *The Reflective Practitioner*, Donald Schön explains the difference between practices that stick to research-based theory and those that do not:

> In the varied topography of professional practice, there is a high, hard ground where practitioners can make effective use of research-based theory and technique, and there is a swampy lowland where situations are confusing 'messes' incapable of technical solution. The difficulty is that the problems of the high ground, however great their technical interest,

are often relatively unimportant to clients or to the larger society, while in the swamp are the problems of greatest human concern. Shall the practitioner stay on the high, hard ground where he can practice rigorously, as he understands rigor, but where he is constrained to deal with problems of relatively little social importance? Or shall he descend to the swamp where he can engage the most important and challenging problems if he is willing to forsake technical rigor?

(Schön 1983: 42)

The risk/need assessment is a first step in understanding individuals under supervision but in and of itself is not enough to truly guide officers on what to do with a person in a given situation. While the interview process of a risk/need assessment presents an opportunity to make sense of complex phenomena, the prevailing conception of risk/need assessments has been mostly relegated to the 'high, hard ground' of professional practice. However, the day-to-day work of a supervision officer happens in the 'swampy lowlands'.

Schön (1983) explains how professionals practice in the 'swampy lowlands' by knowing-in-action, reflection-in-action, and reflection-on-action. Briefly, knowing-in-action is the tacit understanding that drives actions which we do not think so much about but rather just do. Reflection-in-action is triggered by the experience of being surprised as we go about our jobs. Schön (1983) argues, because professional practice includes an element of repetition, the professional's knowing-in-action, 'tends to become increasingly tacit, spontaneous, and automatic' (p. 60). This tendency towards more tacit and spontaneous practices makes it more likely for practitioners to miss opportunities to think about what they are doing and they consequently may find themselves, 'drawn into patterns of error which he cannot correct'. Often the practitioner becomes 'selectively inattentive to phenomena', a state in which the practitioner has 'over-learned' what he knows. The great role of reflection lies in staving off this dangerous state of over-learning in which a practitioner becomes locked into a view of themselves as technical experts.

Schön (1983) describes the process of reflection-in-action in the following steps. First, the practitioner sets or frames the problem in such a way that it lends itself to a method of enquiry that he or she feels able to explore. In trying to solve the problem the reflective practitioner seeks to both understand and change the situation. The practitioner elicits new stories and probes them, 'He tests his evolving understanding and at the same time draws out new phenomena which alters his experience of the situation' (p. 134). In doing this practitioners draw on the fundamental values and theories to which they ascribe. They are successful if their reflection leads to a continuation of the reflective conversation or a change they wanted to see. Importantly, to inform the problem setting and subsequent reflecting the practitioner uses past experience, a 'repertoire of examples, images, understandings, and actions' (p. 138) to contrast with the current experience. This information is crucial to giving the reflective practitioner a 'feel for problems that do not fit existing rules'. So, during the act of reflection practitioners frame a problem based on how the situation differs from previous similar experiences, but do so in a way that they can envision a solution to the problem. They develop a hypothesis and then tests to see if their hypothesis is confirmed. But unlike the objective and removed hypothesis testing of controlled studies, they understand the situation by trying to change it. Essentially, reflective practitioners seek to make the situation conform to their hypothesis, but importantly, remain open to the possibility that it will not, thus avoiding self-fulling prophecy.[7]

So, what does this mean for the coaching relationship? A coach and an officer can reflect on a client contact by creating a 'virtual world' in which they can slow down time, dissect the supervision contact, and hypothesize about the problem behaviour (Schön 1983: 157). This type of reflection-in-action via a virtual world is imperative for supervision officers attempting to become change agents who understand a person's dynamic risk factors and attempt to change behaviour using skills rooted in cognitive behavioural therapy. This type of dialogue between coach and officer ensures that officers are exposed to the opportunity for surprises, as the opportunity to encounter surprises during a supervision contact depends heavily on how willing the officer is to ask questions, dig deeper, set the stage for being surprised, and use discretion to assist the individual in areas that may be outside of public safety (i.e. grief management, food insecurity, housing, etc.). If officers are to become change agents, then they must set the stage for change in duties. This may mean deviating from the official conditions of supervision when those conditions do not broach or align with an individual's criminogenic needs (e.g. sending all drug offenders to some type of drug treatment). And, officers must be willing to drill down when supervision conditions only touch on dynamic risk factors with a vague direction such as 'stay away from antisocial peers'. Agencies do not generally provide guidance on what an officer should talk to a client about. The result is a lot of contacts that look very similar and rarely get past the most perfunctory discussion. This repetition makes officers vulnerable to 'over-learning', which can impede growth in their professional practice.

Reflective conversations are meant to surface and criticize the generally unexamined assumptions or values that impact why an officer does what he or she does. Through conversations with a coach, officers can better reflect on and conceptualize the individuals on their caseloads. They can also explore possibly competing values and choices. Here the coach can help officers explore 'tension points' where old values conflict with new information or where two values seem to be at odds. This reflection may give way to new values or a new way of thinking. The coach is a teacher and mirror. Engaging officers in a reflection exercise is needed to help build competency and capability.

Unlike the technology transfer metaphor of existing coaching models, a more fitting metaphor for a coaching model aimed at developing practical wisdom is the spinning wheel. Plying together the threads of science (risk factors, cognitive behavioural therapy), with individual experience (collecting particulars of a situation), and the guiding values of community corrections (e.g. community well-being, accountability, parsimony) the spinning wheel creates the fabric of supervision practice.

State of knowledge on coaching mechanisms

It seems fairly obvious that having a coach with whom to talk things out is key to developing professional practice, but what makes a person good in this role? What should a person do to ensure that a practitioner is developing critical thinking skills, improving their use of behaviour change practices, and strengthening practical judgement? Much of the research on coaching has been summed up by scholars with the National Implementation Research Network (NIRN), which designated coaching as a key implementation driver. In their education material for organizations they note that coaching is necessary for 'developing skill, judgment, and the artful and individualized use of the new practices or programs'. In their seminal synthesis of implementation research, Fixsen et al. (2005; National Implementation Research Network 2018) conclude with confidence that coaching is crucial to improving knowledge uptake and the use of skills among staff. Yet, beyond the general efficacy of coaching, Fixsen et al. (2005) note that having found no experimental analyses of the functional components of coaching, 'at this point, we know that coaching is important but we do not know (experimentally) what a coach should do or say with a practitioner to be most effective'[8] (p. 46). Fixsen et al. (2005) conclude that the core coaching components seem to be: (1) teaching and reinforcing evidence-based skill development, and (2) adaptations of skills and craft knowledge to fit the personal styles of the practitioners.

One of the most commonly cited reports in support of coaching is a chapter from Bruce Joyce and Barbara Showers's book *Student Achievement Through Staff Development* (2002). Chapter 5, 'Designing Training and Peer Coaching', summarizes a 'rough estimate' of the relationship between training components (study of theory, demonstrations, practice, and coaching) and outcomes (knowledge, skill, transfer). Extrapolating from the research and making judgements from their own extensive experience, the authors provide a table indicating that when trainings include practice and feedback in the training, 5% of participants could be expected to demonstrate the skills in use. When after-training coaching is added, 95% of participants could be expected to demonstrate the skills in use (78). It should be noted that Joyce and Showers support a peer coaching model for teachers that does not involve feedback. It also turns the typical coaching model on its head by having the coach in the role of observer with the coach doing the actual teaching.

A recent experiment in post-training coaching in juvenile justice environments illustrates key features of effective coaching strategies. Taxman and colleagues (2014) randomly assigned four officers in 12 juvenile justice agencies to one of three conditions following a two-day training session on using risk-need information in case planning: (1) creating juvenile justice experts in an office via external facilitators; (2) using booster sessions to refresh the training material; and (3) no post-training coaching except for management memo directing staff to use the risk-need tool information in case plans. External facilitators both developed the in-house juvenile justice experts and delivered the booster sessions. Each office received four on-site booster sessions. The results of the experiment found that the creation of internal juvenile justice experts in case planning, including addressing the social climate to support the new innovation, improved officer perception of the organization and perception of support for the agency (Taxman et al. 2014) and reduced rearrests (Young et al. 2013) compared to the booster sessions or management initiatives. Interestingly, neither the booster sessions or management initiatives had a statistically significant impact on officer perception of the agency or support for the initiative. This randomized study is one effort to illustrate the importance of coaching which supports more reflective practice, rather than merely re-education.

Recommendations for a new coaching model

Accounting for the preceding concerns for a coaching model that addresses feasibility issues and incorporates a wider role for coaches we turn to the work of Derek Milne, and his empirical research on clinical supervision within the field of psychology. Milne (2017) has worked to distil effective components of facilitating professional development of new psychologists (Milne et al. 2008; Milne and James 2000; Milne and Reiser 2017). Milne and Reiser (2017) synthesize the literature on evidence-based clinical supervision and specifically the development of therapists' use of cognitive behavioural therapy. This model is particularly suited for these new evidence-based community supervision models which are rooted in social learning theory and require staff to use skills based on cognitive behavioural therapy.

Milne (2017) offers a theory-based conceptualization of clinical supervision practices supported with the findings from a best-evidence synthesis. Milne et al. (2008) reviewed the literature using a best-evidence synthesis approach in which the authors gleaned best clinical supervision practices from studies that showed an improvement in clinician skills. From this, 26 clinical supervision techniques across 24 studies were identified as well as the mechanisms of action to improve clinician practice. These identified mechanisms of action mapped onto David Kolb's (1984) components of the experiential learning cycle – experiencing, reflecting, conceptualizing, and experimenting. Experiential learning theory states that, 'Learning is the process whereby knowledge is created through the transformation of experience. Knowledge results from the combination of grasping experience and transforming it' (Kolb 1984: 41). Experiential learning theory is best described by the following characteristics as laid out in Kolb's *Experiential Learning: Experience as the Source of Learning and Development*. First, learning is a process, 'Ideas are not fixed and immutable elements of thought but are formed and reformed through experience' (p. 28). Second, learning is grounded in experience 'new ideas stem from the conflict with old beliefs that are inconsistent with them' (p. 28). Third, the process of learning involves resolving conflicts between two dialectically opposed modes of adapting to the word – the conflict between concrete experience and abstract thought and the conflict between contemplating and doing (p. 29). Fourth, learning includes the central elements of experience, reflection, conceptualization, and active experimentation. Fifth, learning involves transactions between the person and the environment. And, sixth, learning is the process of creating knowledge and should be regarded as an oscillation between subjective and objective experiences.

Milne has worked to enhance clinical supervision by clarifying a conceptual model, improving measurement of practices, conducting evaluations, and developing a supervisor development training. To evaluate the competency of clinical supervisors, Milne et al. (2011) developed the Supervision: Adherence and Guidance Evaluation (SAGE). The components of the SAGE form the crux of the coaching components of the coaching model presented here. These components answer the question posed earlier, what makes a person good at coaching? In short, use of the coaching skills outlined below are hypothesized to make a person good at coaching. To understand their applicability to coaching in evidence-based community supervision, it is worth investigating each method as it would apply to coaching officers in community supervision.

1   **Observations and needs assessment.** Coaching should begin with a needs assessment (an understanding of where the officer stands in their level of skill or expertise) and ongoing coaching is most effective when the coach can see the officer operating in real time. Understanding where an officer is in the learning process of using best practices is critical to guide coaching efforts, and the best way to decipher where along the learning continuum an officer may be is to observe them.

2   **Agenda-setting.** Setting goals helps guide the coaching effort. This bridges the needs assessment phase with the coaching process and provides a benchmark against which to evaluate whether the coaching worked to improve officer competency and capability. Goals should be set collaboratively with the officer. This process can also help motivate officers to be involved in the coaching process.

3   **Questioning.** If facilitating individual learning is the crux of coaching, then the use of questions could be considered the crux of facilitating individual learning. Questions serve many purposes, not least of which to encourage reflection. As noted by Yanow and Tsoukas (2009) regarding the process of reflection, 'Such openness requires making one's thinking transparent. . . , which entails setting aside one's ego, as one may not have all the knowledge (or answers) necessary to comprehend a situation (i.e. reflective practice rests on a learned capacity to raise questions, including of oneself, more than on an ability to provide answers)' (p. 1359).

4   **Formulating.** A case formulation can help bridge the risk/need assessment with a case plan. Formulating creates a narrative of developmental, triggering, and maintaining factors of client problems. Tying together the predisposing factors (vulnerabilities), precipitating factors (triggers), perpetuating factors (maintenance), and protective factors in a coherent narrative allows officers to depict the aetiology of dynamic risk factors to predict possible futures and to better individualize treatment plans (Palmer 2016; Vess and Ward 2011).

5   **Prompting.** Prompting involves knowing when to give reminders or cues. This skill includes reminding the officer about relevant material by prompting and cueing them (e.g. 'sounds like your earlier point'). This can include repeating or rephrasing that contains a reference to stated or implied feelings (e.g. paraphrasing).

6   **Teaching, demonstrating, training/experimenting.** Effective coaching involves multiple methods of facilitating learning including symbolic (based on words), iconic (based on images), and enactive (based on actions).

7   **Managing.** An effective coach should scaffold learning. Specifically, the coach should build on the officer's existing knowledge and skills, structure, and pace activities to help the officer learn and get comfortable with new concepts or skills, and set up learning situations. Make sure the coaching session flows smoothly. The Dreyfus model of human learning divides the human learning process into five different levels – novice, advanced beginner, competent performer, proficient performer, and expert (Flyvbjerg 2001). While a review of this model is outside the scope of this chapter, the main takeaway is the placement of both reasoning based on formal logic, and intuition (gained from experience) within human learning. Essentially, a person starts out at the novice phase learning general rules, facts, and characteristics that they try to apply to particular situations, but as they gain more experience the rule-based application of knowledge gets pushed to the background as intuition comes to the foreground. In the model, rational, rule-based deliberation takes precedence in the first three levels (novice, advanced beginner, competent performer), but one cannot become really adept at performing a skill and move up to the top two levels (proficient performer and expert) without genuine human experience. As Flyvbjerg (2001) notes, 'The position of intuition is not beyond rationality but alongside it, complementary to it, and insofar as we speak of experts, above rationality' (p. 23). This understanding of human learning has important implications for coaching officers. Coaches must understand where a person is in his or her learning. A coach would not approach a novice the same way as an expert.

8   **Feedback.** Feedback should highlight gaps between what is expected/required and what has been demonstrated/observed. Feedback should facilitate self-assessment, engage the officer, energize the officer by setting SMART (specific, measurable, achievable, realistic, and time-based)

371

goals, involve dialogue, be backed up by reinforcement, identify next steps, clarify standards/expectation/gaps in performance, and explain how to close gaps (Milne and Reiser 2017: 157).

Additional coaching competencies include possessing knowledge of evidence-based practices, establishing a quality relationship with coaches, effective communication skills (particularly in sensitive conversations), and managing group coaching sessions.

Evaluating coaching models

A coaching model seeks to achieve the larger aim of staff professionalization via the following sub-goals: (1) improve supervisors' coaching skills, (2) improve front-line officers' use of Core Correctional Practices, and (3) improve decision-making of front-line officers. Milne and Reiser (2017) suggest six successive steps to systematically evaluating a coaching intervention. To this point, this chapter has been preoccupied with the first step specifying and justifying a model for the intervention. The next step is to carefully describe and standardize a coach's training with the aid of a training manual and set supervision guidelines. Steps 3–6 include the following: examine the quality of coaching being delivered, examine how coaching is received by those being coached, examine how efforts may be impacting clients, establish a system of feedback on coaching efforts. Measures for steps 3–6 are outlined below.

Measurements

The **delivery of coaching** may be captured a number of ways. The most time-intensive and thorough being in-person observations of coaching sessions. To guide this effort Milne (2011) developed the Supervision: Adherence and Guidance Evaluation, which allows researchers to code the use of coaching skills. Coaching skills may also be captured via self-report, or case vignettes (Minoudis et al. 2013).

Receipt of coaching may include officers' reception to coaching as well as changes in officer professional development, with the latter being also be measured in a variety of ways such as observation of officer-client contact sessions, self-reported use of skills, vignette scoring, and survey items measuring things like changes in wisdom or ethical decision-making (Ardelt 2003; Rest 1975) and the former being measured via an 11 item survey scale – Rating of Experiential Learning and Components of Teaching and Supervision (REACTS) – developed by Milne (2011). In-person observations could be done with the aid of coding sheets that allow the observer to rate the use of skills. STICS, STARR, and EPICS all use such a coding sheet for the CCPs. Table 30.3 provides an example of 20 skills used in SOARING2. Observers rate the officer's

Table 30.3 In-person rating sheet for SOARING2

WORKING RELATIONSHIP SKILLS ($\alpha = 0.87$)

1 Expresses empathy towards the individual. (EMPATHY)

2 Demonstrates a firm but fair supervision style when working with the individual. (FIRM BUT FAIR)

3 Uses authoritative not authoritarian style with the probationer. (EFFECTIVE AUTHORITY)

4 Helps establish a mutual understanding of the purpose and expectations of supervision, the role of the officer, and the part the individual plays in the process. (ROLE CLARIFICATION)

5 Actively listens to what the individual has to say. (ACTIVE LISTENING)

ENGAGEMENT SKILLS ($\alpha = 0.79$)

6 Uses affirmations when appropriate. (AFFIRMATIONS)

7 Expresses confidence that the individual can be successful. (EXPRESSES CONFIDENCE)

8 Encourages individual participation in setting case plan goals. (GOAL ALIGNMENT)

9 Encourages and/or recognizes change talk. (PROMOTES CHANGE TALK)

10 Effectively reinforces compliance, accomplishments, and/or pro-social behaviour. (PROVIDES REINFORCEMENT)

RISK ASSESSMENT AND MANAGEMENT SKILLS ($\alpha = 0.86$)

11 Effectively completes risk/need assessment to get accurate information to inform case plan. (RISK/NEED ASSESSMENT)

12 Effectively discusses and addresses criminogenic needs. (CRIM NEEDS)

13 Addresses changes in an individual's dynamic risk factors that may increase the risk of reoffending. (ACUTE RISK)

14 Helps individual manage triggers. (TRIGGERS)

15 Reinforces stabilizing influences in individual's life. (STABILIZERS)

PROBLEM SOLVING SKILLS ($\alpha = 0.83$)

16 Effectively identifies problem and elicits individual's goals in solving problem. (IDENTIFIES PROBLEM)

17 Elicits from individual immediate, short-term solutions for change that can be realistically completed before the next session. (EXPLORES SHORT-TERM SOLUTIONS)

18 Encourages the individual to examine the pros and cons of possible solutions (or pros and cons of maintaining status quo if individual is reluctant to acknowledge underlying problems). (PROS AND CONS)

19 Helps the individual develop an action plan to achieve goals via the identified solution. (ACTION PLAN)

20 Helps the individual understand the actions, thoughts, and feelings that lead to negative outcomes or criminal behaviour. (BEHAVIOURAL OFFENCE CHAIN)

Source: Center for Advancing Correctional Excellence 2017

use of skills on a rating scale of 0–3 with 0 indicating that the officer had an opportunity to use a skill and simply did not do it, 1 indicating that the officer used the skill but needs significant improvement, 2 indicating that the officer used the skill well but could still use improvement, and 3 indicating that the officer performed mastery use of the skill. The SOARING2 in-person observation rating form has demonstrated good internal validity of the four skill categories it captures: Risk Management ($\alpha = 0.86$), Engagement Skills ($\alpha = 0.79$) Problem Solving Skills ($\alpha = 0.83$), and Working Relationship Skills ($\alpha = 0.87$) (Donohoe et al. 2017, June).

The SAGE also includes a component for assessing officer receipt of coaching. If a coach is using the skills outlined above, if a coach is asking probing questions, helping the officer formulate a narrative of the individual on their case load, prompting the officer when needed to help make connections, then we would expect to see the officer engage in the following methods of experiential learning (see Table 30.4). These can be coded via an in-person observation of a coaching session.

Table 30.4 Indications of officer experiential learning

Reflecting

An officer summarizes relevant events and offer their personal understanding (e.g. describing what happened in the contact session). They actively and explicitly draw on their personal experiences, understanding, and history to make sense of these events. Officer reflecting effectively shows signs of integrating material, assimilating things into a reasoned understanding, and of developing their own understanding.

Conceptualizing

The officer integrates public information with their personal understanding (e.g. realizing how a theory or research finding pulls events together into a clearer formulation). Officers actively conceptualize work to develop a deeper/ richer understanding of relevant material (e.g. asking procedural questions), as opposed to merely labelling it or describing it; using technical terms/concepts to better grasp/comprehend; seeking insight. Officer indicates signs of assimilating information, reasoning something through, integrating material to make sense.

Planning

An officer shows ability to draw on their own understanding to plan relevant action, including problem-solving and decision-making, possibly jointly with coach. Barriers/obstacles/challenges to actions noted and addressed.

Experiencing

The officer processes emotional material. For example, the officer indicates being aware of current sensations; recognizes/identifies/labels own feelings; demonstrates intuition; is in the 'here and now' moment; is aware of emotional or sensory accompaniments to activity (whether in relation to the experience of the supervision, or to discussing their work in supervision). The function of experiencing is to aid the supervisee in grasping (understanding) their sensory/ affective experiences, in supervision and in relation to the material provided in supervision (e.g. recounting incidents in therapy).

And finally, in the cascade of outcomes are those of the client typically measured as further involvement with the criminal justice system. However, capturing **client outcomes** should expand beyond rearrest, reconviction, or re-incarceration to include changes in risk factors, or strengths. For example, days sober, improvements in family dynamics, more pro-social connections, new ways of thinking, just to name a few. Client outcomes should be measured by reassessments of the risk/need assessment as well as specialized forms to capture important short-term goals or stability factors.

Establishing a **system of feedback** is also crucial to studying the implementation of a coaching model. Efforts to study coaching must include a qualitative component that attempts to understand the lived experience of practitioners. To better understand the components of coaching and how they work in actual practice it is necessary to conduct qualitative interviews with both coaches and officers. The interviews should focus on how coaches experienced the training and used the coaching skills in practice, as well as how officers 'received' the coaching (Johnston and Milne 2012). These interviews should contribute to changes in the programme or training when appropriate.

Conclusion

In sum, the nature of what evidence-based supervision models demand of staff and agencies requires attention to the learning process and curricula that better equips supervisors with the necessary skills to incorporate a coaching role into their existing management functions. Core Correctional Practices are psychological practices aimed at changing behaviour. Much of the evidence of their effectiveness comes from group-based, treatment programs; however, RNR scholar Guy Bourgeon and colleagues (2012) note that despite this, 'it is reasonable to expect that these principles are also relevant in the case of one-on-one supervision of offenders in the community' (p. 237). This line of reasoning, combined with growing empirical data on what works to change problem behaviour, and a recognition that traditional supervision practices are little to no better at changing behaviour than having no supervision at all have worked to inflame the popularity of the RNR model (Bonta et al. 2007). However, forgoing methods to integrate science with craft paints a bleak future for the landscape of correctional practice. A leading RNR scholar, Guy Bourgon (2013), likened front-line community supervision officers tasked with taking on new evidence-based skills to foot a soldier in a battle 'who has marched into the battlefield and, tired, weary, and burdened with the ever-changing orders from the generals, *must make crucial decisions all alone*, the community supervision officer "follows" the orders of management' (p. 33, emphasis added). The fact that officers must make crucial decisions all alone, speaks to the need for a method of encouraging critical reflection on practice to improve decision-making and deepen understanding.

Trainers continually bemoan the 'train and hope' method nearly universally employed by most organizations. And yet, the response is typically some sort of additional training sessions that just touches on a concept not explicitly acknowledged – that learners must integrate new knowledge into existing knowledge. Coaching as conceptualized here is defined as an accountable, two-way process, which supports, motivates, and enables the development of good practice for individual correctional workers (Care Council Wales 2011). Coaching that effectively integrates science with craft requires turning experience into knowledge. While the RNR model ostensibly provides guidance to correctional workers on what to do with clients, there remains an enormous need for discretion by the correctional worker. While experience is important, experience alone is far from enough. Coaching professional staff on skills makes sense in light of theories of learning which holds the importance of developing practical wisdom or phronesis.[9] Spouse (2001) notes, 'Without such adaptation of epistemic knowledge, their practice carries imprints of beliefs and values that may bear little relationship with research into effective practice' (p.1).

A coach's role is to improve the probation officer's ability to be a change agent and improve their procedural knowledge, or when to do what. This entails leveraging epistemic knowledge of psychology to understand the individuals on their caseload while also embodying state-sanctioned authority to punish. A coach helps officers learn techniques and skills not in a one-way teacher/student relationship but in a two-way process in which the officer's own experiences create knowledge. A coach also helps officers reflect on values exemplified in particular situations and bridge the gap between the technical-rational and the lived experience of probation officers. As Willis and Mastrofski (2018) so succinctly put it in discussing evidence-based policing,

> To this point, evidence-based policing, similar to evidence-based medicine, has tried to persuade others through the strength and consistency of its arguments on the benefits of scientific research, yet in doing so the needs, habits, and interests of practitioners have been mostly overlooked, underrepresented, or devalued.
>
> (p. 28)

The same sentiment holds for evidence-based supervision. It is clear that reflecting on and enriching officer experience is not only the right thing to do but absolutely necessary if evidence-based practices are to become officers' reality. The practical wisdom of knowing what to do when in complex situations requires a marriage of empirical science with finely honed intuition.

Notes

1 It was estimated that over a third of agencies used a risk tool in 2007 (Taxman et al. 2007) whereas it is not estimated that most agencies use some type of tool (Council of State Government 2018).

2 The authors of RNR and STICS refer to "clinical supervision" as it is referenced in the field psychology. Other supervision models such as PCS, STARR, EPICS, and SUSTAIN refer to 'coaching'. While the two can be thought of as distinct practices, for the purposes of this chapter the goal of both 'clinical supervision' and 'coaching' refer to similar efforts to improve the skills and professional practice of correctional workers.

3 The SOARING2 curriculum is now out of print. The training has been updated with a coaching model that reflects the one advanced in this chapter. The new training is called SUSTAIN.

4 Monthly meeting points were calculated by multiplying points for attendance (5 or fewer meetings=1, 6 or more meetings=2) by a qualitative participation rating assigned by the trainers. Total scores of less than or equal to 3 were assigned a score of 1 for the monthly meeting variable. Total scores higher than 3 were assigned a score of 2 for the monthly meeting variable. For feedback, officers were awarded 2 points when they received feedback on two or more audiotapes, 1 point when they received feedback on one audiotape, and no points if they did not receive any feedback. The third item, Refresher Course, provided officers with 1 point if they attended the refresher course and no points if they did not attend the refresher course.

5 This conceptualization comes from RNR architects Bonta and Andrews (2016). For a review of issues related to the various risk/need assessment instruments see Via et al. (2016).

6 A notable exception is the work of Tony Ward and Shadd Maruna, which calls into question the causal mechanisms in the dynamic risk factors and the RNR model's utility for guiding rehabilitative efforts (see Ward and Maruna 2007).

7 Some scholars have found Schön's conception of reflection in action too cognitive, too separated from a state of being, as if it is an altogether deliberative mental process. Those taking a phenomenological approach have expanded Schön's original conception of 'reflection-in-action' as less a thinking (cognitive) exercise and more so as a being exercise. In other words, being surprised and reacting takes place while one is absorbed in the world and this process of reflection-in-action moves from total absorption to a more deliberate cognitive process depending on the severity of the surprise (Yanow et al. 2009).

8 They do, however, note various factors that can impact coaching. This includes time spent coaching (Diamond et al. 2002; Marks and Gersten 1998; Schoenwald et al. 2000; Kavanagh et al. 2003); the availability of coaches who are expert in the content, techniques, and rationales of the programme, time allotted to do the work, reluctance to seek information from the mentor, role confusion due to the dual role of supervisor and coach, feelings of inadequacy on the part of the mentors, poor match between the coach and practitioner, and lack of availability of coaches in rural areas (McCormick and Brennan 2001); leadership, organizational culture, labor-relations, scheduling, interpersonal relationships, and engagement in participatory planning (Joyce and Showers 2002); training for coaches and organizational leadership (Marks and Gersten 1998); high caseloads and inadequately trained supervisors (Kavanagh et al. 2003); lack of information and skills, lack of time, inadequate staff resources, and a focus on paperwork instead of outcomes (Bond et al., 2001).

9 Scholars have noted the various conceptions of phronesis. For a thorough explanation see.

References

Ardelt (2004) Wisdom as expert knowledge system: A critical review of a contemporary operationalization of an ancient concept. *Human Development*, 47(5), 257–285.

Alexander, M., Palombo, L., Cameron, E. and Wooten, E. (2013) Coaching: The true path to proficiency, from an officer's perspective. *Federal Probation*, 77(2), 64.

Ardelt, M. (2003) Empirical assessment of a three-dimensional wisdom scale. *Research on Aging*, 25(3), 275–324.

Ardelt, M. (2004) Wisdom as expert knowledge system: A critical review of a contemporary operationalization of an ancient concept. *Human Development*, 47(5), 257–285.

Argyris, C. and Schön, D. (1974) *Theory in Practice: Increasing Professional Effectiveness*. San Francisco, CA: Jossey-Bass Publishers.

Bond, G. R., Becker, D. R., Drake, R. E., Rapp, C. A., Meisler, N., Lehman, A. F. et al. (2001) Implementing supported employment as an evidence-based practice. *Psychiatric Services*, 52(3), 313–322.

Bonta, J. and Andrews, D. A. (2007). Risk-need-responsivity model for offender assessment and rehabilitation. *Rehabilitation*, 6(1), 1–22.

Bonta, J. and Andrews, D. A. (2016) *The Psychology of Criminal Conduct*. New York: Routledge.

Bonta, J., Bourgon, G. and Rugge, T. (2017) From evidence-informed to evidence-based: The Strategic training initiative in community supervision. In J. Annison, P. Raynor and P. Ugwudike (Eds.), *Evidence-Based Skills in Criminal Justice: International Research on Supporting Rehabilitation and Desistance*. Bristol and Chicago: Policy Press, p. 169.

Bonta, J., Bourgon, G., Rugge, T., Scott, T. L., Yessine, A. K., Gutierrez, L. K. and Li, J. (2010) *The Strategic Training Initiative in Community Supervision: Risk-Need-Responsivity in the Real World 2010–01*. Ottawa: Public Safety Canada.

Bonta, J., Bourgon, G., Rugge, T., Scott, T. L., Yessine, A. K., Gutierrez, L. and Li, J. (2011) An experimental demonstration of training probation officers in evidence-based community supervision. *Criminal Justice and Behavior*, 38(11), 1127–1148.

Bosker, J., Witteman, C. and Hermanns, J. (2013) Structured decisions about Dutch probation service interventions. *Probation Journal*, 60(2), 168–176.

Bourgon, G. (2013) The demands on probation officers in the evolution of evidence-based practice: The forgotten foot soldier of community corrections. *Federal Probation*, 77, 30.

Bourgon, G., Gutierrez, L. and Ashton, J. (2012) The evolution of community supervision practice: The transformation from case manager to change agent. *Federal Probation*, 76(2), 27–35, 56. Available at: http://search.proquest.com/docview/1223859853/.

Care Council Wales. (2011) *Supervising and Appraising Well: A Guide to Effective Supervision and Appraisal. Care Council Wales*. [Online]. Available at: www.daycaretrust.org.uk/data/files/Projects/Volunteering/Supervising_and_Appraising_Well.pdf.

Center for Advancing Correctional Excellence. (2017, September 1) SUSTAIN In-Person Observation Scoring Guide.

Chadwick, N., Dewolf, A. and Serin, R. (2015) Effectively training community supervision officers: A meta-analytic review of the impact on offender outcome. *Criminal Justice and Behavior*, 42(10), 977–989. https://doi.org/10.1177/0093854815595661.

Clodfelter, T., Holcomb, J., Alexander, M., Marcum, C. and Richards, T. (2016) A case study of the implementation of Staff Training Aimed at Reducing Rearrest (STARR). *Federal Probation*, 80(1), 30–38, 71.

Costa Jr, P. T. and McCrae, R. R. (1992) Four ways five factors are basic. *Personality and Individual Differences*, 13(6), 653–665.

Council of State Government. (2018) *Infographic: The Importance of Implementing Risk and Needs Assessments Successfully*. New York. Available at: https://csgjusticecenter.org/nrrc/publications/infographic-the-importance-of-implementing-risk-and-needs-assessments-successfully/.

Diamond, G., Godley, S. H., Liddle, H. A., Sampl, S., Webb, C., Tims, F. M., et al. (2002) Five outpatient treatment models for adolescent marijuana use: A description of the Cannabis Youth Treatment Interventions. *Addiction*, 97(s1), 70–83.

Donohoe, C., Hiller, M. and Belenko, S. (2017) *Summary of Findings from APPD Staff Focus Groups: Initial In-Depth Analyses.* Philadelphia, PA: BJA Stakeholder Meeting, June.

Dowden, C. and Andrews, D. A. (2004) The importance of staff practice in delivering effective correctional treatment: A meta-analytic review of core correctional practice. *International Journal of Offender Therapy and Comparative Criminology*, 48(2), 203–214.

Edmondson, A. and Moingeon, B. (1998) From organizational learning to the learning organization. *Management Learning*, 29(1), 5–20.

Fixsen, D. L., Naoom, S. F., I, K. A., Friedman, R. M. and Wallace, F. (2005) *Implementation Research: A Synthesis of the Literature.* Tampa, FL: University of South Florida, Louis de la Parte Florida Mental Health Institute, The National Implementation Research Network (FMHI Publication #231).

Flyvbjerg, B. (2001) *Making Social Science Matter: Why Social Inquiry Fails and How It Can Succeed Again.* Cambridge: Cambridge University Press.

Green, L. W. (2008) Making research relevant: If it is an evidence-based practice, where's the practice-based evidence? *Family Practice*, 25(Supplement 1), i20–i24.

Johnston, L. H. and Milne, D. L. (2012) How do supervisee's learn during supervision? A grounded theory study of the perceived developmental process. *The Cognitive Behaviour Therapist*, 5(1), 1–23.

Jones, S. E., Miller, J. D. and Lynam, D. R. (2011) Personality, antisocial behavior, and aggression: A meta-analytic review. *Journal of Criminal Justice*, 39(4), 329–337.

Joyce, B. and Showers, B. (2002) *Student Achievement Through Staff Development*, 3rd edition. Alexandria, VA: Association for Supervision and Curriculum Development.

Kadushin, A. and Harkness, D. (2014) *Supervision in Social Work*, 5th edition. New York: Columbia University Press.

Kavanagh, D. J., Spence, S. H., Strong, J., Wilson, J., Sturk, H. and Crow, N. (2003) Supervision practices in allied mental health: Relationships of supervision characteristics to perceived impact and job satisfaction. *Mental Health Services Research*, 5(4), 187–195.

Kolb, D. A. (1984) *Experiential Learning: Experience as the Source of Learning and Development.* Englewood Cliffs: Prentice-Hall.

Labrecque, R. and Smith, P. (2017) Does training and coaching matter? An 18-month evaluation of a community supervision model. *Victims & Offenders*, 12(2), 233–252.

Landenberger, N. and Lipsey, M. (2005) The positive effects of cognitive – behavioral programs for offenders: A meta-analysis of factors associated with effective treatment. *Journal of Experimental Criminology*, 1(4), 451–476. https://doi.org/10.1007/s11292-005-3541-7.

Latessa, E. J., Smith, P., Schweitzer, M. and Labrecque, R. (2013) *Evaluation of the Effective Practices in Community Supervision Model (EPICS) in Ohio.* Cincinnati, OH: University of Cincinnati, School of Criminal Justice.

Lowenkamp, M. S., Robinson, C. R., Koutsenok, I., and Lowenkamp, C. T. (2012) The importance of coaching: A brief survey of probation officers. *Federal Probation*, 76, 36.

Maass, S. A., Taxman, F. S., Eby, K., Johnson, D. and Wilson, D. (2017) *Individual, Organizational, and Training Design Influences on Supervision Staff's Knowledge and Use of Evidence-Based Practices.* ProQuest Dissertations Publishing. Available at: http://search.proquest.com/docview/1937522745/.

Maass, S. A., Taxman, F. S., Serin, R., Crites, E., Watson, C. A. and Lloyd, C. (2013) *SOARING 2: An Elearning Training Program to Improve Knowledge of EBPs.* Paper Presented at the American Society of Criminology Annual Conference.

Marks, S. U. and Gersten, R. (1998) Engagement and disengagement between special and general educators: An application of Miles and Huberman's cross-case analysis. *Learning Disability Quarterly*, 21(1), 34–56.

McCormick, K. M. and Brennan, S. (2001) Mentoring the new professional in interdisciplinary early childhood education: The Kentucky Teacher Internship Program. *Topics in Early Childhood Special Education*, 21(3), 131–144.

Milne, D. L. (2011) *Evidence-Based CBT Supervision: Principles and Practice*, 2nd edition. Hoboken, NJ: Wiley.

Milne, D. L., Aylott, H., Fitzpatrick, H. and Ellis, M. V. (2008) How does clinical supervision work? Using a "best evidence synthesis" approach to construct a basic model of supervision. *The Clinical Supervisor*, 27(2), 170–190.

Milne, D. L. and James, I. (2000) A systematic review of effective cognitive-behavioural supervision. *British Journal of Clinical Psychology*, 39(2), 111–127.

Milne, D. L. and Reiser, R. P. (2017) *A Manual for Evidence-Based CBT Supervision*. Hoboken, NJ: John Wiley & Sons.

Milne, D. L., Reiser, R. P., Cliffe, T. and Raine, R. (2011) SAGE: Preliminary evaluation of an instrument for observing competence in CBT supervision. *The Cognitive Behaviour Therapist*, 4(4), 123–138.

Minoudis, P., Craissati, J., Shaw, J., McMurran, M., Freestone, M., Chuan, S. J. and Leonard, A. (2013) An evaluation of case formulation training and consultation with probation officers. *Criminal Behaviour and Mental Health*, 23(4), 252–262.

Mischel, W. (1969) Continuity and change in personality. *American Psychologist*, 24(11), 1012.

Mischel, W. and Shoda, Y. (2008) Toward a unified theory of personality. *Handbook of Personality: Theory and Research*, 3, 208–241.

National Implementation Science Network. Coaching. (2018) Available at: https://implementation.fpg.unc.edu/module-2/coaching Executive (Accessed 4 January 2018).

Oleson, J. C., VanBenschoten, S., Robinson, C., Lowenkamp, C. T. and Holsinger, A. M. (2012) Actuarial and clinical assessment of criminogenic needs: Identifying supervision priorities among federal probation officers. *Journal of Crime and Justice*, 35(2), 239–248.

Palmer, L. (2016) *Dynamic Risk Factors and their Utilisation in Case Formulation: A New Conceptual Framework*. (Unpublished master's thesis). Victoria University of Wellington, New Zealand.

Proctor, E., Silmere, H., Raghavan, R., Hovmand, P., Aarons, G., Bunger, A., Hensley, M. (2011) Outcomes for implementation research: Conceptual distinctions, measurement challenges, and research agenda. *Administration and Policy in Mental Health and Mental Health Services Research*, 38(2), 65–76. https://doi.org/10.1007/s10488-010-0319-7.

Rest, J. R. (1975) Longitudinal study of the defining issues test of moral judgment: A strategy for analyzing developmental change. *Developmental Psychology*, 11(6), 738.

Rhine, E. E., Mawhorr, T. L. and Parks, E. C. (2006) Implementation: The bane of effective correctional programs. *Criminology & Public Policy*, 5(2), 347–358.

Robinson, C. R., Lowenkamp, C. T., Holsinger, A. M., VanBenschoten, S., Alexander, M. and Oleson, J. C. (2012) A random study of Staff Training Aimed at Reducing Re-arrest (STARR): Using core correctional practices in probation interactions. *Journal of Crime and Justice*, 35(2), 167–188.

Robinson, C. R., VanBenschoten, S., Alexander, M. and Lowenkamp, C. T. (2011) A random (almost) study of Staff Training Aimed at Reducing Re-Arrest (STARR): Reducing recidivism through intentional design. *Federal Probation*, 75, 57.

Schoenwald, S. K., Sheidow, A. J. and Chapman, J. E. (2009) Clinical supervision in treatment transport: Effects on adherence and outcomes. *Journal of Consulting and Clinical Psychology*, 77(3), 410.

Schön, D. A. (1983) *The Reflective Practitioner: How Professionals Think in Action*. New York: Basic Books.

Senge, P. M. (1998) The leader's new work. *Leading Organizations*, 1, 439–457.

Session on Community Corrections. (2017) *Toward an Approach to Community Corrections for the 21st Century: Consensus Document of the Executive Session on Community Corrections*. Program in Criminal Justice Policy and Management, Harvard Kennedy School.

Schoenwald, S. K., Henggeler, S. W., Brondino, M. J. and Rowland, M. D. (2000) Multisystemic therapy: Monitoring treatment fidelity. *Family Process*, 39(1), 83–103.

Smith, P., Schweitzer, M., Labrecque, R. M. and Latessa, E. J. (2012) Improving probation officers' supervision skills: An evaluation of the EPICS model. *Journal of Crime and Justice*, 35(2), 189–199.

Spouse, J. (2001) Bridging theory and practice in the supervisory relationship: A sociocultural perspective. *Journal of Advanced Nursing*, 33(4), 512–522.

Taxman, F. S. (2008) No illusions: Offender and organizational change in Maryland's proactive community supervision efforts. *Criminology & Public Policy*, 7(2), 275–302.

Taxman, F. S. (2018) The partially clothed emperor: Evidence-based practices. *Journal of Contemporary Criminal Justice*, 34(1), 97–114.

Taxman, F. S., Henderson, C., Young, D. and Farrell, J. (2014) The impact of training interventions on organizational readiness to support innovations in juvenile justice offices. *Administration and Policy in Mental Health and Mental Health Services Research*, 41(2), 177–188.

Taxman, F. S., Perdoni, M. L. and Harrison, L. D. (2007) Drug treatment services for adult offenders: The state of the state. *Journal of Substance Abuse Treatment*, 32(3), 239–254.

Toronjo, H. and Taxman, F. S. (2017) Supervision face-to-face contacts: The emergence of an intervention. In J. Annison, P. Raynor and P. Ugwudike (Eds.), *Evidence-Based Skills in Criminal Justice: International Research on Supporting Rehabilitation and Desistance*. Bristol and Chicago: Policy Press, p. 217.

Trotter, C. (2015) *Working with Involuntary Clients: A Guide to Practice*, 3rd edition. Abingdon, Oxon: Routledge.

Vanbenschoten, S. (2008) Risk/needs assessment: Is this the best we can do? *Federal Probation*, 72(2), 38–42, 91. Available at: http://search.proquest.com/docview/2139 84321/.

Viglione, J. (2017) Street-level decision making: Acceptability, feasibility, and use of evidence-based practices in adult probation. *Criminal Justice and Behavior*, 44(10), 1356–1381.

Viglione, J., Rudes, D. S. and Taxman, F. S. (2015) Misalignment in supervision: Implementing risk/needs assessment instruments in probation. *Criminal Justice and Behavior*, 42(3), 263–285.

Ward, T. and Maruna, S. (2007) *Rehabilitation: Beyond the Risk Paradigm*. London: Routledge.

Ward, T., Melser, J. and Yates, P. M. (2007) Reconstructing the risk – need – responsivity model: A theoretical elaboration and evaluation. *Aggression and Violent Behavior*, 12(2), 208–228.

Willis, J. J. and Mastrofski, S. D. (2018) Improving policing by integrating craft and science: What can patrol officers teach us about good police work? *Policing and Society*, 28(1), 27–44.

Taxman, F. S. and Belenko, S. (2012) *Implementing Evidence-Based Practices in Community Corrections and Addiction Treatment*. New York: Springer.

Taxman, F. S., Henderson, C., Young, D. and Farrell, J. (2014) The impact of training interventions on organizational readiness to support innovations in juvenile justice offices. *Administration and Policy in Mental Health and Mental Health Services Research*, 41(2), 177–188.

Yanow, D. and Tsoukas, H. (2009) What is reflection-in-action? A phenomenological account. *Journal of Management Studies*, 46(8), 1339–1364.

Young, D. W., Farrell, J. L. and Taxman, F. S. (2013) Impacts of juvenile probation training models on youth recidivism. *Justice Quarterly*, 30(6), 1068–1089.

Vess, J. and Ward, T. (2011) Sexual offenses against children. *Forensic Case Formulation*, 173–193.

Via, B., Dezember, A. and Taxman, F. S. (2016) Exploring how to measure criminogenic needs: Five instruments and no real answers. In *Handbook on Risk and Need Assessment*. New York: Routledge, pp. 328–346.

Weick, K. E., Sutcliffe, K. M. and Obstfeld, D. (2005) Organizing and the process of sensemaking. *Organization Science*, 16(4), 409–421.

Willis, J. J.and Mastrofski, S. D. (2018) Improving policing by integrating craft and science: What can patrol officers teach us about good police work? *Policing and Society*, 28(1), 27–44.

Applications of psychotherapy in statutory domestic violence perpetrator programmes

31

Challenging the dominance of cognitive behavioural models

Nicole Renehan

Introduction

Domestic abuse is a global phenomenon which can have far reaching physical, psychological, and social consequences for its victims. It is estimated that one in four women in the UK will experience domestic abuse at some point in their lifetime and two women a week (on average) are killed by a current or former partner. In year ending 2017, 1.1 million domestic abuse-related incidents were recorded by the police in England and Wales, of which 43% were recorded as crimes (Ons 2017). 110,833 cases were referred to the Crown Prosecution Service (CPS) with 70,853 of court-processed cases resulting in successful prosecution. In the current year, 92% of defendants were male with the majority of incidents occurring within intimate heterosexual relationships. Men convicted of domestic abuse-related offences are often repeat offenders (Dobash et al. 1999a), thus domestic violence perpetrator programmes (DVPPs) have been established alongside other criminal justice sanctions which seek to rehabilitate partner-violent men.

The efficacy of such programmes, which are predominantly based on cognitive behavioural approaches has, however, long been debated (Morran 2011; Gadd and Jefferson 2007; Gadd 2004; Fox 1999) and, unfortunately, despite almost four decades of domestic abuse perpetrator rehabilitation, there is little consensus on what causes men to be violent towards their partners let alone what such interventions should 'look like'. This chapter aims to contribute to existing knowledge by highlighting alternative psychotherapeutic approaches that are used to rehabilitate partner-violent men which challenge the dominance of cognitive behavioural interventions. Drawing specifically on psychodynamic theories and the influence of discourse in shaping men's behaviour, it is proposed that there are intangible dynamics at play that are crucial to understanding the aetiology of domestic abuse. Understanding these dynamics is useful for developing rehabilitative interventions and methods for evaluating these.

The chapter begins by outlining two dominant explanations of male-perpetrated domestic abuse from sociology primarily feminist perspectives and psychology, while proposing that both fail to adequately theorize masculine subjectivity when theorizing men's domestic abuse. Examples of how the dominant schools of thought have influenced the current statutory rehabilitative context in England and Wales are provided before describing some of their limitations.

Explaining men's violence against women: a sociological model

Second-wave feminism in 1970s North America and Britain was pivotal in raising awareness of, and politicizing, the issue of men's violence towards women within the home. Women's common experiences of violence at the hands of their husbands were unwittingly discovered within informal community groups with varying degrees of frequency and severity in their accounts (Dobash and Dobash 1992; Dobash et al. 1999a). Domestic abuse can range anywhere from a slap to a more sustained assault – which can also culminate in homicide – and the constellation of violence also consists of non-physical forms of intimidating and controlling behaviour *intended* to cause harm and terrorize (Dobash et al. 1999a). Men's violence towards women more widely has been conceptualized as a 'continuum of violence' (Kelly 1988) which is both normative and functional in maintaining a patriarchal system which oppresses women. Within this feminist sociological model, establishing and maintaining male authority and demanding (sexual) domestic servitude are the prerogatives of men and evidence of their collective social power. Challenges to men's ownership and gendered expectations of women are key sources of conflict in heterosexual relationships (Dobash et al. 1999a). From this sociological perspective, men's violence towards women is instrumental, societally endorsed, and synonymous with masculinity. Whether actively engaged in *legitimated* violence which subordinates women (hegemonic masculinity) or by failing to challenge the status quo (complicit masculinity) *all* men are viewed as beneficiaries of the patriarchal divide (Connell 1995). In other words, there exists a legitimate system of gender hierarchy that privileges men and oppresses women.

While feminist critiques have evolved, this account posits men's behaviour as largely determined and constrained within and by social structures but says little about individual differences or how motivation operates within these. Feminist researcher (Hearn 2013) seeks to addresses this limitation by proposing a more multifaceted analysis of men's social power which can be questioned within systems of oppression, social structures, and multiple disadvantage. Hearn proposes there are also hegemonic masculinities *among* men and the violence of those occupying the most subordinate positions may be explained through their relative and perceived *lack* of power (Hearn 2013). Contradictorily, Hearn also critiques those who look towards these social divisions as explanation of men's domestic abuse for neglecting the agentic subject within this.

Where Hearn falls short here is that he also fails to adequately theorize subjectivity by proposing that men's violence is hegemonic, complicit, or subordinate without explaining *why* or *how* men are differentially invested in these alternative masculinities. Hearn (2013) does propose a theory of autonomy through which violence is mediated but simultaneously cautions against feminist theories which over-rely on a rational, non-gendered subject as conceptualized within Western individualism. Unfortunately, this is a missed opportunity to develop a theory of masculine subjectivity which adequately explains the feelings of loss and relative powerlessness which he identifies within (some) men's accounts (Hearn 2013; Hearn 1998). Instead, Hearn reinforces the notion of rational masculinity, reason, and individualism which he seeks to avoid and fails to adequately explain *why* only *some* men become invested in violent masculinities.

A psychological model

The failure to provide an adequate theory of subjectivity has created a lacuna in feminist research of this nature and has meant that explaining individual differences has predominantly been left to the discipline(s) of 'traditional' psychology. The most widely cited and empirically tested framework is that of Holtzworth-Munroe and Stuart's (1994) domestic abuse 'offender types' using aggregated data from clinical samples. Based upon three dimensions – severity, generality, and psychopathology – they propose three 'types' of offender can be identified: the 'family-only violent', the 'dysphoric/borderline', and the 'generally violent/anti-social'. The 'family-only' violent is posited as exhibiting little or no psychopathology, engages in less severe violence, and has misogyny scores like those of non-violent men (Holtzworth-Munroe et al. 2000; Johnson 2006). The 'dysphoric/borderline' engages in moderate to severe (sexual) violence, and are the most misogynistic, psychologically distressed and emotionally volatile. The 'generally violent/anti-social' engages in moderate to severe (psychological and sexual) violence. Like the former group, these men are likely to abuse substances but are also more likely to be involved in extrafamilial violence and have an extensive criminal record. This research points to both the complexity of domestic abuse offenders and the potential utility of tailoring interventions to psychologically diverse men (Kelly and Johnson 2008; Cavanaugh and Gelles 2005).

While empirically laudable, the construction of such fixed typologies is an oversimplification of lived experience and one must take care to avoid their reification (Gadd and Corr 2018; Gadd and Corr 2017), particularly when front-line responses to domestic abuse rely on self-reports and so-called 'isolated incidents' (Gadd and Corr 2017). Focusing on the psychopathology of offenders fails to explain the aetiology of domestic abuse or provide any theory of (masculine) subjectivity. It also fails to acknowledge the (interpersonal) dynamics of domestic abuse and the role that substances play in creating interdependencies in intimate relationships (Gadd et al. 2019). The issue here is that typological research of this kind obtains its epistemological insights by stripping them of emotional experience and contextual meaning (Hollway 2006) and fails to capture the *meaning* of men's violence at the individual level (Gadd and Corr 2017). Men's sexist entitlement, 'mental states', and misogynism are often reduced to fixed (and inherent) 'personality traits' and 'disorders' which tells us very little about men's motivations, gendered expectations, or the gendered patterns of violence and sources of conflict in heterosexual relationships. Such questions matter if one is to develop an adequate theory of subjectivity which incorporates both the gendered 'structuring of violence' (Messerschmidt 1997) and individual differences in men's investments in its utility.

Dominance of cognitive behavioural DVPPs in sociological and psychological models

Despite the limitations of sociological and psychological models, DVPPs rooted in these first emerged in 1980s North America. Their appearance was initially met with scepticism by the women's movement as targeting relatively few men for treatment was unlikely to bring about wider social change (Dobash and Dobash 1992). There were also concerns that DVPPs would be funded at the expense of women's support services (Phillips 2015; Gadd 2004; Haaken 2010). The Domestic Abuse Intervention Project (DAIP) in Duluth, Minnesota, was developed with these concerns in mind. DAIP is a community coordinated response offering women and children support while simultaneously holding the perpetrator to account. Beyond arrest, many men are also mandated to attend a pro-feminist perpetrator programme which seeks to challenge men's perceived entitlements and teach them egalitarian attitudes within their intimate relationships (Pence and Paymar 1993). The 'Power and Control Wheel' (Pence and Paymar 1993) – central to the 'Duluth model' – is used as a conceptual tool within DVPPs to illustrate the range of abusive tactics men use and to teach them to relinquish their power and control over women. To achieve this, facilitators are required to be suitably challenging to ensure men accept responsibility for their behaviour (Mullender 1996). Pro-feminist approaches typically involved consciousness-raising. However, the idea that men's violence towards women is learned and purposeful is aligned with feminist critiques of masculinities and the scientific discourses of cognitive behavioural therapy (Morran 2016; Gadd 2004). As such, together they form the backdrop of many DVPPs and 'cognitive restructuring' has become a prominent feature within the skills-based component of many such interventions today (Bowen 2011).

The international influence of the 'Duluth model' cannot be overstated. Drawing inspiration from this, the first 'Duluth-type' interventions emerged in Scotland in the 1990s in the form of the CHANGE and Lothian Domestic Violence Probation Project (LDVPP) (Gadd 2004). An evaluation of these programmes (contestably) concluded that men were more amendable to change via court-mandated programmes than alternative criminal justice sanctions (Dobash et al. 1999b). This resulted in a proliferation of 'pro-feminist cognitive behavioural' programmes across the UK. Although practitioners facilitating CHANGE and LDVPP expressed concern and subsequently developed more person-centred approaches (Morran 2016), the Home Office commissioned a Pathfinder programme and ultimately endorsed 'pro-feminist cognitive behavioural' DVPPs based on the 'Duluth model'. While the results of this Pathfinder programme are *still* eagerly anticipated (Gadd 2004; Bowen 2011), in 2003 two 'pro-feminist cognitive behavioural programmes' – the Integrated Domestic Abuse Programme (IDAP) and Community Domestic Violence Programme – were born. These marked the first standardized statutory interventions across England and Wales which Probation Services were compelled to adopt in exchange for necessary funding (Gadd 2004).

The standardization of existing cognitive behavioural programmes such as IDAP emerged within a political culture of 'evidence-based' interventions and accreditation (Morran 2011) and IDAP was met with criticism for adopting a 'one size fits all approach' to explaining, and responding to, partner-violent men (Gadd 2004). There were also concerns that cognitive behavioural therapy – targeting men's 'cognitive distortions' – privileged intellectual insight and failed to engage men on an emotional level (Morran 2013). Evidence suggests that this pedagogical approach often left men feeling resentful while continuing to be abusive (Wolf-Light 2006). Resistance to this 'treatment' style is, arguably, a consequence of seeing men's attempts to deny, minimize, or blame in the context of interventions as indicative of men's refusal to accept responsibility (Gadd and Jefferson 2007). Therefore, how denial is conceptualized within DVPPs has consequences for developing theories of change. On the one hand, denial is conceived as self-serving and rational (cf. Bullock and Condry 2013); on the other, psychotherapeutic approaches, for example, psychodynamic models, usefully recognize that denial is an unconscious (psychic) defence mechanism (cf. Gadd and Jefferson 2007). Highlighting such nuances is crucial if one is to decide on rehabilitation strategies that arm men with a cognitive bag of tools which 'teach' them to 'manage' their 'relationship conflicts'; or whether to adopt psychotherapeutic approaches such as psychodynamic models of treatment through which men's violence, denials, and projections are understood as an expression of their perceived lack of power and feelings of persecutory rage. There has been some evidence to suggest this latter approach is beneficial to the emotionally dependent, dysphoric/borderline in typological research (Saunders 1996).

There are, however, few DVPPs in the UK which adopt psychodynamic models of working. Arguably, this might be a consequence of the 'what works', 'evidence-based' paradigm and criminal justice agenda; and the success of cognitive behavioural therapy within the wider offender population (Bowen 2011; although cf. Hollin et al. 2008; Lipsey et al. 2001 for methodological limitations). However, the marginalization of psychotherapeutic interventions more generally, and the statutory context specifically, might more accurately reflect the relative dearth of psychotherapeutic training and qualifications of those facilitating DVPPs. This is unfortunate as a comparative study of IDAP and a psychodynamic-informed model in the UK (Garfield 2007) highlighted that where men were encouraged to talk about, and develop an understanding of, their emotions and behaviour, this led to an 'identity shift'. This re-evaluation of self has been identified as key to the process in the desisting from crime (Maruna 2001). In contrast, men attending the cognitive behavioural programme talked of learning to 'manage' their violence with little understanding of why they were motivated to be violent in the first place. Similar findings were replicated in a longer-term desistance study in the UK (Morran 2013). These differences in outcome have been attributed to the more flexible programme structure, informed by a psychodynamic model, the therapeutic skills of facilitators, and the strong therapeutic alliance these create between DVPP staff and men (Garfield 2007).

While the standardization of DVPPs was initially met with enthusiasm across probation, the consequences of increasing workloads and bureaucratic procedures has meant that programme delivery has often been left to less skilled staff (Morran 2016). During the implementation of IDAP, concerns were raised regarding facilitator expertise (Bilby and Hatcher 2004). Almost six years later, questions regarding experience and variability in the facilitation of criminal justice interventions for partner-violent men remained unchanged (Bullock 2010). Arguably, this is a consequence of conceptualizing 'programme integrity' as delivering a rigidly structured manual 'as intended' which sees non-programmatic content as surplus. Often as a substitute to facilitators' qualifications, experience, and enthusiasm (Gadd 2004), the monitoring of a heavily manualized programme has been more concerned with the technicalities of programme delivery rather than the holistic engagement with men (Morran 2008). Consequently, the skills and commitment of the facilitators, and the heterogeneity of men, almost exclusively remain within a 'black box' (Gadd 2004).

A recent review of European DVPPs has highlighted the highly skilled and therapeutic task of facilitating men's change (Lilley-Walker et al. 2016). Studies such as Garfield (2007), Wolf-Light (2006), and (Smith 2011) in the UK, and Holma et al. (2006) and Rakil (2006) in Finland might be a starting point for wider discussion on the need for, and recruitment of, qualified psychotherapists in complex treatments of this kind. Granted, such resources will likely come at a handsome sum, but appropriately designed and adequately funded interventions which invest in staff training (well-being) and expertise are likely to recoup such costs through a reduction in the need for public services (cf. Perfect Moment 2010). 'Quick cures' in the form of cognitive behavioural programmes are unlikely to offer a solution to a problem with much wider reach (Gadd 2004).

More recently in 2012, IDAP has been replaced with the cognitive behavioural programme 'Building Better Relationships' (BBR). This shift (or leap) is momentous in that it marks a departure from Duluth-type models to one more aligned with general offending behaviour programmes. Significantly, a gendered analysis has been discarded in favour of a 'general aggression' model which excludes gender as a motivating factor towards individual men's perceptions and appraisals. The rationale behind the development of BBR was to create a programme based on evidence of 'what works' and adopting a 'strengths-based' approach based on principles of Narrative Therapy and Mindfulness (Morran 2016; Weatherstone 2010). Facilitators are expected to adopt a therapeutic, strengths-based solutions-focused approach to men's change. Facilitators are also encouraged to engage men in discussion through critical enquiry about their thoughts, emotions, and relationships through a cognitive framework which connects perceptions, appraisals, and anger arousal.

Despite concerns around investing in good facilitation, the new 'Building Better Relationships' comprises material which is substantially more intellectually demanding than its predecessor (Hughes 2017). Its implementation also coincides with difficult financial times within which Community Rehabilitation Companies (CRCs) – responsible for rehabilitating 'low'- to 'medium'-risk offenders and facilitating offender programmes – are dependent upon government bailouts and have profit-loss forecasts looming (Committee of Public Accounts 2018). While the 'official' rationale for Transforming Rehabilitation was to reduce bureaucracy, and encourage individual discretion and innovation (Burke and Collett 2016), it is questionable whether such aspirations can be achieved in the pursuit of profit. Indeed, (undoubtedly the consequence of rushing through such reforms) the failure of most CRCs to cut the frequency of reoffending has put the very future of CRCs in doubt (House of Commons Justice Committee 2018). An inspection report has also concluded that CRCs are not doing enough to rehabilitate domestically violent men or safeguard domestic abuse victims (HM Inspectorate of Probation 2018). How this current political landscape shapes BBR, its outcomes for men, and the consequences for the staff who deliver this is yet to be researched; as are the implications for 'de-gendering' what has come to be largely evidenced as a form of gender violence.

Proposing a psychosocial model

Having outlined the necessity (and absence) of a theory of subjectivity and the relevance of gender in explaining domestic abuse, a third-way theory is proposed which has received less attention in this field. A psychosocial theory of subjectivity – epistemologically situated within psychoanalysis and Foucauldian post-structuralism – transcends the individual-society/agency-structure dualisms in the perspectives discussed above (cf. Hollway 1989; Hollway and Jefferson 2000; Hollway and Jefferson 2013; Gadd and Jefferson 2007). Making visible the forgotten subject in psychological models, and in contrast to the (overly) rational, calculating subject conceptualized within feminist victimology, the subject of psychosocial research is internally conflicted and motivated to defend against these feelings of angst. In other words, individual differences in what people feel, say, and do are a manifestation and complex interaction of subjective fears and desires which need to be internally resolved. However, motivation for behaviour is not always known or intentional and, in this Freudian view of the unconscious, becomes hidden in the psychic realm, particularly when revealing such motives are threatening to the self (Hollway 1989). Anxiety, desires, 'phantasies' (as spelt in psychoanalysis), and feelings (guilt, shame, and envy) are located within the unconscious but are simultaneously shaped by external forces (structures, power, and discourse). Transcending the individual-society dualism, Gadd and Jefferson (2007: 4) propose that people are 'simultaneously, the products of their own unique worlds and a shared social world'; bridging the agency-structure dualism, Frosh proposes that the subject is:

> both a centre of agency and action (a language user, for example) and the subject of (or subjected to) forces operating from elsewhere – whether that be the 'crown', the state, gender, 'race' and class, or the unconscious.
> (Frosh, cited in Gadd and Jefferson 2007: 4)

Conflicted feelings trigger anxiety and (unconscious) defense mechanisms – denial, 'defensive splitting', and projection – to protect against this. 'Splitting' – a concept located within Kleinian 'Object Relations Theory' – refers to a person's mental state whereby contradictory thoughts about self and other are separated and the inability to hold together the good and bad parts within a coherent whole. Research with domestic abuse perpetrators illustrates how men use these defensive strategies to protect against feelings of vulnerability, fear, and shame and project them 'out there' onto the 'other' (partner) where these can be 'safely attacked' (Gadd 2000, 2002, 2004). These psychological processes are inherent to all, but defenses are uniquely patterned by historical antecedents (trauma, neglect, and abuse) – particularly early childhood experience (Hollway and Jefferson 2013; Hollway and Jefferson 2000; Gadd and Jefferson 2007) – and are central to healthy psychological development and the mental capacity to relate to, and empathize with, others (cf. Benjamin 1988; Fonagy et al. 1993).

For Gadd and Jefferson (2007: 4), the psychoanalytic concept of 'fantasy' is 'crucial to linking the psychoanalytic subject to the social domain of structured power and discourse'. Discourses of the masculine and feminine are psychically invested in through the processes of identification and splitting; people are more likely to invest in empowering discourses and take up subject positions within them that support and protect identity (Hollway and Jefferson 2000, 2013). Masculine discourses which suggest 'boys don't cry' and should 'man up' illustrate the relational aspect of gender (Connell 1995) which equates masculinity with strength, reason, and power, and the feminine with all that is weak. Emotions are thus feminized and denigrated (Seidler 1997; Segal 1997). If we return to Hearn's observations discussed above, this intersubjective theory of gender and motivations for violence might better explain men's projections, feelings of loss, and self-reported accounts of relative powerlessness. Widely endorsed gendered discourses about how men and women should behave can create conflict and anxiety at the individual level. Feeling undermined (rather than entitled) may explain men's investments in 'aggressive masculinities'; particularly when they are positioned within those masculinities which are marginalized and subordinated.

Thus, the relationship between men's social power (masculine) subjectivity, and violence requires a more nuanced analysis which holds together both the (unconscious) intrapsychic and outer (discursive) worlds. It is here where we may uncover the paradoxical position of men's power and powerlessness, and explain the many contradictions in what 'violent men say, feel and do' (Gadd 2000: 431). The foregoing suggests that psychotherapeutic approaches rooted in psychosocial theories can be effective for addressing underlying or intangible correlates of domestic abuse perpetrated by men.

Conclusion

Cognitive behavioural approaches are the favoured intervention for men convicted of domestic abuse-related offences in England and Wales, yet there is little evidence to support their effectiveness in rehabilitating partner-violent men. Influenced by feminist victimology and the sciences, cognitive behavioural approaches assume men's violence is rational and purposeful which can lead to interventions that engage men on a superficial level; teaching them to 'manage' their aggression rather than to develop an understanding of what purpose it serves – then, or in the future. The preoccupation with 'programme integrity' and delivering manuals 'as intended' means that staff qualifications, skills, and enthusiasm, and the context of delivery, are often overlooked. Alternatively, psychodynamic models that go beyond a narrow cognitive framework have been shown to encourage men to reveal and talk about their feelings and develop an understanding of their violence which can result in an 'identify shift'. Such revelations illustrate that people cannot be reduced to their cognitions alone but may be 'acting out' and subject to intangible forces operating from within and elsewhere. It is proposed that interventions should be better developed to deal with this complex and contradictory subject in mind. This will also require programme evaluations that are methodologically capable of capturing and revealing men's unique internal conflicts that shape their behaviour. Only then can we begin to explore what might work, for whom, and under what circumstances.

References

Benjamin, J. (1988) *The Bonds of Love: Psychoanalysis, Feminism, and the Problem of Power.* Pantheon and New York: Google Scholar.

Bilby, C. and Hatcher, R. (2004) Early stages in the development of the Integrated Domestic Abuse Programme (IDAP): Implementing the Duluth Domestic Violence pathfinder. In H. Office (Ed.). Online Report.

Bowen, E. (2011) *The Rehabilitation of Partner-Violent Men.* Published Online: John Wiley & Sons.

Bullock, K. and Condry, R. 2013. Responding to denial, minimization and blame in correctional settings: The 'real world' implications of offender neutralizations. *European Journal of Criminology*, 10, 572–590.

Bullock, K., Sarre, S., Tarling, R. and Wilkinson, M. (2010) The delivery of domestic abuse programmes. An implementation study of the delivery of domestic abuse programmes in probation areas and her Majesty's prison service. M. O. Justice (Ed.) Available at https://www.justice.gov.uk/downloads/publications/research-and-analysis/moj-research/delivery-domestic-abuse-programmes.pdf (Accessed 3 July 2018).

Burke, L. and Collett, S. (2016) Transforming Rehabilitation. *Probation Journal*, 63, 120–135.

Cavanaugh, M. M. and Gelles, R. J. (2005) The utility of male domestic violence offender typologies: New directions for research, policy, and practice. *Journal of Interpersonal Violence*, 20, 155–166.

Committee of Public Accounts (2018) *Government Contracts for Community Rehabilitation Companies.* Available at: https://www.parliament.uk/business/committees/committees-a-z/commons-select/public-accounts-committee/inquiries/parliament-2017/contracts-community-rehabilitation-companies-17-19/ (Accessed 2 September 2018).

Connell, R. W. (1995) *Masculinities.* Cambridge: Polity Press.

Dobash, R. E. and Dobash, R. P. (1992) *Women, Violence and Social Change*. London: Routledge.

Dobash, R. E., Dobash, R. P., Cavanagh, K. and Lewis, R. (1999a) *Changing Violent Men*. London: Sage Publications.

Dobash, R. P., Dobash, R. E., Cavanagh, K. and Lewis, R. (1999b) A research evaluation of British programmes for violent men. *Journal of Social Policy*, 28, 205–233.

Fonagy, P., Moran, G. S. and Target, M. (1993) Aggression and the psychological self. *The International journal of psycho-analysis*, 74, 471.

Fox, K. J. (1999) Changing violent minds: Discursive correction and resistance in the cognitive treatment of violent offenders in prison. *Social Problems*, 46, 88–103.

Gadd, D. (2000) Masculinities, violence and defended psychosocial subjects. *Theoretical Criminology*, 4, 429–449.

Gadd, D. (2002) Masculinities and violence against female partners. *Social & Legal Studies*, 11, 61–80.

Gadd, D. (2004) Evidence-led policy or policyled evidence? Cognitive behavioural programmes for men who are violent towards women. *Criminal Justice*, 4, 173–197.

Gadd, D. and Corr, M. L. (2017) Beyond typologies: Foregrounding meaning and motive in domestic violence perpetration. *Deviant Behavior*, 38, 781–791.

Gadd, D. and Corr, M. L. (2018) On the limits of typologies. *The Routledge Handbook of Gender and Violence*, 12.

Gadd, D., Henderson, J., Radcliffe, P., Stephens-Lewis, D., Johnson, A. and Gilchrist, G. (2019) The dynamics of domestic abuse and drug and alcohol dependency. *The British Journal of Criminology*. DOI:10.1093/bjc/azz011.

Gadd, D. and Jefferson, T. (2007) *Psychosocial Criminology*. Published Online: Sage Publications.

Garfield, S. (2007) *Exploring the Impact of the Therapeutic Alliance and Structural Factors in Treatment Groups for Domestically Abusive Men*. Doctor of Philosophy, London: South Bank University. Available at: http://ethos.bl.uk/Home.do

Haaken, J. (2010) *Hard Knocks: Domestic Violence and the Psychology of Storytelling*. East Sussex: Routledge.

Hearn, J. (1998) *The Violences of Men: How Men Talk About and How Agencies Respond to Men's Violence to Women*. London: Sage Publications.

Hearn, J. (2013) The sociological significance of domestic violence: Tensions, paradoxes and implications. *Current Sociology*, 61, 152–170.

HM Inspectorate of Probation. (2018) Domestic abuse: The work undertaken by Community Rehabilitation Companies. Available at: https://www.justiceinspectorates. gov.uk/hmiprobation/inspections/domestic-abuse-the-work-undertaken-by-community-rehabilitation-companies/ (Accessed 30 September 2018).

Hollin, C. R., Mcguire, J., Hounsome, J. C., Hatcher, R. M., Bilby, C. A. L. and Palmer, E. J. (2008) Cognitive skills behavior programs for offenders in the community – a reconviction analysis. *Criminal Justice and Behavior*, 35, 269–283.

Hollway, W. (1989) *Subjectivity and Method in Psychology: Gender, Meaning and Science*. London: Sage Publications.

Hollway, W. (2006) *The Capacity to Care*. London and New York: Routledge.

Hollway, W. and Jefferson, T. (2000) *Doing Qualitative Research Differently: Free Association, Narrative and the Interview Method*. London: Sage Publications.

Hollway, W. and Jefferson, T. (2013) *Doing Qualitative Research Differently: A Psychological Approach*. Sage Publications.

Holma, J., Partanen, T., Wahlström, J., Laitila, A. and Seikkula, J. (2006) Narratives and discourses in groups for male batterers. *Domestic Violence and Its Reverberations*, 59–83.

Holtzworth-Munroe, A., Meehan, J. C., Herron, K., Rehman, U. and Stuart, G. L. (2000) Testing the Holtzworth-Munroe and Stuart (1994) batterer typology. *Journal of Consulting and Clinical Psychology*, 68, 1000.

Holtzworth-Munroe, A. and Stuart, G. L. (1994) Typologies of male batterers: Three subtypes and the differences among them. *Psychological bulletin*, 116, 476.

House of Commons Justice Committee. (2018) *Transforming Rehabilitation*. Available at: https://publications.parliament.uk/pa/cm201719/cmselect/cmjust/482/48202.htm (Accessed 2 September 2018).

Hughes, W. (2017) Lessons from the integrated domestic abuse programme, for the implementation of building better relationships. *Probation Journal*, 64, 129–145.

Johnson, M. P. (2006) Conflict and control: Gender symmetry and asymmetry in domestic violence. *Violence Against Women*, 12, 1003–1018.

Kelly, J. B. and Johnson, M. P. (2008) Differentiation among types of intimate partner violence: Research update and implications for interventions. *Family Court Review*, 46, 476–499.

Kelly, L. (1988) *Surviving Sexual Violence*. Cambridge: Polity Press.

Lilley-Walker, S. J., Hester, M. and Turner, W. (2016) Evaluation of European domestic violence perpetrator programmes: Toward a model for designing and reporting evaluations related to perpetrator treatment interventions. *International Journal of Offender Therapy and Comparative Criminology*. DOI:10.1177/0306624X16673853.

Lipsey, M. W., Chapman, G. L. and Landenberger, N. A. (2001) Cognitive-behavioral programs for offenders. *The ANNALS of the American Academy of Political and Social Science*, 578, 144–157.

Maruna, S. (2001) *Making Good: How Ex-Convicts Reform and Rebuild Their Lives*. Washington: American Psychological Association.

Messerschmidt, J. (1997) *Crime as Structured Action: Gender, Race, Class, and Crime in the Making*. Sage Publications.

Morran, D. (2008) Firing up and burning out: The personal and professional impact of working in domestic violence offender programmes. *Probation Journal*, 55, 139–152.

Morran, D. (2011) Re-education or recovery? Re-thinking some aspects of domestic violence perpetrator programmes. *Probation Journal*, 58, 23–36.

Morran, D. (2013) Desisting from domestic abuse: Influences, patterns and processes in the lives of formerly abusive men. *The Howard Journal of Crime and Justice*, 52, 306–320.

Morran, D. (2016) Programmes for domestic violence perpetrators. *Beyond the Risk Paradigm in Criminal Justice*, 108.

Mullender, A. (1996) *Rethinking Domestic Violence: The Social Work and Probation Response*. London: Routledge.

ONS. (2017) *Domestic Abuse in England and Wales: Year Ending March 2017*. [Online]. Available at: www.ons.gov.uk/peoplepopulationandcommunity/crimeandjustice/bulletins/domesticabuseinenglandandwales/yearendingmarch2017 (Accessed 2 December 2017).

Pence, E. and Paymar, M. (1993) *Education Groups for Men Who Batter: The Duluth Model*. New York: Springer Publishing Company.

Perfect Moment. (2010) Strength to Change Return on Investment Study.

Phillips, R. (2015) British Domestic Violence Perpetrator Programmes: Programme Integrity Within Service Integrity. London: London Metropolitan University.

Rakil, M. (2006) Are men who use violence against their partners and children good enough fathers? The need for an integrated child perspective in treatment work with men. In C. Humphrey's and N. Stanley (Eds.), *Domestic Violence and Child Protection: Directions for Good Practice*. Philadelphia, PA: Jessica Kingsley Publishers. Domestic Violence and Child Protection, pp. 190–202.

Saunders, D. G. (1996) Feminist-cognitive-behavioral and process-psychodynamic treatments for men who batter: Interaction of abuser traits and treatment models. *Violence and Victims*, 11, 393.

Segal, L. (1997) *Slow Motion: Changing Masculinities, Changing Men*. London: Virago.

Seidler, V. J. J. (1997) *Man Enough: Embodying Masculinities*. London: Sage Publications.

Smith, M. E. (2011) A qualitative review of perception of change for male perpetrators of domestic abuse following Abuser Schema Therapy (AST). *Counselling and Psychotherapy Research*, 11, 156–164.

Weatherstone, P. (2010) *Presentation: Introducing the Building Better Relationships Programme*. NOMS. London.

Wolf-Light, P. (2006) *Duluth Perpetrator Programme – Examined and Amended*. Respect Newsletter, Spring.

32

Arts-based interventions in the justice system

Laura Caulfield and Ella Simpson

The range of arts-based interventions in the justice system

There is a diversity of arts provision in the criminal justice system, and creative practitioners come to this work from an equally varied range of backgrounds and training. From creative writing, drama and theatre, art, music, dance, the list goes on. Arts provision in the justice system takes many forms, and indeed providers often work in a number of different ways. For example, it is not unusual to see an arts organization that works in prisons, in the community, with young people, and adults. Likewise, the type of programme any one organization might run can vary according to the population they are working with and their focus at the time. We provide some examples later in this section.

There is no single agenda or ethical agreement concerning the purpose of arts in prisons (Thompson 2003: 45). This is clearly indicated by the multiple delivery points of arts in prisons, through education departments (Peaker and Vincent 1990), through therapeutically based interventions grounded in the disciplines of forensic psychology, psychoanalysis, and community psychiatry (Laing 1984; Gussack 2009; Cox and Ogelthorpe 2012), and through the work of independent creative practitioners (Peaker and Vincent 1990), some emerging from the radical activism of the 1970s (Johnston 2004: 95), others embodying a conventional artistic training based around notions of fine arts and conservatoire education (Thompson 2003: 46–47). Indeed, many creative practitioners have adapted their practices to the requirements of the professions of teaching or art therapy in order to combine their interests in art and work with prisoners. The introduction of an advocacy agenda in arts in criminal justice (Belfiore and Bennett 2008) has seen practitioners shape their discourses, though not necessarily their practices, to policy requirements (e.g. Mer 2011).

There are too many individuals and organizations working in this area to highlight in this chapter, so below we list a cross-section of organizations and the type of work they undertake:

Organization	Art form	Settings/groups
The Irene Taylor Trust	Music	Prisons, young people in the community, ex-prisoners
Geese Theatre	Theatre and drama	Prison, probation, mental health settings, with young people, with professionals
Rideout	Primarily drama	Prisons, plus European work with a range of audiences
Artist in Residence	Art	HMP Grendon (male prison)
Fine Cell Work	Creative needlework	Prisons
Making for Change	Fashion design (and manufacturing)	HMP Downview (female prison)

Case study: Good Vibrations

Good Vibrations is a charity that uses gamelan percussion music from Indonesia that has been identified as suitable for community or group settings; it has an informal and inclusive approach and includes a variety of instruments that can be played without any prior musical training or knowledge of musical notation. Gamelan is the term for a collection of Indonesian bronze percussion instruments, consisting of a variety of metallophones, gongs, chimes, and drums. It is a particularly communal form of music-making where participants are compelled to work together (Henley 2009). Since its inception in 2003 Good Vibrations has worked with more than 3,300 participants in 53 different secure institutions in the United Kingdom.

Good Vibrations projects typically run over one week for around 15 to 20 individuals on average. They run in prisons, young offender institutions, and in probation services, and are available to any offender in contact with these services (or, in some prisons, to targeted groups, e.g. the unemployed, the very low-skilled, people in touch with mental health teams or personality disorders, vulnerable prisoners). As well as learning how to play traditional pieces of gamelan music, participants create their own compositions as a group. Many also learn about Indonesian culture and associated art forms (e.g. shadow puppetry, Javanese dance), and gain nationally recognized qualifications, e.g. in team-working skills. At the end of the week, participants perform a concert to which staff, peers, family members, and others are invited.

Case study: 'the studio' at the Youth Offending Service

Figure 32.1 Music programme leader and participant at 'the studio'

Birmingham Youth Offending Service (YOS) runs a music programme for young people in contact with their service. The music programme, known locally as 'the studio', has existed for over ten years. The programme began for young people working with the Intensive Supervision & Surveillance team (ISS), but over time its remit has been broadened and it is now open to any young person in contact with the YOS. Referrals are made by a young person's YOS caseworker/programme manager, typically where a young person is seen to have a musical talent and/or interest in music. Overall, the young people taking part in this programme are representative of the wider population of the YOS in terms of age, ethnicity, gender, and offence/sentence type.

The aims of the programme are to: develop the creative, expressive, and musical ability of children and young people; improve children and young people's self-efficacy and resilience; and improve the level of compliance and successful completion of court orders amongst project participants.

Sessions run on a one-to-one basis between the music leader and young person (with their caseworker present where appropriate). A typical level of engagement is one two-hour session per week over a 12-week period. The programme is run in a professional working studio space located near to the centre of Birmingham and young people can work on a variety of music-making activities, including digital composition and production, creative lyric writing, vocal coaching and performance skills (rapping and singing), drum kit tuition, guitar tuition, music theory, deejaying skills; studio sound engineering, and vocal recording techniques.

In the UK, many individual artists, groups, and arts organizations working in the justice system are represented by the National Criminal Justice Arts Alliance (NCJAA). The NCJAA is a network that exists 'to promote, develop and support high quality arts practice in criminal justice settings, influencing and informing government, commissioners and the public' (National Criminal Justice Arts Alliance 2017a). The NCJAA has over 800 members, demonstrating the scale of arts and creative activities in the justice system.

In 2012 the NCJAA launched the Evidence Library. The Evidence Library is 'an online library, housing the key research and evaluation documents on the impact of arts-based projects, programmes and interventions within the Criminal Justice System' (National Criminal Justice Arts Alliance 2017b). Other countries have followed the Evidence Library initiative, setting up their own resources. See, for example, the Prison Arts Resource Project (PARP), which 'is an online library of evidence-based research into U.S. correctional arts programs' (Prison Arts Resources Project 2017).

A brief history of arts-based interventions in the justice system

The relationship between the creative arts and the Criminal Justice System has a long and complex history (Cox and Gelsthorpe 2012). Indeed, the inclusion of artistic and literary content in official prison regimes appear alongside the emergence of the modern penal system. As early as 1837 Foucault notes that at the House of Young Prisoners in Paris, amidst a routine of reveille, hard labour, and austere rations, the rules included:

> Art. 22. School. . . . The class lasts two hours and consists alternately of reading, writing, *drawing* and arithmetic. . . .
>
> Art. 27. At seven o'clock in the summer, at eight in winter, work stops. . . . For a quarter of an hour one of the prisoners or supervisors *reads a passage from some instructive or uplifting work.*
>
> (Faucher 1838, cited in Foucault 1995: 6, our emphasis)

The 'uplifting' nature of this literature, in the context of the period, was predominantly religious rather than aesthetic (Rogers 2013: 10), though it was certainly intended to be morally improving (Fyfe 1992: 18). However, the presence of literature and the arts in prisons was not entirely devoted to scriptural readings, and by the 1830s secular literature was entering prisons through the work of the Society for the Promotion of Christian Knowledge (Fyfe 1992: 9). The Prison Discipline Society included 'leisure reading' as having a role in supporting the reform process (5th Annual Report 1823: 63 cited in Fyfe 1992: 37) and the governor of Coldbath Fields felt that novels were able to effect 'a salutary revolution in the soul *and imagination* of the prisoner' (Pears 1872: 71–72 cited in Hartley 2011: 93, our emphasis).

The combination of religion and erudition in the 1800s are embodied in the activities of Elizabeth Fry, 'the best-known and most influential prison reformer of her sex' (Fyfe 1992: 23). Though she had set out with the intention of providing a school for the children of female prisoners in Newgate, 'the women persuaded her to provide them with needlework and teach them to read and write' (Rogers 2013: 10 citing Foxwell Buxton 1818; Cooper 1981: 683). Nor was Fry alone in these endeavours. Sarah Martin at Yarmouth Jail in the 1800s is also documented as having procured sewing materials to allow both male and female prisoners to engage in craft activities (Carey and Walker 2002: 53). While alone such examples may suggest isolated incidents of maverick practitioners operating below the radar of official approval, by the time Peaker and Vincent (1993) embarked on the first comprehensive survey of arts in British prisons, they found 'a vast diversity of arts available in the majority of prisons' (Brown 2002: 106).

Parkes (2011) identifies the 1980s as a notable period for the delivery of artistic interventions in prisons in the UK, which followed on from similar developments in the US during the 1970s (Currie 1989). In terms of how the arts entered prisons, there is a history of this work through art therapy. Brown (2002: 107) identities the early 1990s as the time when a small number of individuals attempted to make art therapy an established part of prison provision. Reassessing the literature on creative arts in the justice system some 15 years later, Hughes (2005: 24) finds 25 projects out of a total of 200 were delivered via art therapy, dramatherapy, or psychodrama. Although, as Brown (2002: 107) notes, by the beginning of the 21st century there was a more widespread use in secure units. Guidelines specific to the use of art therapies in prisons were published in 1997 (Teasdale 1997 cited in Brown 2002: 107).

The presence of the arts in criminal justice settings has not always been a comfortable fit. Laing (1984: 119) writes about how group therapy sessions were often labelled as 'classes' by prison staff 'thus implying they will be seen as teaching sessions in the scholastic sense'. In the early 1970s there were approximately 100,000 classes organized in prisons with around half of all practical classes consisting of arts, handicrafts, and related hobbies (Brandreth 1972: 32). As late as the 1980s, in a curriculum offering a good deal of variation in subjects and study levels (Laing 1984: 119), education appears to have included a wide range of creative subjects such as pottery, art, and music (Bayliss and Hughes 2008). In response to changes in policy, creative practitioners have adopted educational discourses, as can be seen in responses to the introduction of the Core Curriculum[1] (Bayliss and Hughes 2008: 300), which was followed by a concerted effort on the part of practitioners to demonstrate the relevance of the arts to basic skills education (Home Office Standing Committee for Arts in Prisons 2001; Hughes 2005: 39).

Garland (2001) details the wider context in criminal justice in the 1980s, which saw the treatment or medical model of offender rehabilitation, prevalent from the 1950s, fall out of favour due to 'an astonishingly sudden draining away of support for the ideal of rehabilitation' (Garland 2001). The shift from reform and rehabilitation to a focus on the 'management of prisons' (Mott 1985: 2 cited in Duguid 2000: 75), emerged the 'opportunities approach' (Duguid 2000: 76), which led to the entry of a large number of outside agencies into prisons as prison administrations sought to contract services out (Duguid 2000: 93). Brown (2002) augments Duguid's (2000) 'opportunities' era exposition, claiming that at the end of the 1980s 'there seemed to be feeling that art in prison was about to become a vital new way of helping individuals to change' (Brown 2002: 106). Peaker and Vincent (1990) offer a fuller consideration of how the period came to inform arts provision in prisons. They identify the emergence of participatory arts; a policy commitment from the Arts Council, set out in the *Glory of the Garden* report (ACE 1984), aimed to democratize the arts, along with a number of 'profound' changes in the prison system in terms of management, and a new understanding of prison service purpose. Indeed, Peaker and Vincent's (1990, 1993) research emerged out of this confluence of events which resulted in a grant, jointly funded by the Arts Council and the Home Office, being made to enable an investigation into the uses of creative arts in British prisons (Brown 2002: 106). Out of this work, initially based at Loughborough University and later the University of Kent in Canterbury (Brown 2002), the Unit for Arts and Offenders emerged in 1992. In 1996 the organization became a charitable trust (Brown 2002: 106–107), and changed its name to the Anne Peaker Centre in 2005. It remained a key advocacy organization for arts in prisons until its closure in 2010 due to lack of funding.

More recently the Arts Alliance was established to serve as 'a representative body which will enable practitioners and service users to gain a representative voice to influence policy, a forum to exchange views, and a stand to promote and raise the profile of the arts in criminal justice sector' (Edwards 2008). The Arts Alliance also took over the research function of the Anne Peaker Centre with its Evidence Library. In tandem with the creation of the Arts Alliance, the Ministry of Justice, Department for Innovation, Universities, and Skills and Department for Digital, Culture, Media, and Sport established the Arts Forum which aimed to work in partnership with the Alliance. The Arts Alliance is now called the National Criminal Justice Arts Alliance, as discussed above.

The impact of the arts in the justice system

As Parkes and Bilby (2010: 106) note, the arts can map an 'alternative terrain to traditional concepts of rehabilitation and treatment'. As a general rule, arts programmes in criminal justice settings aim to have a positive impact on participants in a range of ways (Parkes and Bilby 2010), rather than having a direct impact on offending behaviour (Bilby et al. 2013):

> there are strong reasons to consider arts in criminal justice an area of considerable significance and innovation. The value of engaging prisoners in purposeful activity has long been recognised, and is part of the criteria against which prisons are assessed by the inspectorate. Similarly the goals of HM Prison Service include the duty to look after prisoners with humanity, as well as rehabilitating offenders to lead crime-free lives. If we accept that an element of humanity is the need and desire to express ourselves creatively, whether verbally or in other ways, then we must also acknowledge that this demands the provision of creative activities within the prison estate and the wider Criminal Justice System (Parkes & Bilby, 2010).
>
> Bilby et al. (2013: 12)

There is significant evidence that participation in the arts increases confidence and social skills (Baker and Homan 2007; Bilby et al. 2013; Bruce 2015; Cox and Gelsthorpe 2008). For example, in Caulfield's (2011, 2014) longitudinal evaluation of an art residency at HMP Grendon, participants showed significant increases in creativity and technical abilities and subsequently an increase in confidence. Similarly in Cursley and Maruna's (2015) Changing Tunes evaluation, participant's improvements in musical ability appeared to improve their self-confidence in rehearsals and performances. Increases in the confidence of offenders lead to a better, more constructive use of their time.

Within the literature on arts-interventions, confidence is often linked to the reintegration of offenders into education (Viggiani et al. 2013). Indeed

Cox and Gelsthorpe (2008) and Wilson et al. (2009) have found that prisoners taking part in music projects report increased motivation to engage in future education. Winner and Cooper (2000) suggest that participation in the arts uses cognitive structures such as problem-solving and close observation, and that these skills can be applied to other forms of learning in the future. The mechanisms behind the participation in the arts has shown to increase offenders' capability to learn and so in turn can develop important life skills for use after release (Miles and Strauss 2008).

Attitudinal and behavioural changes often arise through self-evaluation and changes in self-concept (Bruce 2015). Several studies have shown that through engagement with arts-based activities, participants learn to foster their emotions in a safe way (Winder et al. 2015) and may use the arts as an emotional outlet for any negative emotions (Cartwright 2013). Arts-based projects are thought to offer a safe space (Cox and Gelsthorpe 2008) away from everyday life challenges (Wilson et al. 2009). The positive regulation of emotions has been linked to increased well-being and decreases in anger and aggression, through participation in arts-based projects (Wilson et al. 2009; Miles and Strauss 2008).

Building and maintaining positive emotions is crucial to counteracting stressful life experiences and building resilience (Rutten 2013). Resilience refers to 'the capacity of a system, enterprise or person to [find] and maintain its core purpose and integrity in the face of dramatically changed circumstances' (Zolli and Healy 2012: 6) and is an important factor in lifelong health and well-being, thought to help explain how individuals deal with challenges throughout life. Existing research has noted that participation in arts-based projects increases offenders' ability to deal with personal problems (Wilson et al. 2009; Henley 2012; Viggiani et al. 2013) and improves coping (Miles and Strauss 2008) – factors core to resilience. Furthermore, Newman (2002) suggests that participation in the arts reduces risk factors and increases protective factors, including social support (Cursley and Maruna 2015) and new role models in their peers and art facilitators (Viggiani et al. 2013). Potentially the most powerful bonds that form may be between the arts facilitators and the offenders, although the literature has only just begun to explore this. Henley (2012) reports the high level of trust and respect observed between participants and the arts facilitator, with social barriers broken in the spaces created (Abrahams et al. 2012). Indeed, a review of 12 studies on music programmes in prison concluded that they 'are perceived by participating prisoners as a liberating process, which encourages participation and allows for noncoercive personal development' (Kougiali et al. 2017: 1).

There evidence to suggest that arts-based interventions within criminal justice settings foster a process of self-evaluation (Caulfield et al. 2016; Davey et al. 2015; Silber 2005), which has been found to positively improve self-concept (Baker and Homan 2007; Berson 2008; Henley 2012). For example, in McKean's (2006) evaluation of a theatre-based project with women in prison, participants reported an enhanced sense of self and a newfound autonomy through freedom to express their emotions. This can be viewed as contributing to secondary desistance (Maruna and Farrall 2004), where 'Desistance is the process by which people who have offended stop offending (primary desistance) and then taken on a personal narrative (Maruna 2001) that supports a continuing non-offending lifestyle (secondary desistance)' (Bilby et al. 2013: 13).

An evaluation of the Changing Tunes music project for ex-prisoners found that participants came to see themselves not primarily as ex-offenders, but as a musicians and individuals with responsibility for their own future (Cursley and Maruna 2015). Similarly, Anderson et al. (2011) report that involvement in arts-based offender interventions in Scotland enabled participants to redefine themselves. These examples, among others (cf. Caulfield et al. 2016; Henley 2012) suggest that arts-based interventions can influence the process of desistance, by creating a sense of personal agency.

While much useful and insightful research has been produced on the role of the Arts in criminal justice, the evidence base has been subject to criticism. For example, the focus of much research in this area has been on self-reported measures. While it is clear that the voice of participants is crucial to understanding how any project works, Burrowes et al. (2013) – in their evidence assessment of intermediate outcomes of arts projects for National Offender Management Services – note that there is a lack of good quality research into the arts in criminal justice, citing a particular lack of robust quantitative data. Even when research has taken a mixed method approach, Burrowes et al. note methodological issues with most research in the area lack any control group to compare results to. In addition, it is rare to see evaluations that use pre-test and post-test scores (Cheliotis et al. 2014; Miles and Clarke 2006), meaning it is hard to clearly establish outcomes in most of the current literature.

Some researchers have, however, argued for the importance of 'intermediate' measures, and measures that tell us something of the experience of those taking part. Indeed, reducing evaluation of the arts to a mere quantitative binary measure may risk losing any insight into the real impact of the arts in criminal justice (Caulfield 2014). As Bilby et al. (2013: 10) note:

> Just as arts practices in the criminal justice system can be seen as innovative projects in themselves, exploring the mechanisms for change in the journey to desistance needs to be innovative too. Methodologies that can measure changes in behaviour (important in primary desistance[2]) as well as changes in personal narratives (important in secondary desistance) need to be adopted. This needs to be recognized and accepted by policy makers.

Indeed, as Caulfield et al. (2016: 412) note,

> it is clearly unreasonable to suggest that such projects can be directly responsible for reducing reoffending – and nor do they seek to be – but it

remains important to consider how a variety of experiences can be relevant in shaping the path an offender takes towards desisting from crime.

Summary

There is a diversity of arts provision in the criminal justice system, and creative practitioners come to this work from an equally varied range of backgrounds and training. In the UK, many individual artists, groups, and arts organizations working in the justice system are represented by the National Criminal Justice Arts Alliance (NCJAA). As a general rule, arts programmes in criminal justice settings aim to have a positive impact on participants in a range of ways (Parkes and Bilby 2010), rather than having a direct impact on offending behaviour, and there is a growing amount of research that demonstrates a range of positive impacts arising from participation in the arts within the justice system.

Notes

1   In prison education in the UK 'learning became a competitive commodity' (Bayliss and Hughes 2012: 300) and the focus shifted significantly away from arts and crafts activities to focus on Skills for Life and the introduction of a Core Curriculum in 1997.
2   Desistance is the process by which people who have committed crimes stop offending (primary desistance) and take on a personal narrative that supports a continuing nonoffending lifestyle (secondary desistance). This essentially refers not only to an individual stopping committing crime, but an individual seeing her-/himself as someone other than 'an offender'.

References

Abrahams, F., Rowland, M. M. and Kohler, K. C. (2012) Music education behind bars: Giving voice to the inmates and the students who teach them'. *Music Educators Journal*, 98(4), 67–73.

Anderson, K., Colvin, S., McNeil, F., Nellis, M., Overy, K. and Sparks, R. (2011) Inspiring change: Final project report of the evaluation team (online). Available at http://www.artsevidence.org.uk/media/uploads/evaluation-downloads/mc-inspiring-change-april-2011.pdf (Accessed 2 November 2017).

Arts Council of Great Britain. (1984) *The Glory of the Garden: The Development of the Arts in England.* London: The Arts Council.

Baker, S. and Homan, S. (2007) Rap, recidivism and the creative self: A popular music programme for young offenders in detention. *Journal of Youth Studies*, 10(4), 459–476.

Bayliss, P. and Hughes, S. (2008) Teachers and Instructors in Prisons. In J. Bennett, B. Crewe and A. Wahidin (Eds.), *Understanding Prison Staff.* Abingdon: Routledge, pp. 298–315.

Belfiore, E. and Bennett, O. (2008) *The Social Impact of the Arts: An Intellectual History.* Basingstoke: Palgrave Macmillan.

Berson, J. (2008) Baring and bearing life behind bars: Pat Graney's "keeping the faith" prison project. *The Drama Review*, 52(3), 79–93.

Bilby, C., Caulfield, L. and Ridley, L. (2013) *Re-Imagining Futures: Exploring Arts Interventions and the Process of Desistance*. London: Arts Alliance.

Brandreth, G. D. (1972) *Created in Captivity*. London: Hodder and Stoughton.

Brown, M. (2002) *Inside Art: Crime, Punishment and Creative Energies*. Winchester: Waterside Press.

Bruce, K. (2015) *Community Exchange Project Between Detainees at Harmondsworth Immigration Removal Centre and Young People at West London YMCA, Hayes*. London: National Foundation for Youth Music.

Burrowes, N., et al. (2013) Intermediate outcomes of arts projects: A rapid evidence assessment. *National Offender Management Services*. Available at: https://pdfs.semanticscholar.org/f6c4/acf85ec4465e40f51cf6c34f749968a0b72e.pdf

Carey, M. and Walker, R. (2002) The Penal Voluntary Sector. In S. Bryans, C. Martin and R. Walker (Eds.), *Prisons and the Voluntary Sector: A Bridge Into the Community*. Winchester: Waterside Press, pp. 50–62.

Cartwright, J. (2013) *An Evaluation of the Irene Taylor Trust's Sounding Out Programme*. London: The Irene Taylor Trust.

Caulfield, L. S. (2011) *An Evaluation of the Artist in Residence at HMP Grendon*. Birmingham: Birmingham City University.

Caulfield, L. S. (2014) *Final Evaluation of the Artist in Residence at HMP Grendon*. Bath: Bath Spa University.

Caulfield, L. S. and Wilkinson, D. J. and Wilson, D. (2016) Exploring alternative terrain in the rehabilitation and treatment of offenders: Findings from a prison-based music project. *Journal of Offender Rehabilitation*, 55(6), 396–418.

Cheliotis, L. K., Jordanoska, A. and Sekol, I (2014) *The Arts of Desistance: Evaluation of the Koestler Trust Arts Mentoring Programme for Former Prisoners*. London: Koestler Trust.

Cooper, R. A. (1981) Jeremy Betham, Elizabeth Fry, and English prison reform. *Journal of the History of Ideas*, 42(4), 6785–6790.

Cox, A. and Gelsthorpe, L. (2008) *Beats & Bars, Music in Prisons: An Evaluation*. London: The Irene Taylor Trust.

Cox, A. and Gelsthorpe, L. (2012) Creative encounters: Whatever happened to the arts in prisons? In L. K. Cheliotis (Ed.), *The Arts of Imprisonment: Control, Resistance and Empowerment*. Farnham: Ashgate, pp. 257–275.

Currie, C. (1989) *Art in Prison: An Evaluation of a New Zealand Programme*. Wellington: University of Wellington.

Cursley, J. and Maruna, S. (2015) *A Narrative-Based Evaluation of "Changing Tunes" Music-Based Prisoner Reintegration Interventions*. Bristol: Changing Tunes.

Davey, L., Day, A. and Balfour, M. (2015) Performing desistance: How might theories of desistance from crime help us to understand the possibilities of prison theatre? *International Journal of Offender Therapy and Comparative Criminology*, 58(8), 798–809.

Duguid, S. (2000) *Can Prisons Work? The Prisoner as Object and Subject in Modern Corrections*. Toronto, Buffalo and London: University of Toronto.

Edwards, B. (2008) *The Fight for Recognition*. Available at: www.artsprofessional.co.uk/magazine/article/fight-recognition (Accessed 3 November 2017).

Foucault, M. (1995) *Discipline and Punish: The Birth of the Prison*, 2nd edition. New York: Vintage Books.

Foxwell Buxton, T. (1818) *An Inquiry, Whether Crime and Misery Are Produced or Prevented, by Our Present System of Prison Discipline*. London: John and Arthur Arch.

Fyfe, J. (1992) *Books Behind Bars: The Role of Books, Reading, and Libraries in British Prison Reform, 1701–1911*. Westport, CT: Greenwood Press.

Garland, D. (2001) *The Culture of Control: Crime and Social Order in Contemporary Society*. Oxford: Oxford University Press.

Gussak, D. (2009) The effects of art therapy on male and female inmates: Advancing the research base. *The Arts in Psychotherapy*, 36(1), 5–12.

Hartley, J. (2011) Reading in ucc. In B. Palmer and A. Buckland (Eds.), *A Return to the Common Reader: Print Culture and the Novel, 1850–1900*. Farnham: Ashgate, pp. 87–102.

Henley, J. (2009) *The Learning Ensemble: Musical Learning Through Participation*. Unpublished PhD thesis, Birmingham City University.

Henley, J. (2012) *Good Vibrations: Music and Social Education for Young Offenders*. London: University of London.

Home Office Standing Committee for Arts in Prisons. (2001) *Including the Arts: The Creatives Arts – the Route to Basic and Key Skills in Prisons*. Manchester: Bar None Books.

Hughes, J. (2005) *Doing the Arts Justice: A Review of Research Literature, Practice and Theory*. Unit for the Arts and Offenders (Arts Council England, Department for Culture, Media and Sport, Department for Education and Skills).

Johnston, C. (2004) The role of the camshaft in offender rehabilitation. In M. Balfour (Ed.), *Theatre in Prison: Theory and Practice*. Bristol: Intellect Books, pp. 95–110.

Kougiali, Z., Einat, T. and Liebling, A. (2017) Rhizomatic affective spaces and the therapeutic potential of music in prison: a qualitative meta-synthesis. *Qualitative Research in Psychology*, 1–28.

Laing, J. (1984) Art therapy in prisons. In T. Dalley (Ed.), *Art as Therapy: An Introduction to the Use of Art as a Therapeutic Technique*. New York: Tavistock, Routledge, pp. 115–128.

McKean, A. (2006) Playing for time in the doll's house. Issues of community and collaboration in the devising of theatre in a women's prison. *Research in Drama Education*, 11, 313–327.

Maruna, S. (2001) *Making Good: How Ex-Convicts Reform and Rebuild Their Lives*. Washington, DC: APA Books.

Maruna, S. and Farrall, S. (2004) Desistance from crime: A theoretical reformulation. *Kölner Zeitschrift für Soziologie und Sozialpsychologie*, 44, 171–194.

Mer, R. (2011) *Arts in Prison: Lessons from the United Kingdom*. Available at: www.artsevidence.org.uk/texts/guides/arts-prison-lessons-united-kingdom/ (Accessed 2 November 2017).

Miles, A. and Clarke, R. (2006) *The Arts in Criminal Justice: A Study of Research of Research Feasibility*. Manchester: Centre for Research on Socio Cultural Change.

Miles, A. and Strauss, P. (2008) *The Academy: A Report on Outcomes for Participants, June 2006-June 2008*. Manchester: University of Manchester.

National Criminal Justice Arts Alliance. (2017a) *About the National Criminal Justice Arts Alliance*. Available at: www.artsincriminaljustice.org.uk/about-us/ (Accessed 30 October 2017).

National Criminal Justice Arts Alliance. (2017b) *Evidence Library: Online Library Showcasing the Impact of the Arts in Criminal Justice Settings*. Available at: www.artsincriminaljustice.org.uk/evidence-library/ (Accessed 30 October 2017).

Newman, T. (2002) *Promoting Resilience: A Review of Effective Strategies for Child Care Services*. Exeter: Centre for Evidence-Based Social Services.

Parkes, R. (2011) Hard times: Is the 'rehabilitation revolution' bad news for enrichment activities with prisoners? *British Journal of Community Justice*, 9(1–2), 125–139.

Parkes, R. and Bilby, C. (2010) The courage to create: The role of artistic and spiritual activities in prisons. *The Howard Journal of Criminal Justice*, 49, 97–110.

Peaker, A. and Vincent, J. (1990) *Arts in Prisons: Towards a Sense of Achievement*. Loughborough: Loughborough University, Centre for Research in Social Policy.

Peaker, A. and Vincent, J. (1993) *Arts Activities in Prisons 1991–1993: A Directory*. Loughborough: The Unit for the Arts and Offenders.

Prison Arts Resources Project. (2017) *Research on U.S. Arts in Corrections: Jails, Prisons and Probation/Parole*. Available at: https://scancorrectionalarts.org/ (Accessed 30 October 2017).

Rogers, H. (2013) Free to Learn? Reading and Writing in the Early Nineteenth-Century Prison. In G. Creer, H. Priest and T. Spargo (Eds.), *Free to Write: Prison Voices Past and Present*. West Kirby: Headland.

Rutten, B., et al. (2013) Resilience in mental health: Linking psychological and neurobiological perspectives. *Acta Psychiatrica Scandinavica*, 128, 2–20.

Silber, L. (2005) Bars behind bars: The impact of a women's prison choir on social harmony. *Music Education Research*, 7(2), 251–271.

Thomson, J. (2003) Doubtful principles in arts in prisons. In R. M. C. Williams (Ed.), *Teaching the Arts Behind Bars*. Boston: Northeastern University Press, pp. 40–61.

Viggiani, N., Daykin, N., Moriarty, Y. and Pilkington, P. (2013) *Musical Pathways: An Exploratory Study of Young People in the Criminal Justice System, Engaged with a Creative Music Programme*. University of the West of England.

Wilson, D., Caulfield, L. and Atherton, S. (2009) Good vibrations: The long-term impact of a prison-based music project. *Prison Service Journal*, 182, 27–32.

Winder, B., Sperling, V., Elliot, H., Lievesley, R., Faulkner, J. and Blagden, N. (2015) *Evaluation of the Use of 'Good Vibrations' Percussion Courses to Improve Motivation to Change and Treatment Readiness with Convicted Sexual Offenders Embarking on Treatment Programmes*. Nottingham: Nottingham Trent University.

Winner, E. and Cooper, M. (2000) Mute those claims: No evidence (yet) for a causal link between arts study and academic achievement. *Journal of Aesthetic Education*, 34(3–4), 11–75.

Zolli, A. and Healy, A. M. (2012) *Resilience: Why Things Bounce Back*. New York: Free Press.

Organizations/webpages mentioned in this chapter

Arts Alliance Evidence Library: www.artsevidence.org.uk
Fine Cell Work: https://finecellwork.co.uk
Geese Theatre: www.geese.co.uk
Good Vibrations: www.good-vibrations.org.uk
The Irene Taylor Trust: https://irenetaylortrust.com
Making for Change: www.arts.ac.uk/fashion/about/better-lives/making-for-change
National Criminal Justice Arts Alliance: www.artsincriminaljustice.org.uk
Prison Arts Resources Project: https://scancorrectionalarts.org
Rideout: www.rideout.org.uk

The use of sport to promote employment, education, and desistance from crime

33

Lessons from a review of English and Welsh prisons

Rosie Meek

Introduction

There are currently in the region of 85,000 people in prison in England and Wales, over 4,000 of whom are women and over 900 of whom are children under the age of 18 (Ministry of Justice 2017). The reoffending of those released from prison custody poses an enormous societal issue: according to official data (which presents its own challenges), at present in England and Wales 29% of adults and 42% of children reoffend within one year, with these rates rising dramatically (50% of adults and 77% of children) for those with 11 or more previous offences (Ministry of Justice 2018). Aside from the singular issue of official rates of reoffending, what takes place in our prisons is very much a public concern, with the physical and psychological well-being of those in prison posing a public health issue. Efforts to promote the physical and psychological well-being of those in prison custody will inevitably then have an impact on broader efforts to create safer communities.

It is widely accepted that those leaving prison need to be motivated to change their behaviour and to be equipped with the necessary skills in order to change. It is also clear that those working with people in prison need to be creative in finding ways to respond to the complex needs of those in their care. Although sport is not the only answer, it can provide some solutions to the long-standing problems of the disengagement, disempowerment, and disaffection of people in prison. As well as being a way to bring together disparate groups, develop communication skills, and learn life lessons, it also has the advantage of being something many people are passionate about. It can be a relatively straightforward way to encourage otherwise reluctant individuals to engage in a whole raft of associated activities, while also serving to improve mental and physical health, reduce violence, and ultimately to tackle reoffending.

Although some positive examples are evident, the utilization of sport across prisons and youth custody is inconsistent and underdeveloped. In my recent independent review of sport in youth and adult prisons (Meek 2018), undertaken on behalf of Dr Phillip Lee MP, then Parliamentary Under Secretary of State for Justice, I identified numerous examples of good practice, many of which were the result of partnerships between prisons and community groups and clubs. On being asked in September 2017 to undertake the review, I started a series of visits to over 20 prisons, young offender institutions, secure training centres, and secure children's homes. I was able to meet with 74 children, women, and men detained within these establishments and I spoke with representatives from a number of other prisons and community organizations, as well as carrying out a public consultation which attracted 87 complete responses. In this chapter I will reflect on some of these findings and the broader issues which they raised, with a particular focus on education and employment opportunities.

Official guidelines and expectations

NHS guidelines recommend at least 60 minutes of moderate to rigorous exercise per day for children (and at least 150 minutes of moderate exercise per week for adults) but prisons are rarely able to support this goal. Prison-based sport and physical activity tends to be classified in different jurisdictions as either a health, a recreation, or an education requirement, but basic provision and access is considered part of the basic principles of prison laws and policies of many countries (van Zyl and Snacken 2002). In England and Wales, as well as national Prison Service Orders and Instructions (see Ministry of Justice 2011), legislation which the UK has signed up to includes that from the United Nations, where the Standard Minimum Rules for the Treatment of Prisoners prescribe that:

Every prisoner who is not employed in outdoor work shall have at least one hour of suitable exercise in the open air daily if weather permits. Young prisoners, and others of suitable age and physique, shall receive physical and recreational training during the period of exercise. To this end space, installations and equipment should be provided.

(Rule 23, United Nations 2015)

The UK has also adopted the European Prison Rules, which recognize the importance of exercise and recreation by stating that:

Recreational opportunities, which include sport, games, cultural activities, hobbies and other leisure pursuits, shall be provided and, as far as possible, prisoners shall be allowed to organise them.

(European Committee for the Prevention of Torture and Inhuman or Degrading Treatment 2006)

Lastly, the UK has also adopted the Havana Rules (United Nations 1990) which apply to children in detention and specify that:

The design of detention facilities for juveniles and the physical environment should be in keeping with the rehabilitative aim of residential treatment, with due regard to the need of the juvenile for privacy, sensory stimuli, opportunities for association with peers and participation in sports, physical exercise and leisure-time activities.

(Rule 32)

Every juvenile should have the right to a suitable amount of time for daily free exercise, in the open air whenever weather permits, during which time appropriate recreational and physical training should normally be provided. Adequate space, installations and equipment should be provided for these activities.

(Rule 47)

Despite an expectation that those held in custodial care should spend time engaged in sports, fitness, and physical activity each week, prisoners consistently report highly sedentary lifestyles in custody, and repeated HM Inspectorate reports confirm that many establishments fail to meet policy expectations in this domain (HM Inspectorate of Prisons 2017). Sedentary behaviour in prisons has been identified as a high-risk health behaviour which contributes to an increased risk of obesity, hypertension, diabetes, cardiovascular disease, and mortality (Battaglia et al. 2013), not only placing a considerable cost burden on healthcare providers both in custody and the community but also acting as a barrier to efforts to rehabilitate. A strong body of evidence confirms that the provision of physical activity represents a simple intervention which can ameliorate the negative health effects of a sedentary lifestyle in prison (see, for example, Meek and Lewis 2012).

As places which house people with an increased likelihood of significant health needs, prisons and other secure settings represent an especially important target for health promotion initiatives. Recognition of the role of physical activity in promoting well-being is reflected in the HM Prison Service (now the HM Prison and Probation Service) Physical Education Prison Service Order (2009), which states that:

> PE plays an important part in a prison regime by providing high quality purposeful activity and engagement with prisoners; in addition, PE can make a major contribution to the physical, mental and social well-being of prisoners.

The benefits of sport in prison: existing evidence

A body of international literature has made the case for the primary benefits of prison-based sport and physical activity in terms of improved physical health (Amtmann and Kukay 2016; Elger 2009) and mental health (Buckaloo et al. 2009; Woods et al. 2017). There is also a growing awareness of a wider psychological – as well as social – benefit, where sport can offer an alternative means of excitement and risk-taking to that gained through engaging in offending behaviour (Meek 2014). Of particular importance for those attempting to leave behind a past which may have involved gang-related offending, sporting activities can also provide access to a pro-social network and positive role models, and the opportunity to gain new experiences and achievements. In sum, participating in sport can offer an alternative to offending which not only has intrinsic value but also provides a relatively easy way to establish a more positive self-identity (Meek 2014). Finally, there is plenty of wider psychological and educational literature on the importance of *play* in healthy child development (see, for example, Frost et al. 2007), particularly in working with those who have experienced trauma and neglect.

A note on collaborative working

Despite previous recommendations from the World Health Organization (2007) to pursue a whole-prison approach to health promotion, and from Public Health England (2016) to pursue the 'make every contact count' (MECC) agenda in supporting behaviour change, prisons still tend to lack a fully integrated well-being strategy, with different departments operating in isolation from one another. This doesn't mean that collaborations between different prison departments are not possible, but with commissioning

Good practice example

The GOOP (Greener on the Outside of Prisons) programme provides a tailored 'green health' programme which promotes mental health, physical activity, and healthier eating. Delivered in a number of youth, adult male and female prisons across the north-west of England as part of a regional 'target wellbeing' initiative, the scheme was funded by the Big Lottery Fund and delivered in partnership with University of Central Lancashire's Healthy & Sustainable Settings Unit. In 2013–2015 the programme had 872 beneficiaries from prison populations, with recorded improvements to knowledge, skills, and uptake regarding physical activity, nutrition, and healthy eating (University of Central Lancashire 2015).

Good practice example

A number of establishments offer annual/ad hoc events aligned with fundraising initiatives (for example Sport Relief, Children in Need) and national/international sporting events (Wimbledon, the Olympics, World Cup competitions, etc.). The reach and impact of these events is reported as being greatest when based on collaborations between the gym and other departments, particularly education and healthcare.

arrangements, and a culture of 'silo mentalities' (Moore and Hamilton 2016) in prisons, examples of genuine partnership working between internal departments remain scarce.

Education and employability

Sport and physical activity have enormous potential in motivating individuals to desist from crime, particularly in increasing employability and in motivating reluctant learners to engage in education when they would otherwise be unwilling or feel unable to participate due to negative experiences of education (Meek et al. 2012). Those in custody are likely to have disrupted and negative experiences of learning prior to incarceration, to lack confidence in their learning abilities, and have a high prevalence of permanent exclusion from school and poorer educational achievements (Ministry of Justice and Department for Education 2016). With such high levels of educational and emotional need, engaging prison learners can be challenging, but represents a critical feature of efforts to support desistance. As a 'hook' for motivating

Good practice example

Rainsbrook Secure Training Centre's creative writing initiative is offered as part of their 'sport project week competition' with the sport element encouraging participation from some of the most difficult, violent, and disengaged children who would otherwise be unlikely to engage but who can be encouraged to do so due to their interest in sports.

In a similar example of a prison-wide coordinated effort to use sport to motivate learners, staff from multiple departments at HMYOI Wetherby organized an establishment-wide Rio Olympics event which was fully imbedded in education as well as gym activities. Engagement with this event by both staff and children was good and the establishment report recorded significantly fewer incidences of violence during the month that the event took place (according to recorded data held by the prison there were fewer instances of assaults on prisoners and on staff during the month of the event, with figures falling below the average for the year).

Good practice example

Throughout the year 2017 a total of 21 Level 1 and Level 2 qualifications in maths and English were achieved by young adult learners between the ages of 18–21 at HMYOI Feltham as part of their structured football and rugby programmes, which was the result of a partnership between the National Careers Service, the prison's education provider, gym staff, and the external rugby and football club partners. As well as the sports activities promoting motivation and engagement for previously reluctant learners, the educational component was tailored to reflect sporting examples.

learners, sport (as with the arts) can be a powerful tool, but it can also be used as a vehicle for delivering 'stealth' educational and therapeutic experiences for even the most reluctant learners by embedding lessons into sports-based activities and examples.

The importance of higher level distance learning in sport and fitness

Although there is no doubt that a significant number of people in custody are capable of engaging in sports and fitness studies to Level 3 (equivalent to an A Level, which is also the level of qualification typically required by employers in the sports and fitness industries), this is rarely seen. This mirrors Dame Sally Coates's (2016) observation that only 0.1% of prison learners in 2014–2015 were participating in Level 3 courses under a prison's education contract, despite 20% of learners saying they would prefer to be studying at a higher level.

The Prisoners Education Trust (PET) supports learners to embark on distance learning in sports and fitness. In Meek (2018), this PET alumna reflects on how sports-based learning transformed his time in prison and prepared him for employment after completing his sentence:

> Having been expelled from school and thrown out of two colleges before the age of 18, I gave up on education. As a young lad I was earmarked early on as a trouble-maker and told often I'd end up in jail. Prison was a huge shock to my system. It was a dark time for me, full of despair, and when the inevitable blows came in the form of a 'Dear John' letter and the long list of restrictions from probation I'd face upon release, I was rapidly abandoning all hope.
>
> It was at this point that a kind English teacher reached out to me and suggested distance learning. He gave me a Stonebridge course prospectus and information about Prisoners' Education Trust. That night I sat reading about all the courses I could take. The following day, I sent off an application for a diploma in Sports Psychology. . . . The course couldn't have come at a better time, while I was at my lowest ebb. Doing this diploma and writing business plans kept my hopes and dreams alive at a time when they'd all but died.
>
> Having been released from custody a few months ago, I am now carving out a career as a personal trainer, specialising in sports psychology. It isn't proving easy, with my tarnished reputation and criminal record holding me back, but I'm determined to rebuild my life.

The impact of sports-based programmes in prison: is it about the people, or the sport?

In sports-based programmes with wraparound services such as mentoring and through-the-gate support, the type of sport being utilized may not be of primary importance as long as it serves as a 'hook' for engaging individuals. As Hartmann (2003) claims, the success of any sports-based intervention may be as much, or more, determined by the strength of the non-sport components, such as the charisma, experience, and engagement technique of the delivery staff involved, and recognizing this.

Recognizing the distinct advantages of different sports and physical activities both within and beyond the gym and sports hall, particularly in promoting participation in education and training and other rehabilitative outcomes,

Good practice example

The Airborne Initiative is a five-day residential programme for young offenders (ages 18–21) which takes place in Dartmoor and is led by serving paratroopers, supported by prison (including PE) staff.

During the course the young men who take part experience map reading and orienteering, caving, river crossing, adventure training, leadership, and team-building exercises. The initiative is linked to the Duke of Edinburgh award scheme as well as further RoTL (release on temporary license) activities.

there is evidence of non-traditional offerings having a positive impact in prison settings, particularly for those who are otherwise reluctant to engage (Chamberlain 2013). For example, aside from the benefits of more traditional football and rugby-based resettlement programmes (see Meek 2012), positive outcomes have been demonstrated in prison populations by offering activities as diverse as chess (Portman 2016), outward bound/wilderness activities (Leberman 2007), and yoga (Muirhead and Fortune 2016).

Summing up

Given the widespread appeal of sport and the gym, and the strong relationships which prison gym staff often develop with those in their care, it is clear that prison sports have a valuable role to play in many elements of prisoner resettlement, including (but not limited to) promoting education and employment opportunities, as well as the obvious mental and physical health benefits of regular exercise.

Specialist and carefully planned methods of delivery can motivate individuals to make positive life changes during their time in prison custody. But there is a need to be creative in promoting engagement from those who are less likely to visit the gym (for example, the unfit, vulnerable, non-sporty, or inactive) and to develop strategies for targeting specific populations, such as vulnerable prisoners, those with mental health or substance misuse issues, and those serving short sentences.

Lastly, the importance of nutrition should of course be considered alongside discussions of physical activity. It is not surprising that diet has a direct impact on the mood and behaviour of those in prisons; for example in a randomized trial of nutritional supplements on 231 young adult prisoners in England, those receiving the supplements for at least two weeks committed an average of 35% fewer behavioural offences (Gesch et al. 2002). Consequently, it is disappointing that very little policy attention is given to the nutritional content of the meals and snacks that are made available to those in custody.

This chapter has highlighted some of the key issues associated with prison sport, and drawn on some of the good practice examples identified in the 2018 independent review of sport and physical activity in youth and adult prisons. In doing so it has drawn attention to the opportunities that exist to utilize sport in promoting rehabilitative efforts, opportunities that to date remain underused across our prisons.

References

Amtmann, J. and Kukay, J. (2016) Fitness changes after an 8-week fitness coaching program at a regional youth detention facility. *Journal of Correctional Health Care*, 22(1), 75–83.

Battaglia, C., et al. (2013) Benefits of selected physical exercise programs in detention: A randomized controlled study. *International Journal of Environmental Research and Public Health*, 10(11), 5683–5696.

Buckaloo, B., Krug, K. and Nelson, K. (2009) Exercise and the low-security inmate: Changes in depression, stress and anxiety. *The Prison Journal*, 89(3), 328–343.

Chamberlain, J. (2013) Sports-based intervention and the problem of youth offending: A diverse enough tool for a diverse society? *Sport in Society*, 16(10), 1279–1292.

Coates, S. (2016) *Unlocking Potential: A Review of Education in Prison*. London: Ministry of Justice.

Elger, B. (2009) Prison life, television, sports, work, stress and insomnia in a remand prison. *International Journal of Law and Psychiatry*, 32, 74–83.

European Committee for the Prevention of Torture and Inhuman or Degrading Treatment. (2006) *European Prison Rules*. Strasbourg: Council of Europe.

Frost, J., Wortham, S. and Reifel, S. (2007) *Play and Child Development*. Hoboken, NJ: Pearson.

Gesch, C., Hammon, S., Hampson, S., Eves, A. and Crowder, M. (2002) Influence of supplementary vitamins, minerals and essential fatty acids on the antisocial behaviour of young adult prisoners. *British Journal of Psychiatry*, 181, 22–28.

Hartmann, D. (2003) Theorising sport as social intervention: A view from the grassroots. *Quest*, 55(2), 118–140.

HM Inspectorate of Prisons. (2017) *Life in Prison: Living Conditions*. London: HMIP.

HM Prison Service. (2009) *Physical Education*. PSO 4250. London: HMPPS.

Leberman, S. (2007) Voices behind the walls: Female offenders and experiential learning. *Journal of Outdoor Education and Outdoor Learning*, 7(3), 113–130.

Meek, R. (2012) *The Role of Sport in Promoting Desistance from Crime: An Evaluation of the 2nd Chance Project Rugby ad Football Academies at Portland Young Offender Institution*. Southampton: University of Southampton.

Meek, R. (2014) *Sport in Prison: Exploring the Role of Physical Activity in Correctional Settings*. Abingdon: Routledge.

Meek, R. (2018) *A Sporting Chance: An Independent Review of Sport in Youth and Adult Prisons*. London: MoJ.

Meek, R. Champion, N. and Klier, S. (2012) *Fit for Release: How Sports-Based Learning Can Help Prisoners Engage in Education, Gain Employment and Desist from Crime*. London: Prisoners Education Trust.

Meek, R. and Lewis, G. (2012) The role of sport in promoting prisoner health. *International Journal of Prisoner Health*, 8(3–4), 117–131.

Ministry of Justice. (2011) *Physical Education (PE) for Prisoners*. PSI 58/2011. London: MoJ.

Ministry of Justice. (2017) *Prison Population and Youth Custody Reports, November 2017*. London: MoJ.

Ministry of Justice. (2018) *Proven Reoffending Statistics Quarterly Bulletin January 2016 to March 2016*. London: Ministry of Justice.

Ministry of Justice and Department for Education. (2016) *Understanding the Educational Background of Young Offenders: Joint Experimental Statistical Report from the Ministry of Justice and Department for Education*. London: MoJ/DfE.

Moore, R. and Hamilton, P. (2016) 'Silo mentalities' and their impact on service delivery in prison-community transitions: A case study of resettlement provision at a male open prison. *The Howard Journal of Crime and Justice*, 55(1–2), 111–130.

Muirhead, J. and Fortune, C. (2016) Yoga in prisons: A review of the literature. *Aggression and Violent Behavior*, 28, 57–63.

Portman, C. (2016) *Chess Behind Bars*. Glasgow: Quality Chess UK.

Public Health England. (2016) *Making Every Contact Count (MECC) Consensus Statement*. London: Public Health England, NHS England, Health Education England.

United Nations. (1990) *Rules for the Protection of Juveniles Deprived of their Liberty ('the Havana Rules')*, UNGA resolution 45/113.

United Nations. (2015) *Standard Minimum Rules for the Treatment of Prisoners ('the Nelson Mandela Rules')*, UNGA resolution 45/113.

University of Central Lancashire. (2015) *Impact Report: Greener on the Outside of Prisons*. Preston: UCLAN/Groundwork UK.

Van Zyl, D. and Snacken, S. (2002) *Principles of European Prison Law and Policy: Penology and Human Rights*. Oxford: Oxford University Press.

Woods, D., Breslin, G. and Hassan, D. (2017) Positive collateral damage or purposeful design: How sport-based interventions impact the psychological well-being of people in prison. *Mental Health and Physical Activity*, 13, 152–162.

World Health Organization. (2007) *Health in Prisons: A WHO Guide to Essentials in Prison Health*. Copenhagen: WHO.

Violent offenders

34

Contemporary issues in risk assessment, treatment, and management

Philip Birch and Jane L. Ireland

The purpose of risk assessment: examining contemporary evidenced-based practice

As identified by Mooney and Sebalo (2018: 3) violent risk assessment approaches are an extension of the Risk-Need-Responsivity (RNR) model provided through the work of Andrews and Bonta (2010). Focusing on both static and dynamic factors associated with an individual's offending, the risk assessment process allows for offender needs, not just violent offenders, to be assessed. Preference currently is for adopting a structured clinical judgement approach to risk assessment as opposed to an actuarial approach or unstructured clinical approach, such as the use of clinical 'gut instinct'. Structured clinical approaches focus on a combination of empirical, historical, dynamic, and projective risk factors connected to risk, avoiding the pitfalls of the other approaches that fail to account for change (i.e. actuarial), or are based on intuition (i.e. unstructured clinical) (see Mooney and Sebalo 2018 for a more detailed illustration of the three main approaches to risk assessment). Structured risk assessments consider a range of factors, including but not limited to the psychological, social, cognitive functioning of an offender along with other risk/management factors that may impact on offending behaviour. Increasingly we are seeing more attention being paid to protective factors, namely those that promote nonoffending, and seeing the integration of these approaches with those solely focusing on risk factors. The ultimate purpose of the more progressive and holistic risk-protective assessment approaches, such as structured clinical, is to inform on appropriate treatment interventions and assess the likelihood of reoffending and/or non-compliance with expectations, which ultimately informs offender management strategies. As surmised by Bartol and Bartol (2008), risk assessments provide a psychosocial evaluation for the criminal justice system in which the management of risk in terms of future offending and the prevention of violence is paramount. It is argued that we can contain the human and financial cost of offending behaviour through risk assessments, which is an important role when considered in relation to the findings of McEvoy and Hideg (2017) who report that 560,000 deaths were caused by interpersonal and collective violence in 2016. This clearly makes violence risk assessment a major concern for all stakeholders.

Risk assessments are used in a number of situations, for decisions relating to moves within and across secure units, for the determination of bail, sentencing, and release, as well as informing on the most appropriate treatment and support services. As a consequence, errors in the process of risk assessment have serious ramifications. For example, offenders can be assigned to incorrect treatment, public protection is compromised due to offenders being incorrectly risk categorized, along with a breach in the civil liberties of offenders, victims, and the wider community as a result of poorly informed and conducted assessments. Risk assessments are not, after all, about getting the 'right' decision, as determining an absolute judgement in this area of practice is notoriously challenging. Rather, it is about having the best considered and informed approach.

Developments in the risk assessment field have aimed to meet this goal through the use of empirically informed risk assessment approaches and in doing so have shaped the practice of a range of professions including those allied to forensic psychology, psychiatry, and community corrections. For example, Lavoie et al. (2009) noted that during the 1970s, liability claims against clinicians who failed to protect potential victims began to increase, making risk assessment approaches an important form of protection for clinicians and their clients, while throughout the 1980s a rise in involuntary treatment within community for 'dangerous' offenders was introduced, again providing an important role for risk assessments in managing 'dangerous' groups such as violent offenders. Such historical developments have led to the use of risk assessment tools becoming a standard, mandatory, practice for clinicians and security providers that inform decision-making outcomes about their 'clients'. Over this period of time we have seen a shift from prediction of risk/future risk to risk *reduction* and risk *management* (Hart 1998; Steadman 2000; Webster et al. 2000). This is of particular significance when considering violent offenders, as the shift to risk reduction resonates with violence being considered a hard to predict and manage behaviour, where informed judgements about trying to understand and predict the behaviour become key. Risk assessments are a process of speculating in an empirically informed manner about the aggressive acts that may be committed. It is more of a process that must be followed in trying to reach an informed judgement. The shift to considering dynamic factors associated with violence (risk reduction), rather than static factors associated with violence (prediction) is key to this process (see the work of Caudy et al. 2013; Hanson et al. 2007; McDermott et al. 2008).

This process approach, of determining risk reduction, is one of management, and therefore the assessment of a range of conditions such as geography, social, and emotional factors that may increase and/or decrease risk rather than take a condition-free prediction of violence offending is engendered. The importance of developing a more informed judgement in identifying the risk status of a violent offender is paramount. The five principles of the risk assessment process outlined by Lavoie et al. (2009) become useful in reaching this goal. The first principle is the *reliable identification of offending risk factors* in which risk factors associated with violence need to be identified in order to determine the level of risk posed by an offender. This principle is intrinsically linked to the second, *comprehensive coverage of offending risk factors*, which relates to the need for all identified risk factors associated with violence to be covered by the risk assessment tool, allowing for the assessor to further capture any specific factors they view to be of significance in individual cases. The third principle is the *reliance of a risk assessment to risk management and risk reduction*. Through this third principle, recommendations for treatment and management of an offender can take place, where the risk status of an offender can be accounted for, namely their propensity to engage in violence at a particular time based on dynamic changes to psychological, biological, and/or social variables. The dynamic factors associated with their violence is further considered in relation to the historical (static/unchanging) factors associated with their behaviour. As a consequence, the assessment process becomes linked to recommendations for their management. The fourth principle for an accurate risk assessment procedure is the need for *clear and logical methods for communicating risk decisions*. Consequently, risk assessments should not only contain a clear descriptive statement of the risk (e.g. increased risk under certain circumstances) but obtain clear advice on how that risk should be reduced. Finally, the fifth principle is a *reviewable and accountable decision-making process*. In practice this element can be neglected, and it refers to the consideration of the assessment by other disciplines, such as lawyers, allowing for them to critically review and determine how such risk assessment decisions were reached. In essence, it lends itself to the importance of the transparency of the process of risk assessment.

Various risk assessment tools are currently in use for violent offenders and it is not the purpose of the current chapter to capture them all (see Mooney and Sebalo 2018, for a review). Nevertheless, in relation to structured clinical risk for general violence risk, the most commonly considered and applied in practice include the Historical Clinical Risk Management-20, Version 3 (HCR-20: V3) (Douglas et al. 2013), and the Short-Term Assessment of Risk and Treatability (START) (Nicholls et al. 2006). While many enhancements to risk assessment tools have occurred over recent years, specific tools have been developed for violent offenders other than men, namely women and adolescents (see Gray et al. 2018; Ireland 2018; Manning 2018; Pressman 2018; Vogel et al. 2018; Ogloff and Daffern 2006). What most of these tools overlook is the importance of protective factors. Many risk assessment tools focus on risk factors at the expense of considering attributes an offender possesses that could enable them to deal with, mitigate, and even eliminate the risk of engaging in behaviours such as violence (see de Vries Robbé et al. 2018). Tools such as the Structured Assessment of Protective Factors of Violence Risk (SAPROF) devised by de Vries Robbé as part of a comprehensive development including a range of other researchers (de Vogel et al. 2011) are evidenced to enhance the accuracy of risk management and treatment planning approaches, as well as desistence strategies (de Vries Robbé et al. 2015, 2018).

In sum, significant advancements in recent years with regards to the risk assessment procedure, in particular for violent offenders, has taken place. The improvements to this practice positively impact on both treatment interventions and management strategies for offenders. The following section moves on to consider the delivery of violent treatment interventions, which are the natural progression for addressing risk needs post evaluation.

Treatment approaches: current practice for violent offender treatment delivery

Offender behaviour treatment programmes have been developed through the prism of cognitive behavioural theory in which thoughts are considered to influence affect and ultimately influence behaviour (Tarrier and Wykes 2007). More recently there has been an acceptance of more integrated therapeutic programmes, where principles from a range of effective therapies, including CBT (cognitive behavioural therapy), are considered but also extended to cover other effective approaches, such as dialectic behaviour therapy (DBT) and cognitive analytic therapy (CAT) (see Ireland and Ireland 2018). This has led to the concept of multi-modal integrated therapy (MMIT: Ireland and Ireland 2018) emerging for a range of offence-related approaches, including those for violence. Within aggression therapy programmes, there has been a focus on social cognition as a key aspect (i.e. Information Processing), emotional management and relapse prevention (Ireland and Batool 2018; Ireland and Ireland 2018), with programmes such as the Life Minus

Violence-Enhanced (LMV-E) emerging (Ireland and Ireland 2018; Daffern et al. 2018). The following section provides an overview of the essential components to violent treatment interventions.

The first essential component for violent treatment interventions is that of Information Processing (i.e. social cognition). Treatment needs here attend to the processing of social information to enable an understanding of the development and maintenance of violence. The most applied and utilized model is the integrated work of Huesmann (1998) and his 'Unified Model of Information Processing' (UMIP). Huesmann's model demonstrates the importance of behavioural scripts as they guide our behaviour and act as a trigger following a stimulus, which can be used to explain the selection of aggressive versus non-aggressive scripts and how affect and the environment can impact on script selection. The UMIP also illustrates the significance of normative beliefs – beliefs held by an individual, who believes others hold the same views; emotions, which impact on the ability to process information; as well as perception/attributional errors, where a bias towards misinterpreting the actions (actual or intended) of others, leading to perceiving hostility in neutral or ambiguous situations. The value of this approach lies in its focus on how these elements all interact, sometimes simultaneously, to lead to aggressive actions. They also tie in well with structured risk assessment approaches, since they attend to the role of beliefs, emotions, and past behaviour (i.e. scripts). The value of models such as UMIP lies in their approach to considering aggression a decision that has been made; consequently, the focus in therapy becomes on the choices made by an individual and what impacts on that choice (i.e. beliefs, emotions, past actions). Treatment then moves to how to widen choices in order to supplement aggressive scripts with non-aggressive scripts (Ireland and Ireland 2018). By accounting also for learning experience and how this impacts on script selection and interpretation, treatment programmes likely to be effective need to consider and encourage offenders to consider how their behaviour has been influenced by past events and their response to environmental cues.

The impact of emotions on an individual's behaviour and the emotional management of such are important to consider and essential to integrate into violence treatment. Emotions can present as triggers, facilitators, and goals for aggression (Ireland and Ireland 2018), with a breadth of research demonstrating associations between aggression and emotions (Ireland 2009), with a significant proportion of this focusing on anger (Baumeister and Bushman 2007). The emotion of anger has dominated treatment programmes concerning aggression, but other emotions have to be considered too and have been considerably neglected (Ireland and Ireland 2018). These include fear, anxiety, pain, shame, guilt, jealousy, pleasure, and frustration (Baumeister and Bushman 2007; Ireland and Ireland 2018) to name but a few. Essentially emotions are nothing more than the label we give to a physiological response, emphasizing further the essential role for cognition, with physiological arousal then impacting negatively on the ability to process information. This is further consistent with the UMIP.

Violent treatment interventions must, therefore, incorporate emotional management. Emotional management is complex and arguably comprises three elements; Acceptance, which is concerned with not suppressing an emotion response; Regulation, namely employing strategies to explicitly or implicitly manage emotions; and Reactivity, where the focus is on how an individual reacts to an aggressive trigger and/or facilitator. All violence treatment must recognize these three core areas, along with the obvious interplay between cognitions and emotions. A restructuring of cognition becomes key in trying to manage an emotional reaction. Within therapy a range of approaches will be adopted to try and teach acceptance, regulation, and to understand reactivity, by using techniques such as role play, mood induction, and group discussion (Ireland and Ireland 2018). Mood Induction Procedures (MIPS) are worthy of a brief commentary as they can be very useful means of identifying and working directly with aroused ('hot') cognition. MIPS (e.g. Burkitt and Barnett 2006) require clients to recall an event they have experienced relevant to the mood being induced (i.e. elaborate memory recall), where there is a focus on where they were when the mood occurred, when the mood occurred, who was involved, what happened, and what induced the mood. Through the mimicking of the mood and exploration of the associated and resulting cognition(s), clients are able to see how their mood has impacted on their cognition processing and resulting decisions they have taken. Once an understanding of the experience is cognitively appraised, insight into how the emotion is linked to the cognition is presented, allowing for restructuring to take place.

Finally, relapse prevention is a central element to violent treatment interventions and should form a fully integrated component of such intervention. It should not appear as an afterthought or placed solely at the end of therapy; rather it should be integrated throughout (Ireland and Ireland 2018). Relapse prevention is closely aligned to the protective factors that are found within structured clinical risk assessment approaches, where we try to determine what factors in the future need to be accounted for. As part of this, relapse prevention considers the triggers and cues that occur prior to a further act of aggression or 'near miss' occurring. A model that has been used to support this process in violence therapy has been the SRM-RP (Self-Regulation Model of Relapse Process), a model outlined by Ward and Hudson (2000). This model recognizes the problems in self-regulation and failure to control behaviour and emotions, leading to ineffective strategies to achieve goals, which in turn can facilitate the occurrence of violence. Immediately the association between this model and that of the UMIP can be considered. When considering relapse prevention, nine stages of the SRM-PR are addressed:

1   Life Events – how do offenders appraise events, which may lead to their offence, e.g. behavioural scripts?
2   Desire for Deviant Act – what creates the desires, which facilitate the maladaptive activity?

3   Offence-Related Goals Established – what is the offenders' desire to engage in maladaptive behaviour?

4   Strategy Selecting – does the offender try to prevent the violence; is it planned?

5   High Risk Situations Entered – what is the offender's access to high-risk victims and situations?

6   Lapse – what is the immediate precursor to the aggression?

7   Offence – what aggression was committed and what emotional state did it lead to?

8   Past Offence Evaluation – how does the offender evaluate what they have done?

9   Attitudes Towards Future Offending.

(Ward and Hudson 2000)

The SRM-RP process contributes to the maintenance awareness of what contributes to lapse and relapse. Therefore, these stages need to be addressed in treatment. Equally, there needs to be attention given to those situations where an offender could have been violent but chose not to do so. The enhancement of positive events and strength becomes key in this regard, since this helps to maximize offender strengths whilst also identifying key protective factors that bring them away from a choice to be aggressive (Ireland and Ireland 2018).

This brief section on violence treatment has highlighted the core components for such interventions as information processing (social cognition), emotional management, and relapse prevention. Addressing these areas in a group setting also has a range of advantages. These become obvious once the importance of social cognition is accepted and the fact that aggression generally occurs in a social context where there are a range of environmental factors likely influencing. Treating aggression in the absence of a social context can be problematic, particularly when the aim is to challenge cognition that is misattributed and/or has a basis in normative beliefs. Aggression is, after all, largely a social problem that needs to be addressed within such a context. This consideration moves the chapter onto the importance of management; intervention is only one part of the risk process, with management and the social components also a key aspect of working with violent offenders.

The management of violent offenders: principles and operational practice

As illustrated thus far, the criminal justice system is concerned with managing offenders through risk assessment and treatment intervention. This process is also extended to the management of offenders, in particular violent offenders, reflected in surveillance techniques, supervision methods, as well as through-care and resettlement practices that primarily occur through probation, community corrections service delivery, and/or secure community health provision. The operational practice for the management of violent offenders, in particular within the 21st century, has been informed by the concept of 'dangerousness' in which it is recognized that a group of individuals require enhanced intervention and management from the criminal justice system (Williams 2018). This is underpinned by the earlier work of Beck (1992) and the concept of the 'risk society' in which the precautionary principle of 'better safe than sorry' prevails and has significantly influenced the management of offenders, in particular those deemed to be the most dangerous, violent offenders. It also parallels more broadly with developments in the risk assessment and intervention field, where focus is not just on the assessment of such individuals but on treatment and management; past are the days where a risk assessment would just determine risk level, with more current thinking (as reflected in structure clinical assessment approaches) focused on what to do with the assessment, i.e. how to intervene and manage. This has also led to a preference for the more dynamic term of 'risk assessment' as opposed to the more static term of 'dangerousness' but the latter is still enshrined as a normative term within the criminal justice field.

Dangerousness and the management of offenders is symbolized by three current penal practices, first, *incapacitation*, in which reforming an individual offender occurs at the same time as the redistribution of the risk away from society into incarceration. Second, *preventative detention*, in particular within the new millennium where criminal justice policy and practice is based on public protection (Nash 2006; Williams 2018). Finally, the third penal practice informing the management of offenders, in particular violent offenders, is that of *profiling*, where risk factors are used to profile likely offenders and likely criminal situations that then lead to targeted interventions such as Intensive Supervision Programmes (ISP) and Intensive Policing Practices (IPP) (Considine and Birch 2009). Such practices reflect an approach to managing offenders that is based on actuarial justice, the avoidance of future risks and harms, and is ultimately concerned with risk reduction, a focus of contemporary risk assessment procedures and treatment interventions.

In terms of surveillance and technology as a management strategy for violent offenders, this approach has been used for some time in working with this cohort, particularly in the community. The introduction of electronic monitoring is a feature of criminal justice practice in over 30 countries (Bartels and Martinovic 2017), whilst ever since 9/11 in 2001 we have seen an overabundance of surveillance strategies and technologies introduced in a bid to manage high-risk offenders. Developments such as 'finger and retinal scans, software which assesses hand geometry and vein patterns, voice and face recognition software' (Hier and Greenberg 2007: 7) have become increasingly commonplace in the management of dangerousness and high-risk offenders, such as violent offenders, in the community. The use of surveillance and new technologies in the management of offenders has enabled criminal justice agencies to monitor and manage their behaviour and daily lives. As a consequence, surveillance and technology has created a panopticon effect, in particular for those violent offenders being managed in the community, in that there is a constant monitoring and visibility of those subject to such sanctions. This is illustrated through the use of GPS to manage violent offenders (Nellis and Shadbolt 2018), albeit engendering a number of ethical and allied dilemmas. The debate within criminological discourse is significant with regards to the breach in the human rights of using such methods as a means of managing offenders (see Cobley 2013; Nash 2006; Nellis and Shadbolt 2018). The perils of surveillance and technology in managing the most dangerous offenders within our community is further exacerbated through questioning the practice of criminal justice agencies and their (over)reliance on using such methods, not only to manage the risk posed by an individual, but also to protect the public from further harm.

The importance of offender supervision is an important feature of managing violent offenders. Evidenced-based practice, as outlined by Trotter (2018) provides a number of strategies shown to be effective in the management of such offenders through supervision. The relationship an offender has with the criminal justice practitioners involved in their management plan is of significance, and Trotter (2018) acknowledges that nonjudgemental and effective communication are essential to the working relationship between practitioner and offender. The strength of this working relationship correlates with the need for the management of violent offenders to involve pro-social modelling. The management of violent offenders through the process of offender supervision requires a non-criminal lifestyle to be reinforced by criminal justice and allied professionals working with this cohort of offenders, in order to reduce the likelihood of further offending. As a consequence, the promotion of pro-social values and behaviours takes place through supervision, drawing similarities between the essential components of violent treatment initiatives, which enhance coping strategies and relapse prevention techniques, and the management of violent offenders. It also draws parallels to the developments in the protective risk assessment field, such as the SAP-ROF, where focus is shifting towards the preventative and protective factors to promoting as opposed to just recognizing and monitoring the risk factors. The supervision of violent offenders needs to take advantage of all of these developments in the field, including identifying and working with the protective factors. However, as Trotter (2018) recognizes, the importance of accurate risk assessment procedures remains paramount, as the process provides the risk status of an offender, which ultimately informs the management strategies adopted through offender supervision and the intensity of the resources they will allocate.

Overall, the role of supervision in the management of violent offenders and the relationship with through-care and resettlement practice is both significant and well evidenced (Bouffard and Bergeron 2006; Griffiths et al. 2007; Serin et al. 2010). Arguably, through-care and resettlement practices are a subsidiary focus when considering the management of offenders, yet Trebilcock and Worrall (2018) contend such practices are important when working with violent offenders. The concept of through-care and resettlement representing an 'afterthought' to intervention and risk assessment is not unique to supervision and management (Ireland and Ireland 2018). Reframing through-care and resettlement as a process, as argued earlier in this chapter for risk assessment, rather than as a single event becomes key. Trebilcock and Worrall (2018) acknowledge the practice focuses on addressing the likelihood of reoffending by dealing with criminogenic factors, including unemployment, housing, and health issues. However, obstacles such as poor partnership working amongst criminal justice and allied professions, the use of extended and indeterminate sentencing as well as adverse media attention given to the management of dangerous offenders (in particular violent offenders), has undermined through-care and resettlement strategies (Trebilcock and Worrall 2018). Nevertheless, initiatives such as the Resettle Program in the UK (Baker et al. 2013) and supported accommodation for violent offenders (Bruce et al. 2014) provide a strong case for through-care and resettlement practices, especially when working with violent offenders. It would just appear that as an area of development it has not yet been afforded as much attention as the process of risk assessment and violence treatment intervention.

In summary, the management of dangerous offenders, namely violent offenders, in particular within the community, is a contentious issue. The principles and theoretical frameworks that have informed the service delivery of this work over time, such as Beck's (1992) 'risk society', has led to practices which arguably impinge on the human rights of offenders and arguably de-skill the work of probation, community correction officers, and allied professionals. There is still, nevertheless, strong evidence that evidences the core practices of service provision offered by criminal justice professionals, such as probation officers, namely offender supervision and through-care and resettlement practices, are effective in working with violent offenders and contribute to recidivism.

Conclusion

Through this chapter the core components of working with violent offenders have been considered: risk assessment procedures, violent treatment interventions, and the management strategies. These three components for working with this cohort are circular, in that the precision of the risk assessment process is paramount in informing treatment, and the impact and outcome of treatment is important when considering the management strategies to be employed. Having considered these three distinct, yet integrated practices on offer when working with violent offenders and acknowledging the respective benefits and challenges of such practice, the most significant challenge in working with this cohort of offender may lie in how the concept of risk is understood. As Kemshall and McIvor (2004) highlighted, the origin of the word risk has two meanings – 'danger' and 'taking a chance'. Considine and Birch (2009) expand on this by stating that risk and dangerousness have become synonymous and almost exclusively conceived as 'danger' or 'threats', overlooking the alternative definition of 'taking a chance'. The conception of risk in the form of danger or threats has particular consequences for shaping the debate on how dangerous offenders should be managed and treated, and is reflected in criminal justice practices such as preventative detention and the undervaluing of through-care and resettlement strategies. If we had a concept of risk meaning 'taking a chance', alongside an increased focus of seeing risk assessment as an ongoing dynamic process, then the implications of working with violent offenders would shift from the current focus, one that centres on actuarial justice to one that centres more boldly on rehabilitation and reintegration, providing an alternate vision of the 'risk society' and how criminal justice and allied professionals work with this cohort of offender.

References

Andrews, D. A. and Bonta, J. (2010) Rehabilitating criminal justice policy and practice. *Psychology, Public Policy, and Law*, 16(1), 39–55.

Baker, V., Johnson, D. and Oluonye, S. (2013) Resettle: A significant new step in an emerging pathway that manages risk and addresses need in high risk personality disordered offenders on their release into the community. *Psychology, Crime & Law*, 19, 449–460.

Bartels, L. and Martinovic, M. (2017) Electronic monitoring: The experience in Australia. *European Journal of Probation*, 9(1), 80–102.

Bartol, C. R. and Bartol, A. M. (2008) *Introduction to Forensic Psychology: Research and Application*. London: Sage Publications.

Baumeister, R. F. and Bushman, B. J. (2007) Angry emotions and aggressive behaviors. In G. Steffgen and M. Gollwitzer (Eds.), *Emotions and Aggressive Behaviour*. Cambridge, MA: Hogrefe and Huber, pp. 61–75.

Beck, U. (1992) *Risk Society*. London: Sage Publications.

Bouffard, J. A. and Bergeron, L. E. (2006) Re-entry works: The implementation and effectiveness of a serious and violent offender re-entry initiative. *Journal of Offender Rehabilitation*, 44(2–3), 1–29.

Bruce, M., Crowley, S., Jeffcote, N. and Coulston, B. (2014) Community DSPD pilot services in South London: Rates of reconviction and impact of supported housing on reducing recidivism. *Criminal Behaviour & Mental Health*, 23, 124–140.

Burkitt, E. and Barnett, N. (2006) The effects of brief and elaborate mood induction procedures on the size of young children's drawings. *Educational Psychology*, 26(1), 93–108.

Caudy, M. S., Durso, J. M. and Taxman, F. S. (2013) How well do dynamic needs predict recidivism? Implications for risk assessment and risk reduction. *Journal of Criminal Justice*, 41(6), 458–466.

Cobley, C. (2013) The legislative framework. In A. Matravers (Ed.), *Sex Offenders in the Community*. Cullompton: Willan Publishing, pp. 69–89.

Considine, T. and Birch, P. (2009) Challenges of managing the risk of violent and sexual offenders in the community. In J. L. Ireland, C. A. Ireland and P. Birch (Eds.), *Violent and Sexual Offenders: Assessment, Treatment and Management*. London: Routledge, pp. 284–302.

Daffern, M., Simpson, K., Ainslie, H. and Chu, S. (2018) The impact of an intensive inpatient violent offender treatment programme on intermediary treatment targets, violence risk and aggressive in a sample of mentally disordered offenders. *The Journal of Forensic Psychiatry & Psychology*, 29(2), 163–188.

De Vogel, V., de Vries Robbé, M., de Ruiter, C. and Bouman, Y. H. (2011) Assessing protective factors in forensic psychiatric practice: Introducing the SAPROF. *International Journal of Forensic Mental Health*, 10(3), 171–177.

De Vogel, V., Wijkman, M. and de Vries Robbé, M. (2018) Violence risk assessment in women: The value of the female additional manual. In J. L Ireland, C. A. Ireland and P. Birch (Eds.), *Violent and Sexual Offenders: Assessment, Treatment and Management*, 2nd edition. London: Routledge, pp. 210–228.

De Vries Robbé, M., Mann, R. E., Maruna, S. and Thornton, D. (2015) An exploration of protective factors supporting desistance from sexual offending. *Sexual Abuse*, 27(1), 16–33.

Douglas, K. S., Hart, S. D., Webster, C. D., Belfrage, H., Guy, L. S. and Wilson, C. M. (2013) Historical-clinical-risk management-20, version 3 (HCR-20V3): Development and overview. *International Journal of Forensic Mental Health*, 13(2), 93–108.

Gray, A. L., Shaffer, C. S., Viljoen, J. L., Muir, N. M. and Nicholls, T. L. (2018) Assessing violence risk in youth. In J. L. Ireland, C. A. Ireland and P. Birch (Eds.), *Violent and Sexual Offenders: Assessment, Treatment and Management*, 2nd edition. London: Routledge, pp. 120–141.

Griffiths, C. T., Dandurand, Y. and Murdoch, D. (2007) *The Social Reintegration of Offenders and Crime Prevention*. Ottawa, ON: National Crime Prevention Centre.

Hanson, R. K., Harris, A. J., Scott, T. L. and Helmus, L. (2007) *Assessing the Risk of Sexual Offenders on Community Supervision: The Dynamic Supervision Project*, Vol. 5, No. 6. Ottawa, ON: Public Safety Canada.

Hart, S. D. (1998) The role of psychopathy in assessing risk for violence: Conceptual and methodological issues. *Legal and Criminological Psychology*, 3(1), 121–137.

Hier, S. P. and Greenberg, J. (Eds.). (2007) *The Surveillance Studies Reader*. Maidenhead: McGraw-Hill.

Huesmann, L. R. (1998) The role of social information processing and cognitive schema in the acquisition and maintenance of habitual aggressive behavior. In R. G. Green and E. Donnerstein (Eds.), *Human Aggression Theories, Research and Implications for Social Policy*. San Diego, CA: Academic Press, pp. 73–109.

Ireland, J. L. (2009) Treatment approaches for violence and aggression: Essential content components. In J. L Ireland, C. A. Ireland and P. Birch (Eds.), *Violent and Sexual Offenders: Assessment, Treatment and Management*. London: Routledge, pp. 153–178.

Ireland, J. L. (2018) Individual assessments of aggression: Accounting for core factors. In J. L. Ireland, C. A. Ireland and P. Birch (Eds.), *Violent and Sexual Offenders: Assessment, Treatment and Management*, 2nd edition. London: Routledge, pp. 231–255.

Ireland, J. L. and Batool, S. (2018) Treatment intervention for aggression: Promoting individual change. In J. L. Ireland, P. Birch and C. A. Ireland (Eds.), *The Routledge International Handbook of Human Aggression*. London: Routledge, pp. 122–134.

Ireland, J. L. and Ireland, C. A. (2018) Therapeutic treatment approaches for violence: Some essential components. In J. L Ireland, C. A. Ireland and P. Birch (Eds.), *Violent and Sexual Offenders: Assessment, Treatment and Management*, 2nd edition. London: Routledge, pp. 319–341.

Kemshall, H. and McIvor, G. (Eds.). (2004) *Managing Sex Offender Risk*. London: Jessica Kingsley Publishers.

Lavoie, J. A., Guy, L. S. and Douglas, K. S. (2009) Violence risk assessment: Principles and models bridging prediction to management. In J. L Ireland, C. A. Ireland and P. Birch (Eds.), *Violent and Sexual Offenders: Assessment, Treatment and Management*. London: Routledge, pp. 3–26.

Manning, N. (2018) Assessing violence and sexual risk among offenders with cognitive intellectual difficulties. In J. L Ireland, C. A. Ireland and P. Birch (Eds.), *Violent and Sexual Offenders: Assessment, Treatment and Management*. London: Routledge, pp. 179–193.

McDermott, B. E., Edens, J. F., Quanbeck, C. D., Busse, D. and Scott, C. L. (2008) Examining the role of static and dynamic risk factors in the prediction of inpatient violence: Variable-and person-focused analyses. *Law and Human Behavior*, 32(4), 325–338.

McEvoy, C. and Hideg, G. (2017) *Global Violent Deaths 2017: Time to Decide*. Switzerland: Small Arms Survey.

Mooney, R. and Sebalo, I. (2018) Violence risk assessment. In J. L Ireland, C. A. Ireland and P. Birch (Eds.), *Violent and Sexual Offenders: Assessment, Treatment and Management*, 2nd edition. London: Routledge, pp. 31–45.

Nash, M. (2006) *Public Protection and the Criminal Justice Process*. Oxford: Oxford University Press.

Nellis, M. and Shadbolt, N. (2018) Managing violent and sexual offenders in contemporary technoculture. In J. L Ireland, C. A. Ireland and P. Birch (Eds.), *Violent and Sexual Offenders: Assessment, Treatment and Management*, 2nd edition. London: Routledge, pp. 504–518.

Nicholls, T. L., Brink, J., Desmarais, S. L., Webster, C. D. and Martin, M. L. (2006) The short-term assessment of risk and treatability (START) A prospective validation study in a forensic psychiatric sample. *Assessment*, 13(3), 313–327.

Ogloff, J. R. and Daffern, M. (2006) The dynamic appraisal of situational aggression: An instrument to assess risk for imminent aggression in psychiatric inpatients. *Behavioral Sciences & the Law*, 24(6), 799–813.

Pressman, D. E. (2018) Risk assessment and management of violent extremists and terrorists: Background, principles, and practice. In J. L Ireland, C. A. Ireland and P. Birch (Eds.), *Violent and Sexual Offenders: Assessment, Treatment and Management*, 2nd edition. London: Routledge, pp. 105–119.

Serin, R. C., Lloyd, C. D. and Hanby, L. J. (2010) Enhancing offender re-entry: An integrated model for enhancing offender re-entry. *European Journal of Probation*, 2(2), 53–75.

Steadman, H. J. (2000) From dangerousness to risk assessment of community violence: Taking stock at the turn of the century. *Journal of the American Academy of Psychiatry and the Law*, 28(1), 265–271.

Tarrier, N. and Wykes, T. (2007) Cognitive therapy. In D. Machin, S. Day and S. Green (Eds.), *Textbook of Clinical Trials*. London: Wiley, pp. 353–376.

Trebilcock, J. and Worrall, A. (2018) The importance of throughcare and resettlement for working with violent and sexual offenders. In J. L Ireland, C. A. Ireland and P. Birch (Eds.), *Violent and Sexual Offenders: Assessment, Treatment and Management*, 2nd edition. London: Routledge, pp. 532–547.

Trotter, C. (2018) Offender supervision and compliance: Managing violent and sexual offenders in the community. In J. L Ireland, C. A. Ireland and P. Birch (Eds.), *Violent and Sexual Offenders: Assessment, Treatment and Management*, 2nd edition. London: Routledge, pp. 481–489.

Ward, T. and Hudson, S. M. (2000) A self-regulation model of relapse prevention. In D. R. Laws, S. M. Hudson and T. Ward (Eds.), *Remaking Relapse Prevention with Sex Offenders: A Sourcebook*. Thousand Oaks, CA: Sage Publications, pp. 79–101.

Webster, C. D., Douglas, K. S., Belfrage, H. and Link, B. G. (2000) Capturing change: An approach to managing violence and improving mental health. In S. Hodgins and R. Müller-Isberner (Eds.), *Violence Among the Mentally Ill*. Dordrecht: Springer, pp. 119–144.

Williams, A. (2018) Preventive detention and extended sentences: A regressive approach to managing violent and sexual offenders? In J. L Ireland, C. A. Ireland and P. Birch (Eds.), *Violent and Sexual Offenders: Assessment, Treatment and Management*, 2nd edition. London: Routledge, pp. 490–503.

35

Effective approaches to working with sex offenders

Tim Warton

Introduction

The literature on sex offender management includes notable models and methods of assessment and treatment that guide what we do with sex offenders post-adjudication. There are also arguments for and against prescriptive, or manualized approaches to treatment (Mann 2009; Hollin 2009). These are all necessary considerations; however, this chapter is less concerned with models and manuals and more concerned with *how* to undertake such approaches. More specifically, some areas of specific professional skill that are useful for success with any given interaction with an offender. For instance, cognitive behavioural therapy has been widely reported in the literature as a successful treatment modality (Marshall and Serran 2004; Marshall et al. 2006; Yates 2009; Marshall and Marshall 2016; Stinson and Becker 2013); however, using CBT can be done with low levels of skill and in isolation from other areas of practice competency necessary for a more significant impact of treatment overall.

This chapter will outline several effective approaches to working with sex offenders with a focus on some of the skills and practices that are useful in the early stages of a working relationship with a sexual offender. Many of these skills and discussions may seem familiar when considering the literature on working with non-sex offenders – this is to be expected as the principles of effective practice can be interchangeable (Hanson et al. 2009; Andrews and Bonta 2010). Having said that, the social responses to sex offending as well as other intrapersonal variances from the non-sex offending population highlight differences in practice required as well as the need for categorical support for workers (Bailey and Sample 2017).

Stigma's effect on practice

One of the more difficult realities to negotiate in the area of sex offender treatment is the influence stigma can have on good practice. Societal expectations and opinion can weigh heavily on the policy of statutory bodies and in turn, the practice of the worker. Many vocal opinions that call for harsh measures and close monitoring of sex offenders (Huffman 2016; Ward 2007; Alexander 2010; Glaser 2003) might influence the attitudes and beliefs of those tasked to work with them. Should a practitioner be influenced by such retributive ideologies, it can be argued that such practice may increase the risk of recidivism. Day et al. (2014) promisingly found that many practitioners hold more useful views about sex offender management than such ideologies would promote.

The notion of stigma is true for all offenders, but people who sexually offend tend to hold a particular place in the list of the stigmatized of society. Generally, last place. Mingus and Burchfield (2012) noted that the 'sex offender' is amongst the most highly stigmatized labels in contemporary societies. In comparison to other offender categories, sex offenders are often seen as more dangerous and persistently predatory (Cain 2008; Andrews and Bonta 2010) and specialized social policies are often introduced to address the perceived risk of recidivism (Hanson and Morton-Bourgon 2009). These blanket policies often miss the mark as sex offenders tend to be regarded as a homogenous group that can all be treated successfully in the same, often restrictive way (Bailey and Sample 2017; Sample and Bray 2006).

These social phenomena can have a marked effect on the practice of someone who has committed sexual offences. Client and worker are both likely aware of society's views on sexual offending, and this can make already difficult conversations harder still. It can blur the purpose of the role of the worker and supervision and treatment. Before working with people who sexually offend, it is critical that the worker have adequate space to reflect on their own potential bias and systems of belief to ensure adherence to best practice principles.

Role clarification

Once in the criminal justice system, the stigma associated with official and unofficial labels can have significant impacts on client outcomes (Tewksbury and Connor 2012). This stigma can affect the client's self-concept as well as the way they believe others perceive them – in turn, this affects social ties, social integration, employment, and related opportunities (Mingus and Burchfield 2012). In brief, the way the offender now perceives the world and the people in it can be dramatically affected by adjudication and the surrounding processes.

Consider a socially isolated sex offender who has withdrawn from new relationships to avoid facing the assumptions of new people (Link et al. 1989). This offender may have well-rehearsed beliefs about what people who find out about the offences think of him and want to do to him. Bailey and Sample (2017) found that clients who experienced negative encounters with their workers assumed it was due to their dislike of sex offenders. These general perceptions are likely to shape what sex offenders may believe supervision to be about and what can be expected from a working relationship. Such a client may assume that the role of the worker is to continue interrogations, maintain a sense of hardship through ongoing scrutiny, exposure, and punishment. These beliefs will significantly influence the nature of the working relationship. Similarly, as noted earlier, if the worker's views about their purpose and role are punitive or strictly about social control, this can also affect the nature of the working relationship (Bailey and Sample 2017).

To address the problems associated with such confusion, role clarification is a necessary and persistent process to undertake. Trotter (2015: 78) states that role clarification is essentially workers helping clients understand the purpose and nature of direct practice processes – it is exploratory and involves more than merely explaining a legal mandate.

Role clarification is a purposeful and specific practice that is carried out, typically at the outset of a legal order and any given supervision session or other interaction that creates a platform of mutual understanding and shared expectations between worker and client (Trotter 2015). It includes clarifying the role of the agency, the individuals within it as well as clear explanation of the expectations of the worker and the client. It is also necessary to clarify the purpose of each supervision session as well as rules and expectations in a custodial environment (Cherry 2014). While client understanding is important, client approval in what the worker is clarifying can also be helpful. Levenson et al. (2010) found that when clients believed that what they were working on in treatment to be important, satisfaction was higher, and clients were more engaged.

What is the role of the worker?

The literature on role clarification highlights the 'dual role' of the worker in a mandated setting – that is, the worker can help with the client's problems despite being an agent of social control (Trotter 2015). Or as Skeem et al. (2007) note, workers have care for and control over involuntary clients. This two-in-one role is perhaps one of the trickiest skills to maintain as it demands that the worker keep a helper role and all that entails, but at the same time necessitates the role of the social control agent. If done poorly this can lead to some particularly negative assumptions that would make progress difficult. When done well, adherence to the dual role can positively affect client worker relationship quality and satisfaction, treatment motivation, and compliance with the rules of legal mandates (Skeem 2007).

To ensure consistency of role clarification, it may be helpful for workers to consider the assumptions or perception of the role from the perspective of the sex offender. For example, does the client view the worker as somewhat like the police who are most concerned with adherence to the sex offender registry? Is the client becoming dependant on the worker or is challenging criminality growing increasingly difficult within a hostile working relationship?

Westwood et al. (2011) discuss the difficulties in working within the tension of a dual purpose that exists between workers and sex offenders specifically. This tension affects the levels of admissions and transparency that clients may choose to generate due to the knowledge of the consequences. One participant of the study summated the tension well by saying:

> They can never trust us utterly because they know, and we have offenders say to us, look . . . I know that you're trying to make things better for me, I know you're trying to get the electronic tag lifted, I know that you're trying to work in my favour, but I know you're a probation officer as well.
>
> (Westwood et al. 2011: 223)

To address this dilemma is not easy; however, it can be effectively managed using purposeful and consistent role clarification throughout interactions. For example, a useful phrase might be 'when you say something that I think will lead to you hurting someone or get you into trouble, I'll bring it up to discuss'.

The working relationship

When working with any mandated client, an effective working relationship allows the worker and client to be cooperative and understand the best way to help and match interventions to the circumstances and needs of the client (Cherry 2014). While there is not a considerable literary base examining the nature of a working relationship with sex offenders, good quality relationship skills remain essential for treatment success (Marshall and Serran 2004). Hughes (2011) found that effective interpersonal contact and relationships between clients and workers are of 'most significance in encouraging compliance and engagement' (Hughes 2011: 49). Unfortunately for those working with sex offenders the model of effective relationships generally stems from voluntary working relationships (Mirick 2018). These models are typically characterized by working with clients who are willing and interested in being engaged in a relationship that is collaborative, warm, and empathetic – sex offenders who are mandated into treatment and not interested in such a relationship are often labelled resistive, and the working relationship is considered poor (Mirick 2018). It is no surprise then that Brown and Tully (2014) found many sex offenders have had bad experiences with professionals. This is not to say that those working with offenders are doomed to have poor working relationships, but rather, more concerted efforts may be required to establish a similar working relationship as those had with voluntary clients.

Again, the above can be considered valid to all mandated clients; however, within the context of adverse stigma, the nature of the working relationship can be argued to be different from the relationships formed with non-sex offenders (Bailey and Sample 2017). Drawing on the experiences of supervision officers working with sex offenders, as well as offenders themselves, Bailey and Sample (2017) found several useful points around the working relationship. One important finding relates to worker beliefs about sex offenders' capacity for manipulation and dangerousness and as a result, staff report to maintain a more 'formal' or detached working relationship with sex offenders (Bailey and Sample 2017). This detached relationship was argued to potentially impede the capacity for workers to help influence offender behaviour (Bailey and Sample 2017), possibly due to the reduced capacity for openness and effective challenging.

Another important distinction in the working relationship between sex offenders and non-sex offenders is their capacity for interpersonal relationships. Evidence suggests that sex offenders have particular deficits around intimacy and relationship issues that are significant treatment targets and are related to recidivism (Hanson and Morton-Bourgon 2005; Marshal and Marshal 2016; Shursen et al. 2008; Bailey and Sample 2017). These deficits may be related to the fact that many sex offenders often have had poor childhood attachments negatively influencing their capacity for the development of meaningful relationships (Bailey and Sample 2017). Whatever the case, Bailey and Sample (2017) make a valuable point that the same deficits that prevent intimate social bonds are likely to also affect any social relationship, including those with correctional staff. Staff, therefore, need to be able to be appropriately responsive to these deficits and avoid labelling clients resistive, unwilling, or manipulative – as doing so may change the nature of the working relationship from a more productive one to a monitoring or detached role.

Concerning approaches to consolidate a sound working relationship with mandated clients, Trotter (2015: 35) offers a helpful list of interpersonal skills including the use of 'empathy and reflective listening, self-disclosure, use of humour and optimism'. It is noted, however, that the effective use of empathy and reflective listening specifically with mandated clients appears to require a decidedly pro-social slant to be effective (Trotter 2015). That is, empathy is not colluding, endorsing or in any way showing approval for attitudes or actions (Cherry 2014). This is particularly important for sex offenders who may be persistently relinquishing responsibility for attitudes, feelings, or actions. Consider expressing empathy using reflective listening with a sex offender on their struggles say, with feeling emotionally 'safe' with children over adults. Without a pro-social challenge after this expression of empathy, there is likely to be an implied condoning of the experiences the offender has. For example, there is a significant difference in the transaction of meaning between 'it must be tough that you feel that way around children' and 'it must be tough that you feel that way around children, but it needs to change'.

In a similar vein, Dowden and Andrews's (2004) well-cited meta-analysis on effective correctional staff practices note that the best outcomes come from staff who are fair, firm, transparent, and unambiguous. While these are undoubtedly sound principles to base a working relationship on, there may be difficulty in translating them to practice due to the subjectivity of interpretation. What may be firm and fair to one person might be punitive and demeaning to another. Again, transparency in explaining a concept to a sex offender may be confused with bluntness or even coercive interactions in practice. This concept of practice subjectivity can be seen as Marshall and Serran (2004) discuss the utility of 'directiveness' in the therapeutic relationship. They note that directiveness is helpful but can easily be 'overdone such that the therapist comes to control the decisions made by the clients' (Marshall and Serran 2004: 315). Developing these skills, therefore, requires more than one worker, that is, effective supervision. It takes a commitment to improve and an openness as a worker to receive critical supervisory feedback as well as being open to self-reflection as key to enhancing practice over time. While training may be helpful, a coaching model may be a far better method of development (Labrecque and Smith 2017).

Confrontation, challenging, and disclosures

When working with sex offenders, difficult conversations are an inevitable part of the role. This section will examine specific features of such interactions, specifically the notion of confrontation or challenging and managing disclosures.

The concept of reacting to criminality in some useful way has been discussed in various ways in the literature. Effective disapproval, for example, refers to the worker, within a warm and open relationship, expressing disapproval of behaviour or attitude and encouraging the client to consider why it is undesirable (Dowden and Andrews 2004; Andrews and Bonta 2010). Similarly, challenging is discussed by workers responding to undesirable or pro-criminal behaviours or comments on a regular basis in what could be described as an exploratory non-blaming manner (Trotter 2015; Trotter et al. 2017). Again Hepworth et al. (2010) use the term 'confrontation' to refer to a process of discussing with clients their thinking, feelings, and behaviour that contributes to their difficulties. This school of thought on the issue presents a continuum of confrontation, ranging from avoidance to abusive interaction – with the levels of reasonable confrontation in between being appropriate (Mirick 2018).

However described, the fact remains that when a sex offender presents a worker with a criminally dangerous sentiment or behaviour, some form of interjection is needed. Ignoring or accepting justifications can be detrimental to the process and is associated with poorer outcomes (Trotter 2015). An argument could easily be made that non-purposeful ignoring of criminal sentiments could inadvertently condone the sentiment (purposeful to address later or avoid 'baiting' for example).

Also, challenging using hostility or within the bounds of a relationship characterized by distrusting or dislike can be counterproductive, and staff must be cautious not to 'overdo' the challenging (Andrews and Bonta 2010; Trotter 2015; Mirick 2018). Andrews and Bonta (2010) and Trotter (2015) discuss the '4 to 1' rule where to every challenge there are four positive statements.

The general offending literature has informed the above discussion, and as noted earlier, it is compatible with sex offender interventions. However, when challenging behaviours or sentiments that support or excuse sexual offending, it is necessary to consider how to structure these conversations without sounding like the rest of society to further stigmatize and jeopardize a well-established working relationship which is necessary for effective challenging (Andrews and Bonta 2010). That is, we obviously do not want to compromise the messages of sexual harm. However, many offenders have a clear and well-rehearsed framework of justification that prevents them from effectively hearing confronting messages – Mirick (2018) refers to such clients as being 'heavily defended'. Such a situation may, in turn, encourage workers to increase levels of severity of the challenge. However, strong confrontation can incite strong defensive responses which can reduce the efficacy of the challenge in the first place (Mirick 2018: 217). It may then be more helpful to defer to a style of challenging that is exploratory (Trotter et al. 2017). That is, rather than expressing disapproval and leaving it at that, follow-up open questions are likely to be useful. For example, 'it seems like thinking that way about women and girls could maintain these problems, could you tell me more about it?'

Disclosures

Even when the expectations of the working relationship are set, disclosures from clients – that is the portrayal of new or once-secret information – can be challenging to negotiate. As with the rest of the therapeutic process, a safe and robust working relationship is paramount in dealing effectively with sexual offending disclosures (Purvis et al. 2013). While client disclosures are not usually expressions of shocking revelatory significance (Westwood et al.

2011), managing them does not always work in the best interest of the client and preparation for both worker and the client should made (Glaser 2003). Drawing on the experience of practitioners, Wood et al. (2010) identified both deliberate or unintentional disclosures on the part of the offender, both with points to consider. For example, if the disclosure is intentional, this should be measured against the offender's motivation to change (Purvis et al. 2013). It is also important to consider if such a disclosure may be viewed as an 'over-disclosure' to be 'overly compliant'. This may be indicative of the person attempting to tell the worker what they believe they would want to hear (Wood et al. 2010). Caution must be used with unintentional disclosures. Information from an unintentional disclosure may need to be used at a more appropriate time rather than at the initial confrontation to ensure the continuation of open discussion (Wood et al. 2010).

Disclosure under Therapeutic Jurisprudence – which is argued to give the law a 'healing' role – may damage a working relationship by disrupting a perceived place of confidentiality (Glaser 2003). While good role clarification can work to prevent this, encouraging clients to see the benefits of disclosure is also of use. Westwood et al. (2011) note that when sex offenders disclose information and experience a poor outcome, it is unlikely they will choose to disclose again and the challenge for the practitioner is the extent to which they can enable offenders to see benefits of disclosures. Two ways to avoid this are: highlighting that not all disclosures lead to a punitive action, particularly within a positive working relationship, positive interactions can endure; and reframing a disclosure as a request for help and intervention can encourage an overall strengths-based approach to a punitive situation encouraging a sense of self-efficacy (Westwood et al. 2011: 224).

There are of course instances where it is advantageous to try to elicit disclosures, and there is literature around this (see Purvis et al. 2013 for more discussion). In brief, however, Westwood et al. (2011) discuss the following strategies and skills to elicit a disclosure successfully; firstly the working relationship must be a safe and permissive environment. Secondly, the worker must have expertise in interviewing and questioning techniques, as well as specialist knowledge of sexual offending risk assessment and victim issues. Finally, the worker must also be able to assess the significance of the disclosure and match it to a potential change in risk (Westwood et al. 2011: 217). Regarding change in risk status, Purvis et al. (2013) note that some of these changes in risk may include substance abuse, victim access, or emotional collapse.

It is important to be mindful that full disclosure may not be a necessary goal. Hanson and Morton-Bourgon (2005: 1159) note that 'few people, however, are inclined to completely reveal their faults and transgressions'. Clients who don't fully disclose all the information are probably doing so because they know their behaviour is wrong and are experiencing shame or embarrassment (Purvis et al. 2013; Hanson and Morton-Bourgon 2005).

Dealing with denial

Dealing with denial, minimizations, or justifications for offending can be difficult for the practitioner to manage. Denial should probably be expected – it is a typical response to being confronted with any wrongdoing, and the expectation that sex offenders would respond differently is unrealistic (Ware and Mann 2012; Yates 2009). While denial has not been shown to be related to recidivism (Yates 2009; Hanson and Morton-Bourgon 2005), a considerable proportion of sex offenders maintain some level of denial – be it total (like 'I wasn't there'), partial, or around specific features like offence planning (like 'I didn't really think about it, it just happened') (Marshall et al. 2003). Denial then can be deemed to relate to outstanding criminogenic needs due to blockages it causes in treatment (Freeman et al. 2010; Yates 2009).

The relationship between empathy and denial can be an essential point for the practitioner to consider when working with a denying client. Despite the debates in the literature around the relationship between empathy and recidivism, empathy development remains one of the critical treatment targets for sex offenders (see Brown et al. 2013; Hanson and Morton-Bourgon 2005). Anderson and Dodgson (2002) note that there may be a relationship between what looks like a lack of empathy and denial. That is, as Marshall et al. (2009) theorize, due to problems with shame, sex offenders may deny offending or deny causing harm to avoid the emotional impacts of empathy. Again, Brown et al. (2013) discuss how offenders create 'psychologically comfortable positions' that enable offending by protecting themselves from the dissonance that empathy for the victims causes. As a result then, it *may* be a promising sign in some sense that a sex offender is stuck in denial as it could indicate intrinsic pro-social beliefs about the harm that they have caused as 'offenders who minimize their crimes are at least indicating that sexual offending is wrong' (Hanson and Morton-Bourgon 2005: 1159).

For direct practice, Yates (2009) offers a helpful and practical summary of effective approaches when dealing with a denying client. Firstly, Yates (2009) notes that, assess the function and purpose of the function of denial (remembering denial may be quite a 'normal' cognitive process) and approach any CBT interventions in a collaborative rather than confrontative (confrontative approaches encourage defensiveness and entrenches denial) manner. Secondly, helping clients to understand the role their thinking plays in their offending or behaviour *generally* or *globally* is said to be helpful (Yates 2009: 194). For example, discussing people's capacity for consent generally, rather than focusing on the offender's victim.

Should a client be a categorical denier, modifications to treatment rationale can be made. Marshall et al. describes a 'deniers treatment programme' where clients are told that they will not be required to admit offending, but all general dynamic factors will be worked on (Yates 2009' Marshall et al. 2006). Following this discussion around the risk factors that led them to be 'falsely accused' can be dealt with as primary risk factors (Marshall et al. 2006).

Another important point to note is the importance of maintaining the working relationship with a denying client. Glaser (2003) notes that denying sex offenders are particularly prone to manipulative behaviour and 'therapist shopping' so persistence is key. Watson et al. (2016) also found that the longer deniers are in treatment, the less resistant and vocal they become about their denial and would still likely to glean some benefit from being involved in mainstream treatment programmes.

Conclusion

This chapter has presented several practice issues and skills that are generally applicable to working effectively with non-sex offenders. However, given the social and characteristic differences that sex offenders have as well as considering the impact of stigma, these approaches were discussed with the consideration of areas of specialization.

The approaches presented are not necessarily attached to any broader framework of intervention – that calls for far more significant discussion. Demonstrated in this chapter are discussions of skills necessary to continue to master as regardless of the framework in which a worker may operate, they still have a person in front of them, under peculiar circumstances, that is generally mandated to have significant levels of interaction.

References

Alexander, R. (2010) Collaborative supervision strategies for sex offender community management. *Federal Probation*, 74(2), 16–19.

Anderson, D. and Dodgson, P. G. (2002) Empathy deficits, self-esteem, & cognitive distortions in sexual offenders. In Y. M. Fernandez (Ed.), *In Their Shoes: Examining the Issue of Empathy Psychology, Crime & Law*. Oklahoma City: Oakwood 'N' Barnes Publishing.

Andrews, D. A. and Bonta, J. (2010) *The Psychology of Criminal Conduct*, 5th edition. London: Anderson Publishing.

Bailey, D. J. and Sample, L. L. (2017) Sex offender supervision in context: The need for qualitative examinations of social distance in sex offender – supervision officer relationships. *Criminal Justice Policy Review*, 28(2), 176–204.

Brown, S. J. and Tully, R. J. (2014) Components underlying sex offender treatment refusal: An exploratory analysis of the treatment refusal scale – sex offender version. *Journal of Sexual Aggression*, 20(1), 69–84.

Brown, S. J., Walker, K., Gannon, T. A. and Keown, K. (2013) Creating a psychologically comfortable position: The link between empathy and cognitions in sex offenders. *Journal of Sexual Aggression*, 19(3), 275–294.

Cain, K. B. (2008) *Managing Convicted Sex Offenders in the Community*. Washington, DC: NGA Centre for Best Practices.

Cherry, S. (2014) *Transforming Behaviour: Pro-social Modelling in Practice*, 2nd edition. New York: Routledge.

Day, A., Carson, E., Newton, D. and Hobbs, G. (2014) Professional views on the management of sex offenders in the community. *Journal of Offender Rehabilitation*, 53, 171–189.

Dowden, C. and Andrews, D. A. (2004) The importance of staff practice in delivering effective correctional treatment: A meta-analytic review of core correctional practice. *International Journal of Offender Therapy and Comparative Criminology*, 48(2), 203–214.

Freeman, J., Palk, G. and Davey, J. (2010) Sex offenders in denial: A study into a group of forensic psychologists' attitudes regarding the corresponding impact upon risk assessment calculations and parole eligibility. *Journal of Forensic Psychiatry & Psychology*, 21(1), 39–51.

Glaser, B. (2003) *Therapeutic Jurisprudence: An Ethical Paradigm for Therapists in Sex Offender.*

Hanson, R. K. and Morton-Bourgon, K. E. (2005) The characteristics of persistent sexual offenders: A meta-analysis of recidivism studies. *Journal of Consulting and Clinical Psychology*, 73(6), 1154–1163.

Hanson, R. K. and Morton-Bourgon, K. E. (2009) The accuracy of recidivism risk assessments for sexual offenders: A meta-analysis of 118 prediction studies. *Psychological Assessment*, 21(1), 1–21.

Hanson, R. K., Bourgon, G., Helmus, L. and Hodgson, S. (2009) The principles of effective correctional treatment also apply to sexual offenders: A meta-analysis. *Criminal Justice and Behavior*, 36(9), 865–891.

Harper, C. A. and Hogue, T. E. (2015) Measuring public perceptions of sex offenders: Reimagining the Community Attitudes Toward Sex Offenders (CATSO) scale. *Psychology, Crime & Law*, 21(5), 452–470.

Hepworth, D. H., Rooney, R., Rooney, G., Strom-Gottfried, K. and Larsen, J. (2010) *Direct Social Work Practice: Theory and Skills*, 8th edition. Belmont, CA: Brooks, Cole, Cengage Learning.

Hollin, C. R. (2009) Treatment manuals: The good, the bad and the useful. *Journal of Sexual Aggression*, 15(2), 133–137.

Huffman, M. K. (2016) Moral panic and the politics of fear: The dubious logic underlying sex offender registration statutes and proposals for restoring measures of judicial discretion to sex offender management. *Virginia Journal of Criminal Law*, 4(2), 217–234.

Hughes, W. (2011) Promoting offender engagement and compliance in sentence planning: Practitioner and service user perspectives in Hertfordshire. *Probation Journal*, 59(1), 49–65.

Labrecque, R. M. and Smith, P. (2017) Does training and coaching matter? An 18-month evaluation of a community supervision model. *Victims & Offenders*, 12(2), 233–252.

Levenson, J. S., Prescott, D. S. and D'Amora, D. A. (2010) Sex offender treatment: Consumer satisfaction and engagement in therapy. *International Journal of Offender Therapy and Comparative Criminology*, 54(3), 307–326.

Link, B. G., Cullen, F. T., Struening, E., Shrout, P. E. and Dohrenwend, B. P. (1989) A modified labeling theory approach to mental disorders: An empirical assessment. *American Sociological Review*, 54(3), 400–423.

Mann, R. E. (2009) Sex offender treatment: The case for mutualisation. *Journal of Sexual Aggression*, 15(2), 121–131.

Marshall, W. L. and Serran G. A. (2004) The role of the therapist in offender treatment. Psychology. *Crime & Law*, 10(3), 309–320.

Marshall, W. L., Serran, G. A., Fernandez, Y. M., Mulloy, R., Mann, R. E. and Thornton D. (2003) Therapist characteristics in the treatment of sexual offenders: Tentative data on their relationship with indices of behaviour change. *Journal of Sexual Aggression*, 9(1), 25–30.

Marshall, W. L. and Marshall, L. E. (2016) The treatment of adult male sex offenders. In D. P. Boer (Eds.), *The Wiley Handbook on the Theories, Assessment and Treatment of Sex Offenders*. Chichester: Wiley Blackwell.

Marshall, W. L., Marshall, L. E., Serran, G. A. and Fernandez, Y. M. (2006) *Treating Sexual Offenders: An Integrated Approach*. New York: Routledge.

Marshall, W. L., Marshall, L. E., Serran, G. A. and O'Brien, M. D. (2009) Self-esteem, shame, cognitive distortions and empathy in sexual offenders: Their integration and treatment implications. *Psychology, Crime & Law*, 15(2), 217–234.

Marshall, W. L. and Serran, G. A. (2004) The role of the therapist in offender treatment. *Psychology, Crime & Law*, 10(3), 309–320.

Mingusa, W. and Burchfield, K. B. (2012) From prison to integration: Applying modified labelling theory to sex offenders. *Criminal Justice Studies*, 25(1), 97–109.

Mirick, R. (2018) Initial phase work with individual involuntary clients. In Rooney, R. H. and Mirick, R.G. (Eds.), *Strategies for Work with Involuntary Clients*, 3rd edition. Columbia.

Purvis, M., Ward, T. and Shaw, S. (2013) *Applying the Good Lives Model to the Case Management of Sexual Offenders*. Brandon, Vermont: The Safer Society Press.

Sample, L. L. and Bray, T. M. (2006) Are sex offenders different? An examination of rearrest patterns. *Australian and New Zealand Journal of Criminology*, 29(1), 29–46.

Shursen, A., Brock, L. J. and Jennings, G. (2008) Differentiation and intimacy in sex offender relationships. *Sexual Addiction & Compulsivity*, 15(1), 14–22.

Skeem, J. L., Louden, J. E., Polaschek, D. and Camp, J. (2007) Assessing relationship quality in mandated community treatment: Blending care with control. *Psychological Assessment*, 19(4), 397–410.

Stinson, J. D. and Becker, J. V. (2013) *Treating Sex Offenders AN Evidence Based Manual*. New York: The Guilford Press.

Tewksbury, R. and Connor, D. P. (2012) Incarcerated sex offenders' perceptions of family relationships: Previous experiences and future expectations. *Western Criminology Review*, 13(2), 25–35.

Trotter, C. (2015) *Working with Involuntary Clients*, 3rd edition. Sydney: Allen & Unwin.

Trotter, C., Evans, P. and Baidawi, S. (2017) The effectiveness of challenging skills in work with young offenders. *International Journal of Offender Therapy and Comparative Criminology*, 61(4), 397–412.

Ward, T. (2007) On a clear day you can see forever: Integrating values and skills in sex offender treatment. *Journal of Sexual Aggression*, 13(3), 187–201.

Ware, J. and Mann, R. E. (2012) How should "acceptance of responsibility" be addressed in sexual offending treatment programs? *Aggression and Violent Behaviour*, 17(4), 279–288.

Watson, S., Harkins, L. and Palmer, M. (2016) The experience of deniers on a community sex offender group program. *Journal of Forensic Psychology Practice*, 16(5), 374–392.

Westwood, S., Wood, J. and Kemshall, H. (2011) Good practice in eliciting disclosures from sex offenders. *Journal of Sexual Aggression: An International, Interdisciplinary Forum for Research, Theory and Practice*, 17(2), 215–227.

Wood, J., Kemshall, H., Westwood, S., Fenton, A. and Logue C. (2010) *Research Summary 6/10*. Investigating Disclosures Made by Sexual Offenders: Preliminary Study for the Evaluation of Mandatory Polygraph Testing, Ministry of Justice.

Yates, P. M. (2009) Is sexual offender denial related to sex offence risk and recidivism? A review and treatment implications. *Psychology, Crime & Law*, 15(2), 183–199.

36

'Five-Minute Interventions' in prison

Rehabilitative conversations with offenders

Charlene Pereria and Phillipa Evans

Therapeutic relationships in correctional programs

Within the helping professions, creating a trusting and nonjudgemental relationship with the client, and collaboratively developing treatment goals and tasks is considered central to establishing a positive working alliance and promoting behaviour change (Hart and Collins 2014). Edward Bordin's theory on the therapeutic working alliance (1979) encompassing three elements: tasks, goals, and bond, augment the importance of the bond. Bordin (1979) identifies this element as the mediator within the worker-client relationship that enables the collaborative agreement on the therapeutic goals and tasks to be addressed (Hart and Collins 2014).

Contemporary correctional practices which embrace psychological research regarding behaviour change acknowledge the importance of the worker-client therapeutic alliance in delivering evidence-based practices (EBPs) proven to promote reduced recidivism (Viglione et al. 2017; Polaschek 2016). The role of the correctional officer has accordingly transitioned from being primarily concerned with custodial/risk management to adopting a function as an 'agent of positive influence' (Johnston 2015). The adoption of the therapeutic working alliance encourages officers to model pro-social behaviour, work collaboratively to aid rehabilitation by supporting the offender with their treatment goals and in their transition from custody to community (Johnston 2015). Sonkin and Dutton (2003) argue that this shift in correctional practice also requires officers to be competent in the application of several skills including reflective listening and empathy, if they are to encourage an offender to view their relationships, self, and offending behaviour from a different perspective. Frazer et al. (2014) concur, suggesting that when an officer demonstrates care about the offender and their future, provides advocacy, and engages the offender in goal setting this helps support and facilitate the desistance process.

Grant and McNeill (2014) undertook a study with English and Scottish community probation officers examining their perspectives of the meaning of quality in offender supervision and its influence on client outcomes. The probation workers interviewed affirmed that establishing good relational bonds as the primary foundation to quality work. Building rapport, listening, respect, building trust, and viewing the person as a 'whole' were identified as other key qualities that enhanced the supervision process. Hart and Collins (2014) conducted a more in-depth exploration of the influence of working alliance on probation supervision and offender outcomes. This study was undertaken in the North of England with ten probation officers and 48 offenders. The link between working alliance and an offender's perception of the success of the probation experience was examined, in addition to the effect of risk level and offence type on working alliance. Offenders were administered the Working Alliance Inventory Short Revised (WAISR) questionnaire measuring their feelings of probation and their probation officer. The Success of Probation Scale (SPS) was also administered measuring impulsivity, empathy, loyalty, and encouragement from probation officers, in addition to problem-solving skills, motivation to change, and perceived helpfulness of probation. Results identified offenders were more likely to maintain the skills, behaviours, and values learnt from supervision when the bond with their officer was strong. This study also concluded that a strong bond with their supervisor contributed to offenders being more equipped to form positive relationships in the future.

Despite research highlighting the importance of the therapeutic working alliance between officers and offenders in generating rehabilitative outcomes, the responsibility for creating a therapeutic culture within the prison environment has been primarily the role of clinical staff. The officer-prisoner relationship has been historically underemphasised due to a strong focus on curriculum learning, programme integrity, and more measurable outcomes associated with recidivism rates (Shively et al. 2016). However it can be argued that the amount of direct time an officer spends with a prisoner places an officer in an influential position to establish a positive working alliance to reward positive behaviours and reinforce treatment goals and concepts learned in clinical treatment programmes (Polaschek 2016).

Shively et al. (2016) propose that in order to foster a therapeutic prison culture, prison officer roles need to be considered complementary to clinical treatment programme staff. Adopting this approach requires officers to use consistent language encouraging consequential thinking, empathy for others, modelling of pro-social behaviour, and offering incentives as a means to motivate the prisoner toward change (Shively et al. 2016). Viglione et al. (2017) further identify that the application of client-centred, collaborative communication techniques are consistent with the responsivity principle and suggest this interaction style contributes to officers engaging in a dual relationship that balances authority and compliance with a therapeutic problem-solving approach.

Research suggests the benefits of adopting therapeutic approaches are bidirectional. Prison officers may start to perceive their role more as educators and mentors, encouraging the uptake of skills to help prisoners reflect and problem-solve, and therefore manage prisoner conflict in non-violent and pro-social ways. This is in turn may contribute to less tension, greater job satisfaction, and work toward helping the prisoner develop internal motivation and support self-efficacy (Smith and Schweitzer 2012).

'Right Track' is an example of one such approach, implemented within a custodial environment in New Zealand in 2012. This approach stemmed from the 'active management' framework which encouraged custodial staff to take an offender-centric approach, be responsive to emerging issues, work in collaboration with other service providers, and it emphasized officers' opportunity to use every contact with the offender to influence the rehabilitation process (Johnston 2015). It is suggested having an intentional plan to guide officers in their interactions, demonstrating a genuine interest in the offender by having a brief conversation while passing them by, delivering on promises, using active listening skills, and reinforcing treatment concepts promotes a shared purpose between officers and clinical staff as change agents (Shively et al. 2016).

The use of evidence-based skills in correctional settings

Examination of workers' use of effective practice skills has been growing in momentum in recent years. A meta-analysis undertaken by Dowden and

Andrews (2004) identified five Core Correctional Practice skills associated with positive outcomes for offenders: effective use of authority, appropriate modelling and reinforcement, problem-solving, use of community resources, and quality of interpersonal relationships. The effectiveness of these skills in community supervision has been shown in a number of studies including Trotter (1996), Trotter and Evans (2012), Taxman (2008), Bonta et al. (2011), Paparozzi and Gendreau (2005), Robinson et al. (2012), and Raynor et al. (2014). Although the definition of effective practice skills mildly varies between these studies, they clearly link workers' use of effective practice skills to better outcomes for the offender (Maguire and Raynor 2016).

Whilst there is evidence to support positive outcomes for offenders when workers use effective practice skills, the majority of this research has been undertaken in community corrections. Within the custodial environment, there is a growing narrative surrounding rehabilitative prison cultures, with staff relationships and interactions with prisoners forming the cornerstone of this debate (Mann et al. 2018). Petersilia (2003) argues that prisons need to be permeated by a pro-social offender management process; however examination regarding prison officers' use of pro-social modelling and other effective practices skills is sparse. McGuire and Raynor (2016) argue that the development of trusting personal relationships between prison officers and prisoners is central to rehabilitative resettlement.

There is some evidence that adult prison officer skills are related to better outcomes. French and Gendreau (2006), for example, concluded from their meta-analysis that prison climate and behaviours are better when workers have a rehabilitative focus. They suggest that good practice in prisons is similar to good practice in community supervision.

There is some research that has been undertaken that suggests that prison officers and prisons would benefit from greater use of effective practice skills in custody. An American study by Marsh and Evans (2009) examined the relationships between prison officers and 543 youth across a number of youth detention centres. They tentatively concluded that there was at least some evidence that relationships with staff lead to better outcomes for youth after they leave custody. They comment on the challenges relating to changing the culture of youth detention but suggest that 'the cost associated with avoiding this challenge, however, is simply too great for society or its most troubled youth' (Marsh and Evans 2009: 64).

Antonio et al. (2009) examined the impacts of a two-hour custodial staff training programme focused on encouraging staff to utilize positive reinforcement in their day-to-day work with prisoners, using rewards and showing disapproval. Pre- and post-training surveys were administered to correctional workers to get a further understanding if the training impacted on staff attitudes regarding offender treatment and rehabilitation. Researchers found that staff became more aware of their own behaviour after attending the training; however the extent to which they used positive reinforcement in practice was not examined.

The five-minute intervention project

Whilst it is clear that prison officers are central to creating a positive prison climate, the research also appears to suggest that effective practice skills can contribute to a positive prison climate for both prison officers and prisoners. Research regarding training for prison officers in effective practice skills is limited. The five-minute intervention project, designed and implemented by the National Offender Management Service (NOMS) in the United Kingdom, was developed to support prison officers in their use of problem-solving skills on a day-to-day basis, taking into consideration the operational requirements of their positions.

Two qualitative studies have been undertaken examining the impact of prison officer training in Five Minute Intervention (FMI) from both the prison officer and prisoner perspective.

Ten prison officers from Her Majesty's Prison and Young Offender Institution (HMP/YOI) Portland participated in two days of training specially focusing on the skills prison officers utilize in their interactions with prisoners. The skills included: structured questioning, giving and receiving feedback, active listening, and giving prisoners hope (Kenny and Webster 2015). Through in-depth quantitative interviews researchers interviewed ten prison guards trained in FMI to further understand the impact of the training. Officers highlighted a number of broader environmental barriers to utilizing the FMI skills including low staff morale, the complexity of the prisoners that they were working with (including serious mental health and behavioural issues), concern regarding the high levels of reoffending and time restrictions that would impact on them having meaningful conversations with the prisoners. Whilst there were some operational issues notes, including the time taken to deliver FMI and the cultural shift in their role to becoming an 'interventionist', prison officers noted several positive aspects of the FMI training model including:

- A focus on building rapport with the prisoner prior to conducting FMI
- Making the time for engagement in meaningful conversations
- Finding time to use FMI

Although this is a small-scale study, this research highlights the operational adaptation of effective practice skills to suit a prison environment. The researchers did note that some prison officers did not engage well with the model and recommended that professional supervision needed to be incorporated into the model.

In a follow-up study, Tait et al. (2017) interviewed ten prisoners to gain a better understanding of their perception of care and rehabilitation from prison officers who had been trained in FMI. Prisoners identified specific qualities of officers trained in FMI. Prisoner officers trained in FMI were perceived as being 'genuinely interested', which researchers noted appeared to facilitate change

(Tait et al. 2017). Prisoners also noticed an increased use of affirmations used by FMI officers, along with encouraging prisoners use of self-reflection.

There were a number of personal qualities noted by prisoners that FMI displayed including being nonjudgemental, a willingness to help, and a reciprocal relationship.

Whilst these studies highlight the impact of staff utilizing effective practice skills in the context of their day-to-day duties, there are limitations including the small sample sizes and short follow-up period. These studies do however give us pause for optimism, suggesting that effective practice skills can be built into the fabric of the prison.

Professional supervision

At its core, professional supervision is concerned with providing a better quality of service to clients by ensuring ethical and professional practice standards are met and interventions are tailored to the individual needs of the client. Within the criminal justice environment, supervision also acts as a mechanism to hold staff accountable, monitor compliance with organizational rules and procedures, and implement interventions to address client needs with a specific focus on reductions in recidivism. However with the re-emergence of offender (case) management emphasizing the importance of the quality of the therapeutic working alliance and application of evidence-based practice skills, this has called for management to revisit the facilitation of supervision as a learning forum to support the correctional officer (supervisee) to increase their competence and confidence in adhering to evidence-based practices to provide a balanced approach to risk management, rehabilitation of offenders, and community safety (Annison et al. 2008; Bonta et al. 2013).

Walker et al. (2018) and Griffin et al. (2012) posit that when professional supervision is provided within a learning culture that supports staff discussion regarding the strains and stress of managing offenders, it may also act as a protective factor. This supervision style is especially important for officers within therapeutic prisons encompassing the dual role of custodian and treatment provider due to their increased likelihood of being exposed to graphic details of offending behaviour and managing extreme emotions and distorted cognitions, that if left unaddressed may affect their personal and occupational well-being. Gornik et al. (1999) further add that a supervision approach that also enforces pro-social values and behaviours within a learning culture not only supports behaviour change in offenders, but contributes to staff being less likely to experience burnout, experience low job satisfaction, and/or use authority inappropriately.

Experiences of prison officers within the Five Minute Intervention Project support and acknowledge the importance of a learning culture within the prison setting and the provision of quality professional supervision to embrace a rehabilitative ethos and keep performance moving in the desired direction through reflective practice discussions on challenges and shared successes (Kenny and Webster 2015). Smith and Schweitzer (2012) purport that within a therapeutic prison environment, training is also required to enable officers and clinical staff to have a better understanding and appreciation for the similarities and differences in their work roles. Cross training and regular clinical supervision act to further embed a learning culture to improve prisoner needs and programme outcomes. In addition, studies exploring perceptions of quality supervision between offender and officer, and between corrections officer and line manager (supervisor) found positive perceptions of the quality of supervision and the supervisor was an important indicator of desistance for offenders, and was linked to increased job satisfaction and commitment for staff (Griffin et al. 2012).

These research findings strongly demonstrate the need for executive levels of management to create and embed a learning culture whereby staff receive regular professional supervision that encourages reflective practice, allows for constructive feedback to keep attention on an offender-centric and collaborative model of intervention, provides a safe and supportive environment to disclose personal and professional problems, but most importantly emphasizes the vital role officers play in offender rehabilitation reinforcing their professional identity as an 'agent of change' working within an integrated correctional strategy (Gornik et al. 1999; Johnston 2015).

References

Annison, J., Eadie, T. and Knight, C. (2008) People first: Probation officer perspectives on probation work. *Probation Journal*, 55(3), 259–271.

Antonio, M. E., Young, J. L. and Wingeard, L. M. (2009) Reinforcing positive behavior in a prison: Whose responsibility is it? *Journal of Offender Rehabilitation*, 48(1), 53–66.

Bonta, J., Bourgon, G., Rugge, T., Gress, C. and Gutierrez, L. (2013) Taking the leap: From pilot project to wide-scale implementation of the Strategic Training Initiative in Community Supervision (STICS). *Justice Research and Policy*, 15(1), 1–18.

Bonta, J., Bourgon, G., Rugge, T., Scott, T., Yessine, A., Gutierrez, L. and Li, J. (2011) An experimental demonstration of training probation officers in evidence-based community supervision. *Criminal Justice and Behavior*, 38(11), 1127–1148.

Bordin, E. (1979) The generalisability of the psychoanalytical concept of the working alliance. *Psychotherapy*, 16, 252–260.

Dowden, C. and Andrews, D. A. (2004) The importance of staff practice in delivering effective correctional treatment: A meta-analytic review of the literature. *International Journal of Offender Therapy and Comparative Criminology*, 48(2), 203–214.

Frazer, L., Drinkwater, N., Mullen, J., Hayes, C., O'Donoghue, K. and Cumbo, E. (2014) Rehabilitation: What does 'good' look like anyway? *European Journal of Probation*, 6(2), 92–111.

French, S. A. and Gendreau, P. (2006) Reducing prison misconducts. *Criminal Justice and Behaviour*, 33, 185–218.

Gornik, M., Bush, D. and Labarbera, M. (1999) *Strategies for Application of the Cognitive Behavioural/Social Learning Model to Offender Programs*. Technical Assistance Proposal.

Washington, DC: National Institute of Corrections. A Cognitive Interpretation of the Twelve-Steps.

Grant, S. and McNeill, F. (2014) The quality of probation supervision: Comparing practitioner accounts in England and Scotland. *European Journal of Probation*, 6(2), 147–168.

Griffin, M., Hogan, N. and Lambert, E. (2012) Doing "people work" in the prison setting. An examination of the job characteristics model and correctional staff burnout. *Criminal Justice and Behaviour*, 39(9), 1131–1147.

Hart, J. and Collins, K. (2014) A 'back to basics' approach to offender supervision: Does working alliance contribute towards success of probation? *European Journal of Probation*, 6(2), 112–125.

Johnston, P. (2015) Twenty years of corrections – the evolution of offender rehabilitation. *Practice: The New Zealand Corrections Journal*, 3(2), December.

Kenny, T. and Webster, S. (2015) *Experiences of Prison Officers Delivering Five Minute Interventions at HMP/OI Portland*. Available at: http://socialwelfare.bl.uk/subject-areas/services-client-groups/adult-offenders/ministryofjustice/175147portlandfmi.pdf (Accessed 25 November 2017).

Maguire, M. and Raynor, P. (2016) *Offender Management in and After Prison: The End of 'End to End'*. Unpublished manuscript.

Mann, R., Fitzalan Howard, F. and Tew, J. (2018) What is a rehabilitative prison culture. *Prison Service Journal* (235), 3–10.

Marsh, S. and Evans, W. (2009) Youth perspectives on their relationships with staff in juvenile correction settings and perceived likelihood of success on release. *Youth Violence and Juvenile Justice*, 7(1), 46–67.

Paparozzi, M. A. and Gendreau, P. (2005) An intensive supervision program that worked: Service delivery, professional orientation, and organizational supportiveness. *The Prison Journal*, 85(4), 445–466.

Petersilia, J. (2003) *When Prisoners Come Home*. New York: Oxford University Press.

Polaschek, D. (2016) Do relationships matter? Examining the quality of probation officers' interactions with parolees in preventing recidivism. *Practice: The New Zealand Corrections Journal*, 4(1).

Raynor, P., Ugwudike, P. and Vanstone, M. (2014) The impact of skills in probation work: A reconviction study. *Criminology and Criminal Justice*, 14(2), 235–249.

Robinson, C., Lowenkamp, C., Holsinger, A., VanBenschoten, S., Alexander, M. and Oleson, J. (2012) A Random Study of Staff Training Aimed at Reducing Re-arrest (STARR): Using core correctional practices in probation interactions. *Journal of Crime and Justice*, 35, 167–188.

Shively, R., Simpson, M. and Nunes, P. (2016) The importance of therapeutic relationships in correctional programs. *Corrections Today*, January–February.

Smith, P. and Schweitzer, M. (2012) The therapeutic prison. *Journal of Contemporary Criminal Justice*, 28(1), 7–22.

Sonkin, D. J. and Dutton, D. (2003) Treating assaultive men from an attachment perspective. *Journal of Aggression, Maltreatment, and Trauma*, 7(1), 105–133.

Tait, H., Blagden, N. and Mann, R. (2017) *Prisoners' Perceptions of Care and Rehabilitation from Prison Officers Trained as Five Minute Interventionists*. Analytical Summary 2017, HM Prison and Probation Service.

Taxman, F. (2008) No illusions: Offender and organizational change in Maryland's proactive community supervision efforts. *Criminology and Public Policy*, 7(2), 275–302.

Trotter, C. (1996) The impact of different supervision practices in community corrections. *Australian and New Zealand Journal of Criminology*, 29(1), 29–46.

Trotter, C. and Evans, P. (2012) Analysis of supervision skills in juvenile justice. *Australian and New Zealand Journal of Criminology*, 45(2), 255–273.

Viglione, J., Rudes, D. and Taxman, F. (2017) Probation officer use of client-centred communication strategies in adult probation settings. *Journal of Offender Rehabilitation*, 56(1), 38–60.

Walker, E., Egan, H., Jackson, C. and Tonkin, M. (2018) Work-life and well-being in U.K. Therapeutic prison officers: A thematic analysis. *International Journal of Offender Therapy and Comparative Criminology*, 62(14), 4258–4544.

The benefits of mindfulness-based interventions in the criminal justice system

37

A review of the evidence

Katherine M. Auty

Introduction

The increasing popularity of mindfulness in criminal justice settings is down to a number of factors. Criminal justice systems in most Western countries are under intensive pressure to reduce budgets and mindfulness meditation programmes have proved attractive, as they are comparatively affordable. Mindfulness programmes are rapidly becoming a credible and evidence-based alternative to psychotherapeutic groups, and mindfulness's focus on the present means that groups are often experienced by participants as less intrusive (Baker et al. 2016), as they shift the focus away from (possibly) traumatic historical events. A recent systematic review and meta-analysis of prison yoga and meditation programmes (Auty et al. 2017) found that participants experienced small increases in their psychological well-being and small improvements to their behavioural functioning. The review also found that less intensive programmes of longer duration had a statistically significant larger effect on the behavioural functioning and psychological well-being of prisoners, compared to the shorter, more intense ones.

Several recent narrative reviews of meditation programmes in correctional settings (Fix and Fix 2013; Himelstein 2011a; Lyons and Cantrell 2015; Shonin et al. 2013) have also identified that the benefits of meditation programmes for participants' psychological well-being are complex and only now starting to become more widely understood. Proponents for their use with offenders in the criminal justice system offer the following reasons and empirical evidence: firstly, mindfulness emphasizes the nonjudgemental observation of emotions by the self, and can undermine angry states (Wright et al. 2009) and engender positive moods (Galantino et al. 2005; Lane et al. 2007; Mackenzie et al. 2006); secondly, mindfulness practices target experiential avoidance, which is thought to be a central motivation for substance misuse (Simpson et al. 2007); thirdly, mindfulness reduces depression, stress, and anxiety (Kabat-Zinn et al. 1992; Samuelson et al. 2007; Teasdale et al. 2000); fourth, 'improved self-awareness and present moment awareness are factors that reduce impulsivity' (Wright et al. 2009); fifth, greater self-awareness means that mindful individuals are more accepting when coping with emotional experiences (Shapiro et al. 2006); sixth, regular practice of meditation fosters inner calm, improves sleep quality, and leads to reductions of autonomic and physiological arousal (Derezotes 2000; Sumter et al. 2009). It is also thought that mindfulness programmes may be particularly helpful for those with substance misuse problems (Himelstein 2011b) and may even contribute to reducing reoffending by increasing the chances that offenders will engage positively with other rehabilitation programmes (Himelstein 2011a). In spite of this, many have cautioned against the wholesale adoption of mindfulness-based practices in the absence of high-quality empirical evidence for its efficacy (Van Dam et al. 2018).

In some senses, the upsurge in interest in meditation programmes in prison mirrors the growing interest in contemplative practices in society more generally. Prison meditation programmes became established in the 1970s when the Prison-Ashram Project and the Siddha Yoga Dham of America (SYDA) Foundation started offering meditation programmes to prisoners in the US. Prisoner meditation programmes have been the focus of much of the research into the use of mindfulness in the criminal justice system. However, as its benefits become more widely recognized, its application within criminal justice has broadened and gained momentum. The majority of studies have been completed with incarcerated populations, but recently there have been studies of mindfulness programmes in the community with parolees with personality difficulties and a history of serious offending (Baker et al. 2016). Mindfulness has also been combined with yoga as part of an Alternatives to Incarceration programme for young offenders in New York City (Barrett 2017). Evidence is starting to accumulate on the efficacy of mindfulness-based interventions for mental ill-health, substance misuse, and reoffending. The research evidence reviewed here is organized into these three areas.

Mindfulness

Mindfulness is a multifaceted concept that many have found is not so easy to define (Block-Lerner et al. 2005; Brown and Ryan 2003). Often mindfulness is taken to mean the mental capacity for being able to purposely pay attention to the present moment and the awareness that emerges from doing so. In this sense it is both a skill and a resultant state (Maull and Crisp 2018). Mindfulness is also thought to be an inherent human characteristic that everyone possesses to a greater or lesser extent (Kabat-Zinn 2003), even if they have never practiced mindfulness and have no understanding of the term.

Mindfulness meditation aims not to alter a person's thoughts, but rather to facilitate the development of a nonjudgemental approach to thoughts as they occur (Teasdale et al. 1995). 'At its core, mindfulness promotes present awareness, acceptance of experience, a quiet mind, and non-judgement' (Malouf et al. 2017: 603). In this respect, mindfulness has something in common with several other therapeutic approaches such as dialectical behaviour therapy (DBT; Linehan 1993) and acceptance and commitment therapy (ACT; Hayes et al. 1999). It is suggested that practicing mindfulness can enhance cognitive change, self-management, relaxation, and acceptance within the self (Baer 2003).

This review will show that much of the evidence for the effectiveness of mindfulness comes from evaluations of prison programmes that incorporate mindfulness techniques (to a greater or lesser extent) with other therapeutic techniques that have a larger evidence base (for example, cognitive behavioural therapy), and due to restrictions placed on incarcerated individuals, many mindfulness programmes often require adaptations. The work of Jon Kabat-Zinn has done much to translate the principles of mindfulness into structured programmes that can be tailored and then delivered to specific populations in the criminal justice system and elsewhere. The three most common programmes are described briefly below.

Mindfulness-Based Stress Reduction (MBSR) was developed by Jon Kabat-Zinn in 1979 with the intention of making meditation techniques accessible for a Western audience who may not be seeking the spiritual elements. MBSR comprises three elements: awareness of breathing whilst meditating in the seated position, the body scan whilst lying down, and Hatha yoga postures (Kabat-Zinn and Hanh 2013). The classes are manualized, led by a teacher, and guided by audio recordings. The classes are typically held over six to eight weeks, and as the weeks progress, the classes become more focused by tailoring the meditation practice to the individual. Mindfulness-Based Relapse Prevention (MBRP) was adapted from MBSR by Alan Marlatt and colleagues to treat substance misuse disorders (Bowen et al. 2011). MBRP integrates cognitive behavioural techniques to challenge substance-misuse related beliefs. MBRP differs from many other relapse prevention strategies, as it focuses on internal cues that may trigger relapse (such as negative affect or craving), rather than identifying specific situations to avoid (Bowen et al. 2014).

Mindfulness-Based Cognitive Therapy (MBCT; Segal et al. 2002) was also developed from MBSR to prevent the reoccurrence of depression. It aims to raise participants' awareness of feelings associated with depressive episodes, approach them practically, and prevent avoidance and self-criticism. MBCT harnesses key mindfulness skills such as self-compassion, acceptance, and awareness of the body to devise a personalized approach to recognizing the onset of a depressive episode and managing it independently.

Mindfulness-based practices may be becoming more ubiquitous in the criminal justice system, but practitioners and researchers have questioned whether highly structured, manualized, and time-limited programmes are the best way to introduce mindfulness to parolees under supervision in the community (Baker et al. 2016). This study also stressed the need for a co-facilitator who 'bridges the gap' between the experienced group facilitator and the beginners, and that this could lead to changes in attitudes towards staff. The study also cautioned that participants with a history of trauma could experience mindfulness-based interventions as unpleasant, particularly those that involve lying down on the floor with the lights off and eyes closed (Baker et al. 2016: 84–85), and that steps should be taken to alleviate any anxieties.

Mindfulness and mental health

Incarcerated populations have a much higher prevalence of mental ill health than the general population (Jenkins et al. 2005; Singleton et al. 2003; Singleton et al. 1998), and this is thought to be due to a combination of importation (vulnerabilities brought in from outside the prison) and deprivation (problems that the prison produces) factors (Armour 2012). Mindfulness's focus on nonjudgemental self-awareness had led to several studies of the impact that it can have on the mental ill health of offenders both in prison and in the community.

Samuelson et al. (2007) report on a large study of 113 MBSR courses involving 1,953 male and female adult prisoners in six Massachusetts correctional facilities. Each weekly session had between 12 and 20 participants; 75% were male and all had substance misuse problems. Sixty-nine percent of the participants completed the course (n = 1,350), which lasted between one and one and a half hours and ran for six to eight weeks. The study also had a wait-list control group (n = 180, approximately), who attended other programmes such as education and exercise. Samuelson et al. (2007) looked at changes in hostility, self-esteem, and mood disturbance for those who attended the MBSR programme. They found changes in the participants' score on the Cook and Medley Hostility Scale (Barefoot et al. 1989), suggesting that participants experienced reductions in hostility. Changes in the Rosenberg Self-Esteem Scale scores (Rosenberg 1979) showed improvements in self-esteem. Finally, participants had lower scores on the Profile of Mood States (McNair et al. 1992), suggesting reductions in mood disturbance. Notably, the percentage reduction in each of the three outcomes was greatest for the female participants. The study ran between 1992 and 1996, and across this period there was considerable variation in how this MBSR programme was delivered. Therefore caution is advised when interpreting the findings.

Similar improvements in psychological well-being have been observed for incarcerated adolescents by Himelstein et al. (2011). In a much smaller study, 32 participants completed a ten-week mindfulness programme. The course was based on the Mind Body Awareness (MBA) project's mindfulness course, but due to institutional limitations, the course had to be adapted for use in a custodial setting. Each class lasted one hour and included group discussions as well as sitting meditation. Participants were encouraged to practice what they had learned between the classes. They completed self-report questionnaires before and after the course revealing significant decreases in perceived stress, as captured using the Perceived Stress Scale (PSS; Cohen et al. 1983) and a significant increase in healthy self-regulation, as captured using the Healthy Self-Regulation Scale (HSR; West 2008). Despite these findings, interestingly, no significant differences in self-reported mindfulness (as captured using the Mindfulness Attention Awareness Scale, MAAS; Brown and Ryan 2003) were observed. The authors attribute this to the lack of mindfulness training between the classes or that the curriculum does not cover mindfulness in sufficient detail, and both of these factors could be due to the adaptations that had to be made, showing the difficulties that often occur when adapting mindfulness programmes for a custodial environment.

In another sample of incarcerated adolescents (aged 16–18), Leonard et al. (2013) investigated whether a combination of cognitive behavioural therapy and mindfulness training (CBT/MT) would have an impact on their attention task performance. Attention is one aspect of the cognitive system necessary for regulating emotions and managing stress and deficits are associated with the development of antisocial behaviour in young people (Teplin et al. 2002). Each dormitory in the prison was randomized to receive Power Source (PS; Casarjian and Casarjian 2003). PS is a group-based programme which blends 'the social-cognitive change components of CBT with the attentional and response modification elements of mindfulness meditation' (Leonard et al. 2013: 3). In small groups, participants are encouraged to develop a repertoire of behaviours that enable them to avoid risky behaviour in various different circumstances. Mindfulness is a key tool in that it supports the reappraisal of stressful situations by encouraging the individual to focus on more neutral stimuli thereby neutralizing its emotional impact, resulting in a more pro-social behavioural response. One hundred and forty-seven male adolescents participated in PS, and 117 received an evidence-based cognitive-perception intervention. They were assessed using the Attention Network Test (ANT; Fan et al. 2002) at baseline and four months later. The results showed that test performance had declined over time for participants in both groups; however this was less so in the PS group. Within the PS group, performance declined for those who did not practice mindfulness exercises independently outside the structured sessions, but remained stable for those that did. The authors tentatively suggest that the CBT/MT programme may have a protective effect on the functional attentional impairments of incarcerated youth, yet concede that motivation levels may have varied between the two groups, due to the differing content of the two programs. When speculating as to the mechanisms responsible for their findings, they highlight the importance of the development of metacognitive skills during the reflective elements of the sessions, which could be encouraging participants to re-evaluate their response to stressful situations, as the researchers had anticipated.

There are only a few studies on the effects of mindfulness training on prisoners in non-Western jurisdictions. Xu et al. (2016) examined the potential benefits to emotional health for participants in a six-week mindfulness training programme. The sample comprised 19 long-term Chinese prisoners (21 prisoners formed a wait-list control group). The training emphasized present-focused and nonjudgemental awareness and was adapted to the prison context; lack of privacy meant that group mindfulness sessions replaced individual practice. The programme was based on MBCT and also incorporated elements of MBSR. Weekly sessions lasting between two and a half and three hours included a body scan, sitting and walking meditation, yoga, and group discussions. The results showed that after the course was completed, those in the mindfulness training group had improved levels of mindfulness (as measured using the Five-Facet Mindfulness Questionnaire; FFMQ) (Deng et al. 2011), and lower levels of anxiety, depression, tension anxiety, depression-dejection, anger-hostility, confusion-bewilderment, and mood disturbance. The authors conclude that mindfulness training has the potential to enhance emotional health through two mechanisms: by helping participants to be less sensitive to emotional distress, and by decreasing their fatigue or increasing their energy levels (see also An et al. 2019).

There are also very few studies of mindfulness techniques being used with offenders under supervision in the community. Henwood et al. (2018) report on a small-scale randomized controlled trial (RCT) of a combined CBT and mindfulness-based anger management intervention called the Individual Managing Anger Programme (I-MAP; Johnson and Gast 2013). The study took place in Malta and incorporated mindfulness into I-MAP through the use of relaxation and visualization techniques, such as the body scan. However, I-MAP differs substantially from many mindfulness-based interventions reviewed here as it was delivered on a one-to-one basis; each participant that had been randomized to the programme group received nine sessions, lasting about 90 minutes each. The study participants were all male (n = 24, mean age=33), and were selected on the basis of their dysfunctional anger and met criteria for clinical or pathological levels of anger. The researchers found significantly lower self-reported dysfunctional anger symptoms (as measured using the Anger Disorder Scales, ADS; Di Giuseppe and Tafrate 2004). The authors note that self-selection bias may have played a part here, as many of the participants were already contemplating or in the early stages of change. However, they do credit much of the programme's success to the one-to-one sessions, which made it possible to personalize the sessions and this distinguishing feature should be explored in further studies of the efficacy of mindfulness.

A weekly yoga and mindfulness programme was offered to males (aged 18–24 years), as part of a larger court-mandated Alternatives to Incarceration project (ATI), which was run by a non-profit organization in New York (Barrett 2017). The evaluation used qualitative methods such as participant/observation and open-ended interviews (n = 10) to discover if the programme had positive effects for the young men. All interview participants had a minimum of eight mindfulness classes. The qualitative interviews revealed that the participants felt that the programme led to significant reductions in the stress of their daily lives; a unique contributory feature of offenders in the community (as opposed to in prison) is the pervasive threat of being incorrectly ID'ed and returned to custody. They also described how the programme had led to them regulating their anger and other emotions more effectively, moving from reacting to responding in their day-to-day lives. The participants were also attending an anger management programme as part of the ATI programme, and were able to clearly articulate the added benefits of the yoga/mindfulness programme; the authors describe this as 'developing and practicing an *embodied responsiveness*' (Barrett 2017: 1731). What is meant by this is that instead of talking about techniques to relax and relieve stress (e.g. breathing in the anger management class), the techniques are central to the practice of mindfulness.

Mindfulness and substance misuse

Substance misuse disorders amongst offending populations are also known to be very high (Fazele et al. 2017). Studies suggest that mindfulness interventions may be particularly helpful with these offenders given mindfulness's focus on experiential avoidance and improved awareness and self-awareness, which is thought to reduce impulsivity – a key predictor of relapse.

A pilot RCT of a mindfulness-based intervention called REVAMP (Re-Entry Values and Mindfulness Programme), which aimed to 'reduce post-release risky behaviour by targeting dimensions of mindfulness (e.g. willingness/acceptance) and associated proximal outcomes/mechanisms of action (emotion regulation, self-control, shame/guilt)' (Malouf et al. 2017: 603), by investigating if REVAMP would affect 14 psychological constructs associated with adaptive behavioural change. Prisoners who were nearing release were randomized to the REVAMP group (n = 21) or treatment as usual (TAU, n = 19). REVAMP is a manualized group intervention for prisoners nearing the end of their sentence. It combines elements from several mindfulness-based interventions (MBIs), such as ACT, MBRP, and DBT. Malouf et al. (2017) found that REVAMP participants reported less substance misuse post release, but this was not found to be statistically significant. The authors explain that REVAMP, as a general re-entry programme 'was not specifically focussed on treating inmates' substance use disorder . . . when substance misuse is a primary concern, it may be beneficial to supplement REVAMP with other empirically supported interventions' (Malouf et al. 2017: 612).

Some more promising results were found in a small-scale RCT in Taiwan (Lee et al. 2011). This study tested the efficacy of MBRP in a sample of ten male prisoners serving short sentences for drug offences (14 prisoners received a comparable TAU). The MBRP was delivered over ten weekly sessions that each lasted 1.5 hours. After completing the programme, the MBRP group had significantly less positive attitudes to substance use as captured by the Drug Use Identification Disorders Test–extended (DUDIT-E; Berman et al. 2007), compared to the TAU group. The MBRP group experienced significantly less depressive symptoms as captured by the Beck Depression Inventory (BDI; Beck et al. 1996), and improved drug refusal self-efficacy as captured using the Drugs Avoidance Self-Efficacy Scale (DASE; Martin et al. 1995). These modest findings should be interpreted with caution. The study seems to suggest that MBRP are appropriate for non-Western populations, yet there are still questions as to whether the research instruments were also culturally appropriate. This, together with the small sample size makes the generalizability of the findings somewhat questionable.

Bowen and colleagues (Bowen et al. 2006; Bowen et al. 2007) have completed a series of studies that example the effects of Vipassana mindfulness meditation on substance misuse in a minimum security adult jail in Seattle housing males and females. Vipassana meditation is typically conducted in standardized ten-day courses, where participants meditate for up to 11 hours a day and watch videos of Buddhist teachings. The courses are gender-segregated and participants are required to maintain silence throughout. In the first study (Bowen et al. 2006), 173 participants completed a post-course assessment (79% were male). This study is unique as follow-up measures were completed three months post release. There was a sizeable attrition rate, but 87 participants remained in the study. Compared to the 90 days prior to their incarceration the meditation group participants reported significantly lower alcohol, crack cocaine, and marijuana use three months post release. In a follow-up study at the same institution of another ten-day Vipassana meditation course Bowen et al. (2007) found that participants reported significant decreases in thought avoidance, but not intrusive thoughts (as measured using the White Bear Suppression Inventory, WBSI; Wegner and Zanakos 1994).

Mindfulness and reoffending

Some have questioned how mindfulness might be related to criminal thinking and whether it has the potential to reduce recidivism. Tangney et al. (2017) asked a sample of 259 male jail inmates to complete a 45-item self-report mindfulness assessment (MI: ND; Harty et al. 2009), which captures six core components of mindfulness: Present Awareness, Metacognition, Quiet Mind, Willingness/Acceptance, Nonjudgement of Self, Nonjudgement of Others and three proximal dimensions that are theoretical outcomes of mindfulness: Distress Tolerance, (lack of) Experiential Avoidance, and (lack of) Emotion-Driven Impulsivity. Inmates also completed the 25-item Criminal Cognitions Scale (CCS: Tangney et al. 2012), which covers five dimensions: Notions of Entitlement, Failure to Accept Responsibility, Short-Term Orientation, Insensitivity to the Impact of Crime, and Negative Attitudes Toward Authority. They found that individuals higher in the core components of mindfulness were less likely to rationalize, excuse, or justify their criminal behaviour. Next, they examined whether inmates' emotional regulation (comprised of the three proximal dimensions) mediated the relationship between mindfulness and criminogenic cognitions. When they included emotional regulation in the model they found that there was now a *positive* direct link between mindfulness and criminogenic cognitions, suggesting that those higher in mindfulness now also showed more criminogenic thinking. They discovered that it was the Nonjudgement of Self component (defined as 'evaluative scrutiny of one's thoughts, feelings, and behaviours' (Tangney et al. 2017: 1420)) that was largely responsible for this finding and concluded that some self-judgement may actually be beneficial when engaging with treatment for incarcerated populations.

In the REVAMP trial (discussed earlier), Malouf et al. (2017) also demonstrated that three months after the programme was completed, the REVAMP group showed statistically significant lower scores on the measure of Non-Judgement of Self, when compared to the TAU group. Scores on Willingness/Acceptance were approaching statistical significance. Increases in scores for shame for the REVAMP group were also observed. Arrests were examined for both groups in the three years following release. The mean arrest rate for the TAU group was almost twice that of the REVAMP group. The TAU group also recidivated earlier, although both of these differences did not quite reach conventional levels of statistical significance.

The increases in self-judgement and shame for the REVAMP group seem contrary to the intentions of mindfulness, which emphasizes nonjudgement and self-compassion. The authors explain that

> this may be the natural ramification of increased willingness/acceptance in a population facing difficult, typically self-imposed circumstances. . . . For REVAMP participants, enhanced willingness/acceptance may have allowed them to overcome this defensiveness in order to openly reflect

on past behaviour and take a good hard (somewhat negative) look at the self.

(Malouf et al. 2017: 611–612)

Furthermore,

willingness/acceptance, enhanced by MBIs, may allow inmates (and others more generally) to make the most of shame in service of adaptive behavioural change going forward, rather than getting mired in experiential avoidance, externalization of blame and denial. . . . In sum, REVAMP may concurrently increase the tendency to experience and tolerate shame and self-judgement

(Malouf et al. 2017: 612)

and 'to develop a reparative plan for the future' (Malouf et al. 2017: 604). It is likely that the small sample size made it difficult to detect statistically significant results, yet one of the study's main strengths is its randomization; participants did not self-select into either treatment or control group.

Conclusions and directions for future research

Mindfulness now appears to be a firm part of the criminal justice landscape, and as this chapter has shown, the findings from studies of mindfulness in offending populations show much promise, especially in the three areas examined here: mental ill-health, substance misuse, and reoffending. However, a note of caution should be added, as many of these studies suffer from methodological flaws and it is these areas that future researchers should focus on when designing new research studies.

The vast majority of studies describe the mindfulness intervention given to the experimental/programme group in detail, but lack sufficient detail when it comes to describing the TAU conditions; as Malouf et al. (2017: 613) state 'future RCTs should include a comparison condition similar in format and time engaged'. Many of the experimental and quasi-experimental studies typically compare outcomes for prisoners attending a meditation programme to 'treatment as usual' (TAU). In practice, this can mean experiencing a 'no frills' prison regime to attending a mix of work, educational, and rehabilitative programmes. This makes it difficult to interpret findings, as they do not represent the effect of the meditation programme in isolation, but rather its added value relative to the regular prison regime. Therefore, 'the nature of research in this area likely downwardly biases any estimate of effectiveness' (Wilson 2016: 214).

There are also difficulties of conducting randomized studies in certain settings, such as prisons; there will always be attrition in follow-up studies as some participants will be released. We should also recognize that findings may not generalize to other populations, for example, female inmates or adolescent offenders. There are also issues with access to confidential criminal justice data reported by some research teams (for example; Himelstein 2011b). Well-designed and methodologically sound studies are crucial if we are to understand the potential of mindfulness in criminal justice populations.

Further reading

Auty, K. M., Cope, A. and Liebling, A. (2017) A systematic review and meta-analysis of yoga and mindfulness meditation in prison. *International Journal of Offender Therapy and Comparative Criminology*, 61(6), 689–710.

Fix, R. L. and Fix, S. T. (2013) The effects of mindfulness-based treatments for aggression: A critical review. *Aggression and Violent Behavior*, 18(2), 219–227.

Himelstein, S. (2011) Meditation research: The state of the art in correctional settings. *International Journal of Offender Therapy and Comparative Criminology*, 55(4), 646–661.

Lyons, T. and Cantrell, W. D. (2015) Prison meditation movements and mass incarceration. *International Journal of Offender Therapy and Comparative Criminology*, 60(12), 1363–1375.

Settle, S., Zephaniah, B. and Morgan, P. (2017) *Peace Inside: A Prisoner's Guide to Meditation*. London: Jessica Kingsley Publishers.

Shonin, E., Van Gordon, W., Slade, K. and Griffiths, M. D. (2013) Mindfulness and other Buddhist-derived interventions in correctional settings: A systematic review. *Aggression and Violent Behavior*, 18(3), 365–372.

References

An, Y., Zhou, Y., Huang, Q., Jia, K., Li, W. and Xu, W. (2019) The effect of mindfulness training on mental health in long-term Chinese male prisoners. *Psychology, Health and Medicine*, 24(2), 167–176. DOI:10.1080/13548506.2018.1510130.

Armour, C. (2012) Mental health in prison: A trauma perspective on importation and deprivation. *International Journal of Criminology and Sociological Theory*, 5(2), 886–894.

Auty, K. M., Cope, A. and Liebling, A. (2017) A systematic review and meta-analysis of yoga and mindfulness meditation in prison. *International Journal of Offender Therapy and Comparative Criminology*, 61(6), 689–710. DOI:10.1177/0306624X15602514.

Baer, R. A. (2003) Mindfulness training as a clinical intervention: A conceptual and empirical review. *Clinical Psychology: Science and Practice*, 10, 125–143.

Baker, V., Young, K. and Wolfe, S. (2016) Incorporating and adapting shared experience of mindfulness into a service for men who have committed serious offences and who have significant personality difficulties. *Probation Journal*, 63(1), 80–87. DOI:10.1177/0264550515620693.

Barefoot, J. C., Dodge, K. A., Peterson, B. L., Dahlstrom, W. G. and Williams, R. B., Jr. (1989) The cook-medley hostility scale: Item content and ability to predict survival. *Psychosomatic Medicine*, 51(1), 46–57.

Barrett, C. J. (2017) Mindfulness and rehabilitation: Teaching yoga and meditation to young men in an alternative to incarceration program. *International Journal of Offender Therapy and Comparative Criminology*, 61(15), 1719–1738. DOI:10.1177/0306624x16633667.

Beck, A. T., Steer, R. A. and Brown, G. K. (1996) Beck depression inventory-II. *San Antonio*, 78(2), 490–498.

Berman, A. H., Palmstierna, T., Kallmen, H. and Bergman, H. (2007) The self-report Drug Use Disorders Identification Test – Extended (DUDIT-E): Reliability, validity, and motivational index. *Journal of Substance Abuse Treatment*, 32, 357–369.

Block-Lerner, J., Salters-Pednault, K. and Tull, M. T. (2005) Assessing mindfulness and experiential acceptance: Attempts to capture inherently elusive phenomena. In S. M. Orsillo and L. Roemer (Eds.), *Acceptance and Mindfulness-Based Approaches to Anxiety: Conceptualisation and Treatment*. New York: Springer, pp. 71–100.

Bowen, S., Chawla, N. and Marlatt, G. A. (2011) *Mindfulness-Based Relapse Prevention for Addictive Behaviors: A Clinician's Guide*. New York: Guilford Press.

Bowen, S., Witkiewitz, K., Clifasefi, S. L., et al. (2014) Relative efficacy of mindfulness-based relapse prevention, standard relapse prevention, and treatment as usual for substance use disorders: A randomized clinical trial. *JAMA Psychiatry*, 71(5), 547–556. DOI:10.1001/jamapsychiatry.2013.4546.

Bowen, S., Witkiewitz, K., Dillworth, T. M., Chawla, N., Simpson, T. L., Ostafin, B. D., et al. (2006) Mindfulness meditation and substance use in an incarcerated population. *Psychology of Addictive Behaviors*, 20(3), 343–347. DOI:10.1037/0893-164x.20.3.343.

Bowen, S., Witkiewitz, K., Dillworth, T. M. and Marlatt, G. A. (2007) The role of thought suppression in the relationship between mindfulness meditation and alcohol use. *Addictive Behaviors*, 32(10), 2324–2328. http://dx.doi.org/10.1016/j.addbeh.2007.01.025.

Brown, K. W. and Ryan, R. M. (2003) The benefits of being present: Mindfulness and its role in psychological well-being. *Journal of Personality & Social Psychology*, 84(4), 822–848.

Casarjian, B. and Casarjian, R. (2003) *Power Source: Taking Charge of Your Life*. Boston, MA: Lionhart Press.

Cohen, S., Karmack, T. and Mermelstein, R. (1983) A global measure of perceived stress. *Journal of Health and Social Behavior*, 24(4), 385–396.

Deng, Y. Q., Liu, X. H., Rodriguez, M. A. and Xia, C. Y. (2011) The five facet mindfulness questionnaire: Psychometric properties of the Chinese version. *Mindfulness*, 2(2), 123–128. DOI:10.1007/s12671-011-0050-9.

Derezotes, D. (2000) Evaluation of yoga and meditation trainings with adolescent sex offenders. *Child and Adolescent Social Work Journal*, 17(2), 97–113. DOI:10.1023/a:1007506206353.

Di Giuseppe, R. and Tafrate, R. C. (2004) *Anger Disorders Scale (ADS): Technical Manual*. North Tonawanda, NY: Multi-Health Systems.

Fan, J., McCandliss, B. D., Sommer, T., Raz, A. and Posner, M. I. (2002) Testing the efficiency and independence of attentional networks. *Journal of Cognitive Neuroscience*, 14(3), 340–347. DOI:10.1162/089892902317361886.

Fazel, S., Yoon, I. A. and Hayes, A. J. (2017) Substance use disorders in prisoners: An updated systematic review and meta-regression analysis in recently incarcerated men and women. *Addiction* 112(10), 1725–1739. DOI:10.1111/add.13877.

Fix, R. L. and Fix, S. T. (2013) The effects of mindfulness-based treatments for aggression: A critical review. *Aggression and Violent Behavior*, 18(2), 219–227. http://dx.doi.org/10.1016/j.avb.2012.11.009.

Galantino, M. L., Baime, M., Maguire, M., Szapary, P. O. and Farrar, J. T. (2005) Association of psychological and physiological measures of stress in health-care professionals during an 8-week mindfulness meditation program: Mindfulness in practice. *Stress and Health*, 21(4), 255–261. DOI:10.1002/smi.1062.

Harty, L., Youman, K., Malouf, E. T., Appel, M., Hall, S., Pilafova, A. and Tangney, J. P. (2009) *Mindfulness Inventory: Nine Dimensions (MIND)*. Fairfax, VA: George Mason University.

Hayes, S. C., Strosahl, K. D. and Wilson, K. G. (1999) *Acceptance and Commitment Therapy: An Experiential Approach to Behavior Change*. The Guilford Press.

Henwood, K. S., Browne, K. D. and Chou, S. (2018) A randomized controlled trial exploring the effects of brief anger management on community-based offenders in Malta. *International Journal of Offender Therapy and Comparative Criminology*, 62(3), 785–805. DOI:10.1177/0306624X16666338.

Himelstein, S. (2011a) Meditation research: The state of the art in correctional settings. *International Journal of Offender Therapy and Comparative Criminology*, 55(4), 646–661. DOI:10.1177/0306624x10364485.

Himelstein, S. (2011b) Mindfulness-based substance abuse treatment for incarcerated youth: A mixed method pilot study. *International Journal of Transpersonal Studies*, 30, 1–10.

Himelstein, S., Hastings, A., Shapiro, S. L. and Heery, M. (2011) Mindfulness training for self-regulation and stress with incarcerated youth: A pilot study. *Probation Journal*, 59(2), 151–165. DOI:10.1177/0264550512438256.

Jenkins, R., Bhugra, D., Meltzer, H., Singleton, N., Bebbington, P., Brugha, T., et al. (2005) Psychiatric and social aspects of suicidal in prisons. *Psychological Medicine*, 35(2), 257–269.

Johnson, J. L. and Gast, L. (2013) *Facilitation Manual of the Individual Managing Anger Programme (I-MAP)*. Bucharest: Developed for the Romanian Ministry of Justice, Irish Probation Service and the Italian Ministry of Justice.

Kabat-Zinn, J. (2003) Mindfulness-based interventions in context: Past, present, and future. *Clinical Psychology: Science and Practice*, 10(2), 144–156. DOI:10.1093/clipsy. bpg016.

Kabat-Zinn, J. and Hanh, T. N. (2013) *Full Catastrophe Living (Revised Edition): Using the Wisdom of Your Body and Mind to Face Stress, Pain, and Illness*. New York: Random House Publishing Group.

Kabat-Zinn, J., Massion, A. O., Kristeller, J., Peterson, L. G., Fletcher, K. E., Pbert, L., et al. (1992) Effectiveness of a meditation-based stress reduction program in the treatment of anxiety disorders. *American Journal of Psychiatry*, 149(7), 936–943. DOI:10.1176/ ajp.149.7.936.

Lane, J. D., Seskevich, J. E. and Pieper, C. F. (2007) Brief meditation training can improve perceived stress and negative mood. *Alternative Therapies in Health and Medicine*, 13(1), 38–44.

Lee, K. H., Bowen, S. and An-Fu, B. (2011) Psychosocial outcomes of mindfulness-based relapse prevention in incarcerated substance abusers in Taiwan: A preliminary study. *Journal of Substance Use*, 16(6), 476–483. DOI:10.3109/146 59891.2010.505999.

Leonard, N., Jha, A., Casarjian, B., Goolsarran, M., Garcia, C., Cleland, C., et al. (2013) Mindfulness training improves attentional task performance in incarcerated youth: A group randomized controlled intervention trial. *Frontiers in Psychology*, 4(792). DOI:10.3389/fpsyg.2013.00792.

Linehan, M. (1993) *Skills Training Manual for Treating Borderline Personality Disorder, First Ed.* New York: Guilford Press.

Lyons, T. and Cantrell, W. D. (2015) Prison meditation movements and mass incarceration. *International Journal of Offender Therapy and Comparative Criminology*. 60(12), 1363–1375. DOI:10.1177/0306624x15583807.

Mackenzie, C. S., Poulin, P. A. and Seidman-Carlson, R. (2006) A brief mindfulness-based stress reduction intervention for nurses and nurse aides. *Applied Nursing Research*, 19(2), 105–109. DOI:10.1016/j.apnr.2005.08.002.

Malouf, E. T., Youman, K., Stuewig, J., Witt, E. A. and Tangney, J. P. (2017) A pilot RCT of a values-based mindfulness group intervention with jail inmates: Evidence for reduction in post-release risk behavior. *Mindfulness*, 8(3), 603–614. DOI:10.1007/s12671-016-0636-3.

Martin, G. W., Wilkinson, D. A. and Poulos, C. X. (1995) The drug avoidance self-efficacy scale. *Journal of Substance Abuse*, 7(2), 151–163. https://doi.org/10.1016/0899-3289(95)90001-2.

Maull, F. and Crisp, K. (2018) Can mindfulness make prison a healthier place? In E. L. Jeglic and C. Calkins (Eds.), *New Frontiers in Offender Treatment: The Translation of Evidence-Based Practices to Correctional Settings*. Cham: Springer International Publishing, pp. 189–208.

McNair, D. M., Lorr, M. and Droppleman, L. F. (1992) *Edits Manual for the Profile of Mood States (POMS)*. San Diego, CA: Educational and Industrial Testing Service.

Rosenberg, M. (1979) *Conceiving the Self*. New York: Basic Books.

Samuelson, M., Carmody, J., Kabat-Zinn, J. and Bratt, M. A. (2007) Mindfulness-based stress reduction in Massachusetts correctional facilities. *The Prison Journal*, 87(2), 254–268. DOI:10.1177/0032885507303753.

Segal, Z. V., Williams, J. M. G. and Teasdale, J. D. (2002) *Mindfulness-Based Cognitive Therapy for Depression, First Edition: A New Approach to Preventing Relapse*. New York: The Guilford Press.

Shapiro, S. L., Carlson, L. E., Astin, J. A. and Freedman, B. (2006) Mechanisms of mindfulness. *Journal of Clinical Psychology*, 62(3), 373–386. DOI:10.1002/jclp.20237.

Shonin, E., Van Gordon, W., Slade, K. and Griffiths, M. D. (2013) Mindfulness and other Buddhist-derived interventions in correctional settings: A systematic review. *Aggression and Violent Behavior*, 18(3), 365–372. http://dx.doi.org/10.1016/j.avb.2013.01.002.

Simpson, T. L., Kaysen, D., Bowen, S., MacPherson, L. M., Chawla, N., Blume, A., et al. (2007) PTSD symptoms, substance use, and Vipassana meditation among incarcerated individuals. *Journal of Traumatic Stress*, 20(3), 239–249. DOI:10.1002/jts.20209.

Singleton, N., Bumpstead, R., O'Brien, M., Lee, A. and Meltzer, H. (2003) Psychiatric morbidity among adults living in private households, 2000. *International Review of Psychiatry*, 15(1–2), 65–73. DOI:10.1080/0954026021000045967.

Singleton, N., Meltzer, H., Gatward, R., Coid, J. and Deasy, D. (1998) *Psychiatric Morbidity Among Prisoners in England and Wales*. London: TSO.

Sumter, M. T., Monk-Turner, E. and Turner, C. (2009) The benefits of meditation practice in the correctional setting. *Journal of Correctional Health Care*, 15(1), 47–57. DOI:10.1177/1078345808326621.

Tangney, J. P., Dobbins, A. E., Stuewig, J. B. and Schrader, S. W. (2017) Is there a dark side to mindfulness? Relation of mindfulness to criminogenic cognitions. *Personality and Social Psychology Bulletin*, 43(10), 1415–1426. DOI:10.1177/0146167217717243.

Tangney, J. P., Stuewig, J., Furukawa, E., Kopelovich, S., Meyer, P. J. and Cosby, B. (2012) Reliability, validity, and predictive utility of the 25-item Criminogenic Cognitions Scale (CCS). *Criminal Justice and Behavior*, 39(10), 1340–1360. DOI:10.1177/0093854812451092.

Teasdale, J. D., Segal, Z. V., Williams, J. M. G., Ridgeway, V. A., Soulsby, J. M. and Lau, M. A. (2000) Prevention of relapse/recurrence in major depression by mindfulness-based cognitive therapy. *Journal of Consulting and Clinical Psychology*, 68(4), 615–623.

Teasdale, J. D., Segal, Z. V. and Williams, J. M. G. (1995) How does cognitive therapy prevent depressive relapse and why should attentional control (mindfulness) training help? *Behaviour Research and Therapy*, 33, 25–39.

Teplin, L. A., Abram, K. M., McClelland, G. M., Dulcan, M. K. and Mericle, A. A. (2002) Psychiatric disorders in youth in juvenile detention. *Archives of General Psychiatry*, 59(12), 1133–1143.

Van Dam, N. T., van Vugt, M. K., Vago, D. R., Schmalzl, L., Saron, C. D., Olendzki, A., . . . and Meyer, D. E. (2018) Mind the hype: A critical evaluation and prescriptive agenda for research on mindfulness and meditation. *Perspectives on Psychological Science*, 13(1), 36–61. DOI:10.1177/1745691617709589.

Wegner, D. M. and Zanakos, S. (1994) Chronic thought suppression. *Journal of Personality*, 62(4), 616–640.

West, A. M. (2008) *Mindfulness and Well-Being in Adolescence: An Exploration of Four Mindfulness Measures with an Adolescent Sample* (Doctoral dissertation). ProQuest (304824868).

Wilson, D. B. (2016) Correctional programs. In D. Weisburd, D. P. Farrington and C. Gill (Eds.), *What Works in Crime Prevention and Rehabilitation*. New York: Springer-Verlag, pp. 193–217.

Wright, S., Day, A. and Howells, K. (2009) Mindfulness and the treatment of anger problems. *Aggression and Violent Behavior*, 14(5), 396–401. http://dx.doi.org/10.1016/j.avb.2009.06.008.

Xu, W., Jia, K., Liu, X. and Hofmann, S. G. (2016) The effects of mindfulness training on emotional health in Chinese long-term male prison inmates. *Mindfulness*, 7(5), 1044–1051. DOI:10.1007/s12671-016-0540-x.

38

Mentoring in the justice system

Gillian Buck

Introduction

Mentoring is now a widely utilized approach in both adult and youth rehabilitation settings (Buck et al. 2015), having recently taken centre stage as one of the primary 'interventions' to reduce reoffending (Hucklesby and Wincup 2014). Central to government proposals to *transform rehabilitation* in the UK was a vision that everybody leaving prison be offered a 'wise friend' to prevent them from reoffending, and that it will often be the 'former offender gone straight' best suited to this role (Grayling 2012). Such 'peer' mentoring is also an increasing feature of direct work with offenders, with peer mentors making up as many as 92% of offender mentors in some parts of England (Willoughby et al. 2013: 7). This chapter will offer a critical introduction to these practices. It will begin by defining 'mentoring' and 'peer mentoring', before looking at some claims that have been made for them and asking some critical questions of mentoring as an adopted approach.

In 2011, the Ministry of Justice (MoJ) and the National Offender Management Service (NOMS) made mentoring a key policy objective, arguing that there are 'roles for offenders acting as mentors [as] they can be particularly effective during the transition from prison to outside world' (Ministry of Justice 2011: 23); the ambition was that 'eventually all offenders in our system will be offered the opportunity of an informal mentor' (National Offender

Management Service 2011: 3). Despite such enthusiasm, mentoring and peer mentoring remain under-researched and diversely defined. Indeed, Bozeman and Feeney (2007) highlighted no fewer than 13 descriptions of mentoring in publications between 1984 and 2005. 'The 'peer' element of the intervention is [also] open to interpretation' (Finnegan et al. 2010: 6), as there is little clarity about what constitutes a 'peer' in these settings. Such diversity poses clear problems in terms of measuring any possible effects of 'mentoring', as in reality the term encompasses a range of approaches.

Despite multiplicity, there are some core definitions available. In the UK, the national Mentoring and Befriending Foundation (MBF) defines mentoring as 'a voluntary, mutually beneficial and purposeful relationship in which an individual gives time to support another to enable them to make changes in their life' (Mentoring and Befriending Foundation (MBF 2014: 2)). Clinks, a charity supporting voluntary organizations that work with offenders, defines *volunteer peer support* as:

> [W]hen people with the same shared experience provide knowledge, experience, or emotional, social or practical help to each other . . . trained individuals volunteering to support people with specific or multiple needs to provide practical advice and guidance.
>
> (Clinks 2012: 8)

In addition to these starting points, there are a number of recurrent themes, or 'truth claims' about mentoring, which run through the literature. These are: that mentoring changes you, that it constitutes an approach which is better than those gone before, and that it is egalitarian. Each of these claims will now be explored, along with some of the critical tensions they produce.

Mentoring changes you

A consistent claim made about mentoring is that it has the potential to change its participants. Unsurprisingly, the claimed *change* is often a reduction in offending. The Princes Trust, for example, declared that '65% of offenders under the age of 25 said that having the support of a mentor would help them to stop re-offending; 71% said they would like a mentor who is a former offender' (Princes Trust 2008: 3). Evaluations commissioned by the St Giles Trust, claim that peer-supported 'Through the Gates'[1] clients reoffend 40% less than the national reoffending rate (Frontier Economics 2009: 15) and 'the reconviction rate for WIRE [female ex-offender led service] participants was 42%, against 51% for the national average for women offenders' (The Social Innovation Partnership 2012: 5). In both of these cases 'reoffending' was measured in binary terms after a period of 12 months. Summarizing the evidence on mentoring more broadly, Jolliffe and Farrington (2007: 3) concluded that mentoring 'reduced subsequent offending by 4 to 11%'. However, they added the caveat that the 'best studies, designed to provide the most accurate assessment of the impact of mentoring, did not suggest that mentoring caused a statistically significant reduction in re-offending' (Jolliffe and Farrington 2007: 3). Rather: 'mentoring was only successful in reducing re-offending when it was one of a number of interventions given, suggesting that mentoring on its own may not reduce re-offending' (Jolliffe and Farrington 2007: 3). This problem of isolating the effects of mentoring was also noted in a rapid evidence assessment by Taylor and colleagues (2013), who argued that the effect of mentoring on reoffending is inconclusive, and because people often engage in mentoring on a voluntary basis, results may be subject to 'selection bias in favour of those most ready and motivated to change' (p. 3).

Mentoring is also claimed to result in 'intermediate outcomes' that may contribute to desisting from crime (Taylor et al. 2013). Such outcomes include mentors acting as a 'bridge' to other services; improving mentee engagement in other programmes and interventions; and improving mentees' employment outcomes, housing situations, and reductions in substance misuse. Tolan et al. (2008) also found mentoring to have a 'modest positive effect for delinquency, aggression, drug use, and achievement' (p. 3). Young people participating in peer mentoring are claimed to be 'less likely to use drugs and alcohol, less likely to be violent, have improved school attendance and performance and improved relationships with their parents and peers' (Parsons et al. 2008: 6). In the UK, peer education has been found to improve attitudes and behaviour relating to substance misuse (Parkin and McKeganey 2000: 302). There are also claims that peer mentoring can increase a sense of 'agency' or self-direction. An evaluation of a female prisoners' programme in Canada, for example, 'found that both the peer counsellors and recipients of the service said the programme decreased feelings of isolation and increased feelings of self-worth and autonomy' (Pollack 2004: 702). This finding is significant, given that the success of people to maintain desistance from crime is often linked to their sense of self-control or agency (Maruna 2001; Zdun 2011).

Whilst there are early signs that mentoring may effect changes in offending and related behaviour, we know less about why that is, leading commentators to note that mentoring theory remains underdeveloped (Bozeman and Feeney 2007; Hucklesby and Wincup 2014). Sullivan and Jolliffe (2012), however, point out that:

> Differential Association Theory (Sutherland, 1947), Social Learning Theory (Akers, 1973) and Social Control Theory (Hirschi, 1969) all suggest that criminal behaviour is more or less likely depending upon those with whom we share the immediate environment, [and that] strategies focused on peer influence are broadly based on these associations.
>
> (Sullivan and Jolliffe 2012: 207)

There are also some early theoretical explanations of peer mentoring. Drawing on the mimetic theory of Girard (1962), Buck (2017) argues that determination to change can be influenced by role models, who inspire a desire to change and sustain desire through the offer of their lived example. A peer, or someone closer to an individual's conception of self, is well placed to act as a model, given they can offer reassurance that change can be managed and that alternative futures are possible (Buck 2019). This is important, given that desisting from crime can present a leap into the unknown, where familiar supports are absent. 'Peer' mentors can provide a sense of ontological security, mutual recognition, and reassurance to accept help, within a context where authority figures are often seen as dangerous (Buck 2019). These arguments imply that the identity of the mentor has a role to play in the mentoring dynamic. Similarly, Asencio and Burke (2011) demonstrated that the strength of the criminal identity and the drug user identity (both deviant identities) were influenced by the reflected appraisals of significant others and peers (though not [prison] guards)' (Asencio and Burke 2011: 177), suggesting that peers in mentoring roles may have more influence than authority figures, in terms of how identity is internalized.

Mentoring is better than what has gone before

The above discussion brings us to another theme from the extant literature, which is that mentoring (particularly peer mentoring) brings something new to the field of criminal justice, not just in terms of effects, but in terms of the *actors* involved and the *knowledges* they bring, elements which are claimed to offer something expressly different to formal 'experts':

> Ex-offender mentors' personal insight into prison life makes it easier for the young people to bond with the volunteers and provides the all-important initial hook with which to engage them in the project.
>
> (Princes Trust 2012: 1)

Peers are claimed to have a credibility that 'professional' rehabilitation workers may not because they have experienced first-hand many of the problems faced by their 'clients' and can relate to the challenges of life after prison (Boyce et al. 2009: viii), they offer 'proof that it is possible to move on and sort your life out' (Boyce et al. 2009: 20). Whilst this philosophy is relatively new to criminal justice, it has been dominant in the field of recovery from substance misuse:

> It is only through recovery forums and peer-led services that people in recovery can become visible. Once these people become visible recovery champions, they can help people to believe that recovery is not only possible but desirable.
>
> (Kidd 2011: 174)

Peers are understood as 'passing on the baton' (Boyce et al. 2009: 29). As one respondent remarked: 'If I'm looking to deter young people from crime, I've got to be that positive change. . . . It wasn't easy, but look what I've done. I've got to inspire people' (Keisha, mentor, cited in Buck 2017: 6). Peer mentoring is not only imagined to be *better* in terms of what it offers mentees, but also what it offers to mentors and the services they work within. The availability of peer mentoring offers a valuable opportunity to people who often find it difficult to obtain work otherwise, due to having a criminal record (Clinks and MBF 2012; Corcoran 2012). This opportunity is important given that 'desistance requires the involvement and cooperation of the offender as well as access to "opportunities"' (Boyce et al. 2009: 27). Mentoring is also claimed to bring benefits for rehabilitation services, given that it involves 'relatively high levels of contact time between mentors and mentees. In contrast, the contacts between professional support workers and their clients are likely to be brief and episodic' (Brown and Ross 2010: 32). Furthermore, whilst each mentoring relationship is unique, Buck (2018) argues that three 'core conditions' of caring, listening, and taking small steps underpin many of these relationships.

> These conditions do not sit comfortably within a punishment framework, yet they offer antidotes to what can often be experienced as disconnected, unhearing and technocratic criminal justice practices. Peer mentoring, in contrast, is claimed to release suffering, to unburden the self of grief and to enable new self-direction. It is seen as a safe space to do this given that mentors [are perceived to] 'genuinely care' and are tolerant of slip-ups.
>
> (Buck 2018: 203)

Mentoring therefore appears to address 'a strong unmet need for support and advice, not only immediately after leaving prison, but for some months afterwards' (Maguire and Nolan 2007: 166). These features are argued to be particularly important for women, as mentoring may facilitate the transition from prison, 'while also offering access to a prosocial source of support, independent from the insecure networks that may be available within the social environments of women offenders' (Rumgay 2004: 415). Whilst volunteers may often offer emotional and social support, and indeed fill gaps in existing services, there is an equally 'strong consensus that volunteer labour should not substitute for paid professional jobs' (Corcoran 2012: 20).

In addition to offering high contact levels and potentially creating sustainable social support, there is some evidence that peer mentors may be *better* at improving compliance with other services. For example, mentors were found to be particularly successful in reintegrating 'young people into education, training and the community' (Finnegan et al. 2010: 10). A recent criminal justice inspection also highlighted that mentoring can bring about 'a greater level of cooperation with supervision than anticipated' (HMIP 2016: 45). In this latter example, however, mentors were not commissioned by community rehabilitation companies (CRCs), but third-sector organizations. These

> non-CRC mentors appeared willing to work with the least motivated offenders, and to have a high level of flexibility and persistence. . . .

> Conversely, in one of the cases allocated a CRC mentor, the offender had failed to attend two appointments, and the service was likely to be removed due to the offender's lack of motivation.
>
> (HMIP 2016: 45)

Persistence, flexibility, and tolerance of slip-ups are therefore important qualities for mentors to have (Buck 2018). Peer mentors' ability to 'separate themselves from authority and officialdom' (Buck 2019) may also be important, given interactions with authority can be fraught for 'offenders', 'people whose relationships with others – often especially with authority figures – have been, at worst, abusive and traumatic and, at best, inconsistent and difficult' (McNeill 2013: 84). This links us directly to the third claim made about mentoring: that it is egalitarian.

Mentoring as egalitarian

Not only is peer mentoring claimed to change people and offer something better than the professionally dominated approach to offender management that precedes it, it is also claimed to be more egalitarian than other forms of rehabilitation. This is not an intervention delivered by an expert 'other', but a peer, purportedly enabling people to engage in less hierarchical relationships. The St Giles Trust Peer Advice Project, for example, tests out 'the concept that prisoners themselves can be an important resource in the rehabilitation and resettlement processes' and, as such, serve 'as a counterbalance to the widespread belief that programmes are something that are "done" to offenders by specialists' (Boyce et al. 2009: vi). This repositioning of 'offenders' as intervening agents as opposed to intervened-upon subjects potentially offers something quite different to the dominant intervention approach, which remains heavily reliant upon teaching 'offenders' cognitive skills (Rex 2011: 68). Rumgay (2004: 405) terms this 'a cognitive deficit model', which views offenders as 'deficient individuals whose faulty thinking requires correction by professionals with special expertise in cognitive training' (Rumgay 2004: 405). When ex-offenders, or even non-specialist befrienders, become the intervenors, however, this constructed divide is destabilized.

This reimagining of who may constitute the providers and users of services is itself part of a broader movement of 'levelling' the field of human services, encapsulated in the 'user engagement' discourse (Hughes 2012: 50). Hughes points to an increasing emphasis on service user engagement, not least because through expert-led 'what works' defined programmes 'we run the risk of pissing [people] off . . . since our methods seem not to match what they see as their primary needs (and most pressing goals)' (Porporino 2010, cited in Hughes 2012: 50). This analysis is furthered by McNeill and Weaver (2010: 10), who argue that a radical desistance supporting approach might 'involve current and former service users in co-designing, co-developing, co-implementing and co-evaluating a desistance-supporting intervention process'. They argue that:

> A strong evidence-based case could be made for this . . . partly because of what the desistance research has to say about the importance of and merits of developing agency, generativity and civic participation and partly because services co-designed by their current or former users may well be more likely to be fit for purpose and thus effective.
>
> (McNeill and Weaver 2010: 10)

The increased inclusion of *user* or *offender* voices invites more *egalitarian* forms of rehabilitation practice, where expertise may reside as much within people's lived experiences as in academic and professional knowledge. Kavanagh and Borrill (2013: 14), for example, have recognized that mentoring can be 'empowering in both prison and probation settings' in contrast to 'previous experiences of feeling powerless'. Peer mentoring can therefore be read as a stylistic rebellion to the stigma and exclusion former offenders often experience, as an activity which politically turns the power of these exclusions on their head.

Peer mentoring is not only claimed to be egalitarian because it includes voices previously excluded from the practice of rehabilitation, but also because mentoring itself aims for a more democratic kind of intervention, one which allows both helper and helped to be afforded a voice. Such egalitarian learning spaces were theorized by critical pedagogue Paulo Freire:

> The fundamental task of the mentor is a liberatory task. It is not to encourage the mentor's goals and aspirations and dreams to be reproduced in the mentees, the students, but to give rise to the possibility that the students become the owners of their own history . . . to transcend their merely instructive task and to assume the ethical posture of a mentor who truly believes in the total autonomy, freedom, and development of those he or she mentors.
>
> (Freire 1997: 324)

Pollack (2004) examined peer support as an example of such practice with women in prison:

> The fact that the group was co-facilitated by prisoners, rather than by professional staff, greatly enhanced a sense of self-reliance and the autonomy of prisoner participants who have so few opportunities to author their own stories and define their own needs.
>
> (Pollack 2004: 703)

Pollack suggests that peer support 'helps counter the notion that women in prison have few skills, are unable to assume responsibilities, cannot be trusted and are emotionally unstable' (Pollack 2004: 704). Consequently it constitutes a move 'away from deficit model to one that emphasizes women's strengths and acknowledges their varied and skilful modes of coping' (Pollack 2004: 704; see also Burnett and Maruna 2006). An important difference in principle between mentoring and other rehabilitative relationships, is that both parties are positioned as collaborators in the problem-solving process. A peer programme in New York, for example, was found to provide:

> leadership, support, and guidance for female offenders, and not only created a prosocial environment, but fashioned an entire community. This community continued outside of the prison walls, provided women with emotional support, and subsequently resulted in increased levels of institutional and post-release success.
>
> (Collica 2010: 314)

Such personal connections represent an increase in 'social capital', those 'relationships, networks and reciprocities within families and communities' (McNeill and Weaver 2010: 20), which can be key to desisting from crime (Farrall 2011). The approach also resonates with 'strengths-based' practices, which 'treat offenders as community assets to be utilized rather than merely liabilities to be supervised' (Burnett and Maruna 2006: 84). The goal of strengths work is to provide opportunities for individuals 'to develop pro-social self-concepts and identity, generally in the form of rewarding work that is helpful to others' (Burnett and Maruna 2006: 84). The idea is that: 'Nobody should be only a receiver. If people are going to feel good and be accomplished and be part of something, they have to be doing something they can be proud of' (Burnett and Maruna 2006: 84). Peer mentoring positions people as valuable resources in their own right, whilst offering opportunities with redemptive capacities.

Some critical points

Whilst there are clearly a number of claims being made for the practice of mentoring within criminal justice, and some early evidence of its worth, there are also some critical tensions.

Mentoring may not result in desired changes

One problem with mentoring is that it can potentially induce unintended changes. As early as the 1930s the 'Cambridge-Somerville Youth study', which examined mentees under the age of 12 who were at risk of delinquency, 'found that bringing young people with similar delinquent backgrounds together might actually increase antisocial behaviors' (cited in Clayton 2009: 6). More recently, Buck (2017) found that peer mentoring can, at times, result in mentees expressing concern, doubts, or a complete rejection of the intended mentors' example. This can be because mentors are assessed to be 'inauthentic' models; 'How can he help me? I've burgled houses with him!' (peer group member, cited in Buck 2017: 1034), because the stigma of past criminality limits the credibility of reformed identities, or because mentees wish to withhold the 'homage' of imitation (Girard 1991). This is problematic for policies aiming to offer mentoring to all as a generic good (National Offender Management Service 2011).

There are also problems providing mentoring on the scale that has been pledged. A 2016 inspection of the government's flagship 'Through the Gate' policy, highlighted serious shortfalls in the promise to provide a mentor to every person leaving prison:

> None of the prisoners had been helped into employment by Through the Gate services and we did not see examples of handover to specialist education or training resources in the community. The low number of mentors available did not match the early promise of CRC contract bids, or the numbers of prisoners who might have benefited from this type of support on release.
>
> (HMIP 2016: 8)

This inspection, and an earlier sector survey (Clinks and MBF 2012), highlight that numbers of suitably motivated and skilled mentors may be insufficient.

Mentoring may not be better than what has gone before

Whilst mentoring can provide a space for inspirational models and support structures, there are concerns that the practice presents a new set of problems, including mismatches of mentor and mentee in terms of expectations, gender, culture, or race; reluctant or over-zealous mentors/mentees; broken confidentiality; obstructions from others; and parameters/boundaries not agreed upon in advance (McKimm et al. 2007: 13–14). Similarly, Spencer (2007) highlighted six factors that contributed to the demise of mentoring relationships, including 'mentor or protégé [mentee] abandonment; perceived lack of protégé motivation; unfulfilled (or mismatched) expectations; deficiencies in mentor relational skills, including the inability to bridge cultural divides; family interference; and inadequate agency support' (p. 331). There are also challenges related to the voluntary sector context specifically, as funding tends to be short term, limiting the time for projects 'to become established and effective' (Boyce et al. 2009: 22), there are problems accessing good quality volunteer managers and difficulties in relation to 'recruitment, selection and retention' (Clinks and MBF 2012: 9–11), and not insignificantly, there are warnings that volunteering, particularly in prison settings, can take a high personal toll with harms including burnout, post-traumatic stress, injury, or even death (see Corcoran 2012: 22).

Further apprehensions relate to the charged contexts in which mentors operate. Buck and Jaffe (2011) for example, highlighted a lack of private places in prisons where confidential discussions can take place. Boyce et al. (2009), outline the potential for the peer advisors to be subject to bullying or pressure to traffic items such as drugs or mobile phones through the system, although they acknowledge that this was a concern about the possible opportunity rather than a worry about the number of such incidents (Boyce et al. 2009: 11). Nonetheless, these concerns were also raised by Devilly et al. (2005), who argued that clarification of the many ethical issues needs to be addressed, issues such as professional conduct, boundaries, abuse of the system, and the passing of information and or/drugs (Devilly et al. 2005: 233). Such concerns highlight how mentors with criminal convictions are frequently perceived in terms of risk, and links directly to the final point.

Mentoring may not be egalitarian

Whilst mentoring may appear to be less authoritarian than other criminal justice relationships, the subjugated position of 'ex-offenders', and elements of mentoring itself, often serve to undermine this potential. Buck (2014) for example highlights how volunteers with criminal histories often experience forms of exclusion in prison and community settings, resulting in restrictions on their practice. There are also limits to how far mentors can 'empower' mentees, given the chaotic nature of offender placements, which often involves people being transferred to other areas (Clinks and MBF 2012: 8). Mentoring in environments where control and punishment dominate poses unique problems, given the propensity of the system to routinely manage and dehumanize people (Gosling and Buck 2015).

Another challenge to the egalitarian claim is that mentoring essentially maintains a hierarchical relationship structure. This is not a space where 'nobody is a receiver' (Burnett and Maruna 2006: 84), but there are intervenors (mentors) and intervened upon (mentees). Mentees, whilst benefitting in practical and social terms, are still subject to a relationship with another who has something to teach them, a way to help them improve. Moreover, mentoring often takes place as part of a broader criminal justice intervention (Ministry of Justice 2011), for example, a prison or community sentence. The sense of mutuality is therefore undermined in both aim and context. In practical terms, this can result in mentoring which conforms to the 'social deficit model rather than providing an alternative' (Hucklesby and Wincup 2014: 15); indeed it is argued that when bolted on to punitive criminal justice processes, reformist interventions can come to bear little resemblance to their original principles, delivering monitoring and social control functions instead (Hucklesby and Wincup 2014: 2–3). In this regard, the institutionalization of mentoring enables the state to appropriate it and extends the reach of the criminal justice system (Hucklesby and Wincup 2014; Hannah-Moffatt 2000, 2002).

In summary, the practices of mentoring and peer mentoring have clear potential to assist people with the difficult process of leaving crime behind and to mediate some of the excluding and limiting practices of the criminal justice system. Mentors who draw upon lived experiences can potentially bond with, relate to, and inspire mentees in a personalized way. Mentors are also able to offer high levels of support and fill gaps in existing services. Despite these claims, however, there are also concerns about the effectiveness and safety of the practice, given the lack of a developed mentoring theory, the potential for relationships to encounter problems, the contradictions and shortfalls within a predominantly punitive criminal justice system, and the prospect of excessive personal demands upon mentors. These are concerns which require attention in order to harness the potentials of mentoring for this field.

Note

1 'Through the Gates' is a charitable project launched by St Giles Trust in partnership with the London Probation Service. The programme assists ex-prisoners returning to London (Frontier Economics 2009).

References

Akers, R. (1973) *Deviant Behavior: A Social Learning Approach*. Belmont: Wadsworth.

Asencio, E. K. and Burke, P. J. (2011) Does incarceration change the criminal identity? A synthesis of labelling and identity theory perspectives on identity change. *Sociological Perspectives*, 54(2), 163–182.

Boyce, I., Hunter, G. and Hough, M. (2009) *The St Giles Trust Peer Advice Project: Summary of an Evaluation Report*. London: The Institute for Criminal Policy Research, School of Law, King's College. Available at: www.icpr.org.uk/media/10363/St%20Giles%20Trust%20peer%20Advice%20evaluation.pdf (Accessed October 2017).

Bozeman, B. and Feeney, M. K. (2007) Toward a useful theory of mentoring: A conceptual analysis and critique. *Administration and Society*, 39(6), 719–739.

Brown, M. and Ross, S. (2010) Mentoring, social capital and desistance: A study of women released from prison. *Australian & New Zealand Journal of Criminology (Australian Academic Press)*, 43(1), 31–50.

Buck, G. (2014) Civic re-engagements amongst former prisoners. *Prison Service Journal* (214), July.

Buck, G. (2017) "I wanted to feel the way they did": Mimesis as a situational dynamic of peer mentoring by ex-offenders. *Deviant Behavior*, 38(9), 1027–1041.

Buck, G. (2018) The core conditions of peer mentoring. *Criminology & Criminal Justice*, 18(2), 190–206.

Buck, G., Corcoran, M. and Worrall, A. (2015) Gendered dynamics of mentoring. In J. Annison, J. Brayford and J. Deering (Eds.), *Women and Criminal Justice: From the Corston Report to Transforming Rehabilitation*. Bristol: Policy Press.

Buck, G. and Jaffe, M. (2011) Volunteering in criminal justice: Seminar report. In *ESRC Seminar Series: The Third Sector in Criminal Justice*. Keele: Keele University.

Burnett, R. and Maruna, S. (2006) The kindness of prisoners: Strengths-based resettlement in theory and in action. *Criminology and Criminal Justice*, 6(1), 83–106.

Clayton, A. N. (2009) *Mentoring for Youth Involved in Juvenile Justice Programs: A Review of the Literature*. MA: University of Massachusetts.

Clinks. (2012) *Volunteer Peer Support: A Volunteering and Mentoring Guide*. London: Clinks.

Clinks and MBF. (2012) *Supporting Offenders Through Mentoring and Befriending: Clinks and MBF Survey Findings September 2012*. Available at: www.mandbf.org/wp-content/uploads/2012/10/Clinks-and-MBF-survey-report-findings-final-version-Sept-2012.pdf (Accessed October 2017).

Collica, K. (2010) Surviving incarceration: Two prison-based peer programs build communities of support for female offenders. *Deviant Behavior*, 31(4), 314–347.

Corcoran, M. (2012) "Be careful what you ask for": Findings from the seminar series on the "Third sector in criminal justice". *Prison Service Journal* (24), 17–22.

Devilly, G. J., Sorbello, L., Eccleston, L. and Ward, T. (2005) Prison-based peer-education schemes. *Aggression and Violent Behavior*, 10, 219–240.

Farrall, S. (2011) Social capital and offender reintegration: Making probation desistance focused. In S. Maruna and R. Immarigeon (Eds.), *After Crime and Punishment: Pathways to Offender Reintegration*. Oxon: Routledge.

Finnegan, L., Whitehurst, D. and Denton, S. (2010) *Models of Mentoring for Inclusion and Employment: Thematic Review of Existing Evidence on Mentoring and Peer Mentoring*. London: Centre for Economic and Social Inclusion.

Freire, P. (1997) *Mentoring the Mentor: A Critical Dialogue with Paulo Freire*. New York: Peter Lang.

Frontier Economics. (2009) *St Giles Trust's Through the Gates: An Analysis of Economic Impact*. London: Pro Bono Economics.

Girard, R. (1962) Marcel Proust. In Girard, R. and Doran, R. (Eds.), *Mimesis and Theory: Essays on Literature and Criticism, 1953–2005*. Stanford, CA; London: Stanford University Press, pp. 56–70.

Girard, R. (1991) Innovation and repetition. In Girard, R. and Doran, R. (Eds.), *Mimesis and Theory: Essays on Literature and Criticism, 1953–2005*. Stanford, CA; London: Stanford University Press, pp. 230–245.

Gosling, H. and Buck, G. (2015) Mentoring: Crossing boundaries with care? *Criminal Justice Matters*, 99(1), 22–23.

Grayling, C. (2012) Justice Minister's 'Rehabilitation Revolution'. *Speech*, 20 November. Available at: www.justice.gov.uk/news/speeches/chris-grayling/speech-to-the-centre-of-social-justice (Accessed October 2017).

Hannah-Moffat, K. (2000). Prisons that empower: Neo-liberal governance in Canadian Women's prisons. *British Journal of Criminology*, 40, 510–531.

Hannah-Moffat, K. (2002). Creating choices: Reflecting on choices. In Carlen, P. (Ed.), *Women and Punishment: The struggle for Justice*. Cullumpton: Willan Publishing.

Hirschi, T. (1969). *Causes of Delinquency*. Berkeley: University of California Press.

HM Inspectorate of Probation (HMIP) and HM Inspectorate of Prisons (2016) An Inspection of Through the Gate Resettlement Services for Short-Term Prisoners. Manchester: Her Majesty's Inspectorate of Probation. Available online at: https://www.justiceinspectorates.gov.uk/cjji/wp-content/uploads/sites/2/2016/09/Through-the-Gate.pdf (Accessed May 2019).

Hucklesby, A. and Wincup, E. (2014) Assistance, support and monitoring? The paradoxes of mentoring adults in the criminal justice system. *Journal of Social Policy*, 43(2), 373–390.

Hughes, W. (2012) Promoting offender engagement and compliance in sentence planning: Practitioner and service user perspectives in Hertfordshire. *Probation Journal*, 59(1), 49–65.

Jolliffe, D. and Farrington, D. P. (2007) *A Rapid Evidence Assessment of the Impact of Mentoring on Re-Offending: A Summary*. London: Home Office.

Kavanagh, L. and Borrill, J. (2013) Exploring the experiences of ex-offender mentors. *Probation Journal*, 60(4), 400–414.

Kidd, M. (2011) A first-hand account of service user groups in the United Kingdom: An evaluation of their purpose, effectiveness, and place within the recovery movement. *Journal of Groups in Addiction & Recovery*, 6(1–2), 164–175.

Maguire, M. and Nolan, J. (2007) Accommodation and related services for ex-prisoners. In Hucklesby, A. and Hagley-Dickinson, L. (Eds.), *Prisoner Resettlement: Policy and Practice*. Oxon: Routledge, pp. 144–174.

Maruna, S. (2001) *Making Good: How Ex-Convicts Reform and Rebuild Their Lives*. Washington, DC: American Psychological Association.

McKimm, J., Jollie, C. and Hatter, M. (2007) *Mentoring Theory and Practice*. London: Imperial College School of Medicine. Available at: www.faculty.londondeanery. ac.uk/e-learning/explore-further/e-learning/feedback/files/Mentoring_Theory_and_ Practice.pdf (Accessed October 2017).

McNeill, F. (2013) Transforming Rehabilitation: Evidence, values and ideology. *British Journal of Community Justice*, 11(2–3), 83–87.

McNeill, F. and Weaver, B. (2010) *Changing Lives? Desistance Research and Offender Management, Research Report 03/2010*. The Scottish Centre for Crime and Justice Research. Available at: www.sccjr.ac.uk/pubs/Changing-Lives-Desistance-Research-and-Offender-Management/255 (Accessed October 2017).

Mentoring and Befriending Foundation (MBF) (2014) *What Is Mentoring and Befriending?* Manchester: Mentoring and Befriending Foundation. Available at: https://www.ncvo.org.uk/component/redshop/1-publications/P177-what-is-mentoring-and-befriending?highlight=WyJ3aGF0Iiwid2hhdCdzIiwiJ3doYXQiLCJ pcyIsIidpcyIsImlzZSIsImlzyIsIm1lbnRvcmluZyIsIm1lbnRvciIsIm1lbnRvcn MiLCJtZW50b3Incyel sIndoYXQgaXMiLCJ3aGF0IGlzIG1lbnRvcmluZyIsImlzI GllbnRvcmluZyJd (Accessed May 2019)

Ministry of Justice (MoJ). (2011) *Making Prisons Work: Skills for Rehabilitation Review of Offender Learning*. London: Department for Business, Innovation and Skills. Available at: www.gov.uk/government/uploads/system/uploads/attachment_data/ file/230260/11-828-making-prisons-work-skills-for-rehabilitation.pdf (Accessed October 2017).

National Offender Management Service (NOMS). (2011) *Mentoring in NOMS*. London: National Offender Management Service. Available at: www.law.leeds.ac.uk/assets/ files/research/ccjs/mentoring/mentoring-in-noms.pdf (Accessed October 2017).

Parkin, S. and McKeganey, N. (2000) The rise and rise of peer education approaches. *Drugs: Education, prevention and Policy*, 7(3), 293–310.

Parsons, C. Maras, P., Knowles, C., Bradshaw, V., Hollingworth, K. and Monteiro, H. (2008) *Formalised Peer Mentoring Pilot Evaluation*. Canterbury: Canterbury Christ Church University.

Pollack, S. (2004) Anti-oppressive social work practice with women in prison: Discursive reconstructions and alternative practice. *British Journal of Social Work*, 34(5), 693–707.

Princes Trust. (2008) *Making the Case: One-to-one Support for Young Offenders*. Princes Trust, Rainer, St Giles Trust, CLINKS, 23 June.

Princes Trust. (2012) *Evaluation Summary: Working One to One with Young Offenders*. Available at: www.icpr.org.uk/media/32465/The%20Prince's%20Trust%20indepen dent%20evaluation%20summary%20of%20121%20pilot%20Jan%202012.pdf (Accessed October 2017).

Rex, S. (2011) Beyond cognitive-behaviouralism? Reflections of the effectiveness of the literature. In A. Bottoms, L. Gelsthorpe and S. Rex (Eds.), *Community Penalties*. Oxon: Routledge.

Rumgay, J. (2004) Scripts for safer survival: Pathways out of female crime. *The Howard Journal of Criminal Justice*, 43(4), 405–419.

The Social Innovation Partnership. (2012) *The WIRE (Women's Information and Resettlement for Ex-offenders) Evaluation Report.* London: The Social Innovation Partnership. Available at: http://site.stgilestrust.org.uk/project/uploads/user_files/files/Support%20for%20vulnerable%20women%20leaving%20prison%20full%20report.pdf (Accessed October 2017).

Spencer, R. (2007). It's not what I expected A qualitative study of youth mentoring relationship failures. *Journal of Adolescent Research*, 22(4), 331–354.

Sullivan, C. J. and Jolliffe, D. (2012) Peer influence, mentoring, and the prevention of crime. In B. C. Welsh and D. P. Farrington (Eds.), *The Oxford Handbook of Crime Prevention*. Oxford: Oxford University Press.

Sutherland, E. H. (1947). *Principles of Criminology,* 4th edition. Philadelphia: Lippincott.

Taylor, J., Burrowes, N., Disley, E., Liddle, M., Maguire, M., Rubin, J. and Wright, S. (2013) *Intermediate Outcomes of Mentoring Interventions: A Rapid Evidence Assessment.* London: National Offender Management Service.

Tolan, P., Henry, D., Schoeny, M. and Bass, A. (2008) Mentoring interventions to affect juvenile delinquency and associated problems. *Campbell Systematic Reviews*, 16.

Willoughby, M., Parker, A. and Ali, R. (2013) *Mentoring for Offenders: Mapping Services for Adult Offenders in England and Wales.* London: Sova.

Zdun, S. (2011) Immigration as a trigger to knife off from delinquency? Desistance and persistence among male adolescents from the Former Soviet Union in Germany. *Criminology and Criminal Justice*, 11(4), 307–323.

39

The contribution of ex-service users

The life and death of a peer mentor employment rehabilitation programme

John Rico

Introduction

As the job title suggests, the purpose of the *Engagement Worker* role was to engage service users, but more specifically, to engage service users with individuals who had shared experiences of the criminal justice system, ethnicity, social class, and life experience. Additionally, whereas some service users would limit their level of engagement with probation officers who were forced into the sometimes-awkward simultaneous roles of therapist and disciplinarian (Miller 2015), Engagement Workers would only attempt therapeutic engagement and leave the disciplinary consequences to the probation officers. Perhaps, it was hoped, these Engagement Workers would be able to engage the more difficult, hard-to-reach service users in a way in which probation officers were not always able to, despite their best intentions.

Using former offenders in mentor roles was, in itself, not new. The London Probation Trust – like other organizations focused on offender engagement – had previously recruited volunteer peer mentors, many of whom had previously been offenders. Research into offender engagement seemed to have proved the benefits of these peer relationships. Fletcher and Batty (2012) produced a paper summarizing the benefits that had thus far been identified:

- Boyce and colleagues (2009) concluded that offenders were more likely to seek help from peers rather than figures within positions of authority.
- Cook and colleagues (2008) reported that inmates who were on the path to rehabilitation and were provided proper training were more likely to be viewed as authentic and were more likely to demonstrate understanding than hired treatment staff.
- Huggins (2010) found that peers provided offenders with successful role models by serving as an actual example of someone from a shared background, who had managed to turn their life around.
- A 2003 study from the United Nations Office on Drugs and Crime found that offenders were more likely to both accept and act on information when it was presented by a figure with whom they could identify.

However, as has been identified within research literature (Kavanagh and Borrill 2013; Foster 2011; Ministry of Justice 2014) peer mentor programmes also had their share of issues, specifically in relation to keeping peer mentors motivated and engaged with the programme, as well as dealing with issues of professional boundaries. The Probation Trust's own experience echoed these findings, with peer mentors having a high turnover rate, and also having episodes where poor awareness of professional boundaries had led to conflict.

As was identified in an evaluation of a Transitional Support Scheme (TSS) in Wales, mentors that received training and support were much less likely to vacate the role (Maguire et al. 2010). With the Engagement Workers, it was hoped that routine supervision, ongoing training, professional development, and full-time pay would allow for the benefits of the mentor role while controlling for the most frequent problems: commitment would be fixed by providing the salary, and the maintenance of appropriate boundaries would be addressed through supervision and professional development. It was this professionalization and integration of the peer mentor role with former offenders that was novel for the Probation Service and had rarely been attempted. In the end, however, nothing would quite go as planned. The programme would barely last a single employment cycle and the Engagement Workers would discover that two years of solid employment did little to compensate for multiple criminal convictions when looking for work.

Identity shift through employment

The Engagement Worker programme did not exist only to benefit current service users. In fact, one of the primary purposes of the programme was to help the Engagement Workers themselves through the offer of employment, which research has linked to desistance (Barnett 2013; Ministry of Justice 2013a) and fewer arrests (Rossi et al. 1980). Employment has also been linked to the creation of normalizing routines (Cohen and Felson 1979; Sampson and Laub 1993) and the development of cultural and social capital (Laub and Sampson 2003). However, not all employment has the same effect on desistance: the effect on desistance is much less for low-skill disposable roles than it is for professional highly skilled roles. The Engagement Worker role being advertised was a white-collar position where those within the role would receive ongoing professional development, attend strategic meetings, and have ancillary avenues to explore in relation to accumulating additional responsibilities. It was a respected role in the community; this was not fast food. The Engagement Worker role seemed to fit all the criteria necessary for serving as a vehicle to facilitate pro-social identity shift.

The first cohort of Engagement Workers to be hired largely came from a pool of peer mentors volunteering for two local voluntary organizations that worked with the London Probation Trust. A mix of women and men, varying in age from young adults to past middle age (and in one instance, nearing retirement age), what they had in common was that each had made the decision to desist from what were sometimes very prolific offending lifestyles. As recent research has demonstrated (Skardhamar and Savolainen 2014), decisions to desist often precede obtaining employment, with employment instead contributing to the ongoing maintenance of desistance. In other words, offenders most often consider getting a job only after they have already made the decision to stop offending.

The Engagement Workers also had something else in common: a realization that they were now suffering from the cumulative damage wrought by a lifetime of missed opportunities. As adults without much in the way of a formal employment history, with little formal education, and a host of criminal convictions, a number of the Engagement Workers could be considered almost unemployable (even for entry-level non-skilled jobs, employers would undoubtedly prefer teenagers or young adults over middle-aged offenders with no history of employment). As has been studied by Heckman (2006), compensating for early-in-life deficits becomes that much more difficult later in life as the opportunities of early adulthood disappear with age, often leaving service users without access to starting opportunities, but insufficiently skilled to work alongside nonoffending peers in adult employment.

In his 1997 book *Violence: Reflections on a National Epidemic*, criminal psychiatrist James Gilligan promoted the theory that offenders, like all people, are primarily motivated by needs for respect and ego validation. Whereas for nonoffenders, that respect is earned through career, financial, or familial achievement, for offenders – for whom many of the traditional pathways to respect and achievement are closed – respect and ego validation is pursued through the development of alternative identities, which lie on paths that are achievable to them. The exaltation of criminal identities and the purposeful denigration of those that play by 'mainstream rules' is an attempt at saving the ego, a re-writing of the rules into a dynamic where they receive ego validation through their chosen identities.

Within this theoretical framework, the Engagement Workers as a group were in a precarious position. They had (at least temporarily) rejected criminal identities and were attempting conventional avenues to success by volunteering as mentors and applying for work. However, continued failure to achieve conventional success would put their desistance at risk (Agnew 1985) as they were being asked to adapt to the rules and norms of a system in which there was no way for them to win, given the early life choices they had made. Desistance was often painful and difficult (Nugent and Schinkel 2016). At some point, a return to an outlaw identity where their ego could be validated could start to seem like the rational choice.

The original programme saw the Engagement Worker role as a way to help former offenders fully make that transition to work. Simultaneously, the role could be a stepping stone into future employment, where it was envisioned that each Engagement Worker would stay in the role about two years, building their CVs and skills, before moving on to new opportunities external to the organization. This departure would then create a vacancy for another former service user. As a programme, it would be an ongoing desistance conveyor belt, a pipeline of opportunity provided to one former service user after another. There were even plans to grow the programme in the future, perhaps doubling or even tripling the number of roles available to former service users. This was the crux of the programme. This entire Engagement Worker experiment, as with much of the work done by Probation, was ultimately about shifting the identity (Hazel 2017) of the Engagement Workers from that of offenders to that of working professionals, through the use of employment.

Fitting in

While the Engagement Worker project had the backing of the Probation Trust's Chief Probation officer, some middle and senior managers were sceptical about the programme and less encouraging. And whereas some staff members applauded the initiative and kept an open mind about the new role, others denounced the idea of having to work side by side with offenders, with some even suggesting that the organization was putting their safety at risk. The scepticism of some staff towards the role seemed a curious perspective, given Probation's purported appreciation for the values of individual transformation and second chances.

In weekly meetings, the Engagement Workers would speak openly about the hostility they received – being openly talked about, being discussed in the third person, and being the only person to be told to leave the room for parts of a team meeting which were considered too sensitive for them to hear. For a group of former offenders with low self-esteem, struggling to fit in, all of this had a significant impact on their self-esteem.

Fortunately, these negative engagements were balanced by an equal number of positive reactions: probation officers who were friendly and eager to show them the ropes of managing offenders, generous supervisors who helped them develop professionally, and the camaraderie and support of the other members of the Engagement Worker team.

Social and cultural capital

As was demonstrated in two ground-breaking books on the subject (*Ain't No Makin' It* by Jay MacLeod [1987] and *Getting Paid* by Mercer L. Sullivan [1989]), one of the biggest obstacles to desistance is the lack of social and cultural capital. Cultural capital is knowledge regarding the unwritten societal rules that must necessarily be mastered for successful integration into the professional world: how to dress, how to act, how to write, etc. Social capital refers to the development of relationships that can be capitalized on for future success (role models, access to working professionals, mentors, etc). Lack of social capital was also an early concern for some of the Engagement Workers. There were issues regarding inappropriate comments to other staff, as well as issues surrounding tardiness and absences, and even issues about how to behave properly in a meeting or needing to be told to take notes prior to receiving a large amount of information. One Engagement Worker was suspended for sexual harassment, another caused scandal through inappropriate comments offered in a team meeting. For some existing probation staff, these examples were considered to be evidence that the hiring of former offenders was a bad idea.

However, despite the initial deficits in cultural capital held by some of the Engagement Workers early on, they still held more cultural capital than some service users who, in some instances, lacked the basic skills to apply for an ID card or open a bank account, all tasks that Engagement Workers would assist them with. It was in these situations where, in addition to one -on-one engagement, intervention groupwork, and running inductions, Engagement Workers found the task for which they would be most valued by their colleagues. Real world success and even a return to prison often pivoted on whether or not something simple like an ID card could be obtained; incredibly, there was no one in Probation to assist with these simple things other than Engagement Workers.

A case study in teaching social capital

Marcus's probation officer told him to drop off an application at the housing office; he was homeless and the new legislation required councils to provide a place for him to live; at least, that was what he was told. Inevitably, Marcus would return to his next appointment not having completed the task. This almost always angered his probation officer who felt that Marcus was not trying very hard. Marcus, in turn, attempted to communicate how he had made an attempt at the housing office, but Marcus did not have the best communication skills and his anger over his probation officer blaming him for the failure ended up erupting and obscuring his explanation. What Marcus struggled to tell his probation officer was that when he had presented himself at the housing office, he had quickly been dismissed by one of the workers who, Marcus felt, had tricked him into admitting he wasn't eligible for housing assistance as the council was no longer responsible for him since he had purposefully left the council when he was sentenced to prison. Marcus would attempt to explain and advocate for himself but was perceived by the housing workers as being hostile and was quickly asked to leave.

What his probation officer did not understand was that young black adults had a different experience in the office than did white middle-class professionals. His probation officer also did not understand that housing workers saw their role as to serve, in part, as gatekeepers for what was a very finite resource, and that often meant trying to discourage individuals from applying. Marcus would not be listed in housing performance figures as someone they were unable to house, because he had been discouraged from even making an application. As with many bureaucracies, the housing office was front-loading their own performance figures, by controlling what would get counted and what would not.

It was in these sorts of situations that Engagement Workers were exceedingly useful. They knew how to speak to the housing worker with a carefully balanced mix of assertiveness and humility. Engagement Workers also knew that regardless of what the legislation said, actual access to resources often depended on personal relationships. In this way, the Engagement Workers' most important job became teaching social capital to the service users they worked with, most specifically: how to put in an application.

An ending . . .

Two years into the programme, the Engagement Workers had largely been not only accepted by staff, but in many instances considered irreplaceable. They were less offenders, and more colleagues. A qualitative review of the programme after a year was mostly glowing. Meanwhile, the Engagement Workers themselves had undergone a remarkable professionalization. As individuals, they were advising on the service users' perspective in strategic top-level management meetings, and they were frequently presenting and running inductions by themselves. They had become trusted professionals able to represent the organization. One recommendation of the review was that Engagement Workers needed to document their contributions better, while also finding a way to categorize and then count the various types of support they offered.

However, to most of the Engagement Workers, this seemed an unnecessary and boring bureaucratic function: they wanted to get on with the work of helping offenders, not trying to count meeting types. In the end, it would, in part, be the failure to perform this 'boring' bureaucratic function that would lead to the ending of the Engagement Worker project.

Unfortunately, like many Probation Trust initiatives, the Engagement Worker programme was realized at the cusp of the Transforming Rehabilitation restructure (Ministry of Justice 2013b) when, all across the country, Probation Trusts were dissolved as their service users were allocated to either the National Probation Service (NPS) or a local Community Rehabilitation Company (CRC). In the London CRC, the new managers were anxious to make their mark and transform the organization. The incoming view of management seemed to be that the Probation Trusts had been bloated, inefficient public organizations, and that in order to transform into agile, lean, corporate entities, they needed to get rid of many of the unnecessary roles that seemed a feature of government bureaucracies. (The extent of the cutting would, in subsequent years, be shown to have been detrimental, as the London CRC would later spend years attempting to rebuild the very infrastructure it had eliminated so early on.)

For the new management team, the Engagement Worker role was an early target for elimination. They did not understand the purpose of the programme. In part, it seemed an expensive form of welfare, effectively paying what was now ten former service users to stay clean and sober. Compared to the 20,000 service users within the London CRC, what was the value of paying for just ten to be successful? It was an allocation of funds that seemed all the more questionable given that the individuals it was helping with formal employment, were – for the most part – no longer probation service users; the programme was spending money to help rehabilitate individuals for whom the organization did not any longer have a responsibility.

All of this was reinforced by the fact that few Engagement Workers had documented their performance as was recommended in the earlier review, making it difficult later on to describe the volumes and types of help they had offered service users. Without performance figures it was impossible to define the scope and scale that the Engagement Workers' contribution had provided; there were a great many anecdotal stories from service users that the Engagement Workers had transformed their lives, but anecdotal stories do not provide a frequency, or a measure of units of engagement. The decision was made to end the programme and the existing team of Engagement Workers. The Engagement Workers were now going to find out how effective their probation roles had been in securing future work.

Expectation raising

With the final two months of employment with the London CRC looming, the Engagement Workers had begun applying for work outside of the organization – work which was still largely within the fields of criminal justice and social work. They applied to voluntary organizations, social welfare drug rehabilitation centres, and other positions where they could rely on their existing experience and work with offenders or other troubled at-risk youth. Their initial attitudes when they began applying for positions had been largely optimistic. A number of different Engagement Workers commented on how impressed potential employers would be when they saw that they had transitioned from service users to staff; it was widely felt that this would demonstrate that they had been rehabilitated. Unfortunately, these estimations would be wrong; not only did potential employers often not even know what the Probation Service did, but the fact that another organization had taken a chance on them did not seem reason to take on a liability themselves. These were roles that dealt with sensitive data security and often required security clearances, which Engagement Workers were unable to secure due to their offending history.

During one of the weekly team meetings, it was explained that they had perhaps held unrealistic expectations regarding how easy securing work would be. Part of this discussion involved explaining that finding employment was extremely difficult even for applicants without offending histories. Furthermore, it was explained that in the roles they were applying for they would be competing with many individuals who not only had more than two years of employment history, but also had university educations and did not have offending histories (Wester 2002). In one study, 65% of employers reported that they would not knowingly hire an ex-offender (Holzer 1996). Ironically, the formal Engagement Worker programme had recently begun focusing more on continued professional development and delivering training modules for which Engagement Workers would receive education certificates. However, this would ultimately be an endeavour which had started too late.

This was arguably a pivotal moment in the desistance pathways of the Engagement Workers; they had felt that they had worked hard and accomplished so much yet were still being told they were not good enough. Self-esteem is an important moderator of feedback in desistance, and the Engagement Workers seemed to be taking the rejections more personally than a nonoffending peer colleague would. It was throughout this period that an unexpected outcome was found. The Engagement Workers had raised their expectations for what they considered a deserved role, a standard against which they would define their own success or failure while on a desistance pathway. The experience obtained in the Engagement Worker role could very well have been helpful in their job search had they been seeking unskilled work in factories or warehouse work or other blue-collar jobs. But now that they had experienced two years of white-collar work, where they worked on a computer, had scheduling flexibility, had participated in meetings that dealt with important strategic issues, and were allowed to pursue their work objectives relatively free of direct supervision, returning to a highly controlled unskilled environment would be considered a failure.

Struggling to change identities

It was also discovered that there was an inherent flaw within the Engagement Worker role that could potentially limit their ability to change their own identity from one of offender to that of professional worker. The role they were hired for was that of the reformed offender. In each meeting they participated in, they were always introduced as the 'reformed offender', never just as a routine employee. The organization's pride in having such a programme, that employed ex-offenders, was frequently paraded to stakeholders and partnering organizations as a visible demonstration of the organization's progressive values. This necessitated that the Engagement Workers attend a great many meetings where they were surrounded by working professionals, as they identified themselves as offenders. Engagement Workers openly discussed how hard it was to transform their identities from offenders to working professionals given that their identity in the organization was that of an offender, albeit reformed.

In the end, partly due to internal criticism from staff who had come to respect and rely on the contributions of the Engagement Workers, the organization allowed them to apply for internal roles, for which they would be favoured. Most managed to get hired as Probation Service Officers, group facilitators, or administrative staff. It is worth noting that the Engagement Worker role was one that made it difficult for them to escape their label of being an 'offender' (given that the role was designed as one of offenders that work with service users), but in these new roles, their past offending history was no longer relevant. In the months to come, their prior offending history would rarely be mentioned. They would manage to transform their identities – in both their own eyes and those of their colleagues – from offenders to colleagues. Ultimately, three of the Engagement Workers chose not to take other positions within the organization and of these three, one ended up reoffending and back in prison.

However, for the period of sustained employment, the reoffending rate for the Engagement Workers had been zero percent.

Acknowledgement

I am grateful to Nigel Hosking, who provided valuable feedback on earlier versions of this chapter.

References

Agnew, R. A. (1985) A revised strain theory of delinquency. *Social Forces*, 64(1), 151–167.
Barnett, E. (2013) *Analysis on the Impact of Employment on Re-Offending*. 18th GSS Methodology Symposium. London: Ministry of Justice.

Boyce, I. Hunter, G. and Hough, M. (2009) *St Giles Trust Peer Advice Project: An Evaluation.* London: St Giles Trust.

Cohen, L. E. and Felson, M. (1979) Social change and crime rate trends: A routine activity approach. *American Sociological Review,* 44(4), 588–608.

Cook, J., McClure, S., Koutsenok, I. and Lord, S. (2008) The implementation of inmate mentor programs in the correctional treatment system as an innovative approach. *Journal of Teaching on the Addictions,* 7(2), 123–132.

Fletcher, D. R. and Batty, E. (2012) *Offender Peer Interventions: What Do We Know?* Sheffield: Sheffield Hallam University.

Foster, J. (2011) *Peer Support in Prison Health Care: An Investigation into the Listening Scheme in One Adult Male Prison.* London: University of Greenwich.

Gilligan, J. (1997) *Violence: Reflections on a National Epidemic.* New York: Pantheon.

Hazel, N. (2017) *Now All I Care About Is My Future.* London: Beyond Youth Custody.

Heckman, J. J. (2006) Skill formation and the economics of investing in disadvantaged children. *Science,* 312, 1900–1902.

Hirschi, T. (1980) Labelling Theory and Juvenile Delinquency: An Assessment of the Evidence. In W. R. Gove (Ed.), *The Labelling of Deviance: Evaluating a Perspective.* New York: Wiley.

Holzer, H. (1996) *What Employers Want: Job Prospects for Less-Educated Workers.* New York: Russell Sage Foundation.

Huggins, R. (2010) *Mentoring for Progression: Prison Mentoring Project. Assessing Strength, Outcomes, and Roll-Out Potential.* Oxford: Oxford Brookes University.

Kavanagh, L. and Borrill, J. (2013) Exploring the experiences of ex-offender mentors. *Probation Journal,* 60(4), 400–414.

Laub, J. H. and Sampson, R. J. (2003) *Shared Beginnings, Divergent Lives: Delinquent Boys to Age 70.* Cambridge, MA: Harvard University Press.

MacLeod, J. (1987) *Ain't No Makin' It.* New York: Routledge.

Maguire, M., Holloway, K., Liddle, M., Gordon, F., Gray P., Smith A. and Wright, S. (2010) *Evaluation of the Transitional Support Scheme (TSS): Final Report to the Welsh Assembly.* Available at: http://wccsj.ac.uk/images/docs/tss-report-en.pdf.

Miller, J. (2015) Contemporary modes of probation officer supervision: The triumph of the "synthetic officer." *Justice Quarterly,* 32(2), 314–336.

Ministry of Justice. (2013a) *Analysis of the Impact of Employment on Re-Offending, Following Release from Custody, Using Propensity Score Matching.* London: Ministry of Justice.

Ministry of Justice. (2013b) *Transforming Rehabilitation: A Strategy for Reform.* Cm 8619. London: Ministry of Justice.

Ministry of Justice. (2014) *Transforming Rehabilitation: A Summary of the Evidence on Reducing Reoffending.* Ministry of Justice Analytical Series. London: Ministry of Justice.

Nugent, B. and Schinkel, M. (2016) The pains of desistance. *Criminology & Criminal Justice,* 16(5), 568–584.

Rossi, P. H., Berk, R. A. and Lenihan, K. J. (1980) *Money, Work, and Crime: Experimental Evidence.* New York: Academic Press.

Sampson, R. J. and Laub, J. H. (1993) *Crime in the Making: Pathways and Turning Points Through Life.* Cambridge, MA: Harvard University Press.

Skardhamar, T. and Savolainen, J. (2014) Changes in criminal offending around the time of job entry: A study of employment and desistance. *Criminology,* 52(2), 263–291.

Sullivan, M. L. (1989) *Getting Paid: Youth, Crime and Work in the Inner City.* Ithaca: Cornell University Press.

United Nations Office on Drugs and Crime. (2003) *Peer to Peer: Using Peer Strategies in Drug Abuse Prevention.* New York: United Nations.

Western, B. (2002) The impact of incarceration on wage mobility and inequality. *American Sociological Review,* 67(4), 526–546.

40

Co-producing outcomes with service users in the penal system

Trish McCulloch

Introduction

Since the 1960s, participatory discourses and practices have steadily moved to the fore in public, political, and academic discourse. Mobilized originally by critiques of liberal and representative democracy (Barber 1984), top-down governance (Hirschman 1970), and a rethinking of the public sphere (Habermas 1962/1969), participatory practices were initially advanced as a mechanism for political and social change through processes of citizen empowerment (Arnstein 1971). By the 1970s, Elinor Ostrom's (1975) work on the role of and relationships between public services and service users in US urban reform prompted particular attention to the participatory dynamic within public service provision and to co-production as an emerging concept and practice.

As is immediately evident, developing ideas of participation and co-production fuse and overlap. Pestoff (2012: 17), for example, discusses co-production as a term used to describe and analyze citizen participation in the provision of publicly financed services. Others describe participation as a component of co-production, and vice versa. Acknowledging the elastic and overlapping nature of these terms (Ewert and Evers 2012), conceptual clarity is important. As some commentators observe, in the absence of definitional clarification, co-production runs the risk of meaning everything and nothing at the same time.

For Ostrom (1996: 1073), co-production describes a process through which 'inputs used to produce a good or service are contributed by individuals who are not in the same organisation'. More recently, Bovaird and Loeffler (2012) describe co-production as the progression of shared outcomes through regular relationships between professionalized service providers, service users, and/or other members of the community, where all parties make substantial resource contributions. Key here is the idea of co-contribution. While participation occurs on multiple levels and may include co-contribution (see, for example, Arnstein's [1971] ladder of citizen participation), co-production can be distinguished conceptually insofar as it speaks to a process which begins with the idea of active co-contribution across organizations, communities, groups, and/or citizens.

Like most socio-political turns, the recent rise of co-production as a 'new' and 'transforming' approach to public service provision can be traced to a number of divergent and coalescing political, economic, and socio-cultural developments, some of which are introduced above. Amidst this play, the idea that public services can only deliver 'personalized' outcomes through an interplay of public and private contribution has become both central and powerful (Bovaird 2007), if also appropriated and tamed (that is conceptualized and applied in instrumental or reductive ways). In a global socio-political landscape of widening inequalities, economic austerity, welfare reductionism, and demographic diversity, the appeal and promise of co-production for the delivery and reform of modern public services appears firm. The facing question is whether public services, and the relationships they depend on, can be remade to respond to this 'new' truth.

If co-production is perplexing for public services generally (Boyle and Harris 2009), its place in criminal justice systems and services is perhaps particularly problematic. In neo-liberal cultures of control, criminal justice systems and sanctions continue to be constructed within an explicitly punitive and coercive frame (Garland 2015). Meanwhile, its subjects, that is, those sentenced, have become the objects upon which justice is done. In this narrow space, the idea of service user co-production as a legitimate approach is questionable to say the least. However, this is only part of the story. Running alongside this dominant punishment narrative is another story of rehabilitation. In this story, crime is a problem to be treated, or corrected, via the application of evidence-based interventions targeted at the level of the individual and beyond. It is within this story that co-production perhaps finds a place (Ward and Maruna 2007). To the extent that rehabilitation is concerned with individually led processes of progression, recovery, desistance, and re-entry, questions of user co-production become pivotal.

The focus of this chapter is on user co-production in justice sanctions. The chapter will consider the question of user co-production within this particular space, attending specifically to questions of 'what', 'why', and 'how'. It begins by providing a review of existing research in this area, followed by a summary of findings from a recent empirical study conducted by the author in Scotland. Together, the findings suggest that co-production may be, for now, an 'imaginary' frame for justice sanctions; that is, an appealing idea that exists mostly in our imagination and is sustained through the negation of less appealing realities and truths (see Carlen 2012 and below). However, its core principles – personhood, participation, empowerment, and co-contribution – emerge as critical to longstanding ideas of 'just' sanctions, and to the processes of recovery and change which make sanctions meaningful. The chapter concludes that these principles require more reflexive consideration by justice actors, connecting to broader socio-political questions of what justice sanctions are for.

Co-production and criminal justice

There is very little research on co-production in criminal justice services and sanctions (McCulloch 2016), less still that speaks to the theme of user co-production within this sphere.

There is a small but growing body of work on the themes of crime, justice, and democracy, reflecting renewed interest in criminal justice policy, practice, and enquiry as a democratic endeavour (Christie 1977; Sparks and Loader 2010). In the main, this work considers the proper role of citizens and/or 'the public' in criminal justice systems and debate and, broadly, advances a more democratic and participatory justice practice. Significantly, with one or two exceptions, people with convictions remain on the margins of this analysis, with constructions of citizens and/or 'the public' typically constrained to law-abiding citizens, victims, and/or communities. However, though not speaking directly to the value of involving people with convictions in justice processes, much of this work foregrounds the longstanding rationales underpinning democratic, participatory, and co-productive practices, across sectors and peoples. Dzur (2012), for example identifies three functions of participatory democracy and responsibility in public life. These include the ways in which participation helps all those involved become better in some way; the importance of extending opportunities for participation, contribution, and collective decision-making into domains commonly thought apolitical, i.e. workplaces, families, and institutions, and the benefits of individuals acquiring responsibility. This body of work also foregrounds the important relationship between social and criminal justice and the inequalities and costs associated with and perpetuated by non-participatory regimes. Many of these arguments connect with more recent UK developments around the 'Big Society' and with global debates regarding the inter-relationships between equality, economics, and well-being. As Dzur (2012: 121) observes, democratic participation is not triggered then by 'a happy-go-lucky impulse for self-development or aimless do-gooding', but by recognition of the value and the specific harms, dangers, and injustices produced when participation is restricted to and between conventional institutions and actors. As these studies conclude: these themes are not irrelevant to effective criminal justice practice but fundamental.

This body of literature also highlights the challenge of progressing a more democratic practice in the criminal justice context. Identified barriers for lay people include: time, conflicts with domestic and work commitments, tokenism, and a sense that sharing responsibility for crime control and prevention is not 'easy to fulfil' (Crawford 2002). Further, Lacey (2007) cautions that the progression of a more democratic justice practice does not necessarily equate with the progression of participatory, inclusive, or restorative justice practices. As is now evident, in an agitated, insecure, and intensely mediated world, democratic responsiveness and social inclusion do not necessarily go hand in hand. As Maruna and King (2008) observe, public participation can exacerbate the social distance that exists between justice actors as public citizens are reconfigured as 'partners against crime' and, by extension, those who commit it.

More recently, questions of participation and co-production have resurfaced within enquiry around compliance and penal legitimacy (McCulloch 2013). Research in this area indicates that if we wish to improve the outcomes of justice sanctions we need to better understand the subjective experience and motivations of those completing sanctions (Bottoms 2001). This work points to the importance of attending to issues of procedural justice, that is the exercise of fair procedures in justice processes (Tyler 1990), to the relational element of interventions (McNeill and Robinson 2013), to the inter-relationship between criminal and social justice (Farrall 2002), and to the importance of cooperative and co-productive approaches (Morgenstern and Robinson 2014). These insights are significant and have done much to reassert the pivotal place of those sentenced in justice sanctions. However, to date, the impact of this new thinking appears constrained by the instrumental and managerial lenses through which these messages are being heard and applied; that is, from a starting point of: 'how can we get offenders to do what we want?'.

Finally, there is a small body of work that speaks directly to the themes of user participation and/or co-production in justice sanctions and services, reflecting the rise of rights-based rationales and evidence-based perspectives. Rights-based rationales start from the foundation that people who offend are citizens and thus, in addition to being held to account for their behaviour, must *also* be afforded the rights and responsibilities of citizenship. Again, this rationale is frequently positioned within a broader social justice framework which advocates a need to acknowledge the broader social factors that can impact on individual decisions to persist and desist. Evidence-based rationales draw on research that suggests that involving, collaborating, and co-producing with people with convictions in the development and/or delivery of justice interventions can enhance the meaning, legitimacy, credibility, and effectiveness of those interventions.

Existing studies in this area highlight the multiple forms on which user participation and co-production occurs, a tendency towards individualized forms and a pattern of mostly shallow forms of participation (Weaver and McCulloch 2012). However, it is clear from the literature that user co-production in justice is not a new phenomenon, indeed some practices, for example the use of prison listeners and councils, have been established for some time (Clinks 2011).

In terms of impact, almost all studies point to positive 'early indicators' with many schemes showing very positive results. However, most reviews note a lack of systematic evidence and conclude that further and systematic evaluation is needed to better understand the dynamics, impact, outcomes, and efficacy of existing approaches in the justice context. Existing studies also highlight various obstacles to advancing user participation and co-production in justice services, citing ideological tensions, a mixed message policy framework, lack of operational guidance, professional resistance and apprehension, attitudinal and cultural barriers, and the 'complexities' of application – including issues of time, money, support, and security (Clinks 2008). Relatedly, though there exist promising examples, there is a distinct lack of strategy with many initiatives appearing to be short lived and dependent on the commitment of individual 'champions' (Clinks 2011).

Again, across this literature, little attention is given to the role of those sentenced in the progression of their *own* sanction, with existing studies focusing mostly on the contributions of 'reformed' or 'ex-offenders'. Exceptions exist though they suggest that there is much to do if this arguably pivotal aspect of co-production is to become normative.

Importantly, very few studies engage with the possible moral and philosophical tensions of advancing user co-production in the context of justice sanctions. Is it reasonable or moral for justice professionals to co-opt, or expect the co-contribution of people with convictions in practices of punishment? To what extent might this differ across prison and community-based sanctions? Do we need to draw a distinction between practices designed to punish and those designed to help and support? And if so, can we promote and advance co-production in one and not the other? Some of these questions are addressed in Carlen's (2012) work which cautions against adopting an idealist or 'imaginary' vision of justice, without engaging with the gross inequalities that characterize modern democratic societies and that play out in the social positions, stigmas, and exclusions experienced by different groups, and by people with convictions in particular. For Carlen, this means drawing a distinction between discriminatory justice practices and empowering and enabling ones. The former, she argues, are about the state keeping risky others in their place while acting to fix the person/problem. The latter involves societies and justice systems taking collective responsibility for creating opportunities for all citizens to share responsibility and make good. As Carlen and others observe, advancing the latter requires more than procedural efforts towards co-production, it requires that notions of criminal justice be subsumed within an overarching state and social commitment to social justice. In this alternative 'penal imaginary', values of citizenship, democracy, and inequality reduction are given primacy.

Amidst these questions, the consistent message arising from this literature is that accounts of user participation in criminal justice provision, far less co-production, are few and far between, particularly in community-based settings. Further, there exists little systematic or comparable research evidence relating to the value of such practices for justice policy and practice. As Weaver and McCulloch (2012: 8) observe, this mostly reflects the fact that, in the criminal justice context, the concept and practice of user co-production has been scarcely advanced, rarely analyzed, and almost never made subject to robust evaluation.

Acknowledging the very limited literature on user-co-production in justice sanctions, we turn in closing to consider the key findings from a recent Scottish case study which sought to understand and unpack user co-production from the perspective of those sentenced.

User co-production in justice sanctions? Stories from Scotland

McCulloch's (2016) study explored the meaning, value, and possibility of co-production in criminal justice sanctions and services. The study employed a co-productive research design and was designed and conducted by an academic and people with lived experience of justice sanctions and of co-production. Data was collected via six in-depth research conversations with people with lived experience of justice sanctions. Data was analyzed using thematic narrative analysis.

Defining and locating co-production

For most participants, the term co-production meant little. The concept however was familiar and connected mostly with experiences outside of the justice system. In this broader context, co-production was a valued and straightforward concept and practice and involved: 'people working together in a practical and even-handed way', 'equality', and 'sharing power'.

Co-production became 'complicated' when considered in the context of statutory criminal justice relationships. Complications revolved principally around issues of power in justice relationships, around the perceived purpose and priorities of justice sanctions, and around the cultures, regimes, failures, and disconnects deemed to flow from these priorities. These issues were felt to significantly obstruct the possibility and potential of co-production within this sphere. Significantly, none of the participants identified co-production as a recognizable feature of their experience of justice sanctions. Further, for many, the idea that their sentence might be constructed in this way was initially surprising and confusing. For these participants, the predominant experience of justice sanctions was of punishment, judgement, humiliation, depersonalization, and a 'total imbalance of power'.

Why co-produce?

Participant reasons for co-producing (or not) within a sentence connected closely with identified aids and obstacles to co-production (see below). Mostly, co-production emerged less as a conscious choice and more as a normative response to the situation, relationships, and/or environment a person found themselves in. Broadly, participants co-produced when they:

1   Possessed *capacity* for co-production;
2   Experienced *opportunity* for co-production; and
3   Recognized the *rewards* of co-production.

Though experiences of user co-production were atypical, for all, co-production emerged as a deeply relevant concept and practice. It was identified as a foundational feature of ongoing journeys of progression, recovery, and desistance and for these reasons was considered a foundational feature of productive and progressive justice sanctions. Within and beyond justice sanctions, participants identified an array of reasons for and benefits of user co-production, including: recovery of worth and identity, self-actualization, opportunity for voice and equality, and the ability to make a difference. Importantly, participants also gave voice to the costs of co-production, an aspect under-explored in the literature.

Aids and obstacles

Identified aids and obstacles to co-production correspond with the reasons for co-production described above. User co-production was significantly aided when the person completing a sentence possessed the basic capital required to co-produce, capital that connected closely with a person's life experience and opportunities. In essence, co-production was aided when participants were 'lucky' enough not to share the life histories, traits, and associated problems common to most involved in persistent offending. Co-production was also aided by empowering human relationships and by safe and supportive environments and spaces.

Identified obstacles to co-production emerged as the inverse of the above and were deemed to be 'everywhere'. They were identified in 'the stuff' that a person brings into the justice system, in the status and stigma of 'being an offender', and in the prejudice encountered as a result of that status. Additional obstacles were identified in the politics and priorities that define the criminal justice experience, in the humiliating, distancing, and disempowering regimes and relationships that flow from that, and in the 'clash' and disconnect of these experienced realities.

Looking forward

Looking forward, participants were ambivalent about the possibility of user co-production in justice sanctions. Progress was seen to depend on:

1   A fundamental and cultural shift within and beyond justice services, including a reconstruction of 'offenders' as people;
2   A more developed and participatory understanding of co-production amongst justice actors and stakeholders; and
3   Investment in real and relevant pathways out of offending and of the justice system.

The above findings draw on a small and situated sample. However they connect and add to emerging research findings in this area. Across the literature, people with experience of justice sanctions speak to the transformative value and potential of co-production within and beyond justice sanctions and in this respect the findings accord with the broader literature on co-production in public services. However, service users and others also express considerable ambivalence around whether co-production is possible within the particular constraints of criminal justice sanctions. This presents a particular conundrum for a public service that lists amongst its key outcomes: personalization, responsibility, recovery, rehabilitation, and re-entry.

Conclusions and questions

The above review indicates that the concept and practice of user co-production in justice sanctions is significantly under-explored in the existing research literature. However, related themes of democracy, user involvement, and participation are not new. Further, though there is broad and deep agreement regarding the value and potential of participatory and co-productive approaches and practices for criminal justice, there is a lack of robust evidence and theorizing. Relatedly, existing conceptualizations and practices appear to privilege the involvement of nonoffending or 'reformed' citizens over, and sometimes to the exclusion of, those completing a sentence. Going forward, research points to the need to attend more meaningfully to the multiple and sometimes competing functions of justice sanctions – i.e. punishment and support – and to whether these functions can usefully co-exist; to the lived experience of justice sanctions; to issues of procedural justice; and to the integration of co-productive approaches and practices (Crawford 2002; Lacey 2007). However, some of the same authors point to the significant obstacles to advancing the above and to the limitations, and for some the 'absurdities' of integrative or procedural approaches to co-production within current cultures of control and exclusion. For these reasons, many point to a need to locate and advance co-productive approaches within a broader framework of social and penal reform. As Weaver (2011) observes, this takes us beyond procedural questions of how to make justice co-productive into more important and challenging territory of how to make co-production just.

References

Arnstein, S. (1971) The ladder of citizen participation. *Journal of the Royal Town Planning Institute*, 57(1), 176–182.

Barber, B. (1984) *Strong Democracy: Participatory Politics for a New Age*. Berkeley: University of California Press.

Bottoms, Anthony (2001) Compliance and community penalties. In Anthony Bottoms, Loraine Gelsthorpe, and Sue Rex (Eds.), *Community Penalties: Change and Challenges.*. Cambridge Criminal Justice Series. Devon: Willan Publishing.Bovaird, T. (2007) Beyond engagement and participation: User and community co-production of public services. *Public Administration Review*, 67(5), 846–860.

Bovaird, T. and Loeffler, E. (2012) From engagement to co-production: How users and communities contribute to public services. In V. Pestoff, T. Brandsen and B. Verschuere (Eds.), *New Public Governance, the Third Sector and Co-Production*. London: Routledge, pp. 35–60.

Boyle, D. and Harris, M. (2009) *The Challenge of Co-Production: How Equal Partnerships Between Professionals and the Public Are Crucial to Improving Public Service*. London: National Endowment for Science, Technology and the Arts.

Carlen, P. (2012) Against rehabilitation: For reparative justice. In E. O'Brien, K. Carrington, J. Tauri and M. Ball (Eds.), *Crime, Justice and Social Democracy: International Perspectives*. London: Palgrave Macmillan, pp. 89–104.

Christie, N. (1977) Conflicts as property. *British Journal of Criminology*, 17, 1–15.

Clinks. (2008) *Unlocking Potential: How Offenders, Former Offenders and Their Families Can Contribute to a More Effective Criminal Justice System*. Available at: www.clinks.org/unlocking-potential (Accessed May 2018).

Clinks. (2011) *A Review of Service User Involvement in Prisons and Probation Trusts*. Available at: www.clinks.org/sites/default/files/Service%20User%20Findings%20Sept%2011.pdf (Accessed 22 September 2015).

Crawford, A. (2002) In the hands of the public? *Relational Justice Bulletin*, 13, 6–8.

Dzur, A. (2012) Participatory democracy and criminal justice. *Criminal Law and Philosophy*, 6(2), 115–129.

Ewert, B. and Evers, A. (2012) Co-production: Contested meanings and challenges for user organisations. In V. Pestoff, T. Brandsen and B. Verschuere (Eds.), *New Public Governance, the Third Sector and Co-Production*. London: Routledge, pp. 61–78.

Farrall, S. (2002) Long-term absences from probation: Officers' and probationers' accounts. *The Howard Journal of Criminal Justice*, 41(3), 263–278.

Garland, D. (2015) *What is wrong with penal populism?* Scottish Centre for Crime and Justice Research, 9th Annual Lecture, 27 May, Edinburgh.

Habermass, J. (1962/1989) *The Structural Transformation of the Public Sphere: An Inquiry into a Category of Bourgeois Society.* Cambridge: Polity Press.

Hirschman, A. O. (1970) *Exit, Voice and Loyalty: Responses to Decline in Firms, Organisations and States.* Cambridge, MA: Harvard University Press.

Lacey, N. (2007) *Criminal Justice and Democratic Systems: Inclusionary and Exclusionary Dynamics in the Institutional Structure of Late Modern Societies.* CES Working Paper, no. 148.

Maruna, S. and King, A. (2008) Selling the public on probation: Beyond the bib. *Probation Journal*, 55(4), 337–351.McCulloch, T. (2013) Re-analysing the compliance dynamic: Towards a co-productive strategy and practice? In P. Ugwudike and P. Raynor (Eds.), *What Works in Offender Compliance? International Perspectives and Evidence-Based Practice.* Basingstoke: Palgrave Macmillan, pp. 44–66.

McCulloch, T. (2016) Co-producing justice sanctions? Citizen perspectives. *Criminology and Criminal Justice*, 16(4), 431–451.

McNeill, F. and Robinson, G. (2013) Liquid legitimacy and community sanctions. In A. Crawford and A. Hucklesby (Eds.), *Legitimacy and Compliance in Criminal Justice.* Cullompton: Willan Publishing, pp. 116–137.

Morgenstern, C. and Robinson, G. (2014) Consent and co-operation of the unfree: Introduction to the special issue. *European Journal of Probation*, 6(3), 203–208.

Ostrom, E. (1975) *The Delivery of Urban Services: Outcomes of Change.* Beverly Hills, CA: Sage Publications.

Ostrom, E. (1996) Crossing the great divide: Coproduction, synergy, and development. *World Development*, 24(6), 1073–1087.

Pestoff, V. (2012) Co-production and third sector social service in Europe: Some crucial conceptual issues. In V. Pestoff, T. Brandsen and B. Verschuere (Eds.), *New Public Governance, the Third Sector and Co-Production.* London: Routledge, pp. 13–34.

Sparks, R. and Loader, I. (2010) *Public Criminology?* London: Routledge.

Tyler, T. (1990) *Why People Obey the Law.* New Haven: Yale University Press.

Ward, T. and Maruna, S. (2007) *Rehabilitation: Beyond the Risk Paradigm.* Oxon: Routledge.

Weaver, B. (2011) Co-producing community justice: The transformative potential of personalisation for penal sanctions. *The British Journal of Social Work*, 41(6), 1038–1057.

Weaver, B. and McCulloch, T. (2012) *Co-Producing Criminal Justice: Executive Summary.* Research Report no. 5/2012. Glasgow: Scottish Centre for Crime and Justice Research.

41

Victim-focused work with offenders

Simon Green

Over the last 30 years there has been a steady growth in 'victim-focused work with offenders'. Yet this phrase itself is vague, conveying little about what such work actually is, and is not (Burrows 2013). If it conjures any meaning at all, it is most commonly associated with victim awareness or empathy programmes designed to help reduce recidivism by improving offenders' understanding about the impact of their harmful behaviour on victims. These programmes are often geared towards the perpetrators of sexual and domestic violence and take place during or as part of a sentence. Yet, if victim awareness and empathy interventions were to be taken as a rudimentary definition of victim-focused work with offenders it could easily include a raft of other activities, including restorative justice, victim impact statements, speed awareness courses, copyright piracy campaigns, and a whole host of charitable and outreach programmes working with prisoners, street gangs and youth clubs, and drug users. Whilst many of these activities would not necessarily define themselves in terms of victim awareness and empathy, many contain a clear element of this within their work. This chapter will therefore seek to provide a framework for understanding the range of activities that include victim-focused work with offenders.

Mental calluses: a brief history of victim-blaming

Where does victim-focused work with offenders come from? To answer this question a short excursion into criminological theory and early victimological research is necessary. In 1957, Sykes and Matza developed their techniques of neutralization, which they used to critique subcultural theories emerging in the United States around the same time (e.g. Cloward and Ohlin 1960; Cohen 1955). This critique was based around their argument that members of street gangs drifted in and out of delinquency which challenged the idea that street gangs generated their own internal, and separate set of cultural norms and values from that of mainstream society. This drift into delinquency is a consequence of a series of interrelated environmental circumstances and internal 'recipes' that provided juvenile delinquents with the mental tools for justifying their criminal behaviour. For Sykes and Matza (1957), gang membership is therefore better understood as a type of soft determinism where people opt in and out of gang activities just as they opt in and out of a range of other non-criminal activities. The mental recipes are the techniques of neutralization that provide five strategies for overcoming feelings and emotions such as guilt and empathy that might constrain delinquent pursuits. The five techniques of neutralization are:

1   Denial of responsibility;
2   Denial of injury;
3   Denial of the victim;
4   Condemnation of the condemners;
5   Appeals to higher loyalties.

These techniques are strategies for denying harm and blaming others for criminality. Whilst these are embedded in the wider social fabric of society, Sykes and Matza (1957) argue that living in conditions of deprivation and despair can have the effect of hardening people to the feelings of others. They develop mental calluses that provide immunization from guilt and these calluses are to some extent shared by us all so that we can function without becoming drowned in self-loathing, shame, or pity. An everyday example might include turning a blind eye to homelessness or begging because they'll just spend it on drugs. Perhaps we don't give to charity because the problem is really with corrupt governments, neo-liberal capitalism, Western foreign policy, or decadent charity workers. Whatever justifications we give ourselves for our actions or inactions they all amount to something that looks suspiciously like techniques of neutralization. Like Sykes and Matza (1957), this is not intended as accusatory: it is intended to draw attention to the normality, indeed necessity, of developing mental toughness for distancing ourselves from the suffering of others – whether we have inflicted that suffering or not. In terms of offending behaviour, part of this toughening up is denying responsibility and denying the victim using thought processes such as 'they had it coming' or 'they'd have done the same to me'.

Around the same time as these criminological insights into offending behaviour, early victimological research emerges with the ideas of Von Hentig (1948), Wolfgang (1957, 1958), and Mendelsohn (1956, 1974) who introduced the concept of victim precipitation. These ideas explore the characteristics and behaviours of victims that predispose, or make the victim culpable for the harm inflicted upon them. Another study using this approach is Hindelang et al. (1978), who argued that the rate of injury is much greater for young male victims who used 'self-protective' measures than for those who did not. And similar approaches have also been applied to robbery by Normandeau (1968) and to rape by Amir (1971):

> the victim actually – or so it was interpreted by the offender – agreed to sexual relations but retracted . . . or did not resist strongly enough when the suggestion was made by the offender. The term also applies to cases in which the victim enters vulnerable situations sexually charged.
>
> (Amir 1971, taken from Morris 1987: 173)

Davies (2017) has argued that approaches like Amir's (1971) lend academic legitimacy to widely held rape myths in society that imply either the attitude, behaviour or appearance of rape victims amounts to something along the lines of 'she was asking for it'. Consequently, in a similar fashion to Sykes and Matza's (1957) techniques of neutralization, victim precipitation interweaves attitudes towards victims with the wider functioning of our social institutions. These early forays in victimology have been heavily criticized for victim-blaming (Walklate 1989) but taken together with techniques of neutralization demonstrate an important, deeper dynamic. This dynamic has a psychosocial (Gadd and Jefferson 2007) aspect that suggests that the behaviour of both offenders and social institutions are intimately connected and share a common derivation in the form of denial of the victim. This denial provides the mental calluses that affords a form of psychic defence against both individual and societal shame and embarrassment about injustice and victimization. It is this tendency that makes it hard to look victims in the eye, to wince and turn away rather than face their suffering. At the level of the criminal justice system the consequence of this until fairly recently has been to deny victims a place in the proceedings; leading to the exclamation that victims were the forgotten 'non-persons' of the criminal justice system (Shapland et al. 1985). By the same token, this also manifests itself in the offender as insensitivity and indifference to the harm caused by their actions.

These connections demonstrate that denial is woven into both institutional and interpersonal reactions to victims. Whilst this denial may have its roots in Locke (1980[1690]) and Rousseau's (1762) concepts of social contract and the rule of law which provide the philosophical grounds by which the state prosecutes on behalf of the victim, we are now witnessing a much wider repositioning (or rebalancing) of the victim within the criminal justice system. Victim-focused work with offenders is just one aspect of this repositioning and can be seen as part of a re-sensitisation of both the system and the offender within it. Whilst victim-focused work with offenders is often understood in terms of cognitive behaviour therapy (CBT) interventions, the roots of this activity stretch much more deeply into a more profound transformation of how victims are treated, engaged, invoked, and supported across society. Karstedt (2011) has referred to this as the re-emotionalization of justice and Green (2011) as the re-engagement of the victim with penal decision-making. Regardless of how it is described, there is now a significant shift in the penal logic of several, predominantly Western, criminal justice systems that is designed to sensitize offenders, courtrooms, and enforcement agencies to the feelings and needs of the victims of crime. The combined effect of this shift may provide the metaphorical equivalent of a pumice stone for the mental calluses that lead to victim-blaming. Yet this invites a cautionary note – calluses toughen for a reason – they provide a degree of protection from harsh environmental conditions. And although we tend to separate victims from offenders we know this is a false dichotomy (Cops and Pleysier 2014; Drake and Henley 2014) and many offenders have their own experiences of victimization. One of the most commonly debated examples of this is the 'cycle of abuse' with regards to child sexual abuse (see Plummer and Cossins 2016), but we also know that victims and offenders are often the same group of people, struggling with the same set of socio-economic deprivations that can lead to the formation of mental calluses as a form of self-defence. If rubbed too vigorously the potential exists to leave raw, sensitive skin exposed to the elements.

Victim awareness programmes: challenging cognitive distortions in offenders

A good starting place to begin exploring specific victim-focused work with offenders is the CBT interventions undertaken with offenders during their sentence. This can be either a custodial or community sentence and is focused on trying to reduce the offender's likelihood of reoffending by sensitizing them about how their actions are likely to have affected victims. The Probation Service and youth offending team may also touch on offender awareness during pre-sentence or specific-sentence reports (PSRs and SSRs) but according to Williams and Goodman Chong (2008), this is not always done as thoroughly as it could be due to limited timescales and information. However, the predominant focus of individual and groupwork victim awareness interventions takes place during the sentence. Founded on the pioneering work of Aaron Beck, CBT was originally developed to tackle clinical depression using an approach based around a cognitive triad of 'self, other (the world) and future' (Beck et al. 1979). Over the last 30 years this approach has been incorporated into work with offenders to reduce reoffending within correctional and custodial settings. Bolstered by a strong evidence base (see, for example, Henwood et al. 2015), CBT provides a framework for interventions with offenders designed to treat the thoughts, choices, and attitudes associated with offending behaviour. Specific CBT programmes are designed to address particular types of offending behaviour and some element of victim awareness is built into most of these and can also be deployed as a standalone intervention.

Most CBT programmes are run with groups over several weeks and are intended to provide improved problem-solving skills using a range of group exercises, role play, intensive feedback, diaries, and worksheets. The aim is to 'restructure' ways of thinking so that offenders can develop more pro-social ways of thinking about themselves, others, and their future. Within the context of victim-focused work with offenders this usually involves a series of activities designed to give the offender a greater appreciation of the consequences of their actions. This involves several stages beginning with the 'ripple effect' of harm that aims to improve offenders' awareness of the impact of their crimes upon a wide range of people beyond the specific person they victimized. This is then often followed with a combination of role play, role reversal, and 'My Victim' exercises that often culminates in writing (though not usually sending) a letter to their victims expressing remorse and empathy to the person they victimized. This style of victim-focused work with offenders often relies on building a meaningful rapport with the offender and motivational interviewing is often used as the method of working with offenders to help build a relationship through which change can occur (Tallant et al. 2008). Developed by Miller and Rollnick (2002 motivational interviewing is built on five key principles designed to confront (without argument) the offender's ideas and statements:

1   Being empathetic and accepting of the individual although not the behaviour;
2   The development of discrepancies in an offender's cognitive distortions leading to the questioning of beliefs;
3   The avoidance of argument through rolling with resistance;
4   Seeing resistance as part of an offender's reaction to discomfort with the realization of their cognitive distortions;
5   Supporting efficacy through building belief in the offender's own abilities.

(adapted from Fleet and Annison 2003: 113–116)

These key principles dovetail very nicely with CBT interventions and taken together provide a very clear benchmark for understanding the ethos and approach of victim awareness CBT interventions. Striking a balance between giving specific feedback, active listening, reflecting back what someone's trying to say to you, open questions, and challenging disruptive behaviour (without recourse to threats, criticisms, or commands) is at the core of these interventions. An example is warranted to demonstrate how this looks in practice:

Practitioner:	Thank you for being punctual. I've noticed that you've been on time the last two sessions. Today we need to look again at your index offences.
Offender:	Again? It's hardly important. They shouldn't have left their bag on the chair like that if they didn't want it taken.
Practitioner:	So you think that it's the victim's fault for not safeguarding their possessions?
Offender:	That's not what I said.
Practitioner:	Explain to me what you meant?
Offender:	It's just that I need to get money and sometimes if it's made easy for me to take something, then I will. They obviously didn't want it that much if they were willing to leave it lying around.
Practitioner:	So you feel the victim wouldn't have much of a reaction to finding that their bag and possessions had been taken?
Offender:	Well, no. I don't know. I've not really thought about it.
Practitioner:	Okay. Let's look at it now. Tell me how you think the victim may have reacted and what they may have felt.
Offender:	I don't know. I'm not doing this, it's pointless.
Practitioner:	No worries. Have you ever had anything taken or stolen from you?
Offender:	Yes.
Practitioner:	Tell me about that, and how you felt.
Offender:	I had my Xbox nicked by a so-called mate. It made me really angry and I was kind of upset as I'd had to save for ages to get it.
Practitioner:	That sounds pretty awful. Especially as it was something you'd worked hard for.
Offender:	Yeah.
Practitioner:	Thinking about the victim of your offence again, how do you think they may have felt?
Offender:	Alright, alright. They might have felt angry and upset too.

(Hussey and Richardson 2013: 13–14)

Specific CBT programmes are usually tied to particular offender risk categories and as such share much in common with Feeley and Simon's (1992) new penology. However, victim-awareness interventions are often most closely associated with the emergence of early domestic violence programmes, especially Duluth and the associated IDAP (Integrated Domestic Abuse Programme) that both had a feminist-inspired philosophy for working with male offenders of domestic violence. These programmes include victim empathy as a core part of their CBT programmes designed to educate men about the relationship between their abuse and the wider patriarchal dynamics of power and control (Rivett and Rees 2008).

Unfortunately, whilst there is a considerable evidence base about the effectiveness of CBT programmes, victim awareness is often lost in the wider emphasis on reducing reoffending and similarly attracts little attention from victimologists who probably see it as offender-focused research. Victim awareness therefore seems to fall between two stalls and has only had sporadic and localized evaluation, and no systematic review or meta-analysis of findings currently exists. This may be partly due to the fact that victim awareness is often integrated into a wider programme designed to address particular offending behaviours (for example, domestic violence) and is therefore difficult to meaningfully disaggregate results that pertain specifically to victim awareness. This raises a question about how to explain the growth of victim-focused work with offenders given the paucity of evidence in support of it. Gadd (2004) has argued that the Duluth and IDAP programmes were driven by political processes rather than evidence they worked and this would fit within a broader critique of the political manipulation of crime victims for electoral gain (Elias 1993; Green 2007). However, there are some studies that do seek to measure victim awareness, or empathy projects and they shed some light on the effectiveness of this approach. In the UK a pilot victim awareness course (VAC) in Hampshire was evaluated by Simkin (2015). This course was designed for offenders who had been given a Penalty Notice for Disorders (PND) or conditional caution and was aimed at understanding take-up and attitudes towards the course. As a pilot study the evaluation was necessarily localized and small but the results demonstrated that 86% of participants stated that the course had helped them think about how a victim might feel as a result of their offending behaviour and 70% said they would definitely behave differently in the future as a result of attending the course (though no follow-up rearrest data was collected).

The main field in which research about victim awareness and empathy has been conducted is in relation to sex offender treatment programmes. For example, in England and Wales, an evaluation by Brown, Harkins, and Beech (2011) found both general empathy and victim empathy on sex offender treatment programmes and in a ten-year follow-up period sex offenders did have improved victim empathy but not general empathy and concluded that this supports wider research findings that sex offenders only suffer an empathy deficit to their specific victims rather than to others in general. Further afield, O'Reilly et al. (2010) cautiously found some positive effect on victim empathy within a small (n = 38) study of an Irish sex offender intervention programme, and in the United States a study by Sedelmaier and Gaboury (2015) undertaken across four states found that a wider pool of general offenders on an

Impact of Crime on Victims programme exhibited increased understanding of victim rights, facts, and sensitivity to victim difficulties. Each of these studies shows that to a greater or lesser extent, when offenders are put on programmes to raise their levels of victim awareness or empathy there are some measurable improvements. Yet frustratingly they don't then compare these findings to reoffending/rearrest rates; although Brown, Harkins, and Beech (2011) tentatively point to an association between a decline in the Victim Empathy Scale (VES) and increased risk of sexual recidivism. In summary, research in this area is patchwork but suggests interventions do generally improve participant victim awareness and empathy but don't conclusively demonstrate that such improvements lead to a reduction in reoffending.

Victim participation, empathy, and emotional literacy

Another way in which offenders often come into contact with victims is through victims increasingly getting involved in the 'business' of criminal justice. Whilst much of this business does not necessarily involve direct engagement between offenders and victims, some of it does and some of it has either an implicit or explicit emphasis in using victims to help offenders. Yet even those types of victim involvement that have no direct relevance to offenders provide indicators of the growing social, political, and legal salience crime victims have in society. For example, the UK now has a Victims' Commissioner, Victims Advisory Panel, Code of Practice for the Victims of Crime, special measures in court for vulnerable victims and witnesses, and a national Victim Support Service. Our media and politicians actively pursue campaigns that have sought penal reform in the name of victims and there are routinely moral panics, terrorist atrocities, and miscarriage of justice campaigns played out in printed and online media drawing our attention to the plight of victims and our likelihood of becoming victims. Much of this is very emotive and much of it arguably distorts the public impression of the risk and seriousness of victimization (Jewkes 2015; Walklate and McGarry 2015) and challenges the authority and competency of our political leaders and legal institutions (Greer and McLaughlin 2017). But it does sensitize our political, legal, and media institutions to victim concerns. Despite the distortion contained with these public debates, the cultural and symbolic salience of the victim has grown considerably in the last 30 years (Garland 2001) and provides an important backdrop for understanding the increasing role of the victim within the criminal justice system.

Driven by a complex range of social, political, and ideological forces, the victim has re-emerged onto the centre stage of criminal justice (see Godfrey 2017). This has created a fertile ground in which more overt victim-focused work with offenders has developed beyond the CBT interventions discussed above. In particular, the phenomenal growth of restorative justice stands out in this regard. Whilst it would be overstating the case to describe restorative justice as victim-focused work with offenders as it fulfils a much wider array of objectives, there is little doubt that some restorative justice initiatives have the overt goal of helping reintegrate and rehabilitate offenders by bringing them face to face with either their direct victims or a wide range of indirect victims. Restorative justice provides the forum for many different strands of victim-offender encounter, and within its broader philosophy (Braithwaite 1989; Johnstone 2011; Zehr 1990) there is clear intention that victims can help rebuild the offender's identity, self-worth, and social acceptance. Alongside restorative justice, rafts of similar or related initiatives that more directly involve the victims of crime with offenders have also emerged. Victim impact (or personal) statements are now used to help inform sentencing decisions and victim awareness work with offenders if they're found guilty. And within the charitable and third sector, innovations like the Restore Programme (www.theforgivenessproject.com) seek to engage prisoners with both victims and perpetrators to open up a safe space to talk about trauma and resilience. And this is just one example of a range of victim involvement charities working with disaffected young people, street gangs, and drug users to explore a combination of their own victimization just as much as the harm they cause others. Even less direct victim involvement initiatives such as speed awareness courses and anti-copyright piracy awareness campaigns invoke real and symbolic victims as a way of sensitizing us to the damage everyday law-breaking can cause people. Consequently, it would be a considerable oversight to limit a discussion of victim-focused work with offenders to CBT interventions run by probation and correctional services.

Conclusion

This short discussion has sought to locate victim-focused work with offenders within the context of theory and research about victim-blaming. Although victim-focused work with offenders conjures images of CBT programmes aimed at victim awareness and empathy, it is less clear what the impact of these particular interventions may be on reoffending rates. However, there is a lot more activity going on across a much wider range of settings that might also fall under the broad mantel of victim-focused work with offenders. This chapter has touched on some of the wider cultural and political forces that help explain the growing importance given to crime victims in society but has stopped short of developing an analysis of these forces. However, the position presented towards the start of this chapter is that offenders develop mental calluses towards victims as a form of self-justification for their harmful behaviour *and* as a form of self-defence against their own harsh experiences. Consequently, victim-focused work with offenders needs to confront not only their criminal behaviour but also their own suffering and hardship if meaningful change is to be achieved.

References

Beck, A. T., Rush A. J., Shaw, B. F. and Emery, G. (1979) *Cognitive Therapy of Depression*. New York: The Guilford Press.

Braithwaite, J. (1989) *Crime, Shame and Reintegration*. Cambridge: Cambridge University Press.

Brown, S., Harkins, L. and Beech, A. R. (2011) General and victim-specific empathy: Associations with actuarial risk, treatment outcome and sexual recidivism. *Sexual Abuse: A Journal of Research and Treatment*, 12(5), 411–430. https://doi.org/10.1177/1079063211423944.

Burrows, J. (2013) Victim awareness: Re-examining a probation fundamental. *Probation Journal*, 60(4), 383–399. https://doi.org/10.1177/0264550513502250.

Cops, D. and Pleysier, S. (2014) Usual suspects, ideal victims and vice versa: The relationship between youth offending and victimization and the mediating influence of risky lifestyles. *European Journal of Criminology*, 11(3), 361–378. https://doi.org/10.1177/1477370813500886.

Cloward, R. A. and Ohlin, L. E. (1960) *Delinquency and Opportunity: A Theory of Delinquent Gangs*. New York: Free Press.

Cohen, A. K. (1955) *Delinquent Boys: The Culture of the Gang*. New York: Free Press.

Davies, P. (2017) Feminist voices, gender and victimization. In S. Walklate (Ed.), *Handbook of Victims and Victimology*, 2nd edition. London: Routledge, pp. 107–123.

Drake, D. H. and Henley, A. J. (2014) Victims' versus 'offenders' in British political discourse: The construction of a false dichotomy. *The Howard Journal*, 53(2), 141–157. https://doi.org/10.1111/hojo.12057.

Elias, R. (1993) *Victims Still: The Political Manipulation of Crime Victims*. London: Sage Publications.

Feeley, M. and Simon, J. (1992) The new penology: Notes on the emerging strategy of corrections and its implications. *Criminology*, 30(4), 452–474. https://doi.org/10.1111/j.1745-9125.1992.tb01112.x.

Fleet, F. and Annison, J. (2003) In support of effectiveness: Facilitating participation and sustaining change. In W. H. Chui and M. Nellis (Eds.), *Moving Probation Forwards: Evidence, Arguments and Practice*. Essex: Pearson, Longman, pp. 129–143.

Gadd, D. (2004) Evidence led or policy led evidence? Cognitive-behavioural programmes for men who are violent towards women. *Criminal Justice*, 4, 173–197.

Gadd, D. and Jefferson, T. (2007) *Psychosocial Criminology: An Introduction*. London: Sage.

Garland, D. (2001) *The Culture of Control: Crime and Social Order in Contemporary Society*. Oxford: Oxford University Press.

Godfrey, B. (2017) Setting the scene: A question of history. In S. Walklate (Ed.), *Handbook of Victims and Victimology*, 2nd edition. London: Routledge, pp. 13–29.

Green, C. and McLaughlin, E. (2017) News power, crime and media justice. In A. Liebling, S. Maruna and L. McAra (Eds.), *The Oxford Handbook of Criminology*, 6th edition. Oxford: Oxford University Press.

Green, S. (2007) Restorative justice and the victims' movement. In G. Johnstone and D. Van Ness (Eds.), *A Handbook of Restorative Justice*. Collumpton: Willan Publishing, pp. 171–193.

Green, S. (2011) Vengeance and furies: Existential dilemmas in penal decision-making. In J. Hardie-Bick and R. Lippens (Eds.), *Crime, Governance and Existential Predicaments*. Basingstoke: Palgrave Macmillan, pp. 61–84.

Henwood, K. S., Chou, S. and Browne, K. D. (2015) A systematic review and meta-analysis on the effectiveness of CBT informed anger management. *Aggression and Violent Behaviour*, 25, 280–292. https://doi.org/10.1016/j.avb.2015.09.011.

Hindelang, M. S., Gottfredson, M. R. and Garofalo, J. (1978) *Victims of Personal Crime*. Cambridge, MA: Ballinger Press.

Hussey and Richardson (2013) *Victim Awareness Workbook*. Oakmore: Bennion Kearny Limited.

Jewkes, Y. (2015) *Media and Crime*, 3rd edition. London: Sage Publications.

Johnstone, G. (2011) *Restorative Justice: Ideas, Values, Debates*, 2nd edition. London: Routledge.

Karstedt, S. (2011) Handle with care: Emotions, crime and justice. In S. Karstedt, I. Loader and H. Strang (Eds.), *Emotions, Crime and Justice*. Oxford: Hart Publishing.

Locke, J. (1980[1690]) *The Second Treatise of Government*. Indianapolis: Hackett Publishing Company Inc.

Mendelsohn, B. (1956) Une Nouvelle Branche de la Science Bio-psycho-sociale: Victimologie. *Revue Internationale de Criminologie et de Police Technique*, 10–31.

Mendelsohn, B. (1974) The origins of the doctrine of victimology. In I. Drapkin and E. Viano (Eds.), *Victimology*. Lexington, MA: Lexington Books.

Miller, W. R. and Rollnick, S. (2002) *Motivational Interviewing: Preparing People for Change*, 2nd edition. London: The Guilford Press.

Morris, A. (1987) *Women Crime and Criminal Justice*. Oxford: Blackwell.

Normandeau. (1968) Patterns in robbery. *Criminologica*, 6.

O'Reilly, G., Carr, A., Murphy, P. and Cotter, A. (2010) A controlled evaluation of a prison-based sexual offender intervention program. *Sexual Abuse*, 22(1), 95–111. https://doi.org/10.1177/1079063209358107.

Plummer, M. and Cossins, A. (2016) The cycle of abuse: When victims become offenders. *Trauma, Violence & Abuse*, 1–19, (online first) https://doi.org/10.1177/1524838016659487.

Rivett, M. and Rees, A. (2008) Working with perpetrators and victims of domestic violence. In S. Green, E. Lancaster and S. Feasey (Eds.), *Addressing Offending Behaviour*. Cullompton: Willan Publishing.

Rousseau, J. J (1762/2008) *The Social Contract*. Translated by Christopher Betts. Oxford: Oxford University Press.

Sedelmaier, G. M. and Gaboury, M. T. (2015) Administering a victim impact curriculum to inmates: A multi-site replication. *Criminal Justice Studies: A Critical Journal of Crime, Law and Society*, 28(2), 226–238. https://doi.org/10.1080/1478601X.2015.1014037.

Simkin, C. (2015) An evaluation of the victim awareness pilot with Hampshire, Commissioned by Victim Support. Available at: www.victimsupport.org.uk/sites/default/files/Victim%20Awareness%20Course%20evaluation%20report.pdf.

Shapland, J., Willmore, J. and Duff, P. (1985) *Victims of Crime in the Criminal Justice System*. Aldershot: Gower.

Sykes, G. and Matza, D. (1957) Techniques of Neutralisation: A theory of delinquency. *American Sociological Review*, 22(6), 664–670.

Tallant, C., Sambrook, M. and Green, S. (2008) Engagement skills with offenders: Best practice or effective practice? In S. Green, E. Lancaster and S. Feasey (Eds.), *Addressing Offending Behaviour*. Cullompton: Willan Publishing, pp. 75–94.

Von Hentig, H. (1948) *The Criminal and His Victim: Studies in the Sociobiology of Crime*. New Haven: Yale University Press.

Walklate, S. (1989) *Victimology: The Victim and the Criminal Justice Process*. London: Unwin Hyman.

Walklate, S. and McGarry, R. (2015) *Victims: Trauma, Testimony and Justice*. London: Routledge.

Williams, B. and Goodman-Chong, H. (2008) Victims. In S. Green, E. Lancaster and S. Feasey (Eds.), *Addressing Offending Behaviour*. Cullompton: Willan Publishing, pp. 305–318.

Wolfgang, M. E. (1957) Victim-precipitated criminal homicide. *Journal of Criminal Law and Criminology and Police Science*, 48, 534–543.

Wolfgang, M. E. (1958) *Patterns of Criminal Homicide*. Philadelphia: University of Pennsylvania Press.

Zehr, H. (1990) *Changing Lenses: A New Focus for Crime Justice*. Scottdale, PA: Herald Press.

Section 5

Overview: resettlement

Section 5 Introduction

In this fifth section, we move on from considering a range of approaches to direct work with people who have offended to exploring one specific context or process in which rehabilitation's successes or failures are thrown into very sharp relief: ex-prisoner resettlement. While we use the English term 'resettlement' here, the various chapters attend to a range of issues raised by the transition from prison to community, and they discuss various stages in this process – from the prison-based process of preparation for release and reintegration to post-release support.

In Chapter 42, Mike Maguire and Peter Raynor focus on preparing prisoners for release, exploring several decades of research concerning the problems that people leaving prison face on release and of practical efforts to assist them in the obstacle-strewn journey to find a home or a way home. Having reviewed issues, practices and experiences in several countries, they conclude soberingly that 'the effective rehabilitation and resettlement of prisoners is a goal that has eluded almost all penal systems throughout their history'. This failure is not, they suggest, the result of a lack of knowledge about what is required (indeed, they sum up the knowledge base in seven key principles). Rather, it results from the difficulty of designing and implementing systems and practices that work 'through the gate' in a way that returning citizens experience, through trusting relationships with their supervisors, as coherent and humane.

John Halushka, in Chapter 43, focuses firstly on the lived experience of prisoner re-entry in the US, finding that it is far from the ideal suggested in the previous chapter; rather, it is an experience marked by severe material deprivation and disproportionately visited on already disadvantaged men of colour from the most deprived communities. Compounding the physical, mental, social, and economic vulnerabilities that they carry as a result of their histories, these men face a range of formal and informal barriers to finding work and housing, and are propelled into engagement with a range of criminal justice and human service agencies seeking to manage risk and enable reintegration. Unable to tackle the profound social and structural issues that these men face, these agencies focus instead on 'teaching participants cognitive and emotional tools to cope with these harsh realities'. Halushka criticizes this narrow and responsibilizing approach to rehabilitation, arguing that the pursuit of desistance is not synonymous with the achievement of reintegration. Rather than 'strong-arm rehab', he suggests – following Bruce Western (2018) – that the answers to the problems of re-entry lie in social policy reforms that would provide for housing, health, education, and a decent income.

In Chapter 44, Keir Irwin-Rogers and Carla Reeves hone in on the issue of accommodation, looking specifically at the role of residential supervision (in hostels and halfway houses) in resettlement and re-entry. Focusing on research from England and Wales, the US, and Canada, they argue that, despite retaining welfarist rhetoric, in all of these jurisdictions, the imperative of managing the behaviour of 'risky' and 'dangerous' populations has displaced the traditional welfarist concern with reintegration. Yet the evidence base around the effectiveness of residential supervision in pursuit of both sets of goals remains very limited. Chapter 45 by Craig Cumming sustains the theme of effective reintegration by exploring the health needs of people leaving prison and emphasizing the importance of assessing these needs pre-release, to inform the work of those helping them to make the transition from prison to the community.

Chapter 46, by Cormac Behan, provides a necessary counter-weight to the preoccupation with managing risk. Focusing on ideals of citizenship (and reprising debates about rights-based rehabilitation raised by Rob Canton in Chapter 4), he argues that, within the wider project of developing and respecting the citizenship of justice-affected people, encouraging prisoners to act as advocates for their rights may play a crucial role in motivating them in the process of transformation within and beyond imprisonment.

In a different but complementary way, Thomas P. LeBel, in Chapter 47, also insists on a positive approach to both transformation and resettlement. Rather than pursuing risk-based or needs-based approaches to re-entry, LeBel argues for a strengths-based approach. Drawing on desistance research, positive criminology and psychology (Ronel and Segev 2015; Seligman and Csikszentmihalyi 2000), and on ideas related to recovery from addictions (Groshkova et al. 2013; Van Wormer and Davis 2018), he suggests that criminal justice needs to learn how to develop, support, and sustain the strengths of returning prisoners; partly by learning more about how and why some become involved in the provision of help and advocacy within social movements. Working out how and why people identify, utilize, and develop their strengths deserves at least much attention, he suggests, as identifying and addressing their deficits.

In the final chapter in this section, Chapter 48, Alice Mills and Rosie Meek explore the role of the third sector in supporting resettlement and reintegration. Noting the long history of charitable efforts to support former prisoners, they examine both the strengths of such forms of provision and the challenges faced by third-sector (or not-for-profit) providers. Such organizations benefit from a degree of independence from more formal criminal justice agencies, they have developed significant experience and expertise, they can play a key role in developing the social capital (or networks and relations) of returning prisoners, and – echoing LeBel's contribution – they often enable peer support and other forms of volunteering or activism. However, the increasing marketization of criminal justice in some jurisdictions threatens their 'distinctive, person-centred culture and value-driven approach'; smaller, local, community-based organizations have become particularly vulnerable in this new landscape.

Taken together, these chapters highlight not just the profound and complex challenges faced by returning prisoners, but also the difficulties faced by correctional agencies, third-sector, and community-based organizations in developing and sustaining systems and practices that can address those challenges. Whilst part of the solution may be to develop the rights-respecting and strengths-based approaches advocated respectively by Behan and LeBel, Halushka's chapter reminds us how often the projects of rehabilitation and reintegration depend on commitments, resources, attitudes, and dispositions that lie beyond the reach of the criminal justice system. It seems that post-prison reintegration requires social movements, social policy reform, and a commitment to social justice; the same may be true of rehabilitation in general (Burke et al. 2018).

References

Burke, L., Collett, S. and McNeill, F. (2018) *Reimagining Rehabilitation: Beyond the Individual*. London: Routledge.

Groshkova, T., Best, D. and White, W. (2013) The assessment of recovery capital: Properties and psychometrics of a measure of addiction recovery strengths. *Drug and Alcohol Review*, 32, 187–194.

Ronel, N. and Segev, D. (2015) *Positive Criminology*. New York: Routledge.

Seligman, M. E. P. and Csikszentmihalyi, M. (2000) Positive psychology: An introduction. *The American Psychologist*, 55(1), 5–14.

Van Wormer, K. and Davis, D. R. (2018) *Addiction Treatment: A Strengths Perspective*, 4th edition. Boston, MA: Cengage Learning.

Western, B. (2018) *Homeward: Life in the Year After Prison*. New York: Russell Sage Foundation.

42

Preparing prisoners for release

Current and recurrent challenges

Mike Maguire and Peter Raynor

Introduction

The bulk of academic literature and research on imprisonment focuses on issues such as prison conditions, the treatment of prisoners, staff-prisoner and intra-prisoner relationships, inmate and staff safety, and so on; in other words, on 'life behind walls' (for example Liebling and Arnold 2004; Crewe 2009). However, essential as it is to keep shining a light on what is a largely hidden world with a highly vulnerable population, it can be easily forgotten that nearly everyone sent to prison will be released at some point and resume life outside, in most cases within quite a short time. This makes it equally important to pay close attention to efforts to maintain links with the outside world and prepare prisoners for life after custody: in short, to activities concerned with 'rehabilitation' and 'resettlement'.

The above terms tend to be associated with two apparently different aims – reduction of the risk of future offending, and reintegration of ex-prisoners into community life – and this distinction is reflected to some extent in institutional structures whereby separate departments and groups of staff are responsible for each. In very broad terms, rehabilitative interventions typically set out to challenge antisocial thinking and attitudes and to help prisoners build and sustain motivation to change, while resettlement work is largely concerned with addressing the immediate practical problems they will face on release. However, it should be emphasized that there are close links and overlaps between these aims and activities. For example, key elements of successful resettlement, such as stable housing and employment, are also associated with reduced reoffending. Vice versa, ex-prisoners are more likely to keep a job and sustain a more settled lifestyle if they have internalized the necessary determination and resilience to overcome setbacks and avoid crime. In short, the two should be regarded as interconnected parts of a larger process.

In this chapter, we first identify necessary ingredients of an effective system for the delivery of rehabilitative and resettlement services to prisoners, in custody and 'through the gate'. We then look at some of the fundamental barriers to achieving this and at various attempts to overcome them. Our main focus will be on recent such attempts in prisons in England and Wales. These include reforms to the system of 'offender management', which usually refers to the planning and delivery of rehabilitative work with individual prisoners throughout their sentence. They also include the establishment of 'resettlement prisons', together with new 'resettlement teams' to work with prisoners shortly before their release. Finally, we shall look briefly at practice in other European countries, before drawing some broad conclusions.

Ideals and barriers

American researchers have been particularly clear about how prisons could in principle contribute to more effective resettlement (or 're-entry', as it is called in the US). A central conclusion has been that it should be seen as a process that starts well before release, and includes work with the offender throughout his or her sentence. In her authoritative overview of the subject, Joan Petersilia (2003) argues that improvements in re-entry require attention to four key areas. Although these are discussed under the heading of re-entry, they actually provide guidance for the whole process of offender management through and beyond the prison sentence; resettlement is part of offender management and should not be separated from it. Her four areas are:

1   Alter the in-prison experience (by creating a prison environment which focuses consistently on rehabilitation, education, and work; promotes life skills rather than allowing criminal attitudes and subcultures to dominate; and, ideally, is permeated by a pro-social offender management process);
2   Change prison release and revocation practices (by which she primarily means introducing a system of discretionary release and recall based on

consistent guidelines and risk assessments – some of which is already present in the UK);

3   Revise post-prison services and supervision (targeting by risk and need);

4   Foster collaborations with the community and enhance mechanisms of informal social control (this resembles some of the conclusions of current British research on desistance from offending, which points out that the 'what works' focus on thinking and attitudes needs to be accompanied by building social capital and access to opportunities – see, for example, Bottoms and Shapland 2011).

A similar understanding of resettlement as a multi-stage process beginning well before release is set out by Faye S. Taxman in her work on engaging offenders' active participation in reintegration (Taxman 2004). Her 'five-step offender active participant model' includes:

1   The 'message to the offender' (concerning personal responsibility, the key decisions are in the offender's own hands, and risk and need assessment must include 'sharing information from the assessment with the offender' to help in action planning);

2   Institutional treatment (during the sentence, including reintegration goals, transitional planning, and motivation);

3   Institutional pre-release (active planning for release, with a focus on survival needs: 'a place to live, a place to work, food on the table, people to love'. Taxman suggests starting this phase 90 days before release, while one of the programmes commended by Petersilia recommends an earlier start);

4   Post release (basically the first month at liberty: learning to survive without offending, and overcoming initial obstacles); followed by

5   Integration (up to two years of 'maintenance and crisis management' and eventual consolidation of a crime-free life in the community).

Both of these American examples show how resettlement is, in effect, an offender case management process which begins early in the sentence and continues through and beyond release, and in which each stage builds on the last. Neither specifies exactly how the process should be managed, but continuity of assessment, planning, and implementation are clearly required. It has also become increasingly emphasized in more recent UK literature that a further vital ingredient is the development and maintenance throughout of trusting relationships between offenders and those working with them (see, for example, McNeill and Weaver 2010).

In very broad terms, then, the research literature suggests that an effective system requires a combination of a rehabilitative prison culture; the development of trusting relations with well-trained staff (before and after release); well-planned case management throughout the whole sentence; work on offenders' thinking, attitudes, and management of emotions; and effective links with mainstream community services to assist them with practical problems.

All of this is, of course, much easier to state than it is to deliver. Many jurisdictions now recognize the need for continuity of case management and services 'through the gate', but find this difficult to deliver because of the separation of prison and community services. As will now be demonstrated, this is nowhere more evident than in England and Wales, where the fundamental problem of 'joining up' these two 'silos' has plagued successive efforts at reform over many years. Such problems are exacerbated by an under-resourced and overcrowded prison system.

Changing arrangements in British prisons

Three sets of major organizational changes to prison and probation services have been introduced in England and Wales since the mid-2000s, in each case heralded by government as a solution to recurrent problems of coordination and continuity in the resettlement of prisoners. Numerous independent commentators, including Inspectorates, agree that two of these have largely failed to achieve this goal (the third is in its early stages of implementation).

The first, the creation of the National Offender Management Service (NOMS) – now renamed Her Majesty's Prison and Probation Service (HMPPS) – took place in 2005 following the publication of the Carter Review (Carter, 2003). The main problems identified in the report – prisons and probation as separate 'silos' with a lack of continuity in the management of individual offenders – were seen by Carter as primarily organizational issues, to be addressed by shared high-level management; his proposed solution, as might be expected from a management expert, was system-centred rather than based on a view of offender management as a human process. NOMS, a new executive agency of the Ministry of Justice, was made responsible for commissioning and providing both prison and probation services in England and Wales, thereby offering the prospect that, in the case of people sent to prison, the planning and delivery of rehabilitative work in custody and after release would be effectively coordinated. Under the NOMS Offender Management Model, which was developed to achieve this, community-based probation officers, re-badged as 'offender managers' (OMs), were tasked with the 'end-to-end' management of prisoners sentenced to 12 months or over. Ideally, the same community-based probation officer would prepare the initial court report, devise and oversee the prisoner's sentence plan while he/she was in custody, and supervise him/her after release. The OM was assisted by a prison-based 'Offender Supervisor', normally a prison officer based in the Offender Management Unit, who oversaw the implementation of the sentence plan (NOMS 2006).

However, within just a few years this arrangement began to attract serious criticism, it being pointed out that, in reality, communication between outside probation officers and prison staff was often poor, and many OMs failed to visit their supervisees and had little knowledge about what they had done in prison. This culminated in a series of damning reports from the Inspectorates of Prisons and Probation. In their final report the Inspectorates 'reluctantly' concluded that:

> the Offender Management Model, however laudable, is not working in prisons. The majority of prison staff do not understand it and the community based offender managers, who largely do, have neither the involvement in the process nor the internal knowledge of the institutions, to make it work. It is more complex than many prisoners need and more costly to run than most prisons can afford. Given the Prison Service's present capacity and the pressures now facing it with the implementation of *Transforming Rehabilitation* and an extension of 'Through the Gate' services, we doubt whether it can deliver future National Offender Management Service expectations. We therefore believe that the current position is no longer sustainable and should be subject to fundamental review.
>
> (HM Inspectorate of Probation and HM Inspectorate of Prisons 2013: 4)

An internal NOMS review was set up in response, leading to plans for significant changes to the offender management system which are currently in the course of implementation. These will be described presently below.

The second major reorganization affecting preparation for release and 'through the gate' arrangements was the Transforming Rehabilitation (TR) initiative, beginning in 2013 (see Ministry of Justice 2013). This included a policy to enable as many prisoners as possible to spend the last few months of their sentence in an institution as close to their home as possible, thereby making it easier to make meaningful links with local agencies to assist their resettlement. To this end, numerous establishments have been designated as local 'resettlement prisons', each of which has a 'resettlement team' tasked with making such links and helping all prisoners to meet their practical needs. These teams are currently managed by Community Rehabilitation Companies (CRCs), largely private companies to which much of the work of probation services was outsourced as part of TR.[1] In addition, a 'through the gate' system has gradually been introduced, whereby mentors managed by the CRCs (many of them volunteers) meet some prisoners as they are released and accompany them to their first appointments with probation, housing agencies, and so on. It is important to add that in May 2019, following serious criticism from the Chief Inspector of Probation, the House of Commons Public Accounts Committee, National Audit Office, and many others, the government announced that the system of part-privatization was not working and that the probation service would be returned to public management (see, for example, http://www.russellwebster.com/reversetr/). However, it is not yet clear how this will affect the prison-based resettlement teams.

While the pending reforms to TR may improve the situation, commentators broadly agree that introduction of resettlement teams has so far been ineffective in terms of providing help to prison leavers. They have been seriously handicapped by shortages of resources, large caseloads, difficulties in building close links with outside agencies, and heavy demands in terms of process targets which often lead them to prioritize bureaucratic tasks (completing assessments, recording information, etc.) over meaningful work with prisoners. In addition, the through-the-gate system allows very little time for mentors to develop any rapport with those they are meeting, or to do anything beyond the day of release (see, for example, Taylor et al. 2017).

The third major re-organization, which is still underway, resulted from the aforementioned internal review set up in response to the serious concerns expressed by the Inspectorates about the ineffectiveness of the NOMS Offender Management Model and its underpinning concept of 'end to end' offender management by community-based probation officers. This concept has now been largely abandoned. Instead, responsibility for the offender management of prisoners will fall entirely to prison-based staff, passing to external probation staff only after release (Ministry of Justice 2018). This can be understood as moving from an 'end to end' to a 'handover' model (Maguire and Raynor 2017). In addition, full-blown offender management will be offered only to prisoners assessed as high risk. To provide this, a considerable number of OMs from the National Probation Service are being appointed to posts inside prisons, where they will work alongside prison staff to plan and oversee high risk prisoners' 'rehabilitative journeys' (devising a sentence plan, engaging in individual supervision sessions with them, referring them to offending behaviour programmes, and so on). On release, responsibility for the case will be handed over to a new OM based in the community. Ideally, the latter will earlier have attended at least one three-way meeting with the prison-based OM and the prisoner, at which he or she will be informed about progress to date and will begin to get to know the prisoner.

By contrast, the great majority of prisoners will no longer be subject to 'offender management' in custody as generally understood; rather, they will receive periodic advice and support from a prison officer in a new role of 'key worker'. The intention is that, over time, the majority of prison staff will be trained to undertake this role and thereby help motivate and empower prisoners to take more responsibility for their own rehabilitation. Each key worker will take on a small caseload of prisoners (Ministry of Justice 2018).

Of course, whether this new system will improve the rehabilitation of prisoners remains to be seen. The arrangements for high-risk prisoners have a certain amount of promise, and it is possible that the disadvantages brought about by removing the potential for productive 'end to end' relationships with external OMs are more than offset by the advantages of regular contact with a well-qualified custody-based OM. The effectiveness of the key worker system for the bulk of prisoners is considerably less certain. It is in many ways a positive and evidence-informed idea, in accord with the concept of a 'rehabilitative prison' in which all staff play a part in assisting prisoners to desist from offending (Maguire and Raynor 2017). The obvious practical concerns, however, are that many current staff may not have the skills or willingness to undertake such a role effectively, and that as prison culture takes a long time to change, the aim of 'empowering' prisoners may be frustrated by the traditional tendency of prison life to suppress individual agency. In the meantime, there is a risk that many medium-term (and even long-term) prisoners will 'drift' through their sentence with little being done to address their rehabilitative needs.

Resettlement systems in other European countries

Having undertaken a review of recent literature and research on resettlement systems in other European countries, including corresponding with a number of researchers,[2] the authors concluded that near-universal difficulties have been experienced in attempts to 'join up' services 'through the gate'. For example, one correspondent might be said to have stated the whole problem in a nutshell:

> In Germany oftentimes the released prisoner meets his probation officer only weeks after the release and many times probation officers know the prisoner from a former probation period but are not integrated in the sentence and the release planning for this prisoner.
>
> (I. Pruin, personal communication, 2014)

Another wrote:

> I visited the prison in X [a major English city] to see how end-to-end management works. In theory the model looks very attractive but in reality it is quite impossible to implement in an accurate way. However, . . . it helped to develop some links between the inside and the outside world. . . . I went to Denmark to see how it works. . . . In most cases the prisoner file goes out to probation only a few weeks prior to release, if not after release.
>
> (I. Durnescu, personal communication, 2014)

A correspondent in France reported that they have probation staff located in prisons and in the community, but communication between the two is often not good, and is hampered by lack of an agreed-upon risk assessment process and by the existence of pools of unallocated cases due to system overload. The result can be that offenders wrongly assessed as low risk are unallocated and unsupervised, which has led to some notorious cases of serious reoffending. This happens in spite of a system of judicial oversight through re-entry courts (M. Herzog-Evans, personal communication, 2014). Various forms of early release are in fact widely practised in Europe (Padfield et al. 2010), sometimes with supervision and sometimes without; a recent overview by Dünkel (2017: 646) states, 'I would . . . not defend a policy of just releasing prisoners without the necessary support of the prison and probation services in an integrated model of transition management'. The almost universal problem is how to manage this integration successfully.

The CEP resettlement project (Durnescu 2011) surveyed resettlement practices in a number of European countries and also included a literature search, mainly but not entirely of English language sources. The final report and a related article (Durnescu and Descarpes 2014) aimed to sum up the current state of research on resettlement (using Taxman's five-stage model outlined previously) and to point to some promising developments. There was general agreement that resettlement should be a 'through the gate' process in which prisons try to help prisoners to acquire some of the skills, attitudes, and thinking which will help them to succeed after release; and in which post-release resettlement supervision helps them to apply what they have learned, supplements it, facilitates access to community resources, and provides personal support and guidance where needed. In addition, there is a generally recognized public protection responsibility where ex-prisoners are judged to present a risk. However, the authors found little evidence of case management approaches which ensure continuity and consistency of engagement with the offender in both prison and community. The project leader's summary was:

> I don't think there is a system in Europe that has a coherent prisoner management combining inside with the outside inputs.
>
> (I. Durnescu, personal communication, 2014)

The EU-funded DOMICE project covered 40 jurisdictions in 34 countries, involving the production of 'system maps', a literature review (Institute for Criminal Policy Research 2011) and a series of meetings and conferences. The overall conclusion summarized on the DOMICE website (www.domice.org/default.asp?page-id=137) is:

> Nowhere is case management designed and delivered as an integrated, system-wide function; nowhere does a single plan for case management span the pre-sentence and post-sentence, and custody and community stages.

However, the project team point to some promising developments: for example, they report that Sweden and Turkey have integrated IT systems covering custody and supervised release. They also describe an approach in Northern Ireland which is not so much a case management innovation as a retention of some very long-standing traditional practices designed to maintain relational continuity:

> In Northern Ireland pre-trial reports are viewed and managed as the start of the case management process rather than as a separate task; wherever possible whoever prepared a pre-sentence report retains responsibility for a case after sentence.

Similar approaches can be identified in other jurisdictions (usually small, whereas England and Wales have the largest penal system in Europe). For example, Jersey in the Channel Islands allocates a probation officer to each prisoner at the start of the sentence, who maintains contact during the sentence and also undertakes the post-release work with the prisoner (B. Heath, personal communication, 2014). In Guernsey, a nominated probation officer is actively involved in offenders' sentence planning from the start of their time in custody and follows through after release (A. Guilbert, personal communication, 2014). Clearly these examples benefit from the high degree of localism and collaboration possible in small communities; it is to be hoped that the development of resettlement prisons in England and Wales might eventually allow the development of a similar focus on the connection between local prison and local community.

A final example from Europe is the 'reintegration guarantee' used in Norway (mentioned under this title in the CEP report, and as the 'return guarantee' in the English version of the relevant Government policy statement: Norwegian Ministry of Justice and Police 2008). This is not directed at case management as such, but at the rehabilitation of the ex-prisoner as a citizen able to access services and resources on the same basis as other citizens. The aim is to identify needs for services well before release and to put into effect a plan to facilitate access to them. This is a clear recognition of the multi-agency support required for successful resettlement, and in effect gives the ex-prisoner a right of access to all normal services and resources. It is emphasized that the aim is to put the prisoner who has served a sentence on an equal footing with other citizens rather than to create special privileges.

Overall the two surveys of European practice, together with a review of other literature, offer no general solutions for the problems and barriers to successful resettlement identified earlier. There are interesting examples of good practice (for example, Finland had 105 Prison Sanctions Officers overseeing the implementation of sentence plans for a prison population just over 3,000 at the time of DOMICE) but there is also evidence of a common set of systemic problems centred around (1) the management of prison sentences in such a way as to meet offending-related needs and (2) the management of transition between prison and community on release. These problems are rooted in social structures: prisons are a sub-system of society which is characterized, for obvious reasons, by separation from normal community life, and effective methods of managing reintegration after the sentence have to try to overcome this. There is some evidence that this is easier to do in jurisdictions where prison is used sparingly, and where regimes are designed to rehabilitate and prepare for release (as in the example from Finland above). Obviously, high-quality regimes are in general more affordable when prisoner numbers are low.

Concluding comments

Achieving the effective rehabilitation and resettlement of prisoners is a goal that has eluded almost all penal systems throughout their history. Knowledge about what is needed to achieve it is not in short supply. An accumulation of research over many years offers a number of key messages, which can be summarized, following Maguire and Raynor (2017) as:

1   Case management in prisons should be seen by all those involved (including the offender) as part of a coherent process, beginning early in the sentence and continuing after release.
2   It should be understood as a 'human service' rather than simply a management system, and founded upon trusting relationships between offenders and those working with them.
3   Sentence planning and its implementation should be seen as collaborative exercises, involving offenders in decisions about how best to progress their rehabilitation.
4   As far as possible, interventions should be tailored to individual risks, needs, strengths, and opportunities rather than 'one size fits all'.
5   To maximize its chances of success, case management requires a holistic approach, with attention both to practical 'resettlement' issues (housing, employment, etc.) and to offending behaviour, thinking, attitudes, and emotions.
6   It should be undertaken as far as possible by skilled practitioners.
7   It is most likely to succeed in a prison environment characterized by a rehabilitative culture throughout the establishment and with sufficient time and resources for staff of all kinds to engage and work with individual offenders.

Clearly, to be effective, rehabilitation and resettlement have to be based on a coherent, holistic process in which attention is paid systematically to a combination of practical, emotional, and cognitive issues. The NOMS Offender Management Model is rightly built around the idea of such a process, which is represented by the acronym ASPIRE, meaning Assess, Sentence Plan, Implement, Review, and Evaluate (NOMS 2006). But while this summarizes the management process, it misses the key point that the change process should be a collaborative, 'human' process, based on *offender-centred* thinking, rather than system-centred thinking. If a new acronym would be helpful to emphasize this point, we would suggest EPICS:[3]

Engage and assess;
Plan together;

Influence and motivate;

Connect to pro-social community resources; and

Support.

However, as we have shown, attempts to turn such principles into practice are confronted by huge obstacles. In the UK, as in many other jurisdictions, these include the perennial practical problems of prison overcrowding, limited facilities and staff shortages, as well as institutional cultures resistant to change. Currently, too, the organizational upheaval caused by the splitting and part-privatization of the probation service has led to more fragmentation and problems of communication within the system, while many community-based OMs in the CRCs are burdened with very high caseloads,[4] leaving them little time to develop more than superficial relationships with their supervisees after release, let alone visit those still in prison (Dominey 2016). There are also indications that the competitive market in services to offenders created by Transforming Rehabilitation has fostered distrust between providers (Burke and Collett 2016), making it more difficult for OMs to coordinate multi-agency work with released prisoners. Whether or not these problems will be ameliorated by the return of probation to public management is yet to be seen.

On the positive side, there is reason to hope that, if they can overcome the problems that have marked their first few years, the advent of resettlement prisons (and prison-based resettlement teams) will make it easier to join up service provision inside and outside custody. However, these arrangements – which do not necessarily involve close liaison with offender managers outside – are focused mainly on immediate practical assistance. Important as this is, they do not address the need for continuity of personal relationships and broader rehabilitative work which research suggests is important to successful resettlement in its fullest sense: what might be called 'rehabilitative resettlement'.

In conclusion, even if current problems of high caseloads and shrinking resources are ameliorated, the fundamental problem remains of how to design and implement an effective coordinated system of offender management 'through the gate' and – equally important – how to ensure that it will be experienced by service users as a coherent and 'human' process, built on trusting relationships with those assisting them. A great deal more innovative thought is needed on this question.

Notes

1 The delivery of probation services to the majority of offenders is currently commissioned by HMPPS (formerly NOMS) on a 'payment by results' basis from 21 Community Rehabilitation Companies (CRCs), leaving only the high risk to be supervised by the public-sector National Probation Service (Ministry of Justice 2013). Some CRCs have sub-contracted resettlement work in prisons to third-sector

organizations. However, as noted in the text, the part-privatization arrangements will end shortly and the probation service will be returned to public management.

2 The authors were able to draw on the resources of two international research networks: the European Society of Criminology Working Group on Community Sanctions, and CREDOS (the Collaboration of Researchers on the Effective Development of Offender Supervision). In addition, we had access to the outputs of two recent Europe-wide projects: a survey of resettlement arrangements funded by CEP (Conférence Permanente Européenne de la Probation, now the Confederation of European Probation), which reported in 2011 (Durnescu 2011); and DOMICE (Developing Offender Management in Corrections in Europe), a European Commission–funded project in which the UK's National Offender Management Service was a lead partner, which aimed to document case management practices with adult offenders across Europe and to identify good practice.

3 This acronym is already used by some researchers to mean 'Effective Practices in Correctional Settings' (Lowenkamp et al. 2012), which makes it quite apt by adding another layer of meaning.

4 This has been caused partly by a significant reduction in government funds allocated to probation, and partly by the extension (under the Offender Rehabilitation Act 2014) of statutory post-release supervision to all prisoners, rather than just those serving 12 months or over.

References

Bottoms, A. and Shapland, J. (2011) Steps towards desistance among male young adult recidivists. In S. Farrall, M. Hough, S. Maruna and R. Sparks (Eds.), *Escape Routes: Contemporary Perspectives on Life After Punishment*. Abingdon: Routledge, pp. 43–80.

Burke, L. and Collett, S. (2016) Transforming Rehabilitation: Organizational bifurcation and the end of probation as we knew it? *Probation Journal*, 63(2), 120–305.

Carter, P. (2003) *Managing Offenders, Reducing Crime: A New Approach*. London: Home Office.

Crewe, D. (2009) *The Prisoner Society: Power, Adaptation and Social Life in an English Prison*. Oxford: Oxford University Press.

Dominey, J. (2016) Fragmenting probation: Recommendations from research. *Probation Journal*, 63(2), 136–143.

Dünkel, F. (2017) European penology: He rise and fall of prison population rates in Europe in times of migrant crises and terrorism. *European Journal of Criminology*, 14(6), 629–653.

Durnescu, I. (2011) *Resettlement Research and Practice: An International Perspective*. Report to Conférence Permanente Européenne de la Probation.

Durnescu, I. and Descarpes, P. (2014) Where are we in resettlement research? *Eurovista*, 3(2), 47–67.

HM Inspectorate of Probation and HM Inspectorate of Prisons (2013) *Third Aggregate Report on Offender Management in Prisons*. London: Criminal Justice Joint Inspection.

Institute for Criminal Policy Research (2011) *DOMICE Literature Review*. London: ICPR.

Liebling, A. and Arnold, H. (2004) *Prisons and Their Moral Performance*. Oxford: Oxfrod University Press.

Lowenkamp, C., Lowenkamp, M. and Robinson, C. (2012) *Effective Practices in Correctional Settings II*. Cincinnati: Published by the Authors.

Maguire, M. and Raynor, P. (2017) Offender management in and after prison: The end of "End to End". *Criminology and Criminal Justice*, 17(2), 138–157.

McNeill, F. and Weaver, B. (2010) *Changing Lives: Desistance Research and Offender Management*. Glasgow: Scottish Centre for Crime and Justice Research. Project Report 03/2010.

Ministry of Justice. (2013) *Transforming Rehabilitation: A Revolution in the Way We Manage Offenders*. London: Ministry of Justice.

Ministry of Justice (2018) *Manage the Custodial Sentence Policy Framework*. London: Ministry of Justice. https://www.gov.uk/government/publications/manage-the-custodial-sentence

NOMS. (2006) *The NOMS Offender Management Model*. London: National Offender Management Service.Norwegian Ministry of Justice and Police. (2008) *Punishment That Works – Less Crime – a Safer Society*. (English summary.) Oslo: Norwegian Ministry of Justice and the Police.

Padfield, N., van Zyl Smit, D. and Dünkel, F. (2010) *Release from Prison: European Policy and Practice*. Cullompton: Willan Publishing.

Petersilia, J. (2003) *When Prisoners Come Home*. New York: Oxford University Press.

Taxman, F. (2004) The offender and reentry: Supporting active participation in reintegration. *Federal Probation*, 68(2). Available at: www.uscourts.gov (Accessed 15 September 2014).

Taylor, S., Burke, L., Millings, M. and Ragonese, E. (2017) Transforming Rehabilitation during a penal crisis: A case study of through the gate services in a resettlement prison in England and Wales. *European Journal of Probation*, 9(2), 115–131.

Prisoner re-entry in the United States

43

John Halushka

Introduction

Every year in the United States, some 650,000 individuals are released from state and federal prisons, and an additional 12 million are released from local jails (Carson 2018; Miller and Stuart 2017).[1] Scholars and policymakers refer to this process of transitioning from incarceration to community as 'prison re-entry' (Miller 2014; Petersilia 2003; Travis 2005). Prisoner re-entry is at once a lived experience as well as a political project: 'something almost all former prisoners do, and something that is done on their behalf' (Miller 2014: 306–307).

As a *lived experience*, prisoner re-entry is typically a life course transition marked by severe material deprivation (Desmond 2015; Western 2018). The population returning home is composed primarily of disadvantaged men of colour, who come from and return to some of America's most racially segregated and economically disadvantaged urban neighbourhoods (Clear 2007). They face a variety of formal and informal barriers to securing stable sources of employment and housing, and disproportionately suffer from a variety of social vulnerabilities, including low-levels of human capital and histories of trauma, substance abuse, physical disability, and mental illness (Harding et al. 2014; Herbert et al. 2015; Western et al. 2015; Western 2015). As a *political project*, prisoner re-entry 'activates the universe of human service actors, criminal justice agencies, and policy and program planners to assist former prisoners in making their transition from prison to their home communities' (Miller 2014: 307). These services reflect a mixture of criminal justice supervision and social service intervention, designed to both manage criminal risk and facilitate community reintegration.

This chapter provides an overview of current literature on prisoner re-entry in the United States with a particular focus on ethnographic studies. The first section explores how former prisoners navigate conditions of severe poverty following incarceration. During the period following release, former prisoners struggle to establish employment and independent housing, and mostly rely on family, friends, and public assistance agencies to meet their basic material needs. This daily grind of poverty survival has a devastating effect on their physical and emotional well-being and ultimately undermines successful reintegration. The next section explores prisoner re-entry as a political project. It begins with an overview of current efforts to get 'smart on crime', particularly efforts to reduce corrections costs by rehabilitating offenders in less costly community settings. The chapter then journeys into various community settings to explore how front-line service providers in parole offices, residential treatment facilities, and workforce development programmes attempt to rehabilitate offenders. The chapter concludes with an analysis and critique of current efforts to reform the criminal justice system. While current efforts to get 'smart on crime' represent a welcome departure from 'tough-on-crime' politics of the past, these reforms do not go nearly far enough to challenge the political roots of mass incarceration (Gottschalk 2015).

Prisoner re-entry as lived experience

Prisoner re-entry is a period of profound instability and uncertainty in the lives of former prisoners. Attaining even basic elements of social integration, such as housing, food, and transportation, can be a significant challenge (Harding et al. 2014; Herbert et al. 2015; Pager 2007; Western et al. 2015). For most people leaving prisons, coming home represents a transition into severe poverty (Western 2018). While we know a great deal about demographic characteristics of offender populations and the negative impact mass incarceration has had on communities of colour (Clear 2007; Patillo et al. 2004; Wakefield and Uggen 2010; Western 2006), we know less about the lived realities of prisoner re-entry. Because former prisoners tend to be weakly attached to stable households, unevenly employed, and sometimes 'on the run' from authorities, they are a difficult population to systematically follow over long periods of time (Western et al. 2015). However, in recent years a growing body of qualitative literature has been able to overcome these logistical challenges. These studies paint a bleak picture of life after incarceration, one characterized by severe material deprivation and social isolation.

In their three-year qualitative study of 22 former prisoners released in Michigan, Harding et al. (2014) found that food and housing insecurity are common experiences among former prisoners. A quarter of study participants (six out of 22), never established stable, independent living situations, and relied on soup kitchens, food pantries, and transitional housing facilities, such as homeless shelters and residential treatment programs, to meet their basic material needs. Other subjects were able to establish more stable living situations, but continued to rely on family members, romantic partners, and public assistance programs for food and shelter. Only a select few who had attended college or secured jobs with prospects of career advancement were able to attain independent economic security and mobility.

Western et al.'s (2015) six-month qualitative study of over 100 former prisoners returning to neighbourhoods in Boston also found that independent housing and full-time employment are rare among returning prisoners. Over a third of study participants stayed in marginal or temporary housing and half were unemployed after six months. Just as in Michigan, former prisoners in Massachusetts relied extensively on public assistance and family support to meet their basic material needs. Two months after release, 70% of the sample had enrolled in food stamps and other benefits. By six months, over half was receiving money, being fed by, or staying with a family member (usually a mother, grandmother, aunt, or sister) or romantic partner (Western et al. 2015: 1537–1538).

Western et al. (2015) found that former prisoners over age 44 and those with histories of substance abuse or mental illness were especially vulnerable to social isolation and material insecurity. Owing to the deterioration of family ties, this group was unable to draw on informal support networks for material assistance or emotional support. As a result, they were more likely to experience housing instability and unemployment and to rely on public assistance programs and transitional housing facilities to meet their basic material needs for food, shelter, and social support (Western et al. 2015: 1538).

The daily grind of poverty survival has a devastating effect on physical and emotional well-being of former prisoners. Urban ethnographers have shown how food and housing insecurity can compromise a person's mental health, triggering symptoms of anxiety and depression and increasing their risk of substance abuse (Desmond 2015, 2016). For former prisoners, this state of acute stress and anxiety is especially consequential. When former prisoners are irritable, anxious, and depressed due to hunger or homelessness, they are less able to think clearly and weigh the long-term costs and benefits of their actions (Western 2018). They may act out impulsively, returning to substance use or criminal behaviour as a means to cope with the stress of severe poverty.

Given the immense challenges former prisoners face in making the transition from incarceration to community, how have policymakers responded? The next section explores the growing movement of scholars and policymakers that has coalesced in recent years to confront the challenges of prisoner re-entry.

Prisoner re-entry as political project

Mass incarceration has emerged as a significant policy problem over the last decade. With the onset of the Great Recession in 2008, state governments from across the US have been struggling to reduce public spending in the face of shrinking revenue and growing budget deficits. In this context, lawmakers simply cannot afford the high costs of maintaining large prison populations. Instead, they are searching for ways to reduce prison populations and curb corrections costs while still maintaining public safety (Aviram 2015; Gottschalk 2015).

Rather than continuing costly and inefficient 'tough-on-crime' policies, the so-called 'fiscal crisis in corrections' has spurred lawmakers to get 'smart on crime' (Vera Institute of Justice 2010). Getting 'smart on crime' means re-orienting criminal justice policymaking around the principles of technical expertise and empirical evaluation, rather than populist outrage, traditional morality, or partisan interest. The goal is to find cheaper and more efficient ways of achieving public safety than simply warehousing offenders in costly, overcrowded prisons. For smart-on-crime reformers, '[i]t is apparent that warehousing prisoners while cutting prison programs, and replacing parole assistance with law enforcement supervision, breeds a churning cycle of recidivism that depletes social capital and bottoms out state funds' (Seeds 2017: 593–594). Thus, one of the primary means by which smart-on-crime reformers aim to improve systems efficiency is to rehabilitate offenders in less costly community settings.

The proliferation of private, 'community-based' prisoner re-entry agencies has been central to this project of recidivism reduction (DeMichele 2014; Halushka 2017; Lucken 1997; Miller 2014). Between 1996 and 2007, the number of community-based prisoner re-entry programs more than tripled, from less than 400 in 1996 to over 1,300 in 2007 (Miller 2014: 312). These organizations provide a range of rehabilitative services designed to reduce former prisoners' risk of recidivism. Such services include substance abuse and mental health treatment, transitional housing placement, workforce development training, welfare case management, and family counselling.

Although smart-on-crime reformers have revitalized faith in the rehabilitative ideal after decades of tough-on-crime hegemony, it is important to emphasize that smart-on-crime reformers justify rehabilitation primarily in terms of risk management and cost savings. The ultimate aim of these interventions is to lower recidivism rates and maximize public safety returns on corrections spending, not necessarily to benefit the welfare of former prisoners or to address the structural conditions that produce criminality (Goddard 2012; Miller 2014; Hannah-Moffat 2005). In this context 'rehabilitation is viewed as a means of managing risk, not a welfarist end in itself' (Garland 2001: 176).

A growing body of ethnographic research explores how 'later modern' rehabilitation operates in practice (Robinson 2008). These studies journey into various institutional settings to explore how governing authorities attempt to transform former prisoners into reformed citizens, including parole offices, residential treatment programs, and community-based employment programmes.

Parole: rehabilitation as risk management

For most of the 20th century, the work of parole officers was oriented toward a social work model of case management that emphasized individualized rehabilitation and community reintegration (Simon 1993; Garland 2001). However, the institution of parole changed dramatically in the closing decades of the 20th century. Beginning in the 1970s, the basic organizing principle of modern corrections, the 'rehabilitative ideal', came under intense scrutiny (Garland 2001). Experts declared that 'nothing works' to rehabilitate offenders, and by the 1980s, parole in the US re-oriented itself as primarily a law enforcement agency. The agency's organizing principle shifted from the 'old penology' of social work and individualized rehabilitation to a 'new penology' focused on risk management and systems efficiency (Feeley and Simon 1992; Lynch 2000; Simon 1993; Werth 2013).

Ethnographers have shown how parole officers continue to pay rhetorical lip service to the rehabilitative ideal, but their interventions tend to come in the form of punitive 'tough love' (Lynch 2000; Werth 2013). These studies find that parole officers tend to conceive of parolees as flawed individuals who lack self-control and good character. Parole officers believe that through close monitoring and punitive sanctions, they can push parolees toward self-discipline and personal responsibility.

Because parole officers view their jobs as limited to managing risk and protecting public safety, they ultimately hold parolees responsible for their own self-reform. For example, parole officers may mandate parolees to attend various rehabilitative programs, such as substance abuse treatment, employment training, or anger management (Lynch 2000; Werth 2013; Herbert et al. 2015). Parole officers primarily justify these rehabilitative interventions in public safety terms. They are a technique for monitoring parolees' daily activities and punishing them for violating the terms of their parole. However, parole officers also view these interventions as a form of 'tough love' meant to push parolees into accepting responsibility for their own self-reform. Two of the most common forms of this 'tough love' are mandated substance abuse treatment and workforce development training, which I explore in the next two sections.

Substance abuse treatment programs: rehabilitation as recovery

Through the expansion of drug courts and other efforts to divert addicts into treatment rather than jail, there has been an explosion of residential substance abuse treatment programs in the US. These facilities not only house individuals diverted from criminal courts, but also former prisoners transitioning back to community life (Whetstone and Gowan 2017). Indeed, many former prisoners with substance abuse issues are released directly to treatment facilities as a condition of parole. Others are mandated to treatment facilities as an 'intermediate sanction' for noncompliance with parole rules, particularly drug or alcohol use (Herbert et al. 2015; Lynch 2000; Werth 2013). Still others rely on the expanding market of private 'sober houses' as a source of housing stability, even though these buildings are often overcrowded and substandard (Fairbanks 2009; Prisoner Reentry Institute 2013).

While most middle-class addicts encounter a form of bio-medical treatment that defines addiction as a metabolic disease, the mostly poor people of colour leaving prison and entering treatment facilities are exposed to a punitive form of rehabilitation that scholars refer to as 'strong-arm rehab' (Gowan and Whetstone 2012). 'Strong-arm rehab' draws heavily from the discourses and practices of Twelve Step programs like Alcoholics Anonymous (AA), but with a distinctly punitive and coercive bent (Whetstone and Gowan 2017; see also Haney 2010; Kay 2013; McCorkel 2013). Where AA focuses on peer fellowship, spiritual self-discovery, and emotional catharsis, 'strong-arm rehab' focuses on breaking down the pathological self of addicts through bodily discipline, public confrontation, and mutual surveillance (Whetstone and Gowan 2017: 85).

In 'strong-arm' treatment programmes, residents are subject to a regimented schedule of chores, therapy sessions, and group meetings (Gowan and Whetstone 2012; Haney 2010; Kaye 2013). Facility staff not only monitor residents' progress toward sobriety through daily therapy sessions, but also through the use of closed-circuit cameras and random drug tests. Staff also enlist residents as active partners in surveillance, encouraging residents to monitor each other's behaviour and to publicly confront peers about perceived breaches of conduct. The front desk serves as a security checkpoint, with guards controlling the flow of residents in and out of the building. Residents must have a written 'pass' to leave the facility, a privilege they must earn by meeting certain treatment milestones.

If a resident fails a drug test, misses an appointment, or otherwise violates facility rules, they face a series of graduated sanctions ranging from extra chores to loss of phone privileges to eviction. These sanctions have significant legal ramifications for residents on parole. Strong-arm rehab facilities have a direct, formal relationship with the criminal justice system, and they are mandated to make regular reports to parole officers about the progress of parolees. If a parole officer receives a report that a parolee is being 'non-compliant' or has been evicted, they can send the parolee back to prison for violating the terms of their parole. Given the surveillance, restricted freedoms, and constant threat of legal sanctions, scholars tend to conceptualize 'strong-arm rehab' as an extension of the state's power to punish, rather than a progressive 'alternative' to the warehousing of prisoners (Haney 2010; Whetstone and Gowan 2017).

The therapeutic content of strong-arm rehab constructs addiction in broad terms, encompassing not only dependence on drugs and alcohol, but also 'addictions' to various lifestyle practices, such as selling drugs, living on the street, being in abusive relationships, or being dependent on welfare (Haney 2010; McCorkel 2013; Kaye 2013). While 'strong-arm rehab' rhetorically embraces the disease model of addiction, in practice it tends to locate the root causes of so-called 'lifestyle addiction' in residents' moral failings and character flaws (Kaye 2013). According to this approach, criminal-addicts lack self-discipline and personal responsibility; they are 'deceitful, manipulative, impulsive, and openly defiant of authority' (Whetstone and Gowan 2017: 92). The mostly poor people of colour who circulate through 'strong-arm rehab' are thought to have developed these personal pathologies through their exposure to a morally deficient 'culture of poverty' that encourages immediate gratification and condones irresponsible behaviour. In group therapy sessions, counsellors publicly confront residents about their personal shortcomings, often berating them for their moral failings, demanding accountability, and accepting no excuses for leading a pathological lifestyle. The ultimate goal is to radically re-socialize residents, stripping them of their former identity and lifestyle, and rebuilding them as self-disciplined, personally responsible citizens (Gowan and Whetstone 2012; Haney 2010; Kaye 2013; see also Rose 1999; Garland 2001).

With more and more returning citizens entering substance abuse treatment facilities, exposure to 'strong-arm rehab' has become a routine aspect of transitioning from incarceration to community. However, even former prisoners who do not reside in residential treatment facilities are nonetheless exposed to the discourses and practices of recovery therapy. While originally designed to treat drug and alcohol dependency, researchers have shown how recovery therapy has moved beyond the walls of support groups and treatment facilities and into a variety of criminal justice and welfare settings, including prisons (McCorkel 2013), homeless shelters (Stuart 2016), welfare offices (Soss et al. 2011), and workforce development programmes, particularly those directed at former prisoners (Halushka 2016, 2017).

Workforce development programmes: rehabilitation as employment

A guiding assumption of smart-on-crime policy is that developing the human capital of former prisoners will keep them sober, employed, and out of prison (Gottschalk 2015; Halushka 2016; Miller 2014). Drawing on many of the practices of welfare-to-work programmes, these workforce development programmes operate from the assumption that 'returning citizens are disadvantaged in the job market because they lack key skills, training, education, or personal traits, such as punctuality, a service-oriented personality, and a will to work' (Gottschalk 2015: 87–88; Miller 2014). As a result, workforce development programmes focus on cultivating former prisoners' 'employability' or 'soft skills'. These include 'interactional skills', such as the ability to 'fit in' with co-workers and generally be friendly. They also include 'motivational skills', such as enthusiasm, punctuality, and willingness to learn (Moss and Tilly 1996).

In my ethnographic study of employment-based re-entry programs in New York City (Halushka 2016, 2017), I illustrate how front-line service providers cultivate 'employability' through a curriculum I call 'work wisdom'. This curriculum included standard lessons on résumé writing and job interview etiquette, but these lessons were tailored to the particular needs of former prisoners. For example, part of the curriculum focused on teaching former prisoners how to convincingly convey remorse during job interviews without revealing 'too much information' about their convictions. Other lessons focused on how to appear 'non-threatening' in work settings by teaching former prisoners how to dress, speak, and act like a 'respectable' citizen.[2]

While the curriculum of work wisdom focused largely on practical advice for getting and keeping a job, front-line staff nonetheless drew heavily on the discourses and practices of recovery therapy to cultivate participants' sense of self-confidence, tenacity, and personal responsibility. Staff members positioned themselves as 'recovery sponsors': older, wiser peers who acted as sympathetic but strict mentors (Soss et al. 2011). Staff members would use themselves as role models to show programme participants that it was possible to overcome the seemingly insurmountable obstacles to employment through hard work and a positive attitude. They encouraged participants to stop blaming the 'system' or the 'white man' for their ongoing unemployment. Instead, taking a page from Twelve-Step philosophy, they encouraged participants to 'look in the mirror' and 'take a personal inventory' to identify the character flaws and personal shortcomings that are preventing them from attaining employment. Rather than 'playing the victim' by sitting around and complaining about racism and inequality, staff members encouraged programme participants to 'take life on life's terms' and to 'accept and adjust' to the harsh realities of re-entry. They must learn to 'accept the things they cannot change', such as structural racism and mass incarceration, and to 'have the courage to change the things they can', such as developing resilience and a positive attitude in the face of hardship.

As former prisoners themselves, staff members knew that maintaining a positive outlook in the face of housing insecurity, labour market exclusion, and criminal justice surveillance is difficult. But they also knew that wallowing in this social suffering would only further discourage programme participants from pursuing re-entry success – and may even provide them with a justification for relapsing. To prevent this from happening, staff members encouraged participants to subjectively reinterpret the objective realities of severe material deprivation and social exclusion. Thorough a process of 'willful cognitive distortion' (Maruna 2001: 9), participants learned to recast themselves as masters of their own destiny, able to overcome whatever obstacles they may encounter in the re-entry process. While this exaggerated sense of agency does not necessarily correspond to the objective realities of severe material deprivation, it serves as a psychological resource that allows former prisoners to remain resilient in the face of hardship and prevents them from relapsing into addiction and crime (Maruna 2001).

Moreover, it was not as if staff members did not *want* to address the structural conditions that limited participants' life chances. Both organizations I studied engaged in advocacy for criminal justice reform and racial justice. However, they lacked the power and resources to abolish legal barriers to employment or licensure; prevent employer discrimination; control the supply of jobs for low-skill workers; or erase participants' histories of neighbourhood disadvantage, trauma, mental illness, or substance abuse. Because staff could do little to address these structural conditions, they focused on teaching participants cognitive and emotional tools to cope with these harsh realities.

Toward a broader vision of reform

Over the last decade smart-on-crime reformers have been able to revive faith in the rehabilitative ideal by reframing rehabilitation as a project of cost savings and risk management. No longer considered a 'soft' approach to crime control, rehabilitation is now positioned as a 'smart' policy choice – one driven by the cold, hard facts of science and market discipline rather than the naïve world views of liberal elites (Gottschalk 2015; Robinson 2008; Garland 2001). While the revival of the rehabilitative ideal is a welcome departure from the vindictive politics of the tough-on-crime era, a growing body of scholarship suggests that the smart-on-crime movement does not go nearly far enough to challenge the political roots of mass incarceration (Gottschalk 2015).

First, the resonance of the smart-on-crime movement is closely linked to the 'fiscal crisis in corrections' (Aviram 2015; Vera Institute of Justice 2010). However, there is no guarantee that smart-on-crime policies will retain their traction once state governments no longer face budget austerity (Gottschalk 2015). Moreover, because rehabilitation is not tied to any broader policy goal beyond cost savings and public safety, should it fail to produce its desired crime reduction effect, policymakers may revert to more reliable approaches, like incapacitation (Robinson 2008). To sustain the smart-on-crime movement beyond the fiscal crisis in corrections, reformers must adopt a broader vision of reform, one that treats prison re-entry as a project of social justice. They must expand their vision of policy success beyond recidivism reduction and cost savings to include former prisoners' well-being and economic security, and they must also look beyond the politics of austerity, recognizing that promoting re-entry success will involve investing in a robust social safety net.

An important first step in sustaining reform is reframing re-entry as a project of social justice. Justifying reform in the name of cost savings and risk management prevents public discussion of the human rights costs of mass incarceration. Rather than confront the rampant civil and human rights violations occurring in America's prisons or acknowledge that former prisoners are a deeply vulnerable population who struggle for basic survival after release, the smart-on-crime movement reframes the deep moral problems of the American penal state as technical problems of systems inefficiency. Shifting this conversation can begin by redefining what we mean by re-entry 'success'.

Under the current framework, successful rehabilitative interventions are those that cause former prisoners to commit fewer crimes, do fewer drugs, and cost the state less money (Currie 2013). However, this narrow and minimalist definition of re-entry 'success' ignores the fact that desisting from criminal behaviour does equate with reintegration. As noted at the beginning of this chapter, former prisoners are a deeply disadvantaged population who must navigate conditions of severe material deprivation on a daily basis. Just because they do not reoffend, does not mean former prisoners are stably housed or employed or are integrated as full rights-bearing citizens. A more robust measure of re-entry 'success' would include indicators of individual well-being (e.g. physical and mental health), economic security (e.g. housing, food security, employment), and civic participation (e.g. voting, volunteering, organizing).

Finally, reformers must recognize that individualized rehabilitation alone does not do nearly enough to facilitate the reintegration of former prisoners. Exposure to 'strong-arm rehab' and workforce development training may help former prisoners control their impulses and make better decisions, but they do not change the ecological conditions under which former prisoners make those choices. Unless these individualized efforts are complimented by a robust social safety net, former prisoners will continue to struggle at the margins of mainstream society. Indeed, as Bruce Western puts it, 'reentry policy cannot successfully substitute for real social policy' (quoted in Gottschalk 2015: 92). In other words, recovery therapy and workforce development training should be complements to, rather than replacements for, public resources like 'affordable housing, free health care, accessible education, or a basic income' (De Giorgi 2017: 95).

Notes

1   In the United States, prisons are administered by state and federal authorities and house individuals with felony conviction serving a sentence of at least one year. Jails are administered by local counties and are used for pre-trial detention and for custodial sentences of less than one year.
2   For a more detailed analysis of this curriculum, see Halushka (2016).

References

Aviram, H. (2015) *Cheap on Crime: Recession-Era Politics and the Transformation of American Punishment*. Berkeley: University of California Press.

Carson, E. A. (2018) *Prisoners in 2016*. Washington, DC: Bureau of Justice Statistics. Available at: www.bjs.gov/content/pub/pdf/p16.pdf (Accessed 9 July 2018).

Clear, T. (2007) *Imprisoning Communities: How Mass Incarceration Makes Disadvantaged Neighborhoods Worse*. New York: Oxford University Press.

Currie, E. (2013) Consciousness, solidarity and hope as prevention and rehabilitation. *International Journal of Crime, Justice, and Social Democracy*, 2(2), 3–5.

De Giorgi, A. (2017) Back to nothing: Prisoner reentry and neoliberal neglect. *Social Justice*, 44(1), 83–120.

DeMichele, M. (2014) Studying the community corrections field: Applying neo-institutional theories to a hidden element of mass social control. *Theoretical Criminology*, 18(4), 546–564.

Desmond, M. (2015) Severe deprivation in America: An introduction. *Russell Sage Foundation Journal of Social Science*, 1(2), 1–11.

Desmond, M. (2016) *Evicted: Poverty and Profit in the American City*. New York: Crown.

Fairbanks, R. (2009) *How It Works: Recovering Citizens in Post-Welfare Philadelphia*. Chicago: University of Chicago Press.

Feeley, M. M. and Simon, J. (1992) The new penology: Notes on the emerging strategy of corrections and its implications. *Criminology*, 30(4), 449–474.

Garland, D. (2001) *The Culture of Control*. Chicago: University of Chicago Press.

Goddard, T. (2012) Post-welfarist risk managers? Risk, crime prevention, and the responsibilization of community-based organizations. *Theoretical Criminology*, 16(3), 347–363.

Gowan, T. and Whetstone, S. (2012) Making the criminal addict: Subjectivity and social control in strong-arm rehab. *Punishment & Society*, 14(1), 69–93.

Gottschalk, M (2015) *Caught: The Prison State and the Lockdown of American Politics*. Princeton, NJ: Princeton University Press.

Halushka, J. (2016) Work wisdom: Teaching former prisoners how to negotiate workplace interactions and perform a rehabilitated self. *Ethnography*, 17(1), 72–91.

Halushka, J. (2017) Managing rehabilitation: Negotiating performance accountability at the frontlines of reentry service provision. *Punishment & Society*, 19(4), 482–502.

Haney, L. (2010) *Offending Women: Power, Punishment, and the Regulation of Desire*. Berkeley, CA: University of California Press.

Hannah-Moffat, K. (2005) Criminogenic needs and the transformative risk subject: Hybridizations of risk/need in penality. *Punishment & Society*, 7(1), 29–51.

Harding, D. J., Wyse, J. J. B., Dobson, C. and Morenoff, J. D. (2014) Making ends meet after prison. *Journal of Policy Analysis and Management*, 33(2), 440–472.

Herbert, C. W., Morenoff, J. D. and Harding, D. J. (2015) Homelessness and housing insecurity among former prisoners. *Russell Sage Foundation Journal of Social Science*, 1(2), 44–79.

Kaye, K. (2013) Rehabilitating the 'drug lifestyle': Criminal justice, social control, and the cultivation of agency. *Ethnography*, 14(2), 207–232.

Lucken, K. (1997) Privatizing discretion: "Rehabilitating" treatment in community corrections. *Crime and Delinquency*, 43(3), 243–259.

Lynch, M. (2000) Rehabilitation as rhetoric: The ideal of reformation in contemporary parole discourse and practices. *Punishment & Society*, 2(1), 40–65.

Maruna, S. (2001) *Making Good: How Ex-Convicts Reform and Rebuild Their Lives*. Washington, DC: American Psychological Association.

McCorkel, J. A. (2013) *Breaking Women: Gender, Race, and the New Politics of Imprisonment*. New York: New York University Press.

Miller, R. J. (2014) Devolving the carceral state: Race, prisoner reentry, and the micropolitics of urban poverty management. *Punishment & Society*, 16(3), 305–335.

Miller, R. J. and Stuart, F. (2017) Carceral citizenship: Race, rights, and responsibility in the age of mass supervision. *Theoretical Criminology*, 21(4), 532–548.

Moss, P. and Tilly, C. (1996) "Soft" skills and race: An investigation of black men's employment problems. *Work and Occupations*, 23(3), 252–276.

Pager, D. (2007) *Marked: Race, Crime, and Finding Work in an Era of Mass Incarceration*. Chicago: University of Chicago Press.

Patillo, M., Weiman, D. and Western, B. (Eds.). (2004) *Imprisoning America: The Social Effects of Mass Incarceration*. New York: Russell Sage Foundation.

Petersilia, J. (2003) *When Prisoners Come Home: Parole and Prisoner Reentry*. New York: Oxford University Press.

Prisoner Reentry Institute. (2013) *Three-Quarter Houses: The View from the Inside*. New York: John Jay College of Criminal Justice. Available at: (http://johnjayresearch.org/pri/files/2013/10/PRI-TQH-Report.pdf) (Accessed 3 September 2016).

Robinson, G. (2008) Late-modern rehabilitation: The evolution of a penal strategy. *Punishment & Society*, 10(4), 429–445.

Rose, N. (1999) *The Powers of Freedom: Reframing Political Thought*. New York: Cambridge University Press.

Seeds, C. (2017) Bifurcation nation: American penal policy in late mass incarceration. *Punishment & Society*, 19(5), 590–610.

Simon, J. (1993) *Poor Discipline: Parole and the Social Control of the Underclass, 1890–1990*. Chicago: University of Chicago Press.

Soss, J., Fording, R. C. and Schram, S. F. (2011) *Disciplining the Poor: Neoliberal Paternalism and the Persistent Power of Race*. Chicago: University of Chicago Press.

Stuart, F. (2016) *Down, Out, and Under Arrest: Policing and Everyday Life in Skid Row*. Chicago: University of Chicago Press.

Travis, J. (2005) *But They All Come Back: Facing the Challenges of Prisoner Reentry*. New York: The Urban Institute.

Vera Institute of Justice. (2010) *The Continuing Fiscal Crisis in Corrections: Setting a New Course*. New York: Vera Institute of Justice.

Wakefield, S. and Uggen, C. (2010) Incarceration and stratification. *Annual Review of Sociology*, 36, 387–406.

Werth, R. (2013) The construction and stewardship of responsible yet precarious subjects: Punitive ideology, rehabilitation, and "tough love" among parole personnel. *Punishment & Society*, 15(3), 219–246.

Western, B. (2006) *Punishment and Inequality in America*. New York: Russell Sage Foundation.

Western, B. (2015) Lifetimes of violence in a sample of released prisoners. *Russell Sage Journal of the Social Sciences*, 1(2), 14–30.

Western, B. (2018) *Homeward: Life in the Year After Prison*. New York: Russell Sage Foundation.

Western, B., Braga, A. A., Davis, J., Sirois, C. (2015) Stress and hardship after prison. *American Journal of Sociology*, 120(5), 1512–1547.

Whetstone, S. and Gowan, T. (2017) Carceral rehab as fuzzy penality: Hybrid technologies of control in the new temperance crusade. *Social Justice*, 44, 83–112.

Post-release residential supervision

Keir Irwin-Rogers and Carla Reeves

44

Introduction

Finding a suitable form of accommodation in the community is a central concern for many people being released from prison. In countries where housing is in short supply, and particularly in cases where support from family members or friends is unavailable, the transition from life in prison to life in the community can be fraught with difficulty. Concerns around housing are sometimes delayed by the requirement or opportunity to reside in supervised accommodation for a fixed, and typically short, period on release.

The scope and nature of post-release residential supervision varies considerably across jurisdictions and time. Many of the buildings that today provide post-release residential supervision were once reserved for people on bail or subject to community sanctions. These buildings are sometimes referred to as 'halfway houses', or hostels, as they represent a mid-point between 'open' conditions in the community and 'closed' conditions in prison. However, given that this terminology is not used universally, we have opted to use the term 'post-release residential supervision', as this term best encapsulates the chapter's focus.

In an attempt to find an appropriate balance between the depth and scope of its coverage, the chapter discusses post-release residential supervision in four countries: England and Wales, the US, and Canada. These particular countries were chosen based firstly on the authors' expertise, and secondly, on the prevalence of post-release residential supervision in each country and the availability of literature on the subject. The chapter proceeds by addressing each country in turn, first providing a brief outline of the history of post-release residential supervision in each respective country, before exploring relevant research and any key policy developments. A concluding section summarizes contemporary approaches to post-release residential supervision in each of the three countries, highlights points of overlap and divergence, and indicates likely future trends.

England and Wales

At the time of writing, hostels in England and Wales are reserved predominantly for post-release residential supervision. Historically, however, they acted as places of residence for people on bail and those subject to community sanctions. Whilst hostels were voluntarily organized, funded, and managed for much of their history, they were placed on a statutory footing and began receiving public funds as a result of the enactment of the Criminal Justice Act 1948. Following the Children and Young Persons Act 1969, which prohibited their use for children and young people, hostels became an established and important part of the adult criminal justice system (Cowe and Reeves 2012).

Since the 1980s, the traditional welfare-oriented approach to working with offenders in hostels has been replaced by one based on principles of risk management. This has mirrored the more general shift in probation work in England and Wales away from the guiding motto of 'advise, assist and befriend', which initially stemmed from the Probation of Offenders Act 1907 and was restated by a report of the Departmental Committee on the Social Services in 1936 (Hill 1993). Documents such as the *Statement of National Objectives and Priorities* for the probation service, published in 1984, served to redirect the focus of probation from supporting 'in need' clients through a social work service, towards the management of people deemed to be potential threats to society (May 1994; Raynor 1988). During the 1990s and up until the present day, hostels have played a key role in the management of 'risky' and 'dangerous' populations leaving prison. Although officially pursuing the dual functions of help and support and monitoring and control, in practice the former has often been overshadowed and undermined by the dominance of risk-management and public protection priorities (Wincup 2003; Irwin-Rogers 2017a).

Contemporary post-release residential supervision

In the present day, post-release residential supervision is overseen by the National Probation Service, part of Her Majesty's Prison and Probation Services (HMPPS, under the auspices of the Ministry of Justice [MoJ]). There are currently 96 Probation Approved Premises (PAPs), also known as probation hostels, which provide over 2,000 residential hostel supervision places (a further 11 are independently managed). The vast majority of PAPs, approved under section 13 of the Offender Management Act 2007, are used to accommodate men leaving prison, with just six PAPs accommodating women. PAPs primarily accommodate people who are deemed to be 'high risk' and have no other appropriate community accommodation (Her Majesty's Inspectorate of Probation 2017). Some people on bail may also be accommodated if they are deemed to require an enhanced level of supervision, but do not warrant imprisonment on remand (NAPA, n.d.). The main purpose of PAPs is to provide residents with an enhanced level of supervision aimed at protecting the public by mitigating the risks of these people committing serious harm in the community (Dame Glenys Stacey, Chief Inspector of Probation: Her Majesty's Inspectorate of Probation 2017).

PAPs generally accommodate between ten and 45 people in a range of single, double, and triple bedrooms within a community-based setting. Residents have access to communal laundry, washing, and cooking facilities, although main meals are usually included for a relatively cheap weekly rent. All people leaving prison in England and Wales are subject to a post-custodial licence – a document which stipulates a set of eight standard conditions (and potentially some additional bespoke conditions), including the requirement to attend regular supervision sessions with a supervising officer, being 'well behaved', and notifying a supervising officer of any changes to accommodation arrangements or employment (National Offender Management Service 2014). In addition to these licence conditions, PAPs typically require residents to respect a set of behavioural standards whilst in the hostel, and abide by certain curfews and prohibitions on visitors, drugs, alcohol, and medications (the latter of which are managed by staff who oversee residents' consumption). People living in hostels are subject to random drug tests and room searches, and may be required to engage in various chores around the hostel, for example, cleaning or gardening. Residents may be required to attend a range of offence-based or life skills programmes, such as anger management or one-to-one work with their probation supervisor or hostel key worker. In addition, residents are encouraged to engage in education, training, or employment, approved through sentence planning sessions and risk assessments. Breaches of these rules and regulations may result in formal warnings, the imposition of additional licence or hostel conditions, and in the most serious cases, recall to prison[1] (Her Majesty's Inspectorate of Probation 2017; Reeves 2016b).

Recent research on post-release residential supervision in England and Wales has highlighted issues around professional role conflict. Reeves (2011,

2013, 2016a), for example, noted that hostel staff varied in their views on the primary purpose of the hostel and their professional roles, but in general tended to resolve the tension by regarding supervision as supporting reintegration and rehabilitation – a sort of 'tough-love' approach – whilst simultaneously protecting the public. However, residents were sceptical of the idea that rehabilitation and reintegration were core hostel purposes, instead considering the primary work of hostels to be control and incapacitation. Research has indicated that hostels may also undermine supportive work by socially segregating and isolating certain groups of residents, thus encouraging the maintenance of offence-related identities (Reeves 2013, 2016a).

Similarly, another recent study observed that whilst hostels can provide supportive environments to aid the reintegration and rehabilitation of people post release, seemingly innocuous variation in hostel policies can significantly influence the likelihood of successful prison-to-community transitions (Irwin-Rogers 2017b). Open or closed staff office door policies, for example, can influence opportunities for residents and staff to interact, thereby enabling or preventing constructive relationships from forming. Irwin-Rogers (2017a) argued that the success of post-residential supervision depends in large part on the establishment of constructive relationships between hostel staff and residents, which in turn depends on procedural justice criteria, such as treating residents with dignity and respect, providing adequate and up-to-date information, and listening to residents' views and concerns before making important decisions.

The future of post-release residential supervision in England and Wales

Hostels, like other areas of probation work, have been affected by the recent Transforming Rehabilitation (TR) agenda in England and Wales, which began in 2014. Among other significant changes, TR heralded the fragmentation and partial privatization of probation services into the National Probation Service (tasked with supervising approximately one-third of the total number of people assessed as high risk) and Community Rehabilitation Companies (tasked with supervising the remaining two-thirds of people assessed as low to medium risk). To date, the implications of TR for hostels have been minimal. As hostels are reserved primarily for people deemed to be high risk, however, they have taken on an increased role and importance in relation to the work of the National Probation Service (Her Majesty's Inspectorate of Probation 2017).

As the probation services have been restructured away from their previous division as regional trusts, hostels have amalgamated into divisional area teams within the nationalized NPS, enabling more efficient sharing and comparison of policies and practices (Williams 2016). Closer working relationships between different hostels, and between hostel and probation staff, have served to highlight inconsistences and improve communication, although to date there has been no noticeable difference in outcomes in terms of compliance rates or occupancy and intervention completions (Williams 2016).

A recent major inspection of probation hostels across England and Wales was conducted by Her Majesty's Inspectorate of Probation (Her Majesty's Inspectorate of Probation 2017). The inspection highlighted the value of hostels with regards to protecting the public and supporting people's rehabilitation and reintegration back into communities and, overall, they were held to 'bridge criminal justice and broader social policy concerns' (Her Majesty's Inspectorate of Probation 2017: 8). Inspectors found that hostel provision is routinely over-subscribed, with occupancy rates of around 92% and an estimated shortfall in provision of 25%, indicating that significant sector growth is required to serve the needs of people post release in the coming years. The implications of residential shortages are threefold: first, that some people may not be released from prison until such safe and secure accommodation is available; second, that people may be accommodated outside of their local area and therefore away from their family or other social support networks that can provide an important source of support during this period of transition; and third, people could have their residency terms cut short to free up spaces for other people leaving prison.

According to the inspection, research evaluating the effectiveness of hostel residency with regards to reoffending rates or broader measures of success such as engagement in education and employment is scarce, with no official attempts to routinely capture data. To address this data deficit, the inspection called for new systems and processes of data gathering and analysis. Whilst noting the concerns of hostel managers about the quality of contracted working arrangements with external partners delivering services such as offence-related interventions, the inspection concluded that hostels remain a 'necessary and credible . . . structured way to protect the public and meet resettlement needs and focus on rehabilitation' (Her Majesty's Inspectorate of Probation 2017: 26).

The inspection not only reported on the current state of probation hostels in England and Wales, but also demarcated a desirable course for the future. In addition to more robust tracking of resident referrals and evidence on hostel effectiveness and good practice, the inspection called for an expansion in hostel provision. This could be achieved through the establishment of new approved premises and partnerships with the voluntary sector, or by expanding existing facilities to create more bed spaces. The notion of 'virtual' hostel placements in people's own homes through the use of curfews, GPS tags, regular visits, and alcohol and drugs tests was also addressed. It was recognized, however, that virtual placements should not replace hostel provision for people who pose the highest risk of serious harm, as they would not provide the continuous or enhanced level of oversight necessary to adequately protect the public. To support the work of hostels and to promote the effective and efficient use of people's period of residency, the inspection called for preparatory work, such as benefits assessments and applications, to be completed before people's release dates.

In short, hostels in England and Wales are expected to grow in scale and importance in the coming years, and look set to continue in their current role of providing a place of residence for people who are perceived to pose a relatively high risk of serious harm as they transition from prisons into the community.

The US

Post-release residential supervision in the US has a long history, dating back to the mid-19th century. The earliest recorded post-release residential facility, the Isaac T. Hopper Home in New York City, opened its doors in 1874 after being purchased by the Women's Prison Association (Landmarks Preservation Commission 2009). Following a significant decline during the Great Depression of the 1930s, the number of residential facilities grew rapidly during the middle of the 20th century. By 1978, almost 400 facilities were in operation across nearly all states comprising a total capacity of around 10,000 bed spaces. In large part, the expansion of residential supervision during this period was driven by support and investment from the federal government (Alarid and del Carmen 2012). Such support and investment coincided with the widespread popularity of the rehabilitative ideal and the idea that criminal justice systems could and should help those who have broken the law to live productive and law-abiding lives. Post-release residential supervision was thought to provide a means of achieving this goal by functioning as a 'decompression chamber', reducing the stress, confusion, and uncertainty of life post release (Allen et al. 1978: 1).

At the time of writing, post-release residential facilities play an important role in most states throughout the US. A range of actors manage these facilities, including states, federal government, private agencies, and third-sector organizations. Whilst the reasons underpinning their expansion during the middle of the 20th century persist today, additional justifications have emerged in recent decades. Mirroring the trend towards the prioritization of public protection in the UK, residential supervision in the US has moved increasingly away from a model centred on the provision of help and support and towards a focus on risk management and the control of 'dangerous offender populations' (Latessa 2012: 199). Indeed, this shift was documented as early as the 1980s, with Hicks (1987) noting that residential facilities were becoming increasingly punitive and aimed at controlling the behaviour of people deemed to pose a risk to the well-being of the general population.

There is considerable variation in post-release residential supervision across the US. In the state of Missouri, for example, the Department of Corrections operates nine post-release residential facilities, providing a total bed capacity of 785. These facilities are reserved primarily for people leaving prison who are deemed to be 'high risk' and in need of a structured environment to manage their transition back into the community. Most people's residency periods are around three months, although for those convicted of sex offences the term is somewhat longer: 6.4 months (Kras et al. 2016). Pathways into residential supervision usually take one of three forms: (1) residency owing to a person's lack of financial means or social support to secure an alternative form of accommodation; (2) residency owing to supervision restrictions, which particularly affect people convicted of sexual offences (for example, the restriction from living within a certain distance of schools or day-care facilities); and (3) residency as a punishment and additional sanction for technical violations of parole.

Far from providing a supportive environment for adapting back into community life, research has provided a relatively negative portrayal of post-release residential supervision, dominated by concerns around risk management and often detrimental to residents' transitions (Kras et al. 2016). Residents reported being forced to occupy a space populated by a high number of drug users, which increased the likelihood of hitherto non-drug users developing addictions. Moreover, residents who could not find work in the community were required to undertake work tasks in the hostel that paid US$1 per day; this was perceived to be more akin to an extension of prison life than a transitional employment opportunity. Other residents went further and argued that residential supervision could be *de*-habilitative, further hindering their successful reintegration into the community. For example, residency requirements prevented some people from leaving the facility during times when their employers asked them to work, resulting in the termination of their employment. Furthermore, the lack of a personal phone number made communication between employers and residents problematic, with some residents suspecting that their case managers were not communicating call-backs effectively. Finally, people argued that the stigma of hostel residency – in relation, for instance, to being labelled as 'high risk' and likely to be recalled to prison – further undermined their prospects with potential employers.

In a recent systematic review of the effectiveness of post-release residential supervision in the US, the reviewers argued that a lack of methodological rigour prevented any firm conclusions from being drawn from existing research (Growns et al. 2017). Whilst they identified a small number of studies that linked residential supervision to favourable outcomes in the form of reduced rates of reconviction and re-incarceration (e.g. Latessa et al. 2010; Routh and Hamilton 2015), they highlighted that most studies found no statistically significant difference between programme and comparison groups, and that some studies indicated that residential supervision could have criminogenic effects (Lowenkamp et al. 2006).

Despite the lack of a positive evidence base, commentators have predicted a continued expansion of post-release residential supervision, in large part due to severe overcrowding in local and state prisons. Such expansion will likely result in further diversification, with residential facilities offering a range of programmes and services, including rehabilitative interventions such as relationships and substance abuse counselling, victim awareness programmes and work release centres, alongside various forms of monitoring and control, facilitated to some extent by the more general growth of electronic monitoring in community corrections (Latessa 2012).

Canada

Whilst residential facilities housing people leaving prison emerged in Canada during the late 19th century, it was not until the middle of the 20th century that these types of facility comprised an official component of sentences of imprisonment (Raush 1968). Early residential facilities focused primarily on providing individualized help and support to those leaving prison. The approach of St Leonard's House, which opened in Ontario in 1962, for example, was not to 'try to force a certain period of [individual counselling] each week', but rather to encourage residents to 'see his own needs and to express these to a selected member of staff' (Libby 1968: 408). The Executive Director of St Leonard's considered the facility to function as a continuous group therapy system, which, while holding specific group sessions from time to time, focused primarily on one-to-one counselling sessions with individuals.

During the 1970s the role of private, non-profit organizations in the delivery of community corrections expanded significantly, as they were perceived to have closer relationships with, and better access to, community resources, as well as more potential to involve local communities in programmes to support those leaving prison (Ekstedt and Griffiths 1988; Outerbridge 1972). The private and third sector continue to play a central role in the delivery of post-release residential supervision at the time of writing, with over 200 Community Residential Facilities (CRFs) operating across Canada. This compares to just 16 Community Correction Centres (CCCs), which are the public sector equivalents of CRFs (Office of the Correctional Investigator 2014). Residency conditions are commonly imposed on people leaving prison and have been increasing in recent years: in 2012–2013, the Parole Board of Canada imposed a residency condition on 42% of people on statutory release, up from 30% in 2008–2009 (Office of the Correctional Investigator 2014).

CRFs have been described as minimum-security facilities that offer a less institutionalized environment than their CCC counterparts, operating on the basis of client-centred and humanistic approaches (Bell and Trevethan 2004; The John Howard Society of Alberta 2011a). All CRFs offer internal caseworker support, typically alongside a range of programmes such as budgeting, substance abuse, and anger management. The facilities often impose relatively stringent conditions during the early part of a person's residency, which are then gradually relaxed if residents appear to be coping well with their transitions (The John Howard Society of Alberta 2011b). A tender notice for a CRF, submitted by the Correctional Service of Canada (CSC) in 2017, stated that the primary requirements of a CRF are: the 'management of offenders during their transition from the institution to the community' and 'ensuring the safety and security of members of the public, victims, staff and offenders in the community' (Public Works and Government Services Canada 2017). To ensure these requirements are met, the CSC outlined a number of more specific tasks, including the provision of outreach services, the establishment of community resource networks, and the provision crisis intervention such as counselling and medical services.

Public sector CCCs are typically responsible for supervising people who are deemed to pose a relatively high risk of serious harm to members of the public, compared to those in CRFs and the population of people released from prison more widely (Axford and Abracen 2011). A recent investigation into CCCs by the Office of the Correctional Investigator (2014) provides some important insights into their scope and nature. The investigation revealed that CCCs provide a total bed capacity of 474, which accounts for around 6% of the approximately 7,750 federally sentenced people overall who are supervised in the community. Whilst periods of residency in CCCs usually last for around five months, a minority of residents serving long-term supervision orders are required to remain for an average of one and a half years.

While all CCCs offer some form of 'correctional programming', concerns were raised by the investigation that too often these were scheduled during daytime working hours, meaning that residents with regular employment were unable to participate. Other concerns included a lack of consistency with regards to rule enforcement in hostels, which undermined residents' trust and confidence in CCC regimes. The investigation called for more rigorous internal monitoring of recall decisions and more transparent mechanisms of accountability. Finally, elements of CCC best practice included an intensive schedule of correctional programmes, the ability to strike a good balance between supervision and assistance, and close collaboration with health agencies, social services, and other community-based organizations (Office of the Correctional Investigator 2014).

Conclusion

Whilst the precise nature and scope of post-release residential supervision varies across each of the countries discussed in this chapter, it is worth noting a number of key points of overlap. Whilst hostel regimes across all three countries were initially welfare-oriented, focusing on the provision of help and support to residents perceived to be 'in need', the role of hostels has shifted in recent decades towards the imperative of managing the behaviour of 'risky' and 'dangerous' populations. Post-release residential supervision in each country professes to balance the provision of help and support with monitoring and control, although studies have highlighted that the practical implications of attempting to do so typically result in help and support being undermined and overshadowed by the priorities of managing risk and protecting the public (Irwin-Rogers 2017a; Kras et al. 2016; Reeves 2011; Wincup 2003). This shift is reflected by the fact that hostels in all three countries focus some or all of their provision on those who are deemed to pose the highest risk of serious harm. Whilst in England and Wales, as with many states in the US, there is little provision for those who fall outside the supposed high-risk category, in Canada, largely owing to the contribution made by non-profit, voluntary organizations, there is also substantial provision for people categorized as medium or low risk.

Although the length that people reside in hostels varies quite substantially, a typical residency period in all three countries appears to be around three to six months. The content of post-release residential supervision across all three countries is broadly similar. For example, hostels usually encourage or require residents to engage in a range of activities, such as programmes addressing issues around drugs, alcohol, employment, and anger management, all of which are designed to reduce people's risk of reoffending whilst also supporting their reintegration into the community. Moreover, residents are usually required to attend regular meetings with supervising officers, abide by strict curfew times, and adhere to a range of conditions stipulated as part of their terms of release from prison, as well as any specific rules imposed by the hostel.

Given the prevalence and importance of post-release residential supervision in each of the countries discussed in this chapter, the lack of robust empirical data evidencing its effectiveness with regards to reoffending rates in particular, or indeed a broader set of criteria, is concerning. Despite lacking a reliable evidence base, recent trends and public statements appear to indicate that hostels in all three countries will remain squarely focused on people who are deemed to pose a 'high risk' of serious harm to members of the public, with the scale of post-release residential supervision set to grow in the coming years (Her Majesty's Inspectorate of Probation 2017; Latessa 2012; Office of the Correctional Investigator 2014).

Note

1 In England and Wales, when a person is recalled, they may be required to serve a fixed term, or the remainder of their sentence, in prison.

References

Alarid, L. F. and del Carmen, R. V. (2012) *Community-Based Corrections*, 8th edition. Belmont, CA: Wadsworth.

Allen, H. E., Carlson, E. W., Parks, E. C. and Seiter, R. P. (1978) *Halfway Houses*. Washington, DC: US Department of Justice.

Axford, M. and Abracen, J. (2011) *Sexual Offenders with an LTSO Designation Residing in Community Correctional Centres (CCC's): Comparison to Other Groups Residing in CCC's*. Ottawa, ON: Correctional Service of Canada.

Bell, A. and Trevethan, S. (2004) *Community Residential Facilities in Canada: A Descriptive Profile of Residents and Facilities*. Available at: www.csc-scc.gc.ca.

Cowe, F. and Reeves, C. (2012) Residential work with sex offenders: Places of collusion and segregation or preparation for resettlement and reintegration? In J. Brayford, F. Cowe and J. Deering (Eds.), *Sex Offenders: Punish, Help, Change or Control? Theory, Policy and Practice Explored*. London: Routledge.

Ekstedt, J. W. and Griffiths, C. T. (1988) *Corrections in Canada: Policy and Practice*, 2nd edition. Toronto: Butterworths.

Growns, B., Kinner, S. A., Conroy, E., Baldry, E. and Larney, S. (2017) A systematic review of supported accommodation programs for people released from custody. *Offender Therapy and Comparative Criminology*, 62(8), 2174–2194.

Hicks, N. (1987) New relationship: Halfway houses and corrections. *Corrections Compendium*, 12(1), 5–8.

Hill, D. (1993) *Intensive Probation Practice: An Option for the 1990s*. London: Probation Monographs. Social Work Monographs.

HMIP (Her Majesty's Inspectorate of Probation). (2017) *Probation Hostels' (Approved Premises) Contribution to Public Protection, Rehabilitation and Resettlement*. Thematic Inspection. Manchester: HMIP. Available at: www.justiceinspectorates.gov.uk/hmiprobation/wp-content/uploads/sites/5/2017/07/Probation-Hostels-2017-report.pdf.

Irwin-Rogers, K. (2017a) Legitimacy on licence: Why and how it matters. *The Howard Journal of Crime and Justice*, 56(1), 53–71.

Irwin-Rogers, K. (2017b) Staff-resident relationships in approved premises: What a difference a door makes. *Probation Journal*, 1–17. DOI:10.1177/0264550517728785.

The John Howard Society of Alberta. (2011a) *Fact Sheet: Just What Are "Halfway Houses"? (1 of 2)*. Edmonton: The John Howard Society of Alberta.

The John Howard Society of Alberta. (2011b) *Fact Sheet: Just What Are "Halfway Houses"? (2 of 2)*. Edmonton: The John Howard Society of Alberta.

Kras, K. R., Pleggenkuhle, B. and Huebner, B. M. (2016) A new way of doing time on the outside: Sex offenders' pathways in and out of a transitional housing facility. *International Journal of Offender Therapy and Comparative Criminology*, 60(5), 512–534.

Landmarks Preservation Commission. (2009) *Ralph and Ann E. Van Wyck Mead House*. Designation List 419 LP-2331. Available at: www.nyc.gov/html/lpc/downloads/pdf/reports/mead.pdf (Accessed 21 September 2017).

Latessa, E. J. (2012) Halfway houses and residential centres. In S. M. Barton-Bellessa (Ed.), *Encyclopedia of Community Corrections*. Thousand Oaks, CA: Sage Publications, pp. 197–208.

Letessa, E. J., Lovins, L. B. and Smith, P. (2010) *Follow-Up Evaluation of Ohio's Community Based Correctional Facility and Halfway House Programs – Outcome Study*. Cincinnati, OH: Centre for Criminal Justice Research, University of Cincinnati.

Libby, T. N. (1968) The residential centre for released prisoners. *Canadian Journal of Corrections*, 10, 406–408.

Lowenkamp, C. T., Latessa, E. J. and Smith, P. (2006) Does correctional program quality really matter? The impact of adhering to the principles of effective intervention. *Criminology and Public Policy*, 5, 575–594.

May, T. (1994) Probation and community sanctions. In M. Maguire, R. Morgan and R. Reiner (Eds.), *The Oxford Handbook of Criminology*. Oxford: Oxford University Press.

NAPA (National Approved Premises Association). (n.d.) *Approved Premises*. Available at: www.napa-uk.org/premises.html.

National Offender Management Service. (2014) *Post-Sentence Supervision Requirements*. Available at: www.justice.gov.uk.

Office of the Correctional Investigator. (2014) *Overcoming Barriers to Reintegration: An Investigation of Federal Community Correctional Centres*. Available at: www.oci-bec.gc.ca.

Outerbridge, W. R. (1972) *Report of the Task Force on Community-Based Residential Centres.* Ottawa, ON. Information Canada.

Public Works and Government Services Canada. (2017) *Community Based Residential Facility – Alternative Housing (21883–17–0012).* Available at: https://buyandsell. gc.ca/.

Raush, H. L. (1968) *Halfway House Movement: A Search for Sanity.* New York: Irvington-Publishers.

Raynor, P. (1988) *Probation as an Alternative to Custody: A Case Study.* Aldershot: Avebury.

Reeves, C. (2011) The changing role of probation hostels: Voices from the inside. *British Journal of Community Justice*, 9(3), 51–64.

Reeves, C. (2013) The others': Sex offenders' social identities in probation approved premises. *The Howard Journal of Criminal Justice*, 52(4), 383–398.

Reeves, C. (2016a) The meaning of place and space in a probation approved premises. *The Howard Journal of Crime and Justice*, 55(1–2), 151–167.

Reeves, C. (2016b) Everyday life in UK probation approved premises for sex offenders. In C. Reeves (Ed.), *Experiencing Imprisonment: Research on the Experience of Living and Working in Carceral Institutions.* London: Routledge.

Routh, D. and Hamilton, Z. (2015) Work release as a transition: Positioning success via the halfway house. *Journal of Offender Rehabilitation*, 54, 239–255.

Williams, R. (2016) Transforming Rehabilitation and approved premises: The effect of ideologically driven change upon probation practice in an institutional setting. *Probation Journal*, 63(2), 202–210.

Wincup, E. (2003) *Residential Work with Offenders: Reflexive Accounts of Practice.* Aldershot: Ashgate.

The health needs of people leaving prison

45

A new horizon to address

Craig Cumming

Introduction

People who are incarcerated experience poor health at higher rates than the general community (Baillargeon et al. 2009; Australian Institute of Health and Welfare 2015; Fazel et al. 2016), resulting in far higher rates of primary and acute health service after release (Somers et al. 2015; Carroll 2017). Despite these high rates of health service use, subjectively this group reports major challenges in maintaining their health once they leave prison, citing a range of logistical and psychosocial factors that contribute to increased stress levels and anxiety that impact on their health outcomes (Binswanger et al. 2011). This has implications for the justice system, as poor health has been shown to predict a return to custody (Thomas et al. 2015; Smith and Trimboli 2010). This means that any risk and need assessments conducted when an individual is being considered for supervised release must consider their health needs to give them the best chance of a successful transition back to the community. It is therefore crucial that community corrections staff who are working with supervisees released back into the community are aware of the specific and unique health-related challenges that people who to go prison are likely to face upon their transition back into the community.

This chapter looks at the needs of those who are incarcerated from a public health perspective, viewing prison and supervised release as an opportunity to address the underlying health problems that this group often experiences (Kinner and Wang 2014). A number of health problems that this group are at an increased risk of experiencing are discussed. These include mental illness, drug use, infectious disease, chronic disease, intellectual disability, and brain injury. This chapter aims to inform those working with supervisees as they transition back into the community where health resources are most needed. The term community corrections officer (CCO) will be used throughout this chapter; this encompasses anyone supervising someone who is subject to orders of the court, including case workers, parole officers, and any other supervisors.

The Health After Release from Prison (HARP) study

This chapter is informed by a number of studies into a range of health issues that impact people who have been to prison across the world. One of the key studies currently underway is the Health After Release from Prison (HARP) study (Kinner et al. 2013). The HARP study has been conducted across two different Australian states (Queensland and Western Australia), with more than 2,700 participants participating in a face-to-face interview in the weeks before their release from prison. Participants also consented to researchers having access to their administrative health records for the five years before and after their prison term, as well as their prison health records. This study has many strengths: the large sample size, the use of cross-sectional and longitudinal data sources, and the use of objective administrative data as well as subjective self-report data are among the most important. The multiple data sources and types mean that the researchers are able to effectively control for potential confounders in ways that are not possible where only one data source or type is used. The unique study design and rich data are facilitating unprecedented research into a population that has often been extremely difficult to engage and follow up.

Prison health screening and management

A key element of any effort to manage the health of supervisees transitioning back into the community is for CCOs to be fully aware of their health status prior to their release from prison. The old economist's adage 'what gets measured gets done' is highly relevant in the context of prisoner health; if health problems are not identified, then planning to manage them during supervised release is unlikely to happen. The implications of this are that although supervised release happens outside of the prison, its success is influenced by how effective prison health services are in identifying health problems prior to release.

In light of the evidence that prisoners experience conditions such as mental illness at high rates, it seems reasonable to expect that health screening would be standard practice in prisons. Unfortunately this is not always the case, even in developed countries such as the United States, where one entire state's prison system was found not to use any evidence-based mental illness screening tools (Scheyett et al. 2009). To complicate matters further, there are often issues with the transfer of medical records between community and prison health services (Cornford et al. 2007), making effective treatment of ongoing health problems in people who cycle in and out of prison a major challenge. These factors all contribute to the environment in which CCOs must work; awareness of these issues is essential so that proactive steps can be taken prior to release to ensure that as much information about each supervisee's health as possible is available for planning purposes.

Multimorbidity and complexity

The health problems that prisoners experience rarely occur in isolation, with many individuals experiencing multiple health problems at the same time (Piselli et al. 2015; Indig 2016; Butler et al. 2011). Often these multiple co-occurring health problems interact, increasing complexity and making management of the individual's health more difficult; this can result in poor health and justice outcomes. For example, research has found that people who experience both a drug use disorder and serious mental illness together are at a far higher risk of both having their parole revoked (Baillargeon et al. 2009), and multiple incarcerations over time (Baillargeon et al. 2010) than people who experience either of these in isolation. It is essential to understand the complexity of health needs that can arise in people who go to prison, as often multiple different types of treatment from different clinicians are needed to address all issues. Failing to do so could mean that any progress made with one condition may be offset by a failure to treat another, resulting in continued poor health and related outcomes for the individual. What this means for the management of supervisees, is that in many cases, CCOs will need to coordinate care from a number of different providers for an individual supervisee in the community. This can often take significant time and material resources to manage, so risk and needs assessment and planning prior to release is essential.

The high-risk period after release from prison

Research suggests that one of the riskiest periods of time for poor health outcomes, including death, is the period just after release from prison (Hobbs et al. 2006; Merrall et al. 2010). There is overwhelming evidence that people who leave prison are at a greatly increased risk of death in the period after release compared to the general population (Hobbs et al. 2006; Binswanger et al. 2007; Farrell and Marsden 2008; Spaulding et al. 2011). Drug overdose is the leading cause of death in this population during the period after release (Binswanger et al. 2013), with drug-related causes such as injury or poisoning and related chronic conditions also playing a major role (Hobbs et al. 2006; Chang et al. 2015). Suicide is also a major contributor to this risk (Hobbs et al. 2006; Binswanger et al. 2007; Chang et al. 2015; Stewart et al. 2004), particularly in the first month after release (Pratt et al. 2006). The factors that contribute to suicide risk include opioid use, being prescribed antidepressants during the most recent incarceration, a history of using alcohol at problematic levels, and having served more than one prison sentence (Spittal et al. 2017). Mental illness and drug use are prominent factors in the risk of post-release death; they are major issues for this population and it is crucial for CCOs to have a sound understanding of them.

Mental illness

People who go to prison experience high rates of severe mental illness compared to the general population, with more than 14% of prisoners across the world experiencing either psychosis or major depression (Fazel and Seewald 2012). Further, Australian research found that 49% of prisoner entrants reported being diagnosed by a clinician with any type of mental health disorder at some point in their life (Australian Institute of Health and Welfare 2015). Similarly, in 2005 half of the United States' inmates were reported to experience a mental illness of some kind (James and Glaze 2006). These figures highlight the necessity of mental health services generally for people leaving prison, particularly as mental illness is associated with an increased risk of an individual being incarcerated multiple times (Baillargeon et al. 2009). In addition to this, co-occurring mental illness is a complicating factor for the management of other health problems, such as HIV and HCV (Springer et al. 2011; Meyer et al. 2011), which if not treated or managed, can result in extremely poor health outcomes and even death.

Self-harm and suicide

One important area of focus for CCOs is the prevention of self-harm and suicide in the period after release from prison. Recent research has found that people leaving prison are at a significantly higher risk of self-harming (Borschmann et al. 2017), and committing suicide (Spittal et al. 2014) than the general community post-release. Research conducted in Australian prisons found that one-third of participants had considered committing suicide, and that one-fifth had attempted suicide (Larney et al. 2012). Factors that correlate with having considered suicide include a history of violent offending, having a brain injury, experiencing depression, self-harming, and having been admitted to a psychiatric hospital (Larney et al. 2012). Other international research found that factors associated with completing suicide included being white, male, previously considering suicide, previously attempting suicide, being diagnosed with a current mental illness, receiving psychiatric medication, and having a history of alcohol problems (Fazel et al. 2008). This illustrates the complex personal histories that many people who are imprisoned have, and provides some guidance to CCOs on factors that may increase the risk of suicide for supervisees transitioning from prison to the community.

Preventing suicide

The effectiveness of suicide prevention interventions for supervisees is an area requiring further research. Without meaningful evidence of the effectiveness of existing interventions in a community corrections setting, guidance must be drawn from research looking at interventions implemented in other settings. For example, there is good evidence that 'gatekeeper training' has been effective in reducing the numbers of people contemplating, attempting, and completing suicide in military personnel and physicians (Isaac et al. 2009). Gatekeepers are people who have primary contact with those at risk of suicide, and identify this risk by observing a number of suicide risk factors (Gould and Kramer 2001; Centers for Disease Control 1992). CCOs are natural gatekeepers in a community corrections context, so undertaking gatekeeper training may improve their ability to identify suicide risk in supervisees, and make the necessary referrals to specialist mental health services.

At a system level, there is evidence that provision of a 24-hour crisis care service that responds to people with acute mental health needs reduced the suicide rate after it was implemented in the United Kingdom (While et al. 2012). Additionally, a trial of post-release specialist support for people with mental illness in Queensland, Australia, found that those receiving support for the longest amount of time were at the lowest risk of being re-incarcerated (Green et al. 2016). CCOs should be aware if the jurisdiction they are working in provides any such similar services or programmes, should inform supervisees about them, and ensure they have the means to seek assistance if required. More generally, it is suggested that improving referral to mental health services and primary care (often a first point of contact for those with mental illness) upon release, should provide opportunities to identify suicide risk, for necessary referrals to be made, and treatment to be provided (Cardarelli et al. 2015). Continuity of mental healthcare in particular is associated with the prevention of suicide (Burgess et al. 2000). Therefore pre-release planning to identify the needs of prisoners with mental illness, and facilitate access to appropriate services post-release is important in reducing the risk of suicide.

CCOs should consider how post-release contact with supervisees can be structured to facilitate access to mental health services, particularly in the period just after release.

Drug use

Drug use is a major issue for people who go to prison, with research consistently showing drug use occurs at far higher rates in this group than the general community (Australian Institute of Health and Welfare 2015; Petersilia 2015; Fazel et al. 2006). Drug use also plays a central role in the increased risk of death in the period after release from prison (Merrall et al. 2010; Farrell and Marsden 2008; Spittal et al. 2017; Andrews and Kinner 2012). A number of factors that may contribute to a return to drug use post-release include poor social support, comorbid health problems, and a lack of economic resources (Binswanger et al. 2012). Accidental overdose may occur due to reduced tolerance, and intentional overdose may be a way of escaping situational stress (Binswanger et al. 2012). Accordingly, CCOs require sound knowledge of the aetiology of dependence, relapse, and the availability of treatment and harm minimization options, as a large number of the people they will be working with will experience drug dependence. There are a number of evidence-based treatment and harm-minimization options for people experiencing drug dependence.

Psychosocial treatment

A comprehensive review of the effectiveness of drug treatment programmes for people who were in prison, or under supervision in the community found that participation in cognitive behavioural therapy (CBT), contingency management (CM), therapeutic communities (TC), and drug courts were effective in reducing the rates of both drug use and criminal activity when participants were compared to those who did not participate in any of these programmes (Bahr et al. 2012). The researchers found that the effectiveness of these programs improved when multiple interventions were provided simultaneously, and also when there were inducements (such as monetary or other rewards) to receive treatment (Bahr et al. 2012). Other key components associated with treatment being effective included the provision of intensive treatment, as well as post-treatment aftercare (Bahr et al. 2012). Perhaps counter-intuitively, the evidence suggests that 12-step programs such as Alcoholics Anonymous and Narcotics Anonymous do not have the same impact as CBT, CM, TC, or the drug courts in reducing crime and drug use (Bahr et al. 2012). For CCOs working with supervisees experiencing drug dependence, it is important to ensure that they are receiving behavioural therapy that is as intensive as resources permit, and that where possible, incentives are incorporated into the programme.

Pharmacotherapy

For those experiencing opioid dependence, buprenorphine or methadone in combination with behavioural therapy or CM was found to be effective in reducing drug use compared to those on behavioural therapy alone. For prevention of opioid overdose death after release from prison, providing take-home naloxone in combination with brief training in administering it was shown to significantly reduce the number of opioid-related overdose deaths in the community (Strang et al. 2013; Bird et al. 2016). Accordingly, where an individual is experiencing opioid dependence, buprenorphine or methadone in combination with behavioural therapy is an option that should be considered. For the prevention of overdose deaths in this group, take-home naloxone with instructions for use in the event of opioid overdose should also be considered as a harm reduction measure, particularly for individuals with a history of opioid dependence.

Chronic and infectious diseases

People that go to prison are more likely to experience chronic disease and be exposed to infectious diseases such as blood-borne viruses (BBVs), tuberculosis, and sexually transmitted infections than the general population (Kinner and Wang 2014). If untreated or unmanaged by a health professional, these can cause serious health problems for those affected. Evidence-based strategies for managing some of the more prevalent and potentially serious diseases are considered below.

Blood-borne viruses

Prisoners are at a particular risk of contracting BBV due to risky injecting drug use (IDU) practices (Fazel et al. 2006; Dolan et al. 2015). Accordingly, people in prison experience significantly higher rates of BBV such as hepatitis B (HBV), HCV, and HIV than the general community (Butler et al. 2015; Mir-Nasseri et al. 2011; Wilper et al. 2009). For those with chronic hepatitis who do not naturally clear the infection and do not respond to treatment, their condition will need to be managed as they transition back to the community.

Hepatitis C

For people with HCV, the development of direct-acting antiviral (DAA) medication has greatly improved their chances of successfully clearing the infection (Pawlotsky et al. 2015). Several medications are available now, and most treatment regimens involve the daily administration of medication and run for either 12 or 24 weeks, and must be completed to maximize the chances of treatment success (Pawlotsky et al. 2015). Recommendations from the American Association for the Study of Liver Diseases and the Infectious Diseases Society of America include that for people with a current HCV infection, they should be assessed by a clinician, and provided with a comprehensive management strategy, including information on the DAA therapy options available. If a CCO is working with a supervisee who has been diagnosed with HCV and is receiving treatment, then the CCO should ensure that the treatment can continue uninterrupted through the release process, and should be aware of the type of treatment, time left until treatment completion, and who the treating physician is for individual supervisees.

HIV

Recent research has provided strong evidence that recent advances in antiretroviral therapy (ART) have made it possible for HIV progression to be prevented, for clinical outcomes to be improved (Temprano 2015; Insight Start Study G 2015), and for better quality of life outcomes (Lifson et al. 2017), when ART is started within two weeks of HIV diagnosis, and then maintained and monitored according to the recommendations of the US Panel of the International Antiviral Society (Günthard et al. 2016). Despite the evidence that effective treatment is available, research conducted in Texas prisons showed that 30% or fewer HIV-positive patients enrolled in HIV care programmes in the period after release from prison (Baillargeon et al. 2009; Baillargeon 2010). Among the reasons for this cited in the research are unstable housing, unemployment, drug use, and mental illness (Haley et al. 2014; Nunn et al. 2010). HIV-positive patients who use drugs or alcohol face difficulties being treated effectively for HIV, resulting in higher rates of mortality for this group (Baum et al. 2009; Kamarulzaman and Altice 2015).

Transitional planning to improve outcomes

For HIV-positive patients who are incarcerated and released, there is a range of evidence suggesting that transitional care planning during incarceration results in a higher proportion of HIV-positive patients accessing ART (Baillargeon et al. 2009), and being administered ART at recommended doses, resulting in fewer ED visits post-release (Teixeira et al. 2015). People with HIV leaving prison also reported that assistance to navigate the health system during transition and after release also resulted in better continuity of HIV care (Fuller et al. 2018). A trial of an intensive case management programme for HIV-positive patients found that there was no increase in utilization of health services after release from prison when compared to less intensive pre-release discharge planning (Wohl et al. 2011). This suggests that standard pre-release discharge planning should be a basic requirement for all supervis-ees who are HIV-positive, and that post-release support to assist this group with navigating the health system (particularly in relation to their HIV-related needs) is essential to ensuring that treatment continues once they have left prison.

Non-communicable diseases

Research conducted around the world suggests that after standardizing for age, prison inmates experience higher rates of hypertension, persistent asthma, obesity, and previous heart attack than their counterparts in the community (Wilper et al. 2009; Herbert et al. 2012). These diseases are often the result of modifiable lifestyle factors, and can be treated or managed through lifestyle change (such as improved diet and exercise), and/or appropriate medication. As has been discussed, identifying these diseases in individuals is the first step in ensuring that they are treated and managed effectively. This is a challenge, as United States research suggests that a substantial number of inmates with chronic conditions at federal, state, and local correctional facilities are not medically examined during incarceration (Wilper et al. 2009), making iden-tification of these conditions difficult in many facilities. More troubling is the disruption in medication for many of those with known existing condi-tions that they were taking medication for prior to incarceration (Wilper et al. 2009). Continuity of care, whether it be ongoing monitoring or treatment of chronic conditions, is essential to ensuring the best possible health outcomes for people moving through the prison system and transitioning back into the community. When CCOs identify that medical examinations are not being routinely or sufficiently performed in prison facilities that their supervisees are leaving, they should prioritize having attendees attend a community health service for a health check upon release, to ensure that any preventable or treatable conditions can be identified as early as possible.

Marginalized sub-groups

Within the prison population, there are sub-groups of people who are particu-larly marginalized who inherently experience poorer health than the general community regardless of their legal status. A prime example is Indigenous people around the world, who experience preventable conditions such as car-diovascular disease, type 2 diabetes, and infectious disease such as tuberculo-sis at higher rates than their non-Indigenous counterparts (Gracey and King 2009). CCOs that are working with people from marginalized sub-groups such as these should be aware that they may be at a greater risk of experiencing particular health conditions than the general prison population, so additional screening and treatment may be necessary in some cases.

Intellectual and cognitive disability and brain injury

People with intellectual and other cognitive disability are over-represented in the prison population (Hayes et al. 2007; Søndenaa et al. 2008; Dias et al. 2013; Hassiotis et al. 2011). Traumatic brain injury (TBI) is also associated with being convicted of an offence (Schofield et al. 2015), with people who have a history of TBI also over-represented in the prison population (Shiroma et al. 2010). A big challenge for this group collectively is having their disability or condition identified and acknowledged during incarceration so that the necessary service planning can be done prior to release from prison (Baldry et al. 2013).

The importance of identifying intellectual disability

Recent Australian research found that people who were identified with intellectual disability prior to their release from prison were more likely to report greater confidence and motivation to self-manage their health needs than people who screened positive for possible intellectual disability that was not identified prior to release from prison (Young et al. 2017). This suggests that identifying intellectual disability prior to release from prison is crucial to ensure that the necessary pre-release planning is done, and links are made with appropriate support services during the period of transition back into the community. Accordingly, screening for possible intellectual disability during a prisoner's sentence should be a priority. These can be done easily in a few minutes using a tool such as the Hayes Ability Screening Index (Hayes 2000). Those identified with possible intellectual disability should then be referred for additional diagnostic testing to ascertain actual intellectual disability, which can then be considered in pre-release planning.

Accessing support

Once intellectual disability has been properly identified, the mechanism for accessing support services differs between countries. For example, Australia launched its National Disability Insurance Scheme (NDIS n.d.) in 2013, a scheme that covers intellectual disability and provides 'reasonable and necessary supports they need to live an ordinary life' to any Australian with 'permanent and significant disability' (NDIS n.d.); a similar scheme is in operation in the United Kingdom (UK Government n.d.). CCOs in jurisdictions with similar schemes to Australia and the United Kingdom should be aware of the support that is available through their respective schemes, who is eligible, and what the process is for accessing it. These processes should be undertaken during the period prior to release from prison, so that supervisees have the necessary support available from the time they are released into the community, making continuity of care possible.

In the United States, no such national scheme is in operation, with intellectual disability support services largely provided by a range of regional services such as The Arc (The Arc n.d.), or the American Association on Intellectual and Developmental Disabilities (AAIDD n.d.). Medicaid is generally available to cover health service costs for people with disability (Medicaid n.d.a); however, non-health disability support services are not included in the mandatory benefits list, and may not be provided in every state (Medicaid n.d.b). Accordingly, CCOs in the United States should be aware of the schemes or services available in their region, and what the process is for eligible supervisees to obtain support upon their release.

Improving access to health services: a simple intervention

To investigate how engagement with health services after release could be improved, a randomized controlled trial of a low-intensity case-management intervention was conducted as part of the HARP study in Queensland, Australia between 2008 and 2010 (Kinner et al. 2016). Each participant receiving case management was provided with a personalized booklet that provided participants with tailored information regarding their treatment needs, and where to find the relevant services in the community (Kinner et al. 2016). In addition to this, each participant in the case-management group received up to four follow-up phone calls in the community to assist participants to access health services based on the needs they identified (Kinner et al. 2016). The participants who received the intervention were more likely to have GP contact at one, three, and six months after release from prison, and were more likely to have contact with a mental health service in the six months after release (Kinner et al. 2016). This suggests that simply providing supervisees with information upon release about where to access community health services, in combination with a follow-up phone call every four to six weeks, would increase their chances of maintaining contact with primary and mental health services. Given that supervisees are generally required to report and maintain contact with CCOs whilst under supervision, ensuring that access to relevant health services is included as part of any needs assessment, and followed up by CCOs during this period would be a step towards ensuring supervisees receive the healthcare they need.

Conclusion

The evidence is clear that people who go to prison often have a multitude of health problems that require treatment. Despite this, prison health services are often not equipped to identify and manage these problems adequately during incarceration, meaning that many individuals are released back into the community with ongoing problems that put them at an increased risk of adverse health events, including death, and also re-incarceration. This means that CCOs supervising this group upon their release into the community must consider risks associated with poor health when conducting risk and needs assessments. To inform this process, this chapter considered some of the most prevalent health problems that people who go to prison experience, as well as possible strategies for managing or treating them during transition from prison to the community. Whilst some of the treatment options discussed are intensive and complex, there is good evidence that even simple broad-based interventions aimed at promoting engagement with primary healthcare after release from prison can be an important step in the identification and treatment of health problems in the period after release.

References

AAIDD. American Association on Intellectual and Developmental Disabilities. (n.d.) Available at: http://aaidd.org/.

Andrews, J. Y. and Kinner, S. A. (2012) Understanding drug-related mortality in released prisoners: A review of national coronial records. *BMC Public Health*, 12(1), 270.

The Arc. (n.d.) *The Arc: For People with Intellectual and Developmental Disabilities*. Available at: www.thearc.org/.

Australian Institute of Health and Welfare. (2015) *The Health of Australia's Prisoners*. Contract No. Cat. No. PHE 207. Canberra: AIHW.

Bahr, S. J., Masters, A. L. and Taylor, B. M. (2012) What works in substance abuse treatment programs for offenders? *The Prison Journal*, 92(2), 155–174.

Baillargeon, J. G., Binswanger, I. A., Penn, J. V., Williams, B. A., Murray, O. J. (2009) Psychiatric disorders and repeat incarcerations: The revolving prison door. *American Journal of Psychiatry*, 166(1), 103–109.

Baillargeon, J. G., Giordano, T. P., Harzke, A. J., Baillargeon, G., Rich, J. D., Paar, D. P. (2010) Enrollment in outpatient care among newly released prison inmates with HIV infection. *Public Health Reports*, 125(Supplement 1), 64–71.

Baillargeon, J. G., Giordano, T. P., Rich, J. D., Wu, Z. H., Wells, K., Pollock, B. H., et al. (2009) Accessing antiretroviral therapy following release from prison. *JAMA*, 301(8), 848–857.

Baillargeon, J. G., Penn, J. V., Knight, K., Harzke, A. J., Baillargeon, G., Becker, E. A. (2010) Risk of reincarceration among prisoners with co-occurring severe mental illness and substance use disorders. *Administration and Policy in Mental Health and Mental Health Services Research*, 37(4), 367–374.

Baillargeon, J. G., Williams, B. A., Mellow, J., Harzke, A. J., Hoge, S. K., Baillargeon, G., et al. (2009) Parole revocation among prison inmates with psychiatric and substance use disorders. *Psychiatric Services*, 60(11), 1516–1521.

Baldry, E., Clarence, M., Dowse, L. and Trollor, J. (2013) Reducing vulnerability to harm in adults with cognitive disabilities in the Australian criminal justice system. *Journal of Policy and Practice in Intellectual Disabilities*, 10(3), 222–229.

Baum, M. K., Rafie, C., Lai, S., Sales, S., Page, B. and Campa, A. (2009) Crack-cocaine use accelerates HIV disease progression in a cohort of HIV-positive drug users. *JAIDS Journal of Acquired Immune Deficiency Syndromes*, 50(1), 93–99.

Binswanger, I. A., Blatchford, P. J., Mueller, S. R. and Stern, M. F. (2013) Mortality after prison release: Opioid overdose and other causes of death, risk factors, and time trends from 1999 to 2009. *Annals of Internal Medicine*, 159(9), 592–600.

Binswanger, I. A., Nowels, C., Corsi, K. F., Glanz, J., Long, J., Booth, R. E., et al. (2012) Return to drug use and overdose after release from prison: A qualitative study of risk and protective factors. *Addiction Science & Clinical Practice*, 7(1), 3.

Binswanger, I. A., Nowels, C., Corsi, K. F., Long, J., Booth, R. E., Kutner, J., et al. (2011) "From the prison door right to the sidewalk, everything went downhill," A qualitative study of the health experiences of recently released inmates. *International Journal of Law and Psychiatry*, 34(4), 249–255.

Binswanger, I. A., Stern, M. F., Deyo, R. A., Heagerty, P. J., Cheadle, A., Elmore, J. G., et al. (2007) Release from prison – a high risk of death for former inmates. *New England Journal of Medicine*, (356), 157–165.

Bird, S. M., McAuley, A., Perry, S. and Hunter, C. (2016) Effectiveness of Scotland's national naloxone programme for reducing opioid-related deaths: A before (2006–10) versus after (2011–13) comparison. *Addiction*, 111(5), 883–891.

Borschmann, R., Thomas, E., Moran, P., Carroll, M., Heffernan, E., Spittal, M. J., et al. (2017) Self-harm following release from prison: A prospective data linkage study. *Australian & New Zealand Journal of Psychiatry*, 51(3), 250–259.

Burgess, P., Pirkis, J., Morton, J. and Croke, E. (2000) Lessons from a comprehensive clinical audit of users of psychiatric services who committed suicide. *Psychiatric Services*, 51(12), 1555–1560.

Butler, T., Callander, D. and Simpson, M. (2015) *National Prison Entrants' Bloodborne Virus and Risk Behaviour Survey 2004, 2007, 2010 and 2013*. Sydney: Kirby Institute, UNSW Australia.

Butler, T., Indig, D., Allnutt, S. and Mamoon, H. (2011) Co-occurring mental illness and substance use disorder among Australian prisoners. *Drug and Alcohol Review*, 30(2), 188–194.

Cardarelli, R., Balyakina, E., Malone, K., Fulda, K. G., Ellison, M., Sivernell, R., et al. (2015) Suicide risk and mental health co-morbidities in a probationer population. *Community Mental Health Journal*, 51(2), 145–152.

Carroll, M., Spittal, M. J., Kemp-Casey, A. R., Lennox, N. G., Preen, D. B., Sutherland, G., et al. (2017) High rates of general practice attendance by former prisoners: A prospective cohort study. *The Medical Journal of Australia*, 207(2), 75–80.

Centers for Disease Control. (1992) *Youth Suicide Prevention Programs: A Resource Guide*. Atlanta, GA: US Department of Health and Human Services.

Chang, Z., Lichtenstein, P., Larsson, H. and Fazel, S. (2015) Substance use disorders, psychiatric disorders, and mortality after release from prison: A nationwide longitudinal cohort study. *The Lancet Psychiatry*, 2(5), 422–430.

Cornford, C., Sibbald, B., Baer, L., Buchanan, K., Mason, J, Thornton-Jones H, et al. (2007) *A Survey of the Delivery of Health Care in Prisons in Relation to Chronic Diseases*. Manchester: Prison Health Research Network, Primary Care.

Dias, S., Ware, R. S., Kinner, S. A. and Lennox, N. G. (2013) Co-occurring mental disorder and intellectual disability in a large sample of Australian prisoners. *Australian & New Zealand Journal of Psychiatry*, 47(10), 938–944.

Dolan, K., Moazen, B., Noori, A., Rahimzadeh, S., Farzadfar, F. and Hariga, F. (2015) People who inject drugs in prison: HIV prevalence, transmission and prevention. *International Journal of Drug Policy*, 26, S12–S15.

Farrell, M. and Marsden, J. (2008) Acute risk of drug-related death among newly released prisoners in England and Wales. *Addiction*, 103(2), 251–255.

Fazel, S. and Seewald, K. (2012) Severe mental illness in 33 588 prisoners worldwide: Systematic review and meta-regression analysis. *The British Journal of Psychiatry*, 200(5), 364–373.

Fazel, S., Bains, P. and Doll, H. (2006) Substance abuse and dependence in prisoners: A systematic review. *Addiction*, 101(2), 181–191.

Fazel, S., Cartwright, J., Norman-Nott, A. and Hawton, K. (2008) Suicide in prisoners: a systematic review of risk factors. *Journal of Clinical Psychiatry*, 69(11), 1721–1731.

Fazel, S., Hayes, A. J., Bartellas, K., Clerici, M., Trestman, R. (2016) Mental health of prisoners: Prevalence, adverse outcomes, and interventions. *The Lancet Psychiatry*, 3(9), 871–881.

Fuller, S. M., Koester, K. A., Maiorana, A., Steward, W. T., Broaddus, M. R., Lass, K., et al. (2018) "I don't have to do this all by myself": Systems navigation to ensure continuity of HIV care for persons leaving prison. *AIDS and Behavior*, 1–11.

Gould, M. S. and Kramer, R. A. (2001) Youth suicide prevention. *Suicide and Life-Threatening Behavior*, 31(Supplement 1), 6–31.

Gracey, M. and King, M. (2009) Indigenous health part 1: Determinants and disease patterns. *The Lancet*, 374(9683), 65–75.

Green, B., Denton, M., Heffernan, E., Russell, B., Stapleton, L. and Waterson, E. (2016) From custody to community: Outcomes of community-based support for mentally ill prisoners. *Psychiatry, Psychology and Law*, 23(5), 798–808.

Günthard, H. F., Saag, M. S., Benson, C. A., Del Rio, C., Eron, J. J., Gallant, J. E., et al. (2016) Antiretroviral drugs for treatment and prevention of HIV infection in adults: 2016 recommendations of the International Antiviral Society – USA panel. *JAMA*, 316(2), 191–210.

Haley, D. F., Golin, C. E., Farel, C. E., Wohl, D. A., Scheyett, A. M., Garrett, J. J., et al. (2014) Multilevel challenges to engagement in HIV care after prison release: A theory-informed qualitative study comparing prisoners' perspectives before and after community reentry. *BMC Public Health*, 14(1), 12–53.

Hassiotis, A., Gazizova, D., Akinlonu, L., Bebbington, P., Meltzer, H. and Strydom, A. (2011) Psychiatric morbidity in prisoners with intellectual disabilities: Analysis of prison survey data for England and Wales. *The British Journal of Psychiatry*. DOI:10.1192/bjp.bp.110.088039.

Hayes, S. C. (2000) *Hayes Ability Screening Index (HASI) Manual*. Sydney, Australia: Department of Behavioural Sciences in Medicine.

Hayes, S. C., Shackell, P., Mottram, P. and Lancaster, R. (2007) The prevalence of intellectual disability in a major UK prison. *British Journal of Learning Disabilities*, 35(3), 162–167.

Herbert, K., Plugge, E., Foster, C. and Doll, H. (2012) Prevalence of risk factors for non-communicable diseases in prison populations worldwide: A systematic review. *The Lancet*, 379(9830), 1975–1982.

Hobbs, M., Krazlan, K., Ridout, S., Mai, Q., Knuiman, M. and Chapman, R. (2006) Mortality and morbidity in prisoners after release from prison in Western Australia 1995–2003. Research and Public Policy Series, no. 71. Canberra: Australian Institute of Criminology.

Indig, D. (2016) *Comorbid Substance Use Disorders and Mental Health Disorders Among New Zealand Prisoners*. Wellington: New Zealand Department of Corrections.

Insight Start Study G. (2015) Initiation of antiretroviral therapy in early asymptomatic HIV infection. *New England Journal of Medicine*, 373(9), 795–807.

Isaac, M., Elias, B., Katz, L. Y., Belik, S. L., Deane, F. P., Enns, M. W., et al. (2009) Gatekeeper training as a preventative intervention for suicide: A systematic review. *The Canadian Journal of Psychiatry*, 54(4), 260–268.

James, D. J. and Glaze, L. E. (2006) *Mental Health Problems of Prison and Jail Inmates*. Bureau of Justice Statistics Special Report.

Kamarulzaman, A. and Altice, F. L. (2015) The challenges in managing HIV in people who use drugs. *Current Opinion in Infectious Diseases*, 28(1), 10.

Kinner, S. A., Alati, R., Longo, M., Spittal, M. J., Boyle, F. M., Williams, G. M., et al. (2016) Low-intensity case management increases contact with primary care in recently released prisoners: A single-blinded, multisite, randomized controlled trial. *Journal of Epidemiology and Community Health*. DOI:10.1136/jech-2015-206565.

Kinner, S. A., Lennox, N., Williams, G. M., Carroll, M., Quinn, B., Boyle, F. M., et al. (2013) Randomised controlled trial of a service brokerage intervention for ex-prisoners in Australia. *Contemporary Clinical Trials*, 36(1), 198–206.

Kinner, S. A. and Wang, E. A. (2014) The case for improving the health of ex-prisoners. *American Journal of Public Health*, 104(8), 1352–1355.

Larney, S., Topp, L., Indig, D., O'Driscoll, C. and Greenberg, D. (2012) A cross-sectional survey of prevalence and correlates of suicidal ideation and suicide attempts among prisoners in New South Wales, Australia. *BMC Public Health*, 12(1), 14.

Lifson, A. R., Grund, B., Gardner, E. M., Kaplan, R., Denning, E., Engen, N., et al. (2017) Improved quality of life with immediate initiation of antiretroviral therapy in the strategic timing of antiretroviral therapy trial. *AIDS*, 31, 953–963.

Medicaid. (n.d.a) *Eligibility*. Available at: https://www.medicaid.gov/medicaid/eligibility/index.html.

Medicaid. (n.d.b) *List of Medicaid Benefits*. Available at: www.medicaid.gov/medicaid/benefits/list-of-benefits/index.html.

Merrall, E. L. C., Kariminia, A., Binswanger, I. A., Hobbs, M. S., Farrell, M., Marsden, J., et al. (2010) Meta-analysis of drug-related deaths soon after release from prison. *Addiction*, 105(9), 1545–1554.

Meyer, J. P., Chen, N. E. and Springer, S. A. (2011) HIV treatment in the criminal justice system: critical knowledge and intervention gaps. *AIDS Research and Treatment*, 2011. DOI:10.1155/2011/680617.

Mir-Nasseri, M. M., MohammadKhani, A., Tavakkoli, H., Ansari, E. and Poustchi, H. (2011) Incarceration is a major risk factor for blood-borne infection among intravenous drug users: Incarceration and blood-borne infection among intravenous drug users. *Hepatitis Monthly*, 11(1), 19.

NDIS. (n.d.) *Our History*. Available at: www.ndis.gov.au/about-us/our-history.html.

Nunn, A., Cornwall, A., Fu, J., Bazerman, L., Loewenthal, H. and Beckwith, C. (2010) Linking HIV-positive jail inmates to treatment, care, and social services after release: Results from a qualitative assessment of the COMPASS program. *Journal of Urban Health*, 87(6), 954–968.

Pawlotsky, J-M., Aghemo, A., Back, D., Dusheiko, G., Forns, X., Puoti, M., et al. (2015) EASL recommendations on treatment of hepatitis C. *Journal of Hepatology*, 63(1), 199–236.

Petersilia, J. (2005) From cell to society: Who is returning home? *Prisoner Reentry and Crime in America*, 15–49.

Piselli, M., Attademo, L., Garinella, R., Rella, A., Antinarelli, S., Tamantini, A., et al. (2015) Psychiatric needs of male prison inmates in Italy. *International Journal of Law and Psychiatry*, 41, 82–88.

Pratt, D., Piper, M., Appleby, L., Webb, R. and Shaw, J. (2006) Suicide in recently released prisoners: A population-based cohort study. *The Lancet*, 368(9530), 119–123.

Scheyett, A., Vaughn, J. and Taylor, M. F. (2009) Screening and access to services for individuals with serious mental illnesses in jails. *Community Mental Health Journal*, 45(6), 439.

Schofield, P. W., Malacova, E., Preen, D. B., D'Este, C., Tate, R., Reekie, J., et al. (2015) Does traumatic brain injury lead to criminality? A whole-population retrospective cohort study using linked data. *PLoS One*, 10(7), e0132558.

Shiroma, E. J., Ferguson, P. L. and Pickelsimer, E. E. (2010) Prevalence of traumatic brain injury in an offender population: A meta-analysis. *Journal of Correctional Health Care*, 16(2), 147–159.

Smith, N. E. and Trimboli, L. (2010) Comorbid substance and non-substance mental health disorders and re-offending among NSW prisoners. *BOCSAR NSW Crime and Justice Bulletins*, 16.

Somers, J. M., Rezansoff, S. N., Moniruzzaman, A., Zabarauckas, C. (2015) High-frequency use of corrections, health, and social services, and association with mental illness and substance use. *Emerging Themes in Epidemiology*, 12(1), 17.

Søndenaa, E., Rasmussen, K., Palmstierna, T. and Nøttestad, J. (2008) The prevalence and nature of intellectual disability in Norwegian prisons. *Journal of Intellectual Disability Research*, 52(12), 1129–1137.

Spaulding, A. C., Seals, R. M., McCallum, V. A., Perez, S. D., Brzozowski, A. K., Steenland, N. K. (2011) Prisoner survival inside and outside of the institution: Implications for health-care planning. *American Journal of Epidemiology*, 173(5), 479–487.

Spittal, M. J., Forsyth, S., Borschmann, R., Young, J. and Kinner, S. (2017) Modifiable risk factors for external cause mortality after release from prison: A nested case – control study. *Epidemiology and Psychiatric Sciences*, 1–10.

Spittal, M. J., Forsyth, S., Pirkis, J., Alati, R. and Kinner, S. A. (2014) *Suicide in Adults Released from Prison in Queensland*. Australia: A Cohort Study. *Journal of Epidemiology & Community Health*. DOI:10.1136/jech-2014-204295.

Springer, S. A., Spaulding, A. C., Meyer, J. P. and Altice, F. L. (2011) Public health implications for adequate transitional care for HIV-infected prisoners: Five essential components. *Clinical Infectious Diseases*, 53(5), 469–479.

Stewart, L. M., Henderson, C. J., Hobbs, M. S. T., Ridout, S. C. and Knuiman, M. W. (2004) Risk of death in prisoners after release from jail. *Australian and New Zealand Journal of Public Health*, 28(1), 32–36.

Strang, J., Bird, S. M. and Parmar, M. K. (2013) Take-home emergency naloxone to prevent heroin overdose deaths after prison release: Rationale and practicalities for the N-ALIVE randomized trial. *Journal of Urban Health*, 90(5), 983–996.

Teixeira, P. A., Jordan, A. O., Zaller, N., Shah, D. and Venters, H. (2015) Health outcomes for HIV-infected persons released from the New York City jail system with a transitional care-coordination plan. *American Journal of Public Health*, 105(2), 351–357.

Temprano, A. S. G. (2015) A trial of early antiretrovirals and isoniazid preventive therapy in Africa. *New England Journal of Medicine*, 373(9), 808–822.

Thomas, E. G., Spittal, M. J., Taxman, F. S., Kinner, S. A. (2015) Health-related factors predict return to custody in a large cohort of ex-prisoners: New approaches to predicting re-incarceration. *Health & Justice*, 3(1), 10.

UK Government. (n.d.) *Disabled People*. Available at: www.gov.uk/browse/disabilities.

While, D., Bickley, H., Roscoe, A., Windfuhr, K., Rahman, S., Shaw, J., et al. (2012) Implementation of mental health service recommendations in England and Wales and suicide rates, 1997–2006: A cross-sectional and before-and-after observational study. *The Lancet*, 379(9820), 1005–1012.

Wilper, A. P., Woolhandler, S., Boyd, J. W., Lasser, K. E., McCormick, D., Bor, D. H., et al. (2009) The health and health care of US prisoners: Results of a nationwide survey. *American Journal of Public Health*, 99(4), 666–672.

Wohl, D. A., Scheyett, A., Golin, C. E., White, B., Matuszewski, J., Bowling, M., et al. (2011) Intensive case management before and after prison release is no more effective than comprehensive pre-release discharge planning in linking HIV-infected prisoners to care: A randomized trial. *AIDS and Behavior*, 15(2), 356–364.

Young, J. T., Cumming, C., Dooren, K., Lennox, N. G., Alati, R., Spittal, M. J., et al. (2017) Intellectual disability and patient activation after release from prison: A prospective cohort study. *Journal of Intellectual Disability Research*, 61(10), 939–956.

Rights, advocacy, and transformation

46

Cormac Behan

Introduction

The modern prison was established as a place of reform. Through its buildings, administration, regimes, and technologies, it hoped to engender change in those it confined (O'Donnell 2016). As soon as the prison was created, the limitations on its potential to create an environment suitable for transformation became apparent. Demands were soon made to make it a more apposite place to promote change. Charles Dickens, on his visit to the Eastern State Penitentiary (1842 [2000]: 82), the early noble experiment in penal transformation recounted how:

> The system here is rigid, strict, and hopeless solitary confinement. I believe in its effects to be cruel and wrong. In its intention, I am well convinced that it is kind, humane and meant for reformation; but I am convinced that those who devised this system of Prison Discipline, and those benevolent gentlemen who carry it into execution, do not know what they are doing. I believe few men are capable of estimating the immense amount of torture and agony which this dreadful punishment, prolonged for years, inflicts upon the sufferers. . . . I am only the more convinced that there is a depth of terrible endurance in it which none but the sufferers can fathom, and which no man has the right to inflict upon his fellow-creature.

Honourable intentions were no guarantee of virtuous outcomes. Over 200 years after the birth of the modern prison, the debates are ongoing about whether the institution is criminogenic, does more harm than good, and is un-reformable (Ryan and Sim 2016). The fading of the optimism of the early reformers has led to a discussion about a more minimalist 21st-century reality, a reformulation of its objectives, with the aim of imprisonment to 'reconstitute the prisoner's spatiotemporal world without causing avoidable collateral damage' (O'Donnell 2016: 39). Nevertheless, while the prison exists, advocates on all sides of the debate call for it to become – either through more austere or liberal conditions and regimes – a place of change, whether that is termed reform, rehabilitation, personal development, or transformation.

This chapter will consider the potential for transformation in prison, utilizing the lens of citizenship. While primarily concentrating on England and Wales the challenges faced in promoting transformation in prison will have resonance elsewhere. The structure of the chapter is as follows: it begins by reviewing a limited number of prisoners' rights, concentrating on opportunities for prisoners to act as agents, with some control over their destiny. It then juxtaposes 'soft' versus 'hard' citizenship activities and explores the prospects for creating a penal culture that allows for both of these within a mosaic of citizenship. The chapter concludes that if prison is to become an institution in which prisoners are to be encouraged to transform their lives, this necessitates changes on a number of levels: removing legal impediments to civic and political participation, reforming prison governance, transforming penal culture, along with social and structural changes to allow former prisoners to reintegrate into society after they have served their time.

Prisoners as citizens

The European Court of Human Rights in the *Hirst* case ruled that 'prisoners in general continue to enjoy all the fundamental rights and freedoms guaranteed under the Convention save for the right to liberty, where lawfully imposed' (*Hirst v. United Kingdom* [No. 2] 2005). Along with this and other jurisprudence in the English courts setting out prisoners' rights (Easton 2011; Scott 2013a), there is an abundance of declarations, policy documents, conventions, and international agreements dealing, either explicitly or implicitly, with prisoners' rights. These date back to the European Convention on Human Rights (1950), along with the International Convention on Civic and Political Rights (1966), and more recently include the revised United Nations Standard Minimum Rules for the Treatment of Prisoners (The Mandela Rules) (2015), European Prison Rules ([EPR] 1987, 2006), and Prison Rules for England and Wales (1999). This section will examine three spheres for prisoners to be bearers of rights: access to the vote, the right to influence the governance of their community, and the right to redress.

Due to the long-running and contested debates on prisoners and voting in the United Kingdom, there has been widespread examination of this issue (see, for example, Behan 2014a; Easton 2009, 2011; Livingstone et al. 2008; van Zyl Smit and Snacken 2009). Despite the European Court of Human Rights's ruling that the UK's blanket ban on all sentenced prisoners from voting contravened the European Convention of Human Rights, successive governments refused to amend legislation in response. Over five years after the judgement, the House of Commons reaffirmed this ban by 234 to 22 (*Hansard*, HC Debates, 10 February 2011, vol. 523, col. 502). The UK government's refusal to comply with the ruling led to it being censured regularly by the Committee of Ministers of the Council of Europe. Ten years after the judgement, the Committee of Ministers 'expressed profound concern that the blanket ban on the right of convicted prisoners in custody remains in place' and further, 'reaffirmed, that as with all Contracting Parties, the United Kingdom has an obligation . . . to abide by judgments of the Court' (Committee of Ministers 2015).

Twelve years after the ruling the UK government gave their response to the *Hirst* judgement. The Secretary of State for Justice, David Lidington, was determined that, despite the judgement, the government would not depart 'from the principle that it is reasonable to clearly tell someone who has been sentenced to prison . . . that they have forfeited the right to vote as a consequence'. However, the United Kingdom would uphold its obligations 'consistent with British values of rights and responsibilities'. The ban on prisoners in custody voting would be maintained, but prisoners who are on release on temporary licence (ROTL) and registered would now be allowed to vote if they were not in prison on election day. This permits approximately 100 prisoners out of just under 86,000 (ICPR 2017) to vote. The measure, David Lidington assured the House of Commons, required 'no changes to the Representation of the People Act 1983, but instead will entail a change to Prison Service guidance' (*Hansard*, HC Debates, 2 November 2017, vol. 630, col. 1008). These administrative changes and alterations in guidance finally resolved the issue to the satisfaction of the Committee of Ministers (Bowcott 2017).

Despite the overwhelming majority of sentenced prisoners not having the prospect of voting, there are other opportunities for them to act as citizens. Prisoner councils allow prisoners to participate in the governance of their immediate community. As part of a deliberative process, prisoner councils give a voice to prisoners, allow them to assert their agency by conveying and in some cases representing their views on prison conditions and treatment more generally to prison authorities (Bishop 2006). Prisoner councils are allowed under the 2006 EPR (Rule 50), and were promoted by the Woolf Report as means for prisoners 'to contribute to and be informed of the way things are run' (Woolf, cited in Solomon and Edgar 2004: 3).

Another way for prisoners to express their agency within their communities is through engagement with accountability and oversight bodies. This allows prisoners to assert and protect their rights, which can lead to improvements in their conditions of confinement and enhance prison life for themselves, their fellow prisoners, and prison staff. In England and Wales, a tripartite model of accountability and oversight consists of Independent Monitoring Boards, Her Majesty's Chief Inspector of Prisons, and the final arbiter of complaints adjudication, the Prisons and Probation Ombudsman ([PPO] Behan and Kirkham 2016). In the first instance, prisoners in England and Wales can try to resolve local issues through engagement with their Independent Monitoring Board. Failure to find a resolution locally can eventually lead to an appeal to the Prisons and Probation Ombudsman. While Her Majesty's Inspectorate of Prisons does not deal with individual complaints, it carries out whole prison inspections which assess the conditions of confinement and provide benchmarks by which to judge the standards within individual institutions. Ultimately, prisoners can appeal to the courts to seek redress for particularly serious issues.

'Soft' and 'hard' citizenship

Citizenship activities and civic engagement do not take place in a vacuum. In any society, they occur in a social, political, and legal context. In terms of prisoners, there is the added penal context. By its very nature, prison limits freedom of choice and movement, and restricts an individual's agency, thereby undermining their potential to pursue activities associated with citizenship.

This section identifies two different types of citizenship in prison: 'soft' citizenship, where prisoners are encouraged to participate in volunteering and even organize charitable events approved by prison authorities, and 'hard' citizenship, where prisoners, as bearers of rights, become advocates and even activists in asserting their political and civil rights. While 'hard' citizenship rights are restricted by imprisonment, even where they do exist, prisoners do not always feel confident when attempting to translate these 'rights on the books' into 'rights in action'.

In England and Wales, many prisoners participate in charitable and volunteering activities associated with active citizenship (Burnett and Maruna 2006; Faulkner 2002, 2003; Levenson and Farrant 2002; Prison Reform Trust 2017; Pryor 2002). Some institutions provide opportunities for various types of purposeful activity, programme participation, and activities that promote civic engagement. These include Listener Schemes (Levenson and Farrant 2002), volunteering (Behan 2014a; Burnett and Maruna 2006), the Paws for Progress programme (Scott 2013b), educational pursuits (Behan 2014b), and active citizen forums (Prison Reform Trust 2017). These are some examples of what may be termed 'soft' citizenship. While recognizing that these 'strengths-based practices . . . provide opportunities . . . to develop pro-social self-concepts and identity' (Burnett and Maruna 2006: 84), they are within the parameters set out by the prison regime, either nationally or locally.

Few would oppose these citizenship activities and most would commend prisoners who participate and thereby demonstrate the potential of harnessing their time, energy, and commitment in pursuit of the greater good.

However, when the debate moves into the realm of prisoners as bearers of citizenship rights – for the purposes of this chapter termed hard citizenship – it becomes more complex. For example, the compromise offered by the UK government on prisoner voting may satisfy the Committee of Ministers and the ECtHR, but it is a minimalist approach that adheres to the letter rather than the spirit of the judgement. It signals to confined and free citizens alike, that even when the highest court to which they could appeal finds against them, when it comes to prisoners as bearers of rights, the UK government will do the minimum necessary to adhere to such judgements.[1]

Although they do not operate in all prisons in England and Wales, prisoner councils have functioned with mixed results, depending on a number of factors including the category of prison and attitude of the local prison management. While prisoners have a right to representative associations, it is a qualified right (Prison Service Order 4480: Prisoners Representation Association). There are strict limitations on the role and powers of prisoner councils. They cannot be facilitated through cross-institutional representation and have no standing outside individual institutions. Prisoner councils have no right to negotiate with national authorities. Governors and prison directors must be allowed to take account of good order and/or discipline in their operation and personal and security issues are outside the remit of prisoner councils (PSO 4480).

While the tripartite model of prison oversight and accountability has led to improvements in prison governance, concerns have been reported by prisoners that their 'rights on the books' do not always translate into 'rights in action'. These relate to how prisoners access accountability and monitoring bodies, procedural fairness, trust, independence and legitimacy, and ultimately fear of negative consequences (Behan and Kirkham 2016). In his 2014–2015 Annual Report, HM Chief Inspector of Prisons for England and Wales (2015: 12) admitted that 'prisoners had little confidence in the complaints system'. In one PPO study, one young participant said that even if he had a complaint, he would 'just get on with it' (cited in Prisons and Probation Ombudsman 2015: 14). Both women and young prisoners felt that because they had broken the law and ended up in prison, they did not have a right to complain and would just have to put up with ill treatment (Prisons and Probation Ombudsman 2015: 14). Many prisoners feared that to be seen to be complaining could have negative consequences for their sentence, with the threat of being 'ghosted' (or transferred) to another prison.

The mosaic of citizenship

The facilitation of activities traditionally associated with freedom and necessary for participative citizenship is problematic in prisons, which are 'the ultimate places of social exclusion' (Stern 2002: 138). It presents challenges on a number of levels, not only for confined citizens, but also for those who are tasked with running prisons. However, the modern prison is not a monolith. As outlined above, there are practices and places in prisons that allow for soft, and less frequently, hard citizenship activities and rights. Nevertheless, both hard and soft elements of citizenship are essential to complete what is termed, for the purposes of this chapter, the mosaic of citizenship. In a modern polity, citizenship is more than just about the responsibility to give back to the community for breaking the law as demonstrated through volunteering and charitable activities; it must also allow for opportunities to participate in, and contribute to, civil and political society. 'Citizenship is not about rights and membership of a polity, but is a matter of participation in the political community . . . citizenship concerns identity and action' (Delanty 2003: 602). There are a number of ways that prisoners could be supported to *identify* as citizens, thus encouraging them to *act* as citizens, and vice versa.

Prisoners in many of the UK's European neighbouring jurisdictions are allowed to vote, without undermining the democratic polity or eroding respect for the rule of law (Behan 2014a: 43–44). If this right was extended to prisoners in the UK, it might act as one of 'hooks for change' identified in the desistance process (Giordano et al. 2002). Denying prisoners the right to vote is not only an added punishment beyond the denial of liberty, it reduces their identity as a citizen and it undermines the potential to participate in one of the most expressive ways in a democratic polity. Although not the only way of engaging in civic and political society, voting is one of most significant demonstrations of citizenship, and is indicative of further engagement (or disengagement). Lijphart (1997: 10) found a 'spill-over effect' from voting to participation in the workplace, churches, and voluntary organizations and vice versa. Civic participation led to higher levels of voting which, according to Putnam (2000: 35) is 'an instructive proxy measure of broader social change'. He continued:

> Compared to demographically matched non-voters, voters are more likely to be interested in politics, to give to charity, to volunteer, to serve on juries, to attend community school board meetings, to participate in public demonstrations, and to co-operate with their fellow citizens on community affairs. It is sometimes hard to tell whether voting causes community engagement or vice versa, although some recent evidence suggests that the act of voting itself encourages volunteering and other forms of good citizenship.

Allowing prisoners to vote may also encourage participation in more soft citizenship activities. It not only empowers citizens; it can also be another element in the transformative process of developing a pro-social identity when, on election day, individuals act as citizens rather than prisoners, identifying with other members of the polity.

Despite their limitations, prisoner councils offer prisoners an opportunity to participate in the governance of their community, improve prison culture, and engage in conflict resolution. The act of participating can be part of the process of transformation. Advocating for the more widespread adoption of prisoner councils, Solomon and Edgar (2004: 35) concluded that they are more than just representative opportunities for prisoners, but challenge society to see prisoners:

> in a new light, as citizens and individuals who have a right to make choices. Having a say about the conditions in which they are held and the politics that regulate their lives is a vital process of fostering personal responsibility. It is a recognition that prisoners are not powerless, but are members of a community which requires their consent if it is to exercise its authority legitimately.

In any organization or bureaucracy, reform from the top is important, but must be interlinked and make possible contributions from below. A prison management training manual in England and Wales argues that human rights consciousness 'suffuses all aspects of good prison management and is integral to it', and it emphasizes the 'importance of managing prisons within an ethical context which respects the humanity of everyone involved in a prison: prisoners, prison staff and visitors' (cited in Coyle 2009: 9). While undoubtedly those who exercise power in penal institutions have an obligation not to transgress the rights of prisoners in the exercise of their duties, the ultimate guarantors of rights in any context are those whom they affect most. This entails creating a culture where prisoners have the confidence to assert their rights. Prisoner councils can encourage prisoners to be active in protecting these rights and contribute to the improvement of prison life and community relations.

Promoting enhanced prisoner engagement with accountability and oversight bodies might encourage prisoners to take greater responsibility for their immediate community and encourage them to act out citizenship through participation. Interaction with the accountability and oversight bodies should be seen as a positive activity and a demonstration of active citizenship within the confines of prison walls. Drawing on Harbermas's (2001) idea of a deliberative democracy, engagement with these bodies might be interpreted as a civic activity to be encouraged inside. Such a move would require the reconfiguring of power relations in prison, at least in the context of complaints. Only then could prisoners be encouraged to complain, both formally and informally, confident in the knowledge that the act of complaining will not result in any negative consequences. This approach might lead to more complaints being made, but dealt with informally, without recourse to accountability frameworks. In turn, this might create an environment which encourages prisoners to become advocates. It might even reduce the need for professionalized structures in favour of resolving disputes through facilitating individual and community agency within the prison society.

Citizenship activities cover a wide mosaic. They encompass both soft and hard elements. Richardson (1983: 55) suggested that participation 'not only enhances the individual's ability to cope intelligently with a new range of issues' but also increases 'self-confidence to tackle problems in other spheres'. 'Participation' she concludes, 'is about making more fully developed human beings'. Legal changes and practical supports that encourage participation in a range of citizenship activities are necessary to enable and enhance active citizenship which is a learning process that has the potential to encourage transformation (Delanty 2003: 602). If the ultimate goal of imprisonment is to create law-abiding and transformed individuals, this chapter does not argue that changes in legislation alone will achieve this, because desistance from crime (essentially what governments and prison authorities term rehabilitation, or more widely viewed as change and/or transformation) is 'both an event and a process' (Maruna et al. 2004: 5). However, legislative changes including enfranchisement, have the potential to awaken the 'slumbering citizen' while recognizing the 'importance of maturation, positive social ties and the re-crafting of (stigmatized) identities in securing change' (McNeill and Velasquez 2017).

Conclusion

Civil and political restrictions have wider implications than just legal restraints; they can undermine prisoners' individual and collective agency. In order to strengthen and enhance the potential for transformation through citizenship, changes are necessary on a number of levels: prisoners should be allowed to vote; the role and powers of prisoner councils should be expanded, giving prisoners a greater say in their community. Penal culture needs to be rebalanced, with prisoners confident in exercising their right to engage with the accountability and oversight bodies and ultimately, the courts, without the fear of negative consequences. Where they do exist, greater efforts must be made to translate 'rights on the books' into 'rights in action'. Rights without the opportunity to affirm and exercise them can become meaningless. The best person/s to establish and assert their rights are the bearer of these rights. If citizens, even though confined, do not feel confident in resolving issues through established procedures, they can feel disempowered and/or civilly dead, reducing their sense of agency. Alternatively, if they feel the only avenue to guarantee political and civil rights is to resort to legal action, this erodes the power of the citizen to participate in, and influence decisions that affect their lives. The importance of political and civic activity is weakened, reducing the role of citizen as a human agent, with consequent undermining of their potential for active political participation and civic engagement. And, as Scott (2013a: 238) cautions, the judiciary in England and Wales have tended to be sympathetic to prison administrators in the application of the law, so 'any optimism and zeal for penal transformation through the courts must be qualified'.

Encouraging participation in a range of soft and hard citizenship activities recognizes both are important in the mosaic of citizenship. Supporting prisoners to become agents in asserting their hard citizenship rights means the emphasis becomes 'focused less on enabling prisoners know their place in society and more on enabling them to re-conceptualise their place in society' (Costelloe 2014: 33). Enhancing rather than restricting rights for prisoners is both a real and symbolic indication from government and society that it recognizes the possibilities for transformation through identifying, and acting out citizenship as part of that re-conceptualization. If one of the 'hooks for change' (Giordano et al. 2002) is through participation in a range of hard and soft citizenship activities, this requires more than just alterations in legislation and penal codes. It challenges governments, penal authorities, and society to see prisoners in a different light: as bearers of rights, with the capacity to be agents for change and the potential for transformation.

Note

1 At the time of writing, the Scottish Parliament through its Equality and Human Rights Committee is considering prisoners and voting in Scotland. A number of contributors to this book (including this author) have made oral and written submissions. See www.parliament.scot/parliamentarybusiness/CurrentCommittees/1060 33.aspx.

References

Behan, C. (2014a) *Citizen Convicts: Prisoners, Politics and the Vote*. Manchester: Manchester University Press.

Behan, C. (2014b) Learning to escape: Prison education, rehabilitation and the potential for transformation. *Journal of Prison Education and Re-Entry*, 1(1), 20–31.

Behan, C. and Kirkham, R. (2016) Monitoring, inspection and complaints adjudication in prison: The limits of prison accountability frameworks. *Howard Journal of Crime and Justice*, 55(4), 432–454.

Bishop, N. (2006) Prisoner participation in prisoner management. *Penal Field*, 3, 1–12.

Bowcott, O. (2017) Council of Europe accepts UK compromise on prisoner voting rights. *The Guardian*, 7 December.

Burnett, R. and Maruna, S. (2006) The kindness of strangers: Strengths-based resettlement in theory and action. *Criminology and Criminal Justice*, 6(1), 83–106.

Committee of Ministers. (2015) *Interim Resolution CM/ResDH (2015) 251*. Adopted by Meeting of Ministers Deputies 1234rd Meeting, 8–9 December.

Costelloe, A. (2014) Learning for liberation, teaching for transformation: Can education in prison prepare prisoners for citizenship? *Irish Journal of Applied Social Studies*, 4(1), 30–36.

Coyle, A. (2009) *A Human Rights Approach to Prison Management: Handbook for Prison Staff*. London: International Centre for Prison Studies.

Delanty, G. (2003) Citizenship as a learning process: Disciplinary citizenship versus cultural citizenship. *International Journal of Lifelong Learning*, 22(6), 579–605.

Dickens, C. (1842 [2000]) *American Notes*. London: Penguin.

Easton, S. (2009) The prisoner's right to vote and civic responsibility: Reaffirming the social contract? *Probation Journal*, 56, 224–237.

Easton, S. (2011) *Prisoners' Rights: Principles and Practice*. Oxford: Routledge.

Faulkner, D. (2002) Turning prisons inside-out. *Relational Justice*, 16, 1–3.

Faulkner, D. (2003) Taking citizenship seriously: Social capital and criminal justice in a changing world. *Criminal Justice*, 3(3), 287–315.

Giordano, P., Cernkovitch, S. and Rudolph, J. (2002) Gender, crime and desistance: Toward a theory of cognitive transformation. *American Journal of Sociology*, 107(4), 990–1064.

Habermas, J. (2001) *The Postnational Constellation*. Cambridge: Polity Press.

HM Chief Inspector of Prisons for England and Wales. (2015) *Annual Report 2014–15*. London: The Stationery Office.

Institute for Criminal Policy Research. (2017) *World Prison Brief*. Available at: www.prisonstudies.org/country/united-kingdom-england-wales (Accessed 30 November 2017).

Levenson, J. and Farrant, F. (2002) Unlocking potential: Active citizenship and volunteering by prisoners. *Probation Journal*, 49, 195–204.

Lijphart, A. (1997) Unequal participation: Democracy's unresolved dilemma. *American Political Science Review*, 91(1), 1–14.

Livingstone, S., Owen, T. and McDonald, A. (2008) *Prison Law*, 4th edition. Oxford: Oxford University Press.

Maruna, S., Immarigeon, R. and LeBel, T. (2004) Ex-offender re-integration: Theory and practice. In S. Maruna and R. Immarigeon (Eds.), *After Crime and Punishment: Pathways to Offender Re-Integration*. Cullompton: Willan Publishing.

McNeill, F. and Velasquez, J. (2017) *Prisoners, Disenfranchisement and Sleeping Citizenship*. Available at: https://sccjrblog.wordpress.com/2017/11/14/prisoners-disenfranchisement-and-sleeping-citizenship/ (Accessed 18 April 2018).

O'Donnell, I. (2016) The aims of imprisonment. In Y. Jewkes, J. Bennett and B. Crewe (Eds.), *Handbook on Prisons*, 2nd edition. London: Routledge.

Prison Reform Trust. (2017) *A Different Lens: Report on a Pilot Programme of Active Citizen Forums in Prison*. London: Prison Reform Trust.

Prisons and Probation Ombudsman. (2015) *Learning from PPO Investigations: Why Do Women and Young People in Custody Not Make Formal Complaints*. London: Prisons and Probation Ombudsman.

Pryor, S. (2002) The responsible prisoner. *Relational Justice*, 15, 1–3.

Putnam, R. (2000) *Bowling Alone: The Collapse and Revival of American Community*. New York: Simon and Shuster.

Richardson, A. (1983) *Participation*. London: Routledge, Keegan and Paul.

Ryan, M. and Sim, J. (2016) Campaigning for and campaigning against prisons: Excavating and reaffirming the case for prison abolition. In Y. Jewkes, J. Bennett and B. Crewe (Eds.), *Handbook on Prisons*, 2nd edition. London: Routledge.

Scott, D. (2013a) The politics of prisoner legal rights. *Howard Journal of Criminal Justice*, 52(3), 233–250.

Scott, K. (2013b) How dogs are teaching young offenders new tricks. *The Guardian*, 18 September. Available at: www.theguardian.com/society/2013/sep/17/how-dogs-teaching-young-offenders (Accessed 5 November 2016).

Solomon, E. and Edgar, K. (2004) *Having Their Say: The Work of Prisoner Councils*. London: Prison Reform Trust.

Stern, V. (2002) Prisoners as citizens: A comparative view. *Probation Journal*, 49, 130–139.

Van Zyl Smit, D. and Snacken, S. (2009) *Principles of European Prison Law and Policy: Penology and Human Rights*. Oxford: Oxford University Press.

Strengths-based re-entry and resettlement

47

Thomas P. LeBel

Introduction

Efforts to assist in the re-entry and resettlement of prisoners back into society have typically been either risk based or need based. However, strengths-based re-entry has been gaining traction in the 21st century as a 'third way', or new paradigm, for reducing recidivism and improving the quality of life of formerly incarcerated persons. There has been increasing recognition of the importance of strengths in many disciplines related to criminal justice including: strengths-based social work (Saleebey 2012), positive psychology (see Seligman and Csikszentmihalyi 2000), and addiction treatment, counselling, and 'recovery capital' (see Groshkova et al. 2013; Van Wormer and Davis 2018). Although strengths-based practices have received relatively limited attention in the criminal justice literature, scholars have increasingly called for the integration of this approach when engaging with correctional clients, especially those returning home from prison (see e.g. Maruna and LeBel 2003, 2009; Miller 2006; Van Wormer 2001; Ward and Stewart 2003). Recently, Ronel and Elisha 2011; Ronel and Segev 2015) proposed the concept of positive criminology that focuses on the personal strengths of offenders, and emphasizes protective factors. Similarly, Hucklesby and Hagley-Dickinson (2007: 294) argue that 'resettlement work should play to prisoners' strengths, working to empower prisoners to contribute positively to society and not concentrating exclusively on what they lack or are not doing'. As Ward (2017: 20) succinctly states, 'there has been a renewed attention to approaches oriented around resilience, protection, strengths, and positive psychology'.

Some scholars have suggested that strengths-based theories have arisen from research on how individuals 'go straight' or desist from crime 'on their own' or outside of structured interventions (Maruna et al. 2004). Maruna and LeBel (2003, 2009) discuss an approach that has been labelled as 'strengths based' or alternatively 'restorative re-entry' as it is based on principles fundamental to the restorative justice movement (see also Burnett and Maruna 2006; Maruna et al. 2003; Bazemore and Stinchcomb 2004). As opposed to risk- or need-based interventions, the focus is less on controlling or helping ex-prisoners and instead on treating them as individuals with talents and abilities to contribute to society. Strengths-based interventions recognize this by providing opportunities for individuals who have offended to make amends or 'earn redemption' (Bazemore 1999). This strengths model is premised both on a normative theory of justice based around restitution (see especially Eglash 1977), and an empirical theory of criminal recidivism based on labelling theory (overcoming stigma) or the 'looking-glass' self-concept (Maruna et al. 2004). Importantly, this strengths-based approach, as it relates to individuals involved with the criminal justice system, largely emerged from the perspective of 'success stories' themselves. Indeed, Clark (2012: 134) argues that '[t]he strengths perspective could well be construed as a "science" of utilizing an offender's perspective'.

Below a summary is provided of the extant literature on the implementation of prisoner re-entry-related strengths-based practices such as screening and assessment and other interventions. Moreover, how individuals desist from crime by engaging in strengths-based roles that explicitly involve help-giving (professional ex- or wounded healer) and/or advocacy efforts to contribute positively to their communities and society is examined.

Strengths-based screening and assessment

Serin et al. (2016: 157) suggest that the corrections 'field has generally embraced the importance of client strengths', although a clear consensus on terminology and definitions of these strengths is lacking. Ward (2017: 26) for example, posits 'that protective factors are the internal and external capacities and personal priorities that enhance individuals' well-being and reduce the likelihood that they will harm others or themselves'. In fact, the expanded Risk-Need-Responsivity (RNR) Model of Offender Assessment and Treatment (Andrews et al. 2011) now acknowledges the importance of offenders' strengths and motivations in successful rehabilitation practices. Bonta and Andrews (2017: 177) include 'strength' under the Core RNR Principles and Key Clinical Issues, and write that this principle requires one to 'assess strengths to enhance prediction and specific responsivity effects'.

Several assessment instruments for criminal justice-involved individuals have incorporated strengths including the Inventory of Offender Risk, Needs, and Strengths (IORNS; Miller 2006, 2015), the Service Planning Instrument (SPIn; Orbis Partners 2003; Jones et al. 2015), the Positive Psychological States (PPS; Woldgabreal et al. 2014, 2016), and the Dynamic Risk Assessment of Offender Reentry (DRAOR; Serin 2007). (See Serin et al. 2016 for a more detailed review of some of these assessment tools.) The IORNS developed by Miller (2006) includes a 26-item Protective Strength Index (PSI). Recently, in a study of sexual offenders, Miller (2015) found that self-perceived protective strengths were significantly (negatively) related to sexual, violent, and general recidivism. Jones and colleagues (2015) examined the role of strengths (over and above risk/needs) in predicting recidivism among an adult correctional population. Using data from the Service Planning Instrument (SPIn) Pre-Screen, they found that the inclusion of strengths added uniquely to the prediction of recidivism (Jones et al. 2015). Moreover, a significant interaction between the strength and risk scores indicated that higher strength scores were especially effective in reducing recidivism among the most high-risk adult offenders.

In an application of positive psychology to the assessment of criminal justice populations, Woldgabreal and colleagues (2014, 2016) examined the relationship between dimensions of Positive Psychological States (PPS) (i.e. psychological flexibility, self-efficacy, optimism, and hope) and offender supervision outcomes including technical violations, charges, reconviction, and imprisonment. This research found that offenders with higher PPS have fewer criminogenic risk factors and are less likely to have negative supervision outcomes (Woldgabreal et al. 2016). Importantly, they also concluded that the four dimensions of psychological states contribute to a single higher order factor that 'may buffer against risk of recidivism' (p. 713). Based on the limited but growing research in this area, the continued study and inclusion of strengths and protective/promotive factors in the assessment and treatment of prisoners and former prisoners is certainly warranted as it can potentially change the interaction between correctional staff and clients 'from one of risk avoidance and monitoring to one of challenging and supporting change and growth' (Serin et al. 2016: 164).

Other strengths-based applications and interventions

The Good Lives Model (GLM) was first proposed by Ward and Stewart in 2003. In the past 15 years it has been further developed by Ward and his colleagues (e.g. see Purvis and Ward, this volume; Chu and Ward 2015; Laws and Ward

2011; Ward and Fortune 2013; Ward and Maruna 2007). The GLM has been defined as a 'contemporary, strength-based approach to offender rehabilitation that emphasizes the promotion of individuals' personal goals, together with the reduction or management of their risk of future offending' (Chu and Ward 2015: 144). The GLM posits that as part of any risk assessment of offenders it is important to 'discover individuals' personal aspirations and core values, and their areas of existing skills and strengths' (Ward and Fortune 2013: 33). From this assessment, correctional personnel can develop intervention plans (Good Lives plans) to assist persons under supervision in acquiring the capabilities to achieve personally meaningful goals. Hunter and colleagues (2016) describe a strengths-based case management approach to service provision both before and after release from prison that draws upon the GLM model. Although only providing qualitative data to support this strengths-based case management approach, they argue that more research is needed about how correctional staff can more effectively interact with clients in order to improve re-entry and resettlement outcomes (Hunter et al. 2016).

It appears that the assessment of strengths complements other interventions used with criminal justice-involved individuals such as motivational interviewing (National Institute of Corrections 2012). Stinson and Clark (2017: 28), in their book *Motivational Interviewing with Offenders: Engagement, Rehabilitation, and Reentry*, argue that

> the spirit of MI . . . aligns with strengths-based approaches in that you trust that people already have within them what is needed for positive change. The goal is to help them activate it. MI calls you to draw forth their aspirations, values, and competencies, or that which makes them distinctly and individually human.

(See Norton in this volume for more about MI.) Anstiss et al. (2011) found that offenders who received MI were reconvicted and reimprisoned at significantly lower rates compared to a control group receiving treatment as usual. In particular, they argue that the use of motivational interviewing may have a positive impact on offenders' 'agency, competency, and responsibility' (Anstiss et al. 2011: 706). In contrast, Polaschek (2017: 69) notes that a key difference between some other strengths-based approaches such as those described by Serin and colleagues (2016) and MI is that unlike MI '[i]t does not assume that the assets, skills or resources the offender needs to draw on to desist are already available and simply need to be "rediscovered"'. That is, correctional personnel working with clients can assist in the development of strengths that can lead to successful re-entry and resettlement (see e.g. Jones et al. 2015; Woldgabreal et al. 2014: 37).

Several interventions involving the use of 'circles' of volunteers that support and guide individuals returning from prison to the community emphasize the importance of a strengths-based approach (see e.g. Fox 2016; Höing et al. 2015; Walker 2015). Fox (2016), for example, argues that Circles of Support and Accountability (CoSA) 'deemphasize risk and focus on strengths and shared values' (p. 88) in order to promote desistance and successful reintegration. Fox (2016: 89) notes that similar to the GLM, 'The CoSA model acknowledges the importance of self-determination for offenders and the pursuit of human, positive goals rather than simply avoidance of criminal activity'. In a similar vein, Walker (2015: 137) describes the implementation of strength-based 're-entry circles' in Hawaii that provide soon to be released prisoners 'with the opportunity to express and receive "acceptance, compassion, encouragement" and the other "positive components" that positive criminology emphasizes'. She notes that these re-entry circles focus on 'reconciliation' and make the participant the 'driving force for planning the direction of her life' (Walker 2015: 132).

Researchers have also suggested drawing upon the literature about post-traumatic growth (PTG) (Tedeschi and Calhoun 2004) to improve re-entry and resettlement outcomes (see e.g. Guse and Hudson 2014; LeBel and Richie 2019; Mapham and Hefferon 2012). Several dimensions of PTG such as the discovery of hidden strengths and abilities, strengthened relationships and new priorities are thought to be especially relevant to prisoner re-entry and resettlement (Mapham and Hefferon 2012). For example, Guse and Hudson (2014) found that former prisoners discussed the importance of psychological strengths such as hope, gratitude, and spirituality in contributing to their successful re-entry from prison to the community. These findings support those from the desistance literature indicating that higher levels of hope and optimism are associated with reductions in recidivism (see e.g. Bahr et al. 2010; LeBel et al. 2008; Martin and Stermac 2010; Visher and O'Connell 2012). In fact, in utilizing hope as an intervention target with sexual offenders, researchers found that increasing levels of hope enhanced engagement in treatment and led to reductions in recidivism (Marshall et al. 2008; Marshall and Marshall 2012).

Strengths-based roles of the professional ex-/wounded healer and activist

Maruna and LeBel (2003, 2009) suggest that perhaps the primary challenge facing the returning prisoner is overcoming stigma (LeBel 2012) and the need to prove him- or herself to be worthy of forgiveness. In recognition of this re-entry obstacle, researchers have begun to examine a more proactive and strengths-based stigma management strategy among recovering substance users and formerly incarcerated persons involving becoming a 'professional ex-' (Brown 1991) or a 'wounded healer' (Heidemann et al. 2016; LeBel 2007; LeBel et al. 2015; Maruna 2001). This focus builds on Brown's (1991) assertion that it is important to consider how one might 'adopt a legitimate career premised upon an identity that embraces one's deviant history' (p. 220). Maruna and LeBel (2003, 2009) discuss this approach as strengths-based or alternatively 'restorative re-entry' as it is based on principles fundamental to the restorative justice movement (see also Bazemore and Stinchcomb 2004; Burnett and Maruna 2006; Maruna et al. 2003). As opposed to risk- or need-based interventions, the focus here is less on controlling or removing the deficits of ex-prisoners and instead on treating them as individuals with talents and abilities to contribute to society. As Bazemore and Stinchcomb (2004) argue, 'only by taking responsibility for making things right with victims and victimized communities can offenders change either the *community's image* of them or their perceptions of themselves' (p. 16, italics in original).

This strength-based role is often accomplished by sharing one's experiences, strength, and hope; acting as a role model; mentoring others; and, for some, making a career of assisting others who are not as far along in the recovery and/or reintegration process. Many formerly incarcerated persons, across a wide range of roles (e.g. 'life coaches', Schinkel and Whyte 2012; members of mutual aid groups, Bellamy et al. 2012), and by type of offender (e.g. lifers, Liem 2016; Munn 2011), express an interest and/or active involvement in helping others. In particular, preliminary evidence suggests that many staff members working for prisoner re-entry programmes are, in fact, formerly incarcerated persons (see e.g. Irwin 2005; LeBel et al. 2015). The benefits of assuming the role of helper are thought to include increased feelings of interpersonal competence, a sense of meaning and purpose in their lives, improved self-esteem, a sense of accomplishment, and social approval (see e.g. Aresti et al. 2010; Maruna 2001). Thus, becoming a professional ex- or wounded healer may allow stigmatized individuals to overcome the 'ex-con' label and reconcile with society for their past crimes, while also contributing to changes in the persons' self-identity.

LeBel and colleagues (2015) examined if, how, and why formerly incarcerated staff members of prisoner re-entry programmes differ from the clients. Importantly, in the course of data collection, several staff members expressed that 'this is the only job where my criminal record is viewed as an asset'. When compared to clients, having a current staff position was positively related to perceiving less personal stigma, higher self-esteem and satisfaction with life, more pro-social attitudes/beliefs and positive relationships with family members, and using active coping strategies such as advocacy (LeBel et al. 2015). Similarly, in a study of previously incarcerated women, Heidemann and colleagues (2016) found that a helper/wounded healer orientation enhanced self-esteem, increased pro-social activity, and improved pro-social connections. Moreover, staff members were much less likely to forecast that they would get arrested in the next three years (LeBel et al. 2015).

Although research in this area is limited, Burnett and Maruna (2006) provide a strengths-based case study of an innovative project that involved prisoners in the United Kingdom as 'citizens advisors' at a Citizens Advice Bureau (CAB). This initiative involved prisoner volunteers receiving daytime release to work out of the bureau's call centre. This qualitative research found that the prisoner volunteers were accepted and that their contributions were warmly appreciated by both the citizens who were seeking assistance and the other volunteers (see Welsh and Wyies in this volume for more about the perspectives and important contributions of ex-offenders).

As a note of caution, Heidemann and colleagues (2016: 20) suggest that the professional ex-/wounded healer role may be one of the only options available for a person to exit a 'deviant career'. That is, formerly incarcerated persons remain extremely marginalized by society, and have few opportunities to use their strengths to improve their own lives and those of the communities in which they return. To address this marginalization, Maruna and LeBel (2009; LeBel 2009) have discussed going a 'third mile' as moving beyond the helping roles of the professional ex-/wounded healer to engaging in more direct efforts at stigma reduction through 'reintegration advocacy' to address social justice issues at a political level. They argue that this is a natural next step in efforts towards destigmatization of formerly incarcerated persons. Some prisoner re-entry organizations, such as the Fortune Society (2017) in New York City, engage in both roles, with formerly incarcerated persons working as professional-exes in counselling other former prisoners, as well as engaging in advocacy work to change laws restricting ex-prisoner access to jobs as well as other rights lost due to the civil disabilities of having a felony conviction. Others have gone further and suggested that the perspective of formerly incarcerated persons should be at the forefront of the wider policy debate regarding criminal justice reform and re-entry (see e.g. Nixon 2017; LSPC 2017; WPA 2017; JLUSA 2017). Organizations like All of Us or None, the Women's Prison Association (WPA), and JustLeadershipUSA (JLUSA) seek to develop 'a group of leaders equipped to craft solutions to the problems facing incarcerated and formerly incarcerated persons' (Women's Prison Association [WPA] 2017). JustLeadershipUSA (JustLeadershipUSA 2017) provides an example of entry into the realm of advocacy work, and their website indicates the 'goal is to amplify the voice of the people most impacted, and to position them as reform leaders. . . . JLUSA is based on the principle that people closest to the problem are also the people closest to its solution'. JLUSA attempts to accomplish these goals through advocacy campaigns and leadership training. Thus, these organizations clearly believe that formerly incarcerated persons have many positive attributes and strengths that can be utilized to elevate social justice endeavours.

LeBel's (2009) quantitative research provides some evidence of the benefits of involvement in advocacy as a coping orientation for formerly incarcerated persons. His survey research found that having a stronger advocacy orientation is positively associated with psychological well-being, and in particular satisfaction with life as a whole. This research found a significant negative correlation between one's advocacy orientation and criminal attitudes and behaviour, indicating that this coping strategy may help to maintain a person's pro-social identity and facilitate ongoing desistance from crime. These findings suggest that the stigma management strategies of helping others and becoming involved in advocacy-related activities may assist some formerly incarcerated persons in utilizing their strengths to successfully re-enter society and give meaning, purpose, and significance to their lives (Heidemann et al. 2016; LeBel et al. 2015; Maruna and LeBel 2009).

The transformation of formerly incarcerated individuals from being part of the problem into part of a solution requires mechanisms in which their lives can become useful and purposeful. If helping others has adaptive consequences, then an argument can be made to make opportunities to engage in reciprocal processes of mutual support (i.e. mutual-help groups and volunteering, peer mentoring) more widely available to prisoners and former prisoners (Maruna et al. 2003). Concrete steps that corrections could adopt include allowing successful formerly incarcerated persons to provide newly released prisoners with an introduction to life in the community and help them to deal with the plethora of problems related to re-entry and reintegration. In addition, to create more professional exes, policies can be developed to reduce legal restrictions to employment for felons, and to provide monetary support to promote the completion of certification programs and college degrees (LeBel et al. 2015; Heidemann et al. 2016).

Conclusion

Based on the preliminary findings discussed above, there is growing support for increasing the number of interventions that assess and enhance strengths of incarcerated and released individuals in order to reduce recidivism and improve the quality of their lives. Clark (2012) argues that 'the field of criminal justice will need to learn how to elicit, amplify, and reinforce . . . strengths' and that these 'methods will need to become both customary and expected' (p. 139). Moving forward, longitudinal research, using longer assessment time frames, combining qualitative, quantitative, and more interdisciplinary work is needed to provide a more in-depth understanding of the role of (specific) strengths in successful re-entry and resettlement. In particular, research is needed to learn how and why formerly incarcerated persons become involved in help-giving and advocacy-related activities, to study the strengths of leaders of these types of strengths-based activities, and to document the development of this growing social movement. In conclusion, as Jones and colleagues (2015: 332) suggest, 'correctional researchers and practitioners need to expend at least as much time and energy identifying offender strengths as they spend identifying their deficits'.

References

Andrews, D. A., Bonta, J. and Wormith, J. S. (2011) The Risk-Need-Responsivity (RNR) model: Does adding the Good Lives Model contribute to effective crime prevention? *Criminal Justice and Behavior*, 38, 735–755.

Anstiss, B., Polaschek, D. L. and Wilson, M. (2011) A brief motivational interviewing intervention with prisoners: When you lead a horse to water, can it drink for itself? *Psychology, Crime & Law*, V, 689–710.

Aresti, A., Eatough, V. and Brooks-Gordon, B. (2010) Doing time after time: An interpretative phenomenological analysis of reformed ex-prisoners' experiences of self-change, identity and career opportunities. *Psychology, Crime & Law*, 16(3), 169–190.

Bahr, S. J., Harris, L., Fisher, J. K. and Armstrong, A. H. (2010) Successful re-entry: What differentiates successful from unsuccessful parolees? *International Journal of Offender Therapy and Comparative Criminology*, 54, 667–692.

Bazemore, G. (1999) After shaming, whither reintegration: Restorative justice and relational rehabilitation. In G. Bazemore and L. Walgrave (Eds.), *Restorative Juvenile Justice: Repairing the Harm of Youth Crime*. Monsey, NY: Criminal Justice Press, pp. 155–194.

Bazemore, G. and Stinchcomb, J. (2004) A civic engagement model of re-entry: Involving community through service and restorative justice. *Federal Probation*, 68(2), 14–24.

Bellamy, C. D., Rowe, M., Benedict, P. and Davidson, L. (2012) Giving back and getting something back: The role of mutual aid groups for individuals in recovery from incarceration, addiction, and mental illness. *Journal of Groups in Addiction & Recovery*, 7, 223–236.

Bonta, J. and Andrews, D. A. (2017) *The Psychology of Criminal Conduct*, 6th edition. New York: Routledge.

Brown, J. D. (1991) The professional ex-: An alternative for exiting the deviant career. *Sociological Quarterly*, 32, 219–230.

Burnett, R. and Maruna, S. (2006) The kindness of prisoners: Strengths-based resettlement in theory and in action. *Criminology & Criminal Justice*, 6, 83–106.

Chu, C. M. and Ward, T. (2015) The Good Lives Model of offender rehabilitation: Working positively with sexual offenders. In N. Ronel and D. Segev (Eds.), *Positive Criminology*. New York: Routledge, pp. 140–161.

Clark, M. D. (2012) The strengths perspective in criminal justice. In D. Saleebey (Ed.), *The Strengths Perspective in Social Work Practice*, 6th edition. Boston: Pearson, pp. 129–148.

Eglash, A. (1977) Beyond restitution: Creative restitution. In J. Hudson and B. Galaway (Eds.), *Restitution in Criminal Justice*. Lexington, MA: D.C. Heath, pp. 91–129.

Fortune Society. (2017) *Homepage*. Available at: https://fortunesociety.org/.

Fox, K. J. (2016) Civic commitment: Promoting desistance through community integration. *Punishment & Society*, 18(1), 68–94.

Groshkova, T., Best, D. and White, W. (2013) The assessment of recovery capital: Properties and psychometrics of a measure of addiction recovery strengths. *Drug and Alcohol Review*, 32, 187–194.

Guse, T. and Hudson, D. (2014) Psychological strengths and posttraumatic growth in the successful reintegration of South African ex-offenders. *International Journal of Offender Therapy & Comparative Criminology*, 58(12), 1449–1465.

Heidemann, G., Cederbaum, J. A., Martinez, S. and LeBel, T. P. (2016) Wounded healers: How formerly incarcerated women help themselves by helping others. *Punishment & Society*, 18(1), 3–26.

Höing, M., Vogelvang, B. and Bogaerts, S. (2015) "I am a different man now" – sex offenders in circles of support and accountability: A prospective study. *International Journal of Offender Therapy and Comparative Criminology*, 61(7), 751–772.

Hucklesby, A. and Hagley-Dickinson, L. (2007) Conclusion: Opportunities, barriers, and threats. In A. Hucklesby and L. Hagley-Dickinson (Eds.), *Prisoner Resettlement: Policy and Practice*. Cullompton: Willan Publishing, pp. 289–299.

Hunter, B. A., Lanza, A. S., Lawlor, M., Dyson, W. and Gordon, D. M. (2016) A strengths-based approach to prisoner reentry: The fresh start prisoner reentry program. *International Journal of Offender Therapy & Comparative Criminology*, 60(11), 1298–1314.

Irwin, J. (2005) *The Warehouse Prison: Disposal of the New Dangerous Class*. Los Angeles, CA: Roxbury Publishing Company.

Jones, N. J., Brown, S. L., Robinson, D. and Frey, D. (2015) Incorporating strengths into quantitative assessments of criminal risk for adult offenders: The service planning instrument. *Criminal Justice & Behavior*, 42(3), 321–338.

JustLeadershipUSA. (2017) *About Us*. Available at: www.justleadershipusa.org/about-us/.

Laws, D. R. and Ward, T. (2011) *Desistance from Sex Offending: Alternatives to Throwing Away the Keys*. New York: Guilford Press.

LeBel, T. P. (2007) An examination of the impact of formerly incarcerated persons helping others. *Journal of Offender Rehabilitation*, 46(1–2), 1–24.

LeBel, T. P. (2009) Formerly incarcerated persons' use of advocacy/activism as a coping orientation in the reintegration process. In B. M. Veysey, J. Christian and D. J. Martinez (Eds.), *How Offenders Transform Their Lives*. Cullompton: Willan Publishing, pp. 165–187.

LeBel, T. P. (2012) Invisible stripes? Formerly incarcerated persons' perceptions of stigma. *Deviant Behavior*, 33, 89–107.

LeBel, T. P., Burnett, R., Maruna, S. and Bushway, S. (2008) The "chicken and egg" of subjective and social factors in desistance from crime. *European Journal of Criminology*, 5(2), 130–158.

LeBel, T. P. and Richie, M. (2019) The psychological effects of contact with the criminal justice system. In B. M. Huebner and N. Frost (Eds.), *ASC Division on Corrections and Sentencing Handbook Volume 3: Handbook on the Consequences of Sentencing and Punishment Decisions*. New York: Routledge, pp. 122–142.

LeBel, T. P., Richie, M. and Maruna, S. (2015) Helping others as a response to reconcile a criminal past: The role of the wounded healer in prisoner reentry programs. *Criminal Justice and Behavior*, 42(1), 108–120.

Legal Services for Prisoners with Children (LSPC). (2017) *All of Us or None*. Available at: www.prisonerswithchildren.org/our-projects/allofus-or-none/.

Liem, M. (2016) *After Life Imprisonment: Reentry in the Era of Mass Incarceration*. New York: New York University Press.

Mapham, A. and Hefferon, K. (2012) "I used to be an offender – Now I'm a defender": Positive psychology approaches in the facilitation of posttraumatic growth in offenders. *Journal of Offender Rehabilitation*, 51(6), 389–413.

Marshall, L. E., Marshall, W. L., Fernandez, Y. M., Malcolm, P. B. and Moulden, H. M. (2008) The Rockwood preparatory program for sexual offenders: Description and preliminary appraisal. *Sexual Abuse: A Journal of Research and Treatment*, 20, 25–42.

Marshall, W. L. and Marshall, L. E. (2012) Integrating strength-based models in the psychological treatment of sexual offenders. *Sexual Abuse in Australia & New Zealand*, 4(1), 53–58.

Martin, K. and Stermac, L. (2010) Measuring hope: Is hope related to criminal behavior in offenders? *International Journal of Offender Therapy and Comparative Criminology*, 54, 693–705.

Maruna, S. (2001) *Making Good: How Ex-Convicts Reform and Rebuild Their Lives*. Washington, DC: American Psychological Association.

Maruna, S., Immarigeon, R. and LeBel, T.P. (2004) Ex-offender reintegration: Theory and practice. In S. Maruna and R. Immarigeon (Eds.), *After Crime and Punishment: Pathways to Offender Reintegration*. Cullompton: Willan Publishing, pp. 3–26.

Maruna, S. and LeBel, T. P. (2003) Welcome home? Examining the "reentry court" concept from a strengths-based perspective. *Western Criminology Review*, 4, 91–107.

Maruna, S. and LeBel, T. P. (2009) Strengths-based approaches to reentry: Extra mileage toward reintegration and destigmatization. *Japanese Journal of Sociological Criminology*, 34, 59–80.

Maruna, S., LeBel, T. P. and Lanier, C. (2003) Generativity behind bars: Some "redemptive truth" about prison society. In E. de St. Aubin, D. McAdams and T. Kim (Eds.), *The Generative Society: Caring for Future Generations*. Washington, DC: American Psychological Association, pp. 131–151.

Maruna, S., LeBel, T. P., Mitchell, N. and Naples, M. (2004) Pygmalion in the reintegration process: Desistance from crime through the looking glass. *Psychology, Crime and Law*, 10(3), 271–281.

Miller, H. A. (2006) A dynamic assessment of offender risk, needs, and strengths in a sample of pre-release general offenders. *Behavioral Sciences & the Law*, 24(6), 767–782.

Miller, H. A. (2015) Protective strengths, risk, and recidivism in a sample of known sexual offenders. *Sexual Abuse: A Journal of Research & Treatment*, 27(1), 34–50.

Munn, M. (2011) Living in the aftermath: The impact of lengthy incarceration on post-carceral success. *Howard Journal of Criminal Justice*, 50(3), 233–246.

National Institute of Corrections. (2012) *Motivational Interviewing in Corrections: A Comprehensive Guide to Implementing MI in Corrections*. Washington, DC: National Institute of Corrections.

Nixon, V. D. (2017) Learning to lead in the decarceration movement. In M. W. Epperson and C. Pettus-Davis (Eds.), *Smart Decarceration: Achieving Criminal Justice Transformation in the 21st Century*. New York: Oxford University Press, pp. 90–100.

Orbis Partners. (2003) *Service Planning Instrument (SPIn)*. Ottawa, ON: Orbis Partners.

Polaschek, D. L. L. (2017) Protective factors, correctional treatment and desistance. *Aggression & Violent Behavior*, 32, 64–70.

Ronel, N. and Elisha, E. (2011) A different perspective: Introducing positive criminology. *International Journal of Offender Therapy and Comparative Criminology*, 55, 305–325.

Ronel, N. and Segev, D. (2015) *Positive Criminology*. New York: Routledge.

Saleebey, D. (Ed.). (2012) *The Strengths Perspective in Social Work Practice*, 6th edition. Boston: Pearson, pp. 278–304.

Schinkel, M. and Whyte, B. (2012) Routes out of prison using life coaches to assist resettlement. *The Howard Journal of Criminal Justice*, 51(4), 359–371.

Seligman, M. E. P. and Csikszentmihalyi, M. (2000) Positive psychology: An introduction. *The American Psychologist*, 55(1), 5–14.

Serin, R. C. (2007) *The Dynamic Risk Assessment Scale for Offender Re-Entry (DRAOR)* (Unpublished scale). Ottawa, ON: Carleton University.

Serin, R. C., Chadwick, N. and Lloyd, C. D. (2016) Dynamic risk and protective factors. *Psychology, Crime & Law*, 22(1–2), 151–170.

Stinson, J. D. and Clark, M. D. (2017) *Motivational Interviewing with Offenders: Engagement, Rehabilitation, and Reentry*. New York: Guilford Press.

Tedeschi, R. G. and Calhoun, C. G. (2004) Posttraumatic growth: Conceptual foundations and empirical evidence. *Psychological Inquiry*, 15, 1–18.

Van Wormer, K. (2001) *Counseling Female Offenders and Victims: A Strengths-Restorative Approach*. New York: Springer Publishing Company, Inc.

Van Wormer, K. and Davis, D. R. (2018) *Addiction Treatment: A Strengths Perspective*, 4th edition. Boston, MA: Cengage Learning.

Visher, C. A. and O'Connell, D. J. (2012) Incarceration and inmates' self perceptions about returning home. *Journal of Criminal Justice*, 40, 386–393.

Walker, L. (2015) Applied positive criminology: Restorative reentry and transition planning circles for incarcerated people and their loved ones. In N. Ronel and D. Segev (Eds.), *Positive Criminology*. New York: Routledge, pp. 128–139.

Ward, T. (2017) Prediction and agency: The role of protective factors in correctional rehabilitation and desistance. *Aggression & Violent Behavior*, 32, 19–28.

Ward, T. and Fortune, C. (2013) The Good Lives Model: Aligning risk reduction with promoting offenders' personal goals. *European Journal of Probation*, 5(2), 29–46.

Ward, T. and Maruna, S. (2007) *Rehabilitation: Beyond the Risk Paradigm*. London: Routledge.

Ward, T. and Stewart, C. A. (2003) Criminogenic needs and human needs: A theoretical model. *Psychology, Crime & Law*, 9, 125–143.

Woldgabreal, Y., Day, A. and Ward, T. (2014) The community-based supervision of offenders from a positive psychology perspective. *Aggression and Violent Behavior*, 19, 32–41.

Woldgabreal, Y., Day, A. and Ward, T. (2016) Linking positive psychology to offender supervision outcomes: The mediating role of psychological flexibility, general self-efficacy, optimism, and home. *Criminal Justice and Behavior*, 43(6), 697–721.

Women's Prison Association (WPA). (2017) *Homepage*. Available at: www.wpaonline.org/.

The role of third-sector organizations in supporting resettlement and reintegration[1]

Alice Mills and Rosie Meek

Introduction

Third-sector organizations[2] (TSOs) have a long history of assisting people leaving prison to resettle and reintegrate into society. In the UK, Discharged Prisoners' Aid Societies were officially established in 1862, and in the late 19th century, volunteers from the Church of England Temperance Society became police court missionaries, the forerunner to the modern probation service (Carey and Walker 2002). Developments in New Zealand followed a similar pattern. The first Patients' and Prisoners' Aid Society (later to become the Prisoners' Aid and Rehabilitation Society [PARS]) was established in Dunedin in 1877 and the first probation volunteers in New Zealand, linked to local branches of PARS, were licenced in 1913 (Tennant 2007). TSOs now play a wide variety of roles in the resettlement process, from providing accommodation, training, and employment services to substance misuse treatment, peer support, and mentoring. This chapter will draw upon research and initiatives from England and Wales and New Zealand to discuss how TSOs can not only meet offenders' practical resettlement needs but also help to develop their social capital and promote social reintegration. It will then briefly examine the potential strengths of TSO provision before exploring the challenges faced by TSOs working in resettlement and reintegration.

Third-sector involvement in resettlement and reintegration and the marketization of criminal justice

Although the third sector has long been a trailblazer for the provision of resettlement services (Hucklesby and Worrall 2007), it is only in recent years that the benefits of working in partnership with TSOs to tackle the seemingly intractable problem of reoffending by ex-prisoners have been recognized by the British and New Zealand governments. In 2012 the New Zealand Ministry of Justice announced a target to reduce reoffending by 25% by 2017 (New Zealand Ministry of Justice 2012) and noted the value and necessity of TSOs in attempting to achieve this goal (Mills 2015). Similarly in England and Wales, the Third Sector Reducing Re-Offending Action Plan stated:

> The third sector has a critical role to play as advocates of service users and communities, as partners in strategy and service development, and as service providers. We value their role as enablers of effective community engagement, volunteering and mentoring.
>
> (Ministry of Justice/National Offender Management Service [NOMS] 2008: 7)

The marketization of criminal justice in England and Wales, envisaged by the Carter Report (Carter 2003) and the creation of NOMS in 2004 has enabled third-sector and private providers to become increasingly involved in the provision of criminal justice and resettlement services. Following the Corston Report (Corston 2007), TSOs were funded to develop a network of women's centres to provide community support services for women offenders and women at risk of offending. A 'Payment by Results' (PbR) pilot project at HMP Peterborough involved a number of TSOs and private companies working in partnership to reduce reoffending amongst short-sentence prisoners. Under the Transforming Rehabilitation programme, services formerly provided by the probation service to supervise all low- and medium-risk adult offenders on community sentences or post-release licence have been outsourced to 21 Community Rehabilitation Companies (CRCs), whilst high-risk offenders remain the responsibility of a newly constituted National Probation Service

(Martin et al. 2016).[3] Most CRCs are led by large private sector corporations which manage various partners and subcontractors including TSOs[4] (National Audit Office [NAO] 2016). CRCs are incentivized to reduce rates of reoffending through the use of PbR and, as a result of the Offender Rehabilitation Act 2014, offenders serving prison sentences of less than 12 months will receive post-release supervision for the first time (NAO 2016). 'Through the gate' services, provided by CRCs, are intended to support prisoners in the last three months of their sentence and then in the community on their release. Both CRCs and the National Probation Service have also continued to refer service users to TSO services with whom they do not have a contractual relationship (Clinks 2016).

In England and Wales nearly 1,500 TSOs work predominantly with offenders, ex-offenders, and their families (Centre for Social Justice 2013). However, the position of these TSOs is somewhat polarized. Most are small, locally based, and heavily reliant on volunteers (Clinks 2017). More than a half (51%) have an annual turnover or income of £150,000 or less and 24% have no full-time equivalent employees. At the other end of the scale, 3% of these organizations have an annual turnover or income of more than £5 million and 4% have more than 100 full-time equivalent employees (Centre for Social Justice 2013). It is these large 'semi-corporate' (Mills 2015) organizations which have benefitted the most from recent policy changes to open up the criminal justice market (Maguire 2016). Simultaneously grant funding upon which small, local TSOs are more likely to rely, continues to decline (Clinks 2017).

The roles of TSOs in supporting prisoner resettlement and reintegration

TSOs in England and Wales provide a range of resettlement/reintegration services. Table 48.1 indicates the proportion of TSOs listed in the Clinks[5] Directory of Offender Services[6] involved in various areas of resettlement, based on the resettlement pathways set out in the Reducing Re-Offending National Action Plan (Home Office 2004).

Alongside the provision of practical support to meet offenders' social needs, TSOs also specialize in helping ex-prisoners to build social capital and develop meaningful relationships, thus fostering social integration, which research has suggested is central to the promotion and motivation of desistance (Maguire and Raynor 2017; McNeill 2006; Farrall 2002; Maruna 2001). One approach to this is mentoring by volunteers from the community. In New Zealand, PARS Inc recruits volunteer mentors to befriend, support, and advocate for people recently released from prison (PARS 2019). Arooj, a UK TSO which runs a resettlement programme for black and minority ethnic and Muslim offenders, provides mentors to establish a trusting relationship with offenders whilst they are still in prison and work with prisoners' families to

Table 48.1 Resettlement services provided by TSOs in the Clinks Directory

Area of resettlement work	Proportion of TSOs (n = 929)
Housing and accommodation	19%
Education	20%
Training	61%
Employment	46%
Health	20%
Substance misuse	40%
Finance, benefit, and debt	27%
Children and families	48%
Attitudes, thinking, and behaviour	9%
Domestic and sexual violence[7]	25%
Sex work	2%

facilitate communication and encourage the acceptance of the offender back into family life (Hough 2016).

Many of these social reintegration initiatives are faith based and may involve faith-based volunteers visiting people in prison with a view to continuing these relationships on release. One notable example is Circles of Support and Accountability (CoSA), initially associated with the Quakers in the UK. A small group of trained volunteers ('circle') meets regularly with a recently released sex offender ('core member') to address risk and reintegration issues. The volunteers provide practical and social support, befriending the core member and helping them to develop appropriate hobbies and interests with the aim of reducing social isolation and building healthy, meaningful, honest adult relationships to reduce the risk of reoffending (McCartan et al. 2014). According to Bates et al. (2014: 865), CoSA has proven to be 'the practical embodiment' of strengths-based interventions using theoretical constructions such as the Good Lives Model (Ward and Stewart 2003 cited in Bates et al. 2014) and desistance theory. A non-faith based example of the social reintegration function of TSOs is that of the Women's Institute (WI) branch at HMP Bronzefield, which hosts talks and invites local WI members into the prison for coffee mornings. The prison funds a year's membership of the WI which can then be transferred to the prisoner's local branch on release from prison (HM Chief Inspector of Prisons 2013), enabling them to connect with their local community. By bringing the community into prisons and representing the community to prisoners, TSOs can help to break down misconceptions amongst both parties (Mills and Meek 2016).

Several TSOs have acknowledged the value of peer support in resettlement as prisoners and ex-prisoners have first-hand experience of the problems faced by their peers. St Giles Trust, for example, trains offenders to deliver housing advice services in prisons and then employs them, initially on a voluntary basis, as mentors to support ex-prisoners after their release. Around a third of St Giles staff are ex-offenders (Boyce et al. 2009). Through engaging in 'generative activities' such as peer support, particularly where this involves volunteering to help others, offenders may achieve a sense of redemption, helping to promote process of desistance, as successfully reintegrated ex-offenders tend to be significantly more care-orientated than active offenders (Maruna 2001, 2007).

Moreover, resettlement-based TSOs have been established by ex-prisoners as a consequence of their own experiences. Vision Housing (now part of the Forward Trust) aims to provide stable housing for people released from prison or on community sentences. It was founded by Annys Darkwa, an ex-prisoner who noticed that many returning prisoners identified the lack of accommodation as the main barrier to successful resettlement (Castro 2013). Based in London, Vision Housing offers a guaranteed security bond and rent to private landlords who are willing to house ex-prisoners. It employs ex-offenders to carry out monthly property inspections and provide social mentoring, and can refer service users to various other TSO support services. Tenants can stay in their accommodation for at least six months and Vision Housing is usually able to house them on the day of release, avoiding the need for transitional housing (Vision Housing 2015). A study in 2013 found an 11% reduction in reoffending amongst Vision Housing tenants with higher reductions for women and more serious offenders (Ellison et al. 2013).

Finally, TSOs provide specialized services for specific groups of prisoners. In New Zealand, the indigenous Māori population is substantially over-represented in the prison population and is more likely to reoffend on release (Johnson 2016). Culturally informed reintegration services are provided by *iwi* (tribe) and *hapu* (sub-tribe) groups in addition to mainstream and criminal justice TSOs. For example, A3K runs a *tikanga Māori* (Māori custom) based reintegration programme for high-risk male Māori offenders which offers intensive support for nine months pre-release and three months post release. The programme helps with accommodation and employment and also assists offenders to reconnect and develop strong relationships with their *whānau* (extended family) to enable them to contribute positively to their *whānau* and wider community (Sullivan et al. 2016).

Strengths of third-sector involvement in resettlement and reintegration

TSOs are deemed to have a number of strengths in their resettlement and reintegration provision. These are well rehearsed in the previous literature on this topic (see, for example, Mills et al. 2011; Fradd and Wyton 2009; Silvestri 2009) and are briefly summarized here. Firstly, their relative independence from the criminal justice system can have several benefits. It may ensure that offenders view them as more approachable and trustworthy than criminal justice staff. A two-year study on the role of TSOs in work with offenders in England and Wales carried out by the authors,[8] found that the independence of TSOs, and the willingness of volunteers to give up their time to talk and listen to prisoners and build relationships with them, was deeply appreciated by prisoners, particularly those who had been shunned by criminal justice agencies. Prisoners reported being more likely to engage with TSO services, and to be honest with volunteers, who were perceived as empathetic and nonjudgemental (Mills and Meek 2016). The independence of TSOs may also enable them to act as advocates, representing the views and needs of service users to criminal justice and other agencies. It may allow considerable diversity and innovation, permitting TSOs to provide a wider range of services, which prioritize the needs of offenders and communities (Martin et al. 2016).

Secondly, TSOs have considerable expertise in resettlement and working with offenders. By being community based they tend to have excellent knowledge of and connections to services located where prisoners are likely to live on release (Mills and Meek 2016). Through these links TSOs can utilize their substantial social capital to facilitate the resettlement of offenders, for example, by using their local connections to source employment opportunities (Hough 2016).

Thirdly, as noted above, TSOs can a play a fundamental role in helping offenders to develop their own social capital, which is seen as a vital component of successful and sustained desistance (Maguire and Raynor 2017; McNeill 2006). A significant part of successful reintegration and rehabilitation relies on the strength of the relationship between offenders and those who are there to help them (McNeill et al. 2005; Asay and Lambert 1999). TSOs tend to specialize in empathetic, person-centred work, building rapport with individuals, working with their strengths and fostering their social capital by creating strong, meaningful relationships between those who have offended, their families, and the wider community (Martin et al. 2016).

Finally, the opportunities that TSOs may provide for offenders themselves to volunteer and/or engage in peer support can have a number of benefits, including gaining new skills and work experience, improved self-confidence, and potentially a work reference in preparation for paid employment (Boyce et al. 2009; Levenson and Farrant 2002).

Challenges of TSOs' involvement in resettlement and reintegration

TSOs also face a number of challenges in working in resettlement and reintegration, particularly when seeking to provide services commissioned by the state or private providers, leading to concerns that their traditional strengths are under threat. In the drive to be competitive and meet the requirements of commissioners, it is feared that TSOs will lose their distinctive, person-centred culture and value-driven approach (Maguire 2016). Such contracts often do not appreciate, and therefore do not fund, the wider relationship building and community development work conducted by TSOs, focusing instead on narrow measurable outcomes (Mills 2015; Mills et al. 2011). In England and Wales, for TSOs working in CRCs or on other contracts with a PbR element, they may be pressurized to focus on those least likely to reoffend, neglecting those with complex needs in order to demonstrate results (Maguire 2016), or to concentrate on ensuring a reduction in reoffending within a short period of time rather than engaging with more expensive, complex processes which support long-term desistance (Hough 2016). Furthermore, in accepting contracts from the state, particularly those involving what have traditionally been state functions such as risk management or punishment, TSOs may lose their perceived independence and come to be viewed as 'shadow state apparatus' (Wolch 1990) or 'little fingers of the state' (Nyland 1993), potentially losing the trust of service users. In such circumstances, some TSOs may actively seek to eschew state funding to avoid potential threats to their autonomy (Mills 2015).

The existence of smaller, local TSOs which specialize in working with offenders may be particularly threatened by the decline in grant funding and increasing use of service contracts. They may lack expertise or resources to bid for contracts or demonstrate the effectiveness of their services (Martin et al. 2016; Hucklesby and Worrall 2007). Most specialist resettlement TSOs lack the capacity to fulfil national or even regional service specifications. Instead, large semi-corporate generalist social service TSOs and private corporations, with little experience of working with offenders, are moving into the criminal justice market and gaining an increasing share of contracts (Maguire 2016). This is exemplified by CRCs in England and Wales, and the contracts for regional Out of Gate resettlement services in New Zealand which were granted to organizations with little experience of prisoner reintegration such as Healthcare New Zealand, rather than smaller, more specialist organizations such as Prison Fellowship New Zealand or Prisoners' Aid and Rehabilitation Trust (Mills 2015).

Additionally, funding for resettlement and reintegration services run by TSOs has remained patchy and unstable. In England and Wales, even for those TSOs named in the bids for the CRCs, the actual pace of change has been glacially slow and their future funding and service provision is far from certain. Some of these TSOs have had no communication from the relevant CRC (Clinks 2016), suggesting that they may have been used as 'bid candy' to increase the attractiveness of the bid, then sidelined once the contract has been won (Maguire 2016).

Finally, it should be noted that the provision of resettlement services by TSOs does not necessarily mean that they will be used by offenders. A survey of prisoners in eight prisons in England and Wales found that despite an average of 20 TSOs working in each prison, on average prisoners had heard of just four and had engaged with no more than one (Meek et al. 2013). This low awareness may be due to poor publicity, difficulties establishing a continued presence in the prisons due to lack of space, and disinterest from prison staff (Meek et al. 2013).

Conclusion

TSOs can play a fundamental role in the resettlement of offenders through the provision of services to meet offenders' practical and social needs. Through their position in the community, and emphasis on building relationships and stronger communities, they can also help to motivate sustained desistance by assisting offenders with social reintegration and developing their own social capital. However, commissioners and contractors, including private providers, may be more concerned with what they can acquire from TSOs rather than their broader community development work (Nowland-Foreman 1997). The recent marketization of some criminal justice services in England and Wales risks subjecting TSOs, particularly smaller, specialist organizations, to 'incremental colonisation' (Mythen et al. 2013: 363), whereby 'measures of reconviction and value for money come to supersede the principle of "moral good" that has historically underpinned activities and policymaking in the sector' (Mythen et al. 2013: 364). The continued existence of the distinctive, 'added value' that TSOs can bring to their work with offenders cannot therefore be taken for granted.

Notes

1 In the UK, the term 'resettlement' is used to refer to pre- and post-release assistance and support which aims to enable ex-prisoners and their families to adjust to life after prison without reoffending (Moore 2011). In New Zealand and Australia, the term 'reintegration' is preferred, most likely because 'resettlement' is linked with the notion of 'settlement' and thus colonization. Both 'resettlement' and 'reintegration' are somewhat flawed concepts as many prisoners have felt neither 'settled' nor 'integrated' into the community prior to imprisonment (Social Exclusion Unit 2002).
2 A range of terms have been utilized to describe these organizations including 'voluntary and community organizations', 'charities', 'non-government organizations', and 'non-profit organizations'. These terms all emphasize different attributes of the sector (Buckingham 2009), but all have limitations. In this chapter, we use the term 'third-sector organizations', as this carries few assumptions about the characteristics of these organizations but also best accommodates their diversity (Buckingham 2009).
3 At the time of going to press the Ministry of Justice has announced plans to renationalize probation services.
4 Seventy-five percent of the subcontractors named in the successful bids are TSOs (Clinks 2016). Only one of the CRCs, Durham Tees Valley, was won by a contractor from outside the private sector.
5 Clinks is an infrastructure organization which aims to support TSOs which work with offenders and their families in England and Wales.
6 www.clinks.org/directory.
7 Two additional pathways for women, domestic violence and sex work, were added in 2008 following the Corston Report (Corston 2007).
8 See Mills and Meek (2016) for details of the methodology used in this research.

References

Asay, T. P. and Lambert, M. J. (1999) The empirical case for the common factors in therapy: Quantitative findings. In M. A. Hubble, B. L. Duncan and S. D. Miller (Eds.), *The Heart and Soul of Change: What Works in Therapy*: Washington, DC: American Psychological Association, pp. 33–56.

Bates, A., Williams, D., Wilson, C. and Wilson, R. J. (2014) Circles South East: The first 10 years 2002–2012. *International Journal of Offender Therapy and Comparative Criminology*, 58(7), 861–885.

Boyce, I., Hunter. G. and Hough, M. (2009) *St Giles Trust Peer Advice Project: An Evaluation*. Institute for Criminal Policy Research. Available at: www.icpr.org.uk/media/10363/St%20Giles%20Trust%20peer%20Advice%20evaluation.pdf (Accessed 15 December 2017).

Buckingham, H. (2009) Competition and contracts in the voluntary sector: Exploring the implications for homelessness service providers in Southampton. *Policy and Politics*, 37(2), 235–254.

Carey, M. and Walker, R. (2002) The penal voluntary sector. In S. Bryans, C. Martin and R. Walker (Eds.), *Prisons and the Voluntary Sector*. Winchester: Waterside Press, pp. 50–62.

Carter, P. (2003) *Managing Offenders, Reducing Crime: A New Approach*. London: Prime Minister's Strategy Unit.

Castro, D. (2013) Askoha Fellow Annya Darkwa: Better housing and less recidivism. *Innovate Podcast*, 28 April. Available at: http://innovatepodcast.org/ashoka-fellow-annys-darkwa-better-housing-and-less-recidivism/ (Accessed 8 January 2018).

Centre for Social Justice. (2013) *The New Probation Landscape: Why the Voluntary Sector Matters If We Are Going to Reduce Reoffending*. Available at: www.centreforsocialjustice.org.uk/library/new-probation-landscape-voluntary-sector-matters-going-reduce-reoffending (Accessed 29 May 2018).

Clinks. (2016) *Change & Challenge: The Voluntary Sector's Role in Transforming Rehabilitation*. Available at: www.clinks.org/sites/default/files/basic/files-downloads/clinks_track-tr_changechallenge_final-web.pdf (Accessed 10 January 2018).

Clinks. (2017) *The State of the Sector*. Available at: www.clinks.org/sites/default/files/clinks_state-of-the-sector-2017_final-web1.pdf (Accessed 18 January 2018).

Corston, J. (2007) *The Corston Report: A Review of Women with Particular Vulnerabilities in the Criminal Justice System*. London: Home Office.

Ellison, M., Fox, C., Gains, A. and Pollock, G. (2013) An evaluation of the effect of housing provision on reoffending. *Safer Communities*, 12(1), 27–37.

Farrall, S. (2002) *Rethinking What Works with Offenders: Probation, Social Context and Desistance from Crime*. Cullompton: Willan Publishing.

Fradd, A. and Wyton, R. (2009) *Breaking the Cycle: Charities Working with People in Prison and on Release*. London: New Philanthropy Capital.

HM Chief Inspector of Prisons. (2013) *Report on an Unannounced Inspection of HMP Bronzefield*. London: HM Inspectorate of Prisons. Available at: www.justiceinspectorates.gov.uk/prisons/wp-content/uploads/sites/4/2014/03/bronzefield-2013.pdf (Accessed 12 January 2018).

Home Office. (2004) *Reducing Re-Offending National Action Plan*. London: Home Office.

Hough, C. V. (2016) Transforming Rehabilitation on its impact on a locally-based rehabilitation programme for black and minority ethnic and Muslim offenders. *European Journal of Probation*, 8(2), 68–81.

Hucklesby, A. and Worrall, J. (2007) The voluntary sector and prisoners' resettlement. In A. Hucklesby and L. Hagley-Dickinson (Eds.), *Prisoner Resettlement: Policy and Practice*. Cullompton: Willan Publishing, pp. 174–196.

Johnson, A. (2016) *Moving Targets: State of the Nation Report 2016*. Wellington: Salvation Army and Social Policy Unit.

Levenson, J. and Farrant, F. (2002) Unlocking potential: Active citizenship and volunteering by prisoners. *Probation Journal*, 49(3), 195–204.

Maguire, M. (2016) Third tier in the supply chain? Voluntary agencies and the commissioning of offender rehabilitation services. In A. Hucklesby and M. Corcoran (Eds.), *The Voluntary Sector and Criminal Justice*. Basingstoke: Palgrave Macmillan, pp. 43–70.

Maguire, M. and Raynor, P. (2017) Offender management in and after prison? The end of "end to end"? *Criminology and Criminal Justice*, 17(2), 138–157.

Martin, C., Frazer, L., Cumbo, E., Hayes, C. and O'Donoghue, K. (2016) Paved with good intentions: The way ahead for voluntary, community and social enterprise sector organisations. In A. Hucklesby and M. Corcoran (Eds.), *The Voluntary Sector and Criminal Justice*. Basingstoke: Palgrave Macmillan, pp. 15–42.

Maruna, S. (2001) *Making Good: How Ex-Convicts Reform and Rebuild Their Lives*. Washington DC: American Psychological Association.

Maruna, S. (2007) *Why Volunteerism 'works' as Prison Reintegration: Rehabilitation for a 'bulimic society'*. The 18th Edith Kahn Memorial Lecture, House of Lords, 24 April.

McCartan, K., Kemshall, H., Westwood, S., Solle, J., MacKenzie, G., Cattell, J. and Pollard, A. (2014) *Circles of Support and Accountability: A Case File Review of Two Pilots*. Available at: www.gov.uk/government/uploads/system/uploads/attachment_data/file/293400/cosa-research-summary.pdf (Accessed 12 January 2018).

McNeill, F. (2006) A desistance paradigm for offender management. *Criminology and Criminal Justice*, 6(1), 39–62.

McNeill, F., Batchelor, S., Burnett, R. and Knox, J. (2005) *21st Century Social Work: Reducing Re-Offending: Key Practice Skills*. Edinburgh: The Scottish Executive.

Meek, R., Gojkovic, D. and Mills, A. (2013) The involvement of non-profit organizations in prisoner reentry in the UK: Prisoner awareness and engagement. *Journal of Offender Rehabilitation*, 52(5), 338–357.

Mills, A. (2015) A gentle thaw or continued deep freeze? Relationships between voluntary and community organisations and the state in criminal justice in New Zealand. *Third Sector Review*, 21(1), 121–141.

Mills, A. and Meek, R. (2016) Voluntary work in prisons: Providing services in the penal environment. In A. Hucklesby and M. Corcoran (Eds.), *The Voluntary Sector and Criminal Justice*. Basingstoke: Palgrave Macmillan, pp. 143–169.

Mills, A., Meek, R. and Gojkovic. D. (2011) Exploring the relationship between the voluntary sector and the state in criminal justice. *Voluntary Sector Review*, 2(2), 193–211.

Ministry of Justice and NOMS. (2008) *Working with the Third Sector to Reduce Re-Offending: Securing Effective Partnerships 2008–2011*. London: Ministry of Justice.

Moore, R. (2011) Beyond the prison walls: Some thoughts on prisoner 'resettlement' in England and Wales. *Criminology and Criminal Justice*, 12(2), 129–147.

Mythen, G., Walklate, S. and Kemshall, H. (2013) Decentralizing risk: The role of the voluntary and community sector in the management of offenders. *Criminology & Criminal Justice*, 13(4), 363–379.

National Audit Office. (2016) *Transforming Rehabilitation*. London: National Audit Office.

New Zealand Ministry of Justice. (2012) *Delivering Better Public Services: Reducing Crime and Re-Offending Result Action Plan*. Wellington: Ministry of Justice.

Nowland-Foreman, G. (1997) Can voluntary organisations survive the bear hug of government funding under a contracting regime? A view from Aotearoa New Zealand. *Third Sector Review*, 3, 5–39.

Nyland, J. (1993) Little fingers of the state: Aggressive instrumentalism in the Australian welfare state. In *Power, Politics and Performance: Community Management in the 90s – Conference Proceedings*, Vol. 1. Sydney: Centre for Australian Community Organisations and Management.

PARS (2019) *Volunteer*. https://pars.co.nz/volunteer (Accessed 29 May 2019).

Silvestri, A. (2009) *Partners or Prisoners? Voluntary Sector Independence in the World of Commissioning and Contestability*. London: Centre for Crime and Justice Studies.

Social Exclusion Unit. (2002) *Reducing Re-Offending by Ex-Prisoners*. London: Social Exclusion Unit.

Sullivan, T., McDonald, M. and Thomson, T. (2016) Offender case management: Reducing the rate of reoffending by Māori. *Australian and New Zealand Journal of Criminology*, 49(3), 405–421.

Tennant, M. (2007) *The Fabric of Welfare: Voluntary Organisations, Governmental and Welfare in New Zealand, 1840–2005*. Wellington: Bridget Williams Books.

Vision Housing. (2015) *Our Housing Offer*. Available at: http://visionhousing.org.uk/visionhousing.org.uk/our-housing-offers/index.html (Accessed 12 January 2018).

Wolch, J. (1990) *The Shadow State: Government and Voluntary Sector in Transition*. New York: The Foundation Center.

Section 6

Application to specific groups

Section 6 Introduction

This section provides insights into a much-neglected aspect of rehabilitative work and this pertains to the issue of what constitutes effective practice with diverse groups. Thus, chapters in this section focus on rehabilitative work with women, BAME people, foreign nationals, young people, and older people. The impact of punishment on families is also examined.

With respect to working with women, it is generally acknowledged that women involved in the system have unique needs and therefore require bespoke or gender-sensitive rehabilitative work (see Gelsthorpe, Chapter 50 in this volume). A range of factors underlies this contention. For example, a gender gap in offending exists in most societies and it is characterized by the reality that men commit far more crimes than women, are involved in more serious offending, and tend to be more persistent in their offending (example, Ministry of Justice 2016). Furthermore, in England and Wales for instance, there is evidence that a high proportion of women involved in the system experience or have experienced several (sometimes intersecting) adversities. Examples include a history of care and general exploitation alongside violence in intimate relationships (Corston 2007). These problems sometimes manifest as mental disorder; involvement in substance abuse; low self-esteem; as well as self-harm and suicide in custody (Hawton et al. 2014; Ministry of Justice 2016; Prison and Probation Ombudsman 2017).

For these reasons, many have called for gender-responsive approaches to working with women. These are approaches that are tailored to suit the unique needs of women in the system. It is also argued that the approaches should be supportive not punitive and should be delivered outside custodial settings (Chapters 49–52 of this volume address these issues; see also United Nations Rules for the Treatment of Women Prisoners and Non-custodial Measures for Women Offenders – Bangkok Rules).

Indeed, in a widely cited review of the experiences of women in custody established across England and Wales, Corston (2007: 79) called for a 'distinct, radically different, visibly-led, strategic, proportionate, holistic, women-centred, integrated approach' for women involved in the system. It is however argued that research and policy in this area remain underdeveloped (see, for example, Annison et al. 2018). But it is worth noting that several research-ers have made useful inroads in the effort to develop gender-responsive approaches. Furthermore, recent policy developments reflect a growing inter-est in ensuring that rehabilitative work is adapted to suit the conditions and circumstances that appear to affect women quite disproportionately (see, for example, Ministry of Justice 2018). Key examples of emerging research and policy developments in this area are provided by the chapters in this section.

BAME people represent another typically ignored group; there is a paucity of theoretical, empirical, and policy development in relation to rehabilitative work with this group. That said, in Chapters 53–57, several authors explore the much-ignored issue of effective rehabilitative work with BAME people. The overarching theme underpinning the chapters is the need for approaches that are sensitive to their circumstances. Thus, whilst it is important to recognize that BAME people are not a homogenous group, their unique experiences, including their historical experience of racial discrimination and the impact this could have on criminalization and rehabilitative work, are addressed by the chapters. Thus, issues linked to the nexus of race and rehabilitative work are examined and key examples include the suitability of risk assessment tools and rehabilitation programmes, and the adequacy of diversity training programmes available to staff.

Diversity issues relating to age are also explored and Chapters 58–64 focus on effective approaches to working with young people in diverse policy con-texts and across a range of jurisdictions. In England and Wales for instance, youth justice policy has tended to oscillate between a welfare-focused or justice-oriented (just deserts) approach, or a combination of both (Bateman, Chapter 58 in this volume). The intricacies of this justice/welfare dualism are explored in detail by some chapters whilst other chapters focus on the actual content of rehabilitative work with young people in custody and the commu-nity. In this respect, the pioneering work of Chris Trotter on effective supervi-sion skills is examined alongside key research on the impact of skills such as pro-social modelling and relationship building skills.

Added to the nature and impact of rehabilitative work with women, BAME people, and young people, other dimensions of diversity are also explored. Thus, Chapter 65 examines the issues affecting rehabilitative work with foreign nationals involved in the justice system; Chapter 66 focuses on end-of-life prisoners; and the remaining chapters address the role and experiences of families affected by punishment. Together, these chapters discuss effective front-line practice with these diverse groups.

References

Annison, J., Auburn, T., Gilling, D. and Hanley Santos, G. (2018) The ambiguity of therapeutic justice and women offenders. In P. Ugwudike, P. Raynor and J. Annison (Eds.), *Evidence-Based Skills in Criminal Justice: International Research on Supporting Rehabilitation and Desistance*. Bristol: Policy Press.

Corston Report. (2007) *Review of Women with Particular Vulnerabilities in the Criminal Justice System*. London: Home Office.

Hawton, K., Linsell, L., Adeniji, T., Sariaslan, A. and Fazel, S. (2014) Self-harm in prisons in England and Wales: An epidemiological study of prevalence, risk factors, clustering, and subsequent suicide. *The Lancet*, 383(9923), 1147–1154.

Ministry of Justice. (2016) *Statistics on Women and the Criminal Justice System 2015: A Ministry of Justice Publication Under Section 95 of the Criminal Justice Act 1991*. London: Ministry of Justice.

Ministry of Justice. (2018) *Female Offender Strategy, Cm 9642*. London: Ministry of Justice.

Prison and Probation Ombudsman. (2017) *Self-Inflicted Deaths Among Female Prisoners*. Available at: www.ppo.gov.uk/app/uploads/2017/03/PPO-Learning-Lessons-Bulletin_ Self-inflicted-deaths-among-female-prisoners_WEB.pdf.

United Nations Rules for the Treatment of Women Prisoners and Non-Custodial Measures for Women Offenders. Available at: www.penalreform.org/wp-content/ uploads/2016/07/BangkokRules-Updated-2016-with-renumbering-SMR.pdf.

More sinned against than sinning

Women's pathways into crime and criminalization

Gilly Sharpe

Introduction

Women's involvement in crime is closely bound up with their gendered experiences of social life. Two factors in particular constitute a contextual backdrop to many women's pathways into the criminal justice system. First, patriarchal cultures and structures both facilitate gendered violence and ration justice and therapeutic support to those who endure it; second, women's caring responsibilities over-determine female poverty and low-paid or precarious employment. Most of our current knowledge about the characteristics of women in conflict with the law derives from studies of convicted (and usually imprisoned) women. However, patterns of arrest and sentencing are influenced by class and 'race', such that middle-class and white women tend to escape the policing and penal punishments to which their working-class and black, Asian, and minority ethnic (BAME) counterparts are more frequently subjected (Feilzer and Hood 2004; Hedderman and Gelsthorpe 1997).

Nonetheless, a fairly consistent picture of the nature of women's crimes and their life circumstances and histories emerges from both statistical data and empirical research with female lawbreakers.

Patterns of female lawbreaking and characteristics of female lawbreakers

Women make up a minority of lawbreakers, constituting just 16% of arrestees and 27% of those prosecuted in England and Wales in 2015 (Ministry of Justice 2016).[1] Women who do offend tend to commit less serious offences, less frequently, and have shorter criminal 'careers' than their male counterparts. A notable exception here is following a custodial sentence, when imprisoned women are slightly more likely than men to reoffend after release (Ministry of Justice 2016). Women defendants outnumber men in only a small number of crimes, all of which are related to poverty and/or women's responsibilities for their children. These include TV licence evasion – which accounted for a very substantial 36% of female prosecutions in 2015 compared with 6% of those of men – benefit fraud, child cruelty or neglect, and failure to secure a child's attendance at school (Ministry of Justice 2016).

Empirical studies of criminalized women have consistently shown that they are highly likely to experience poverty and economic marginalization, and to be the victims/survivors of gendered violence. A large proportion have difficulties relating to homelessness or insecure housing, are unemployed or underemployed, and left school early with few formal qualifications or none at all (Sheehan et al. 2011). Many live with the painful emotional legacy of a history of state care and welfare neglect. Physical ill health and substance misuse problems are common, as are mental health needs. A recent report of the Chief Inspector of Prisons in England and Wales (Her Majesty's Chief Inspector of Prisons 2017: 57) found that 65% of women prisoners (compared with 42% of men) said they had mental health issues, reflecting earlier research (e.g. Light et al. 2013). It is important to note that women offenders' mental ill health is frequently related to 'the structural and cultural practices that intersect and shape [their] lives' (Player 2017: 578), such as their experiences of trauma and abuse, and not a sign of pathology, disorder, or individual deficiency. Related to these multiple disadvantages, female prisoners report higher levels of Class A drug use prior to their reception into custody than male prisoners (Light et al. 2013).

Although there are large gender differences in rates of lawbreaking, with women offending far less than men in almost all crime categories, broad motivations for offending are often similar for both genders. However, the situational contexts of crime and the strategies used in crime commission show marked gender differences. For example, when women deal drugs, they typically occupy lower and less powerful positions than men in drug hierarchies (Fleetwood 2014). When they are violent, women use weapons less frequently and cause fewer injuries than men (Miller 1998). And although young women who fight do so in the face of provocation, in the defence of respect, and due to anger and rage, as do young men, the contexts of disrespect and provocation are gendered and characterized by unequal power relationships and a sexual double standard (see Miller and White 2004).

Women's pathways into crime

Feminist theorists of crime, law, and justice from the late 1970s onwards (Daly and Chesney-Lind 1988; Heidensohn 1996; Smart 1976, inter alia) have argued that in order to understand women's lawbreaking, theorizing gender – the nature and meaning of gender relations – is just as important as theorizing crime. According to Daly's (1998) influential conceptual schema four broad approaches (which frequently overlap or intersect with one another) can be discerned in research which aims to explain gendered patterns of lawbreaking. First, the *gender ratio* approach examines gender differences, or why men and boys offend more than women and girls. Second, *gendered crime*, or 'rates' of lawbreaking, focuses on the context of illegal acts and how specific crimes are organized according to gender. Third, a *gendered pathways* approach examines the factors in women's and men's biographies or life courses which lead them into – or away from – conflict with the law. And fourth, *gendered lives* similarly addresses life course trajectories, but from a broader perspective: namely, how does gender organize social life, including identity, behaviour, basic survival, and social activities, such as finding shelter and caregiving? Below, following the gendered pathways approach, I review evidence relating to what are arguably the two most central influences in women's routes into crime and criminalization: poverty and victimization.

Poverty and economic marginalization

The role of economic necessity in women's frequently mundane and low-value thefts has long been clear from biographical accounts (e.g. Carlen 1988; Cook 1997) and the majority of women in prison or subject to community sanctions are affected by poverty, structural disadvantage, and an absence of power. Persistent poverty, which affects women, and particularly BAME women, disproportionately (Bennett and Daly 2014), and is in part a function of lower involvement in waged labour by women due to the demands of caring for children and others, may sometimes result in acquisitive crime becoming a necessary or 'rational' choice (Carlen 1988).

The political landscape constraining the choices of poor and marginalized women has changed in important ways in recent years. The increasing punishment of poverty by the state (Wacquant 2009) has particularly gendered effects, as criminalized women frequently move between welfare and criminal justice systems (Povey 2017). In societies subject to austerity measures, the impact on women of cuts to support services and welfare conditionality has been substantial. Welfare budget cuts, a deepening of social security retrenchment and an increasingly punitive welfare benefits system with stringent eligibility criteria affect women, and particularly mothers, disproportionately. In England and Wales in recent years, for example, lone parents (the majority of whom are women) have experienced large financial losses due to changes in benefits and taxation (Fawcett Society 2012) and welfare sanctions against lone parents have increased (Rabindrakumar 2017). One review of the 'triple jeopardy' for women under austerity highlighted the combined impact of benefits cuts, cuts to services including children's social care and health provision, and the fact that women are most likely to plug the gaps left by the withdrawal of state welfare and health services by undertaking unpaid care (Fawcett Society 2012). This may narrow some women's options so much as to compel them into acquisitive or other crimes. Data from England and Wales in 2010–2011 indicate that women who were apprehended for offending were more likely than men to be on welfare benefits (the reverse of the pattern in the general population), and that women lawbreakers who were employed earned less than males (Ministry of Justice 2014: 15), providing further support that female lawbreaking is frequently motivated by financial hardship.

In addition to its material and potentially criminogenic impact on already-marginalized groups, austerity has damaging emotional effects, producing humiliation, anxiety, shame, harassment, stigma, and depression. Inequality has been shown to result in a decrease in empathy and a hardening of attitudes towards those perceived to be 'at the bottom' (Savage et al. 2015). In other words, those lower down the class hierarchy may make downward social comparisons with those even worse off than themselves, such as benefits claimants, those perceived to be claiming state welfare undeservingly, and those with a criminal record. Poor women with other markers of a spoiled past (Goffman 1963), such as being (too) young, single mothers, and affected by drug misuse, are likely to encounter intense and overlapping forms of gendered surveillance and social control (and resultant stigma) across multiple sites of state governance (Sharpe 2015).

Gendered victimization

Women in conflict with the law have frequent experiences of victimization and gendered violence as children, adults, or both (Sheehan et al. 2011; Sharpe 2016). Moreover, they may be victims (of crime, violence, abuse, or neglect) and offenders simultaneously, with complex and shifting 'victim' and 'perpetrator' identities. In the context of women's victimization experiences, lawbreaking may constitute an attempt to resist, accommodate, or escape victimization. Conversely, a woman's involvement in crime might increase her risk of victimization through association with criminal associates or the possibility of retaliatory assault. In addition, imprisoned women are frequently homeless or precariously housed on their release, which increases their vulnerability to violence and sexual exploitation by men: for example, being pressured to exchange sex for a place to stay.

Prospective longitudinal research has found that girlhood experience of abuse significantly increases a woman's likelihood of arrest and conviction in adulthood (Cernkovich et al. 2008; Widom and Maxfield 2001). The association between trauma and loss and later criminal behaviour – the psychological and criminogenic sequelae of victimization experiences – is well documented yet undertheorized. Longitudinal research by Halsey (2018), focusing on second- and third-generation male prisoners in Australia and drawing on Fairbairn's (1943) conceptualization of the 'repression and return of bad objects', posits that unresolved trauma may create internalized pain or rage which is later manifested in externalized violence. However, as Trauffer and Widom (2017) remind us, the relationship between child maltreatment and lawbreaking is not deterministic: many maltreated girls do not subsequently break the law. This draws attention to the role of support and treatment – or an absence thereof – in victimized women's pathways into the criminal justice system.

Explanations of the victimization-crime nexus must also look upstream to the ways in which girls and women are regulated, or left unsupported, by state institutions beyond the criminal justice system. Qualitative research with justice system-involved girls has revealed systemic failings by the state to recognize (and, even where it does, to act upon) their frequent and often multiple experiences of victimization at home, on the streets, at school, and in state care (Sharpe 2016). Feminist scholars have highlighted the role played by the justice system in criminalizing girls' and women's survival strategies (Chesney-Lind 1989), including running away from home, involvement in sex work, substance misuse, and theft, as well as offending as a 'cry for help' where welfare support is not forthcoming (Phoenix 2012).

A history of abuse or neglect can also work against women in criminal justice risk assessment practices. For example, the likelihood of incarceration is far greater for young women with current or previous contact with child welfare agencies than for those in the general population (Goodkind et al. 2006), in effect punishing victimization. And while victimization may be conceptualized as a gendered dynamic risk factor warranting sensitive and gender-responsive criminal justice intervention (Hannah-Moffat 2010), a more just response is diversion from criminalization altogether. Indeed, where the state has failed to protect, support, and meet the basic economic needs of women who break the law, there is a compelling case that the state does not have the right to punish them (Carlen 1983).

Choice within constraint

It is unwise to generalize about the causes of offending for *all* women or to essentialize female lawbreakers. Social relations, as well as identities, are organized not only according to gender, but also according to 'race', class, and generation, amongst other variables, and lawbreaking is entered into (or not) in particular economic, historical, and cultural contexts. Consequently, situated and contextualized analyses of women's involvement in crime are essential in increasing understanding of *when* and *how* gender matters, and also how gender interacts with other aspects of identity.

As outlined above, 'feminist pathways' research on the central role played by abuse and victimization in women's routes into crime has made major advances in criminological theorizing. By contrast, recent explorations of girls' and women's agency and identity – how crime commission is structured by gender, or how women lawbreakers 'do gender' through crime – have been more limited (Fleetwood 2015; however, see Batchelor 2011; Jones 2010; Maher 1997; Miller 2001). De Coster and Heimer (2017) propose a theoretical framework of 'choice within constraint' in an attempt to go beyond the (sometimes) deterministic view of the relationship between structural disadvantage and lawbreaking. Such a framework requires theorizing how social structures that are unequal with respect to gender, class, race/ethnicity, and sexuality shape human behaviour in multiple, interactive, and situationally specific ways. In other words, how does gender intersect with place, poverty, and race to shape offending decisions? As De Coster and Heimer explain:

> regardless of gender, people sometimes *choose* crime to meet reputational, identity, and practical needs in situations where choices are limited by intersecting inequalities of opportunities and constraints.
>
> (2017: 7)

Thus, as active agents, women (and men) negotiate structural barriers and opportunities in ways which render lawbreaking a more or less attractive or necessary course of action. In some circumstances, women's options may be so constrained that offending becomes almost impossible to avoid.

Numerous studies have drawn attention to coercion as a pathway into crime for women (e.g. Barlow 2016; Richie 1996). There is some evidence that women who co-offend with men are more likely to commit serious crimes, as well as gender atypical offences, such as robbery (Becker and McCorkel 2011; Koons-Witt and Schram 2003). However, one review of the literature concluded that 'the belief that men play a pivotal role in the initiation of female crime' has little empirical support (Blanchette and Brown 2006: 13). It seems that the influence of men is more likely to be indirect. In her seminal work on the 'gender entrapment' of women of colour, Richie (1996) argued that a combination of intimate partner violence, culturally expected gender roles, and structural disadvantage coalesce to 'compel' African American women into crime. The situation for women of colour has worsened 'during an era in which public policy has virtually locked them into desperate and often dangerous situations' (Richie 2012: 7) and penal policy has led to their imprisonment in ever-greater numbers (although a cruel irony here is that the more frequent and longer imprisonment of black men has improved – at least temporarily – the safety of the black women towards whom they have been violent).

Richie's claim that 'women of color are more likely to be treated as criminal than as victims when they are abused' (2012: 7) was echoed in a recent case in England, when a pregnant woman who reported to the police that she had been raped and kidnapped in Germany over a six-month period was arrested on immigration charges while she was still being looked after in a sexual assault referral centre (Siddique and Rawlinson 2017). This example also attests to the gendered fallout of political climates and practices that are deliberately hostile to immigrants. British research on foreign national women in prison (Hales and Gelsthorpe 2012) reveals blurred boundaries between women's 'victim' and 'offender' identities. Hales and Gelsthorpe interviewed 103 women in four prisons and one immigration detention centre in England. More than half had been trafficked or smuggled into the UK or experienced work under slavery or servitude-like conditions after their arrival. The majority of the trafficked women and slavery victims had worked in the sex trade, in cannabis production, or domestic servitude prior to their incarceration, and most did not see it as a safe or viable option to seek help from the police due to concerns about their own safety.

Women's (arduous) routes out of crime

Longitudinal research on desistance from crime demonstrates that many internal processes are common to both men and women attempting to leave crime behind. Moreover, the same structural disadvantages which over-determine women's and men's pathways *into* crime may well also impede or derail their routes *out* (see e.g. Farrall et al. 2011; Halsey et al. 2017). However, scholars have also highlighted the salience of gender in processes of 'cognitive transformation' (Giordano et al. 2002), and in the distinctively gendered meanings attached to life events, as well as to crime itself.

The most gendered life event of all, becoming a mother, may be assumed to have substantial crime-inhibiting potential, either through a process of cognitive change, whereby a woman's identity as a mother provides new motivation to go straight, and/or through changes in routine activities, such as spending less time outside the home and more time engaged in outings and appointments with one's children. Research evidence on the impact of motherhood on lawbreaking paints a more complex picture, however: some studies have found little or no crime-reducing effect (e.g. Bachman et al. 2016; Giordano et al. 2002), while others have revealed a more or less rapid impact on crime cessation or reduction (e.g. Edin and Kefalas 2011; Kreager et al. 2010; Sharpe 2015). For example, for many of the women in Sharpe's (2015) study of young mothers with a criminal past, the ultimate maternal 'feared self' (Paternoster and Bushway 2009) – the mother whose children are taken into state care – was a powerful inhibitor of further lawbreaking. The extent of a woman's past involvement in the criminal justice system may also be important. Motherhood may have less impact on offending for women with a history of imprisonment (Giordano et al. 2002; Kreager et al. 2010; Leverentz 2014): with no help from family members and without the benefit of structural supports, caring for children and supporting them financially may cause additional strain (Giordano et al. 2011).

Structural barriers to desistance, as well as cultural definitions of behavioural expectations and norms, are also gendered. A growing body of research points to the *continued* salience of marginalization, poverty, and victimization as women attempt to leave crime behind. Overcoming structural barriers to (re)gaining a home, an income and one's own children for a woman with a criminal past and little social or state support may be nearly impossible (Bachman et al. 2016; Baldry 2010; Opsal and Foley 2013). Even where maternity causes a woman to leave crime behind by providing a pro-social 'replacement self' (Giordano et al. 2002), a formerly criminalized mother's spoiled identity may be the source of continued stigma and social opprobrium. Involvement in crime is rarely status-enhancing for women in ways that it sometimes is for marginalized men, and time spent in prison rarely affords a woman kudos or respect from her peers or community.

Societal responses to women who offend are important for an individual woman's self-concept and motivation to go straight, and also potentially in relation to ongoing scrutiny and assessment by state and other agencies of her parenting capabilities, eligibility for state financial support, and suitability for employment. Stigma may serve both to reinforce a women's criminal identity and, once internalized, produce intense shame and despair. For women with a history of custody, imprisonment and resettlement are likely to involve repeated episodes of incarceration alternated with serial periods of release, resulting in painful struggles for survival and negotiation of the legacy of shame, trauma, self-loathing, and self-injury (Carlton and Segrave 2011). Even amongst female *ex*-offenders, for whom criminal labels are extremely sticky, their past conduct frequently attracts judgements of enduring bad character, and their femininity and mothering capabilities may continue to be called into question (Sharpe 2015).

Concluding reflections

This necessarily selective overview of knowledge about women's routes into and out of crime has highlighted the salience of economic marginalization and victimization in over-determining women's pathways into the criminal justice system, as well as the need for policymakers and practitioners to recognize and take into account the structural contexts that surround women's lawbreaking. Moreover, the same structural contexts and barriers – exacerbated by the possession of a criminal record and by the widespread stigma and social condemnation conferred upon female lawbreakers – invariably continue to impede women's efforts to leave crime behind, frequently frustrating attempts to desist (Baldry 2010; Carlton and Segrave 2013). This points to the limits of individualized rehabilitative strategies in helping women to desist from crime, as well as an important role for advocacy for/with criminalized women who have been repeatedly failed by the state both as victims and as impoverished and marginalized citizens.

Note

1   The rather higher proportion of female defendants than arrestees is driven by prosecutions for TV licence evasion, which cannot be dealt with by the police.

References

Bachman, R., Kerrison, E., Paternoster, R., Smith, L. and O'Connell, D. (2016) The complex relationship between motherhood and desistance. *Women & Criminal Justice*, 26(3), 212–231.

Baldry, E. (2010) Women in transition: From prison to. . . *Current Issues in Criminal Justice*, 22(2), 253–267.

Barlow, C. (2016) *Coercion and Women Offenders: A Gendered Pathway into Crime*. Bristol: Policy Press.

Batchelor, S. (2011) Beyond dichotomy: Towards an explanation of young women's involvement in violent street gangs. In B. Goldson (Ed.), *Youth in Crisis? 'Gangs', Territoriality and Violence*. Abingdon: Routledge.

Becker, S. and McCorkel, J. (2011) The gender of criminal opportunity: The impact of male co-offenders on women's crime. *Feminist Criminology*, 6(2), 79–110.

Bennett, F. and Daly, M. (2014) *Poverty Through a Gender Lens: Evidence and Policy Review on Gender and Poverty*. Oxford: University of Oxford, Department of Social Policy and Intervention.

Blanchette, K. and Brown, S. L. (2006) *The Assessment and Treatment of Women Offenders: An Integrative Perspective*. Chichester: Wiley.

Carlen, P. (1983) On rights and powers: Some notes on penal politics. In D. Garland and P. Young (Eds.), *The Power to Punish: Contemporary Penality and Social Analysis*. London: Heinemann.

Carlen, P. (1988) *Women, Crime and Poverty*. Milton Keynes: Open University Press.

Carlton, B. and Segrave, M. (2011) Women's survival post-imprisonment: Connecting imprisonment with pains past and present. *Punishment & Society*, 13(5), 551–570.

Carlton, B. and Segrave, M. (2013) *Women Exiting Prison: Critical Essays on Gender, Post-Release Support and Survival*. Abingdon: Routledge.

Cernkovich, S., Lanctôt, N. and Giordano, P. (2008) Predicting adolescent and adult antisocial behavior among adjudicated delinquent females. *Crime & Delinquency*, 54(1), 3–33.

Chesney-Lind, M. (1989) Girls' crime and woman's place: Toward a feminist model of female delinquency. *Crime and Delinquency*, 35, 5–30.

Cook, D. (1997) *Poverty, Crime and Punishment*. London: Child Poverty Action Group.

Daly, K. (1998) Women's pathways to felony court: Feminist theories of lawbreaking and problems of representation. In K. Daly and L. Maher (Eds.), *Criminology at the Crossroads: Feminist Readings in Crime and Justice*. New York: Oxford University Press.

Daly, K. and Chesney-Lind, M. (1988) Feminism and criminology. *Justice Quarterly*, 5(4), 497–538.

De Coster, S. and Heimer, K. (2017) Choice within constraint: An explanation of crime at the intersections. *Theoretical Criminology*, 21(1), 11–22.

Edin, K. and Kefalas, M. (2011) *Promises I Can Keep: Why Poor Women Put Motherhood Before Marriage*. Berkeley, CA: University of California Press.

Fairbairn, W. R. D. (1943) The repression and the return of bad objects (with special reference to the 'war neuroses'). *Psychology and Psychotherapy*, 19, 327–341.

Farrall, S., Sharpe, G., Hunter, B. and Calverley, A. (2011) Theorizing structural and individual-level processes in desistance and persistence: Outlining an integrated perspective. *Austrian and New Zealand Journal of Criminology*, 44, 218–234.

Fawcett Society. (2012) *The Impact of Austerity on Women*. London: Fawcett Society.

Feilzer, M. and Hood, R. (2004) *Differences or Discrimination? Minority Ethnic Young People in the Youth Justice System*. London: Youth Justice Board.

Fleetwood, J. (2014) *Drug Mules: Women in the International Cocaine Trade*. Basingstoke: Palgrave Macmillan.

Fleetwood, J. (2015) A narrative approach to women's lawbreaking. *Feminist Criminology*, 10(4), 368–388.

Giordano, P., Cernkovich, S. and Rudolph, J. (2002) Gender, crime and desistance: Toward a theory of cognitive transformation. *American Journal of Sociology*, 107(4), 990–1064.

Giordano, P., Seffron, P., Manning, W. and Longmore, M. (2011) Parenthood and crime: The role of wantedness, relationships with partners, and SES. *Journal of Criminal Justice*, 39(5), 405–416.

Goffman, E. (1963) *Stigma: Notes of the Management of Spoiled Identity*. Harmondsworth: Penguin.

Goodkind, S., Ng, I. and Sarri, R. (2006) The impact of sexual abuse in the lives of young women involved or at risk of involvement with the juvenile justice system. *Violence Against Women*, 12(5), 456–477.

Hales, L. and Gelsthorpe, L. (2012) *The Criminalisation of Migrant Women*. Cambridge: Institute of Criminology, University of Cambridge.

Halsey, M. (2018) Child victims as adult offenders: Foregrounding the criminogenic effects of (Unresolved) trauma and loss. *British Journal of Criminology*, 58(1), 17–36.

Halsey, M., Armstrong, R. and Wright, S. (2017) 'F*ck It!': Matza and the mood of fatalism in the desistance process. *British Journal of Criminology*, 57(5), 1041–1060, 1 September.

Hannah-Moffat, K. (2010) Sacrosanct or flawed: Risk, accountability and gender-responsive penal politics. *Current Issues in Criminal Justice*, 22, 193–215.

Hedderman, C. and Gelsthorpe, L. (Eds.). (1997) *Understanding the Sentencing of Women*. London: HMSO.

Heidensohn, F. (1996) *Women and Crime*, 2nd edition. Basingstoke: Palgrave Macmillan.

Her Majesty's Chief Inspector of Prisons. (2017) *Annual Report 2016–17*. London: HM Inspectorate of Prisons.

Jones, N. (2010) *Between Good and Ghetto: African American Girls and Inner-City Violence*. New Brunswick: Rutgers University Press.

Koons-Witt, B. and Schram, P. (2003) The prevalence and nature of violent offending by females. *Journal of Criminal Justice*, 31, 361–371.

Kreager, D., Matsueda, R. and Erosheva, E. (2010) Motherhood and criminal desistance in disadvantaged neighbourhoods. *Criminology*, 48(1), 221–258.

Leverentz, A. (2014) *The Ex-Prisoner's Dilemma: How Women Negotiate Competing Narratives of Reentry and Desistance*. New Brunswick: Rutgers University Press.

Light, M., Grant, E. and Hopkins, K. (2013) *Gender Differences in Substance Misuse and Mental Health Amongst Prisoners: Results from the Surveying Prisoner Crime Reduction (SPCR) Longitudinal Cohort Study of Prisoners*. London: Ministry of Justice.

Maher, L. (1997) *Sexed Work: Gender, Race and Resistance in a Brooklyn Drug Market.* Oxford: Oxford University Press.

Miller, J. (1998) Up it up: Gender and the accomplishment of street robbery. *Criminology,* 36(1), 37–66.

Miller, J. (2001) *One of the Guys: Girls, Gangs, and Gender.* New York: Oxford University Press.

Miller, J. and White, N. (2004) Situational effects of gender inequality on girls' participation in violence. In C. Alder and A. Worrall (Eds.), *Girls' Violence: Myths and Realities.* Albany: University of New York Press.

Ministry of Justice. (2014) *Statistics on Women and the Criminal Justice System 2013.* London: Ministry of Justice.

Ministry of Justice. (2016) *Statistics on Women and the Criminal Justice System 2015.* London: Ministry of Justice.

Opsal, T. and Foley, A. (2013) Making it on the outside: Understanding barriers to women's post-incarceration reintegration. *Sociology Compass,* 7(4), 265–277.

Paternoster, R. and Bushway, S. (2009) Desistance and the 'Feared Self': Toward an identity theory of criminal desistance. *Criminology,* 99(4), 1103–1156.

Phoenix, J. (2012) *Out of Place: The Policing and Criminalisation of Sexually Exploited Girls and Young Women.* London: The Howard League.

Player, E. (2017) The offender personality disorder pathway and its implications for women prisoners in England and Wales. *Punishment & Society,* 19(5), 568–589.

Povey, L. (2017) Where welfare and criminal justice meet: Applying Wacquant to the experiences of marginalised women in austerity Britain. *Social Policy and Society,* 16(2), 271–281.

Rabindrakumar, S. (2017) *Paying the Price: Still 'Just About Managing'?* London: Gingerbread.

Richie, B. (1996) *Compelled to Crime: The Gender Entrapment of Black Battered Women.* New York: Routledge.

Richie, B. (2012) *Arrested Justice: Black Women, Violence, and America's Prison Nation.* New York: New York University Press.

Savage, M., Cunningham, N., Devine, F., Friedman, S., Laurison, D., McKenzie, L., Miles, A., Snee, H. and Wakeling, P. (2015) *Social Class in the 21st Century.* London: Penguin.

Sharpe, G. (2015) Precarious identities: 'Young' motherhood, desistance and stigma. *Criminology & Criminal Justice,* 15(4), 407–422.

Sharpe, G. (2016) Re-imagining justice for girls: A new agenda for research. *Youth Justice,* 16(1), 3–17.

Sheehan, R., McIvor, G. and Trotter, C. (Eds.) (2011) *Working with Women Offenders in the Community.* Cullompton: Willan Publishing.

Siddique, H. and Rawlinson, K. (2017) Rape victim arrested on immigration charges after going to police. *The Guardian,* 28 November.

Smart, C. (1976) *Women, Crime and Criminology: A Feminist Critique.* London: Routledge and Kegan Paul.

Trauffer, N. and Widom, C. S. (2017) Child abuse and neglect, and psychiatric disorders in nonviolent and violent female offenders. *Violence and Gender,* 4(4), 137–143.

Wacquant, L. (2009) *Punishing the Poor: The Neoliberal Government of Social Insecurity.* Durham, NC: Duke University Press.

Widom, C. and Maxfield, M. (2001) *An Update on the 'Cycle of Violence'.* Washington, DC: National Institute of Justice.

What works with women offenders? An English and Welsh perspective

Loraine Gelsthorpe

Introduction

There are three legal jurisdictions in the UK: England and Wales, Scotland, and Northern Ireland. Attention to women offenders has been at a different pace in each of these jurisdictions, but broadly speaking, there has been an awakening to women offenders' needs since the 1970s, bearing in mind the claim that women have very often been 'correctional afterthoughts' (Ross and Fabiano 1986). There have been some positive steps forwards to address offending behaviour over the past 30 years in particular, especially since the early 1990s with the expansion of the database to include meta-analytic studies. Indeed, the research base now strongly recognizes that effective work with offenders is entirely possible (Hollin and Palmer 2006a). But there have also been some reverses or steps backwards as political dimensions and paradoxes of initiatives have come to light, and fights for funding have intensified. Tensions between a tight focus on initiatives which might reduce offending behaviour and reconviction rates, and a broader focus on facilitating the development of confidence and social capital amongst women have emerged.

Women and their crime-related needs

Prior to the 1960s women were more or less ignored in criminological theorizing or they were pathologized, seen as 'abnormal' or as 'doubly deviant', both biologically and socially. We have moved a long way from this to acknowledge that not only is offending behaviour often situationally controlled, but that assumptions about single causal factors which produce criminal behaviour are short-sighted. There are multiple routes into crime, not least poverty and vulnerability. Women themselves often indicate that there was seemingly no choice but to commit crime, sometimes out of need to care for family members, sometimes under duress, sometimes because of complicated power relationships, sometimes because the crime opportunity seemed a rational choice, sometimes under the influence of alcohol or drugs. There is need to acknowledge that 'crime-related needs' are sometimes socially constructed and relate to gender and culture expectations. This is certainly a challenge in a criminal justice system where there is emphasis on 'risks' and 'needs' and where there is neglect of the risk factors most relevant to women (Hannah-Moffat 2004).

Addressing various criticisms relating to the limitations of previous assessments of crime-related needs, recent research focusing on the dynamic predictors of reconviction for women identifies poor problem-solving skills, impulsivity, and unemployment as the most prevalent criminogenic needs amongst women offenders (Travers and Mann 2018). Unemployment, regular activities which encourage offending, binge drinking, Class A drug use, and impulsivity emerge as the strongest predictors of reoffending.

Women who are in conflict with the law in the UK typically commit property-related offences and have fewer criminal convictions than men; they commit fewer and less serious offences, and persist in offending less often than men (Ministry of Justice 2018a). There have been consistent messages from the research literature, and from experienced service providers and service users, that women offenders tend to have histories of unmet needs in relation to sexual and violent victimization, physical and mental health, housing and income, and training and employment (Sheehan et al. 2007). Substance misuse and childcare responsibilities often compound these problems (Women in Prison 2017). Service providers and service users in prisons and in probation/community-based provision, support claims that there may well be indirect relationships between abuse and mental health, labour market participation, and substance abuse, all of which are associated with the risks of reoffending (Hollin and Palmer 2006b). Put simply, 'victimization' creates psychological sequalae which can lead to offending behaviour. This leads to the question of 'what is needed', and 'what works with women'.

Rapid evidence assessments: what is needed?

The first rapid evidence assessment in the UK was carried out by the National Offender Management Service (Lart et al. 2008). The research findings were limited insofar as they emerged from just 16 North American and Canadian studies (in the main) and three meta-analyses. They did not really go beyond the rather general claim that targeting women's antisocial attitudes, and general educational needs might be useful, especially if combined with residential treatment after prison.

The second rapid evidence assessment was completed in 2015 (Stewart et al.) The authors suggest that substance abuse treatment interventions in prisons, in particular, or structured therapeutic community-based programmes which apply cognitive behavioural practices focusing on skills development, are helpful. There is also suggestion that a gender-responsive cognitive behavioural programme with emphasis on existing strengths and competencies, as well as skills acquisition, is useful to facilitate pathways out of crime. Further, community-based opioid maintenance can result in reduced offending patterns whilst women are in treatment. Booster programmes and treatment reflecting gender-responsive approaches show promise relative to gender-neutral programmes.

What works? Offending-related policy and programmes for women: initiatives in the UK

Following renewed recognition that the women's prison population was growing at a greater rate than that of men in England and Wales in the 1990s and into the 2000s, yet with no evidence that women were committing more crime or more serious crime, the government produced a Women's Offending Reduction Programme (WORP; Home Office 2004). The Women's Policy Team (2006) subsequently encouraged the development of guidance concerning services for women on probation, and lent support to existing initiatives to improve community-based responses to women's mental health needs. The Policy Team negotiated £9.15 million to build on best practice developed by small-scale initiatives such as the 218 Centre in Scotland (Loucks et al. 2006) and the Asha Centre in England and Wales (Rumgay 2004). It supported a demonstration programme *Together Women* (TW; five projects across two regions of the country) which sought to provide holistic support for women who were former or current offenders or whose social exclusion needs were thought to put them at risk of offending (Hedderman et al. 2008).

The Ministry of Justice's own analysis of the implementation of community services for women offenders introduced between late 2006 and early 2007 suggested that TW was seen by local stakeholders as filling an important gap in provision (notwithstanding concerns about the supply of suitable accommodation, access to counselling, and mental health out-reach services). Most service users interviewed early on were optimistic about their chances of avoiding further offending, though later interviews introduced a note of caution as women recognized that progress would not be straightforward (Hedderman et al. 2008: 16). Service users who had sustained contact with TW in its first year of operation valued the assis-tance provided and the facilitated access to other agencies (Hedderman et al. 2011).

In 2007, the suicides of six women in HMP Styal prompted the Labour Government to commission Baroness Corston to review women 'with partic-ular vulnerabilities' in the criminal justice system. She interpreted her brief broadly, seeing most women in prison as 'vulnerable'. Drawing on the exper-tise of practitioners and the experiences of women in prison whom she met, Corston produced 43 recommendations which revolved around the need for holistic care of women in the community (Annison et al. 2015). Readiness for action was reinforced by the Fawcett Society's commissioned survey of existing community centres and services which might be adapted for women offenders (Gelsthorpe et al. 2007), published within weeks of the publication of the Corston Report. The report identified nine lessons to be taken into account in providing for women in the community. Drawing on a wide range of literature on women's needs and 'what works' with women, it was thought that services should:

1   Be women-only to foster safety and a sense of community and to enable staff to develop expertise in work with women (i.e. women-centred);
2   Integrate offenders with nonoffenders so as to normalize women offend-ers' experiences and facilitate a supportive environment for learning;
3   Foster women's empowerment so they gain sufficient self-esteem to directly engage in problem-solving themselves, and feel motivated to seek appropriate employment;
4   Utilize ways of working with women which draw on what is known about their effective learning styles;
5   Take a holistic and practical stance to helping women to address social problems which may be linked to their offending;
6   Facilitate links with mainstream agencies, especially health, debt advice, and counselling;
7   Have the capacity and flexibility to allow women to return to the centre or programme for 'top up' of continued support and develop-ment where required;
8   Ensure that women have a supportive milieu or mentor to whom they can turn when they have completed any offending-related pro-grammes, since personal support is likely to be as important as any direct input addressing offending behaviour;

9   Provide women with practical help with transport and childcare so that they can maintain their involvement in the centre or programme.

(Gelsthorpe et al. 2007: 54)

Thus there was huge momentum for change. Drawing on the initial favourable impact of the TW project, expertise from practitioners,[1] and with support from the Equalities Office and the Corston Independent Funders Coalition,[2] the Ministry of Justice found funding to promote the extension of work in women's centres around the country to provide service interventions for women in contact with the criminal justice system. With recognition that a strategic approach was needed, in May 2011, with support from the Ministry of Justice, Government Equalities Office, and the Corston Independent Funders Coalition, Women's Breakout,[3] a national network to help coordinate community services for women was born. Shortly after the publication of the Corston Report, the National Offender Management Service[4] issued a National Service Framework for Women Offenders (NOMS 2008) which set out the kinds of services which were to be provided (subsequently replaced by a NOMS Women and Equalities Group authored report: *A Distinct Approach: A Guide to Working with Women Offenders* (NOMS 2012)). By 2016, Women's Breakout[5] reported a membership of nearly 50 organizations. Other positive developments include the development of guidance on regimes and standards of care in prisons and, more recently, we have seen the development of trauma-informed work (privately sponsored, but publicly supported by the Prison Service) to ensure that women offenders are not further brutalized and that their vulnerability is fully acknowledged.[6] We have witnessed parallel positive developments in probation with recognition that women are 'equal but different' (HM Inspectorate of Probation 2011).

Learning about what works from the women's centres

Building on *Unlocking Value*, published in 2008, the New Economics Foundation strongly suggested that we *all* benefit from investing in alternatives to prison for women offenders. The authors went so far as to indicate that using women's centre provision as an alternative to custody can deliver £14 of social value for every £1 invested. Later research from the New Economics Foundation (Nicholles and Whitehead 2012) investigated the impact of the 'Women's Centres' on women offenders across five sites, and suggested a positive direction of travel in relation to women's optimism, autonomic and self-efficacy, and establishing supportive relationships.

The Inspire Women's Project in Northern Ireland, established in October 2008, aimed 'to develop and deliver in the community a new, enhanced range of women-specific services which directly contribute to reducing women's offending through targeted community based interventions' (DOJ 2010).

The evaluation involved analysis of a cohort of women (between 20 and 49 years of age) who were referred to Inspire between October 2008 and July 2010, with the majority of the women being on community sentences (89%) (Easton and Matthews 2011). Most of the women were compliant with their community sentences (72%), and the women were positive about the provision available to them, both in relation to the quality of supervision and the variety of support options available. Women were grateful for the women-only provision and physical space and the nonjudgemental attitude of their probation officers at Inspire. Peer support and practical help around specific issues such as debt, housing, and attending court were also mentioned positively (Easton and Matthews 2011: 5). Interviews with some of the women indicated that 78% (29 out of 37) indicated that they had not committed any further offences since engaging with Inspire.

Holloway and Brookman's (2010) evaluation of the *Turnaround Project in Wales* and McCoy et al.'s (2013) evaluation of the *Liverpool Women's Turnaround Project* reveal positive experiences of nonjudgemental support, improvements in the use of alcohol, physical and mental health, relationships, offending, and social skills, for instance. Looking at a range of community centres for women in England and Wales, Radcliffe, Hunter, and Vass (2015) concluded from qualitative analysis of interviews with service users that relationships with key workers and peers and the education and employment opportunities available are crucial in supporting desistance from crime. The Inspire project at Brighton Women's Centre has produced a similar positive story, with 90% of women successfully completing their Community Orders through the support of the Centre and with reductions in reoffending (Inspire 2017).

Looking further

The *Probation Journal* ran a special issue devoted to Women and the Criminal Justice System in 2009 within which Worrall and Gelsthorpe reviewed the development of work with women offenders in the previous 30 years. They suggested that there had been a number of 'bottom up' initiatives from within Probation (groupwork programmes and so on) which helped to identify what works with women. Jill Annison et al. (2015) chart developments since the publication of the Corston Report; contributors note positive initiatives regarding 'what works' in Wales, work with older women, and the impact of 'serious therapy' for serious female offenders in the therapeutic community at HMP Send.

At the same time that community-based services were being developed via the Together Women initiative, in 2006, Jenny Cann examined the impact of 'enhanced thinking skills' programmes (a programme shaped by cognitive social learning theory) on women as compared with men. She found that there were no statistically significant differences in the one- and two-year reconviction rates between female offenders who participated in the prison-based cognitive skills programmes delivered between 1996 and 2000 and a matched comparison group of men (leaving aside methodological limitations in terms of targeting and the 'purity' of the matched comparison group of men). Her first interpretation led to a conclusion that 'what works for men works for women too'. But whilst Veronica Hollis produced further research hot on the heels of that of Cann, indicating no clear differences between men and women in regard to the impact of the General Offender Behaviour Programme on reconviction rates (GOBP – another intervention shaped by cognitive social learning theory), this was later challenged by Martin et al. (2009). Martin et al. (2009) found that despite some similarities, the predictors of programme completion not only varied for men and women, but operated differently between them, thus supporting the claim that gender-responsiveness is important in shaping what works with women.

In Scotland, the introduction of a presumption against short sentences has arguably benefitted women given that so many women are given short sentences, though the overall impact is debatable because of a coincidental decline in offending rates (Roberts and Tipple 2019). This said, there have been positive developments in regard to community services for women (Scottish Government 2015) beyond the notable impact of Centre 2018 (as described earlier). But as the Prison Reform Trust (2017a) has noted, there is a ways to go.

Towards *Better Outcomes*

A NOMS (2015) report on *Better Outcomes for Women Offenders* reflects a wider remit and draws on wide-ranging evidence on 'what works' with women to live safe, offending-free lives, promoting desistance and management of the effects of domestic violence. This report seems altogether grounded in women's lived experiences, and reflects Corston's (2007) recognition of the need for a holistic approach to assist women. There is also recognition that women are not an homogenous group and that future guidance on improving outcomes for black, Asian, and minority ethnic offenders is needed (see Prison Reform Trust 2017b). *Better Outcomes* of course goes beyond what works in terms of reducing reoffending, but relates to broad factors which impact on reoffending. The report identifies the need to stabilize substance misuse via cognitive behavioural programmes (as outlined by Stewart and Gobeil 2015), expedite access to health services for mental health issues including anxiety, depression, 'personality disorder', trauma, and post-traumatic stress disorder (via advocacy interventions, social support, mentoring, and trauma-focused cognitive behavioural programmes) and offer short-term trauma-focused counselling.

Another priority need concerns ways of helping women build skills to control impulsive behaviour and destructive emotions – again, cognitive behavioural programmes are thought to help here, alongside mindfulness techniques and dialectical behaviour therapy. *Better Outcomes* includes:

(1) the need for women to develop a pro-social identity – via opportunities to build positive, robust relationships and activities which enable people to do good for others or for their community; such activities help people to describe themselves other than as 'an offender'; (2) the need for women to be in control of their daily lives and develop goals for life (with opportunity to develop confidence to achieve personal goals and be self-efficacious; (3) the need for women to maintain or develop supportive family relationships (via supportive facilitation), and resettle and build social capital (improving money management skills and employability via services which help women to gain the skills that they need to secure stable accommodation and meaningful employment). Thus 'what works' in this context relates to what is *most likely* to be effective. The same report indicates what is *less likely* to be effective: services aimed solely at improving awareness of the effects of substance misuse; services which merely signpost to other services; long-term non-specific counselling; services which aim solely to increase awareness of the effects of crime on others, fuelling a negative view of the self; services which focus solely on building self-esteem through 'attractiveness' or other external characteristics; services or activities which simply facilitate contact without a concomitant focus on the quality of the contact/relationships; and finally, services which have no focus on developing skills to sustain involvement in resettlement activities.

Concluding reflections

Much has been achieved in terms of identifying what women need and 'what works', whether this be in relation to reoffending or more broadly to what women want or what practitioners who work closely with women offenders say. What is delivered on the ground to address what seems to work varies according to the vicissitudes of political will and financial constraints (Gelsthorpe and Russell 2018). Every now and again, there is renewed interest in setting out a strategy for women offenders delivering what might work (Ministry of Justice 2018b) but aspirations are tempered by financial realities on the ground and by the need to take intersectionality into account. Longitudinal studies of girls through to adulthood are needed, with opportunity to analyze risk factors and protective factors; so too is a systematic review of what works with women (at least one is in process). More case studies would also be beneficial. Analyzing 'what works with women' is sometimes hampered by small numbers if we think that quantitative evidence is what really matters in measuring the impact of interventions; yet at the same time women service users' stories of 'what works' speak volumes.

Notes

1   For example, Women at the Well: www.watw.org.uk; Women in Prison: www.women inprison.org.uk.

2   This was a collaboration of grant-making trusts and foundations who wanted to see action following the report.
3   Women's Breakout: http://womensbreakout.org.uk. Women's Breakout became the representative voice for the 47 organizations that were providing community services for women within the criminal justice system, strategically aiming to influence government in regard to the use of community penalties instead of custody, and increase sentencers' understanding of women's vulnerability and needs, as well as promoting the need for gender-specific services in the community in particular, but in prisons too.
4   From April 2017, renamed as Her Majesty's Prison and Probation Service (HMPPS).
5   Women's Breakout: http://womensbreakout.org.uk. The organization merged with Clinks, a national umbrella organization for third-sector parties involved in criminal justice, in September 2017.
6   See One Small Thing: www.onesmallthing.org.uk/about/. One Small Thing is an initiative sponsored by Lady Edwina Grosvenor to ensure trauma-informed practice in women's prisons. The training is now being rolled out in men's prisons, too.

References

Annison, J. Brayford, J. and Deering, J. (Eds.). (2015) *Women and Criminal Justice: From the Corston Report to Transforming Rehabilitation*. Bristol: Policy Press.

Cann, J. (2006) *Cognitive Skills Programmes: Impact on Reducing Reconviction Among a Sample of Female Prisoners*. Home Office Research Findings 276. London: Home Office.

Corston, Baroness. (2007) *The Corston Report: A Review of Women with Particular Vulnerabilities in the Criminal Justice System*. London: Home Office.

Department of Justice (DOJ). (2010) *Women's Offending Behaviour in Northern Ireland: A Strategy to Manage Women Offenders and Those Vulnerable to Offending Behaviour 2010–2014*. Belfast: Department of Justice.

Easton, H. and Matthews, R. (2011) *Evaluation of the Inspire Women's Project*. London: London South Bank University.

Gelsthorpe, L. and Russell, J. (2018) Women and penal reform: Two steps forwards, three steps backwards? *Political Quarterly*, 89(2), 227–236, April–June.

Gelsthorpe, L., Sharpe, G. and Roberts, J. (2007) *Provision for Women Offenders in the Community*. London: Fawcett Commission.

Hannah-Moffat, K. (2004) Criminogenic need and the transformative risk subject: Hybridizations of risk/need in penality. *Punishment & Society*, 7, 29–51.

Hedderman, C., Gunby, C. and Shelton, N. (2011) What women want: The importance of qualitative approaches in evaluating work with women offenders. *Criminology and Criminal Justice*, 11(1), 3–19.

Hedderman, C., Palmer, E. and Hollin, C. (2008) *Implementing Services for Women Offenders and Those 'at risk' of Offending: Action Research with Together Women*. Ministry of Justice Research Series 12/08. London: Ministry of Justice.

HM Inspectorate of Probation. (2011) Thematic Inspection Report, *Equal But Different? An Inspection of Alternatives to Custody for Women Offenders*. Manchester: HM Inspectorate of Probation. Available at: www.justiceinspectorates.gov.uk/probation/wp-content/uploads/sites/5/2014/03/womens-thematic-alternatives-to-custody-2011.pdf.

Hollin, C. and Palmer, E. (2006a) *Offending Behaviour Programmes. Development, Application and Controversies*. Chichester: Wiley.

Hollin, C. and Palmer, E. (2006b) Criminogenic need and women offenders: A critique of the literature. *Legal and Criminological Psychology*, 11, 17–195.

Hollis, V. (2007) *Reconviction Analysis IAPS*. London: RDS, NOMS, December.

Holloway, K. and Brookman, F. (2010) *An Evaluation of the Women's Turnaround Project*. Final Report Prepared for NOMS Cymru. Available at: https://wccsj.ac.uk/images/docs/report.pdf (Accessed 10 June 2019).

Home Office. (2004) *Women's Offending Reduction Programme (WORP). Action Plan.* London: Home Office.

Inspire. (2017) *Brighton Women's Centre.* Available at: www.womenscentre.org.uk/services/inspire/ (Accessed 2 May 2018).

Lart, R., Pantazis, C., Pemberton, S., Turner, W. and Almeida, C. (2008) *Interventions Aimed at Reducing Re-Offending in Female Offenders: A Rapid Evidence Assessment (REA).* Ministry of Justice Research Series 8/08. London: Ministry of Justice, NOMS.

Loucks, N., Malloch, M., McIvor, G. and Gelsthorpe, L. (2006) *Evaluation of the 218 Centre.* Edinburgh: Scottish Executive.

Martin, J., Kautt, P. and Gelsthorpe, L. (2009) What works for women? A comparison of community-based general offending programme completion. *British Journal of Criminology,* 49(6), 879–899.

McCoy, E., Jones, L. and McVeigh, J. (2013) *Evaluation of the Liverpool Women's Turnaround Project.* Liverpool. Available at: www.psspeople.com/app/uploads/2014/10/Evaluation-of-the-Liverpool-Turnaround-Project-7.pdf (Accessed 18 July 2018).

Ministry of Justice. (2018a) *Statistics on Women and the Criminal Justice System 2017.* London: Ministry of Justice. Available at: https://assets.publishing.service.gov.uk/government/uploads/system/uploads/attachment_data/file/759770/women-criminal-justice-system-2017.pdf (Accessed 10 June 2019).

Ministry of Justice. (2018b) *Female Offender Strategy for Women in the Criminal Justice System.* London: Ministry of Justice. Available at: www.gov.uk/government/publications/female-offender-strategy (Accessed 18 July 2018).

National Offender Management Service (NOMS). (2008) *Offender Management Guide to Working with Women.* London: Ministry of Justice, NOMS.

National Offender Management Service (NOMS). (2012) *A Distinct Approach: A Guide for Working with Women Offenders.* London: NOMS.

National Offender Management Service (NOMS). (2015) *Better Outcomes for Women Offenders.* London: NOMS.

New Economics Foundation. (2008) *Unlocking Value.* London: New Economics Foundation.

Nicholles, N. and Whitehead, S. (2012) *Women Community Services: A Wise Commission.* London: New Economics Foundation.

Prison Reform Trust. (2017a) Why focus on reducing women's imprisonment in Scotland? *Prison Reform Trust Briefing.* Available at: http://www.prisonreformtrust.org.uk/Portals/0/Documents/Women/Why%20women_Scotland_2017.pdf (Accessed 10 June 2019).

Prison Reform Trust. (2017b) *Counted Out: Black, Asian and Minority Ethnic Women in the Criminal Justice System.* London: PRT.

Radcliffe, P., Hunter, G. and Vass, R. (2015) *The Development and Impact of Community Services for Women Offenders: An Evaluation.* London: The Institute for Criminal Policy Research, School of Law, Birkbeck College.

Roberts, M. and Tipple, C. (2019) *What Could England and Wales Learn from Scotland's Approach to Justice? A Study of the Impact of a Presumption against Custodial Sentences of Three Months or Less in Scotland.* Crest Advisory. Available at: https://static.wixstatic.com/ugd/b9cf6c_6ee60c5e60014ae6b3ffb7020ccf3739.pdf (Accessed 10 June 2019).

Ross, R. and Fabiano, E. (1986) *Female Offenders: Correctional Afterthoughts.* Jefferson, NC: McFarland.

Rumgay, J. (2004) *The Asha Centre: Report of an Evaluation.* Worcester: Asha Centre.

Scottish Government. (2015) *Evaluation of Sixteen Women's Community Justice Services in Scotland.* The Scottish Government. Research Findings 60/2017. Available at: https://www.gov.scot/binaries/content/documents/govscot/publications/research-and-analysis/2015/09/evaluation-sixteen-womens-community-justice-services-scotland-research-findings/documents/evaluation-sixteen-womens-community-justice-services-scotland/evaluation-sixteen-womens-community-justice-services-scotland/govscot%3Adocument (Accessed 10 June 2019).

Sheehan, R., McIvor, G. and Trotter, C. (2007) *What Works with Women Offenders*. Cullompton: Willan Publishing.

Stewart, L. and Gobeil, R. (2015) *Effective Interventions for Women Offenders: A Rapid Evidence Assessment*. London: National Offender Management Service Analytical Summary, July.

Travers, R. and Mann, R. (2018) *The Dynamic Predictors of Reconvictions for Women*. Analytical Summary. London: Her Majesty's Prison and Probation Service.

Women in Prison. (2017) *Corston+10. The Corston Report 10 Years on*. London: Women in Prison.

Women's Policy Team. (2006) *Women's Offending Reduction Programme: Review of Progress*. London: Home Office.

Worrall, A. and Gelsthorpe, L. (2009) 'What works' with women offenders: The past 30 years. *Probation Journal*, 56, 329–345.

Gender-responsive approaches for women in the United States

51

Nena P. Messina, Barbara E. Bloom, and Stephanie S. Covington

Introduction

A large body of literature shows that there are dramatic differences between justice-involved men and women (Bloom and Covington 2008; Bloom et al. 2003, 2004; Browne et al. 1999; Chesney-Lind and Pasko 2004; Owen and Bloom 1995; Singer et al. 1995). The women are more likely to have co-occurring substance use disorders and mental health issues, to have chronic physical health issues, to be primary caretakers of minor children, and to be victims of intimate partner violence, as opposed to their male counterparts. Pregnant and postpartum women also require additional specialized treatment and care. Justice-involved women are also more likely than men to report extensive histories of trauma, including emotional, physical, and sexual abuse as children, adolescents, and adults (Langan and Pelissier 2001; Messina et al. 2007; Pollock 2002).

The complex histories and needs of justice-involved women require specific criminal justice policies, practices, and approaches to their rehabilitation and recovery. In fact, the differential impact of incarceration on men and women has been outlined in the literature. Disproportional mental health problems among women offenders are often exacerbated during incarceration, particularly for women with children and a history of victimization (Wolf et al. 2007). The disruption of families and the burden on child welfare systems is alarming when imprisonment is the result of low-level offences for mothers with minor children.

Over two decades of research has shown that justice-involved women are predominantly low-level offenders convicted of drug and property crimes, whose needs may better be served in the community with specialized treatment programmes (Bloom et al. 2003). The challenge is the need to create alternative custody policies for low-level offenders that contribute to their successful recovery and that better achieve societal goals.

Pathways of addiction and crime

The 'pathways perspective' is one approach to understanding addiction and criminality among women (Bloom et al. 2003). Research that follows this perspective suggests that specific life experiences of men and women are differentially relevant to crime and addiction. For girls and women, these critical events include childhood trauma and abuse, mental illness, poverty, homelessness, and destructive relationships (Belknap 2007; Chesney-Lind and Pasko 2004; Colman and Kim 2009; Deschenes et al. 2007; Hamburger et al. 2008). In contrast, primary predictors of criminal behaviour for men include criminally active peers, extensive prior offending, and financial gain (Messina et al. 2000). Men often have more employment opportunities and experience than women prior to incarceration. Thus, men often supplement their income from illegal activities, whereas illegal activities are the primary source of income for many justice-involved women (Messina et al. 2003).

The gender-responsive approach

The National Institute of Corrections *Gender-Responsive Strategies: Research, Practice and Guiding Principles for Women Offenders* report documents the need for a new vision for the criminal justice system (Bloom et al. 2003: 75):

> Gender-responsive means creating an environment through site selection, staff selection, program development, content, and material that reflects an understanding of the realities of women's lives and addresses the issues of the participants. Gender-responsive approaches are multidimensional and are based on theoretical perspectives that acknowledge

women's pathways into the criminal justice system. These approaches address social (e.g. poverty, race, class and gender inequality) and cultural factors, as well as therapeutic interventions. These interventions address issues such as abuse, violence, family relationships, substance use and co-occurring disorders. They provide a strength-based approach to treatment and skill building. The emphasis is on self-efficacy.

The *Gender-Responsive Strategies* report (Bloom et al. 2003) indicates that female crime rates, with few exceptions, are much lower than male crime rates and women's crimes tend to be less serious than men's crimes. The gender differential is most pronounced in violent crime, for which women's participation is profoundly lower. Recognizing the behavioural and social differences between female and male offenders has specific implications for gender-responsive policy and practice changes in the criminal justice system.

Trauma in the lives of women

The consistent finding that justice-involved women report a high prevalence of lifelong trauma and abuse has justifiably led to an increase in research assessing the long-term impact of such adverse events.

Exposure to childhood trauma[1]

Extensive research on female jail and prison populations indicates an overwhelming prevalence of childhood histories of exposure to traumatic events, affecting between 77% and 90% of incarcerated women (Battle et al. 2003; Greene et al. 2000; Kubiak et al. 2016; Messina et al. 2003; Messina and Grella 2006; Messina et al. 2007; Owen and Bloom 1995; Wolff and Shi 2012). Between 59% and 90% of incarcerated women also report continued patterns of physical and sexual abuse by intimate partners in their adolescent and adult relationships (Berzofsky et al. 2013; Bloom et al. 1994; Grella et al. 2005; Messina et al. 2007; Owen et al. 2017; Wilson-Cohn et al. 2002). Messina and colleagues (2007) compared the occurrence of adverse childhood events reported by 427 incarcerated men and 315 women. Women offenders had significantly greater exposure to the childhood traumatic events than did men. Advocates for trauma-informed programmes suggest that these issues should be discussed in a safe environment for women (Bloom et al. 1994; Brown 2018).

Childhood trauma and mental health

Few efforts have attempted to explain the factors that contribute to the disproportionate prevalence of mental health problems among women offenders.

Findings have repeatedly linked childhood trauma to later problems in psychosocial functioning, personality disorders, depression, post-traumatic stress disorder (PTSD), panic disorders, eating disorders, and other forms of psychopathology among women offenders (Bronson and Berzofsky 2017; Brown 2018; DeHart et al. 2014; Grella 2003; Haller and Miles 2004). Messina and Grella (2006) directly explored the effect of cumulative childhood traumatic experiences on the adult mental health problems of 500 women parolees. Results showed that the impact of childhood trauma on adult mental health outcomes was strong and cumulative. A key finding in this literature is the general lack of appropriate mental health treatment available in correctional settings, as well as the elevated risk of recidivism associated with untreated co-occurring mental health and substance use disorders (Messina et al. 2006).

Childhood trauma and substance use disorders

Evidence has shown that the trauma that results from childhood physical and sexual abuse is a key contributor to alcohol and drug dependence in adolescence and adulthood among women and girls (Brems et al. 2004; Greene et al. 2000; Grella et al. 2005; Mejía et al. 2015). In fact, childhood traumatic experiences and re-victimization rates are proportionately higher among female inmates undergoing treatment for substance abuse (Mejía et al. 2015; Wilson-Cohn et al. 2002; Wolff and Shi 2012). Messina and Grella (2006) assessed the cumulative impact of childhood abuse on adolescent and adult behaviours among 500 women parolees. This study showed that among women parolees, greater exposure to multiple childhood traumatic experiences was associated with histories of substance use, homelessness, and adolescent conduct disorder (between 62% and 76% of women who reported five or more types of childhood trauma reported such histories).

Childhood trauma and criminality

There is also empirical support for the relationship between early childhood trauma and adult criminality (Battle et al. 2003; Grella et al. 2005; Ireland and Widom 1994; Kubiak et al. 2016; Widom and Ames 1994; Wolff and Shi 2012). Messina and Grella (2006) found that women parolees with more exposure to childhood trauma also had earlier and greater criminal histories. Women with five or more childhood traumatic experiences were all between the ages of 15 and 20 when they engaged in their first criminal behaviours, compared with those who reported no childhood trauma, who were between the ages of 21 and 27 when they first engaged in such behaviours. In addition, women with five or more types of childhood traumatic experiences reported an average of 22.9 prior arrests compared to 12.8 prior arrests reported by those with no reported traumatic event. Additional studies have found that trauma histories specifically have a stronger influence on adult offending patterns and adult traumatic distress in women, compared with men (Messina et al. 2007; Moloney et al. 2009).

Physical health problems

Justice-involved women often suffer from a variety of chronic physical health problems, including TB, hepatitis, toxaemia, anaemia, hypertension, diabetes, and asthma (Anderson et al. 2002; Pollock 2002; Stevens and Glider 1994). Incarcerated women also cite dental problems and obesity as recurring health problems (Fickenscher et al. 2001). Women's more complex reproductive systems also increase their risk of health problems and other female-specific disorders, and some women may be pregnant and in need of prenatal and postpartum care (Grella 1999). Messina and Grella (2006) found that histories of childhood trauma were significantly and positively related to 12 of the 18 health problems assessed among 500 women parolees (i.e. eating disorders, prostitution, hepatitis, sexually transmitted diseases, gynaecological problems, alcoholism, asthma, ulcers, frequent migraines/headaches, poor overall health, and tuberculosis), and effect sizes ranged from a 15% increase in the odds of having had gynaecological problems or poor health to a 40% increase in the odds of having had mental health treatment.

Intergenerational cycle of trauma, substance use, and criminality

Women offenders typically come from highly dysfunctional families with histories of mental illness, suicide, violence, and addiction (Brown 2018; Langan and Pelissier 2001; Berzofsky et al. 2013). Exacerbating the need for appropriate rehabilitative programs for women offenders is the fact that most of them have children under the age of 18 and they are typically the primary childcare provider, creating a detrimental effect on families (Brown 2018; Henderson 1998). Greene and associates (2000) found that a number of criminogenic influences experienced by women offenders were replicated in the lives of their children, including sexual/physical abuse in childhood, adolescence, and adulthood; poverty; and violence. This is an important factor in terms of the societal impact of rehabilitation for women offenders. Historically, trauma has not been addressed in treatment settings and has not been included in assessments measuring risk and need factors for appropriate individual treatment plans. Various assessment tools have been employed to identify the criminogenic needs of male offenders; however, their relevance to female offenders remains questionable (Bloom 2000; Wright et al. 2012).

Becoming trauma informed, trauma responsive, and trauma specific

Many individuals involved in the criminal justice system were often victims before they were offenders (Miller and Najavits 2012; Widom and Maxfield 2001). When women enter custodial settings, they arrive with their personal histories of trauma exposure, and they may experience additional trauma while in custody. Routine correctional practices (i.e. strip searches, pat downs) may trigger previous trauma and increase trauma-related symptoms and behaviours, such as impulsive acts and aggression, that may be difficult to manage within the prison or jail (Covington 2008; Moloney et al. 2009). Therefore, trauma-informed practice is important.

In their seminal work on trauma-informed services, Fallot and Harris (2006) articulate five core values: safety (both physical and emotional), trustworthiness, choice, collaboration, and empowerment. The following three definitions differentiate the levels of work associated with developing services for women. Given the high rates of trauma in the lives of justice-involved women, it is impossible to be gender responsive if you are not trauma informed (Covington 2012, rev. 2018; Kubiak et al. 2017).[2]

> *Trauma informed:* Being trauma informed means having universal knowledge about trauma and adversity. All staff in correctional settings need to understand the process of trauma and its link to mental health problems, substance use disorders, behavioural challenges, and physical health problems in women's lives. Staff also need to understand trauma as it relates to childhood experiences and brain development, and how individuals may be affected by and cope with trauma and victimization.

> *Trauma responsive:* After becoming trauma informed with the knowledge of trauma and its impact, a facility then needs to become trauma responsive by reviewing policies and practices in order to incorporate this information into all operational practices. This involves all administration and staff in most, if not all, facilities to create a culture change.

> *Trauma specific:* To become trauma specific, custodial settings for women provide actual therapeutic approaches that focus on trauma.

After staff became trauma informed and created a trauma-responsive institutional environment in the mental health unit at the Framingham facility in Massachusetts, there was a 62% decrease in inmate assaults on staff and a 54% decrease in inmate-on-inmate assaults (Bissonnette 2013; National Resource Center on Justice Involved Women [NRCJIW] 2014). There was also a decrease in other behavioural and mental health situations: a 60% decline in the number of suicide attempts, a 33% decline in the need for one-on-one mental health watches, and a 16% decline in petitions for psychiatric services. See the next section for more specific information on trauma-informed (and trauma-specific) programmes.

Available evidence-based programmes and settings

The number of evidence-based, gender-responsive, and trauma-informed (and trauma-specific) curricula and materials has grown with the increased understanding of women's unique pathways to crime and their treatment needs. These curricula and materials have been tested with women in a variety of criminal justice settings.

Helping Women Recover: A Program for Treating Addiction (Covington 1999, rev. 2008, 2019) addresses substance use by integrating theories of women's psychological development, trauma, and addiction. This programme was examined through a randomized experimental study with incarcerated women in either a *Helping Women Recover* programme or a standard prison-based therapeutic community for substance use treatment. Women who received *Helping Women Recover* had improved psychological well-being, greater reductions in drug use, greater likelihoods of staying in aftercare after release from prison, and lower odds of recidivism than those who received standard, non-gender-responsive programming (Messina et al. 2010).

Moving On (Van Dieten 2008) is a programme based on cognitive behavioural theory, relational theory, and motivational interviewing. It provides women with opportunities to expand their strengths and strategies for improving their lives, and mobilize and access resources within community and personal networks. It incorporates cognitive behavioural techniques with motivational interviewing and relational theory. Positive outcomes have been found for this programme for women on probation in terms of lower rearrests and conviction rates for women who completed this programme than for women who did not receive it during probation (Gehring et al. 2010).

Beyond Trauma: A Healing Journey for Women (Covington 2003, rev. 2016) is a 12- session programme that uses psycho-educational, cognitive behavioural, expressive arts, mindfulness, and relational therapeutic approaches to help women develop coping skills and emotional wellness. A six-session version of this programme is called *Healing Trauma: A Brief Intervention for Women* (Covington and Russo 2011, rev. 2016). Studies evaluating the effectiveness of *Helping Women Recover* and *Beyond Trauma* (as well as *Healing Trauma*), which are gender-responsive and trauma-informed programmes with explicit foci on and foundation in a strengths-based approach, show that participants had reductions in PTSD and depression symptoms (Covington et al. 2008; Messina et al. 2012). These studies had samples of women in residential substance use treatment units, of which half were mandated to treatment (mainly through the criminal justice system). A majority of the women (99% at the end of treatment and 97% at the six-month follow-up point) reported no involvement in criminal activities (Covington et al. 2008). Also, a follow-up study of a randomized control trial of women involved in drug courts showed that women's involvement in these programs was significantly connected to improved well-being, low rates of rearrest, high levels of participation in treatment, and reductions in PTSD symptoms (Messina et al. 2012).

Beyond Violence: A Prevention Program for Criminal Justice-Involved Women (Covington 2013) is an evidence-based curriculum for women in criminal justice settings who have histories of aggression and/or violence. This group-based model of violence prevention considers the complex interplay between individual, relationship, community, and societal factors. Within a Midwestern prison, researchers have studied the programme's feasibility and fidelity (Kubiak et al. 2014), short- and long-term outcomes (Kubiak et al. 2016; Kubiak et al. 2012), and outcomes with specific populations (Fedock et al. 2017; Kubiak et al. 2014), and have found consistently positive results of lowered mental health symptoms and low recidivism rates for women who completed the programme. In addition, the programme has been tested in two California women's prisons, and similar positive results have been found, with medium to high effect sizes for women who are serving long or life sentences (Messina et al. 2016). Significant reductions were found in PTSD, anxiety, serious mental illness symptoms, and anger and aggression in women serving time for violent offences. These groups were tested using peer educators (i.e. incarcerated women serving life sentences) to deliver the intervention, which is a model that is both cost-effective and evidence based. While the studies related to this curriculum studied mental health and recidivism measures, a core premise of the programme is developing, building upon, and sustaining women's strengths, and women who have gone through the programme have expressed that they gained a deep sense of meaning through it, despite being in prison (Covington and Fedock 2015).

Seeking Safety (Najavits 2002) treats the co-occurring disorders of trauma, PTSD, and substance use, based on research from cognitive behavioural treatment of substance use disorders and post-traumatic stress treatment. It is a programme that focuses on women building coping strategies and addresses multiple concerns. Zlotnick et al. (2003) evaluated *Seeking Safety* in a sample of incarcerated women with co-occurring PTSD and substance use disorders; 53% of the women no longer met the criteria for PTSD after completing treatment, and 46% still no longer met the criteria three months after treatment. Another study from Gatz et al. (2007) found that women receiving *Seeking Safety* improved significantly more on symptoms of PTSD and use of coping skills compared to women in the comparison group. Another randomized controlled trial of *Seeking Safety* with incarcerated women found that women had improvements in their mental health, with their average depression scores changing to below the clinically significant level and lower scores of PTSD (Tripodi et al. 2017).

Summary of outcome studies research

Findings from over ten extensive field studies culminating in a diverse sample of over 3,000 justice-involved women (i.e. incarcerated or on parole/probation) are summarized below. Participants were sampled from various treatment settings (i.e. jail/prison, re-entry aftercare, drug court, California's Prop 36, etc.). Datasets include retrospective self-reports covering participants' lifetimes and encompass a wide range of domains (e.g. substance use, criminal activity, trauma exposure, mental/physical health, family functioning, treatment, and health service utilization) and administrative data on treatment participation (e.g. setting, modality, and services) and criminal justice interactions (arrest and incarceration history).

Research findings report consistent factors that are associated with justice-involved women's successful rehabilitation and recovery. They include:

- Reuniting with children, which can reduce the risk of recidivism for women (Benda 2005)
- Involvement with child welfare, which is associated with higher motivation for recovery (Grella and Rodriguez 2011)
- Engagement and retention in treatment, which is enhanced when there are services that are gender-responsive and that attend specifically to histories of trauma (Messina et al. 2010)
- Community-based aftercare treatment upon release, which is significantly associated with reduced recidivism, more so than prison treatment alone (Grella and Greenwell 2007; Messina et al. 2006)
- Gender-responsive programmes (specialized programmes with wrap-around services for women and children) and longer retention rates, which are strongly associated with post-treatment abstinence (Grella 1999; Grella et al. 2000; Prendergast et al. 2011)
- Strong family support and a stable living situation, which is associated with reductions in recidivism (Griffin and Armstrong 2003)

Defining potential predictors of successful recovery among women offenders has greatly informed the criminal justice system and guided the development of appropriate legislation, policies, programmes, and services for this historically underserved population of offenders.

A new vision: guiding principles and strategies for effective system change

The following research-based principles and strategies have been incorporated into strategic plans, as well as state, national, and international criminal justice standards. They have been widely accepted by the scientific, policy, and practice fields and provide a new vision for promoting best practices for justice-involved women.

Guiding principle 1: acknowledge that gender makes a difference

The foremost principle in responding appropriately to women offenders is to acknowledge the implications of gender throughout the criminal justice system.

The criminal justice field purports to provide equal treatment to everyone. However, this does not mean that the same treatment is appropriate for both women and men.

Strategy

- Allocate both human and financial resources to create women-centred services.
- Designate a high-level administrative position for oversight of management, supervision, and services for women offenders.
- Recruit and train personnel and volunteers who have both the interest and the qualifications needed for working with women under criminal justice supervision.

Guiding principle 2: create an environment based on safety, respect, and dignity

Research from a range of disciplines (e.g. health, mental health, and substance use) has shown that safety, respect, and dignity are fundamental to behavioural change. To improve behavioural outcomes for women, it is critical to provide a safe and supportive setting for all services.

Strategy

- Conduct a comprehensive review of the institutional or community environment in which women are supervised to provide an ongoing assessment of the current culture.
- Develop policy that reflects an understanding of the importance of emotional and physical safety.
- Establish protocols for reporting and investigating claims of misconduct.
- Understand the effects of childhood trauma to avoid further traumatization.

Guiding principle 3: develop policies, practices, and programmes that are relational and promote healthy connections to children, family, significant others, and the community

Understanding the role of relationships in women's lives is fundamental because connections and relationships to children, family, significant others, and the community are important threads throughout the lives of women in the justice system.

Strategy

- Develop training for all staff and administrators in which relationship issues are a core theme. Such training should include the importance of relationships, staff-client relationships, professional boundaries, communication, and the mother-child relationship.
- Examine all mother and child programming through the eyes of the child (e.g. child-centred environment, context), and enhance the mother/child connection and the connections of the mother to child caregivers and other family members.
- Promote supportive relationships among women offenders.
- Develop community and peer-support networks.

Guiding principle 4: address substance abuse, trauma, and mental health issues through comprehensive, integrated, and culturally relevant services and appropriate supervision

Substance abuse, trauma, and mental health are three critical, interrelated issues in the lives of women offenders. These issues have a major impact on both women's programming needs and successful re-entry. Although they are therapeutically linked, these issues have historically been treated separately. One of the most important developments in healthcare over the past several decades is the recognition that a substantial proportion of women have a history of serious traumatic experiences that play a vital and often unrecognized role in the evolution of a woman's physical and mental health problems.

Strategy

- Service providers need to be cross-trained in three primary issues: substance use, trauma, and mental health.
- Resources, including skilled personnel, must be allocated.
- The environment in which services are provided must be closely monitored to ensure the emotional and physical safety of the women being served.

Guiding principle 5: provide women with opportunities to improve their socio-economic conditions

Generally, justice-involved women are underemployed or unemployed, work fewer hours than men, make less per hour than men, and are often employed in temporary, low-level occupations with little chance for advancement.

Criminal behaviour by women is closely tied to their socio-economic status, and rehabilitation often depends on their ability to become financially independent.

Strategy

■ Allocate resources within both community and institutional correctional programmes for comprehensive, integrated services that focus on the economic, social, and treatment needs of women. Ensure that women leave prison or jail with provisions for short-term emergency services (e.g. subsistence, lodging, food, transportation, and clothing).

■ Provide traditional and non-traditional training, education, and skill-enhancing opportunities to assist women in earning a living wage.

Guiding principle 6: establish a system of community supervision and re-entry with comprehensive, collaborative services

Women face specific challenges as they re-enter the community from jail or prison, and women on probation also face challenges in their communities. In addition to the stigma of being formerly incarcerated, they may carry additional burdens such as single motherhood, low income and limited employment prospects, the absence of services and programmes targeted for women, responsibilities to multiple agencies, and a general lack of community support.

Strategy

■ Create an individualized support plan and wrap the necessary resources around the woman and her children.

■ Develop a 'one-stop shopping' approach to community services, with the primary service provider also facilitating access to other needed services.

■ Use a coordinated case management model for community supervision and programming.

Guiding future directions

The pathways and profiles of justice-involved women consistently reveal factors that should be central to any form of supervision and treatment for women. The importance of understanding and addressing the full spectrum of substance use and criminal activity, and their consequences, for women and their children cannot be overstated. Gender-responsive policy and practices target women's pathways to criminality by providing effective interventions that address the intersecting issues of trauma, criminal behaviour, substance use, mental health, and economic marginality, as well as providing specific services for mothers and their children (Bloom 2015).

Experiences of trauma have been identified repeatedly as issues that need to be addressed within rehabilitative programmes, whether in the community or in prison. Regardless of the treatment setting, staff training on the appropriate response to trauma histories and how to effectively avoid re-traumatization is imperative. The benefits of a trauma-informed organization are compelling. Prisons that have implemented trauma-informed services and become trauma responsive have experienced substantial decreases in institutional violence (NRCJIW 2014). However, treatment programmes in prison may not be able to address all of the complex needs of women offenders due to funding and security constraints. Evidence continues to demonstrate that justice-involved women come in contact with multiple service systems prior to and after release from correctional settings (e.g. drug treatment, criminal justice, mental health, welfare, primary healthcare), necessitating an integrated and comprehensive approach to addressing their specific needs.

As criminal justice officials consider implementing treatment options for justice-involved women, it is vitally important to incorporate the above core guiding principles in developing effective criminal justice policies and practices. Furthermore, criminal justice officials can gain insight from the growing body of empirical evidence to determine the critical factors associated with onset, persistence, and desistence of substance use and crime and the types of settings, services, and approaches that are optimal to enhance long-term outcomes for justice-involved women.

Notes

1 Traumatic events are stressful or traumatic events including emotional, sexual, and physical abuse and neglect. They may also include household dysfunction such as witnessing domestic violence, out-of-home placement, or growing up with family members who have substance use disorders or who have been incarcerated.
2 The following set of training materials is available to assist criminal justice professionals in becoming trauma informed: *Becoming Trauma Informed: Working with Women in Correctional Settings* (Covington 2012, rev. 2018) and *Moving from Trauma Informed to Trauma Responsive: A Training Program for Organizational Change* (Covington and Bloom 2018).

References

Anderson, T. B., Rosay, A. and Saum, C. (2002) The impact of drug use and crime involvement on health problems among female drug offenders. *Prison Journal*, 82(2), 50–68.

Battle, C., Zlotnick, C., Najavits, L., Gutierrez, M. and Winsor, C. (2003) Posttraumatic stress disorder and substance use disorder among incarcerated women. In P. Ouimette and P. J. Brown (Eds.), *Trauma and Substance Abuse: Causes, Consequences, and Treatment of Comorbid Disorders*. Washington, DC: American Psychological Association, pp. 209–225.

Belknap, J. (2007) *The Invisible Woman: Gender Crime and Justice*, Revised edition. Cincinnati, OH: Wadsworth.

Benda, B. B. (2005) Gender differences in life-course theory of recidivism: A survival analysis. *International Journal of Offender Therapy and Comparative Criminology*, 49(3), 325–343.

Berzofsky, M., Krebs, C., Langton, L., Planty, M. and Smiley-McDonald, H. (2013) *Female Victims of Sexual Violence, 1994–2010*. Washington, DC: US Department of Justice, Office of Justice Programs, Bureau of Justice Statistics.

Bissonnette, L. (2013) *Personal Communication with Lynn Bissonnette*, 17 April. Available at: www.cjinvolvedwomen.org/innovator-massachusetts-correctional institution-at-framingham.

Bloom, B. (2000) Beyond Recidivism: Perspectives on evaluation of programs for female offenders in community corrections. In M. McMahan (Ed.), *Assessment to Assistance: Programs for Women in Community Corrections*. Lanham: International Community Corrections Association, p. 122.

Bloom, B. (2015) *Meeting the Needs of Women in California's County Justice Systems: A Toolkit for Policymakers and Practitioners*. Oakland, CA: Californians for Safety and Justice.

Bloom, B., Chesney-Lind, M. and Owen, B. (1994) *Women in California Prisons: Hidden Victims of the War on Drugs*. San Francisco: Center on Juvenile and Criminal Justice.

Bloom, B. and Covington, S. (2008) Addressing the mental health needs of women offenders. In R. L. Gido and L. Dalley (Eds.), *Women's Mental Health Issues Across the Criminal Justice System*. Upper Saddle River, NJ: Prentice Hall.

Bloom, B., Owen, B. and Covington, S. (2003) *Gender-Responsive Strategies: Research, Practice, and Guiding Principles for Women Offenders*. Washington, DC: US Department of Justice, National Institute of Corrections. Available at: http://nicic.org/pubs/2003/018017.pdf.

Bloom, B., Owen, B. and Covington, S. (2004) Women offenders and gendered effects of public policy. *Review of Policy Research*, 21(1), 31–48.

Brems, C., Johnson, M. E., Neal, D. and Freemon, M. (2004) Childhood abuse history and substance use among men and women receiving detoxification services. *American Journal of Drug and Alcohol Abuse*, 30(4), 799–821.

Bronson, J. and Berzofsky, M. (2017) *Indicators of Mental Health Problems Reported by Prisoners and Jail Inmates, 2011–12*. Washington, DC: US Department of Justice, Office of Justice Programs, Bureau of Justice Statistics.

Brown, V. (2018) *Through a Trauma Lense. Transforming Health and Behavioral Health Systems*. New York: Routledge.

Browne, B., Miller, B. and Maguin, E. (1999) Prevalence and severity of lifetime physical and sexual victimization among incarcerated women. *International Journal of Law and Psychiatry*, 22(3–4), 301–322.

Chesney-Lind, M. and Pasko, L. (2004) *The Female Offenders: Girls, Women, and Crime*, 2nd edition. Thousand Oaks, CA: Sage Publications.

Colman, R. A. and Kim, D. H. (2009) Delinquent girls grown up: Young adult offending patterns and their relation to early legal, individual, and family risk. *Journal of Youth and Adolescence*, 38, 355–366.

Covington, S. S. (1999, revised 2008, 2019) *Helping Women Recover: A Program for Treating Substance Abuse: Special Edition for Use in the Criminal Justice System*. San Francisco, CA: Jossey-Bass.

Covington, S. S. (2003, revised 2016) *Beyond Trauma: A Healing Journey for Women*. Center City, MN: Hazelden Publishing Company.

Covington, S. S. (2008) Women and addiction: A trauma-informed approach. *Journal of Psychoactive Drugs*, 40, 377–385.

Covington, S. S. (2012, revised 2018) *Becoming Trauma Informed: Working with Women in Correctional Settings*. La Jolla, CA: Author.

Covington, S. S. (2013) *Beyond Violence: A Prevention Program for Criminal Justice-Involved Women*. Hoboken, NJ: John Wiley & Sons.

Covington, S. S. and Bloom, S. (2018) *Moving from Trauma Informed to Trauma Responsive: A Training Program for Organizational Change*. Center City, CA: Hazelden Publishing.

Covington, S. S., Burke, C., Keaton, S. and Norcott, C. (2008) Evaluation of a trauma-informed and gender-responsive intervention for women in drug treatment. *Journal of Psychoactive Drugs*, 40(Supplement 5), 387–398.

Covington, S. S. and Fedock, G. (2015) Beyond violence: Women in prison find meaning, hope, and healing. In *Trauma Matters, Fall*. Hamden, CT: Connecticut Women's Consortium and the Connecticut Department of Mental Health and Addiction Services in support of the Connecticut Trauma Initiative, p. 1.

Covington, S. S. and Russo, E. (2011, revised 2016) *Healing Trauma: A Brief Intervention for Women*. Center City, MN: Hazelden Publishing.

DeHart, D., Lynch, S., Belknap, J., Dass-Brailsford, P. and Green, B. (2014) Life history models of female offending: The roles of serious mental illness and trauma in women's pathways to jail. *Psychology of Women Quarterly*, 38(1), 138–151.

Deschenes, E. P., Owen, B. A. and Crow, J. (2007) *Recidivism Among Female Prisoners: Secondary Analysis of the 1994 BJS Recidivism Data Set*. A Report Prepared for the US Department of Justice. Long Beach, CA: California State University Long Beach, Department of Criminal Justice.

Fallot, R. and Harris, M. (2006) *Trauma-Informed Services: A Self-Assessment and Planning Protocol*. Washington, DC: Community Connections.

Fedock, G., Kubiak, S. and Bybee, D. (2017) Testing a new intervention with incarcerated women serving life sentences. *Research on Social Work Practice*. DOI:1049731517700272.

Fickenscher, A., Lapidus, J., Silk-Walker, P. and Becker, T. (2001) Women behind bars: Health needs of inmates in a county jail. *Public Health Reports*, 116, 191–196.

Gatz, M., Brown, V., Hennigan, K., Rechberger, E., O'Keefe, M., Rose, T. and Bjelajac, P. (2007) Effectiveness of an integrated, trauma-informed approach to treating women with co-occurring disorders and histories of trauma: The Los Angeles site experience. *Journal of Community Psychology*, 35(7), 863–878.

Gehring, K., Van Voorhis, P. and Bell, V. (2010) "What works" for female probationers? An evaluation of the Moving On program. *Women, Girls, and Criminal Justice*, 11(1), 6–10.

Greene, S., Haney, C. and Hurtado, A. (2000) Cycles of pain: Risk factors in the lives of incarcerated mothers and their children. *Prison Journal*, 80(1), 3–23.

Grella, C. E. (1999) Women in residential drug treatment: Differences by program type and pregnancy. *Journal of Health Care for the Poor and Underserved*, 10(2), 216–229.

Grella, C. E. (2003) Effects of gender and diagnosis on addiction history, treatment utilization, and psychosocial functioning among a dually-diagnosed sample in drug treatment. *Journal of Psychoactive Drugs, SARC Supplement*, 1, 169–179.

Grella, C. E. and Greenwell, L. (2007) Treatment needs and completion of community-based aftercare among substance-abusing women offenders. *Women's Health Issues*, 17(4), 244–255.

Grella, C. E., Joshi, V. and Hser, Y. (2000) Program variation in treatment outcomes among women in residential drug treatment. *Evaluation Review*, 24(4), 364–383.

Grella, C. E. and Rodriguez, L. (2011) Motivation for treatment among women offenders in prison-based treatment and longitudinal outcomes among those who participate in community aftercare. *Journal of Psychoactive Drugs*, 43(Supplement 1), 58–67.

Grella, C., Stein, J. and Greenwell, L. (2005) Associations among childhood trauma, adolescent problem behaviors, and adverse adult outcomes in substance-abusing women offenders. *Psychology of Addictive Behaviors*, 19(1), 43–53.

Griffin, M. L. and Armstrong, G. S. (2003) The effect of local life circumstances on female probationers' offending. *Justice Quarterly*, 20(2), 213–239.

Haller, D. and Miles, D. (2004) Personality disturbances in drug-dependent women: Relationship to childhood abuse. *American Journal of Drug and Alcohol Abuse*, 30(4), 269–286.

Hamburger, M. E., Leeb, R. T. and Swahn, M. H. (2008) Childhood maltreatment and early alcohol use among high-risk adolescents. *Journal of Studies of Alcohol and Drugs*, 69(2), 291–295.

Henderson, D. (1998) Drug abuse and incarcerated women. *Journal of Substance Abuse Treatment*, 15(6), 579–587.

Ireland, T. and Widom, C. S. (1994) Childhood victimization and risk for alcohol and drug arrests. *International Journal of the Addictions*, 29(2), 235–274.

Kubiak, S. P., Brenner, H., Bybee, D., Campbell, R. and Fedock, G. (2016) Reporting sexual victimization during incarceration: Using ecological theory as a framework to inform and guide future research. *Trauma, Violence, & Abuse*. DOI:10.1177/152483 8016637078.

Kubiak, S. P., Covington, S. and Hiller, C. (2017) Trauma-informed corrections. In D. Springer and A. Roberts (Eds.), *Social Work in Juvenile and Criminal Justice Systems*, 4th edition. Springfield, IL: Charles C. Thomas.

Kubiak, S. P., Fedock, G., Kim, W. J. and Bybee, D. (2016) Long-term outcomes of a RCT intervention study for women with violent crimes. *Journal of the Society for Social Work and Research*, 7(4), 661–676.

Kubiak, S. P., Fedock, G., Tillander, E., Kim, W. J. and Bybee, D. (2014) Assessing the feasibility and fidelity of an intervention for women with violent offenses. *Evaluation and Program Planning*, 42, 1–10.

Kubiak, S. P., Kim, W. J., Fedock, G. and Bybee, D. (2012) Assessing short-term outcomes of an intervention for women convicted of violent crimes. *Journal of the Society for Social Work and Research*, 3(3), 197–212.

Langan, N. and Pelissier, B. (2001) Gender differences among prisoners in drug treatment. *Journal of Substance Abuse*, 13(3), 291–301.

Mejía, B., Zea, P., Romero, M. and Saldívar, G. (2015) Traumatic experiences and re-victimization of female inmates undergoing treatment for substance abuse. *Substance Abuse Treatment, Prevention, and Policy*, 10(1), 5.

Messina, N., Braithwaite, J., Calhoun, S. and Kubiak, S. P. (2016) Examination of a violence prevention program for female offenders. *Violence and Gender Journal*, 3(3), 143–149.

Messina, N., Burdon, W., Hagopian, G. and Prendergast, M. (2006) Predictors of prison TC treatment outcomes: A comparison of men and women participants. *American Journal of Drug and Alcohol Abuse*, 32(1), 7–28.

Messina, N., Burdon, W. and Prendergast, M. (2003) Assessing the needs of women in institutional therapeutic communities. *Journal of Offender Rehabilitation*, 37(2), 89–106.

Messina, N., Calhoun, S. and Warda, U. (2012) Gender-responsive drug court treatment: A randomized controlled trial. *Criminal Justice and Behavior*, 39(12), 1539–1558.

Messina, N. and Grella, C. E. (2006) Childhood trauma and women's health: A California prison population. *American Journal of Public Health*, 96(10), 1842–1848.

Messina, N., Grella, C. E., Burdon, W. and Prendergast, M. (2007) Childhood adverse events and current traumatic distress: A comparison of men and women prisoners. *Criminal Justice and Behavior*, 34(11), 1385–1401.

Messina, N., Grella, C. E., Cartier, J. and Torres, S. (2010) A randomized experimental study of gender-responsive substance abuse treatment for women in prison. *Journal of Substance Abuse Treatment*, 38(2), 97–107.

Messina, N., Wish, E. and Nemes, S. (2000) Predictors of treatment outcomes in men and women admitted to a therapeutic community. *American Journal of Drug and Alcohol Abuse*, 26(2), 207–228.

Miller, N. A. and Najavits, L. M. (2012) Creating trauma-informed correctional care: A balance of goals and environment. *European Journal of Psychotraumatology*, 3. DOI:10.3402/ejpt.v3i0.17246.

Moloney, K. P., van den Bergh, B. J. and Moller, L. F. (2009) Women in prison: The central issues of gender characteristics and trauma history. *Public Health*, 123, 426–430.

Najavits, L. (2002) *Seeking Safety: A Treatment Manual for PTSD and Substance Abuse*. New York: The Guilford Press.

National Resource Center on Justice Involved Women. (2014) *Trauma-Informed Practices: A Strategy for Enhancing Safety and Security in Female Correctional Facilities*. Available at: http://cjinvolvedwomen.org/massachusetts-correctional-institution-at-framingham/.

Owen, B. and Bloom, B. (1995) Profiling women prisoners: Findings from national surveys and a California sample. *Prison Journal*, 75(2), 165–185.

Owen, B., Wells, J. and Pollock, J. (2017) *In Search of Safety: Confronting Inequality in Women's Imprisonment*. Oakland, CA: University of California Press.

Pollock, J. (2002) *Women, Prison, and Crime*, 2nd edition. Belmont, CA: Wadsworth Thomson Learning.

Prendergast, M., Messina, N., Hall, N. and Warda, N. (2011) The relative effectiveness of women-only vs. mixed-gender substance abuse treatment. *Journal of Substance Abuse Treatment*, 40(4), 336–348.

Singer, M. I., Bussey, J., Song, L-Y. and Lunghofer, L. (1995) The psychosocial issues of women serving time in jail. *Social Work*, 40(1), 103–113.

Stevens, S. J. and Glider P. J. (1994) Therapeutic communities: Substance abuse treatment for women. In F. M. Tims, G. De Leon and N. Jainchill (Eds.), *Therapeutic Community: Advances in Research and Application*. National Institute on Drug Abuse (NIDA) Research Monograph 144. Rockville, MD: NIDA, pp. 162–180.

Tripodi, S. J., Mennicke, A. M., McCarter, S. A. and Ropes, K. (2017) Evaluating seeking safety for women in prison: A randomized controlled trial. *Research on Social Work Practice*. DOI:1049731517706550.

Van Dieten, M. (2008) *Moving on*. Center City, MN: Hazelden Publishing Company.

Widom, C. S. and Ames, M. A. (1994) Criminal consequences of childhood sexual victimization. *Child Abuse & Neglect*, 18(4), 303–318.

Widom, C. S. and Maxfield, M. G. (2001) An update on the "cycle of violence." *Research in Brief*, 1–8.

Wilson-Cohn, C., Strauss, S. M. and Falkin, G. P. (2002) The relationship between partner abuse and substance use among women mandated to drug treatment. *Journal of Family Violence*, 17(1), 91–105.

Wolf, A., Silva, F., Knight, K. and Javdani, S. (2007) Responding to the health needs of female offenders. In R. Sheelan (Ed.), *What Works with Women Offenders*. Devon: Willan Publishing.

Wolff, N. and Shi, J. (2012) Childhood and adult trauma experiences of incarcerated persons and their relationship to adult behavioral health problems and treatment.

International Journal of Environment Research and Public Health, 9, 1908–1926. DOI:10.3390/ijerph9051908.

Wright, E. M., Van Voorhis, P., Salisbury, E. J. and Bauman, A. (2012) Gender-responsive lessons learned and policy implications for women in prison: A review. *Criminal Justice and Behavior*, 39(12), 1612–1632.

Zlotnick, C., Najavits, L. M., Rohsenow, D. J. and Johnson, D. M. (2003) A cognitive-behavioral treatment for incarcerated women with substance abuse disorder and posttraumatic stress disorder: Findings from a pilot study. *Journal of Substance Abuse Treatment*, 25(2), 99–105.

Women's experiences of the criminal justice system

52

Megan Welsh

Trends in women's criminal justice involvement

Across the globe, women's criminal justice involvement has increased substantially in recent decades. Although women continue to comprise a minority (10% or less in most countries) of incarcerated prisoners, the female incarceration rate has increased faster than the male incarceration rate on every continent. Put another way, the number of women incarcerated in prisons across the world has grown by 50% since the year 2000 (Penal Reform International [PRI] 2017). In the United States, women's incarceration rate increased 646% from 1980 to 2010, while men's incarceration grew by 419%. Further, although women account for a small fraction of the US prison population, they comprise 25% of people on probation and 13% of those on parole (Kaeble and Bonczar 2017; Mauer 2013), a reflection of the fact that many more people under correctional supervision are supervised in the community than in institutions (Glaze et al. 2010). Between 1995 and 2006, the growth rate of women on probation or parole increased by 56%, far outpacing that of men (Glaze and Bonczar 2007; Moorish 2010).

In the US, these statistics are largely the legacy of punitive drug policies implemented in past decades: between 1986 and 1991 alone, the number of women incarcerated in state prisons for drug crimes increased 433%, while men's incarceration for the same offences increased 283% (Bush-Basket 2010: 40; see also Sudbury 2002). Internationally, women are likely to be incarcerated for low-level, non-violent crimes related to poverty, including property and drug-related offences (PRI 2017). According to the most recent national data, which is over a decade old, of women in US local jails, 32% are there for a property offence; 29% for drug offences; and 21% for 'public order' offences (James 2004; see also Swavola et al. 2016).

Research suggests that this is part of a larger trend toward the 'net-widening' that has been a consequence of "broken windows" policing tactics involving arrests for low-level, misdemeanour offences deemed threats to 'quality of life' (Harcourt 2001; Barrett and Welsh 2018). Indeed, in part due to the types of offences for which women are often arrested, the number of women held in local jails – which, in the US context, comprise the 'front door' to incarceration – has grown exponentially, from fewer than 8,000 in 1970 to close to 110,000 in 2014 (Swavola et al. 2016). Notably, these trends persist in the US despite declining and even historically low rates of crime in recent years (Grawert and Cullen 2017; Gramlich 2018).

Who are criminalized women?

As other chapters in this book discuss in greater depth, poverty and racism are major structural elements of criminal justice involvement for both men and women. Like their male counterparts, criminalized women often struggle with economic disadvantage, mental health and/or substance abuse issues, and histories of interpersonal violence and trauma. Several decades of research have endeavoured to disentangle the extent to which these factors affect women more frequently and/or severely, and the extent to which women may report them more so than men. To the extent possible, this review highlights these distinctions.

Criminal justice contact can be both a cause and an effect of women's poverty. Women tend to have experienced greater economic disadvantage than men prior to criminal justice involvement (Heilbrun et al. 2008). At the time they enter the system, 60% of women in jail do not have full-time employment before they were arrested; for men, this rate is 40% (James 2004). Stunningly, close to half of all single black and Hispanic women have zero or negative net wealth (Chang 2010); criminal justice involvement, through both the imposition of fines and fees, as well as the risk of losing employment and/or public assistance (welfare), can send anyone, but women especially, further into financial crisis (Swavola et al. 2016). Post-incarceration, women living in poverty are at a much higher risk of future criminal justice contact (Holtfreter et al. 2004). In seeking public assistance, criminalized women can have the added difficulty of not fitting into defined need categories. For example, women seeking to reunite with their children and needing to demonstrate an ability to 'provide' for their children in order to get custody often encounter difficulty qualifying for the welfare assistance to do so because they do not have custody. Likewise, criminalized women struggle to fulfil welfare work requirements while also complying with the demands of family court and community supervision (Welsh 2015; Welsh and Rajah 2014).

Criminalized women have serious mental illness at a rate (30 to 45%) double that of criminalized men, and six times that of women in the general population (Lynch et al. 2012; Swavola et al. 2016). In a randomly selected sample of incarcerated women from rural and urban jails, Lynch et al. (2012) find that 82% of women meet the lifetime criteria for drug or alcohol dependence. Further, a third of criminalized women report having experienced symptoms of PTSD in the past year, more than half have experienced PTSD symptoms at some point in their lives, and 86% report having experienced sexual violence at some point in their life (Lynch et al. 2012). It is likely that many of these statistics may be lower than in reality, as mental health screening in jails has been criticized for failing to accurately identify women who need treatment (National Commission on Correctional Health Care [NCCHC] 2014).

Nearly 80% of women in jail are mothers (Swavola et al. 2016), and similar statistics have been reported for women in prison (Mumola 2000). Compared to men, women are far more likely to be caring for children – and to be doing so alone, as single parents – prior to their incarceration (Heilbrun et al. 2008). This has reverberations through the next generations: children with at least one incarcerated parent are at higher risk of not only problems in school, but also physical and mental health issues that can follow them into adulthood (Murphey and Cooper 2015). Intuitively aware of these negative effects of their criminal history, criminalized mothers utilize an array of 'motherwork' strategies to anticipate, cope with, and respond to threats to their parenting and to protect their children from the risks of state intervention (Gurusami 2018; see also Aiello and McQueeney 2016).

Lastly, race/ethnicity is a substantial – and dynamic – factor in patterns of criminal justice involvement. In the US context, it is estimated that two-thirds of criminalized women are non-white (Greenfeld and Snell 1999), though in some local jurisdictions, this ratio is even higher (Swavola et al. 2016: 11). While the US continues to have the highest documented incarceration rate in the world, in 2010 there was a decline in US prison populations for the first time since 1972 (Guerino et al. 2012). Alongside this reversal in a 30-year-long trend, racial/ethnic disparities appear to be changing. For example, in 2000, black women were incarcerated at a rate six times that of white women; by 2009, this ratio shrank by 53%, to 2.8 to 1. Incarceration rates for black men and women have declined, Hispanic men's rates have declined slightly, Hispanic women's rates have risen substantially – by 23.3% – and white men's and women's incarceration rates have risen by 8.5% and 47.1% respectively (Mauer 2013).

There likely is no one single explanation for these changing trends in incarceration rates by race/ethnicity, but rather a combination of factors related to changes in offending patterns, law enforcement approaches, as well as broader socio-economic changes. Some research suggests that the increasing use and distribution of methamphetamine and prescription drugs may contribute to these trends; indeed, a substantial reduction in incarceration of black women for drug offences appears to be a major driver of these trends (Mauer 2013). While racial disparities persist in life expectancies, and while women overall continue to have a longer life expectancy than men, the life expectancy for poor white women with less than a high school diploma has declined by more than five years over the past three decades (Olshansky et al. 2012). As Mauer (2013) observes, 'the cumulative social disadvantage experienced by certain groups, and for less-educated white women in particular, may contribute to greater likelihood of involvement in substance abuse and crime' (p. 17).

Neglect of research on criminalized women

Although women have comprised the fastest-growing prison demographic for decades (Mauer 2013), discourses around criminal justice involvement continue to be predominantly about men (Richie 2012). Loïc Wacquant, for example, a prominent critical theorist, reinforces this 'separate spheres' notion. Wacquant argues that while the incarceration and prisoner re-entry systems control poor, criminalized men's lives, the welfare system similarly controls the lives of the women and children who are these men's 'mothers, sisters, wives, and offspring' in a 'gendered division of control' (2010: 616). Wacquant (2012) recognizes an important fact about what Beth Richie calls America's 'prison nation': that the penal and welfare systems work together to control and marginalize poor people, particularly poor people of colour.

However, Wacquant's argument positions women as bystanders to mass incarceration, when in reality, thousands of women are themselves swept up into the criminal justice system every year. In this way, our popular and academic discourses around the welfare and penal systems have neglected the experiences of criminalized women. This is not to discount insightful research that has documented criminalized men's experiences (e.g. Goffman 2014; Miller 2014; Stuart and Miller 2017) as well as women's experiences as the friends, partners, co-parents, and other family members of criminalized men (e.g. Comfort 2003, 2007; Christian 2005). Rather, it is important to highlight the discourses that have enabled the continued marginalization of research on women's encounters with the criminal justice system, and to recognize how these gaps in the research have limited our ability to theorize criminal offending patterns in ways that are inclusive of gender differences *and* similarities as well as the broader paradigms of gender politics that sustain such patterns (Kruttschnitt 2016).

The essentializing of gender differences runs throughout the criminal justice system. Criminalized women are often portrayed in popular media as either 'mad' – mentally unstable – or 'bad' – manipulative or in defiance of gender role expectations (Brennan and Vandenberg 2009). Thus, criminalized women are in a 'double bind' (Heidensohn 1989; see also Lloyd 1995) in which they are punished both for their criminal behaviour as well as their deviation from gendered expectations of their behaviour, which prescribe that women should be well behaved and law abiding. Further, when women engage in violent or otherwise 'unfeminine' crimes, they are punished more harshly (Chesney-Lind et al. 2008; Grabe et al. 2006). Lastly, because women are associated with emotions – which are considered to be unpredictable and uncontrollable and thus in need of intervention – while men are associated with reason (Jaggar 1992), rehabilitation programming for criminalized women often centres around controlling women's emotions and policing their relationships (Haney 2010; McCorkel 2003, 2013; McKim 2008, 2014). Meanwhile, men's rehabilitation is often framed in economic terms – finding gainful employment. As Wyse (2013) observes, this approach gives short shrift to both men and women, who need attention to and help with rebuilding all facets of their lives. For women especially, the net result of these stereotypes is that women's experiences of the criminal justice system are frequently rendered invisible – either through assumptions that women don't experience criminal justice contact, or that those who do deserve it.

Women's experiences of policing

There is a growing understanding, as reviewed above, of the gendered factors that contribute to women's criminal justice involvement and that suggest approaches to effective rehabilitative services (see also Belknap and Holsinger 2006; Bloom et al. 2003; DeHart et al. 2014). There is also increasing awareness of women's gendered experiences of incarceration, including sexual assault, limited access to gynaecologic and obstetric healthcare, and inhumane practices around childbirth in carceral settings, including shackling (Raeder 2013; Swavola et al. 2016; NCCHC 2014). However, less attention has been paid to women's encounters with police. Ritchie (2017) argues that it is precisely these encounters that should be a focal point, given that the police are typically the 'entry point' to the rest of the criminal justice system. The remainder of this chapter focuses on the gendered – and frequently racialized – dynamics of police-citizen encounters in the US, and how policing has increasingly become involved in post-incarceration supervision processes.

As Ritchie (2017) notes, women's experiences with the police have been 'erased within broader discourses surrounding the drug war, racial profiling, police violence, and mass incarceration' (p. 11). While the stories and images of black men such as Rodney King, Eric Garner, Freddie Gray, and Philando Castile have embodied police violence against men of colour over recent decades, the many cases of police-inflicted violence against women have gone largely unnoticed by the general public. Only very recently, starting in July 2015, when video footage of Sandra Bland's violent arrest, and coverage of her subsequent death while in police custody, have women's encounters with police started to receive national attention (Lai et al. 2015; Montgomery 2015; Ritchie 2017).

Beth Richie's (2012) violence matrix (p. 133) offers a conceptual framework for how violence against women of colour persists in multiple contexts – in intimate relationships as well as in communities and state/governmental institutions. At all levels, this violence can take the forms of not only physical and sexual assault, but also emotional manipulation. Importantly, Richie's matrix allows us to see how interpersonal violence and sexual abuse is connected to a broader social environment that is especially hostile to women of colour, and this includes state or institutional violence in which women of colour are 'assaulted, manipulated, and not protected by institutions and the individuals that act on their behalf' (p. 135).

The limited evidence that exists on the relationship between gender and police contact suggests that racial disparities persist across gender for police stops (Lundman and Kaufman 2003) and arrests (Chauhan et al. 2014). Overall, women are much less likely than men to be the subjects of traffic or pedestrian stops, though there are exceptions: in the year preceding Michael Brown's death, black women in Ferguson, Missouri, experienced traffic stops more frequently than any other category of driver (State of Missouri 2013: 359), and reported similar experiences of police violence as did black men (US Department of Justice, Civil Rights Division 2015).

In a seminal study on the effect of gender on police arrest decisions, Visher (1983) finds that women are only treated more leniently by police if they 'display appropriate gender behaviors and characteristics' (p. 5). Thus, the so-called 'chivalry hypothesis' – that police are more likely to be lenient to women than to men – only holds for older, white, and deferential women: younger women receive harsher treatment than older women, and women of colour are significantly more likely to be arrested than white women or men. Across gender, citizens who are perceived by officers to be disrespectful or otherwise noncompliant are generally viewed to be more worthy of punishment and, potentially, to have force used against them (Crawford and Burns 1998; Engel et al. 2010; Reisig et al. 2004; Van Maanen 1978). It may be that, in some circumstances, women whose demeanour is perceived to be hostile to the police are punished both for their lack of deference and for defying gender-normative behaviour, though much more research is needed to determine how and when this happens.

Because of these complex gender dynamics, in an encounter with police, women may be relatively less concerned than men about that encounter culminating in violence, but more concerned about sexual harassment or assault. In one of the very few studies on this topic, Brunson and Miller (2006) shed light on how gender stereotypes play out in the policing of black youth in poor urban communities. While black young men are routinely treated by police as suspects regardless of their criminal involvement and are also frequently victims of aggressive physical contact, young women are routinely stopped for status offences (offences that are only crimes for young people under the age of 18, such as curfew violations). Young women may be more likely than young men to challenge police misconduct because they are less fearful than are young men of physical aggression from police officers (see also Fine et al. 2003). Young women also report encounters with officers that are sexually harassing in nature if not outright sexually abusive. Simultaneously, young women report a systematic refusal by police to take women's reports of sexual victimization seriously (Brunson and Miller 2006). This evidence supports Richie's (2012) and Ritchie's (2017) contention that police violence against women can take the form of not only sexual exploitation and assault by police officers (see Perry 2014; Queally 2017 for examples of recent cases; see also Yoder 2016) but also emotional manipulation that creates a hostile social environment in which women don't feel safe and supported by their communities to report intimate violence and other forms of victimization.

Women's experiences of the policing-community supervision nexus in California

In my own research with formerly incarcerated women living at one re-entry home in California, I discovered another unexpected way in which policing can violate women's sense of safety. I did not set out to study women's encounters with the police; rather, my study focused on how women experience the 'back end' of the criminal justice system: post-conviction community supervision (parole or probation), and how women manage the demands of this supervision, which often compete with other post-incarceration work women must do to rebuild their lives, such as finding employment, gaining resources through public assistance/welfare, and reuniting with children and other family members (Welsh and Rajah 2014; Welsh 2015, 2017). I discovered, however, that in California, some of the work of community supervision is 'outsourced' to local police departments, and that this has an array of negative consequences for women who have already been previously criminalized.

The state of California underwent a massive change to its correctional system in 2011, with the passage of the Public Safety Realignment Act, also known as Assembly Bill 109, which sought to reduce extensive prison overcrowding by shifting responsibility for people convicted of certain low-level offences from the state to the local counties. People convicted of these offences, who previously would have been served time in state prison and then released on state parole supervision, now serve time in local jail and/or on Post-Release Community Supervision (PRCS), a new form of supervision administered by county probation departments. Given what we know about women's criminal justice involvement, AB 109 stands to have a substantial effect on criminalized women in California (Owen and Mobley 2012).

In my study, eight women were on PRCS, and 16 were on conventional state parole. I wanted to understand whether and how women's experiences of being on PRCS might differ from that of being on parole. I found that women's experiences across the two supervision types were more similar than different, with supervision often constraining rather than facilitating women's efforts at rehabilitation. However, I also found that how the two forms of supervision uphold their goal of ensuring public safety meant different lived experiences of supervision.

State parole agents are sworn peace officers, meaning they carry firearms in the field. Teams of armed parole agents regularly conduct checks of parolees' homes and workplaces to verify parolees' whereabouts. In contrast, California's 58 counties differ on whether and how many of their probation officers are armed. Thus, in counties where probation officers are not armed, local police departments have taken on the added responsibility of conducting compliance checks to verify that people on PRCS are living at the addresses to which they were released (Petersilia 2013). During the period in which I conducted fieldwork at the re-entry programme, the police attempted or completed compliance checks on all eight of the women in my sample who were on PRCS. It is also important to note that throughout my study, I neither witnessed nor heard mention of parole agents doing similar searches of any of the women who were on parole, likely because the parole agency knew and trusted the programme to enforce its own rules and to report to parole when women were no longer staying at the programme.

In interviews with me, women repeatedly described how upsetting it was not only to be the subjects of these compliance checks, but also to have them happen despite regularly meeting with their probation officers and otherwise complying with the conditions of supervision. Women recounted stories of being woken up in the early hours of the morning to police officers kicking down their bedroom doors, shining flashlights in their faces, and being watched by police as they climbed out of bed and put clothes on. Given that people's encounters with the police are typically in the context of crime prevention or investigation, women understandably struggled to make sense of why the police were looking for them *after* their release from incarceration.

Then there was the manner in which these checks unfold, which is rooted in police procedures and training: two or more cars containing four or more police officers and/or armed probation officers would park in front of one of the re-entry programme's houses, which are all single-family homes in a residential neighbourhood. A woman would be handcuffed outside of her residence and questioned by a pair of officers while the other officers searched the premises, flipping over mattresses and emptying dresser drawers. For the women in my study, this meant that their neighbours now knew that they have some sort of involvement with the police, thus perpetuating the stigma of being formerly incarcerated. One mother, who lived at the programme with her two young children, expressed a concern that the police would 'handcuff me in front of my children and go in and destroy my room looking for guns and weapons'. This fear was compounded by the image of male officers barging into a home for women, which is supposed to be a safe space for women in recovery from not only substance abuse, mental health issues, and various forms of trauma, but also from the accumulation of experiences related to their criminal justice involvement. Another woman who recounted her experience of these checks disclosed to me that she sleeps in the nude, which made her early morning encounter with several male police officers all the more upsetting, though not surprising, given that men on average comprise 83% of American police forces (Reaves 2015). As this woman put it, 'if you're looking for females why don't you have female officers, when you're coming into a female facility? So if you're looking for females, why is it all men and not no women?'

Notably, these police encounters seemed otherwise disconnected from the supervision process. When one woman notified her PRCS officer of a disruptive compliance check in which she felt intimidated and bullied by the officers involved, her PRCS officer implied a deferential relationship between probation and the local police; according to the woman, 'she was like, "as long as you was in compliance don't worry about it. They gonna do what they do"'. Probation's deference to the police may be due to the perception that people on PRCS 'should' be incarcerated, if not for the new law guiding their release, and thus are in need of law enforcement's heavy-handed approach.

Interestingly, however, I found that women on PRCS overall felt more positively about their supervision experience than did women on conventional parole. This may be due to a few reasons, including intense public pressure placed on county probation departments to ensure that PRCS is a success, as well as differences in the training and prior work experience of some PRCS officers compared to parole agents (Welsh 2018). Women on PRCS uniformly described their PRCS officers as genuinely caring about their success, and this was communicated to them through small gestures, such as providing bus directions to the PRCS office. Women on parole, on the other hand, widely varied in their perceptions of their parole agents, with some women describing a strong 'working alliance' (Bordin 1979) with their agents, and others equating their agents to the police – as contact to be minimized and avoided at all costs (Welsh 2017). Across both supervision types, women consistently articulated a fundamental lack of substantive assistance toward rehabilitation, with women having to take on the many forms of work necessary to surmount the many institutionally constructed barriers to rebuilding their lives.

Conclusion

Given that criminalized women are even more likely than their male counterparts to have histories of mental illness, trauma, and poverty, and to confront systemic issues related to their gender post-incarceration, feminist criminologists have long argued for rehabilitative programming that holistically accounts for and effectively addresses these issues. This chapter has summarized some of the trends in both women's criminal involvement and institutional responses to women's criminalization. Drawing on my research in California, I have highlighted the tensions that have emerged alongside efforts to reduce the incarcerated population, which have been met with a scaling up of police involvement in the community supervision of previously incarcerated people.

This chapter has also highlighted the need to reconsider police practices, particularly as they relate to women. Three specific ways in which feminist researchers and advocates are currently pushing for reform to reduce negative encounters between police and female citizens are through decriminalization of behaviours that unnecessarily bring women into contact with the police, police accountability models, and the increased use of non-police interventions. As Ritchie (2017) argues, to end police violence against women, 'the most effective measure is to reduce opportunities for law enforcement officers to engage and hold power over women of color' (p. 123). This can be accomplished in part through decriminalizing low-level drug- and poverty-related behaviours, as well as activities such as prostitution, for which women are often criminalized. Second, much more work can be done around police accountability; alarmingly, for example, a majority of the largest US police departments have no policies explicitly defining and prohibiting police sexual misconduct (Ritchie and Jones-Brown 2017; Yoder 2016). Ellen Pence's work on safety and accountability audits through the 'Duluth model' of addressing domestic violence also suggests ways in which criminal justice professionals and community advocates can work together to bolster police accountability (Pence 2001; Praxis International 2018). Third, increasing the use of non-police interventions, especially for circumstances involving mental illness, has the potential to increase women's safety and reduce police violence. Such non-police responses can include peer counsellors, mental health crisis professionals, and an array of diversion programmes (for example, see Bernd 2016). Lastly, the use of police to monitor people on supervision and to thereby project an image of public safety should be reconsidered, not only for the stigmatizing effects on crime-processed people (and the gendered nature of such effects), but also for the drain on police resources and the potentially harmful effect of such checks on police-community relations more broadly.

References

Aiello, B. and McQueeney, K. (2016) "How can you live without your kids?" Distancing from and embracing the stigma of "incarcerated mother". *Journal of Prison Education and Reentry*, 3(1), 32–49.

Barrett, C. and Welsh, M. (2018) Petty crimes and harassment: How community residents understand low-level enforcement in three high-crime neighborhoods in New York city. *Qualitative Sociology*, 41(2), 173–197.

Belknap, J. and Holsinger, K. (2006) The gendered nature of risk factors for delinquency. *Feminist Criminology*, 1, 48–71.

Bernd, C. (2016) Community groups work to provide emergency medical alternatives, separate from the police. In M. Schenwar, J. Macaré and A. Price (Eds.), *Who Do You Serve, Who Do You Protect? Police Violence and Resistance in the United States*. Chicago: Haymarket Books.

Bloom, B., Owen, B., Rosenbaum, J. and Deschenes, E. (2003) Focusing on girls and young women: A gendered perspective on female delinquency. *Women and Criminal Justice*, 14, 117–136.

Bordin, E. (1979) The generalizability of the psychoanalytic concept of the working alliance. *Psychotherapy: Theory, Research, & Practice*, 16, 252–260.

Brennan, P. and Vandenberg, A. (2009) Depictions of female offenders in front-page newspaper stories: The importance of race/ethnicity. *International Journal of Social Inquiry*, 2(2), 141–175.

Brunson, R. and Miller, J. (2006) Gender, race, and urban policing: The experience of African American youths. *Gender & Society*, 20(4), 531–552.

Bush-Baskette, S. (2010) *Misguided Justice: The War on Drugs and the Incarceration of Black Women*. Bloomington, IN: iUniverse.

Chang, M. (2010) *Lifting as We Climb: Women of Color, Wealth, and America's Future*. Oakland, CA: Insight Center for Community Economic Development. Available at: www.mariko-chang.com/LiftingAsWeClimb.pdf.

Chauhan, P., Fera, A., Welsh, M., Balazon, E. and Misshula, E. (2014). *Trends in Misdemeanor Arrest Rates in New York*. Report presented to the Citizens Crime Commission, New York.

Chesney-Lind, M. and Irwin, K. (2008) *Beyond Bad Girls: Gender, Violence, and Hype*. New York: Routledge.

Christian, J. (2005) Riding the bus: Barriers to prison visitation and family management strategies. *Journal of Contemporary Criminal Justice*, 21(1), 31–48.

Comfort, M. (2003) In the tube at San Quentin: The "secondary prisonization" of women visiting inmates. *Journal of Contemporary Ethnography*, 32(1), 77–107.

Comfort, M. (2007) *Doing Time Together: Love and Family in the Shadow of the Prison*. Chicago: University of Chicago Press.

Crawford, C. and Burns, R. (1998) Predictors of the police use of force: The application of a continuum perspective in Phoenix. *Police Quarterly*, 1, 41–63.

DeHart, D., Lynch, S., Belknap, J., Dass-Brailsford, P. and Green, B. (2014) Life history models of female offending: The roles of serious mental illness and trauma in women's pathways to jail. *Psychology of Women Quarterly*, 38, 138–151.

Engel, R., Klahm, C. and Tillyer, R. (2010) Citizens' demeanor, race, and traffic stops. In S. Rice and M. White (Eds.), *Race, Ethnicity, and Policing: New and Essential Readings*. New York: New York University, pp. 287–308.

Fine, M., Freudenberg, N., Payne, Y., Perkins, T., Smith, K. and Wanzer, K. (2003) "Anything can happen with police around": Urban youth evaluate strategies of surveillance in public places. *Journal of Social Issues*, 59, 141–158.

Glaze, L. and Bonczar, T. (2007) *Probation and Parole in the United States, 2006*. Washington, DC: Bureau of Justice Statistics.

Glaze, L., Bonczar, T. and Zhang, F. (2010) *Probation and Parole in the United States, 2009*. Washington, DC: Bureau of Justice Statistics.

Goffman, A. (2014) *On the Run: Fugitive Life in an American City*. Chicago: University of Chicago Press.

Grabe, M. E., Trager, K. D., Lear, M. and Rauch, J. (2006) Gender in crime news: A case study test of the chivalry hypothesis. *Mass Communication and Society*, 9(2), 137–163.

Gramlich, J. (2018) *5 Facts About Crime in the U.S.* Washington, DC: Pew Research Center. Available at: www.pewresearch.org/fact-tank/2018/01/30/5-facts-about-crime-in-the-u-s/.

Grawert, A. and Cullen, J. *Crime in 2017: A Preliminary Analysis*. New York: New York University School of Law, Brennan Center for Justice. Available at: www.brennancenter.org/publication/crime-2017-preliminary-analysis.

Greenfield, L. and Snell, T. (1999) *Women Offenders*. Washington, DC: Bureau of Justice Statistics.

Guerino, P., Harrison, P. and Sabol, W. (2012) *Prisoners in 2010*. Washington, DC: Bureau of Justice Statistics.

Gurusami, S. (2018) Motherwork under the state: The maternal labor of formerly incarcerated black women. *Social Problems*. DOI:10.1093/socpro/spx045.

Haney, L. (2010) *Offending Women: Power, Punishment, and the Regulation of Desire*. Berkeley: University of California Press.

Harcourt, B. (2001) *Illusion of Order: The False Promise of Broken Windows Policing*. Cambridge, MA: Harvard University Press.

Heidensohn, F. (1989) *Crime and Society*. Basingstoke: Palgrave Macmillan, pp. 85–111.

Heilbrun, K., Dematteo, D., Fretz, R., Erickson, J., Yasuhara, K. and Anumba, N. (2008) How "specific" are gender-specific rehabilitation needs? An empirical analysis. *Criminal Justice & Behavior*, 35(11), 1382–1397.

Holtfreter, K., Reisig, M. and Morash, M. (2004) Poverty, state capital, and recidivism among women offenders. *Criminology & Public Policy*, 3(2), 185–208.

Jaggar, A. (1992) Love and knowledge: Emotions in feminist epistemology. In Alison M. Jaggar and Susan R. Bordo (Eds.), *Gender/Body/Knowledge*. New Brunswick: Rutgers University Press.

James, D. (2004) *Profile of Jail Inmates, 2002*. Washington, DC: U.S. Department of Justice, Office of Justice Programs, Bureau of Justice Statistics.

Kaeble, D. and Bonczar, T. (2017) *Probation and Parole in the United States, 2015*. Washington, DC: US Department of Justice, Bureau of Justice Statistics.

Kruttschnitt, C. (2016) The politics, and place, of gender in research on crime. The 2015 presidential address to the American society of criminology. *Criminology*, 54(1), 8–29.

Lai, K., Park, H., Buchanan, L. and Andrews, W. (2015) Assessing the legality of Sandra Bland's arrest. *The New York Times*, 22 July. Available at: www.nytimes.com/interactive/2015/07/20/us/sandra-bland-arrest-death-videos-maps.html.

Lloyd, A. (1995) *Doubly Deviant, Doubly Damned: Society's Treatment of Violent Women*. London: Penguin Books.

Lundman, R. and Kaufman, R. (2003) Driving while black: Effects of race, ethnicity, and gender on citizen self-reports of traffic stops and police actions. *Criminology*, 41(1), 195–220.

Lynch, S., DeHart, D., Belknap, J. and Green, B. (2012) *Women's Pathways to Jail: The Roles and Intersections of Serious Mental Illness & Trauma*. Washington, DC: Bureau of Justice Assistance. Available at: www.bja.gov/publications/women_pathways_to_jail.pdf.

Mauer, M. (2013) *The Changing Racial Dynamics of Women's Incarceration*. Washington, DC: Sentencing Project. Available at: https://sentencingproject.org/wp-content/uploads/2015/12/The-Changing-Racial-Dynamics-of-Womens-Incarceration.pdf.

McCorkel, J. (2003) Embodied surveillance and the gendering of punishment. *Journal of Contemporary Ethnography*, 32(1), 41–76.

McCorkel, J. (2013) *Breaking Women: Gender, Race, and the New Politics of Imprisonment*. New York: New York University Press.

McKim, A. (2008) 'Getting gut-level': Punishment, gender, and therapeutic governance. *Gender & Society*, 22(3), 303–323.

McKim, A. (2014) Roxanne's dress: Governing gender and marginality through addiction treatment. *Signs*, 39(2), 433–458.

Miller, R. (2014) Devolving the carceral state: Race, prisoner reentry, and the micro-politics of urban poverty management. *Punishment & Society*, 16(3), 305–335.

Montgomery, D. (2015) New details released in Sandra Bland's death in Texas jail. *The New York Times*, 20 July. Available at: www.nytimes.com/2015/07/21/us/new-details-released-in-sandra-blands-death-in-texas-jail.html.

Morash, M. (2010) *Women on Probation and Parole: A Feminist Critique of Community Programs and Services*. Boston: Northeastern University.

Mumola, C. J. (2000) *Incarcerated Parents and Their Children*. Washington, DC: Department of Justice, Office of Justice Programs, Bureau of Justice Statistics.

Murphey, D. and Cooper, P. M. (2015) *Parents Behind Bars: What Happens to Their Children*. Bethesda, MD: Child Trends. Available at: www.childtrends.org/wp-content/uploads/2015/10/2015-42ParentsBehindBars.pdf.

National Commission on Correctional Health Care. (2014) *Position Statement: Women's Health Care in Correctional Settings*. Chicago. Available at: www.ncchc.org/womens-health-care.

Olshansky, S., et al. (2012) Differences in life expectancy due to race and educational differences are widening, and many may not catch up. *Health Affairs*, 31(8), 1803–1813.

Owen, B. and Mobley, A. (2012) Realignment in California: Policy and research implications. *Western Criminology Review*, 13(2), 46–52.

Penal Reform International. (2017) *Global Prison Trends 2017*. London: Penal Reform International. Available at: https://cdn.penalreform.org/wp-content/uploads/2017/05/Global_Prison_Trends-2017-Full-Report-1.pdf.

Pence, E. (2001) Safety for battered women in a textually mediated legal system. *Studies in Cultures, Organizations, and Societies*, 7, 199–229.

Perry, T. (2014) San Diego to pay $5.9 million to woman assaulted by officer. *LA Times*, 25 September. Available at: www.latimes.com/local/lanow/la-me-ln-san-diego-cop-20140925-story.html.

Petersilia, J. (2013) *Voices from the Field: How California Stakeholders View Public Safety Realignment*. Stanford, CA: Stanford Law School, Stanford Criminal Justice Center.

Praxis International. (2018) *Institutional Analysis: Changing Institutional Responses to Violence Against Women*. Duluth, MN. Available at: http://praxisinternational.org/institutional-analysiscommunity-assessment-2/.

Queally, J. (2017) Accuser in Oakland police sex abuse scandal settles claim for nearly $1 million. *LA Times*, 31 May. Available at: www.latimes.com/local/lanow/la-me-ln-oakland-sex-scandal-settlement-20170531-story.html.

Raeder, M. (2013) *Pregnancy- and Child-Related Legal and Policy Issues Concerning Justice-Involved Women*. Washington, DC: US Department of Justice, National Institute of Corrections. Available at: https://s3.amazonaws.com/static.nicic.gov/Library/027701.pdf.

Reaves, B. (2015) *Local Police Departments, 2013: Personnel, Policies, and Practices*. US Department of Justice, Office of Justice Programs, Bureau of Justice Statistics. Available at: www.bjs.gov/content/pub/pdf/lpd13ppp.pdf.

Reisig, M., McCluskey, J., Mastrofski, S. and Terrill, W. (2004) Suspect disrespect toward the police. *Justice Quarterly*, 21, 241–268.

Richie, B. (2012) *Arrested Justice: Black Women, Violence, and America's Prison Nation*. New York: New York University Press.

Ritchie, A. (2017) *Invisible No More: Police Violence Against Black Women and Women of Color*. Boston: Beacon.

Ritchie, A. and Jones-Brown, D. (2017) Policing race, gender, and sex: A review of law enforcement policies. *Women and Criminal Justice*, 27(1), 21–50.

State of Missouri. (2013) *Racial Profiling Data 2013*. Available at: http://ago.mo.gov/docs/default-source/public-safety/2013agencyreports.pdf?sfvrsn=2.

Stuart, F. and Miller, R. (2017) The prisonized old head: Intergenerational socialization and the fusion of ghetto and prison culture. *Journal of Contemporary Ethnography*, 44(6), 673–698.

Sudbury, J. (2002) Celling black bodies: Black women in the global prison industrial complex. *Feminist Review*, 70, 57–74.

Swavola, E., Riley, K. and Subramanian, R. (2016) *Overlooked: Women and Jails in an Era of Reform*. New York: Vera Institute of Justice. Available at: https://storage.googleapis.com/vera-web-assets/downloads/Publications/overlooked-women-and-jails-report/legacy_downloads/overlooked-women-and-jails-report-updated.pdf.

US Department of Justice, Civil Rights Division. (2015) *Investigation of the Ferguson Police Department*. Washington, DC. Available at: www.justice.gov/sites/default/files/opa/press-releases/attachments/2015/03/04/ferguson_police_department_report.pdf.

Van Maanen, J. (1978) The asshole. In P. Manning and J. Van Maanen (Eds.), *Policing: A View from the Street*. Chicago: Goodyear, pp. 221–238.

Visher, C. (1983) Gender, police arrest decisions, and notions of chivalry. *Criminology*, 21(1), 5–28.

Wacquant, L. (2010) Prisoner reentry as myth and ceremony. *Dialectical Anthropology*, 34, 605–620.

Welsh, M. (2015) Categories of exclusion: The transformation of formerly-incarcerated women into "Able-Bodied Adults Without Dependents" in welfare processing. *Journal of Sociology & Social Welfare*, 42(2), 55–77.

Welsh, M. (2017) How formerly incarcerated women confront the limits of caring and the burdens of control amid California's carceral realignment. *Feminist Criminology*. Online first. Available at: http://journals.sagepub.com/doi/abs/10.1177/1557085117698751.

Welsh, M. (2018) Conceptualizing the personal touch: Experiential knowledge and gendered strategies in community supervision work. *Journal of Contemporary Ethnography*. Online first. Available at: https://doi.org/10.1177/0891241618777304.

Welsh, M. and Rajah, V. (2014) Rendering invisible punishments visible: Using institutional ethnography in feminist criminology. *Feminist Criminology*, 9(4), 323–343.

Wyse, J. (2013) Rehabilitating criminal selves: Gendered strategies in community corrections. *Gender & Society*, 27(2), 231–255.

Yoder, S. (2016) Officers who rape: The police brutality chiefs ignore. *Al-Jazeera*, 19 January. Available at: http://america.aljazeera.com/articles/2016/1/19/sexual-violence-the-brutality-that-police-chiefs-ignore.html.

Working with black and minority ethnic groups in the penal system

53

Theo Gavrielides

Introduction

The literature on race and the criminal justice system is rich both in its theoretical and empirical aspects (e.g. see Mason 2003; Rollock 2009). Yet, despite such extensive debate, we are far from fully understanding key concepts that are necessary for reaching a basic consensus among those working in this field. This chapter is not going to engage with this debate. Certain truths have to be accepted a priori and these include firstly, the fact that we are not living in an equal society and, secondly, that racism is embedded within our criminal justice institutions and society (Mason 2003; Rollock 2009). We also accept that there is disproportionality in the criminal justice system (Cabinet Office 2017).[1]

Consequently, this chapter focuses on current best practice in probation services with a specific focus on black and minority ethnic (BAME) users. In this chapter, the term 'probation services' refers to the production of reports for sentencers, the management of community sentences, working with released prisoners, and working with victims and families. 'Users' means offenders and victims who are served by probation agencies.

The chapter aims to make two contributions. First, it aspires to inform criminal justice policy and practice in the UK and beyond. Second, it will provide a practical tool for involving BAME users in criminal justice service provision. To these ends, the chapter has been divided into four parts. First, it will attempt some conceptual agreements that will allow us to proceed with its key argument. Subsequently, the chapter will present what research findings have shown in terms of effective practice for resettling offenders and achieving reductions in recidivism. The third section will proceed with the design of a practical tool that aims to support practitioners and policymakers in involving BAME users. The chapter will then conclude with some key arguments on user involvement.

Conceptual agreements

Before we proceed, it is important that certain concepts are agreed upon. One such agreement should include an understanding of the term 'race'. Concepts develop and are redefined by society and the times within which we are living. The same applies to the term 'race'. As a protected characteristic the Equality and Human Rights Commission (EHRC) states that the term refers to a group of people defined by their race, colour, and nationality (including citizenship), ethnic, or national origins.[2]

In this chapter, the term 'race' is used in its analytical context, rather than its descriptive context. To elaborate, the term is used to refer to the process of power that 'racializes' groups and identities. Patel and Tyler (2011: 2) explain that this process of power 'impacts upon all of us in different but significant ways, for example how Muslims as a seemingly religious community are still racialised as a group'.

For the more descriptive needs of the arguments presented in the chapter, the term 'black and minority ethnic' (BAME) will be used but whenever our findings refer to a specific group within this term (e.g. black Caribbean, black African, and Asian), the relevant distinction will be made. Further distinctions also need to be made in relation to age and gender as certain issues are more likely to be relevant to BAME subgroups.

We also need to be clear who the users and who the customers of probation services are. It is more likely that improving outcomes for probation customers might be a different exercise from improving outcomes for users. The probation service is based on certain utilitarian assumptions of rehabilitation and punishment. Von Hirsch explains: 'Rehabilitation is the idea of curing an offender of his or her criminal tendencies. It consists, more precisely, of changing an offender's personality, outlook, habits, or opportunities so as to make him or her less inclined to commit crimes' (1998: 1). Von Hirsch continues: 'Often, rehabilitation is said to involve helping the offender, but a benefit to the offender is not necessarily presupposed: those who benefit are other persons, ourselves, who become less likely to be victimised by the offender' (1998: 1).

How are these assumptions pursued by probation services? Who are they aiming to please? Offenders do not decide whether to have contact with probation. The sentencers or courts do this for them, and under the utilitarian model of rehabilitation, offenders are simply instructed to comply and if they breach those instructions, then there are furthermore punitive 'just deserts' penalties. Put another way, offenders use the probation service because they have to. They are not customers; they are users of probation services. However, this should not impact on the fact that they can still report on how well the service worked for them. Moreover, it shouldn't affect any qualitative or quantitative analysis of service progress and outcomes.

BAME users' perspectives on resettlement and recidivism

Much research has been conducted into the factors which aid desistance from crime and successful reintegration into the community (see, for example, Maruna 2001, 2004). These processes tend to be generic rather than ethnically specific with all offenders facing similar problems on their path to resettlement. Here, we highlight areas that relate to BAME probation service users specifically.

Accessing informal support networks

Informal support networks (such as those provided by religious groups, family, and community organizations) play a vital role in the resettlement of offenders (Gavrielides and Blake 2013). However, when it comes to family and social networks there are noticeable differences between BAME individuals and their white counterparts (Gavrielides and Blake 2013). Looking at existing probation practices, these differences may work either against or in favour of reintegration. For example, the support provided by social relationships complements the work of offender managers by aiding BAME offenders' reintegration into society and creating opportunities for a life without crime. We also know that the support networks available to each offender will vary based on individual circumstances and so it is important for probation workers to be well-informed about the personal situations reflected in their caseloads. This is particularly pertinent for BAME users as some may lack a family and friends infrastructure (e.g. foreign nationals). However, for others, unusually strong social and family networks can hinder reintegration (e.g. by creating a feeling of shame and rejection).

Family members can provide one of the most basic but invaluable support networks to offenders independently of their background. It has been observed that an offender's reliance on different support networks shifts as they progress through the criminal justice system and that family support plays the most important role upon release from prison (England et al. 2007) but also while they are in prison.

The process of family formation and rebuilding relationships with one's children has also been identified as a key influence upon desistance. This is particularly true for offenders with cultural backgrounds that are informed by strong family ties. The desire to set a good example for their children has frequently been cited by male offenders as a motivation for moving away from crime (Jacobson et al. 2010). Therefore, it is important for the criminal justice system to provide a space for these familial relationships to strengthen and develop. Furthermore, providing support for offending parents also addresses the needs of their children. There is an established relationship between a child growing up with an absent parent and experiencing a tendency towards crime (Rakt et al. 2012). Focusing on black males, this trend is especially evident (House of Commons 2007). However, it is necessary to point out that the matter is complex and that the role that a BAME offender's family might play in facilitating rehabilitation varies according to differences in family structures and cultural practices.

Community support

Another key source of support for offenders can be provided by either the community into which they are resettling or their own community of culture. However, this matter is complex. There is evidence that community can also act as a pressure and as a stigmatizing factor of shame and control (Gavrielides and Blake 2013). BAME offenders may feel isolated from their own communities as a result of their offending behaviour. Others have, however, pointed out that 'Experiencing a sense of community is linked to informal social control and improves prospects of social reintegration' (England et al. 2007: 8). Positive engagement in civic life and social institutions will encourage an offender to move away from crime and aid their rehabilitation into society (Calverley 2009).

Community and faith-based institutions that work in partnership with probation can provide accessible community networks for many BAME offenders (Gavrielides and Blake 2013). Nevertheless, whilst religion may play an important role in the rehabilitation of some BAME offenders, statutory bodies, including probation services, should not rely upon it. For example, research on Muslim prisoners undertaken in 2009 revealed that upon release Muslim ex-prisoners tended to receive less support in finding accommodation and reintegrating into the community than non-Muslims. Rather than having these needs met through religious associations, many of the offenders found themselves rejected from their mosques and ostracized by the community (McNeill and Weaver 2010).

Overall, it appears that the voluntary and community sector is 'crucial' to the delivery of effective resettlement services. Voluntary organizations are specially disposed to provide for groups of offenders with specialist needs and it has been suggested that this should be reflected in the commissioning arrangements when developing services for BAME groups. Service providers are giving increasing recognition to the important role the third sector can play in the resettlement process (Jacobson et al. 2010). However, there is evidence to believe that this valuable resource has traditionally been underutilized by statutory bodies (Nacro 2005).

Employment

Engaging in gainful employment is another important factor in the resettlement of offenders independently of their background. Fieldwork that was conducted with over 100 BAME prisoners and ex-prisoners revealed that the two elements the offenders felt were most critical to their rehabilitation were finding employment and accommodation (Jacobson et al. 2010).

Employment demands discipline from the worker and imposes time structures which reduce opportunities for engaging in criminal behaviour. Economic remuneration and the sense of self-worth gained from work are also conducive to desistance from crime as offenders are given opportunities to construct a new social identity.

There are some employment-focused initiatives that are either triggered or integrated within formal criminal justice structures. For example, employment advice may be available to some prisoners as they prepare for release and to offenders on probation. Supervision orders which include accredited opportunities like unpaid work requirements and offender behaviour programmes can help increase the social capital[3] and self-worth of individual offenders (Bain and Parkinson 2010).

King of my castle?

Accommodation provides another key influence on desistance. Securing stable and suitable accommodation is most important to offenders who have just been released from prison. It is estimated that having accommodation arranged on release can reduce prisoner's reconviction rates by up to 20% (Stevens et al. 2011). A survey of BAME prisoners revealed that they valued accommodation as the most essential requirement after leaving prison (Jacobson et al. 2010). Without a fixed address, offenders are limited in their ability to access support services, apply for jobs, and claim benefits (Nacro 2005).

Racial prejudice and economic marginalization means that black people are more likely to be dependent upon social housing and has contributed to high rates of homelessness among black households (Nacro 2007). Calverley

(2009) has noted how patterns of weak kinship networks and the dominance of small, geographically disparate families amongst his black and dual heritage sample put these offenders at greater disadvantage compared with Asian and Bangladeshi offenders when seeking accommodation. Unable to meet their housing requirements through their own means or by utilizing social networks, some black offenders rely heavily on the support of statutory bodies and voluntary-sector organizations (Calverley 2009). Resettlement workers should be aware that distinct issues can be associated with accommodating offenders from BAME groups. For certain groups of offenders, such as those whose offences are gang related or heavily influenced by their surrounding environment, it is important that they are rehoused away from their old neighbourhoods (Gavrielides and Blake 2013).

However, there is evidence that it is better not to resettle BAME offenders in unfamiliar and potentially less diverse communities where they are at risk of isolation and unable to draw on the support of family and friends (Gavrielides and Blake 2013). This should be taken into account if better outcomes are to be achieved. Cultural and religious factors also have an impact on housing needs. For example, attention should be paid to the specialist needs of Muslim offenders and their resettlement arrangements should take into account the need to attend a mosque several times a day.

The additional barriers that BAME offenders may face in finding and maintaining stable accommodation presents a key concern for offender managers engaged in the rehabilitation of BAME offenders. Stronger links between prisons, local authorities, and the probation service would be beneficial for service providers and offenders, allowing for housing needs to be identified and met more quickly. Whilst general indicators of BAME disadvantage have been identified, variation in patterns of homeowning and family structures among the ethnic groups serve as a reminder that offenders must at all times be treated as individuals and that offender managers must take the time to understand the particular circumstances of each case.

Self-image and positive thinking

Good practice in relation to developing positive thinking and a self-image has also been highlighted in research (Gavrielides and Blake 2013). A combination of social and economic disadvantage, racial discrimination, and historical exploitation may affect the self-image of some BAME groups and impact upon their conceptions of self-worth and the ability to move on. This is particularly true for young black offenders (Sender et al. 2006).

BAME experiences within the criminal justice system can exacerbate low feelings of self-worth. Particular attention has been given to the effect of imprisonment on BAME self-identity. Cowburn and Lavis (2009) maintain that Western forms of identity, such as being European, are being forced on to BAME prisoners, causing them to lose some of their sense of cultural identity and adding to feelings of isolation. It has also been said that prisons negatively address ethnicity and fail to provide BAME prisoners with opportunities to create positive identities based on their race (Cheliotis and Liebling 2006). Eurocentric service provision, discrimination, and staff prejudice can therefore leave BAME prisoners particularly vulnerable to isolation and feelings of negative self-identity. For these reasons, Gavrielides (2015) and Gavrielides and Worth (2014) have criticized the Risk-Need-Responsivity (RNR) model on which parts of our current criminal justice system are based. RNR's focus is on reducing and managing risk as well as on studying the process of relapse. Pathology-focused research and intervention have consequently been developed as tools for RNR-based approaches to rehabilitation. Despite being criticized by clinicians and researchers, RNR is generally accepted as the benchmark against which rehabilitation programmes should be measured and tested (Mapham and Hefferon 2012). The fact that the model emphasizes empirically supported therapies makes its scientific approach appealing.

Gavrielides and Worth (2014) advocate for alternative approaches such as those based on the Good Lives Model. They argue that for any individual to develop their potential and thrive, first there needs to be a sense of self-pride and a set of personal goals. Remove these, and independently of the social, societal, biological, political factors that may be evoked, we should not expect to see any desistance (Gavrielides and Worth 2014). According to classic theories of human development, we acquire and foster these goals and aspirations though a mixture of factors such as our parents, role models, peers, and teachers (Salkind 2004). But we first have to believe in ourselves (Gavrielides 2015).

Involving BAME users in probation services: a practical tool

BAME user involvement is complex and can include strands from ex-offenders helping to review and monitor the service, to sitting on a decision-making board, speaking at events, or participating in delivering the service as employees – for instance, in the role of Engagement Workers, mentors, and volunteers.

The principles of BAME service user involvement

Working together to increase understanding of BAME service users' experiences requires having a set of principles for engagement. Principles are the stepping-stones for effective service user involvement and illuminate the core values, beliefs, and attitudes essential for meaningful engagement. Engagement requires a long-term commitment to building partnership arrangements between probation services users and probation officers. Based on the findings of recent research (see Gavrielides and Blake 2013), this chapter proposes the following key principles of engagement:

1   Respecting the individual uniqueness of people and challenging negative stereotypes surrounding BAME offenders;
2   Consulting with different groups of BAME service users to explore different topics in order to ensure their diverse voices are heard;
3   Helping BAME service users to become active in the rehabilitation process and supporting them to develop their own ideas of desistance;
4   Being flexible and open to different ways of working;
5   Ensuring the rights of BAME service users to decide where and how they want to get involved – wherever possible within the limits imposed by the statutory nature of criminal justice interventions;
6   Believing in the value of BAME service users' contributions to design and delivery of services;
7   Demonstrating a commitment to welcome and include BAME service users' in all aspects of the work;
8   Willingness to change the equilibrium of power towards BAME service users to demonstrate open policy and procedures that promote engagement;
9   It is recommended that the right to be informed/involved in decision-making processes (Article 6 of the Human Rights Act) be used to foster a human rights culture within the institution. Embedding such a culture can increase BAME user confidence and engagement as users become better informed about decisions that impact on them.

The toolkit

Apart from the principles of engagement cited above, those listed below can be used to produce a toolkit for practitioners who wish to involve BAME users in their service delivery, and the principles derive from the findings of a study conducted by the author and some colleagues (see Gavrielides and Blake 2013).

Achieving user-to-user support

Black male offenders may benefit from mentoring schemes and support groups as a way of expanding their social networks and informal support systems for reintegration. Mentoring and peer mentoring schemes are noted for their ability to increase the participant's involvement in education, training, and employment.

Actions:

1   Ex-offenders get together (more informal than focus groups), with the service users facilitating it, and probation officers present.

2   Group discussions that are properly managed. Service users and staff need to be fully prepared. Service users may need rehearsal, training, and support to deliver their message. Flexibility is needed to accommodate the preferences of service users, and debriefing is vital when people have shared sensitive information about their lives. As discussed above, group-work programmes that directly address race and self-image could enable BAME offenders to build more positive social and cultural identities.

3   Choice of family involvement when requested by a service user. This must take into account cultural background of an ex-offender, and be implemented in a nonjudgemental and non-intrusive way.

4   Cultural appropriateness of temporary accommodation, e.g. enabling family and friends to visit ex-offenders there. Resettlement workers should also be aware that distinct issues can be associated with accommodating offenders from BAME groups. For certain groups of offenders, such as those whose offences were gang related or heavily influenced by their surrounding environment, it is important that they are rehoused away from their old neighbourhoods.

Changing the organizational culture

To meaningfully achieve user involvement, the whole organization must believe in the value of doing so. Actions to be taken:

1   Staff training and development including supporting race equality staff initiatives.

2   BAME ex-offenders input to business planning, consultations, presentations, training (especially on equality and diversity), membership panels, joint staff and users events (e.g. team meetings, away days, and team open days where ex-offenders are invited).

3   Showcase best practice models of BAME involvement and advise on how such mechanisms can be built into future design and delivery.

4   Involvement of BAME ex-offenders in designing monitoring and evaluation feedback forms.

5   Exit meetings for feedback. Probation officers should ask if they provided adequate help to a user; then it should be fed back to managers. Family member/friend could attend those exit meetings.

6   BAME ex-offenders' feedback on court reports.

7   Court user forums where magistrates would meet offenders and listen to their life stories. This practice provides a wider context to someone's criminal history and helps to humanize an offender.

8   Recruitment of Engagement Workers who feedback to the team and managers. They should be involved in the process on a regular basis, not only when there's a risk of licence breach. It is important for group inductions to be led by Engagement Workers where BAME ex-offenders learn about their rights and entitlements, including complaints procedures.

9 Learning from other professions. Some BAME service users who were interviewed for the project said that the role of a probation officer should be akin to that of a social worker or a GP.

10 Relationship with probation officer should be motivational and engaging, rather than control oriented. Ex-offenders should be involved in setting goals for supervision.

11 BAME user involvement initiatives must be people-centred, have incentives and clear outcomes for ex-offenders.

BAME user involvement checklist (see also Gavrielides and Blake 2013)

1 Does the organization have a commitment to value BAME user involvement and does it welcome the views of BAME service users?

2 Is there an active BAME service users' engagement strategy? Is it audited/ evaluated? Who is involved in this process?

3 Who is the senior manager responsible for progressing BAME engagement?

4 How will probation officers seek the views of BAME service users about engagement?

5 What mechanisms are in place to ensure that what probation officers agree with BAME service users will be followed up?

6 In what ways do probation officers value the expertise and time of BAME service users?

7 Are probation officers clear about the purpose for BAME service user involvement?

8 What arrangements do probation officers have in place to involve the widest possible range of ex-offenders from BAME backgrounds, including those who are hard to reach/vulnerable?

Notes

1 By disproportionality, we refer to the circumstances in which particular groups of people are represented at lower or higher levels relative to their representation in the general population.

2 See www.equalityhumanrights.com/advice-and-guidance/new-equality-act-guidance/protected-characteristics-definitions/ (accessed March 2013).

3 Social capital is a relatively recent concept encompassing social support, social networks, and social cohesion (Almedom and Glandon 2008). Social capital theory teaches us that there is much to be gained, even for those in prison or offenders, as it has been shown to improve quality of life through greater access to resources that may not otherwise be available to an individual acting alone (Shortt 2004).

References

Almedom, A. M. and Glandon, D. (2008) Social capital and mental health. In: I. Kawachi, S. Subramanian and D. Kim (Eds.), *Social Capital and Health*. New York: Springer.

Bain, A. and Parkinson, G. (2010) Resettlement and social rehabilitation: Are we supporting success? *Probation Journal*, (57), 63.

Cabinet Office. (2017) *Race Audit*. London: Cabinet Office.

Calverley, A. (2009) *An Exploratory Investigation into the Process of Desistance Amongst Minority Ethnic Offenders*. PhD Thesis, Keele University.

Cheliotis, L. K. and Liebling, A. (2006) Race matters in British prisons: Towards a research agenda. *The British Journal of Criminology*, (46), 286–317.

Cowburn, M. and Lavis, V. (2009) Race relations in prison: Managing performance and developing engagement. *British Journal of Community Justice*, 7(3), 77–89.

England, J., Deakin, J. and Spencer, J. (2007) *Investigating the Community Networks of Black and Minority-Ethnic Ex-Prisoners: An Exploratory Study*. Manchester: University of Manchester.

Gavrielides, T. (2015) *Offenders No More: An Interdisciplinary Restorative Justice Dialogue*. New York: Nova Science Publishers.

Gavrielides, T. and Blake, S. (2013) *Race in Probation: Achieving Better Outcomes for Black and Minority Ethnic Users of Probation Services*. London: The IARS International Institute and The London Trust.

Gavrielides, T. and Worth, P. (2014) Another push for restorative justice: Positive psychology & offender rehabilitation. In *Crime: International Perspectives, Socioeconomic Factors and Psychological Implications*. New York: Nova Science Publishers.

House of Commons Home Affairs Committee. (2007) *Young Black People and the Criminal Justice System*. London: House of Commons.

Jacobson, J., Phillips, C. and Edgar, K. (2010) *'Double Trouble'? Black, Asian and Minority Ethnic Offender's Experiences of Resettlement*. London: Clinks and the Prison Reform Trust.

Mapham, A. and Hefferon, K. (2012) "I used to be an Offender - now I'm a Defender": Positive psychology approaches in the facilitation of Posttraumatic Growth in offenders. *Journal of Offender Rehabilitation*, 51(6), 389–413.

Maruna, S. (2001) *Making Good: How Ex-Convicts Reform and Rebuild Their Lives*. Washington, DC: American Psychological Association Books.

Maruna, S. (2004) Pygmalion in the reintegration process: Desistance from crime through the looking glass. *Psychology, Crime and Law*, 10(3), 271–281.

Mason, D. (2003) *Explaining Ethnic Differences: Changing Patterns of Disadvantage in Britain*. Bristol: The Policy Press.

McNeill, F. and Weaver, B. (2010) *Changing Lives? Desistance Research and Offender Management*. Glasgow: Scottish Centre for Crime and Justice Research.

Nacro. (2005) *Integrated Resettlement: Putting the Pieces Together*. London: Nacro.

Nacro. (2007) *Black Communities, Mental Health and the Criminal Justice System*. Available at: https://3bx16p38bchl32s0e12di03h-wpengine.netdna-ssl.com/wp-content/uploads/2015/05/Black-communities-mental-health-and-the-criminal-justice-system.pdf.

Patel, T. and Tyler, D. (2011) *Race, Crime and Resistance*. London: Sage Publications.

Rakt, M., Murray, J. and Nieuwbeerta, P. (2012) The long-term effects of paternal imprisonment on the criminal trajectories of children. *Journal of Research in Crime and Delinquency*, 49(1), 81–108.

Rollock, N. (2009) *The Stephen Lawrence Inquiry 10 Years On: An Analysis of the Literature*. London: Runnymede.

Salkind, N. (2004) *An Introduction to Theories of Human Development*. London: Sage Publications.

Sender, H., Littlechild, B. and Smith, N. (2006) Black and minority ethnic groups and youth offending, *Youth and Policy*, (93), 61–76.

Shortt, S. E. D. (2004) Making sense of social capital, health and policy. *Health Policy*, 70(1), 11–22.

Stevens, P., Baly, K. and Chatfield, J. (2011) Resettlement of residents from approved premises: Results of a London probation NHS collaboration case study. *Probation Journal*, 58(2).

von Hirsch, A. and Ashworth, A. J. (1998) *Principled Sentencing*. Oxford: Hart Publishing.

54 'Race', rehabilitation, and offender management

Bankole Cole and Paula McLean

Introduction

Black, Asian, and minority ethnic peoples (BAME) are disproportionately represented in the British criminal justice systems but this disproportionality is yet to be matched by proportionate provisions to address the offending and reoffending rates of this group (Sharp et al. 2006; Jacobson et al. 2010). There is increasing recognition of the need for criminal justice interventions to acknowledge and address ethnic diversity in offender management, more so after the 2008 Race Review (MoJ/NOMS 2008a) had identified the significantly inadequate attention that had been paid to 'race' in the rehabilitation of offenders. Despite this, little development has occurred (see Lammy Report 2017).

This chapter examines how 'race' has progressed in offender management in Britain. The chapter assesses the suitability of the assessment tools used to predict criminogenic risks and needs of BAME offenders and examines how well rehabilitation work with these offenders is tailored to meet their needs and circumstances. The chapter will also assess developments since the onset of Transforming Rehabilitation (TR) in order to ascertain the impact on 'race' since this agenda was introduced in 2014.

The tools *'don't work'*

The journey to rehabilitation often starts with the diagnosis of the defendant's offending behaviour in pre-sentence reports (PSR) and, upon conviction, in subsequent analysis of their risk and needs using OASys. In both of these significant processes, studies have shown that BAME offenders have been disadvantaged. For example, several studies regarding PSRs written by probation officers (POs) for BAME offenders have revealed that racist stereotyping and prejudicial explanations often appeared in their reports purporting a pejorative link between offending and ethnicity (Denney 1992; Hudson and Bramhall 2005; Vanstone 2006). PSRs guide the courts to the appropriate sentences which, in turn, determine the types of intervention. Studies have further shown that PSRs for BAME defendants tend to be thinner and of low quality indicating limited or inadequate understanding of BAME offending and that this had contributed to BAME defendants being disproportionately imprisoned by the courts (see Voakes and Fowler 1989; Hood 1992; Her Majesty's Inspectorate of Probation 2000). A recent study on PSRs has revealed a decline in written PSRs in favour of oral reports to the courts and this can only mean less engagement with complex issues such as the impact of 'race' on offending (see Centre for Justice Innovation 2018).

Upon conviction, BAME offenders face an additional hurdle and this relates to whether or not they will be properly assessed for intervention. The assessment process includes analyses of their criminogenic risk factors and needs using OASys. Key to this is the fact that no 'race'-related changes have been made to OASys since it was first introduced in 2001. This is despite widespread criticism that OASys does not adequately prepare practitioners to address a key risk factor that has been identified for BAME people, namely how their experience of structural inequalities and racism, for example in education, employment, and housing can correlate with offending behaviour (see Calverley et al. 2004; Cole 2008).

In contrast, attempts to 'racialize' assessment tools have been made in other countries such as Canada and Australia, to prioritize factors that are known or thought to influence specifically the offending behaviour of minority ethnic people and to address these in offender programmes (see Cole 2008 for a detailed review). Although there is no conclusive evidence that a 'racialized' risk and needs assessment instrument would work better for minority ethnic offenders than a 'generic' one, it is, nevertheless, acknowledged that assessment instruments developed for the 'general population' are not always necessarily appropriate for all cultures and indigenous groups (Worrall 2000; Hannah-Moffat 2005).

In assessing the appropriateness of this approach, a Canadian study conducted by Dell and Boe (2000) warned against 'over-emphasising' the ethnicity element in risk and needs assessment; that much more would be achieved if interventions were focused on criminogenic factors (risks and needs) that are known to affect offending irrespective of 'race' (see also

Rugge 2006). Vanstone (2006) has argued against this view. He maintains that it is a view that has underlined the 'what works' agenda in Britain which had produced a lack of sensitivity to diversity and promoted an individualistic approach to understanding offending that is devoid of the social context.

Interventions are not fully relevant to 'race'

It would be incorrect to argue that 'race' has never featured in offender management. Much work has been done in Britain to address 'race' as a managerial and operational issue in terms of accommodating accessibility and responsivity in the provision and delivery of interventions to BAME offenders and staff (see Powis and Walmsley 2002; Durance and Williams 2003). A significant development was the introduction of the black- and Asian-only programmes in the 1990s, many of which have since been discontinued. Black empowerment programmes focused on the relevance of 'race' to offending. They did so in the following ways:

1   By encouraging participants to be change agents rather than having a victim mentality and for them to have more responsibility for themselves and others, with the aim of helping them feel more embedded in the community and reach their goals in a legitimate pro-social manner.
2   By including items such as the historical context of racism and discrimination coupled with content about positive black role models, culture, and black history presented in a format that was understood. Thus, the programmes had the potential to engender hope and a sense of pride in BAME offenders, resulting in positive self-definition and identity. To feel empowered meant that they were less likely to reoffend as they would respect themselves and others; and the revolving door of offending is less likely to occur.
3   By giving the individual 'an opportunity to identify strategies for coping with events that influence his/her lifestyle but for which he/she does not have ultimate control for change' (Duff 2002: 10, cited in Williams 2006: 151; see Williams 2006: 149–154 for details).

The empowerment programmes were short lived for many reasons, including:

■   Organizational failings such as the lack of managerial support for black and Asian programmes, lack of commitment by senior management, lack of black managers and tutors, and a lack of professionally trained specialists;
■   Inadequate training of staff to deliver these programmes and low or decreasing numbers of staff from BAME backgrounds (see Walmsley and Stephen 2006).

There is no evidence that 'race' has 're-emerged' as a key area in the development of accredited programmes. Programmes incorporating a 'race' element are usually in the 'other' category of programmes (see West Yorkshire Community Rehabilitation Company [CRC] 2017).

Notwithstanding this, there is no conclusive empirical evidence that a separate provision for BAME offenders reduces their reoffending (Walmsley and Stephens 2006). In New Zealand, for example, an evaluation of culturally based programmes for Māori offenders showed that although the offenders had improved pro-social behaviour and were more motivated to address the underlying causes of their offending, the programmes alone were ineffective in changing offending behaviour. More success was achieved where culturally based programmes were used to complement proven mainstream treatment processes (State Services Commission New Zealand 2005, cited in Cole 2008: 415). What is significant in this context was that the offenders' circumstances were not undermined, underplayed, or ignored in the intervention.

Transforming Rehabilitation and 'race'

In April 2014, the Coalition government introduced the Transforming Rehabilitation (TR) strategy to reform the National Probation Service. These reforms included part privatization and the introduction of a Payment by Results (PbR) mechanism to measure outcomes (MOJ 2013a). A part of the rationale for these changes was the need to create a smoother and more effective transition for offenders leaving prison, as previous academic research and government reports had indicated that offender resettlement services had been very poor and inadequate (Social Exclusion Unit 2002; Jacobson et al. 2010). To this end, as part of TR, 'Through the Gate' (TTG) was introduced and developed as a means of addressing the deficiencies in service delivery and also to make risk factors such as unemployment, homelessness, poor educational achievement, substance misuse, and mental health issues a priority for resettlement services (MOJ 2013b; Offender Rehabilitation Act 2014). TTG operates through having a TTG Resettlement Team based in the local prison who conducts initial risk assessments to identify prisoner needs. Thereafter, the information is relayed to the relevant PO in the community to recommend post-release interventions. TTG promotes seamless, end-to-end management of the prisoner from sentence to release, aiming to lessen the likelihood of reoffending.

However, consultations with stakeholders raised concerns regarding the lack of consideration for equality and diversity issues (MOJ 2013c). These fears were further reinforced by the noticeable absence of equality and diversity in the TR Target Operating Model (MOJ 2013d). Stakeholders feared that private contractors utilizing a PbR model may develop a homogeneous approach to offending that was counterproductive with scant evidence that this had been accounted for. The government responded that they were aware of this and that mechanisms would be put in place to ensure private contractors did give considerations to diversity needs (MOJ 2013c). However, Baroness Young, in her report on young black men and Muslim prisoners in the CJS, revealed that diversity only accounted for 5% of the weighting in the bids for probation services (Young 2014). There was also no consultation with offenders from minority groups regarding TR.

Existing literature indicates that community reintegration post-custody has always been challenging, additionally so when layered with 'protected characteristics' such as 'race', gender, and disabilities (see HMIPP 2001). Nevertheless, several official and independent research reports have been published on the resettlement of BAME offenders. These reports range from those investigating the resettlement needs of black offenders in particular areas (Sharp et al. 2006) to reports targeting whether 'ethnic culture' played a role in the resettlement of black offenders (Jacobson et al. 2010), and specifically on the resettlement of black and Muslim men (Young 2014).

Several recurring themes have emerged from these reports: (1) the consensus that resettlement provision both in prison and the community is either non-existent, difficult to access or if accessed is unhelpful, lacking any clear strategy, and is affected by government cuts; (2) that racism and discrimination impact on the ability to resettle such as in finding employment and that a criminal record compounds these difficulties; and (3) that offenders feel that a probation or prison worker from the same 'race'/ethnic background is desirable as they could better understand their needs (see also Cole and Wardak 2006).

In a rapid evidence assessment (REA) conducted to explore the research evidence in relation to the effectiveness of rehabilitative correctional interventions in reducing reoffending among BAME people, Shingler and Pope (2018) found ample evidence of research in support of the view that for rehabilitative services to be 'effective' for BAME offenders, it is important that they are:

- Culturally aware, sensitive, and inclusive
- Delivered by culturally aware and sensitive staff
- Delivered by staff from similar ethnic backgrounds to their clients

While it is accepted that providing for 'all' ethnicities may be an arduous task, it is important to take seriously the need to increase the numbers of BAME offenders taking up interventions; ensure that treatment materials are relevant to BAME groups; and do more to actively engage with and respect cultural experiences and differences. It is also important to be aware of the barriers to effective engagement with BAME offenders that may interfere with them starting, completing, or engaging in treatment, such as experiences or fear of racism/discrimination, any fear or resistance associated with feeling isolated or misunderstood, and the perception and possible reality that the intervention will not be culturally relevant (see Shingler and Pope 2018: 2).

Poor service delivery

Recently published reports have evidenced that the implementation of TTG nationally has been poor (HMIP 2016; National Audit Office 2016; User Voice 2015). Much has been blamed on cuts in probation funding especially post-TR which has led to reductions in staffing and reduced services; for example, in access to drug treatment, anger violence provisions, and women-specific programmes (Owen, 2010). This correlates with the findings of the User Voice (2015) survey of offenders who also thought that service delivery had worsened under TR. Historically, where criminal justice funding and resources have been reduced, it is usually the provisions for minority groups that are either down-sized, 'harmonized' with mainstream provisions, or discontinued. This is likely to happen more with TR (BTEG 2011; Maguire 2016).

Despite the insistence of the government that BAME charities and third-sector organizations should be embedded into the rehabilitation of offenders (see MoJ 2008; MoJ and NOMS 2008b; NOMS and YJB 2007; Home Office 2009), this has not happened since the introduction of the TR agenda and many of these organizations have been financially squeezed out. Furthermore, funding for BAME organizations has been reduced far more than mainstream charities (see Baring Foundation 2015). The reality of the current situation in Britain is that initiatives that were developed between probation and black community-based groups – and are known to have had a positive impact (such as HIMMAT and Arooj) – have lost funding since the inception of TR (BTEG 2011; Hough 2016; HIMMAT n.d.).

In addition, an action research undertaken by the Association of Black Probation Officers (ABPO) has alluded to the fact that a large number of black staff left the Probation Service post-TR (ABPO et al. 2015) which is detrimental to offenders for whom 'race' is important to their rehabilitation. Staff shortages and budget cuts have led to a loss of interventions, particularly any that are 'race'-specific both in prison and the community (Maguire 2016); this could lead to feelings of hopelessness and invisibility amongst BAME offenders under probation supervision.

Conclusion

The Lammy Review (2017) is a timely report in the sense that it was published at a time when concerns about 'race' disproportionality and discriminatory practices in the British criminal justice system (CJS) were being highlighted again, despite these concerns having remained constant for decades. It would appear that privatization of the Probation Service and other cuts to criminal justice agencies have only served to undermine the facts and ignore the evidence. Thus, the report should be read as a reminder of the reality of being a BAME offender and criminal justice practitioner in 21st-century Britain. The revelation that the over-representation of black people in the CJS costs the British taxpayer £309 million per year should have been an incentive for the government to take 'race' more seriously in TR (MoJ 2017). Interestingly, in early TR documents, the MoJ acknowledged that minority groups were likely to be negatively impacted by TR; however it did not put any systems in place to address the issue (MoJ 2013c).

It has been argued in this chapter that in spite of various official responses and legislation, 'race' is yet to get the necessary positive input it deserves in rehabilitation and offender management. There certainly is a lack of support for efforts that might alleviate the key barriers, such as:

1   Inadequate staffing.
2   Inadequate training: anti-racism/anti-discriminatory practice training no longer exists. Rather, it has been subsumed under the 'diversity' agenda which does not pay particular attention to 'race', not to mention the politics of 'race' and criminal justice in Britain. Probation officer training on 'race' is rather poor, delivered mostly online or in very fast condensed half-day 'walk through' sessions (HMPPS 2018). Beyond this training, there is no staff development on 'race'.
3   Links with many black community groups have been severed due to cuts in probation funding and cuts to their own funding.
4   Offending behaviour programmes for black offenders no longer exist and there is no indication that these will ever be brought back.

In order to improve practice, it is important to add 'race'-specific elements to the Through the Gate (TTG) resettlement strategy. More knowledge of 'race' and offending is required in probation training and more 'race' elements should be included in OASys. In addition, more funding and support is required for 'race'-specific or 'race'-sensitive community organizations working in the resettlement sector and more efforts should be made to encourage more BAME people to choose probation as a profession.

References

ABPO, NILE and NAPO. (2015) *National Survey of BAME Probation Staff*. Final Report. Joint Action Research Initiative.

The Baring Foundation. (2015) *Funding for Black, Asian & Other Minority Ethnic Communities, Bridging the Gap in Funding for the BAME Voluntary and Community Sector*. London: The Baring Foundation.

Black Training and Enterprise Group (BTEG). (2011) *Race in the Criminal Justice System*. London: BTEG.

Calverley, A., Cole, B., Kaur, G., Lewis, S., Raynor, P., Sadeghi, S., Smith, D., Vanstone, M. and Wardak, A. (2004) *Black and Asian Offenders on Probation Home Office Research Study 277*. London: Home Office.

Centre for Justice Innovation. (2018) *The Changing Use of Pre-Sentence Reports*. London: Centre for Justice Innovation.

Cole, B. (2008) Working with ethnic diversity. In S. Green, E. Lancaster and S. Feasey (Eds.), *Addressing Offending Behaviour*. Cullompton: Willan Publishing, pp. 402–425.

Cole, B. and Wardak, A. (2006) Black and Asian men on probation: Social exclusion, discrimination and experiences of criminal justice. In S. Lewis, P. Raynor, D. Smith and A. Wardak (Eds.), *Race and Probation*. Cullomption: Willan Publishing, Chapter 5, pp. 81–99.

Dell, C. A. and Boe, R. (2000) *An Examination of Aboriginal and Caucasian Women Offender Risk and Needs Factors*. Ottawa: Research Branch. Correctional Services of Canada.

Denney, D. (1992) *Racism and Anti-Racism in Probation*. London: Routledge.

Durrance, P. and Williams, P. (2003) Broadening the agenda around what works for black and Asian offenders. *Probation Journal*, 50,(3), 211–224.

Hannah-Moffat, K. (2005) Criminogenic needs and the transformative risk subject. *Punishment & Society*, 7(1), 29–51.

Her Majesty's Inspectorates of Prison and Probation (HMIPP). (2001) *Through the Prison Gate*. A Joint Thematic Review. London: HMIP.

Her Majesty's Inspectorate of Probation (HMIP). (2000) *Thematic Inspection Report: Toward Race Equality*. London: HMIP.

Her Majesty's Inspectorate of Probation (HMIP). (2016) *Quality and Impact Inspection: The Effectiveness in Probation Work in the North of London*. London: HMIP.

Her Majesty's Prison and Probation Service (HMPPS). (2018) *Train to Be a Probation Officer*. Available at: www.traintobeaprobationofficer.com/about-the-training/.

HIMMAT. (n.d) *Working Together with the National Probation Service and Community Rehabilitation Companies and the Youth Offending Team to Protect the Public Halifax: Himmat*. Available at: www.himmat.org/.

HM Government. (2014) *Offender Rehabilitation Act, 2014*. London: HMSO, Chapter 11.

Home Office. (2009) *Engaging Communities in Criminal Justice*. London: HMSO.

Hood, R. (1992) *Race and Sentencing: A Study in the Crown Court – A Report for the Commission of Racial Equality*. Oxford: Clarendon Press.

Hough, C. V. (2016) Transforming Rehabilitation and its impact on a locally-based rehabilitation programme for black and minority ethnic and Muslim offenders. *European Journal of Probation*, 8(2), 68–81.

Hudson, B. and Bramhall, G. (2005) Assessing the 'Other': Constructions of 'Asianness' in risk assessments by probation officers. *British Journal of Criminology*, 45(5), 721–740.

Jacobson, J., Phillips, C. and Edgar, K. (2010) *Double Trouble? Black, Asian and Minority Ethnic Offenders Experiences of Resettlement*. London: Clinks, The Prison Reform Trust.

Lammy, D. (2017) *The Lammy Review: An Independent Review into the Treatment of, and Outcomes for, Black, Asian and Minority Ethnic Individuals in the Criminal Justice System*. London: HMSO.

Maguire, M. (2016) Third tier in the supply chain? Voluntary agencies and the commissioning of offender rehabilitation services. In A. Hucklesby and M. Corcoran (Eds.), *The Voluntary Sector and Criminal Justice*. London: Palgrave Macmillan, pp. 43–70.

Ministry of Justice (MoJ). (2008) *Third Sector Strategy: Improving Policies and Securing Better Public Services Through Effective Partnerships (2008–2011)*. London: Ministry of Justice.

Ministry of Justice. (2013a) *Transforming Rehabilitation: A Revolution in the Way We Manage Offenders*. Consultation Paper CP1/2013. London: The Stationery Office.

Ministry of Justice. (2013b) *Transforming Rehabilitation: A Strategy for Reform*. Response to Consultation CP(R)16/2013. London: The Stationery Office.

Ministry of Justice. (2013c) *Consideration of Equalities Impacts: Rehabilitation Programme. Transforming Rehabilitation*. London: The Stationery Office.

Ministry of Justice. (2013d) *Target Operating Model: Rehabilitation Programme*. London: The Stationery Office.

Ministry of Justice. (2017) *An Exploratory Estimate of the Economic Cost of Black, Asian and Minority Ethnic Net Over Representation in the Criminal Justice System in 2015*. London: MoJ.

Ministry of Justice (MoJ) and National Offender Management Service (NOMS). (2008a) *Race Review 2008. Implementing Race Equality in Prisons: Five Years on*. London: MoJ, NOMS.

Ministry of Justice (MoJ) and National Offender Management Service (NOMS). (2008b) *Working with the Third Sector to Reduce Re-Offending: Securing Effective Partnerships (2008–2011)*. London: Ministry of Justice.

National Audit Office. (2016) *Transforming Rehabilitation*. London: National Audit Office.

National Offender Management System (NOMS) and the Youth Justice Board (YJB). (2007) *Believing We Can: Promoting the Contribution Faith-Based Organisations Can Make to Reducing Adult and Youth Re-Offending: A Consultative Document*. London: NOMS and YJB.

Owens, E. (2010) *Exploring the Experiences of Minority and Ethnic Women in Resettlement: What Role, If Any, Does Ethnic Culture Play in the Resettlement of Black (African-Caribbean) Women Offenders in the UK?* London: The Griffins Society.

Powis, B. and Walmsley, R. K. (2002) *Programmes for Black and Asian Offenders on Probation: Lessons for Developing Practice*. Home Office Research Study 250. London: Home Office.

Rugge, T. (2006) *Risk Assessment of Male Aboriginal Offenders: A 2006 Perspective*. Canada: Public Safety and Emergency Preparedness.

Sharp, D., Atherton, S. and Williams, K. (2006) *Everybody's Business: Investigating the Resettlement Needs of Black and Minority Ethnic Ex-Offenders in the West Midlands*. Centre for Criminal Justice Policy and Research – University of Central England. Birmingham: Government Office for the West Midlands.

Shingler, J. and Pope, L. (2018) *The Effectiveness of Rehabilitative Services for Black, Asian and Minority Ethnic People: A Rapid Evidence Assessment*. Ministry of Justice Analytical Series. London: Ministry of Justice, HM Prison and Probation Service.

Social Exclusion Unit. (2002) *Reducing Reoffending by Ex-Prisoners – Report by the Social Exclusion Unit*. London: Office of the Deputy Prime Minister.

State Services Commission, New Zealand. (2005) *Briefing Papers and Report – Review of Targeted Policies and Programmes (1) Corrections: Briefing Paper to Minister on Eight Programmes*. Wellington: State Services Commission.

User Voice. (2015) *"Transforming Rehabilitation" The Operational Model from the Service Users Perspective*. A Report to the National Audit Office. London: User Voice.

Vanstone, M. (2006) Room for Improvement: A History of the Probation Service's Response to Race. In L. Lewis, P. Raynor, D. Smith and A. Wardak (Eds.), *Race and Probation*. Devon: Willan Publishing, pp. 13–25.

Voakes, R. and Fowler, Q. (1989) *Sentencing, Race and Social Enquiry Reports*. Bradford: West Yorkshire Probation Service.

Walmsley, R. K. and Stephens, K. (2006) What Works with Black and Minority Ethnic Offenders? Solutions in Search of a Problem. In L. Lewis, P. Raynor, D. Smith and A. Wardak (Eds.), *Race and Probation*. Devon: Willan Publishing, pp. 164–181.

West Yorkshire Community Rehabilitation Company (CRC). (2017) *Guide to Interventions: Community Orders & Suspended Sentence Orders*. Wakefield: West Yorkshire CRC.

Williams, P. (2006) Designing and delivering programmes for minority ethnic offenders. In S. Lewis, P. Raynor, D. Smith and A. Wardak (Eds.), *Race and Probation*. Devon: Willan Publishing, pp. 145–163.

Worrall, A. (2000) What works at one arm point? A study in the transportation of a penal concept. *Probation Journal*, 47, 243–249.

Young, Baroness Lola. (2014) *The Young Review: Improving Outcomes for Young Black and/or Muslim Men in the Criminal Justice System Final Report*. London: The Young Review.

Hamlet's dilemma

55

Racialization, agency, and the barriers to black men's desistance

Martin Glynn

Introduction – Hamlet's dilemma

> To be, or not to be, that is the question, whether 'tis nobler in the mind to suffer the slings and arrows of outrageous fortune, or to take arms against a sea of troubles, And by opposing end them.
>
> (Shakespeare 1603)

Hamlet's dilemma as he contemplates suicide is an important metaphor for black offenders' desistance. Namely, 'to desist or not to desist?'. Maruna (2010) argues that reintegration of prisoners back into the community requires well-orchestrated rituals. Maruna further argues that prisoner reintegration as it is currently practiced is a failing ritual based on a series of racialized systemic restrictions that blocks black offenders' overall 'agency'. On concluding a prison sentence, a 'former' offender will be released to 're-enter' the community, and then hopefully be ready for a life free from crime. To successfully desist, a 'former' prisoner must be equipped with the necessary tools to 'reintegrate' back into the community by being reformed as a consequence of experiencing (pro)-social rehabilitative processes. Previous studies suggest that successful desistance occurs due to one or several number of factors. These factors include things such as becoming a father and thereby recognizing one's responsibilities to others (Maruna 2011); faith-based conversion that can give one's life meaning and purpose (Giordano et al. 2002); or employment that can improve self-esteem, offer legitimate financial gain, and enable one to develop a stronger sense of one's social capital (Maruna 2011). I argue that the desistance trajectories for many black offenders are best understood by themselves. Like Hamlet, the ongoing dilemma for many black offenders is the uncertainty about pursuing their desistance, or staying on the familiar road of (re)offending. Hamlet knew that if he did commit suicide, he could not return from the dead to live again. Likewise, many black offenders (and offenders in general?) know that continued involvement in criminal lifestyles, metaphorically speaking, means they cannot go back to a 'crime-free life'.

Methodology

My research started from an interpretivist perspective. That is, it focused on the meanings that black offenders gave to their lived experiences in relation to their desistance (McAdams 1985). The research focused on black offenders in the city of Baltimore (US) during August/September 2010, as part of a Winston Churchill International Travel Fellowship. Each interview lasted approximately one hour, culminating in some occasional 'unstructured conversation' that was at times not recorded, merged with some participant observation. Each interviewee's identity has been kept hidden in the text that follows, but for ease of reference they have been identified by a randomly chosen letter.

Findings

The results within this strand of the research have been triangulated with two significant studies exploring the experiences of black men in US inner city areas. Glasgow (1981), writing in *The Black Underclass*, examines poverty, entrapment of ghetto youth, and black men on the margins of urban society, whilst Elijah Anderson (1990) in his book *Streetwise* investigates the understandings and insights of race, class, and social change in an urban black community. Each study explores the impact of the stigma of race, social alienation, and the barriers towards black offenders' desistance trajectories.

Grounded theory

The interviews were then transcribed in preparation for the data analysis that used an adapted form of grounded theory (Strauss and Corbin 1997; Charmaz 2006). Grounded theory consists of systematic yet flexible guidelines for collecting and analyzing qualitative data to 'construct theories grounded in the data themselves' (Charmaz 2006: 6). The following themes emerged:

- Code of the streets
- Effects of incarceration
- Street cool
- Re-entry

Code of the streets

A prevalent feature of many black offenders I encountered was the way in which the 'code of the streets' created a Darwinian 'survival of the fittest' mind-set. 'The code' tended to revolve around the ability to navigate the perils of violence, gang culture, drugs, and extreme social deprivation. Individuals who understood and could maintain 'the code' would at times use extreme menace and intimidation to control who could gain access and street credibility. There were no hard and fast rules about survival on the streets, other than you had to survive at all costs. The interviews would suggest that the 'code of the street' is less about planning a future, or looking back, but more of living in the moment, as you never know what is around the corner. The desire to get off the streets and being connected to the problems associated with being black would suggest that the streets are a place to have some control over their life. Although many of those interviewed intimated that they would like to get off the streets, the wider problem with the 'code of the streets' is that it demands loyalty, leaving little room for exit strategies. Most acknowledged the difficulty of street life, and fatalistically accepted that there was no way out. This type of deterministic view gives rise to the view that many young black men in Baltimore involve themselves in extreme violence to protect their own small patch of ground (turf) in the community as a way of gaining respect. Another significant feature of 'the code' is the constant struggle with education where poor schooling drove many of the participants onto the streets. Katz (1988) puts forward a view that some individuals are seduced by street life and criminal activity. Katz further argues that researchers who have never engaged with those individuals at times fail to look critically at that seduction and spend more time trying to disprove any notion that some criminals actually like being involved with crime. The idea that for some young men I encountered in Baltimore saw themselves as soldiers, defending their territory suggests that the streets become the territory for an alternative police force, designed to keep order in the community, with a strong sense of duty and loyalty. Being physically and psychologically tough therefore equates to the currency of survival on the streets of Baltimore.

Death also seems to be casually accepted as a by-product of occupying the streets. So the ability to be around death without it affecting you is equally as important. It appears on the surface that there is a casual acceptance of death as inevitable. However, the 'code of the streets' centres more on survival. Using menace to gain status would not be seen as a legitimate way to gain respect. Although the code of the streets places some value on achieving respect, the means through which such respect is attained should be consistent with the accepted but loosely defined rules of survival on the streets.

Effects of incarceration

Those interviewed have spent many years in prison where the experience of incarceration has had a significant impact on their lives. They see the system as unfair and a violation of their human rights and locate the loss of liberty as a human rights violation that ultimately diminishes their psychological state and mental well-being. Many questioned whether the system worked and suggested that incarceration had a more sinister motive, namely damaging the psyche of prisoners. Alexander (2010) argues the same point, citing prisons as the new slavery. Her analogy rests on the understanding that destroying the minds of slaves made them compliant, controlled, and incapable of contemplating any challenge to their captors. Many expressed the view that prison was worse than the streets, but conceded that they carried the same type of behaviour in prison as they did when they were free. I would argue that prison behaviour is at times motivated by the need for psychic preservation from being overtaken by the oppression of the prison system and ultimately becoming sedated by one's deteriorating mental condition. Equally as important was educating the mind whilst incarcerated. Sanity on the streets and in prison have parallels. They are both ruled by fear, codes of violence, and respect. The word 'respect' becomes important here. Although rehabilitative processes can enable a prisoner to learn about respect as a possible factor required in the trajectory towards desistance, the separation from friends and family can push some prisoners deeper into a state of regression. This continuous exposure to the prison environment can lead to a shift in mood state that at times would be seen as depressive. This state of affairs would suggest that the wider structural concerns can and do render the possibility for some ex-offenders pointing the way towards their own desistance obsolete. A recurring theme was the anger that emerged when interviewees saw attempts to rehabilitate prisoners as empty gestures. Equally important here was in the recognition about how the humanity of those who have offended is not always as a result of a conscious act of criminality, but as the result of poor choices. As Alexander (2010) points out, prison is a control mechanism which has as its purpose the goal of subordinating people of colour. This leads me to consider the importance of social and community bonds in relation to creating a stronger pathway towards desistance than incarceration.

Street cool

How then do black offenders rise above negative experiences to chart a pathway towards their desistance? The unfolding narrative clearly demonstrates that the weakening of social bonds can lead an individual into a life of crime and constructing notions of 'street cool' to cope with the pressure of both incarceration and street life. Using fear to gain respect can be seen as cool in relation to the 'code of the streets'. Being bad isn't enough. There's a style that accompanies it, that gains the respect. This benchmark of 'street cool' masks another important issue, that of 'father absence'. The desire to demonstrate manhood without being shown adequate masculine guidance can lead to many destructive behaviours. By normalizing this type of behaviour in the name of being cool can only serve to create more tension on the streets, the community, and society as a whole. Many questioned the role of parents in their life. The problem here is having no sense of community created a legion of isolated individuals, connected by loss and no sense of belonging. Hence, the propensity to join a gang. If the gang then becomes the replacement family and becomes part of the normal socialization then it fractures the possibility of developing meaningful and positive social bonds required to create a pathway towards desistance. By constructing a street persona defined as cool may be construed as a coping strategy in light of their circumstances but the absence of guidance from family and community only seeks to drive them further into seeing crime as a way out. A closer examination of the constraints or opportunities that can be created by re-entry back to the community is important here.

Re-entry

Although many of those interviewed revelled in their experiences of being released, the lack of preparation or ability to adjust to a new situation would suggest that rehabilitative processes if they were present whilst incarcerated were not put in place on release. The inability to manage the prison experience posed a significant threat to maintaining a successful re-entry back to the community. This view reaffirms what Alexander (2010) fears is a culture of neglect, and a failure to provide a duty of care to returning black offenders may be fuelling the notion that prisons are the new slavery. Not having anyone to meet you on release can be debilitating for men returning back to the community. The stories of those interviewed is a sad indictment on so-called community service providers who should be making some provision for returning prisoners. This state of affairs is also compounded when the returning offender, excited by the prospect of a new life, realizes that they are returning to an

unchanged environment. Knowing that things have gotten worse and not better can be at worst both dehumanizing and demoralizing in equal measure.
These testimonies highlight the continuing failure of a criminal justice system that unsuccessfully restricts productive processes designed to give black
offenders a fair chance of making headway towards desistance trajectories.

Discussions

Emerging from the analysis are a range of key issues that form the basis of this
discussion section. The themes represented are not exhaustive, but represent
some of the important matters arising from the shared testimonies.

Dilemmas

All of those interviewed were wrestling with a series of personal dilemmas: the
difficulty of living, the fear of death, the uncertainty of the future, combined
with a significant amount of recurring existential crises.

Services

Services engaging with black offenders are required but they must continue to
call upon black offenders' insights and understandings of their attitudes and
behaviours in relation to their engagement with the criminal justice system.
Accessing these insights and understandings should not purely centre on further diagnosis, risk, or needs assessment.

Achieving desistance

Achieving desistance for black offenders is often very difficult and requires
interventions and support that will promote the skills, competencies, and
skill sets that will enable them to reduce any previous risks posed, leading to
a crime-free life. This position would suggest it is about the (re)construction
of self, requiring services providers to consider, address, and take into consideration individual, relational, and contextual factors, attending to both
personal characteristics and social environments.

The structural context

The structural context of many black offenders' lives combined with the level
of social disorganization they face on re-entry is also a problem. Important
here is to consider the influence of local cultures and how membership of

powerful street cultures fractures the possibility of desistance in inner-city communities in places such as Baltimore. Before black offenders are willing to give up their working identity as a lawbreaker, they must begin to perceive their old identity as unsatisfying, thus weakening their commitment to it.

Social networks

Unless the participants are embedded into new social networks that not only support a new identity and tastes but can also isolate them from those who would oppose them quitting crime or induce them to continue in their criminal ways, then desistance is highly unlikely. These aspirations are built on two premises: firstly, all black offenders have skills, abilities, and talents that can and should be used for the benefit of the community; and secondly, that rather than seeing them as 'community liabilities', the communities need to view, enlist, and deploy them as 'community assets'. Enabling and supporting black offenders to desist is about providing them with what has been missing from their lives. To promote a successful, positive change the community must target their negative value system in ways that will increase their appreciation for the challenges facing the communities they have affected, connected to real and meaningful opportunities. However, the increasingly rising 'hyper-masculine' stance suggests that at this moment in time they are unwilling to consider a shift in their personal identity for fear of losing control of aspects of their lives which they don't trust.

'Safe space'

Many black offenders require a 'safe space' to work out their anxieties, frustrations, and difficulties if they are to successfully reintegrate back into the community. But to do so they need encouragement, opportunities, and structures through which they can function as full and bona fide members of the community and make a positive contribution to community life. If they cannot fulfil their potential based on the erosion of their self-concept, it is questionable whether they can maintain a focus that will enable them to desist from crime. There needs to be a shifting emphasis of service delivery for black offenders, away from diagnosis and prescriptions, to screening, accurate assessment, and identification of immediate needs. Service providers that do not see, acknowledge, or understand the impact of fractured social bonds and poor socialization in black offenders will only serve to perpetuate the difficulties that they experience.

Conclusion

If culture is underpinned by collective meaning and identity, then an assessment of the cultural rehabilitation of black offenders is warranted here. Friere

(1970) points out that the *oppressed* are better placed at times to understand their oppression, and argues their voices must speak and be heard. Denzin (2010) similarly points out that for 'subordinated and oppressed voices' to be heard, they must be assisted in their desire to 'transcend their silences'. Desiring to break from crime may be motivated at first by a strong aversion to viewing one's self as negative and not liking what they have become. Black offenders seeking to break from crime slowly begin to consider a new identity and move towards a more pro-social life. However, in places like Baltimore's inner city the word 'pro-social' seems to be too idealistic. The development of a 'community-led model of desistance' for black offenders would therefore critically assess how the racialization of the social structure post release enhances or impedes the functioning of returning black offenders, in relation to offenders as a whole.

References

Alexander, M. (2010) *The New Jim Crow – Mass Incarceration in the Age of Colorblindness*. New York: The New Press.

Anderson, E. (1990) *Streetwise: Race, Class, and Change in an Urban Community*. Chicago: University of Chicago Press.

Charmaz, K. (2006) *Constructing Grounded Theory*. London: Sage Publications.

Denzin, N. K. (2010) *The Qualitative Manifesto*. Walnut Creek: Left Coast Press.

Giordano, P., Cernkovich, A. and Rudolph, J. (2002) Gender, crime, and desistance: Toward a theory of cognitive transformation, *AJS*, 107(4), 990–1064.

Glasgow, D. G. (1981) *The Black Underclass*. San Francisco: Jossey-Bass.

Katz, J. (1988) *Seductions of Crime: Moral and Sensual Attraction of Doing Evil*. New York: Perseus Books.

McAdams, D. (1985) *Power, Intimacy, and the Life Story*. London: Guilford Press.

Maruna, S. (2011) Reentry as a rite of passage. *Punishment & Society*, 13(1), 3–28.

Strauss, A. and Corbin, J. (1997) *Grounded Theory in Practice*. London: Sage.

Applications of risk prediction technologies in criminal justice

56

The nexus of race and digitized control

Pamela Ugwudike

Introduction

Risk management and the application of digital risk prediction technologies are key features of rehabilitative work in contemporary penal systems across several Western and non-Western jurisdictions. Indeed, it is now generally accepted that risk management is the prevailing penal orthodoxy in Western countries such as the United Kingdom and the United States, with some scholars stating that risk has become the 'key organising principle of correctional practice and offender management' (Maurutto and Hannah-Moffat 2005: 438) or the 'dominant organising lexicon traversing penal discourses in advanced capitalist jurisdictions' (Ugwudike 2012: 244). Reflecting this, a constellation of digital prediction technologies are currently being mobilized internationally to inform key penal decisions, including the content and intensity of rehabilitative work. Some of these technologies possess Machine Learning capabilities and are as such able to accomplish timely and efficient analyses of complex and multidimensional 'big data' (Berk and Bleich 2013).

This chapter focuses on the intersection of digitized risk prediction and race. It argues that studies endorsing the reliability and validity of risk technologies appear to equate predictive accuracy with fairness (example, Flores et al. 2016; Skeem and Lowenkamp 2016). In this context, the tools are technically fair even if they produce racially disparate outcomes. This can, for instance, occur when risk technologies rely on sociostructural predictors which operate as proxies for race. Examples include deficiencies in education and employment (Harcourt 2015). Given their vulnerability to racial discrimination, black people in particular are disproportionately affected by these issues compared to other groups, and may consequently be more susceptible to over-prediction or false positives. This places them at greater risk of racially disparate outcomes such as excessive penal intervention, with implications for their rights and civil liberties. But the studies focusing on predictive accuracy do not address the problem of racially disparate outcomes. Meanwhile, other studies have shown that some of the commonly used general risk assessment techs are over-predicting the recidivism risks of black people (see Angwin and Larson 2016; Jimenez et al. 2018; but cf. Dieterich et al. 2016; Skeem and Lowenkamp 2016). On the issue of the vulnerability of racialized groups,[1] particularly black people, to over-prediction, penological perspectives on the emergence of risk management as a key penal objective are instructive. The perspectives draw attention to the possibility that risk technologies are instruments of control targeted at specific populations, including racialized groups (Garland 2001; Feeley and Simon 1992). The perspectives also emphasize that the technocratic imperative of applying technologies which augment efficient and cost-effective risk management is a hallmark of the prevailing risk-focused penal agenda. Therefore, utilitarian objectives, for example the predictive accuracy of the risk techs or their capacity to support the efficient categorization and management of target populations, supersede deontological concerns such as the ethical implications of relying on socio-structural proxies for race, which can unfairly elevate the risk scores ascribed to racialized people.

Although studies investigating the validity of risk techs focus on what can be described as the objective or technical fairness of the technologies (primarily their predictive accuracy) (see for example Dieterich et al. 2016), the issue of subjective or perceived fairness also deserves attention.[2] This relates to the perceptions of racialized people affected by the inequitable impact of technically fair predictions. It is an aspect of risk management that has not received sufficient criminological attention. Thus, the perceptual character of fairness and the implications for rehabilitative work have been ignored. To explore these issues, this chapter draws on social psychological studies of procedural justice which highlight the intersections of subjective fairness, legitimacy, and compliance in criminal justice settings, including the contexts of rehabilitative work. In particular, the studies suggest that systemic racial discrimination (for example, the application of risk technologies which are perceived as capable of producing racially disparate outcomes) can pose implications for the perceived legitimacy of authority. This can in turn undermine the processes and outcomes of rehabilitative work.

Thus, the chapter synthesizes penological perspectives on the utility of risk technologies (which are capable of producing racially unequal outcomes) as instruments of racialized control, with social psychological perspectives on procedural justice within the context of rehabilitative work. Synthesizing these perspectives expands understandings of the application of digital risk technologies in the justice system. It also highlights the implications of biased predictions for procedural justice and the outcomes of rehabilitative work.

Risk consciousness, modernity, and the racialization of risk

Risk prediction technologies are transforming the criminal justice landscape in many countries. In policing contexts in the UK, they underpin some predictive policing practices including the identification of crime 'hot spots' (Moses and Chan 2016). They also inform bail and remand decisions (Oswald et al. 2018). Furthermore, in court, they sometimes influence sentencing decisions (Sentencing Council 2016), and in penal contexts such as probation and prison settings, they are expected to inform the content and intensity of rehabilitative work (HM Inspectorate of Probation 2018; National Offender Management Service Public Protection Manual 2016).

In some ways, the prominence of a risk management discourse in several justice systems reflects a key theme within the sociology of risk which is that in modern society, transforming future uncertainties into manageable entities has become the primary approach to dealing with social problems. For example, the sociologist Beck (1992) maintained that a risk society marked by a high degree of risk consciousness emerged in the shift towards modernity. Writing shortly after the Chernobyl nuclear incident, Beck (1986) limited his analysis initially to concerns about the ecological risks of advances in science and technology and the social changes triggered by the advent of globalization. He believed that these features of modernization gave rise to new uncertainties and heightened risk consciousness alongside a preoccupation with managing risks in global society. Beck's (1986) thesis and other contributors to the sociological literature on risk drew attention to the importance of paying attention to the damaging consequences of the scientific, technological, and other features of modernization (see also Beck et al. 1994; Giddens 1991).

The claim that a global risk society has emerged and is unified in the concern to identify and manage risks has been challenged on several grounds. For example, it is argued that the account focuses rather narrowly on ecological risks (Lidskog and Sundqvist 2012) and there is also the argument that in many Western societies, the preoccupation with managing risks is far from novel (O'Malley 2010). Nevertheless, a corpus of penological perspectives influenced by insights from the sociology of risk has emerged. Central to this penological scholarship is the contention that the discourse of risk and its underpinning principles of surveillance and incapacitation have since the 1970s and 1980s evolved into a punitive 'new penology' (Feeley and Simon 1992, 1994). This penology is rooted in actuarial justice and involves the carceral 'warehousing' or penal containment of a 'dangerous class' of primarily racialized populations on the basis of past behaviour and predicted criminality (see also Garland 2001). According to Feeley and Simon (1992: 452): 'The new penology is concerned with techniques to identify, classify, and manage groupings sorted by dangerousness. The task is managerial, not transformative'. It is therefore a pre-emptive, rather than reactive, mode of penal regulation and it is underpinned by the principle of prudentialism. The latter emphasizes the morality of taking pre-emptive or proactive action to prevent a negative future event or occurrence. In this respect, punishment is imposed, not on the basis of the morality of the penal subject's offence, but on the basis of what s/he might do, and this in essence involves punishing 'pre-criminals' (O'Malley 2017: 532).

Within this risk-focused penal framework, the aim of penal practice is systemic and geared towards rationalizing the system: 'it pursues systemic rationality and efficiency' (Feeley and Simon 1992: 452). It is as such, a technocratic penal approach in which the systemic aims of cost-effective and efficient management of risky populations are accorded greater priority than transformative aims, of which rehabilitation represents an example. Managerialist imperatives of monitoring practice to ensure accountability through demonstrable compliance with standardized cost-effective and efficient practices inform the new penology. Individuals involved in the system are no longer depicted in penal discourses as people requiring individualized transformative interventions underpinned by social objectives such as rehabilitation, but as risky or dangerous groups who should be targeted using standardized risk tools, and collectively subjected to penal control (Feeley and Simon 1992). Thus, the new penology 'sorts individuals into groups according to the degree of control warranted by their risk profiles' (p. 459). Risk-focused penal regulation is as such, an instrument of control. Beyond this, some scholars draw on Foucauldian governmentality to argue that risk and its management constitute a form of governmentality or a mode of governance. It primarily involves the application of mechanisms such as sophisticated risk technologies which enable governments to steer citizens into conformity without exerting visible force (Rose and Miller 2010). Target populations who fail to comply with established norms are designated as risky and subjected to penal control measures to equip them with the self-management skills required for insulating themselves from risky behaviour (Rose and Miller 2010). Risk scores and categories, for instance, become the means of holding citizens accountable for how well they accomplish the risk reduction role imposed on them. Risk is thus denuded of its socio-structural dimensions and reframed as a feature of individual responsibility. The state's role in managing risk is de-emphasized, instead the strategy of 'governing at a distance' responsibilizes individual citizens by placing the onus of risk management and other securitized functions on them (p. 271). This individualization of risk reflects broader neo-liberal principles of attributing the problems associated with structural inequalities to individual deficiencies rather than structural deficiencies.

The Foucauldian concept of governmentality also informs the work of scholars who maintain that risk-focused penal regulation is an instrument of control since it entails 'governing through crime'. This, it is argued, involves politicians and policymakers redefining social problems associated with structural deprivations as crime and responding to the problems with crime control measures such as penal incapacitation (Simon 2007).

Sustaining this argument, Garland (2001) notes that risk-focused penal discourse (and regulation) is a form of expressive justice which nation-states, unable to control crime in times of social and economic difficulty and declining political support, but keen to reassert their sovereignty, employ. It is animated by punitive rhetoric and severe penal sanctions which are targeted at a population portrayed as a 'dangerous' and typically racialized group. Politicizing the risk discourse this way represents an attempt to leverage (for political advantage) public fears and anxieties about groups who have been historically depicted as 'dangerous'. To this end, states introduce policies that are excessively punitive but nevertheless politically expedient. This is because they derive legitimacy from a fearful public keen to support control measures that are targeted at subpopulations who have been depicted in political and other discourses as the source of their anxieties. This primarily racialized subpopulation is portrayed as possessing essentialized atypical traits. They are portrayed as a 'criminal type, the alien other' who pose an intractable threat to mainstream society (Garland 2001). Feeley and Simon (1992) elaborated on these themes earlier with the observation that the risk-focused new penology is in part a response to the growing population of a socio-economically excluded racialized subpopulation. In the US, this subpopulation comprises black and Hispanic groups residing in deprived inner city or urban areas. They are deemed pathologically 'dangerous' or 'high risk' and unable to contribute to mainstream society even at the lowest level of the production process where the reserve or surplus pool of labour is concentrated. Managing this permanently marginal (and primarily racialized) subpopulation is fundamental to the new penology and constitutes the 'managerial task that provides one of the *most powerful* sources for the imperative of preventive management in the new penology' (p. 468 emphasis added).

The racial dynamics of risk-focused digitized control

In contemporary criminal justice systems, the risk technologies which animate the risk-focused penality to which the aforementioned penological perspectives allude have become mainly digitized. We can therefore expand on the concept of the new penology which according to Feeley and Simon (1992) underpins actuarial justice, by pointing to the advent of a digitized penology which is risk-focused and underpinned by digital justice. This is a form of justice that is dispensed through digital technologies which automate key phases of the justice system such as court trials and the allocation, design, and delivery of punishment.

Digital justice is central to the emergence of what can be classified as a digital justice system in many jurisdictions. In the UK for instance, the Ministry of Justice has revealed its digital justice strategy which seeks to digitize many parts of the system as part of its modernization project (Ministry of Justice 2012). From a sociological perspective, the term digital justice has been used to explore how conditions in the social world and the digital world intersect. For example, some maintain that digital technologies are fomenting digital injustice by reproducing structural inequalities (Halford and Savage 2010) including racial injustices.

We contend here that a digitized penology rooted in digital injustice has emerged alongside advances in digital technology which have since the 1980s paved the way for the creation and development of risk prediction technologies. An example is the OASys tool which is the core risk technology used by Prison and Probation Service for adults aged 18 and over in England and Wales (Howard and Dixon 2012; Moore 2015). The LSI-R is another example and it is applied internationally in the US, Canada, Australia, and other jurisdictions.

These risk technologies appear to disadvantage racialized groups, particularly black people, quite disproportionately. Primarily, studies and reports have found that the technologies can over-predict their recidivism risks compared with other groups (see, for example, Angwin and Larson 2016; Hannah-Moffatt and Maurutto 2010; Jimenez et al. 2018; Singh and Fazel 2010; but cf. Skeem and Lowenkamp 2016). Other studies suggest that they have strong predictive accuracy and are therefore technically fair, even if they ignore the structural and other factors that can render racialized groups vulnerable to over-prediction (see for example Skeem and Lowenkamp 2016). Meanwhile, the extent to such over-prediction is fueling the influx of some racialized people into the prison system has been ignored. Official statistics consistently show that black people, for example, are over-represented in criminal justice statistics across Western jurisdictions where these technologies are applied, such as Canada, the United Kingdom, and the United States (Canadian Centre for Justice Statistics 2018; Ministry of Justice 2017; Bureau of Justice Statistics 2018). There is indeed evidence that the risk threshold for imposing severe sentences is lower for black and Asian people than other groups (Raynor and Lewis 2011).

A conclusion that could be drawn from this is that these racially disparate outcomes are being discountenanced as long as the prediction technologies are able to achieve the broader aim to which the aforementioned penological perspectives allude, which is the risk-focused control of typically racialized populations. In this respect, the risk technologies can be classified as instruments of digitized control. Greater priority is given to their fundamental function which is to aid the efficient and cost-effective categorization, management, and control of target subpopulations. It could be argued that this is particularly the case where the technologies are used beyond the penal contexts for which they were originally designed, which is in the context of rehabilitative work, specifically for identifying areas that should be targeted for intervention. Extending their use to the initial phases of the criminal justice process, primarily the pre-trial (police bail/remand) or post-trial (sentencing) phases, moves the tools beyond the benign identification of deprivations that should be targeted for intervention, to the pernicious identification of those who should be condemned to selective incapacitation.

Digital risk technologies, subjective fairness, and legitimacy: implications for rehabilitative work

Studies highlighting the capacity for risk technologies to achieve predictive accuracy whilst producing racially disparate outcomes bear upon the objective fairness of the technologies. This issue of objective fairness (and how its parameters should be measured) has been the subject of much debate (see, for example, Dressler and Farid 2018). Whilst it is an important debate, the subjective fairness of the technologies also deserves attention. Wang (2018) rightly notes that the subjective fairness of risk technologies has been ignored in the extant literature. Although Wang (2018) focuses on public opinion about the legitimacy of prediction technologies, I specifically explore the ways in which racially biased predictions pose implications for the perceived legitimacy of authority during rehabilitative work. The connection between this form of systemic discrimination and the outcomes of rehabilitative work has received limited attention although it is a form of discrimination that can create several problems. First, it can trigger perceptions of unfair treatment which can in turn provoke negative attitudes towards authority and generate high risk of recidivism scores. This is because such attitudes are defined as one of the 'big four' risk predictors (Bonta and Andrews 2017). Second, studies suggest that perceived unfair treatment (for example, biased decision-making) can trigger non-compliance during interactions with authorities, including during rehabilitative work (Rowe et al. 2018; Robinson and Ugwudike 2012; Ugwudike 2010). It can also provoke non-compliance with the law in general (Tyler 2005).

The quality of treatment received during the criminal justice process relates to the broader issue of procedural justice or the subjective fairness of the process. Procedural justice or procedural fairness in this context refers to the quality of decision-making processes within criminal justice institutions. It is for instance defined as the 'fairness of the processes through which the police [and other representatives of authority] make decisions and exercise authority' (Sunshine and Taylor 2003: 514).

Broadly, procedural justice theory provides a useful theoretical backdrop against which the importance of procedurally fair decision-making including risk assessment decision-making can be understood. Scholars have explored the nature and impact of procedural justice in criminal justice contexts from a social psychological perspective. Pioneered by Tyler (2005), studies in this field suggest that procedural justice manifests itself, or is animated by, people's perceptions of the quality of treatment and decision-making process during interactions with criminal justice institutions and their representatives. The quality of treatment received affects perceived legitimacy and the decision to defer to the authority in question.

Impartial/unbiased or non-discriminatory decision-making, showing respect, and earning the trust of citizens are key dimensions of good quality treatment (Tyler 2005). According to Tyler (2010: 130) the dimensions of procedural fairness or procedural justice are 'opportunities for participation, a neutral forum, trustworthy authorities, and treatment with dignity and respect'. Thus, biased risk predictions and lack of participation in determining the processes and outcomes of risk assessment are examples of procedural issues that could provoke feelings of unfair treatment.

Procedural justice is an antecedent of perceived legitimacy which has been described as a normative mechanism of compliance since it is based on the perception that the representatives of authority have the moral right to exercise their authority, therefore one has an obligation to comply with their directives (Tyler 2005). Legitimacy in this context is defined as 'the belief within the members of society that there are adequate reasons to voluntarily obey the commands of authorities' (Tyler 1997: 323). Studies have found evidence that procedural justice affects perceived legitimacy and compliance in policing contexts (Hough et al. 2010), in court (Tyler and Sevier 2013), in prison (Jackson et al. 2010), and in probation contexts (Ugwudike 2010).

However, studies of the perceptions of BAME people during their interactions with criminal justice officials have found that they are less likely to view their treatment as fair and the officials' authority as legitimate in a range of jurisdictions such as the US, UK, and Australia (Brunson and Miller 2006; Gau 2013; Johnson et al. 2017; Tyler et al. 2010; Huq 2017; Murphy et al. 2015). There is indeed evidence that perceived racial bias during criminal justice processing undermines the perceived legitimacy of the entire system amongst BAMEs (Rocque 2011) and can discourage compliance with decisions made within the system. Their discontent can also manifest as a defiant attitude towards law enforcement officials. As noted earlier, this attitude can increase their vulnerability to high risk scores.

Following the involvement of BAME people in the justice system, the harms caused by the system, such as negative labelling which limits access to participation in education, employment, and other structural avenues or opportunities for social participation (Apel and Sweeten 2010; Loeffler 2013), can lead to perceived injustice which in turn fuels defiance against the law and its enforcement officials (Tyler 2010). This reaction to unfair discrimination is consistent with the findings of studies which identify procedural justice or procedural fairness as a key antecedent of the perceived legitimacy of authority (Tyler 2005). The latter, in turn, enhances the belief that an authority or the law in general is legitimate and deserves compliance.

Participation and subjective fairness

Participation in decision-making processes is, as noted earlier, another fundamental dimension of good quality treatment or procedural justice which is linked to perceived legitimacy and the decision of whether or not to comply with the directives of people in authority. Thus, alongside fair decision-making procedures (for example impartial or non-discriminatory risk assessments and predictions), actual participation in decision-making processes is a vital dimension of procedural justice (Tyler 2010). However, the degree to which BAME populations and indeed other people undergoing risk assessments are able to participate in the process of determining the accurate level of risk is open to question. Digitized risk technologies come with pre-programmed and weighted predictors, and algorithmic scoring systems. Users (typically practitioners), and the people being assessed, have little or no say in the creation of aspects of the technologies – for example, the choice of predictors integrated into the technologies. Consequently, some have called for the creation and development of risk technologies to be democratized, to facilitate public participation in defining risk and the level of risk that can be tolerated before criminal justice intervention becomes necessary (see, for example, Eaglin 2013). This, it is contended, would attenuate the dangers of ceding epistemic control over accepted knowledge of risk and its management, to the state and unregulated non-state actors (Eaglin 2013).

It is worth noting that in England and Wales, the OASys risk assessment tool comprises a self-assessment questionnaire which should be used to collect information about an individual's self-perception and views of their offending behaviour. Other information that should be generated using the self-assessment section include the individual's perception of problems to do with accommodation, employment, relationships, attitudes, beliefs, reasoning, and so forth. However, a review of 101,240 self-assessment questionnaires found that the perceptions of individuals being assessed differed from the assessment outcomes computed by the tool's algorithmic scoring system. For example, 'Many offenders were more optimistic regarding their future desistance than indicated by their OASys scores, or at least were keen to portray themselves as optimistic' (Moore 2007). There is also evidence that factors such as the predictors inscribed in risk technologies inform practitioners' professional judgements about risk levels, more than subjective factors such as people's assessment of their own needs (see Hannah Moffat 2005). Some have rightly argued that risk assessment practice should be expanded to include the perceptions of people being risk assessed, particularly their perceptions of systemic legitimacy and also the legitimacy of the risk assessment process itself and the prediction produced by the process (see, for instance, Kempany and Kaiser 2016). This could help integrate procedural justice principles into the application of risk technologies, to ensure that people undertaking court orders view interventions (such as rehabilitative work) based on them as legitimate and deserving of compliance.

Conclusion

In the context of rehabilitative work, the importance of paying attention to the subjective fairness of digitized risk prediction technologies cannot be overstated. Social psychological perspectives on procedural justice, for instance, indicate that perceived bias and lack of participation during risk assessment can fuel feelings of unfair treatment. For racialized people, these and other systemic biases, along with structural discrimination, are factors that can undermine perceptions of procedural justice and views about the legitimacy of authority. Indeed, there is evidence that the impact of perceived procedural injustice can persist over an extended period of time, long after the triggering event occurred. A study of ex-probationers found that 40 years after their experiences, the participating ex-probationers still recounted 'with great indignation their sense of betrayal and injustice' (McNeill 2009 cited in McNeill and Weaver 2010: 42). We have seen that a sense of unfair treatment and injustice can affect the perceived legitimacy of penal authorities. Furthermore, studies consistently show that perceived legitimacy is crucial for compliance with the key goals and objectives of rehabilitative work, and it has also been linked to longer-term positive outcomes such as desistance from offending.

As prediction technologies become increasingly digitized and powered by algorithms and other digitized features which are not readily amenable to public scrutiny, it becomes even more pertinent to review their validity for diverse populations and jurisdictions. Two key implications arise from applying risk technologies that produce racially disparate outcomes. First, it raises serious ethical questions regarding the civil rights and liberties of affected populations. Only robust independent evidence of their suitability for diverse groups can resolve these ethical issues. Second it reinforces the claim that the risk discourse and risk management technologies are operating as instruments of control (in this case, instruments of digitized control). As such, the broader aim of managing and controlling target groups supersedes concerns about the ethical implications and overall fairness of the technologies.

Notes

1   In this chapter, the term 'racialized groups' refers to people of non-white descent who have historically experienced one form of discrimination or the other because of the race ascribed to them. They are not a homogenous group and their experiences of racial discrimination have not always been similar. But, a unifying feature they all share is the experience of racial discrimination.
2   This chapter focuses on risk technologies which rely on the static (immutable) and dynamic (mutable) predictors derived from the Risk-Need-Responsivity model of rehabilitation. These predictors are integrated into the technologies commonly used in a range of Western and non-Western countries such as the UK, US, Canada, Australia, Singapore, Japan, New Zealand, and Pakistan. The predictors are criminal history, accommodation, employment training and education, relationships, lifestyle and associates, substance misuse, and personal attributes – thinking and attitudes (Bonta and Andrews 2017).

References

Angwin, J. and Jeff Larson, J. (2016) *Bias in Criminal Risk Scores Is Mathematically Inevitable, Researchers Say*. Available at: www.propublica.org/article/bias-in-criminal-risk-scores-is-mathematically-inevitable-researchers-say (Accessed June 2018).

Apel, R. and Sweeten, G. (2010) The impact of incarceration on employment during the transition to adulthood. *Social Problems*, 57(3), 448–479.

Australian Bureau of Statistics. (2018) *Persons in Corrective Services*. Available at: www.abs.gov.au/AUSSTATS/abs@.nsf/Lookup/4512.0Main+Features1June%20quarter%20 2018?OpenDocument (Accessed November 2018).

Beck, U. (1992) *Risk Society: Towards a New Modernity*. London: Sage Publications.

Beck, U., Giddens, A. and Lash, S. (1994) *Reflexive Modernization. Politics, Tradition and Aesthetics in the Modern Social Order*. Stanford: Stanford University Press.

Berk, R. A. and Bleich, J. (2013) Statistical procedures for forecasting criminal behaviour: A comparative assessment. *Criminology & Public Policy*, 12, 513–544.

Bonta, J. and Andrews, D. A. (2017) *The Psychology of Criminal Conduct*, 6th edition. Abingdon: Routledge.

Brunson, R. K. and Miller, J. (2006) Young black men and urban policing in the United States. *British Journal of Criminology*, 46(4), 613–640.

Bureau of Justice Statistics. (2018) *Prisoners in 2016*. Available at: www.bjs.gov/content/ pub/pdf/p16_sum.pdf (Accessed November 2018).

Canadian Centre for Justice Statistics. (2018) *Adult and Youth Correctional Statistics in Canada, 2016/2017*. Available at: https://www150.statcan.gc.ca/n1/en/pub/85-002-x/2018001/article/54972-eng.pdf?st=-60eEXbF (Accessed November 2018).

Dieterich, W., Mendoza, C. and Brennan, T. (2016) *COMPAS Risk Scales: Demonstrating Accuracy Equity and Predictive Parity: Performance of the COMPAS Risk Scales in Broward County*. Technical Report. Traverse City, MI: Northpointe Inc.

Dressler, J. and Farid, H. (2018) The Accuracy, Fairness and Limits of Predicting Recidivism. Available at: http://advances.sciencemag.org/content/4/1/eaao5580.full (Accessed August 2018).

Eaglin, J. M. (2013) *Against Neorehabilitation*. Articles by Maurer Faculty, 1665. Available at: www.repository.law.indiana.edu/facpub/1665 (Accessed June 2018).

Feeley, M. and Simon, J. (1992) The new penology: Notes on the emerging strategy of corrections and its implications. *Criminology*, 30, 449–474.

Feeley, M. and Simon, J. (1994) Actuarial justice: The emerging new criminal law. In D. Nelken (Ed.), *The Future of Criminology*. London: Sage Publications, pp. 172–201.

Flores, A. W., Bechtel, K. and Lowenkamp, L. K. (2016) False positives, false negatives, and false analyses: A rejoinder to "Machine bias: There's software used across the country to predict future criminals. And it's biased against blacks." *Federal Probation*, 80, 38.

Garland, D. (2001) *The Culture of Control: Crime and Social Order in Contemporary Society*. Oxford: Oxford University Press.

Gau, J. M. and Brunson, J. K. (2013) Procedural justice and order maintenance policing: A study of inner-city young men's perceptions of police legitimacy. *Justice Quarterly*, 27(2), 255–279.

Giddens, A. (1991) The *Consequences of Modernity*. Cambridge: Polity Press.

Halford, S. and Savage, M. (2010) Reconceptualizing digital social inequality. *Information, Communication & Society*, 13(7), 937–955.

Hannah-Moffat, K. (2005) Criminogenic needs and the transformative risk subject: Hybridizations of risk/need in penality. *Punishment & Society*, 7, 29–51.

Hannah-Moffat, K. and Marutto, P. (2010) Restructuring pre-sentence reports: Race, risk, and the PSR. *Punishment & Society*, 12(3) 262–286.

Harcourt, B. (2015) Risk as a proxy for race: The dangers of risk assessment. *Federal Sentencing Reporter*, 27(4), 237–243.

HM Inspectorate of Probation. (2018) The Quality of Service User Assessment (Probation Services) HMIP Research and Analysis Bulletin 2018/01. Available at: https://www.justiceinspectorates.gov.uk/hmiprobation/wp-content/uploads/sites/ 5/2018/09/2018-01-The-quality-of-service-user-assessment-probation-services-final. pdf (Accessed December 2018).

Hough, M., Jackson, J., Bradford, B., Myhill, A. and Quinton, P. (2010) Procedural justice, trust, and institutional legitimacy. *Policing: A Journal of Policy and Practice*, 4(3), 203–210.

Howard, P. and Dixon, L. (2012) The construction and validation of the OASys violence predictor: Advancing violence risk assessment in the English and Welsh correctional services. *Criminal Justice and Behaviour*, 39(3), 287–307.

Huq, A. Z. (2017) Dignity, not deadly force: Why procedural justice matters for modern policing and democracy. *World Policy Journal*, 34(2), 8–42.

Jackson, Jonathan, Tyler, Tom R., Bradford, Ben, Taylor, Dominic and Shiner, Mike. (2010) Legitimacy and procedural justice in prisons. *Prison Service Journal*, 191.

Jimenez, A. C., Hazel Delgado, R., Vardsveen, T. C. and Wiener, R. L. (2018) Validation and application of the LS/CMI in Nebraska probation. *Criminal Justice and Behaviour*, 45(6), 863–884.

Johnson, D., Wilson, D. B., Maguire, E. R. and Lowrey-Kinbergg, B. V. (2017) Race and perceptions of police: Experimental results on the impact of procedural (In) justice. *Justice Quarterly*, 1184–1212.

Kempany, K. and Kaiser, K. A. (2016) Incorporating procedural justice into the RNR model to improve Risk-Need Assessment. In F. Taxman (Ed.), *Handbook of Risk and Need Assessment: Theory and Practice*. Abingdon: Routledge.

Lidskog, R. and Sundqvist, G. (2012) The sociology of risk. In S. Roeser, R. Hillerbrand, P. Sandin and M. Peterson (Eds.), *Handbook of Risk Theory*: *Epistemology, Decision Theory, Ethics, and Social Implications of Risk*. London: Springer.

Loeffler, C. E. (2013) Does imprisonment alter the life course? Evidence on crime and employment from a natural experiment. *Criminology*, 51(1), 137–166.

Lum, K. and Isaac, W. (2016) To predict and serve? *Significance*, 13, 14–19.

Maurutto, P. and Hannah-Moffat, K. (2005) Assembling risk and the 'Restructuring of Penal Control'. *British Journal of Criminology*, 46, 438–454.

McNeill, F. and Weaver, B. (2010) *Changing Lives? Desistance Research and Offender Management*. Glasgow: School of Social Work, The Scottish Centre for Crime and Justice.

Ministry of Justice. (2012) *Ministry of Justice Digital Strategy: A Strategy Setting Out How the Ministry of Justice Will Digitally Transform Services*. Available at: www.gov.uk/government/publications/ministry-of-justice-digital-strategy.

Ministry of Justice. (2017) *Statistics on Race and the Criminal Justice System 2016: A Ministry of Justice Publication Under Section 95 of the Criminal Justice Act 1991*. Available at: https://assets.publishing.service.gov.uk/government/uploads/system/uploads/attachment_data/file/669094/statistics_on_race_and_the_criminal_justice_system_2016_v2.pdf.

Moore, R. (2007) *Adult Offenders' Perceptions of Their Underlying Problems: Findings from the OASys Self-Assessment Questionnaire*. Home Office Findings 284. Available at: www.ohrn.nhs.uk/resource/policy/OASys.pdf.

Moore, R. (2015) *A Compendium of Research and Analysis of the Offender Assessment System (OASys) 2009–2013*. London: National Offender Management Service.

Moses, L. B. and Chan, J. (2016) Algorithmic prediction in policing: Assumptions, evaluation, and accountability. *Policing and Society*, 1–17.

Murphy, K., Sergeant, E. and Cherney, A. (2015) The importance of procedural justice and police performance in shaping intentions to cooperate with the police: Does social identity matter? *European Journal of Criminology*, 12(6), 719–738.

National Offender Management Service Public Protection Manual. (2016) Available at: https://www.justice.gov.uk/downloads/offenders/psipso/psi-2016/psi-18-2016-pi-17-2016-public-protection-manual.pdf (Accessed November 2016).

O'Malley, P. (2010) *Crime and Risk*. London: Sage Publications.

Oswald, M., Grace, J., Urwin, S. and Barnes, G. (2018) Algorithmic risk assessment policing models: Lessons from the Durham HART model and 'experimental' proportionality. *Information & Communications Technology Law*, 27(2), 223–250.

Raynor, P. and Lewis, S. (2011) Risk – need assessment, sentencing and minority ethnic offenders in Britain. *British Journal of Social Work*, 41, 1357–1371.

Robinson, G. and Ugwudike, P. (2012) Investing in 'toughness': Probation, enforcement and legitimacy. *Howard Journal of Criminal Justice*, 51(3), 300–316.

Rocque, M. (2011) Racial disparities in the criminal justice system and perceptions of legitimacy: A theoretical linkage. *Race and Justice*, 1(3), 292–315.

Rose, N. and Miller, P. (2010) Political power beyond the state: Problematics of government. *British Journal of Sociology*, 61(1), 271–303.

Rowe, M., Irving, A. and Soppitt, S. (2018) The legitimacy of offender management programmes in a post-TR landscape. *Safer Communities*, 17(2), 69–80.

Sentencing Council (2016) Imposition of Community and Custodial Sentences: Definitive Guidelines. Available at: https://www.sentencingcouncil.org.uk/wp-content/uploads/Imposition-definitive-guideline-Web.pdf (Accessed January 2018).

Simon, J. (2007) *Governing Through Crime: How the War on Crime Transformed American Democracy and Created a Culture of Fear*. New York: Oxford University Press.

Singh, J. P. and Fazel, S. (2010) Forensic risk assessment: A metareview. *Criminal Justice and Behaviour*, 37(9), 965.

Skeem, J. and Lowenkamp, C. (2016) Risk, race & recidivism: Predictive bias and disparate impact. *Criminology*, 54(4), 680–712.

Sunshine, J. and Taylor, T. R. (2003) The role of procedural justice and legitimacy in shaping public support for policing. *Law and Society Review*, 37(3), 513–547.

Tyler, T. R. (1997) The psychology of legitimacy: A relational perspective on voluntary deference to authorities. *Personality and Social Psychology Review*, 1(4), 323–345.

Tyler, T. R. (2005) *Why People Obey the Law*. Princeton, NJ: Princeton University Press.

Tyler, T. R. and Sevier, J. (2013) How do the courts create popular legitimacy – the role of establishing the truth, punishing justly, and/or acting through just procedures. *Albany Law Review*, 77, 1095.

Tyler, T. R., et al. (2010) Legitimacy in corrections: Policy implications. *Criminology and Public Policy*, 9(1), 127–134.

Ugwudike, P. (2010) Compliance with community penalties: The importance of interactional dynamics. In F. McNeill, P. Raynor and C. Trotter (Eds.), *Offender Supervision: New Directions in Theory, Research and Practice*. Cullompton: Willan Publishing.

Ugwudike, P. (2012) Mapping the interface between contemporary risk-focused policy and frontline enforcement practice. *Criminology and Criminal Justice*, 11(3), 242–258.

Wang, A. J. (2018) *Procedural Justice and Risk-Assessment Algorithms*. Available at: http://dx.doi.org/10.2139/ssrn.3170136 (Accessed July 2018).

Wormith, J. S. (2012) *The Predictive Validity of Aboriginal Offender Recidivism with a General Risk/Needs Assessment Inventory*. Available at: www.usask.ca/cfbsjs/research/pdf/research_reports/LSI-OR%20Aboriginal%20Paper%20w%20Abstract.pdf (Accessed December 2018).

57

Cultural competency in community corrections

Jessica J. Wyse

Introduction

African American and Latino populations remain starkly over-represented across the spectrum of criminal justice institutions (Pettit and Western 2004; Wakefield and Uggen 2010; Western 2006). For instance, among adult males, one of every 106 white men is imprisoned, but among African American men, this is the true of one in 15 (Pew 2008). Within the context of justice institutions (e.g. courts, law enforcement, corrections), a large literature has sought to uncover racial and ethnic disparities in treatment that may help explain this over-representation and, as such, focuses largely on justice system practices that disadvantage people of colour (Beckett et al. 2006; Bridges and Steen 1998; Everett and Wojtkiewicz 2002; Rios 2011). In contrast, very little research has addressed differential justice system treatment that stems from beneficent motivations, namely, the voiced desire to provide more effective treatment to clients from minority racial or cultural groups. Yet, particularly within the rehabilitative arm of the correctional system, the movement to tailor treatment to justice-involved participants' racial and ethnic group membership in what is known as 'culturally competent practice' has become increasingly common (Cornett-DeVito and McGlone 2000; Kapoor et al. 2013; Primm et al. 2005).

Cultural competency can be defined as work practices that take into account race, ethnicity, and cultural background, and adapt treatment (e.g. interactions, processes, interventions) in response to these factors. The underlying motivation of the practice is the notion that treating all clients or patients identically ignores real differences between members of social groups, e.g. in communication styles or historical experiences with governmental institutions. For this reason, proponents argue, equitable treatment requires attention to these differences and a tailored approach. While widely advocated, the implications of such an approach for workplace practice remains little understood. This chapter begins to fill this gap, investigating the following: How does cultural competency take shape in the everyday practice of community corrections officers? How is the practice reflective of officers' racial beliefs and perspectives? And what is the significance of such practice for the individuals who are subject to it?

Drawing on interviews conducted with community corrections officers and observations of routine meetings between officers and probationers/parolees, I argue that, given the lack of uniform understanding of the term 'cultural competency', or clear direction from management as to what constitutes a culturally competent approach, the interpretation and consequent meaning of the term is defined through the lens of individual officers' racial beliefs and perspectives.

Building upon Frankenberg's (1993) distillation of racial frames, I identify three prominent categories of race-thought among the officers I interviewed, and link these categories with distinct approaches to cultural competency. I designate these approaches *Superficial and Symbolic*, *Culturally Constrained*, and *Racially Reflexive*. In the first, officers signal recognition of the symbolic elements of clients' cultural practice (food, holidays), but neglect the structural elements of racial-ethnic inequality. In the second, officers verbally acknowledge inequality and the significance of racially situated perspective but, struggling to understand how such knowledge should impact their work, remain focused on differences in cultural practices. In the third, racial inequality, discrimination, and the historical tensions between law enforcement and communities of colour are recognized and addressed in interactions.

Shifting racial discourses and ideologies

Racial ideologies and discursive frames, while contradictory and contingent, evidence historical patterns that evolve over time. Frankenberg (1993) classifies three discursive stages of race-thought: essentialist racism, colour-blind/power evasion, and race cognizance. She explains that, while these discursive frames arose independently at particular historical moments, each remains available to be drawn upon in the contemporary period. In the first, race was understood as biologically based and hierarchically organized. In the second, race began to be defined in social and cultural terms, though biological elements lingered. In the third stage, which unfolded in the late 1960s, social movements advocating cultural nationalism and radical antiracism emphasized racial and cultural minority groups' differences from mainstream white culture, and sought to revalue these differences in positive terms (Skrentny 2002). In the contemporary period, scholars of race have argued that the dominant discourse that whites rely upon to explain and make sense of race-relations and realities is that of colour-blindness (Berrey 2015; Bonilla-Silva 2006; Mueller 2017). Denying the significance of race for life experiences, the discourse reinforces existing social and structural arrangements that privilege whites (Mueller 2017).

Data and methods

This chapter draws upon interviews with community correctional officers and observations of meetings between officers and their clients collected within two county community corrections systems within a western US state. I refer to these counties as Greendale and Riverside. Both counties are growing rapidly and have a white, non-Hispanic population between 71 and 74%, with Latinos composing the largest minority group (US Census Bureau 2008). The counties border one another and are the two most populous counties in the state.

I selected these counties in part because of their strong commitment to employing a culturally competent approach. In both, the language of cultural competency is pervasive, cited in organizational literature, trainings, addressed in hiring, even posted on websites. This commitment extends to client management as well, in that some officers' caseloads are made up entirely of clients of a particular race and/or cultural groups, for instance Spanish-speaking and Latino, or African American clients. The stated purpose of this approach is to allow officers to learn the management style and techniques that work best with their clients, as well specific community resources available to them.

Across the two counties, I interviewed 27 officers and staff in a single office in Greendale County and 23 officers and staff across five free standing offices in Riverside County. White officers composed the majority of interviewees (39/50), and more women (27) than men (23) were interviewed. The sociodemographic profile of those interviewed reflected the sociodemographic profile of officers generally within each county system. Interviews averaged between 45 minutes and one hour. Interviews aimed to gain a broad understanding of what it means in practice to be a community corrections officer, the type of caseload officers supervised (and reasons for this assignment), and probed their thoughts regarding differences between groups, focusing on beliefs about group-specific needs and paths to reform. Each interview was audiotaped and transcribed verbatim.

In Greendale, I also observed over 50 meetings between community correc-tions officers and their clients after obtaining consent from the officers. These meetings averaged between 15 and 45 minutes. In each case, I approached clients in the lobby as they waited for their appointment, and sought their consent to observe the meeting; no one declined. Clients seemed relatively indifferent to my presence, although some enquired about the project or my field of study.

Atlas.TI Qualitative Analysis Software was utilized for data organization and coding. Each transcript was carefully read to identify key themes and subsequently coded. Text linked with key codes was systematically reviewed and compared both within and across interviews to identify patterns.

In the course of interviews, I found that asking officers to address issues of race, culture, and the ways in which their practice engaged these topics was often challenging. As has been documented, race, discrimination, and cultural difference remain difficult topics for white Americans to discuss (Bell and Hartman 2007). Officers were frequently at a loss for words with which to respond to questions about the challenges faced by people of colour in the criminal justice system, or the specific treatment needs required by racial and cultural minorities. White officers tended to respond to such questions with one-word answers, with silence, or provided answers couched in cave-ats along the lines of 'I don't want to stereotype, but. . .'. Ultimately, these strained responses became useful data in the analysis phase, as I detail in the results.

Superficially symbolic practice

Derrick[1] is a white officer on the Spanish-speaking team, whose approach to cultural competency was hinted at by the objects on display within his oth-erwise bare office. On the walls hung large, Navajo-themed textiles, on his desk a small radio played Andean music, while on the shelf above his desk, a framed picture of a smiling Hispanic woman faced out. These visual repre-sentations were intended to signal his familiarity and comfort with Latino culture, despite his white skin. In the interview, he explained that clients often assumed he knew little about Latino culture; he had to prove himself to them to gain their trust.

> It's been a struggle for me as an Anglo person who speaks Spanish and is not Hispanic at all, there is [pause] sometimes some clients have, I have felt, have looked at me like, 'who are you to tell me because I'm a minority and you don't understand what I've had to go through', and so, you have to have an understanding. I sometimes have had to explain to clients how I may be Anglo, however I grew up in a very predominantly Hispanic community. I was the minority in the community and I have an understanding of how things are in the Hispanic culture.

Derrick explains that some of his clients contest his knowledge of Hispanic culture; they make assumptions based upon the colour of his skin. He clarifies for me, as he does for his clients, that in fact he has a very high level of Hispanic cultural knowledge. To reassure clients, he signals knowledge through office decorations, mentioning his Latina wife and bicultural family in conversation and by weaving Spanish words into his English speech. He believes these practices show his clients, 'that it's just not, for the lack of a better term, a white person telling a Hispanic person what to do'. While not absent, power is strongly downplayed in Derrick's account. In the quote above, he recognizes that some of his clients view their interactions with him through a lens of race hierarchy. Because, for him, cultural competency is about knowledge of cultural practices, he believes that once clients know the depth of his cultural knowledge, the racial dynamic is essentially resolved.

Officers employing a *Superficial and Symbolic* approach to cultural competency focused on the visible differences between groups in cultural practices and, in interviews, explained that cultural competency entailed respecting these differences and setting aside personal biases or assumptions. Frankenberg's concept of a colour-blind/power-evasive racial understanding underlies this approach, in its focus on the superficial differences between groups. While not exclusive to white officers, white officers were the primary proponents of this approach.

Later in the interview as Derrick identifies the differences between Anglo and Hispanic culture, he reveals that he holds a negative valuation of these cultural differences. This is evident in his response to my question, 'what do you think causes people to become involved with the criminal justice system in the first place?' He responds with evident difficulty:

> Um, the type of cases that I mostly supervise are Hispanic domestic violence cases. And um there is a lengthy um [pause] cultural, what do I, how do I want to say this, I want to try to be sensitive to the subject, but there is, there is a, in the Hispanic culture for many, many, many, many, many years, eons, centuries maybe, um domestic violence has been somewhat accepted if not, if not at least ignored. And many, many, many people grow up in homes where domestic violence is just how it is.

One prominent difference between Hispanic and mainstream American culture for Derrick is acceptance of domestic violence.[2] Derrick's earlier comment about having an 'understanding' of Hispanic culture is read differently once we recognize how Derrick himself identifies a key difference. Yet how such negative beliefs about Hispanic culture should be incorporated into a culturally competent approach remains unclear. Exclusive focus on cultural differences, without consideration of the implications of structural forces on clients' lives and behaviours, means that the negative implications of forces like discrimination are then attributed to differences in cultural practices. *Superficial and Symbolic* officers are thus caught in the uncomfortable position of professing to respect cultural practices they clearly think problematic, as in the case of Derrick's perception of Hispanic domestic violence.

Other interview participants as well highlighted superficial cultural differences in discussion of cultural competency, which allowed them to skirt more difficult considerations about power and racial inequality. This was evident in comments made by Lane, a white officer, who contests the notion that the African American Program should be staffed by African American officers:

> One of the perceptions is that I as a white PO couldn't work in the African American program. . . . I don't know anyone who has said anything that these African American clients have a need or something different that these African American POs are able to give to them because they speak the same language or come from the same country, or eat the same [food] . . . that's sort of lost on me . . . because one: my friends, growing up; it's a very diverse background. And a lot of my family is Southern. So there's a lot of things culturally that with my black friends we relate.

Lane implies that the system of supervision practiced in the prisoner re-entry programme, a system that pairs African American officers with African American clients, is itself biased because it fails to recognize that a white officer might have the cultural knowledge necessary to make him a good fit for the team. Focusing on visible and material cultural differences, Lane fails to acknowledge less easily visible but nonetheless significant differences in racial experiences and perspective.

Culturally Constrained

The category of *Culturally Constrained* marks but a half-step away from the *Superficial and Symbolic* practice described above. In interviews, officers initially appeared well-versed in the significance of race and cultural dynamics for their clients, yet behind this verbal acknowledgement there was limited understanding of how such knowledge should impact their work. In response, and like the *Superficial and Symbolic* approach, these officers focused on acknowledging and respecting differences in cultural practices, but put greater emphasis on remaining open to new information and learning from their clients.

I classify the racial frame as 'constrained' because of how difficult it was for these officers to answer questions about the significance of race and culture for those justice-involved. Each time I asked a question I steeled myself for the look of discomfort, the awkward silence, or the nervous giggle that so often followed. Explicitly talking about race appeared to be quite uncomfortable for these officers, who seemed to lack the language necessary to do so. Though these officers verbally acknowledged the realities of discrimination and inequality for their clients of colour, they were generally unable to voice concretely either how these burdens affected their clients, or how this knowledge should be integrated into their correctional work. Peeking behind the verbal acknowledgement thus revealed a culturally based word-lessness.

Here, Lisa, an officer on the women's team, strongly acknowledges that discrimination affects probationers/parolees of colour, but responds with puzzlement to a follow-up question I pose requesting specifics:

Do you think among your clients, clients of different races have different issues or challenges on probation or parole?
Well, I would say absolutely yes just because I think any person of colour in the United States has different issues and different difficulties because discrimination is still so prevalent.
But anything particular about being released from prison or anything like that that you can think of?
Um [long pause] um, I don't know, I don't know how to answer that, um. Yeah.

Other officers as well, who were otherwise quite verbose, answered this question with one-word responses, 'Probably' or 'Sure', which I had to probe to elicit additional details. Officers even viewed this question as a trap of sorts. Following up on one staff member's response that 'Some [issues] are the same and some are different', I probed for details and she responded, laughing, 'You're not going to get that from me!'

Even acknowledging differences in experiences between groups seems dangerous to these officers, who view themselves as racially progressive. I suggest that this is because their racial understanding is shaped by a white normative world view; a world view that says that, to the extent that cultural or racial traits and practices differ from the white norm, these differences will largely be negative. Immersed in this culture of whiteness, the differences officers conjure up tend to be negative stereotypes about people of colour. Thus, subjects wedded to their racially progressive narrative are left speechless. Indeed, those I press to respond do tend to voice negative stereotypes:

Would you think that women from different race groups have different issues or challenges that they face?
Probably. [laugh]
[laugh] Do you know what that might be or have any thoughts on that?
Well you know women who were in the Hispanic community . . . have to probably deal with um more [pause] see and I don't want to be stereotypical. . . . You know women are viewed lower than men in the Hispanic community. . . .

The challenges faced by Latina women that she identifies stem from her perceptions of dynamics *within* Latino culture rather than dynamics at play between majority white and minority cultures (e.g. discrimination, structural inequality). Because such a verbal admission challenges officers' self-concepts, or at least self-presentations, as progressive racial thinkers, to the extent possible officers avoided answering these questions.

Despite this apparent anxiety, *Culturally Constrained* officers did voice a desire to learn more about their clients, whether through discussion, coursework, or trainings. One officer explained that, to him, culturally competent work meant 'You don't pretend to know more than you do', while another officer noted that she tried to 'Explore the differences and ask'. In their openness to new information, this approach diverges from officers classified as *Superficial and Symbolic*, many of whom presumed to 'know it all' already.

Yet while officers *Culturally Constrained* believed it important to learn about and remain open to new perspectives, they did not necessarily endorse or understand this perspective. White officer Deborah exemplifies this:

> If I'm doing, taking classes about um [pause] Black American studies, that gives me certain information or a frame of reference for working with those clients, because you know particularly with blacks, whites don't understand, um [pause] the depth of their um sense of race and racism, you know we have no comprehension about, I mean in terms of what is the most important thing about a person. For them it's always them being black, nothing else is even remotely close to that and you have to accept it that that's their frame and you have to be respectful of that.

For Deborah, practicing cultural competency meant accepting that black clients view experiences through a racial lens; in contrast her own racial lens is neither acknowledged nor visible. Rather than seeing herself implicated in the racial dynamics of supervision, she sees racial knowledge as external to her, a practice to be learned.

Racially Reflexive

For *Racially Reflexive* officers, cultural competency entailed, not recognition of differences in cultural practices, but rather recognition of differences in group perspective and experiences born of social inequality. Here Gloria, a Latina officer, exemplifies this as she expands upon her statement that culture can be one root cause of crime:

You said that there's different cultural reasons you think people get involved [in crime]?
Well, cultural reasons meaning the lack of opportunities. And for people of various cultures, and I can speak right now for the Latino culture in language issues and barriers, discrimination. And I could say that, too, for African American kids and even Asian kids, that there is discrimination. It does exist in our system and in our society.

713

Officers recognized that these experiences of oppression and discrimination had effects, both psychological and structural, that in important ways could contribute to group members' likelihood of entering the criminal justice system and their success in exiting it. Central to this approach is officers' recognition of the way in which both their own perspective, and that of their clients, was shaped by race and cultural membership.

Racially Reflexive officers drew liberally upon their own experiences to inform their work with clients. In interviews, officers of colour told personal stories about being ignored, dismissed, or discriminated against because of their race or culture, and explained how they carried these experiences with them into their work. White officers' practice was similarly informed by personal experiences, knowledge from trainings or classes, or experiences of friends and relatives who had experienced discrimination or racial 'otherness'.

Among white officers, culturally competent interactions consisted of acknowledging clients' perspective and world view, listening to and learning from clients, and recognizing that they might have to work harder to connect with clients of colour to earn their trust. Eliza, a white officer who had worked for many years in a field office located in a historically African American neighbourhood, explains:

> One big way that you're responsive is that you listen . . . just because this . . . is a person of colour certainly their experiences are not all the same. And so that really is by listening. If you're working with someone who feels very victimized by the system, you need to take that into account. . . . Because if you want to build a relationship with this person, then you need to understand how this person is viewing themselves in society . . . as a white person working in a system . . . with a good part of my caseload being people of colour . . . you do have to understand that trust is gonna take a while to build . . . there is a distrust for law enforcement, for police. And it's justly so. There's a lotta discrimination out there.

Eliza recognizes that discrimination is a potent force in her clients' lives, and that she must acknowledge and respond to this reality when working with clients of colour.

While some aspects of practice were similar across white and non-white officers, officers of colour's strategies differed in that they additionally understood culturally competent practice to mean serving as a racial ally to their clients or working to empower them.

Sylvia is a Latina officer on the Spanish-speaking team who identifies her own competency to work with Latino clients as stemming from a childhood growing up in a segregated Latino community. She explains,

> I have an awareness of what it's like to live in a Mexican community . . . and where there's a lot of poverty, there's a lot of struggling with bureaucracies,

there's a lot of using your children to help translate for you, there's a fear of authority and a fear of police and fear of deportation.

Thus for her, cultural competency signifies knowledge of the challenges faced by poor and immigrant Latinos living as minorities in a predominantly white society.

She views her role and mission to be that of acting as a liaison between the community corrections system and the Latino community:

> And in working with the Hispanic community it's a lot about giving back to my community, and having the knowledge that many times an oppressed people can alienate themselves or cut themselves off from the majority or from the mainstream because they don't feel they have any kind of investment in . . . the dominant community.

Sylvia, like other officers, consciously worked to overcome these divisions between communities of colour and law enforcement, which she saw as self-defeating. An important part of this approach was the joint recognition that people of colour face greater scrutiny by the police, and that experiencing oppression itself can lead to criminality, motivated by hopelessness.

Racially Reflexive officers also saw their clients' identification with them as fellow race-mates as a significant part of what made their practice culturally competent. 'It's huge', said one African American officer. Some officers expressed the belief that probationers/parolees who were supervised by someone of their own race or cultural group were comforted by this and even inspired, perhaps seeing in their officers' middle-class status a 'nugget of hope' for their own future, as one officer explained. They believed that probationers/parolees identified more easily with officers of colour and were more likely to form a trusting, open relationship with them, thereby making them more effective correctional officers.

Conclusion

This chapter was motivated by a desire to understand the meaning and consequence of a directive to practice cultural competency within a community correctional setting. Findings suggest that targeting treatment to probationer/ parolees' race and cultural group may have important implications for clients of colour. While it is certainly not inappropriate to learn differences in rules and norms between cultures, exclusive focus on these differences absent a recognition of systemic and structural inequalities between groups won't, on its own, substantially impact the trust and rapport of the supervisory relationship. Further, if the cultural difference identified is stigmatized or devalued in the officer's mind, attention to this difference is unlikely to improve the officer-client dynamic. In contrast, when officers understand cultural difference as significant primarily in relation to probationer/parolees' experiences of discrimination and/or structural inequality, and view cultural competency as implicating their own racial positionality as well, it may well result in more individually responsive and, ultimately, equitable treatment. Research has shown that establishing trust and a collaborative relationship between client and worker facilitates behaviour change across a wide variety of outcomes, including criminal behaviours (Andrews et al. 1990; Bonta and Andrews 2007). Thus, officers seeking to build trust with probationers/parolees may usefully consider the approaches voiced by racially reflexive officers, from listening and acknowledging clients' perspective to sharing their own knowledge of, and experiences with, discrimination.

The diversity of ways in which culturally competent practice was interpreted and enacted by the officers I interviewed suggests an important role for leadership in making explicit the actions and behaviours that are expected from culturally competent staff. Absent such direction, these interviews suggest that officers will fill in the blanks with their own beliefs and experiences, which may not align with leaders' intentions. Clear definition may also help establish staff buy-in, by counteracting the belief that cultural competency is a buzzword, and lacking in real content and meaning. It is important to acknowledge, however, that such efforts may founder. Even given explicit direction, some officers may reject the premises on which culturally competent practice is based, and fail to implement it as requested. This may be the case, for instance, for officers who see the world in 'colour blind' terms, ascribing their own and others' successes and failures largely to individual achievement and responsibility, rather than social and structural forces.

There are caveats to the findings presented here. First, this research took place within a criminal justice context, a racially charged setting that may well have evoked a particularly negative conception of cultural competency. It is also possible that officers were hesitant to challenge discriminatory police practices or injustices of the justice system, given their positioning within the system. While possible, the fact that officers readily critiqued other aspects of the community correctional system, and management practices explicitly, argues against this interpretation. Finally, reflecting the sociodemographic patterns of the counties in which I conducted this research, the majority of interviewees were white; research conducted with a more racially diverse sample might yield different results. Future work should evaluate whether these findings are unique to this context or likewise characterize other sites that promote cultural competency.

Notes

1   All names are pseudonyms.
2   Notably, the Bureau of Justice Statistics reports that African Americans experience intimate partner violence at a significantly higher rate than either whites or Hispanics. No statistically significant difference in experiences of intimate partner violence was found between whites and Hispanics (Rennison and Welchans 2000).

References

Andrews, D. A., Bonta, James and Hoge, R. D. (1990) Classification for effective rehabilitation: Rediscovering psychology. *Criminal Justice and Behavior*, 17(1) 19–52.

Beckett, K., Nyrop, K. and Pfingst, L. (2006) Race, drugs, and policing: Understanding disparities in drug delivery arrests. *Criminology*, 44(1), 105–137.

Bell, J. M. and Hartmann, D. (2007) Diversity in everyday discourse: The cultural ambiguities and consequences of "happy talk". *American Sociological Review*, 72(6), 895–914.

Berrey, E. (2015) *The Enigma of Diversity: The Language of Race and the Limits of Racial Justice*. Chicago: University of Chicago Press.

Bonilla-Silva, E. (2006) *Racism Without Racists: Color-Blind Racism and the Persistence of Racial Inequality in the United States*. Lanham: Rowman & Littlefield Publishers Inc.

Bonta, J. and Andrews, D. A. (2007) Risk-Need-Responsivity model for offender assessment and rehabilitation. *Rehabilitation*, 6.

Bridges, G. S. and Steen, S. (1998) Racial disparities in official assessments of juvenile offenders: Attributional stereotypes as mediating mechanisms. *American Sociological Review*, 63, 554–570.

Cornett-DeVito, M. M. and McGlone, E. L. (2000) Multicultural communication training for law enforcement officers: A case study. *Criminal Justice Policy Review*, 11(3), 234–253.

Everett, R. S. and Wojtkiewicz, R. A. (2002) Difference, disparity, and race/ethnic bias in federal sentencing. *Journal of Quantitative Criminology*, 18(2), 189–211.

Frankenberg, R. (1993) *White Women, Race Matters: The Social Construction of Whiteness*. Minneapolis: University of Minnesota Press.

Kapoor, R., Dike, C., Burns, C., Carvalho, V. and Griffith, E. E. (2013) Cultural competence in correctional mental health. *International Journal of Law and Psychiatry*, 36(3), 273–280.

Mueller, Jennifer C. (2017) Producing colorblindness: Everyday mechanisms of white ignorance. *Social Problems*, 64(2), 219–238.

Pettit, B. and Western, B. (2004) Mass imprisonment and the life course: Race and class inequality in US incarceration. *American Sociological Review*, 69(2), 151–169.

Pew Charitable Trusts. (2008) *One in 100 Behind Bars in America*. 28 February.

Primm, A. B., Osher, F. C. and Gomez, M. B. (2005) Race and ethnicity, mental health services and cultural competence in the criminal justice system: Are we ready to change? *Community Mental Health Journal*, 41(5), 557–569.

Rennison, C. M. and Welchans, S. (2000) *Intimate Partner Violence: Bureau of Justice Statistics Special Report*. Washington, DC: US Department of Justice.

Rios, V. M. (2011) *Punished: Policing the Lives of Black and Latino Boys*. New York: New York University Press.

Skrentny, J. D. (2002) *The Minority Rights Revolution*. Cambridge, MA and London: Belknap University Press.

US Census Bureau. (2008) *American Community Survey*.

Wakefield, S. and Uggen, C. (2010) Incarceration and stratification. *Annual Review of Sociology*, 36, 387–406.

Western, B. (2006) *Punishment and Inequality in America*. New York: Russell Sage Foundation.

58

Responding to youth offending

Historical and current developments in practice

Tim Bateman

Introduction

It is frequently contended that crime is a social construction since criminality is determined by activities proscribed by law rather than anything inherent in the behaviour itself (Mahoney 2017). Legislative provisions, themselves, shift in line with social mores and political imperatives. For example, possession of what would today be classed as 'Class A' drugs was legal in England and Wales until the early part of the 20th century; conversely, the banning of what are referred to as 'legal highs' in 2016 increased the range of substance-related behaviours that can contravene the criminal law (Bateman 2017). What constitutes a crime in one period may not be considered so at another and vice versa. In a similar vein, it is often contended that the notion of childhood is also socially constructed rather than denoting a universal role (James et al. 1998). Expectations of children are variable and shaped by the cultural context in which they live rather than reflecting a constant understanding of pre-adulthood.

These insights have particular ramifications for understanding responses to youth offending since youth justice sits at the intersection of the two constructions. The meaning of youth justice is fluid and the contours of the system constantly shift to accommodate these fluctuations in meaning. The appropriate treatment of children who fall within that system's ambit is correspondingly a site of ongoing contestation and responses to youth offending and can, in other words, only be properly understood when 'considered within a broad socio-political context' (Hendrick 2015: 3). Indeed, from an historical perspective, adolescence has only recently been marked as a distinct developmental stage. As Muncie (2015: 51) argues, 'juvenile delinquency as a distinctive social problem' only emerged in the early part of the 19th century, as a consequence of increased political concern about the perceived threat to the social order posed by the children of the poor in the context of uncertainties that accompanied the triumph of the new urban, industrial, capitalist landscape (Hendrick 2015). Youth justice is thus a relatively recent phenomenon since prior to the discovery of 'young offenders', there could be no requirement for a separate system of justice for that group (Arthur 2010).

Youth justice: a recent invention

Until the mid-19th century, the criminal legislative framework and institutional provisions for children were identical to those for adults, though it was accepted that there should be some mitigation for youth (Arthur 2010). The development of separate custodial facilities for children from the 1850s onwards marked the beginning of a process of differentiation which culminated in the establishment, by early in the next century, of a separate system of justice for those who had yet to attain adulthood (Pitts 2005). Perhaps most significant in this regard was the creation of the juvenile court as the primary venue for criminal proceedings against children aged 7–16 years by the Children Act 1908. (The new court also dealt with care proceedings, an issue discussed below.) This defining moment came in the wake of the Probation of Offenders Act 1907 which had already introduced probation as a statutory function and provided for a body of specialist probation staff with a remit to work with children (Arthur 2010).

Narratives of welfare, justice, and beyond

With the bones of a youth justice architecture in place, questions could legitimately be asked about how best to deal with children who came to the attention of the new system. The ensuing debates are most commonly portrayed as undulating around paradigms of 'welfare' and 'justice', each reflecting a different understanding of the aetiology of youth offending and generating different sets of principles to inform direct work with children who engage in it (Hazel 2008). The welfare model understands delinquency as a manifestation of underlying need and emphasizes the considerable overlap in the backgrounds and characteristics of children in trouble and those who require care and protection. In this sense, the creation of the juvenile court accommodating *both* care and criminal proceedings is indicative of the welfarist leanings that underpinned the Children Act 1908. The justice model, by contrast, is less interested in the underlying causal mechanisms that give rise to offending behaviour which it maintains should be addressed outside of the criminal justice arena. It highlights the potential injustices that can arise for both populations of children where care and crime are conflated and endorses the principle of 'just deserts': criminal justice interventions should be proportional to the seriousness of the child's offending rather than the social circumstances which may give rise to it. The influence of a justice lobby is thus evident in the Children Act 1989 which established a family proceedings court separate from the juvenile court, severing the conceptual link between children who offend and those in need of care and support, and signalling a shift from welfarist assumptions to precepts of justice.

While the welfare-justice narrative provides a useful starting point for analysis, the dichotomy which it implies fails to capture the intricacies of policy and practice. In England and Wales, at least, the welfare-justice divide presents itself as a continuum wherein the nature of rehabilitative work with children at any given period will manifest elements of both approaches, sometimes in contradictory ways. The architects of the Children Act 1908 regarded the juvenile court as a mechanism for the 'rescue as well as the punishment of juveniles', embedding 'conflict and ambivalence' at the heart of youth justice from its inception (Gelsthorpe and Morris 1994: 951). Similarly, while the Children Act 1989 established a criminal jurisdiction for children separate from that dealing with care-related matters, it did not overturn the longstanding requirement, introduced by the Children and Young Persons Act (CYPA) 1933, that the juvenile court must have regard to the welfare of the child in determining sentence, thereby retaining a vestige of welfarism (Great Britain 1933).

It is apparent too that there are variants of both welfare and justice so that each paradigm may be consistent with radically different outcomes, leading to uncertainty as to how to characterize particular periods in terms of the model. For instance, the 'back to justice' movement of the 1980s is sometimes credited with having achieved a dramatic reduction in the number of children incarcerated during that decade (Allen 1991). Conversely, a rising custodial population over the following ten years has been attributed to a retreat from welfare (Hopkins Burke 2008). Furthermore, more recent developments suggest that the welfare-justice framework does not fully exhaust the range of available youth justice models. The New Labour government, elected in 1997, claimed that the introduction of a statutory aim for the youth justice system of preventing offending by children, dissolved the tensions inherent in the welfare-justice debate (Graham and Moore 2008). Commentators have also pointed to the recent influence of restorative justice, diversionary mechanisms and actuarial modes of practice, the latter predicated on addressing assessed 'risk factors' for offending, as adding to the discernible range of youth justice 'modes' (McAra and McVie 2015).

Such considerations suggest that credible analysis of the shifting sands on which responses to youth offending are founded should avoid simplistic categorization and overgeneralization. Nonetheless, when considering youth justice in the post-WW2 period, it is possible, without doing too much damage to the subtleties that would accompany a more detailed investigation, to identify four distinct chronological phases, each embodying different understandings of how children in conflict with the law should be treated.

The 'welfare imperative' and unintended consequences: 1950–1979

The establishment of juvenile court as a single jurisdiction for care and crime signalled an incipient commitment to a welfare model of justice, albeit one that retained possibilities of punishment, and the history of the first half of the 20th century can be seen as driven by a 'strong welfarist imperative' (Morgan and Newburn 2007: 1025).

The aforementioned principle that courts must have regard to the child's welfare in both criminal and care cases was enshrined in the CYPA 1933 (Great Britain 1933). The Act heralded a child-centred approach to children who broke the law that became increasingly ascendant in the following decades (Pitts 2005). This development, itself an embodiment of the optimism of an era of broader social reform and the rise of social work and allied professions, gained further impetus with a modest increase in the age of criminal responsibility from eight to ten years in 1963 (Bateman 2012a) and reached its apogee in the late 1960s.

The Labour administration that came to power in 1964 was heavily influenced by emerging social sciences that promised 'technical' solutions to the consequences of social inequality (Pitts 1988). In opposition the Party had commissioned the Longford Commission which developed a radical argument for the abolition of the juvenile court: if a child's offending was minor, branding him or her as a criminal was repugnant; if conversely, the behaviour involved was more serious, that was prima facie evidence of a need for skilled help and guidance (Labour Party's study group 1964). In either case, prosecution was indefensible. Consistent with that logic, the report recommended the abolition of the juvenile court and the subsequent 1965 white paper *The Child, the Family and the Young Offender* advocated the court's replacement by a system of family councils composed of social workers and other relevant childcare professionals (Bottoms 2002: 221). The distinction between responses to welfare need and youth crime was to be eliminated.

In the event, for reasons of political compromise, the juvenile court survived and, in retrospect, it is apparent that the Longford Commission represented the highpoint of welfarist aspirations. The CYPA 1969 embodied something of a fudge, introducing 'criminal' care orders and supervision orders intended to replace existing custodial provision in due course. The legislation was supported by a new form of intervention, known as 'intermediate treatment' (IT) (Morgan and Newburn 2007), through which the latest care-orientated disposals would be delivered. It was anticipated that IT would stimulate the withering away of incarceration as the superiority of treatment over punishment was demonstrated (Rutherford 1992).

The expectation that custody would waste away proved overly optimistic: the new measures were simply grafted onto to existing arrangements, expanding both the number of children removed from home and subject to supervision in the community (Thorpe et al. 1980). Indeed IT became part of the problem for a number of reasons.

The welfarist imperative dictated that IT should not be reserved for adjudicated offending since it addressed need rather than rigid contours of due process. In practice, IT evolved into groupwork programmes, potentially available to all disadvantaged youngsters, with no distinctions between care and criminal cases (Haines 1996). Conversely, the prospect that criminal justice would deliver treatment rather than punishment increased its attraction to police and other professionals, leading to net widening – a process whereby children are increasingly subject to formal processing for behaviour that would not previously have been criminalized. Where a child brought before the court had previously had IT, magistrates saw little merit in repeating such intervention at sentencing stage, particularly as they regarded IT as youth work, which offered enjoyable activities as a reward for offending. More punitive sentencing ensued. Finally, where IT had been tried on a voluntary basis, further offending was frequently considered by social work professionals as evidence of the failure on the part of the child to respond to treatment (Haines and Drakeford 1998). One study established that social workers were three times more likely than probation officers to recommend custody (Thorpe et al. 1980).

These unintended consequences combined to ensure that the number of children convicted of criminal offences rose, from 79,300 in 1974 to 96,000 in 1978 (Home Office 1984), while youth imprisonment rose exponentially to a level that Millham (1997) described as being without historical precedent.

Back to justice and minimum intervention: 1980–1992

The apparently punitive outcomes associated with welfare led to increasing disillusion among some practitioners, stimulating the development of specialist juvenile justice teams who rejected the 'generic social work dogma of the 1970s' (Rutherford 1992: 20) which they considered to be imbued with an undue focus on deficits in the individual child and his or her family. Staff within those teams sought to replace the 'profound indifference' (Haines and Drakeford 1998: 50) to context associated with such individualistic forms of explanation, by an interest in evidence as to the role of social and systemic structures. Academics at Lancaster University, in particular, developed a critique of welfare alongside promotion of a model that understood the youth justice system as a series of related decision points, susceptible to practitioner influence though effective gatekeeping. Such criticism of welfarist pretensions was buttressed by a recognition of the utility of justice-premised arguments which contended that compulsory intervention should never exceed that which was proportionate to the gravity of the child's offending. Given the minor nature of most youth crime, this amounted to a call for less intrusion by criminal justice agencies in children's lives (Thorpe et al. 1980).

This new breed of practitioner combined an antipathy to welfare interventions whose rehabilitative benefits were unproven and potentially damaging, a belief that children, if left to themselves would grow out of crime, advocacy of minimum necessary intervention, and a 'crusading zeal' (Allen 1991: 49) against the use of child imprisonment. A radical, vociferous, occupational culture that took inspiration from Edwin Shur's defence of 'radical non-intervention', rapidly emerged whose tenets were: 'Abolish the work, abolish custody, do your best for the kids' (practitioner cited in Haines and Drakeford 1998: 56). Achieving desired outcomes, however, sometimes required establishing credibility with the very agencies – notably the police, the courts, and social services – responsible for net widening and incarceration. Such tensions led to the development in some areas of a 'correctional curriculum' (Denman 1982) – effectively offence-focused work – that might prove more attractive to sentencers, and other decision makers, than vague notions of social work treatment.

Paradoxically, this model of practice met with approval from the Conservative government of Margaret Thatcher, which had come to power on a law and order agenda and was thus potentially more sympathetic to the language of justice than welfare. Pitts points out that Thatcherite project was also wedded to a reduction in state expenditure. A contracting youth justice population helped 'to balance the books' (Pitts 2003: 81). Certainly, government encouraged cautioning rather than prosecution and introduced statutory thresholds which had to be crossed before custody was imposed on young people in 1982 and again in 1991 (Rutherford 2002).

The result of this alliance was a spectacular reduction in child convictions, from 89,900 in 1980 to 24,600 in 1991, accompanied by an even sharper fall in custodial sentences, from 7,500 to 1,400 (Home Office 1989, 1993). As noted above, the apparent success of the justice model received systemic recognition with the separation of criminal and care jurisdictions in 1989.

Tough justice and a risk-oriented lens: 1993–2008

Any complacency that punitive approaches had been superseded was rapidly dispelled when, in wake of the murder of two-year-old James Bulger by two boys aged ten in 1993, levels of child imprisonment ballooned, rising by 90% over the next 15 years. Prosecutions also soared even though detected youth crime continued to fall, signifying the abandonment of diversionary practice (Nacro 2003). The Bulger case is frequently regarded as a catalyst that crystallized an already emerging shift in political mood in alignment with a 'new punitiveness' that triggered an array of successive legislative changes. These reduced entitlements to bail, lowered the minimum age for custody in the (now renamed) youth court from 15 to 12 years, and made it easier to lock up older children for longer (Goldson 2002). Although a clear reversal of trends in the previous decade, this was no reversion to welfare, but proof that justice tenets could come in lenient or tough guises.

The punitive turn, unlike the earlier back to justice movement, was not instigated by practitioners and there is evidence that youth justice staff remained committed to principles of 'progressive minimalism' while custody rose (Haines and Drakeford 1998). But it would be unrealistic to suppose that front-line staff could remain immune to the 'baleful influence of the punitive climate' (Bateman 2005: 99). The challenge to practice was all the greater because of limitations of the justice-philosophy. The erosion of welfarist modes of understanding youth crime was consistent with a denial of *any* extenuating social context for the behaviour of children who broke the law and the adoption of increasingly harsh measures in the absence of that context. The call to address welfare need outside the justice system appeared shallow against a background of public sector cuts, and attracted accusations of 'benign neglect' (Cohen 1988: 102) that made an interventionist stance more likely the moment youth crime became a burning political issue. In the event, such politicization, when it occurred, coincided with an increasing tendency within the criminal justice arena towards 'managerialism' that reduced the space for reflective practice by equating effectiveness with adherence to centrally mandated national standards and process-driven interventions (Eadie and Canton 2002). This propensity was taken to new heights with the election of a New Labour government in 1997.

Labour's reforms are sometimes credited as sufficiently radical to institute a 'new youth justice' (Goldson 2000) but this overlooks continuities with what went before. Fionda (1999) argues that the Crime and Disorder Act 1998 repackaged much of the previous administration's approach: the main impact of the shift in government was to consolidate existing interventionist and punitive tendencies. The title of the white paper preceding the legislation, *No More Excuses*, made plain that Labour had no sympathy for welfarist assumptions and the content extolled the virtues of holding children accountable for their behaviour, early formal youth justice intervention to 'nip offending in the bud', and 'effective' custody (Home Office 1997, paragraphs 5.15 and 6.1), assumptions indicative of a harsh justice-orientated paradigm, despite the government's protestations to have moved beyond the welfare-justice debate.

New Labour was however responsible for at least three important, if not always welcome, innovations. Managerialist oversight of practice was consolidated though the proliferation of performance indicators that required reporting more than 3,000 data items to the newly created Youth Justice Board (National Audit Office 2010). Service delivery was relocated from social services and probation to multi-agency youth offending teams (YOTs), that included police, health, and education representation, and guaranteed that any vestiges of progressive minimalism among practitioners would struggle to survive (Souhami 2007). Finally, addressing assessed risk factors became the centrally mandated priority for youth justice practice through the introduction of standardized assessment processes that gave numeric scores to children's risk of reoffending and national standards that linked supervisory intervention to those assessments. This was a model that located the causes of offending in children's deficits and saw rehabilitation as fixing those deficits. Practice increasingly conformed to the precepts of what has been called an actuarial mode of youth justice that views the child as a repository of risk and carefully calibrates intervention 'in proportion to risk posed' (McAra 2010: 291), thereby limiting, considerably, scope for professional discretion (Pitts 2001).

Contemporary youth justice: 2008–2017

A further, and final, policy and practice about-face can be discerned with the introduction, in 2008, of a government target to reduce the number of children entering the youth justice system for the first time, by 20% by 2020 (Home Office 2008). The new measure had immediate impact and was met within 12 months of its introduction, indicating how adept the system had become at responding to performance indicators. Between 2007 and 2016, the number of first time entrants (FTEs) time fell dramatically by 84% from 110,801 to 18,263. There has been a corresponding decline in the overall volume of detected youth crime, with a beneficial knock-on effect on the average child custodial population, which fell from 2,932 in 2007/2008 to 959 in 2015–2016 (Bateman 2017).

Such large-scale reductions are suggestive of a 'reinvention of diversion' that mirrors in important respects trends during the 1980s (Smith 2014), confirming perhaps Bernard's (1992) thesis that youth justice policy tends to progress through alternately harsh and lenient cycles. Given Pitt's argument in relation to the Thatcher government's tolerance of minimum intervention, the timing of the introduction of the FTE target as recession kicked in, and governments subsequently affirmed the necessity of austerity measures, is hard to ignore (Bateman 2012b).

This is not however simply an instance of 'back to the future'. There is a distinct absence, for instance, of a practitioner movement driving current diversionary impulses, which derive largely from centrally imposed targets. No doubt these impulses have allowed a more lenient and child-friendly practice but that practice, arguably, lacks a coherent philosophical basis such as that which informed the practitioner lobby of 30 years ago. Despite more frequent references to the welfare of the child, a desire to realign youth justice with children's services, and an incipient interest in future-oriented, strengths-based practice that draws on desistance theory (McNeill 2009), 'risk thinking' – concerned with past offending behaviour and addressing the risk factors that are assessed as having given rise to it – continues to exert a powerful sway over much diversionary activity, imbuing it with an interventionist tone that distinguishes it from the minimalism of the Thatcher era. Rather than aiming to 'leave kids alone wherever possible' as Schur (1973: 155) advocated, rehabilitation in contemporary youth justice often means diverting children into informal risk-focused programmes that look, and are experienced as being, similar to those that previously accompanied formal sanctions. There are, as Kelly and Armitage (2015) observe, diverse forms of diversion.

Conclusion: conflict and ambivalence unresolved?

The foregoing brief overview of youth justice history over the past 70 or so years demonstrates, if nothing else, that rehabilitation of children in trouble cannot be understood as a neutral endeavour. Although contemporary debates in youth justice are less frequently framed in terms of the competing principles associated with welfare and justice, those tensions have never been fully resolved. Indeed, developments since the early 1990s have tended to mitigate against philosophical clarity in this arena with the result that youth justice policy and practice is vulnerable to sharp periodic reversals triggered by pragmatic responses to short-term pre-occupations rather than the long-term benefits for children's well-being. The conflict and ambivalence that Gelsthorpe and Morris (1994) detected in youth justice's founding moment are no less present more than 100 years after the creation of the juvenile court.

References

Allen, R. (1991) Out of jail: The reduction in the use of penal custody for male juveniles 1981–1988. *Howard Journal of Criminal Justice*, 30(1), 30–52.

Arthur, R. (2010) *Young Offenders and the Law*. London: Routledge.

Bateman, T. (2005) Reducing child imprisonment: A systemic challenge. *Youth Justice*, 5(2), 91–105.

Bateman, T. (2012a) *Criminalising Children for No Good Purpose: The Age of Criminal Responsibility in England and Wales*. London: NAYJ.

Bateman, T. (2012b) Who pulled the plug? Towards an explanation of the fall in child imprisonment in England and Wales. *Youth Justice*, 12(1), 36–52.

Bateman, T. (2017) *The State of Youth Justice 2017*. London: NAYJ.

Bernard, T. J. (1992) *The Cycle of Juvenile Justice*. Oxford: Oxford University Press.

Bottoms, A. (2002) On the decriminalisation of the English juvenile courts. In J. Muncie, G. Hughes and E. McLaughlin (Eds.), *Youth Justice: Critical Readings*. London: Sage Publications, pp. 216–227.

Cohen, S. (1988) *Against Criminology*. Abingdon: Routledge.

Denman, G. (1982) *Intensive Intermediate Treatment with Juvenile Offenders: A Handbook of Assessment and Groupwork Practice*. Lancaster: Lancaster University.

Eadie, T. and Canton, R. (2002) Practising in a context of ambivalence: The challenge for youth justice workers. *Youth Justice*, 2(1), 14–26.

Fionda, J. (1999) New Labour, old hat: Youth justice and the crime and disorder act 1998. *Criminal Law Review*, 36–47.

Gelsthorpe, L. and Morris, A. (1994) Juvenile justice 1945–1992. In M. Maguire, R. Morgan and R. Reiner (Eds.), *The Oxford Handbook of Criminology*. Oxford: Oxford University Press, pp. 949–993.

Goldson, B. (Ed.). (2000) *The New Youth Justice*. Lyme Regis: Russell House.

Goldson, B. (2002) New punitiveness: The politics of child incarceration. In J. Muncie, G. Hughes and E. McLaughlin (Eds.), *Youth Justice: Critical Readings*. London: Sage Publications, pp. 386–400.

Graham, J. and Moore, C. (2008) Beyond welfare versus justice: Juvenile justice in England and Wales. In J. Junger-Tas and S. H. Decker (Eds.), *International Handbook of Juvenile Justice*, 1st edition. New York: Springer, pp. 65–92.

Great Britain. (1933) *Children and Young Persons Act 1933: George V*. London: HMSO, Chapter 12.

Haines, K. (1996) *Understanding Modern Juvenile Justice*. Aldershot: Avebury.

Haines, K. and Drakeford, M. (1998) *Young People and Youth Justice*. Basingstoke: Palgrave Macmillan.

Hazel, N. (2008) *Cross National Comparison of Youth Justice*. London: Youth Justice Board.

Hendrick, H. (2015) Histories of youth crime and justice. In B. Goldson and J. Muncie (Eds.), *Youth Crime and Justice*, 2nd edition. London: Sage Publications, pp. 30–36.

Home Office. (1984) *Criminal Statistics for England and Wales 1983*. Cmnd 9349. London: HMSO.

Home Office. (1989) *Criminal Statistics: England and Wales 1988*. Cmnd 847. London: HMSO.

Home Office. (1993) *Criminal Statistics: England and Wales 1992*. Cmnd. 2410. London: HMSO.

Home Office. (1997) *No More Excuses: A New Approach to Tackling Youth Crime in England and Wales*. London: Home Office.

Home Office. (2008) *Youth Crime Action Plan*. London: Home Office.

Hopkins Burke, R. (2008) *Young People, Crime and Justice*. Cullompton: Willan Publishing.

James, A., Jenks, C. and Prout, A. (1998) *Theorizing Childhood*. Cambridge: Polity Press.

Kelly, L. and Armitage, V. (2015) Diverse diversions: Youth justice reform, localized practices and a 'new interventionist diversion'. *Youth Justice*, 15(2), 117–133.

Labour Party's Study Group. (1964) *Crime: A Challenge to Us All*. London: Labour Party.

Mahoney, I. (2017) Definitions and counting of crime. In J. Harding, P. Davies and G. Mair (Eds.), *An Introduction to Criminal Justice*. London: Sage Publications, pp. 40–60.

McAra, L. (2010) Models of youth justice. In D. Smith (Ed.), *A New Response to Youth Crime*. Cullompton: Willan Publishing, pp. 287–317.

McAra, L. and McVie, S. D. (2015) The case for diversion and minimum necessary intervention. In B. Goldson and J. Muncie (Eds.), *Youth Crime and Justice*, 2nd edition. London: Sage Publications, pp. 119–136.

McNeill, F. (2009) Supervising young offenders: What works and what's right. In M. Barry and F. McNeill (Eds.), *Youth Offending and Youth Justice*. London: Jessica Kingsley, pp. 132–153.

Millham, S. (1997) Intermediate treatment: Symbol or solution? *Youth in Society*, 26, 22–24.

Morgan, R. and Newburn, T. (2007) Youth justice. In M. Maguire, R. Morgan and R. Reiner (Eds.), *The Oxford Handbook of Criminology*, 4th edition. Oxford: Oxford University Press.

Muncie, J. (2015) *Youth and Crime*, 3rd edition. London: Sage Publications.

Nacro. (2003) *A Failure of Justice: Reducing Child Imprisonment*. London: Nacro.

National Audit Office. (2010) *The Youth Justice System in England and Wales: Reducing Offending by Young People*. London: NAO.

Pitts, J. (1988) *The Politics of Juvenile Crime*. London: Sage Publications.

Pitts, J. (2001) Korrectional karaoke: New labour and the zombification of youth justice. *Youth Justice*, 1(2), 3–16.

Pitts, J. (2003) *The New Politics of Youth Crime: Discipline or Solidarity*. Lyme Regis: Russell House.

Pitts, J. (2005) The recent history of youth justice in England and Wales. In T. Bateman and J. Pitts (Eds.), *The RHP Companion to Youth Justice*. Lyme Regis: Russell House, pp. 2–11.

Rutherford, A. (1992) *Growing Out of Crime*, 2nd edition. Winchester: Waterside Press.

Rutheford, A. (2002) Youth justice and social inclusion. *Youth Justice*, 2(2), 100–107.

Schur, E. (1973) *Radical Non Intervention: Rethinking the Delinquency Problem*. Englewood Cliffs: Prentice Hall.

Smith, R. (2014) Reinventing diversion. *Youth Justice*, 14(2), 109–121.

Souhami, A. (2007) *Transforming Youth Justice: Occupational Change and Identity*. Cullompton: Willan Publishing.

Thorpe, D. H., Smith, D., Green, C. J. and Paley, J. H. (1980) *Out of Care: The Community Support of Juvenile Offenders*. London: George Allen and Unwin.

Youth justice in Wales 59

Susan Thomas

Introduction

In recent years, increasing attention has been given to whether youth justice policy and practice in England and in Wales are different. The National Assembly for Wales was created in 1999 and the ensuing devolution settlement for Wales contained 20 areas for which the Welsh Government would have responsibility. This included social policy, but not policing and criminal justice (including youth justice), which remained 'reserved' to the UK Government (Davies and Williams 2009). While youth justice is not devolved in Wales, there is a strong interface with devolved services, because some of these agencies are statutory members of youth offending teams (YOTs), notably education, health and children's services, and others, such as housing, are providers of services to which young people in the youth justice system may require access. Youth justice is in some respects an anomaly as the Welsh Government has responsibility for all other areas of children and young people's policy (Drakeford 2010).

The opportunity which devolution created saw the emergence of strategic differences between Wales and England. Welsh Government policies for children and young people are based on social inclusion and access to rights. For example, *Extending Entitlement* (National Assembly for Wales 2000) identified ten entitlements which all young people in Wales aged 11 to 15 years should receive, including young people in the justice system (Welsh Assembly Government 2004). The United Nations Convention on the Rights of the Child

(UNCRC)[1] was incorporated into domestic legislation through the Rights of Children and Young Persons (Wales) Measure 2011.

Since December 2010, the UK Government has had due regard for the Convention, but has not incorporated it into statute, as in Wales. However, investigation into the extent to which due regard is applied, found that government departments did not always consider compliance with the UNCRC when developing policy and legislation, citing the Ministry of Justice amongst others (Joint Committee on Human Rights 2015). The Convention contains a series of rights (in the form of 54 articles) which promote the 'best interests' of children (article 3) and young people, 'non-discrimination' (article 2), and 'participation' in matters which affect them (article 12). Welsh Government policy has impacted on youth justice, with Haines (2010) suggesting that it has been 'dragonised', meaning that it has features which relate to the wider Welsh Government agenda of rights and entitlements (Drakeford 2010; Edwards and Hughes 2009; Muncie 2011), in contrast to England, which at the time, was characterized as punitive, risk-led, deficit-focused and unfairly responsibilizing children (Goldson 2002; Case 2006; Muncie 2008; Pitts 2008; Gray 2009).

The need to reconcile the approaches of the UK Government and Welsh Government resulted in the *All Wales Youth Offending Strategy (AWYOS)* (Welsh Assembly Government/YJB 2004). It integrated the different government viewpoints, set out an approach on which there was consensus about youth justice, laid the foundations for the strategic direction in Wales and incorporated how devolved services could support and contribute to the prevention of offending (Cross et al. 2003). This gave youth justice in Wales its own identity (National Assembly for Wales 2009). However, there were differing opinions about how well the UK Government and Welsh Government viewpoints were integrated. Williams (2007) suggested there had been limited accommodation of the Welsh Government perspective and Haines (2010) wrote that while the *AWYOS* was presented as a joint document there was a lack of clear alignment of the strategies of the UK and Welsh Governments. For example, public protection, early intervention, and appropriate punishment were UK Government goals, whereas maximum diversion, minimal formal intervention, and penal reduction were Welsh Government objectives.

However, rights-based principles were included in the *AWYOS*, such as treating young people as 'children first and offenders second' and enabling children and young people to participate in decisions which affect them (Welsh Government/YJB 2004). The commitment to 'children first, offenders second' signalled the biggest difference, when comparing the policies of Wales to England (Cross et al. 2003; Welsh Assembly Government/YJB 2004; Haines 2010). The *AWYOS* stated there was no contradiction between protecting the welfare of children who had offended and the prevention of offending and reoffending (Welsh Government/YJB 2004), indicating a welfare-based approach, where reduced offending would be a by-product of improved well-being. This contrasted with *No More Excuses*, New Labour's vision for the youth justice system at the time, which contended there was no 'conflict between protecting the welfare of a young offender and preventing that individual from offending again' (Home Office 1997: 7). This was a justice-based policy, which separated addressing offending behaviour from concerns about welfare.

'Children first' embodied that welfare should be a predominant concern in Wales. A Welsh Government cabinet paper in 2011 stressed the importance of addressing the 'holistic needs of children and young people, rather than their offending behaviour' in order to improve their welfare, well-being, and offending needs (Welsh Assembly Government 2011: 3). Policy concentrated on strengthening the support local authorities and others should provide to young people in contact with the justice system, to realize their rights and extend entitlements. Consultations took place on a Welsh Prevention of Offending Bill (Welsh Government 2012, 2014), which aimed to reinforce the planning and accountability from mainstream services in improving outcomes for young people. However, the Welsh Government withdrew the Bill shortly after the Silk Commission[2] recommended that youth justice should be devolved (Commission on Devolution in Wales 2014). The *AWYOS* was succeeded by *Children and Young People First* (Welsh Government/YJB 2014), which continued to adopt the 'children first' principle and to present a positive and distinctly Welsh approach to youth justice (Haines and Case 2015).

Delivering youth justice in Wales

Whilst the *AWYOS* and *Children and Young People First* sets out a strategic commitment to 'children first', it is important to consider whether this is reflected and delivered in front-line practice. As a principle 'children first' could be open to different interpretations. Haines and Case (2015) suggest the key ingredients are that decision-making should be child-focused, child-friendly, and child-appropriate, with opportunities for diversion from the formal system and promotion of positive behaviour and outcomes. However, as indicated the Welsh Government also stressed the importance of welfare and well-being as significant considerations. For example, a Welsh Government cabinet paper on the devolution of youth justice (Welsh Assembly Government 2011) explored whether children and young people in the youth justice system who met the 'children in need' criteria under the Children Act 1989[3] should be directly supported by Children's Services. The paper also contained proposals to ensure that all children and young people remanded or sentenced to custody received looked-after status (as defined by the Children Act 1989). The Legal Aid, Sentencing Punishment of Offenders Act 2012 introduced this provision for remanded young people in England and Wales, but the UK Government had no plans to extend the arrangements to sentenced young people. Further, a Welsh Government green paper on youth justice discussed how the system could be more effective in improving pre-court and community provision through preventative interventions (Welsh Government 2014). These examples raise the question of whether there is a more welfare-led and less risk-based practice in Wales.

Some commentators concluded that there is a welfare culture in some YOTs in Wales (Cross et al. 2003; Field 2006). However, when compared to studies of YOTs in England, the findings were similar in that despite a post Crime and Disorder Act 1998 shift from wider social welfare-orientated practice to the narrower focus of addressing offending behaviour (the 'punitive turn'), concern for young people's welfare continues to be important, is not ignored, and well-being needs are addressed in tandem with offending behaviour (Burnett and Appleton 2004; Ellis and Boden 2005; Field 2006; Briggs 2013). This does not indicate there is a clear-cut national divide with Wales taking an exclusively 'children first' approach and England a wholly 'offender focused' one, suggesting that team culture and practice is far more nuanced.

Further, it is not clear whether the 'children first' approach in Wales is derived from 'top-down' implementation of national policy (initially the *AWYOS*), or 'bottom-up' team culture. Practitioners can be aware of a policy, but this does not mean familiarity with its contents or how it applies to them, as they rely on their managers to draw attention to relevant issues (Thomas 2015). Whilst the *AWYOS* set out the expectations of what youth justice should look like, it did not detail how 'children first' practice might be achieved and what would explicitly demarcate practice in Wales from that in England. *Children and Young People First* (Welsh Government/YJB 2014) provides a more explicit framework, based on several key activities. These are a well-designed partnership approach, early intervention, prevention and diversion, reducing reoffending, effective use of custody, and resettlement and reintegration at the end of a sentence.

Discussion of practice culture within YOTs has focused on the nature of multi-agency working. The change from youth justice being the responsibility of a single agency (children's services) to a multi-agency service (containing criminal justice and welfare agencies) has not guaranteed that the statutory agencies which make up the YOT (the police, probation service, health, education, and social care) would have or adopt a social work ethic (youth justice's traditional base). Multi-agency working introduced different ideas about how to address offending behaviour (Souhami 2007) and the assortment of agencies and individuals involved and the negotiation this requires around practice (Field 2015) did not ensure all would necessarily be pro 'children first' or understand what it meant.

Further, whilst welfare-based practice was claimed, some of the actions taken by practitioners, whilst justified as being in young people's 'best interests', have consequences that place them at risk of greater criminal justice sanctions, punishment, and custody. Field and Nelken's (2010) research (in Wales) found that a young person's eligibility for a welfare-based response from the YOT depended on the practitioner feeling they could work with them (because of the demonstration of a positive attitude) and moral judgements about the offence (understandable in the circumstances). In contrast if practitioners were less well disposed to young people, they would highlight 'deeds' rather than 'needs', and describe young people's backgrounds in terms of 'risk and hopelessness'. Practice shifts are also discernible with breach becoming an accepted and unquestioned norm in modern youth justice practice and erosion of the pre-YOT 'crusading zeal' to divert children and young people from custody (Bateman 2011), resulting in custody being recommended if not directly, then by inference (Field and Nelken 2010).

The system has also been manipulated in the interests of justice or welfare. For example, Asset, the youth justice assessment tool,[4] required practitioners to numerically score criminogenic risks and to develop intervention plans to address high-scoring areas. Risks would be deflated to downgrade a problem or inflated to ensure needs were addressed (Briggs 2013), which could place children at greater risk of receiving more contact with the criminal justice system than was warranted and of breach should they fail to comply (Phoenix 2009). So, although there might be a policy aspiration to deliver a 'children first' service, the reality is more challenging. Practitioners can be selective about what sort of service they provide to children and young people irrespective of consequence. Concern about children's welfare and well-being are not necessarily always preserved in practice and actions may not always be in their 'best interests' even though they are presented as such by practitioners, either because of individual beliefs about how practice should be delivered or because the youth justice system has driven practice in a particular direction.

The dragon and Saint George

In terms of testing this out further, a comparative study was undertaken of two YOTs in England and two in Wales to ascertain whether their attitudes and values were similar or different, and to establish if a 'children first' approach has primacy in Wales, and if so, what that it might mean in practice. Sixty-five practitioners took part in surveys and interviews, which were evenly split between the two countries. An initial ranking exercise was developed from the five typologies of youth justice identified by Cavadino and Dignan (2009). These are welfare, justice, minimum intervention, restorative, and neo-correctionalism.

In summary, welfare approaches focus on the needs of young people and what is in their best interests, with the aim of assisting those who offend to get appropriate help and support rather than being punished for their actions. Justice responses tackle deeds rather than welfare needs and focus on culpability and proportionate punishment. Minimum intervention is based on the notion that contact with the criminal justice system can place young people at risk of engaging in further criminal activity, which can be reduced by 'managing the system' to reduce the risk of criminalization, the use of unwarranted interventions, avoidance of prosecution, and use of custody. Restorative justice places emphasis on the harm done to victims by crime and of young people making amends either directly or indirectly for their actions. The prevention of offending is predominant in neo-correctionalism, which is characterized by early intervention to address antisocial behaviour and crime, the identification and delivery of effective interventions, and the minimization and management of risk (Cavadino and Dignan 2006).

The ranking exercise took the distinctive features from these approaches and presented them in ten statements, which practitioners were asked to list in order of importance to give an indication of practice priorities. When the responses were aggregated, it showed that the top three rankings in England and in Wales were 'acting in the best interests' of children and young people, 'protecting the public', and 'early intervention', whereas at the bottom of the scale only 'promote public confidence' was common to both. 'Prevent offending' was ranked lower (fourth) than best interests in both countries. Where there were more pronounced differences, it was because there was greater priority of 'public protection', 'proving a proportionate response' and 'risk-led' practices in England, in contrast to Wales where there was more emphasis on young people 'taking responsibility for their actions' and 'improving parenting'. Using 'restorative approaches' were given equal status in both countries. If acting in the best interest of children and young people is taken as a proxy measure of the intent to deliver a 'children first' approach, this analysis demonstrated that practitioners (in England and in Wales) had very similar views about its importance.

It is also noteworthy that the Welsh YOTs showed a greater inclination to 'responsibilization' which is a factor associated with neo-correctionalism and risk-based culture than rights-based practice. The notion of responsibility is viewed very differently in each approach. Neo-correctionalism regards offending as a matter of individual choice for which individuals must take responsibility and face appropriate punishment when transgressions occur (Cavadino and Dignan 2006). Whereas responsibility in rights-based terms relates to the role agencies and government have in ensuring that individuals have unconditional access to their entitlements (Goldson 2002). Neo-correctionalism suggests that an individual may become less deserving of help and support because of their actions, whereas rights-related approaches take the opposite approach and seek to ensure that rights are delivered regardless. The stance adopted will influence the way in which the criminal justice system responds to children and young people, how they are treated, and what opportunities are made available to them.

Qualitative interviews revealed more about the ethos of the four teams and their characteristics. England A had gone through a profound cultural change because a new manager questioned the extent to which the YOT was achieving good outcomes for children and young people, as there were high rates of use of custody and breach, which suggested otherwise. An inspection report by Her Majesty's Inspectorate of Probation (HMIP) also drew attention to the lack of attention to children's welfare in team practice. The YOT manager redirected the team to deliver a more child-centred approach, with priorities on building relationships with children, connecting them to educational opportunities, and promoting their participation in decision-making, as strategies to reduce recidivism. It is noteworthy that this change in approach did not arise from central prescription or a national strategy advocating for it, but because the manager wanted the team to be more child-focused and to achieve better outcomes for the children and young people it was supervising.

Wales A had also experienced a change in approach, although not as profound. The YOT had traditionally taken a predominantly risk-led approach to practice, but an inspection of the service highlighted that certain welfare practices were not as prominent as they should have been. As a result, the YOT was moving towards more holistic practice and endeavouring to find a balance between using risk to identify need and target resources effectively and the importance of safeguarding the children they were working with. England B had a consistent ethos, without any obvious change. The stability of the team, shared values, and cohesive working practices contributed to this. Those interviewed described the team as child-focused with offending being a by-product of unmet welfare needs, which stood in contrast to the possible stereotype of an English YOT being solely risk-focused. England B also stressed the importance of relational working with children and of working with mainstream services as necessary to improve outcomes for children.

In Wales B, practitioners described the team as welfare focused, but there was division about the extent to which this should be the case and how welfare needs were balanced with justice considerations. The YOT had been criticized in a past inspection for being too welfare-orientated and recommended to adopt more risk-focused practice. However, there were very different opinions within the team about whether children's well-being and welfare or risk management and minimization should have primacy. This created tensions which did not appear to have been totally resolved. Consequently, a different ethos flourished and a wide range of ideas about how practice should be delivered were co-located in the same team.

These findings raise the question of whether there can be complete acceptance across a team of a specific culture or approach; in each team, there was at least one practitioner who questioned whether this was possible. Practice might look similar on the surface, but fundamental differences existed in the style of delivery and the rationale for it. For example, one of the contested areas was in the use of breach – how many chances should be given to a child/young person to comply. Each practitioner thought their own practice was correct and were critical of colleagues who they considered to be too punitive or lax. There did not appear to be a clear-cut model of practice which existed in Wales which was distinct from that in England. There were similar ideologies between the four YOTs and no obvious divergence between the countries; rather the site of any individual difference was at a local level or between individuals within the team. Wales did not wholly emerge as welfare-focused nor England as purely risk-focused; both approaches co-existed and practice was adapted at various points to one or other approach. There was consensus amongst the four YOTs that 'best interests' should be a priority, with the aforementioned caveats about how it is interpreted, that it may mean different things to different people, and that responses to children and young people should go beyond the narrow confines of simply addressing their offending behaviour. All YOTs stressed the importance of relational working to get to know children and young people, understand their backgrounds and behaviour, to establish trust, and form a basis to effectively engage with and assist them. None of the YOTs laid claim to their practice being rights-led, but all considered that it reflected a 'children first' philosophy. The YOT manager emerged as very influential as they could mediate national policy in favour of a particular approach (as in England A) and determined and directed what they wanted their team's practice to look like. HMIP inspections also played an important function in regulating practice; two YOTs were recommended by the Inspectorate to become more welfare-orientated and one more risk-led; all three were at various stages of trying to achieve this.

Examples of a 'children first' approach

Pre-court diversion

The Swansea Bureau was a practitioner-led initiative developed in 2009, which applied 'children first' principles to pre-court diversion (Haines et al. 2013). It was based on a model of multi-agency pre-court diversion which was established in Northamptonshire in the 1993, involving the police and youth justice service. The Northamptonshire model included the options of using informal actions (now known as non-criminal disposals) and offers of voluntary interventions to address the causes and impact of offending. It was cited as a model of good practice by the Audit Commission in 1996 (Kemp et al. 2002). The Swansea Bureau had similar features. It adopted a 'children first' approach as it diverted children and young people who had committed low-level first-time offences from the system thereby avoiding unnecessary criminalization. This aligns with article 40 of the UNCRC, which states that a variety of proportionate options should be available to children and young people to prevent them from entering the criminal justice system (UNICEF 1990). The development of the Swansea Bureau was significant as it was before the wider system moved in a more diversionary direction because of the Legal Aid Sentencing and Punishment of Offenders Act 2012. Evaluation of the Swansea Bureau demonstrated that it accelerated reductions in first time entrants to the youth justice system and showed promising results in reducing offending (see Haines et al. 2013 for further discussion).

The youth justice community in Wales is a small one, with the key actors well known to one another and meeting regularly in a range of related fora. There are 17 YOTs; the Welsh YOT managers have their own association – YOT Managers Cymru; the Wales Youth Justice Advisory Panel is jointly hosted by the YJB and Welsh Government and advises on policy and implementation. A YJB-led practice forum (Hwb Doeth), supported by the Welsh Centre for Crime and Social Justice, YOTs, and the Welsh Government encourages practice development and evaluation. These arrangements enabled multiple discussions about the Swansea Bureau in formal and informal settings, and increased confidence in it as an approach. As a result, other Bureaus were established across Southern Wales[5] in 2011 and to YOTs in west, mid, and north Wales in 2014. It could therefore be said that Wales has a national approach to pre-court diversion, underpinned by the principle of 'children first'. The size of the youth justice community in Wales was key and it is debatable whether this would have been achieved in the same way with around 140 YOTs in England and the multitude of agencies and individuals involved. Further, the scale of youth justice in Wales enabled focused examination of practice, so there was more certainty about how pre-court diversion was delivered and the principles which underpinned it, which has not been captured in the same way on a YOT-by-YOT basis for England.

Enhanced case management

One of the challenges for the youth justice system has been how to address the needs of children and young people who progress further into the youth justice system, who have complex needs and may be a risk to themselves or others, but also vulnerable because of traumatic histories and experiences. This has become more acute as the effectiveness of pre-court diversion has resulted in a distilled population of young people with these characteristics occupying the youth justice system. Complexity means that young people are experiencing several co-existing and interrelated difficulties, which cannot be resolved by a single agency. They may have a long-term history of problems with mental health conditions, cognitive disabilities, problematic drug or alcohol use, and a background of emotional trauma and adverse childhood experiences (Rosengard et al. 2007).

Those in the youth justice system may struggle to engage with what is required of them, placing them at risk of breach and increasing criminal sanctions. Reoffending rates are high for those with cumulative experience of the system; 76% for those who have committed 11 offences or more, compared to 25% for those without a previous criminal history (YJB and Ministry of Justice (2018).

YJB Cymru recognized this, and was interested in the Trauma Recovery Model (TRM), which was developed by Skuse and Matthew (2015) for use in a Secure Children's Home, and whether it could be applied for use in the community. This led to the development of the Enhanced Case Management (ECM) project which is a trauma-informed approach to practice, targeting young people who repeatedly offend and who have complex needs. The ECM is the application of the TRM in a community justice setting. A key component is that it is clinical psychology-led and underpinned by multi-agency case formulation. Clinical supervision is used to support YOT case workers to tailor and sequence interventions to the young person's developmental and mental health needs, recognizing the trauma and adverse events they have experienced (Cordis Bright 2017). YJB Cymru developed the ECM approach in several YOTs, with the support of the Welsh Government, the Wales Forensic Adolescent Consultation and Treatment Service (FACTS), South Wales Police and Crime Commissioner, and Public Health Wales.

The ECM is a highly individualized approach as case formulations are bespoke to the young person and their experiences; youth justice interventions and methods of working are tailored to be the most appropriate and effective for that individual. It is not a deficit model, which responds to children as a problem, but a supportive one, which helps them to build resilience to cope with the problems and stresses they have experienced. This aligns to article 40 of the UNCRC which identifies that assisting young people to lead a constructive role in life is a necessary component of post-offending reintegration and article 39, that providing appropriate treatment for those who have experienced neglect, exploitation, or abuse because of adverse childhood experiences and events, contributes to this. Evaluation of the ECM pilot found there were improvements in young people's relationships, higher levels of engagement, and enhanced outcomes which were strengths-based and desistance focused. There were reductions in breach and in the frequency and/or seriousness of offending or complete cessation during the period of the order and positive indications that relational working was a contributory factor (Cordis Bright 2017).

Moving forward

In recent years, the 'children first' philosophy has gained more traction across England as well as Wales. The YJB's mission statement sets out a vision for a child-centred and distinct approach to youth justice (YJB 2015) and the development of its participation strategy for engagement with children (YJB 2016) is a visible commitment to ensuing that the child's voice is at the forefront of practice. The Charlie Taylor report was a significant review of the youth justice system which will shape what it will look like in the immediate years, talked about the aspiration for a youth justice system in which young people are treated as children first (Taylor 2016). The National Police Officer's strategy for the policing of children and young people discussed those below the age of 18 being treated as 'children first', not as 'mini adults', and of the importance of non-criminalization and diversion from the criminal justice system (NPCC 2015). The thematic inspection of YOTs and public protection work (HMIP 2017) recommended that more emphasis be given to understanding children's traumatic histories and how to respond to them, advocating for 'simple' uncomplicated interventions, the building of relationships between children, young people, and their case managers, and the necessity of addressing underlying issues before progressing to offence-focused work. The ECM approach in Wales was cited as one of the examples of where this was happening in practice.[6]

The importance of developing trauma-informed practice has also been highlighted by Public Health Wales in research which identified that individuals who have four or more adverse childhood experiences (ACEs) are 15 times more likely to have committed a violent act against another person and 20 times more likely to have been incarcerated at any point in their lifetime, thereby recognizing that ACEs contribute to health-harming behaviours (Public Health Wales 2015). The Welsh Government supported the setting up of an ACEs hub to help individuals, organizations, and communities to become ACE aware (www.aceawarewales.com), to improve the health and well-being of children who have experienced adverse and stressful experiences, aligning this work to the objectives of the Well-being of Future Generations Act 2015 and *Prosperity for All: The National Strategy* and programme for government (Welsh Government 2017). Further, in 2017 the Police Transformation Fund awarded the four Welsh Police forces, Public Health Wales, Her Majesty's Prison and Probation Service, NSPCC, and Barnardos, £6.8 million for three years to develop a national ACE approach to policing.

The youth justice system has been through several distinct phases since its creation in 2000, driven by different UK government policies. The early years were characterized by interventionist approaches arising from *No More Excuses* (Home Office 1997). This continued with the Youth Crime Action Plan in 2008, which featured the 'triple track approach' of enforcement and punishment, tackling the root causes of crime and early intervention and non-negotiable support and intervention (HM Government 2008). *Breaking the Cycle* (Ministry of Justice 2011) moved in a different direction by introducing freedoms and flexibilities, which led to significant increases in the use of out-of-court disposals and an overall reduction in the youth justice population. The Taylor review in 2016 proposed wider reform of the system, a 'children first' approach, use of diversion, and the unnecessary escalation of young people through the system. This stands in contrast to the youth justice system of *No More Excuses*, which separated justice from welfare, to the present one which 'moves away from justice with some welfare, to a welfare system with justice' (Taylor 2016: 49). This suggests that youth justice has moved a significant distance away from the 'punitive turn', and in a 'children first' direction, with more concern for improving welfare, well-being, and life chances. This is characterized by the emphasis on preventing criminalization, of understanding the impact of adverse childhood events on behaviour, and of developing responses which are commensurate with children's and young person's needs and chronological, social, and emotional development.

Notes

1 For further information on the UNCRC, go to www.unicef.org.uk/what-we-do/un-convention-child-rights/.
2 The Silk Commission was set up to review the constitutional arrangements in Wales.
3 This has been replaced in Wales by the Social Services and Well-being (Wales) Act 2014.
4 Now replaced by AssetPlus.
5 Two YOTs in South Wales have a different model of pre-court diversion.
6 The ECM has also been cited in the UK Government's Serious Violence Strategy (HM Government 2018).

References

Bateman, T. (2011) 'We Now Breach More Kids in a Week Than We Used to in a Whole Year': The punitive turn, enforcement and custody. *Youth Justice*, 11(2), 115–133.

Briggs, D. (2013) Conceptualising risk and need: The rise of actuarialism and the death of welfare? Practitioner assessment and intervention in the youth offending service. *Youth Justice*, 13(1), 17–30.

Burnett, R. and Appleton, C. (2004) Joined-up services to tackle youth crime. *British Journal of Criminology*, 44, 34–54.

Cordis Bright. (2017) *Evaluation of the Enhanced Case Management Approach*. Cardiff: Welsh Government.

Case, S. (2006) Young people at risk of what? Challenging risk-focused early intervention as crime prevention. *Youth Justice*, 6(3), 171–179.

Cavadino, M. and Dignan, J. (2006) *Penal Systems a Comparative Approach*. London: Sage Publications.

Cavadino, M. and Dignan, J. (2009) Comparative youth justice. In T. Newburn (Ed.), *Key Readings in Criminology*. Cullompton: Willan Publishing, pp. 698–707.

Commission on Devolution in Wales. (2014) *Empowerment and Responsibility: Legislative Powers to Strengthen Wales*. Cardiff: Commission on Devolution in Wales.

Cross, N., Evans, J. and Minkes, J. (2003) Still children first? Developments in youth justice in Wales. *Youth Justice*, 2(3), 151–162.

Davies, N. and Williams, D. (2009) *Clear Red Water and Socialist Policies*. London: Francis Bootle Publishers.

Drakeford, M. (2010) Devolution and youth justice in Wales. *Criminology and Criminal Justice*, 10, 137.

Edwards, A. and Hughes, G. (2009) The preventative turn and the promotion of safer communities in England and Wales: Political inventiveness and governmental instabilities. In A. Crawford (Ed.), *Crime Prevention in Europe: Comparative Perspectives*. Cullompton: Willan Publishing, pp. 62–85.

Ellis, T. and Boden, E. (2005) *Is There a Unifying Professional Culture in Youth Offending Teams?* A research note, British Society of Criminology 2004, Volume 7. Conference Proceedings.

Field, S. (2006) Practice cultures in the 'New' youth justice in England and Wales. *The British Journal of Criminology*, 47, 311–330.

Field, S. (2015) Developing local cultures in criminal justice policy-making: The case of youth justice in Wales. In M. Wasik and S. Santatzoglou (Eds.), *The Management of Change in Criminal Justice*. London: Palgrave Macmillan.

Field, S. and Nelken, D. (2010) Reading and writing youth justice in Italy and (England and) Wales. *Punishment & Society*, 12(3), 287–308.

Goldson, B. (2002) New labour, social justice and children: Calculation and the deserving-undeserving schism. *British Journal of Social Work*, 22(6), 683–695.

Gray, P. (2009) The political economy of risk and the new governance of youth crime. *Punishment & Society*, 11, 443.

Haines, K. and Case, S. (2015) *Positive Youth Justice Children First, Offenders Second*. Bristol: Policy Press.

Haines, K. (2010) The dragonisation of youth justice. In W. Taylor, R. Earle and R. Hester (Eds.), *Youth Justice Handbook Theory, Policy and Practice*. Devon: Willan Publishing.

Haines, K., Case, S., Davies, K. and Charles, A. (2013) The Swansea bureau: A model of diversion from the youth justice system. *International Journal of Law, Crime and Justice*, 1–21.

HM Government. (2008) *Youth Crime Action Plan 2008*. London: HM Government.

HM Inspectorate of Probation. (2017) *The Work of Youth Offending Teams to Protect the Public*. Manchester: HMIP.

Home Office. (1997) *No More Excuses – A New Approach to Tackling Youth Crime in England and Wales*. London: The Stationery Office.

Joint Committee on Human Rights. (2015) *The UK's Compliance with the UN Convention on the Rights of the Child*. London: The Stationery Office.

Kemp, V., Sorsby, A., Liddle, M. and Merrington, S. (2002) *Assessing Responses to Youth Offending in Northamptonshire*. London: Nacro Ministry of Justice.

Ministry of Justice. (2011) *Breaking The Cycle: Government Response*. London: Ministry of Justice.

Muncie, J. (2008) The 'Punitive Turn' in juvenile justice: Cultures of control and rights compliance in Western Europe and the USA. *Youth Justice*, 8, 107–121.

Muncie, J. (2011) Illusions of difference comparative youth justice in the devolved United Kingdom. *British Journal of Criminology*, 51, 40–57.

National Assembly for Wales. (2000) *Extending Entitlement: Supporting Young People in Wales*. Report by the Policy Unit, The National Assembly for Wales. Cardiff: The National Assembly for Wales.

National Assembly for Wales. (2009) *Transcript Youth Justice Board for England and Wales*. Cardiff: National Assembly for Wales, 7 May.

The National Police Chief's Council. (2015) *National Strategy for the Policing of Children and Young People*. London: NPCC.

Phoenix, J. (2009) Beyond risk assessment: The return of repressive welfareism? In *Youth Offending and Youth Justice*. London: Jessica Kingsley.

Pitts, J. (2008) Too grand, bland and abstract: The limitations of 'youth governance' as an explanatory schema for contemporary governmental responses to socially deviant young people. *Youth and Policy*, (99), 67–89.

Public Health Wales. (2015) *Adverse Childhood Experiences and Their Impact on Health-Harming Behaviours in the Welsh Adult Population*. Cardiff: Public Helath Wales.

Rosengard, A., Laing, I., Ridley, J. and Hunter, S. (2007) *A Literature Review on Multiple and Complex Needs*. Edinburgh: Scottish Executive Social Research.

Skuse, T. and Matthew, J. (2015) The trauma recovery model: Sequencing youth justice interventions for young people with complex needs. *Prison Service Journal*, 220, 16–25.

Souhami, A. (2007) *Transforming Youth Justice Occupational Identity and Cultural Change*. Cullompton: Willan Publishing.

Taylor, C. (2016) *Review of the Youth Justice System in England and Wales*. London: MoJ.

Thomas, S. (2015) *Children First Offenders Second an Aspiration or a Reality for Youth Justice in Wales*. Thesis submitted for Professional Doctorate in Leadership in Children and Young People's Services, University of Bedfordshire, Luton.

UNICEF. (1990) *The United Nations Convention on the Rights of the Child*. London: UNICEF.

Welsh Assembly Government. (2004) *Children and Young People: Rights to Action*. Cardiff: Welsh Assembly Government.

Welsh Assembly Government. (2011) Devolution of youth justice. *CAB: Criminal Assets Bureau*, (10–11), 50.

Welsh Assembly Government and YJB. (2004) *The All Wales Youth Offending Strategy*. Cardiff: Welsh Assembly Government.

Welsh Government. (2012) *Proposals to Improve Services in Wales to Better Meet the Needs of Children and Young People Who Are at Risk of Entering, or are Already in the Youth Justice System*. Cardiff: Welsh Government, September.

Welsh Government. (2014) *Prevention of Offending by Young People*. Cardiff: Welsh Government.

Welsh Government. (2017) *Prosperity for All: The National Strategy*. Cardiff: Welsh Government.

Welsh Government and YJB. (2014) *Children and Young People First*. Cardiff: Welsh Government.

Williams, J. (2007) Incorporating children's rights: The divergence in law and policy. *Legal Studies*, 27(2), 261–287, June.

YJB. (2015) *Youth Justice Board for England and Wales Strategic Plan 2015–18*. London: YJB.

YJB. (2016) *Participation Strategy Giving Young People a Voice in Youth Justice*. London: YJB.

YJB and Ministry of Justice. (2018) *Youth Justice Statistics England and Wales*. London: Ministry of Justice.

'Rights-based' and *'Children and Young People First'* approaches to Youth Justice

60

Patricia Gray

Introduction

The Committee on the Rights of the Child (see CRC 2007) monitors the extent to which youth justice systems across the world comply with the principles laid out in the 1989 United Nations Convention on the Rights of the Child (United Nations General Assembly 1989). This chapter will explore the extent to which youth justice in England and Wales[1] protects the rights and well-being of children in conflict with the law in compliance with the Convention. The first part of this chapter outlines the key features of international and European children's rights standards as they apply to youth justice. The second part begins with a brief history of youth justice in England and Wales since the United Kingdom (UK) became a signatory to the Convention in 1991. Throughout this period right up to the most recent report published in

2016, the CRC has been highly critical of the youth justice system in England and Wales for its failure to adequately safeguard the rights and well-being of young people who offend.

The third part of this chapter will focus on the dramatic changes that have taken place in recent years in policy and practice directed at young people who offend. This is reflected in a significant drop in 'first time entrants' (FTEs)[2] to the youth justice system and the numbers sentenced to youth custody. In response to these changes and reductions in public spending brought about by the financial crisis, the delivery of services to young people who offend have been restructured. Research shows that three main models have emerged, that is 'offender management', 'targeted intervention', and 'children and young people first' (Smith and Gray 2018). This section will compare and contrast the key characteristics of each of these models before going on to consider whether or not they offer a more rights-compliant approach to youth justice, and therefore move closer to the principles of the Convention.

The final part of this chapter will focus specifically on youth offending services that follow a 'children and young people first' (CYPF) model. Such services claim to pursue a distinctly different, 'child-friendly', and progressive attitude to youth justice, which is explicitly guided by the 1989 Convention. In this section it will be argued that while youth justice agencies which adopt a CYPF approach do indeed offer a more rights-compliant approach, the extent to which such agencies fully uphold the principles of the Convention in the sense of addressing young people's social welfare rights based on social justice principles is questionable.

International and European children's rights standards

The 1989 United Nations Convention on the Rights of the Child (United Nations General Assembly 1989) sets out the basic principles or standards which are expected to act as benchmarks to assess the extent to which youth justice systems in countries throughout the world protect and promote young people's human rights and 'best interests'. The Convention defines a child as a person below the age of 18 years, and in this chapter the words child and young person will be used interchangeably to describe this age group. The Convention is supported by a number of other international human rights instruments, which specifically apply to young people in conflict with the law. The most significant of these are the United Nations Standard Minimum Rules for the Administration of Juvenile Justice (United Nations General Assembly 1985: the 'Beijing Rules'), the United Nations Rules for the Protection of Juveniles Deprived of their Liberty (United Nations General Assembly 1990a: the 'Havana Rules'), and the United Nations Guidelines for the Prevention of Juvenile Delinquency (United Nations General Assembly 1990b: the 'Riyadh Guidelines').

The Committee on the Rights of the Child (see CRC 2007) is charged with the task of monitoring how countries are implementing the Convention. All countries that have signed up to the Convention are periodically subject to review, and the reports are open to public scrutiny. There are 54 articles in the Convention which draw together children's economic, social, cultural, and political rights, but the most important from a youth justice perspective is article 3, which states that 'the best interests of the child shall be a primary consideration' in all proceedings against children in conflict with the law (Goldson and Muncie 2015: 230). This concept can be interpreted in different ways, but according to the CRC guidelines (2007), which were written to clarify how the principles of the Convention should be applied to youth justice, this is understood to mean that the welfare or well-being of the child should be given top priority at all stages of the youth justice process. However, as Muncie (2015: 375) argues, while the Convention is 'the most ratified of all international human rights directives . . . it is also the most violated'.

The articles of the Convention[3] which are considered to be crucial in the context of youth justice state that:

Article 12 – The right to be heard
'every child has the right to express his/her views freely, in all matters affecting the child';

Article 19 – Protection from abuse and violence
'children should be protected from all forms of physical or mental violence, injury or abuse, neglect or negligent treatment, maltreatment or exploitation';

Article 37(a) – Inhumane treatment
'no child shall be subjected to . . . cruel, inhuman or degrading treatment or punishment';

Article 37(b) – Last resort and shortest time
'the arrest, detention or imprisonment of a child . . . shall be used only as a measure of last resort and for the shortest appropriate period of time';

Article 37(c) – Humanity, respect and dignity
'every child deprived of liberty shall be treated with humanity and respect for the inherent dignity of the human person, and in a manner which takes into account the needs of persons of his or her age';

Article 40(i) – Dignity and worth
'every child alleged as, accused of, or recognised as having infringed the penal law to be treated in a manner consistent with the promotion of the child's sense of dignity and worth'.

The UNCRC does not explicitly state the minimum age of criminal responsibility (MACR) at which a child who commits an offence can be formally charged and dealt with through criminal procedures. However, the CRC (2007) guidelines make clear that an MACR below the age of 12 years is not acceptable by international standards as it fails to take into account the special status of the child by reason of their emotional, mental, and intellectual maturity. In England and Wales the age of criminal responsibility is ten years.

In Europe the UNCRC is supported by a number of Council of Europe directives to encourage a more 'child-friendly' youth justice. The most important of these are the *European Rules for Juvenile Offenders Subject to Sanctions or Measures* (Council of Europe 2009) and the *Guidelines for Child-Friendly Justice* (Council of Europe 2010). The latter expresses a commitment to the idea that young people who offend must be treated first and foremost as children, and that youth justice policies and processes must be child-friendly with the child's well-being, protection, and safety as their first priority. The European Commission prioritized child-friendly justice in its 2011 EU Agenda for the Rights of the Child (International Juvenile Justice Observatory 2017). This reinforced its concern to prioritize the Council of Europe's Guidelines on child-friendly justice, with a particular emphasis on promoting the child's right to participation.

Goldson and Muncie (2015: 233) conclude that together the UNCRC and the Council of Europe human rights standards provide 'a well-established "unifying framework"' to guide rights-compliant and child-friendly youth justice policy and practice. However, in reality, these standards have simply become moral obligations that 'lack teeth' as they have not been translated into domestic law and so are not legally binding and enforceable.

Compliance with international and European youth justice standards

To what extent is youth justice in England and Wales 'child-friendly' and directed at protecting the 'best interests' or well-being of the child in compliance with the UNCRC and Council of Europe guidelines? To answer this question, it is useful to compare a brief history of youth justice since the beginning of the 1990s with the findings of the periodic reviews that were conducted by the CRC in 2002, 2008, and 2016. Cunneen et al. (2017) argue that there have been three distinct periods in the recent history of juvenile justice, and coincidentally each of them matches the timing of the main CRC periodic reviews (see also Goldson and Muncie 2012).

The first period between 1991 and 1997 is described by Cunneen et al. (2017: 4) as 'burgeoning punitiveness', when the murder of James Bulger in 1993 acted as a catalyst to politicize youth crime and demonize any young person involved in it, no matter how minor the criminal act. This resulted in a rapid increase in the rate of youth custody, which rose by 90% between

1992 and 2002 (Bateman 2012). Needless to say, the CRC periodic review for 2002 was highly critical of the failure of England and Wales to comply with article 37(b) by ensuring that youth custody was used only as a 'measure of last resort' (United Nations Committee on the Rights of the Child 2002).

The second period between 1998 and 2008 was marked by the implementation of New Labour's flagship legislation, the *1998 Crime and Disorder Act*, which led to a complete transformation in youth justice policy and practice. New Labour promised to be 'tough on crime, tough on the causes of crime', but in practice the emphasis was more on the 'consolidation and intensification of punitiveness' (Cunneen et al. 2017: 4) than on addressing the high levels of socio-economic disadvantage experienced by the vast majority of young people who offend (Goldson 2010). The 'risk factor prevention paradigm' (RFPP) underpinned thinking about youth crime during this period (see Farrington 2000). This claimed to be able to identify the individual and social factors that increased young people's risk of offending and advocated early intervention to stop offending as quickly as possible (Case and Haines 2009).

The RFPP was subject to scathing criticism as it emphasized individual risk factors and underplayed social structural constraints such as lack of educational and employment opportunities (Case and Haines 2009). This resulted in the criminalization of social need as young people's social welfare difficulties were viewed as pathological, individual deficits in need of correction in order to reduce the risk of offending (Goldson 2013: 123). Overall, the individualization and dematerialization of young people's welfare needs, the conflation of these needs with the risk of offending, and the focus on early intervention led to net widening and net strengthening. Increasing numbers of young people were drawn into the youth justice system, and subjected to more intrusive forms of correctional intervention. Hence the rapid rise in youth custody continued unabated until the mid-2000s (Goldson 2010).

The continued failure of the UK to translate the standards of the UNCRC, particularly the principle of safeguarding the child's 'best interests', into youth justice policy and practice was heavily criticized in the 2008 CRC report. The key target of New Labour's youth justice reforms to 'nip offending in the bud' had simply legitimated excessive criminalization as large numbers of young people who offend were sucked into the youth justice system and hastily driven towards custody. Once again custody was not being used as a 'measure of last resort' and treatment inside custody remained 'degrading and inhumane' (United Nations Committee on the Rights of the Child 2008; see also Gray 2011).

The final period, 2009 to 2016, appears to have been one of 'penal moderation' (Cunneen et al. 2017: 4). This has been evidenced by a dramatic drop in first time entrants (FTEs) of 83% between March 2006 and March 2016 (Ministry of Justice, Youth Justice Board and National Statistics 2017). In the same period, there was an equally significant reduction in the rate of youth custody, falling by 73% (Ministry of Justice, Youth Justice Board and National Statistics 2017). These changes lead Bateman (2017: 4) to talk about the 'shrinkage' or 'slimming down' of youth justice. However, like a number of other critics (Smith 2014; Kelly and Armitage 2015), Bateman (2017) challenges the progressiveness of these developments. He argues that they are unlikely to be an informed response to the research evidence on the dangers of criminalizing young people by drawing them into the formal youth justice process (see McAra and McVie 2010), and are more likely to be a response to changes in police recording practices, a drop in recorded youth crime, and the cuts in public expenditure set in place by the last two governments. Correctional measures, particularly youth custody, become expensive policy options in times of austerity.

Research also shows that during this era of 'penal moderation' there has been a more concerted effort to protect the child's 'best interests' or welfare. A number of researchers had noted that a strong undercurrent of welfare was already evident in policy and practice in the earlier period (Field 2007; Phoenix 2009), suggesting that Cunneen et al. (2017) may have exaggerated the level of punitiveness in youth justice under New Labour between 1998 and 2008. Since the early 2000s, multi-agency youth offending teams in partnership with a range of social service agencies progressively attempted to target young people's complex welfare problems, not just concentrating on their offending. However, overall the research shows that throughout this period the social welfare needs of young people who offend, for example those needs relating to family, education, training and employment, and mental health and well-being, were not being adequately met (Soloman and Garside 2008; Carlile, 2014; Gray 2016). The reasons for this are complex. The negative impact of the audit and managerialist culture set in place by New Labour created tensions and conflicts over targets between YOTs and their partners in the social welfare sector. More recently, these tensions and conflicts have worsened as a result of the public spending cuts imposed by both the Coalition and Conservative governments. YOT budgets were reduced by more than 25% between 2011 and 2016 (Bateman 2017).

While recognizing some improvements in the last decade, particularly the drop in FTEs and the rate of youth custody, the most recent CRC report (United Nations Committee on the Rights of the Child 2016) on UK's compliance with the Convention remained critical of its failure to translate key principles into its childcare and youth justice policy and practice. Repeating comments from previous reports, the 2016 report again criticized the UK for its low age of criminal responsibility which criminalized young people from an early age and was out of step with acceptable international standards. The rate of custody was still considered to be too high, with custody not being used only as a 'last resort', and involving a disproportionate number of ethnic minority and 'looked after' children. Conditions inside custody remained a source of concern, with the use of painful physical constraints and solitary confinement, and the prevalence of high levels of violence and bullying infringing the child's right to be treated with 'dignity and respect' (article 37c) and not to be subject to 'degrading and inhumane treatment' (article 37a).

However, the core issue which emerged from the 2016 CRC report was the overall failure of the UK government to give sufficient attention to protecting the child's 'best interests' or well-being by addressing their welfare needs and social rights. Particular concerns were expressed about the high levels of poverty and homelessness suffered by children from disadvantaged backgrounds. The inequalities in the distribution of resources to meet young people's mental health needs and improve their educational attainment were also noted. This was mainly blamed on public spending cuts, which had had a disproportionately unfair and unjust impact on 'children's enjoyment' (United Nations Committee on the Rights of the Child 2016: 3) of their social rights in these areas. This problem was exacerbated by the failure to comply with article 12 by respecting and listening to the views of young people and meaningfully involving them in decision-making.

The changing contours of youth justice services

Drawing on the findings from the most recent CRC report, McAra (2017: 961–962) concludes that there are 'major shortcomings' in the way the youth justice system protects the well-being and 'best interests' of the child. While she is willing to concede that the upsurge in diversion is to be commended because it reduces the 'criminogenic effect' of system contact, and that there has been some movement towards improving the child-friendliness of youth justice processes, she feels that not enough is being done in 'tackling poverty and promoting a wide social justice agenda'.

In this section I would like to consider whether there is any likelihood of the development of 'child-friendly' youth justice which protects the child's best interests in accord with the principles of social justice. In response to the significant drop in the number of young people entering the youth justice system and reductions in public spending, the delivery of services to young people who offend have been restructured. Over the last two years I, along with a colleague, have been conducting research which is mapping and modelling changes in the structure and delivery of youth offending team services, and their implications for policy and practice (Smith and Gray 2018). Our research suggests that three main models of youth justice are emerging, which we have called 'offender management', 'targeted intervention', and 'children and young people first'.

'Offender management' teams take a similar approach to young people who offend as appeared in the New Labour era and therefore can be subject to the same criticisms. They focus on managing offending behaviour through the supervision of young offenders on out-of-court and court-ordered disposals. Their core objective is to achieve the three main performance targets of reducing FTEs, reducing the use of custody, and reducing reoffending. Although desistance theory and research which stress a more strength-based, positive approach to young people's offending is now in vogue (see HM Inspectorate of Probation 2016), 'offender management' teams continue to draw upon the 'risk factor prevention paradigm'. This means that the 'criminalization of need' remains as young people's needs are individualized, and conflated with risks of offending. Overall, while some of these teams have developed some innovative and creative interventions in partnership with a variety of community-based social welfare providers, in the main they continue to adopt a risk-orientated, 'deficit' mindset which 'pathologizes' and 'medicalizes' the problems of young people who offend.

'Targeted intervention' teams are guided by the same three performance targets as 'offender management teams', and are similarly concerned with young people's behaviour. However, these teams also tend to take a broader perspective in dealing with young people who offend, and see themselves as part of a set of specialist youth support services, with whom they are frequently co-located, which address different aspects of young people's social welfare problems. Whilst influenced by the 'risk factor prevention paradigm', these teams also tend to take a holistic view of young people's welfare difficulties.

Youth offending teams that follow a 'children and young people first' (CYPF) model pride themselves on pursuing a distinctly different, 'child-friendly', and progressive approach to young people who offend, which is explicitly guided by the UNCRC and the Council of Europe guidelines[4]. Young people involved in crime are seen as being first and foremost children and CYPF teams explicitly seek to protect their rights under the Convention. Young people's problems are viewed holistically such that the dynamic interaction between the psychological and the social is given prominence. Diverting young people from the youth justice system to avoid criminalization and stigmatization is prioritized and achieved through close collaboration with the police. Diversion from criminalization is strengthened by social inclusion or supporting young people who offend to access mainstream, universal social services to which all children are entitled. Overall, CYPF teams aim to provide holistic, integrated, universal support, or 'one-stop shops' to meet the complex social problems that young people who offend frequently face.

Whither social justice in an era of 'children first' youth justice?

In recent years CYPF agencies have faced significant budget cuts and have also been subject to performance management and inspection criteria suited mainly to 'offender management' rather than 'children first' criteria (Smith and Gray 2018). Commendably, despite these obstacles, they have strived to offer a more principled 'child-friendly' service that is non-criminalizing and engages collaboratively with all disadvantaged children, not just those who offend (Byrne and Case 2016; Haines and Case 2015). Undoubtedly, they provide a positive and benevolent experience of youth justice which is more rights-compliant than the other two models. But the extent to which such agencies fully uphold the wider principles and spirit of the UNCRC by, as suggested by McAra (2017: 962), 'tackling poverty and promoting a wide social justice agenda', is questionable. This failure to work more assertively towards social justice is evidenced by the way CYPF teams assess the problems of young people who offend and the way they interpret 'effective practice'.

CYPF agencies place the spotlight on the child, not their offending, which does avoid 'othering', labelling, and criminalization. The assessment of need is not conflated with risk of offending, as in the RFPP but takes account of the wider contours of the child's 'whole' personal and social situation, and supports access to universal entitlements. Nevertheless, the child's problems still tend to be blamed on individual and family deficits, with social constraints given only limited attention. Hence, while in this process system contact is less damaging and harmful than in 'offender management' type agencies and the impact of social disadvantage is taken into account, it could be argued that from a social justice perspective more could be achieved by fundamentally challenging and tackling structural inequalities.

Similar arguments can be made about the way CYPF agencies understand 'effective practice'. Desistance theory and research are influential in their thinking in this area (HM Inspectorate of Probation 2016). 'Effective practice' is viewed in terms of building young people's strengths, resilience, and motivation rather than being obsessed by deficits and pathologies as in the 'offender management' model. The core principle of 'effective practice' is to divert the young person away from formal processing through the youth justice system into universal provision which should be available to all children. This prevents criminalization. Restorative type interventions are lauded as yet another fundamental component of 'effective practice'. However, interest in such interventions is not driven by concerns about 'responsibilization' or holding the young person accountable as in 'offender management' teams. Instead, the focus of restorative practice is about 'social inclusion' or supporting young people to be restored into the mainstream of community life, for example, by returning to school or finding employment. Finally, article 12 of the UNCRC, which obligates 'giving young people a voice' by engaging them in the change process, underlies all aspects of 'effective practice' (United Nations General Assembly 1989).

Overall, the above understanding of 'effective practice' is very narrow, process orientated, and avoids facing up to the challenges posed in order to achieve 'just' and 'equitable' outcomes. The achievement of the latter would necessitate a greater commitment to advocacy work and social action to confront the negative effects of socio-economic disadvantage.

Despite the criticisms that can be directed at the limitations of CYPF agencies in the way they assess young people's problems and interpret 'effective practice', there are two aspects of their structure and style of delivery which places them in a strategic position to engage in more progressive forms of practice in the future which better uphold the 'socially just' spirit of the UNCRC. First, guided by their 'child first' principle, they have established partnerships with a wide network of social welfare providers to offer integrated 'one-stop shop' youth support services with access to universal entitlements. Second, in response to public spending cuts and government demands for greater localization and flexibility, they have shown themselves to be capable of delivering some innovative and creative intervention packages. Both of these features could readily be adapted to work more stridently towards social justice ideals and equitable outcomes for disadvantaged young people who offend.

Conclusion

Newly emerging agencies such as those inspired by CYPF principles are in a stronger position to adhere to the principles laid out in the UNCRC and Council of Europe guidelines than at any other time in the history of youth justice. This is not simply in the sense of promoting the 'best interests' or 'well-being' of the child, but also of, as McAra suggests, moving beyond being 'child-friendly' to achieve outcomes which are socially just and actually confront social disadvantage and structural inequalities. The key question is do these agencies have the desire to move beyond 'talk' to engage in 'social action', or is this to place unrealistic expectations on them at a time when they continue to be funded and inspected according to 'offender management' logic?

Notes

1 The CRC reports cover the whole of the United Kingdom, which includes Scotland and Northern Ireland. Although the broader criticisms of the CRC apply to all four countries in the UK, the legislation in each is slightly different and therefore for the purposes of clarity and length the chapter will only focus on England and Wales.
2 That is, those young people receiving a formal caution or court disposal for the first time.
3 The language has been simplified for the purpose of clarity. See United Nations General Assembly (1989).
4 These teams are informed by the 'positive youth justice' movement. See Case and Haines (2015a); Byrne and Case (2016); Case and Haines (2015b); Haines and Case (2015).

References

Bateman, T. (2012) Who pulled the plug? Towards an explanation of the fall in child imprisonment in England and Wales. *Youth Justice*, 12(1), 36–52.

Bateman, T. (2017) *The State of Youth Justice 2017*. London: National Association for Youth Justice.

Byrne, B. and Case, S. (2016) Towards a positive youth justice. *Safer Communities*, 15(2), 69–81.

Carlile, A. (2014) *Independent Parliamentarians' Inquiry into the Operation and Effectiveness of the Youth Court*. London: National Children's Bureau.

Case, S. and Haines, K. (2009) *Understanding Youth Offending: Risk Factor Research, Policy and Practice*. Devon: Willan.

Case, S. and Haines, K. (2015a) Children first, offenders second positive promotion. *Youth Justice*, 15(3), 226–239.

Case, S. and Haines, K. (2015b) Children first, offenders second: The centrality of engagement in positive youth justice. *Howard Journal*, 54(2), 57–175.

Committee on the Rights of the Child (CRC). (2007) *General Comments No. 10: Children's Rights in Juvenile Justice*. Geneva: United Nations.

Council of Europe. (2009) *European Rules for Juvenile Offenders Subject to Sanctions or Measures*. Strasbourg: Council of Europe Publishing.

Council of Europe. (2010) *Guidelines of the Committee of Ministers of the Council of Europe on Child Friendly Justice*. Strasbourg: Council of Europe Publishing.

Cunneen, C., Goldson, B. and Russell, S. (2017) Human rights and youth justice reform in England and Wales, *Criminology and Criminal Justice*, Online First, 1–26.

Farrington, D. (2000) Explaining and preventing crime: The globalisation of knowledge. *Criminology*, 38(1), 1–24.

Field, S. (2007) Practice cultures and the 'new' youth justice in England and Wales. *British Journal of Criminology*, 47(2), 311–330.

Goldson, B. (2010) The sleep of (criminological) reason: Knowledge–policy rupture and new labour's youth justice legacy. *Criminology and Criminal Justice*, 10(2), 155–178.

Goldson, B. (2013) Unsafe, unjust and harmful to wider society: Grounds for raising the minimum age of criminal responsibility in England and Wales. *Youth Justice*, 13(2), 111–130.

Goldson, B. and Muncie, J. (2012) Towards a global 'child friendly' juvenile justice?'. *International Journal of Law, Crime and Justice*, 40(1), 47–64.

Goldson, B. and Muncie, J. (2015) Children's human rights and youth justice with integrity. In B. Goldson and J. Muncie (Eds.), *Youth Crime and Justice*, 2nd edition. London: Sage.

Gray, P. (2011) Youth custody, resettlement and the right to social justice. *Youth Justice*, 11(3), 235–249.

Gray, P. (2016) 'Child friendly' international human rights standards and youth offending team partnerships. *International Journal of Law, Crime and Justice*, 45, 59–74.

Haines, K. and Case, S. (2015) *Positive Youth Justice: Children First, Offenders Second*. Bristol: Policy Press.

HM Inspectorate of Probation. (2016) *Desistance and Young People*. Manchester: HMIP.

International Juvenile Justice Observatory (2017) *Can Anyone Hear Me? Participation of Children in Juvenile Justice*. Brussels: IJJO.

Kelly, L. and Armitage, V. (2015) Diverse diversions: Youth justice reform, localised practices, and a 'new interventionist diversion'? *Youth Justice*, 15(2), 117–133.

McAra, L. (2017) Youth justice. In A. Liebling, S. Maruna, and L. McAra (Eds.), *The Oxford Handbook of Criminology*, 6th edition. Oxford: Oxford University Press.

McAra, L. and McVie, S. (2010) Youth crime and justice: Key messages from the Edinburgh study of youth transitions and crime. *Criminology and Criminal Justice*, 10(2), 179–209.

Ministry of Justice, Youth Justice Board and National Statistics. (2017) *Youth Justice Statistics 2015/16*. London: Ministry of Justice.

Muncie, J. (2015) *Youth and Crime*, 4th edition. London: Sage.

Phoenix, J. (2009) Beyond risk assessment: The return of repressive welfarism. In M. Barry, and F. McNeill (Eds.), *Youth Offending and Youth Justice*. London: Jessica Kingsley Publishers.

Smith, R. (2014) Re-inventing diversion. *Youth Justice*, 14(2), 109–121.

Smith, R. and Gray, P. (2018) The changing shape of youth justice: Models of practice. *Criminology and Criminal Justice*, Online First, 1–18.

Soloman, E. and Garside, R. (2008) *Ten Years of Labour's Youth Justice Reforms: An Independent Audit*. London: Centre for Crime and Justice Studies.

United Nations Committee on the Rights of the Child. (2002) *Thirty-first Session: Consideration of Reports Submitted by States Parties Under Article 44 of the Convention – Concluding Observations: United Kingdom of Great Britain and Northern Ireland*. Geneva: United Nations.

United Nations Committee on the Rights of the Child. (2008) *Forty-ninth Session: Consideration of Reports Submitted by States Parties Under Article 44 of the Convention – Concluding Observations: United Kingdom of Great Britain and Northern Ireland*. Geneva: United Nations.

United Nations Committee on the Rights of the Child. (2016) *Committee on the Rights of the Child – Concluding Observations on the Fifth Periodic Report of the United Kingdom and Northern Ireland*. Geneva: United Nations.

United Nations General Assembly. (1985) *United Nations Standard Minimum Rules for the Administration of Juvenile Justice*. New York: United Nations.

United Nations General Assembly. (1989) *United Nations Convention on the Rights of the Child*. New York: United Nations.

United Nations General Assembly. (1990a) *United Nations Guidelines for the Prevention of Juvenile Delinquency*. New York: United Nations.

United Nations General Assembly. (1990b) *United Nations Rules for the Protection of Juveniles Deprived of Their Liberty*. New York: United Nations.

Effective supervision of young offenders[1]

61

Chris Trotter

Literature review

A review of research (Trotter 2015) suggested that the following worker skills are related to reduced offending and increased compliance by those under supervision:

- The worker is clear about their role. This includes helping the client to understand the dual social control and helping aims of supervision, and other issues such as confidentiality and what is expected of the client.
- The worker models and reinforces pro-social values and actions, and makes appropriate use of challenging or confrontation. In other words, the worker is reliable and fair, and questions rationalizations for offending.
- The worker helps offenders with problems that are identified by the client rather than the worker.
- The worker encourages clients to focus on problems or issues that are related to the person's offending (e.g. drugs, peers, employment, family issues).
- The worker helps clients to develop strategies to address these issues. These strategies focus on practical issues and may include cognitive behavioural and/or relapse prevention strategies.

- The worker takes a holistic approach to client issues rather than focusing on just one or two specific problems or symptoms.
- The worker develops a therapeutic alliance with the client. In other words, they work in a collaborative, friendly, optimistic way so that the client develops trust in the worker as someone who can genuinely help them with their problems.

These principles are consistent with the best practices principles enunciated and researched by others in the field (e.g. Dowden and Andrews 2004; Raynor et al. 2010; Robinson et al. 2011). This is not to say that there is universal agreement on best practice principles in offender supervision. Bonta and Andrews (2010) place particular emphasis on focusing on high-risk offenders, on using actuarial tools to assess levels of offender risk and needs, and on the use of predominantly cognitive behavioural approaches to assist offenders to address their risk-related needs.

By contrast, Ward et al. (2007) have argued that the focus on risk and risk assessment has been at the expense of opportunities for offenders to develop 'good lives' on their own terms. He and others (e.g. McNeill et al. 2005) have emphasized the importance of therapeutic alliance and the worker/client relationship, which they argue may be compromised by a focus on risk factors that may be defined by workers rather than clients.

Several studies have specifically examined the relationship between worker skills and reoffending rates of clients. Some of these studies have also examined the extent to which training has influenced the use of the skills by workers. One study also looked at the relationship between use of the skills, education in social work and welfare, and further offending. These studies are briefly reviewed below.

Andrews et al. (1979) published a seminal study conducted on probation in Ontario, Canada, which focused on the use of skills in the routine community supervision of offenders. They found that probation officers who made use of pro-social modelling and reinforcement, problem-solving, and who had high levels of empathy had clients with significantly lower recidivism. A further study undertaken in Victoria (Trotter 1996) offered training to 12 community corrections officers in role clarification, problem-solving, pro-social modelling, and relationship skills. Those who received training were significantly more likely to make use of skills (as determined by examination of file notes) and had significantly lower reoffence rates in their client groups at 18 months and four-year follow-up by comparison with a control group of clients of officers who had not received training.

A study undertaken in adult probation in Canada (Bonta et al. 2011) found similar results with similar training, although the Canadian training placed greater emphasis on cognitive behavioural interventions. They found that those under the supervision of the trained officers had significantly lower rates of recidivism after controlling for client risk levels. The clients of those officers who made maximum use of ongoing clinical supervision had a recidivism rate of only 15%. It was found that the most influential skills in terms of reduced offending were those relating to cognitive behavioural principles by contrast with relationship and other skills which were not significantly related to recidivism.

A larger study with similar aims was conducted by Robinson et al. (2011), with US courts and the Middle District of North Carolina. They used a sample of 41 officers in the trained experimental group and 26 in the control group, and a total of more than 1,000 pre-trial and post-conviction adult clients. They found that those in the experimental group (offenders supervised by trained officers) were more likely to use the effective practice skills when tapes of interviews were analyzed and had significantly lower recidivism.

The evidence is mounting therefore that the skills offered by supervisors to offenders sentenced to community supervision make a difference to the reoffending rates of the offenders. The studies undertaken to date have focused on adult offenders in Australia, the United States, and Canada. No studies of this type have focused specifically on young offenders in Australia or elsewhere. Further, the studies conducted to date have used analysis of file notes or coding of audiotapes of interviews to determine the nature of skills used by workers. None have observed interviews in person – a method that might provide information about non-verbal interactions. The various studies have also used different definitions of skills. In addition, none of the studies have considered the relationship between levels of education of staff in counselling skills or their specific designated role as a counsellor versus worker. There is also some uncertainty as to which aspects of the effective practice principles have the most impact, with one earlier Australian study (Trotter 1996) pointing to pro-social modelling and reinforcement as most strongly related to positive outcomes, by contrast with the Canadian study (Bonta et al. 2011), which found the use of cognitive techniques to be the most influential. Some of these issues are addressed in this study.

Methodology

Aims

To examine the relationship between the use of effective practice skills by supervisors in Juvenile Justice New South Wales and reoffence rates by clients.

To consider which of the skills, if any, have the most impact on reoffending rates.

Sample

This study was undertaken in the Department of Juvenile Justice in New South Wales. Community-based supervision represents the primary form of intervention with young offenders in New South Wales, as well as throughout

Australia (AIHW 2011). Aboriginal and Torres Strait Islander young people continue to be over-represented in community supervision, as well as in detention (AIHW 2011).

After receiving university and NSW Department of Juvenile Justice ethics approval, juvenile justice staff with responsibility for direct supervision of young offenders were invited to be involved in the project. Forty-eight staff members initially volunteered. For each worker, the next five clients allocated to them became eligible for the study. Interviews between the staff members and young people were then observed within three months of the young person receiving their court order. In total, 117 interviews were observed by 46 workers over a period of four years. In some cases, five interviews were observed for each worker; however, in other cases, only one or two interviews could be observed due to staff and client turnover. All interviews were with different clients.

Fifteen Juvenile Justice Counsellors were involved in 32 of the interviews and 33 Juvenile Justice Officers conducted the remaining 84 interviews. Juvenile Justice Counsellors and Juvenile Justice Officers each provide direct supervision to young offenders on probation, parole or other community-based supervision orders. Juvenile Justice Counsellors have relevant tertiary qualifications and have a counselling or problem-solving role, whereas Juvenile Justice Officers are not required to have tertiary qualifications and are generally expected to focus more on compliance and practical issues.

The 117 young people had an average age of 15.82 years, with the youngest being 12 years old and the oldest being 18 years old. They were all on court orders of some type, usually probation or parole. The most common offences for which they received the current order included assaults (n = 33), break and enter (n = 23), robbery (n = 12), theft (n = 11), and property damage (n = 11). Twenty-three percent (n = 27/117) identified as Aboriginal.

Coding

A coding manual was developed following collaboration with other researchers on similar projects (Bonta et al. 2011; Raynor et al. 2010), although it was different in some respects to the coding manuals used on those projects. The manual reflected the effective practice skills referred to in the literature review and outlined in Trotter (2015). The manual was framed to define the skills, and assist in the accuracy and reliability of the estimates of the extent to which the skills were used in interviews. It was divided into 15 sections including setup of the interview, structure of the interview, role clarification, needs analysis, problem-solving, developing strategies, relapse prevention/cognitive behavioural techniques, pro-social modelling and reinforcement, nature of the relationship, empathy, confrontation, termination, use of referral/community resources, non-verbal cues, and incidental conversations. For the skill to be rated high, it needed to be implemented in a way that was consistent with the research about good practice referred to in the literature review.

Each of the interviews was coded either by the researcher who observed the interview or subsequently by another researcher from an audiotape of the interview. When the coding was undertaken from an audiotape, the coder also had access to a non-verbal checklist, which was completed by the observer following each interview. The non-verbal checklist provided information about the body language and non-verbal interactions between the workers/counsellors and the clients.

Inter-rater reliability

Three research officers conducted field observations. Ninety-seven observations were completed by the first research officer, who was employed continuously on the project for a period of four years. Sixteen observations were completed by an Indigenous research officer and four were completed by another research officer. The project purposefully employed an Indigenous research officer because of the large number of Indigenous young offenders in NSW Juvenile Justice and because it was anticipated that an Indigenous research officer might help to identify skills that were of particular relevance to Indigenous clients. The coding was undertaken by three coders. The second and third coders did not observe the interviews but coded from the tapes and the non-verbal cues checklist.

Twenty of the interviews were coded by the research officer who observed the interview and subsequently cross-coded by another research officer using the audiotapes and the non-verbal checklist. There was a high degree of consistency in the ratings. For example, the correlation on the overall global skill score between first and second coders was .741 ($p<.000$), on time spent discussing role clarification it was .548 ($p<.006$), on time spent on problem-solving it was .626 ($p<.002$), and on pro-social modelling .561 ($p<.005$).

Global score

The global score is a score out of 10 relating to the interview as a whole. If, for example, the worker did not use any of the effective practice principles in the interview, then a score of one would be allocated. If the worker showed some use of the effective practice principles, they would be given a score of five. If the worker used all of the principles in the interview, then they could be scored at 10.

For the overall global score to be rated high, the worker would display high-level skills in role clarification, pro-social modelling, problem-solving, and relationship, and each of the skills would be used in a collaborative way. It would be rated low if the worker did not reinforce the young person's pro-social comments, identified problems with minimal input from the client, made no attempt to help the young person understand the purpose of supervision, and if the worker appeared to be punitive or blaming.

The coders attempted to score the interviews independently of the offender's response. In other words, if the worker was using high-level skills but the client was not engaged, the skills scores would still be high. This approach acknowledged that clients might be disengaged for reasons other than workers' skills, such as poor language skills, or earlier experiences with services.

Recidivism

The recidivism measure reported in this chapter is *any further offence, for which the young person was found guilty by a court, within two years of receiving their order*. The data was taken from police records. The two-year period was used based on the evidence that most young people who reoffend do so within a period of two years (Carcach and Leverett 1999). While there are obvious limitations to using only one measure, there was a significant correlation between this measure and other recidivism measures used in the study; for example, placement in detention or prison within two years (r .351 $p<.000$).

Results

Use of skills by workers and client recidivism

There was a positive relationship between the linear global score on use of the skills and reduced reoffending using a comparison of means in SPSS (Global Score 6.07 for those supervisors of young people who did not reoffend and 5.56 for those who did reoffend). This was, however, outside statistical levels of significance.

Similarly, when a dichotomous score was used, it was found that workers with high global skill scores (6 or above) had clients with lower rates of reoffending after two years compared with those with low global scores (see Table 61.1). However, the differences were outside the .05 level of statistical significance.

There was, however, a statistically significant association between the recidivism rates of clients of supervisors who had particularly low global scores when compared with the other clients. As shown in Table 61.2, if the probation officers were allocated a score of less than 5, their clients offended significantly more often than the clients of other probation officers. That is, those supervised by workers with more skills survived two years without reoffending at almost twice the rate of those whose workers who displayed fewer skills.

Table 61.1 Overall use of skills by workers (scored 6 or more and 5 or less) by any further offence in 24 months by clients

	Reoffended in two years
Skills score 5 or less	74% (39/53)
Skills score 6 or more	62.5% (40/64)

Table 61.2 Overall use of skills by workers (scored 5 or more and 4 or less) by any further offence in 24 months by young people

	Reoffended in two years
Skills score 4 or less	81% (26/32)
Skills score 5 or more	62% (52/85)
One tailed Fischer's exact test p <.04	

Table 61.3 Logistic regression analysis of overall use of skills by workers (scored 5 or more and 4 or less) by any further offence in 24 months by clients including client risk levels

		B	S.E.	Wald	df	Sig.	Exp(B)
Step 1[a]	Skill score	−1.088	.553	3.869	1	.049	.337
	YLSI	.116	.029	15.690	1	.000	1.123
	Constant	.642	1.056	.370	1	.543	1.901

[a] Variable(s) entered on step 1: gs4, FR.YLSI_score

This significant difference was also evident when a regression analysis was undertaken in SPSS, taking account of the assessments derived from the YLSI (the standard risk assessment measure used in NSW Juvenile Justice). In other words, the differences cannot be explained by the risk levels of the clients as shown in Table 61.3. When Indigenous status of the client was taken into account in the regression analysis, the differences remained within significant levels.

The use of other skills and client recidivism

Most of the skills coded during the observations were related to lower reoffending by clients. In most cases, however, this did not reach statistically significant levels. For example, the more time workers were involved with clients undertaking problem-solving, the lower the recidivism rates of the clients. When strategies were developed in the sessions to address problems, this was related to reduced offending, particularly where the young people developed the strategies themselves, rather than the worker. In each instance, when the workers used cognitive behavioural skills and relapse prevention skills, the clients had lower rates of recidivism. Workers who used pro-social modelling and relationship skills also had clients with lower reoffending rates. Workers who were rated as open and honest, non-blaming, optimistic, enthusiastic, used appropriate self-disclosure and who were friendly all had clients with lower reoffending.

None of these measures, however, reached conventional levels of statistical significance. The two worker skills that were most strongly related to reduced further offending were the use of rewards by the worker and a non-blaming approach. Fifty-five percent (n = 27/49) of the young people reoffended when the use of rewards by the worker was scored 3 or more on the 5-point scale, compared with 76% (n = 52/68) when the use of rewards was scored two or less. This was significant at the $p<.05$ level on a chi-square analysis, although it was not statistically significant when the YLSI was included in a regression analysis. High scores were given on this item if the worker identified the client's pro-social actions and comments (victim empathy for example) and praised the client or provided concrete rewards (reduced frequency of appointments for example) in response to the pro-social actions and comments of the client.

Those who scored above 2 on the 5-point scale for the non-blaming measure had a recidivism rate of 61% (n = 40/66) compared with 76.5% (n = 39/51) for those who scored two or below. This was just outside the conventional significance level (p = .056) after taking risk into account in the regression analysis. The non-blaming item was scored high if the worker explored the young person's circumstances (work, family, or drug use for example) and did not inadvertently or directly attribute blame to the young person for their situation.

Staff role and qualifications

As mentioned earlier, Juvenile Justice Workers may be employed as Juvenile Justice Counsellors or as Juvenile Justice Officers. The counsellors made more use of the effective practice skills, being twice as likely to be rated above 5 on the global score (45%, n = 38/84 for workers and 80%, n = 26/33 for counsellors; $p<.01$).

They also had clients with lower recidivism (54.5%, n = 18/33 for counsellors, compared with 73%, n = 61/84 for officers), yet the counsellors supervised clients who were higher risk (i.e. scored higher on the LSI-R). The differences in recidivism between the groups was statistically significant ($p<.05$) after taking risk levels into account through the regression analysis as shown in Table 61.4. The statistically significant differences between the staff groups remained if other variables such as client gender or Indigenous status were included in the analysis.

Table 61.4 Regression analysis of staff position (JJ Officer or JJ Counsellor) client risk level and any further offence in two years

		B	S.E.	Wald	df	Sig.	Exp(B)
Step 1[a]	FR.YLSI_score	.126	.030	17.354	1	.000	1.134
	Staff_position	−1.269	.501	6.403	1	.011	.281
	Constant	.205	.726	.080	1	.788	1.227

[a] Variable(s) entered on step 1: FR.YLSI_score, Staff_position

Discussion

A growing number of studies have indicated that correctional interventions characterized by certain features lead to reduced levels of recidivism. More specifically, a small group of studies has found that the nature of the skills used by supervisors in the routine supervision of offenders on community-based orders relates to the recidivism of offenders under supervision (Trotter 1996; Bonta et al. 2011; Robinson et al. 2011). These studies have also shown that supervisors are more likely to use these skills if they have received specific training and supervision based on the skills. One study (Trotter 2000) also found that supervisors who had completed social work and welfare qualifications (courses in which these skills are commonly taught) were more likely to use the skills and more likely to have clients with lower recidivism. There is some doubt, however, about the precise nature of the effective practice skills, with some studies supporting the importance of cognitive behavioural skills and others placing more emphasis on relationship skills (Bonta et al. 2011; Trotter 1996; Ward 2010). The studies to date have also focused on adult offenders rather than young offenders and they have used various methods to assess the use of skills.

This study aimed to examine the relationship between the use of skills in youth justice and client recidivism using observation of interviews and a detailed coding manual. It was found that when the observers rated the workers as having good skills, the clients had fewer further offences in the two-year follow-up period, although this only reached statistically significant levels when the clients of workers who were rated as making minimal use of the skills were compared with the clients of other workers. The workers with few skills seemed to be particularly ineffective.

The study found the skills with the strongest associations with reoffending were the use of rewards and a non-blaming approach. The relationship between the use of rewards by supervisors and low reoffending is consistent with earlier research on pro-social modelling and reinforcement (Trotter 1996), and with the various 'what works' meta-analyses (Bonta and Andrews 2010). It seems clear that it is a core skill in work with offenders. Similarly, the importance of the client-worker relationship and of collaboration between worker and client (arguably the antithesis of a blaming approach) has been consistently emphasized in the research on effective supervision (Andrews and Bonta 2008; McIvor and Raynor 2008; McNeill et al. 2005). Again, the ability to be non-blaming seems to be a core skill in effective offender supervision.

This study has a number of limitations. In particular, the sample was dependent on volunteers. It may be that those workers who volunteered were more skilled than other workers. Also, workers may have behaved under observation in a different way to the way they would usually behave. They might have used more skills under observation than they would usually use. The requirement to undertake research under ethical guidelines makes it difficult to control for these factors.

Nevertheless, when the results of this study are considered alongside the earlier research, it does support the hypothesis that workers with certain skills will have clients with lower recidivism and that the extent to which those skills are used by individual workers can be determined through a process of observation. It also provides support for the view that workers who have qualifications in social work or psychology and who are given a counselling role are likely to make more use of effective practice skills and have clients with lower recidivism.

These findings have implications for selection, training, and the roles of youth justice staff. There is potential for widespread reductions in recidivism if juvenile justice organizations prescribe a counselling role to supervisors and employ staff with relevant qualifications. Ongoing training and supervision focused on effective practice skills may provide for further reductions in reoffending. The benefits are likely to be further increased if training and supervision is accompanied by regular observation and analysis of interviews between juvenile justice workers and their supervisors, and with feedback, discussion, and coaching in order to provide for ongoing skill development.

Acknowledgements

The assistance of Phillipa Evans and Tamara Saunders, who undertook the data collection, is acknowledged, along with the support provided by Juvenile Justice NSW and the Australian Criminology Research Council.

Note

1 This chapter has been adapted from an article published in Trotter, C. (2012). Effective supervision of young offenders trends and issues. *Criminal Justice*, 448, 1–9.

References

Andrews, D. A. and Bonta, J. (2008) *The Psychology of Criminal Conduct*. Cincinnati: Anderson Publishing.

Andrews, D. A., Keissling, J. J., Russell, R. J. and Grant, B. A. (1979) *Volunteers and the One-to-One Supervision of Adult Probationers.* Toronto: Ontario Ministry of Correctional Services.

Australian Institute of Health and Welfare (AIHW). (2011) *Australia's welfare 2011.* Canberra: AIHW. Available at: http://www.aihw.gov.au/publication-detail/?id=10737420537.

Bonta, J. and Andrews, D. (2010) Viewing offender assessment and rehabilitation through the lens of the Risk-Needs-Responsivity model. In F. McNeil, P. Raynor and C. Trotter (Eds.), *Offender Supervision: New Directions in Theory, Research and Practice.* Devon: Willan Publishing.

Bonta, J., et al. (2011) An experimental demonstration of training probation officers in evidence-based community supervision. *Criminal Justice and Behavior,* 38(11), 1127–1148.

Carcach, C. and Leverett, S. (1999) *Recidivism Among Juvenile Offenders: An Analysis of Times to Reappearance in Court.* Research and Public Policy series no. 17. Canberra: Australian Institute of Criminology. Available at: http://aic.gov.au/publications/current%20series/rpp/1-20/rpp17.aspx.

Dowden, C. and Andrews, D. A. (2004) The importance of staff practice in delivering effective correctional treatment: A meta-analytic review of the literature. *International Journal of Offender Therapy and Comparative Criminology,* 48(2), 203–214.

McIvor, G. and Raynor, P. (Eds.) (2008) *Developments in Social Work with Offenders.* London: Jessica Kingsley.

McNeill, F., Batchelor, S., Burnett, R. and Knox, J. (2005) *21st Century Social Work: Reducing Re-Offending: Key Practice Skills.* Edinburgh: Scottish Executive.

Raynor, P., Ugwudike, P. and Vanstone, M. (2010) Skills and strategies in probation supervision: The Jersey Study. In F. McNeil, P. Raynor and C. Trotter (Eds.), *Offender Supervision: New Directions in Theory, Research and Practice.* Devon: Willan Publishing.

Robinson, C., Vanbenschoten, S., Alexander, M. and Lowenkamp, C. (2011) A random (almost) study of staff training aimed at reducing re-arrest (STARR): Reducing recidivism through intentional design. *Federal Probation,* 75(2), 57–63.

Trotter, C. (1996) The impact of different supervision practices in community corrections. *Australian and New Zealand Journal of Criminology,* 29(1), 29–46.

Trotter, C. (2000) Social work education, pro-social orientation and effective probation practice. *Probation Journal,* 47, 256–261.

Trotter, C. (2015) *Working with Involuntary Clients.* Sydney: Allen & Unwin.

Ward, T. (2010) The Good Lives Model of offender rehabilitation. In F. McNeil, P. Raynor and C. Trotter (Eds.), *Offender Supervision: New Directions in Theory, Research and Practice.* Devon: Willan Publishing.

Ward, T., Melser, J. and Yates, P. M. (2007) Reconstructing the Risk-Need-Responsivity model: A theoretical elaboration and evaluation. *Aggression and Violent Behavior,* 12, 208–228.

62

Working with young people in prison

Phillipa Evans and Chris Trotter

Introduction

The detention of young people in custody in Australia has received consider-able recent community and media attention. The publicized use of physical restraint mechanisms in Don Dale Detention Centre in the Northern Territory is a compelling example of this media attention, and led to the establishment in 2016 of a Royal Commission into the protection and detention of children in the Northern Territory. The report by the Commission (Royal Commission 2017: 4) found that:

> The centres are neither fit for rehabilitation nor suitable workplaces for staff. They are not fit for accommodating, let alone rehabilitating, chil-dren and young people . . . children were subject to verbal abuse, physical control and humiliation.

The report refers to excessive use of force and of isolation of young people causing 'likely, in some cases lasting, psychological damage' (Royal Commis-sion: 8). The Royal Commission refers specifically to the need for a new model for secure detention of young people in custody.

Concerns about youth detention are not limited, however, to the North-ern Territory. For example, the Victorian Parliament Legal and Social Issues

Committee is currently undertaking an Inquiry into two Victorian youth justice centres following behavioural disturbances, riots, and damage at the centres. The Inquiry's terms of reference look to 'the security and safety of staff, employees and young offenders'; to 'the culture, policies, practices and reporting of management at the centres'; and, to the 'role of the Department of Health and Human Services in overseeing practices at the centres' (Parliament of Victoria 2017). Similarly, Victoria undertook a comprehensive review of the youth justice system that emphasized shortcomings in rehabilitation efforts (Armytage and Ogloff 2017). Concerns about youth detention are also prevalent internationally. A recent Inspectors' report regarding Oakhill Secure Training Centre in England, for example, referred to 'violence, vandalism and weapons' and recommended an immediate review of practices (HM Inspectorate of Prisons 2017).

Background

There is negligible research on how to develop rehabilitative environments in youth detention. There is, however, a growing body of research focused on community-based supervision of offenders, both young and adult, placed on court orders or parole. This research can assist in the development of a framework for creating a rehabilitative environment in youth detention as it demonstrates the impact youth justice workers can have on engaging young people and how they can improve their antisocial behaviour.

A growing body of research dating back to the 1970s (Andrews et al. 1979) suggests that when probation officers or others who supervise offenders in the community have good interpersonal skills, offenders will be positively engaged in supervision and have low recidivism rates. The various studies have used different methods to examine the relationship between workers' use of interpersonal skills and offender outcomes including interviews with workers and offenders to ask about the skills used and observation of interviews, or of audiotapes of interviews, in order to identify the skills.

Two reviews of the research have considered the overall impact of worker skills in community corrections supervision and the specific nature of those skills: a systematic literature review (Trotter 2013) and a meta-analysis (Chadwick et al. 2015). An earlier meta-analysis (Dowden and Andrews 2004) also considered the relationship between core practice skills and recidivism in corrections generally. Two of the studies included in these reviews were undertaken in Australia (Trotter 1996, 2012). Each of these research reviews came to similar conclusions – that workers with good skills had clients who were engaged with their workers and had low rates of recidivism, often up to 50% lower than control groups. The skills include modelling and reinforcing pro-social values (e.g. respect for the law, fair treatment of others) and reinforcing of those values in the offenders; role clarification (e.g. helping offenders to understand the dual helping and social control role of the worker);

problem-solving skills (e.g. addressing problems such as family breakdown or drug use); effective challenging (respectful questioning of pro-criminal comments or rationalization); use of cognitive techniques (e.g. teaching offenders about how address distorted thinking); and appropriate empathy for the offender's situation.

A number of studies have also suggested that while workers generally make minimal use of effective practice skills (Bonta et al. 2008; Trotter and Evans 2012), training, group coaching, supervision which includes observations of practice and feedback, and organizational support and reinforcement leads to an increase in the use of skills (Robinson et al. 2011; Trotter 1996, 2013).

Worker skills in youth detention

There is less research relating to worker skills in youth detention. There is some evidence, however, that workers do not instinctively use effective practice skills in detention settings any more than they do in community settings. This is certainly evident from Inquiries such as the Northern Territory Royal Commission (Royal Commission 2017), the Victorian Youth Justice Review (Armytage and Ogloff 2017), and from other research.

A Swedish study in juvenile detention highlighted the complex populations and situations that youth officers are commonly presented with. They examined the training and backgrounds of youth workers to get a better understanding of the organizational conditions impacting on the provision of care offered to young people in detention. Researchers found that there was significant diversity amongst the staff in terms of their educational background and the training and support offered to staff whilst employed with the organization. In addition to these findings, the majority of staff did not feel competent in performing their daily work and many had never been offered any in-service education (Ahonen and Degner 2014).

On the other hand, there is some evidence that workers in detention settings can be encouraged to use effective practice skills. Research undertaken by the National Offender Management Service in the UK (Kenny and Webster 2015) aimed to develop a more rehabilitative environment in a prison and young offender institution. The project involved training ten prison/youth officers in 'Five Minute Interventions'. The trained officers were then compared to a comparison group who also volunteered for training but did not receive the training. The training involved teaching the staff to turn everyday conversations into rehabilitative interventions. The training involved an introduction to skills similar to the skills identified in the community-based research – positive feedback, active listening, and encouragement of residents. Interviews with the officers before and after the training indicated that the trained officers had improved relationships with residents, higher job satisfaction, improvements in prisoner/resident thinking skills, self-efficacy, and problem-solving abilities. This is a small study and does not report statistical significance; nevertheless it is consistent with the outcomes in the community-based studies. In a separate study, researchers examined the experiences of prisoners who participated in 'Five Minute Intervention' conversations with trained prison officers (Tate, Blagden, and Mann 2017). Again, the sample size for this study was small (ten prisoners); however a number of positive changes were identified by the prisoners that they believed occurred from the 'Five Minute Intervention' conversations. These included changes to their thinking skills and self-efficacy (Tate et al. 2017). Prisoners also reported a change in their perception towards the prison officers, believing that they had been shown humanity and a caring attitude towards them.

There is also some evidence that effective practice skills used by custodial youth workers can lead to lower recidivism in addition to improved relationships in custody. A US study by Marsh and Evans (2009) examined staff/youth relations of 543 young people in secure correctional settings in a number of youth institutions and concluded that there was at least tentative evidence that relationships with staff lead to better outcomes for youth after they leave custody. They comment on the challenges relating to changing the culture of youth detention but suggest that 'the cost associated with avoiding this challenge, however, is simply too great for society or its most troubled youth' (Marsh and Evans 2009: 64).

There is also some evidence that adult prison officer skills are related to better outcomes. French and Gendreau (2006), for example, concluded from a meta-analysis that prison climate and behaviours are better when workers have a rehabilitative focus. They suggest that good practice in prisons is similar to good practice in community supervision.

McQuire and Raynor (2017: 146) summarize this issue in a recent publication:

> Recent research in prisons has placed the relationship between prison staff and prisoners at the centre of our understanding of what makes a good prison. . . . Prison staff are now told that every contact matters . . . and are being encouraged to use personal skills more purposefully and systematically in new initiatives like Five Minute Interventions.

This comment is supported by the Victorian Youth Justice review by Armytage and Ogloff (2017):

> The relationship between staff and young people is critical for the prompt identification of their risks, issues, needs and triggers. In an effective operating model, these relationships form part of daily operations, led by the key worker or case manager function. The relationship between custodial staff and young people is powerful and influential, given young people spend a minimum of 12 hours each day looking to staff as role models. These relationships provide the platform for the key risks/issues of the

clients, their history, their family, their acquaintances and their interpersonal issues.

(p. 223)

In summary, there have been a number of concerns expressed about the good order, security, and rehabilitative environment in both Australian and overseas youth detention centres. These issues have received a significant profile in Australia in recent years. It is clear that the practice skills of youth justice workers have an impact on the engagement and recidivism of young offenders; and that youth justice workers make more use of practice skills when given training, coaching, and organizational support. Whilst much of the research on this has been undertaken in community-based settings, the evidence suggests that similar principles also apply to youth detention settings.

An evidence-based framework for effective practice in youth detention

Research is currently being undertaken in youth detention centres in NSW Australia examining the impacts of training, supervision, and coaching on the development of worker skills in juvenile detention. This research is specifically examining how the development of effective practice skills relates to specific outcome measures including: the level of positive interactions between staff and young people, the well-being of staff and young people, and the good order of the centres.

The training model occurs over six months, with staff participating in a two-hour module each month. Each module covers a specific effective practice skill including role clarification, pro-social modelling, brief problem-solving, and relationship skills. The training also addresses some of the background to criminal behaviour including trauma. This training has been designed to introduce staff to a specific skill then practice the skill in between sessions, with senior practitioners providing real-time feedback about the staff's use of the skills in practice.

This study aims to advance knowledge about how to develop more rehabilitative custodial environments by examining the following research questions:

1   Do workers demonstrate an increase in their use of appropriate interpersonal skills in their interactions with residents following the training, coaching, and supervision intervention?

2   If so, is there an improvement on the outcome measures (such as positive interactions between staff and residents, well-being of staff and residents, and the good order of the centre), in comparison to before the intervention and in comparison to a control group which has not been offered the intervention?

3   What is the relationship between use of the specific skills and outcome measures?
4   What are the implications of the findings for youth detention in Australia?

The template for effective practice in youth detention produced by the research is likely to influence policy in Australia and internationally with long-term benefits for youth justice staff and for the rehabilitation of residents.

Procedure

The research focuses on three youth detention centres across NSW, two metropolitan centres, and one regional centre. The research involves a mixed methods study using quantitative and qualitative methods. It uses a pre-test/post-test design within the experimental sites and in addition to comparative groups design in relation to three control group sites (Rubin and Babbie 2005). The research uses qualitative methods to explain the quantitative findings through interviews with workers and staff and through focus groups with key stakeholders. The focus groups will also provide data on the practical implications of the findings. The methodology also includes the use of triangulation with multiple data sources (interviews, videotape transcripts, and department records) and use of more than one researcher for coding of videotapes to enhance the validity and reliability of the study.

Staff response to training

The training has been successfully delivered and completed at one NSW detention centre, Reiby. After each module, staff were required to complete a feedback form regarding their satisfaction with the training and also how useful they felt the module was in terms of assisting them to do their day-to-day job.

Workers generally agreed that module 1, offending behaviour and human development, met their expectations, with 52.6% agreeing with this statement.

	Frequency	Valid percent
Strongly disagree	0	0
Disagree	0	0
Neutral	3	15.8
Agree	10	52.6
Strongly agree	6	31.6
Total	19	100.0

Workers also typically agreed that module 1 would help them go about their day-to-day role, with 63.2% of workers agreeing with this statement.

	Frequency	Valid percent
Strongly disagree	0	0
Disagree	0	0
Neutral	1	5.3
Agree	12	63.2
Strongly agree	6	31.6
Total	19	100.0

Workers were introduced to the concept of role clarification in module 2, whereby the concept of the dual role and being a helper and having security responsibilities was introduced. Again, staff were mostly positive about this module with 83.4% either agreeing or strongly agreeing that this module met their expectations.

	Frequency	Valid percent
Strongly disagree	0	0
Disagree	1	2.8
Neutral	5	13.9
Agree	15	41.7
Strongly agree	15	41.7
Total	36	100.0

86.1% of workers either agreed or strongly agreed that this module would assist them in their day-to-day job.

	Frequency	Valid percent
Strongly disagree	0	0
Disagree	0	0
Neutral	5	13.9
Agree	16	44.4
Strongly agree	15	41.7
Total	36	100.0

Module 3, interpersonal skills, worked through a number of relationship skills that can assist workers with establishing rapport with young people in a positive manner. This module also examined the use of humour and self-disclosure in the helping relationship. Workers were positive in their experience of this module with most workers agreeing that the module met their expectations.

	Frequency	Valid percent
Strongly disagree	0	0
Disagree	0	0
Neutral	2	7.7
Agree	14	53.8
Strongly agree	10	38.5
Total	26	100.0

96.1% of workers reported that this module would help them with their daily duties.

	Frequency	Valid percent
Strongly disagree	0	0
Disagree	0	0
Neutral	1	3.8
Agree	11	42.3
Strongly agree	14	53.8
Total	26	100.0

This preliminary feedback indicates that staff are finding the training helpful and applicable to their day-to-day interactions with young people.

Discussion

Workers' acquisition and development of effective practice skills needs to be well supported outside the training environment to ensure it is firmly embedded in day-to-day practice. Workers need to see a benefit to the skills that they are being trained in and persuaded that this way of working will be beneficial to both themselves and young people. The training and support model being piloted in NSW moves beyond a typical training approach, supporting workers to utilize the skills between the sessions. Preliminary feedback from workers after attending the introductory modules suggests that these modules are being received positively and workers feel that the content will better assist them to do their day-to-day job.

Conclusion

It is clear that youth workers in detention have a significant role to play in the management of young people. Whilst research in this area is quite sparse, the available research indicates benefits to both workers and young people when workers utilize effective practice skills in their daily interactions with young people. The research presented in this chapter provides an overview of a training and coaching package designed to support the implementation of these skills in three juvenile justice centres across NSW. The underpinnings of the training and support model are to further encourage and facilitate positive relationships between workers and young people.

References

Ahonen, L. and Degner, J. (2014) Working with complex problem behaviors in juvenile institutional care: Staff's competence, organizational conditions and public value. *International Journal of Prisoner Health*, 10(4), 239–251.

Andrews, D. A., Keissling, J. J., Russell, R. J. and Grant, B. A. (1979) *Volunteers and the One-to-One Supervision of Adult Probationers*. Toronto: Ontario Ministry of Correctional Services.

Armytage, P. and Ogloff, J. (2017) *Youth Justice Review and Strategy: Meeting Needs and Reducing Offending*. Available at: www.justice.vic.gov.au/home/justice+system/youth+justice/youth+justice+review+and+strategy+meeting+needs+and+reducing+offending (Accessed 2 November 2017).

Bonta, J., Rugge, T., Scott, T., Bougon, G. and Yessine, A. (2008) Exploring the black box of community supervision. *Journal of Offender Rehabilitation*, 47(3), 248–270.

Chadwick, N., DeWolf, A. and Serin, R. (2015) Effectively training supervision officers – a meta-analytic review of the impact on offender outcome. *Criminal Justice and Behaviour*, 42(10), 977–989.

Dowden, C. and Andrews, D. A. (2004) The importance of staff practice in delivering effective correctional treatment: A meta-analytic review of the literature. *International Journal of Offender Therapy and Comparative Criminology*, 48(2), 203–214.

French, S. A. and Gendreau, P. (2006) Reducing prison misconducts. *Criminal Justice and Behaviour*, 33, 185–218.

HM Inspectorate of Prisons. (2017) *Inspection of Secure Training Centres. Inspection of Oakhill*. Available at: www.statewatch.org/news/2017/nov/uk-ofsted-hmic-cgc-oakhill-secure-training-centre-inspection-report-21-11-17.pdf (Accessed 6 December 2017).

Kenny, T. and Webster, S. (2015) *Experiences of Prison Officers Delivering Five Minute Interventions at HMP/OI Portland*. Available at: http://socialwelfare.bl.uk/subject-areas/services-client-groups/adult-offenders/ministryofjustice/175147portland-fmi.pdf (Accessed 25 November 2017).

Marsh, S. and Evans, W. (2009) Youth perspectives on their relationships with staff in juvenile correction settings and perceived likelihood of success on release. *Youth Violence and Juvenile Justice*, 7(1), 46–67.

McGuire, M. and Raynor, P. (2017) Offender management in and after prison – the end of 'end to end'. *Criminology and Criminal Justice*, 17(2), 138–157.

Parliament of Victoria. (2017) *Victorian Parliament Legal and Social issues Committee Inquiry into Youth Justice Centres in Victoria*. Available at: www.parliament.vic.gov.au/lsic/inquiries?showyear=0&section_id=489&cat_id=453 (Accessed 1 November 2017).

Robinson, C., Van Benschoten, S., Alexander, M. and Lowenkamp, C. (2011) A random (almost) study of staff training aimed at reducing re-arrest: Reducing recidivism through intentional design. *Federal Probation*, 75(2), 57–63.

Royal Commission. (2017) *Royal Commission into the Protection and Detention of Children in the Northern Territory*. Report Overview. Available at: https://childdetentionnt. royalcommission.gov.au/Pages/Report.aspx (Accessed 26 November 2017).

Rubin, A. and Babbie, E. (2005) *Research Methods for Social Work*. Belmont: Thompson Brooks, Cole.

Tate, H., Blagden, N. and Mann, R. (2017) Prisoner's perceptions of care and rehabilitation from prison officers trained as 5 minute interventionists: Analytical summary, HM Prison & Probation Service. Available at http://irep.ntu.ac.uk/id/ eprint/32345/1/9882_Blagden.pdf (Accessed 27 May 2019).

Trotter, C. (1996) The impact of different supervision practices in community corrections. *Australian and New Zealand Journal of Criminology*, 29(1), 29–46.

Trotter, C. (2012) Effective supervision of young offenders. *Trends and Issues in Criminal Justice*, 448, 1–8.

Trotter, C. (2013) Reducing recidivism through probation supervision – what we know and don't know from four decades of research. *Federal Probation*, 77(2), 43–46.

Trotter, C. and Evans, P. (2012) Analysis of supervision skills in juvenile justice. *Australian and New Zealand Journal of Criminology*, 45(2), 255–273.

63 Prevention work with young people

Anne Robinson

Introduction

Many areas around youth justice are difficult and contentious. Even so, prevention stands out as a special case. Youth justice services are charged with preventing young people's involvement in crime or antisocial behaviour whilst being positioned alongside other children's services in the effort to engage with young people in tackling the myriad problems they may face in life, and in contributing to their positive development and resilience (McAra 2010). What prevention means for youth justice is consequently a vexed question and one that has been understood differently and given varying degrees of emphasis across its history (Muncie 2015). A narrow view focuses on behaviours that break the law and social norms, and it is largely this version that informed the 'preventative turn' (Muncie 2015) which took hold in the wake of the Crime and Disorder Act 1998 in England and Wales. Broader perspectives refer to preventing potential poor outcomes for young people, for example, in education, mental health, and social relationships, enhancing their capacities and assisting their transitions to adulthood and full citizenship (Hall et al 1998). Here I explore these broader notions with examples of preventative work by youth workers, illustrating key characteristics of relationships, social learning, and active participation conducive to growth.

Under New Labour, it was certainly recognized that young people's personal and social circumstances have a bearing on what they do and the way they behave, including potential offending, drug use, and aggression. However, connections that are often complex and subtle were framed within the much-criticized Risk Factor Prevention Paradigm (RFPP) and separated out as 'criminogenic risk factors' (O'Mahoney 2009; Paylor 2011). The RFPP over-simplifies causes and effects, such as the influence of poor parenting or family stress (Case and Haines 2015), eschewing a holistic view of young people and their interrelated needs. The RFPP nevertheless proved useful to the Youth Justice Board in justifying intervention targeted at particular individuals, geographical 'hot spots', or groups, such as care leavers. The Labour government directed a great deal of money at prevention activities under the aegis of youth offending teams (Blyth and Soloman 2009) but these arguably risked defeating their own purpose. First,

> the language of 'prevention' is problematic in itself, in that it generates a pre-emptive concern with 'problems' and 'risk' rather than focusing on universal aspirations and broadly 'inclusive' goals.
>
> (Smith 2011: 175)

Practice may have been more variable, but the surrounding discourse was firmly on deficits, not healthy growth and fulfilling lives. Second – and relatedly – prevention projects were largely funded on outcomes and the numbers of young people from target populations who participated, encouraging projects to over-emphasize the riskiness or vulnerability of the young people they were working with (Kelly 2012), hardly a recipe for inclusive and non-stigmatizing practice.

Over this period, youth work itself was subject to pressures over performance and managerial prescription in the same way as youth justice, with strikingly similar expressions of pain and frustration from practitioners (Mason 2015). Its ambiguous and ill-defined professional status has caused it to struggle even more to maintain a sense of identity (Bradford and Finn 2014). Youth work activity has been drastically cut in the austerity regimes of the Coalition and Conservative governments (Mason 2015; Price 2017) but the 'shape-shifting capacity' (Bradford and Finn 2014) of youth work and the many contexts in which it takes place – allied to religious communities, sporting clubs, schools and colleges, guides and scouts – ensures its continued existence. The National Youth Agency articulates key aims for a heterogenous workforce:

> Youth work focuses on working holistically with young people. It's about building resilience and character and giving young people the life skills (often totally misleadingly described as 'soft') they need to live, learn, work and interact successfully with other people.
>
> (www.nya.org.uk/about-us/ourpurpose)

This chapter explores how youth work seeks to do this, based on my experience in three youth work projects as part of my doctoral research. Whilst not ignoring the current difficulties taken up by the *In Defence of Youth Work* campaign (https://indefenceofyouthwork.com/), I suggest that the best youth work practice is instructive in how to engage with young people in ways that are empowering and participatory. Three particular themes are of note – relationships of trust, learning from social groups, and citizenship – and these each raise questions about the appropriate location and perimeters of prevention work with young people who may come into conflict with the law.

Despite common interest in young people and their well-being, the principles underpinning youth work differ from those of youth justice practice. Whilst it does vary according to the specific context and different traditions within youth work (Jeffs and Smith 2002), historically youth work is based on voluntary participation, social education, relationships, and community (Jeffs and Smith 2008). In essence, this means working with young people with attention to the democratic processes and socialization that takes place within groups. However, it is evident that the distinction between youth work and the casework methods of social work and youth justice is being eroded. Despite the worthy intentions of *Positive for Youth* (HM Government 2011) recent youth policy has promoted targeted youth support and work with partner agencies, curtailing youth workers' autonomy in how and when they intervene with young people. That said, whilst maintaining an ethos that favours universal provision, youth work practice has traditionally directed attention to those young people who are most disadvantaged or in need (Williamson 2009). This is now simply more explicit and youth work is pushed to compromise its principle of voluntarism in dealings with contracting organizations or with partnerships (Mason 2015).

While I was aware that these tensions existed in the wider organizations where I volunteered, they were not overriding concerns for the specific youth projects themselves, which offered group settings and informal relationships with supportive youth workers. Briefly, the three projects were

- 'The conservation project' – a partnership initiative hosted by an established children's organization in the voluntary sector. This lasted ten months and was grant-funded to improve young people's mental health by connecting them with local and accessible outside spaces. The project involved older peer mentors alongside the main group who were mostly 13–14 years old.
- 'The church hall group' – a long-standing weekly open access session which attracts a more fluid group of young people aged 15–17. Again, most of the young people have relationships outside of the sessions from attending the same school and/or living locally.
- 'The boys group' – run in a training centre for young men unable to attend conventional college. This was the only one of the three where members came to the project by referral, typically arising from psychological or

mental health conditions. The group explored masculinity and group members' transitions as young men over 12 weeks. It was led by a male worker from the same voluntary sector organization as the 'conservation project', and I acted as co-worker.

These three projects are very different and illustrate the diversity in prevention work and, indeed, the 'ills' that they are aiming to prevent. In many respects they exemplify the type of 'progressive prevention-promotion' (Haines and Case 2015) that focuses on positive behaviours and outcomes and young people's rights and entitlements. There have been difficulties in determining the effectiveness of prevention activity, particularly given the tendency for risk assessment to over-predict negative outcomes (Haines and Case 2015). Unqualified claims for the success of prevention should be treated with caution. There is no certain way of knowing whether the absence of offending or ASB is due to pre-emptive intervention. Separating out the effects of prevention activity from other factors, such as police recording or charging practices, is also tricky (CJJI 2010). The measurement of positive growth and resilience is not straightforward either, at least not in the quantitative terms favoured by policy makers. However, there are qualitative indicators of participation and well-being that may provide rich evidence of the value of intervening early to prevent later problems, as I found in my fieldwork.

In this regard, Spence et al. (2006) highlight the importance within youth work of negotiated relationships between young people and youth workers based on mutual respect. Such relationships are seen as empowering for young people and potentially transformative (Hart 2016). Trust is a key element underpinning credibility and legitimacy. Here the positioning of those youth work projects that sit apart from statutory agencies may be critical. For example, one of Hart's (2016) research sites was a homework club partly funded by a school who asked to be provided with the names of the young people who attended. The young people unanimously said that they did not want this information passed to the school: they valued the homework club as a separate entity. Elsewhere, ethnographic research found young people campaigning for new youth facilities despite having an established youth centre in the area: 'The youth club is not the place for these young people. The activities do not appeal and, for Sarah at least, the fact that the club is run by a policeman speaks volumes' (Hall et al. 1999: 508).

Trust is not an overnight phenomenon and 'like respect, has to be earned through processes of interaction, often over a sustained and lengthy period' (Hart 2015: 62). Whilst this is true, in the two projects where I was present from the outset, I observed the skilled process of building trust and attachment, with relationships of trust developing surprisingly quickly and then strengthening over time. Young people were given choices: the young men in 'the boys group' set the agenda for the full series of sessions, identifying subjects significant and relevant to them. The perimeters of sessions – break times, refreshments, one-to-one time as well as group activity – were also agreed and carried forward over the weeks. The workers thus demonstrated their trust-worthiness and they enhanced their position of trust through the manner in which they responded to issues arising in the projects in relation to well-being and security. This was evident when several young people were asked to leave one of the projects and the youth worker was at pains to explain the reasons for his actions to the remaining group in a way that increased their sense of ownership and responsibility for the project space.

The relational practices at the heart of youth work mean that boundaries tend to be more flexible than for youth justice practitioners. Rigid boundaries may be experienced as barriers by the very hard-to-reach young people that professionals are seeking to engage (Hart 2016). The challenge for the worker is to develop a relationship that is personal, intimate, and emotionally engaged, whilst at the same time protecting areas of life and feelings that are private. Self-disclosure can be used to demonstrate understanding and empathy or for the purposes of social learning. I have witnessed one practitioner sharing experiences of homelessness and precarious employment and another discussing their own sexual identity, both doing so consciously and purposefully in context. Nevertheless this is personal information that would seem less comfortable to reveal in a youth justice setting:

> The boundaries between personal and professional life in youth work are narrower than other professions, but the quantity of information one is expected to disclose and the quality of information – the type of information one is expected to disclose is greater. Who you are as a person, as well as a professional, is of vital importance in youth work.
>
> (Ord 2007: 54 cited in Hart 2016: 872)

Looking further at relationships of trust, Ani Wierenga's (2009) ethnographic research in rural Tasmania offers real insights. She explores how and why young people engage so differently in the process of what she terms 'making a life'. By this she means creating possibilities for future livelihood, meaning, and social connectedness, all of which are fundamentally of interest in prevention work. She followed a cohort of 32 young people through their adolescence and towards adulthood, benefitting from her previous history in that community as youth worker and the relationships of trust already gained. The stories that young people told about their lives are therefore remarkably candid and, combined with observations and knowledge of the community over more than ten years, these enable Wierenga to reflect in depth on the relationships that matter and how differently young people use them to access resources.

In her analysis resources may be material in the sense of housing, transport, and social contacts, but may also be less tangible things connected to culture, communication, and shared practices of story-telling as a means of making sense of life and developing future directions. While young people may have different types and varying quantities of 'resources-at-hand', Wierenga suggests that there is a common theme in terms of resources being accessed through relationships of trust. Roles such as coach, mentor, interpreter, translator may therefore be greatly significant in young people's lives. And where these are not readily available in social and family networks, professionals or volunteers may play a critical part by providing the 'human bridges' that enable young people to access the resources and social capital that they need.

Wierenga (2009) also emphasizes that the trusted relationships that matter to young people are not necessarily restricted to personal relationships, but may involve groups, institutions, or systems. Aspects of trust operate at all sorts of levels from the macro to the very personal but it is the relationships that help make a resource seem relevant to the young person that matter. These may involve role models that show that a particular activity or occupation is accessible for 'someone like me', connections to other locations that therefore become 'knowable', or opportunities for exposure to, and engagement with, new experiences. Here Wierenga talks about 'resource flows', by which she means the channels through which resources of all types are made available. This is not just about what is on offer: she refers to creating meaningful possibilities and enabling young people to try things out so that there is a 'been there, can do it again' attitude to moving further. By way of illustration, one member of the 'boys group' has been inspired to start voluntary work with other young people because of the example shown by the youth worker. He has accepted invitations to participate in other groups and to begin to lead activities. The 'conservation project' provides another striking example as some of the young women prepared presentations about the project that they then delivered to school assemblies and in local primary schools. At the start of the project, they would never have envisaged feeling confident and able to talk publicly in that way.

There is learning here for a youth justice system that has been notably instrumental in its approach to relationships but also questions about the potential for developing these sorts of relationships of trust in situations where there are degrees of coercion or at least the possibility of young people's non-engagement with prevention activity being cited if they come into contact with police or courts. Moreover, while youth justice workers are just as interested in young people's growth and development as youth workers, they are often also expected to reduce the impact of their behaviours on others. These both impinge on their ability to create the close and intimate relationships with young people that youth workers seek and to be young person-centred in the way that the best youth work practice achieves. If we also recognize the feelings of mistrust that young people may have towards authority, based on their own or their peers' experiences, the arguments for locating all prevention work outside of the criminal justice system surely become compelling.

One further aspect to consider is the ability of youth work to connect with young people in groups and to use the group process as a means of learning. In 'the church hall group' the workers are reactive and focused on joint problem-solving but work more directly to encourage participation, leadership, and so on in 'the boys group', building skills and social confidence. Here the value of group identities and identification (Jenkins 2014) comes to light and certainly in 'the conservation project' loyalty played a crucial part in keeping the core participants engaged. The project was not aimed at any particular ethnicity but from the outset attracted an established friendship group of South Asian young women who quickly formed a collective attachment to project workers and volunteers, then to the wider organization that hosted the project. They enjoyed the visits to outdoor locations and the activities that formed part of the project but perhaps benefitted even more from the time they spent together in informal settings that allowed them to explore new roles and ways of relating. Arguably they would not have become involved individually in some of the more challenging and personally stretching aspects of the project that they were willing to take on together. By the end of the ten months they were observably more autonomous as individuals and more self-aware, as well as more tightly bonded as a supportive friendship group.

Friendship and peer groups are treated with ambivalence at best in youth justice and this seriously underplays their role in adolescent development. As France et al. note,

> Pre-occupation with 'at risk' youngsters' identifications with 'delinquent' or anti-social peers precludes attention to how peers and peer practices are also important to individual identity work through the positioning of self and 'others' (Hey 1997) and engagement in (normative) youth cultural pursuits.
>
> (2012: 81)

Youth work, in contrast, recognizes the value of peer groups for safety, for self-exploration, and for identity. Their function in providing transitional opportunities for young people as they move away from families of origin may have been exaggerated (Jones 2009) but they nevertheless provide social connectedness and sites of learning. They may also be enablers of social capital and support, allowing young people to find collective ways of coping with situations of economic, social, or racial disadvantage (Bottrell 2009; MacDonald and Marsh 2005).

It seems that youth work is better able (and certainly more willing) to respond to young people in all the various groups that they occupy and to recognize the positive aspects of their interrelations. It understands that young people seek a degree of control over their lives and want to feel powerful even if, at that moment, they are doing this in maladaptive ways. For Ungar (2004) the key is recognizing the strengths, capacities, and energies that young people may be evidencing whilst they are acting out, rebelling, or perhaps taking prominent roles in a gang. In ostensibly negative situations, these are positive qualities and capacities that can be nurtured through a health-enhancing approach with the aim of developing resilience. It might be too optimistic to suggest that present day youth work has the capability to do this and to make an appreciable difference given its diminished status in the current configuration of children's services. However, its core beliefs are focused on empowerment and promoting resilience, and we can draw from practice examples of proactive engagement with groups that could provide valuable insights for youth justice and other services that remain stubbornly problem-focused.

Of course, the ultimate aim of youth work is to enable young people to participate in society and to become active citizens. The informality of the youth group or project can be conducive to a sharing of power and practicing democratic processes in decision-making and communication – effectively citizenship in microcosm. Citizenship, however, is a tricky and contested concept, specifically within the discourses of morality or 'rights and responsibilities' that have come to dominate the citizenship curriculum. In contrast, Hall et al. argue for a wider conception of citizenship and the importance of having not just formal rights, such as the right to vote, but also the capacity to exercise them. They suggest that

> The *practice* of youth work – incorporating participative activity, community involvement, the acquisition of skills and competences – contains much that bears strongly on elements of citizenship. Indeed, youth work, as broadly conceived, may be viewed as a 'playground' for the learning of citizenship.
>
> (1998: 309)

Both Hall et al. (1998) and Thomson and colleagues (2004; Henderson et al. 2007) talk about citizenship in the context of achieving adult status and associated feelings of independence, autonomy, and agency. The *Inventing Adulthoods* study also shows how some young participants stressed the relational aspects of adulthood involved in caring and taking responsibility for others which may be particularly important as conventional age-related markers and institutional rites of passage carry increasingly less meaning. Young people appreciate their competence and contribution being recognized and benefit from opportunities to develop agency. Although the youngest of the three groups in my fieldwork, members of 'the conservation project' conducted panel interviews for workers for a new project being run by the children's organization and enjoyed the praise they received for taking that responsibility seriously. Trust and respect were key ingredients in enabling them to take a role in recruitment which resonates with all that is known about best practice in youth work and, it must be said, youth justice.

As I have illustrated through glimpses of my fieldwork, best practice can still be found. Nevertheless, we are facing a challenging scenario. Youth justice – flawed as it is in terms of prevention – has largely withdrawn in favour of other statutory work (Bateman 2017) whilst youth work and other projects are neither comprehensively nor adequately resourced. This is worrying in the light of Williamson's view that

> Where once 'benign neglect' was the desired position for youth justice . . .
> now this is tantamount to malign indifference in the context of difficult
> transitions to adulthood and the ways in which social exclusion has a
> clustering and persistent effect.
>
> (2009: 14)

In sum, the present puzzle for prevention is no longer what should be prioritized and what risks, vulnerabilities, and potentialities are of most concern.
The conundrum is, first, how we identify spaces of time and contexts where
relationships of trust and possibilities for enhancing young people's resilience
can be nurtured, and, second, how we maximize their impact. The three projects described here may help us find a way forward. The two projects focused
on target groups demonstrate how thoughtful positioning in host organizations can enhance the positive effects of project work. The reach of these projects far exceeded the limited number of young people involved, in the case of
the 'boys group' by developing relationships with staff in the training centre
and influencing their practice as well as their relationships with participants.
For 'the conservation project' the dissemination activities meant that news
of the project and the outdoor spaces that young people could visit for peace
and healing reached a large number of children and young people. A little
intervention at strategic points can thus go a long way but demands care in
planning, clarity of purpose, and skills in delivery, all of which were arguably
lacking in the rushed expansion of crime-related prevention in the 'nough-
ties'. Prevention in the contemporary context of austerity needs to justify its
existence and to go beyond crude metrics to do so.

Finally, we must end by revisiting the importance of space for young people that allows them to develop peer relationships as well as relationships of
trust with adults and with organizations that offer opportunities for growth.
Growth comes from commitment and participation, which for young people
is often about learning about respect, responsibilities, and reciprocity through
membership of groups and their interactions. Prevention activity that isolates
or individualizes young people may provide a degree of protection from risk
but does not enable young people to take appropriate risks that allow them to
move on into their futures. Belonging, community, and inclusion are difficult
concepts for youth justice practice. Yet they are central for holistic prevention
work which I argue should be actively supported as a separate, valued entity
in environments – and through relationships – which are friendly and accessible to young people.

References

Bateman, T. (2017) *The State of Youth Justice 2017: An Overview of Trends and Developments*.
London: NAYJ.

Blyth, M. and Soloman, E. (Eds.). (2009) *Prevention and Youth Crime: Is Early Intervention
Working?* Bristol: Policy Press.

Bottrell, D. (2009) Dealing with disadvantage: Resilience and the social capital of young people's networks. *Youth and Society*, 40, 476–501.

Bradford, S. and Cullen, F. (2014) Positive for youth work? Contested terrains of professional youth work in austerity England. *International Journal of Adolescence and Youth*. DOI:1080/02673843.2013.863733.

Case, S. and Haines, K. (2015) Risk management and early intervention: A critical analysis. In B. Goldson and J. Muncie (Eds.), *Youth Crime and Justice*, 2nd edition. London: Sage Publications.

CJJI. (2010) *A Joint Inspection of Youth Crime Prevention*. Available at: www.justiceinspectorates.gov.uk/hmiprobation/inspections/a-joint-inspection-of-youth-crime-prevention/.

France, A., Bottrell, D. and Armstrong, D. (2012) *A Political Ecology of Youth and Crime*. New York: Palgrave Macmillan.

Government of the United Kingdom. (2011) *Positive for Youth*. Available at: www.youthpolicy.org/national/United_Kingdom_2011_Youth_Policy_Framework.pdf.

Haines, K. and Case, S. (2015) *Positive Youth Justice: Children First, Offenders Second*. Bristol: Policy Press.

Hall, T., Williamson, H. and Coffey, A. (1998) Conceptualising citizenship: Young people and the transition to adulthood. *Journal of Education Policy*, 13(3), 301–315.

Hall, T., Coffey, A. and Williamson, H. (1999) Self, space and place: Youth identities and citizenship. *British Journal of Sociology of Education*, 20(4), 501–513.

Hart, P. (2016) Young people negotiating and maintaining boundaries in youth work relationships: Findings from an ethnographic study of youth clubs. *Journal of Youth Studies*, 19(7), 869–884.

Henderson, S., Holland, J., McGrellis, S., Sharpe, S. and Thomson, R. (2007) *Inventing Adulthoods: A Biographical Approach to Youth Transitions*. London: Sage Publications.

Hey, V. (1997) *The Company She Keeps: An Ethnography of Girls' Friendships*. Buckingham: Oxford University Press.

Kelly, L. (2012) Representing and preventing youth crime and disorder: Intended and unintended consequences of targeted youth programmes in England. *Youth Justice*, 12(2), 101–117.

Jeffs, T. and Smith, M. (2002) Individualisation and youth work. *Youth and Policy*, 76, 39–65.

Jeffs, T. and Smith, M. (2008) Valuing youth work. *Youth and Policy*, 100, 277–230.

Jenkins, R. (2014) *Social Identity*, 4th edition. Abingdon: Routledge.

Jones, G. (2009) *Youth*. Cambridge: Polity Press.

MacDonald, R. and Marsh, J. (2005) *Disconnected Youth? Growing Up in Britain's Poor Neighbourhoods*. Basingstoke: Palgrave Macmillan.

Mason, W. (2015) Austerity youth policy: Exploring the distinctions between youth work in principle and youth work in practice. *Youth and Policy*, 114, 55–74.

McAra, L. (2010) Models of youth justice. In D. Smith (Ed.), *A New Response to Youth Crime*. Abingdon: Routledge, pp. 287–317.

Muncie, J. (2015) *Youth and Crime*, 3rd edition. London: Sage Publications.

O' Mahoney, P. (2009) The risk factor prevention paradigm and the causes of youth crime: A deceptively useful analysis? *Youth Justice*, 9(2), 99–114.

Paylor, I. (2011) Youth justice in England and Wales: A risky business. *Journal of Offender Rehabilitation*, 50(4), 221–233.

Price, M. (2017) Youth practitioner professional narratives: Changing identities in changing times. *British Journal of Education Studies*. DOI:10.1080/00071005.2017.1332334.

Smith, R. (2011) *Doing Justice to Young People: Youth Crime and Social Justice*. Abingdon: Willan Publishing.

Spence, J., Devanney, C. A. and Noonan, K. (2006) *Youth Work: Voices of Practice*. Leicester: National Youth Agency.

Thomson, R., Holland, J., McGrellis, S., Bell, R., Henderson, S. and Sharpe, S. (2004) Inventing adulthoods: A biographical approach to understanding youth citizenship. *The Sociological Review*, 52(2), 218–239.

Ungar, M. (2004) *Nurturing Hidden Resilience in Troubled Youth*. Toronto: University of Toronto Press.

Wierenga, A. (2009) *Young People Making a Life*. Basingstoke: Palgrave Macmillan.

Williamson, H. (2009) Integrated or targeted youth support services: An essay on 'prevention'. In M. Blyth and E. Solomon (Eds.), *Prevention and Youth Crime: Is Early Intervention Working?* Bristol: Policy Press, pp. 9–20.

Realizing the potential of community reparation for young offenders

64

Nicholas Pamment

Introduction

Reparation has been defined as 'any action taken by the offender to repair the harm s/he has caused' (Wilcox and Hoyle 2004: 17). There are two types of reparation available for young offenders. 'Direct' reparation occurs when an offender has some level of contact with the victim and this can be through a letter of apology, face-to-face meeting, or practical activity. Alternatively, community reparation, which is the focus of this chapter, involves unpaid work for the general benefit of the local community, such as painting and decorating, litter picking, and graffiti removal (Wilcox and Hoyle 2004; Pamment 2016: 2).

Community reparation remains a major part of the youth justice landscape within England and Wales (E&W), available through the Reparation Order, Referral Order, and Youth Rehabilitation Order (YJB 2014; YJB and MOJ 2018). Previously promoted to the public under the banner of 'making good' (YJB 2010), it has been classed as 'partly restorative' due to the lack of victim involvement and focus on offender responsibilization[1] (see also Walgrave 1999; Roche 2001; Barry et al. 2009). Consequently, it has been claimed that community reparation is ineffective at preventing recidivism, fulfilling a punitive function only (Holdaway et al. 2001: 37).

This conveys very little of what positive involvement may mean for the offender (Marshall 1999; Zedner 1994). Certainly, the notion is conceptually anomalous, with clear tensions between reparation which is reintegrative and reparation which is punitive (see Zedner 1994; Sumner 2006). By its definition, reparation must be a constructive and reintegrative process, whereby there is a lasting change in the attitude of the offender (Braithwaite and Pettit 1990). Whilst this chapter focuses primarily on community reparation for juveniles, the disposal was introduced at a time when retribution was the main focus established for adult community service (CS), within E&W. Therefore, the following section charts the development of unpaid work for both adult and young offenders (for a comprehensive overview, see Pamment 2016).

The development of unpaid work

Adult community service

The Community Service Order (CSO) was introduced in 1972, later defined as a 'penal sanction in which convicted offenders are placed in unpaid positions with non-profit or governmental agencies' (Pease 1985: 1). Initially, it was hoped that the disposal would be reintegrative *and* [emphasis added] rehabilitative, acting as a credible alternative to custody (Advisory Council on the Penal System 1970; Hine and Thomas 1996; Rex and Gelsthorpe 2002). In fact, a subcommittee of the Advisory Council on the Penal System (1970, para 34) was confident that it would contribute to a changed outlook on the part of the offender. Furthermore, it was stated that CS should not be seen as 'wholly negative or punitive', providing an opportunity to gain employability skills and a work ethic (see also McIvor 1993). However, as McCulloch (2010: 4) identified, 'the initial vision of CS is barely recognisable in the practice that followed – a practice which, at least officially, has tended to capitalise on the punitive aspects and appeal of CS'.

Under the Criminal Justice Act 1991, there was a rejection of the 'alternatives to custody model' (Wasik 2008; Muncie 1999). Adult CS was re-conceptualized as a distinctive sanction and rebranded, placing particular emphasis on its 'tough' punitive function (McIvor 2002; Worrall and Hoy 2005). The Act also introduced the Combination Order, reinforcing and combining a distinction between probation as *rehabilitation* and CS as *punishment*. Thus, the disposal quickly became synonymous only with its retributive element (McIvor 1993; Ellis, Hedderman and Mortimer 1996; Rex and Gelsthorpe 2002; Gelsthorpe and Rex 2004; Wasik 2008; Faulkner and Burnett 2011).

In 2000, the Criminal Justice and Court Services Act was introduced and under section 44 (1), the adult CSO was renamed the Community Punishment Order (CPO), once again re-emphasizing the punitive, rather than reintegrative aspects of completing unpaid work (Rex and Gelsthorpe 2002; McIvor 2002). However, through the Criminal Justice Act 2003 and a more flexible sentencing framework, unpaid work is now a condition of a generic Community Order (CO), promoted to the public under the label of 'Community Payback', whereby offenders wear highly visible orange vests[2] to identify and shame them (Maruna and King 2008; see also Pamment and Ellis 2010). Moreover, the work undertaken must be demanding, 'not something the public would choose to do themselves' (Casey 2008: 55). This politically inspired initiative has firmly positioned adult CS as a 'marginalized' retributive disposal in E&W, where little attention is now paid to the possibility that it may have greater reintegrative and rehabilitative potential for offenders (McIvor 2002; Rex and Gelsthorpe 2002; Maruna and King 2008; Pamment and Ellis 2010; National Association of Probation Officers, NAPO 2008).

Youth Justice Community Reparation (YJCR)

YJCR has a much shorter history, introduced by New Labour under the CDA 1998 (Crime and Disorder Act 1998, Section 67). Crucially, YJCR was developed when punishment was the major focus for adult CS, discussed above (Rex and Gelsthorpe 2002; Maruna and King 2008; Wasik 2008). Thus, since its inception, it has developed in a similar manner. In particular, the Youth Rehabilitation Order (YRO) has placed community reparation as an option, providing a further distinction between *rehabilitation* and *punishment*. Additionally, the 'Making Good' scheme, whereby members of the public identified reparative activities, mirrored the 'Community Payback' strategy within adult CS, demonstrating the political imperative for increased visibility (Casey 2008; YJB 2010; see also Pamment and Ellis 2010).

Perhaps most importantly, YJCR is prematurely dismissed before its potential benefits have been considered. Holdaway et al. (2001: 101) argue that community reparation is the least valuable disposal for offenders, the work more associated with retribution. Furthermore, Stephenson et al. (2007: 164) stress that only face-to-face contact with victims (i.e. fully restorative) leads to reductions in reoffending (see also McCold and Wachtel 2003). Certainly, there is a clear inference here that community reparation is ineffective, due to its limited status as a restorative sanction (Pamment 2016). However, this is only one facet and it misses the possibility that the disposal may develop employability skills, a far greater factor correlated with the 'what works' evidence base (Rutter et al. 1998; McGuire 1995; Farrall 2002; Hollin and Palmer 2006). The following section aims to address this, by briefly exploring how the completion of unpaid work may support offenders in the acquisition of employability skills (Gelsthorpe and Rex 2004; Home Office 2004).

The acquisition of employability skills

Although unpaid work is rejected for its limited RJ status (Holdaway et al 2001: 101; Stephenson et al. 2007), academics have recognized that the intervention represents a 'natural environment' for the acquisition of employability skills, a far greater factor correlated with the 'what works' literature (Rex 2001: 80; Carter and Pycroft 2010: 14–16). For the purposes of this chapter, employability skills refer to the following broad categories: *transferable, problem-solving, team working*, and *communication skills* (adapted from Carter and Pycroft 2010: 14–16; see also Work Foundation 2010; Chartered Institute of Personnel and Development, CIPD 2004).

Firstly and perhaps most importantly, unpaid work *could* enhance transferable skills, whereby offenders are gaining knowledge of key vocational trades such as concreting, fencing, painting, or decorating. Upon completion of the activities, offenders *could* gain certificates and qualifications in preparation for employment (Carter and Pycroft 2010: 228). The work may also encourage offenders to adopt a problem-solving approach, by identifying advantages or disadvantages of varying techniques and by following health and safety guidelines (McIvor 2002: 4; Carter and Pycroft 2010: 228). Ultimately, this could lead to increased confidence, self-efficacy, and motivation to change (Gelsthorpe and Rex 2004: 235; see also Advisory Council on the Penal System 1970: 13).

Unpaid work *may* also encourage team-working skills, where the activities develop trusting relationships between co-workers and supervisors, whilst working within potentially hazardous environments (Carter and Pycroft 2010: 228). This may enhance communication and develop socially responsible behaviour (see also Advisory Council on the Penal System 1970: 13; Tallant et al. 2008: 79).

In summary, the focus of unpaid work is neither specifically on offending behaviour nor on restorative justice (Holdaway et al. 2001; Stephenson et al. 2007; McCulloch 2010). Crucially however, the practical setting and nature of the communication that takes place: 'might well offer learning experiences at least as powerful as an approach that directly tackles offending behaviour' (Rex 2001: 80; McIvor 2002; Chapman and Hough 1998; McCulloch 2010).

Recognizing such potential, Rex and Gelsthorpe (2002) argued the need to rediscover the rehabilitative and reintegrative potential of unpaid work, the pursuit of which would take the sanction back to its origin (p. 311; Advisory Council on the Penal System 1970: para 34; McCulloch 2010). They stated that the retributive focus should not exclude the reintegrative aims, advocating harmonization between work and the development of skills suitable for employment (Rex and Gelsthorpe 2002: 311; see also McIvor 1991, 1992). However, to end on a cautionary note, this would necessitate the provision of a *range* of meaningful and engaging tasks, which encourage and facilitate the acquisition of employability skills. The next section discusses the research evidence base for YJCR.

Research evidence base

There is a paucity of research into community reparation for young offenders. This could be due to the lack of priority historically afforded to unpaid work (Ellis et al. 1996; Rex and Gelsthorpe 2002) and difficulty accessing young offenders during and after their community reparation (Delens-Ravier 2003: 156). Nevertheless, the findings of the relevant studies are summarized in Table 64.1. Most importantly, most of these studies have only touched on community reparation as part of wider ranging evaluations of youth justice

Table 64.1 Summary of studies into YJCR

Study	Sample size and offender profiles	Methodology	Summary of selected findings
National evaluation of the pilot youth offending teams (Holdaway et al. 2001)	▪ 602 reparation orders ▪ 85% male ▪ Mean age 14.3 (range 10–18) ▪ 62% in school or further education ▪ 52% had one or two minor convictions ▪ Theft/dishonesty most common offence (48%)	▪ Analysis of case files ▪ Case study interview data with offender, staff, and parents ▪ Sentencing statistics ▪ Data collection varied by each YOT and record-keeping considered 'poor'	▪ Community reparation most common intervention ▪ Offenders did not understand the order ▪ Offenders given limited range of activities ▪ Little connection between work and offender/offence
National evaluation of the YJB's RJ projects (Wilcox and Hoyle 2004)	▪ Data available for 42 RJ projects, 6,800 offenders ▪ 76% male ▪ Age range 14–17 ▪ 90% white ▪ Theft most common offence (30%), followed by violence (23%) ▪ Offenders in 'early stages of criminal career'	▪ Questionnaires for victims and offenders ▪ Significant variation in methodologies adopted by 'local' evaluators' ▪ 1/3 of projects unable to provide basic data	▪ Over-reliance on community reparation ▪ Primarily perceived as a punishment by offenders with no clear benefit to victims or community ▪ Placements not relevant to crimes committed
'Local' evaluation of an RJ project in the South West of England (Gray et al. 2003; Gray 2005)	▪ 214 young offenders ▪ 81.3% male ▪ Average age 14.5 years (range 10–18) ▪ 96.1% white ▪ Theft most common offence (37.8%) ▪ 78.3% no previous convictions	▪ Quantitative data obtained from YOT database and Asset ▪ Interviews with 41 offenders and 21 victims	▪ Primarily perceived as a punishment by offenders, in place to deter future offending ▪ Community reparation unfair to victims ▪ Offenders disappointed that they could not make amends directly

(Continued)

Table 64.1 Continued

Study	Sample size and offender profiles	Methodology	Summary of selected findings
Evaluation of the Intensive Supervision and Surveillance Programme (ISSP) (Gray et al. 2005)	■ 3,384 ISSP cases recorded ■ 93% male ■ Mean age 16.4 years ■ 83.5% white ■ Average of nine previous offences ■ Burglary most common offence (24.7%)	■ Qualitative data: interviews with 173 offenders, 144 staff, and 33 parents	■ Offenders unable to relate to menial tasks, including litter picking and leafleting ■ Activities with a lack of purpose considered 'pointless' and a 'waste of time'
Community Reparation for Young Offenders: Perceptions, Policy, and Practice (Pamment 2016)	■ 97 young offenders ■ 74% male ■ Average age 15.6 years ■ Majority of offenders subject to Referral Orders (67%), followed by Reparation Orders (20%) and ISSPs (8%) ■ Actual Bodily Harm (ABH) was the most common offence, followed by theft (21.9%) and drug possession (9.4%)	■ Assisted questionnaires with 97 young offenders (see Holt and Pamment 2011); semi-structured interviews with 12 supervising staff ■ Restricted analysis of case file data	■ Formulaic approach to workplace provision ■ Over-reliance on menial tasks. 76.3% of sample completed non-skills-based activities, including shrub clearance, litter picking, and 'kindling preparation' ■ Offenders and supervisors frustrated and disappointed at lack of skills provision ■ Rarely an identifiable beneficiary ■ Offenders unable to fully make amends ■ Offenders not interested, stimulated, or challenged by placements

Source: Adapted from Pamment (2016: 48)

sanctions. Thus, they contain a distinct lack of data relating specifically to the intervention. Additionally, several of the reports were written for the Home Office or YOT management and the varying methodologies and numbers involved remain imprecise, resulting in limited and descriptive analyses (Holdaway et al. 2001; Wilcox and Hoyle 2004). Nonetheless, they are discussed, in turn, further below.

In 2001, Holdaway et al. published an assessment of the pilot YOTs in West London, Sheffield, Wessex, and Wolverhampton. Of most significance here is the brief examination that was undertaken into the court orders introduced within the CDA 1998, including reparation. According to Holdaway et al.

(2001: 91), young people on community reparation were given a very limited range of menial tasks to complete, consisting primarily of 'unchallenging' gardening or shrub clearance work. Moreover, there was little correlation between the tasks, offender, and offence. During interviews with YOT staff, supervisors acknowledged the difficulty in establishing adequate numbers of 'quality placements', although the reasons for this remain unclear. However, as the researchers indicate, it would appear that the implementation of general 'unskilled' tasks were far easier to organize than meaningful placements, capable of facilitating the acquisition of skills (Holdaway et al. 2001: 91).

Holdaway et al. (2001) warned that community reparation was degenerating into a 'tokenistic response', whereby offenders gain little from the process (p. 38). It was concluded that young people on the intervention should be allocated to a range of engaging activities which are closely linked to the offence, allowing them to see the connection. Most importantly, tasks should relate to the interests of offenders and develop new skills, which can lead to reductions in reoffending (McGuire 1995; Farrall 2002; Hollin and Palmer 2006).

Three years later, the YJB funded an assessment of 46 restorative justice interventions (Wilcox and Hoyle 2004). In response to growing concerns at the time regarding the quality of community reparation, possibly due to the negative results outlined above (Holdaway et al. 2001), *Crime Concern* (then national supporters of the approach) provided the evaluators with guidelines regarding 'best practice'. Although it is difficult to establish the origin of these guidelines, it was stated that placements should: relate to the offence, develop or enhance young persons' skills and interests, encourage offenders to consider the consequences of their actions on victims and the community, and address issues such as unstructured/unsupervised leisure time (*Crime Concern*, cited by Wilcox and Hoyle 2004: 35).

The evaluators state that only four projects (out of a possible 42) adhered to the good practice guidelines provided by *Crime Concern* (Wilcox and Hoyle 2004: 35). Although there were 'several' examples of positive placement provision, including the restoration of prosthetic limbs for landmine victims, results were described as 'unfavourable'. In particular, it was discovered that offenders were being allocated to a limited range of menial activities, which were primarily perceived as a punishment by offenders and of no value to victims or the wider community. Furthermore, the tasks were not relevant to the crimes committed. Recognizing the potential of community reparation as a creative disposal, Wilcox and Hoyle (2004: 35) stressed the importance of engaging placements, facilitating skills acquisition.

As part of the national study of restorative justice interventions outlined above (Wilcox and Hoyle 2004), Gray et al. (2003; Gray 2005) published a 'local' evaluation of projects developed by a YOT in the south-west of England. Of most interest to this chapter are the extremely limited and negative qualitative findings that emerged from 41 offender interviews (Gray 2005: 942). Although there is no information on the placement activities provided, offenders who undertook community reparation perceived no personal benefit from the disposal. Instead, they viewed its primary purpose as punishment which is in place to deter further offending. Young offenders were also concerned regarding the unfairness of community reparation to the victim, and the fact that they were unable to make amends directly (Gray 2005: 945).

Later research into the effectiveness of the Intensive Supervision and Surveillance Programme (ISSP) for severe and persistent offenders also briefly explored the impact of community reparation upon young offenders (see Gray et al. 2005; Ellis et al. 2009). According to the researchers, young people who undertook community reparation completed a range of projects including gardening, recycling, and environmental improvements. Crucially however, offenders preferred being involved in constructive and engaging activities where they could work with other people and develop new skills. For instance, one young person stated: 'We've done gardening and DIY stuff; it's taught me how to do things I haven't done before'. Conversely, offenders were unable to relate to menial activities such as litter picking, shrub clearance, and leafleting, describing them as a 'waste of time' and 'boring'. Therefore, Gray et al. (2005: 118) concluded by warning against the utilization of 'pointless' and non-stimulating placements, which lack direct purpose.

The first fully researched examination of community reparation further supports the findings identified above (Pamment 2016). It uncovered serious inadequacies and failings regarding the organization and delivery of the disposal, which severely limited any potential to reduce reoffending. In particular, the YOT 'case study' area adopted a formulaic approach to workplace provision, providing a narrow range of low-cost placements. There was an over-reliance on menial tasks, with 76% of participants completing shrub clearance, litter picking, or 'kindling preparation'. As a result, both offenders and their supervisors were frustrated and disappointed that such placements did not facilitate the acquisition of employability skills.

The low skills content and menial nature of three-quarters of YJCR work meant that the majority of offenders were unable to fully 'make amends' for their offending. Furthermore, they were not interested, stimulated, or challenged by the placements, which rarely had any identifiable beneficiary. YOT staff also experienced disillusionment and nine of the 12 supervisors had considered leaving the YOT. One supervisor likened the activities to 'voluntary refuse collection'. Thus, instead of being considered a 'worthwhile' or 'helpful' process, YJCR was perceived primarily as a punitive experience by all participants and to a large extent, even the staff (see also Holdaway et al. 2001; Wilcox and Hoyle 2004; Gray et al. 2005).

If the intention is purely retributive, as the changes discussed above in legislation over a long period tend to indicate (see Faulkner and Burnett 2011: 127–128), this might be seen positively. However, punishment alone does not contribute to long-term desistance from crime (McSweeney et al. 2006; Worrall 1997) and the evidence base presented suggests that it would be more profitable to focus on worthwhile activities that can engage and motivate offenders and on facilitating direct contact with beneficiaries as a positive reintegrative process, encouraging lasting behavioural change (McIvor 1992, 2002; Gray et al. 2005: 945).

Conclusion

Consecutive legislative changes have emphasized the punitive power of unpaid work, ignoring the rehabilitative and reintegrative potential. Through the completion of unpaid work, offenders can gain skills suitable for employment (Varah 1981; McIvor 1991, 1992; Rex et al. 2003), a well-established key factor associated with reductions in reoffending (Rutter et al. 1998; McGuire 1995; Farrall 2002; Hollin and Palmer 2006). Placements can also motivate offenders, facilitating positive behavioural change and the work itself can provide the opportunity to fully 'make amends' (Rex et al. 2003; Curran et al. 2007; McIvor 1991, 1992; Wilcox and Hoyle 2004).

Available research, however, demonstrates that community reparation is not being operated effectively by YOTs, through a formulaic approach to workplace allocation and an over-reliance on low-cost menial tasks. Indeed, as this chapter has shown, there are important detailed qualifications relating to the delivery and organization of the disposal, which, if not in place will reduce the chances of successful outcomes.

As summarized in Figure 64.1, the evidence base shows that offenders must be provided with a variety of 'meaningful' work placements, which are not perceived as menial, repetitive, or boring by offenders and/or supervisors (Varah 1981; McIvor 1992; Holdaway et al. 2001; Wilson and Wahidin 2006). To be successful, unpaid work placements must also facilitate the acquisition of employability skills and they should be engaging, involving a level of problem-solving and stimulation (Wilcox and Hoyle 2004; Curran et al. 2007). The work should also maximize contact with beneficiaries, ensuring that the process is perceived by offenders as worthwhile and helpful to the community (McIvor 1991, 1992; Gray 2005).

There are currently no evidence-based guidelines on the effective delivery of YJCR, leading to reductions in reoffending. Crucially, previous guidance provided to YOTs by the YJB on how to develop reparation, as part of the Youth Crime Action Plan, have merely focused on improving the visibility of the disposal, rather than outlining key elements of supervision most likely to lead to successful outcomes (see YJB 2008, 2014). Therefore, there is certainly a need to develop an evidence-based best practice model using the criteria outlined above, in order to develop more effective inspection criteria.

Such a model should also be disseminated to sentencers. Indeed, the courts need a greater level of understanding of YJCR and its reintegrative potential. This could positively affect sentencing behaviour, diverting young offenders away from the damaging environment of custody (Carlile Inquiry 2006; Faze et al. 2005; Goldson 2006) and other ineffective disposals, such as Intensive Supervision and Surveillance (ISS) (Ellis et al. 2009; Howard League for Penal Reform 2011). Emphasizing the effectiveness of YJCR would enable sentencing

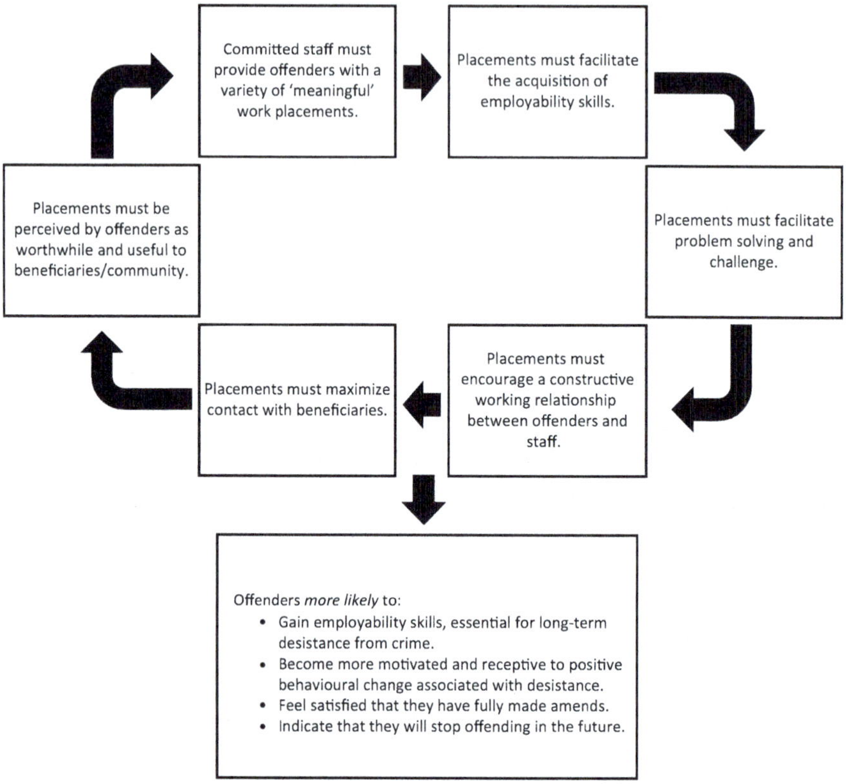

Figure 64.1 Summary of evidenced-based principles for the delivery of unpaid work most likely to lead to successful outcomes

Source: Pamment (2016: 77)

and the allocation of YOT budgets to be harmonized (see also Sutton 2010), but it will also empower sentencers to demand YJCR orders that have evidence-based content and delivery (Pamment 2016).

Notes

1   Described as the 'new rehabilitation' of the risk era (for a comprehensive discussion see Kemshall 2002; Robinson 2002; O'Malley 2001; Gray 2005). It is closely linked to the notion of communitarianism, emphasizing that the solution to crime is the responsibility of communities and individuals (Dugmore et al. 2006; Barry et al. 2009).
2   Dubbed the 'vests of shame' by the popular press (see Roper 2008).

References

Advisory Council on the Penal System. (1970) *Non-Custodial and Semi-Custodial Penalties*. London: HMSO.

Barry, M., McNeil, F. and Lightowler, C. (2009) *Youth Offending and Youth Justice* (Briefing paper). Available at: www.sccjr.ac.uk/pubs/Youth-Offending-and-Youth-Justice/162.

Braithwaite, J. and Pettit, P. (1990) *Not Just Deserts: A Republican Theory of Criminal Justice*. Oxford: Oxford University Press.

Carlile Inquiry. (2006) *An Independent Inquiry into the Use of Physical Restraint, Solitary Confinement and Forcible Strip Searching of Children in Prisons, Secure Training Centres and Local Authority Secure Children's Homes*. London: Howard League for Penal Reform.

Carter, C. and Pycroft, A. (2010) Getting out: Offenders in forestry and conservation work settings. In J. Brayford, F. Cowe and J. Deering (Eds.), *What Else Works? Creative Work with Offenders*. Uffculme: Willan Publishing, pp. 211–236.

Casey, L. (2008) *Engaging Communities in Fighting Crime: A Review*. London: Cabinet Office.

Chapman, T. and Hough, M. (1998) *Evidence Based Practice: A Guide to Effective Practice*. London: HMIP.

CIPD. (2004) *Employing Ex-Offenders: A Practical Guide*. London: CIPD.

Curran, J., MacQueen, S., Whyte, B. and Boyle, J. (2007) *Forced to Make Amends: An Evaluation of the Community Reparation Orders Pilot*. Crime and Justice Research Findings No. 95. Available at: www.scotland.gov.uk/Resource/Doc/195674/0052459.pdf.

Delens-Ravier, I. (2003) Juvenile offenders' perceptions of community service. In L. Walgrave (Ed.), *Repositioning Restorative Justice*. Portland, OR: Willan Publishing, pp. 149–166.

Dugmore, P., Pickford, J. and Angus, S. (2006) *Transforming Social Work Practice: Youth Justice and Social Work*. Exeter: Learning Matters.

Ellis, T., Hedderman, C. and Mortimer, E. (1996) *Enforcing Community Sentences: Supervisors' Perspectives on Ensuring Compliance and Dealing with Breach*. Home Office Research Study, 158. London: Home Office.

Ellis, T., Pamment, N. and Lewis, C. (2009) Public protection in youth justice? The intensive supervision and surveillance programme (ISSP) from the inside. *International Journal of Police Science and Management*, 11(4), 393–413.

Farrall, S. (2002) *Rethinking What Works with Offenders: Probation, Social Context and Desistance from Crime*. Cullompton: Willan Publishing.

Faulkner, D. and Burnett, R. (2011) *Where Next for Criminal Justice?* Bristol: Policy Press.

Faze, S., Benning, R. and Danesh, J. (2005) Suicides in male prisoners in England and Wales 1978–2003. *The Lancet*, 366, 1301–1302.

Gelsthorpe, L. and Rex, S. (2004) Community service as reintegration: Exploring the potential. In G. Mair (Ed.), *What Matters in Probation*. Cullompton: Willan Publishing, pp. 229–254.

Goldson, B. (2006) Damage, harm and death in child prisons: Questions of abuse and accountability. *The Howard Journal of Criminal Justice*, 45(5), 449–467.

Gray, E., Roberts, C., Merrington, S., Waters, I., Fernandez, R. and Hayward, G. (2005) *ISSP: The Final Report*. London: Youth Justice Board.

Gray, P. (2005) The politics of risk and young offenders' experiences of social exclusion and restorative justice. *British Journal of Criminology*, 45(6), 938–957.

Gray, P., Moseley, J. and Browning, R. (2003) *An Evaluation of the Plymouth Restorative Justice Programme*. Plymouth: University of Plymouth.

Hine, J. and Thomas, N. (1996) Evaluating work with offenders: Community service orders. In G. McIvor (Ed.), *Working with Offenders*. London: Jessica Kingsley.

Holdaway, S., Davidson, N., Dignan, J., Hammersley, R., Hine, J. and Marsh, P. (2001) *New Strategies to Address Youth Offending – The National Evaluation of the Pilot Youth Offending Teams*. RDS Occasional Paper No. 69. London: Home Office.

Hollin, C. R. and Palmer, E. J. (Eds.). (2006) *Offending Behaviour Programmes: Development, Application and Controversies*. Chichester: John Wiley & Sons.

Home Office. (2004) *Reducing Re-Offending National Action Plan*. London: Home Office.

Holt, A., and Pamment, N. (2011) Overcoming the challenges of researching 'young offenders': using assisted questionnaires – a research note. *International Journal of Social Research Methodology*, 14(2), 125–133.

Howard League for Penal Reform. (2011) *Life Outside: Collective Identity, Collective Exclusion*. Available at: https://howardleague.org/wp-content/uploads/2016/05/Life_outside.pdf.

Kemshall, H. (2002) Effective practice in probation: An example of 'advanced liberalism responsibilisation'. *Howard Journal*, 41(1), 41–58.

Marshall, T. (1999) *Restorative Justice: An Overview*. London: Home Office.

Maruna, S. and King, A. (2008) Selling the public on probation: Beyond the bib. *The Journal of Community and Criminal Justice*, 55(4), 337–351.

McCold, P. and Wachtel, T. (2003) *In Pursuit of Paradigm: A Theory of Restorative Justice*. Paper Presented at the XIII World Congress of Criminology, Rio de Janeiro, Brazil. Available at: www.iirp.org/pdf/paradigm.pdf.

McCulloch, T. (2010) Exploring community service: Understanding compliance. In F. McNeill, P. Raynor and C. Trotter (Eds.), *Offender Supervision: New Directions in Theory, Research and Practice*. Cullompton: Willan Publishing, pp. 228–236.

McGuire, J. (Ed.). (1995) *What Works: Reduce Re-Offending – Guidelines from Research and Practice*. Chichester: Wiley.

McIvor, G. (1991) Community service work placements. *The Howard Journal*, 30, 19–29.

McIvor, G. (1992) *Sentenced to Serve*. Burlington: Ashgate.

McIvor, G. (1993) Community service by offenders: Agency experiences and attitudes. *Research on Social Work Practice*, 3, 66–82.

McIvor, G. (2002) *What Works in Community Service?* CJSW Briefing Paper 6. Edinburgh: Criminal Justice Social Work Development Centre.

McSweeney, T., Stevens, A., Hunt, N. and Turnbull, P. J. (2006) Twisting arms or a helping hand? Assessing the impact of coerced and comparable voluntary drug treatment options. *British Journal of Criminology*, 47(3), 470–490.

Muncie, J. (1999) Institutionalised intolerance: Youth justice and the 1998 crime and disorder act. *Critical Social Policy*, 19(2), 147–175.

NAPO. (2008) *Call for Withdrawal of Distinctive Clothing for Community Payback*. London: NAPO.

O'Malley, P. (2001) Risk, crime and prudentialism revisited. In K. Stenson and R. Sullivan (Eds.), *Crime, Risk and Justice: The Politics of Crime Control in Liberal Democracies*. Devon: Willan, pp. 83–103.

Pamment, N. (2016) *Community Reparation for Young Offenders: Perceptions, Policy and Practice*. Basingstoke: Palgrave Macmillan.

Pamment, N. and Ellis, T. (2010) A retrograde step: The potential impact of high visibility uniforms in youth justice. *Howard Journal*, 49(1), 18–30.

Pease, K. (1985) Community service orders. In M. Tonry and N. Morris (Eds.), *Crime and Justice*. Chicago: University of Chicago Press.

Rex, S. (2001) Beyond cognitive-behaviouralism? Reflections on the effectiveness literature. In A. Bottoms, L. Gelsthorpe and S. Rex (Eds.), *Community Penalties: Change and Challenges*. Cullompten: Willan Publishing, pp. 67–87.

Rex, S. and Gelsthorpe, L. (2002) The role of community service in reducing offending: Evaluating pathfinder projects in the UK. *The Howard Journal*, 41(4), 311–325.

Rex, S., Gelsthorpe, L., Roberts, C. and Jordan, P. (2003) *Crime Reduction Programme: An Evaluation of Community Service Pathfinder Projects: Final Report 2002*. RDS Occasional Paper 87. London: Home Office.

Robinson, G. (2002) Exploring risk management in probation practice. *Punishment & Society*, 4, 5–25.

Roche, D. (2001) The evolving definition of restorative justice. *Contemporary Justice Review*, 43(3–4), 341–353.

Roper, M. (2008) *Community Service Offenders Forced to Wear New Hi-Vis 'vest of shame'.* Available at: www.mirror.co.uk/.

Rutter, M., Giller, H. and Hagell, A. (1998) *Antisocial Behaviour by Young People.* Cambridge: Cambridge University Press.

Stephenson, M., Giller, H. and Brown, S. (2007) *Effective Practice in Youth Justice.* Cullompton and Devon: Willan Publishing.

Sumner, M. (2006) Reparation. In E. McLaughlin and J. Muncie (Eds.), *The Sage Dictionary of Criminology.* London: Sage Publications, pp. 351–352.

Sutton, P. (2010) *Unpaid Work by 16 &17 Year Olds: A Feasibility Study for YJB, NOMS and YJPU.* London: YJB.

Tallant, C., Sambrook, M. and Green, S. (2008) Engagement skills: Best practice or effective practice? In S. Green, E. Lancaster and S. Feasey (Eds.), *Addressing Offending Behaviour: Context, Practice and Values.* Devon: Willan Publishing, pp. 75–92.

Varah, M. (1981) What about the workers? Offenders on community service orders express their opinions. *Probation Journal,* 120–123.

Walgrave, L. (1999) Community service as a cornerstone of a systemic restorative response to (Juvenile) crime. In G. Bazemore and L. Walgrave (Eds.), *Restorative Juvenile Justice: Repairing the Harm of Youth Crime.* Monsey, NY: Criminal Justice Press, pp. 129–154.

Wasik, M. (2008) The legal framework. In S. Green, E. Lancaster and S. Feasey (Eds.), *Addressing Offending Behavior: Context, Practice and Values.* Cullompton: Willan Publishing, pp. 3–24.

Wilcox, A. and Hoyle, C. (2004) *The National Evaluation of the Youth Justice Board's Restorative Justice Projects.* London: YJB.

Wilson, D. and Wahidin, A. (2006) *"Real Work" in Prison: Absences, Obstacles and Opportunities.* Birmingham: Centre for Criminal Justice Policy and Research, UCE. Available at: www.bcu.ac.uk/.

Work Foundation. (2010) *Employability and Skills in the UK: Redefining the Debate.* Available at: https://curve.coventry.ac.uk/cu/file/f7a0974d-4548-4f07-bf0b-553504cc6888/1/Employability%20and%20Skills%20in%20the%20UK%20report.pdf.

Worrall, A. (1997) *Punishment in the Community: The Future of Criminal Justice.* London and New York: Addison Wesley Longman.

Worrall, A. and Hoy, C. (2005) *Punishment in the Community: Managing Offenders, Making Choices,* 2nd edition. Cullompton: Willan Publishing.

YJB. (2008) *To Develop and Improve Reparation, as Part of the Youth Crime Action Plan. Good Practice for Youth Offending Teams (YOTs).* Available at: www.gov.uk/government/organisations/youth-justice-board-for-england-and-wales.

YJB. (2010) *Making Good.* Available at: www.gov.uk/government/organisations/youth-justice-board-for-england-and-wales.

YJB. (2014) *Guidance: Use Community Interventions: Section 6 Case Management Guidance.* Available at: www.gov.uk/government/publications/use-community-interventions/use-community-interventions-section-6-case-management-guidance.

YJB and MOJ. (2018) *Youth Justice Statistics 2016/17.* Available at: file:///C:/Users/pammentn/Documents/youth_justice_statistics_2016–17.pdf.

Zedner, L. (1994) Reparation and retribution: Are they reconcilable? *The Modern Law Review,* 57, 228–250.

65

Foreign national prisoners

Precarity and deportability as obstacles to rehabilitation

Sarah Turnbull and Ines Hasselberg

Introduction

As of the end of March 2017, 9,791 foreign nationals were incarcerated in England and Wales, constituting 11% of the total prison population. Of these, 1,650 were on remand, 6,735 were sentenced prisoners, and 1,406 were 'non-criminal' foreign nationals (Ministry of Justice 2017). After British nationals, the most common prisoner nationalities are Polish (9%), Irish (8%), Albanian (7%), Romanian (6%), and Jamaican (5%) (Ministry of Justice 2017). Men account for 96% of the foreign national prison population (Allen and Watson 2017), although the proportion of female foreign national prisoners is greater than their male counterparts (Prison Reform Trust 2012).[1] Britain (along with Norway) is unique amongst Western European countries in having separate 'specialist' prisons solely for those defined as foreign nationals (Pakes and Holt 2017; Kaufman 2013, 2015; Ugelvik and Damsa 2017).

Over the past decade, the 'foreign criminal' has emerged as a 'doubly damned modern British folk-devil' (Griffiths 2017: 1), an especially deviant, and dehumanized, penal subject produced through the increasing merger of immigration and crime control measures. Griffiths (2017: 2) argues that polices and legislation over the last ten years are marked by 'fundamentally shifting the landscape: making more people criminal and (certain) people more foreign'. Since 2000, the foreign national prisoner population has risen by 98% while the number of British nationals has increased by 25% (Barnoux and Wood 2013). According to Banks (2011: 186), the 'growth in the foreign national prison population has been fuelled by substantial increases in both the number of foreign nationals receiving immediate custody and the number of foreign nationals subject to untried reception into custody'. The prison, as Pakes and Holt (2017: 63) observe, 'has recently become an acute site of crimmigration', reflecting a growing intersection of criminal justice and immigration. Consequently, the foreign national prisoner is subject both to penal power through the criminal sentence and to immigration power through deportation (or the threat thereof) (Pakes and Holt 2017; Turnbull and Hasselberg 2017).

The majority (70%) of foreign national prisoners are defined as non-white and comprise 40% of 'ethnic minorities' in prison (Barnoux and Wood 2013). Indeed, the notion of the 'foreign national prisoner' needs deconstructing (Ugelvik 2012). Most obviously, a foreign national prisoner is an individual who is serving a prison sentence in a country in which they do not have citizenship. Yet, more insidiously, racialized understandings of 'foreignness' mean that 'nationality is confused with ethnicity, and assumptions (frequently erroneous) are made about residence, religion, culture and language' (Pakes and Holt 2017: 67; Kaufman 2015).

Section 32(5) of the UK Borders Act 2007 *requires* the Home Secretary to make a deportation order against a non-European Economic Area (EEA) 'foreign criminal', which the Act defines as an individual who has been sentenced to 12 months or more of imprisonment as a consequence of a conviction (Nason 2017a). For an EEA national, a sentence of imprisonment is likely to result in deportation proceedings brought against them, but they are afforded a number of protections not available to their non-EEA counterparts – although this is likely to change if and when the United Kingdom (UK) leaves the European Union (EU) (Nason 2017b).

Foreign national prisoners are generally seen to have different needs than the citizen prisoner population. Many will face language barriers, separation from their families overseas, and isolation (Bosworth et al. 2016) as well as have gendered needs associated with their pathways into prison and responsibilities as parents (Prison Reform Trust 2012). Whether they have been long-term residents in the country or arrested at a port of entry, due to their lack of citizenship they are deportable subjects, which generates further anxiety and uncertainty over their futures. Foreign nationals represent 'nearly a quarter of self-harm incidents and self-inflicted deaths' amongst prisoners (Barnoux and Wood 2013: 240), underscoring the particular vulnerabilities for this prisoner population.

As Canton and Hammond (2012: 8) observe, much of the dominant framing of rehabilitation in sentencing and penal policy 'ignores the predicament of foreign nationals' and the particular 'standing to which they are to be restored'. They contend that non-citizens' 'different rights and legal entitlements as well as varying needs and periods of settlement' affect how they can avoid reoffending in the pursuit of reformed selves (Canton and Hammond 2012: 8). Warr (2016) and Ugelvik and Damsa (2017) argue that the 'pains of imprisonment' for foreign nationals are different, impacting how this particular group experiences their incarceration. For Warr, the lack of certitude, legitimacy, and hope are additional pains that dominate foreign national prisoners' carceral and post-carceral lives, while Ugelvik and Damsa point to issues of discrimination, long-distance relationships, and deportability.

This chapter focuses on the rehabilitative ideal in relation to the unique situation of foreign national prisoners who are facing deportation. As we have previously shown (Turnbull and Hasselberg 2017), the lack of citizenship has important implications for how these prisoners experience their incarceration and what follows. In particular, many foreign national prisoners may be subsequently subject to immigration detention and deportation and experience their (re)integration phase as marked by great uncertainty and precarity. This chapter details how citizenship (and lack thereof) works to shape access to and the type of rehabilitative programming for foreign national prisoners, while also influencing how they transition from prison to the community. It also examines foreign nationals' perceptions of the rehabilitative efforts directed specifically at them as deportable subjects during custody. The British government's responses to foreign national prisoners reflect Aas's (2014: 521) notion of 'border penality', a 'legally regulated, but differentiated, two-tier system of justice' along the lines of formal citizenship. This bifurcated justice has important implications for how foreign national prisoners do their time and make sense of the rehabilitative process.

Drawing on ethnographic fieldwork with male foreign nationals in custody (both prison and immigration detention) and after release, this chapter connects the penal goal of rehabilitation to broader political concerns about the 'foreign criminal' (Griffiths 2017), showing how 'deportability' – the possibility of deportation (De Genova 2002) – impacts the rehabilitative ideal for this diverse group of prisoners. We bring together qualitative data from two research projects: Turnbull's research at four immigration removal centres (IRCs) – Campsfield House, Yarl's Wood, Colnbrook, and Dover – between 2013 and 2014, and Hasselberg's research at HMP Huntercombe over the course of four months in 2013. For each project, we were granted full access to the facilities such that we had the opportunity to engage freely with detainees/prisoners and staff. Although we conducted formal semi-structured interviews, our method was primarily ethnographic. More specifically, Turnbull spent 149 days of fieldwork across the four field sites and Hasselberg spent 30 days at HMP Huntercombe. The projects similarly explored research questions related to participants' migratory paths, their time spent in the UK, feelings of belonging, and issues of identity like gender and race in relation to these themes and to the daily lived experience of confinement.[2] The data, comprised of interview transcripts and fieldnotes, were analyzed inductively and deductively for analytic themes using the qualitative software programme NVivo. All names of participants are pseudonyms. In this chapter, we focus solely on male participants' narratives.

The rehabilitation of foreign nationals in prison

In England and Wales prior to 2006, foreign national prisoners progressed through their sentences much in the same manner as their citizen counterparts. Nationality was not taken into account in prison allocation and there were no HM Prison Service policies and practices specific to foreign national prisoners (Bhui 2004a; Hammond 2007). Upon release, probation and supervision arrangements did not differ for this segment of the prisoner population. Deported prisoners were not required to be under any form of supervision following their removal from the country. Yet, this was not tantamount to enjoying equal access to rehabilitative activities or support with resettlement; indeed, a number of research publications and inspection reports were already concerned with the circumstances of foreign nationals in prison (see Bhui 2004a, 2004b; Her Majesty's Inspectorate of Prisons 2006; Hammond 2007).

In 2006, a foreign national prisoner 'crisis' resulted in the development and implementation of specific policies targeting foreign national prisoners, including the predominant focus on deportation going forward (Webber 2009). This crisis emerged when it came to public and political attention that over 1,000 foreign national prisoners were released to society upon the end of their sentences without being considered for deportation.[3] Ultimately, the crisis led to the passing of the UK Borders Act 2007, which, as noted above, introduced the provisions for automatic deportation, and demanded tighter collaboration between the Prison Service and the then UK Border Agency in identifying foreigners serving custodial sentences and considering them for deportation. Additionally, the crisis sparked the development of a 'hubs and spokes' system in which special prisons for foreign nationals were established (Kaufman 2013). These 'specialist' prisons involve the permanent placement of immigration officials to expedite deportation proceedings and are (assumedly) better equipped to attend to the particular needs of this segment of the prison population. In practice, however, these policies have legally sanctioned the differential treatment of foreign nationals (Aliverti 2016) and changed the experiences of punishment for foreign nationals serving custodial sentences (Kaufman and Bosworth 2013; Kaufman 2015; Turnbull and Hasselberg 2017). Foreign national-only prisons also disrupt traditional meanings of rehabilitation and (re)integration vis-à-vis punishment,[4] for what can be said of these principles when prisoners are intended for deportation rather than release?

Today, foreign national prisoners cannot be said to enjoy equal access to rehabilitative and resettlement activities compared to prisoners who possess British citizenship. Foreign national prisoners are often given lower priority in education and work allocation as they are not meant to be relocated nor (re)integrated in British society. Furthermore, in practice, foreign national prisoners are typically assessed as a higher risk of absconding, which jeopardizes their access to a whole set of rehabilitative and resettlement opportunities, such as progressing to semi-open and open conditions, participating in home visits, and accessing work or recreational activities that may involve exiting the premises of the prison (Bhui 2004a; Hammond 2007; Turnbull and Hasselberg 2017). Language barriers also work as impediments to taking up work positions and participating in vocational training (see e.g. Martynowicz 2016). Despite these barriers, foreign national prisoners are often motivated to engage in paid work whilst in prison, as often this is their only source of income and one that may enable them to send money to their families, domestically or overseas (Bhui 2004a; Hammond 2007). Recreational activities, such as sport and art, have been found to be especially appreciated by foreign national prisoners, particularly amongst those struggling with language issues, as these provide opportunities for non-verbal social contact and expression, thus easing their isolation (Hammond 2007).

Recent research by Kaufman (2015) on male foreign national prisoners in the hubs and spokes system found a general perception, on the part of both prisoners and staff, that the range and quality of rehabilitative activities (such as vocational training, offending behaviour programmes, and life skills courses) were limited precisely because of the assumption that these prisoners would not be returned to British society (Kaufman 2015: 128; Hammond 2007). 'This second-class system', Kaufman (2015: 129) writes, 'provides a window into the nationalist boundaries of the penal project'. Likewise, the data and analysis presented below show how the logic of rehabilitation remains bound to the nation-state and citizen penal subjects.

Rehabilitation, resettlement, and deportability

Elsewhere (Turnbull and Hasselberg 2017) we explore the carceral trajectories of foreign national offenders in the UK, moving from the prison as sentenced prisoners to immigration detainees held in one of Britain's IRCs. This work shows how immigration detention is often a second carceral site for non-citizens facing deportation as a consequence of their criminal convictions. We discuss how the UK's increasingly punitive response to so-called foreign criminals challenges the traditional purposes of punishment by discounting prisoners' rehabilitative efforts and denying them the 'second chances' given to British citizens. Here, we expand on some of these themes to demonstrate how citizenship remains tied not just to the enforcement of punishment, but also to opportunities for rehabilitative work. We show how male foreign national offenders' perceptions of the rehabilitative work directed at them as deportable subjects are often at odds with their own aspirations and future plans, instilling feelings of unworthiness, irredeemability, and, ultimately, frustration with their inability to put to work what they accomplished while in prison.

Destined for elsewhere

By the time we conducted our own research, some of the concerns related to the second-class system for foreign nationals highlighted above were being addressed by the Prison Service. HMP Huntercombe, for instance, which re-rolled to a male-only foreign national prison in 2012, was and still is a training prison where a range of vocational and work activities are available to all prisoners, which, at present, are wholly foreign nationals. The work activities and vocational courses at HMP Huntercombe were adapted when it re-rolled, and rehabilitation is now oriented towards the presumed needs of offenders once 'successfully' deported to their countries of origin. Available activities include courses in IT, business management, English as a second language (ESL), industrial cleaning, gardening, and waste management.

For many of those wanting to return to their countries of origin, these activities offered important opportunities and were much appreciated. Not only did they provide welcome distraction and kept prisoners engaged, but prisoners also found them useful in planning their futures. IT and business management courses were particularly sought after as many considered setting up their own businesses upon their return. The chance to improve their English language skills through ESL courses was also important as prisoners believed this would give them a competitive edge on the job market in their countries of origin. For instance, Mauro (late twenties, Latin America, HMP Huntercombe), did his best to take full advantage of the opportunities for training and advancement that were at his disposal at HMP Huntercombe. Not wanting to remain in the UK, he was uncertain at what prospects awaited him upon his return. As such, his strategy was to diversify and do as many courses as possible to ensure he would broaden the scope of potential work opportunities. In this regard, Mauro greatly appreciated the spectrum of options available at HMP Huntercombe.

Conversely, for those wanting to remain in the UK, especially those who had been in the country for long periods of time, the range of available activities seemed largely irrelevant. Instead, these prisoners raised concerns over their rehabilitation and their ability to progress through their sentences with an eye to resettlement in British society. Some remarked how the 'good courses' were no longer available at the specialist prison. By 'good', they meant courses that enabled them to develop skills that were in demand outside, like welding, carpentry, and double-glazing, which would afford them work opportunities upon re-entry in their local (read: British) communities. Aleksei's (late thirties, Eastern Europe, HMP Huntercombe) words here further point to resulting feelings of being discriminated against due to the lack of citizenship:

> Prison is prison. But if you are British in prison you get enhanced prison. They give you chance to improve your situation. D-Cat. If they divide British prisoners from foreigners then that is discrimination, because British prisoners have future, they can improve. . . . I really want D-Cat, I want to go back to society and be a good member. But as a foreigner they [the Home Office] don't care because they try to send you to a different society . . . so I don't have future in this sentence.

For Jeremiah (late twenties, Caribbean, HMP Huntercombe), the array of available options was both preposterous and humiliating: 'Waste management? What the fuck is waste management?' He felt that the courses on offer at HMP Huntercombe, like waste management and industrial cleaning, reflected wider societal perceptions of the kind of work foreigners ought to be doing: 'clean up white people's mess'. Jeremiah could not understand how a training prison failed to provide a single option that he, and others like him, found to be of use. This perception was exacerbated by the lack of any Level 3 courses available in the prison.[5]

A second key issue raised by prisoners wanting to remain in the UK, and one pointed out in Aleksei's quote above, was the limited access to progress to semi-open and open custodial conditions whilst incarcerated at HMP Huntercombe. In fact, since its start as a foreign national prison, staff were concerned with expected restrictions in trying to release on temporary license (ROTL) foreign nationals to outside work and maintaining the established work placements the prison had previously secured with 16 local employers. Re-categorization to Category D (open conditions) was constantly denied to prisoners on account of their immigration status, with prisoners simply being told that immigration had an 'interest' in them. Immigration officers, on the other hand, reassured prisoners that they had no say in these matters. Prisoners were lobbed back and forth between immigration and the Offender Management Unit, which left them feeling frustrated and unsure of how to progress through their sentences and attain the much-coveted re-categorization. For those wanting to remain in the UK, serving time at HMP Huntercombe was perceived as jeopardizing their personal development and future aspirations because the rehabilitative programming to which they were entitled was viewed as inadequate to their needs.

Experiencing irredeemability

Foreign national offenders are served with deportation orders on the grounds that their removal from the country is conducive to the public good (Nason 2017a). Consequently, many of our participants felt the tension between the state's efforts at deporting them and the rehabilitative work they had undertaken whilst in prison. Narratives of irredeemability on account of a criminal conviction were frequently articulated. As Antoine (mid-thirties, West Africa, detained in an IRC) painfully observed, there were no second chances: 'It's not right. They [the authorities] should have consideration. Say, "okay, he's done this. Let's give him a chance". But, but in a way, they're not giving me no chance'. He desperately wanted another opportunity to prove his new, rehabilitated self:

> To be honest with you, I think they should give me a chance, Sarah. I've changed. I've changed, Sarah. I've done, I've done courses. I've done anger-management. I've done my art. I've done everything, Sarah. Healthy living. Know what I mean? . . . That old person is gone. This is a new and improved person now. But that's what they don't seem to want to believe, that I've changed.

Despite serving his time, Antoine's foreign national status trumped his efforts at rehabilitation during his imprisonment and his good behaviour at the IRC, along with his long history of residence in, and personal and familial ties to, the UK.

Participants expressed frustration at the Home Office's insistence on their irredeemability even as they had done the work of reform. The fact that both efforts – rehabilitation *and* deportation – were deployed by the same government was all the more puzzling. Terry (late thirties, Caribbean, detained in IRC), for instance, questioned how the Home Office could 'see that I'm a reformed person, my past life is behind me' but still decide that 'it is best for them to separate me from my kids because my threat I pose to the public outweighs the kids [having their father] by far'. Such incongruity was exceedingly frustrating for men like Terry who were sent from prison to immigration detention, and thus caught between two systems with opposing goals (see Turnbull and Hasselberg 2017).

Being transferred to immigration detention had implications for how several participants made sense of their rehabilitation whilst in prison. One participant, Samson (mid-twenties, Caribbean, detained in an IRC), found detention to be very stressful because there were no 'constructive' activities to occupy his time, which he contrasted to his time as a sentenced prisoner:

> In prison, at least they have a routine, there's more constructive things. You can do trades, you can do courses. In detention you can't do nothing. So, in my eyes if you're really looking to benefit yourself, detention is a very bad option.

Although he tried to keep busy by working at the IRC and studying mathematics, Samson was discouraged at the lack of opportunities to improve himself while he awaited a resolution to his immigration case.

Indeed, as immigration detainees, former prisoners are not being rehabilitated nor prepared for life 'outside'; rather, they are awaiting removal, which is tantamount to full exclusion from British society. This element is prevalent in the experiences of immigration detention amongst former prisoners. Furthermore, foreign national offenders who are granted bail from immigration detention while their immigration cases are being adjudicated are faced with the loss of entitlement to work, study, bank, rent, and drive in the context of Britain's 'hostile environment' (Aliverti 2015: 217). Not only are these former prisoners prevented from supporting themselves and their families, they feel unable to move on with their lives and to put to use the rehabilitative work they developed whilst in prison (Hasselberg 2014).

Despite the British government's preoccupation with expelling 'foreign criminals', deportation is not a straightforward process. Various legal safeguards exist to protect non-citizens' human rights against the power to deport, including the right to family and private life under Article 8 of the European Convention on Human Rights (Nason 2017a). The legislation and policy on the deportation of foreign national offenders insists that expulsion is in the 'public interest', but many foreign national prisoners have long histories of residence in Britain and significant personal and familial ties that deportation threatens to disrupt, often permanently, through bans on re-entry and the mandatory exclusion of people with criminal records from legal entry.[6] The process of appealing against deportation can take years, leaving foreign nationals (and their families) in suspended states of being characterized by uncertainty and precarity (Hasselberg 2016), difficult situations that are further compounded by often repeated detentions at an IRC and/or the challenging circumstances of surviving enforced destitution within Britain's hostile environment. It is not surprising that many of our participants felt as if they were being set up to 'fail' (i.e. reoffend), which would then be further 'proof' to the Home Office that they were, indeed, irredeemable.

Conclusions

This chapter has shown how deportability produces important implications for rehabilitation for people categorized and treated as foreign national prisoners. For those who will leave the country, being given low priority to engage in rehabilitative activities in 'regular' (i.e. non-specialist) prisons further limits their options upon return to their countries of origin. At HMP Huntercombe, however, the rehabilitative work undertaken by prisoners was deemed to be potentially very useful by those wishing to leave the UK. It follows that rehabilitative efforts should be adapted to the needs of particular populations, which, in this case, HMP Huntercombe provided to those wishing to take advantage of voluntary return programmes. But, in making available only rehabilitative activities institutionally viewed as 'useful' to post-deportation life overseas, HMP Huntercombe did not provide adequate rehabilitation to those who want to, and/or will (eventually), stay in the UK. For these foreign national prisoners, limited access to adequate rehabilitative opportunities hinders their chances of 'successful' resettlement and adds to their sense of being discriminated against as foreigners. In hindering access to rehabilitation (and (re)integration) for an increasing segment of the prison population, what remains of the traditional purposes of punishment? As we have highlighted in this chapter, foreign national prisoners constitute a diverse and unique population to which the incongruous penal goals of rehabilitation and deportation are applied. The fact that many foreign national prisoners will end up in immigration detention further underscores the need to think critically about the carceral trajectories of this population.

Notes

1 The Prison Reform Trust (2012) indicates that 15% of the female prison population is classified as foreign national compared to 13% of the male prison population.
2 Due to space limitations in this chapter, we cannot provide adequate consideration of the gendered and racialized experiences of female and male foreign national prisoners. We recognize this is an important limitation.
3 For detailed discussions of the 'crisis', see Bhui (2007) and Kaufman (2013).
4 As Van Zyl Smit and Snacken (2009) note, in the context of imprisonment, the twin penal aims of rehabilitation and social (re)integration are traditionally inclusionary rather than exclusionary. See also Barker (2017).
5 A Level 3 qualification is the minimum requirement for higher education and jobs that demand further detailed study.
6 Many of our participants had come to Britain as children and were permanent residents (possessing what is termed 'indefinite leave to remain'). Some never got around to applying for naturalization, while others believed their indefinite leave was a secure legal status. As Gibney (2013) notes, in daily life, there is little that distinguishes the rights of British citizens from those of permanent residents. Yet, once in conflict with the law and receiving convictions for criminal offences, formal citizenship is the only protection against deportation.

References

Aas, K. F. (2014) Bordered penality: Precarious membership and abnormal justice. *Punishment & Society*, 16(5), 520–541.

Aliverti, A. (2015) Enlisting the public in the policing of immigration. *British Journal of Criminology*, 55(2), 215–230.

Aliverti, A. (2016) Doing away with decency? Foreigners, punishment and the liberal state. In A. Eriksson (Ed.), *Punishing the Other: The Social Production of Immorality Revisited*. London: Routledge, pp. 124–144.

Allen, G. and Watson, C. (2017) *UK Prison Population Statistics*. Briefing Paper Number SN/SG/04334. London: House of Commons Library.

Banks, J. (2011) Foreign national prisoners in the UK: Explanations and implications. *The Howard Journal of Criminal Justice*, 50(2), 184–198.

Barker, V. (2017) Penal power at the border: Realigning state and nation. *Theoretical Criminology*, 21(4), 441–457.

Barnoux, M. and Wood, J. (2013) The specific needs of foreign national prisoners and the threat to their mental health from being imprisoned in a foreign country. *Aggression and Violent Behavior*, 18(2), 240–246.

Bhui, H. S. (2004a) *Going the Distance: Developing Effective Policy and Practice with Foreign National Prisoners*. London: Prison Reform Trust.

Bhui, H. S. (2004b) The resettlement needs of Foreign national offenders. *Criminal Justice Matters*, 56(1), 36–44.

Bhui, H. S. (2007) Alien experience: Foreign national prisoners after the deportation crisis. *Probation Journal*, 54(4), 368–382.

Bosworth, M., Hasselberg, I. and Turnbull, S. (2016) Punishment, citizenship and identity: An introduction. *Criminology and Criminal Justice*, 16(3), 257–266.

Canton, R. and Hammond, N. (2012) Foreigners to justice? Irregular migrants and foreign national offenders in England and Wales. *European Journal of Probation*, 4(3), 4–20.

De Genova, N. P. (2002) Migrant 'illegality' and deportability in everyday life. *Annual Review of Anthropology*, 31(1), 419–447.

Gibney, M. (2013) Deportation, crime, and the changing character of membership in the United Kingdom. In K. F. Aas and M. Bosworth (Eds.), *The Borders of Punishment: Migration, Citizenship, and Social Exclusion*. Oxford: Oxford University Press, pp. 218–236.

Griffiths, M. (2017) Foreign, criminal: A doubly damned modern British folk-devil. *Citizenship Studies*, 21(5), 527–546.

Hammond, N. (2007) United Kingdom. In A. M. Van Kalmthout, F. B. A. M. Hofstee-Van Der Meulen and F. Dünkel (Eds.), *Foreigners in European Prisons*. Nijmegen: Wolf Legal Publishers, pp. 811–854.

Hasselberg, I. (2014) Whose security? The deportation of foreign-national offenders from the UK. In M. Maguire, N. Zurawski and C. Frois (Eds.), *The Anthropology of Security: Perspectives from the Frontline of Policing, Counter-Terrorism and Border Control*. London: Pluto Press, pp. 139–157.

Hasselberg, I. (2016) *Enduring Uncertainty: Deportation, Punishment and the Everyday Life*. Oxford: Berghahn.

Her Majesty's Inspectorate of Prisons. (2006) *Foreign National Prisoners: A Thematic Review*. London: Her Majesty's Inspectorate of Prisons.

Kaufman, E. (2013) Hubs and spokes: The transformation of the British prison. In K. F. Aas and M. Bosworth (Eds.), *The Borders of Punishment: Migration, Citizenship, and Social Exclusion*. Oxford: Oxford University Press, pp. 166–182.

Kaufman, E. (2015) *Punish and Expel: Border Control, Nationalism, and the New Purpose of the Prison*. Oxford: Oxford University Press.

Kaufman, E. and Bosworth, M. (2013) The prison and national identity: Citizenship, punishment and the sovereign state. In D. Scott (Ed.), *Why Prison?* Cambridge: Cambridge University Press, pp. 170–188.

Martynowicz, A. (2016) Not so multicultural prison: Polish prisoners in a transitional prison system. *Criminology and Criminal Justice*, 16(3), 337–349.

Ministry of Justice. (2017) *Offender Management Statistics Bulletin, England and Wales*. London: Ministry of Justice.

Nason, N. (2017a) What is the law on the deportation of non EU foreign criminals and their human rights? *Free Movement* [online]. Available at: www.freemovement.org.uk/what-is-the-law-on-the-deportation-of-non-eu-foreign-criminals-and-their-human-rights/.

Nason, N. (2017b) What is the law governing the deportation of EU nationals? *Free Movement* [online]. Available at: www.freemovement.org.uk/what-is-the-law-governing-the-deportation-of-eu-nationals/.

Pakes, F. and Holt, K. (2017). Crimmigration and the prison: Comparing trends in prison policy and practice in England & Wales and Norway. *European Journal of Criminology*, 14(1), 63–77.

Prison Reform Trust. (2012) *No Way Out: A Briefing Paper on Foreign National Women in Prison in England and Wales*. London: Prison Reform Trust.

Turnbull, S. and Hasselberg, I. (2017) From prison to detention: The carceral trajectories of foreign-national prisoners in the United Kingdom. *Punishment & Society*, 19(2), 135–154.

Ugelvik, T. (2012) The dark side of a culture of equality: Reimagining communities in a Norwegian remand prison. In T. Ugelvik and J. Dullum (Eds.), *Penal Exceptionalism? Nordic Prison Policy and Practice*. Abingdon: Routledge, pp. 121–138.

Ugelvik, T. and Damsa, D. (2017) The pains of crimmigration imprisonment: Perspectives from a Norwegian all-Foreign prison. *The British Journal of Criminology*. Published online, 31 October 2017.

Van Zyl Smit, D. and Snacken, S. (2009) *Principles of European Prison Law and Policy: Penology and Human Rights*. Oxford: Oxford University Press.

Warr, J. (2016) The deprivation of certitude, legitimacy and hope: Foreign national prisoners and the pains of imprisonment. *Criminology and Criminal Justice*, 16(3), 301–318.

Webber, F. (2009) *Segregating Foreign National Prisoners* [online]. Institute of Race Relations. Available at: www.irr.org.uk/news/segregating-foreign-national-prisoners/.

66 End of life in prison

Challenges for prisons, staff, and prisoners

Marina Richter, Ueli Hostettler, and Irene Marti

Introduction

In most cases and apart from countries where the death penalty constitutes a legal sentence, prisons are built to punish and reform offenders. Thus, prisons are geared towards people who are sentenced to stay incarcerated for a definite period of time. Because of therapeutic or security measures, the period of detention for some categories of prisoners is currently prolonged in many countries. However, the long-term aim to rehabilitate offenders nevertheless remains. Although reoffending occurs after release, causing prisoners to re-enter the system, sentences are generally still pronounced for a definite period of time. But, in some countries such as the US, mandatory minimum sentencing policies permit the permanent incarceration of those who have been convicted of a third crime.

Further, prisons are usually built and conceptualized for able-bodied people. Stairs and long aisles require mobile prisoners. The quality of furniture is as sturdy and secure as possible to last long and withstand any attempt of dismantling and using for other purposes. Health facilities are basically meant to cure ill prisoners to bring them back to the regular running system, rather than keeping them for long periods of care.

If prisons are built neither for sick nor old people, they are even less built for dying prisoners and the provisions of end-of-life care or for what is debated as 'good death'. As deaths in prison were in most cases rather seen as accidents, they were also for a long time overlooked in research (Liebling 1996, 1998). The term 'good death' refers to the idea that there are many ways to die and that some are considered as being 'better' than others. Some of the most salient aspects of current definitions of good death include 'being in control, being comfortable, sense of closure, affirmation/value of the dying person recognized, trust in care providers, recognition of impending death, beliefs and values honored, burden minimized, relationships optimized, appropriateness of death, leaving a legacy, and family care' (Kehl 2006: 277). In short, good death should be self-determined, free of pain, and humane (Schneider 2005). But, the concept has also been highly criticized as it imposes a certain attitude towards dying and a certain model of dying (Hart et al. 1998).

In prisons, suicide, homicide, or also accidents do occur. In contrast to these 'deaths without dying' (Liebling 2017), where death comes unexpectedly without a prior process of dying, we concentrate in this chapter on deaths that are preceded by an evening of life and a period of dying. Because of the deteriorating health condition of the prisoner observed by staff and fellow prisoners, they know that he/she is reaching a terminal phase that will inevitably end with the death of that person. The duration of this process can be shorter or longer, but implies that the institution can and should pay attention and provide support during this time. To discuss the challenges dying prisoners constitute for the prison system, we will first outline the reasons for the increase in end-of-life cases in prisons. Bearing in mind that prisons were originally not built for dying inmates, we will then discuss what it means for the system, for staff, and for co-inmates to work and live with dying prisoners. Finally, after a prisoner's death, bereavement and other forms of personal and institutional coping remain important.

Increasing numbers of end-of-life cases in prisons worldwide

Across the globe, the numbers of prisoners who expect to experience their end of life in prison are increasing. In the United States, approximately 3,500 prisoners die every year of a natural death (Bureau of Justice Statistics). This means that every year one of 450 prisoners dies in custody (0.22%). In other countries, the rate is comparable or rather lower while the absolute numbers differ considerably. In England and Wales there were 122 natural deaths in custody in 2015, which represents 0.14% of the prison population (Eurostat, Inquest). In countries such as Switzerland where the absolute numbers are very low – 14 persons died in custody in 2015 (Swiss Federal Statistical Office) – the rate oscillates arbitrarily.

The situation in every country is different and the numbers of end-of-life cases show that the development is much more advanced in countries such as the United States or the UK. Nevertheless, there are a couple of general trends that lead to an increase in prisoners dying of non-sudden natural deaths in prisons in many parts of the Western world, if not on a global scale (Penal Reform International 2018). These trends also make the case of end-of-life prisoners an urgent topic, relevant to all countries, but to a different extent.

There is, first, a change in the sentencing and release practices that leads to longer confinement and to more frequent lifelong custody. Although there are alternatives available, such as electronic monitoring, there is a general increase in the prison population worldwide (Johnston 2008); exceptions include some societies considered as less punitive such as Canada or Scandinavian countries (Pratt et al. 2005). This increased sentencing is coupled with an increased imposing of longer sentences. Not only are there more people sentenced to prison, but also for longer periods of time. Furthermore, there are various possibilities of imposing long periods of custody for security reasons. This so-called punitive turn (Garland 2001) is followed by a trend that could be termed the securitive turn that not only tends towards valuing punishment higher than rehabilitation, but also follows the idea of maximizing the security of society (Loader 2009; Schuilenburg 2015). Prisoners are preventively excluded from society on the basis of an attributed risk for future offending. This penal intensification leads to a greater occurrence of different forms of indefinite and lifelong confinement.

Second, there is a general increase in the number of older prisoners (Crawley 2005). The general ageing of the population also changes the composition of prison population with regard to age. In addition to the phenomenon of hyper ageing that prisoners experience in custody (Dubler 1998; Fazel et al. 2001), there is also an increasing number of older and elderly prisoners due to demographic changes in the general population. Another factor that further supports this trend is the increase in the number of offenders who commit crimes at a later age or whose crimes were prosecuted only many years after they had been committed (in many jurisdictions statutory limitations for sex-related offences have been lifted; for more details, see Ulmer and Steffensmeier 2014). The increase in elderly prisoners coupled with longer sentences and with a restrictive practice of release and security measures leads to more people dying in prisons of natural non-sudden deaths.

On the one hand, this increase in cases of end-of-life situations in prison challenges established practices of handling prisoners and of running prisons. On the other hand, the fact that death occurs in a foreseeable way because of natural reasons has also fuelled a debate on ethical issues. In countries such as Germany or Switzerland, where end of life in prison is a rather new and not yet a frequent phenomenon, the ethical debate includes a basic argument: should the prison at all be a place to die? From a legal-philosophical position, an individual should always be dying as a human being and not as a prisoner, in peace and, particularly, in freedom (Kinzig 2012; Wulf and Grube 2012). Freedom thereby implies, in particular, the possibility to choose about relevant issues, such as where and when to die and who shall be accompanying this process. In many countries, there exist legal possibilities to release prisoners who are facing their end of life. Compassionate release is applicable when legal principles of security and prevention do not apply anymore. The freedom of choice can also imply to die in prison, if it is the prisoner's wish. The point is not where prisoners die, but that they are given free will to decide where this shall happen (Kinzig 2012).

In the face of an increasingly punitive and security-focused penal regime, the ethical issues remain for prisoners who cannot expect to be released towards the end of their lives. In countries, such as the United States, where end-of-life situations in prison are in general an acknowledged fact, the ethical discussion centres on ethical principles of dying inside the walls of confinement (Cohn 1999; Byock 2001; Taylor 2002). The humanitarian argument states that society should care about dying inmates and provide end-of-life care in order to ensure a humane treatment (Cohn 1999; Maull 2005). Many consider this as a basic human right (Maschi et al. 2014; Maschi and Richter 2017). The social contract argument states that because of the equivalence of all members of society, grounded in the social contract of modern democratic states, the society has the obligation to care for every one of its members, also for those in prison (Byock 2001; Handtke et al. 2012).

Prisoners facing end of life in confinement have usually lived for many years in secured settings, without having any perspective of eventually leaving confinement. Their lives take place inside the walls; their lifeworlds have melted down to what happens inside the prison. Moreover, they have to find new ways in dealing with time in prison, as there is no way out and no possible change in sight (Marti 2017). This situation has crucial implications for the prisoners themselves, as well as for their fellow prisoners who share their daily lives in the same spaces. But the situation not only impacts on prisoners; their long-term stay in prison, the lack of any perspective, and the prospect of dying in prison also strongly influences the prison as an institution, how it is organized, and, additionally, the work of prison staff (Marti et al. 2017).

Experiencing end of life in prison

End of life in prison challenges the prisoners, staff, and the system in many ways. There are challenges that occur on the normative level of the penitentiary system, challenges on the organizational level of the single prison, challenges for the day-to-day work of staff, and challenges for fellow prisoners as well as for the dying prisoners themselves. We outline each of these challenges in more detail.

As end of life refers not only to the mere moment of dying but also includes the time span that leads towards this moment, there are implications beyond death itself. In recent years, palliative care has been developed to accompany this process. In dealing with end-of-life situations, palliative care takes the patient with his or her necessities as a point of reference. The aim is not to extend life, but to improve the quality of the remaining lifetime as much as possible. This entails measures of treating symptoms such as pains, suffocation, or other physical problems. At the same time, it also includes spiritual and social care. It therefore addresses questions regarding the accompaniment by other persons and the bereavement of all the affected people as well (Ratcliff 2000).

Prisons are governed by strict rules about the usage of time and space with little possibility to adapt the prison regime to the needs of prisoners requiring end-of-life care. Issues such as continuous medical care (especially palliative care), assistance of fellow prisoners, or flexible visiting schemes often encounter systematical barriers. Yet, there are various approaches to addressing these problems. One is to install specific units for end-of-life care in prisons. Such prison hospices have first been established in the United States (Cahal 2002; Maull 2005). Another approach is to open the prison to ambulatory end-of-life care teams (Turner and Payne 2011). However, the question remains whether prisoners at their end of life still need to be treated, without any exception, according to the rules established for prisoners who are serving a sentence.

At the organizational level, end-of-life cases challenge prisons in many ways. Usually, prisons are neither built nor organized to accommodate dying prisoners. The infrastructural elements in retirement homes, such as medical beds, floors, and rooms without thresholds or other impediments for restricted mobility, such as handles, as well as other helping features for people with impediments are often missing. Prisons have to adapt their infrastructure if they have to keep elderly prisoners in the evening of their lives and eventually also their end of life. Also, the organization as a whole needs to adapt. Prison staff has either to be trained or supported by external specialists for end-of-life care (Howe and Scott 2012). Above all, as end of life in the sense of non-sudden natural death is foreseeable, the prison as an organization has a time-frame to plan and to provide solutions either inside their walls or in cooperation with external specialized institutions such as retirement homes or hospices (Hostettler et al. 2016).

The daily work routine of staff is challenged by end-of-life situations in a very profound way. A good example is the rule to keep a (physical and emotional) distance, to which staff in most countries adhere. Physical distance between staff and prisoners reduces the possibility of physical violence and assaults. But at the end of life, care often requires physical contact as well as emotional closeness. Staff needs to provide treatment such as ointments or the patient may require help with personal hygiene. Working with end-of-life prisoners challenges the professional definition of prison staff (Howe and

Scott 2012). Instead of securing, controlling, and rehabilitating, they suddenly need to take care of the dying person and his or her body in need of care. Not all members of staff can imagine providing (end-of-life) care for a prisoner. Therefore, also specialized personnel and cooperation across professions are needed. As palliative care is a holistic approach towards physical, spiritual, and social questions, there is a need for health professionals, chaplains, social workers, and other prison staff to collaborate closely (Cloyes et al. 2016).

Fellow prisoners are also affected (Supiano et al. 2014). They fear that eventually they will die in similar conditions and might want to help because they know the dying inmate, or simply because the prison cannot provide a 24-hour assistance and fellow prisoners would be willing to help out. In some prisons, prisoners are not only accepted to assist in providing end-of-life care, but are even trained to provide professional care for their dying fellow prisoners (Cloyes et al. 2014). There is a big difference in allowing voluntary help by prisoners who feel that they want to do something for the prisoner who has been living with them for years, or in training prisoners specifically for this task. On the one hand, the training allows prisoners to provide professional care, and, as examples have shown, also provides the caregivers with the opportunity to pursue an important and meaningful task. On the other hand, however, it substitutes the state's obligation to provide care and constitutes a less expensive solution.

After death

Death means the end of life of the dying person. For all the other persons involved, this moment marks the turn from acting, caring, and accompanying this person to a period of mourning and bereavement (Charlton 2002). The challenges related to end-of-life prisoners, therefore, do not end with death, but continue during the period of bereavement. The people involved are family members and friends, but also prison staff and, in particular, fellow inmates. In short, it involves the dead person's social network. As these prisoners usually spent many years in the prison system it includes rather people from within the system than from outside. Often, there are only very few relatives left who used to maintain contact with the prisoner. In many cases, contact with the outside world gets completely lost over time.

Those people from the world outside the walls, such as family members, relatives, friends, or voluntary visitors who kept in touch with the prisoner, need access and time to empty the cell and take with them some of the prisoner's belongings as they would do if they were emptying his or her house. The economic logic of a prison expressed in the reflex to re-occupy the cell as fast as possible must be put on hold. It is a question of dignity and respect towards the prisoner who has died as well as his or her social network, to not empty the cell immediately as if the prisoner was just a number that now exited the system (Hostettler et al. 2016).

For prisoners who have spent many years in the prison system and feel more and more alienated from the world outside, the people inside the prison, staff, and fellow prisoners, represent a sort of family or community – although by force. This community then also needs moments, places, and symbols of mourning and bereavement (Supiano et al. 2014). An important element, in particular for fellow prisoners, is clear and early communication and information. As prisoners usually mistrust the system and fear that they do not get adequate care at the right moment, it is important to inform promptly and openly to prevent rumours. In addition to communication, there is also a need for rituals, for instance organized by the prison chaplain, or symbols like a burning candle, or to leave the cell unoccupied for some time. Prisoners who usually cannot leave the prison to participate in a burial need therefore places, rituals, and symbols inside the walls that support their period of mourning and bereavement (Hostettler et al. 2016).

Conclusions

Although originally, prisons have not been built as spaces for practices of 'good death', the current increase in end-of-life cases in prisons worldwide calls for an adaption of prison organization and practice. The reasons for this increase in end-of-life cases merits a discussion in their own right. However, the fact that there are more and more prisoners who are facing the prospect of dying in custody, urgently requires a reaction of prisons and of the prison system as a whole. We have discussed this adaptation in several ways:

First, although there are more cases of end of life in prison, this does not mean that prisons should generally be transformed into hospices. For many prisoners there are legal options, such as compassionate release, or release due to the bad health condition of the inmate, that allow an end of life outside of confinement. In many countries there exist such legal options, but their usage is still rather scarce. In short, the search for alternatives, to provide a 'good death' outside confinement is also a form of adaptation.

Second, there are many specialized institutions in the community that are already taking care of elderly and dying people. In particular for countries with small numbers of prisoners and therefore also limited numbers of cases of end of life in confinement, it can be easier to cooperate with institutions of the general community to provide solutions for dying prisoners than to create a special unit.

Third, as already practiced in countries such as the United States or the UK, it is possible to provide 'good' death in prison. Again, there are organizational variations that are mediated by the history and culture of a national prison system but also by the numbers of prisoners at stake. Palliative care can be offered in special sections within the prison or in separated prison hospices or by mobile caring teams of internal and external staff and be provided upon request and when needed.

Finally, the challenges for the system do not end at the organizational level, but also touch the prison as an organization as well as its staff. Beyond that, the fellow inmates as part of the social environment and network of the dying inmate are also affected and challenged by an inmate's death. In general, end of life does not only concern the dying person and therefore challenges the organization in order to allow for a 'good death', but it also involves all persons of the social network of the dying person, including family and friends, voluntary visitors, fellow inmates, and often also prison staff.

End-of-life situations in prison may vary significantly across prison systems and differ quite clearly from the situation of dying people outside prison walls. These differences exist. However, prisoners have the same concerns about death and dying like any other person. One and, maybe, the most common concern is the wish to die at home, which in the prison context can often be translated into the wish to die in the prison where a prisoner has spent his or her last ten or 20 years and where he or she literally feels at home. At the same time, being in prison always means being deprived of one's basic rights, to decide when, where, how, and in who's company to die.

References

Byock, I. R. (2001) Dying well in corrections: Why should we care. *Journal of Correctional Health Care*, 9(2), 107–117.

Cahal, W. (2002) The birth of a prison hospice program. *Journal of Correctional Health Care*, 9(2), 125–129.

Charlton, R. (Ed.). (2002) *Primary Palliative Care. Dying, Death and Bereavement in the Community*. Oxon: Radcliffe Medical Press.

Cloyes, K. G., Rosenkranz, S. J., Berry, P. H., Supiano, K. P., Routt, M., Shannon-Dorcy, K. and Llanque, S. M. (2016) Essential elements of an effective prison hospice program. *American Journal of Hospice & Palliative Medicine*, 33(4), 390–402.

Cloyes, K. G., Rosenkranz, S. J., Wold, D., Berry, P. H. and Supiano, K. P. (2014) To be truly alive: Motivation among prison inmate hospice volunteers and the transformative process of end-of-life peer care service. *American Journal of Hospice & Palliative Medicine*, 31(7), 735–748.

Cohn, F. (1999) The ethics of end-of-life care for prison inmates. *Journal of Law, Medicine & Ethics*, 27(3), 252–259.

Crawley, E. (2005) Institutional thoughtlessness in prisons and its impacts on the day-to-day prison lives of elderly men. *Journal of Contemporary Criminal Justice*, 21(4), 350–363.

Dubler, N. N. (1998) The collision of confinement and care: End-of-life care in prisons and jails. *Journal of Law, Medicine & Ethics*, 26(2), 149–156.

Fazel, S., Hope, T., O'Donnell, I., Piper, M. and Jacoby, R. (2001) Health of elderly male prisoners: Worse than the general population, worse than younger prisoners. *Age and Ageing*, 30, 403–407.

Garland, D. (2001) *The Culture of Control: Crime and Social Order in Contemporary Society*. Chicago: University of Chicago Press.

Handtke, V., Bretschneider, W., Wangmo, T. and Elger, B. (2012) Facing the challenges of an increasingly ageing prison population in Switzerland: In search of ethically acceptable solutions. *Bioethica Forum*, 5(4), 134–141.

Hart, B., Sainsbury, P. and Short, S. (1998) Whose dying? A sociological critique of the "good death". *Mortality*, 3(1), 65–77.

Hostettler, U., Marti, I. and Richter, M. (2016) *Lebensende im Justizvollzug. Gefangene, Anstalten, Behörden*. Bern: Stämpfli Verlag.

Howe, J. B. and Scott, G. (2012) Educating prison staff in the principles of end-of-life care. *International Journal of Palliative Nursing*, 18(8), 391–395.

Johnston, H. (2008) Concluding remarks: The 'punitive turn': The shape of punishment and control in contemporary society. In Helen Johnston (Ed.), *Punishment and Control in Historical Perspective*. London: Palgrave Macmillan, pp. 235–241.

Kehl, K. A. (2006) Moving toward peace: An analysis of the concept of a good death. *American Journal of Hospice & Palliative Medicine*, 23(4), 277–286.

Kinzig, J. (2012) Sterben in geschlossenen Einrichtungen des Maßregelvollzugs. In Michael Anderheiden and Wolfgang U. Eckart (Eds.), *Handbuch Sterben und Menschenwürde*. Berlin: De Gruyter, pp. 1595–1617.

Liebling, A. (Ed.). (1996) *Deaths in Custody: Caring for People at Risk*. London: Whiting & Birch.

Liebling, A. (Ed.). (1998) *Deaths of Offenders: The Hidden Side of Justice*. London: Waterside Press.

Liebling, A. (2017) The meaning of ending life in prison. *Journal of Correctional Health Care*, 23(1), 20–31.

Loader, I. (2009) Ice cream and incarceration: On appetites for security and punishment. *Punishment & Society*, 11(2), 241–257.

Marti, I. (2017) Doing (With) time: Dealing with indefinite incarceration in Switzerland. *Tsantsa*, 22, 68–77.

Marti, I., Hostettler, U. and Richter, M. (2017) End of life in high-security prisons in Switzerland: Overlapping and blurring of "care" and "custody" as institutional logics. *Journal of Correctional Health Care*, 23(1), 32–42.

Maschi, T., Marmo, S. and Han, J. (2014) Palliative and end-of-life care in prisons: A content analysis of the literature. *International Journal of Prisoner Health*, 10(3), 172–197.

Maschi, T. and Richter, M. (2017) Human rights and dignity behind bars: A reflection on death and dying in world prisons. *Journal of Correctional Health Care*, 23(1), 76–82.

Maull, F. (2005) The prison hospice movement. *Explore: The Journal of Science and Healing*, 1(6), 477–479.

Penal Reform International. (2018) *Global Prison Trends 2018*. London: Penal Reform International. Available at: https://s16889.pcdn.co/wp-content/uploads/2018/04/PRI_Global-Prison-Trends-2018_EN_WEB.pdf.

Pratt, J., Brown, D., Brown, M. and Hallsworth, S. (2005) *The New Punitiveness: Trends, Theories, Perspectives*. Milton Park and New York: Routledge.

Ratcliff, M. (2000) Dying inside the walls. *Journal of Palliative Medicine*, 3(4), 509–511.

Schneider, W. (2005) Der "gesicherte" Tod – zur diskursiven Ordnung des Lebens in der Moderne. In Hubert Knoblauch and A. Zingerle (Eds.), *Thanatosoziologie: Tod, Hospiz und die Institutionalisierung des Sterbens*. Berlin: Duncker & Humboldt, pp. 55–79.

Schuilenburg, M. (2015) *The Securitization of Society: Crime, Risk and Social Order*. New York and London: New York University Press.

Supiano, K. P., Cloyes, K. G. and Berry, P. H. (2014) The grief experience of prison inmate hospice volunteer caregivers. *Journal of Social Work in End-of-Life & Palliative Care*, 10(1), 80–94.

Taylor, P. B. (2002) End-of-life care behind bars. *Illness, Crisis, & Loss*, 10(3), 233–241.

Turner, M. and Payne, S. (2011) Palliative care for prisoners. In David Oliviere, Barbara Monroe and Sheila Payne (Eds.), *Death, Dying and Social Differences*. Oxford: Oxford University Press, pp. 200–206.

Ulmer, J. T. and Steffensmeier, D. (2014) The age and crime relationship: Social variation, social explanations. In Kevin M. Beaver, J. C. Barnes and Brian B. Boutwell (Eds.), *The Nurture Versus Biosocial Debate in Criminology: On the Origins of Criminal Behavior and Criminality*. New York: Sage Publications, pp. 377–396.

Wulf, R. and Grube, A. (2012) Sterben im Gefängnis. In Michael Anderheiden and Wolfgang U. Eckart (Eds.), *Handbuch Sterben und Menschenwürde*. Berlin: De Gruyter, pp. 1571–1594.

Older prisoners

A challenge for correctional services

Susan Baidawi

Definition of an older prisoner

Researchers, policymakers, and corrections administrators have yet to reach a consensus as to what constitutes an 'older offender' and definitions vary substantially, ranging from 45 years and above to 65 years and above (Stojkovic 2007). The issue of definition is essential for comparative research and a lack of consensus can impede the development of a sound evidence base concerning older prisoners and related issues, such as offence types, recidivism rates, health concerns, and prison management issues. Despite the variability of definition, many writers and researchers have adopted a functional definition of 'older prisoners' as being those who are 50 years of age and over (Kerbs and Jolley 2007; Stojkovic 2007). The utilization of 50 years and older as an appropriate gauge for 'old age' in prison is based on research findings that identify a 10- to 15-year differential between the health of prisoners and that of the general population (Fazel et al. 2001; Loeb et al. 2008). Accelerated ageing among prisoners is generally attributed to a combination of their pre-prison lifestyles (including poor nutrition, substance misuse, and a lack of medical care) and the understanding that prison environments may escalate age-related illnesses and conditions (Stojkovic 2007; United Nations Office on Drugs and Crime 2009).

An ageing inmate population

Older prisoners are the fastest growing age group of inmates in various prison systems around the world (Aday and Krabill 2012; Baidawi et al. 2011; Office of the Correctional Investigator Canada 2018; Sturge 2018). In Australia, prisoners aged 50 years and older represented 13% of the total (sentenced and un-sentenced) prisoner population in 2018 (or 5,554 prisoners), compared to 9.5% in 2005 and around 6% in 1994 (Australian Bureau of Statistics 1997, 2005, 2018b). Similarly, older prisoners are increasing in number across several jurisdictions globally, including Canada, the United States, United Kingdom, and New Zealand (see Table 67.1).

In England and Wales, inmates aged 50 years and older formed 7% of the prisoner population in 2002, and 16% in 2018 (Sturge 2018). It is predicted that by 2030, one-third of all prisoners in the United States will be over the age of 55 years (Kerbs and Jolley 2009). Similarly, New Zealand experienced a 94% increase in the number of prisoners aged 50 years and over from 2000 to 2009 (New Zealand Department of Corrections 2010).

Why are the numbers of older prisoners increasing?

While in general Western populations are ageing, it has been postulated that changes in prosecution and sentencing laws and practices – including man-

Table 67.1 Proportion of older prisoners by country

Country	Proportion of prisoners aged 50 years and older
Australia	13%
England and Wales	16%
Northern Ireland	17%
New Zealand	17%
United States*	19%
Canada	25%

* Proportion of prisoners in the US aged 51 years and older

Sources: Australian Bureau of Statistics (2018b), United States Federal Bureau of Prisons (2018), New Zealand Department of Corrections (2018), Office of the Correctional Investigator Canada (2018), Sturge (2018)

datory minimum sentencing and reduced options for early release – have also contributed to older prisoner population growth (Aday and Krabill 2012; Kerbs and Jolley 2009). This is also indicated by comparison of prisoner and community demographic statistics. For instance, the Australian population aged 50 years and older increased by 31% from 2000 to 2010, a comparatively smaller figure than the 84% increase observed in the older prisoner population over the same period (ABS 2001, 2010). Ageing of the general population alone cannot account for older prisoner population growth. Additionally, higher proportions of older prisoners are convicted of offences that attract long sentences (e.g. sex offences, homicide, and drug-related offences), contributing to their rising numbers (Aday and Krabill 2012; Baidawi 2016; Wahidin 2011).

Types of older prisoners

In describing their diversity, researchers have identified four main groups of older prisoners based on offending history (Aday 2006; Goetting 1984):

- First-time prisoners, incarcerated at an older age
- Ageing recidivist offenders who enter and exit prison throughout their lifetime and return to prison at an older age
- Prisoners serving a long sentence who grow old while incarcerated
- Prisoners sentenced to shorter periods of incarceration late in life

According to Stojkovic (2007: 101), the experience of prison is different for each of these groups of people, but linked by the 'overwhelming stress' of incarceration.

Older prisoner minority groups

Attention needs to be paid to both female prisoners and Indigenous prisoners (in relevant jurisdictions) as notable minority groups within the older inmate population.

Older female prisoners

Though the number of female prisoners is far smaller than that of males, the growth observed in the female prisoner population since 2000 far exceeds that observed for males (53% and 20% respectively) (Walmsley 2017). This rise in female prisoner numbers is further emphasized among older females compared to the overall female prisoner population. For example, in Australia the number of female prisoners aged 50 years and over nearly quadrupled over the period 2000–2018 (an increase of 370%), far exceeding the percentage growth in the female prison population aged under 50 years (approximately 151%) (ABS 2000, 2018b). Similarly in the US, the number of sentenced female prisoners under 50 years old decreased between 2010 and 2016, compared to a 19% increase in the number of female prisoners aged 50 years and older over the same period (Carson 2018; Guerino et al. 2011).

Researchers have drawn attention to older female prisoners as an overlooked minority (Aday and Krabill 2011; Wahidin 2011). Authors have emphasized that male and female prisoners are incomparable due to differences in criminal history profiles and adjustment to prison, and the unique rehabilitation, health, and transitional support needs of female inmates (Baidawi and Trotter 2016; Wahidin 2004). Several studies have now found that older female prisoners face substantially greater physical, mental, and functional health morbidity compared to older males, including serious health problems such as cardiac, degenerative, and respiratory illnesses (Baidawi 2016; Baidawi and Trotter 2016; Kerbs and Jolley 2009; Leigey and Hodge 2012). Accordingly, gender-specific responses have been suggested as more appropriate to address the particular healthcare needs of older female inmates (HMIP 2008; Wahidin 2003).

Older Indigenous prisoners

In jurisdictions such as Australia and Canada, Indigenous peoples are over-represented among those in contact with the criminal justice system, particularly in prisons (Australian Human Rights Commission 2008; Office of the Correctional Investigator Canada 2018). In Australia, Indigenous peoples comprised 28% of the 2018 adult prisoner population, despite making up only 2% of the national population aged 18 years and older (Australian Bureau of Statistics 2018b).

While constituting an important subgroup, the Indigenous inmates comprise a relatively lower proportion of older inmates, representing only 14% of males and 16% of females aged 50 years and over in Australian prisons in 2018 (ABS Australian Bureau of Statistics 2018b). This perhaps reflects the lower median age of death of Indigenous Australians compared with non-Indigenous Australians (59.7 years compared to 82 years in 2018; ABS 2018a). Indigenous prisoners would therefore be expected to be affected by age-related health issues at a younger age than other prisoners and this can be accounted for in research and practice (e.g. by altering the definition of 'older' for Indigenous prisoners to 45 years and over) (Baidawi et al. 2011; Leach and Neto 2011).

While the Indigenous populations of Canada are similarly over-represented among the national prisoner population, the issue of defining 'older' as it relates to this population is not discussed in the literature (e.g. Greiner and Allenby 2010). This may be because the Canadian Indigenous life expectancy gap is far smaller than the Australian Indigenous life expectancy gap (AIHW; Australian Institute of Health and Welfare 2011).

Issues in the management of older prisoners

The rising number and proportion of older prisoners has implications for planning, policy, and service delivery across the correctional system.

Health concerns

As with older people in general, the most immediate issues facing older prisoners are often those related to ageing and associated declines in physical and cognitive health and functioning. Furthermore, considering the accelerated biological ageing process, a prisoner who is chronologically 50 years of age is generally expected to display the onset of age-related health concerns of a 60-year-old in the general population. Such concerns include coping with chronic disease and/or terminal illness, fear of dying, pain management, reduced levels of mobility, disability, loss of independence, and cognitive impairments (Baidawi and Trotter 2016; Fazel et al. 2001; Williams et al. 2006). The rising numbers of older prisoners has implications for prison health services (e.g. in screening, preventative healthcare, and chronic disease management) and for custodial management of older prisoners (e.g. accommodation needs and programme delivery).

Mental health and adjustment

Although older prisoners are generally less disruptive than younger prisoners, a considerable number experience depression and other psychological problems (Baidawi 2016; Kakoullis et al. 2010). Historically, little attention has been paid to issues relating to older prisoners, partly due to the perception of prison staff that older prisoners are 'compliant' and therefore, not (overtly) a 'problem' (Crawley 2005; Wahidin 2004). This is reflected in national and international research concerning older prisoners' mental health, of which there is 'strikingly little' (Kakoullis et al. 2010: 696; Kingston et al. 2011).

Yet approximately 40 to 50% of ageing prisoners experience mental health issues, including a high prevalence of depression (Baidawi and Trotter 2016; Fazel et al. 2001). Further, the prevalence of mental illness among older prisoners is likely to be higher than estimates derived from prison records for several reasons. First, mental illness may develop during the course of incarceration after initial screenings are completed and second, prisoners may not disclose symptoms due to fear of consequences, such as eligibility for parole and fear of judgement (Kakoullis et al. 2010; Potter et al. 2007). This may have implications for older prisoners upon release, particularly those with unidentified mental health needs, who may be unable to access various health and social services, leaving them vulnerable and at risk of reoffending (LeMesurier et al. 2010; Williams et al. 2010).

Increasing costs

Corresponding with the rise in older prisoner numbers, an increase in associated healthcare costs has been a concern for policymakers and prison administrators (Human Rights Watch 2012; Maschi et al. 2013). Research in both Australia and the US identified that the cost of accommodating older prisoners is significantly greater than it is for younger prisoners (up to three times in some jurisdictions) (Aday 2003; Trotter and Baidawi 2013). In addition to actual and potential costs, many prison administrators are considering, or have responded to, older prisoners' health needs through hiring specialized staff, or the creation of nursing or 'older prisoner' units (Anno et al. 2004; Her Majesty's Inspectorate of Prisons [HMIP] 2008). The rising numbers of older inmates therefore has implications for correctional budgets, and there is a subsequent imperative to identify cost-effective strategies, particularly in relation to healthcare, for this prisoner group.

Prison environment, regime, and programmes

Correctional environments are primarily designed for the young and able-bodied, who comprise the majority of prisoners (Aday 2003; Kerbs and Jolley 2009). Older prisoners' health concerns are seen to be exacerbated by unsuitable prison environments and regimes which poorly cater for the needs of older prisoners with physical disabilities, such as limited mobility (e.g. requiring the use of ramps, wheelchairs, or walking frames), hearing or vision impairments, infirmity, or incontinency (Baidawi and Trotter 2016; PRT 2008; Williams et al. 2006).

A lack of appropriate and meaningful programs for older prisoners has also been noted across a range of programme areas including education, vocation, and exercise (Sterns et al. 2008; Wahidin and Aday 2005). Many prison education programs are often focused on basic literacy and numeracy skills (targeting younger prisoners), and the physical education provided may be too challenging or unsuitable for older prisoners, who may also have to contend with younger prisoners dominating exercise equipment (HMIP 2004; Trotter and Baidawi 2015). Some have described this situation as a 'double punishment', concluding that difficulties with, or lack of access to, prison facilities and programs creates a harsher prison environment for older prisoners (PRT 2014; Stojkovic 2007).

Vulnerability to victimization

The literature indicates that older prisoners – especially those with limited mobility, frailty, or disability – are perceived as more vulnerable to victimization than their younger, generally stronger counterparts (Kerbs and Jolley 2009; Trotter and Baidawi 2015). Older prisoners with functional impairments appear to experience the greatest fear of victimization (Trotter and Baidawi 2015). An HM Inspectorate report for England and Wales (2004) found that prison staff were not trained or willing to push wheelchairs, thereby predisposing wheelchair-dependent prisoners to victimization from other prisoners on whom they relied for assistance – in some cases by 'paying' helpers. Likewise a study involving interviews with older prisoners in the United Kingdom outlined that 'almost half the men had experienced bullying and intimidation' and 'over 60 percent . . . felt unsafe' (Prison Reform Trust 2008: 7–8). A large proportion of older (male) prisoners are also sex offenders, predisposing them to victimization based on their offence category (Kerbs and Jolley 2009).

Release and resettlement issues

Difficulties in post-release planning and support for older prisoners have also been identified (Crawley 2004; Williams et al. 2010). The causes underlying this shortcoming include a lack of coordination between prisons, community correctional services, and community agencies; priority being provided to younger inmates (either due to their higher risk of reoffending or greater perceived chances of successful rehabilitation and reintegration); and a lack of strategies to address the needs of older prisoners, combined with restrictive criteria for the early medical release of terminally or chronically ill prisoners (Maschi et al. 2013; Rikard and Rosenberg 2007; Stojkovic 2007).

The need for support in transitioning from prison may be amplified for older prisoners experiencing chronic illness (Crawley 2004). In addition, those incarcerated for longer periods are likely to have more difficulty adjusting to community living, particularly if they have lost family and social support, as well as housing, possessions, and employment capacity (Aday and Krabill 2012; Crawley 2004; Prison Reform Trust 2008).

Strategies and solutions

A number of strategies have been suggested and implemented with a view to managing the issues surrounding older prisoners.

Nursing home prisons, prison hospices, and special needs units

Several examples exist of specialized prisons designed to accommodate older prisoners with chronic health concerns and/or terminal illnesses, including Laurel Highlands, a geriatric and special needs facility in central Pennsylvania, and a 50-bed prison in Singen, Germany (Anno et al. 2004; Kucharz 2008). Such prisons can provide specialized intensive services required by ill and infirm prisoners, while reducing costs through centralization of resources. Such facilities may also reduce victimization of older inmates and provide staffing and environment better tailored to the older prisoner population.

Other correctional facilities have instead established special needs units within prisons to service older populations (Anno et al. 2004; Fry and Howe 2005). The reported benefits of such units are similar to that of the nursing home prisons, with centralized resources reducing costs associated with staffing, medical care, and transport, and age-segregation of prisoners alleviating issues around prisoner victimization and enabling more targeted programming and rehabilitation efforts (Fry and Howe 2005; Kerbs and Jolley 2009).

While there is much support for age segregation in correctional settings, others have noted that prisons sometimes see a value in 'mainstreaming' or intermingling of older and younger prisoners to help calm and stabilize the younger prisoner population (Aday 2006; Kerbs and Jolley 2009). Research also indicates variation among older prisoners in their preference for segregation or mainstreaming (Dawes 2009).

Staffing, services, and programmes

Many strategies implemented with a view to managing older prisoner populations have been developed at the local level, rather than being directed by policy frameworks. Such initiatives have utilized assessment, collaboration with community agencies, case management, mentoring, and advocacy to identify and address issues affecting older prisoners; for example, developing more appropriate exercise and day programmes and coordinating transitional support (Aday and Krabill 2012; Trotter and Baidawi 2013). Implemented strategies have included developing an elderly register, training and employing prisoners as carers, and utilizing older inmates as advisors on ageing issues within prisons (Baidawi 2015).

Other institutions have opted to hire specialist staff with training in aged care, gerontology, and nursing to provide appropriate care to the ageing prison population (Baidawi 2015). Prisons have also provided training to custodial staff to improve their capacity to understand, respond to, and empathize with inmates with mental, cognitive, or physical impairments (Baidawi and Trotter 2016; Gaseau 2004; Williams et al. 2012). The need for health promotion programmes and education for elderly inmates has also been highlighted

(Williams et al. 2014), as has the benefits of group consultation with older prisoners in the form of committees and forums (Cooney and Braggins 2010).

Parole and early release

Although older offenders generally pose a lower risk of reoffending, there remains reluctance from government and prison administrators to consider early release or promote the use of community corrections as an alternative to imprisonment for older low-risk offenders (Kerbs and Jolley 2009). Early release and parole options for older prisoners also attract opposition from victims' advocacy groups, victims, and their families. One argument for 'early' or 'compassionate release' or medical/geriatric parole is the reduction in costs of providing medical care in prison (Williams et al. 2011). However opponents have pointed out that these same costs will simply be borne by a different government sector, such as health or aged care, as many inmates are unwanted by family or have out-lived their relatives (Yorston and Taylor 2006). In Louisiana, the POPS (Project for Older Prisoners) programme utilizes law students to work with older prisoners who meet various selection criteria, who then investigate community placements available and consult with the prisoners' victims before advocating for release with the Louisiana Parole and Pardon Boards (Martin 2001). By 2001, the programme had assisted close to 300 inmates to gain release 'without a single act of recidivism' (Martin 2001).

Implications

The rise in numbers of older prisoners is expected to continue to impact a range of correctional domains.

- Prison health services are likely to experience increased requirements for specialist services and chronic disease management services, as well as screening and treatment for age-related illnesses (including dementia and terminal illness).
- A greater need for accommodation arrangements suitable for prisoners with frailty and mobility issues is also likely. Correctional services may experience greater requirements for personal care, therapeutic equipment, and modifications to cells and facilities for older prisoners.
- There are implications for programme delivery, given that many older inmates may be either medically unfit for work or past retirement age. Prisons may need to assess the availability of appropriate social, educational, and recreation programmes for this prisoner group.
- As a result, there are implications for correctional budgets, including costs associated with catering for older prisoners with higher healthcare needs, or where alternative transport and accommodation are required.

■ Finally, there are implications for correctional research. Information about the needs of older prisoners and the extent to which the current trends will continue is vital for prison service planning.

Conclusion

Numerous and significant issues related to older prisoners exist, which are pertinent to the prisoners themselves, their families, the wider community, corrections administrators, healthcare professionals, and policymakers. The growth of the older prisoner populations will continue to necessitate more systematic approaches towards planning for and addressing their needs.

Acknowledgements

This chapter is adapted from a manuscript first published in *Trends and Issues in Crime and Criminal Justice* (Baidawi et al. 2011), reproduced with permission from the Australian Institute of Criminology.

References

Aday, R. H. (2003) *Aging Prisoners: Crisis in American Corrections*. Santa Barbara, CA: Praeger Publishers.

Aday, R. H. (2006) Aging prisoners. In B. Berkman and S. D'Ambruoso (Eds.), *Handbook of Social Work in Health and Aging*. Santa Barbara, CA: Oxford University Press, pp. 231–244.

Aday, R. H. and Krabill, J. J. (2011) *Women Aging in Prison: A Neglected Population in the Criminal Justice System*. Boulder, CO: Lynne Rienner.

Aday, R. H. and Krabill, J. J. (2012) Older and geriatric offenders: Critical issues for the 21st century. In L. Gideon (Ed.), *Special Needs Offenders in Correctional Institutions*. Thousand Oaks, CA: Sage Publications, pp. 203–232.

Anno, B. J., Graham, C., Lawrence, J. E., Shansky, R., Bisbee, J. and Blackmore, J. (2004) *Correctional Health Care: Addressing the Needs of Elderly, Chronically Ill and Terminally Ill Inmates*. Middletown: National Institute of Corrections.

Australian Bureau of Statistics. (1997) *Australian Social Trends 1997*. Australian Bureau of Statistics. Available at: www.ausstats.abs.gov.au/ausstats/free.nsf/0/3105281F7F04C4 ACCA25722500049550/$File/41020_1997.pdf.

Australian Bureau of Statistics. (2000) *Prisoners in Australia 2000 (no. 4517.0)*. Canberra: Australian Bureau of Statistics.

Australian Bureau of Statistics. (2001) *Population by Age and Sex. (no. 3201.0)*. Canberra: Australian Bureau of Statistics. Available at: www.abs.gov.au/AUSSTATS/abs@.nsf/ DetailsPage/3201.0Jun%202001?OpenDocument.

Australian Bureau of Statistics. (2005) *Prisoners in Australia 2005 (no. 4517.0)*. Canberra: Australian Bureau of Statistics.

Australian Bureau of Statistics. (2010) *Australian Demographic Statistics (no. 3101.0)*. Canberra: Australian Bureau of Statistics.

Australian Bureau of Statistics. (2018a) *Deaths, Australia 2018 (no. 3302.0)*. Canberra: Australian Bureau of Statistics.

Australian Bureau of Statistics. (2018b) *Prisoners in Australia 2018 (no. 4517.0)*. Canberra: Australian Bureau of Statistics.

Australian Human Rights Commission. (2008) *A Statistical Overview of Aboriginal and Torres Strait Islander Peoples in Australia*. Sydney: Australian Human Rights Commission.

Australian Institute of Health and Welfare. (2011) *Comparing Life Expectancy of Indigenous People in Australia, New Zealand, Canada and the United States*. Canberra: Australian Institute of Health and Welfare.

Baidawi, S. (2015) *Managing the Health of an Ageing Prison Population – A Review of the Challenges to Be Addressed by Effective Models of Care*. Sydney: The Sax Institute.

Baidawi, S. (2016) Older prisoners: Psychological distress and associations with mental health history, cognitive functioning, socio-demographic and criminal justice factors. *International Psychogeriatrics*, 28(3), 385–395.

Baidawi, S. and Trotter, C. (2016) Psychological distress among older prisoners: Associations with health, healthcare utilisation and the prison environment. *Journal of Correctional Health Care*, 22(4), 354–366.

Baidawi, S., Turner, S., Trotter, C., Browning, C., Collier, P., O'Connor, D. W. and Sheehan, R. (2011) Older prisoners – a challenge for Australian corrections. *Trends and Issues in Crime and Criminal Justice*, (426), 1–8.

Carson, E. A. (2018) *Prisoners in 2016*. Washington, DC: Bureau of Justice Statistics. Available at: www.bjs.gov/content/pub/pdf/p16.pdf (Accessed 19 December 2018).

Cooney, F. and Braggins, J. (2010) *Doing Time: Good Practice with Older People in Prison – the Views of Prison Staff*. London: Prison Reform Trust. Available at: www.prisonreformtrust.org.uk/Portals/0/Documents/doing%20time%20good%20practice%20with%20older%20peop,.pdf.

Crawley, E. (2004) Release and resettlement: The perspectives of older prisoners. *Criminal Justice Matters*, 56, 32–33.

Crawley, E. (2005) Institutional thoughtlessness in prisons and its impacts on the day-to-day prison lives of elderly men. *Journal of Contemporary Criminal Justice*, 21(4), 350–363.

Dawes, J. (2009) Ageing prisoners: Issues for social work. *Australian Social Work*, 62(2), 258–271.

Fazel, S., Hope, T., O'Donnell, I. and Jacoby, R. (2001) Hidden psychiatric morbidity in elderly prisoners. *British Journal of Psychiatry*, 179, 535–539.

Fazel, S., Hope, T., O'Donnell, I., Piper, M. and Jacoby, R. (2001) Health of elderly male prisoners: Worse than the general population, worse than younger prisoners. *Age and Ageing*, 30(5), 403–407.

Fry, D. and Howe, D. (2005) Managing older prisoners at HMP Wymott. *Prison Service Journal*, 160.

Gaseau, M. (2004) Caring for the aging inmate: Solutions for corrections. *Corrections Connection (Online magazine)*, 6 December. Available at: www.corrections.com/news/article/3718 (Accessed 17 January 2011).

Goetting, A. (1984) The elderly in prison: A profile. *Criminal Justice Review*, 9, 14–24.

Greiner, L. and Allenby, K. (2010) *A Descriptive Profile of Older Women Offenders*. Ottawa: Correctional Service of Canada.

Guerino, P., Harrison, M. H. and Sabol, W. J. (2011) *Prisoners in 2010*. Washington, DC: Bureau of Justice Statistics. Available at: www.bjs.gov/content/pub/pdf/p10.pdf (Accessed 19 December 2018).

Her Majesty's Inspectorate of Prisons. (2004) *'No Problems – old and quiet': Older Prisoners in England and Wales: A Thematic Review by HM Chief Inspector of Prisons*. London: HMIP.

Her Majesty's Inspectorate of Prisons (HMIP). (2008) *Older Prisoners in England and Wales: A Follow-Up to the 2004 Thematic Review by HM Chief Inspectorate of Prisons.* London: HMIP.

Human Rights Watch. (2012) *Old Behind Bars: The Aging Prison Population in the United States.* New York: Human Rights Watch.

Kakoullis, A., LeMesurier, N. and Kingston, P. (2010) The mental health of older prisoners. *International Psychogeriatrics,* 22(5), 693–701.

Kerbs, J. and Jolley, J. (2007) Inmate-on-inmate victimization among older male prisoners. *Crime and Delinquency,* 53(2), 187–218.

Kerbs, J. and Jolley, J. (2009) A commentary on age segregation for older prisoners: Philosophical and pragmatic considerations for correctional systems. *Criminal Justice Review,* 34(1), 119–139.

Kingston, P., Le Mesurier, N., Yorston, G., Wardle, S. and Heath, L. (2011) Psychiatric morbidity in older prisoners: Unrecognized and undertreated. *International Psychogeriatrics,* 23(8), 1354–1360.

Kucharz, C. (2008) Germany: Prison specializes in older prisoners. *Seniors World Chronicle.* Available at: www.seniorsworldchronicle.com/2008/03/germany-prison-specializes-in-older.html.

Leach, J. and Neto, A. (2011) *Offender Population Trends: Aged Offenders in NSW.* Sydney: Corrective Services New South Wales.

Leigey, M. E. and Hodge, J. P. (2012) Gray matters: Gender differences in the physical and mental health of older inmates. *Women and Criminal Justice,* 22, 289–308.

LeMesurier, N., Kingston, P., Heath, L. and Wardle, S. (2010) *A Critical Analysis of the Mental Health Needs of Older Prisoners: Final Report.* Staffordshire: Staffordshire University.

Loeb, S., Steffensmeier, D. and Lawrence, F. (2008) Comparing incarcerated and community-living older men's health. *Western Journal of Nursing Research,* 30(2), 234–249.

Martin, K. (2001) The POPS program: Providing a voice for older inmates. *Corrections Connection (Online magazine),* 19 February. Available at: www.corrections.com/news/article/7449 (Accessed 16 January 2011).

Maschi, T., Morrissey, M. B. and Leigey, M. E. (2013) The case for human agency, well-being, and community reintegration for people aging in prison: A statewide case analysis. *Journal of Correctional Health Care,* 19(3), 194–210.

Maschi, T., Viola, D. and Sun, F. (2013) The high cost of the international aging prisoner crisis: Well-being as the common denominator for action. *The Gerontologist,* 53(4), 543–554.

New Zealand Department of Corrections. (2010) *Offender Volumes Report 2009.* Wellington: New Zealand Department of Corrections.

New Zealand Department of Corrections. (2018) *Prison Facts and Statistics – September 2018.* Available at: www.corrections.govt.nz/resources/research_and_statistics/quarterly_prison_statistics/prison_stats_june_2018.html (Accessed 17 December 2018).

Office of the Correctional Investigator Canada. (2018) *Annual Report 2017–18.* Ottawa: Office of the Correctional Investigator. Available at: www.oci-bec.gc.ca/cnt/rpt/pdf/annrpt/annrpt20172018-eng.pdf (Accessed 17 December 2018).

Potter, E., Cashin, A., Chenoweth, L. and Jeon, Y. (2007) The healthcare of older inmates in the correctional setting. *International Journal of Prisoner Health,* 3(3), 204–213.

Prison Reform Trust. (2008) *Doing Time: The Experiences and Needs of Older People in Prison.* London: Prison Reform Trust. Available at: www.prisonreformtrust.org.uk/Portals/0/Documents/Doing%20Time%20the%20experiences%20and%20needs%20of%20older%20people%20in%20prison.pdf.

Prison Reform Trust. (2014) *Prison for Old People Can Be Double Punishment.* Prison Reform Trust. Available at: www.prisonreformtrust.org.uk/PressPolicy/News/ItemId/210/vw/1 (Accessed 31 October 2016).

Rikard, R. and Rosenberg, E. (2007) Ageing inmates: A convergence of trends in the American criminal justice system. *Journal of Correctional Health Care*, 13(3), 150–162.

Sterns, A. A., Lax, G., Sed, C., Keohane, P. and Sterns, R. S. (2008) The growing wave of older prisoners: A national survey of older prisoner health, mental health and programming. *Corrections Today*, 70(4), 70–72, 4–6.

Stojkovic, S. (2007) Elderly prisoners: A growing and forgotten group within correctional systems vulnerable to elder abuse. *Journal of Elder Abuse and Neglect*, 19(3), 97–117.

Sturge, G. (2018) *Briefing Paper: UK Prison Population Statistics.* London: House of Commons Library. Available at: http://researchbriefings.files.parliament.uk/documents/SN04334/SN04334.pdf (Accessed 18 December 2018).

Trotter, C. and Baidawi, S. (2013) *A Strategic Framework for the Management of Australia's Ageing Offenders.* Melbourne: Monash University.

Trotter, C. and Baidawi, S. (2015) Older prisoners: Challenges for inmates and prison management. *Australian and New Zealand Journal of Criminology*, 48(2), 200–218.

United Nations Office on Drugs and Crime. (2009) *Handbook on Prisoners with Special Needs.* New York: United Nations.

United States Federal Bureau of Prisons. (2018) *Inmate Age.* Federal Bureau of Prisons. Available at: www.bop.gov/about/statistics/statistics_inmate_age.jsp (Accessed 19 December 2018).

Wahidin, A. (2003) *We Are a Significant Minority: Old Women in English Prisons.* Paper Presented to British Criminology Conference, Bangor, June.

Wahidin, A. (2004) *Older Women in the Criminal Justice System: Running Out of Time.* London: Jessica Kingsley Publishers.

Wahidin, A. (2011) Ageing behind bars, with particular reference to older women in prison. *Irish Probation Journal*, 8, 109–123.

Wahidin, A. and Aday, R. H. (2005) The needs of older men and women in the criminal justice system: An international perspective. *Prison Service Journal*, 160, 13–22.

Walmsley, R. (2017) *World Female Imprisonment List.* London: International Centre for Prison Studies.

Williams, B. A., Ahalt, C. and Greifinger, R. (2014) The Older Prisoner and Complex Chronic Medical Care. In S. Enggist, L. Møller, G. Galea and C. Udesen (Eds.), *Prisons and Health.* Copenhagen, Denmark: World Health Organization Europe, pp. 165–170.

Williams, B. A., Lindquist, K. L., Sudore, R. L., Strupp, H. M., Willmott, D. J. and Walter, L. C. (2006) Being old and doing time: Functional impairment and adverse experiences of geriatric female prisoners. *Journal of the American Geriatrics Society*, 54(4), 702–707.

Williams, B. A., McGuire, J., Lindsay, R. G., Baillargeon, J., Cenzer, I. S., Lee, S. J. and Kushel, M. (2010) Coming home: Health status and homelessness risk of older pre-release prisoners. *Journal of General Internal Medicine*, 25(10), 1038–1044.

Williams, B. A., Stern, M. F., Mellow, J., Safer, M. and Greifinger, R. B. (2012) Aging in correctional custody: Setting a policy agenda for older prisoner health care. *American Journal of Public Health*, 102(8), 1475–1481.

Williams, B. A., Sudore, R. L., Grelfinger, R. and Morrison, R. S. (2011) Balancing punishment and compassion for seriously ill prisoners. *Annals of Internal Medicine*, 155(2), 122–126.

Yorston, G. and Taylor, P. (2006) Commentary: Older offenders – no place to go? *Journal of the American Academy of Psychiatry and Law*, 34(3), 333–337.

The role of offenders' family links in offender rehabilitation

Anna Kotova

> An offender's family are the most effective resettlement strategy.
>
> (HM Inspectorate of Prisons, HMP Inspectorate of
> Probation and Ofsted, 2014)

Introduction

Criminologists are becoming increasingly interested in the experiences of offenders' families, and more and more research is being conducted into how punishment reaches into all facets of these families' lives (e.g. Condry 2007; Condry et al. 2016). We have also become interested in the various roles these families can play when it comes to offender rehabilitation. This is not surprising, as people who offend are often parts of familial networks: they are mothers, fathers, sons, siblings, cousins, and so on. In England and Wales, over half of male prisoners have at least one minor child and about one quarter had lived with a partner prior to imprisonment (Ministry of Justice 2012). It has been estimated that about 200,000 children in England and Wales experience parental imprisonment each year (Ministry of Justice 2012). This is but an estimate, as no formal data on this population of children is collected, and it is entirely possible that this number is in fact higher.

This chapter will explore the various roles the family can play in offender rehabilitation. It will discuss the evidence to support the claim that families can have a part to play in reducing reoffending, and discuss the reasons for the correlation between sustained family links and the reduction in reoffending. However, it will also argue that we need to approach this issue with some caution. Offenders' families are often financially and socially vulnerable themselves (see Condry et al. 2016), and the burden of supporting an offender may, for some, be unduly onerous. The challenges faced by offenders' families should not be ignored simply because the family can play an important part in supporting offenders and can help them lead law-abiding lives.

Family ties and reoffending – the evidence

The strengthening of family ties has long become a feature of offender treatment in England and Wales. The National Reducing Re-offending Delivery Plan includes a Children and Families Pathway (NOMS 2014), and states that 'children and families can play a significant role in supporting an offender to make and sustain changes which reduce re-offending' (NOMS 2014: 40). In 2016, the HM Inspectorate of Prisons (2016) also reinforced the importance of family ties in the context of young offender institutions, stating that it is its expectation that 'prisoners can maintain contact with the outside world through regular and easy access to mail, telephones and other communications' (2016: 5).

Research has certainly shown that there is a correlation between sustained family links and a reduction in reoffending (see Famer 2017 for an overview). Even though many of these studies were conducted in the context of imprisonment specifically, many of the themes raised are also applicable to rehabilitation of those who were not given a prison sentence. It is important to note that all of the studies on family links showed a small or moderate link between strong family ties and better post-release outcomes for prisoners (e.g. Holt and Miller 1972; Visher and Travis 2003). Crucially, no study has shown a negative correlation between family ties and reoffending. Research looking at specific family-focused programs has also found this correlation to be true. In the US, a study on family visits found that 21% of those who participated in an overnight family visit were arrested or imprisoned again, compared to 36% of those who received no overnight or ordinary visits. In the UK, Markson et al. (2015: 433) concluded that 'family relationships are important for developing resilience after release from prison and therefore may have an impact on the desistance process'.

This is not to say, of course, that all family ties are inherently positive. For example, Leverentz (2006) in the US found that in the cases of women who offended, the male partners were often central to the offending behaviour.

Female offenders are especially vulnerable in this respect, with many suffering from abuse and violence (Corston 2007) perpetrated by those close to them. However, there is no evidence to show that the majority of familial relationships are abusive, or that family contact is more harmful for families and children of offenders than not. Although there is certainly a need to be wary of a blanket assumption that family contact is good for everyone involved (Comfort 2008), we should also not assume that it is harmful. Farmer (2017), in his overview of the evidence about prisoners' family ties, concluded that there is no evidence to support the view that prisoners' families are 'bad', or that prisoners make bad fathers.

Offenders' family links are, therefore, important for our society more generally. If they help reduce offending, these links could help make our communities safer places for us all. We therefore all have a vested interest in ensuring that positive, stable relationships between offenders and their families are sustained.

Why are family links important for offenders?

There has been comparatively little research into *why* or *how* family links work in the context of resettlement and reintegration of offenders (Mills and Codd 2008). It is, however, critical that we try and understand these processes and the reasons why or how families could be important in maximizing offenders' rehabilitative efforts. Understanding the role(s) families play could help policymakers and practitioners design and implement targeted, effective programs and support mechanisms for offenders and families alike.

One key concept in this context is social capital. This refers to the 'everyday fabric of social connections between individuals and the tacit co-operation that such connections entail' (Mills and Codd 2008: 11). For example, stable employment, which is both a source and a result of social capital (Halpern 2005), can assist the person who offended in his or her resettlement through mobilizing their social capital and therefore helping the former offender re-establish his or her own. Families could play a key role in helping him or her enter gainful employment, be it by employing them directly or by providing help and advice when it comes to job searching. Families may be able to draw on their extended social networks in order to help their relative find work, thus mitigating the hardship of finding work with a criminal record. In fact, the 2003 Home Office survey found that more than half of prisoners had plans for employment or a place on an education or training scheme arranged through families and friends (in Mills and Codd 2008). It should be noted, however, that such social capital may manifest itself in quasi-legal employment such as cash-in-hand employment rather than fully legitimate work (Mills and Codd 2008).

Moreover, families can provide emotional and moral support (Mills and Codd 2008). Studies suggest that the state of prisoners' mental health is correlated with the extent to which they sustain contact with relatives outside. Richards (1978) found that for long-term prisoners, especially, maintaining family ties played a key role in the management of mental health. Numerous studies (e.g. Richard 1978; Hulley et al. 2016; Sykes 1958) found that 'missing somebody' was a key pain of imprisonment felt by prisoners. Helping prisoners cope with this pain via sustained, positive family contact, therefore, may be important for ensuring their mental health does not deteriorate significantly. Poor mental health, after all, could hinder rehabilitation efforts after imprisonment. This function of family links could be especially pertinent in light of the fact that many offenders have numerous mental health needs: the Social Exclusion Unit (2002) found that over 70% of male and female prisoners suffered from one or more mental health disorders. Providing a supportive family environment for those with such vulnerabilities could help offenders in their rehabilitative efforts.

Nonetheless, a positive, enduring family relationship could also be a source of anguish for the offender. Being removed from their family could be stressful and upsetting, and they may worry about how their family is faring (Farmer 2017). We know that some men prefer their children not visit them in prison because they do not wish to expose their children to a harsh and stressful environment (Farmer 2017). Instead, they attempt to remove themselves from their families, a coping strategy known as 'hard-timing'.

Importantly, families cannot simply be expected to provide this support. When a prisoner is released, especially after serving a long sentence, the system needs to ensure that the family, where appropriate, is involved in his or her resettlement planning, yet this is rarely done (Farmer 2017). Families may need information, help, and support in order to best provide the sort of assistance the offender may need upon release. We cannot simply assume that someone returning to a family home will automatically be given practical and emotional support, as families may feel 'highly conflicted about a returning ex-prisoner' (Farmer 2017: para 186 page 72).

Thirdly, families can motivate the person who offended to lead law-abiding lives. In their seminal study, Sampson and Laub (1993) showed that people with stronger social bonds, such as strong marriages, were less likely to offend than those who were less strongly attached. They argued that such bonds 'create interdependent systems of obligations and restraint' (Sampson and Laub 1993: 141). In other words, if the person who offended is strongly bonded to his or her relatives, they may avoid reoffending because they may fear disappointing or upsetting their relatives. They may, moreover, wish to set a good example for their children. Families could also persuade the man or woman who offended to stay away from negative influences and former co-offenders, attend relevant addiction treatment programs, comply with parole requirements, and so on (Markson et al. 2015).

We need to recognize that people who offend make their own choices. However, family links could help them re-orientate their identities towards more 'legitimate' ones. Families could help people who offend to see themselves as husbands, wives, mothers, fathers, and so on, bolstering this deep, identity-level change via strong family links (Visher and Travis 2003). Schemes in England and Wales such as *Storybook Dad* and *Storybook Mum* help to illustrate this. These schemes are aimed at helping men and women in prison to strengthen their identities as parents by engaging in storybook reading and other parental activities with their children. It is argued that 'doing something positive and tangible for their child increases [prisoners'] self-esteem and belief in themselves as a valued parent' (*Storybook Dads*, n.d.).

However, different family members may provide different kinds of support and motivation (Markson et al. 2016). Parents, for example, may be better placed to help the person who offended find employment because they may have a longer employment history and wider social networks. Partners may be better placed to provide day-to-day practical support and motivation, as well as accommodation. Children may be sources of motivation to lead law-abiding lives and reformulate former offending identities towards those of parenthood and being a good role model. Again, however, this analysis needs to come with a word of caution. Not all families will be able to motive the offenders to change, and some families may in fact do the opposite – for example, relatives who are themselves engaged in criminal behaviour.

We also need to bear in mind that for ethnic minorities, the meaning of family may be somewhat different. For instance, people from certain ethnic groups often place very strong cultural emphasis on the family (Chao and Tseng 2002, writing in the context of Asian ethnicities). This could in turn result in these families being more proactive in sustaining family ties to the people who offended. On the other hand, traditional conceptions of family could also result in a greater level of familial shame and result in such families shunning or cutting off the person who offended altogether.

Why are family links important for families of offenders?

When we talk about offenders' family links, we usually discuss their importance to the offender and the criminal justice system. An important question to ask is why, and to what extent, might they also be important to the family? In what ways might the family benefit from maintaining contact with the offender?

Where the relationship in question was generally positive and close, punishing the offender, especially through imprisonment, could put significant stress on the relationship. It has been found that imprisonment puts a significant amount of strain on marital relationships (see Hairston 1991 for an overview). Partners and other relatives may miss the prisoners and experience feelings of loss and grief (Hairston 1991; Comfort 2008; Condry 2007). Maintaining close links with the prisoner may, therefore, help such families in that they will continue to sustain a relationship with their loved ones and therefore help mitigate some of these feelings of loss and grief.

Children are especially affected by a parent's offending in general and parental imprisonment specifically. Studies have indicated that parental imprisonment is correlated with poor school performance and negative behaviour (Lowenstein 1986), as well as other behavioural, social, and mental health problems. Murray and Farrington (2008: 133) found that parental imprisonment is correlated with 'child anti-social behaviour, offending, mental health problems, drug abuse, school failure, and unemployment'. It is very difficult to ascertain whether imprisonment or pre-existing disadvantage (including poverty, poor pre-existing familial relationships, etc.) are causally linked to these poor outcomes for children, yet qualitative evidence certainly shows that maintaining relationships with imprisoned parents is beneficial for many children (e.g. see Scharff Smith 2014). Moreover, parental imprisonment may be all the more confusing for children, as they are sometimes not told the full truth about the imprisoned parent's circumstances (see Condry et al. 2016). Sustaining positive relationships in this context could help reassure the child that their parent is faring well, that he or she still cares for them, and mitigate their fears and feelings of loss.

However, we cannot assume all families will benefit from sustaining family ties with offenders. For some families, such as those who had experienced the offender's violence, addiction problems, or domestic abuse, severing these ties may be a positive change indeed (see Comfort 2008). There is a need for careful consideration of the offenders' prior family history and of the families' and children's welfare. In fact, one study (Swan 1981) found that children were more affected by parental imprisonment when the pre-existing relationship with the imprisoned parent was a close one and when they had spent more time together prior to imprisonment.

Risks and opportunities: a word of caution

As discussed above, there is certainly good evidence to support the view that stable, positive family links are important for offender resettlement and rehabilitation, especially when the person who offended is being released from prison. Families can provide emotional, practical, and financial support and can be a source of motivation for the person who offended to lead a law-abiding life.

However, we need to consider the costs of supporting a person who offended. It has long been shown that families of offenders experience a wide range of difficulties and deprivations (see Condry et al. 2016 for an overview). Sustaining family links with an offender sometimes comes with significant financial and temporal costs, especially when they need to visit him or her in prison (Morris 1965; Condry 2007), and many families experience stigma (Condry 2007). Moreover, the families have to negotiate complex, sometimes contradictory emotions. Visiting a prisoner can be stressful, exciting, and joyous, all at once (see Comfort 2008; Arditti 2012), for instance. Visiting prisons can also expose families to stigmatization from prison staff and result in emotional trauma (Mills and Codd 2007). As I have argued elsewhere, therefore, families of prisoners experience a range of social injustices (Kotova 2014). Finally, it may be completely inappropriate to expect families to sustain such family links in cases when these families were themselves victims of the acts of the person in question.

The above is especially true in the context of prisoners' children. Maintaining contact with prisoners should not be seen simply as good by default. Children may find visiting stressful and upsetting, even if the relationship with the imprisoned parent is a positive one. Children may feel sad and upset after visits, as they have to leave their parent in the prison. They may feel intimidated by the searching process and the rigorous rules that prison visitors need to follow (see Arditti 2012).

We must, therefore, be very careful when we talk about offenders' families as being useful resettlement resources that the criminal justice system can draw upon. There is no central government body responsible for engaging with the complex needs of these families, and they often receive little support. Most have to rely on charities and NGOs, which are more often than not small, local, and under-staffed, and lack secure long-term funding (Mills and Codd 2008). We need to strike a careful balance between harnessing family links within offender rehabilitation programs and ensuring we do not put an undue, unfair burden on families already experiencing a range of social injustices. Moreover, we should not imply that the family has a duty to ensure their relative does not offend again (and, by extension that they are 'bad' families if he or she does offend). It is ultimately the duty of the state to ensure effective resettlement and rehabilitation for offenders, not the family. The challenge is to recognize and harness the role of the family when appropriate, but also to ensure we realize that this should not mean outsourcing the duties of professionals to vulnerable and socio-economically excluded families. This outsourcing may seem especially attractive at a time of challenging criminal justice budgets, but needs to be resisted (see Farmer 2017).

It should also be noted that if we only envisage families as important rehabilitation tools, many vulnerable families in need of support will be left out. For example, when someone is serving a very long sentence, the issue of rehabilitation does not arise for many years. In this time, we will have little imperative to engage with the family. Likewise, we will have little reason to engage with those families who decide to cease to have any contact with the person who offended. Nonetheless, these families may still need financial, practical, and emotional support regardless of whether they can help the offender in his or her rehabilitative efforts or not.

Finally, it is critical that we recognize that that effective offender rehabilitation cannot be achieved without adequate funding, staffing, and staff training (Farmer 2017). The issue is one that goes far beyond ensuring offenders and families sustain meaningful, positive relationships. Our criminal justice system cannot be saved by positive family links alone. Lord Farmer, in his recent report on prisoners' families ties, explicitly recognized that he found it impossible 'not to be aware of the deep and pervasive problems endemic across the prison estate, which have to be alleviated if rehabilitation is to be a realistic aim. These include understaffing and overcrowding' (Farmer 2017: 8). If rehabilitation is to be taken seriously, therefore, a wholesale programme of rehabilitation-focused reform needs to be undertaken.

References

Arditti, J. A. (2012) *Parental Incarceration and the Family: Psychological and Social Effects on Children, Parents, and Caregivers*. New York: New York University Press.

Chao, R. and Tseng, V. (2002) Parenting of Asians. In M. H. Bornstein (Ed.), *Handbook of Parenting: Social Conditions and Applied Parenting*, 2nd edition. Mahwah, NJ: Lawrence Erlbaum Associates.

Comfort, M. (2008) *Doing Time Together: Love and Family in the Shadow of the Prison*. Chicago: University of Chicago Press.

Condry, R. (2007) *Families Shamed: The Consequences of Crime for Relatives of Serious Offenders*. Abingdon: Willan Publishing.

Condry, R., Kotova, A. and Minson, S. (2016) Social Injustice and Collateral Damage: The Families and Children of Prisoners. In Y. Jewkes, J. Bennett and B. Crewe (Eds.), *Handbook on Prisons*. Abingdon: Routledge.

Corston, J. (2007) *The Corston Report: A Review of Women with Particular Vulnerabilities in the Criminal Justice System*. London: Home Office.

Farmer, Lord. (2017) *The Importance of Strengthening Prisoners' Family Ties to Prevent Reoffending and Reduce Intergenerational Crime*. London: Ministry of Justice.

Hairston, C. F. (1991) Family ties during imprisonment: Important to whom and for what. *Journal of Sociology and Social Welfare*, 18, 87–104.

Halpern, D. (2005) *Social Capital*. Oxford: Polity Press.

HM Inspectorate of Prisons. (2016) *Life in Prison: Contact with Families and Friends* [online]. Available at: www.justiceinspectorates.gov.uk/hmiprisons/wp-content/uploads/sites/4/2016/08/Contact-with-families-and-friends-findings-paper-2016.pdf (Accessed 17 October 2017).

HM Inspectorate of Prisons, HM Inspectorate of Probation and Ofsted. (2014) *Resettlement Provision for Adult Offenders: Accommodation and Education, Training and Employment* [online]. Available at: www.justiceinspectorates.gov.uk/cjji/wp-content/uploads/sites/2/2014/09/Resettlement-thematic-for-print-Sept-2014.pdf (Accessed 3 November 2017).

Holt, N. and Miller, D. (1972) *Explorations in Intimate-Family Relationships*. Sacramento, CA: California Department of Corrections.

Hulley, S., Crewe, B. and Wright, S. (2016) Re-examining the problems of long-term imprisonment. *The British Journal of Criminology*, 4(1), 769–792.

Kotova, A. (2014) Justice and prisoners' families. *Howard League What Is Justice? Working Papers*, May [online]. Available at: http://howardleague.org/wp-content/uploads/2016/04/HLWP_5_2014_2.pdf.

Leverentz, A. (2006) The love of a good man? Romantic relationships as a source of support or hindrance for female ex-offenders. *Journal of Research in Crime and Delinquency*, 43, 459–488.

Lowenstein, A. (1986) Temporary single parenthood – the case of prisoners' families. *Family Relations*, 35(1), 79–85.

Markson, L., Losel, F., Souza, K. and Lanskey, C. (2015) Male prisoners' family relationships and resilience in resettlement. *Criminology & Criminal Justice*, 15(4), 423–441.

Ministry of Justice. (2012) *'Prisoners' childhood and family backgrounds: Results from the Surveying Prisoner Crime Reduction (SPCR) longitudinal cohort study of prisoners.* Ministry of Justice Research Series 4/12. [Available online] https://assets.publishing. service.gov.uk/government/uploads/system/uploads/attachment_data/file/278837/ prisoners-childhood-family-backgrounds.pdf (Accessed 30 May 2019).

Mills, A. and Codd, H. (2007) Prisoners' families. In Y. Jewkes (Ed.), *Handbook on Prisons*. Cullompton: Willan Publishing.

Mills, A. and Codd, H. (2008) Prisoners' families and offender management: Mobilising social capital. *Probation Journal*, 55(1), 9–24.

Morris, P. (1965) *Prisoners and Their Families*. New York: Hart Publishing Co.

Murray, J. and Farrington, D. P. (2008) The effects of parental imprisonment on children. *Crime and Justice*, 37(1), 133–206.

NOMS. (2014) *The National Reducing Re-Offending Delivery Plan*. London: National Offender Management Service.

Richards, B. (1978) The experience of long-term imprisonment. *British Journal of Criminology*, 10(2), 162–169.

Sampson, R. J. and Laub, J. H. (1993) *Crime in the Making: Pathways and Turning Points Through Life*. Cambridge, MA: Harvard University Press.

Scharff Smith, P. (2014) *When the Innocent Are Punished: The Children of Imprisoned Parents*. Basingstoke: Palgrave Macmillan.

Social Exclusion Unit. (2002) *Reducing Re-Offending by Ex-Prisoners*. London: Social Exclusion Unit.

Storybook Dads. (undated) *About Us* [online]. Available at: www.storybookdads.org.uk/ about.html (Accessed 1 November 2017).

Swan, L. A. (1981) *Families of Black Prisoners: Survival and Progress*. Boston, MA: G. K. Hall.

Sykes, G. (1958) *The Society of Captives: A Study of a Maximum Security Prison*. Princeton, NJ: Princeton University Press.

Visher, C. A. and Travis, J. (2003) Transitions from prison to community: Understanding individual pathways. *Annual Review of Sociology*, 29, 89–113.

69

The impact of imprisonment on families

Helen Codd

Introduction

During the last ten years there has been a very significant and rapid expansion in research and debate around prisoners, families, and penal policy, such that within the academic sphere it is no longer appropriate to refer to prisoners' family members as 'forgotten', 'invisible', or 'hidden' victims (Morris 1965; Codd 1998; Jardine 2017). That said, this research is still limited in its scope, and thus there are some family members about whom little is known, such as the families of older and LGBTQ+ prisoners. Similarly, whilst there is now a substantial body of research documenting and analyzing the experiences and needs of prisoners' partners and children in many European countries, Australia, New Zealand, and North America (Philbrick et al. 2014; Scharff Smith and Gampell 2011), research on Asian, African, and South American jurisdictions is less developed and thus there are some significant regional and jurisdictional gaps in the literature. Relationships between prisoners and their families, especially between parents and children, are now matters of global concern, especially in the context of human rights (Liefaard 2015; Scharff Smith and Gampell 2011; Robertson 2007; Donson and Parkes 2016).

This expansion in research and policy debate has not, however, led to root-and-branch reforms in sentencing and custodial regimes, and the impacts of imprisonment on prisoners' family members, including children, are very often negative and harmful. Although there has been a substantial expansion in the published research and policy literature, this has not always been translated into greater awareness of prisoners' families and their needs and experiences in the criminal justice system and beyond. For example, whilst the impact of parental imprisonment on children is well documented, there is wide variation in school and teacher awareness and responsiveness to the needs of prisoners' children. Gwyneth Boswell argues that, with a few exceptions, little has changed for imprisoned fathers and their children in England and Wales (Boswell 2018). Indeed, little seems to have changed in practice for prisoners and their children in most, if not all, jurisdictions around the world.

Prisoners' families

Since Pauline Morris's pioneering work in the 1960s (Morris 1965), the term 'prisoner's family' has been most commonly applied to include spouses and intimate partners (mainly heterosexual partners), and children. Some attention has been paid to parents, and less to siblings. Reflecting the gendered composition of the prison population, most of the research and policy documentation has focused on the family relationships of imprisoned men, with the exception of research exploring imprisoned mothers and the challenges of mothering 'from the inside' (Ferraro and Moe 2003; Golden 2005; Enos 2001). Little is known about the adult children of prisoners, including the adult children of older prisoners.

Compared to other work on family structures and the sociology of the family, research with prisoners' families has remained curiously resistant to change, and only very recently has this research begun to question the meaning of 'family' itself (Jardine 2017). The report of the review conducted by Lord Farmer (Farmer 2017) stresses that there should not be an undue emphasis on the biological or nuclear family, and this approach is to be welcomed in the context of the complexities of contemporary family, kin, and friendship networks. Jardine's innovative and important ethnographic work (Jardine 2017) adopts an approach which explores family as constructed by people themselves and explores family practices and displays, recognizing that families are 'diverse, fluid and highly individual' (Jardine 2017). Jardine (2017) argues that failing to look beyond the boundaries of the traditional nuclear family not only risks underestimating the impacts of imprisonment but also perpetuates a model of family life which is simply not relevant to many people. The term 'prisoners' family' is thus perhaps most usefully applied in a brief chapter such as this one as a shorthand term for the diverse range of people who maintain close relationships and ongoing contact with prisoners, these relationships being significant both to the prisoner and also to those 'on the outside'.

Whatever definition of the family is adopted, increased use of imprisonment coupled with longer average sentence lengths has meant that in the US and the UK more and more individuals, families, and communities are affected by imprisonment, sometimes experiencing the incarceration of more than one family member. Although it is difficult to assess exact numbers, it is estimated that around 200,000 children in the UK experience the imprisonment of a parent every year, more than the number of children affected by divorce or in care (Williams et al. 2012). In some communities, as has been especially visible in some urban US areas, many families are living with multiple family members absent through imprisonment, including the imprisonment of mothers, and entire community structures are challenged and weakened by these 'collateral consequences' which impact not only on individuals and families but on entire communities, which, in the US, and to a lesser extent the UK, often maps onto inequalities of race and ethnicity (Braman and Wood 2003; Braman 2004).

The impacts of imprisonment on families

Whilst for some families the imprisonment of a family member benefits that family, for many partners, children, and parents of prisoners the prison sentence brings with it many challenges, and social, financial, and emotional consequences which are usually negative (Murray et al. 2014; Condry et al. 2016). It is important to recognize the nuances of these impacts – a family, for example, may benefit from the imprisonment of a violent, drug-dependent, and drug-dealing parent, but at the same time experience negative financial impacts of the loss of an income, even if that income was generated by drug-dealing and other criminal activity. The imprisonment of a family member may involve the loss of an income – and a criminally obtained income is still an income; the loss of housing due to rent or mortgage arrears; stigma and fear of stigma, combined with profound impacts on physical, psychological, emotional, and mental health.

Children may suffer severe emotional upset at the loss of contact with a much-loved parent, even if that parent was a prolific offender outside the home. Children may not understand how or why their parent is absent, and it is still common for children not to be told the truth, or to be lied to, as to where their absent parent is. The situation becomes even more challenging for the child when they are told the truth by other people, such as friends at school, or when they discover the truth for themselves, as then they may believe that the non-imprisoned parent may themselves not know the true location of the prisoner, and feel obliged to continue to maintain the pretence. Children may blame themselves for their parent's imprisonment, especially if they themselves are the victim, or develop suspicion and mistrust of authority figures including the police and teachers. Children may experience difficulties at school, and increased absence from school either because of visiting on weekdays, or having to care for other siblings whilst the non-imprisoned parent goes to visit. The consequences of the sentence can be exacerbated by unfamiliar and unclear visiting policies and procedures, the challenges of visiting prisons in remote locations with poor public transport, and unfamiliar security rules and routines. That said, there is wide variation in visiting policies, practices, and procedures, and there are some outstanding examples of good practice in encouraging and supporting visitors, although these can be contrasted with examples of visiting where families perceive that they are unwelcome and treated with suspicion and hostility.

The impacts of imprisonment on families are gendered, with women usually bearing the burdens of caring 'from the outside' regardless of the gender of the inmate (Codd 2008). This is not necessarily the case in all communities, as anecdotal evidence suggests that in some British Muslim communities women are discouraged from visiting prisons, but on a global level it is women who support prisoners in both practical and emotional terms (Codd 2008). For most men in prison, their children continue to be cared for by female partners, and when women are imprisoned children are most likely to be cared for by other female relatives (Codd 2008). Family members may change and adapt family routines and practices in order to comply with the rules, regulations, and routines of the prison, with work commitments and children's school attendance sometimes having to play a secondary role to pre-booked visits and expected telephone call times.

Grandparents, particularly grandmothers, may find themselves caring for the children of their imprisoned offspring, particularly the children of imprisoned daughters. There are theoretical questions as to the desirability of children being cared for by grandparents, especially if the family could be described as a crime-support or criminogenic environment, and there are also practical concerns. Whilst not all grandparents are 'older' or 'elderly', some are, and thus may be shouldering the 'double burden' of taking responsibility for caring for children at the same time as having to care for their own elderly parents, sometimes also coping with their own ill health. Where they are not the main children's carers, grandparents of prisoners' children can play a key role where the relationship between the prisoner and another parents has broken down, such as after divorce, helping facilitate contact between the prisoner and his/her children and taking the children to visit.

The impacts of imprisonment do not end automatically once the person imprisoned is released, as at that point new challenges emerge in terms of return and reintegration into the family and the community and the dynamics of decision-making and authority in the family have changed. Children may no longer respond to the returned prisoner as an authoritative parental figure. Women who have experienced responsibility for all family decision-making may not want to return to the situation prior to the sentence, and for some women the absence of their partner means that they have developed new interests of their own, including employment or college courses. Whilst the belief in the family and home may provide a sustaining image and aspirational ideal for the prisoner during the sentence, the experience of living through the sentence may leave the family's structures and processes altered fundamentally. When the prisoner is released, the family may have to deal with restrictions due to electronic monitoring and probation supervision, for example, and also cope with the frustrations of the returned family member who may find it challenging to comply with their licence limitations. The returning former prisoner may also experience unemployment, mental health difficulties, and social hostility and stigma, and thus the process of return has been described by some family members as 'the second sentence'. For some families, such as the families of sex offenders, the family structure may be changed fundamentally as the imprisoned parent may be prevented from returning to live in the family home, or there could be strict limitations on contact with any children. This can mean that the long-awaited return of an imprisoned family member may represent not just the closing of one chapter in the life of the family but the beginning of a whole new volume of challenges. Of course, bearing in mind high post-prison reoffending rates, this process is one which many families go through more than once, sometimes on multiple occasions and with multiple family members.

Families during remand and custody

> This report is not sentimental about prisoners' families, as if they can, simply by their presence, alchemise a disposition to commit crime into one that is law abiding. However, I do want to hammer home a very simple principle of reform that needs to be a golden thread running through the prison system and the agencies that surround it. That principle is that relationships are fundamentally important if people are to change.
>
> (Farmer 2017: 4)

Family members often provide practical, financial, and emotional support throughout remand and imprisonment, assistance ranging from paying for clothes, telephone calls, leisure activities and hobbies, to writing letters and emails, and visiting. Family members can act as a link between the prison and the prison establishment, through contacting the chaplaincy, for example, if they feel their partner is in need of support, or contacting the prison governor and the Independent Monitoring Board if they have concerns about the regime or environment in which their family member is being held.

Visits continue to be highly significant for both prisoners and family members. Although outside the prison new communications technologies and social media are in common usage, in UK prisons the legitimate and approved use of such technologies is highly proscribed, although of course smuggled mobile phones in prisons continue to be a prized commodity.[1] There is wide variation between institutions. In some prisons, the visiting experience would be familiar to families visiting over 40 years ago, as little has changed. In others, initiatives such as designated visitors' centres, some managed by outside agencies, combined with initiatives such as extended family visits and family days, mean that prisoners and their families can experience far more enriching contacts. Access to these opportunities can be limited, however, due to pressures of resources, and this can mean limits on numbers of prisoners who can participate and limits on frequency of participation. Prisons can view families more as a threat to security than as providing valuable support, according prisoners' families low priority status within a framework of decision-making dominated by security and risk. In England, the tendency has been for most prisons to frame supporting visitation and family contact ideologically as a privilege rather than a right, which McCarthy and Adams (2017) contrast with the development of visitation in Scotland, which they characterize as justifying visiting policies and practices with a strong focus on human rights, against a backdrop of a greater historical acceptance of penal welfarism.

Women may endeavour to make the imprisoned family member feel as if they are still an important part of the family, engaging them in decision-making and relocating family events and traditions, such as birthday celebrations, into the prison visiting environment. A particular role is fulfilled by parents, particularly mothers, who may be the only long-standing visitor to continue to support a prisoner who is serving a long sentence, for a stigmatized offence, and who continue to support the prisoner long after romantic attachments have ended. Prison visits have been linked to improved prisoner well-being and increased chances of successful re-entry after release, and also help prisoners' children maintain relationships with their imprisoned family member, even though in some institutions visiting can be stressful and scary (Kalkan and Smith 2014). Prison visits centres play a key role in facilitating what family members call a 'good' visit, contributing to the well-being of both prisoners and their visiting family members (Woodall and Kinsella 2018). That said, visits are not experienced as universally positive and beneficial interactions (Turanovic and Tasca 2017) and some prisoners who do not receive visits decide to 'opt out', choosing not to receive visits either because of the perceived social and economic costs and stresses caused to their visitors, stress to themselves, or as a choice guided by their own sense of agency and self-identity (Pleggenkuhle et al. 2017).

Families, release, and resettlement

Historically, criminological research has explored the potential criminogenic role of the family. Longitudinal research, including the Cambridge Study in Delinquent Development, has analyzed and evaluated the impacts or otherwise of parental imprisonment on the likelihood of children, particularly boys, going on to offend and be imprisoned in later life, and psychological research has assessed parental factors, including mothering, in relation to particular offence types, including sexual offences and violence. A number of studies have found links between parental imprisonment and the likelihood of children experiencing a range of difficulties in later life, including mental ill health and antisocial behaviour (Murray and Farrington 2008).

Alongside this, somewhat paradoxically, an extensive and growing body of research has explored the links between strong supportive family ties and a decreased likelihood of reoffending after release, a tranche of studies supporting the view that supportive family ties play a key role, and sometimes the most significant role, in promoting successful community reintegration after release, and decreased recidivism (Brunton-Smith and McCarthy 2017; Farmer 2017; Social Exclusion Unit 2002). Jardine's research (2017) adopts relational perspectives focusing on the meaning prisoners attach to family ties and it seeks to reconcile the benefits of families supporting inmates with the negative burdens placed upon them. The mechanisms by which family ties are linked to successful re-entry and reduced risk of reoffending are the subject of ongoing research, some commentators interpreting strong family ties in terms of social capital and others drawing links with social bonding theories.

Prison policy in England and Wales has reiterated that prisons need to include family members throughout the sentence and pre-release planning process (Farmer 2017). The expectation that families play an active role in supporting imprisoned family members whilst inside and through the gate is, however, in direct opposition to the gated, secure, and exclusionary nature of some prisons, where there is still a tendency to view families as threats to security above all else.

Conclusions: good practice in working with families

The Farmer report (2017) provides a set of proposals for embedding family relationships throughout the penal system, advocating strongly for increased spending on the prison estate, staffing, and resources so as to embed consideration of the family in the sentence and how it is experienced: whether the recommendations of this report are implemented remains to be seen.

There is no single agency responsible for prisoners' families, leading to family issues being at a low level of priority. Institutional priorities in offender management which place monitoring and managing risk at the centre of decision-making, as in probation practice, mean that families can feel displaced or ignored, unless they are actual or potential victims.

A number of well-established schemes exist to assist prisoners in maintaining contact, especially with children. Some, such as the 'storybook' reading schemes, are well established and embed not only parenting and literacy but also, for those involved in the editing and sound recording, employability skills.

Educational and training courses, such as 'Family Man', encourage imprisoned fathers to reflect on their role, both inside and after release. A beacon of good practice, HMP Parc, in South Wales, has created a pioneering multi-agency 'through the gate' approach to maintain relationships between prisoners and their families, adopting a 'whole family' approach in its 'Invisible Walls Wales' (IWW) provision (Clancy and Maguire 2017). However, the nature of prison governance in England and Wales can mean a lack of continuity when prisoners move from one prison to another, and a lack of consistency and continuity in opportunities to maintain relationships, especially with children.

Outside prisons, a wide range of professionals can be significant in signposting family members to sources of help of which they may be unaware. Whilst the most obvious professionals to come into contact with prisoners' families are those such as prison, probation, and rehabilitation staff, teachers, GPs, health visitors, school nurses, and social workers can also, if they are appropriately aware, assist and support family members through the sentence. There is, however, wide variation in how schools approach parental imprisonment, which can make it easier for families to let schools know if a child is living with an impending trial or sentence hearing within the family, or experiencing a family member's imprisonment.

A number of local, regional, and national non-statutory third-sector organizations provide information and support for families, some running visitors' centres. The internet and social media are also important sources of information, support, and sometimes self-help for family members, the potential to remain pseudonymous on social media sites allowing family members to seek help and discuss their situation in a nonjudgemental, accepting, and safe space run by and for other family members.

Supporting imprisoned family members imposes burdens on families already often living lives characterized by disadvantage, hardship, and exclusion. After all, prisoners themselves are most likely to have come from backgrounds of social exclusion and, as has been said of the children of imprisoned mothers, the imprisonment of a mother is not usually the only challenge in their lives – it is the latest in a long line of challenges (Golden 2005). This is a core paradox at the heart of the links between prisons, families, rehabilitation, and resettlement. Families themselves have documented the many challenges of visiting prisons – then at the same time families are supposed to be involved throughout the sentence and afterwards, governmental policies reiterate the role of family members as agents of resettlement. Against a backdrop of drastic cuts in public spending and shifts in the focus of probation work to offender monitoring and management, prisoners' family members are being co-opted as unpaid – and untrained – rehabilitation workers.

In conclusion, imprisonment can have a profound and often negative impact on prisoners' family members, including children. However, ongoing supportive relationships between prisoners and their families have been identified as playing a key role in preventing reoffending and promoting rehabilitation. Whilst there has been much progress in the development of research exploring and documenting the impacts of imprisonment on families, and an expansion in official recognition of the value of maintaining inmates' family ties, there is still much room for improvement, so as to translate this extensive research into real-life policies and practices which benefit prisoners and their families without imposing unreasonable burdens and responsibilities.

Note

1   For a discussion of technological initiatives in US prisons, see Johnson and Hail-Jares (2016).

References

Boswell, G. (2018) Imprisoned fathers and their children: A reflection on two decades of research. *Child Care in Practice*, 24(2), 212–224.

Braman, D. (2004) *Doing Time on the Outside: Incarceration and Family Life in Urban America*. Ann Arbor: University of Michigan Press.

Braman, D. and Wood, J. (2003) From one generation to the next: How Criminal sanctions are reshaping family life in urban America in. In J. Waul Travis and M. Waul Travis (Eds.), *Prisoners Once Removed: The Impact of Incarceration and Reentry on Children, Families and Communities*. Washington, DC: The Urban Institute Press, pp. 157–188.

Brunton-Smith, I. and McCarthy, D. J. (2017) The effects of prisoner attachment to family on re-entry outcomes: A longitudinal assessment. *The British Journal of Criminology*, 57(2), 463–482.

Clancy, A. and Maguire, A. (2017) Prisoners and their children: An innovative model of 'whole family' support. *European Journal of Probation*, 9(3), 210–230.

Codd, H. (1998) Prisoners' families: The 'Forgotten Victims'. *Probation Journal*, 45(3), 148–154.

Codd, H. (2008) *In the Shadow of Prison: Families, Imprisonment and Criminal Justice*. Cullompton: Willan.

Condry, R., Kotova, A. and Minson, S. (2016) Social injustice and collateral damage: The families and children of prisoners. In Y. Bennett, J. Crewe and B. Jewkes (Eds.), *Handbook on Prisons*. London: Routledge, pp. 622–640.

Donson, F. and Parkes, A. (2016) Weighing in the balance: Reflections on the sentencing process from a children's rights perspective. *Probation Journal*, 63(3), 331–346.

Enos, S. (2001) *Mothering from the Inside: Parenting in a Women's Prison*. Albany, NY: SUNY Press.

Farmer, M. (2017) *The Importance of Strengthening. Prisoners' Family Ties to Prevent Reoffending and Reduce Intergenerational Crime*. London: Ministry of Justice.

Ferraro, K. J. and Moe, A. M. (2003) Mothering, crime and incarceration. *Journal of Contemporary Ethnography*, 23(1), 9–40.

Golden, R. (2005) *War on the Family: Mothers in Prison and the Families They Leave Behind*. New York: Routledge.

Jardine, C. (2017) Constructing and maintaining family in the context of imprisonment. *British Journal of Criminology*, 58(1), 114–131.

Johnson, R. and Hail-Jares, K. (2016) Prisons and technology: General lessons from the American context. In Y. Bennett, J. Crewe and B. Jewkes (Eds.), *Handbook on Prisons*. London: Routledge, pp. 284–306.

Kalkan, G. and Smith, N. (2014) *Just Visiting: Experiences of Children Visiting Prisons*. London: Barnardos.

Liefaard, T. (2015) Rights of children of incarcerated parents: Towards more procedural safeguards. *European Journal of Parental Incarceration*, 1(1), 13–15.

McCarthy, D. and Adams, M. (2017) Prison visitation as human 'right' or earned 'privilege'? The differing tales of England/Wales, and Scotland. *Journal of Social Welfare and Family Law*, 39(4), 403–416.

Morris, P. (1965) *Prisoners and Their Families*. London: Allen & Unwin.

Murray, J. and Farrington, D. P. (2008) The effects of parental imprisonment on children. *Crime and Justice*, 37(1), 133–206.

Murray, J., Bijleveld, C. C. J. H., Farrington, D. P. and Loeber, R. (2014) Effects of Parental Incarceration on Children: Cross-National Comparative Studies. Washington, DC: American Psychological Association.

Philbrick, K., Ayre, L. and Lynn, H. (2014) *Children of Imprisoned Parents: European Perspectives on Good Practice*, 2nd edition. Paris: Children of Prisoners Europe.

Pleggenkuhle, B., Huebner, B. M. and Summer, M. (2017) Opting out: The role of identity, capital, and agency in prison visitation. *Justice Quarterly*, 35(4), 726–749.

Robertson, O. (2007) *The Impact of Parental Imprisonment on Children*. Geneva: Quaker United Nations Office.

Scharff Smith, P. and Gampell, L. (Eds.). (2011) *Children of Imprisoned Parents*. Denmark: Danish Institute for Human Rights, European Network for Children of Imprisoned Parents, University of Ulster and Bambinisenzasbarre.

Social Exclusion Unit. (2002) *Reducing Re-Offending by Ex-Prisoners*. London: Social Exclusion Unit.

Turanovic, J. and Tasca, M. (2017) Inmates' experiences with prison visitation. *Justice Quarterly*. DOI:10.1080/07418825.2017.13858.

Williams, K., Papadopoulous, V. and Booth, N. (2012) *Prisoners' Childhood and Family Backgrounds*. London: Ministry of Justice.

Woodall, J. and Kinsella, K. (2018) Striving for a "good" family visit: The facilitative role of a prison visitors' centre. *Journal of Criminal Psychology*, 8(1), 33–43.

Section 7

Control and surveillance

Section 7 Introduction

This section considers key themes of control and surveillance in rehabilitative work in criminal justice. The dynamics of 'care *and* control' in supervisory relationships are complex. If the intensity and severity of control and surveillance is too great, or applied in cases that do not need it, regardless of benevolent intentions, there is real potential for practitioners and justice institutions to do more harm than good. However, if there is insufficient control and surveillance in cases of people who are assessed as needing it, there is real potential for not only non-compliance but for those people to go on and do harmful things, with implications for those who supervise them and for victims and communities. Such a balancing act is of perennial concern for practitioners and policymakers in criminal justice systems around the world. While brief in length and few in number, the chapters in this section navigate headline issues through clear-sighted distillation of international literatures. They largely steer away from focusing on the institution of the prison, mostly situating their analyses in probation and community justice contexts in Europe.

Time emerges as a way of nuancing understandings of compliance with supervisory enforcement and surveillance practices, including the use of penal technologies such as electronic monitoring. In their chapter, Ugwudike and Phillips (Chapter 71) provide an overview of theoretical literature and empirical research on compliance during penal supervision. While it is expected that the individual agency and personal engagement of service users is influential, Ugwudike and Phillips's analysis of international evidence shows that professionals have the strongest influence in constructing and compelling compliance. What can be expected while under penal supervision cannot necessarily be expected to endure in the same way or to the same extent over time after penal supervision has ceased. In other words, meanings and motivations of compliance can change over time (see also Boone and Maguire 2017).

The theme of time also mediates the intensity of rehabilitative work and integration between different types of service provision and supervision. Worrall and Mawby's chapter (Chapter 74) examines the emergence and evaluation of Integrated Offender Management (IOM) initiatives in England and Wales, involving intensive supervision of prolific and persistent adult offenders in the community. IOM initiatives seek to balance the relative immediacy of control and surveillance including swift breach and enforcement action in the event of non-compliance, with multifaceted interdisciplinary supports for rehabilitation that can be sustained long term. Worrall and Mawby critically reflect not only on service provision and effectiveness of IOM for those subject to it, but also the dynamics of multi-agency partnership work involving the police and recent policy and contextual influences such as Transforming Rehabilitation and the semi-privatization of probation services in England and Wales.

Uses of technology with those who offend or are otherwise caught up in criminal justice processes is the subject of renewed interest in the field, with moves towards more technical approaches to social control influencing people's experiences of rehabilitative processes and practitioners' sense of rehabilitative work (Burke et al. 2018). Another theme in this section is proportionality or disproportionality, intrinsic to chapters such as Ugwudike and Phillips's and more apparent in Beyens and Roosen's chapter. Beyens and Roosen (Chapter 73) explore different contemporary approaches to using electronic monitoring (EM) technologies in the Netherlands, Belgium, and England and Wales, offering an analysis well grounded in European penological thought. Beyens and Roosen draw upon empirical findings of one of the first comparative studies of uses of electronic monitoring in Europe, of which they were part (Hucklesby et al. 2016a, 2016b). Their chapter and the international literature informing it illustrates how integrated and proportionate uses of EM can be goal-oriented and purposeful, including but not limited to goals of control and surveillance (see Graham and McIvor 2015; Boone et al. 2017). Conversely, punitive and disproportionate uses of enforcement practices and surveillance technologies can frustrate the very goals and purposes informing why rehabilitative work is done. Beyens and Roosen rightly conclude that electronic monitoring is not rehabilitative in and of itself, but it can be used in ways which facilitate rehabilitative processes. Such an insight spans the range of issues covered in this brief section – enforcement and surveillance practices can be used effectively and ethically in rehabilitative processes, but they are not necessarily rehabilitative in and of themselves and, importantly, can be anti-therapeutic and anti-rehabilitative if used coercively and disproportionately. Fitzalan Howard (Chapter 72) is similarly clear in her emphasis of the relational dynamics of adjudication and discipline, tracing the importance and influences of procedural justice on subsequent outcomes and engagement and foreshadowing what can happen if procedural justice is not prioritized. Relationships are the fulcrum in which these things are balanced.

References

Boone, M. and Maguire, N. (Eds.). (2017) *The Enforcement of Offender Supervision in Europe: Understanding Breach Processes*. London: Routledge.

Boone, M., van der Kooij, M. and Pas, S. (2017) The highly reintegrative approach of electronic monitoring in the Netherlands. *European Journal of Probation*, 9(1), 46–61.

Burke, L., Collett, S. and McNeill, F. (2018) *Reimagining Rehabilitation Beyond the Individual*. London: Routledge.

Graham, H. and McIvor, G. (2015) *Scottish and International Review of the Uses of Electronic Monitoring*. Stirling: Scottish Centre for Crime and Justice Research (SCCJR), University of Stirling.

Hucklesby, A., Beyens, K., Boone, M., Dünkel, F., McIvor, G. and Graham, H. (2016a) *Creativity and Effectiveness in the Use of Electronic Monitoring: A Case Study of Five Jurisdictions*. Leeds: University of Leeds and Criminal Justice Programme of the European Commission.

Hucklesby, A., Beyens, K., Boone, M., Dünkel, F., McIvor, G. and Graham, H. (2016b) Creativity and effectiveness in the use of electronic monitoring: A case study of five jurisdictions. *Journal of Offender Monitoring*, 27(2), 31–47.

Approaches to working with young people

70

Encouraging compliance

Mairead Seymour

Introduction

Despite growing interest in the area of offender compliance during community supervision (Robinson 2013), less research attention has been given to exploring approaches that support young people's compliance. Yet, the logic put forward for heightened interest in compliance as a policy and practice issue in adult community supervision applies equally in youth justice. Public credibility and judicial confidence in community supervision is compromised when those under supervision do not comply. Furthermore, it is difficult to envisage how its purposes, including the potential for rehabilitation and desistance, can be achieved without young people's involvement. Robinson (2013: 27) encapsulates the point succinctly in arguing that 'where an offender fails to comply with a community sanction it is (in the absence of any enforcement action) tantamount to having imposed no penalty at all'. Unlike in other areas of their lives, failure to cooperate with community supervision places young people at increased risk of further immersion in the criminal justice system, especially where custodial sentences are utilized in response to non-compliance. Strategies to promote compliance are therefore central to support young people's transition through community supervision and away from offending behaviour. This chapter focuses on such strategies. It begins by defining compliance and exploring how the concept is constructed and operationalized in practice. The unique challenges of working with young people on community supervision are outlined, before moving on to discuss the types of skills and practices used to encourage young people's compliance. The chapter concludes with discussion on the relevance of fostering social and psychological legitimacy to encourage compliance, as well as consideration of future possibilities to enhance practice.

Understanding compliance

The most commonly reported types of non-compliance on community supervision include failing to attend appointments, refusing to communicate at supervision, limiting the disclosure of information, failing to abide by curfews, and turning up under the influence of alcohol or drugs (Grandi and Adler 2016; Rex 1999). Robinson and McNeill (2010: 369) identify that compliance is a complex notion with multiple nuanced layers of meaning. They make a distinction between what is termed 'formal' and 'substantive' compliance on community supervision. Formal compliance refers to a supervisee's adherence to the minimum 'technical' requirements of supervision such as attending supervision appointments. Substantive compliance, on the other hand, is the type of compliance that involves active engagement in the supervision process.

In Seymour's (2013) study of young people's compliance on community supervision in Ireland and Northern Ireland, practitioners reported that identifying what constituted compliance when working with supervisees required consideration of young people's age, maturity, learning difficulties, level of risk, and their stage and progress in supervision. According to what practitioners said, interpreting young people's behaviour involved working out the nuances between behaviour characteristic of their developmental stage, and more discernible resistance and unwillingness to engage. Making sense of young people's actions and behaviours on supervision required in-depth knowledge of their social and psychological development and reliance on professional skills. It also involved consultation with colleagues and managers in exercising discretion as to what was categorized as compliance and what was not (ibid.). Canton and Eadie (2008) assert that the use of professional discretion is central to an equitable response on community supervision given the diversity of individuals' personal and life circumstances. They caution against unrestricted discretion and suggest that broad discretion, coupled with a high level of accountability, provides the basis for the most responsive model of decision-making practice (ibid.). Without such balance and attention to 'professionally defensible' decision-making, the legitimacy of community supervision may be negatively impacted (Robinson 2013: 40).

Mechanisms of compliance

Bottoms's (2001) oft-cited theoretical framework on compliance is a useful basis from which to explore the types of strategies that encourage compliance on community supervision. The framework consists of four principal mechanisms underpinning compliant behaviour. Constraint-based compliance refers to compliance arising from the imposition of structural or other limitations such as an electronic tag, while compliance based on routine or habit results from established conventional behaviours and practices. Instrumental compliance occurs where individuals are motivated to comply by an external influence, which in the context of community supervision could be the threat of breach proceedings or a period of custodial detention. In contrast to instrumental compliance, normative compliance is based on an internalized sense of obligation to comply and includes personal norms and values about acceptable behaviour, positive attachments to others, and an acceptance of the legitimacy of requests made for compliance (ibid.). The latter draws on an established body of research that demonstrates individuals are more likely to comply with the requests of legal authorities when they perceive that they are treated fairly by them (Tyler 1990). This is especially relevant to the supervisory relationship where young people work closely with their supervisors in fulfilling the requirements of the community order.

The challenges of compliance for young people on community supervision

It is well documented that young people struggle with compliance and studies report on their sense of hopelessness and pessimism about successful completion of community supervision (Cox 2013; Nolan et al. 2018). Most young people have not reached full developmental maturity when commencing community supervision and therefore may encounter difficulties in exercising self-restraint and/or comprehending the consequences of their behaviour (Grisso 2000; Cauffman and Steinberg 2000a). There has been limited empirical investigation into the types of compliance stances young people adopt. The available evidence suggests that they are more likely than adults to adopt less subtle, and sometimes more confrontational approaches in demonstrating resistance to supervision; examples include refusing to speak to supervisors, departing early and abruptly from sessions, or conversely, vigorously protesting against requests, or situating themselves in stand-off situations

(Cesaroni and Alvi 2010; Seymour 2013). Although the argument is made that those aged 16 years and older have more advanced cognitive and psychosocial skills than their younger counterparts, chronological age is seen as an unreliable indicator of young people's maturity levels (Cauffman and Steinberg 2000b). Young people develop at different stages and factors that are prevalent in youth justice populations such as childhood trauma, exclusion, mental health, intellectual disability, and other learning difficulties are likely to impede the process.

Kazdin (2000) highlights the need to explore young people's decision-making against their life circumstances and interpersonal relationships. Decision-making is often located within contexts characterized by difficult family backgrounds, educational exclusion, marginalized communities and few positive social opportunities. The power dynamics inherent in community supervision between supervisor and supervisee have an added dimension with young people as they are consolidated within the differential positions of power that exist in society between young people and adults (Smith et al. 2009; Seymour 2013). Furthermore, Raby (2005: 168) suggests that power and identity are distinct for young people because 'they experience a temporary inequality that intersects with other significant identifications . . . are shaped by discourses of a fluid, becoming self, and are also diversely shaped through the material inequalities of their diverse lives'. The desire for greater autonomy, coupled with the mandatory requirements of the criminal justice system, is an inherent challenge for young people on community supervision.

Strategies to encourage compliance

For some young people, the threat of breach proceedings or custodial detention is sufficient to encourage compliance. For others, particularly the most marginalized young people, the impact of such deterrence-based responses, of themselves, is likely to be limited. This is borne out in the high proportions of young people detained in custody in England and Wales when deterrence-based approaches were to the fore in enforcing compliance (Bateman 2011). The challenge rests therefore in motivating young people to comply over and above their legal obligation to do so. The remainder of this chapter examines the types of approaches identified in the effective practice and other literatures to encourage young people's compliance.

Developing positive working relationships

Building relationships with young people on supervision very often commences from a low baseline characterized by young people's poor insight into what supervision involves, limited stakes in conformity, few relevant supports in their lives, and a high level of distrust towards criminal justice professionals

(Cox 2013; Seymour 2013). Young people who have poor experiences of interpersonal, familial, and professional relationships are likely to resist practitioners' efforts to work with them and consequently relationship building takes considerable time and a high degree of perseverance by practitioners (Chablani and Spinney 2011; Nugent 2015). The types of practical strategies identified in previous research to engage young people at the early stages of supervision involved outreach visits and proactive communication with regular phone and text message communication, in addition to face-to-face supervision meetings (Nugent 2015; Seymour 2013).

Practitioner attributes that hold most leverage in supporting compliance in the supervisor-supervisee relationship include conveying openness, encouragement, empathy, respect, and a nonjudgemental approach (Trotter and Evans 2010; Seymour 2013). Trotter's (2013) observation and analysis of juvenile justice workers' skills with young people in New South Wales, Australia, found that practitioners who used relationship skills had clients with lower levels of reoffending. Seymour (2013) found that the dynamics of the supervisory relationship changed in a positive way for young probationers as they came to recognize the benefit arising from having someone to talk to, to listen in a nonjudgemental way, and to provide practical assistance and advocacy in addressing their many challenges and issues.

Drake et al. (2014: 33) describe the development of relationships with young people as 'the basis for making change in their lives'. Previous research has demonstrated that the establishment of positive working relationships is the foundation upon which requests for young people's cooperation are more readily accepted and acted upon (Chablani and Spinney 2011; Seymour 2013). They provide a platform from which practitioners can model pro-social behaviour with supervisees (Ugwudike 2013). There is also evidence to suggest that supervisees are more receptive to being challenged about their behaviour when a positive alliance has been developed (Robinson 2013). Perhaps one of the most promising benefits in terms of compliance is that an established relationship has the potential to engage individuals psychologically in supervision, thereby extending their motivation to comply beyond the parameters of legal or deterrent obligations (McCulloch 2010; Ugwudike 2010).

Communicating roles and expectations: 'front-end compliance'

Existing research identifies the need to outline roles and expectations to young people from the beginning of supervision as a proactive strategy to encourage compliance. Seymour (2013: 96) uses the term 'front-end compliance' to explain practitioners' description of the practice of communicating clear messages to young people about the expectations on them and the consequences of failing to comply from the early stages (front-end) of supervision. According to practitioners, front-end compliance involves regular and ongoing reminders about supervision expectations and consequences of non-compliance. 'Front-end compliance' resonates with what Ugwudike (2013: 171) outlines as the practice of 'pro-active rule clarification' to encourage compliance. It also aligns with elements of Trotter's (1996) description of 'role clarification' which involves discussion about the negotiable and non-negotiable aspects of community supervision, the expectations of the parties involved in the process, and the supervisor's dual and potentially conflicting social control and helper roles (Trotter and Evans 2010). Such practices have also been associated with effective practice in reducing offending (Dowden and Andrews 2004).

Addressing barriers to compliance and building future capacity

Grandi and Adler (2016) report that young people who breached their supervision conditions had more problematic personal and social circumstances than other supervisees. This lends credence to the argument that a core task of supervision involves addressing the reasons for, and obstacles to, compliance (Eadie and Canton 2002; Ugwudike 2013). Reasons identified for young people's non-compliance on community supervision are not dissimilar to adults and include lack of motivation, scheduling of appointments, transportation difficulties, lack of structure in their lives, and personal and social problems (McCulloch 2010; Seymour 2013). While limited investigation has been undertaken into the nature of one-to-one supervision with young people, Seymour's (2013) analysis demonstrates that addressing barriers to compliance with young people involves action-orientated strategies. Practitioners described advocating on young people's behalf to access services, and working with them to maintain their placements, as strategies to support compliance. They also explained that working with young people entailed more direct involvement with their families and/or guardians than in adult supervision cases. Crises such as breakdowns in family relationships were seen as triggers to non-compliance and managing crises involved intensive work with young people, their families, and external agencies to prevent breakdown of the supervision order (ibid.). Problem-solving with young people is relevant to supporting compliance in light of its links to reduced offending and is therefore an integral part of effective supervision (Trotter 2013; Dowden and Andrews 2004). There is also growing recognition of the importance of adopting a strengths-based approach and supporting young people to access meaningful and legitimate opportunities as alternatives to offending behaviour (Hampson 2018; McNeill 2006). Nugent (2015: 274) describes how young people released from custody in Scotland valued being recognized in their own right 'as a whole person rather than a litany of needs'.

Ownership and participation in the supervision process

When young people perceive that they are listened to and have their voices heard in decisions made about them, they are more likely to view their treatment as fair (Rap and Weijers 2014). One of the core principles under Article 12 of the United Nations Convention on the Rights of the Child (UNCRC) states that young people have the right to participate in decision-making that impacts their lives and that due weight should be given to these views in accordance with their age and maturity. Despite this, participation as understood from a rights perspective has not featured to any great degree in the youth justice policy and practice sphere. Hart and Thompson (2009: 10) argue that where participation is referred to in youth justice policy discourse, it is limited to young people providing feedback on initiatives or '*joining in* a particular activity rather than *having a say* in decisions'. While participation is not formalized as a principle of community supervision in the youth justice system, there is some evidence to suggest that aspects of participatory approaches are utilized in practice. Seymour (2013), for example, reports on practitioners' emphasis on giving young people a sense of ownership in fulfilling their supervision requirements as part of encouraging compliance:

> Some kids see a power struggle in that we (probation officers) . . . can go back to court . . . if they're saying 'well I'm not attending my appointments, because they're at nine o'clock on a Monday morning forget it', I'll be 'okay . . . if you're telling me that that's the issue I'll put it in for three o'clock on a Tuesday'. So you're facilitating them and letting them assert themselves. . . . So it's negotiating things with them . . . and giving them a say.
>
> (Probation Officer, Site 1 in Seymour 2013: 99)

Griffin and Kelleher (2010: 38) use the term 'participatory probation supervision' to describe the approach whereby [probation] officers link 'with the expertise of probationers, who can define both the difficulties they face and the solutions most likely to be effective for them'. This type of participatory strategy involves what Raynor, Ugwudike, and Vanstone (2010: 117) describe as 'the collaborative identification of problems, goals and possible solutions' and is linked to effective practice on community supervision and successful completion (Eadie and Canton 2002; Trotter 2013). A number of researchers have identified the need for enhanced opportunities for young people, and others, to meaningfully participate in co-creating interventions to support their pathways through supervision and away from offending behaviour (McMahon and Jump 2018; Ugwudike 2017). By creating the conditions for ownership and empowerment, it offers promise for more positive outcomes in terms of compliance (ibid.).

Compliance-orientated responses to non-cooperation

Responding to incidents of non-compliance is an inevitable aspect of supervisory practitioners' work and an important part of supporting compliance in the longer term. Flexible strategies that allow for individualized responses to offenders' non-compliance offer more promise than rigid and prescriptive enforcement practices (Ugwudike 2013). Such strategies cross the realm of responses from renegotiating rules, to providing reminders about consequences, motivating supervisees through encouragement and reflection on progress to date, and/or providing enhanced practical and emotional support (Seymour 2013; Ugwudike 2013). Being responsive to non-compliance involves consideration of supervisees' circumstances but does not involve 'overlooking, ignoring or "turning a blind eye" to non-compliance' (Robinson 2013: 36). Prompt responses to incidents of non-compliance are also identified with having a more positive impact in encouraging compliance. This is especially relevant for young people where consequences may be more challenging to comprehend (Seymour 2013). Finally, consistency of approach in responding to non-compliance is a necessary element in supervisees' perception of the system as procedurally fair (McIvor 2002).

Conclusion

In light of the well-established evidence that most young people grow out of crime and those that do not benefit from the least intrusive interventions, the argument follows that community supervision should support young people's maturation and minimize their risk of further immersion in the criminal justice system. At the heart of such an approach is the need to encourage young people's 'substantive compliance' to ensure that meaningful change extends beyond the supervision period. It requires that practitioners have specific knowledge and skills about young people's social and psychological development so that any decision-making reflects their developmental stage relative to their adult counterparts. It also requires the types of action-based strategies which seek to inform and challenge young people about the expectations of compliance, provide support to overcome barriers, build future opportunities, and respond to incidents of non-compliance in a flexible, but consistent manner. These types of strategies are likely to promote young people's sense of legitimacy in the process if they consider themselves treated in a procedurally fair manner. Fostering legitimacy has central relevance in light of the body of evidence demonstrating positive links between individuals' perceptions of legitimacy and their willingness to comply with the law (Fagan and Tyler 2005; Tyler 1990). Furthermore, compliance underpinned by internalized factors such as perceptions of legitimacy is more likely to be sustained in the longer term as it does not rely on the ongoing presence of external incentives or threats to encourage compliance (Bottoms 2001; Robinson and McNeill 2010).

Effective practice and related skills employed by practitioners during community supervision with young people offer promise in promoting compliance. While much of the literature is based on adult offenders, there is emerging evidence to link skills with reduced reoffending (Trotter 2013). Further empirical investigation to consolidate the validity of this research across more diverse populations of young people will strengthen the evidence base in this area. With regard to future developments, there is scope to enhance young people's opportunities for meaningful participation and further utilize strengths-based approaches to improve compliance on community supervision (Hart and Thompson 2009; Hampson 2018). Broader shifts in policy and practice are required for this to occur, but if appropriately resourced and implemented, they offer potential to enhance the legitimacy and effectiveness of community supervision.

References

Bateman, T. (2011) "We now breach more kids in a week than we used to in a whole year": The punitive turn, enforcement and custody. *Youth Justice*, 11(2), 115–133.

Bottoms, A. (2001) Compliance and Community Penalties. In A. Bottoms, L. Gelsthorpe and S. Rex (Eds.), *Community Penalties: Change and Challenges*. Cullompton: Willan Publishing.

Canton, R. and Eadie, T. (2008) *Accountability, Legitimacy, and Discretion: Applying Criminology in Professional Practice*. London: Sage Publications.

Cauffman, E. and Steinberg, L. (2000a) (Im)maturity of judgment in adolescence: Why adolescents may be less culpable than adults. *Behavioral Sciences and the Law*, 18(6), 741–760.

Cauffman, E. and Steinberg, L. (2000b) Researching Adolescents' Judgment and Culpability. In T. Grisso and R. Schwartz (Eds.), *Youth on Trial: A Developmental Perspective on Juvenile Justice*. Chicago: University of Chicago Press.

Cesaroni, C. and Alvi, S. (2010) Masculinity and resistance in adolescent carceral settings. *Canadian Journal of Criminology and Criminal Justice*, 52(3), 303–320.

Chablani, A. and Spinney, E. (2011) Engaging high-risk young mothers into effective programming: The importance of relationships and relentlessness. *Journal of Family Social Work*, 14(4), 369–383.

Cox, A. (2013) New visions of social control? Young people's perceptions of community penalties. *Journal of Youth Studies*, 16(1), 135–150.

Dowden, C. and Andrews, D. (2004) The importance of staff practice in delivering effective correctional treatment: A meta-analytic review of core correctional practice. *International Journal of Offender Therapy and Comparative Criminology*, 48(2), 203–214.

Drake, D., Fergusson, R. and Damon, B. (2014) Hearing new voices: Re-viewing youth justice policy through practitioners' relationships with young people. *Youth Justice*, 14(1), 22–39.

Eadie, T. and Canton, R. (2002) Practising in a context of ambivalence: The challenge for youth justice workers. *Youth Justice*, 2(1), 14–26.

Fagan, J. and Tyler, T. (2005) Legal socialization of children and adolescents. *Social Justice Research*, 18(3), 217–242.

Grandi, L. and Adler, J. (2016) A study into breaches of youth justice orders and the young people who breach them. *Youth Justice*, 16(3), 205–225.

Griffin, M. and Kelleher, P. (2010) Uncertain futures: Men on the margins in Limerick city. *Irish Probation Journal*, 7, 24–45.

Grisso, T. (2000) What We Know About Youths' Capacities as Trial Defendants. In T. Grisso and R. Schwartz (Eds.), *Youth on Trial: A Developmental Perspective on Juvenile Justice*. Chicago: University of Chicago Press.

Hampson, K. (2018) Desistance approaches in youth justice – the next passing fad or a sea-change for the positive. *Youth Justice*, 18(1), 18–33.

Hart, D. and Thompson, C. (2009) *Young People's Participation in the Youth Justice System*. London: NCB.

Kazdin, A. (2000) Adolescent Development, Mental Disorders and Decision Making of Delinquent Youth. In T. Grisso and R. Schwartz (Eds.), *Youth on Trial: A Developmental Perspective on Juvenile Justice*. Chicago: University of Chicago Press.

McCulloch, T. (2010) Exploring Community Service, Understanding Compliance. In F. McNeill, P. Raynor and C. Trotter (Eds.), *Offender Supervision: New Directions in Theory, Research and Practice*. Abingdon: Willan Publishing.

McIvor, G. (2002) *What Works in Community Service?* CJSW Briefing Paper 6. Edinburgh: Criminal Justice Social Work Development Centre for Scotland, University of Edinburgh.

McMahon, G. and Jump, D. (2018) Starting to stop: Young offenders' desistance from crime. *Youth Justice*, 18(1), 3–17.

McNeill, F. (2006) Community Supervision: Context and Relationships Matter. In B. Goldson and J. Muncie (Eds.), *Youth Crime and Justice*. London: Sage Publications.

Nolan, D., Dyer, F. and Vaswani, N. (2018) 'Just a wee boy not cut out for prison': Policy and reality in children and young people's journeys through justice in Scotland. *Criminology and Criminal Justice*, 18(5), 533–547.

Nugent, B. (2015) Reaching the 'Hardest to Reach'. *Youth Justice*, 15(3), 271–285.

Raby, R. (2005) What is resistance? *Journal of Youth Studies*, 8(2), 151–171.

Rap, S. and Weijers, I. (2014) *The Effective Youth Court: Juvenile Justice Procedures in Europe*. The Hague: Eleven International Publishing.

Raynor, P., Ugwudike, P. and Vanstone, M. (2010) Skills and Strategies in Probation Supervision: The Jersey Study. In F. McNeill, P. Raynor and C. Trotter (Eds.), *Offender Supervision: New Directions in Theory, Research and Practice*. Abingdon: Willan Publishing.

Rex, S. (1999) Desistance from offending: Experiences of probation. *Howard Journal of Criminal Justice*, 38(4), 366–383.

Robinson, G. (2013) What Counts? Community Sanctions and the Construction of Compliance. In P. Ugwudike and P. Raynor (Eds.), *Offender Compliance: International Perspectives and Evidence-Based Practice*. Basingstoke: Palgrave Macmillan.

Robinson, G. and McNeill, F. (2010) The Dynamics of Compliance with Offender Supervision. In F. McNeill, P. Raynor and C. Trotter (Eds.), *Offender Supervision: New Directions in Theory, Research and Practice*. Abingdon: Willan Publishing.

Seymour, M. (2013) *Youth Justice in Context: Community, Compliance and Young People*. Abingdon: Routledge.

Smith, H., Applegate, B., Sitren, A. and Springer, N. (2009) The limits of individual control? Perceived officer power and probationer compliance. *Journal of Criminal Justice*, 37(3), 241–247.

Trotter, C. (1996) The impact of different supervision practices in community corrections. *Australian and New Zealand Journal of Criminology*, 29(1), 29–46.

Trotter, C. (2013) Effective supervision of young offenders. In P. Ugwudike and P. Raynor (Eds.), *Offender Compliance: International Perspectives and Evidence-Based Practice*. Basingstoke: Palgrave Macmillan.

Trotter, C. and Evans, P. (2010) Supervision skills in juvenile justice. In F. McNeill, P. Raynor and C. Trotter (Eds.), *Offender Supervision: New Directions in Theory, Research and Practice*. Abingdon: Willan Publishing.

Tyler, T. (1990) *Why People Obey the Law*. New Haven, CT: Yale University Press.

Ugwudike, P. (2010) Compliance with community penalties: The importance of interactional dynamics. In F. McNeill, P. Raynor and C. Trotter (Eds.), *Offender Supervision: New Directions in Theory Research and Practice*. Abingdon: Willan Publishing.

Ugwudike, P. (2013) Compliance with community orders: Front-line perspectives and evidence-based practices. In P. Ugwudike and P. Raynor (Eds.), *Offender Compliance: International Perspectives and Evidence-Based Practice*. Basingstoke: Palgrave Macmillan.

Ugwudike, P. (2017) Understanding compliance dynamics in community justice settings: The relevance of Bourdieu's habitus, field, and capital. *International Criminal Justice Review*, 27(1), 40–59.

71

Compliance during community-based penal supervision

Pamela Ugwudike and Jake Phillips

Introduction

In England and Wales, compliance whilst undertaking a community-based order is a relatively under-researched aspect of rehabilitative practice. This has resulted in a surprising gap in knowledge given that, as Bottoms (2013: 89) rightly observes, 'effectiveness and compliance are, in the field of community penalties, topics that are inextricably linked'. Furthermore, compliance is an important aspect of the government's agenda for community-based supervision in England and Wales, as in many other jurisdictions. Perhaps indicating the importance of compliance and service user engagement[1] during supervision, the National Offender Management Service (now known as HM Prison and Probation Service) introduced the Offender Engagement Programme (OEP) in 2010 to explore how to enhance service user compliance and engagement, and how to develop research-based skills and practices (Copsey 2011). However, studies consistently indicate that the rate at which service users fail to comply with their order or complete mandatory rehabilitative programmes in the community is high and that there are links between non-compliance and increased risks of reconviction (see, for example, Hatcher et al. 2012). There is also evidence that, over the years, enforcement action for non-compliance has inflated the prison population (Gyateng et al. 2010). Furthermore, missed appointments (formal non-compliance) and enforcement action have been linked to other forms of reoffending (Wood et al. 2015). All of this suggests that an understanding of the factors that encourage compliance is required. To this end, this chapter provides an overview of the existing theoretical literature as well as an empirical account of compliance dynamics.

Compliance during penal supervision: theoretical developments

In his much-cited theoretical framework on the nature of compliance, Bottoms (2013: 89) notes that complying with the requirements of a community order, and successfully completing the order may be described as 'short-term requirement compliance'. Bottoms (2013: 89) differentiates this form of compliance from 'longer-term legal compliance' after the order ends. In their exploration of compliance during community-based supervision, Robinson and McNeill (2008), and others, have extended Bottoms's (2013) analysis by drawing conceptual distinctions between short-term 'formal' or technical compliance and more sustainable 'substantive' compliance (see also Ugwudike 2008; Ugwudike and Raynor 2013). Formal or technical compliance manifests behaviourally and is the act of complying with the minimum requirements of a court order, mainly by attending statutory appointments without necessarily engaging with the objectives of the order. In contrast, substantive compliance entails active participation and commitment to the aims and objectives of the order (Robinson and McNeill 2008; Ugwudike 2008). Thus, substantive compliance signifies service-user engagement[2] and involves more than attendance. It includes an attitudinal element that finds expression in engagement with the supervision process. In other words, it equates to what some describe as cooperation (Serin et al. 2013: 94).

Key models of supervision in criminal justice contexts, for example, desistance-based models, the Good Lives Model of desistance, and the Risk-Need-Responsivity (RNR) model all stress that service user participation and their exercise of agency[3] are vital components of engagement (and are manifestations of substantive compliance), and even of longer-term positive change (Bonta and Andrews 2017; Maruna 2004; McNeill 2014; Ward and Fortune 2013).

Writing from a desistance[4] perspective, Maruna (2015) draws parallels between the desistance literature on the important role of service user agency, and the extensive research on medical rehabilitation which suggests that human agency is central to decisions to address addiction and a variety of medical conditions. McNeill (2014: 10) similarly emphasizes the agentic dimension of desistance and remarks that service users:

> have strengths and resources that they can use to overcome obstacles to desistance – both personal strengths and resources and strengths and resources in their social networks. Supervision needs to support and develop these capacities.

According to Ward and Fortune (2013: 31): 'the Good Lives Model (GLM) is a strengths-oriented rehabilitation approach that is responsive to service users' particular interests, abilities, and aspirations'. Ward and Fortune (2013) imply that intervention plans and processes should be designed and implemented collaboratively, with the service user playing a meaningful role. Similarly, proponents of the Risk-Need-Responsivity (RNR) model[5] emphasize the importance of enabling service user participation in identifying and implementing the goals of supervision (Bonta and Andrews 2017). Aligned to this, several studies of supervision in community justice settings suggest that service user participation in the planning and delivery of a community order is vital for substantive compliance (Hughes 2012; Rex 1999; Weaver and Barry 2014).

Despite the primacy that key models of supervision accord to service user agency and participation, and the finding that it is a *sine qua non* of substantive and sustained compliance, the few existing empirical studies of compliance tend to see compliance as emerging from the roles and activities of practitioners (see, for example, Blasko et al. 2015; Lewis 2014; Skeem et al. 2007). Collectively, these studies focus on the role of practitioners in managing relational, practical structural and policy-related contradictions to achieve compliance. In this context, the concept of 'contradictions' is borrowed from Pearson's (1975) theoretical analysis of social work practice, and it denotes the relational, practical structural and policy-related conditions that shape front-line practice in a variety of settings. According to Pearson (1975), it is necessary to study these contradictions in order to develop a contextualized understanding of the dynamics and outcomes of practice. As we shall see, in probation practice, compliance is linked to the actions of practitioners in managing several contradictions and in the next section of this chapter, we describe the contradictions, focusing mainly on our own studies of compliance.

One of the studies was conducted in nine offices within a Welsh Probation Area and this chapter focuses on the data generated from one-to-one qualitative interviews with 19 probation practitioners, observations of supervision sessions, and analysis of case management records (Ugwudike 2008, 2010, 2013). The second study entailed an extended period of observation and 32 semi-structured interviews with probation practitioners in England (Phillips 2011). Interactions with service users were also observed and the researcher sat in on staff meetings. Both studies explored the processes of securing compliance and although the studies were conducted in different locations (one in England and the other in Wales), as we shall see below, the data generated across the two studies contained important similarities and a certain level of homogeneity.

Empirical analysis of compliance dynamics

Several studies identify the relational element of supervision as a factor that can affect compliance and both of our studies highlight the role of practitioners in forging good working relationships with service users (see generally Blasko et al. 2015; Kennealy et al. 2012; Lewis 2014; Phillips 2011; Skeem et al. 2007; Sorsby et al. 2017; Ugwudike 2010, 2013, 2016, 2017). In Ugwudike's (2010) study, for instance, the relational element of compliance was a contradiction practitioners sought to manage in order to secure compliance. Most of the practitioners believed that a negative relationship was an obstacle to compliance (see also Phillips 2011, 2016). Therefore, there was a perception that cultivating good relationships with service users was necessary to avert the contradiction that could be posed by a negative relationship which, in the practitioners' view, was likely to discourage compliance.

Ugwudike's (2008, 2010) study also found that compliance was primarily defined as attendance, and the compliance achieved stemmed mainly from the actions of practitioners in managing practical obstacles to attendance (see also Phillips 2011, 2016). A practical problem that several practitioners in Ugwudike's (2008, 2010) study identified as an obstacle to compliance was substance misuse. This fuelled chaotic lifestyles and affected the ability of service users to attend routine appointments. In response, some practitioners sent reminders and scheduled flexible appointments. Another practical problem some practitioners sought to manage in order to produce compliance (primarily attendance) was the problem posed by travel costs, and participants in both Ugwudike's (2008, 2010), and Phillips's (2011) studies of compliance described how they worked to overcome these difficulties. For example, practitioners in both studies employed breach avoidance techniques such as making home visits to alleviate the service users' travel costs which then obviated the need for service users to attend appointments and helped them achieve compliance. This finding, which has been recorded by other studies (see Hucklesby 2017 for an overview) reveals one of the ways in which practitioners play a key role in the construction of compliance.

There is also evidence that practitioners seek to manage structural contradictions such as a lack of adequate accommodation and other deprivations by referring service users to relevant agencies. Policy-related contradictions are also sometimes addressed to achieve compliance. For example, some practitioners overlook prescriptive enforcement policies by devising more flexible responses to non-compliance that are responsive to individual circumstances (Ugwudike 2008, 2010). In both Ugwudike's (2010) and Phillips's (2011) studies, there was a generalized view among the practitioners that most service users were experiencing several problems and deprivations that made it difficult for them to lead 'normal lives' or maintain lifestyles that would enable them to conform with routine reporting arrangements. The prevailing idea seemed to be that flexible compliance strategies (not tough enforcement practices) were vital for ensuring attendance. Importantly, flexible enforcement strategies served the pragmatic purpose of maintaining good supervision relationships, reducing breach rates, and increasing completion targets. The latter was particularly crucial given the pressure on services to produce cost effective and measurable results such as high compliance rates (Robinson 2013; Robinson and Ugwudike 2013). Key examples of these strategies were sending text message reminders, telephoning service users, and making home visits to follow up absences. Indeed, this tendency to employ flexible enforcement strategies to facilitate compliance is a recurring theme in several compliance studies (Hucklesby 2017).

It could be argued that the practitioners' actions in managing obstacles and problems and in adopting flexible enforcement strategies serves the pragmatic objective of producing outcomes that act as proxies for compliance, such as high rates of attendance and completion. However, some of the practitioners may also be motivated by the humanitarian concern to remain responsive to the problems that tend to affect the lives of many service users. Furthermore, there is evidence that enforcement approaches that are unresponsive to obstacles that impede compliance can undermine the perceived legitimacy of authority and trigger non-compliance (Ugwudike 2008, 2010).

The studies cited above enhance our understanding of compliance. Nevertheless, they see compliance as stemming mainly from the practitioners' actions in managing or attempting to work with problems posed by relational, practical, and structural contradictions (obstacles to compliance) to facilitate attendance, or maintain contact with the service users in some way. This implies that, unlike substantive compliance, which manifests as active service user participation and engagement, the compliance that is frequently achieved does not derive primarily from the active participation of the service user or their strengths and 'competencies' as key 'agents of change' (Serin et al. 2013: 96). Rather, it is a form of compliance that fits the description of formal or technical compliance as described earlier (see Robinson and McNeill 2008; Ugwudike 2008).

Managing contradictions and fostering benevolent paternalism

As noted earlier, the practitioners' actions in managing contradictions to secure compliance might be motivated by the pragmatic objective of attaining high completion rates and a humanitarianism that is borne out of the concern to be responsive to the service users' difficult circumstances. However, by assuming the primary role in the production of compliance, practitioners may also be motivated by benevolent paternalism (Glaser 2011). This is particularly likely to be the case where the practitioners believe that service users are unable to comply unaided because of the problems that affect their lives.

The failure to develop and harness the service user's role might be indicative of a paternalistic view of his or her capabilities. As a philosophical concept, paternalism (even where it is motivated by altruism) is inherently unjust as it involves imposing a decision on someone or a group against their will and consequently limits the ability of the those affected to exercise their autonomy. Thus, paternalism can result in the infantilization of penal subjects and has been described as 'intervening unjustly' in an individual's life because it does not foster a subject's agency (Menger and Donker 2014: 285). According to Glaser (2011: 331), in medical practice, paternalism could manifest as a 'doctor knows best' approach to practice. Thus, paternalism might be inspired by the assumption that the professional's judgement and actions should be prioritized, and are morally justified because they are beneficial to the service user even if they usurp the service user's role, undermine human agency and autonomy, and infringe on human rights (Glaser 2011).

Most likely, in probation supervision contexts, where paternalism exists, it is motivated by a humanistic concern to promote what the practitioner perceives to be the service user's best interests. Indeed, studies of supervision practice have consistently revealed an enduring humanitarian commitment (amongst many practitioners) to promoting the service user's welfare (Annison et al. 2008; Worrall and Mawby 2014). But where some practitioners, even if motivated by humanitarianism, assume the dominant role in seeking to 'produce' compliance, it is possible that their humanitarianism co-exists with a degree of benevolent paternalism which obscures the service user's role, infantilizes him or her and prioritizes the practitioner's power and expertise. This is an approach to practice that can fuel passivity and dependency amongst service users.

Participatory practice as a mechanism of substantive compliance

We contend that, quite unlike paternalistic approaches, participatory strategies that actively encourage service user participation are more likely to engender commitment and engagement (substantive compliance). Thus, we propose a co-productive approach which involves both parties working collaboratively to secure compliance. Bovaird's much-cited (2007: 847) definition of co-production seems relevant here. He defines the concept as:

> The provision of services through regular, long-term relationships between professionalized service providers (in any sector) and service users or other members of the community, where all parties make substantial resource contributions.

This definition implies that co-production relies on dialogue, negotiation, mutual trust, and reciprocal respect between the practitioners, service users, and other stakeholders such as the service users' families (Ugwudike 2016, 2017; Weaver 2014). Importantly, a co-productive approach to encouraging compliance relies on the service user's active participation, which according to the models of supervision cited earlier, is linked to long-term positive change. Therefore, we contend that it is a goal worth pursuing.

We do acknowledge that some practitioners in compliance studies appear to engage in participatory practice by encouraging service user participation during sentence planning sessions. In Ugwudike's (2008, 2010) study, some of the practitioners made conscious efforts to ensure that supervision plans were drawn up with the service users. Phillips's (2011, 2016) study also found that some practitioners enable service user participation in supervision planning. This would suggest that service users are given the opportunity to participate in defining supervision goals, and there is evidence that service user participation in goal setting can encourage commitment to the goals (substantive compliance) (see Ugwudike 2016 for an overview).

However, in Phillips's (2011) study, there was limited evidence that service users actively participated in setting supervision goals. They seemed willing to accept the practitioner's recommendations with no amendment. This indicates a degree of dependency rather than participation and engagement as active agents; this might perhaps reflect a reaction to experiencing paternalism. There was also evidence that although some practitioners sought to enable service user participation in sentence implementation, this was mainly in cases where the service users were themselves motivated and committed to participation. What is less clear is whether the practitioners did the same with less committed service users. Indeed, several studies of service user participation during probation supervision suggest that service user participation in the design and implementation of service delivery goals is quite limited, and is linked to limited participation and lack of engagement (see, for example, Hughes 2012; Weaver and Barry 2014).

Discussion and concluding comments

This chapter has presented an overview of key theoretical and empirical studies of compliance and it argues that two key implications arise from the lack of service user participation as capable agents who can play a significant role in the production of compliance. Firstly, lack of participation may reflect or foster paternalism which could in turn breed a sense of dependency among service users. This sense of dependency is unlikely to motivate active engagement which is associated with substantive compliance. Aligned to this, where compliance is the product of practitioners' efforts to manage obstacles and problems, the compliance achieved is likely to be formal in nature (Phillips 2016; Ugwudike 2008, 2010, 2013). The longevity of this form of compliance might be curtailed by the inevitable reduction of supportive provision once an order ends. Furthermore, compliance studies reveal that compliance is typically defined in terms of attendance and practitioners' efforts are usually geared towards enabling attendance or maintaining some form of contact whilst in the process, avoiding breach action for non-compliance. These practices might facilitate short-term compliance with the requirements of an order (or formal compliance), which is not a sustainable form of compliance (Robinson and McNeill 2008; Ugwudike 2008).

It is however useful to place the forgoing in the wider context of contemporary probation policy, particularly given the demands on services to produce quantifiable outcomes such as improved attendance and completion rates. The quest to attain these targets could in part underscore the noted primacy of attendance and other forms of measurable compliance. Other studies of compliance in community justice settings also reveal that compliance is often defined as meeting reporting (primarily attendance) requirements (see, for example, Farrall 2002); and much of the work that occurs to produce compliance is usually geared towards facilitating attendance and avoiding breach action in order to attain compliance and completion targets (Phillips 2011; Ugwudike 2008, 2010, 2013).

Nevertheless, attending appointments without participation and engagement exemplify merely formal compliance. This might in some cases evolve into substantive compliance but, in itself, formal compliance is unlikely to produce positive effects beyond the term of the order. By contrast, substantive compliance which, as noted earlier, stems from commitment and manifests as engagement with short-term and long-term supervision goals, may better produce longer-term effects, including compliance with the law more generally.

We would argue that the knowledge that has been generated from our overview, in conjunction with insights from compliance studies, suggests that a more participatory form of supervision that harnesses the service users' strengths and capabilities as capable and active agents should be attempted.

Notes

1 Engagement in this context may be defined as:

> The active engagement and co-operation of the offender with the requirements of his or her order. It is achieved when (for example) the offender subject to community service works hard and diligently; or when the offender on probation shows a genuine desire to tackle his or her problems.
>
> (Robinson and McNeill 2008: 434)

2 In this chapter, we follow Maruna (1999: 8) to define agency as the ability to engage in purposeful behaviour – human beings demonstrate agency by engaging in 'intentional and purposeful behaviour'. For example, those who wish to desist might exercise their agency by actively engaging in action that supports desistance.

3 There are diverse desistance perspectives. For example, whilst some desistance scholars emphasize the role of agency (Maruna 2004), others acknowledge the role of agency but emphasize the impact of structure in the form of social influences or key transitions in the life course (for example, gaining employment or getting married), or in the form of poverty and unemployment (Sampson and Laub 2005).

4 Please refer to Bonta and Andrews (2017) for an incisive description of the RNR model.

5 There is evidence that family members also play a useful role in encouraging compliance (see, for example, Farrall 2002).

References

Annison, J., Eadie, T. and Knight, C. (2008) People first: Probation officer perspectives on probation work. *Probation Journal*, 55(3), 259–271.

Blasko, B., Friedman, P. D., Rhodes, A. G. and Taxman, F. (2015) The parolee – parole officer relationship as a mediator of criminal justice outcomes. *Criminal Justice and Behaviour*, 42(7), 722–740.

Bonta, J. and Andrews, D. A. (2017) *The Psychology of Criminal Conduct*, 6th edition. New York: Routledge.

Bottoms, A. (2013) Compliance and community penalties. In A. Bottoms, L. Gelsthorpe and S. Rex (Eds.), *Community Penalties*. Abingdon: Routledge.

Bovaird, T. (2007) Beyond engagement and participation: User and community coproduction of public services. *Public Administration Review*, 67, 846–860.

Copsey, M. (2011) *The Offender Engagement Programme: An Overview from Programme Director, Martin Copsey*. London: Ministry of Justice. Available at: www.essexprobationtrust.org.uk/doc/The_Offender_Engagement_Programme_Overview_July_11.pdf (Accessed 10 October 2012).

Farrall, S. (2002) Long-term absence from probation: Officers' and probationers' accounts. *Howard Journal of Criminal Justice*, 41(3), 263–278.

Glaser, B. (2011) Paternalism and the Good Lives Model of sex offender 'rehabilitation'. *Sexual Abuse: A Journal of Research and Treatment*, 23(3), 329–345.

Gyateng, T., McSweeney, T. and Hough, M. (2010) *Key Predictors of Compliance with Community Supervision in London*. Available at: www.icpr.org.uk/media/10306/Key%20predictors%20in%20compliance%20mcsweeney%20gyateng%20hough.pdf (Accessed 10 March 2015).

Hatcher, R. M., McGuire, J., Bilby, C. A. L., Palmer, E. J. and Hollin, C. R. (2012) Methodological considerations in the evaluation of offender interventions: The problem of attrition. *International Journal of Offender Therapy and Comparative Criminology*, 56(3), 447–464.

Hucklesby, A. (2017) Non-compliance and the breach process in England and Wales. In M. Boone and N. Maguire (Eds.), *The Enforcement of Offender Supervision in Europe*. London: Routledge.

Hughes, W. (2012) Promoting offender engagement and compliance in sentence planning: Practitioner and service user perspectives in Hertfordshire. *Probation Journal*, 59, 49–65.

Kennealy, P. J., Skeem, J. L., Manchak, S. M. and Eno Louden, J. (2012) Firm, fair, and caring officer relationships protect against supervision failure. *Law and Human Behavior*, 36(6), 496–505.

Lewis, S. (2014) Learning from success and failure: Deconstructing the working relationship within probation practice and exploring its impact on probationers, using a collaborative approach. *Probation Journal*, 61(2), 161–175.

Maruna, S. (1999) *Desistance and Development: The Psychosocial Process of 'going straight'*. The British Criminology Conferences: Selected Proceedings, Volume 2. Papers from the British Criminology Conference, Queens University, Belfast, 15–19 July 1997, Published 1999. Available at: http://britsoccrim.org/volume2/003.pdf (Accessed January 2001).

Maruna, S. (2004) Pygmalion in the reintegration process: Desistance from crime through the looking glass. *Psychology, Crime and Law*, 10(3), 271–281.

Maruna, S. (2015) Qualitative research, theory development and evidence-based corrections: Can success stories be "evidence"? In J. Miller and W. R. Palacios (Eds.), *Qualitative Research in Criminology*. London: Transaction Publishers.

McNeill, F. (2014) Changing lives, changing work: Social work and criminal justice. In I. Durnescu and F. McNeill (Eds.), *Understanding Penal Practice*. Abingdon: Routledge.

Menger, A. and Donker, A. (2014) Sources of professional effectiveness. In I. Durnescu and F. McNeill (Eds.), *Understanding Penal Practice*. Abingdon: Routledge.

Pearson, G. (1975) Making social workers: Bad promises and good omens. In R. Bailey and M. Brake (Eds.), *Radical Social Work*. London: Arnold.

Phillips, J. (2011) *The Exercise of Discretion in the Probation Service and Bottoms' Model of Compliance*. The Howard League for Penal Reform. Available at: www.howardleague. org/fileadmin/howard_league/user/pdf/Research/Jake_Phillips__article.pdf (Accessed 3 June 2012).

Phillips, J. (2016) Myopia and misrecognition: The impact of managerialism on the management of compliance. *Criminology and Criminal Justice*, 16(1), 40–59.

Rex, S. (1999) Desistance from offending: Experiences of probation. *Howard Journal*, 38(4), 366–383.

Robinson, G. (2013) What counts? Community sanctions and the constructions of compliance. In P. Ugwudike and P. Raynor (Eds.), *What Works in Offender Compliance: International Perspectives and Evidence-Based Practice*. Basingstoke: Palgrave Macmillan.

Robinson, G. and McNeill, F. (2008) Exploring the dynamics of compliance with community penalties. *Theoretical Criminology*, 12, 431.

Robinson, G. and Ugwudike, P. (2013) Investing in 'toughness': Probation, enforcement and legitimacy. *Howard Journal of Criminal Justice*, 51(3), 300–316.

Sampson, R. and Laub, J. H. (2005) A life-course view of the development of crime. *Annals of the American Academy of Political and Social Science*, 602(1), 12–45.

Serin, R., Lloyd, C. D., Hanby, L. J. and Shturman, M. (2013) What and who might enhance offender compliance: Situating responsibilities. In P. Ugwudike and P. Raynor (Eds.), *What Works in Offender Compliance: International Perspectives and Evidence-Based Practice*. Basingstoke: Palgrave Macmillan.

Skeem, J., Louden, J. E., Polasheck, D. and Camp, J. (2007) Assessing relationship quality in mandated treatment: Blending care with control. *Psychological Assessment*, 19, 397–410.

Sorsby, A., Shapland, J. and Durnescu, I. (2017) Promoting quality in probation supervision and policy transfer: Evaluating the SEED programme in Romania and England. In P. Ugwudike, P. Raynor and P. Annison (Eds.), *Evidence-Based Skills in Criminal Justice: International Research on Supporting Rehabilitation and Desistance*. Bristol and Chicago: Policy Press.

Ugwudike, P. (2008) Developing an Effective Mechanism for Encouraging Compliance with Community Penalties. PhD thesis, Swansea University.

Ugwudike, P. (2010) Compliance with community penalties: The importance of interactional dynamics. In F. McNeill, P. Raynor and C. Trotter (Eds.), *Offender Supervision: New Directions in Theory, Research and Practice*. London: Willan Publishing.

Ugwudike, P. (2013) Compliance with community orders: Front-line perspectives and evidence-based practices. In P. Ugwudike and P. Raynor (Eds.), *What Works in Offender Compliance: International Perspectives and Evidence-Based Practice*. Basingstoke: Palgrave Macmillan.

Ugwudike, P. (2016) The dynamics of service user participation and compliance in community justice settings. *Howard Journal of Crime and Justice*, 55(4), 455–477.

Ugwudike, P. (2017) Understanding compliance dynamics in community justice settings: The relevance of Bourdieu's habitus, field, and capital. *International Criminal Justice Review*, 27(1), 40–59.

Ugwudike, P. and Raynor, P. (2013) *What Works in Offender Compliance: International Perspectives and Evidence-Based Practice*. Basingstoke: Palgrave Macmillan.

Ward, T. and Fortune, C. (2013) The Good Lives Model: Aligning risk reduction with promoting offenders' personal goals. *European Journal of Probation*, 5(2), 29–46.

Weaver, B. (2014) Co-Producing desistance – who works to support desistance? In I. Durnescu and F. McNeill (Eds.), *Understanding Penal Practice*. Abingdon: Routledge.

Weaver, B. and Barry, M. (2014) Managing high-risk service users in the community: Compliance, cooperation and consent in a climate of concern. *European Journal of Criminology*, 6(3), 278–295.

Wood, M., Cattell, J., Hales, G., Lord, C., Kenny, T. and Capes, T. (2015) *Reoffending by Service Users on Community Orders: Preliminary Findings from the Offender Management Community Cohort Study*. London: Ministry of Justice.

Worrall, R. and Mawby, A. (2014) *Doing Probation Work: Identity in a Criminal Justice Occupation*. Abingdon: Routledge.

The impact of adjudications and discipline

72

Flora Fitzalan Howard

Introduction

Securing the compliance of people in custody is essential if prisons are to be stable, ordered, and peaceful environments. Keeping staff and prisoners safe, protecting the well-being of people in custody, and helping them to desist from reoffending in the future are legal requirements or priorities for most prison services. Rule breaking can bring instability, a lack of safety, and considerable distress for people who live and work in prisons.

In English and Welsh prisons most misconduct is dealt with informally. Disciplinary adjudications are a formal process used in response to more serious rule breaking (NOMS[1] 2018). Following being charged for breaking a prison rule, court-like adjudication hearings allow for enquiry into the charge, the presentation of evidence, and the right to a defence and legal advice. If found guilty prisoners can be issued with punitive sanctions (punishments). There are a finite number of punishments, which can be given singly or in combination. Punishments range in how constraining or severe they are; for example, days being added to a person's sentence, cellular confinement, forfeiture of privileges, and loss of earnings. Adjudicators are guided on the proportionate punishment for different rule breaking but retain discretion in their decision-making. Punishments can be activated immediately or suspended, typically when the adjudicator offers the prisoner a chance to change their behaviour, and if they are successful for a set period of time, they avoid the issued sanction.

Disciplinary adjudications occur often daily and at high frequencies in English and Welsh prisons. Prison Service Instruction 47/2011 (NOMS 2018) identifies the key outcomes of adjudications to be that the use of authority is proportionate, lawful, and fair; a safe, ordered, and decent prison is maintained; and that prisoners understand the consequences of their behaviour and consider and address the negative aspects of their behaviour as a result. Their effectiveness has largely been taken for granted. However, despite the dearth of research on adjudications it is possible to draw from the little work that has been done along with the wider psychological and correctional evidence to consider how and when adjudications might effectively facilitate behaviour change, and in doing so contribute to better outcomes, including prison order and safety. This includes research on the effect of punishment, rehabilitation, and procedural justice. The next sections discuss each of these in turn, followed by the implications of this evidence for adjudication practice.

Punishing misconduct

Punishment is an important way for society to show its members how important some rules are. In the Criminal Justice System (CJS) there are a number of ways in which people hope punishment will make society safer: retribution (signalling societal disapproval of the act and ensuring punishment is just and proportionate), incapacitation (physically stopping the person from repeating the act), general deterrence (discouraging others from acting in the same way), individual deterrence (discouraging the person from repeating the act), and rehabilitation (helping the person to change their behaviour and desist from crime).

The wider literature on the effects of punishment strongly suggests that it is not very successful at discouraging a person from repeating criminal acts, or at helping them to change their behaviour and desist from crime. For example, studies comparing imprisonment to non-custodial sanctions paint a pretty consistent picture that imprisonment does not effectively reduce crime in comparison to community alternatives, and may in fact increase reoffending rates (for example, Cochran et al. 2014; Mews et al. 2015; Villettaz et al. 2015). Longer sentences have not been found to improve outcomes, and at times suggest worsening effects too (Smith et al. 2002). Research on prison conditions has similarly indicated that harsher or poorer prison conditions, such as lack of privacy, noise, litter, dirt and clutter, insects and rodents, and poor sanitation supplies are related to significantly higher rates of serious prison violence (Bierie 2012). Further, the considerable amount of research evaluating the effect of interventions designed to reduce reoffending, including several large and robust systematic reviews and meta-analyses, identifies more punitive interventions based primarily on surveillance, control, or deterrence and discipline to not be effective (for example, see Amos et al. 2006; Barnett and Fitzalan Howard 2018; Lipsey and Cullen 2007; Mackenzie and Farrington 2015).

Although adjudications, a primarily punishment-focused process, have not received much research attention, contingency management schemes in a number of settings have. These schemes are based on the principle that when reinforcement and punishment are immediately made contingent upon behaviour, then the behaviour in question will be strengthened or supressed. A meta-analysis of the impact of such schemes in varied settings (prisons, training schools, closed residential units, and psychiatric settings) showed overall significant positive effects on behaviour, including institutional adjustment (aggression, antisocial attitudes, fighting, stealing) (Gendreau et al. 2014). The authors identified a number of principles of effective contingency management schemes, including that positive reinforcement predominates over punishment. The weakest effect observed was from the only study of a punishment scheme. In English and Welsh prisons, the Incentives and Earned Privileges (IEP) scheme is a form of contingency management; it allows for privileges to be earned through demonstrating responsible behaviour, participation in work or other constructive activity, and rehabilitation (NOMS 2019). Good behaviour is incentivized and bad behaviour is challenged with loss of incentives. An evaluation (Liebling 2008) found that contrary to expectations its introduction led to increased misbehaviour in prison, and prisoners' perceptions of the fairness of the system and staff deteriorated. The unwanted effects were thought to be caused by the overly strong emphasis on the punitive aspects of the scheme. Prisoners who felt treated unfairly by IEP quickly became defiant and resentful.

Although the impact of adjudications has not be quantitatively tested, the impact of one of the possible punishments (cellular confinement, typically in a segregation unit) has been examined in prisons in the United States (albeit this was for periods typically longer than it is used in England and Wales) (Lucas and Jones 2017; Medrano et al. 2017). When segregation is used as a punishment for prison misconduct it does not appear to deter people from further rule breaking (major or minor rule infractions).

Together this evidence indicates that punishment, as used by the CJS, is not an effective method of helping people to change their behaviour. There are a number of possible explanations for this. The choice to commit crime or break rules is not always as rational as people think – it is often not preceded by a rational cost-benefit assessment which would lead us to think that increased or more severe punishment would drive people to make different decisions (Robinson and Darley 2004). For example, when someone is angry or upset, or drunk or on drugs, they become less capable of making considered decisions. Studies have shown that people who commit crime tend to under-estimate the chances of being punished and overestimate the rewards of crime (Nagin and Pgarsky 2004). Further, the pre-frontal cortex of the brain, the part responsible for planning, impulse control, understanding others, and weighing consequences, does not finish developing until the mid- or late twenties (Casey 2013), which has implications for conduct of younger people. The experience of traumatic brain injury is also thought to be prevalent in prison populations, which may affect thinking, behaviour, and effective responses to this (Durand et al. 2017), and additionally it has been suggested that spending time in prison may slow the development of maturity (Dmitrieva et al. 2012). This raises important implications for how we help people to obey rules in prison, and why punishment-focused schemes may not be effective.

Research has identified a number of necessary conditions for punishment to successfully supress behaviour (Andrews and Bonta 2010). These include, amongst others, that punishment is severe, immediate, and certain. Within the CJS these conditions can be very difficult to meet, which is also the case when using adjudications in response to rule breaking in prison. Misconduct can go unreported or undetected (so it is not certain that punishment will follow), adjudications can often be delayed for procedural reasons (so punishment is not immediate), and punishments are issued proportionately to the misconduct (and are therefore unlikely to be most severe, although the severity of a punishment is partly subjective). Of these principles, the certainty of detection appears to be vastly more important than the severity of the punishment in successfully deterring people from repeating criminal acts (National Institute of Justice 2016); however, this is not something prisons can very easily achieve.

This evidence would suggest that a scheme in prison that is premised on punishment, and delivers punishment in the way that adjudications do, is unlikely to be an effective method of helping people to desist from rule breaking and learn to behave differently. Of course there are other reasons for punishing rule breaking in prisons; it is important that prisons send clear signals about what is and is not acceptable behaviour, and punishment for misbehaviour supports notions of justice and fairness that there are consequences for antisocial behaviour. However, based on related evidence, it does not stand to reason that punitive adjudications are likely to improve conduct. This begs the question then, how can adjudications be conducted in a way that offers the best chance of effectiveness?

Rehabilitation

Recently researchers have suggested methods of making prisons more rehabilitative by focusing on their climate and environment, and that prisons can provide rehabilitative experiences through daily life as well as through structured programmes. Smith and Schweitzer (2012) described an environment built on the principles of effective rehabilitation, where evidence-based interventions were supported by clearly articulated goals and staff practicing a range of rehabilitative behaviours in daily interactions, such as pro-social modelling, reinforcement of new behaviours, skills-building interactions, and open and respectful communication between staff and prisoners. Furthermore, Dowden and Andrews (2004) described what are known as 'Core Correctional Practices' (p. 204) – the skills which, when used by corrections staff, are associated with reduced recidivism. They demonstrated that effective treatment is delivered by staff with high-quality relationship skills in combination with high-quality structuring skills. Relationships are characterized as respectful, caring, enthusiastic, collaborative, and valuing personal autonomy. Structuring skills include pro-social or anti-criminal modelling, effective reinforcement and disapproval, cognitive restructuring, structured skill building, problem-solving, effective use of authority, advocacy/brokerage, and motivational interviewing. When staff incorporate Core Correctional Practices when delivering clinically relevant and psychologically informed treatment, the effects of the treatment are greater. The evidence for these practices, together with research showing that short (e.g. five-minute) daily interventions can produce a surprisingly strong impact (Dau et al. 2011), suggests that the quality and nature of formal and informal interactions between prisoners and those in authority have the potential to impact positively on rehabilitation, even if the contact lasts for only a short time.

It is recognition of this potential that informed the choice of Her Majesty's Prison and Probation Service (HMPPS) Public Sector Prisons' catchphrase 'Every Contact Matters', and the Five Minute Intervention (FMI) project conceived at HMP Portland. This project trained custodial staff to respond differently to prisoners during everyday conversations, using these as opportunities to employ some of the skills and practices listed previously, and in doing so contribute to developing a rehabilitative culture (Webster and Kenny 2015). A qualitative evaluation of FMI (Tate et al. 2017) reported that prisoners describe a number of positive changes that they believed had occurred through the FMI conversations, including changes to their thinking skills and self-efficacy. They also reported some important reciprocal effects where they advocated on FMI officers' behalf, because they perceived the officers to have shown humanity and caring towards them. It appears that the FMI approach can enable meaningful interactions between prison officers and prisoners.

Inspired by this, Fitzalan Howard (2018) explored the rehabilitative potential of adjudications specifically. Given how frequently adjudications take place, Fitzalan Howard hypothesized that they could offer a valuable opportunity to facilitate behaviour change and contribute to the rehabilitative culture of prisons if adjudicators utilized rehabilitative skills during hearings. Content analyzing the behaviours of adjudicators and prisoners in 13 adjudications in four prisons, giving particular attention to the rehabilitative change and skills used to achieve this, the findings showed that adjudicators can, and some already do, use skills that facilitate or support rehabilitative change,

Table 72.1 Rehabilitative skills in adjudications

Socratic questions	Demonstrating empathy
Active listening	Warmth and humour
Praise and reinforcement	Giving choices and fostering hope
Respectful treatment and tone	Being collaborative and transparent

despite adjudications being a traditionally investigative and punishment-focused process. The rehabilitative skills observed that appeared to be associated with engagement, reflection, and change are presented in Table 72.1, although these are certainly not an exhaustive list of rehabilitative skills that may be valuable to integrate into adjudication practice.

The use of these skills was not found to be consistent across adjudicators, with some using rehabilitative skills more frequently than others, and some necessary skills being used infrequently by all participants. Similarly, prisoner behaviour varied, and responses to rehabilitative attempts were not always successful. Whilst a causal relationship between adjudicator and prisoner behaviours was not tested, associations between them were identified. Particularly important was the finding of missed rehabilitative opportunities. These were opportunities in which adjudicators could have used rehabilitative skills to carefully challenge rule-breaking behaviour to facilitate learning and insight, or to reinforce and support progress. Fitzalan Howard (2018) concluded that taking a rehabilitative approach to adjudications is certainly possible and does not need to detract from the primary purpose of adjudications: investigating charges and (if proved) conveying punishment. Rather, these aims can be complementary, with rehabilitative skills being used throughout the process, whilst investigating charges, considering and giving sanctions, and in looking to the future by facilitating learning and behaviour change.

Using authority in a procedurally just way

Procedural justice theory argues that experiencing fair and just procedures (how people make decisions and apply policies, rather than what the outcome is) leads people to view the law and authority figures as more legitimate, and to greater compliance with, and commitment to obey, rules and law (Lind and Tyler 1988; Tyler 1990) and vice versa. Procedural justice involves four principles: neutrality, respect, trustworthiness, and voice (Tyler 2008). People need to see authority figures as neutral and principled decision makers, who apply rules consistently and are not swayed by personal opinion or bias. People need to feel respected and treated courteously, and believe that their rights are considered equal to those of others and that their issues will be taken seriously. People need to see authority figures as having trustworthy motives, who are sincere and authentic, who care and try to do what is right for everyone involved. Finally, people need to have the chance to tell their side of the story and to feel that authority figures will sincerely consider this before making a decision.

A large body of research on procedural justice exists, particularly in court and police settings, which has provided empirical support for the relationship between justice perceptions and compliance with the law and orders (see, for example, Mazerolle et al. 2013; Sunshine and Tyler 2003; Tyler 2001). In prison settings specifically, the benefits of procedural justice have also been demonstrated and the evidence base is growing. Studies from England, Slovenia, North America, and the Netherlands have investigated, and consistently supported, a relationship between perceptions of procedurally unfair and unjust treatment and misconduct in custody. This relationship has been demonstrated for self-reported and officially reported misconduct (Reisig and Mesko 2009), and includes misconduct in many forms, such as violence, non-violent rule breaking, organized defiance, and institutional resistance (Day et al. 2015; Steiner and Wooldredge 2018). Incidences of disrespect or personal indignity have been identified as immediate triggers for violence (Butler and Maruna 2009), and when prisoners' grievances are dealt with in ways that might be perceived to be procedurally unjust, it predicts significantly higher rates of serious violence in subsequent months (Bierie 2013). A recent longitudinal study (Beijersbergen et al. 2015) identified a causal relationship between procedural justice and institutional adjustment and compliance. Accounting for previous misbehaviour, prisoners who perceived their treatment to be procedurally just reported significantly less rule breaking or misconduct three months later, and they were significantly less often charged with violating prison rules.

In relation to prison adjudications specifically, Butler and Maruna (2016) sought to understand why some prisoners in Northern Ireland appeared to be punished more routinely than others and why deterrents appeared to be ineffective for a small number of routinely punished prisoners. The study considered two forms of punishment mechanisms, one of which was adjudications. Interviews with 34 prisoners across four prisons, including people who had experienced prolific cycles of punishment and those who had not, were conducted. The findings shed light on how procedurally unjust this process appeared to be, which may explain the seeming lack of impact on behavioural outcomes. Prisoners reportedly saw adjudications as lacking legitimacy and justice, that they were 'kangaroo courts' (p. 7) that inevitably resulted in a guilty verdict, and feeling that they were not listened to or treated with respect during these procedures.

The implication of this research is that if adjudications (and any other uses of authority) are conducted in a way that is perceived to be procedurally just, then even in the face of a punitive or unfavourable outcome, this could lead to greater respect for rules and authority, acceptance of adjudication decisions, and better subsequent rule compliance. This is not to say that these principles are absent in all adjudication practice, but one of the difficulties with procedural justice is that many features of people, situations, or the environment can interfere with consistently behaving in ways that help others to perceive processes and practices as fair – for example, being in a rush, feeling stressed, irritable or irritated by someone, out of habit or because it is not the 'typical' or 'traditional' way of doing a particular task, or if a person in authority believes that certain procedural justice principles are not deserved or warranted because of the person's location, behaviour, or status.

Implications for disciplinary adjudication practice

The evidence on adjudications, punishment, rehabilitation, and procedural justice can inform how adjudications are conducted that hopefully gives them the best chance of effectively changing prisoners' behaviour and contributing to safety and order in prisons. The extensive research on punishment suggests that reliance on adjudications sanctions is unlikely to successfully reduce or prevent misconduct. However, conducting the adjudication process in a way that is perceived to be procedurally just and using evidence-based rehabilitative skills (or Core Correctional Practices) to help people to think and behave differently may help achieve the desired outcomes. Further, in line with the principles of effective punishment, ensuring that adjudication hearings are conducted in a timely way, and that processes for the detection and reporting of misconduct are as effective (i.e. certain) as possible, is important.

Adjudications, adjudicators, and prison staff generally are more likely to be respected, trusted, and cooperated with if, for example, prisoners have the chance to tell their story, are sincerely listened to and not interrupted (voice); if the process of the adjudication and how and why decisions are made is clear and in line with rules rather than informed by personal opinion or bias (neutrality); if the reasons for the existence of adjudications – the intended purpose and value of this in prisons – are trustworthy and sincere (trustworthy motives); and if people are treated with courtesy and respect, and that their rights are protected and valued (respect).

The way questions are phrased can affect how much people learn; Socratic questions help people to think more deeply about an issue, to help them to analyze it and learn something new. These questions can be used during adjudications, for example, to develop perspective taking, consequential thinking, challenge antisocial beliefs, or prompt consideration about how else the person could behave. Using praise and reinforcement helps people to know what behaviours are valued, helps teach people what to do (rather than focusing what not to do) and motivates them to repeat those behaviours. No one's behaviour is entirely negative, and so despite adjudications focusing primarily on rule breaking, there may be opportunities to reinforce other positive or valued behaviours (such as engagement in activities, or new insight gained during the discussion). Conducting adjudications in a collaborative way can help prisoners to engage and understand better, and believe that staff are treating them fairly. This can help adjudications to feel 'done with' rather than 'done to' prisoners, which may facilitate cooperation and respect. Offering choices, communicating hope, and fostering autonomy can help people to take control of their behaviour and see change as possible. Helping people to reason things out for themselves and make their own choices can be far more powerful than telling people what to do, even if this is done with the best of intentions. Being warm and using humour can help put people at ease, build rapport, and diffuse difficult or emotional interactions that might otherwise lead to conflict or the person disengaging from the adjudication process. Demonstrating care and concern for the person's well-being, and being understanding and empathic about their circumstances (without necessarily condoning their behaviour or decisions) can help make interactions more human and compassionate, whilst still remaining professional.

These are just some examples of how evidence may be integrated into adjudication practice, although the impact of this has not yet been empirically tested to see if these components during adjudications have a measurable effect on the frequency or severity of misconduct in prison. Incorporating these skills and behaviours consistently takes conscious and deliberate effort, and may not always be easy. Prisons can be under enormous and varied pressures, and if facing large numbers of adjudications and the need for these to be conducted according to certain timeframes, any time added by focusing on rehabilitation has potential knock-on effects.

The impact of adjudications conducted in a rehabilitative and procedurally just way is likely to be greater and more durable if they form one component of a broader focus of rehabilitation throughout a prison. HMPPS is promoting and actively working to develop the rehabilitative culture of prisons, including training staff in FMI. Rehabilitative and procedurally just adjudications are entirely consistent with this cultural initiative. Of course while adjudications aim to tackle rule breaking at an individual level, situational features of prisons can contribute to misconduct also (Franklin et al. 2006; Gadon et al. 2006; McGuire 2018; Steiner et al. 2014). These additional features are not something that adjudications can address directly and so they would also need to be considered as part of a wider strategy to tackle misconduct in prison.

In summary, there is considerable evidence that can be drawn upon to inform effective responses to custodial misconduct, and which can be integrated into the existing adjudication process. Cultural or organizational-level support, as well as the dedicated efforts of individual adjudicators, will be needed to do this successfully.

Note

1 Her Majesty's Prison and Probation Service (HMPPS) was formerly known as the National Offender Management Service (NOMS).

References

Andrews, D. A. and Bonta, J. (2010) *The Psychology of Criminal Conduct*, 5th edition. London: Routledge.

Aos, S., Miller, M. and Drake, E. (2006) *Evidence-Based Adult Corrections Programs: What Works and What Does Not.* Olympia: Washington State Institute for Public Policy.

Barnett, G. and Fitzalan Howard, F. (2018) What doesn't work to reduce reoffending? A review of reviews of ineffective interventions for adults convicted of crimes. *European Psychologist*, 23, 111–129. https://doi.org/10.1027/1016-9040/a000323.

Beijersbergen, K. A., Dirkzwager, A. J. E., Eichelsheim, V. I. and Van der Lann, P. H. (2015) Procedural justice, anger, and prisoners' misconduct. *Criminal Justice and Behavior*, 42(2), 196–218. https://doi.org/10.1177%2F0093854814550710.

Bierie, D. M. (2012) Is tougher better? The impact of physical prison conditions on inmate violence. *International Journal of Offender Therapy and Comparative Criminology*, 56(3), 338–355. https://doi.org/10.1177%2F0306624X11405157.

Bierie, D. M. (2013) Procedural justice and prison violence: Examining complaints among federal inmates (2000–2007). *Psychology, Public Policy, and Law*, 19(1), 15–29. http://psycnet.apa.org/doi/10.1037/a0028427.

Butler, M. and Maruna, S. (2009) The impact of disrespect on prisoners' aggression: Outcomes of experimentally inducing violence-supportive cognitions. *Psychology, Crime & Law*, 15(2–3), 235–250. https://doi.org/10.1080/10683160802190970.

Butler, M. and Maruna, S. (2016) Rethinking prison disciplinary processes: A potential future for restorative justice. *Victims & Offenders*, 11(1), 126–148. https://doi.org/10.1080/15564886.2015.1117997.

Casey, B. J. (2013) The teenage brain: An overview. *Current Directions in Psychological Science*, 22(2), 80–81. https://doi.org/10.1177%2F0963721413486971.

Cochran, J. C., Mears, D. P. and Bales, W. D. (2014) Assessing the effectiveness of correctional sanctions. *Journal of Quantitative Criminology*, 30, 317–347. https://doi.org/10.1007/s10940-013-9205-2.

Dau, W., Schmidt, A., Schmidt, A. F., Krug, T., Lappel, S. E. and Banger, M. (2011). Fünf Minuten täglich: Kompass – eine stationäre Kurzintervention für junge Cannabis-Partydrogenpatienten nach dem Bonner Modell. *Junge Sucht. Sucht*, 57(3), 203–214.

Day, J. C., Brauer, J. R. and Butler, H. D. (2015) Coercion and social support behind bars. Testing an integrated theory of misconduct and resistance in US prisons. *Criminal Justice and Behavior*, 42(2), 133–155. https://doi.org/10.1177%2F0093854814546352.

Dmitrieva, J., Monahan, K. C., Cauffman, E. and Steinberg, L. (2012) Arrested development: The effects of incarceration on the development of psychosocial maturity. *Development and Psychopathology*, 24(3), 1073–1090. https://doi.org/10.1017/S0954579412000545.

Dowden, C. and Andrews, D. A. (2004) The importance of staff practice in delivering effective correctional intervention: A meta-analytic review of core correctional practice. *International Journal of Offender Therapy and Comparative Criminology*, 48(2), 203–214. https://doi.org/10.1177%2F0306624X03257765.

Durand, E., Chevignard, M., Ruet, A., Dereix, A., Jourdan, C. and Pradat-Diehl, P. (2017) History of traumatic brain injury in prison populations: A systematic review. *Annals of Physical and Rehabilitation Medicine*, 60(2), 95–101. https://doi.org/10.1016/j.rehab.2017.02.003.

Fitzalan Howard, F. (2018) *Investigating Disciplinary Adjudications as Potential Rehabilitative Opportunities*. London: HMPPS. Available at: https://assets.publishing.service.gov.uk/government/uploads/system/uploads/attachment_data/file/661909/investigating-disciplinary-adjudications.pdf.

Franklin, T. W., Franklin, C. A. and Pratt, T. C. (2006) Examining the empirical relationship between prison crowding and inmate misconduct: A meta-analysis of conflicting research results. *Journal of Criminal Justice*, 34(4), 401–412. https://doi.org/10.1016/j.jcrimjus.2006.05.006.

Gadon, L., Johnstone, L. and Cooke, D. J. (2006) Situational variables and institutional violence: A systematic review of the literature. *Clinical Psychology Review*, 26(5), 515–534. https://doi.org/10.1016/j.cpr.2006.02.002.

Gendreau, P., Listwan, S. J., Kuhns, J. B. and Exum, M. L. (2014) Making prisoners accountable: Are contingency management programmes the answer? *Criminal Justice and Behavior*, 41(9), 1079–1102. https://doi.org/10.1177%2F0093854814540288.

Liebling, A. (2008) Incentives and earned privileges revisited: Fairness, discretion and the quality of prison life. *Journal of Scandinavian Studies in Criminology and Crime Prevention*, 9(1), 25–41. https://doi.org/10.1080/14043850802450773.

Lind, E. A. and Tyler, T. R. (1988) *The Social Psychology of Procedural Justice*. New York: Plenum Press.

Lipsey, M. W. and Cullen, F. T. (2007) The effectiveness of correctional rehabilitation: A review of systematic reviews. *Annual Review of Law and Social Science*, 3, 297–320. https://doi.org/10.1146/annurev.lawsocsci.3.081806.112833.

Lucas, J. W. and Jones, M. A. (2017) An analysis of the deterrent effects of disciplinary segregation on institutional rule violation rates. *Criminal Justice Policy Review*, 1–23. https://doi.org/10.1177%2F0887403417699930.

Mackenzie, D. L. and Farrington, D. P. (2015) Preventing future offending of delinquents and offenders: What have we learned from experiments and meta-analyses? *Journal of Experimental Criminology*, 11, 565–595. https://doi.org/10.1007/s11292-015-9244-9.

Mazerolle, L., Bennett, S., Davis, J., Sargeant, E. and Manning, M. (2013) Procedural justice and police legitimacy: A systematic review of the research evidence. *Journal of Experimental Criminology*, 9, 245–274. https://doi.org/10.1007/s11292-013-9175-2.

McGuire, J. (2018) *Understanding Prison Violence: A Rapid Evidence Assessment*. London: HMPPS. Available at: https://assets.publishing.service.gov.uk/government/uploads/system/uploads/attachment_data/file/737956/understanding-prison-violence.pdf.

Medrano, J. A., Ozkan, T. and Morris, R. (2017) Solitary confinement exposure and capital inmate misconduct. *American Journal of Criminal Justice*, 42(4), 863–882. https://doi.org/10.1007/s12103-017-9389-3.

Mews, A., Hillier, J., McHugh, M. and Coxon, C. (2015) *The Impact of Short Custodial Sentences, Community Orders and Suspended Sentence Orders on Re-Offending*. London: Ministry of Justice. Available at: https://assets.publishing.service.gov.uk/government/uploads/system/uploads/attachment_data/file/399389/impact-of-short-custodial-sentences-on-reoffending.PDF.

Nagin, D. S. and Pogarsky, G. (2004) Time and punishment: Delayed consequences and criminal behaviour. *Journal of Quantitative Criminology*, 20(4), 295–317. https://doi.org/10.1007/s10940-004-5866-1.

National Institute of Justice. (2016) *Five Things About Deterrence*. Washington DC: US Department of Justice.

NOMS (2018) *Prison Service Instruction 47/2011: Prisoner Discipline Procedures (re-issue)*. London: NOMS.

NOMS (2019) *Prison Service Instruction 2013/30: Incentives and Earned Privileges (6th revision)*. London: NOMS.

National Offender Management Service. (2013b) *Prison Service Instruction 30/2013: Incentives and Earned Privileges*. London: NOMS.

Reisig, M. D. and Mesko, G. (2009) Procedural justice, legitimacy, and prisoner misconduct. *Psychology, Crime & Law*, 15(1), 41–59. https://doi.org/10.1080/10683160802089768.

Robinson, P. H. and Darley, J. M. (2004) Does criminal law deter? A behavioural science investigation. *Oxford Journal of Legal Studies*, 24(2), 173–205. https://doi.org/10.1093/ojls/24.2.173.

Smith, P., Goggin, C. and Gendreau, P. (2002) *The Effects of Prison Sentences and Intermediate Sanctions on Recidivism: General Effects and Individual Differences (User Report 2002–01)*. Ottawa: Public Safety and Emergency Preparedness.

Smith, P. and Schweitzer, M. (2012) The therapeutic prison. *Journal of Contemporary Criminal Justice*, 28(1), 7–22. https://doi.org/10.1177%2F1043986211432201.

Steiner, B., Butler, H. D. and Ellison, J. M. (2014) Causes and correlates of prison inmate misconduct: A systematic review of the evidence. *Journal of Criminal Justice*, 42(6), 462–470. https://doi.org/10.1016/j.jcrimjus.2014.08.001.

Steiner, B. and Wooldredge, J. (2018) Prison officer legitimacy, their exercise of power, and inmate rule breaking. *Criminology*, 1–30. https://doi.org/10.1111/1745-9125.12191.

Sunshine, J. and Tyler, T. R. (2003) The role of procedural justice and legitimacy in shaping public support for policing. *Law & Society Review*, 37(3), 513–547. https://doi.org/10.1111/1540-5893.3703002.

Tate, H., Bladgen, N. and Mann, R. M. (2017) *Prisoners' Perceptions of Care and Rehabilitation from Prison Officers Trained as Five Minute Interventionists*. London: HMPPS. Available at: https://assets.publishing.service.gov.uk/government/uploads/system/uploads/attachment_data/file/662699/prisoners-perception-of-care-from-prisoner-officers-trained-5-minute-interventionists.pdf.

Tyler, T. R. (1990) *Why People Obey the Law*. New Haven: Yale University Press.

Tyler, T. R. (2001) Public trust and confidence in legal authorities: What do majority and minority group members want from the law and legal institutions? *Behavioral Sciences & the Law*, 19(2), 215–235. https://doi.org/10.1002/bsl.438.

Tyler, T. R. (2008) Procedural justice and the courts. *Court Review*, 44(1–2), 26–31. Available at: https://digitalcommons.unl.edu/cgi/viewcontent.cgi?article=1254&context=ajacourtreview.

Villettaz, P., Gillieron, G. and Killias, M. (2015) The effects on re-offending of custodial vs. non-custodial sanctions: An updated systematic review of the state of knowledge. *The Campbell Collaboration*, 1. Available at: www.campbellcollaboration.org/media/k2/attachments/Killias_Custodial_Update.pdf.

Webster, S. D. and Kenny, T. (2015) *Experiences of Prison Officers Delivering Five Minute Interventions at HMP/YOI Portland*. London: National Offender Management Service. Available at: www.gov.uk/government/uploads/system/uploads/attachment_data/file/448854/portland-fmi.pdf.

Electronic monitoring and rehabilitation

73

Kristel Beyens and Marijke Roosen

Introduction

The use of electronic monitoring (EM) has grown rapidly in Europe and elsewhere and is likely to continue to do so. This chapter briefly considers two models of using electronic monitoring giving examples from the Netherlands, Belgium, and England and Wales in order to understand the (alleged) rehabilitative potential of EM.

Nellis (2014a: 489) defines EM as 'the use of remote surveillance technologies to pinpoint the locations and/or movements of offenders and/or defendants'. Restrictions can be used to limit an individual's presence to a particular place during a certain number of hours per day over a period of time, or to exclude them from particular places, permanently or during a determined period (Nellis 2013). To do so, EM relies on technologies of remote control, ranging from radio frequency (RF) tagging or voice verification to control a person's presence at a certain place at a certain time, through to satellite tracking, using global positioning systems (GPS tracking) to continuously control the location and movements of people. EM can be used at all stages of the criminal justice process: pre-trial, sentencing, sentence execution, and post sentence.

Electronic monitoring was first applied in practice on a larger scale in the United States in the 1980s (Bonta et al. 2000). It did not take long before the United Kingdom and subsequently the rest of Western Europe followed.

The introduction of EM has to be situated in a broader evolution in community punishments. The decline of the rehabilitative ideal in the 1970s, as a result of the *'nothing works'* movement, led to a renewed search for the legitimacy of community sentences. Its moral legitimacy from before the 1970s movement was then replaced by pragmatic legitimacy, which emphasized the systemic goals of community sentences (e.g. their cost-efficiency) and their potential to alleviate prison overcrowding. Furthermore, community sanctions were presented as 'tough' or harsh on offenders, in order to gain a new symbolic legitimacy and be accepted by the public (Robinson et al. 2013). The result is what Bottoms et al. (2004) labelled the *new generation of community penalties*, which are increasingly punitive, rely on technology and new public management techniques, and where responsibilities are transferred to other bodies via inter-agency cooperation.

In order to provide an analysis of the way of perceiving community sanctions, Robinson et al. (2013) developed a typology of visions on community sanctions. They distinguish four visions: firstly, a rehabilitative vision focusing on rehabilitation; secondly, a punitive vision relating to the expressive function of the sanction, where retribution is the primary goal; thirdly, a managerialist vision, being concerned with providing efficient punishments; and fourthly, a reparative vision centred around making something right, either towards the individual victim or towards society in general. Elsewhere, we have argued that the use of EM can be situated within the first three visions, but that the emphasis in most countries is primarily on the managerialist vision. This is particularly the case when EM is introduced in the context of rising prison populations, with the aim to provide a cheap alternative to alleviate prison overcrowding (Beyens and Roosen 2013).

Even though EM was – and still is – surrounded by scepticism, it has been pragmatically accepted in most European countries (Nellis 2014b). Its applications in practice vary. EM can be a standalone sentence or part of an integrated measure. In the first instance, the technical control is an end in itself, whereas in the second instance, it intends to serve other rehabilitation-oriented goals and practices (Beyens and Roosen 2017; Boone et al. 2017).

While some authors favour the rehabilitative potential of surveillant control (Padgett et al. 2006), others argue for the necessity of adding a supervisory component, not just because this might provide better results, but also because it is ethically more 'right' (Nellis 2006).[1] Also rule 8 of the recommendations on electronic monitoring of the Council of Europe (2014) state that in order to ensure longer-term desistance, EM should be combined with other professional interventions and supportive measures aimed at the social integration of the EM subject.[2]

Two models of EM use

EM automatically generates information about (non-)compliance (Jones 2000), leading to automated forms of enforcement (Paterson 2009) and a diminished necessity for human contact between those in control and those subject to control. This form of control impacts on how compliance with sentences is achieved. Nellis (2006: 104) created a typology of compliance in community supervision, where he distinguishes five forms of compliance. Firstly, 'incentive-based compliance' offers a desirable outcome at the end of the supervision – literacy, employability, early revocation of the order, the relaxation of otherwise stringent conditions. Second, 'trust-based compliance' instills 'a sense of obligation in the heads of the supervisees to honor a promise (e.g. to be of good behavior, not to enter certain zones and to avoid certain associates) made to the supervisor or court'. Third, 'threat-based compliance' instills fear for the consequences of non-compliance, and fourth, 'surveillance-based compliance', is where the supervisees are aware that they are monitored and that their behaviour is traceable and retrievable from databases. Finally, 'incapacitation-based compliance' refers to 'the actual deprivation, not just the restriction, of liberty and choice, the complete inhibition of desired action'. According to Nellis (2006), elements of incentive-based, trust-based, threat-based, and surveillance-based compliance can be found in uses of EM. In this chapter, we argue that the importance of the different types of compliance depends, among other things, on how EM is applied. The importance of incentive- and trust-based compliance can be related to the additional supervisory contacts which can be, but are not always, part of EM.

Different countries apply different models of EM, which can roughly be distinguished into two models: the models where EM is part of an integrated sentence and where EM is applied in combination with other supervisory conditions that are followed up by probation officers, and those where EM is a standalone measure (Beyens 2017). We use the application of EM in the Netherlands, Belgium, and England and Wales to illustrate the difference between the two 'models'.

In the Netherlands, EM is explicitly used as part of an integrated sentence (Boone et al. 2017). Reintegrative objectives are the main purpose of EM, together with the goal of achieving behavioural change. EM is part of the supervision provided by the Probation Service. The Probation Service is thus always involved in the execution of EM in the Netherlands, and this occurs in several ways. The Probation Service gives advice about the desirability of EM and conducts a feasibility study. Furthermore, a probation officer is present during the installation of the equipment. During the EM measure, the probation officer makes all the decisions regarding the breach procedure, which is linked to the situation of the monitored individual rather than to the type of violation, indicating an individualized approach. Monitored individuals are categorized according to their supervision level, which determines the number of contacts with the probation officer. Level 3 is the highest supervision level. Supervised subjects in this category have two fixed contacts a week. Level 2 supervisees are seen once a week and level 1 supervisees have one meeting every two weeks (Boone et al. 2017).

A different approach is used in Belgium and England and Wales. In Belgium, two models co-exist. In the integrated model justice assistants (Belgian probation officers) conduct social enquiry reports and organize meetings with the monitored individuals. The intensity of these meetings varies according to the necessities of the monitored individuals, as estimated by the justice assistants. Justice assistants administer the curfews together with the monitored individuals, in order for it to be adjusted to their needs related to their professional or educational activities. This model has been identified as 'controlling-reintegrative' by Beyens and Devresse (2009). However, for the largest group of monitored individuals today in Belgium, this model no longer applies. Over the years, the additional supervisory conditions have been abandoned for individuals who are sentenced to a prison term of up to three years and who are serving this sentence under EM. For those EM is used as a standalone measure, with a main aim to provide a cheap alternative for imprisonment, in order to alleviate prison overcrowding. This means that the monitored individuals have to comply with the technical control of their curfew conditions, but no additional supervisory conditions are imposed (unless exceptionally, which has to be motivated by the prison director who has the authority to impose such conditions). Justice assistants are only involved at the start of EM, where they provide information to the monitorees about EM, and in the breach procedure, after three or more curfew violations have been committed. Monitored individuals can request meetings with justice assistants but must take the initiative to do so (Beyens and Roosen 2017).

In England and Wales, EM is also used as a standalone measure. Typical for England and Wales is the private sector involvement, which is more extensive than in other Western European countries. Whereas elsewhere the private sector is usually only involved in the delivery of the equipment, in England and Wales the private sector involvement extends to the execution of EM (Hucklesby and Holdsworth 2016). This creates a dynamic which is specific for the English case. There is said to be tension between delivering a criminal justice service and having to meet financial demands which are always at stake in the private sector. In particular, there is a tension between time restrictions and the provision of high-quality services (Paterson 2009 and see Nellis 2014b for a discussion on the negative consequences of the privatization of EM, relating to alleged fraud being committed by private sector companies).

EM is used in England and Wales to strive for different objectives, but focuses mainly on cost-efficiency. As EM is used as a standalone measure, staff are trained to deal with matters relating to curfew conditions and violations, but not with other issues which might emerge while the monitorees are under EM, such as issues with regard to suicide or self-harm in which case emergency services are contacted (Hucklesby and Holdsworth 2016).

Electronic monitoring, supervision, and support

The different models of EM have different rehabilitative ambitions. In line with Hucklesby et al. (2016), we distinguish supervision from support. Supervision relates to individualized supervisory conditions which can be imposed in addition to the technical control provided by EM. Support, on the other hand, relates to provision of information and practical assistance. Support without supervision can also be seen as 'EM style of rehabilitation' (Beyens 2017). Support is usually provided by the monitoring staff and can be part of EM as a standalone measure (Nellis 2013). Of interest in this context is the concept of 'assisted compliance', a term developed by Nellis and used by McNeill (2015, 2017), referring to controllers (or authorities) sending reminders to monitored individuals in order to facilitate their compliance with conditions imposed on them. Typically characteristic of this kind of assistance is that all it seeks is 'mere obedience' but it does not address the needs of the controlled subjects.

Linked to the distinction between support and supervision, Beyens and Roosen (2017) have distinguished active rehabilitation from passive rehabilitation. 'Active' rehabilitation refers to actively working on the underlying problems and difficulties that are linked to previous offending. The aim is to achieve change, in order to prevent reoffending and increase monitored peoples' general well-being. Monitored persons have to comply with individualized supervisory conditions in addition to their curfew conditions and are supervised by probation officers. 'Passive' rehabilitation, on the other hand, refers to practices without supervision. EM is merely used as a substitute for detention (prison sentence or pre-trial detention) and is therefore not as much an instrument to improve *re*integration, but just a means for the monitored individuals to remain in society.

Research by Hucklesby (2008, 2009) shows that the use of EM as a standalone order allows monitored people to keep their job, to maintain social contact, and participate in rehabilitative or educational programmes in society. Curfew orders are seen as tools to increase offenders' social capital, while at the same time reducing antisocial capital, as EM facilitates the disconnection from criminal networks. Furthermore, EM can enhance pro-social community ties, such as those with family and work, although it can sometimes also disrupt these pro-social ties. For instance, monitorees may be unable to work during certain working hours when under EM, such as working in shifts, starting really early or finishing late.

EM is furthermore seen as a responsibilizing sentence where the responsibility for the successful execution and administration of the sentence is transferred to the monitored individuals and their cohabitants. Research by Vanhaelemeesch and Vander Beken (2014) indicates that cohabitants are to a large extent involved in the execution of EM and they can experience some of its discomforts together with the monitorees. Cohabitants furthermore can play different roles, such as being like assistants, social workers, and controllers. Due to the importance placed on the responsibility for the successful execution of EM with the monitorees themselves, standalone EM is not appropriate for everybody as certain individuals lack the necessary capacities and the social network (e.g. illiteracy, not speaking and understanding the official language).

Whether EM is used as a standalone measure or as part of an integrated sentence influences breach. In Belgium, when EM is part of an integrated sentence, non-compliance with the technical control of the curfew conditions does not necessarily lead to the start of a breach procedure and compliance with the other supervisory conditions are taken into account to decide about starting breach procedure. However, when EM is used as a standalone sentence, non-compliance with the curfew conditions suffices for the EM measure to be revoked. This, however, does not mean that every curfew violation will automatically initiate a breach procedure. Research in Belgium shows that there is always some human judgement involved in EM breach decision-making and that breach decisions are never taken on an automated basis (Beyens and Roosen 2017). Before deciding, there will always be a phone contact with the monitored individuals, in order to gauge for the circumstances in which the violations took place. This kind of information is however much more superficial than face-to-face conversations with probation officers. The breach decision is taken by the EM management, based on this information. So, dialogue mainly happens in situations of violations or breach and at a distance, without face-to-face contact.

Discussion and conclusions

The introduction and use of EM has been linked to a decreasing belief in the rehabilitative ideal of community sentences and EM easily fitting within a managerialist approach. Because of the importance of providing a cheap alternative to imprisonment, EM is often used as a standalone measure, without striving for active rehabilitation or long-term change. In some countries, such as Belgium, the rationale and application of EM has shifted. Where previously the penological goals of facilitating rehabilitation and avoiding prison harm were prioritized, systemic goals have become increasingly important at the expense of the penological goals. As a result, individualized approaches are replaced by highly standardized methods. Even though individualized supervisory conditions may not always be required to assist desistance and increase the monitorees' personal well-being, we believe that decisions regarding the necessity of additional supervision should be taken based on individual needs and not in a standardized manner, as is currently the case in Belgium (e.g. Beyens 2017).

We can conclude that EM is not rehabilitative in itself but is able to facilitate other rehabilitative measures (Nellis 2015). This can be linked to Jones's (2014) 'new rehabilitation', which is characterized by a striving for self-actualization, using technology and mentoring. Offenders become responsible for their own 'reform', where self-discipline is expected. This connects with the Eliasian 'civilized' way of sanctioning, pointing at an increasing expected level of self-inhibition (Beyens et al. 2007). Active rehabilitation can be strived for by adding supervisory conditions aiming for changing lifestyles. When EM is part of an integrated sentence, it is used to tighten supervision and it is a way to add an element of surveillant control to supervision, thereby aiming to increase compliance (Beyens 2017). Active rehabilitation can also install a form of trust-based compliance. This assistance is lacking in the case of passive rehabilitation, where follow-up of the sentence is limited to mere compliance with curfews. In this case, one can wonder to what extent EM is aimed at achieving self-actualization. Here, trust-based compliance is more and more abandoned for threat-based and surveillance-based compliance. One of the potential pitfalls of using EM as a standalone measure is that it strives for formal compliance and does not facilitate substantive compliance which leads to long-term desistance. EM is thus primarily aimed at facilitating short-term goals (McNeill 2015, 2017).

The issue of rehabilitation can thus not be isolated from the use of technology. For Belgium, for instance, we can see how the use of technology shifted from being a means to an end towards being a means in itself. In 2010, Annie Devos, director-general of the Belgian Houses of Justice, stated that technology should be used to provide information about compliance with curfew orders, to enable justice assistants to better assess potential risks or discuss situations of non-compliance. Information from the technical control is thus seen as an instrument to support the supervision and the 'pedagogical space' which is so needed to develop active and social reintegration. She further argued that the goal of technical control was to sharpen a sense of responsibility with the monitorees in a broader framework of supervision (Devos 2010: 31–32; Daems 2013).

McNeill (2017) uses the term 'surveillant adaptation of supervision' to capture the tendency of omitting human supervision and moving towards mere surveillance. He warns for the tendency of creating dehumanization, objectification, distancing, and categorization. Also Daems (2013) considers automation as a way to eliminate the humane, discretionary, and thus unpredictable element of sentence implementation. Individuals are reduced to alarms, which are depersonalized and do not include context in themselves. As the knowledge that is generated about individuals under EM is reduced and decontextualized, EM can alter the interaction between the monitored individuals and their controllers (Beyens 2017).

Nellis (2015) argues that EM as a standalone measure can be useful for low-risk monitored people, for whom imprisonment would be excessive and for whom financial penalties would have too much of a negative impact. On the other hand, using EM for low-risk monitorees might also lead to net-widening, when it is not used as a real replacement of a prison sentence (Nellis 2015).

Applying electronic monitoring as a standalone measure has implications for the monitorees' interactions with the criminal justice system and their contacts with criminal justice professionals. EM as a form of remote surveillant control does not necessarily imply any face-to-face contact with professionals and is mainly limited to telephone contacts with the staff of the monitoring centre, who have a different professional profile and training than probation officers. As the monitorees still have voice-to-voice phone contact with the EM officers, dialogue is not entirely removed from EM. However, compared to meetings with probation officers, the interactions with the EM officers are much more limited, both in terms of content and duration.

Notes

1 See also Recommendation CM/Rec(2014)4 of the Committee of Ministers to Member States on electronic monitoring.
2 Recommendation CM/Rec(2014)4 of the Committee of Ministers to Member States on electronic monitoring.

References

Beyens, K. (2017) Electronic monitoring and supervision: A comparative perspective. *European Journal of Probation*, 9(1), 3–10.

Beyens, K., Bas, R. and Kaminski, D. (2007) Elektronisch toezicht in België. een schijnbaar penitentiair ontstoppingsmiddel. *Panopticon*, 28(3), 21–40.

Beyens, K. and Devresse, M-S. (2009) Elektronisch toezicht in België tussen 2000 en 2005. Een terugblik op de toekomst? In T. Daems, S. De Decker, L. Robert and F. Verbruggen (Eds.), *Elektronisch toezicht. De virtuele gevangenis als reële oplossing?*. Leuven: Universitaire Pers Leuven, pp. 61–74.

Beyens, K. and Roosen, M. (2013) Electronic monitoring in Belgium: A penological analysis of current and future orientations. *European Journal of Probation*, 5(3), 56–70.

Beyens, K. and Roosen, M. (2017) Electronic monitoring and reintegration in Belgium. *European Journal of Probation*, 9(1), 11–27.

Bonta, J., Wallace-Capretta, S. and Rooney, J. (2000) Can electronic monitoring make a difference? An evaluation of three Canadian programs. *Crime & Delinquency*, 46(1), 61–75.

Boone, M., van der Kooij, M. and Pas, S. (2017) The highly reintegrative approach of electronic monitoring in the Netherlands. *European Journal of Probation*, 9(1), 46–61.

Bottoms, A., Rex, S. and Robinson, G. (Eds.). (2004) *Alternatives to Prison. Options for an Insecure Society*. Cullompton and Devon: Willan Publishing.

Daems, T. (2013) Functies en functionarissen van het elektronisch toezicht. In T. Daems, T. Vander Beken and D. Vanhaelemeesch (Eds.), *De machines van justitie. Vijfien jaar elektronisch toezicht*. Antwerpen: Maklu, pp. 75–126.

Devos, A. (2010) Balans van het tienjarig bestaan van de justitiehuizen en perspectieven voor de komende jaren. In A. Devos (Ed.), *Tien jaar justitiehuizen: Balans en perspectieven*. Brussel: Federale Overheid Justitie, pp. 13–43.

Hucklesby, A. (2008) Vehicles of desistance? The impact of electronically monitored curfew orders. *Criminology & Criminal Justice*, 8(1), 51–71.

Hucklesby, A. (2009) Understanding offender's compliance: A case study of electronically monitored curfew orders. *Journal of Law and Society*, 36(2), 248–271.

Hucklesby, A., Beyens, K., Boone, M., Dünkel, F., McIvor, G. and Graham, H. (2016) Creativity and effectiveness in the use of electronic monitoring: A case study of five jurisdictions. *Journal of Offender Monitoring*, 27(2), 31–47.

Hucklesby, A. and Holdsworth, E. (2016) *Electronic Monitoring in England and Wales*. Available at: http://28uzqb445tcn4c24864ahmel.wpengine.netdna-cdn.com/files/

2016/06/EMEU-Electronic-monitoring-in-England-and-Wales.pdf (Accessed 1 May 2018).

Jones, R. (2000) Digital rule. Punishment, control and technology. *Punishment & Society*, 2(1), 5–22.

Jones, R. (2014) *The Electronic Monitoring of Serious Offenders: Is There a Rehabilitative Potential?* Edinburgh School of Law Research Paper No. 2014/03.

McNeill, F. (2015) *'Dangling conversations' about supervision: Reflections on the Athens Conference*. Available at: www.offendersupervision.eu/blog-post/dangling-conversations-about-supervision-reflections-on-the-athens-conference (Accessed 1 May 2018).

McNeill, F. (2017) Post-script: Guides, guards and glue – electronic monitoring and penal supervision. *European Journal of Probation*, 9(1), 110–112.

Nellis, M. (2006) Surveillance, rehabilitation and electronic monitoring: Getting the issues clear. *Criminology & Public Policy*, 5(1), 103–108.

Nellis, M. (2013) Surveillance-based compliance using electronic monitoring. In P. Ugwudike and P. Raynor (Eds.), *What Works in Offender Compliance. International Perspectives and Evidence-Based Practice*. Hampshire: Palgrave Macmillan.

Nellis, M. (2014a) Understanding the electronic monitoring of offenders in Europe: Expansion, regulation and prospects. *Crime, Law and Social Change*, 62(4), 489–510.

Nellis, M. (2014b) Upgrading electronic monitoring, downgrading probation: Reconfiguring 'offender management' in England and Wales. *European Journal of Probation*, 6(2), 169–191. DOI:10.1177/2066220314540572.

Nellis, M. (2015) *Standards and Ethics in Electronic Monitoring. Handbook for Professionals Responsible for the Establishment and Use of Electronic Monitoring*. Strasbourg: Council of Europe.

Padgett, K. G., Bales, B. D. and Blomberg, T. G. (2006) Under surveillance. An empirical test of the effectiveness and consequences of electronic monitoring. *Criminology & Public Policy*, 5(1), 61–91.

Paterson, C. (2009) *Understanding the Electronic Monitoring of Offenders. Commercial Criminal Justice in England and Wales*. Saarbrucken: VDM Verslag Dr. Muller Aktiengesellschaft & Co.

Robinson, G., McNeill, F. and Maruna, C. (2013) Punishment in society: The improbable persistence of probation and other community sanctions and measures. In J. Simon and R. Sparks (Eds.), *The Sage Handbook of Punishment & Society*. London: Sage Publications, pp. 321–340.

Vanhaelemeesch, D. and Vander Beken, T. (2014) Between convict and ward: The experiences of people living with offenders subject to electronic monitoring. *Crime Law and Social Change*, 62(4), 389–415.

74

Integrated Offender Management and rehabilitation for adult offenders in England and Wales

Anne Worrall and Rob Mawby

Introduction

> It doesn't have to be harmonious . . . it's the pull and tug that makes it so successful (IOM probation worker).
>
> (Worrall and Corcoran 2015: 269)

For nearly two decades, the government in England and Wales has insisted that a very small proportion of offenders (around 10%) are committing a very large proportion of crime (around 50%) at any point in time (Home Office 2003). Although this received wisdom has been challenged (Hopkins and Wickson 2013), it is in this context that we focus in this chapter on a specific model of multi-agency intensive supervision programmes for persistent and prolific offenders. The underlying principle of such programmes is that a combination of greater control and surveillance, together with help and treatment, offers the best opportunity to reduce the risk of reoffending of this group of predominantly (though not exclusively) young, male, non-violent offenders. The main criticisms of the programmes are that they are resource-intensive, expensive, and unproven. Evaluations, though increasing in number, are based on small samples and are inconclusive in their results. At the same time, these programmes represent an imaginative and alternative opportunity for the rehabilitation and social inclusion of particular offenders, whom agencies commonly have difficulties in engaging (Senior 2014).

In this chapter, first, we place Integrated Offender Management (IOM) within its historical context. Secondly, we identify key common characteristics of IOM programmes. Thirdly, drawing on our own research (Worrall and Mawby 2004; Worrall and Corcoran 2014) and that of others, we examine the evaluation of the programmes, drawing out the main findings and issues. Finally, we draw a number of conclusions about the future of IOM in the context of the radical changes that the probation service has undergone in recent years in England and Wales.

The context of intensive supervision

Intensive supervision programmes for prolific and persistent offenders in England and Wales can be viewed as both a recent innovation – emerging from the convergence of intelligence-led policing and evidence-based probation, modelled on a European initiative (Chenery and Pease 2000) and given impetus by the 1998 Crime and Disorder Act – and as the latest incarnation of a much older penal preoccupation with persistent offending and intensive supervision dating back to the 1970s (Worrall and Mawby 2004; Farrall et al. 2007).

In England and Wales it is possible to identify four 'generations' of intensive supervision initiatives for adult offenders: those that involved 'matched' supervision in the 1970s; those aimed to reduce prison overcrowding in the 1980s and early 1990s; those that emerged in the late 1990s as Prolific and Other Priority Offender Projects (PPOs); and, finally, the latest iteration – Integrated Offender Management.

Although earlier intensive supervision programmes received fairly damning evaluations and failed to meet their stated goals, it has been noted that they achieved a 'series of latent goals' (Tonry 1990, cited in Mair 1997: 67) – organizational, professional, and psycho-political. They enhanced the credibility of probation by appearing to demonstrate a 'change of culture' and a 'reduced tolerance of crime and disorder'. This, in turn, attracted more resources to probation and raised the esteem – and self-esteem – of probation officers. As Clear (1997: 130) puts it: 'the very fact that intensive supervision programmes proliferate is the evidence of their success'.

The latest incarnation extends beyond the Prolific and Other Priority Offender (PPO) Projects of the early 2000s (Home Office 2009).

Integrated Offender Management has been an attempt by the Ministry of Justice to provide a 'strategic umbrella' to coordinate all multi-agency approaches to intensive supervision. It has attempted to operationalize the concept of 'end-to-end offender management' introduced by the Carter Report (2003) with a key aim of 'disrupting' an offender's criminal activity and thus reducing the risk of reoffending. Integrated Offender Management is now the nationally recognized framework for local multi-agency collaboration in working with offenders (Ministry of Justice 2010).

Key characteristics of PPO and IOM programmes

PPO programmes for adult offenders were originally concerned with the reduction of volume property crime, predominantly theft and burglary, although more recent IOM programmes now accept offenders with some form of current or past violence in their records. The central feature of such programmes has been the combination of intensive attention from both the police and probation services.

The other characteristics of the programmes derive from this central feature. First, the project is staffed by designated police and probation personnel, co-located on either police or probation premises (Senior 2014; King et al. 2018). Secondly, participants in the project are required to meet local criteria that categorize them as 'prolific' – that is, among the most persistent offenders in the locality. Thirdly, they are subject to formal court orders of supervision or post-custodial licence though, importantly, IOM programmes now include substantial numbers of non-statutory offenders who are not subject to current court orders, which raises some interesting ethical issues about state intervention (Senior 2014). Fourthly, participants are subject to high levels of police monitoring (McCahill and Finn 2013) and programmes of intensive probation supervision which seek to address their offending behaviour and also to assist with other offending-related needs such as housing, substance misuse, leisure, education, and employment. Fifthly, in order to achieve this, there has to be an agreed mechanism of information exchange between participating agencies (police, probation, prisons, health, and voluntary/not-for-profit organizations). Finally, there is an agreed procedure for swift enforcement in the event of non-compliance or further offending. The fact that swift enforcement (rather than rehabilitation) also counts as 'success' complicates evaluation, as we shall see.

The supervision regime

Here we provide an example of the framework of supervision at one IOM programme (Worrall and Corcoran 2014), based at a police station. Offenders are referred to the programme from a variety of sources including police intelligence, probation, and other partner agencies. Their suitability for the programme is assessed using a scoring schema for serious acquisitive crime. The supervision regime for offenders on the programme consists of five broad categories of activities: individual office appointments; programmes; purposeful leisure activities; appointments with partner and community agencies; and home visits. The underpinning philosophy is that reoffending can be reduced by support and attention to offenders' needs regarding: housing; education, training, and employment; health; drugs and alcohol; finance management; families; attitudes and behaviour; sexual abuse; and violence prevention (the 'pathways' to desistance). Alongside this support, however, are elements of control which strengthen incentives to comply with the programme. Failure to comply results in breach proceedings or rearrest, both of which are implemented more speedily than might be the case for offenders not subject to IOM.

The supervision regime described aspired to a framework of support that was different from other programmes, providing a flexible, responsive service that drew on a range of specialists who would work on a one-to-one basis. Participants considered the project to be unlike their previous experiences of probation and community service. The differences they perceived related to the intensity of contact and the level of support from the project team. The participants were also in agreement that they valued the combination of the project's different elements and activities. They perceived the project to have additional objectives to preventing reoffending, namely assisting reintegration into society and providing support across a range of areas, particularly helping with drugs problems (Worrall and Corcoran 2014: 48–49).

In addition to supervising the participants' lifestyles through the regime of appointments, the police would monitor participants closely. A crime analyst constantly scanned for reported crimes that met the *modus operandi* of participants; incoming intelligence on their movements and associations was constantly reviewed, and the offenders continued to be watched carefully by local policing unit officers.

Evaluations

Hopkins and Wickson (2013) raise the question of *testability* in respect of PPO programmes. They ask how success is measured and how it informs our knowledge of what works with offenders. Drawing on five national evaluations of programmes, as well as their own smaller scale evaluation, they conclude that, while programmes are 'testable' (and 'tested') credibly, pressure from the government for short-term solutions to long-term problems means that there has been very little follow-up of project participants and no evidence of significant long-term impact. They argue that programmes offer opportunities for transition from offending to desistance but do not, of themselves, provide any 'quick fixes'.

For the past decade or more, one of the most influential methodological approaches to the evaluation of social and public policy provision has been that of *realist evaluation* (Pawson 2013). This approach has resulted in the combination of both quantitative and qualitative methods of data collection and analysis and also the distinction between *process* and *outcome* evaluation. The former focuses on the way in which new provision is implemented while the latter is concerned with more traditional 'findings' or 'results'. Realist evaluation emphasizes the complexity of interventions in the social world and demands that evaluations take account of the full range of factors that are likely to influence the success or failure of a programme. Pawson (2013) provides a 'complexity checklist' that covers *inter alia* the choices, pathways, contexts, timescales, contestations, and unintended consequences that should form part of any attempt to evaluate a programme. This approach has proved popular with both evaluators and those responsible for programmes, but has been less popular with governments that desire quick and clear findings to inform their short-term funding decisions.

The body of evaluation research on these programmes is neither large nor conclusive. However, the number of studies is increasing, comprising a mixture of independent evaluations by academics, often on a limited budget (Chenery and Pease 2000; Hope et al. 2001; Worrall et al. 2003; Vennard and Pearce 2004; Hopkins and Wickson 2013; Worrall and Corcoran 2014) and larger scale national or multi-site evaluations undertaken by Home Office and Ministry of Justice researchers (Homes et al. 2005; Dawson and Cuppleditch 2007; Senior et al. 2011). Evaluators have typically had to work with small sample sizes and, in some cases, without a matched comparison group. The resulting reports and their conclusions tend to be highly qualified in relation to reduced offending and cost-effectiveness. Nevertheless, many of the evaluations emerging in the UK have provided optimism that PPO and IOM programmes can be effective in reducing the offending of the participant group. This message, however, tentatively expressed, has been politically expedient for governments. In 2014, a joint inspection of IOM by HM Inspectorate of Probation and HM Inspectorate of Constabulary concluded that the IOM approach gives rise to cautious optimism, though 'the absence of a structured and systematic approach to evaluation' undermines efforts to assess and report effectiveness (2014: 4).

However, the programmes are complex in terms of their multi-agency nature and the needs of their clientele. Their value should be judged beyond crime rates and cost-effectiveness, though these are of course important. Other criteria which should be taken into account include, on the one hand, health, educational, and social benefits for participants and, on the other hand, improved multi-agency working and information exchange between project partners, and improved intelligence on prolific offenders. Participants in an early project (Worrall and Mawby 2004: 278) identified the following benefits:

■ Stopped or reduced their offending whilst they were on the project
■ Kept them occupied

- Provided them with a sense of purpose
- Helped with their drugs problems
- Built their confidence in doing everyday things, e.g. finding accommodation, dealing with the utility companies, social interaction
- Helped the rebuilding of relationships with families (partners, children, and parents)

From a theoretical perspective, programmes might be judged on the basis of their contribution to 'desistance' from offending (Farrall et al. 2007). Here there is a distinction to be made between 'primary' and 'secondary' desistance. The distinction defines 'primary' desistance as 'any lull or crime-free gap', whereas 'secondary' desistance involves 'the assumption of a role or identity of a non-offender' – becoming a 'changed person' (Maruna and Farrall 2004). Evaluations suggest that intensive supervision programmes at their best buttress 'primary' desistance and prepare an offender for 'secondary' desistance, but that the latter will only occur when other personal, social, and economic factors are favourable. Programmes working intensively with prolific offenders might be best regarded as being of a maintenance nature rather than a short sharp intervention that acts as a cure-all. Accordingly they should be assessed primarily on how well they maintain and motivate participants during the 'on project' period. The extent to which programmes contribute to secondary desistance is a different, but related issue, as Hopkins and Wickson (2013) highlight, and programmes also need to be judged on how they affect participants over time – which might involve several relapses and returns to the project.

Since there is no clear definition of what counts as 'success' for the IOM, it is unsurprising that both central and local government have become increasingly anxious to prove either the effectiveness or the lack of effectiveness of IOM, once and for all. As Wong puts it: 'Evidencing the impact and cost effectiveness of IOM has become the holy grail for local agencies and government' (2013: 60). But the impossibility of identifying exactly what it is that IOM aims to achieve, over and above other interventions – or 'assessing additionality' (Wong 2013: 63) – means that the 'holy grail' has become more of a 'fool's errand' (Wong 2013).

Lessons and issues

Early evaluations of PPO programmes identify lessons or issues which might be summarized (Worrall and Mawby 2004: 285–286) as:

- Embedding the project and establishing its credibility, securing long-term funding
- Having clear mechanisms for recruitment, selection, and de-selection of participants

- Demonstrating effective multi-agency practices, while recognizing the distinctive contributions of each agency and resisting the blurring of agency boundaries
- Planning for team development and for human resource contingencies, so that the levels of stress experienced by staff involved in such intensive work are minimized
- Developing a challenging but supportive supervision regime with linked exit strategies, so that participants are not 'set up to fail' by the imposition of unrealistic multiple demands
- Identifying and addressing the communications needs specific to the project, so that the aims and objectives of the project are widely understood among partner agencies
- Evidencing impact in the funding period

King et al. (2018), drawing on Kotter's model, argue that IOM may fail to fulfil its potential because it has failed to address the eight criteria for successful organizational change: establishing a sense of urgency, forming a powerful guiding coalition, creating a vision, communicating the vision, empowering others to act on the vision, planning and creating short-term wins, consolidating performance and producing still more change, and institutionalizing new approaches.

We now highlight two issues that have implications beyond the programmes themselves – professional boundaries and intensive supervision for female offenders.

Implications for professional boundaries

The key component of PPO and IOM programmes is the closeness of the working relationship between the police and probation services. Historically mutually distrustful, the two services have undergone a cultural shift in their attitudes to working together, partly as a result of these programmes (Mawby and Worrall 2013). Physical co-location has produced much greater mutual understanding and there is now considerable evidence about the benefits of such cooperation. However, there have been concerns about the blurring of professional boundaries and the possible emergence of a 'polibation' officer (Nash 1999) who embodies not necessarily the best aspects of the two cultures, but merely the least contentious (Mawby and Worrall 2004). A further concern is that the partnership is unequal with the stronger police service becoming increasingly dominant. Having enthusiastically embraced the culture shift towards rehabilitation, those police officers involved in intensive supervision programmes have now become key players in the government's future plans. With the current fragmentation of probation service provision, IOM programmes have been allocated to the newly privatized branch of the probation service, leaving the police as the most experienced partners.

Cooperation between statutory and non-statutory agencies is also critical to establishing efficient working practices which allow workers from different agencies to discharge their roles within their respective remits. It is critical to retain a clear sight as to the core values and objectives of each participating agency. The division of roles and functions underlines clarity and trust between agencies with a different service ethos, operational cultures, and obligations. By contrast, the process of adjusting to working not only within criminal justice, but with statutory agencies that have different styles and approaches is challenging for voluntary sector agencies. The statutory-community sector relationship is underpinned by the expectation that the voluntary sector provides specialist or 'niche' services which enhance, rather than take over, the role of existing statutory services. Although apparently a soft 'marginal' aspect, this is in fact a critical 'glue' or 'cement' to the work being undertaken at the statutory level (Worrall and Corcoran 2015: 271).

Intensive supervision for female offenders

We have noted that the majority of offenders on IOM programmes are male. This is because most programmes target prolific or persistent offenders and very few such offenders are women. Nevertheless, there is a long tradition in England and Wales of making separate, and often intensive, supervision arrangements for women (Worrall and Gelsthorpe 2009; Gelsthorpe 2011; Hedderman 2011; Annison and Brayford 2015). It has long been recognized that female offenders are subject to discrimination within the criminal justice system and that their small numbers (approximately 20% of all known offenders, 10% of all serious offenders, and 5% of the prison population) limit the range of rehabilitative programmes available to them in practice. There are numerous academic, governmental, and charitable reports on the differing needs of female offenders, both in prison and in the community, the most recent and arguably most influential being the Corston Report (2007), which argued strongly for improved alternatives to custody for the vast majority of women offenders. Since the Corston Report, the government has been more willing to fund multi-agency initiatives, colloquially known as 'one-stop shops', which encourage a holistic approach to women offenders and enable them to access a full range of help under one roof. Unfortunately, in the present economic climate, such funding is continually under threat, and while local councils and voluntary organizations have often stepped in to enable the programmes to continue, too many are now being closed.

The future of intensive supervision

A decade or so ago, prolific property offenders – burglars, shoplifters, and car thieves – were the bane of the criminal justice system and local politics.

Locally driven, intensive, multi-agency 'carrot and stick' work caught the professional imagination. Despite equivocal evaluations, those working on the front line *'knew'* that this work was effective in terms of changing lives and creating the social and personal conditions conducive to reducing reoffending. Proving it beyond doubt to a sceptical public and to local politicians was more difficult but everyone enjoyed hearing successful case studies and the work touched a chord.

Unfortunately, this 'feel-good factor' is no longer sufficient to guarantee the sustainability of such programmes and the IOM finds itself in the much harder-edged, competitive world of commissioning. Moreover, property crime has fallen dramatically in England and Wales in the past decade, for reasons that probably have little to do with intensive supervision – though that may have played its part. Central government criminal justice policy has shifted and IOM programmes are being called upon to tackle violent offenders (including domestic violence perpetrators), sex offenders, and gangs. The suitability of the IOM model for dealing with different types of offenders and offences is now being scrutinized. Worrall and Corcoran (2015) found that some workers argued that the model is wholly inappropriate for high-risk violent and sex offenders. They pointed out that, while a multi-agency approach to such offenders may be appropriate, the IOM model is not the only one available – MAPPA (Multi-Agency Public Protection Arrangements), for example, having been around for a long time (see chapter 18 in this volume). They were concerned that the specific IOM model will become either overwhelmed by the demands or so diluted in practice as to be meaningless. Others suggested that IOM could be viewed as the equivalent of 'acute medicine' for a range of offenders. Offenders could be allocated to the intensive programme for a finite period before being moved on to 'normal wards' or lower levels of supervision and monitoring. Either way, it is possible to distinguish between the *principles* of IOM – which may be widely applicable – and the *interventions* that need to be considered afresh and tailored for each new cohort of offenders.

The future of IOM in the privatized branch of the probation service is difficult to predict, especially in relation to co-location and information exchange (Worrall and Corcoran 2014: 53). Annison et al. (2015) have opened up a fascinating discussion on the significance of criminal justice 'brands' such as IOM for the rebuilding of probation identities. They suggest that 'brands' may be a way of 'ethically orienting' practitioners in times when 'restless' national criminal justice policymaking results in the blurring of organizational boundaries. But they warn that 'brands' cannot be expected to 'work' without appropriate resourcing and structural underpinning. IOM, through the phases we earlier identified, has always operated in a sceptical and changing context; whether it consolidates and survives as a brand through to a fifth generation of intensive supervision provision remains to be seen. Given the current fragmented, under-resourced, and turbulent operating context, there are grounds for pessimism. However, at best the enduring elements of IOM can bind very different partners (enforcement and rehabilitative, statutory and voluntary) into a humane and ethical brand that, despite inconclusive evaluation, is valued by practitioners, organizations, and participants.

IOM, as discussed here, has developed in the specific context of England and Wales but in its origins was influenced by a small-scale European project (Farrall et al. 2007: 354). As with that early project in Dordrecht, subsequent incarnations have been difficult to evaluate. Nevertheless, and especially in times of turbulent criminal justice policy, strong core principles have emerged – not least the joint working of agencies and a humane but realistic relationship with offenders – that may resonate beyond a single jurisdiction.

References

Annison, H., Bradford, B. and Grant, E. (2015) Theorizing the role of "the brand" in criminal justice: The case of integrated offender management. *Criminology and Criminal Justice*, 15(4), 387–406.

Annison, J. and Brayford, J. (2015) Corston and beyond. In J. Annison, J. Brayford and J. Deering (Eds.), *Women and Criminal Justice: From the Corston Report to Transforming Rehabilitation*. Bristol: Policy Press, pp. 1–20.

Carter, P. (2003) *Managing Offenders, Reducing Crime: A New Approach*. London: Home Office.

Chenery, S. and Pease, K. (2000) *The Burnley/Dordrecht Initiative Final Report*. Burnley: University of Huddersfield/Safer Cities Partnership, unpublished.

Clear, T. R. (1997) Evaluating intensive probation: The American experience. In G. Mair (Ed.), *Evaluating the Effectiveness of Community Penalties*. Aldershot: Avebury.

Corston, J. (2007) *The Corston Report: A Report by Baroness Jean Corston of a Review of Women with Particular Vulnerabilities in the Criminal Justice System*. London: Home Office.

Dawson, P. and Cuppleditch, L. (2007) *An Impact Assessment of the Prolific and Other Priority Offender Programme*. Home Office Online Report 08/07. London: Home Office.

Farrall, S., Mawby, R. C. and Worrall, A. (2007) Persistent offenders and desistance. In L. Gelsthorpe and R. Morgan (Eds.), *Handbook of Probation*. Cullompton: Willan Publishing.

Gelsthorpe, L. (2011) Working with women offenders in the community: A view from England and Wales. In R. Sheehan, G. McIvor and C. Trotter (Eds.), *Working with Women Offenders in the Community*. Cullompton: Willan Publishing, pp. 127–150.

Hedderman, C. (2011) Policy developments in England Wales. In R. Sheehan, G. McIvor and C. Trotter (Eds.), *Working with Women Offenders in the Community*. Cullompton: Willan Publishing, pp. 26–44.

HM Inspectorate of Probation and HM Inspectorate of Constabulary. (2014) *A Joint Inspection of the Integrated Offender Management Approach*. London: Home Office, Ministry of Justice.

Home Office. (2003) *Narrowing the Justice Gap and the Persistent Offender Scheme*. National Probation Service Briefing, Issue 14. London: Home Office, July.

Home Office. (2009) *Prolific and Other Priority Offender Programme Five Years on: Maximising the Impact*. London: Home Office, Ministry of Justice.

Homes, A., Walmsley, R. K. and Debidin, M. (2005) *Intensive Supervision and Monitoring Schemes for Persistent Offenders: Staff and Offender Perceptions*. RDS Home Office Development and Practice Report 41. London: Home Office.

Hope, T., Worrall, A., Dunkerton, L. and Leacock, V. (2001) *The Newcastle Prolific Offenders Project Final Evaluation Report*. Keele University, Staffordshire Probation Area, unpublished.

Hopkins, M. and Wickson, J. (2013) Targeting prolific and other priority offenders and promoting pathways to desistance: Some reflections on the PPO programme using a theory of change framework. *Criminology and Criminal Justice*, 13(5), 594–614.

King, S., Hopkins, M. and Cornish, N. (2018) Can models of organizational change help to understand "success" and "failure" in community sentences? Applying Kotter's model of organizational change to an integrated offender management case study. *Criminology and Criminal Justice*, 18(3), 273–290.

Mair, G. (1997) Evaluating intensive probation. In G. Mair (Ed.), *Evaluating the Effectiveness of Community Penalties*. Aldershot: Avebury.

Maruna, S. and Farrall, S. (2004) Desistance from crime: A theoretical reformulation. *Kolner Zeitschrift fur Soziologie und Sozialpsychologie*, 43, 171–194.

Mawby, R. C. and Worrall, A. (2004) Polibation revisited: Policing, probation and prolific offender projects. *International Journal of Police Science and Management*, 6(2), 63–73.

Mawby, R. C. and Worrall, A. (2013) *Doing Probation Work: Identity in a Criminal Justice Occupation*. Abingdon: Routledge.

McCahill, M. and Finn, R. L. (2013) The surveillance of prolific offenders: Beyond docile bodies. *Punishment & Society*, 15(1), 23–42.

Ministry of Justice. (2010) *Breaking the Cycle: Effective Punishment, Rehabilitation and Sentencing of Offenders*. London: Ministry of Justice.

Nash, M. (1999) Enter the "polibation officer". *International Journal of Police Science and Management*, 1(4), 360–368.

Pawson, R. (2013) *The Science of Evaluation: A Realist Manifesto*. London: Sage Publications.

Senior, P. (2014) Integrated offender management: Pooling resources and expertise and creating effective working partnerships. *Irish Probation Journal*, 11, 7–28.

Senior, P., Wong, K., Culshaw, A., Ellingworth, D., O'Keeffe, C. and Meadows, L. (2011) *Process Evaluation of Five Integrated Offender Management Pioneer Areas*. Research Series 4/11. London: Ministry of Justice and Home Office.

Vennard, J. and Pearce, J. (2004) *The Bristol Prolific Offender Scheme: An Evaluation*. Bristol: University of Bristol.

Wong, K. (2013) Integrated offender management: Assessing the impact and benefits – holy grail or fool's errand? *British Journal of Community Justice*, 11(2–3), 59–82.

Worrall, A. and Corcoran, M. (2014) *Integrated Offender Management Research Project Final Report*. Keele: Keele University Research Institute for Social Sciences, p. 92.

Worrall, A. and Corcoran, M. (2015) Integrated offender management: A microcosm of central and local criminal justice policy turbulence. In M. Wasik and S. Santatzoglou (Eds.), *The Management of Change in Criminal Justice: Who Knows Best?* Basingstoke: Palgrave Macmillan, pp. 259–274.

Worrall, A. and Gelsthorpe, L. (2009) What works with women offenders: The past 30 years. *Probation Journal*, 56(4), 239–245.

Worrall, A. and Mawby, R. C. (2004) Intensive projects for prolific/persistent offenders. In A. Bottoms, S. Rex and G. Robinson (Eds.), *Alternatives to Prison: Options for an Insecure Society*. Cullompton: Willan Publishing, pp. 268–289.

Worrall, A., Mawby, R. C., Heath, G. and Hope, T. (2003) *Intensive Supervision and Monitoring Projects*. Home Office Online Report 42/03. London: Home Office.

Section 8

The many hats of probation

Practice ethos and practitioners' perspectives

Section 8 Introduction

Probation has a long trajectory of meeting varying socio-political needs. Probation workers are required to conduct probation work in the spirit of rehabilitation, deterrence, incapacitation, and/or pure monitoring goals. In many contexts, the goals of probation are mixed with conflicting or competing goals. And probation work varies considerably in different countries, with probation staff having different identities, backgrounds, and responsibilities. To add to the complexity, demands on probation staff vary considerably by the different socio-political environments, particularly as probation assumed an emphasis on punishment. The chapters in this section reflect on the history, current practices, and future directions of probation work as it relates to the various socio-political environments.

John Augustus, in his creation of the field of probation, began from a benevolent perspective, with probation steeped in social work traditions of helping an individual. The formulation of probation as a discipline, and also as a legitimate sanction, emphasized the helping component which differed from other sanctions of incarceration or community service. Probation was designed to help individuals that had problems – alcohol, drugs, employment – become productive citizens. Early on, Augustus recognized the importance of support services, housing, and employment as the cornerstone of probation work. His own version of probation work included caring for the person in need. The institutionalization of probation as a sanction offered by the state included helping the individual, sans housing which was not viewed as a responsibility of the justice system. The social work framework dominated during the first century, and in many countries this framework still persists. In Scotland, probation is referred to as criminal justice social work to reinforce an emphasis on social work (McNeill 2005). As the United Kingdom has gone through various means of delivering probation services, from government to privatized to contractual government services, the tradition and role of social work has persisted.

An enforcement model of probation emerged as part of the sanctioning aspect of probation to serve various sentencing goals. A rehabilitation framework combines judicial orders for treatment with the demands of being on supervision. In this model, probation work is to refer the individual to treatment programmes and to ensure that the person complies with treatment conditions.

A deterrence model emphasizes compliance with the conditions, where sanctions are used to hold the probationer accountable. An incapacitative model includes a number of conditions attached to the sanction where probation is more like 'prison without walls' and the probation work is focused on compliance. And a retributive model uses community service or conditions of supervision to ensure that an individual follows through on the sanction requirements. Regardless of the goal of sentencing, probation work is focused on compliance with the conditions attached to probation by the court, or in some cases programs or services run by the probation agency. Social work features were overrun with an emphasis on holding the individual accountable and providing sanctions (more punishment) if the individual did not meet such conditions. In the United States, the enforcement model included increasing conditions of supervision to exert a myriad of psychological, physical, and financial restrictions that now average around 17 per person (Taxman and Breno 2017; Taxman 2012). The enforcement model has also been associated with increasing the revocation rate from probation which contributes to incarceration. In fact, in the United States revocation from probation accounts for 350,000 new intakes into prison each year (Pew Public Safety Performance Project 2018).

A social work-enforcement hybrid model has been proffered given the recognition that probation can maintain its role as a helping profession but also meet the demands of ensuring accountability. Accountability emerged as a construct to explain that part of a sanction is to ensure that the probation meets the demands of the imposed requirements, and if an individual is not accountable (i.e. compliant), then the punishment has not achieved its goal (regardless of which sentencing goal was desired). Accountability in many ways legitimized the emphasis on compliance and enforcement work associated with probation. As part of the hybrid model, a search for helping to provide blended approaches occurred. The Risk-Needs-Responsivity model applied to supervision (see Taxman et al. 2004; Taxman 2008) coupled with Core Correctional Practices (Andrews and Bonta 2010) legitimized a hybrid approach where client-centred approaches could be intertwined with boundary-setting strategies to define probation work. That is, the 'what works' literature crafted a set of principles that defined probation work in a new way where probation work consists of social work *and* enforcement. The challenge is probation staff being able to use the 'tools of the trade' in a blended manner where the punitive aspects of accountability (compliance) do not override the important aspects associated with the helping profession (social work).

In this section, the contributions examine the legacy of probation work from social work to enforcement to hybrid models to understand where probation now sits. Emphasis is on further defining the hybrid model that recognizes the value of probation, but minimizes the over-emphasis on accountability and the punitive aspects associated with mass supervision policies and practices. That is, as probation has emerged as a sanction, the growth has been characterized by more requirements (liberty restrictions) on individuals, which has contributed to both an overuse of probation sanction and an overindulgence in punitive conditions that make probation difficult to be successful in (Phelps 2013). The hybrid approach, in a mass supervision era, also suffers from the need for probation work to ensure that the punitive aspects of supervision are pronounced, which means that that probation work requires complex skills, and these skills are applied in complex socio-political environments. The way forward in hybrid social work-enforcement is not only through training but also in providing organizational and environmental support for the emphasis on social work or helping probationers succeed during the period of supervision. It also affects the identity that probation workers will assume, and how this affects the work that they engage in.

Anne Worrall and Rob Mawby focus on the theme of 'probation worker identity'. Their chapter explores the ways in which probation and/or community corrections officers construct their working identities.

The chapter by John Deering discusses organizational changes in England and Wales during this period and how probation has changed from a number of semi-autonomous local organizations to a single centralized 'national service' and then to a situation where, since 2014 and Transforming Rehabilitation, a unified service no longer exists.

Ronald P. Corbett, Jr and Edward E. Rhine suggest that in the United States, the focus on evidence-based practices (EBPs) has led to a 'correctionalist narrative'. They suggest revisiting the content of supervision and officers' relationships with those they supervise, and the integration of 'what works' with 'what is just'.

Gwen Robinson in her chapter identifies key themes for workers including working relationships; resources; individualization and flexibility; goals and outcomes; attributes, skills, and values; and support. She argues that it is important to consider how practitioners understand quality in their work.

Jill Viglione, Christina Burton, and Sherah L. Basham consider roles of probation officers (POs) and how these are changing with the new EBP expectations. Some POs still see probation as law enforcement and some are hesitant to take on a social service role particularly with probationers who are resistant to change. For some the role of change agent with expertise in cognitive behavioural treatment and other skills is difficult.

The final chapter in the section by Lina Marmolejo, James Byrne, and Faye S. Taxman discusses what is needed for staff to take on new roles, including, for example, support from the agency's leadership and management, engagement of mid-level and front-line staff, support for collaborative partnerships, and the need to listen and include the perspectives of probationers.

An equal emphasis is on the future and how probation organizations can move forward in growing and supporting probation staff that use evidence-based principles that are founded in good empirical and clinical science in the helping professions. While Andrews and Bonta (2010) made it clear that a necessary component of delivering Core Correctional Practices was a human service environment to support probation work, more attention is needed in helping probation organizations move from a punitive, compliance-driven model to a human service environment. This is no small task, but the chapters illustrate that there are principles that can be used to support this effort, and that probation work is steeped in social work and helping profession traditions that make this transformation possible. The emphasis on the organization, building a vision of the goals of probation, and staff skills coalesce into a recipe for remaking supervision, much in the tradition that John Augustus would recognize with the emphasis on helping individuals be (or become) productive citizens.

References

Andrews, D. A. and Bonta, J. (2010) *The Psychology of Criminal Conduct.* New York: Anderson.

McNeill, Fergus. (2005) Remembering probation in Scotland. *Probation Journal,* 52, 23–28.

Pew Public Safety Performance Project. (2018) *Probation and Parole Systems Marked by High Stakes, Missed Opportunities.* Washington, DC: Pew Charitable Trusts. Available at: www.pewtrusts.org/-/media/assets/2018/09/probation_and_parole_systems_marked_by_high_stakes_missed_opportunities_pew.pdf.

Phelps, Michelle S. (2013) The paradox of probation: Community supervision in the age of mass incarceration. *Law & Policy,* 35(1–2), 51–80.

Taxman, Faye S. (2008) No illusion, offender and organizational change in Maryland's proactive community supervision model. *Criminology and Public Policy,* 7(2), 275–302.

Taxman, Faye S. (2012) Probation, intermediate sanctions, and community-based corrections. In Joan Petersilia and Kevin Reitz (Eds.), *The Oxford Handbook of Sentencing and Corrections.* New York: Oxford University Press, pp. 363–385.

Taxman, Faye S. and Breno, Alex. (2017) Alternatives to incarceration. In *Oxford Research Encyclopedia of Oxford Research Encyclopedia of Criminology and Criminal Justice.* New York: Oxford University Press.

Taxman, Faye S., Shephardson, Eric and Byrne, James. (2004) *Tools of the Trade: A Guide to Implementing Science into Practice.* Washington, DC: National Institute of Corrections. Available at: www.nicic.org/Library/020095.

Probation worker identities

75

Responding to change and turbulence in community rehabilitation

Anne Worrall and Rob Mawby

I think offenders are great . . . if you don't like them, this will be a miserable job and you'll be scared of them and they'll know. (Chief Probation Officer)

(Mawby and Worrall 2013: 117)

Introduction

Compared with police and prison officers, there are very few studies of the ways in which probation workers construct their working identities. Drawing principally on our own research in England and Wales (Mawby and Worrall 2013), updated with more recent studies, we examine three specific areas of probation worker identity that may resonate beyond the geographical and socio-political context of the UK. We argue, first, that probation work is socially 'dirty work', since it involves work with people who are generally considered to be undeserving of society's help and support. Second, utilizing our interview-based data on the characteristics and motivations of probation workers, we construct three 'ideal types', and, third, we explore individual probation worker responses to change and turbulence in organizational structures and working conditions. In particular, we propose that some aspects of probation work can be described as being 'edgework' because they involve workers in consciously taking risks by using their skills to control the boundaries between order and chaos in the context of both criminal and social justice in the community. We conclude the chapter by considering the early indications of the impact of privatization policy agendas on probation worker identities.

In the following sections, we draw on a study involving interviews with 60 former and current probation workers (Mawby and Worrall 2013). Our sample comprised a mix of age and experience and we sought to elicit how this range of probation workers perceived their working lives and how they constructed their occupational identities.

Probation work as 'dirty work'

One of the dilemmas that emerged during our interviews was the extent to which workers felt that the social status of the probation officer had changed from that of being 'an authoritative person' to being 'a waste of time'. The image of the probation officer as 'almost priest-like' has been transformed to that of someone who is doing society's dirty work and should probably be ashamed, rather than proud, of themselves, for working with the 'undeserving'.

Ashforth and Kreiner's (1999) concept of 'dirty work' describes those occupations that society regards as 'necessary evils' – jobs that someone has to do but which are considered to be unpleasant and/or morally questionable. People who undertake such work are attributed with a stigma or negative identity as 'dirty workers', who may be physically, socially, or morally tainted. Within this model, it is not too difficult to identify probation workers as being socially tainted. On behalf of society, they engage regularly with stigmatized people and run the risk of being stigmatized themselves. Alongside the work of other criminal justice occupations such as police, prison guards, and criminal lawyers, society reluctantly accepts the necessity for probation work; as one interviewee noted, 'People just want that reassurance that there's somebody doing it'. On numerous occasions during our research, however, people told us that the public really did not know what the work was about so the taint was, in their view, based on both limited knowledge or experience and in many cases, after initial curiosity, a reluctance to find out more. Not everybody regards probation work as 'tainted', and some people retain traces of the earlier respect and appreciation; however others, and particularly some sections of the popular press, see probation workers as representatives of a tendency to be 'soft' on offenders.

There is nothing new about arguing that personal or occupational stigma has negative consequences, resulting in a spoiled identity. For Ashforth and Kreiner (1999), however, the research conundrum is that stigma can result in a *positive* identity among dirty workers. Their model of dirty work gives rise to a number of processes whereby dirty workers construct positive work identities. For example, they develop ideologies that reframe, recalibrate, and refocus the purpose and value of their work. They reframe by foregrounding the virtues and benefits of the work (for example, the traditional probation motto of 'advise, assist, and befriend' becomes updated to 'enforcement, rehabilitation, and public protection'), recalibrate by adjusting the standards that evaluate the extent of 'dirt' (for example, selectively emphasizing statistics which show reductions in reoffending), and refocus by emphasizing the rewarding aspects of the work over the dirty ones (for example, concentrating on 'good news' stories about the offenders who have been successfully rehabilitated rather than the 'bad stories' of those who commit serious further offences).

The 'dirty work' model allows us to gain insight into the social context of probation work and the ways in which probation workers can routinely construct and maintain for themselves a positive work identity. Next we sketch out three ideal types who are drawn towards, and operate within, the sphere of probation work.

Three ideal types: lifers, second careerists, and offender managers

Recognizing the common characteristics of the probation worker and, at the same time, acknowledging the cultural complexity of the role, we constructed three ideal types in order to draw out differences and similarities and to understand the cultural richness of probation work. The title of each type is taken from self-descriptions among our interviewees.

First there was the 'the lifer' – predominantly over 40 years of age, who had spent most of their working life with the probation service. For them, probation was often regarded as being a vocation, a lifelong commitment and their one main career. Members of this group often discovered an interest in probation work at a young age. With a postgraduate social work qualification, lifers had a structural understanding of society, a social work approach to individuals, and believed in the importance of the relationship between probation worker and probationer as a therapeutic resource.

Next, there was 'the second careerist' whose defining characteristic was that they had forged a previous career in an unrelated, or marginally related, occupation. In their prior occupations, the second careerists had developed transferable skills suitable, they believed, for employment in the probation service. They wanted to make a difference and to use their transferable 'people skills'. They also believed in the importance of the relationship with offenders as a vehicle for pro-social modelling and humanistic support.

Finally, we called our third distinctive group 'offender managers'. Predominantly under 40 years of age, they tended to be more recent recruits. To some of this group, the term 'offender manager' was as familiar as 'probation officer'. Many of this group shared much of the motivation of lifers and second careerists, with common values and a capacity for critical thinking and reflection, but they saw their daily job differently in at least three ways: it was dominated by computer-based risk assessment rather than engaging in face-to-face work with offenders; it did not involve any significant time visiting offenders at home or in the community; and inter-agency collaboration was regarded as essential and uncontentious (see Chapter 74). We also found an additional dimension among the offender managers. On the surface, we saw a pragmatism, a sense that working for a public sector organization offered job status, security, and promotion. They had a public protection ethos with little investment in social work culture. Beneath the surface, however, was a principled rehabilitative approach to working with offenders. While pragmatic, our offender managers were committed to their work and many had been pulled towards probation work through their commitment to helping people less fortunate than themselves.

Having set up these ideal types to demonstrate the cultural richness of probation work, we now turn to individual probation worker responses to change and turbulence in organizational structures and working conditions. To help understand these responses, we use first a model developed by Hirschman (1970) and expanded by others and, secondly, the concept of 'edgework'.

Exit, voice, loyalty, neglect, cynicism, and expedience

Hirschman's (1970) 'exit, voice, and loyalty' model has been used widely to analyze and compare employees' responses to adverse workplace conditions. He posited responses of 'exit' (employees leaving the organization or thinking seriously about doing so), 'voice' (employees expressing their concerns and dissatisfaction to management and others), and 'loyalty' (employees retaining an attachment to the organization and waiting for better times). A fourth component of 'neglect' (employees withholding effort through lax behaviour such as persistent lateness, absenteeism, or poor performance) was subsequently added (Farrell 1983).

More recently, Naus et al. (2007) extended the EVLN model by adding a fifth dimension of 'organizational cynicism', in which employees adopt a negative attitude towards their employer based on beliefs that the organization lacks integrity. Consequently they respond negatively toward the organization and tend to disparage it. While organizational cynicism can result in apathetic and alienated behaviour, it can also be a critical but caring voice of conscience. A sixth response of 'organizational expedience' (McLean Parks et al. 2010) moves us more clearly into the arena of 'rule breaking', describing 'workers' behaviours that (1) are intended to fulfil organizationally prescribed or sanctioned objectives but that (2) knowingly involve breaking, bending or stretching organizational rules, directives, or organizationally sanctioned norms' (2010: 703). Arising from the subjective experiences of role overload, emotional exhaustion, tension, and/or task conflict, expedient behaviour can result in increased organizational effectiveness but may also result in workers 'acting out their roles as if they understand expectations and doing whatever it takes to look successful' (2010: 714).

Below, we use our research data to illustrate these six responses, but we argue that this model alone does not entirely capture some aspects of that data. While the concept of 'organizational expedience' comes closest to providing an explanation of contemporary probation work, we suggest that there are some elements of the work that can only be explained in terms of 'voluntary risk-taking'. In an organization obsessed with risk assessment and risk management, we argue that it is relevant to draw upon the sociological concept of 'edgework' to extend our understanding.

Exit

Among our participants were those who left the service at retirement age, those who left to move into academic posts, those who were on the verge of retiring, and younger workers who had decided that they were unlikely to spend many more years in the service. Those in the first category talked about careers of fulfilling work in different posts, adapting to change (giving examples of loyalty), and then, as managerialist practices dominated, experiencing a gradual wearing down and mental exiting, referring to themselves as 'dinosaurs'.

Those who moved to academic posts were more positive, feeling that they could retain their attachment to the service without compromising their principles or values. Those on the verge of retiring were among our most disillusioned interviewees, expressing cynicism (see below) about the organization's integrity and its treatment of experienced workers. But there were younger workers, even trainees, who were already thinking about their exit if things did not improve.

Voice

The absence of 'voice' at every level within the organization was one of the most frequent complaints we heard in interviews. The greatest concern among Chief Officers was the absence of any significant probation voice at the highest level within the National Offender Management Service (NOMS). There was a widespread view that NOMS was prison-dominated and that the consequent organizational culture was one of 'command and control', with probation being regarded as 'troublesome' because it 'wouldn't do what it was told'.

Some participants, however, found their voice through union membership. Interviewees who were probation workers in the 1970s and 1980s remember NAPO (National Association of Probation Officers) as being a powerful influence on probation cultures, providing an alternative and critical vision of the service. Most experienced workers that we interviewed were members of NAPO and those who remained active were clearly committed, believing that, despite being a small union, NAPO 'punches above its weight'.

Loyalty

Most of our participants were, by definition, displaying loyalty by remaining in the organization and, by and large, speaking very positively about their work with offenders. Even those who disliked the general direction of change were finding ways to cope and achieve job satisfaction. They were drawn to the job through common values which include: a belief in the possibility of change and their own ability to effect it (to 'make a difference'); a faith in both offenders and colleagues which may be, but more often is not, a religious faith; and an ethos of service or vocationalism (that the work is a 'calling').

The 'loyalists', even the cynics and world-weary workers, regard probation as more than just a job; they need to make sense of why they do probation work. They need to do meaningful work and the cultural locators or filters for this include: an intellectualism that values thinking and reflection; a commitment to social equality and a respect for social diversity; a political positioning that historically has been overtly left-leaning (though less so currently); and a protective stance on the threatened domain of probation work. They construct themselves as professionals with a legitimate desire to be autonomous (though that desire is often perceived to be thwarted by the organization). They draw on an institutional memory that values a golden age of probation when workers *were* autonomous (while at the same time acknowledging that not all autonomous practice was best practice). As we shall see below, they also construct for themselves moments of action when they are called upon to test out their professional skills in situations that are potentially chaotic or dangerous and introduce into their work a creativity (or departure from the script) that they believe the organization prohibits (but which the organization is implicitly dependent on).

Neglect

We did not hear many stories about the withholding of effort. However disillusioned our participants might have been with the organization, they saw themselves as having a higher loyalty to offenders. They would work long hours and endure the tedium of spending a high proportion of their time in front of computers if they could justify it as being in the interests of their 'clients', as many still insisted on calling offenders. Withholding effort predominantly took the forms of taking sick leave as a mechanism for coping with stress.

Organizational cynicism and organizational expedience

While some interviewees were undoubtedly cynical about the organization and 'management', they would also emphasize that they were doing things their own way to counter perceived lapses in organizational integrity. But for others, the challenge of reconciling the meeting of organizational objectives with carrying out meaningful work with offenders was motivating in itself. We heard stories of workers who bent or resisted the rules in order to work effectively, while avoiding organizational censure. As one interviewee said, 'You can be creative because, the way I see it, when I'm in that room, nobody knows what I'm doing'.

Much of our research data can be adequately analyzed in terms of 'loyalty' and 'expedience', with pockets of 'exit', 'neglect', and 'cynicism', and a somewhat alarming absence of 'voice'. Nevertheless, there remains data that cannot be captured within this framework. In the next section we argue that some elements of probation work can only be understood as examples of 'edgework'.

Edgework in probation

Edgework refers to activities that involve voluntary risk-taking, where there is a 'clearly observable threat to one's physical or mental well-being or one's sense of an ordered existence' (Lyng 1990: 857). It is most easily illustrated in dangerous pastimes such as sky-diving, solo rock climbing, or even criminal behaviour, but the 'edge' can be any boundary where the actor, potentially, can lose control and harm themselves. Controlling this boundary involves the deployment of a specific skill 'to maintain control over a situation that verges on complete chaos, a situation most people would regard as entirely uncontrollable' (Lyng 1990: 859). Edgework tests this skill by getting as close as possible to the edge without crossing it but it is not gambling, recklessness, or the result of a psychological predisposition to take risks (Lyng 2009). Probation workers may not generally be regarded as obvious edgeworkers, but our research suggests that it is possible to identify elements of edgework in some probation work and that it is only by acknowledging this that we can obtain a complete picture of what it means to be a probation worker in an uncertain and potentially uncontrollable environment.

Many probation workers in England and Wales spend the majority of their time in front of computers in open-plan offices, undertaking important but routine risk assessment and risk management. The rest of their time is spent interviewing offenders in the security-conscious environment of anonymous public sector offices away from the places where offenders live. The work is demanding and the consequences of making mistakes could be serious but opportunities for 'action' are very few. Yet probation work is as much about controlling the boundaries between order and chaos as is police work, albeit on a smaller and more specific scale.

Many of our respondents expressed the desire for 'action' and 'autonomy'. This was emphatically not about behaving recklessly or disregarding the organization's objectives. Nor was it necessarily about a nostalgic return to a mythical golden age of probation. Rather it was about putting their skills to the test 'on the edge'. Here we identify four possible aspects of probation edgework.

First, *liking offenders and vicarious rule breaking – the lure of notoriety*: probation edgeworkers enjoy controlling the boundary between getting close to offenders (establishing rapport, showing empathy, and so on), in order to do effective work, and maintaining distance or behaving 'professionally' towards someone who has broken the law and is disapproved of. This involves what one interviewee described as actively choosing to *like* offenders. Taking a step further towards the 'edge' were those probation workers who suggested that it was not only *offenders* that they found attractive, but *offending* itself. Drawn towards behaviour regarded as deviant or 'other', they control this through working with offenders while not crossing the boundary into illegality themselves.

Second, *danger and the threat of violence – the sensation of omnipotence*: although not routinely in harm's way in the same way as police or prison officers, probation workers are often in the position of negotiating the boundary between controlling a 'risky' offender and the situation getting out of hand, resulting in violence, harm, or loss of professional face.

Third, *fast and exciting – performing probation*: we had not anticipated that even the most committed probation worker would describe their work as 'exciting', but a number did. Some probation workers appear to get a kick out of being on their mettle, using their skills to control a situation that could fall apart if they mess up.

Fourth, *creativity and intensity of work – the ambiguity of innovation*: in situations that verge on chaos, where things might just fall apart, professional skills are tested to keep things together. The work may be intensive, there may be a need for creativity, and it requires intellectual and emotional investment. Through taking risks and being creative, probation workers regain agency and achieve feelings of authenticity and self-actualization. They are being true to themselves and their occupation and 'making a difference', realizing some of the motivations and hopes that led them into the career in the first place.

Getting it wrong: edgework and failure

These examples illustrate how edgework can be exhilarating and empowering, but probation workers live in fear of 'getting it wrong', of miscalculating the risk of an offender reoffending, either in terms of frequency or, more significantly, in terms of the harm done. It is the spectre of the 'serious further offence' (SFO) that inhibits routine voluntary risk-taking by probation workers. In situations where offenders under supervision commit murder or serious sexual assault, the repercussions for practitioners who have not followed risk assessment procedures to the letter may be dire (Fitzgibbon 2011), despite the paradox that 'only a willingness to work outside the tick-box methods and grasp the "situational context" in which . . . offenders are located, enables reliable estimates of real risk' (2011: 144).

The impact of privatization on probation worker identities: the durable penal agent?

Prior to 2015, the period in which our research was undertaken, the Probation Service of England and Wales had been located within the public sector. However, following a dramatic change in government policy (see Chapters 13 and 76 in this volume), the service was split in two, with the majority of probation workers being allocated to 21 Community Rehabilitation Companies (CRCs), dominated by the private sector. The impact of this change on probation worker identities is only slowly becoming apparent and there is, as yet, very little research to draw on. Nevertheless, there are several indicators of the direction of change.

First, there have been changes in the qualifying training for probation officers. Cracknell (2016) experienced training in the crucial transitional period prior to the split and expresses concerns about the ability of training to equip workers with a full set of skills to work creatively across two organizations with a full variety of offenders. But the change is not only in the content and possibly ethos of the training programme itself. There is a question about the willingness of private sector employers to fund training places for their staff. Since all those wishing to work as probation officers with the public sector National Probation Service must undergo both academic and vocational training lasting at least 15 months, their sense of identity is, arguably, likely to remain relatively unfractured. However, CRCs are not obliged to employ qualified staff for many supervisory tasks and this may well dilute any strong sense of identity, especially among new recruits.

Second, Teague (2011, 2016) paints a rather bleak picture of the impact of privatization on 'for profit' supervision in some American states, where offenders are charged for the privilege of non-custodial supervision. Revenue generation has become a key performance indicator for probation workers' pay and this, together with the controversial arming of some probation and parole officers, suggests a very different identity – one denuded of the obligation to 'attempt to engage with relevant criminogenic issues' (2016: 105) – and hopefully provides a cautionary tale for probation workers in England and Wales.

Third, research by Burke et al. (2017) into the changing identities of probation workers who were 'migrated' to CRCs provides significant early indications of the impact of privatization on workers who had previously been employed in the public sector. Newly 'migrated' workers appear to fall into two broad categories – those (the 'liberated') who saw CRCs as an opportunity to re-engage in the kind of core work with offenders that they felt was disappearing with the public sector emphasis on public protection, and those who felt 'marooned' in a new organization that de-skilled and devalued them. The latter group could be further divided into the 'leavers' who were likely to 'exit' – either physically or psychologically – and the 'defiantly resilient' who were displaying what Worrall (2015) described as 'civil courage' – determinedly upholding a recognizable 'probation identity' in the face of adversity.

Despite constant policy turbulence, research suggests that probation worker identities have remained remarkably consistent. Utilizing concepts from Bourdieu, Grant (2016) constructs the 'durable penal agent', arguing that probation workers, of whatever generation, have particular 'dispositions' that attract them to the work. These dispositions – towards welfare, social justice, and rehabilitation – appear to protect them and enable them to endure and persist in punitive environments.

References

Ashforth, B. E. and Kreiner, G. E. (1999) "How can you do it?" Dirty work and the challenge of constructing a positive identity. *Academy of Management Journal*, 24(3), 413–434.

Burke, L., Millings, M. and Robinson, G. (2017) Probation migration(s): Examining occupational culture in a turbulent field. *Criminology and Criminal Justice*, 17(2), 192–208.

Cracknell, M. (2016) Reflections on undertaking the probation qualifying framework scheme during the Transforming Rehabilitation changes. *Probation Journal*, 63(2), 211–218.

Farrell, D. (1983) Exit, voice, loyalty, and neglect as responses to job dissatisfaction: A multidimensional scaling study. *Academy of Management Journal*, 26(4), 596–607.

Fitzgibbon, W. (2011) *Probation and Social Work on Trial: Violent Offenders and Child Abusers*. Basingstoke: Palgrave Macmillan.

Grant, S. (2016) Constructing the durable penal agent: Tracing the development of habitus within English probation officers and Scottish criminal justice social workers. *British Journal of Criminology*, 56(4), 750–758.

Hirschman, A. O. (1970) *Exit, Voice and Loyalty: Responses to Decline in Firms, Organizations and States*. Cambridge, MA: Harvard University Press.

Lyng, S. (1990) Edgework: A social psychological analysis of voluntary risk taking. *The American Journal of Sociology*, 95(4), 851–886.

Lyng, S. (2009) Edgework, risk, and uncertainty. In J. O. Zinn (Ed.), *Social Theories of Risk and Uncertainty: An Introduction*. Oxford: Blackwell, pp. 106–137.

Mawby, R. C. and Worrall, A. (2013) *Doing Probation Work: Identity in a Criminal Justice Occupation*. Abingdon: Routledge.

McLean Parks, J., Ma, L. and Gallagher, D. G. (2010) Elasticity in the "rules" of the game: Exploring organizational expedience. *Human Relations*, 63(5), 701–730.

Naus, F., van Iterson, A. and Roe, R. (2007) Organizational cynicism: Extending the exit, voice, loyalty, and neglect model of employees' responses to adverse conditions in the workplace. *Human Relations*, 60(5), 683–718.

Teague, M. (2011) Probation in America: Armed, private and unaffordable? *Probation Journal*, 58(4), 317–332.

Teague, M. (2016) Profiting from the poor: Offender-funded probation in the USA. *British Journal of Community Justice*, 14(1), 99–111.

Worrall, A. (2015) Grace under pressure: The role of courage in the future of probation work. *The Howard Journal of Criminal Justice*, 54(5), 508–520.

76

Probation values in England and Wales

Can they survive Transforming Rehabilitation?

John Deering

Introduction

The professional values of probation practitioners in England and Wales have been debated over the past 30 years or so and such debates have considered what the service's 'corporate' values *have* and *should* have been, whilst also assessing practitioners' values, thereby throwing some light on the relationship between these and those of the probation service itself. In this period, probation governance has changed from it being a number of semi-autonomous local organizations, to a single centralized 'national' service and finally to a situation where, since 2014 and Transforming Rehabilitation (TR), a unified service no longer exists within the public sector.[1] Such a level of upheaval is unprecedented since probation's creation in 1907 and poses questions

about the impact of such radical change upon personal professional and organizational values.

This chapter considers how practitioners' values might have evolved
to meet changing circumstances and whether there has been a divergence
between practitioners on the one hand and government (and to some degree
probation management) on the other (see, for example, Annison et al. 2008;
Deering 2011; Deering and Feilzer 2015; Mawby and Worrall 2013; NAPO
2006). It further looks at how TR may have accelerated any divergence and
whether there can now be said to be a set of extant 'probation values' that
are generally recognizable within probation[2] and the wider criminal justice
sector.

The argument here is that the values and beliefs of many practitioners
throughout this period might be seen as 'traditional', but that these have
come under pressure from government attempts to shift them towards a law
enforcement, punishment, and risk management agenda, resulting in traditional values being amended to varying degrees.

Traditional values are defined here as being related to social work, humanitarian, and involving valuing the individual, whilst seeking behavioural
change via the provision of 'help' in its broadest sense, although it has also
been argued that issues of care and control have never been far beneath the
surface (Raynor 1985; Vanstone 2004; Whitfield 1998). Furthermore they
encompass a range of values and beliefs about how the service should operate: that working with people should be empathic and based on a firm belief
in the ability of individuals to change and in the probation service's ability
to facilitate that change; that this can result in the reduction of reoffending
and in many cases this may be seen as synonymous with rehabilitation. More
broadly, crime is seen as occurring within social, economic, and personal
contexts, rather than as the result of rational free will and thus most likely
to occur when individuals have experienced multiple disadvantage that has
resulted in them making 'bad choices' leading to offending.

Governance, purposes, and the probation values debate

It is perhaps an accepted wisdom that for most of its history, the values of
the probation service have been traditional within a rehabilitative working
model, but that in recent decades it has accepted successive governments
changing its functions to those of a law enforcement agency working to
protect the public via risk assessment and management. These changes are
said to be the result of increasing levels of government interference in both
the practice and governance of probation but also of some theoretical criticisms of the service's interventionist, 'treatment'-based rehabilitative model
(Vanstone 2004).

Late modern theories attribute such changes to the criminal justice system becoming more punitive and intolerant of crime and offenders (Garland 2001; Pratt et al. 2005; Newburn 2003). From the 1970s, the 'nothing works' era had the effect of reducing the government's confidence about the service's ability to facilitate behavioural change in its supervisees (Lipton et al. 1975; Martinson 1974) and led to it producing a Statement of National Objectives and Priorities (SNOP) in 1984 which aimed to move the service into other areas such as crime prevention and the provision of alternatives to custody (Mair and Burke 2013). Moreover, others also suggested that the service should move from a 'treatment'-based approach to a more collaborative model that emphasized appropriate help for supervisees and the provision of alternatives to custody (Bottoms and McWilliams 1979). Despite these influences, rehabilitation probably remained the *raison d'être* of many practitioners working within a largely casework model (Vanstone 2004) and the theoretical debate about rehabilitation as a 'moral good' continued (McWilliams and Pease 1990). In the mid-1990s Williams gave an overview of what probation values might or should be: opposition to custody; opposition to oppression; commitment to justice for offenders; commitment to the client's right to confidentiality and openness; valuing of clients as unique and self-determining individuals; aim to ensure that victims and potential victims are protected; belief that 'purposeful professional relationships can facilitate change in clients' (Williams 1995: 12–20, cited in Deering 2011: 43).

The 1991 Criminal Justice Act saw the acceleration of government efforts to recast the work of the service. The Act made the probation order 'punishment in the community' and the first and subsequent versions of National Standards for the Supervision of Offenders (Home Office 1992) set out clear controls on probation officers' discretion in terms of levels of contact with supervisees and also expectations in terms of returning those who did not comply to court under breach proceedings. Since then the debate about what the purpose of the service should be has encompassed a wide range of theories and practices, including restorative justice, community justice, and human rights, but also public protection and accountability to the court (Farooq 1998; Nellis 1999, 2002; Nellis and Gelsthorpe 2003; Harding 2000). More recently, emerging of desistance theories have argued that the work of the probation service should be recast as being about promoting desistance rather than the prevention of recidivism (Raynor 2004; Farrall 2002; McNeill 2006). These debates and changes in practices, aims, and objectives inevitably had an impact on how the service was viewed in terms of its values, but it is far less clear how individual practitioners were affected. For its part, throughout this period, the trade union and professional association NAPO maintained a commitment to traditional values and purposes and argued that individuals have the ability to change, setting out the following values to which it was committed: respect and trust when working with perpetrators and victims; open and fair treatment for all; empowerment of individuals in order to reduce the risk of harm to themselves and others; promotion of equality and anti-discrimination; promotion of the rights of both perpetrators and victims; building on individuals' strengths as a vehicle for change (NAPO 2006: 5).

Empirical studies

Empirical studies have been relatively rare, but do provide an insight into mainly practitioner beliefs that can be compared to theoretical and political views. After the 1991 Criminal Justice Act, one study reported that probation officers saw their role in terms of providing alternatives to custody (Humphrey and Pease 1992) whilst another concluded that practitioners promoted the 'holy trinity' of public protection, rehabilitation (defined as reducing reoffending), and enforcement (Robinson and McNeill 2004) with an overall aim of protecting the public. The argument was that during the 1990s and into the 21st century, practitioners were adapting their values in order to reflect to some degree the changing priorities of government in terms of law enforcement, the protection of the public, and the rise of risk (Kemshall 2003; Raynor and Vanstone 2002; Vanstone 2004).

However, later studies suggested that whilst practitioners recognized government priorities and worked within them, their underlying values were more traditional than focusing on law enforcement, risk, and punishment. Some conducted with former probation trainees suggested that they had joined the service for reasons related to the 'advising, assisting and befriending' of supervisees (Annison 2006; Annison et al. 2008) and another conducted with over 100 trainees concluded that they had joined the service:

> to offer 'help' in the widest sense with a view to assisting individuals to achieve behavioural change. Whilst respondents recognised the government's agenda they do not appear to have joined to follow it to the letter, but rather to acknowledge and work with it, with something of a different emphasis, particularly around what they regard as the purposes of the system and their role as practitioners.
>
> (Deering 2010: 23)

This study also revealed a further element in the values debate; that of a level of resistance to government plans and intentions for the service. This phenomenon had also been suggested by a study looking at the morale of experienced staff (Farrow 2004) and by more recent research.

One such considered practitioners' views about 'quality' in practice (Robinson et al. 2014) and argued that a divergence in the views of practitioners from those of senior management and the Government had been taking place. Practitioners defined quality as: professionalism in relationships; a humanistic approach; and individual 'progress' in their supervisees. This contrasted with a management regarding it more as task completion and timeliness (Robinson et al. 2014: 127–134). Deering (2011) investigated a range of practitioner views about probation practice and found a similar divergence in view, although interestingly this was not acknowledged or even recognized by managers in the sample. Practitioners' reasons for joining the service were more traditional, but acknowledged responsibility to the court and the protection of the public. Risk management was also seen as important but, in the majority of cases, the reduction in the risk of reoffending by facilitating change was seen as the most efficient way to protect the public, as opposed to a more limited monitoring and surveillance role, which was seen as applying to a relatively small number of higher-risk-of-harm individuals (Deering 2011). Indeed, the government's promoting of the service as a law enforcement agency primarily concerned with 'punishment in the community' and public protection was the source of some disquiet:

> Practitioners, as represented by these respondents, continue to join the service to develop effective professional relationships with individual offenders to try and promote personal change, something that the literature does indicate can be effective, whether from a 'what works' or a desistance based approach. As such, they represent something of a continuum from older forms of practice, although one that operates within a greatly changed overall framework. However, the extent to which they will be able to continue to practice based on these ideals remains very much in the balance.
>
> Deering (2011: 187)

Looking primarily at probation cultures, Mawby and Worrall (2013) concluded that many practitioners remained optimistic about probation work. They saw a service continuing to be based in its traditions and humanitarianism, whilst taking on risk assessment and public protection in a skilful manner that went beyond a law enforcement approach. Mawby and Worrall categorized three ideal types of practitioner: 'Lifers' – baby boomers who went to university from school and joined the service soon afterwards and who were idealist, left-leaning, and saw the job as a vocation; 'Second Careerists' – had previous occupations, including social work and the armed forces, and who were not always graduates, were politically more pragmatic than the lifers but wanting to 'make a difference'; 'Offender Managers' – more recent entrants to the service, often previous graduates trained via the Diploma in Probation Studies, who were overwhelmingly female, politically pragmatic, and with a public protection orientation (Mawby and Worrall 2013: 20–42). Although they identified these ideal types, the overall sample were seen to share certain core values such as: seeing an effective professional relationship with supervisees as fundamental; a belief in the individual's ability to change; the worth of engaging with people in the community; the importance of the social and personal context for crime. All of this was set within the context of public protection and the victim perspective. Finally, and echoing Deering (2011) above they noted that practitioners engaged in what they described as 'edgework', which was the process of practicing in a way that was acceptable to their own values in an environment where there was tension with those practices and values that the probation service had come to espouse, at least at senior management and government levels (Mawby and Worrall 2013).

To what extent did these developments lead to a level of resistance, based upon practitioners' continuing commitment to more traditional values? Of course such detail is very difficult to draw out, but the broad conclusion of the studies outlined above was:

> practitioners were generally not openly hostile or resistant to government policies, however, they clearly had a significant difference in emphasis when considering their underlying values, the purposes of probation (as they felt they should be) and, to some degree, the ways in which they practiced. The influence of managerialism, as expressed by a law enforcement and target-driven agenda was seen as particularly problematic.
>
> (Deering 2016: 105)

Such resistance may be regarded as everyday and small scale, but it is likely to have real impact upon supervisees' lives. As Mawby and Worrall (2013) showed, practitioners 'crafted' their jobs in order for them to achieve a best possible fit between practice and their own values, an example of them resisting changes by 'adaptively and strategically interpreting, evaluating, [and] reconstructing' central priorities (Cheliotis 2006: 324).

Government and change – the road to Transforming Rehabilitation

Since the mid-1980s and prior to TR in 2014, successive government became increasingly proactive in trying to change the practice of the probation service and thereby the fundamental values of practitioners. However, this did not mean that rehabilitation (perhaps generally synonymous with reducing reoffending) was completely abandoned by government. The 1991 Criminal Justice Act was meant to bring the service 'centre stage' and take on more cases as the prison population was reduced (Raynor 2012) and at this time the emergence of the 'what works?' movement, whilst not universally welcomed, gave rise to optimism about the potential for cognitive behavioural approaches to effect behavioural change (McGuire 2001). Despite this, prior to the 1997 general election the continued supervisory function of the service did come under threat (Home Office 1995, 1996) from the then Home Secretary Michael Howard, who abolished social work training for probation officers in a clear attempt to change the type of person entering the profession (Newburn 2003).

Perhaps the election of the New Labour government in 1997 did 'save rehabilitation', but there was no simple return to more traditional approaches.

Whilst probation officer training was reintroduced by the Blair Labour government, it was separated from social work and intended to provide a new generation of probation officers who could:

> focus on Probation's top priority role of protecting the public and reducing crime through effective work with offenders.
>
> (Straw 1997)

Although Labour invested heavily in accredited programmes (Home Office 1998), their commitment to 'modernisation' (Senior et al. 2007) meant further and increasingly intrusive intervention and eventually to a position of perhaps even hostility to the national service that they had themselves created only in 2001 (Burke and Collett 2010). Via the creation of the National Offender Management Service (NOMS) in 2004 and the Offender Management Act 2007, the Labour government laid the foundations for a marketized service, which ultimately led to TR (Deering and Feilzer 2015).

The impact of Transforming Rehabilitation

Transforming Rehabilitation (TR) has been regarded as an ideological change, imposed by a Justice Secretary, Christopher Grayling, acting without evidence that it would improve the overall performance of the probation service, or benefit those under probation supervision, the criminal justice system, or the public (Deering and Feilzer 2015). The TR proposals (Ministry of Justice 2013) were realized initially in June 2014 when the National Probation Service for England and Wales, set up in only 2001, was replaced by a new National Probation Service (NPS) and 21 Community Rehabilitation Companies (CRCs). In February 2015, the latter passed into the hands of new owners, made up of a mixture of private, voluntary, and third-sector organizations (Deering and Feilzer 2015). The impact of these changes on the culture of probation, its organizational values and those of probation practitioners will probably not fully emerge for some time, but it was seen as almost exclusively negative by samples of staff within a few empirical studies. An online survey with probation staff conducted just before the split of the service in June 2014 had over 1,300 responses, and concluded that:

> What is clear from this research was the unequivocal opposition to the majority of the proposals within the TR document, the most fundamental of which have now come into operation . . . there is no doubt that TR's fundamental design and intentions were opposed in terms that revealed the anger, feelings of betrayal, and sadness about the destruction of the unified, public probation service.
>
> (Deering and Feilzer 2015: 101)

It was evident that the majority of the sample had joined the service for the same traditional reasons that have been outlined above. Respondents saw the service as having a role in addressing personal and social factors that were seen as the root of much offending and this was seen as legitimizing its practice. However, practice was also seen as operating within the context of protection of the public, law enforcement, and accountability to the courts.

It noteworthy that respondents also drew attention to the pressure upon traditional values that had been coming from government and senior management prior to TR. However, TR was seen as likely to exacerbate these trends and to introduce a completely new dynamic, that of the introduction of private and third-sector organizations into the 'business' of probation. Never an issue prior to TR, this had assumed a central importance:

> respondents had a clear antipathy to the involvement of the private sector and also, although to a lesser degree to the third sector. This was based upon a range of beliefs about governance and values. The private sector was regarded as being inevitably responsible to its shareholders and the need to make a profit and this was seen as one of the major reasons why it would be unable to provide an appropriate service. There was clearly no agreement with government assertions that the marketisation of services will improve innovation via the disciplines of competition and this idea was regarded as ideological and without any empirical foundation.
>
> (Deering and Feilzer 2015: 101)

In a study that observed the formation of a CRC over a lengthy period of time, Robinson et al. (2016) looked at professional identity. They identified a number of themes but concluded that 'liminality' – of being caught between the 'old' and the 'new' – was the most important. Some of their respondents felt the CRC lacked a clear identity and that their membership of the 'honourable profession' of probation might be compromised because of private sector values and priorities. They concluded that staff within the CRCs were likely to experience ambivalence for some time until they arrived at some more settled view of their identity within the new system, whether that be positive or negative.

Deering and Feilzer reconsidered their online survey taken in 2014 (Deering and Feilzer 2015) and developed it primarily in terms of the feelings of self-legitimacy of practitioners (Deering and Feilzer 2017). Whilst clearly engaged in crystal ball gazing at a very difficult time, respondents had concerns about the continuation of a set of organizational values that were in line with their own. They feared that the erosion of traditional values and an increasing emphasis on punishment, law enforcement, and case management would not only continue but would be exacerbated, alongside a managerialist approach that eschewed quality for outputs and the attainment of targets (Deering and Feilzer 2017).

Adding to the feeling of dislocation was the belief that the two new organizations would fail to perform as efficiently as probation had been doing before TR (NOMS 2014). Respondents were concerned about communication between the NPS and CRCs, professional relationships, workloads, concentration on only lower or higher risk of harm cases, and general fragmentation. These issues suggested that their feelings about the legitimacy of probation practice and their own place within it would be placed in question.

Unfortunately, many of these concerns have been borne out, with official reports and research indicating considerable disquiet about some poor performance by CRCs related to supervisory work and public protection, professional supervision, and relations between CRCs and the NPS (Her Majesty's Inspectorate of Probation [HMIP] 2016; National Audit Office 2016). Moreover, practice appears to be changing and fragmenting to some degree, which is perhaps inevitable given the number of different CRCs with different owners and presumably, therefore, differing priorities (HMIP 2016a). Additionally, evidence has emerged that in some CRCs those regarded as low risk of harm have been moved to a 'reporting only' regime via biometric technology (Travis 2015) and HMIP criticized one CRC for supervising some 'low risk' individuals by telephone once every six weeks (HMIP 2017). Moreover, one of the key elements of TR, the post custody supervision of short-term prisoners by CRCs, has been found to be ineffective (Her Majesty's Inspectorate of Probation and Her Majesty's Inspectorate of Prisons 2017). As a result of the level of concern, in 2017 the House of Commons Justice Committee conducted its own inquiry into the impact of TR, producing a critical report (House of Commons Justice Committee 2018). Subsequent to this, in July 2018 the Ministry of Justice (Ministry of Justice 2018) announced that the existing contracts with the CRCs would be terminated two years earlier than planned. The Ministry launched a consultation, asking for comments on its intended remodelling, which would result in a reduction of the CRC contracts from 21 to ten covering England. In an interesting exception, the intention is to create a single, unified public sector probation service in Wales, with the transfer of the CRC caseload to the NPS in Wales (Ministry of Justice 2018). Whilst this is a clear indication of the government's acknowledgement of real flaws in TR, it seems that it remains wedded to the fundamental TR model of a divided and marketized probation service in England.

Academic research around the impact of TR has also reached largely negative conclusions. For example, Dominey (2016) argues that due to the NPS/CRC split and increased workloads, TR is likely to damage relationships between practitioners and those on supervision (Dominey 2016: 141), something that a number of earlier studies indicate would be inimical to many practitioners (e.g. Annison et al. 2008; Deering 2011; Mawby and Worrall 2013) who regarded their role as far more than a reductive monitoring one. In an article based upon the same study conducted by Robinson et al. (2016) above, Burke et al. (2017) considered the impact upon occupational cultures of the migration of staff from the unified public probation service to a CRC.

Drawing on studies of privatizations in other public sector organizations, one of their conclusions was that the probation experience differed in that it was not a wholesale transfer from the public sector, but rather one where part of the organization moved out of the public sector and into the CRCs. This split they felt raised issues of the relationship between the two new organizations and the idea that the NPS, concentrating as it does on higher risk of harm cases and court work, would be seen to be 'proper' probation, with the CRCs as somewhat second class, something identified by respondents to Deering and Feilzer's earlier study (2015). Moreover Burke et al. (2017: 205) felt that their respondents going into the CRC wanted to hold on to their public service ethos but that perceived threats to this were the cause of anxiety and perhaps one of the reasons why a number of staff were seeking to or had left the CRC after January 2015. They also noted that those most likely to leave related to Mawby and Worrall's (2013) 'lifers' and 'second careerists' (see above) whilst the 'offender managers' – younger and regarded as less likely to see probation as a vocation – were least likely to leave. Burke et al. concluded that whilst those staff transferred to the CRC would continue to aspire to (more traditional) probation values, the 'imperatives and language' of the private sector (2017: 205) might make that more difficult with the passage of time.

Conclusion

This chapter has considered pressure over a considerable period from government upon what I have called traditional values. This has been done via legislation and executive action, but also by efforts to alter the culture and values of the service, by not only attritional change, but also by attempting to recruit a different type of person to the job.

This latter attempt has largely failed, because whilst there is evidence discussed above that practitioners have taken on elements of these changes, namely by recognizing and working with risk assessment and public protection, they have not accepted, to any significant degree the law enforcement and reductive case management agenda. Individuals have continued to join the service for traditional reasons.

Prior to TR, it appears that such values were proving to be resilient and that practitioners were devising ways to work creatively around some elements of the new government agenda that allowed them to practice in ways that fitted with their values. However, the game seems to have irrevocably changed with TR. It did reverse one of the trends of previous decades, that of increased government intervention in practice, but in doing so it delivered over half of practitioners into a system of practice that was ultimately based in different priorities, namely the commercial concerns of the market. Whilst its real impact upon cultures and values will not be known for some time, there seems little doubt that the marketization of part of the service has placed traditional values and the 'probation ideal' (Deering and Feilzer 2015) in real jeopardy. Moreover, the current consultation process and likely reorganization of TR announced in 2018 seems unlikely to fundamentally change the situation, given that the intention seems to be to reduce the number of CRC contracts, whilst retaining the model of a divided, part-marketized service.

As noted, other challenges to traditional values had begun before TR, but many fear it will accelerate them, even within the new NPS, as it is more centrally controlled as part of the civil service and more focused on risk management, given the higher risk of harm status of its supervisees. A further variable is the apparent divergence of views between practitioners and managers. This schism is a further threat to the continued existence of a coherent, collective organization's values and a shared idea of what probation is 'about' – of what defines its values.

More optimistically, practitioners have continued to join probation for traditional reasons and perhaps they will continue to do so, particularly to the NPS. However, quite who will be attracted to the so-called second class CRCs remains to be seen. Under the terms of TR, CRCs are not required to employ professionally qualified staff, but only to ensure they are 'suitably' trained (Ministry of Justice 2013) and the overall effect of this on recruitment and professional values will take time to emerge.

Of course, should the 'usual suspects' continue to be recruited to the NPS and the CRCs, it remains to be seen how long they would wish to remain in the new organizations, or to the extent to which their values would change to suit their working environment. As a result of these dynamics, it is difficult to be optimistic for the future in this regard; how long will probation practitioners share a sense of being a member of a 'collective of professionals doing an important job well' (Ugelvik 2016: 226) and for how long and in what form will a level of collective values survive?

Notes

1   Under Transforming Rehabilitation, the previous public sector probation service became divided between the public sector National Probation Service (NPS) and the marketized and partly privatized Community Rehabilitation Companies (CRCs).
2   For convenience, post Transforming Rehabilitation, I refer to 'probation' as including both the NPS and the CRCs.

References

Annison, J. (2006) *Career Trajectories of Graduate Trainee Probation Officers*. Plymouth: University of Plymouth.

Annison, J., Eadie, T. and Knight, C. (2008) People first: Probation officer perspectives on probation work. *Probation Journal*, 55(3), 259–272.

Bottoms, A. and McWilliams, W. (1979) A non-treatment paradigm for probation practice. *British Journal of Social Work*, 9, 159–202.

Burke, L. and Collett, S. (2010) People are not things: What new labour has done to probation. *Probation Journal*, 57(3), 232–249.

Burke, L., Millings, M. and Robinson, G. (2017) Probation migration(s): Examining occupational culture in a turbulent field. *Criminology and Criminal Justice*, 17(2), 192–208.

Cheliotis, L. (2006) How iron is the iron cage of new penology? The role of human agency in the implementation of criminal justice policy. *Punishment & Society*, 8(3), 313–340.

Deering, J. (2010) Attitudes and beliefs of trainee probation officers – a new breed? *Probation Journal*, 57(1), 9–26.

Deering, J. (2011) *Probation Practice and the New Penology: Practitioner Reflections*. Aldershot: Ashgate.

Deering, J. (2016) Voices from practice – what probation has been and what it could become. In M. Vanstone and P. Priestley (Eds.), *Probation and Politics: Academic Reflections from Former Practitioners*. London: Palgrave Macmillan.

Deering, J. and Feilzer, M. Y. (2015) *Transforming Rehabilitation: Is Privatisation the End of the Probation Ideal?* Bristol: Policy Press.

Deering, J. and Feilzer, M. Y. (2017) Questions of legitimacy in probation practice after Transforming Rehabilitation. *Howard Journal of Criminal Justice*, 56(2), 158–175.

Dominey, J. (2016) Fragmenting probation: Recommendations from research. *Probation Journal*, 63(2), 136–143.

Farooq, M. (1998) Probation, power and change. *Vista*, 3(3), 208–220.

Farrall, S. (2002) *Rethinking What Works with Offenders*. Cullompton: Willan Publishing.

Farrow, K. (2004) Still committed after all these years? Morale in the modern-day probation service. *Probation Journal*, 51(3), 206–220.

Garland, D. (2001) *The Culture of Control*. Oxford: Oxford University Press.

Harding, J. (2000) A community justice dimension to effective probation practice. *Howard Journal of Criminal Justice*, 39(2), 132–149.

Her Majesty's Inspectorate of Probation. (2016a) *Quality and Impact Inspection: The Effectiveness of Probation Work in Durham*. London: HMIP.

Her Majesty's Inspectorate of Probation. (2016b) *Transforming Rehabilitation. Early Implementation 5*. London: HMIP.

Her Majesty's Inspectorate of Probation. (2017) *Quality and Impact Inspection: The Effectiveness of Probation Work in Gwent*. London: HMIP.

Her Majesty's Inspectorate of Probation and Her Majesty's Inspectorate of Prisons. (2017) *An Inspection of Through the Gate Resettlement Services for Prisoners Serving 12 Months or More*. London: HMIP.

Home Office. (1992) *National Standards for the Supervision of Offenders in the Community*. London: Home Office.

Home Office. (1995) *Strengthening Punishment in the Community*. London: HMSO.

Home Office. (1996) *Protecting the Public*. London: HMSO.

Home Office. (1998) *Effective Practice Initiative: Probation Circular 35/98*. London: Home Office.

House of Commons Justice Committee. (2018) *Transforming Rehabilitation*. London: House of Commons.

Humphrey, C. and Pease, K. (1992) Effectiveness measurement in probation – a view from the troops. *Howard Journal of Criminal Justice*, 31(1), 31–52.

Kemshall, H. (2003) *Understanding Risk in Criminal Justice*. Maidenhead: Open University Press.

Lipton, D., Martinson, R. and Wilks, J. (1975) *The Effectiveness of Correctional Treatment*. New York: Praeger.

Mair, G. and Burke, L. (2013) *Redemption, Rehabilitation and Risk Management: A History of Probation*. London: Routledge.

Martinson, R. (1974) What works? Questions and answers about prison reform. *The Public Interest*, 35, 22–54.

Mawby, R. C. and Worrall, A. (2013) *Doing Probation Work: Identity in a Criminal Justice Occupation*. London: Routledge.

McGuire, J. (2001) What works in correctional intervention? Evidence and practical implications. In G. Bernfeld, D. Farrington and A. Leschied (Eds.), *Offender Rehabilitation in Practice: Implementing and Evaluating Effective Programs*. Chichester: Wiley.

McNeill, F. (2006) A desistance paradigm for offender management. *Criminology and Criminal Justice*, 6(1), 39–62.

McWilliams, W. and Pease, K. (1990) Probation practice and an end to punishment. *Howard Journal of Criminal Justice*, 29(1), 14–24.

Ministry of Justice. (2018) *Strengthening Probation, Building Confidence*. London: Ministry of Justice.

Ministry of Justice. (2013) *Transforming Rehabilitation, a Revolution in the Way We Manage Offenders*. London: Ministry of Justice.

NAPO. (2006) *Probation Values: Commitment to Best Practice*. London: NAPO.

National Audit Office. (2016) *Transforming Rehabilitation*. London: National Audit Office.

National Offender Management Service. (2014) *Probation Trusts' Annual Performance Rating, 2013/14*. Available at: https://www.gov.uk/government/uploads/system/uploads/attachment_data/file/338962/probation-trust-perf-ratings-2013-14.Pdf; 11/02/2015.

Nellis, M. (1999) Towards the field of corrections: Modernising the probation service in the late 1990's. *Social Policy*, 33(3), 302–323.

Nellis, M. (2002) Community justice, time and the new national probation service. *Howard Journal*, 41(1), 59–86.

Nellis, M. and Gelsthorpe, L. (2003) Human rights and the probation values debate. In W. Chui and M. Nellis (Eds.), *Moving Probation Forward*. Harlow: Pearson.

Newburn, T. (2003) *Crime and Criminal Justice Policy*. Harlow: Longman.

Pratt, J., Brown, D., Brown, M., Hallsworth, S. and Morrison, W. (2005) *The New Punitiveness: Trends, Theories, Perspectives*. Cullompton: Willan Publishing.

Raynor, P. (1985) *Social Work, Justice and Control*. Oxford: Blackwell.

Raynor, P. (2004) Rehabilitative and reintegrative approaches. In A. Bottoms, S. Rex and G. Robinson (Eds.), *Alternatives to Prison. Options for an Insecure Society*. Cullompton: Willan Publishing.

Raynor, P. (2012) Community penalties, probation and offender management. In M. Maguire, R. Morgan and R. Reiner (Eds.), *The Oxford Handbook of Criminology*. Oxford: Oxford University Press.

Raynor, P. and Vanstone, M. (2002) *Understanding Community Penalties: Probation, Policy and Social Change*. Buckingham: Open University Press.

Robinson, G., Burke, L. and Millings, M. (2016) Criminal justice identities in transition: The case of devolved probation services in England and Wales. *British Journal of Criminology*, 56(1), 161–178.

Robinson, G. and McNeill, F. (2004) Purposes matter: Examining the 'Ends' of probation. In G. Mair (Ed.), *What Matters in Probation*. Cullompton: Willan Publishing.

Robinson, G., Priede, C., Farrall, S., Shapland, J. and McNeill, F. (2014) Understanding 'quality' in probation practice: Frontline perspectives in England and Wales. *Criminology and Criminal Justice*, 14(2), 123–142.

Senior, P., Crowther-Dowey, C. and Long, M. (2007) *Understanding Modernisation in Criminal Justice*. Buckingham: Open University Press.

Straw, J. (1997) *'Commons Written Reply': Hansard*. London: House of Commons.

Travis, A. (2015) 'Probation officers face redundancy with plans to replace them by machines', *Guardian*, 30 March.

Ugelvik, T. (2016) Techniques of legitimation: The narrative construction of legitimacy among immigration detention officers. *Crime, Media, Culture*, 12(2), 215–232.

Vanstone, M. (2004) *Supervising Offenders in the Community: A History of Probation Theory and Practice*. Aldershot: Ashgate.

Whitfield, D. (1998) *Introduction to the Probation Service*. Winchester: Waterside.

Williams, B. (1995) *Probation Values*. London: Venture Press.

77

Probation and parole – shaping principles and practices in the early 21st century

A US perspective

Ronald P. Corbett, Jr and
Edward E. Rhine

Introduction

The justice system in America is an outlier relative to other nations, one that has become comparatively punitive given its dramatic expansion under the imperative of 'penal control' (Garland 2017). This distinctive form of punishment expresses what is already well known: the striking growth in prison populations for nearly four decades (Travis et al. 2014; Gottschalk 2015). Yet the boundaries of this unprecedented moment, frequently referred to as mass incarceration,[1] also encompass the emergence of a comparable phenomenon recognized increasingly as mass community (probation and parole) supervision

(Alper et al. 2016; Corda et al. 2016; Corda and Phelps 2017; Rhine and Taxman 2018; Van Zyl Smit and Corda 2018).[2] These features, when joined with others (e.g. collateral consequences), represent a unique historical instance of American exceptionalism in the severity of punishments imposed (Reitz 2018).[3]

Within this context, probation and parole serve as the paramount form(s) of community-based supervision (Kaeble and Glaze 2016).[4] This chapter starts by observing that with the ascendance of penal control, those subject to probation and parole often experience their time under supervision as intrusive and punitive. This is an acknowledgement that begins, but does not end, the discussion that follows.

The chapter goes on to consider the degree to which the arena of supervision – despite the accent on penal control – has retained a neo-rehabilitation or 'correctionalist narrative' in the process embracing evidence-based practices (Phelps and Curry 2017). These comments provide the foundation for subsequent sections calling for revisiting the content of supervision and officers' relationships with those they supervise, and the integration of 'what works' with 'what is just'. The chapter concludes with a series of 'prescriptions for practice': reforms that are central to the reconstruction of community supervision.

The experience of supervision and 'the burdens of leniency'

Probation and parole supervision share numerous features in common, yet there is one overriding characteristic both display that often goes unnoticed: those subject to this form of penal control experience it as highly constraining and punitive (Durnescu 2011; Corbett 2015; Doherty 2016; Fitzgibbon et al. 2016; Phelps and Curry 2017). In an ethnography discussing the 'pains of probation' in Romania, Durnescu (2011) notes that there are eight interlocking deprivations associated with being on supervision.[5] These include restrictions on offender autonomy, the reorganization of one's daily routine, limits on privacy as well as family life, and time management. They also involve daunting financial costs, the constancy of stigmatization, the need to repeatedly revisit the crime of conviction, and the threat of return to prison.[6]

The pains of probation apply with equal force to parole or post-release supervision. Werth's (2011) ethnographic research shows a supervision system in California that intends to be 'up close' through its regulation of parolees' everyday conduct.[7] Like their counterparts on probation, these individuals live with the ever-present possibility of failure, revocation, and incarceration.

These experiences are exacerbated by another constraining element associated with probation and parole, namely, the conditions of supervision. Whether issued by a judge at sentencing or by a paroling authority upon release, offenders are typically subject to ten to 20 standard conditions of supervision (Taxman 2012; Ruhland et al. 2016). Standard conditions are required for everyone, regardless of offence, risk, or need. Of particular salience, augmenting longstanding financial sanctions such as fines, restitution, and court costs, offenders are now expected to pay monthly supervision fees, and programme, treatment, and specialized assessment fees. As an increasing number of conditions are layered on, especially economic sanctions, they can overwhelm an offender's bandwidth and capacity to comply (Corbett 2015; Jacobson et al. 2017). This heightens the prospect of revocation at the same time it highlights the extent to which mass community supervision in the form of probation and parole functions squarely within the continuum of penal control (Klingele 2013).

Contesting the dominance of penal control on the ground – probation and parole: the repurposing of the correctionalist narrative

As the era of mass incarceration unfolded, probation and parole shifted towards a more pronounced emphasis on surveillance-oriented, control-based strategies of offender supervision. Aligned with the 'New Penology', the purpose and content of supervision embraced an emergent risk-management framework to be achieved largely through more contacts, more enforcement, and more sanctioning of non-compliance (Feeley and Simon 1992). The organizational culture in numerous agencies came to be and remains centred on 'watching, catching, and sanctioning probationers [and parolees] when they don't follow the rules' (Burrell 2010).

It is notable that probation and parole in some jurisdictions retained a visible commitment to what Phelps and Curry (2017) refer to as neo-rehabilitation or a 'repurposing of correctionalist narratives'. They argue that the adoption of new *discourses* of punishment under the New Penology may have been more dramatic than its corresponding impact on *practices*. In some instances, probation and parole officers and their agencies contested the dominating logic of penal control. The officers did so by continuing to offer then and now rehabilitative support and services for those on their caseloads (Cullen 2013; Goodman et al. 2017). They found ways to balance rehabilitation with public safety rather than attending to the demands of risk-based supervision alone.

From 'what works' to evidence-based practice

During the latter decades of the 20th century, community corrections witnessed the steady, but contested reinsertion of 'neo-rehabilitation' sparked by a growth in research that became known as 'what works'. Since then there has been a transition to 'Evidence-Based Practice' or more recently, to the Risk-Need-Responsivity model (Cullen 2013). Probation and parole reflect this trend in seeking to apply its strategies and tools to offender supervision (Burrell and Rhine 2013). However, the implementation of this movement's key principles and practices has been uneven across the field. Even more, its rollout remains framed by a predominant concern for sorting and managing offender risk (Burrell 2016). Offender accountability continues to be accented over offender change.

Nonetheless, evidence-based practices and the Risk-Need-Responsivity model offer an affirmative road map for facilitating offenders' pathways to the successful termination of supervision, and sustainable pro-social conduct. Through the Justice Reinvestment Initiative, a total of 33 states have enacted legislative and policy changes affecting community corrections – reforms that are aligned with the principles and actions discussed above (PEW 2016). More is needed though that speaks to the actual content and interaction that occurs during supervision.

Revisiting the content of supervision within an era of evidence-based practice

As Klingele (2016) argues, the reforms associated with evidence-based practices are not inherently benign, but inform a tenuous duality between rehabilitation efforts and the enforcement power exercised by probation and parole officers. To address this tension, it is essential that attention be devoted to the content of supervision both in its community dimension and relative to the relationships probation and parole officers form with those they supervise.

The strategies associated with evidence-based practice must, of necessity, be tailored to function within a more expansive model of supervision that is community engaged. All too often, offender supervision occurs exclusively within an office setting, thereby fostering passivity in case management. The efficacy of supervision is enhanced when probation and parole officers invest an appreciable amount of time supervising offenders in the neighbourhoods where they live. They must do so in a manner that is responsive to offenders' risk levels, criminogenic needs, and the requisites of community re-entry and reintegration (Probation Reinvention Council 2000; Solomon et al. 2008).

Such efforts must also reconfigure the nature of the interaction between probation and parole officers and those they supervise while attending to the duality of the roles they play. This requires that officers engage offenders in a firm, fair, and caring manner. The routines of supervision in real-world settings typically focus officers' attention on offender risk and the enforcement of conditions. This limits interactions that might otherwise encourage offender change. It is essential that probation and parole officers acquire a better understanding of offenders' narratives and the worlds that shape their lives. Doing so is likely to contribute to more successful supervision outcomes whether measured by fewer violations, or a reduction in criminal activity or recidivism (Lowencamp et al. 2012).

Integrating 'what works' with 'what is just'

As McNeill (2009) argues, the purpose and content of community supervision, its motivating vision, cannot centre simply on 'what works'. It must also incorporate 'what is just'. Recent scholarship suggests how this integration might be achieved. Simon (2014) discusses the consequences of mass incarceration in California that sparked litigation over the medical and mental health harms experienced by the inmate population. Finding the state's prison system unconstitutional, the US Supreme Court in a landmark ruling, Brown v. Plata (2011), declared that the animating interest of the 8th Amendment resides in ensuring the dignity of individuals in confinement.

Though this ruling pertains to imprisonment, its findings are relevant to community supervision. Recall that the expectations of supervision are experienced through the twin lenses of deprivation and punishment. One immediate implication of Brown v. Plata is that the obligation to preserve offenders' dignity arguably applies to those subject to the controlling interventions of supervision as well. Officers' interactions with supervisees invariably carry the prospect of imposing a grievous loss on their continued freedom evidenced by the vicissitudes of revocation and the ever-present threat they may be returned to prison or jail (Rhine 2012). Offenders under community supervision are vulnerable to being criminally sanctioned for a wide variety of non-criminal conduct (Doherty 2016). Whether acting in a public safety or rehabilitative capacity, probation and parole officers must take affirmative steps responsive to the dignity of supervisees.

The preceding argument brings to the fore the importance of procedural justice and individuals' perceptions of the legitimacy of their treatment under the rule of law. Tyler (2003) argues that an expressed commitment to procedural justice by criminal justice officials may impact on individual behaviour in a manner that fosters desired pro-social outcomes. In terms of supervision practice, it requires continually modelling the rule of law in tone and substance, and the display of respect by officers across the whole of their interactions with probationers and parolees.[8]

Six 'best practices' in community corrections

In the preceding section, we have provided an intellectual backdrop and foundation, tracking the most compelling scholarly currents and cross-currents that inform the contemporary correctional world. What follows considers the implications of those ideas and insights for community corrections practices.

948

We suggest there are six key 'best practices' that probation and parole agencies should adopt, informed by the literature reviewed above and directed toward the end of maximizing effective practice.

Probation and parole agencies should adopt evidence-based practice

The first practice has special status as a superordinate principle, informing and subsuming many of the others that follow. It calls for probation and parole agencies to adhere to the principles of the scientific method whenever undertaking a practice that is susceptible to data collection, testing, and statistical proof of validity.

It might be asked why community corrections has not always adhered to this principle, as it seems so obvious and commonsensical. The answer lies in the recognition that for many professions – until the revolution in practice of the last two decades – tradition, conventional wisdom, practitioner preferences and insights, and the prevailing climate of opinion dictated how most agencies approached their work. The world of research and practice occupied a parallel universe, where academicians published reports while often lamenting their lack of impact on the real world.

The situation began to change in the 1990s, as a result of many forces, chief among them the 'reinventing government' movement (Osborne and Gaebler 1993) – one that pressed public agencies to demonstrate that the results that flowed logically from their mission were actually being achieved. This new pressure on agency leaders drove them into the arms of the research community where the skills of data collection and analysis suddenly had great currency. The recognition that results would be measured had as its corollary a commitment to discovering what extant research could offer a conscientious agency head about proven practices in the community corrections domain. This context gave birth over time to the era of evidence-based practice.

The following two key principles, developed by the National Institute of Corrections, capture the essence of evidence-based practices:

> The professional judgment of criminal justice system decision makers is enhanced when informed by evidence-based knowledge.

> The criminal justice system will continually learn and improve when professionals make decisions based on the collection, analysis, and use of data and information.
>
> (National Institute of Corrections 2013)

The adoption of evidence-based practice as a governing principle in the management of community correctional agencies brings with it an obligation to provide the guidance and means for full implementation. This requires the establishment of properly staffed research departments committed to look both externally to cull from the best of what is being published and to labour internally to continually study and evaluate the impact of agency operations.

Commit to employing the least restrictive alternative measure

In recognition of the truly coercive power the state can exercise over offenders, the principle of seeking the least intrusive and onerous punishment consistent with justice has long been recognized in the jurisprudence of corrections. Its essence can be stated as follows: whenever government passes legislation that curtails a fundamental personal liberty, it must employ the least restrictive alternative measure possible to achieve its purpose. Justice Potter Stewart breathed constitutional life into this principle in his dicta in the US Supreme Court decision Shelton v. Tucker (1960): 'In a series of decisions, this Court has held that, even though the government purpose be legitimate and substantial, that purpose cannot be pursued by means that broadly stifle personal liberties when the end can be more narrowly achieved'.

What implications might this principle have for community corrections? This question may be answered against the backdrop of recent revisionist accounts of probation – analyses that are sceptical that probation is in fact the grant of leniency it has been customarily considered to be. They show that in determining which offenders must receive the full complement of obligations, what proportionate length of time should be served under what is now seen as a frequently onerous regimen, and what sanctions should be imposed for a violation of supervision conditions, the principle calling for the Least Restrictive Alternative Measure must be invoked for those subject to probation and parole.

In their accounts, Klingele (2013) and Corbett (2015) observe that the scope and intensity of probation obligations can be overwhelming and unsustainable for many individuals. An agency's adherence to this principle leads to three propositions for practice.

- Not all of those currently placed on supervision, particularly if their offence is comparatively minor, deserve the full panoply of conditions when a more limited sanction (e.g. the imposition of 50 hours of community service as the sole condition) could suffice to achieve a proportionate correctional purpose.
- The length of what is often a multi-year sentence to probation should be shortened to reduce the time of exposure to further penalties imposed on the probationer.
- The breach of one of the technical requirements of probation should almost always be met with a sanction that does not include confinement.[9]

Exercise parsimony when imposing conditions of supervision

During the annual meeting of the American Probation and Parole Association in 2017, a 'Statement on the Future of Community Corrections' was issued growing out of 'Papers from the Executive Session on Community Corrections' (Jacobson et al. 2017). Its purpose was to enunciate key principles for a reformed and revitalized community corrections. The third recommendation in the statement noted the importance of: 'Exercising parsimony in the use of supervision conditions to no more conditions than required to achieve the objectives of supervision'. The symmetry with the previously discussed least restrictive principle is apparent.

Conventional usage defines parsimony as 'economy in the use of means to an end'. It is essential to emphasize parsimony in the imposition of conditions (legally binding requirements) on probationers and parolees so they have a decent prospect of fulfilling their obligations and completing their terms successfully.

The conditions of supervision imposed often number in the double digits and exact a daily regime on offenders that constitutes 'mission impossible'. It is evident that being required to pay fees and fines (though these individuals are commonly indigent), and keep regular appointments with probation and parole officers, treatment counsellors, drug testers, community service supervisors, and AA meetings demands a feat of coordination that would challenge the most organized professional – all of which is undertaken with limited, if any, reliable transportation. The volume of individuals who are incarcerated for violating one or more of these 'technical conditions' is significant given the 'load' placed on most supervisees. They are often without the money or personal wherewithal to keep supervisees up or comply with multiple and often conflicting obligations (Corbett 2016).

We recommend staunching the growth of probation and parole obligations in favour of crafting supervision conditions limited to perhaps two–three obligations, carefully designed to focus on the most urgent needs presented by the offender (e.g. drug testing and treatment, victim restitution). The adoption of such parsimony should seek to make the successful completion of a supervision term something offenders have a realistic chance to achieve.

Incorporate procedural justice and fairness into community supervision

The work of Tyler (2003, 2013) and Meares (2013) centring on procedural justice has begun to gain great traction in the criminal justice world.[10] Across a variety of publications, their research has operationalized procedural justice to four core behaviours or actions to be displayed by criminal justice officials (Meares 2013).

- These officials give the subjects of their control (arrestees, defendants) an opportunity to be heard and explain their perspective on the incident, the charges, and more
- These officials take care to reach a fair decision, one that employs procedures that incorporate the signs and symbols of fairness (e.g. careful attention to both sides, no sign of bias toward agents of the state, no discriminatory actions)
- The officials treat the subjects of their attention with conspicuous dignity and respect
- They convey a sense of benevolence and compassionate consideration for those with whom they are dealing

Together, these behaviours embody 'procedural fairness'. And perhaps of most significance, as Meares (2013, 1865) states: 'A robust body of social science evidence from around the world shows that people are more likely to voluntarily obey the law (when subjected to procedural fairness)'.

The applicability of procedural justice to community supervision is striking. The behaviours enumerated above form (or should form) essential ingredients of effective probation and parole work to be incorporated into routine practice. Suggestive research on the qualities and behaviours of an effective probation officer relative to the elements of procedural justice notes that:

> When an officer is considerate, listens to an offender, and provides him or her with an opportunity to take part in on-going decisions, the offender may feel responsible to follow the law and help the officer to do their job.
> (Kennealy et al. 2012)

These findings provide guidance showing how probation and parole officers may facilitate pro-social behaviour and enhanced compliance with supervision expectations. The results suggest new boundaries for the conduct of one-on-one supervision.

Promote supervision compliance through the application of incentives

The community corrections system has long relied almost exclusively on the use of negative reinforcements – penalties up to and including revocation and incarceration – to promote compliance with the requirements of supervision. Though probationers and parolees are alert to the peril they face should they fall out of compliance with their obligations, it is far more prudent to offer incentives for cooperation. Research shows that positive reinforcement is a far more effective tool in shaping behaviour.

A comprehensive summary, supported by research for over 50 years, argues that when faced with making changes in behaviour, 'human beings appear to respond better and maintain learned behaviors for longer periods of time when approached with carrots rather than sticks' (Crime and Justice Institute 2004: 6). This research also recommends a ratio of four positive to every one negative reinforcement to optimize behavioural change. Instituting this sort of ratio and regime will require profound change in the practices of most community corrections agencies.

Despite the difficulties, the importance of adopting this reform is bolstered by a recent study focusing on community corrections validating the use of positive reinforcements. A review of an intensive supervision programme (ISP) for a population of 283 probationers and parolees in Wyoming found that supervision practices that utilized both rewards and sanctions led to higher success rates (as measured by successful completion of ISP) then when sanctions were used alone. Moreover, the best results were obtained when rewards were used in proportionally higher numbers than sanctions (Wodahl et al. 2011).

How might rewards be introduced into systems not currently employing them? The simplest approach is to offer a reduction of time served under supervision (perhaps a 25% reduction) for compliant, crime-free behaviour. Other incentives might include waived fee payments, reduced community service hours, or a decrease in reporting requirements. Consistent with the requisites of procedural justice, the supportive, encouraging message that is communicated given positive feedback for constructive behaviour changes the tenor of officers' relationships with supervisees providing greater pro-social dividends.

Seek to minimize financial sanctions

Few policies or practices in sentencing do more violence to logic, equity, or basic ideas of fairness and justice than the routine imposition of financial penalties on indigent probationers and parolees. Those living in poverty must either face the prospect of incarceration for failure to pay or as often happens, find counterproductive means for obtaining the needed funds (e.g. deferring basic needs like prescription costs, or resorting to illegal means to secure money). As Harris (2016) found in Washington State, most offenders have little money – some have none.

Demanding that these individuals produce monthly what amounts to 'user fees' for the right to be on probation or parole undercuts the very purpose of community supervision: getting offenders back on their feet by focusing on issues such as drug treatment, further education, and job training. The reality is that none of these reintegrative measures can be consistently pursued if probationers and parolees must undertake a daily search for a few dollars to apply toward their financial obligations.

As a solution, financial sanctions should be 'means-tested', and any fines and fees imposed should be based on offenders' ability to pay determined by a

953

sliding as opposed to a fixed scale. Fees that are fixed constitute a blatant case of a regressive tax. Were such a system instituted, a decent measure of fairness and equity would be introduced. We recognize that government coffers would suffer but accomplishing the ends of justice would be the winner.

Conclusion: prospects for reform in an era of implosive equilibrium

The principles and practices for reconstructing community supervision discussed above have the potential to exert a meaningful impact as the US enters an era of 'implosive equilibrium' (Tonry 2013). The present era is one of progressive, reform-oriented work, especially at the state level, aimed at addressing the consequences produced by unprecedented harshness and punitivity. Yet it is also one that remains governed by the vast infrastructure embedded within the laws, policies, discourses, and practices tied to mass penal control. There exists a tangible fragility to the changes that have been accomplished to date (Enns 2016). It is our belief that the prescriptions for practice proposed herein offer a durable road map for navigating through this era in a manner that improves the effectiveness, fairness, and justice accorded those subject to probation and parole supervision.

Notes

1 There is a widespread academic consensus that '[the] growth of the US carceral state is without comparison. The United States now incarcerates a greater proportion of its population than any other country in the world' (Enns 2016: 5, citing Walmsley 2009).

2 Comparatively, the average rates of probation and parole supervision dwarf those of Europe. In 2013 the rate of US probation supervision exceeded that of Europe fivefold, with 1,605 on probation compared to 297 per 100,000 adults. For parole, the overall rates were more modest, but they still showed that the US rate at 350 was four times that of the European rate at 77, again per 100,000 adults (Corda and Phelps 2017).

3 Both Reitz (2018) and Garland (2017) argue that a full understanding of this phenomenon requires that it be connected in a causal manner to the prominence of crime levels, violence, and social problems in the United States.

4 While probation remains the most common criminal disposition of choice, despite its population dipping modestly for nearly a decade, parole or post-release supervision has shown steady, incremental growth since the turn of the century. At year end 2015, and accounting for jail and prison populations, the figures show nearly 70% of the correctional population is under community supervision (Kaeble and Glaze 2016).

5 The author's use of this term draws on a classic book in the sociology of prisons by Sykes (1958), which includes a chapter on the 'pains of imprisonment'.

6 Durnescu (2011) suggests that the 'pains of probation' have applicability to other countries citing studies showing the similarity of experiences of those under community supervision. With respect to parolees, coping with the expectations of supervision is compounded by the immediacy of meeting the habilitation requisites necessary for a successful re-entry transition (Leverentz 2014; Mears and Cochran 2015).

7　In an extension of his earlier fieldwork, Werth (2013) illustrates how a punitive ideology governs supervision grounded in an aggressive approach to surveillance, and the sanctioning of parolee misconduct.

8　Recent research suggests there may be a benefit in considering offenders' perceptions of legitimacy during justice system involvement and consequent rehabilitative interventions as a criminogenic need. The translation of procedural justice may itself be viewed as a central component of the responsivity principle (Kempany and Kaiser 2016).

9　The discussion of this principle and its propositions is also applicable to parole supervision.

10　Tyler, a sociologist, first undertook his work examining judicial and police officer behaviour to discover what fostered compliance with the instructions and orders of those two criminal justice officials.

References

Alper, Marie, Corda, Alessandro and Reitz, Kevin R. (2016) *American Exceptionalism in Probation Supervision*. Minneapolis: Robina Institute of Criminal Law and Criminal Justice, University of Minnesota Law School.

Burrell, William D. (2010) Probation in the U.S. *Transnational Criminology*, 3, 721–739.

Burrell, William D. (2016) Risk and need assessment in probation and parole: The persistent gap between promise and practice. In Faye S. Taxman (Ed.), *Handbook on Risk and Need Assessment: Theory and Practice*. London: Routledge.

Burrell, William D. and Rhine, Edward E. (2013) Implementing evidence-based practice in community corrections: A review essay. *Justice Research and Policy*, 15(1), 143–157.

Corbett, Ronald P. Jr. (2015) The burdens of leniency: The changing face of probation. *Minnesota Law Review*, 99(5), 1697–1732.

Corbett, Ronald P. Jr. (2016) Probation and mass incarceration: The ironies of correctional practice. *Federal Sentencing Reporter*, 28(4), 278–282.

Corda, Alessandro, Alper, Marie and Reitz, Kevin. (2016) *American Exceptionalism in Parole Supervision*. Minneapolis: Robina Institute of Criminal Law and Criminal Justice, University of Minnesota Law School.

Corda, Alessandro and Phelps, Michelle. (2017) American exceptionalism in community supervision. In *Perspectives*. Lexington, KY: American Probation and Parole Association, Spring.

Crime and Justice Institute. (2004) *Implementing Evidence-Based Practice in Community Corrections*. Washington, DC: National Institute of Corrections, US Department of Justice.

Cullen, Francis T. (2013) Rehabilitation: Beyond nothing works. In Michael Tonry (Ed.), *Crime and Justice: A Review of Research*, 42, 299–376.

Doherty, Fiona. (2016) Obey all laws and be good: Probation and the meaning of recidivism. *Georgetown Law Review*, 104(2), 291–354.

Durnescu, Ioan. (2011) Pains of probation: Effective practice and human rights. *International Journal of Offender Therapy and Comparative Criminology*, 55(4), 530–545.

Feeley, Malcom and Simon, Jonathon. (1992) The new penology: Notes on the emerging strategy of corrections and its implications. *Criminology*, 30(4), 449–474.

Fitzgibbon, Wendy, Graebsch, Christine and McNeill, Fergus. (2016) Pervasive punishment: Experiencing supervision. In Michelle Brown and Eamonn Carrabine (Eds.), *Handbook of Visual Criminology*. London: Routledge.

Enns, Peter. (2016) *Incarceration Nation: How the United States Became the Most Punitive Democracy in the World*. Cambridge: Cambridge University Press.

Garland, David. (2017) Penal power in America: Forms, functions and foundations. *Journal of the British Academy*, 5, 1–35.

Goodman, Philip, Page, Joshua and Phelps, Michelle. (2017) *Breaking the Pendulum: The Long Struggle Over Criminal Justice*. New York: Oxford University Press.

Gottschalk, Marie. (2015) *Caught: The Prison State and the Lockdown of American Politics*. Princeton, NJ: Princeton University Press.

Harris, Alexis. (2016) *A Pound of Flesh: Monetary Sanctions as Punishment for the Poor*. New York: Russell Sage Foundation.

Jacobson, Michael P., Schiraldi, Vincent, Daly, Reagan and Hotez, Emily. (2017) *Less Is More: How Reducing Probation Populations Can Improve Outcomes*. Cambridge, MA: Program in Criminal Justice Policy and Management, Harvard Kennedy School.

Kaeble, Danielle and Glaze, Lauren. (2016) Correctional populations in the United States, 2015. In *Bureau of Justice Statistics*. Washington, DC: US Department of Justice.

Kempany, Katherine Ginsburg and Kaiser, Kimberly A. (2016) Incorporating procedural justice and legitimacy into the RNR model to improve Risk-Need Assessment. In Faye S. Taxman (Ed.), *Handbook on Risk and Need Assessment: Theory and Practice*. London: Routledge.

Kennealy, Patrick J., Skeem, Jennifer L., Manchak, Sarah M. and Louden, Jennifer E. (2012) Firm, fair and caring officer-offender relationships protect against supervision failure. *Law and Human Behavior*, 36(6), 496–505.

Klingele, Cecelia. (2013) Rethinking the use of community supervision. *Journal of Criminal Law and Criminology*, 103(4), 1015–1070.

Klingele, Cecelia. (2016) The promises and perils of evidence-based corrections. *Notre Dame Law Review*, 91(2), 537–584.

Leverentz, Andrea M. (2014) *The Ex-Prisoner's Dilemma: How Women Negotiate Competing Narratives of Reentry and Desistance*. New Brunswick: Rutgers University Press.

Lowencamp, Christopher T., Alexander, M. Holsinger, Robinson, Charles, and Cullen, Francis T. (2012) When a person isn't a data point: Making evidence-based practice work. *Federal Probation*, 76(3), 11–21.

McNeill, Fergus. (2009) What works and what's just. *European Journal of Probation*, 1(1), 21–40.

Meares, Tracey L. (2013) The good cop: Knowing the difference between lawful or effective policing and rightful policing: And why it matters. *William and Mary Law Review*, 54(6), 1865–1886.

Mears, Daniel P. and Cochran, Joshua C. (2015) *Prisoner Reentry in the Era of Mass Incarceration*. Washington, DC: Sage Publications.

National Institute of Corrections. (2013) *Evidence-Based Decision Making: From Principle to Practice*. Washington, DC: US Department of Justice.

Osborne, David and Gaebler, Ted. (1993) *Reinventing Government: How the Entrepreneurial Spirit Is Transforming the Public Sector*. New York: Plume.

PEW Charitable Foundation. (2016) *33 States Take on Criminal Justice Reform Through Justice Reinvestment*.

Phelps, Michelle and Curry, Caitlin. (2017) Supervision in the community: Probation and parole. In *Oxford Research Encyclopedia of Criminology*. Online Publication Date, April.

Probation Reinvention Council. (2000) *Transforming Probation Through Leadership: The "Broken Windows" Model*. New York: Center for Civic Innovation, Manhattan Institute.

Reitz, Kevin R. (Ed.). (2018) *American Exceptionalism in Crime and Punishment*. New York: Oxford University Press.

Rhine, Edward E. (2012) The present status and future prospects of parole boards and parole supervision. In Joan Petersilia and Kevin R. Reitz (Eds.), *The Oxford Handbook of Sentencing and Corrections*. New York: Oxford University Press.

Rhine, Edward E. and Taxman, Faye S. (2018) American exceptionalism in community supervision: A comparative analysis of probation in the United States, Scotland, and

Sweden. In Kevin R. Reitz (Ed.), *American Exceptionalism in Crime and Punishment*. New York: Oxford University Press.

Ruhland, Ebony, Rhine, Edward E., Robey, Jason P. and Mitchell, Kelly Lyn. (2016) *The Continuing Leverage of Releasing Authorities: Findings from a National Survey*. Minneapolis: The Robina Institute of Criminal Law and Criminal Justice, University of Minnesota Law School.

Simon, Jonathan. (2014) *Mass Incarceration on Trial: A Remarkable Court Decision and the Future of Prisons in America*. New York: The New Press.

Solomon, Amy L., Winterfield, Jenny W. L., Elderbroom, Brian, Burke, Peggy, Stroker, Richard P., Rhine, Edward E. and Burrell, William D. (2008) *Putting Public Safety First: 13 Parole Supervision Strategies to Enhance Reentry Outcomes*. Washington, DC: The Urban Institute.

Sykes, Gresham. (1958) *Society of Captives: A Study of a Maximum Security Prison*. Princeton, NJ: Princeton University Press.

Taxman, Faye S. (2012) Probation, intermediate sanctions, and community-based corrections. In Joan Petersilia and Kevin R. Reitz (Ed.), *The Oxford Handbook of Sentencing and Corrections*. New York: Oxford University Press.

Tonry, Michael. (2013) *Sentencing in America, 1975–2025*. Legal Studies Research Paper Series, Research Paper No. 13–44, 1–58. Minneapolis: University of Minnesota Law School.

Travis, Jeremy, Western, Bruce and Redburn, Steve. (Eds.). (2014) *The Growth of Incarceration in the United States: Exploring Causes and Consequences*. Washington, DC: National Academy Report.

Tyler, Tom R. (2003) Procedural justice, legitimacy, and the effective rule of law. In Michael Tonry (Ed.), *Crime and Justice*, 30, 283–357.

Tyler, Tom R. (2013) *Why People Obey the Law*. Princeton, NJ: Princeton University Press.

Van Zyl Smit, Dirk and Corda, Alessandro. (2018) American exceptionalism in parole release and supervision. In Kevin R. Reitz (Ed.), *American Exceptionalism in Crime and Punishment*. New York: Oxford University Press.

Walmsley, Roy. (2009) *World Prison Population List*, 8th edition. Ann Arbor: University of Michigan Press.

Werth, R. (2011) I do what I'm told sort of: Reformed subjects, unruly citizens, and parole. *Theoretical Criminology*, 16(3), 329–346.

Werth, R. (2013) The construction and stewardship of responsible yet precarious subjects: Punitive ideology, rehabilitation, and "tough love" among parole personnel. *Punishment & Society*, 15(3), 219–246.

Wodahl, Eric, Garland, Brett and Culhane, Scott E. (2011) Utilizing behavioral interventions to improve supervision outcomes in the community. *Criminal Justice and Behavior*, 38(4), 386–405.

Cases cited

Brown v. Plata 131 S.Ct. 1910 (2011).
Shelton v. Tucker 364 U.S. 479 1960.

78

How practitioners conceptualize quality

A UK perspective

Gwen Robinson

Introduction

'Quality' is a contested concept. In other words, it is a subjective attribute which may be understood differently by different people. This is the case regardless of context, and it certainly applies in respect of direct work with offenders. What 'counts' as quality is likely to differ across time and place and between people with different roles within and without the organizations which are responsible for delivering offender supervision. This subjectivity may be one reason why there has been so little research that has directly addressed the issue of quality in offender supervision. A review of the international literature on quality in probation settings by Shapland et al. (2012) confirmed that researchers had only very rarely addressed this topic, although the concept could be regarded as implicit to understandings of 'effectiveness', 'best practice', and 'values', which have interested researchers for decades.

Shapland et al. (2012) found that, to the extent that researchers had examined quality explicitly, this had mostly been in relation to discrete aspects or artefacts of practice, such as the quality of programme delivery (e.g. Goggin and Gendreau 2006) or of pre-sentence reports (e.g. Raynor et al. 1995) rather than 'ordinary', face-to-face supervision (though for a recent exception, see Raynor et al. 2014). In these specific contexts, quality had been understood in relation to criteria decided by researchers and then applied through the observation or auditing of practice. Other 'top-down' constructions of quality can be found in many jurisdictions in the form of practice standards and/or performance indicators decided by managers, inspectors, or other regulatory bodies. However, constructions of quality such as these have been criticized as attempts to control (rather than enhance the quality of) practice (e.g. Oldfield 1994), and/or because they have tended to pay more attention to quantitative 'inputs' than to qualitative (and less easy-to-measure) aspects of practice that might connect more intuitively with ideas of quality among practitioners (e.g. Davies and Gregory 2010). Therefore, it should not be assumed that official constructions of quality in offender supervision will, in any jurisdiction, correspond with how those responsible for delivering supervision understand or think about quality in relation to their own or others' practice. Yet it is the latter (i.e. how practitioners understand quality) which is potentially of critical importance in shaping day-to-day offender supervision.

An English study

With this in mind, a team of UK-based researchers sought to design a study that would shed much needed light on the neglected topic of how probation practitioners understood quality in the context of 'ordinary', one-to-one supervision of offenders subject to statutory supervision in the community. The study, which was commissioned by the National Offender Management Service in 2010, was conducted with practitioners in three of the 35 locally based Probation Trusts which at that time constituted the probation service in England and Wales. A total of 116 participants took part in an individual or focus group interview. The majority were current practitioners who had different types and lengths of experience of offender supervision, but the research included a small number of middle managers, administrators, and reception staff.

The research adopted an innovative approach which drew upon the methodology of *appreciative inquiry* (AI) which had previously been used to good effect by researchers interested in understanding the quality of prison life (Liebling 2004). Best known for its applications in organizational settings, AI has been described as 'a focus on best experiences . . . a way of looking at an organization, which concentrates on strengths, accomplishments, best practices, and peak moments' (Liebling 2004: 132–133). In this vein, the research team sought to explore participants' views about quality by asking them to talk about concrete examples of practice – both from their own experience and within their team or Trust (see Robinson et al. 2013). For example, in the individual interviews, participants were asked to describe in detail a 'peak moment' in their probation career, during which they had felt particularly positive about their practice. They were also asked to identify and describe a specific case or piece of work which they felt was illustrative of their best quality practice. The research also incorporated a multiple choice exercise, in which participants were given a list of 19 items drawn up by the research team to sort and rank in accordance with their views about quality. The qualitative data (from the interviews) and the quantitative data (from the multiple choice exercise) were analyzed together to build a picture of practitioners' perspectives on quality.

A key finding of the research was that there was a considerable degree of consensus about the 'ingredients' of quality probation practice among the sample. For the interviewees in the study, quality probation practice could be distilled into six dimensions or aspects, all of which were considered to be relevant to work with a variable population of offenders and in the context of different types and lengths of supervision. In this jurisdiction, then, it was found that there was a 'front-line perspective' on quality that was largely shared, albeit that it had rarely (if ever) been articulated or exposed before (for a detailed account of the findings, see Robinson et al. 2014).

Six key themes

Firstly, staff in all roles saw *good working relationships* as vital to good quality work. Of particular importance to those we interviewed were their relationships with offenders, which were emphasized as the backbone or foundation of good quality supervision. As one participant put it, 'The relationship is the fundamental thing. The better the relationship you have with a person, the more successful the outcome; it makes it easier for people to comply' (PO3, Trust 1). Reinforcing the perception of the one-to-one relationship as a crucial element of quality work, the results of the multiple choice exercise revealed that two items explicitly concerned with the one-to-one relationship ('Really engaging with the individual' and 'A relationship based on mutual trust/respect') were among the five most popular choices of participants when they were asked to select items which, for them, were the most important to quality work.

In their descriptions of engaging and establishing good working relationships with offenders, participants emphasized a variety of factors that they considered important, such as: building rapport, treating the offender respectfully, listening, being open and honest, following up on promised actions, taking time to get to know the person, being consistent, involving the offender in setting goals, establishing boundaries, and building trust. To a large degree, participants understood good relationships in very similar ways – albeit that some explicitly acknowledged that their own 'good' relationships with offenders were not necessarily all identical. As one practitioner put it, 'It's difficult to [define] what a good relationship is because that will vary from case to case. In some cases you will take a different stance to another' (PO46, Trust 3). So the 'particulars' of 'good' relationships could vary, according to characteristics of the particular offender (who might pose higher or lower levels of risk, be male or female, older or younger, more or less motivated, more or less vulnerable, etc.). For example, many of our participants described to us good working relationships which clearly featured commitment to and care for the offender in question, whilst others (a minority) described good working relationships that involved working with people who had committed very serious violent or sexual offences which rendered them hard to empathize with.

It was not however only in their direct work with offenders that participants saw the value of relationships to quality work. Also of significance were relationships with other agencies involved in supporting offenders on their caseload or with which probation staff might otherwise need to liaise in the broader context of their work. As one participant succinctly put it, 'You need to network as a probation officer' (PO27, Trust 2). Several of our interviews included examples of very positive work alongside other professionals, and several emphasized the importance of inter-professional relationship-building skills. Good relationships and communication with other agencies were also frequently cited by participants as examples of 'best practices' in the Trusts in which they worked.

The second theme was *resources*. Like relationships, resources were mentioned very frequently indeed as key to the production of good quality practice. Chief among participants' priorities was time, and in particular having enough time for the following activities: getting to know and working with the offender face to face, preparing for and planning supervision meetings, and reflecting on and discussing casework with colleagues and supervisors. In our multiple choice exercise, 'Having enough time to work with individuals' was ranked third in importance by our participants, and comments such as the following were common: 'I think I could make more of a difference if I had more time' (PO12, Trust 1). Although some participants questioned the need for 'more' time (as opposed to the more productive use of the available time) to do 'quality work', when describing examples of their best practice, interviewees often talked about 'making time' or 'going the extra mile' for an individual, which sometimes meant having to work extra hours to get other things done.

Time was not the only resource considered important to the production of quality work: participants also mentioned the need for resources for staff training, and many talked about the importance of access to the resources of specialist colleagues and other agencies relevant to the needs of the offenders on their caseload. When we asked participants (in the context of both individual and focus group interviews) to provide examples of what they considered to be 'best practices' in their Trust, training provision and local resources (provided in-house or by partnership agencies) were frequently cited. These included resources relevant to accommodation, employment, and female offenders in particular. Several participants commented that 'We don't work in an isolated fashion and quite rightly so. I tap into whatever's available that's pertinent to this person' (PO5, Trust 1). Others emphasized the importance of liaison and referrals to other agencies with specialist skills or resources (e.g. in relation to helping offenders find employment or tackle their drug use). However, it was acknowledged that such resources were not always available and, for some, this was mentioned as a key barrier to delivering quality work.

The third theme was *individualization and flexibility*. For those participants whose work involved most direct contact with offenders (reception staff as well as practitioners), these notions meant expecting the unexpected and being able to respond calmly and effectively to people presenting a variety of emotional states, practical problems, and sometimes crises. For practitioners it also meant knowing what was appropriate and realistic in relation to the individual offender, and his or her risks, needs, and circumstances – all of which were prone to change over time. In the multiple choice exercise, the item 'Responding to the individual's changing needs/situation' was ranked fourth in importance by participants. Quality work was also seen to require, for participants of all grades, having access to relevant and up-to-date knowledge and information, both about the individual (risks, needs, strengths, social circumstances, families, etc.) and about local resources available to deal with those needs.

Notions of individualization and flexibility also involved some discussion of the use of professional discretion and, as a corollary of that, issues around prescription in the context of probation practice. Thus, several of the cases chosen by practitioners to illustrate their best quality work included their use of discretion in deciding how to work with an individual; and, conversely, participants consistently told us that compliance with what they regarded as inflexible practice standards (in force at that time) was not, for them, linked with quality. Indeed, in the multiple choice exercise, 'Complying with national standards' was the item which was most often regarded as irrelevant to quality in probation practice.

One of the issues which the research team sought to explore was the extent to which probation staff associated quality work with 'processes' and/or 'outcomes'. Care was taken in designing the research to ensure that there were ample opportunities for participants to express views about both, and they did so. It was found that both processes and outcomes were important for most practitioner grade staff, and that they were seen as very much connected parts of quality supervision. In other words, good quality outcomes were unlikely to be achieved in the absence of good quality processes, and without the foundation of a good working relationship. Reflecting this consensus, the fourth theme was the *goals and outcomes* of supervision. The perceived importance of goals and outcomes among participants was best illustrated in the multiple choice exercise, in which 'reducing risk', 'seeing progress', and 'having a good sentence plan' were among the nine most popular choices. The first of these, in particular, was frequently mentioned. For example, 'If you're not reducing risk, you're not doing your job properly' (PO42, Trust

3); 'That's very important, whether it's the risk of reoffending or the risk of harm' (PO6, Trust 1). It was however acknowledged that risk reduction was not always as realistic as risk management, or harm minimization, particularly among those working with very high-risk individuals. In a similar vein, comments were also made, not infrequently, about how 'seeing progress' or 'producing a good outcome' could sometimes mean very small steps toward change which were nonetheless significant in the context of working with a particular individual.

The fifth theme was the *attributes, skills, and values which staff bring to their work*. In the individual interviews, participants were asked to talk about what they felt they brought or contributed to their own 'best quality' work. Although training and/or skills were mentioned, participants placed much more emphasis on the values, personal qualities, and experiences which they brought to their work and which often also accounted for their desire to join the probation service. So for example participants talked about the role of life experience and maturity, aspects of their own backgrounds and biographies which they felt enabled them to relate to offenders, personal qualities (e.g. having energy and enthusiasm, having a positive outlook, commitment), and values (e.g. believing in people's ability to change, seeing the individual as a whole person and not just an offender). As one practitioner explained:

> The sort of people that do this work are, the majority are positive people, and if you didn't believe that people had the ability to change and for things to be better you wouldn't be able to do this job.
>
> (PO, Focus Group, Trust 3)

Participants tended to describe themselves as 'the right kind of people' for the job, and quality work was seen by staff as something delivered by people with the right values, virtues, qualities, and experiences, rather than something delivered by a highly trained and technically proficient workforce with specific techniques at their disposal. Indeed, when discussing quality work, very little emphasis was given to specific techniques, interventions, or ways of working, although some participants mentioned things like 'doing motivational work' and 'acting pro-socially', and a very small minority referred to specific approaches that they had been trained to deliver and tried to use as much as possible (e.g. neuro-linguistic programming; transactional analysis). Whether this consensus was an indication of a deficit of appropriate training for one-to-one work and, perhaps, feelings around 'deskilling' among staff, was unclear, although some of our participants hinted that this might be the case. For example, one manager (senior probation officer) told us:

> There's a lot of training in probation, about what I call 'Thou shalt', [which is] about procedures and processes. There's less about different ways of [doing] face-to-face work with offenders.
>
> (SPO3, Trust 1)

The sixth and final theme was *support*. Participants consistently noted that quality work did not happen without support of various kinds. In the words of one participant, 'You can't operate in isolation as a probation officer' (PO9, Trust 1). Sources of support that were valued varied, and included colleagues in formal and informal support roles. For example, among practitioners, other practitioner colleagues were valued for their knowledge and advice, for cover during holidays and absences, but also for friendship and 'camaraderie'. Knowledgeable and efficient administrators were also mentioned by practitioners as key to their best quality work. Good support from managers tended to mean having a manager who was approachable, knowledgeable, and made time for 'traditional' supervision, which meant enabling practitioners to discuss their cases, their progress, and any difficulties encountered. However, such support was perceived to be in short supply, and managers were often described as spending too much time focusing on 'things that had gone wrong', or targets that had not been met, at the expense of potentially useful discussions about casework.

The other main source of support which participants mentioned came from other agencies. This included statutory and non-statutory organizations, both within and beyond the criminal justice sector. The support of other agencies was most commonly mentioned in teams where more complex or high-risk cases were the norm. In many instances practitioners chose 'best cases' which involved close liaison with the police, social services, and drug and alcohol or other services. Participants sometimes commented that they felt, as probation practitioners, that they often had to be the driving force or lynchpin in ensuring that people were sharing information and that the offender's needs and risks were being effectively managed. Overall there was quite significant enthusiasm for the idea of co-located services, or 'one-stop shops' for offenders.

Comparing perspectives on quality across jurisdictions

As noted above, the English study was the first to explicitly investigate practitioners' views about quality in the context of one-to-one offender supervision, but it was quickly adapted to explore the views of criminal justice social workers in Scotland (Grant and McNeill 2015). The Scottish study was smaller in scale, and entailed focus group interviews with 25 practitioners in one local authority area. The focus groups adopted a similar approach to those in the English study, including the use of the multiple choice exercise (with some minor adaptations to reflect local terminology). When the researchers compared their findings with those from the English study, they found a very high degree of similarity in the perspectives of the two groups of participants – despite some important differences between them in terms of professional training, organizational, and policy contexts (see Grant and McNeill 2014).

For example, in the multiple choice exercise there was a perfect correspondence between the two samples in their selection and rank ordering of the five most important items (from the choice of 19). These were: 'Really engaging with the individual', 'Reducing risk', 'Having enough time to work with individuals', 'Responding to the individual's changing needs/situation', and 'A relationship based on mutual trust/respect'. Four of these items indicated that both English and Scottish practitioners viewed relational processes as being strongly associated with quality, with offender engagement seen as the most significant item in both jurisdictions. Further evidence that practitioners in both jurisdictions had similar conceptions of quality came from the focus groups, from which the researchers distilled seven themes, which converged substantially with the six English themes (reviewed above). Indeed, very little divergence was noted:

> in both sites, practitioners gave little weight to quality as related to what they are expected or instructed to do by their agencies (as per national guidelines and standards). . . . Given the consensus in findings across the two jurisdictions, we might conclude that both English and Scottish practitioners operate with degrees of resistance to managerial pressure to perform, and political or cultural pressure to submit to populist punitiveness. Both groups of practitioners displayed a certain weary resilience that appeared to help them cope with seemingly endless reforms, policy shifts and increasing managerialism. According to these practitioners, quality is not located in or helped by setting targets for performance; quality is not the object and subject of production in the supervisory process; rather, quality resides in an approach that embodies a combination of values and principles that lean towards notions of humanity and social justice.
>
> (Grant and McNeill 2014: 163)

The Scottish researchers concluded their comparative analysis by suggesting that further replications of the research in other jurisdictions could be extremely interesting, and could test a working hypothesis that constructions of quality between practitioners working face to face with offenders may transcend the structural and organizational differences between them.

Conclusion

How those involved in the delivery of offender supervision understand 'quality' in the context of their everyday practice is an important issue. Firstly, it is of theoretical importance because it tells us a great deal about the contemporary culture or 'habitus' of practice in any given jurisdiction. In other words, *quality discourse* can serve as a sort of cultural barometer, capable of revealing commonly held assumptions (and, potentially, differences of opinion) about what matters to the practitioner community. But practitioner perspectives on quality are also of practical significance, particularly for those who wish to change or improve practice. Constructions of quality are normative in the sense that they represent an 'ideal' of practice: that is, a vision or template of what practice ought to look like. Attempts to change practice, then, are likely to fail unless they engage with these existing 'ideals', and succeed in either challenging them or persuading practitioners that new ways of working are consistent with their current understandings of what quality work is.

References

Davies, K. and Gregory, M. (2010) The price of targets: Audit and evaluation in probation practice. *Probation Journal*, 57(4), 400–414.

Goggin, C. and Gendreau, P. (2006) The implementation and maintenance of quality services in offender rehabilitation programmes. In C. Hollin and E. Palmer (Eds.), *Offending Behaviour Programmes*. Chichester: Wiley.

Grant, S. and McNeill, F. (2014) The quality of probation supervision: Comparing practitioner accounts in England and Scotland. *European Journal of Probation*, 6(2), 147–168.

Grant, S. and McNeill, F. (2015) What matters in practice? Understanding 'Quality' in the routine supervision of offenders in Scotland. *British Journal of Social Work*, 7(1), 1985–2002.

Liebling, A. (2004) *Prisons and Their Moral Performance: A Study of Values, Quality and Prison Life*. Oxford: Clarendon Press.

Oldfield, M. (1994) Talking quality, meaning control: McDonalds, the market and the probation service. *Probation Journal*, 41(4), 186–192.

Raynor, P., Gelsthorpe, L. and Tisi, A. (1995) Quality assurance, pre-sentence reports and the probation service. *British Journal of Social Work*, 25, 477–488.

Raynor, P., Ugwudike, P. and Vanstone, M. (2014) The impact of skills in probation work: A reconviction study. *Criminology and Criminal Justice*, 14(2), 235–249.

Robinson, G., Priede, C., Farrall, S., Shapland, J. and McNeill, F. (2013) Doing "strengths-based" research: Appreciative inquiry in a probation setting. *Criminology and Criminal Justice*, 13(1), 3–20.

Robinson, G., Priede, C., Farrall, S., Shapland, J. and McNeill, F. (2014) Understanding "quality" in probation practice: Frontline perspectives in England & Wales. *Criminology and Criminal Justice*, 14(2), 123–142.

Shapland, J., Bottoms, A., Farrall, S., McNeill, F., Priede, C. and Robinson, G. (2012) *The Quality of Probation Supervision – A Literature Review: Summary of Key Messages*. Research Summary 2/12. London: Ministry of Justice. Available at: www.justice.gov.uk/downloads/publications/research-and-analysis/moj-research/quality-of-probation-supervision.pdf.

The balancing act of probation supervision

79

The roles and philosophies of probation officers in the evidence-based practice era

Jill Viglione, Christina Burton, and Sherah L. Basham

Introduction

Probation, a form of community corrections used as an alternative to prison (Petersilia 1998), is the most commonly used punishment in the United States (Globokar and Toro 2017). In 2015, approximately 3.8 million adults were under probation supervision in the United States (Kaeble and Bonczar 2017). In 2016, there were over 91,000 probation officers (POs) in the United States (US Department of Labor, Bureau of Labor Statistics 2018). A small body of research focuses on POs to better understand their attitudes toward their work and the probationers they supervise (e.g. Clear and Latessa 1993; Klockars 1972; Ohlin et al. 1956; Paparozzi and Gendreau 2005). This research finds POs vary in terms of which aspects of the job they emphasize, influencing their role orientation, or the 'working philosophy of the probation officer' (Klockars 1972: 550). The role a PO enacts is often used as a justification for behaviours and decisions (Rudes et al. 2011; Taxman 2002) and can influence probationer outcomes and success (Paparozzi and Gendreau 2005; Skeem and Manchak 2008; Taxman 2002, 2008).

Additional research suggests the important relationship that may exist between PO roles and their acceptance of and use of evidence-based practices (EBPs) (Fulton et al. 1997; Rudes et al. 2011; Taxman et al. 2004). In this chapter, we present a brief history of probation followed by a discussion of the traditional PO roles discussed in the literature. Next, we present the contemporary research on PO roles and their relationship to EBP implementation. We then present a case study examining PO perceptions of their role orientation within an agency that had been implementing best practices for over eight years. Lastly, we offer some discussion about the implications EBPs' use in probation work has for the development and modification of PO roles.

History of probation

The practice of probation in the United States can be traced back to John Augustus in 1841. Augustus, a Boston shoemaker, requested a deferred sentence for an individual charged with being a common drunk. With the judge's approval, Augustus took the man into his custody in the hopes of saving his soul from his own 'passions' (Augustus 1852/1972; Dressler 1962). This probationary period provided time for the accused to alter his ways and at the end of the deferred sentence, Augustus was able to convince the judge of his reform, resulting in a fine rather than a jail sentence (Dressler 1962; Petersilia 1997). Augustus continued working with individuals charged with alcohol offences in an effort to rehabilitate them mostly through supervision and pledges of abstinence from alcohol (Lindner 2007). This early practice of deferred sentencing to supervise individuals in the community with the goal of reform laid the groundwork for what eventually became the practice of probation (Vanstone 2004).

Following the model set forth by Augustus, probation services in the United States were first established at the state level for juveniles in 1878 in Massachusetts and in 1901 for adults in New York (Petersilia 1997). Despite numerous attempts to institute probation at the federal level, it was not until 1925 that the Federal Probation Act authorized the federal probation system (Globokar and Toro 2017). And, even with early acceptance at the state level, juvenile and adult probation was not established in all states until 1956 (Petersilia 1997). Even though the system of probation was created from a desire to support reform, the conflicting goals of punishment and rehabilitation plagued probation work from the start (McAnany et al. 1984). While early 'probation officers' were volunteers desiring to aid diverted offenders from prison in the hopes of reforming their soul, they eventually turned into paid positions due to increasing caseload sizes (Dressler 1962). Paid POs were commonly recruited from the law enforcement field and worked directly for judges, eventually becoming known as the 'eyes and ears of local court' (Rothman 1980: 244), contributing to goal conflict. These early clashes between the goals of punishment and rehabilitation resulted in unclear goals and missions of probation work from its inception (McAnany et al. 1984).

The underlying goals and philosophies supporting probation work influence the behaviour of POs and how they supervise probationers. While punitive philosophies focus on surveillance and control of probationers, rehabilitative ideologies involve treatment and provision of social services aimed at easing the transition back into general society (Clear and Latessa 1993; Klockars 1972). How probation officers achieve compliance with their clients can vary between stringent use of rules and regulations (law enforcement strategy) and individualized treatment (rehabilitative strategy) (Ricks and Eno Louden 2015). The 'tough on crime' criminal justice policies during the 1970s and 1980s encouraged an increased focus on control and public safety over support services, an effect POs have experienced with increased interest in drug testing, documentation of violations (Gordon 1991), electronic monitoring, and intensive supervision probation/parole (ISP) (Taxman 2008). Furthermore, the Martinson Report (1974) validated shifts from rehabilitation to a focus on delivering more punishments that were tough on crime in conjunction with political calls for retribution. In this way, POs operated within the 'get tough' policies rather than separate from them, alongside shifts from penal-welfarism to the more punitive measures of the 'get tough' era (Garland 2001).

Conflicts can arise between these two competing ideologies (punishment and rehabilitation) when they are used together in standard practice, especially when POs seek to hold individuals responsible for their actions while also obtaining help for their specific needs. Thus, probation officers must balance the underlying goals of community corrections with their own professional role orientation when supervising offenders on their caseload (Clear and Latessa 1993; Klockars 1972; Taxman 2008). Previous research defines a role as 'a collection of patterns of behavior which are thought to constitute a meaningful unit and deemed appropriate to a person occupying a particular status' (Turner 1956: 316). In this regard, the existing research has identified several varying roles associated with probation supervision.

Probation officer roles

Traditionally, probation officer roles have been delineated into two distinct categories – law enforcement and social workers (Klockars 1972). Probation officers aligned with the law enforcement role traditionally value compliance, authority, regulation, and protecting the public. In contrast, officers classified as fulfilling the social worker role act as a 'therapeutic agent' (Klockars 1972: 551) focusing on the administration of treatment as well as supporting and guiding offenders in the hopes of improving their condition. A combination of law enforcement and social work roles, also referred to as a 'synthetic officer' (Klockars 1972: 552), focuses on maintaining an authoritative role with the client while also trying to help them through therapeutic services. Additionally, research identifies a 'resource broker' role, in which POs assess client needs and link them to appropriate services, rather than direct service provision (Carlson and Parks 1979). Research on these roles finds POs more commonly embrace the social service and resource broker roles (Sluder et al. 1991; Whitehead and Lindquist 1992). Across these studies, POs were least likely to support the law enforcement role (Sluder et al. 1991) and de-emphasize punishment in their approach to their job (Whitehead and Lindquist 1992).

Several research studies suggest a relationship between probation officer role orientation and outcomes. In fact, research finds probation officer role orientation can influence decision-making as well as the development of relationships. For example, POs aligned with a hybrid approach have lower violation rates compared to officers aligned with a law enforcement or social work role (Paparozzi and Gendreau 2005; Skeem and Manchak 2008). And, officers engaging in a balanced approach are more likely to form quality relationships with probationers, which is related to lower recidivism rates (Kennealy et al. 2012; Skeem et al. 2007; Skeem and Manchak 2008). Further research suggests the role orientation of an officer can influence their beliefs regarding offenders and their ability to comply with supervision conditions and perceptions of offender risk levels (Ricks et al. 2016) as law enforcement-oriented officers are often highly concerned with liability and take on a risk-averse supervision approach (Skeem et al. 2003). Thus, it is critical to understand both how role orientations influence decisions of POs and also factors that influence the development and alignment with various role orientations.

Research identifies numerous individual characteristics (i.e. age, race, gender) that influence a PO's role orientation. For example, research finds younger POs are more likely to support the law enforcement role (Reese et al. 1988) and overall support for the law enforcement aspects of the job decline with age (Shearer 2002; Ward and Kupchik 2010). Black POs are more likely to support the social work role compared to white POs (Ward and Kupchik 2010). Lastly, Vidal and Skeem (2007) found female POs are more likely to align with a rehabilitative approach as they more commonly recommend treatment and counselling for youth probationers on their caseloads compared to male POs.

Additional research findings suggest POs can support multiple roles simultaneously. As previously noted, blending the two main strategies of surveillance and treatment has been viewed as the most effective means of supervision to tackle short-term monitoring needs with larger goals of reintegration and reduced recidivism (Skeem and Manchak 2008; Whetzel et al. 2011). Schwalbe (2012) found that POs often make decisions regarding how to supervise a case based on their entire caseload, often implementing strategies aligned with multiple roles depending on the case (Schwalbe and Maschi 2009). Other research findings suggest POs rely on multiple roles and enact the role most appropriate for a particular probationer or situation (Murphy and Lutze 2009). This body of research suggests POs have flexible role orientations with the ability to perform responsibilities aligned with both punishment and rehabilitation.

Contemporary research on probation officer roles

Recent research on PO roles has continued to explore the three traditional orientations: law enforcement (or control), balanced (or synthetic), and social work (or counsellor) (see Miller 2015; Skeem et al. 2007). This body of research suggests the majority of modern POs identified themselves as balanced (Kunkel et al. 2014; Ricks and Eno Louden 2015). Ricks and Eno Louden (2015) found that POs' role orientations are not static; rather they change based on the circumstances. While the majority of officers self-reported a balanced orientation of control and social work, upon being faced with scenarios in which probationers exhibited repeated non-compliance, officers shifted toward control strategies (Ricks and Eno Louden 2015). Similarly, Miller (2015) found little evidence of solely law enforcement- or social work-oriented probation officers. Rather, Miller (2015) redefined the categorical data related to degrees of engagement towards clients (such as low engagers, high engagers, and medium engagers-traditional) and found each of these classes were associated with a 'synthetic' orientation, combining multiple strategies.

Probation officer roles and evidence-based practices

Over the last 30 years, research has increasingly emphasized the importance of implementing evidence-based practices (EBPs) to improve outcomes in the corrections system (Andrews et al. 1990; Lowenkamp et al. 2006). As a result, many correctional agencies, including probation, are implementing practices proven by scientific research to improve outcomes (Henderson et al. 2009). The Risk-Need-Responsivity (RNR) model has significantly influenced changes in probation supervision, with its emphasis on identifying who should receive interventions (those who pose a higher risk), what interventions should address criminogenic needs, and how interventions should be structured (cognitive behavioural) (Bonta and Andrews 2016). Probation supervision aligned with the RNR model requires POs to adopt an individualized supervision approach, assessing each individual's risk for recidivism and their criminogenic needs that may influence future engagement in criminal behaviour (Taxman 2018). In probation, this typically means the integration of several practices: (1) use of validated, standardized risk and needs assessment instruments, (2) evidence-based cognitive behavioural programming, (3) use of swift and certain incentives and sanctions to encourage compliance, and (4) effective communication and therapeutic relationships between POs and probationers (Andrews and Bonta 2010; Hawken 2016; Taxman 2002, 2018). This emphasis has brought attention back towards a rehabilitative focus in probation supervision, requiring the use of individualized treatment and programming in combination with the surveillance and control mechanisms emphasized during the 'tough on crime' era (Taxman 2008). As a result, probation today is often characterized as a hybrid approach, in line with Klockar's (1972) synthetic officer (Taxman 2008).

Despite the increased integration of EBPs into probation supervision over the last decade, little research specifically examines how EBPs influence probation officer role orientations. One recent study examined the relationship between probation officer role orientations and supervision decisions, finding officers aligned with a law enforcement role were more likely to overestimate recidivism risks of low-risk offenders (Ricks et al. 2016). This research suggests role orientation is related to the successful implementation of risk assessments in probation practice. This is an important consideration, as research highlights the importance of risk assessment in appropriately classifying and treating offenders (Bonta and Andrews 2016). A number of additional research studies report challenges with successful implementation of risk and needs assessments in probation practice and associated treatment matching (e.g. Bonta et al. 2008; Ferguson 2002; Miller and Maloney 2013; Viglione et al. 2015). Recent research notes the more general challenge in implementing EBPs in correctional settings, finding correctional agencies typically do not achieve the outcomes they expect or staff buy-in surrounding the use of EBPs such as risk assessment (Taxman 2008).

One unaddressed issue in relation to the implementation of EBPs is a consideration for the ways in which the introduction of practices such as risk assessment, treatment matching, and cognitive behavioural programming alters the expected responsibilities and role perceptions of probation officers. This is a key issue not to be ignored, given POs are at the front line and are the primary implementers of policy change, like the implementation of a risk and needs assessment (Lynch 1998; Viglione 2017). In a recent study, Viglione (2017) set out to examine how POs implement EBPs with probationers they supervise. The following section will present data stemming from this project to examine role orientations of POs in a correctional agency that had been implementing EBPs for over eight years.

PO roles post-EBP implementation case study method

The current case study relies on data derived from a larger mixed methods project designed to examine the implementation of EBPs in an adult probation agency. This project involved 1,084 hours of qualitative observations and interviews as well as surveys with probation staff across 12 probation offices in one mid-Atlantic state from January 2012 until October 2014. During this time, researchers observed 200 POs (including supervisors) as they took part in all work activities, conducting informal interviews throughout the course of observations. While collecting qualitative data, the researchers did not record fieldnotes but rather typed complete notes as soon as possible after leaving the field each day, standard practice in ethnographic research (Emerson 2001; Emerson et al. 1995; Morrill 1995). Once completed, typed fieldnotes were linked to Atlas.ti, a commonly used data management software, for coding and analysis (Muhr 1991). Coding began with an inductive line-by-line coding strategy where each line of text was linked to a series of codes (Charmaz 1995).[1] Once this process was complete, iterative thematic coding was used to identify specific themes relating to probation officer role orientation. This analysis yielded over 350 instances across 87 unique probation staff in which POs described their perception of their role orientations. Finally, researchers conducted a second round of iterative thematic coding to develop typologies of probation staff role orientations. When coding was complete, the researchers queried the data for emergent themes and patterns surrounding probation officer roles.

Results

Coding and analysis revealed five role orientations prevalent across probation staff. As seen in Table 79.1, the most common role articulated was the social service role (46.0%). These conceptualizations of one's role aligned clearly with that of previous research, with social service POs emphasizing the use of treatment and rehabilitative strategies in addressing probationer needs. Given the emphasis on EBPs in this agency, it was not surprising that social service POs emphasized the use of EBPs in supervising their probationers. In this light, POs described their role as ensuring they talk to probationers to help them and better understand their problems rather than focus on compliance and violations. Interestingly, there were no POs who perceived their role to be solely that of a resource broker, as suggested by previous research. Instead, linking probationers to appropriate treatment programs and services was a common responsibility many social service-oriented POs argued they took part in. This finding is not surprising given the emphasis of the RNR model on identification of probationer needs and linkage to appropriate treatment.

Table 79.1 Probation officer role orientations (n = 87)

Social service	Hybrid	Law enforcement	People processor
40 (46%)	22 (25%)	19 (22%)	6 (7%)

During analysis, it was clear that within the social service typology, there was a subclass of POs who perceived their role as more than the traditional social worker role, but who perceived their role as that of a change agent (5.7%). Change agent POs perceived their role to involve actively trying to address thinking errors and generate long-term behaviour change amongst probationers. The following example from fieldnotes highlights these findings:

> In terms of her probation strategy, PO Lewis argued you cannot just try to change someone's behavior without trying to change the way they think. A lot of my job is trying to work with people to change their thinking patterns. Their thinking is really at the root of the problem. For example, if I can get to their thinking behind drug use, then I can start to work on changing their drug-using behavior.

Thus, the change agent strategy extends the role of the social worker beyond simply helping probationers by also engaging in complex cognitive behavioural techniques and strategies.

The second most common typology of POs were those who fulfilled a hybrid role. Probation staff aligned with this approach identified their role as incorporating both rehabilitative and law enforcement components. Hybrid POs maintained a flexible orientation, using multiple techniques when deemed appropriate. Hybrid POs often mentioned the competing tensions between the desire to implement EBPs and rehabilitative strategies with the fact that they are required by the judiciary to monitor probation conditions and hold probationers accountable. In this regard, hybrid POs argued they had to use a combination of approaches and a variety of 'tools' (e.g. treatment programmes and violations) to best supervise their caseload. For example, PO Len argued 'a good PO can balance punitive and rehabilitative strategies and what is best for the probationer and the community'.

Hybrid probation staff articulated a number of contingencies that influenced whether they use strategies aligned with the social service or law enforcement role. Probation staff would not use a social service approach with probationers if they were disrespectful, did not articulate the desire to change, 'burned' them in the past, or did not put in effort. In these circumstances, POs preferred to draw upon the law enforcement role. Probation staff commonly argued that probationers must be willing to work hard and must want to make change, stating that it is ultimately the choice of the probationer which role the PO enacts. For example, PO July frequently told her probationers, 'we [POs] can't work harder at this than you are'. Often, POs argued they wanted to help probationers on their caseloads, but they would not put in a disproportionate amount of effort. In another representative example, PO Dewey argued,

> I will continue to work hard for probationers if they show they are willing to work hard, too. But, if they burn me by not doing what they are

supposed to or not willingly accepting my help, then I wash my hands of them and let them fail on their own.

These examples highlight the expectations POs have of probationers on their caseload and the ways in which probationer behaviour dictates their role orientation.

The third most prevalent role orientation amongst POs in the current study was the law enforcement role (21.8%). Under this role, POs argued that the main way they manage their caseloads was with violations and revocations, emphasizing compliance with probation conditions. Law enforcement POs often stressed the need to protect community safety while enforcing court orders as their top priority. Interestingly, many law enforcement officers conceptualized their role as working directly for the court and judges. The following example highlights this finding:

> PO Adams talked about one of his probationers who is not putting his probation first. The court ordered him to complete substance abuse treatment but the probationer said he needed to do this over the summer so he could finish his classes this semester. PO Adams told the probationer he did not care about his classes and needed to get into treatment because that is what the court wants. It was not his job to care about school or classes, but it was his job to care about the court orders.

Another law enforcement-oriented PO argued 'it is on the probationers to follow conditions or go back to jail' while another described that he is 'more a "on the books", lock-em-up kinda guy'. Law enforcement POs commonly worked closely with local law enforcement, with some POs noting they share personal contact information to better keep track of probationers during off hours and weekends. While the majority of POs in the current study did not commonly wear their protective vest and/or carry a gun, those who did all aligned with the law enforcement orientation.

One final category of POs surfaced worth noting, despite representing only 7% of the sample – the people processor. Probation staff aligned with this role were focused on the paperwork and data entry aspects of the job. People processing POs stated the importance of being personally and emotionally detached from the job. This strategy allowed them to focus on the necessary completion of the hours of paperwork and data entry they often faced. The following representative example highlights this role:

> PO Ray complained they have so much paperwork. When it comes down to it, the department makes you do all this paperwork and check boxes that there is no way you can really talk to someone. You will never, ever get in trouble for the way you talk to someone, but you will get in trouble for not checking boxes, and he has. As a result, he focuses on paperwork and not on talking to people.

Probation staff aligned with the people-processing role highlight the tensions between the data entry aspect of the job and the requirements of EBP-focused supervision. Individuals in this category preferred to protect themselves by focusing on documenting everything clearly and in a timely fashion. This emphasis often resulted in the inability to spend time with probationers, as PO Ray described above.

Discussion

The examples presented from this case study highlight the prevalence of the social service role in an agency that has been implementing EBPs for over eight years. Many EBPs implemented in this agency, such as motivational interviewing and cognitive behavioural therapy, require POs to serve as an agent of change, encouraging change in both thinking and behaviours of their probationers. This pushes the role beyond that of simply helping probationers in a therapeutic way to a role that specifically requires focus and attention to generating change. In line with these reforms in the agency, the presence of a more nuanced social service role was identified – that of the change agent – suggesting a new role orientation within adult probation work.

Successful implementation of these EBPs often requires POs to promote individual change amongst probationers who may be resistant to change (Walters et al. 2007). While the existence of the hybrid role aligns with previous research and reflects necessary responsibilities associated with the job (e.g. monitoring compliance and writing violations), it also suggests potential areas that may complicate EBP implementation. This includes the hesitancy of POs to enact their social service role with probationers resistant to change, yet these may be the very individuals who need the most help (Viglione 2017). Future research should seek to further illuminate the way which the hybrid role unfolds in daily probation work, including a more thorough understanding of PO decision-making regarding which 'hat' they choose to wear in certain situations.

Given the strong emphasis on EBPs within this agency, it is surprising that approximately 22% of the sample aligned with a pure law enforcement role while another 7% aligned with the people-processing role. Given the push towards use of EBPs, future research must identify the ways in which these orientations can influence both implementation as well as probationer outcomes. While beyond the scope of the current study, next steps in this project will include an examination of the relationship between identified PO roles and use of best practices. Evidence-based practices used in probation introduce complex concepts and skills and require officers to understand and implement highly clinical skills, including conducting, interpreting, and addressing screening and assessment tools. These skills run counter to the role orientations identified by 29% of probation staff in the current study and suggest a potential barrier to successful implementation.

Conclusion

Existing research highlights the important relationship between offender behavioural outcomes and their interactions with their community supervision officers (Andrews and Kiessling 1980; Palmer 1995; Skeem et al. 2007; Taxman 2008). For example, Andrews and Kiessling (1980) found decreased recidivism when community supervision officers were trained in interpersonal communication and anti-criminal modelling and reinforcement. And, Skeem and colleagues (2007) found that when probation officers used behavioural management techniques (aligned with the role of a change agent), probationers were less likely to fail while on supervision. Similarly, Taxman (2008) found positive effects when community supervision focused on improvement of the interactions between officers and offenders through use of a variety of behavioural management techniques. That is, when community supervision officers focused on motivating offenders to change their behaviour, offenders were less likely to be rearrested and receive a technical violation (Taxman 2008). This body of research suggests that the role of POs influences the working relationship between officers and probationers, interpersonal communication techniques, and ultimately offender outcomes. Thus, previous research supports the change agent role identified in the current case study as a potential positive facilitator of behavioural change, in line with the EBP movement.

It is expected that moving forward, POs will be required to incorporate EBPs into all aspects of their activities, utilizing data and research to conduct risk assessments, enforce expectations and consequences of violations, supply rehabilitative resources, and adjust their professional role orientation to accept and practice these critical responsibilities. Furthermore, the attempts at introducing EBPs is tempered by the process of infiltrating its use within the organization, a process described as being '"washed through" the filters of staff values and personal orientation' (Whetzel et al. 2011: 8). In this way, new practices are introduced through the existing frameworks of the agency, potentially altering the original concept to one that better suits the organizational goals (such as a more control-oriented mission or one centred on treatment). Thus, identifying and understanding individual role orientations can serve as an important mechanism to better understand EBP implementation challenges commonly observed in correctional settings.

Acknowledgements

This study was funded by the National Institute of Justice, #2014-IJ-CX-2004, National Science Foundation, SES-1420311, and Bureau of Justice Assistance, #2011-DB-BX-K010. All opinions are those of the authors and do not represent the opinions of the National Institute of Justice, National Science Foundation, or Bureau of Justice Assistance or any governmental agency.

Note

1   For a more detailed explanation of project background, data collection, and coding strategies, please see Viglione (2017).

References

Andrews, D. A. and Bonta, J. (2010) *The Psychology of Criminal Conduct*, 5th edition. New Providence, NJ: Lexis Nexis Matthew Bender.

Andrews, D. A. and Kiessling, J. J. (1980) Program structure and effective correctional practices: A summary of the CaVIC research. *Effective Correctional Treatment*, 439–463.

Andrews, D. A., Zinger, I., Hoge, R. D., Bonta, J., Gendreau, P. and Cullen, F. T. (1990) Does correctional treatment work? A clinically relevant and psychologically informed meta-analysis. *Criminology*, 28(3), 369–404.

Augustus, J. (1852/1972) *John Augustus: First Probation Officer*. Montclair, NJ: Patterson Smith.

Bonta, J. and Andrews, D. A. (2016) *The Psychology of Criminal Conduct*, 6th edition. New York: Taylor & Francis.

Bonta, J., Rugge, T., Scott, T. L., Bourgon, G. and Yessine, A. K. (2008) Exploring the black box of community supervision. *Journal of Offender Rehabilitation*, 47, 248–270.

Carlson, E. and Parks, E. (1979) *Critical Issues in Adult Probation: Issues in Probation Management* (NCJRS No. 057667). Washington, DC: US Department of Justice.

Charmaz, K. (1995) The body, identity, and self. *The Sociological Quarterly*, 36, 657–680.

Clear, T. and Latessa, E. (1993) Probation officers' roles in intensive supervision: Surveillance versus treatment. *Justice Quarterly*, 10(3), 441–462.

Dressler, D. (1962) *Practice and Theory of Probation and Parole*. New York: Columbia University Press.

Emerson, E. (2001) *Challenging Behaviour*. New York: Cambridge University Press.

Emerson, E., Fretz, R. I. and Shaw, L. L. (1995) *Writing Ethnographic Fieldnotes*. Chicago: University of Chicago Press.

Ferguson, J. L. (2002) Putting the "What Works" research into practice. *Criminal Justice and Behavior*, 29, 472–492.

Fulton, B., Stichman, A., Travis, L. and Latessa, E. (1997) Moderating probation and parole officer attitudes to achieve desired outcomes. *The Prison Journal*, 77(3), 295–312.

Garland, D. (2001) *The Culture of Control: Crime and Social Disorder in Contemporary Society*. Chicago: University of Chicago Press.

Globokar, J. L. and Toro, M. (2017) The politics of punishment: A study of the passage of the 1925 federal probation act. *Journal of Offender Rehabilitation*, 56(8), 534–551.

Gordon, D. (1991) *The Justice Juggernaut: Fighting Street Crime, Controlling Citizens*. New Brunswick: Rutgers University Press.

Hawken, A. (2016) All implementation is local. *Criminology & Public Policy*, 15(4), 1229–1239.

Henderson, C. E., Young, D. W., Farrell, J. and Taxman, F. S. (2009) Associations among state and local organizational contexts: Use of evidence-based practices in the criminal justice system. *Drug and Alcohol Dependence*, 1035, 523–532.

Kaeble, D. and Bonczar, T. P. (2017) *Probation and Parole in the United States, 2015*. Office of Justice Programs, Bureau of Justice Statistics. Washington, DC: US Department of Justice.

Kennealy, P. J., Skeem, J. L., Manchak, S. M. and Eno Louden, J. (2012) Firm, fair, and caring officer-offender relationships protect against supervision failure. *Law and Human Behavior*, 36(6), 496.

Klockars, C. B. (1972) A theory of probation supervision. *The Journal of Criminal Law, Criminology, and Police Science*, 63(4), 550–557.

Kunkel, T. L., Cheesman, F. L., Javian, K., Shames, A. and White, M. T. (2014) *Preliminary Findings from the Evidence Based Practices Implementation and Organization Assessment*. Williamsburg, VA: National Center for State Courts.

Lindner, C. (2007) Thacher, Augustus, and Hill – the path to statutory probation in the United States and England. *Federal Probation*, 71(3), 36–41.

Lowenkamp, C. T., Latessa, E. J. and Holsinger, A. M. (2006) The risk principle in action: What have we learned from 13,767 offenders and 97 correctional programs? *Crime & Delinquency*, 52(1), 77–93.

Lynch, M. (1998) Waste managers? The new penology, crime fighting, and parole agent identity. *Law & Society Review*, 32, 839–870.

Martinson, R. (1974) What works? Questions and answers about prison reform. *The Public Interest*, 35, 22–54.

McAnany, P., Thomson, D. and Fogel, D. (1984) *Probation and Justice: Reconsideration o Mission*. Cambridge, MA: Oelgeschlager, Gunn and Hain.

Miller, J. (2015) Contemporary modes of probation officer supervision: The triumph of the "synthetic" officer? *Justice Quarterly*, 32(2), 314–336. DOI:10.1080/07418825.2013.770546.

Miller, J. and Maloney, C. (2013) Practitioner compliance with Risk/Needs Assessment tools: A theoretical and empirical assessment. *Criminal Justice and Behavior*, 40, 716–736.

Morrill, C. (1995) *The Executive Way*. Chicago: University of Chicago Press.

Muhr, T. (1991) Atlas.ti – a prototype for the support of text interpretation. *Qualitative Sociology*, 14, 349–371.

Murphy, D. and Lutze, F. (2009) Police-probation partnerships: Professional identity and the sharing of coercive power. *Journal of Criminal Justice*, 37(1), 65–76.

Ohlin, L. E., Piven, H. and Pappenfort, D. M. (1956) Major dilemmas of the social worker in probation and parole. *National Probation & Parole Association Journal*, 3, 211–225.

Palmer, T. (1995) Programmatic and nonprogrammatic aspects of successful intervention: New directions for research. *Crime & Delinquency*, 41(1), 100–131.

Paparozzi, M. A. and Gendreau, P. (2005) An intensive supervision program that worked: Service delivery, professional orientation, and organizational supportiveness. *The Prison Journal*, 85(4), 445–466.

Petersilia, J. (1997) Probation in the United States. *Crime and Justice*, 22, 149–200.

Petersilia, J. (1998) Probation and parole. In M. Tonry (Ed.), *The Handbook of Crime and Punishment*. New York: Oxford University Press, pp. 563–588.

Reese, W. A., Curtis, R. L. and Whitworth, J. R. (1988) Dispositional discretion or disparity: The juvenile probation officer's role in delinquency processing. *Journal of Applied Behavioral Science*, 24(1), 81–100.

Ricks, E. P. and Eno Louden, J. (2015) The relationship between officer orientation and supervision strategies in community corrections. *Law and Human Behavior*, 39(2), 130–141. DOI:10.1037/lhb0000098.

Ricks, E. P., Eno Louden, J. and Kennealy, P. J. (2016) Probation officer role emphases and use of risk assessment information before and after training. *Behavioral Sciences and the Law*, 34, 337–351. DOI:10.1002/bsl.2219.

Rothman, D. J. (1980) *Conscience and Convenience: The Asylum and Its Alternatives in Progressive America*. Boston, MA: Little, Brown & Company.

Rudes, D. S., Viglione, J. and Taxman, F. S. (2011) Juvenile probation officers: How the perception of roles affects training experiences for evidence-based practice implementation. *Federal Probation*, 75, 3.

Schwalbe, C. S. (2012) Toward an integrated theory of probation. *Criminal Justice and Behavior*, 39(2), 185–201.

Schwalbe, C. S. and Maschi, T. (2009) Investigating probation strategies with juvenile offenders: The influence of officers' attitudes and youth characteristics. *Law of Human Behavior*, 33(5), 357–367.

Shearer, R. A. (2002) Probation strategies of juvenile and adult pre-service trainees. *Federal Probation*, 66(1), 33–37.

Skeem, J. L., Encandela, J. and Louden, J. E. (2003) Perspectives on probation and mandated mental health treatment in specialized and traditional probation departments. *Behavioral Sciences & the Law*, 21(4), 429–458.

Skeem, J. L., Eno Louden, J., Polaschek, D. and Camp, J. (2007) Assessing relationship quality in mandated community treatment: Blending care with control. *Psychological Assessment*, 21(4), 429–458.

Skeem, J. L. and Manchak, S. (2008) Back to the future: From Klockars' model to effective supervision to evidence-based practice in probation. *Journal of Offender Rehabilitation*, 47(3), 220–247.

Sluder, R. D., Shearer, R. A. and Potts, D. W. (1991) Probation officers' role perceptions and attitudes toward firearms. *Federal Probation*, 55(3), 3–11.

Taxman, F. S. (2002) Supervision – exploring the dimensions of effectiveness. *Federal Probation*, 66(2), 14.

Taxman, F. S. (2008) No illusion, offender and organizational change in Maryland's proactive correctional facility: Challenges to the culture. *Journal of Offender Rehabilitation*, 50, 467–491.

Taxman, F. S. (2018) The partially clothed emperor: Evidence-based practices. *Journal of Contemporary Criminal Justice*, 34(1), 97–114.

Taxman, F. S., Shepardson, E. S. and Byrne, J. M. (2004) *Tools of the Trade: A Guide to Incorporating Science into Practice*. Baltimore, MD: National Institute of Corrections.

Turner, R. (1956) Role-taking, role standpoint and reference-group behavior. *The American Journal of Sociology*, 61(4), 316–328.

US Department of Labor, Bureau of Labor Statistics. (2018) Probation officers and correctional treatment specialists. *Occupational Outlook Handbook*. Available at: www.bls.gov/ooh/community-and-social-service/probation-officers-and-correctional-treatment-specialists.htm.

Vanstone, M. (2004) *Supervising Offenders in the Community: A History of Probation Theory and Practice*. Burlington, VT: Ashgate Publishing Company.

Vidal, S. and Skeem, J. (2007) Effect of psychopathy, abuse, and ethnicity on juvenile probation officers' decision-making and supervision strategies. *Law and Human Behavior*, 31(5), 479–498.

Viglione, J. (2017) Street-level decision making: Acceptability, feasibility, and use of evidence-based practices in adult probation. *Criminal Justice and Behavior*, 44(10), 1356–1381.

Viglione, J., Rudes, D. S. and Taxman, F. S. (2015) Misalignment in supervision: Implementing Risk/Needs Assessment instruments in probation. *Criminal Justice and Behavior*, 42(3), 263–285.

Ward, G. and Kupchik, A. (2010) What drives juvenile probation officers? Relating organizational contexts, status characteristics, and personal convictions to treatment and punishment orientations. *Crime & Delinquency*, 56(1), 35–69.

Walters, S. T., Clark, M. D., Gingerich, R. and Meltzer, M. L. (2007) *Motivating Offenders to Change: A Guide for Probation and Parole*. Washington, DC: US Department of Justice, National Institute of Corrections.

Whetzel, J., Paparozzi, M., Alexander, M. and Lowenkamp, C. T. (2011) Goodbye to a worn-out dichotomy: Law enforcement, social work, and a balanced approach (A survey of federal probation officer attitudes). *Federal Probation*, 75(2), 7–12.

Whitehead, J. T. and Lindquist, C. A. (1992) Determinants of probation and parole officer professional orientation. *Journal of Criminal Justice*, 20(1), 13–24.

80

Innovations to transform probation supervision

An examination of experiences across 11 US agencies

Lina Marmolejo, James Byrne, and Faye S. Taxman

Introduction

Mass incarceration refers to the United States having less than 5% of the world's population but having nearly 25% of the world's prisoners. The US incarceration rate is the world's highest at 698 prisoners per 100,000 of national population, followed by Turkmenistan (583), El Salvador (492), Thailand (461), Belize (449), and Russia (445), just to mention a few (Walmsley 2016). On the other hand, mass supervision (Phelps 2016, 2017) refers to the utilization of community supervision to extend penal control in the community where the US also has one of the biggest populations under community supervision – in 2014 there were approximately 4.7 million adults under either probation or parole. Probation accounted for about 3.8 million or 82% of the total population under supervision in the US (Kaeble et al. 2015) while during 2015 there were a total of 1.2 million individuals under the supervision of probation agencies in 47 states across Europe (Aebi and Chopin 2016).

During the upturn of mass supervision, supervision agencies have been asked to transform from a law enforcement approach (i.e. compliance management) to utilization of evidence-based practices and treatments (EBP) (behavioural management, treatment, Core Correctional Practices, etc.). The EBP approach requires supervision agencies to alter their practices with modified public safety goals that focus on offender rehabilitation. The supervision organizations, which have practiced various forms of compliance management and enforcement, must put in place strategies to advance EBP. This chapter presents findings from interviews of grantees from the Bureau of Justice Assistance (BJA is a federal US Department of Justice agency that awards grants to improve operations). BJA funded smart supervision strategies and grant programmes for community corrections agencies between fiscal years 2012 and 2016. The main purpose of this research is to learn how these organizations pursued the improvement in supervision using grant resources. The interviews focused on common themes and noteworthy practices such as characteristics of the implemented innovation, partners involved in the project, major facilitators or barriers faced during the implementation, and measures used to assess project outcomes. The chapter synthesizes information gathered from interviews with different stakeholders from across six counties and five states.

Theoretical/conceptual framework

Evidence-based community supervision: what the research tells us

One important and recent advancement in the criminal justice system has been the quest to embrace the notion of EBP. From social policy to corrections, from a health, sociological, and criminological approach, the research about what works and what does not to prevent, control, and reduce crime is increasing and it continues to fill knowledge gaps. Innovations, in service delivery and organizations, are defined by Greenhalgh et al. (2004: 582) as 'a novel set of behaviors, routines and ways of working that are directed at improving health outcomes, administrative efficiency, cost-effectiveness, or users' experience and that are implemented by planned and coordinated actions'.

Introducing and adopting EBP is not an easy task. Once an evidence-based intervention is identified and selected, the process of implementing it in criminal justice settings is complex and often takes a long time, since 'the institutional imperative is to continue to do business using familiar practices and processes' (Taxman and Belenko 2011: 3). It challenges the status quo of everyday work, including the common and traditional decision-making process. Often the existing way of business is not based on research, evaluation, and analysis and often reflects personal experiences, emotions, discretion, and gut feelings – one that does not necessarily link empirical evidence to achieving outcomes of crime prevention in a cost-effective manner.

Extensive research in community corrections has led scholars and practitioners to support and embrace a set of core evidence-based practices and principles that have shown to be effective in reducing offender risk and recidivism and improving public safety (Guevara and Solomon 2009). These include (1) use of a standardized, validated risk and needs assessment tool to identify risk to recidivate and criminogenic needs; (2) use of techniques to enhance intrinsic motivation; (3) targeting interventions considering the Risk-Need-Responsivity model and focus resources on higher-risk rather than lower-risk offenders; (4) skill training with directed practice, which comprises the use of cognitive behavioural treatment methods that have shown to be effective in reducing recidivism; (5) increasing positive reinforcement, or incentives to help the offender, rather than only focusing on sanctions and punishment; (6) engaging ongoing support in natural communities; (7) measuring relevant processes/practices, gathering data about offenders' progress as well as officer performance results of extreme importance when assessing outcomes of implementing evidence-based practices; (8) providing measurement feedback – this principle is directly linked to the previous one. Putting in place regular feedback mechanisms for both offenders and officers improves motivation to change, outcomes, and accountability.

These principles emerge from studies that find that deterrence-oriented community corrections programmes do not reduce recidivism, and may actually be iatrogenic (Petersilia and Turner 1993). More contemporary research finds that offenders who are at higher risk are better suited for more intensive, structured interventions (Taxman and Thanner 2006). Interventions closely adhering to RNR principles can result in a 26% difference in recidivism rates (Bourgon and Gutierrez 2012) and it has shown far greater results than intensive supervision without treatment, which has no detectable effects on recidivism rates (Miller et al. 2013). These principles call for an assessment of the probationer-officer relationship and interactions based solely on surveillance and control for one that helps the offender to change, is more rehabilitative (Taxman and Belenko 2011), and improves social bonds with family members, friends, and pro-social community members as a way to increase the likelihood of offenders' rehabilitation and reintegration (Guevara and Solomon 2009).

Implementation science: a framework to understand innovations in probation practices

Scholars from different disciplines – public policy, business management, social services, healthcare, public health, organizational development, and criminal justice, among others – have recognized the challenges and complexities of the implementation process of EBP. They have built a set of theories and frameworks with common organizational, contextual, and individual variables that influence the process of implementing EBP effectively (Rogers 2003; Greenhalgh et al. 2004; Fixsen et al. 2005; Proctor et al. 2009; Aarons et al. 2011; Taxman and Belenko 2011). Within this framework, implementation science has aimed at precisely bridging this gap between practices that have shown to work based on research, and how these are implemented in specific contexts. According to Proctor (2009: 26), implementation science can be defined as 'the systematic study of how a specific set of activities and designated strategies are used to successfully integrate an evidence-based public health intervention within specific settings'.

Within implementation science, several frameworks have been developed to better understand the process by which new ideas are put into practice and to explore the black box of implementation. For instance: (1) the diffusion of innovation framework (Rogers 2003) considers the process of technology transfer a dynamic one that is conditioned by the attributions of innovations (relative advantage, compatibility, complexity, trialability, and observability), information exchange among different stakeholders, and the ability to adapt; (2) Greenhalgh et al. (2004) was the first one to propose that institutions have inner (organizational antecedents and organizational readiness for innovation, etc.) and outer (socio-political climate, environmental stability, interorganizational networks, etc.) contexts that can facilitate or impede the implementation of innovations; and (3) based on this work, Taxman and Belenko (2011) built the evidence-based interagency implementation model that provides key elements and tools to integrate EBP within the specific field of community corrections where it is recognized that there are strong external stakeholders (i.e. judges, jails, treatment providers, etc.) that affect the operations of community corrections.

These frameworks facilitate the advancement of implementing EBP. In particular, Taxman and Belenko (2011) identify key factors that can influence, either positively or negatively, the successful adoption, implementation, and sustainability of EBP. For example, factors related to a successful implementation include (1) the organization, such as committed leadership and political will, for integration of EBP in the organizational values and mission; (2) the staff, which relates to skills and knowledge and training of probation officers and line supervisors, as well as their understanding of the EBP and its relevance to their work; (3) the system environment, which refers to the collaboration with other criminal justice and treatment agencies, service providers, researchers, and other stakeholders; and (4) quality and monitoring, which implies a feedback system, performance benchmarks, and outcome measures. On the other hand, challenges associated with the implementation of EBP include achieving staff understanding of EBP and organizational change that it implies, overcoming staff resistance, and funding constraints (Taxman and Belenko 2011). These are used to analyze the findings from the interviews of BJA grantees, and to grasp a better understanding of key factors influencing the adoption and implementation of innovations in community correction agencies.

Innovations in probation agencies

BJA's innovation in supervision initiative

This research was conducted as part of BJA's Innovations Suite programmes, a strategic federal effort to promote and expand the use and adoption of EBP and advance the field of community corrections. It promotes practitioner-researcher partnerships that prioritize data-driven and evidence-based innovations to address crime challenges ('Innovation Suite', n.d.). Within this framework, the Innovation in Supervision Initiative (formerly known as Smart Supervision and Smart Probation) was launched in 2012, in order to improve the capacity and effectiveness of community supervision agencies, both probation and parole, in improving the success rate, reducing recidivism, and increasing public safety through the application of technology and evidence-based practices. Since its conception, and until 2017, ISI has awarded a total of $27,148,034 to 44 grantees and their research partners (Innovation in Supervision Initiative n.d.). The funds of this initiative can be used to improve supervision by developing and testing interventions that are innovative and cost-effective, using evidence-based practices, building institutional capacity, developing information and communication technology systems, increasing strategic partnerships with other law enforcement agencies and with researchers, and conducting evaluations of the interventions, among others (Innovation in Supervision Initiative n.d.).

Research methodology

BJA requested that the Center for Advancing Correctional Excellence (ACE!) at George Mason University examine the projects implemented by states and counties that were Smart Supervision grantees during fiscal years 2012 to 2016. There were a total of 36 grants awarded during this period of time. In-depth structured phone interviews (see Appendix) were conducted, and additional documents provided by the interviewees were reviewed. The interview questionnaire consisted of seven sections with a total of 22 open-ended questions covering (1) the characteristics of the grant funded, (2) the internal partners involved in the project, (3) the external partners supporting the project, (4) the major accomplishments of the project to date, (5) the major facilitators and barriers faced during implementation of the project, (6) the measures used to assess project outcomes, and (7) the overall lessons learned from the project.

Sample of grant projects

Interviews were conducted between 24 July and 23 August 2017. This convenience sample included 11 out of 36 (30%) BJA grantees between 2012 and 2016, who were self-selected based on their responses to the email requesting an interview about their grant project. Interviewees included grant managers, directors of probation departments and community corrections, academic research partners, evaluators, and probation officers, among other stakeholders.

As seen in Table 80.1, the 11 grantees included in this examination vastly differ in terms of their organizational structure, the amount of awarded funds, and the size of the agency, defined by number and rate of population under supervision. For instance, Minnesota, Maine, and Wisconsin have a centralized corrections structure in which the Department of Corrections manages all services including probation, parole, and prisons. On the other hand, states like New York, Georgia, Pennsylvania, and Colorado have a decentralized structure with an agency detached from the Department of Corrections in charge of overseeing probation supervision. In other states, such as Arizona and California, probation is the responsibility of local county agencies.

Furthermore, there is great variability in the amounts awarded, ranging from $499,000 to up to $750,000 for a period of 36 months. Four agencies, Colorado, Georgia, Maricopa County, Arizona, and Wisconsin, attained the maximum grant amount of $750,000 and Minnesota obtained $499,000. These funds are not conditioned to the size of the agency; however, a look at the size of the agencies provides a clear picture of how federal grants are serving a diverse pool of probation institutions. The largest funded agency was Georgia with 223,407 adults under probation (2018), followed by the states of Minnesota and Colorado, which have almost four times fewer persons under supervision, 98,000 and 78,000 respectively. The grantee jurisdictions with a smaller size of persons on probation include Somerset County, Pennsylvania (217), Coconino County, Arizona (1,376), and Salinas City, California (4,466).

Findings

This section provides a summary of the findings from the interviews with key stakeholders involved in the design and implementation of the 11 BJA grants selected for the analysis. It is worth highlighting that in several cases the

Table 80.1 Participating BJA grantees

	County/ state	Project name	Fiscal year	Amount awarded	Org. structure	Probation population[1]
1	Minnesota State	Smart Probation	FY12	$499,305	Centralized	Count: 98,258 Rate*: 2,328
2	Coconino County, AZ	Online Probation Education Program	FY13	$608,966	County government/ judicial branch	Count: 1,376
3	Monroe County, NY	Female Offenders Can Ultimately Succeed	FY13	$574,255	Decentralized Division of Criminal Justice Services	
4	Colorado State	Behavioral Shaping Model and Reinforcement Tool	FY13	$749,889	Decentralized Office of Community Corrections	Count: 78,883 Rate: 1,860
5	Maine State	Maine Integrated Risk Reduction Model	FY14	$573,620	Centralized Correctional Services	Count: 6,700 Rate: 2,102
6	Georgia State	GDC Smart Supervision Project	FY14	$750,000	Decentralized department of community supervision	Count: 223,407 Rate: 2,142
7	Maricopa County, AZ	Smart Thinking: Expanding Thinking for a Change Capacity through Collaboration	FY14	$749,998	County government/ judicial branch	Count: 25,827
8	Somerset County, PA	Somerset County Day Reporting Center	FY15	$637,634	Decentralized board of probation and parole	Count: 217
9	Allegheny County, PA	Smart Accountability Project	FY15	$685,920	Decentralized board of probation and parole	Count: 6,533
10	Salinas City, CA	Assessing and Implementing Evidence-based Practices for Probationer Services in Salinas	FY15	$557,734	Decentralized	Count: 4,466
11	Wisconsin State	Technical Assistance and Fidelity Coaches	FY16	$750,000	Centralized correctional services	Count: 46,144 Rate: 1,028

* Rate is the rate of population under supervision

Smart Supervision grants served as a complement to other efforts of implementing EBP within a probation agency. The interviews did not cover other broader initiatives and it is not a comprehensive study of all probation innovations within a particular jurisdiction. Rather, it is a snapshot in time of how community correction agencies are using grant funds to improve their supervision practices through the implementation of EBP.

Characteristics of the innovations

Overall, the innovations discussed in this chapter are aligned with the eight EBP principles for community corrections detailed in the second section of this chapter. In particular, agencies emphasize treatment and rehabilitation as means of promoting public safety, over mere surveillance and control (Table 80.2 summarizes key project characteristics).

Grant funds targeted advancements in probation as a system that invests in the social, emotional, and physical well-being of clients. Efforts at improving services and treatment to probationers include the use and implementation of different strategies, risk, and need assessment tools (principle #1); targeting medium- and high-risk offenders rather than placing lower-risk clients into intensive supervision (principle #3); addressing specific needs of special probation populations such as women and tribal communities (principle #3); the provision of evidence-based interventions such as Thinking for a Change (T4C), motivational interviewing (MI), and Moral Recognition Therapy (MRT) (principles #2 and #4); and ensuring the use of both sanctions and incentives to address noncompliance and encourage progress (principle #5). In addition, probation agencies are dedicating grant funds to strengthening organizational management and decision-making, through the development of new managerial tools, such as Compstat for community corrections, that help measure baseline and outcome indicators; toolkits for performance-based supervision; and interactive dashboards that provide real-time information on probationers and their cases. Finally, grants resources were used in intensive training of personnel (principle #7).

Besides close attention to principles of EBP and effective intervention, another common trait across studied agencies is the use of both hard and soft technologies innovations (Byrne and Rebovich 2007; Pattavina and Taxman 2007). In Allegheny County, Pennsylvania, hard technologies (i.e. mobile devices, telephones, laptops, tablets, and apps) are transforming the probation department to have a mobile workforce that can better supervise individuals in the field and not only from a physical office. Coconino County, Arizona, through its COPE programme, is using telemedicine technology to improve access to treatment and educational opportunities for people under supervision in remote rural areas of the county. On the other hand, soft technologies such as third or fourth generations of risk-need assessment tools (LS-CMI, LSI-R, COMPAS, ORAS, etc.) are being used by the totality of the agencies; case management information technologies and workload software are also being implemented to improve decision-making processes on levels of supervision, specialized treatment, case plans, and to inform the use of sanctions and incentives. For example, Georgia developed a set of tools including the

Table 80.2 BJA project description and characteristics

State/county	Project description	Project related activities	Target populations	EBP tools utilized		Treatment
				RNA	Treatment	
Minnesota State	The Minnesota Department of Corrections is addressing specific risks and needs of American Indian probationers by developing culturally adapted tools and evidence-based programme curricula that better suit the needs of this population.	-Staff training -Case management system -Adapt RNA tools -Train service providers on EBP	High-risk offenders (200 offenders)	LS/CMI	-Thinking for a Change (T4C) -Motivational interviewing (MI)
Coconino County, AZ	The Coconino Online Probation Education (COPE) programme aims at delivering treatment and services to probationers living in outlying rural areas. The online platform allows clients to participate in mentoring sessions, CBT interventions, etc.	-Staff training -Online platforms	Medium- to high-risk clients (excluding sex offenders)	Offenders Screening Tool (OST)	-Moral Recognition Therapy (MRT)
Monroe County, NY	The FOCUS project (Female Offenders Can Ultimately Succeed) provides intensive probation supervision and linkage to medical, mental health, and substance abuse services to medium- and high-risk female offenders.	-Case management system -Training of community health workers (CHW) and probation officers	Medium- to high-risk adult female offenders with six to nine months in jail; 130 women in 3 years	COMPAS	-Self-determination Theory of Motivation Trauma Recovery and Empowerment model used by CHWs and POs
Colorado State	The Colorado Division of Criminal Justice is implementing and evaluating the Behavioral Shaping Model and Reinforcement Tool (BSMART), which aims at standardizing the decision-making process for probation and correctional staff of halfway houses.	-Develop an evidence-based sanctions and incentives tool -Staff training	BSMART does not consider risk level; sanctions and incentives are applied in 18 halfway houses	LSI	-Use of graduated sanctions and incentives to address noncompliance and encourage progress
Maine State	This grant aims at implementing the Maine Integrated Risk Reduction Model (MIRRM) with fidelity and improving enhanced supervision skills of probation officers.	-Case management system -Staff training	Regional correctional managers, regional correctional administrators, and probation officers	LSI-R	-Use of graduated sanctions and incentives to address noncompliance and encourage progress

Jurisdiction	Description	Services	Target population	Assessment tool	Programmes/practices
Georgia State	The goal of this project is to support re-entry services by providing training to post-prison supervision staff and community partners to implement more collaborative supervision services to high-risk/high-need probationers using a train-the-trainer model.	-Staff training -Use of body-worn cameras	High-risk and high-need offenders	Next Generation Assessment	-Motivational interviewing -Effective Practices in Community Supervision (EPICS 2)
Maricopa County, AZ	The Maricopa Adult Probation Department is targeting antisocial behaviour and criminal thinking of medium- and high-risk probationers, by providing T4C programme in the community.	-Staff training -Partnerships with community organizations	Medium- and high-risk probationers	Offender Screening Tool	-T4C -Continuing care
Somerset County, PA	The Day Reporting Center (DRC) is a one-stop shop that centralizes a variety of services for medium- and high-risk offenders. The DRC is a highly structured, non-residential programme.	-Staff training	Medium- to high-risk offenders	COMPAS	-Motivational interviewing -CBT -Comprehensive treatment services -Aftercare
Allegheny County, PA	Allegheny County Adult Probation and Parole Department is implementing the Smart Accountability Project aiming at improving supervision practices by strengthening the agency's management and operations.	-Staff training -Online platforms (dashboard) -Equipment for mobile workforce	Medium- and high-risk offenders	LSI-R	-Treatment dosage
Salinas City, Monterey County, CA	The city of Salinas, in partnership with the Monterey County Probation, is improving the use of evidence-based practices for re-entry services to the AB109 population. The main objective of the project is to improve supervision success rates by providing training and technical assistance to service providers using evidence-based programmes and strategies.	-Staff training -Assessment of programs -Prescription plans -Technical assistance	-High-risk offenders coming out of prison to probation (AB109) -Service providers (GEO; Turning Points; Kickstart; Behavioral Health)	Ohio Risk Assessment System (ORAS)	-Transitional housing and employment assistance -Employment, workforce developing programme -CBT, family counselling, mental and emotional assistance
Wisconsin State	The Wisconsin Department of Corrections is developing a dosage-based probation project, aiming at reducing technical violations and reoffending by ensuring probationers have a determinate term of community supervision.	-Staff training on dosage, quality of supervision, and behavioural change	Medium- and high-risk offenders or even very high risk	COMPAS	-Supervision dosage

Next Generation Assessment and the Personalized Responses for Offender Adjustment and Community Transition Matrix as part of a strategic management approach to use the best available data to identify, prioritize, and refer offenders to appropriate programming, and to respond to offender behaviour during supervision in a manner that is swift, certain, and proportionate to the behaviour.

Internal and external factors facilitating the adoption of innovations

Implementation researchers and practitioners agreed on key internal and external factors to the organization that can affect, positively or negatively, the implementation of EBP. The inner setting refers to elements within the organization that can motivate inner change, such as organizational goals, mission, culture and climate, staff and managers, and readiness for change (Greenhalgh et al. 2004). Other important internal resources can improve the adoption of the innovation, and in terms of fidelity and outcome measures, are related to the availability of technical assistance and researchers to work hand in hand with the agency (Taxman and Belenko 2011).

Internal partners

Results from the interviews echo previous research findings related to the importance of leadership. As seen in Table 80.3, eight out of 11 (73%) interviewees highlighted the importance of having a strong leadership at the managerial level that understands and supports the innovation. Others found it necessary to be able to have a top-down supportive message that engages line staff, motivates participation in the process, and achieves buy-in of the EBP. As noted by Bero et al. (1998), innovations that emerged from a consensus are more likely to be successful than those that are imposed from the top. Involvement of leaders in the design of the implementation strategy, in key implementation activities, and throughout the process are seen as key ingredients to encourage participation, support and sustainability.

Other inner organization issues that emanated from the interviews relate to the need of having middle managers and line staff involved in the implementation process in early stages. Seventy-three percent of the agencies viewed this as an important contributor to achieve organizational change. Since the implementation of EBP might require changes in policies and practices affecting every routine activity, there is a need to proactively engage staff and increase their understanding of the innovation, its benefits, and implications. Focus groups, committees, and regular town hall meetings are key strategies to involve line staff (Lerch et al. 2009).

Table 80.3 Internal and external partners involved in the project

State/county	Inner organization				Outer organization			
	Management leadership	Support from senior and line staff	Programme/ grant managers	Board/ operation committees	Collaboration with other CJ/ health orgs.	Community/ service providers	Technical assistance	Research partners
Minnesota State	X	X	X	X	X	X		X
Coconino County, AZ	X	X	X		X	X		X
Monroe County, NY	X	X		X	X	X		X
Colorado State		X		X				X
Maine State	X		X					X
Georgia State	X				X		X	X
Maricopa County, AZ	X	X	X		X	X	X	X
Somerset County, PA	X	X				X		X
Allegheny County, PA	X	X		X	X			X
Salinas City, CA				X	X	X	X	X
Wisconsin State		X	X		X	X	X	

Lastly, four out of 11 (36%) agencies mentioned the importance of the organizational culture of the agency that not only supports the innovation, but is also ready for it, and has an understanding and history of dealing with EBP. For example, probation agencies in Colorado, Maine, Georgia, and Coconino, Maricopa, and Allegheny Counties were identified as early adopters (Rogers 2003) of EBP with a long trajectory of favourable attitudes and support for new ideas and learning processes. These organizations have been implementing different innovations for more than a decade with efforts on fidelity, quality, and effectiveness. With more or lesser challenges, they have embraced EBP in their organizations' values and objectives, as well as in day-to-day work. This is important because early adopters have the potential to significantly influence and support other agencies to engage in innovations.

External partners

The organization's outer setting includes networks or collaboration with other agencies, academic institutions, and professional associations, among others. It also includes the socio-political climate in which the organization functions; incentives and regulatory and legal mandates; and environment stability and interorganizational norm setting (Greenhalgh et al. 2004). Research on the influence of these factors in the adoption and implementation of innovations suggests that support from multiple stakeholders' agencies is a key element for generating internal change (Taxman and Belenko 2011). More specifically, Young et al. (2009) highlighted the importance of also engaging different levels of government criminal justice agencies because local agencies are often influenced by statewide initiatives that support the use of EBP. High-level leaders both within the agency and at the state level are important players when developing alliances with key stakeholders such as policymakers, researchers, criminal justice institutions, and community organizations.

As summarized in Table 80.3, five agencies emphasized the value of having policy-level committees or advisory boards linked to the programmes. These groups gathered key stakeholders, from policymakers to community organizations and criminal justice agencies. They usually met regularly and were involved in the design and implementation of the innovations, which according to respondents was a key factor in overcoming future barriers.

In Minnesota, the advisory board of the Smart Probation project included supervisors, the director of probation, director of field services, grant coordinator, travel judge, non-travel judge, representatives from the American Indian reservations, and the research team. The purpose was to broaden the net and provide an opportunity for different stakeholders to have input. Specially, the board tried to be inclusive of the tribal community and their agencies from the beginning of the programme. The board was dissolved after the programme finished. In Colorado, the Division of Criminal Justice led a statewide steering committee that was composed by volunteers from state and local governments, as well as representatives from the community and the private sector. The group acted as a policy advisory team by informing and guiding the design and implementation of the programme, and providing problem-solving support along the way.

Almost all agencies (90%) reported to have created a strategic alliance with a research institution. These partnerships vary in the level of engagement of the researchers in the project. Some agencies work hand in hand with the researcher from early stages of project implementation and performing different tasks (data gathering, training, evaluation, etc.), while others limit their practitioner-researcher relationship to the evaluation of the innovation. For example, Maine and Maricopa, Monroe, and Allegheny Counties have had the researchers at the table from the beginning of the programme and they have supported implementation by providing critical input in strategic planning, personnel training, and programme evaluation.

Other key partnerships cited by respondents were those with criminal justice agencies (72%), service providers (63%), and members of the community (28%). As mentioned above, a collaborative working relationship with these stakeholders can positively impact the design, planning, and implementation of the innovation. At the same time, involvement of justice and law enforcement stakeholders can improve public safety and offenders' outcomes. Working together, probation agencies and other governmental agencies can jointly provide a comprehensive and integrated selection of services that could not be offered by a single organization. In addition to the network of services, connecting offenders with their families and the community can enhance behavioural change and reduce recidivism.

The Female Offenders Can Ultimately Succeed (FOCUS) project in Monroe County, New York, has its basis on a collaborative alliance. It provides intensive supervision combined with enhanced care management and connections with medical, mental health, and substance abuse services to medium- and high-risk female offenders returning from jail to the community. In addition, the programme works collaboratively with probation agencies, courts, and community partners such as housing services, HIV clinics, transgender counselling, human trafficking courts, drug courts, domestic violence services, and housing, among others.

In a similar way, the city of Salinas is strengthening supervision, treatment, and re-entry services for offenders coming out of prison by providing training and technical assistance to community-based organizations in using evidence-based treatment and improving fidelity of programs. The project led by the city authorities has partnered with the probation department and four service providers that deliver six different types of programmes: a day reporting centre and a 30-day re-entry programme, workforce developing programme and housing services, and family counselling and mental health assistance.

Challenges faced during implementation of innovations

Implementation scholars have identified a significant number of organizational challenges that affect the successful adoption, implementation, and sustainability of innovations. For example, the availability of resources, such as funding, staff, and time; staff resistance to change (Taxman and Belenko 2011) and staff understanding of the purpose of change; and organization climate and structure that supports innovation (Viglione et al. 2017).

With many internal and external barriers that can affect programme implementation, respondents identified four main challenges (see Table 80.4): 90% of agencies viewed staff resistance as the main factor impeding adoption and implementation of EBP, followed by 45% of interviewees that acknowledged limited financial resources. Lastly, 45% and 18% of respondents considered resistance from clients and caseloads, respectively, as important barriers to implementation.

For example, during the implementation of the Day Reporting Center (DRC) in Somerset County, Pennsylvania, the Department of Probation experienced resistance from line staff. The new DRC is managed by one manager and two probation officers, who were assigned by the managerial team directly to these functions as internal transfers rather than opening a competitive hiring process to other staff members. This procedure caused resistance in the first place, but it was later overcome when the DRC was fully functioning, and probation officers were showing positive results with their clients. Somerset County found that limited financial resources were impeding the creation of its own DRC. Somerset is a rural county, with a high rate of unemployment of 5.9%. It is hard for community members to grasp the concept of helping a current offender or an ex-offender. The DRC would probably not have been in existence if Somerset had not attained the BJA grant. Once the grant is completed, Somerset will need to look for additional funding to ensure sustainability of daily activities of the DRC and transportation for clients.

In Maricopa County, the implementation of Thinking for a Change (T4C) programme in the community has experienced staff resistance. Similarly, some resistance has occurred from clients of the programme. They did not understand or like some treatment mechanisms such as role playing or identifying their feelings or giving feedback. This tends to occur during the first sessions of the programme, but as they experience the programmes the clients get used to these techniques.

Limited staff and high caseloads were mentioned by agencies as an obstacle that they needed to address consistently during implementation. Redistribution and reduction of caseload of probation officers was a strategy to deal with this challenge. In others, grant funds were utilized to hire additional staff or pay overtime to probation officers to undertake additional tasks related to the project. The Maine Department of Corrections identified high caseloads as an impediment for probation officers to engage in other activities, related to the implementation and sustainability of their Risk Reduction Model. There are

Table 80.4 Barriers to implementing innovations

	Inner organization					Outer organization		
	Management leadership	Funding	Staff training/ qualifications	Resistance from staff/staff turnover	Resistance from clients	Lack of cooperation from external partners	Lack of support from community/ service providers	Technical assistance
Minnesota State				X				
Coconino County, AZ				X	X		X	
Monroe County, NY		X		X	X			X
Colorado State	X			X		X		
Maine State				X				
Georgia State		X	X	X	X			
Maricopa County, AZ		X		X	X			
Somerset County, PA		X		X				
Allegheny County, PA		X		X				
Salinas City, CA								X
Wisconsin State				X	X		X	

around 70 probation officer positions statewide but full implementation of the Risk Reduction Model would require around 150 probation officers. The plan was to reduce the caseload by half, so that they could focus on coaching and supervising fidelity implementation of EBP throughout the regional offices. These probation officers received extensive training on the concepts, principles, and strategies for successfully implementing EBP within community corrections. Not having enough human capital represents a barrier to planning and implementing new projects. Lastly, the FOCUS programme in Monroe County, New York, faced implementation challenges due to turnover among probation staff, probation leadership, and technical assistance staff. There was also resistance from clients related to their stress, trauma, substance use, transportation, and time limitations.

Performance indicators

Reliable and accurate performance measures are critical for probation agencies implementing EBP. Performance measures constitute a key decision-making tool for monitoring short-term and long-term planning (budget, staffing), day-to-day programme operations, and evaluating cost-effectiveness of supervision. Assessing how staff and the overall agency performs can increase oversight and management of probation operations, as well as identify programme needs, gaps in services, etc. Although performance measurement and monitoring were viewed by most agencies as a key factor for assessing results, and ensuring sustainability of their projects, there is a lot of variation in the way they are systematically measuring management, line staff, client, and overall system performance. Several commonly used performance measures are identified and summarized in Table 80.5.

Table 80.5 Performance measures

Managers	Line staff	Clients	Overall system
Annual performance assessments/reviews	Annual performance assessments/reviews	Recidivism rates (rearrest, reconviction)	Recidivism rates (rearrest, reconviction)
Quarterly performance evaluation	Video or audio recordings	Probationers that stay sober, test negative for drugs	Probationers that successfully complete probation
Customer service surveys from clients	Observation forms	Probationers who are employed	Decrease in caseloads of officers
Participant's feedback	Participant's feedback	Probationers that graduated programmes, completed treatment, or finished probation	New felony convictions under supervision
Self-assessments	Feedback system, peer learning groups	Probationers with risk level/scores reduced	Programme fidelity

Management and line staff performance

Performance of individual staff is a key factor influencing services provided by the agency, as well as overall system performance. Probation supervision agencies have developed performance-based measures to improve accountability of staff for delivering the services or products that are being provided and also to better understand the strengths and weaknesses, and needs of the staff in terms of training, feedback, and coaching (Boone and Fulton 1996).

From this study, nine out of 11 (80%) linked staff performance to the development and usage of specialized skills, because of specific training. They reported several strategies to ensure performance monitoring of line staff, such as feedback systems based on data collected from observation forms and video recordings on the utilization of new skills and how clients are responding to them. Other strategies include annual performance assessments or reviews, and feedback from clients or participants. For example, the Wisconsin Department of Corrections is implementing a feedback system based on peer learning groups. Probation officers are being trained on the concept and strategies of dosage, as well as other evidence-based practices such as motivational interviewing. During a three-day training they learn and understand the communication skills needed the most with client interactions. Staff who has been trained on MI before getting together in a community of practice or peer learning group work together with new trainees on reviewing their MI skills and providing feedback and coaching.

And, probation officers within the Georgia Department of Community Supervision are wearing body cameras to capture interactions between officers and offenders. They are using the footage to get a better picture of the interactions, provide more detailed feedback, and improve the agency's training tools and supervision quality.

Client and overall system performance

Six out of 11 agencies (54%) include recidivism rates as a key measure for both client and system performance. From these, approximately half rely solely on this measure to document and demonstrate effectiveness. The utility of recidivism rate as a performance measure has been questioned and it has even been considered insufficient for assessing programme outcomes (King and Elderbroom 2014). Other agencies have complemented such measures with intermediate outcomes that capture pro-social changes, such as if probationers are employed, how often they are tested drug-free, and if they are completing treatment. These findings are in line with those of recent studies that have explored different strategies to construct alternative performance measures to recidivism that better reflect EBP within supervision agencies. Blasko et al. (2016) suggest that administrative data constitutes a rich source of information from which to build process measures that reflect evidence-based supervision, such as clients receiving referrals or not; following contact requirements and special conditions; and completing supervision, employment, drug testing, etc. These measures serve to identify programme needs and gaps in services and develop interventions to address such needs.

The Allegheny Adult Probation Department is implementing the Smart Accountability project, an organizational change strategy that aims at improving supervision practices through several activities: developing performance benchmarks for supervision, implementing dosage probation supervision based on risk and needs, developing online dashboards that provide real-time information on performance benchmarks to probation officers and supervisors, implementing tools that help monitor fidelity to EBP in real time and emphasize quality of casework rather than quantity of contacts, and improving the quality of interactions based on EBP, such as motivational interviewing. In addition, the agency partnered with the Urban Institute to support the design and implementation of benchmarks and performance matrices and to utilize dashboards.

Lessons learned from implementing innovations

The lessons learned discussed below stem from the experience of the 11 community corrections agencies examined in this chapter. These highlight a number of issues to consider when implementing innovative strategies or EBP within probation supervision. Six key lessons learned were identified as:

1   *Support from the agency's leadership and management* is essential to the entire process of implementing EBP. From identifying and selecting a practice to looking for funding, designing an implementation plan and executing it, and engaging partners, having buy-in, backing, and direction from upper management will solidify the process and make it smoother.
2   *Engagement of mid-level and front-line staff* is key to the organizational change process. Middle managers constitute the link between upper management and line staff. The responsibility of disseminating change through the organization lies with them. It is clear that an implementation strategy based solely on a top-down approach is not effective. The change process should be embraced at all levels of the organization.
3   *Cultivate and support collaborative partnerships* throughout the change process. It is critical to engage key stakeholders throughout the planning, development, and implementation process of innovations; this will contribute to instil confidence in and gain support for the new practice. As mentioned before, one mechanism used by many agencies to bring together key partners and gain consensus on new policies and practices is the establishment and convening of steering committees or policy advisory boards. This can be an effective venue for educating stakeholders about EBP.

4   *Listen and include the perspectives of probationers.* In addition to proba-
     tion officers and other criminal justice personnel, it is key to provide an
     opportunity for offenders to express their opinions and concerns about
     how the new practice is affecting them. This will help officers to pro-
     vide positive support to their clients and promote compliance. This was
     particularly important for agencies engaging in the implementation of
     incentives and sanctions grids.

5   *Sustain efforts over time.* The implementation of EBP is an ongoing process
     that requires intentional sustaining efforts. It is important to create a
     viable plan for how new practices become routine and common prac-
     tice within the organization. Some of the strategies considered by the
     interviewees included consistent messaging from the organization's lead-
     ership, recurring cycles of training and learning, and developing instru-
     ments for applicability of the EBP into everyday work.

6   *Assessing processes and outcomes is essential in understanding both the imple-
     mentation process and the innovation results.* Agencies should include an
     evaluation plan from the outset to assess the processes of implementa-
     tion and adherence to the programme design, as well as the outcomes of
     the intervention. Having evidence that agency staff are adhering to the
     programme design (fidelity), and that the implementation of the model
     is having the desired effect (outcomes), is essential to gain support from
     stakeholders, increase public trust and confidence, and secure financial
     resources.

Note

1   State probation population as of 31 December 2015. Sources: Kaeble and Bonczar
    (2016), Probation and Parole in the United States (2015), Bureau of Justice Statis-
    tics, US Department of Justice. Probation population for Georgia includes offend-
    ers under state felony supervision (source: DCS, data as of August 2018). County
    probation population: Coconino County (county probation population as of 31
    July 2018. Source: APETS Adult Probation Population Statistics Report); Maricopa
    County (source: Adult Probation Narrative Summary, FY 2016); Allegheny and Som-
    erset Counties, PA (source: County Adult Probation and Parole, Annual Statistical
    Report 2014); Salinas City/Monterey County (source: Chief Probation Officers Dash-
    board, County Probation Data, June 2016).

References

Aarons, G. A., Hurlburt, M. and Horwitz, S. M. (2011) Advancing a conceptual model of
    evidence-based practice implementation in public service sectors. *Administration and
    Policy in Mental Health and Mental Health Services Research*, 38, 4–23.
Adult Probation Narrative Summary. (2016) *Arizona Case Activity by County*. Available at:
    www.azcourts.gov/Portals/39/2016DR/AdultProbation.pdf#page=5.
Aebi, M. and Chopin, J. (2016) *Council of Europe Annual Penal Statistics (SPACE II). Persons
    Serving Non-Custodial Sanctions and Measures in 2015*. Lausanne, Switzerland: Unit of
    Criminology, School of Criminal Justice, University of Lausanne.

Bero, L. A., Grilli, R., Grimshaw, J. M., Harvey, E., Oxman, A. D. and Thomson, M. A. (1998) Closing the gap between research and practice: An overview of systematic reviews of interventions to promote the implementation of research findings. *BMJ: British Medical Journal*, 317(7156), 465–468.

Blasko, B., Souza, K., Via, B., Del Principe, S. and Taxman, F. S. (2016) Performance measures in community corrections: Measuring effective supervision practices with existing agency data. *Federal Probation*, 80(3), 26–32.

Boone, H. and Fulton, B. (1996) *Implementing Performance-Based Measures in Community Corrections*. Washington, DC: National Institute of Justice, Department of Justice.

Bourgon, G. and Gutierrez, L. (2012) The general responsivity principle in community supervision: The importance of probation officers using cognitive intervention techniques and its influence on recidivism. *Journal of Crime and Justice*, 35(2), 149–166.

Byrne, J. M. and Rebovich, D. (2007) *The New Technology of Crime, Law and Social Control*. Monsey, NY: Criminal Justice Press.

Fixsen, D., Naoom, S., Blase, K., Friedman, R. and Wallace, F. (2005) *Implementation Research: A Synthesis of the Literature*. Tampa, FL: University of South Florida, Lous de la Parte Florida Mental Health Institute, The National Implementation Research Network.

Greenhalgh, T., Robert, G., Macfarlane, F., Bate, P. and Kyriakidou, O. (2004) Diffusion of innovations in service organizations: Systematic review and recommendations. *Milbank Quarterly*, 82(4), 581–629.

Guevara, M. and Solomon, E. (2009) *Implementing Evidence-Based Policy and Practice in Community Corrections*, 2nd edition. Washington, DC: Crime and Justice Institute and National Institute of Corrections.

Innovation Suite. (n.d.) *Center for Research Partnerships and Program Evaluation, Bureau of Justice Assistance*. Available at: www.bja.gov/Programs/CRPPE/innovationssuite. html.

Innovation in Supervision Initiative: Building Capacity to Create Safer Communities. (n.d.) *Bureau of Justice Assistance*. Available at: www.bja.gov/ProgramDetails. aspx?Program_ID=122#horizontalTab1.

Kaeble, D., Maruschak, L. and Bonczar, T. (2015) *Probation and Parole in the United States, 2014*. Washington, DC: Bureau of Justice Statistics, Office of Justice Programs, US Department of Justice.

Kaeble, D. and Bonczar, T. (2016) *Probation and Parole in the United States, 2015*. Washington, DC: Bureau of Justice Statistics, Office of Justice Programs, US Department of Justice.

King, R. and Elderbroom, B. (2014) *Improving Recidivism as a Performance Measure*. Washington, DC: Urban Institute.

Lerch, J., James-Andrews, S., Eley, E. and Taxman, F. S. (2009) "Town Hall" strategies for organizational change. *Federal Probation*, 73(3), 2–9.

Miller, M., Drake, E. and Nafziger, M. (2013) *What Works to Reduce Recidivism by Domestic Violence Offenders?* (Document No. 13-01-1201). Olympia, Washington: State Institute for Public Policy.

Pattavina, A. and Taxman, F. S. (2007) Community corrections and soft technology. In J. Byrne and D. Rebovich (Eds.), *The New Technology of Crime, Law and Social Control*. Monsey, NY: Criminal Justice Press, pp. 327–346.

Petersilia, J. and Turner, S. (1993) *Evaluating Intensive Supervision Probation/Parole: Results of a Nationwide Experiment*. Washington, DC: National Institute of Justice.

Phelps, M. S. (2016) Mass probation: Toward a more robust theory of state variation in punishment. *Punishment & Society*, 19(1), 53–73.

Phelps, M. S. (2017) Mass probation and inequality: Race, class and gender disparities in supervision and revocation. In J. Ulmer and M. Bradley (Eds.), *Handbook on*

Punishment Decisions: Locations and Disparities. The ASC Division on Corrections & Sentencing Handbook Series, Vol. 2, pp. 43–63. Lansing, MI: Michigan State University.

Proctor, E., Landsverk, J., Aarons, G., Chambers, D., Glisson, C. and Mittman, B. (2009) Implementation research in mental health services: An emerging science with conceptual, methodological, and training challenges. *Administration and Policy in Mental Health and Mental Health Services Research*, 36, 24–34.

Rogers, E. M. (2003) *Diffusion of Innovations*, 5th edition. New York: The Free Press.

Taxman, F. S. and Belenko, S. (2011) *Implementing Evidence-Based Practices in Community Corrections and Addiction Treatment*. New York: Springer.

Taxman, F. S. and Thanner, M. (2006) Risk, need, and responsivity (RNR): It all depends. *Crime & Delinquency*, 52(1), 28–51.

Viglione, J., Blasko, B. and Taxman, F. (2017) Organizational factors and probation officer use of evidence-based practices: A multilevel examination. *International Journal of Offender Therapy and Comparative Criminology*, 1–20.

Walmsley, R. (2016) *World Prison Population List*, 11th edition. London: Institute for Crime Policy Research.

Young, D., Farrell, J., Henderson, C. and Taxman, F. (2009) Filling service gaps: Providing intensive treatment services for offenders. *Drug and Alcohol Dependence*, 103(Supplement 1), S33–S42.

Appendix

Interview instrument

Name of the agency:			
Overview statement	**Interview date and time**	**Participants**	**Contact information**

Areas of enquiry

(1) Characteristics of the project:

1 Can you provide a brief overview of your project?
2 How did it get started?
3 What is your key project goal?
4 What are the key project timeframes?
5 What are the key project milestones?

(2) Internal partners:

1 Who in your organization is directly involved in this project?
2 How many line staff?
3 What are the roles and responsibilities of staff?

(3) External partners:

1   What other agencies, organizations, and groups are involved in this project?
2   Who is at the table, in terms of planning and project management?
3   Who is NOT at the table? Why? Who is missing?

(4) Accomplishments thus far:

1   What are your major accomplishments to date?
2   What has been the key to your project's success (so far)?

(5) Barriers to implementation:

1   Which of the following are the most significant internal challenges you
     face?

     __ Funding
     __ Staff training and/or qualifications
     __ Resistance from line staff and managers
     __ Resistance from programme participants

2   Which of the following are the most significant external challenges you
     face?
     __ Lack of cooperation from key external partners
     __ Lack of community support

(6) Performance indicators:

1   How do you measure line staff performance?
2   How do you measure management performance?
3   How do you measure client performance?
4   How do you measure overall system performance?

(7) Lessons learned:

1   What are the key lessons learned from your involvement in this project?
2   What recommendations can you offer about how to improve this initia-
     tive?

Section 9

Lived experiences from the lens of individuals involved in the justice system and practitioners

Section 9 Introduction

Probation supervision is a complex enterprise, authorized by the state, where probation workers (whether they are officers or social workers) exert control over individuals in the community. The individuals are required to attend probation meetings and are required to adhere to the conditions of probation, which vary considerably depending on the jurisdiction and the special requirements that the judge and/or parole board may have imposed. In the United States, these requirements can stretch to be up to 25 standard conditions in some probation settings that include a myriad of financial payments (i.e. probation fees, drug testing fees, restitution, court fees, etc.), spatial restrictions (i.e. curfews, house arrest, limitations on areas that a person can go, requirements to get permission to leave an area), and psychological restrictions (i.e. evaluation and testing for psychological conditions, treatment requirements, meeting requirements, etc.). (See Taxman and Breno 2017 for a discussion of these varied types of restrictions.) Both the probation worker and the probationer are exposed to these requirements and they impact the experience that the individual has of supervision in untold ways. We are just beginning to undercover what this lived experience from the lens of the probation worker and the probationer is, and how it affects the legitimacy of the probation sanction.

The pains of punishment were coined by Gresham Sykes's (1958) *The Society of Captives* to describe how prisons are punitive. In his description, Sykes characterized the concept of 'deprivation' which occurred as a result of incarceration to be a series of liberty restrictions such as movement (physical limits) around the facility, limited access to goods and services and support services, ability to make decisions, and security from other prisoners. Hayes, in his chapter, expands on this argument and helps us understand contemporary incarceration. Durnescu (2011) extended this characterization to describe the pains of probation which similarly focuses on how the conditions of probation are punitive, and impact the daily existence of a person. These pains can be conceptualized as a series of requirements placed on individuals where the liberty restrictions affect their daily thoughts and physical movements. The untold impact of these restrictions on the individual is unknown in terms of how individuals experience probation. But several questions are raised that need attention – do these conditions (or pains of probation) affect the legitimacy of the sanction and does the legitimacy affect the degree to which the individual is compliant with the requirements of probation? Since the consequence of failure to comply is high in terms of more liberty restrictions, including the loss of liberty through incarceration, an appreciation for understanding the pains of probation is needed. This is the topic of the Durnescu, Lattimore, and DeMichele chapters in this section that provide both a theoretical argument for more exploration for understanding the pains of probation, as well as the methods by which we can assess how much 'pain' is being felt.

The pains of incapacitation and/or probation, as measured by the burdens of conditions, can also be conceptualized as a problem that affects the trajectory of being successful under crminal justice control. The more requirements for an individual, the more likely the person is not going to meet the requirements in full. Compliance is a thorny issue in that it places the person at jeopardy for more liberty restrictions, and potentially the loss of liberty through incarceration; if incarcerated, it can lead to solitary confinement. The patterns of compliance on supervision are not well understood – both in terms of the types of behaviours that probationers engage in that are in violation of the conditions of probation and the types of responses from probation workers. The challenge associated with how to address compliance is poorly understood; often it is perceived as a 'yes/no' scenario but in fact compliance can be fluid with many ebbs and flows. And, this creates a consternation for probation workers as to the right (or best or most appropriate or most effective) way to address the noncompliance with the conditions of supervision. This is an area that is unexplored in the research, and is addressed in this section for both probation and imprisonment.

Probation workers, and in their experience on the job, form an underresearched area. While there is much emphasis on the use of Core Correctional Practices, and the tools of doing evidence-based, Risk-Need-Responsivity supervision, there is little attention to the related issues of helping probation workers process their experience as officers (or social workers) working with individuals that they have tremendous authority over. The decisions that probation workers make regarding what to communicate to the probationer cannot be taken lightly – workers have to help probationers understand what aspect of their behaviour is undesirable and needs to change. In many cases, this is often done absent the socio-economic environments that probationers live in, which makes some of the changes more challenging when individuals have substance use disorders, mental illness, and/or histories of violence, trauma, or other experiences that may affect how individuals process the world around them. Probation workers must be ready to address work with individuals, not just dictate orders. The skills of evidence-based supervision or Core Correctional Practices may assume that workers/officers have the capabilities to work with varied personalities and experiences but few training programmes focus on developing these types of skills. Little research has delved into the work experience of being a probation worker, and how these experiences shape decisions.

This section benefits from three readings that highlight the importance of understanding the context by which criminal justice control is practised. Ioan Durnescu discusses the pains of probation by examining the experience of a community-based sanction. Pamela K. Lattimore and Matthew DeMichele expand our appreciation for the lives of individuals involved in community supervision by examining how compliance with requirements occurs. And David Hayes's conceptual history of Sykes's pains of imprisonment argument usefully highlights the association of these pains with the harms of punishment. Collectively, these chapters help us appreciate the physical, psychological, and financial demands that the criminal justice experience has on individuals, as well as those that have the responsibility for carrying out the state-sanctioned punishments.

In this set of readings, the theme is to better understand the lived experience from justice workers and those impacted by the justice system. This can best be achieved through mixed method studies that focus attention on understanding context, and how context affects the choices that probationers make and the decisions that workers/officers make. As a people business, decisions are affected by the behaviour of inmates/probationers and workers/officers. While the research tends to favour the notion that it is inmates/probationers that decide whether to comply or not to the conditions of confinement/probation, studies have not been devoted to whether the conditions are legitimate or the worker/officer response is legitimate. In the end, it is critical to understand the multipronged issue to better understand what being under correctional control truly involves, from the individual and worker/officer perspectives.

References

Durnescu, Ioan. (2011) Pains of probation: Effective practice and human rights. *International Journal of Offender Therapy and Comparative Criminology*, 55(4), 530–545.

Sykes, Gersham. (1958) *The Society of Captives: A Study of a Maximum Security Prison*. Princeton, NJ: Princeton University Press.

Taxman, Faye S. and Breno, Alex. (2017) Alternatives to incarceration. In *Oxford Research Encyclopedia of Oxford Research Encyclopedia of Criminology and Criminal Justice*. New York: Oxford University Press.

81

Experiencing community-based supervision

The pains of probation

Ioan Durnescu

Introduction

Before we even commence it might be useful to say a few words about who the probationers are. In most countries, the profile provided by Walsh and Sexton (1999) – 'a young, single male who is unemployed (or underemployed) with poor educational qualifications and vocational skills and is living in the parental home' (p. 97) – probably still make sense. Beside the differences in the level of risk, probationers seem to be rather male, mostly young, first-time offenders and socially disadvantaged. In terms of the crimes they committed, probationers tend to be responsible for property crimes, mildly violent crimes, drug-related crimes, and increasingly for drunk driving or white-collar crimes.

Now that we know who the probationer is, we can start discussing why their perception is important and for whom. 'User's voice' has quite a long history in the social work literature. This interest was originally justified by one of the most important values of social work – the recognition of self-determination

(Biestek 1961). In that sense, listening to clients and taking into account their motivations and preferences were perceived as a logical step. The rise of the radical social work paradigm amplified this perception to a point where social workers were defined as client's allies against the state oppression (Ferguson 2008). However, this paradigm was short-lived and soon was replaced by the new right ideologies where the focus was on 'policing' the poor and the dangerous groups and not on providing them with welfare services. At the end of the 1990s a new ideology came to replace or at least to alter the previous one – the modernization movement. Central to this movement was the concept of good governance where, in order to be effective, the service provider needs to develop partnerships with the service users. The 'service user' was redefined away from the paternalistic view expressed by the concept of 'client'. On the contrary, the 'service user' was the one who knows best what his or her needs are and how they should be responded to.

As probation practice evolved to a certain extent from the social work theory and practice, the interest in what probationers think about the supervisor and the supervision process was quite prevalent. More recently, scholars such as Weaver and Barry (2014) argued that the outcomes of supervision cannot be achieved without the offender's participation and active involvement. Ansems and Braam (2016) noted that offender's involvement is important for their motivation for change and probation officers began to acknowledge this in their daily practice.

Research on compliance (Tyler 1990; Bottoms et al. 2004; Robinson and McNeill 2008; McCulloch 2013, etc.) argues in the same vein. It seems that what supervision should aim for is substantive compliance – a form of compliance that is long term and involves the offender's active and meaningful engagement with the supervision – and not a naked instrumental compliance that involves a simple obedience with the measures and obligations imposed by the court. Substantive compliance, however, appears to be fostered by probation officers who are perceived as fair, positive, and respectful (Ugwudike 2010; Phillips 2011).

Linked to compliance, the concept of legitimacy plays an important role in the sense that offenders are more likely to comply, engage, and progress if they perceive the state authority as fair, just, and reasonable (Bottoms et al. 2004; McIvor 2009; Robinson and McNeill 2008).

All this research provides us with convincing evidence that how probationers perceive supervision and the supervisors is essential to how they will engage with the process and, eventually, whether they will consider even to start the change process. Therefore, the lived experience is important for both the probationer and the probation staff.

How is the 'lived experience' of supervision?

This is most definitely a wide and difficult question to answer in a simple manner. As argued by some scholars, the experience of supervision is most often shaped by what sort of supervision we are talking about, what kind of obligations are involved, for how long, and so on. Hammerschick, Pelikan, and Pilgram (1994), for instance, noted that 85% of the offenders (out of 699 cases referred by the public prosecutor or the judge in 1991 in Austria) responded positively when asked about their participation in the victim offender mediation process. Colman et al. (2011) interviewed offenders on drug treatment and observed that the sanction was considered by the offenders as an opportunity to get back their lives and avoid prison. De Wree et al. (2008) in Belgium noted that the lack of information and too many appointments at the beginning of supervision created some frustration among some offenders under the drug treatment. Those under electronic monitoring seem to share more or less the same perceptions. They seem to be satisfied with avoiding imprisonment and live a 'similar to normal life' (Hammerschick et al. 1994). In the same time they are able to keep distance from their antisocial peers, spend more time with the family, and are able to continue their treatment. While experiencing these advantages, many probationers under electronic monitoring report also considerable psychological pressure in terms of stress, fear, temptation (Vanhaelemeesch and Beken 2012), and self-discipline (Stassart et al. 2000). Electronic monitoring puts also a lot of pressure on the social life and affects third parties (Jorgensen 2011).

Community service is another area that inspires mixed feelings. On one hand, offenders tend to report good experiences, an opportunity to gain something (in terms of a new skill or more prospects for finding a job) or a constructive context to increase self-esteem (Beyens 2010; McIvor 1992; Dantinne et al. 2009). On the other hand, they also report the work as boring or dirty (van den Dorpel et al. 2010).

Post-release supervision is most often reported as arbitrarily focused on constraining criminality rather than promoting progress. As the people who leave prisons are economically vulnerable, indebted, disconnected from the labour market, with low social status and with fractured identities, parole supervision seems to increase rather than to decrease the pains. Werth (2017) and Jefferson (2017) demonstrate in two distinct geographical areas that post-prison 'over-governance' perpetuates the circuits of exclusion rather than fostering social inclusion. When parole supervision is perceived as helpful is when the parole staff is forging positive relationships and makes an extra step to help parolees on their ways to freedom. Autonomy and co-production were also described as positive experiences of parole in Scotland (Schinkel 2017).

Apart from these normative aspects of supervision, the lived experience is also determined by the way the supervision is conducted by the professional staff.

Ditton and Ford (1994), Mair and Mills (2009), Kyvsgaard (1998), Rex (1999), and others noted that supervision in general was perceived as a positive experience when it was delivered in a respectful way, by competent, reasonable, open, and flexible professionals. The 'relationship' factor is mentioned many times in the literature as playing a crucial role in what is usually defined as a good supervision (Ditton and Ford 1994; Burnett and McNeill 2005).

But the experience of supervision seems to be shaped also by who the probationers are. According to Malloch and McIvor (2011) the lived experience is a gendered experience; they argue that the quality of the relationship is important in particular for women offenders. Furthermore, they suggest that enhancing self-efficacy is a critical element for a positive experience among women. Calverley et al. (2006) interviewed 483 black and Asian offenders in England and Wales and concluded that they perceived the probation officers as 'someone they could talk to, who listen, and who was helpful' (p. 34). That was what made their experience under probation supervision a constructive one.

How supervision is experienced in general terms by the offenders is the object of another line of research. Durnescu (2011), for instance, interviewed 43 probationers in Romania and identified eight pains of probation, grouped in six categories: deprivation of autonomy, deprivation of time, financial costs, stigmatization effects, forced return to the offence, and life under tremendous threat. The first pain – the deprivation of autonomy – was divided into two main deprivations: pain of reorganizing the daily routine around the sanction and the deprivation of private family life. Some of them are intentional but some are rather unintentional, or incidental punishments, as described by Walker (1991). Based on these observations, Hayes (2015) interviewed nine probationers in England and identified six major groups of pain of supervision: pains of rehabilitation (the more requirements the more painful the experience is), pains of liberty deprivation (punishment through breach), penal welfare issues (the more vulnerability one has the more painful the supervision is), pains of external agency interventions (the more agencies are involved the more difficult the supervision process is perceived), process pains, and stigma. One important contribution of Hayes (2015) is that some pains are intensified by the supervisory relationship (e.g. pains of rehabilitation and pains of deprivation of liberty) while others can be ameliorated (e.g. penal welfare issues) or not affected by it (e.g. stigma).

The most critical probationers are those who were recalled. Although there is not much research on this subject, probationers seem to believe that probation staff have too much power and the parole conditions are too unreasonable so that they were 'set up to fail' (Padfield 2013). After interviewing 20 recalled prisoners, Digard (2010) concluded that some of them were recalled for minor transgressions or for subjective reasons. It does not come as a surprise therefore to observe that many recalled prisoners developed deep mistrust feelings towards their case managers.

As can be noted, the experience of supervision depends significantly on: how supervision is designed; the content and outcome of supervision; the probation staff; the quality of the relationship; and the supervisee. More research is needed to capture the extent to which the organizational climate or other internal or external factors may influence the lived experience of supervision.

Ways towards the future

Most of the methodologies employed for identifying the lived experience of supervision were based on interviews with the supervisees. However, as with other marginalized groups, offenders often have low educational achievements and poor literacy skills which may inhibit their capacity to verbally articulate what they experience or feel (McNeill et al. 2011). Recently, there has been some progress in measuring or capturing the lived experience of supervision using some innovative approaches such as visual methods.

One such initiative was the 'Supervisible' project, which collected and analyzed images taken by supervisees to represent their experiences of supervision. The project was part of the COST Action – Offender Supervision in Europe.[1] The pictures were discussed and analyzed together with the probationers in different jurisdictions and also with an art therapist. For instance, the women under supervision in England described their experience in terms of: rubbish, health and well-being, judgement and representations, help and support, time, money and cost, hope, growth, and nature.[2] The photographs and the subsequent discussions facilitated access of the researchers to the pains of probation, covering moments when the supervision is active but also those in between supervision sessions. By doing so, the researchers had access to a better understanding of the 'pervasive nature of the all-seeing eye of punishment in community' (Howard League of Penal Reform, n.d.: 4). Overall, the perception of some of these women was that their real lives are suspended and exposed to the others who have power over them.

A second initiative of the same COST Action was a questionnaire – Experiencing Supervision Barometer – that is capable of measuring and comparing the experience of supervision across different jurisdictions. Exploring the lived experience in a comparative fashion brings many benefits to research and practice. First, different aspects of the lived experience could be compared and contrasted between different jurisdictions. In the context of an increased mobility of supervision across European states this comparison may avoid misunderstandings and failed expectations. Second, the tool may be used at different moments in time and this could facilitate a better understanding of a certain dynamic. In this respect, the tool could be used in the same jurisdictions but at different moments. Comparing and measuring the lived experience in different jurisdictions may also provide useful correlations with the outcomes of supervision. It may be, for instance, that jurisdictions that report more practical help or better relationships register better compliance and reconviction rates.

The tool was piloted in 11 jurisdictions on non-representative samples and the psychometric of the scale proved to be acceptable (Cronbach alpha score above .60).

The barometer was built based on the literature review and the Council of Europe recommendations including themes that seem to be relevant to the experience of supervision. Eight broad themes were part of the questionnaire, namely supervision-general aspects, supervision and the supervisor, the relationship with the supervisor, supervision and practical help, supervision and compliance, supervision and breach, supervision and rehabilitation, and supervision and participation.

The tool needs further refinement and testing on real representative samples.

However, these examples show that more types of methodologies could be used to capture the subjective and pervasive nature of supervisions.

Notes

1 For more information about this COST Action, please visit: www.offendersupervi sion.eu/experiencing-supervision.
2 For more information on this project, please visit: http://howardleague.org/wp-con tent/uploads/2016/04/Supervisible.pdf.

References

Ansems, L. and Braam, I. (2016) It takes two to tango: Offenders' involvement in decisions regarding sanctions, measures and conditions in light of the ERCSM and the ERProb. A Dutch case study. *European Journal of Probation*, 8(1), 16–29.

Beyens, K. (2010) From 'community service' to 'autonomous work penalty' in Belgium. What's in a name? *European Journal of Probation*, 2, 4–21.

Biestek, F. P. (1961) *The Casework Relationship*. London: Unwin University Books.

Bottoms, A., Shapland, J., Costello, A., et al. (2004) Towards desistance: Theoretical underpinnings for an empirical study. *Howard Journal of Criminal Justice*, 43(4), 368–389.

Burnett, R. and McNeill, F. (2005) The place of the officer-offender relationship in assisting offenders to desist from crime. *The Journal of Community and Criminal Justice*, 52(3), 221–242.

Calverley, A., Cole, B., Kaur, G., Lewis, S., Raynor, P., Sadeghi, S., Smith, D., Vanstone, M. and Wardak, A. (2006) Black and Asian probationers: Implications of the Home Office study. *Probation Journal*, 53(1), 24–37.

Colman, C., De Ruyver, B., Vander Laenen, F., Vanderplasschen, W., Broekaert, E., De Keulenaer, S. and Thomaes, S. (2011) *De drugbehandelingskamer: een andere manier van afhandelen. Het proefproject geëvalueerd*. Antwerpen: Maklu.

Dantinne, M., Duchêne, J., Lauwaert, K., Aertsen, I., Bogaerts, S., Goethals, J. and Vlaemynck, M. (2009) *Peine de travail et vécu du condamné. Beleving van de veroordeelde tot een werkstraf*. Liège – Leuven: Université de Liège; Katholieke Universiteit Leuven, unpublished.

De Wree, E., De Ruyver, B., Verpoest, K. and Colman, C. (2008) All in favour? Attitudes of stakeholders and drug users towards judicial alternatives. *European Journal on Criminal Policy and Research*, 14, 431–440.

Digard, L. (2010) When legitimacy is denied: Offender perceptions of the prison recall system. *Probation Journal*, 57(1), 160–163, Sage Publications.

Ditton, J. and Ford, R. (1994) *The Reality of Probation: A Formal Ethnography of Process and Practice*. Aldershot: Avebury.

Durnescu, I. (2011) Pains of probation: Effective practice and human rights. *International Journal of Offender Therapy and Comparative Criminology*, 55(4), 530–545.

Ferguson, I. (2008) *Reclaiming Social Work: Challenging Neoliberalism and Promoting Social Justice*. London: Sage.

Hammerschick W., Pelikan, C. and Piligram, A. (1994) Von der Fallzuweisung zum Abschluß des Außergerichtlichen Tatausgleichs – die praktischen Ergebnisse des Modellversuchs [From case assignment to the conclusion of out-of-court offence compensation proceedings: The practical results of the pilot project]. In F. McNeill and K. Beyens, *Offender Supervison in Europe, 2013*. London: Palgrave Macmillan.

Hayes, D. (2015) The impact of supervision on the pains of community penalties in England and Wales: An exploratory study. *European Journal of Probation*, 7, 85–102, August. DOI:10.1177/2066220315593099.

Howard League for Prison Reform. (n.d.) *Supervisible: Exploring Community Supervision Using Photovoice*. Available at: http://howardleague.org/wp-content/uploads/2016/04/Super visible.pdf.

Jefferson, A. M. (2017) Exacerbating deprivations: Trajectories of confinement in Sierra Leone. In R. Armstrong and I. Durnescu (Eds.), *Parole and Beyond. International Perspectives*. London: Palgrave Macmillan, pp. 243–269.

Jorgensen, T. T. (2011) *Afsoning I hjemmet. En effektevaluering af fodlaenkeordningen*. Denmark: Ministry of Justice.

Kyvsgaard, B. (1998) *Kriminalforsorg i Frihed*. Copenhagen: Direktoratet for Kriminal-forsorgen.

Mair, G. and Mills, H. (2009) *The Community Order and the Suspended Sentence Order Three Years on: The Views and Experiences of Probation Officers and Offenders*. London: Centre for Crime and Justice Studies.

Malloch, M. and McIvor, G. (2011) Women and community sentences. *Criminology and Criminal Justice*, 11(4), 325–344.

McCulloch, P. (2013) Re-analysing the compliance dynamic: Towards a co-productive strategy and practice? In P. Ugwudike and P. Raynor (Eds.), *What Works in Offender Compliance? International Perspectives and Evidence-Based Practice*. Basingstoke: Palgrave Macmillan, pp. 44–64.

McIvor, G. (1992) *Sentenced to Serve: The Operation and Impact of Community Service by Offenders*. Aldershot: Avebury.

McIvor, G. (2009) Therapeutic jurisprudence and procedural justice in Scottish drug courts. *Criminology and Criminal Justice*, 9(1), 29–49.

McNeill, F., Anderson, K., Colvin, S., Overy, K., Sparks, R. and Tett, L. (2011) Inspiring desistance? Arts projects and 'what works?' *Justitiele verkenningen*, 37(5), 80–101.

Padfield, N. (2013) *Understanding Recall 2011*. Paper no. 2. Available at: http://papers. ssrn.com/sol3/papers.cfm?abstract_id=2201039.

Phillips, Jake. (2011) Target, audit and risk assessment cultures in the probation service. *European Journal of Probation*, 3(3), 108–122.

Rex, S. (1999) Desistance from offending: Experiences of probation. *The Howard Journal of Criminal Justice*, 38(4), 366–383, Blackwell.

Robinson, G. and McNeill, F. (2008) Exploring the dynamics of compliance with community penalties. *Theoretical Criminology*, 12(4), 431–449.

Schinkel, M. (2017) Experiences of parole in Scotland: Stalled lives. In R. Armstrong and I. Durnescu (Eds.), *Parole and Beyond. International Perspectives*. London: Palgrave Macmillan, pp. 219–242.

Stassart, E., Peters, T. and Parmentier, S. (2000) *Elektronisch toezicht. Een belevingsonderzoek bij de eerste groep van deelnemers*. Eindrapport. Brussel: Ministerie van Justitie – K.U. Leuven, unpublished.

Tyler, T. R. (1990) *Why People Obey the Law: Procedural Justice, Legitimacy and Compliance*. New Haven: Yale University Press.

Ugwudike, P. (2010) Compliance with Community Penalties: The Importance of Interactional Dynamics. In F. McNeill, P. Raynor and C. Trotter (Eds.), *Offender*

Supervision: New Directions in Theory, Research and Practice. Abingdon: Willan Publishing, pp. 325–343.

Van den Dorpel, H., Kamp, E. and Van der Laan, P. (2010) *Amsterdamse Werkgestraften aan het Woord. Eerste Indrukken van een Onderzoek naar de Werkstraf in Amsterdam.* Nederlands: Studiecentrum Criminaliteit en Rechtshandhaving.

Vanhaelemeesch, D. and Vander Beken, T. (2012) Electronic monitoring: Convicts' experiences in Belgium. In M. Cools, B. De Ruyver, M. Easton, L. Pauwels, P. Ponsaers, G. Vande Walle, T. Vander Beken, F. Vander Laenen and G. Vynckier (Eds.), *Social Conflicts, Citizens and Policing.* Antwerpen: Maklu.

Walker, N. (1991) *Why Punish?* Oxford: Oxford University Press.

Walsh, D. and Sexton, P. (1999) *An Empirical Study of Community Service Orders in Ireland.* Dublin: The Stationery Office.

Weaver, B. and Barry, M. (2014) Managing high risk offenders in the community: Compliance, cooperation and consent in a climate of concern. *European Journal of Probation*, 6(3), 278–295.

Werth, R. (2017) Breaking the rules the right way: Resisting parole logics and asserting autonomy in the USA. In R. Armstrong and I. Durnescu (Eds.), *Parole and Beyond. International Perspectives.* London: Palgrave Macmillan, pp. 141–169.

82

Experiencing probation

Results from the Honest Opportunity Probation with Enforcement (HOPE) demonstration field experiment: US perspective

Pamela K. Lattimore and Matthew DeMichele

Introduction

Nearly 3.8 million of the 6.7 million individuals under correctional supervision in the United States in 2016 were on probation (Kaeble and Cowhig 2018). Individuals on probation remain in the community if they meet the conditions of their supervision – conditions set by the sentencing judge and, in some cases, by probation department policy. These conditions can include complying with drug testing, refraining from substance use, performing community service, working or looking for employment, and paying fees and fines. Failure to meet conditions can lead to violations and consequences, including revocation to prison (or jail).

Although probation is common, relatively little is known about the *experience* of probation at the individual level. Assessment of probation effectiveness is often conducted by looking at failure on probation – new arrest or revocation – and conduct on probation – violations of conditions. Researchers typically study probationer behaviour in three ways: (1) determining whether probationers experience any negative event (e.g. arrest, violation) during a fixed time (e.g. over two years); (2) comparing the number of times a negative event occurs (e.g. the number of arrests) during a fixed period (or controlling for variable exposure times); and (3) studying the time to an event (e.g. how long to first arrest). These events – and the lack of these events – occur within a variety of contexts that influence the risk of the events occurring. Specifically, at a minimum, a probationer will be either free in the community; in the community but constrained by curfews, electronic monitoring, or house arrest; or 'off the street' in jail or residential treatment. Community supervision ends with successful completion of probation or, unsuccessfully, with incarceration because of revocation or sentencing for new crimes.

The evaluation of the Honest Opportunity with Enforcement (HOPE) demonstration field experiment provided an opportunity to collect the data needed to examine the experience of probation for eight distinct groups of probationers – HOPE-eligible probationers in four sites who were randomly assigned to either HOPE supervision or to probation as usual (PAU). Because of local variation in policy and practice, PAU varied among the four sites.[1] HOPE was implemented per prescribed principles, but local variation also impacted some experiences. For example, one HOPE judge had access to a residential substance abuse treatment programme operated by the state Department of Criminal Justice and was an avid supporter of this programme – resulting in more than half of the HOPE probationers in that site being sent to residential treatment, substantially more cases than were referred in the other three sites.

For the 1,504 individuals randomly assigned to either a HOPE programme or PAU, complete data were available on time in the community, residential drug treatment, jail, and prison. Also available were the dates of all arrests and probation violations. These data allowed the mapping and examination of the experience of probation for the individuals in these eight groups. Results suggest considerable variation in how probation was experienced – with, for example, substantial differences in numbers of violations and time spent in jail. There was also considerable variation in the characteristics of the probationers across the sites – suggesting that not only did they have different probation experiences but that, across the sites, the types of individuals who were exposed to the probation regimens were different – particularly with respect to prior criminal histories. Despite these differences, recidivism outcomes were not only similar between groups within sites but were largely similar across sites – with roughly half of all groups experiencing either revocation or new arrest during follow-up.

HOPE

The HOPE programme originated as Hawaii's Opportunity Probation with Enforcement (Hawaii HOPE) in Oahu, Hawaii, in 2004, with a goal of holding probationers accountable to their conditions of supervision through swift, certain, and fair responses to any violations, including positive drug tests (Hawken and Kleiman 2007, 2009). HOPE supervision includes:

- A warning hearing by a HOPE judge during which individuals are advised that any violation of conditions will result in an immediate response – most likely a short, immediate jail stay
- Random drug testing at least twice per week initially followed by less frequent testing with repeat negative test results
- Issuance of a warrant and conduct of a violation hearing for any missed appointment, missed drug test, positive test, or other failure to comply with supervision conditions
- Short jail stays following any violation
- Substance abuse treatment only after repeated positive tests
- Revocation only after repeated violations

HOPE was presented in contrast to PAU, envisioned as permitting multiple violations until 'a final straw' results in revocation, often to lengthy prison terms. The hypothesized effects of HOPE are that rapid response to violations deters future violations; drug use and recidivism falls; and fewer revocations result in fewer prison days (and lower prison costs).

The initial evaluation of the Hawaii HOPE programme showed large reductions in positive drug tests and missed appointments; fewer arrests at three, six, and 12 months; about the same number of jail days for violations (more but shorter terms); and about one-third as many days in prison on revocations or new convictions (Hawken and Kleiman 2009). More recent findings, including long-term follow-up of the original Hawaii HOPE participants, were less positive. In a 76-month follow-up of the original study participants, Hawken and Colleagues (2016) found HOPE participants were equally likely to have a new charge, less likely to have multiple charges (primarily due to fewer drug charges), and less likely to be revoked; the Hawaii HOPE participants also had fewer probation violations (6.3 versus 7.1; $p = 0.09$). In a randomized controlled trial of a HOPE-like programme for Delaware probationers, O'Connell et al. (2016) found no impact on a variety of recidivism measures.

The HOPE model was then tested in a four-site demonstration field experiment that included randomized controlled trials conducted in Saline County, Arkansas; Essex County, Massachusetts; Clackamas County, Oregon; and Tarrant County, Texas. Results from the evaluation showed that while HOPE was implemented with fidelity in the four sites, HOPE probationers were no more successful than PAU probationers on a variety of recidivism measures (arrest, revocation, arrest/revocation, and reconviction) while revocations were higher in two sites and reconvictions higher in one site (Lattimore et al. 2016).

Data and methods

Administrative data from local and state agencies were obtained for all 1,504 evaluation participants.[2] These data included demographic information, information on criminal history (prior arrests, convictions), probation violations (date, type, response), substance abuse treatment (placement dates, residential or outpatient), and recidivism (probation revocation date and length of term; conviction date, offence, and disposition; and incarceration dates, offence, and length of term).

Using these data, a history record was constructed for each individual showing when the individual was on the street, in jail, in residential treatment (RSAT), or revoked to prison. The timing of arrests, violations, and deaths were also recorded. These histories provide detailed information on the variability among individual probation experiences. The analyses rely on a method to visualize these data using horizontal line plots.[3] Each probationer is represented by one horizontal line. Grey scale on the line indicates where the individual was during the time periods (e.g. on the street or in jail) with the length of the grey scale segments reflecting the length of time in the state. Events (arrests and violations) are superimposed on the lines using symbols (e.g. circles, x's, plus signs). Participants' lines are stacked and sorted to show the variety of experiential patterns that probationers had during the study. The plots are stratified by group and site to examine site and group differences.

Transition matrices were also constructed and examined that showed transitions from the first to the second state, the second to the third state, and so on. This approach provided descriptive characterizations of transitions while ignoring the duration in each transition.

Study participants

A total of 1,504 individuals comprised the final study-eligible sample (743 HOPE and 761 PAU).[4] Table 82.1 shows the distribution of eligible study subjects overall and by site. At the site level, distribution of cases between HOPE and PAU mirrored the distribution of cases overall.

Table 82.1 Subjects enrolled in the DFE by site and group

Site	HOPE N	HOPE %	PAU N	PAU %	Total N	Total %
Arkansas	179	52.3	163	47.7	342	22.7
Massachusetts	189	48.2	203	51.8	392	26.1
Oregon	190	48.2	204	51.8	394	26.2
Texas	185	49.0	191	51.0	376	25.0
Total	743	49.4	761	50.6	1,504	100.0

Table 82.2 Characteristics of subjects enrolled in the DFE, overall and by group

Characteristic	Overall % (SD)	HOPE % (SD)	PAU % (SD)
Age at intake (mean)	31.0 (10.37)	30.6 (10.06)	31.5 (10.66)
Male = 1	0.81 (0.40)	0.81 (0.39)	0.80 (0.40)
Race			
White	0.69 (0.46)	0.69 (0.46)	0.68 (0.47)
Black	0.16 (0.37)	0.16 (0.37)	0.16 (0.37)
Hispanic	0.13 (0.34)	0.13 (0.33)	0.13 (0.34)
Other	0.02 (0.15)	0.02 (0.14)	0.02 (0.15)
Age at first arrest (mean)	22.1 (7.78)	21.9 (7.64)	22.4 (7.91)
Number of prior arrests (mean)	7.3 (8.13)	7.4 (8.46)	7.3 (7.82)
Has a prior person charge	0.56 (0.50)	0.57 (0.50)	0.56 (0.50)
Has a prior property charge	0.74 (0.44)	0.75 (0.43)	0.74 (0.44)
Has a prior drug charge	0.66 (0.48)	0.66 (0.47)	0.65 (0.48)
Has a prior public order/other charge	0.77 (0.42)	0.75 (0.43)	0.79 (0.41)
Number of prior convictions (mean)	3.5 (4.42)	3.6 (4.80)	3.4 (4.01)
Study offence			
Person	0.24 (0.42)	**0.21[†] (0.41)**	**0.26[†] (0.44)**
Property	0.30 (0.46)	0.31 (0.46)	0.29 (0.46)
Drug	0.31 (0.46)	0.30 (0.46)	0.32 (0.47)
Public order/other	0.15 (0.36)	**0.18[‡] (0.38)**	**0.13[‡] (0.33)**
N	1504	743	761

[†] HOPE and PAU differ at $p<0.05$
[‡] HOPE and PAU differ at $p<0.01$

The baseline characteristics of the full study sample were identified from administrative data. HOPE and PAU study participants were similar in their pre-study characteristics (Table 82.2). They were, on average, about 31 years old, male, and white, with seven prior arrests and three plus prior convictions. Most had a history of arrest for a variety of offences. Individuals in the study were on probation for a drug (31%), property (30%), person (24%), or public order/other (15%) offence. The PAU group was significantly more likely than the HOPE group to have a person charge (26% versus 21%) and less likely to have a public order/other charge (13% versus 18%).

There were significant differences in characteristics among the sites, although with few exceptions there were no differences between the HOPE and PAU groups within each site. Table 82.3 shows the characteristics by site (overall, not by group, as there were few differences between groups). Mean age varied from 27 to 34 and percentage male varied from 73% to 88%. The percentage who were identified as white varied from 35% in Texas to 88% in Oregon. There were large variations in criminal history, in terms of age at first arrest, and number and type of prior charges. There was also variation among

Table 82.3 Subject characteristics by site

Characteristics	Arkansas % (SD)	Massachusetts % (SD)	Oregon % (SD)	Texas % (SD)
Age at intake (mean)***	32.3 (10.21)	33.7 (11.14)	30.8 (9.91)	27.5 (9.10)
Male = 1***	0.73 (0.44)	0.88 (0.32)	0.83 (0.38)	0.77 (0.42)
Race				
White***	0.85 (0.36)	0.68 (0.47)	0.88 (0.33)	0.35 (0.48)
Black***	0.14 (0.35)	0.08 (0.26)	0.05 (0.22)	0.38 (0.49)
Hispanic***	0.01 (0.08)	0.18 (0.39)	0.06 (0.23)	0.27 (0.45)
Other***	0.01 (0.08)	0.06 (0.24)	0.02 (0.13)	0.01 (0.05)
Age at first arrest (mean)***	27.2 (9.63)	20.0 (6.53)	22.9 (6.17)	19.0 (5.95)
Number of prior arrests (mean)***	4.4 (3.38)	13.0 (11.87)	6.0 (6.05)	5.4 (4.70)
Has a prior person charge***	0.52 (0.50)	0.86 (0.35)	**0.48† (0.50)**	**0.38† (0.49)**
Has a prior property charge***	0.69 (0.46)	0.81 (0.39)	0.69 (0.46)	0.77 (0.42)
Has a prior drug charge***	0.59 (0.49)	0.57 (0.50)	**0.73† (0.440)**	0.73 (0.44)
Has a prior public order/other charge***	0.74 (0.44)	0.93 (0.26)	**0.76† (0.43)**	0.65 (0.48)
Number of prior convictions (mean)***	1.7 (1.13)	5.8 (6.45)	4.3 (3.91)	2.1 (2.51)
Study offence				
Person***	0.23 (0.42)	0.50 (0.50)	0.20 (0.40)	0.01 (0.10)
Property***	0.37 (0.48)	0.22 (0.42)	0.16 (0.36)	0.48 (0.50)
Drug***	0.24 (0.43)	0.11 (0.31)	0.44 (0.50)	0.44 (0.50)
Public order/other***	0.16 (0.36)	0.17 (0.38)	**0.20† (0.40)**	0.08 (0.26)
N	342	392	394	376

*** Subject characteristics differed across sites (p<0.001)
† HOPE and PAU differ at p<0.05

the sites in the current offence – with 50% of the Massachusetts sample having a current person charge compared with only 1% of those in Texas.

HOPE probationers were more likely than PAU probationers to have at least one probation violation (659 of 743 HOPE probationers and 623 of 761 PAU probationers; chi-square=13.93; $p<0.01$). Overall, the HOPE probationers had 3,770 violations compared with 3,124 for the PAU probationers. On average HOPE probationers had 5.07 (standard deviation=4.43) violations compared with 4.12 (standard deviation=4.40) violations by the PAU probationers ($t = -4.20$; $p<0.01$).

Tables 81.4 and 81.5 show the prevalence of violations by type, site, and group. Overall, 89% of HOPE probationers compared with 82% of PAU probationers had at least one violation. HOPE probationers were more likely than PAU probationers to have a drug-related violation – either failing to abstain from use or missing a drug test – and to have a violation for failing to appear in court. These are consistent with the principles of HOPE in which HOPE probationers are (1) subjected to frequent random testing and, thus, more likely to test positive or to miss a test and (2) required to attend a court hearing with any violation. HOPE probationers were less likely than PAU probationers to have a violation for missing a probation officer visit or for failing to pay fees and fines. HOPE probationers were also less likely to have a violation for a new charge.

There are significant differences in the prevalence of violations for drug-related events between the HOPE and PAU groups in all four sites, with HOPE probationers much more likely to have a drug-related violation. Again, this is a function of the nature of the HOPE programme and an indication that the random drug testing and adherence to violations in response to any positive

Table 82.4 Prevalence of violations by type, site, and group (mean and standard deviation)

Site	Group	Any	Fail to abstain from drugs	Missed drug test	Fail to appear: PO visit	Fail to appear: court	N
All	HOPE	0.89‡ (0.32)	0.60‡ (0.49)	0.58‡ (0.49)	0.30‡ (0.46)	0.18‡ (0.23)	743
	PAU	0.82‡ (0.39)	0.34‡ (0.47)	0.09‡ (0.29)	0.44‡ (0.50)	0.06‡ (0.23)	761
AR	HOPE	0.92‡ (0.28)	0.62‡ (0.49)	0.54‡ (0.50)	0.27 (0.45)	0.05 (0.22)	179
	PAU	0.72‡ (0.45)	0.21‡ (0.41)	0.02‡ (0.13)	0.32 (0.47)	0.05 (0.22)	163
MA	HOPE	0.76 (0.43)	0.31‡ (0.46)	0.39‡ (0.49)	0.23 (0.42)	0.08 (0.27)	189
	PAU	0.72 (0.45)	0.20‡ (0.40)	0.02‡ (0.16)	0.24 (0.43)	0.07 (0.26)	203
OR	HOPE	0.91 (0.29)	0.71‡ (0.45)	0.75‡ (0.43)	0.20‡ (0.40)	0.16† (0.37)	190
	PAU	0.87 (0.33)	0.50‡ (0.50)	0.04‡ (0.21)	0.68‡ (0.47)	0.08† (0.28)	204
TX	HOPE	0.97 (0.18)	0.76‡ (0.43)	0.63‡ (0.48)	0.49 (0.50)	0.42‡ (0.49)	185
	PAU	0.94 (0.23)	0.42‡ (0.50)	0.28‡ (0.45)	0.50 (0.50)	0.01‡ (0.10)	191

† HOPE and PAU differ at $p<0.05$
‡ HOPE and PAU differ at $p<0.01$

Table 82.5 Prevalence of violations by type, site, and group, continued (mean and standard deviation)

Site	Group	Fail to complete programme/ treatment	Fail to complete community service	Fail to pay fees/fines	Other	Multiple	New charge	N
All	HOPE	0.22 (0.41)	0.05 (0.21)	**0.11[‡] (0.32)**	**0.23[‡] (0.42)**	**0.24[†] (0.43)**	**0.22[‡] (0.41)**	743
	PAU	0.19 (0.39)	0.06 (0.25)	**0.18[‡] (0.39)**	**0.17[‡] (0.38)**	**0.30[†] (0.46)**	**0.28[‡] (0.45)**	761
AR	HOPE	0.05 (0.22)	0.05 (0.22)	0.22 (0.41)	**0.32[‡] (0.47)**	0.24 (0.43)	**0.09[‡] (0.29)**	179
	PAU	0.06 (0.23)	0.02 (0.13)	0.23 (0.42)	**0.10[‡] (0.30)**	0.31 (0.46)	**0.31[‡] (0.62)**	163
MA	HOPE	0.14 (0.35)	0.01 (0.07)	**0.03[†] (0.16)**	0.14 (0.35)	0.25 (0.44)	0.34 (0.47)	189
	PAU	0.11 (0.32)	0.01 (0.10)	**0.08[†] (0.28)**	0.11 (0.32)	0.23 (0.42)	0.33 (0.47)	203
OR	HOPE	0.24 (0.43)	0.01 (0.07)	**0.00[†] (0.00)**	0.23 (0.42)	**0.00[‡] (0.00)**	**0.33[‡] (0.47)**	190
	PAU	0.20 (0.40)	0.02 (0.16)	**0.02[†] (0.14)**	0.28 (0.45)	**0.10[‡] (0.30)**	**0.47[‡] (0.50)**	204
TX	HOPE	0.42 (0.50)	0.14 (0.34)	**0.22[‡] (0.41)**	0.24 (0.43)	0.49 (0.50)	0.10 (0.30)	185
	PAU	0.37 (0.48)	0.20 (0.40)	**0.42[‡] (0.50)**	0.19 (0.40)	0.58 (0.49)	0.07 (0.25)	191

[†] HOPE and PAU differ at $p<0.05$
[‡] HOPE and PAU differ at $p<0.01$

or missed tests were followed by the sites. Differences were even greater for violations for missing a drug test – 75% of HOPE probationers in Oregon, 63% of those in Texas, 54% of those in Arkansas, and 39% of those in Massachusetts had at least one violation for missing a drug test.[5] These percentages compare with 28% of those on PAU in Texas, 4% of those on PAU in Oregon, and 2% of those on PAU in Arkansas and Massachusetts who had at least one violation for missing a drug test. Except for Texas, very few individuals on PAU had a violation for a missed test, likely reflecting the fact that there was little testing done in these sites under probation as usual.

The overall difference between HOPE and PAU on failure to appear for probation officer visits was driven by a substantial difference in prevalence in Oregon – only 20% of HOPE probationers had a violation for missing a probation officer visit compared with 68% of PAU probationers. The threefold difference between HOPE and PAU overall on a violation for failing to appear for court (18% versus 6%) was due to the very large difference in Texas (42% versus 1%) and to a lesser degree the difference in Oregon (16% versus 8%). In three of the four sites, the HOPE groups were less likely than the PAU groups to have a violation for failing to pay fees and fines. In Arkansas and Oregon, HOPE probationers were less likely than PAU probationers to have a violation for a new charge.

Recidivism outcomes by site and group (as well as overall) are shown in Table 82.6. There were few statistically significant differences – and the three cases of significant differences revealed worse outcomes for those on HOPE supervision. Specifically, HOPE had higher rates of revocation in Arkansas and

Table 82.6 Bivariate recidivism outcomes by site and group

Site	Group	Mean length of follow-up (days)	Any arrest charge	Revocation	Revocation or arrest	Conviction	N
AR	**HOPE**	619.4	0.38	**0.33**‡	0.49	**0.39**‡	178
	PAU	592.4	0.44	**0.13**	0.45	**0.22**	162
MA	**HOPE**	577.5	0.43	0.19	0.44	0.23	188
	PAU	590.8	0.48	0.23	0.50	0.24	203
OR	**HOPE**	723.9	0.43	**0.17**†	0.48	0.35	190
	PAU	723.6	0.45	**0.09**	0.47	0.39	204
TX	**HOPE**	693.4	0.37	0.35	0.52	0.16	181
	PAU	668.8	0.41	0.41	0.55	0.19	190
Overall	**HOPE**	653.8	0.40	0.26	0.49	0.28	737
	PAU	646.4	0.44	0.22	0.50	0.26	759

† HOPE and PAU differ at $p<0.05$
‡ HOPE and PAU differ at $p<0.01$

Oregon and higher rates of new convictions in Arkansas than those on PAU. Overall, 40% of those on HOPE and 44% of those on PAU had at least one new arrest charge; 26% of HOPE and 22% of PAU were revoked. On the combined revoked/new arrest measure, 49% of HOPE compared to 50% of PAU experienced at least one incident of arrest or revocation. Finally, new conviction rates were also similar – 28% of HOPE and 26% of PAU had at least one new conviction.

Focusing on the revocation or arrest measure, we see rates that range between 44% for Massachusetts' HOPE to 55% for Texas PAU. There were no significant differences within site on this combined measure. Overall, the results are remarkably stable, with about half of all groups experiencing arrest or revocation during the study follow-up.

Results

The evaluation collected detailed data on where participants were throughout the evaluation and the arrest and violation events that occurred. This information included data on time spent in the community, jail, residential treatment, and prison; as well as the date of each arrest and violation. These data permit examination of how probation was experienced by each of our eight study groups over the course of the evaluation – nearly 1,000 days for some.

For example, one individual was on the street 898 days with three violations (and no jail days). These data look like this:

■ 23 Street Days . . . Violation . . . 203 Street Days . . . Violation . . . 245 Street Days . . . Violation . . . 427 Street Days . . . End of Follow-up

Another individual had seven violations, 89 days in jail, and 816 days on the street:

- 19 Street Days . . . Violation . . . 4 Jail Days . . . 39 Street Days . . . Violation . . . 4 Jail Days . . . 83 Street Days . . . Violation . . . 16 Jail Days . . . 74 Street Days . . . Violation . . . 28 Jail Days . . . 125 Street Days . . . Violation . . . 32 Jail Days . . . 189 Street Days . . . Violation . . . 189 Street Days . . . Violation . . . 5 Jail Days . . . 35 Street Days . . . End of Follow-up

A third individual had nine violations, two arrests, three jail days, and 900 days on the street:

- 13 Street Days . . . Arrested . . . 3 Jail Days . . . 5 Street Days . . . Violation . . . 7 Street Days . . . Violation . . . 28 Street Days . . . Violation . . . 63 Street Days . . . Violation . . . 77 Street Days . . . Violation . . . 7 Street Days . . . Violation . . . 112 Street Days . . . Violation . . . 35 Street Days . . . Arrested . . . 84 Street Days . . . Arrested . . . 28 Street Days . . . Violation . . . 70 Street Days . . . Violation . . . 371 Street Days . . . End of Follow-up

A fourth individual had six violations, one arrest, 65 residential treatment days, 40 jail days, 699 prison days, and 101 days on the street:

- 8 Street Days . . . Violation . . . 10 Street Days . . . Violation . . . 4 Jail Days . . . 2 Street Days . . . Violation . . . 5 Jail Days . . . 7 Street Days . . . Violation . . . 65 Residential Treatment Days . . . 20 Street Days . . . Violation . . . 20 Jail Days . . . 21 Street Days . . . Violation . . . 33 Street Days . . . 16 Jail Days . . . 62 Prison Days . . . Arrested . . . 637 Prison Days . . . End of Follow-up

Of course, it is difficult to process these sequences for four individuals much less for 1,504 participants, so a graphical analysis was conducted. Figure 82.1 shows where study participants in the Arkansas PAU group were during the first 100 days of their participation in the HOPE DFE. Each line in the graphic represents one study participant. The line is dark grey for time on the street, grey for days in residential treatment, light grey for days in jail, and black for prison days (referred to as 'revoked', although some prison days may have followed a new conviction). Violations are indicated with a circle and arrests with a '+'.

Several things are apparent from the graphic about the experience of PAU for this group of Arkansas subjects: (1) more than half of the subjects experienced no intervening events or experiences – they spent the first 100 days in the study on the street with no violations or arrests; (2) only a couple of individuals were sent to prison as indicated by the dark lines; and (3) jail time was rare during this early period for the PAU group. There were few violations and only a handful of arrests.

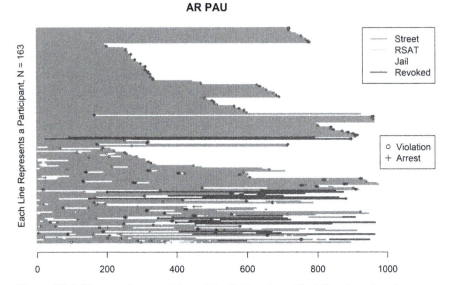

Figure 82.1 Time on the street, in residential treatment, in jail, or in prison/revoked for probation as usual in Arkansas, first 100 days

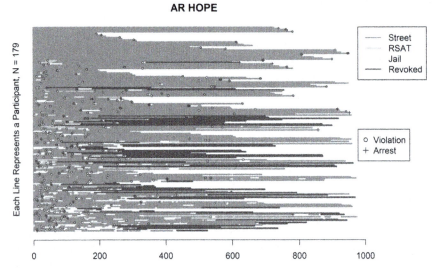

Figure 82.2 Time on the street, in residential treatment, in jail, or in prison/revoked for HOPE probationers in Arkansas, first 100 days

Figure 82.2 shows the initial 100 days for the Arkansas HOPE group. The operationalization of the HOPE model meant increased surveillance – indicated here by the results of many, many violations recorded for these individuals – and the certainty of response – indicated by the large number of jail terms imposed following violations (or new arrests) by these individuals. In contrast with the PAU group, we also see that numerous HOPE participants were sent to residential drug treatment (yellow segments). Consideration of these two figures together suggest that PAU and HOPE resulted in very different probation experiences for these individuals in Arkansas.

Extending the analyses to all four sites and the full study follow-up period provides the graphics presented in Figure 82.3. Each 'bar' consists of a set of lines with each line representing one study participant for each of the eight study groups. Because of the rolling enrolment in the study, the length of follow-up varied for participants, as is evidenced by the shorter lines for some subjects. (There were a few deaths among our subjects, which are reflected in the shorter lines in the graphics.)

These graphs demonstrate that the eight groups had distinct experiences. The variation in the density of lines show that HOPE cases experienced more jail (as we knew) than PAU groups. Oregon PAU, where probation has the authority to send probationers to jail for short periods in response to violations, also had relatively high numbers of jail days. The prevalence of the 'street' time and absence of the 'revoked' time in the Arkansas and Massachusetts PAU groups visually demonstrates the relatively low revocation rates observed for these two groups. In contrast, Texas PAU's high revocation rate is visible with the density of dark lines that occur beginning rather early in the study period.

Figure 82.3 also includes violation and arrest events. The greater density of violations for the HOPE groups compared to the PAU groups is easily visible – particularly for Arkansas and Texas and, to a lesser extent, Oregon. There are few observable differences in arrests.

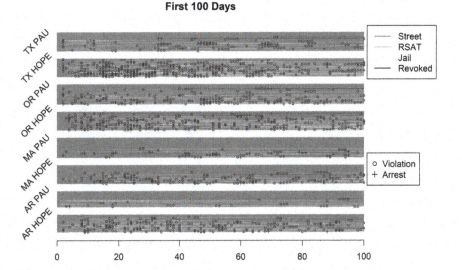

Figure 82.3 Time on the street, in residential treatment, in jail, or in prison/revoked for all HOPE evaluation participants by site and group

A second set of analyses focused on the patterns of transition between states and events for the subjects. Figure 82.4 shows the first place-based transitions by site and group. Everyone began on the street, so these are street-to-next-place.[6] For HOPE participants in all four sites and PAU participants in two sites (Oregon and Texas), the most likely first transition was from the street to jail. In Arkansas and Massachusetts, PAU probationers were most likely to move directly to the study end ('Censor') without intervening jail, residential treatment, or prison revocation. (This is apparent in the previous three exhibits by the dominance of 'bars' for these two groups.)

If we include the events (violation and arrest) in addition to the places, more than 50% of all groups had a violation as the first experience (Figure 82.5). Arrests prior to a violation were rarer for the HOPE groups than the PAU groups. Notable numbers – particularly Arkansas PAU and Massachusetts probationers – transitioned out of the study without experiencing any event.

HOPE was designed to ensure that a violation was followed by a consequence. Figure 82.6 shows the transition from an initial violation to another violation or to jail (other outcomes not shown). HOPE probationers who violated were more likely to go to jail following an initial violation while PAU probationers were more likely to have a second violation without an intervening jail stay. Across the four groups, the likelihood that a violation would be followed by jail varied from 7% (Arkansas PAU) to 84.5% (Oregon HOPE).

Individuals in the HOPE study population experienced up to 70 transitions during the evaluation period. Tables 82.7 and 82.8 show all transitions summed for the HOPE and PAU groups. Each transition matrix shows the summation of all matrices across all transitions for each group – from state 1 to state 2, from state 2 to state 3, and so forth. (These transition summaries

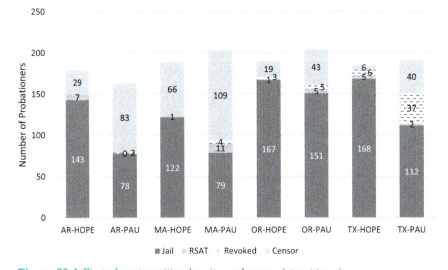

Figure 82.4 First place transition by site and group (street to. . .)

Note: RSAT is residential substance abuse treatment; censor indicated end of follow-up

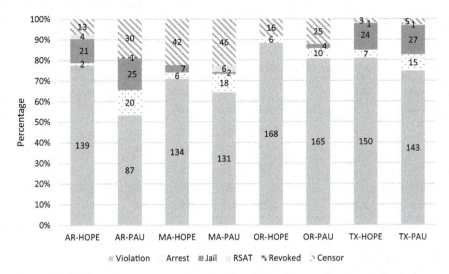

Figure 82.5 First place or event transition by site and group (street to. . .)

Note: RSAT is residential substance abuse treatment; censor indicated end of follow-up

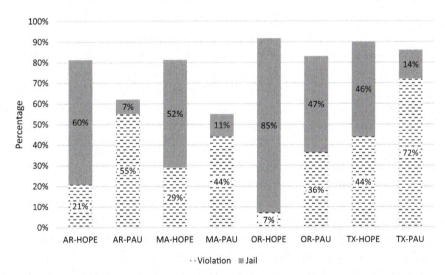

Figure 82.6 Transition from an initial violation to a second violation or to jail by site and group

Note: Other transitions from violation (to arrest, RSAT, revoked, or censor) not shown

ignore the final transitions to 'censor' or end of study.) For example, the 743 HOPE probationers had a total of 3,058 transitions from the street to other states/events (Table 82.7). The most common transition from the street was to a violation (2,479 occurrences). The most common response to a violation was jail – consistent with HOPE principles – 2,217 violations were followed by jail with only 815 followed by another violation and only a handful followed by something else. Most jail stays (2,175) were followed by release to

Table 82.7 HOPE probationer transitions summed

From:	To:							
	Violation	Jail	Street	Arrest	Res. Tx	Revoked	Death	Total
Street	2,479	310	0	107	124	33	5	3,058
Violation	815	2,217	249	243	44	62	2	3,632
Jail	339	73	2,175	43	78	70	1	2,779
Arrest	83	197	45	73	3	26	0	427
Res. Tx	39	2	190	2	1	0	0	234
Revoked	7	0	0	49	0	0	0	56
Total	3,762	2,799	2,659	517	250	191	8	10,186

Table 82.8 PAU probationer transitions summed

From:	To:							
	Violation	Jail	Street	Arrest	Revoked	Res. Tx	Death	Total
Street	1,221	115	0	141	9	28	2	1,516
Violation	1,541	737	135	348	78	19	2	2,860
Jail	145	16	804	30	35	35	0	1,065
Arrest	191	198	22	70	43	2	1	527
Res. Tx	14	1	61	2	0	0	0	78
Revoked	11	0	0	35	0	0	0	46
Total	3,123	1,067	1,022	626	165	84	5	6,092

the street. In total, the 743 HOPE probationers experienced 3,762 violations, 2,799 jail stays, 517 arrests, and 191 revocations. Eight HOPE probationers died during the study.

In comparison, Table 82.8 shows that the 761 PAU probationers experienced 3,123 violations, 1,067 jail stays, 626 arrests, and 165 revocations – with sequential violations much more common that violation-jail transitions (1,541 versus 737). As with the HOPE probationers, the most likely transition from jail was back to the street (804).

Table 82.9 provides site-level information on the probability of jail following a violation (other outcomes not shown). We see a considerable range over the eight groups, from about 13% for PAU in Arkansas and Texas to 75% for HOPE in Oregon. Overall, 61% of violations by HOPE probationers were followed next by a jail stay. This is consistent with HOPE's focus on responding to violations with a (short) jail stay; however, the 61% figure is well below 100%. In Texas, the HOPE group had a relatively large number of violation-to-violation transitions (34%). This was most likely due to a local policy that allowed probationers to turn themselves in if they missed a drug test or office visit;

Table 82.9 Probability of jail following a violation, overall and by site

	Overall	Arkansas	Massachusetts	Oregon	Texas
HOPE	61.0%	63.3%	55.8%	75.3%	51.2%
PAU	25.8%	13.5%	19.4%	45.9%	12.8%

Table 82.10 Probability of another violation following a violation, overall and by site

	Overall	Arkansas	Massachusetts	Oregon	Texas
HOPE	22.4%	21.4%	24.0%	6.8%	34.2%
PAU	53.9%	58.1%	44.8%	34.0%	73.7%

however, if they failed to turn themselves in within 24 hours, they received violations for the missed test/visit and for failing to turn themselves in.

Table 82.10 shows the probability that a violation was followed immediately by another violation. Again, we see considerable variation. Overall, about 22% of HOPE probationers compared with almost 54% of PAU probationers had sequential violations. The variation is large – with the chance of sequential violations among PAU ranging from 74% to 34% and among HOPE ranging from 34% to 7%. Thus, within the HOPE study, there is an observation of large differences in response to probation violations, which may sit at the core of issues related to how probationers experience probation.

Discussion and conclusions

Probation, with nearly four million adults supervised, is the most widely used criminal justice sanction in the United States. Although many have studied the causes and consequences of mass incarceration, there has been little attention to the simultaneous growth in probation (DeMichele 2014). There have been a few studies analyzing the experience of probation. Payne and Gainey (1998) interviewed probationers and learned that they manage their daily lives to navigate stigma related to probation. Others found that probationers are hampered by a contradictory set of conditions that are so numerous that probationers are unlikely to live up to all of them (Lucken 1996).

Our analyses provide a new way to consider the probation experience by looking at the individual-level transitions from the street to sanctions (e.g. jail, revocation) or rehabilitative responses (i.e. treatment). This approach moves away from the overly simplified question of whether probationers succeed or fail. Rather, the transition matrices provide an opportunity to visualize the challenging nature of navigating probation. This approach offers something of an interactive view to see probationer behaviour and probation officer response.

In the past, probation has been experienced with much uncertainty for those on supervision. Violations of conditions are overlooked, and they accumulate until 'the last straw' results in a revocation. The results from the probationers on PAU provide some support for this accumulation effect in which probationers were cited for several violations before a sanction was administered. This is not to challenge officer discretion and their in-depth knowledge of the appropriate response to each violation. Rather, the goal is to contribute to a larger conversation about the probationer experience and how to study probation in ways that lead to more thoughtful and realistic policies and practices. Further, it is important to consider the cognitive assumptions placed in the traditional deterrence model in which probationers are told that violations will be met with some sanctions (e.g. curfews, jail). Such an approach is rooted in rational thinking models that require forward thinking to weigh consequences related to behaviour. But is it reasonable to assume that humans in general, and probationers more specifically, are rational?

A central premise of the HOPE model is that certain responses to any probation violation should be met with a certain penalty, specified as a short jail stay. The HOPE logic model suggests that this certainty will lead to improved outcomes – increased compliance, reduced recidivism. However, that is not what was observed here. Overall recidivism rates, measured by the broad indicator of any arrest or revocation during follow-up, were amazingly similar across the groups with about 50% failure. If we look simply at any new arrest, about 40% overall across both groups experienced at least one new arrest.

Among the eight study groups, two had relatively few violations, arrests, or jail time. Many of the individuals on PAU in Arkansas and Massachusetts mainly served their time on the street. Conversely, the HOPE probationers in these sites experienced many more violations and arrests and, in the case of Arkansas, many more revocations. Revocations were more likely among the HOPE group in Oregon, although PAU there also experienced lots of violations and many jail stays potentially suggesting some unique organization effects. These results challenge some of the initial optimistic findings for the original Hawaii model of HOPE, and, instead, suggest the potential for 'old wine in new bottles'. Specifically, HOPE probationers experienced a higher level of surveillance and enforcement of even tiny infractions (e.g. being late for an office visit) that naturally resulted in increased punitive officer responses. This is similar to what was found nearly three decades ago by Petersilia and Turner (1993) in their study of intensive supervision probation.

Simply, probationer success is often a matter of how officers are instructed to define situations and the level of tolerance they give to probationer conduct. When officers are told that showing up late to appointments, missing a treatment session, and other minor infractions are to result in jail time, then, increased revocations and jail time is a natural outcome. What these findings may signal, however, is that enforcement, accountability, and punishment may not be what probationers need. Rather, they may need redirection, support, and mechanisms that address cognitive and material needs in their lives. The accumulation of negative responses to minor violations may serve to delegitimize probation more generally for some probationers. There is a growing body of law enforcement and legal literature that demonstrates that how people are treated matters to how they behave. That is, procedural justice researchers have shown that the procedure matters. So, here too, it is quite possible that probationers become frustrated at frequent violations that then diminishes their trust and legitimacy with officers.

These issues raise a variety of questions about exactly what may increase the effectiveness of probation. As noted, there was some difference across the study sites in terms of the characteristics of the HOPE-eligible, with some more criminally involved than others. There were differences in probation practices locally as discussed by Zajac et al. (2015) and addressed by Lattimore et al. (2016). For example, some of the sites considered Risk-Needs-Responsivity to be their PAU model. In Texas, the judge made ample use of a residential treatment programme, while in two of the sites very few individuals were sent to treatment. These differences – nor the overlay of the HOPE model onto these PAU practices – appear to have made little difference in recidivism outcomes. More research is needed to examine how individuals experience probation to complement the group outcome assessments of usual probation studies.

Notes

1   The evaluation of the Honest Opportunity Probation with Enforcement (HOPE) Demonstration Field Experiment (DFE) was funded by grant 2011-RY-BX-0003 from the National Institute of Justice, Office of Justice Programs, US Department of Justice. The opinions, findings, and conclusions or recommendations expressed are those of the authors and do not necessarily reflect those of the US Department of Justice. See Lattimore et al. (2018).
2   Site-specific data use agreements were executed with the Arkansas Department of Community Corrections, Clackamas County Community Corrections, and Tarrant County Community Supervision and Corrections Department, and a research agreement was executed with the Massachusetts Office of the Commissioner of Probation. Individual-level electronic probation data were not available in Massachusetts; electronic PDF documents of District Court probation case summaries were obtained in September 2015 and Superior Court probation officers' notes scanned to PDF documents were obtained in February 2016. Information from these documents were abstracted into Excel spreadsheets. In Oregon, local data repositories were manually searched, and relevant data were abstracted in December 2014. In Texas, probation violation data were sourced from individual-level electronic data maintained by Tarrant County Community Supervision and Corrections Department. These data were merged with information about sanctions abstracted from hardcopy court orders and manually recorded; data entry was completed in September 2015.
3   For more information on horizontal line plot methodology, see Tueller et al. (2016). The package longCatEDA was developed by Tueller (2016) and implemented in the R package (R Core Team 2016).
4   A total of 1,580 individuals were randomly assigned to HOPE (794) or PAU (786) and 1,504 individuals comprised the final study-eligible sample (743 HOPE and

761 PAU). The remaining 76 individuals were study ineligible, including 68 who were deemed programme ineligible, and eight who were randomized twice.

5 Not everyone in HOPE in Massachusetts was subject to random drug testing because this condition had to have been imposed at sentencing (prior to assignment to HOPE) or following a significant event that could result in new conditions being imposed. Thus, the lower prevalence rates in Massachusetts for HOPE may simply reflect the fact that fewer individuals had required random tests.

6 A small handful of cases were in jail at the time of their random assignment to HOPE. Their transitions were reset to begin following their initial release.

References

DeMichele, M. (2014) Studying the community corrections field: Applying neo-institutional theories to a hidden element of mass social control. *Theoretical Criminology*, 18(4), 546–564.

Hawken, A. and Kleiman, M. (2007) HOPE for reform: What a novel probation program in Hawaii might teach other states. *The American Prospect*, 10 April. Available at: http://prospect.org/cs/articles?articleId=12628.

Hawken, A. and Kleiman, M. (2009) *Managing Drug Involved Probationers with Swift and Certain Sanctions: Evaluating Hawaii's HOPE*. Washington, DC: US Department of Justice, National Institute of Justice.

Hawken, A., Kulick, J., Smith, K., Mei, J., Zhang, Y., Jarman, S., Yu, T., Carson, C. and Vial, T. (2016) *HOPE II: A Follow-Up to Hawai'i's HOPE Evaluation* (Report # 2010-IJ-CX-0016). Washington, DC: US Department of Justice, National Institute of Justice.

Kaeble, D. and Cowhig, M. (2018) *Correctional Populations in the United States, 2016*. NCJ 251211. Washington, DC: US Department of Justice, Bureau of Justice Statistics, April.

Lattimore, P. K., Dawes, D., MacKenzie, D. L. and Zajac, G. (2018) *Evaluation of the Honest Opportunity with Enforcement Demonstration Field Experiment (HOPE DFE) Final Report*. Washington, DC: US Department of Justice, National Institute of Justice. Available at: www.ncjrs.gov/pdffiles1/nij/grants/251758.pdf.

Lattimore, P. K., MacKenzie, D. L., Zajac, G., Dawes, D., Arsenault, E. and Tueller, S. J. (2016) Outcome findings from the HOPE demonstration field experiment. *Criminology and Public Policy*, 15(4), 1103–1141. DOI:10.1111/1745-9133.12248.

Lucken, K. (1996) Dynamics of penal reform. *Crime, Law, and Social Change*, 26(4), 367–384.

O'Connell, D. J., Brent, J. J. and Visher, C. A. (2016) Decide your time. *Criminology & Public Policy*, 15, 1073–1102.

Payne, B. and Gainey, R. (1998) A qualitative assessment of the pains experienced on electronic monitoring. *International Journal of Offender Therapy and Comparative Criminology*, 422, 149–163.

Petersilia, J. and Turner, S. (1993) *Evaluating Intensive Supervision Probation/Parole: Results of a Nationwide Experiment*. Washington, DC: National Institute of Justice.

R Core Team. (2016) *R: A Language and Environment for Statistical Computing*. Vienna, Austria: R Foundation for Statistical Computing. Available at: www.R-project.org/.

Tueller, S. J. (2016) *LongCatEDA: Package for Plotting Categorical Longitudinal and Time-Series Data*. R Package Version 0.21. Available at: https://cran.r-project.org/web/packages/longCatEDA/index.html.

Tueller, S. J., Van Dorn, R. A. and Bobashev, G. V. (2016) *Visualization of Categorical Longitudinal and Times Series Data* (Report No. MR-0033–1602). Research Triangle Park, NC: RTI Press.

Zajac, G., Lattimore, P. K., Dawes, D. and Winger, L. (2015) All implementation is local: Initial findings from the process evaluation of the honest opportunity probation with enforcement (HOPE) demonstration field experiment. *Federal Probation*, 79(1), 31–36.

83

Pain, harm, and punishment

David Hayes

Introduction: punishment, pain, and civilization

A conventional history of criminal punishment goes something like this: in the beginning, punishment was the arm of an authoritarian state, which displayed its supremacy by visiting horrors upon the body of those who dared to violate the king's commandments (Foucault 1977: 3–69). Punishment was purposefully painful, in order to serve the needs of a barbarically hierarchical socio-political order. However, historical efforts at penal reform have civilized the penal system, abandoning crude capital and corporal punishment and taking on loftier aims based on achieving good for society as a whole (Foucault 1977; Ignatieff 1978; Garland 1990: 177–276; compare Ignatieff 1981). Orthodox advocates of punishment do not see pain as the *point* of punishment, but an unfortunate necessity that we should avoid where we can. The criminal justice systems of the 'civilized' world, in this humanitarian age, are intended to punish, but not to cause pain. But regardless of the claimed intentions of penal policymakers, sentencing authorities, and practitioners, one cannot deny that modern Western penal systems are engaged in substantial and routine 'pain delivery' (Christie 1982: 19). Punishment hurts – as a matter of sociological reality, if not of political design. Criminology has produced a wide-ranging and growing literature devoted to the study of these 'pains of punishment', out of general scientific interest in the nature of punishment today, but also with the aim of either recognizing those pains when developing penal policy, or helping to minimize and eradicate them.

This chapter reviews that literature. It begins by comparing the concepts of 'pain' and 'harm', to clarify what the 'pains of punishment' literature is concerned with. It then charts a brief history of pain-based analysis, from its starting point in prisons research to its modern, extra-custodial, and extra-penal reach. This sets the stage for a discussion of the uses of pains, and particularly the development of a *dimensional* approach to pains that enables them to be more consistently compared and appraised. We conclude with a return to the questions of pain as against harm, considering the advantages and drawbacks that pain-based analyses of criminal punishment offer.

Pain and harm: separating out some ideas

Punishment should be something that we think *at least usually* involves a negative experience. Whether or not we could punish without causing pain in the future is debatable (compare, e.g. Bronsteen et al. 2010: 1469–1473 with Matravers 2016), but for the moment, we must recognize that unpleasantness *does* routinely follow from the sorts of things that the penal state does today, and that sentencing authorities and penal policymakers know that punishment imposes conditions that are 'normally considered unpleasant' (Hayes 2017: 2–3). But what do we mean by 'unpleasantness'? To explain the distinction, we must consider the related but separate concepts of 'pain' and 'harm'.

Harm is a major concept in the theorization of both crimes and punishments. Proportionate punishments are typically calculated with regard to the *seriousness* of the offence, which in turn is some product of the *harm* the crime causes, and the offender's *culpability* for that harm. 'Harm' in this sense usually means some *objectively negative experience* that damages one's overall interests – one's possessions, one's quality of life, and one's ability to put one's autonomous desires into practice (e.g. von Hirsch and Jareborg 1991; compare Feinberg 1984). But harm is distinct from *pain*, at least sometimes. That which hurts can be helpful, and that which harms might not cause pain, at least not at the time. In other words, something may be an objectively positive influence on our lives, but involve at least some subjective negative experiences.

If harm is an objective, aggregate setback to the injured party, then pain is inherently subjective and polyvalent. 'Pain' is not necessarily limited to physical suffering; it might also be mental anguish or emotional trauma. A broken arm and a broken heart both hurt, although the pain they cause is qualitatively different. Moreover, the experience of pain is inherently individual and subjective: '[l]iterature is full of heroes so great that pain becomes small, or cowards so small that almost everything becomes pain' (Christie 1982: 9). To try to get at a *quantum* of pain would require a metric that is neither objective nor fully subjective, but *inter-subjective*, speaking to individual experiences in a way that enables qualitatively different life experiences to be meaningfully compared (Hayes 2016). For this reason, studies of pain have struggled to meaningfully quantify the experience of pain, and tend to merely catalogue tendencies in penal subjects' experiences (compare Gainey and Payne 2000; Crewe 2015).

In short, *harm* should be understood as the overall social 'cost' of punishment – to the punished person, to third parties affected by the punishment (Walker 1991: 106–110), and indeed to the punishing society itself. Pain, by contrast, is a *subjective* negative experience of physical, mental, and/or emotional suffering, in response to a stimulus that may be harmful, but might also be beneficial (or neutral). Different approaches to punishment might see pain as inherently problematic, a necessary evil to be minimized (Durnescu 2011), or even a means of achieving penal aims (Hayes 2016). But what is certain is that pain is an intrinsic feature of penal interventions. This much is revealed by the literature on the 'pains of punishment'.

The pains of punishment: an overview

The study of the 'pains of punishment' traces its heritage back to Gresham Sykes's *The Society of Captives* (1958). Sykes attempted to develop as broadly and fully descriptive a catalogue as possible of what made prisons punitive – what gave them their character as punishment. For Sykes (1958: 64), the pains of imprisonment consist of 'the deprivations and frustrations of prison life', providing a general schematic for describing the challenges of imprisonment from the prisoner's own experience. Specifically, Sykes (1958: 65–78) identified five broad categories of 'deprivation' imposed by imprisonment: of *liberty* of movement both outside and within the institution; of *access to goods and services*; of *access to heterosexual relationships*; of *autonomous control* over one's daily life; and of *security* from other prisoners.

These pains are situated in time and place, and determined to at least some extent by prison policy, the actual practices of prisoners and prison staff, and by the wider place of the prison within broader society. Thus, the pains imposed by a minimum-security prison in Norway can be expected to differ drastically from those of a maximum-security prison in New Jersey (Shammas 2014; compare Flanagan 1980; Ugelvik and Damsa 2018). By the same token, a US prison in 1958 looks radically different to one in 2014, after half a century of penal expansion and 'mass imprisonment' (Fleury-Steiner and Longazel 2014). Likewise, one would expect the pains of imprisonment to differ along demographic lines such as gender (e.g. Crewe et al. 2017), given the effect that one's ethnicity, gender, sexuality, and other personal characteristics can have upon one's experiences of life in a diverse and uneven society.

Ultimately, the pains of imprisonment provide a more textured and nuanced vocabulary for describing what prison life is like, and how far that matches our beliefs about what prison should be like (and should be *for*). In particular, they remind us that prison cannot be spoken of simply in terms of liberty deprivation, the orthodox shorthand for how serious a punishment is in liberal societies (Sykes 1958: 78–79). The pains of imprisonment give a richer and deeper account of the psychological stresses of imprisonment, enabling us to pinpoint precisely what makes imprisonment hurt, and whether (and to what extent) we want it to do so (e.g. Johnson and Toch 1982). They provide meaningful data for both descriptive and evaluative research, and have particularly tended to support humanitarian research agendas aimed at promoting the 'civilization' of prison conditions and the effectiveness of their efforts to reduce reoffending (ibid.; Sykes 1958: 78–79; compare De Vos and Gilbert 2017).

However, it is only over the last two decades there has been any attempt to apply pains-based analysis to non-custodial forms of punishment – and indeed, to activities of the criminal justice state that are not directly related to the punishment of convicted offenders (e.g. Harkin 2015, exploring the pains of policing). In particular, studies of the pains of non-custodial punishment have tended to focus upon *probation supervision* (e.g. Durnescu 2011; Hayes 2015) and *electronic monitoring* (e.g. Payne and Gainey 1998; Gainey and Payne 2000). So the pains of community punishment literature thus far might be described, reductively, as the study of the *pains of oversight* – whether by technological monitoring or human supervision. The pains revealed by these studies reflect the substantial differences between custodial and non-custodial sentences, but they also challenge the conception that non-custodial sentences are 'soft options' that possess no punitive potential (Hayes 2015, 2017). In particular, they emphasize three major differences in the experience of different sorts of pains, concerning: the *diminished significance* of liberty deprivation; the importance of *process* and *values* in the occurrence and intensity of pains; and the impact of the more *penetrative* nature of non-custodial punishment.

The first point is that the experience of both electronic monitoring and probation supervision is characterized by a lesser objective deprivation of the offender's liberty. As a result, whilst offenders under both forms of oversight do report pains associated with the loss of liberty, they tend to be less important than other pains in determining the penal subject's sense of how severe their sentence was (e.g. Payne and Gainey 1998: 155–156; Hayes 2015: 93–94). More important were pains associated with the loss of *autonomy* – that is, freedom of choice and the concomitant impact of lifestyle change, impact on family relationships, and stigmatization effects (Payne and Gainey 1998: 153–155; Durnescu 2011: 534–538). Focusing on the pains of community sanctions suggests that liberty deprivation is an even poorer means of capturing non-custodial sentences' punitive 'bite' than it is for imprisonment (Hayes 2015: 98–99).

The second major issue raised by studies of the pains of non-custodial sentences is the importance of *process* and *values* in terms of the experience of pain. 'Process' includes both the experience of the wider criminal justice system (Hayes 2015: 96–97; compare Feeley 1979; Harkin 2015), and the specific processes by which community penalties are imposed (compare, for instance, the threat of incarceration as a far more immediate feature in Durnescu's [2011: 538] Romanian study than in Hayes's [2015: 93–94] English one). Values also shaped the experience of pains of punishment for (non-custodial) penal subjects, determining the extent to which subjects felt 'punished' at all (van Ginneken and Hayes 2017). Offenders' attitudes and expectations about punishment naturally colour their experience of being punished, exposing them to different pains in different degrees (Hayes 2015: 91; compare Sexton 2015). In particular, probationers who were willing to engage with rehabilitative efforts tended to experience distinct (and relatively severe) pains associated with shame and lifestyle change. This was partly because of the professional values and approaches of their supervising probation officers, which emphasized probationers' personal agency and responsibility for changing their offending behaviour. Whilst showing an admirable respect for probationers as human beings, rather than merely as clusters of criminogenic risks and needs, this approach also tended to put pressure on probationers to make sometimes extreme lifestyle changes, and could come into conflict with their own coping strategies for dealing with their formal identification as 'offenders' (Hayes 2015: 91–93). These 'pains of rehabilitation' (ibid.; compare Nugent and Schinkel's [2016] 'pains of desistance') underscore the difference between pain and harm. Being formally labelled as needing correction, and acted upon by state agents (for better or worse), entails significant attacks on offenders' subjective sense of self-worth and identity, exposing them to pain even if that pain is not objectively harmful overall (McNeill 2019).

Finally, rather than interrupting a penal subject's 'normal' life as incarceration in a total institution would, non-custodial punishments *penetrate* that normal life to a much greater extent, creating new opportunities for pain caused by the interaction of penal and non-penal social forces (Hayes 2015: 96–98; compare Cohen's [1985] 'dispersal of discipline'). This mutual exposure and interconnection of the penal and social worlds undermines the traditional conception of punishment as something that takes place beyond and apart from the subject's civic life, and reveals a complex web of pain-producing interactions between state and non-state actors, as well as between agents of penal and social welfare systems. It is simply not possible to talk of the pains of punishment as being separate from other pains in one's life (Hayes 2017: 5–12).

None of these distinctions mean that community-based pain infliction is worse than prison, only that it is *different*. The expansion of the focus of pains literature beyond the prison wall, as part of the general widening of penology's myopic focus on the prison as the only noteworthy site of punishment, enables a fuller and franker discussion about the place of non-custodial sanctions within penal (and punitive) sentencing hierarchies, and a confrontation with how these sanctions fit with our conception of civilized and humane punishment (compare Durnescu 2011: 539–543).

The dimensions of pain: comparative and intersubjective approaches

For most of their history, the pains of punishment were explored in largely binary terms: one either felt them, or one did not. To be sure, it was possible to say, roughly, that certain pains seemed to be more significant than others, but the qualitative nature of the pains of punishment made it practically impossible to compare two subjects' experiences of the same painful stimulus. However, more recently, various attempts have been made to find ways to discuss pains in less binary terms. These efforts have crystallized in a body of work led by Ben Crewe on the *dimensionality* of pain. Using an extended spatial metaphor, Crewe (2015) attempts to map pain to four major axes of painfulness: *depth*, *weight*, *tightness*, and *breadth*. Briefly: 'depth' acts as a metaphor for the extent to which a punishment constrains, controls, and isolates the subject from wider society; 'weight' represents the level of oppressiveness and psychological trauma caused to the inmate by their incarceration; 'tightness' measures the extent to which the exercise of power within the prison regime is coercive and authoritarian; and 'breadth' is the level of what I have called *penetration* of penal control into the subject's everyday life, before, during, and after punishment (Crewe 2011, 2015; Crewe et al. 2014; see also Downes 1988; King and McDermott 1995). These dimensions are really a series of binary oppositions. They cannot tell us *precisely* how deep, or heavy, or tight, or broad a particular punishment is, but they do enable comparisons (for instance, prison X is 'heavier' than prison Y, or 'tighter' for prisoner A than for prisoner B). These oppositions can at least tell us *something* about the relative shape and dimensions of the pains experienced by a particular penal subject (there being no reason to limit Crewe's framework to imprisonment), and consider the ways in which changes in penal policy and practice affect penal experiences.

Sexton (2015) adds to this analysis a concern with the subjective *salience* of punishment, emphasizing the role that the expectations of the penal subject have in shaping the subjective experience of objective deprivations. Her analysis suggests that punishment hurts more where deprivations are symbolically loaded, involving the imposition of stigma or the expression of authority. Again, this analysis ultimately rests upon a series of binary oppositions, but it provides the germ of a more nuanced index for comparing subjective experiences in a way that could inform policymaker and sentence understandings of penal severity (Hayes 2016: 739–740). Efforts on the part of Crewe and Sexton enable us to move in the direction of using pain as a *metric* for exploring penal severity, and whilst they are relatively limited in this respect by their binary nature, they can inform our thinking on a much broader level about how much pain is desirable, and indeed, appropriate within our penal systems.

Conclusions: pain, harm, and humanity

In sum, the pains of punishment have expanded well beyond the broadly descriptive catalogue of the frustrations involved in maximum-security incarceration in 1950s New Jersey. They have been explored across a range of penal contexts, and exposed a variety of differences in the experience of prisoners of different backgrounds, ethnicities, genders, and sexualities. They have also begun to show the potential for an effectively intersubjective approach to measuring penal severity – understanding pain as an intrinsic part of what makes a sentence punitive. How far one should go in taking pain into account for the purposes of sentencing decision-making and penal policy is a matter of some debate (see e.g. Markel and Flanders 2010; Bronsteen et al. 2010; Hayes 2017: 2–4). However, at the very least the pains of punishment remind us of the difficult terrain in which work with offenders is practiced, by prison and probation officers. Even when a sentence involves no longer-term harm, and indeed, even when it does demonstrable good, that is not to say that it does not involve the conscious and deliberate infliction of pain by the state against individual human beings. That might not be a reason to stop trying to use the penal system to do good, but it is at the least a salutary reminder that we ought not to rely upon it too much (compare Christie 1982: 11, 100–101).

However, the literature to date is not without limitations. In particular, many of the studies involved are small scale and exploratory, and those that are not are necessarily limited to particular times, policies, and places (Durnescu 2011; Hayes 2015; De Vos and Gilbert 2017; van Ginneken and Hayes 2017). This is not to say that only quantitatively generalizable data are capable of telling us something valid about penal systems. Indeed, the pains of punishment are as revealing as they are precisely because of the relative depth and texture of the data they provide relative to quantitative, flat metrics (Crewe 2015; Hayes 2016). But those data cannot tell us everything about the state of the penal system today, and future research into the pains of punishment must engage with a wider range of research methods and populations. Too much reliance on qualitative data is just as much a sin as too much focus on quantitative generalizability.

The pains of punishment literature must also expand its scope more broadly, to considering the pains that punishment causes to third parties – particularly dependents and other family members of penal subjects. The experience of third parties affected by punishment is under-researched generally (Durnescu et al. 2013: 31–36), and would enable an engagement with the question that this chapter started on – on the relationship between *pains* and *harms*. After all, even if pain does not necessarily equate to harm in the punishment of the (formally) guilty penal subject, it is far harder to objectively justify the pain that punishment causes to innocent dependents, family members, and other third parties to punishment (ibid.).

Even to the extent we accept pain as a feature of punishment, we should not allow that to become an excuse to ignore or excuse the harms of punishment. After all, we are all of us responsible for the infliction of harm, as well as pain – and to the innocent as well as to the guilty – because in a democratic society, it is inflicted in our name (Ristroph 2011). The greatest potential strength of pains-based analysis is that it allows us to strip away the euphemistic 'shield of words' and confront punishment as a process that involves subjective and objective downsides, as well as benefits (Christie 1982: 13–19). A confrontation with the pain we cause when we work with offenders encourages us to consider where we might go next, and how we might find other alternative, less painful and less harmful ways to achieve the values we pursue when we do criminal justice.

References

Bronsteen, John, Buccafusco, Christopher and Masur, Jonathan. (2010) Retribution and the experience of punishment. *California Law Review*, 98(5), 1463–1496.

Christie, Nils. (1982) *Limits to Pain: The Role of Punishment in Penal Policy*. Oxford: Martin Robinson.

Cohen, Stanley. (1985) *Visions of Social Control: Crime, Punishment and Classification*. Cambridge: Polity Press.

Crewe, Ben. (2011) Depth, weight, tightness: Revisiting the pains of imprisonment. *Punishment & Society*, 13(5), 509–529.

Crewe, Ben. (2015) Inside the belly of the penal beast: Understanding the experience of imprisonment. *International Journal for Crime, Justice, and Social Democracy*, 4(1), 50–65.

Crewe, Ben, Hulley, Susie and Wright, Serena. (2017) The gendered pains of life imprisonment. *British Journal of Criminology*, 57(6), 1359–1378.

Crewe, Ben, Liebling, Alison and Hulley, Susie. (2014) Heavy-light, absent-present: Rethinking the "Weight" of imprisonment. *British Journal of Sociology*, 65(3), 387–410.

De Vos, Helene and Gilbert, Elli. (2017) Freedom, so close but yet so far: The impact of the ongoing confrontation with freedom on the perceived severity of punishment. *European Journal of Probation*, 9(2), 132–148.

Downes, David. (1988) *Contrasts in Tolerance*. Oxford: Clarendon Press.

Durnescu, Ioan. (2011) Pains of probation: Effective practice and human rights. *International Journal of Offender Therapy and Comparative Criminology*, 55(4), 530–545.

Durnescu, Ioan, Enengl, Christina and Grafl, Christian. (2013) Experiencing supervision. In Fergus McNeill and Kristel Beyens (Eds.), *Offender Supervision in Europe*. Basingstoke: Palgrave Macmillan, pp. 19–50.

Feeley, Malcolm. (1979) *The Process is the Punishment: Handling Cases in a Lower Criminal Court*. Russell Sage Foundation.

Feinberg, Joel. (1984) *The Moral Limits of the Criminal Law, Volume One: Harm to Others*. Oxford: Oxford University Press.

Flanagan, Timothy. (1980) Pains of long-term imprisonment: A comparison of British and American perspectives. *British Journal of Criminology*, 20(2), 148–156.

Fleury-Steiner, Benjamin and Longazel, Jamie. (2014) *The Pains of Mass Imprisonment*. London: Routledge.

Foucault, Michel. (1977) *Discipline and Punish: The Birth of the Prison*. Translated by Alan Sheridan. London: Penguin.

Gainey, Randy and Payne, Brian. (2000) Understanding the experience of house arrest with electronic monitoring: An analysis of quantitative and qualitative data. *International Journal of Offender Therapy and Comparative Criminology*, 44(1), 84–96.

Garland, David. (1990) *Punishment and Modern Society: A Study in Social Theory*. Oxford: Oxford University Press.

Ginneken, Esther van and Hayes, David. (2017) "Just" punishment? Offenders' views on the meaning and severity of punishment. *Criminology and Criminal Justice*, 17(1), 62–78.

Harkin, Diarmaid. (2015) The police and punishment: Understanding the pains of policing. *Theoretical Criminology*, 19(1), 43–58.

Hayes, David. (2015) The impact of supervision on the pains of community punishment in England and Wales: An exploratory study. *European Journal of Probation*, 7(2), 85–102.

Hayes, David. (2016) Penal impact: Towards a more intersubjective measurement of penal severity. *Oxford Journal of Legal Studies*, 36(4), 724–750.

Hayes, David. (2017) Proximity, pain and state punishment. *Punishment & Society*, 20(2): 235–254.

Hirsch, Andrew von and Jareborg, Nils. (1991) Gauging criminal harm: A living-standard analysis. *Oxford Journal of Legal Studies*, 11(1), 1–38.

Ignatieff, Michael. (1978) *A Just Measure of Pain: The Penitentiary in the Industrial Revolution, 1750–1850*. New York: Pantheon Books.

Ignatieff, Michael. (1981) State, civil society and total institutions: A critique of recent social histories of punishment. *Crime and Justice*, 3(1), 153–193.

Johnson, Robert and Toch, Hans. (Eds.). (1982) *The Pains of Imprisonment*. London: Sage Publications.

King, Roy and McDermott, Kathleen. (1995) *The State of Our Prisons*. Clarendon Press.

Markel, Dan and Flanders, Chad. (2010) Bentham on stilts: The bare relevance of subjective experience to retributive justice. *California Law Review*, 98(3), 907–988.

Matravers, Matthew. (2016) Punishment, suffering and justice. In Stephen Farrall, Barry Goldson, Ian Loader and Anita Dockley (Eds.), *Justice and Penal Reform: Re-Shaping the Penal Landscape*. London: Routledge, pp. 27–46.

McNeill, Fergus. (2019) Mass supervision, misrecognition and the "Malopticon". *Punishment & Society*, 21(2), 207–230.

Nugent, Briege and Schinkel, Marguerite. (2016) The pains of desistance. *Criminology and Criminal Justice*, 16(5), 568–584.

Payne, Brian and Gainey, Randy. (1998) A qualitative assessment of the pains experienced on electronic monitoring. *International Journal of Offender Therapy and Comparative Criminology*, 42(2), 149–163.

Ristroph, Alice. (2011) Responsibility for the criminal law. In R. A. Duff and Stuart Green (Eds.), *Philosophical Foundations of Criminal Law*, 107–124.

Sexton, Lori. (2015) Penal subjectivities: Developing a theoretical framework for penal consciousness. *Punishment & Society*, 17(1), 114–136.

Shammas, Victor. (2014) The pains of freedom: Assessing the ambiguity of Scandinavian penal exceptionalism on Norway's prison island. *Punishment & Society*, 16(1), 104–123.

Sykes, Gresham. (1958) *The Society of Captives: A Study of a Maximum Security Prison*. Princeton, NJ: Princeton University Press.

Ugelvik, Thomas and Damsa, Dorina. (2018) The pains of crimmigration imprisonment: Perspectives from a Norwegian all-Foreign prison. *British Journal of Criminology*, 58(5), 1025–1043.

Walker, Nigel. (1991) *Why Punish?* Oxford: Oxford University Press.

Section 10

The development of an evidence base

Section 10 Introduction

How can rehabilitative work contribute to outcomes such as reductions in offending? What can be done to harmonize rehabilitative work and research evidence? Evaluations of practice, using robust social science methodologies, can help answer these questions. However, debates about the constitution of robust evaluation methodologies abound although the randomized control trial (RCT)[1] design is typically cited as the gold standard in evaluation research for several reasons explored by some chapters in this section. For example, properly conducted RCTs are said to have strong internal validity since they are designed to establish whether an intervention causes a given outcome (causality), and the degree to which the intervention causes the observed outcome (treatment effect size).

Evaluations of practice involving the use of other methods such as qualitative methods and quasi-experimental methods lack similar levels of internal validity since they cannot control for the range of factors such as systematic differences between groups which could also explain observed results. It is however worth noting that properly designed quasi-experimental studies which use comparison and experimental groups and try to match the groups across key variables, can produce reliable results. Indeed, the outcomes of RCTs may not always be quite as relevant to policy and practice development as is commonly believed. RCTs are typically conducted using highly trained staff in a controlled environment which may not reflect real-life practice settings. But, it could be argued that if properly conducted, what they lack in ecological validity[2] they may make up for in internal validity. Additional methodologies employed by evaluation studies include systematic reviews and meta-analyses. Both use social science methodologies to summarize existing research and help develop the evidence-base underpinning effective practice.

In many Western jurisdictions, there is a long history of evaluating rehabilitative work.[3] Evaluation research in several Western jurisdictions including the UK and the US did however undergo a hiatus from the 1970s onwards, following the reviews of rehabilitative work conducted in the 1970s, which concluded that 'nothing works' in the sense that rehabilitative work did not appear to reduce recidivism (see, for example, Martinson 1974). This finding, alongside the 'law and order' politics of the 1970s and 1980s, was a key factor in the decline of rehabilitation as a fundamental penal ideal and a loss of official interest in evaluating the effectiveness of rehabilitative work in penal settings.

In the 1990s, however, the emergence of the Risk-Need-Responsivity (RNR) model, known colloquially as the 'what works' approach, reignited official interest in evaluation research. The model was underpinned by several principles which were said to produce measurable reductions in reconviction rates (Bonta and Andrews 2017). In the UK, the promise of quantifiable outcomes complemented the New Labour government's modernization agenda and the underpinning managerialist ideals of focusing on practices which were demonstrably efficient. As part of the effort to roll out the model nationally, the New Labour government launched its Crime Reduction Programme (CRP). Under the rubric of the CRP, the first large-scale evaluations of 'what works' programmes in England and Wales were commissioned. The evaluations and their findings have been reviewed extensively elsewhere (see, for example, Raynor 2004).

Although the findings of the evaluations were inconclusive regarding the effectiveness of the RNR model, they usefully highlighted implementation problems that could undermine effectiveness. Examples were high attrition rates, and a lack of programme integrity or the failure to deliver programmes according to their design or underlying principles (Raynor 2004; Harper and Chitty 2005). These evaluations and others also reveal additional barriers that can limit the scope and impact of evaluations and these are covered in this section. Examples include the methodological issues mentioned earlier and the undue influence of commissioning bodies including policymakers.

Evaluation studies have slowly gained ascendency since the late 1990s and the 2000s when the first set of 'what works' programmes were evaluated, and the studies have revealed further insights. For example, it is clear that evaluation studies share a number of features in common regardless of their methodologies. For example, they can trigger policy change, help develop an evidence base which may inform effective practice, and help bridge gaps between practice and research. Additionally, evaluations can facilitate knowledge exchange through dialogue between researchers, policymakers, and services.

Several chapters in this section examine the many dimensions of evaluation research in the field of rehabilitative work. Chapter 84, which is the first chapter in the section, draws on the findings of evaluation studies to highlight key features of effective programmes in prison, and Chapter 85 discusses approaches to measuring effective supervision practice, with particular emphasis on the utility of performance measures derived from administrative databases.

In Chapter 86, there is an analysis of visual methods that have been used to evaluate probation practice and Chapter 87 focuses on observation methods. These chapters reveal that as evaluation research has evolved, innovative methodologies, including audiovisual and visualization methods, have emerged. In Australia, Trotter and colleagues (2015) have used audio recordings of frontline supervision practise to evaluate the nature and impact of supervision skills. In the UK, Raynor and colleagues (2014) have used video-recorded interviews for the same purpose. These innovative methods, which allow researchers to observe and assess supervision sessions without being physically present during the sessions in real time, have helped researchers transcend spatial and temporal barriers to access and unlock the black box of one-to-one supervision.

The remaining chapters in this section explore how to tailor evaluation research to suit specific groups and contexts. In Chapter 88, there is a description of an innovative gender-responsive approach to evaluating women's programmes. Chapters 89 and 90 focus on approaches to evaluating group programmes, and Chapter 91 provides an analysis of evaluation research targeted at improving outcomes in custodial institutions. The final chapter focuses on historical and contemporary developments in evaluation research in British probation contexts.

Notes

1   There are ethical problems associated with the RCT design in criminal justice settings. For example, the design involves selecting a group of people and then applying a treatment to some within the group whilst denying others in the group the same treatment in order to observe whether the treatment produces an impact (reduction in reconviction).
2   An evaluation lacks ecological validity if its conclusions do not reflect typical real-life practices within a service. This is more likely to occur if the evaluation alters a

service's natural setting by, for example, focusing only on highly trained staff members and evaluating their activities within a controlled environment set up for the purpose of the evaluation.

3 There are several examples in the UK, for instance (see Folkard and colleagues 1976; Radzinowicz 1958; Wilkins 1958; and see generally Raynor 2018).

References

Bonta, J. and Andrews, D. A. (2017) *The Psychology of Criminal Conduct*, 6th edition. Abingdon: Routledge.

Folkard, M. S., Smith, D. E. and Smith, D. D. (1976) *Impact Volume II: The Results of the Experiment*. Home Office Research Study 36. London: HMSO.

Harper, G. and Chitty, C. (Eds.). (2005) *The Impact of Corrections on Re-Offending: A Review of 'what works'*, 3rd edition. Home Office Research Study 291. London: Home Office.

Martinson, R. (1974) What works? Questions and answers about prison reform. *The Public Interest*, 35, 22–34.

Radzinowicz, L. (Ed.). (1958) *The Results of Probation. A Report of the Cambridge Department of Criminal Science*. London: Palgrave Macmillan.

Raynor, P. (2004) The probation service 'pathfinders': Finding the path and losing the way? *Criminal Justice*, 4(3), 309–325.

Raynor, P. (2018) The search for impact in British probation: From programmes to skills and implementation. In P. Ugwudike, P. Raynor and J. Annison (Eds.), *Evidence-Based Skills in Criminal Justice: International Research on Supporting Rehabilitation and Desistance*. Bristol: Policy Press.

Raynor, P., Ugwudike, P. and Vanstone, M. (2014) The impact of skills in probation work: A reconviction study. *Criminology and Criminal Justice*, 14(2), 235–249.

Trotter, C., Evans, P. and Baidawi, S. (2015) The effectiveness of challenging skills in work with young offenders. *International Journal of Offender Therapy and Comparative Criminology*, 61(4), 397–412.

Wilkins, L. T. (1958) A small comparative study of the results of probation. *British Journal of Delinquency*, 8, 201–209.

84

Features of effective prison-based programmes for reducing recidivism

Dominic A. S. Pearson

Introduction

Prisons exist to deter offenders from crime but also to reduce their likelihood of harming victims, both past and future. Yet prisons everywhere have a revolving door: a high proportion of released inmates reoffend and are re-incarcerated. Official statistics for England and Wales indicate that 48% reoffend within a year of release, rising to 64% for prisoners given sentences of less than a year (Ministry of Justice 2018). International reviews report rates of reoffending as ranging between 20% for Norway through 52% for the United States, to 62% for Ireland (Pell Center for International Relations and Public Policy 2014). Re-incarceration rates are also high. In England and Wales for example the annual custody rate is between 44% and 48% of prisoners (Ministry of Justice 2013).[1] International data suggest between 24% and 50% of prisoners are re-incarcerated within three years (Fazel and Wolf 2015). Thus a heavy proportion of prisoners are not being deterred from crime and are creating new victims post release.

These observations are supported by a body of evidence suggesting that imprisonment does not, by itself, lead to reduced rates of recidivism (see White 2017 for a brief policy review). There is, therefore, a need to investigate the potential for implementing evidence-based interventions that can be offered in custody to reduce risk, combined with through-care models to manage that risk post-release. The present chapter argues that success factors do exist but well-designed prison-based programmes should be integrated within a wider 'implement to evaluate' rehabilitative institutional culture with embedded researcher-practitioners. Research and development cultures support prison programmes all too rarely, outside of occasional researcher-monitored 'demonstration' projects.

Much has been learned over the past four decades about how to reduce offender recidivism. This is due to the proliferation of systematic reviews (SRs),[2] enabling researchers to integrate and evaluate the effectiveness literature. SRs have helped synthesize the relevant literature, while emphasizing the importance of high-quality primary studies that maximize comparability between groups and therefore attribution of effects. Study quality is typically rated against the Maryland Scientific Methods Scale (see Farrington et al. 2002). Higher quality, or more methodologically rigorous, studies are randomized trials or strong quasi-experiments with equivalent comparison groups. Lower quality studies have incidental/unmatched or no comparison groups.

This chapter aimed to learn from recent reviews, 2005–2017, of the effectiveness of programmes for incarcerated adult offenders. The reviews discussed below all used meta-analysis to summarize results quantitatively across studies of acceptable quality,[3] and examined effectiveness in reducing recidivism of prison-based intervention compared to minimal/no treatment. Due to space limitations, only the following key areas were considered: substance-misuse rehabilitation, general offending behaviour programmes, and sexual offender treatment. The intention was also to review the effectiveness of interventions for intimate partner violence (IPV); however, literature searches failed to uncover a single SR involving prison-based IPV programmes.

Reducing substance-related recidivism

Drug rehabilitation programmes

These programmes, based on the cognitive behavioural model, involve the assessment and treatment of the physical and psychological needs of participants who are recovering from substance addiction. The assumption is that reducing substance dependency and associated issues will reduce the likelihood of reoffending. Reviews of the literature indicate that substance misuse problems are highly correlated with criminal behaviour among offender populations (Bennett et al. 2008). One recent SR was found (Mitchell et al. 2012).

This updated an earlier 2007 review which itself extended a review by Pearson and Lipton (1999).

Mitchell et al. (2012) reviewed the effect of treatment for substance abusers on drug relapse and post-release recidivism. A variety of interventions were examined including therapeutic communities (TCs), structured counselling, narcotics maintenance, and boot camps. Only six evaluations were true experiments; the remainder involved non-equivalent comparison group designs. The meta-analysis synthesized 74 effect sizes from 69 studies. Results showed an overall positive effect of treatment on recidivism but that this varied depending on the type of programme.

The strongest positive evidence was found for concept-based TCs. These are treatment units that segregate participants ('residents') from mainstream non-participating inmates. Residents are typically involved in running the treatment activities, e.g. leading group sessions, monitoring rule-compliance, maintaining the environment, and resolving disputes. Confrontation with rule violators is encouraged, accompanied by support for efforts toward positive changes. The treatment model views drug use as symptomatic of more general personal problems, thus the target of change is not drug abuse itself but the underlying psychological problems. A typical concept-based TC lasts between 6 and 12 months.

Consistent modest effects of TCs on both drug relapse and recidivism emerged. For post-release recidivism the odds ratio (OR) was 1.40 which was statistically significant, representing a recidivism reduction from 35% to 28%. Importantly, the results were robust to variations in research design and sample characteristics. Thus, evidence of TC effectiveness is not undermined by support only coming from weaker research designs that cannot exclude alternative explanations, and TCs are applicable to a wide range of participants. The only programme feature that exhibited a significant relationship to effect size was voluntary participation: TCs where all participants were volunteers were more effective than other TCs. There was also a trend for longer treatment to be more effective, but this fell short of statistical significance. Relatively fewer TC evaluations examined effects on drug relapse. Overall the evidence suggests that prison-based TCs are effective at reducing recidivism.

For counselling programmes Mitchell et al. (2012) found mixed results. Counselling included a diverse range of interventions, including group counselling such as Alcoholics/Narcotics Anonymous, cognitive skills training, as well as individual therapy. Although these programmes had a mean OR of 1.53 equating to a recidivism reduction from 35% to 26%, this effect comes from weak studies: the minority of evaluations rated higher in methodological rigour showed smaller non-significant effects than those rated lower. Moderator analyses linked larger effects to programmes of longer duration, where participation is voluntary, but with mandatory aftercare post-release – consistent with the findings for TCs. Overall the evidence for prison-based counselling programmes reducing recidivism among drug abusers is promising but unreliable.

The final two programme types reviewed were prison-based narcotics maintenance programmes (NMPs) and boot camps. Prison-based NMPs, such as methadone maintenance, prescribe synthetic opioid medication to block the euphoric high or suppress opiate withdrawal symptoms. Medication is either reduced gradually or maintained long term. The aim is to reduce the harms associated with heroin addiction including criminality and risky injection behaviours. Boot camps, meanwhile, are a military-style intervention designed to deter criminal conduct and instil self-discipline by immersion in a structured regime involving staff confrontation. The mean ORs for both boot camps and NMPs indicated that neither was associated with statistically significant reductions in recidivism. When outliers were not excluded analyses suggested that prison-based NMPs actually increased recidivism.

In summary, Mitchell et al. (2012) found that prison-based substance-misuse programmes are modestly effective in reducing recidivism with positive effects limited to TCs and some counselling programmes. However, effects are not always followed by a reduction in drug use relapse. Regardless of variations in methodology, sample, or treatment characteristics, prison-based drug treatment did not generally reduce measures of post-release drug use. Interestingly however, across all analyses, mandatory aftercare magnified positive recidivism effects compared to optional/no aftercare. Thus continuity of treatment, within prison and post release, may be an important programme component.

Reducing general recidivism

Educational and vocational programmes

Since most prisons offer education, these are probably the most common programme type. However, the rationale linking educational intervention and reducing recidivism is unclear: whether to increase employability skills to reduce dependency on illegitimate income, or, to reduce antisocial identities and cognitive skills deficits that are linked to offending. Three meta-analyses considered the effectiveness of prison-based education and/or vocational programmes (Ellison et al. 2017; French and Gendreau 2006; MacKenzie 2006).

MacKenzie (2006) reviewed prison education, life skills, vocational programmes, and prison industries (i.e. jobs aimed at producing goods and services for the state or general public). Overall the methodological quality was weak, with few experiments or strong quasi-experiments. The typical comparison group was naturally occurring programme non-participants, liable to selection bias. Meta-analysis of 16 educational programmes found that compared to non-participants the odds of recidivating were 16% lower in participants. However, no clear effect emerged in seven of the component studies, including in the one randomized trial.

Regarding life skills programmes, across three studies a positive but non-significant treatment effect emerged. The seven tests of vocational programmes showed a significant positive mean effect with participants' odds of recidivism reduced by 36% compared to non-participants. However, again the effect was not reliable in the two most robust randomized trial evaluations. Across the two studies of prison industries a significant positive effect emerged, but this was due to the lower quality study; the other study was statistically ineffective. MacKenzie (2006) concluded that the evidence for educational and vocational programmes was favourable, while that for life skills and prison industries was inconclusive.

Ellison et al. (2017) reviewed evaluations of prison-based education. Studies were published between 1994 and 2015, and, to include non-US studies, the reviewers relaxed eligibility criteria for study quality.[4] Notwithstanding, the majority were US studies, and 18/28 had data suitable for meta-analysis. Results suggested educational programmes reduced the likelihood of recidivism by one-third. However, two of the 18 studies were inconclusive, and study quality generally was weak with no randomized trials. Therefore, echoing MacKenzie (2006) it is possible that the positive findings stem from something other than the programme activities, e.g. motivational differences between the participants and the non-participants. Ellison and colleagues concluded that the evidence for prison-based education is favourable.

In a review of 104 controlled tests of the effect of treatment on institutional misconducts, French and Gendreau (2006) found that educational/ vocational programmes had no impact. This contrasted with behavioural programmes which reduced misconduct by 26%. Research suggests that misconducts are a reasonable predictor of recidivism in the community (e.g. Cochran et al. 2014). Indeed from analysis of 23 tests with recidivism outcomes, French and Gendreau showed that programmes in the 'high misconduct reduction' category were associated with a 13% reduction in recidivism, while non-behavioural programmes that were less successful in reducing misconducts had a non-significant negative effect. Relatedly, programmes that did not target criminogenic 'needs' (antisocial attitudes, behaviour, and associates) did not impact misconducts. Thus the effectiveness of educational and vocational programmes may be contingent on the extent to which these purposeful activities address the underpinning antisocial cognitions, behaviour, and identity.

Cognitive behavioural programmes

Cognitive behavioural treatment (CBT) programmes are based on the premise that cognitive skills deficits, such as poor reasoning and problem-solving, explain criminal behaviour and can be enhanced. Generally, CBT programmes are structured, short term, manualized, and designed to engage offenders. One example is Reasoning & Rehabilitation (R&R) (Ross et al. 1988), and another is Moral Reconation Therapy (MRT) (Little and Robinson 1988). Landenberger and Lipsey (2005) provided a meta-analysis of CBT programmes, while two reviews focused on the effectiveness of R&R (Tong and Farrington 2008; Wilson et al. 2005) and one focused on MRT (Wilson et al. 2005). Due to space limitations and substantively similar findings, only the broad-based review is discussed below (Landenberger and Lipsey 2005).

Landenberger and Lipsey (2005) included evaluations of programmes for prisoners or probationers, adults or juveniles. They identified 58 high-quality studies with recidivism outcomes, generally within 12 months. CBT was found to significantly reduce recidivism, from 40% to 30%. However, due to the range of programmes included, the findings were highly variable and so the focus was moderators of effectiveness. Importantly, results were robust to the methodological rigour of the primary studies. Results varied however according to whether the analysis was by 'intent-to-treat' or 'treatment received' (TR), with TR producing inflated effects. This is unsurprising because TR biases group comparison by excluding typically riskier non-completer cases. There was no superiority for any particular brand-name CBT programme, and programmes were equally effective in prison or community. Differential effects were, however, found for particular elements. Optimal treatment included delivery to moderately high-risk offenders, delivery over 16+ weeks, zero attrition, and distinct anger control and interpersonal problem-solving programme components. Programmes that included sessions on victim impact were linked to *worse* outcomes. With 'optimal treatment' variables coded into the analysis, matching studies were twice as effective as non-matching studies, cutting recidivism rates from 40% to 19%.

These reviews considered an unrestricted general offender population. Instead, Jolliffe and Farrington (2007) conducted a review of programme effectiveness with specifically violent offenders. Violent offenders tend to have longer offence histories than general offenders and are more difficult to engage in treatment (Jolliffe and Farrington 2007). The reviewers identified just 11 studies that compared reconviction rates of a programme group to those of a control group, eight of which reported impact on violent recidivism. Although, overall, interventions reduced violent reoffending significantly, only two studies reported a statistically significant reduction in violent recidivism.[5] Moreover the studies that were more likely to be biased were associated with larger effects. Overall, impact equated to a reduction in violent recidivism of 7–8%,[6] but individual study features were important as the variation in effects was greater than would be expected by sampling error alone.

After controlling for methodological quality, promising features associated with larger effects included: cognitive skills, role play, and relapse prevention methods. Interventions that used all three features were associated with an 18% reduction in reoffending. There was also some evidence favouring treatment of longer duration, and *not* providing empathy training. However none of the features were independently related to a reduction in violent recidivism when controlling for study rigour. Notwithstanding, these results are consistent with the hypothesis that strong influence methods, typically cognitive social learning practices, should be used with higher-risk offenders and treatment of these prisoners' multifaceted criminogenic needs should be intensive. The Correctional Service of Canada Anger and Emotions Management programme (Dowden et al. 1999) illustrates the effective features.

Reducing sexual recidivism

Psychosocial programmes

These are a broad category of therapeutic intervention, often based on the CBT model. Therapeutic targets include reducing deviant sexual attitudes, improving self-control, enhancing intimacy skills, promoting perspective taking, and coping with stressors. Two recent meta-analyses of the effectiveness of psychosocial programmes were identified (Hanson et al. 2009; Schmucker and Lösel 2017). The majority of programmes reviewed were designed specifically for sexual offenders. Evaluations of pharmacological treatment, i.e. chemical castration, did not meet the minimum study quality level in either review.[7]

Hanson et al. (2009) aimed to examine whether the principles of effective intervention for general offenders (Bonta and Andrews 2007) apply to sexual offender treatment. These principles are that (1) more intensive treatment should be targeted at higher risk offenders (*risk*), (2) treatment should target needs that are empirically supported dynamic risk factors for recidivism (*need*), and (3) cognitive behavioural and social learning approaches should be employed, with treatment design and delivery matching offender learning styles and abilities (*general and specific responsivity*). Twenty-three studies of psychosocial sex offender programmes were included, the majority rated weak quality and only four randomized trials. Overall, Hanson and colleagues found evidence of the effectiveness of these programmes, both in terms of sexual recidivism and general recidivism. Effectiveness was robust to methodological quality and treatment setting (institution/community). The effect size for violent nonsexual recidivism, although positive, was smaller and statistically non-significant. Analyses of sexual recidivism outcomes supported adherence of treatment to the Risk-Need-Responsivity principles. Effects were consistently low/negative for studies adhering to none of the principles, and consistently large for those adhering to all three.

Schmucker and Lösel (2017) reviewed the effectiveness of treatment of male sexual offenders. This updated an earlier review (Lösel and Schmucker 2005), tightening their eligibility criteria to exclude studies with non-equivalent comparison groups. All 27 studies included evaluated psychosocial programmes, mostly CBTs – only eight were in other categories. The majority of studies were quasi-experiments; only six randomized trials were identified. Results indicated an overall positive statistically significant effect on sexual ($OR = 1.41$) and general ($OR = 1.45$) recidivism. Compared to non-participants this equates to a reduction from 13.7% to 10.1% and from 41.2% to 32.6% for each type of recidivism, respectively. Although methodological quality did not influence effect sizes, findings were highly variable, inhibiting a generally positive conclusion.

Individual study features having a strong impact included: medium- to high-risk offenders, CBT programmes, more individualized treatment, studies with small samples (N≤50, published or unpublished), and good descriptive validity. Although the reviewers did not code for the Risk-Need-Responsivity principles, they comment that the first feature relates to the 'risk' principle, while the second and third relate to treatment 'responsivity'. The final two may indicate programme 'integrity', or the delivery of services as designed, since the reviewers presumed that both small sample size and a coherent treatment concept predicted proper resourcing and monitoring.

Although there was no significant difference by treatment setting, unlike community and hospital settings there was insufficient evidence to draw conclusions regarding the effectiveness of treatment in prisons. Prison-based treatment yielded a lower and non-significant mean effect. Nevertheless, one of the few significant effects in the dataset came from a prison-based programme (Duwe and Goldman 2009).

Conclusion and implications

While it is generally accepted that prison by itself does not reduce recidivism (Marsh et al. 2009; White 2017), in the UK only a small fraction (5–7%) of prisoners attend cognitive behavioural programmes (Hopkins and Brunton-Smith 2014). As not all prison-based rehabilitation programmes are effective, the measures below are recommended for research-governed practical investment.

Provide TCs for substance-misusing offenders

A reason for TCs' effectiveness may be the more rehabilitative prison environment due to the isolation of treatment units from the main prison. Accordingly, meta-analysis has found enhanced effects of programmes on prisoner misconducts when participants are housed separately (r = .33), compared to within (r = .05), the general prison population (French and Gendreau 2006). 'Contamination effects' in the prison subculture was one possible reason for the lower effects of prison-based treatment of sex offenders relative to community/hospital settings (Schmucker and Lösel 2017). A distinct environment for treatment volunteers may assist prison management and support rehabilitation.

Indeed, voluntariness was the key moderator underpinning the success of TCs for drug rehabilitation. This is illustrated in an evaluation of a cognitive restructuring programme for violent offenders which accepted referrals on a voluntary basis (Baro 1999). Compared to volunteers for other self-help programmes, Baro (1999) reported a reduction in misconducts, even among participants who had not completed the full CBT programme. However, after the programme became mandatory across a wider prisoner group, there was no impact on the number of misconducts (Hogan et al. 2012). This consistency with the meta-analyses of drug rehabilitation signals that voluntariness may be more broadly relevant to prison-based treatment effectiveness. Indeed, meta-analysis of the effect of coercion on offender treatment suggests that prison-based treatment is more effective in reducing reoffending when truly voluntary (Parhar et al. 2008). Unlike community settings, in prisons this was the only circumstance in which treatment was effective: here there was no effect of coerced treatment, including when treatment was offered with the incentive of early release. In a study of prisoner views of CBT programmes for example, prisoners reported sometimes feeling coerced to participate, perhaps for a favourable parole report, even though they knew programmes were purportedly voluntary (Clarke et al. 2004).

Design and monitor 'best practice' factors in rehabilitation programmes

Particular programmatic features are associated with effectiveness in reducing recidivism. These include: moderately high-risk offender target group, intensive delivery, multiple treatment targets addressing dynamic risk factors, cognitive behavioural treatment with individualized elements, and no attrition (French and Gendreau 2006; Hanson et al. 2009; Jolliffe and Farrington 2007; Landenberger and Lipsey 2005; Schmucker and Lösel 2017). These features correspond to the Risk-Need-Responsivity principles, and meta-analytic results consistent with these principles have emerged regarding treatment for sex offenders (Hanson et al. 2009), general offenders (Landenberger and Lipsey 2005), and substance-misusing offenders (Prendergast et al. 2013).[8]

Some reviews highlighted a positive association between effectiveness and small sample size (Landenberger and Lipsey 2005; Schmucker and Lösel 2017). This has been linked to researcher involvement which has benefits for a clearly defined target group, careful selection, training and ongoing support of staff, close monitoring of adherence to the intervention plan, and ensuring low treatment dropout rates. These are features of programme integrity (Bonta and Andrews 2007), but weaker results in larger studies suggest 'integrity' is harder to achieve in programmes rolled out in routine practice. The small sample size effect could be attributed to publication bias, where only successful small sample studies surface, while unfavourable larger-scale evaluations are more readily submitted/accepted. It cannot be known how many reports on unsuccessful small sample studies are hidden. A less cynical explanation is that small-scale programmes that are subject to evaluation (with a view to publication) would have better outcomes due to closer monitoring of staff and programme delivery.

Build-in aftercare and community continuity

All moderator analyses in Mitchell et al. (2012) indicated that drug rehabilitation programmes that mandated aftercare produced larger effect sizes than those that did not. Similarly, with sex offenders there was a tendency for outpatient hospital treatment to fare better than treatment in prisons (Schmucker and Lösel 2017). Reasons suggested include negative effects of the prison subculture, dissipated treatment gains with delayed transfer of learning to the world outside, and resettlement difficulties. These results therefore suggest the importance of integration of 'through the gate' services into prison-based programme design for maximizing its effectiveness.

Conduct more controlled evaluations of routine practice

A substantial limitation in interpreting the benefit of programmes, particularly educational and vocational interventions, is the absence of well-controlled studies. While a range of research designs is welcomed, the relative absence of randomized trials is all too apparent, especially when the effects observed in the weaker studies are not supported in the few randomized trials (MacKenzie 2006; Mitchell et al. 2012 for counselling programmes). Confidence in results is also reduced where positive effects are only observed in trials of 'demonstration programmes' by the programme developers, not independent trials of routine practice. This is particularly relevant to the state of the evidence regarding programmes for sex offenders (Schmucker and Lösel 2017) and violent offenders (Jolliffe and Farrington 2007).

Incorporate more systematic process evaluations

All reviews bemoaned the paucity of information in primary studies regarding the nature and context of evaluated programmes. One review coded 'descriptive validity' and found stronger effects associated with better documentation (Schmucker and Lösel 2017). Clear and explicit documentation of service process may signify programme integrity which is likely to positively impact effectiveness (Lowenkamp et al. 2006). Conducting and reporting process evaluations linked to outcome evaluation studies may therefore facilitate greater understanding and monitoring of integrity. Furthermore, process data might offer insight into potentially moderating contextual factors such as the technological support systems available (McDougall et al. 2017) or the institutional climate (Woessner and Schwedler 2014).

Test the effect of programme setting

The positive evidence for TCs suggests that an appropriately designed prison community can enable therapeutic change, provided participants are volunteers and agree to take responsibility for their own behaviour as well as challenging others'. While this implies that the mainstream prison subculture may exert a neutralizing effect on otherwise 'best practice' programmes, it also signals that such programmes might further excel when participants reside in a separate therapeutic unit. A final recommendation of this review is therefore the need to test programme setting, given that controlled outcome studies have not directly compared the effect of the same treatment in different settings.

Consistent with the Risk-Need-Responsivity principles, the most promising effects come from using cognitive behavioural approaches incorporating interpersonal problem-solving skills training to address the multiple problems of higher-risk offenders preparing for release. Given the lack of attention to context, the effectiveness of prison-based programmes, even those with 'best practice' features, remains a hypothesis to test with organizational and research support.

Acknowledgement

Thank you to Adrian Needs for his comments on a final draft of this chapter.

Notes

1 The lower re-incarceration rate was for prisoners sentenced to less than 12 months custody, while the higher rate was for matched prisoners sentenced to between one and four years custody (Ministry of Justice 2013).
2 In a systematic review 'a specific and reproducible method is used to identify, select and appraise studies of a previously agreed level of quality' (Booth et al. 2016: 11).
3 The majority of meta-analyses reviewed in this chapter had inclusion criteria that limited eligibility to those studies with control groups and excluded studies with pre-post one-group designs. The exception was in reviews of educational and vocational programmes.
4 Ellison et al.'s (2017) meta-analysis included evaluations without a control group, e.g. predicted versus actual recidivism.
5 Two studies reported a non-significant increase in recidivism.
6 The reduction in general (any) reoffending among the violent offenders was 8–11%.
7 Offenders must volunteer for these programmes and therefore non-randomized evaluations are particularly vulnerable to selection bias. Volunteers for castration are likely to be different from the non-volunteers in the comparison group.

8   The meta-analysis by Prendergast et al. (2013) was not included in the current review as it did not moderate the results by correctional setting, and only 11% of the studies included related to prison-based treatment.

References

Baro, A. L. (1999) Effects of a cognitive restructuring program on inmate institutional behaviour. *Criminal Justice and Behavior*, 26(4), 466–484.

Bennett, T., Holloway, K. and Farrington, D. (2008) The statistical association between drug misuse and crime: A meta-analysis. *Aggression and Violent Behavior*, 13(2), 107–118.

Bonta, J. and Andrews, D. A. (2007) *Risk-Need-Responsivity Model for Offender Assessment and Rehabilitation*. Corrections Research User Report No. 2007–06. Ottawa, ON: Public Safety.

Booth, A., Papaioannou, D. and Sutton, A. (2016) *Systematic Approaches to a Successful Literature Review*, 2nd edition. Thousand Oaks, CA: Sage Publications.

Clarke, A., Simmonds, R. and Wydall, S. (2004) *Delivering Cognitive Skills Programmes in Prison: A Qualitative Study*. Home Office Online Report 27/04. Available at: http://tinyurl.com/yb4qkgac.

Cochran, J. C., Mears, D. P., Bales, W. D. and Stewart, E. A. (2014) Does inmate behavior affect post-release offending? Investigating the misconduct-recidivism relationship among youth and adults. *Justice Quarterly*, 31(6), 1044–1073.

Dowden, C., Blanchette, K. and Serin, R. (1999) *Anger Management Programming for Federal Male Inmates: An Effective Intervention*. Research Report R-82. Ottawa, ON: Correctional Service of Canada. Available at: www.csc-scc.gc.ca/research/r82e-eng.shtml.

Duwe, G. and Goldman, R. A. (2009) The impact of prison-based treatment on sex offender recidivism: Evidence from Minnesota. *Sexual Abuse: A Journal of Research and Treatment*, 21(3), 279–307.

Ellison, M., Szifris, K., Horan, R. and Fox, C. (2017) A rapid evidence assessment of the effectiveness of prison education in reducing recidivism and increasing employment. *Probation Journal*, 64(2), 108–128.

Farrington, D. P., Gottfredson, D. C., Sherman, L. W. and Welsh, B. C. (2002) The Maryland scientific methods scale. In L. W. Sherman, D. P. Farrington, B. C. Welsh and D. L. MacKenzie (Eds.), *Evidence-Based Crime Prevention*. London: Routledge, pp. 13–21.

Fazel, S. and Wolf, A. (2015) A systematic review of criminal recidivism rates worldwide: Current difficulties and recommendations for best practice. *PLoS One*, 10(6), e0130390. http://doi.org/10.1371/journal.pone.0130390.

French, S. A. and Gendreau, P. (2006) Reducing prison misconducts: What works! *Criminal Justice and Behavior*, 33(2), 185–218.

Hanson, R. K., Bourgon, G., Helmus, L. and Hodgson, S. (2009) The principles of effective correctional treatment also apply to sexual offenders: A meta-analysis. *Criminal Justice and Behavior*, 36(9), 865–891.

Hogan, N. L., Lambert, E. G. and Barton-Bellessa, S. M. (2012) Evaluation of change, an involuntary cognitive program for high-risk inmates. *Journal of Offender Rehabilitation*, 51(6), 370–388.

Hopkins, K. and Brunton-Smith, I. (2014) *Prisoners' Experience of Prison and Outcomes on Release: Waves 2 and 3 of SPCR (Results from the Surveying Prisoner Crime Reduction (SPCR) Longitudinal Cohort Study of Prisoners)*. London: Ministry of Justice Analytical Series.

Jolliffe, D. and Farrington, D. P. (2007) *A Systematic Review of the National and International Evidence on the Effectiveness of Interventions with Violent Offenders*. Ministry of Justice Research Series 16/07. London: Ministry of Justice, Research Development Statistics.

Landenberger, N. A. and Lipsey, M. W. (2005) The positive effects of cognitive - behavioral programs for offenders: A meta-analysis of factors associated with effective treatment. *Journal of Experimental Criminology*, 1(4), 451–476.

Little, G. L. and Robinson, K. D. (1988) Moral reconation therapy: A systematic step-by-step treatment system for treatment resistant clients. *Psychological Reports*, 62(1), 135–151.

Lösel, F. and Schmucker, M. (2005) The effectiveness of treatment for sexual offenders: A comprehensive meta-analysis. *Journal of Experimental Criminology*, 1(1), 117–146.

Lowenkamp, C. T., Latessa, E. J. and Smith, P. (2006) Does correctional program quality really matter? The impact of adhering to the principles of effective intervention. *Criminology & Public Policy*, 5(3), 575–594.

MacKenzie, D. L. (2006) *What Works in Corrections: Reducing the Criminal Activities of Offenders and Delinquents*. New York: Cambridge University Press.

Marsh, K., Fox, C. and Sarmah, R. (2009) Is custody an effective sentencing option for the UK? Evidence from a meta-analysis of existing studies. *Probation Journal*, 56(2), 129–151.

McDougall, C., Pearson, D. A. S., Torgerson, D. J. and Garcia-Reyes, M. (2017) The effect of digital technology on prisoner behavior and reoffending: A natural stepped-wedge design. *Journal of Experimental Criminology*, 13(4), 455–482.

Ministry of Justice. (2013) *2013 Compendium of Reoffending Statistics and Analysis. Ministry of Justice Statistics Bulletin*. London: Author. Available at: www.gov.uk/ government/uploads/system/uploads/attachment_data/file/278133/compendium-reoffending-stats-2013.pdf.

Ministry of Justice. (2018) *Proven Reoffending Statistics Quarterly Bulletin, April 2016 to June 2016*. London: Author. Available at: https://assets.publishing.service.gov. uk/government/uploads/system/uploads/attachment_data/file/702789/proven_ reoffending_bulletin_April_to_June_16.pdf.

Mitchell, O., MacKenzie, D. and Wilson, D. (2012) The effectiveness of incarceration-based drug treatment on criminal behavior: A systematic review. *Campbell Systematic Reviews*, 18.

Parhar, K. K., Wormith, J. S., Derkzen, D. M. and Beauregard, A. M. (2008) Offender coercion in treatment: A meta-analysis of effectiveness. *Criminal Justice and Behavior*, 35(9), 1109–1135.

Pearson, F. S. and Lipton, D. S. (1999) A meta-analytic review of the effectiveness of corrections-based treatments for drug abuse. *The Prison Journal*, 79(4), 384–410.

Pell Center for International Relations and Public Policy. (2014) *Incarceration and Recidivism: Lessons from Abroad*. Newport, RI: Salve Regina University. Available at: http://salve.edu/sites/default/files/filesfield/documents/Incarceration_and_Reci divism.pdf.

Prendergast, M. L., Pearson, F. S., Podus, D., Hamilton, Z. K. and Greenwell, L. (2013) The Andrews' principles of risk, needs, and responsivity as applied in drug treatment programs: Meta-analysis of crime and drug use outcomes. *Journal of Experimental Criminology*, 9(3), 275–300.

Ross, R. R., Fabiano, E. A. and Ewles, C. D. (1988) Reasoning and Rehabilitation. *International Journal of Offender Therapy and Comparative Criminology*, 32, 29–35.

Schmucker, M. and Lösel, F. (2017) Sexual offender treatment for reducing recidivism among convicted sex offenders. *Campbell Systematic Reviews*, 8.

Tong, L. S. and Farrington, D. P. (2008) Effectiveness of 'Reasoning and Rehabilitation' in reducing reoffending. *Psicothema*, 20(1), 20–28.

White, H. (2017) *The Effects of Sentencing Policy on Reoffending: A Summary of Evidence from 12 Campbell Systematic Reviews*. Campbell Policy Briefs, 4. Available at: www.campbellcollaboration.org/media/k2/attachments/Campbell_Policy_Brief_4_Sentencing.pdf.

Wilson, D. B., Bouffard, L. A. and MacKenzie, D. L. (2005) A quantitative review of structured, group-oriented, cognitive-behavioral programs for offenders. *Criminal Justice and Behavior*, 32(2), 172–204.

Woessner, G. and Schwedler, A. (2014) Correctional treatment of sexual and violent offenders: Therapeutic change, prison climate, and recidivism. *Criminal Justice and Behavior*, 41(7), 862–879.

85

Performance measure in community corrections

Measuring effective supervision practices with existing agency data[1]

Brandy L. Blasko, Karen A. Souza, Brittney Via, and Faye S. Taxman

In recent years, community supervision in the United States has been changing dramatically, as corrections populations have mounted and philosophies have shifted accordingly to accommodate more evidence-based supervision. There are currently 6.8 million adults under some form of correctional supervision in the United States (Kaeble et al. 2016). During the 1970s' 'tough on crime' movement, probation supervision practices emphasized surveillance, authority, and control. These law enforcement-oriented practices prevailed for three decades, despite mounting evidence against their effectiveness at reducing recidivism (Bonta et al. 2008; Drake 2011; Nagin et al. 2009; Taxman 2002, 2009). Today, growing attention to the ineffectiveness of punishment-oriented responses to criminal behaviour and the associated financial strain (Bonta et al. 2008; Nagin et al. 2009; Taxman 2002) has led to a renewed emphasis on rehabilitation ideals. But these ideals are cloaked in efforts to advance the use of science to identify effective practices. As a result, researchers and practitioners increasingly emphasize Core Correctional Practices using proactive and behavioural management approaches in community supervision.

A core set of community supervision practices has been defined as effective in reducing recidivism. Referred to as evidence-based practices (EBPs), these core practices are:

- Standardized, validated assessment instruments to assess risk and identify service needs.
- Matching of offenders to treatment and referrals made according to identified risk and needs.
- Provision of more treatment and referrals to offenders who pose the highest risk for reoffending.
- Use of a human service environment.
- Use of cognitive behavioural and social learning approaches to work with clients. While the use of proactive and behavioural management approaches to supervision has gained currency in recent years, embedding EBPs within routine community supervision practices has presented significant challenges for researchers and practitioners alike.

A major drawback to the advancement of practice is that there are few reliable measures to describe these practices. We propose a series of measures of supervision that may be gleaned from administrative databases. In this chapter, we review the administrative data from four community supervision agencies to explore the measures and highlight their utility. We then discuss the implications of using these performance measures.

Evidence-based practices in community corrections

Growing evidence on the ineffectiveness of control-oriented supervision practices has led to an emphasis on EBPs – that is, practices that are empirically tied to recidivism reduction (Petersilia and Turner 1993; Taxman 2002, 2008). In general, EBPs refer to the combined use of rigorous research and best available data to guide policy and practice decisions that improve outcomes for individuals under supervision (Bourgon 2013). When applied to supervision specifically, EBPs refer to a core set of correctional practices found to be associated with effective intervention and reductions in recidivism (Dowden and Andrews 2004). In one of the few meta-analytic studies on the topic, Chadwick and colleagues (2015) found that offenders supervised by trained officers in these skills had a 13% reduction in recidivism. This is promising given that in the most recent major national-level study by the Bureau of Justice Statistics (BJS), 43% of prisoners were rearrested within one year of release to the community (see Durose et al. 2014), and 40% of probationers are unsuccessful on supervision (Taxman 2012). While adherence to evidence-based supervision strategies results in positive outcomes among individuals involved in the criminal justice system, we know little about the supervision process and its effectiveness due to a lack of research evidence (Bonta et al. 2011; Taxman 2002, 2008).

An untapped resource: administrative data in community supervision

An important but often overlooked aspect to establishing meaningful measures of performance is administrative databases (i.e. management information systems) that are routinely used by probation agencies. Administrative databases collect routine intake, process, and discharge information at the client level; they are used by the agency to manage the population and, in many instances, serve as a supplement to case files. They are a source of data that can be used to determine progress towards successful implementation of evidence-based supervision. These data can be used to evaluate the effectiveness of an agency's programmes and policies (Drake and Jonson-Reid 1999; English et al. 2000; Raybould and Coombes 1992). An agency's monitoring of administrative data can help to ensure compliance with 'what works' at a system level (Miller and Maloney 2013). However, the functional utility of administrative data is very much contingent on the quality and completeness of the data collected by the agencies, and whether or not the agencies are using the data to construct meaningful measures that are both valid and reliable.

The present study

The aims of the present study are to:

- Develop a set of process measures related to evidence-based supervision that might be measurable in administrative data.
- Assess the quality and completeness of existing administrative data from four community corrections agencies.
- Compare the measures across different sites to assess their robustness. If community corrections agencies can assess how the staff and agency perform in relation to evidence-based practices, then they can more readily

monitor the quality and cost-effectiveness of supervision. They can also then assess what practices need more attention to improve supervision.

Method

Background

The data in this study were collected as part of a larger project that involved assisting justice professionals in translating evidence-based research into practice. Self-selection sampling was used to select the four study sites. All sites are located within the United States in different geographical areas. According to 2010 census data, the percentage of urban population (as compared to rural) within the four selected jurisdictions ranged from 68% to 100% (U.S. Census Bureau 2010).

Sample

Table 85.1 presents the case characteristics of individuals under supervision across the four study sites. The majority were male (range=76% to 94%) and the mean age ranged from 30.6 (SD = 11.4) to 39.4 (SD = 10.1). The study sites provide a mix of racial and ethnic groups, with the white population ranging from 3% to 80%, the black population ranging from 1% to 54%, and the Hispanic population ranging from 0% to 97%. Results from chi-square tests of independence and between-subjects t-tests indicated that, in addition to the characteristics above, offenders differed significantly across sites in terms of educational levels, risk and supervision levels, days on supervision, and history of prior supervision.

Measures and procedure

The jurisdictions were all trained on the 'Skills Offender Assessment and Responsivity in New Goals' (SOARING2) eLearning system (www.gmuace.org/tools) through George Mason University's Center for Advancing Correctional Excellence (ACE!). SOARING2 is an innovative eLearning training platform for professionals working with individuals involved in the criminal justice system to learn about EBPs and to enhance their case management skills. The SOARING2 programme contains five self-guided modules on Risk-Need-Responsivity, motivation and engagement, case planning, monitoring and compliance, and desistance. Recent modifications include segments for criminal thinking and lifestyles, substance abuse disorders, mental illness, emerging adults, and intimate partner violence. The process measures were developed based on these five areas of evidence-based supervision. Table 85.2 provides the variables extracted from the administrative data to develop the five domains for the current analyses.

Table 85.1 Case characteristics by site

	Site 1 %/M(SD)	Site 2 %/M(SD)	Site 3 %/M(SD)	Site 4 %/M(SD)
Male	77%	76%	94%	85%
Age	30.6 (11.4)	30.8 (11.4)	39.4 (10.1)	38.8 (12.0)
Race				
White	44%	3%	79%	32%
Black	54%	1%	14%	52%
Hispanic	0%	96%	5%	9%
Other	2%	0%	2%	7%
Education level				
No diploma	36%	54%	31%	46%
Diploma	64%	30%	25%	42%
GED	0%	0%	42%	0%
Some college	0%	14%	2%	6%
Risk level				
Low	25%	30%	15%	-
Medium	48%	47%	20%	-
High	13%	23%	66%	-
Supervision level				
Low	7%	21%	15%	-
Medium	57%	55%	20%	-
High	30%	24%	66%	-
Days on supervision	353.4 (237.3)	251.2 (201.0)	210.7 (163.4)	417.3 (256.0)
Prior supervision	38%	100%	89%	41%
Current offence				
Violent	9%	10%	19%	23%
Property	15%	20%	19%	27%
Drug	22%	54%	25%	32%
Other	21%	16%	36%	18%

Data are from the 2010 United States Census Bureau

Note: Site 1 N=821 probationers, Site 2 N=2,296, Site 3 N=288, Site 4 N=2,490. Some agencies have more than three levels so these totals may not add up to 100

Domain 1: Risk-Need-Responsivity

The Risk-Need-Responsivity (RNR) domain is the operating principle of Andrews and Bonta' s (2010) model of correctional treatment. According to the RNR model, those at highest risk for recidivism should receive the most intensive programming, offender programmes should target dynamic

Table 85.2 List of measures by the five domains

Domain	Variables
Risk-Need-Responsivity	Risk/need assessment
	Supervision level assigned
	Risk and supervision level match
	Total number of reassessments
	Total contacts during supervision period
	Rate of contact (monthly) on supervision
	Rate of identified needs to treatment placement
	Reduction in number of criminogenic needs
Motivation and engagement	Referral and start date for treatment
	Initial treatment less than 14 days from referral date
	Number of days from referral to treatment
	Number of days between first and third treatment sessions
Case planning	Number of days between intake and assessment
Monitoring and compliance	Revocations
	Special conditions given
	Number of special conditions given
Desistance	Successfully completed supervision
	Negative drug test
	Employed during supervision

criminogenic needs, and correctional interventions should be tailored to meet the individual needs of offenders. Evidence suggests that the principles delineated in the RNR framework also apply to treatment outcomes for interventions with sexual offenders.

Based on the available administrative data, eight measures were created to assess how well agency staff are adhering to RNR principles. The risk/needs assessment variable is a dichotomous variable (yes/no) that was used to record whether a formal risk-need assessment was carried out on each offender. The supervision level assigned variable refers to the clients' assigned supervision level based on their level of risk, which was divided into three categories: low, medium, and high. The risk and supervision level match variable was a dichotomous variable (yes/no) that recorded whether the clients' risk level matched the assigned level of supervision. For instance, if a client was identified as low risk by a risk-need assessment and he or she was subsequently supervised at low level, this constituted a match (yes = 1). Total number of reassessments measured the number of reassessments that were carried out on each individual over the course of supervision. Total contact over supervision refers to the total amount of contact clients had with their probation/parole officers during their supervision. The types of contact included in this variable were telephone, e-mail, letters, and face to face at home, in the office, or in the community. It included 'collateral' contact, which refers to contact with anyone else regarding the offenders' supervision (e.g. treatment providers, family members). The total contact over supervision was divided by the length of time the individual was on supervision to create the variable rate of monthly contact on supervision. The variable 'rate of identified needs to treatment placement' refers to the number of identified needs that matched the number of treatment placements. Finally, needs reduction was a dichotomous variable (yes/no) that recorded whether the clients' number of needs, as determined by a needs assessment, reduced over the course of their supervision.

Domain 2: motivation and engagement

Engaging clients in their community supervision experience and motivating them to make pro-social choices is important to the success of outcomes (Garnick et al. 2014). To this end, three variables were used to measure the constructs of motivation and engagement: referral and treatment start dates, amount of time between referrals and start of treatment (and also if this was less than 14 days), and the number of days between the first and third treatment sessions. Although administrative data have a limited capacity to directly measure these intrinsically driven concepts, these proxy measures were developed based on the understanding that referrals start the process of engagement in care, and that early initiation of treatment with regular follow-up treatment sessions (typically monthly) can increase the odds of better client engagement (Garnick et al. 2014).

Domain 3: case planning

Given that case plans drive the supervision process, it is important to develop a plan early in the supervision process (Taxman et al. 2004). The effective use of case planning was assessed by the number of days between the intake date and the date of assessment. Of course, other aspects of case planning such as goal setting, feedback, and reinforcement are also important to supervision success (Alexander et al. 2014); however, these factors are not typically gathered in management information systems.

Domain 4: monitoring and compliance

To ensure that clients are complying with the terms and conditions of their supervision, it is necessary to know what terms and conditions have been imposed on them by the agencies and courts, and whether or not they were violated. Based on the available data for this sample, three measures were constructed to reflect this domain: special conditions given (yes/no), number of special conditions given, and number of revocations and violations.

Domain 5: desistance

The success of community supervision is often judged by the degree to which it affects recidivism, and this is often measured by rearrest, reconviction, or re-incarceration. However, this is rather short-sighted, as other factors that support the goal of desistance can also be used as markers for re-entry success. For instance, employment and abstinence from substances have been identified as two important elements for re-entry success (James 2014). In the present study, three dichotomous desistance measures were created: whether the client successfully completed supervision, whether the client drug tests were negative, and whether the client was employed.

Findings and discussion

Through the process of data harmonization, we were able to collate the information from multiple administrative management information systems to create measures that could be used consistently across sites. One important learning point is that the ability to create process measures using administrative data is very much contingent on the type and quality of information collected by the agencies.

Findings indicate that of the five domains, data related to RNR domain were the most frequently available (range=0% to 100%) in the management information systems. Except for site 4, all of the sites had the ability of having RNR-related variables (see Table 85.3). Further investigation revealed that the site's policy was to utilize risk assessment information from past supervision. In other words, current clients on supervision were being managed according to their prior risk assessment information. This is problematic according to the RNR principle, as programming should be matched to the clients' current risk-needs appraisal (Andrews and Bonta 2010). Data on the rate of identified needs to treatment placement was the least available in the RNR domain.

The second domain, motivation and engagement, had the least amount of data available across all four sites. While we were able to pull from the data whether or not clients had received a referral, the fact that the agencies did not track any information about these referrals (e.g. client attendance, completion of programme requirements) limits our ability to tap motivation and engagement. Part of the problem may be that administrators are recording information according to the policies and procedures of their agency. Therefore,

Table 85.3 Percentage of administrative data available by site

	Site 1 N=821	Site 2 N=2,296	Site 3 N=288	Site 4 N=2,490
RNR				
Risk/need assessment	86%	100%	100%	45%
Supervision level assigned	86%	100%	100%	45%
Risk and supervision level match	83%	100%	100%	45%
Total contact over supervision	100%	100%	100%	100%
Rate of contact (monthly) on supervision	100%	100%	100%	100%
Rate of identified needs to treatment placement	24%	66%	57%	–
Total number of reassessments	86%	100%	100%	100%
Needs reduction	38%	100%	51%	0%
Motivation and engagement				
Referral and start date	–	9%	27%	–
Initial treatment less than 14 days from referral	–	9%	100%	–
Number of days from referral to treatment	0%	9%	31%	0%
Number of days between first and third treatment sessions	0%	9%	100%	0%
Case planning				
Number of days between intake and assessment	86%	100%	100%	4%
Monitoring and compliance				
Revocations	100%	100%	100%	100%
Special conditions given	100%	100%	60%	–
Number of special conditions given	100%	100%	67%	0%
Desistance				
Successfully completed supervision	33%	32%	100%	17%
Drug test negative	–	100%	85%	–
Employed	100%	100%	100%	

Note: Dashes denote that data were not available for that site

if an agency's responsibility is primarily to refer clients and the onus is on referral programs to track their own client information, it may not be feasible to acquire much information about this domain using agency administrative data.

Case planning was measured by the number of days between intake and assessment. Apart from site 4, which did not track this information, these data were available more than two-thirds of the time across sites. Of course, case planning also involves elements such as goal setting, expectations, rewards, and sanctions, but these data were not available for the agencies. One could speculate that this is in part because such elements involve more of an interactive process between probation officers and clients that is not typically documented. It may be possible, however, to obtain this information from other sources such as single coordinated care plans (SCCPs).

Data for the monitoring and compliance measure were largely available across sites. This is not surprising given the supervisory role of community corrections agencies. Because it is highly likely for individuals under community supervision to have some sort of general supervision conditions (e.g. contact requirements, abstinence from substances), agencies may not deem the tracking of this information as important as tracking special conditions (e.g. no-contact orders, treatment conditions). Not all individuals are given special conditions, but for those who are, findings revealed that this information is not documented reliably. For example, special conditions data were available 60% of the time for site 3, but it was unclear whether the remaining 40% of cases had no special conditions or whether the special conditions were simply not recorded, as in site 4.

For the fifth domain, supervision completion and abstinence from illicit substances are logical desistance measures. However, data were not consistently available across sites. Supervision completion data were recorded in less than one-third of cases (range=17% to 33%) and 50% of sites provided substance use screening data. The latter data were limited due to both the outsourcing of substance use testing by sites and also the quality of data records (e.g. recorded qualitatively as a string variable, inconsistent recording).

The principles of RNR suggest that matching treatment to clients' risk levels and associated needs is the key to treatment success (Andrews and Bonta 2010; Taxman 2008). In comparing the process measures that each site was able to construct with existing data (see Table 85.4), we found that sites 1 through 3 are, for the most part, carrying out risk and needs assessments with clients. The absence of recorded assessment data in more than 50% of clients in site 4 is cause for concern, given that this is a crucial first step to interventions. This means that some clients' needs may not be properly identified, which is reflected in the fact that site 4 had the lowest percentage of the population with a decrease in needs. The implication here is that an examination of the agency's assessment and triage policies is much needed.

Another important principle for the RNR domain is that contact rate while on supervision should correspond with the clients' risk level. As such, one would expect higher risk clients to receive more frequent contacts. While this is true for sites 2 through 4, for site 1, the monthly contact rate was lowest for the *high-risk* clients. In fact, the total average number of contacts over the supervision period was relatively low for this site for all risk levels, which suggests a need to examine the agency's policies of supervision and how clients are being monitored.

Table 85.4 Performance measures by site

	Site 1 N=821	Site 2 N=2,296	Site 3 N=288	Site 4 N=2,490
RNR				
% of population assessed for risk/needs	87%	100%	100%	47%
Assessment level				
Low	28%	30%	14%	18%
Medium	55%	48%	19%	37%
High	17%	23%	68%	45%
Total average contacts over supervision	0.6 (1.1)	2.0 (17.8)	4.0 (3.0)	1.9 (9.0)
Contact rate per month on supervision				
Low	0.1 (0.2)	1.0 (1.5)	2.2 (1.4)	2.0 (0.0)
Medium	0.9 (1.2)	1.6 (15.1)	3.9 (2.8)	–
High	0.1 (0.5)	3.8 (28.3)	4.4 (3.2)	2.3 (0.0)
Rate of identified needs to treatment placement	35%	56%	63%	–
% of population with matched risk and supervision level	58%	90%	100%	98%
% of population with decrease in needs	1%	22%	9%	0%
Total average number of reassessments over supervision	1.3 (0.6)	1.6 (0.9)	1.5 (0.5)	0.5 (0.5)
Average reassessments per risk level				
Low	1.2 (0.5)	1.3 (0.5)	2.0 (0.0)	1.0 (0.1)
Medium	1.3 (0.6)	1.6 (0.8)	1.5 (0.5)	1.0 (0.0)
High	1.4 (0.6)	2.1 (1.2)	1.4 (0.5)	1.0 (0.0)
Motivation and engagement				
% with both a referral and start date	–	9%	28%	–
Average days from referral date to treatment start date	–	302.5 (167.7)	2.4 (7.8)	–
Average days between first and third treatment sessions	–	24.6 (19.4)	14.9 (14.7)	–
Average days between all treatment sessions	–	24.7 (19.8)	14.1 (13.9)	–
Initial treatment <14 days from referral	–	4%	14%	–
Case planning				
Average days between intake and assessment	14.6 (66.2)	16.0 (62.0)	44.9 (82.0)	171.5 (134.2)
Monitoring and compliance				
% revoked	16%	2%	30%	17%
% of population given special conditions	29%	74%	61%	–
Average number of special conditions given	0.5 (1.0)	1.2 (1.0)	6.2 (3.3)	–
Desistance				
% successfully completed supervision	19%	30%	100%	1%
% drug test negative	–	85%	92%	–
% employed	14%	42%	64%	66%

Note: Dashes denote that data were not available for that site

The findings for the case planning domain indicate that, on average, clients are waiting anywhere from around two weeks to six months to receive an assessment after initial intake. This may pose a problem if the goal is to start clients on the road to rehabilitation as quickly as possible. As previously mentioned, information on motivation and engagement is generally lacking in agency administrative data. However, the findings for site 2 show a large average gap between clients receiving a referral and the start of their treatment process (around ten months). This is highly problematic given that research suggests that early initiation of treatment is positively associated with client engagement (Garnick et al. 2014). While this may indicate a problem with the triage procedures of that agency, it could also reflect the lack of resources and local treatment options available.

In regard to desistance, surprisingly, only one site (site 3) had complete data on clients who had successfully completed supervision. For the other three sites, this ranged from 1% to 30%. This is surprising given that rehabilitative success hinges in part on whether clients can successfully adhere to the requirements of their probation. As for the other indicators of success measured in this study, half of the sites in our sample do not track information on drug testing, and employment data was only tracked between 14% and 66% of the time.

Conclusion and implications

In this chapter, we explored the feasibility of developing a set of measures that reflect evidence-based supervision processes. The measures were based on the five domains within the SOARING e-learning system: Risk-Need-Responsivity (RNR), motivation and engagement, case planning, compliance and monitoring, and desistance. Findings suggest it is possible to create evidence-based process measures to identify quality supervision; however, some measures (e.g. treatment referral and identified needs) are unlikely to be available given that the data is not in the database. Of the four sites, six of 19 measures had less than 50% of the data available for two or more sites. These six measures were: rate of identified needs to treatment placement, needs reduction, referral and start date, initial treatment less than 14 days for referral, successfully completed supervision, and negative drug test. This demonstrates that it is possible to construct process measures using administrative data; however, this is a work in progress and further development is needed for some of the items within the model. For example, motivation and engagement was the most problematic domain. The implication is that information about clients' progress is not well documented. The reason may be that motivation and engagement reflects a mindset and individual attitudes (and thus, are intrinsic), which makes it unlikely to be available in administrative data. Therefore we may need to reconsider how to measure this component of evidence-based supervision.

Based on our findings, we offer agencies several suggestions for collecting administrative data for creating process measures that reflect evidence-based supervision practices:

- Create mandatory data fields that must be filled in before moving to the next entry.
- Add dropdown menus to provide clarity for data entered in text fields (e.g. selecting 'no special conditions' in dropdown format as opposed to having a blank text field). It can also increase consistency in data entry within and between staff. Moreover, to maximize effectiveness, response options should be as comprehensive as possible.
- Supervision completion is often recorded dichotomously (yes/no) but could benefit from greater specificity by recording not just whether supervision was completed successfully but also why. For instance, we were unable to differentiate between those who completed supervision in full (i.e. fulfilled all conditions and requirements) without violations versus those who completed supervision but did not fulfil all treatment requirements and/or violated any conditions of their supervision (currently, both groups would be recorded as having 'successfully completed supervision').
- Better tracking of information for client referrals and/or any outsourced treatment. This would require probation/parole staff to be more involved in the supervision process.
- And finally, in general, better staff training on how to use their data systems and what information needs to be recorded and why.

In sum, administrative data contain a wealth of information but are currently under-utilized by community supervision agencies. Using these data to create a set of process measures that reflect evidence-based supervision can aid community supervision agencies in identifying any gaps in service provision and inform policies and procedures for best practice. Future follow-up studies are also needed to validate these measures against client outcomes.

Note

1 This chapter is reprinted from Blasko, B. L., Souza, K. A., Via, B. and Taxman, F. S. (2016) Performance measures in community corrections: Measuring effective supervision practices with existing agency data. *Federal Probation*, 80(3), 26–32.

References

Alexander, M., Whitley, B. and Bersch, C. (2014) Driving evidence-based supervision to the next level: Utilizing PCRA, drivers, and effective supervision techniques. *Federal Probation*, 78, 2–8.

Andrews, D. A. and Bonta, J. (2010) Rehabilitating criminal justice policy and practice. *Psychology, Public Policy, and Law*, 16, 39–55.

Bonta, J., Bourgon, G., Rugge, T., Scott, T. L., Yessine, A. K. and Gutierrez, L. (2011) An experimental demonstration of training probation officers in evidence-based community supervision. *Criminal Justice and Behavior*, 38, 1127–1148. DOI:10.1177/0093854811420678.

Bonta, J., Rugge, T., Scott, T. L., Bourgon, G. and Yessine, A. K. (2008) Exploring the black box of community supervision. *Journal of Offender Rehabilitation*, 47, 248–270.

Bourgon, G. (2013) The demands on probation officers in the evolution of evidence-based practice: The forgotten foot soldier of community corrections. *Federal Probation*, 77, 30–35.

Chadwick, N., Dewolf, A. and Serin, R. (2015) Effectively training community supervision officers: A meta-analytic review of the impact on offender outcome. *Criminal Justice and Behavior*, 42, 977–989.

Dowden, C. and Andrews, D. A. (2004) The importance of staff practice in delivering effective correctional treatment: A meta-analytic review of core correctional practice. *International Journal of Offender Therapy and Comparative Criminology*, 48, 203–214.

Drake, B. and Jonson-Reid, M. (1999) Some thoughts on the increasing use of administrative data in child maltreatment research. *Child Maltreatment*, 4, 308–315.

Drake, E. K. (2011) *"What works" in Community Supervision: Interim Report*. Olympia, WA: Washington State Institute for Public Policy.

Durose, M. R., Cooper, A. D. and Snyder, H. N. (2014) *Recidivism of Prisoners Released in 30 States in 2005: Patterns from 2005 to 2010*. Washington, DC: Bureau of Justice Statistics.

English, D. J., Brandford, C. C. and Coghlan, L. (2000) Data-based organizational change: The use of administrative data to improve child welfare programs and policy. *Child Welfare*, 79, 499–515.

Garnick, D. W., Horgan, C. M., Acevedo, A., Lee, M. T., Panas, L., Ritter, G. A. and Wright, D. (2014) Criminal justice outcomes after engagement in outpatient substance abuse treatment. *Journal of Substance Abuse Treatment*, 46, 295–305. DOI:10.1016/j.jsat.2013.10.005.

James, N. (2014) *Offender Reentry: Correctional Statistics, Reintegration into the Community, and Recidivism*. Washington, DC: Congressional Research Service.

Kaeble, D., Glaze, L., Tsoutic, A. and Minton, T. (2016) *Corrections Populations in the United States, 2014*. Washington, DC: Bureau of Justice Statistics.

Miller, J. and Maloney, C. (2013) Practitioner compliance with risk/needs assessment tools: A theoretical and empirical assessment. *Criminal Justice and Behavior*, 40, 716–736. DOI:10.1177/0093854812468883.

Nagin, D. S., Cullen, F. T. and Jonson, C. L. (2009) Imprisonment and reoffending. *Crime and Justice*, 38, 115–200.

Petersilia, J. and Turner, S. (1993) Intensive probation and parole. *Crime and Justice*, 281–335.

Raybould, S. and Coombes, M. G. (1992) The research potential of administrative data: An illustrative example of the utility of register information in spatial analysis. *Environment and Planning B: Planning and Design*, 19, 131–142. DOI:10.1068/b190131.

Taxman, F. S. (2002) Supervision – exploring the dimensions of effectiveness. *Federal Probation*, 66, 14–27.

Taxman, F. S. (2008) No illusions: Offender and organizational change in Maryland's proactive community supervision benefits. *Criminology & Public Policy*, 7, 275–302. DOI:10.1111/j.1745-9133.2008.00508.x.

Taxman, F. S. (2009) Effective community punishments in the United States: Probation. *Criminal Justice Matters*, 75, 42–44.

Taxman, F. S. (2012) Probation, intermediate sanctions, and community-based corrections. In J. Petersilia and K. Reitz (Eds.), *Oxford Handbook on Sentencing and Corrections*. New York: Oxford University Press, pp. 363–388.

Taxman, F. S., Shepardson, E. S. and Byrne, J. M. (2004) *Tools of the Trade: A Guide to Incorporating Science into Practice*. Washington, DC: US Department of Justice, National Institute of Corrections.

U.S. Census Bureau (2010). *Decennial Census of Population and Housing*. Washington, DC: U. S. Census. Available at: https://census.gov/decennial-census.

Visual methods and probation practice

86

Nicola Carr

Introduction: visual research methods

The 'visual turn' in social research has generated a plethora of approaches. One of the key distinctions made in visual research methodology is between the analysis and investigation of so-called found images – visual representations and artefacts – and researcher-initiated means of visual data production (Pauwels 2017). The former may for example involve the analysis of media representations, films, archive materials, and so on, while the latter includes the generation of visual data as part of the research process. This may involve video or photo-documentation by the researcher or more participatory research approaches, where research subjects are active in the generation of visual imagery. Visual methods are often combined with other research approaches. For instance, participant-generated imagery may be combined with follow-up interviews exploring the meaning and significance of the images created (e.g. through a photo-elicitation technique).

Proponents of visual methods argue that they can provide a different perspective on the world, and in particular can provide insights into difficult, emotional, or otherwise sensitive issues and experiences (Clark and Morris 2017). However, there are important questions to be considered in relation to the uses of visual methodology – not least questions of theory, methodological orientation, and ethical engagement (Rose 2012; Clark 2013; Brown

2014). One site of debate centres on whether the visual provides a mode of enquiry or a means of representation; however, Pauwels (2012) for one criticizes such dualism arguing that it is necessarily reductive. Attention to what Rose (2012) characterizes as the three critical sites of visual imagery – the site of production (the context of the research), the site of the image (the image itself), and the site of the audience (the researcher, and others' interpretations) – can help to delineate some of the epistemological and ethical concerns at stake.

Ethics of visual research

Visual research methods raise particular ethical considerations in relation to the politics of interpretation and representation. Proponents of visual research methods have sometimes made claims regarding the potential of such methods to be participatory and emancipatory (Clark and Morris 2017). Participatory, by the fact that research subjects may be involved in the creation and interpretation of imagery that is reflective of particular aspects of their life experiences (e.g. Copes et al. 2018) and emancipatory in the sense that such processes may lead to greater understanding of complex issues and possible change as a result (Wilson and Milne 2016). However, as with all research, and potentially even more so with visual data, the question of interpretation is inherently subjective and arguably it cannot be meaningfully undertaken without reference to wider cultural frames. For this reason Clark and Morris (2017: 39) caution that it is necessary 'to understand the institutions, structures, and cultures, that participants and researchers interact with, and which may come to bear on how and why certain images get produced'.

This touches upon wider ethical issues relating to visual data, for instance how such data is made available to other audiences and therefore further and multiple interpretations that may be removed from the original context (Bourgois and Schonberg 2009). Questions of image ownership (particularly in the case of participant-generated imagery) and confidentiality and anonymity also arise. What for instance does informed consent mean in relation to the potential manifold use of imagery and for how long does such consent apply (Copes et al. 2018)? Consider for instance a person subject to probation supervision who may consent to their image being captured in a study of probation and subsequently displayed, but who many years after the study does not want their image reappearing and thereby their identity becoming fixed in this way. To put it another way, at what point does a person desist from being a research participant? This connects with some broader epistemological and ontological challenges relating to visual research, such as whether it is possible or desirable to interpret visual data without reference to other information such as verbal text. And if other data is used to explain the visual, an inevitable question is whether the 'visual' can be seen as standalone method?

Applications of visual research

Within the broader sphere of social work research there has been an increased application of creative and multi-modal approaches aimed at excavating the 'craft, themes, and substance of social work' (Clark and Morris 2017: 30). This has included the use of a broad range of visual research methods, which are typically combined with other approaches. Leigh (2015), for instance, uses photographs in her comparative ethnography of child protection social work practice to document differences in the material dimensions of practice in two different countries (Belgium and England). Other research studies have used visual methods to explore dimensions of social work service users' experiences and aspects of identity; for example, in research exploring young people's experiences of belonging in the care system (Wilson and Milne 2016) and older LGBT people's experiences of ageing (Fenge and Jones 2012).

Within the contiguous field of probation research there are fewer examples of the use of visual and creative methods. A review of extant European research on *practices of offender supervision* reported the predominant use of interview-based methods, with the inherent limitation that such a method relies on practitioners' accounts of their own practice (Robinson and Svensson 2013).[1] Such practice discourses are of course important, but the over-reliance on such methods undoubtedly limits the purview of the field. Similarly there has been surprisingly limited research on subjective *experiences of offender supervision*, that is, the experiences of those who are the subjects of probation practice, and the research which exists again tends towards interview-based or survey methodologies (Durnescu et al. 2013).

Visual methods and effectiveness research

One exception to the broader occlusion of visual methods in research exploring probation practice have been a small number of studies which have utilized video recordings of supervision sessions with probation practitioners and their supervisees to explore practice (e.g. Raynor et al. 2014; Durnescu 2014). Situated within a broader research focus about what constitutes 'effectiveness' in offender supervision, these studies have been particularly concerned with identifying the key ingredients of effective supervisory relationships, where effectiveness is understood as having an impact on recidivism (Raynor et al. 2014). One of the most notable examples of this approach is the 'Jersey Supervision Skills Study', which used video recordings to categorize and describe the skills used by probation staff in their meetings with supervisees (Raynor et al. 2010; Vanstone and Raynor 2012; Raynor et al. 2014). The videos of supervisory sessions were analyzed by researchers using a constructed observational checklist, derived from Andrews and Kiessling's (1980) 'Core Correctional Practices', which includes dimensions such as appropriate use of authority and pro-social modelling. Another example of research employing this method is Durnescu's (2014) study of probation supervisors in Romania, where video recordings and follow-up interviews were used to explore the skills and characteristics deployed by probation staff in their supervision sessions with clients. A further area of analytical interest in Durnescu's (2014) study was the interface between prior educational backgrounds and the professional socialization of practitioners.

In the Jersey Study, Raynor et al. (2014) describe the utility of video recordings in research of practice, highlighting that video recordings are less intrusive than direct observations and also less resource intensive in terms of researcher time and travel. (In support of this view, and for a discussion about the challenges and utility of observational research, see Boxstaens et al. 2015.) Furthermore videos, in contrast to audio recordings, enable the analysis of non-verbal communication between probation staff and supervisees. Video recordings can also form an archive of practice, in that the audiovisual record becomes a research artefact that can be analyzed and re-analyzed providing greater utility than a more ephemeral observation. This potential permanency or at least increased longevity brings other ethical considerations to this type of research. It is interesting to note for instance that studies exploring similar terrains – e.g. Bourgon et al.'s (2014) research on the implementation of the Strategic Training Initiative in Community Supervision and Trotter et al.'s (2017) research on effective practice in youth justice – both utilized audio recordings in their studies' practice.[2] Bourgon et al. (2014) report that part of the rationale for using audiotapes in preference to video recordings was that audio recordings were perceived to be 'relatively unobtrusive and non-threatening compared to video-tapes or observers sitting in on sessions' (Bourgon et al. 2014: 101).

Visual methods and practice contexts

One of the metaphors that has regularly been used to characterize probation practice is that of the 'black box' (Worrall et al. 2017). A 'black box' is an airplane's flight recorder that contains information on the flight trajectory and conversations within the cockpit. The fact that we only ever hear about a 'black box' in the context of an aviation accident makes it a curious metaphor to use, but nevertheless the point intended is clear – that somehow there is a way in which practice can be illuminated by opening it up to scrutiny. This metaphor is deployed by Raynor et al. (2014) in the aforementioned study to describe one of the aims of their research seeking to explore what constitutes 'effectiveness' in supervision of people subject to probation supervision. Part of the impetus for the use of videos in the Jersey Study was the need to render visible the interactions of probation staff and their supervisees in order to explore the ingredients of effectiveness in the supervisory relationship. This reflects a particular epistemological approach that has been driven in part by a challenge to the 'what works' agenda, which in its earlier iterations conceived of effectiveness in narrower and proscribed terms, most notably through the delivery of evidence-based accredited offender behaviour programmes (McNeill et al. 2014).

The lack of visibility of probation practice was also part of the impetus for an exploratory comparative study using visual methods to analyze a different practice context – the places and contexts in which probation supervision takes place. Having identified the predominant use of interview-based methods and a limited number of comparative research studies, the Practising Offender Supervision Working Group of the COST Action conducted three pilot studies to explore the utility of different methods in comparative research. These pilot studies used (1) observational methods, (2) practitioner diaries, and (3) visual methods. The overall results of this research are reported in Robinson and Svensson (2015). Amongst the key issues noted are the potential of different approaches to render probation practice more open to interrogation. In comparative research terms, different methods implemented in a number of countries allow for an analysis of areas of commonality and divergence in the practices of 'offender supervision', and whether indeed one can speak of core features or characteristics of practice. For instance, the use of diaries completed by practitioners outlining their daily tasks, in five different countries (England, France, Norway, Malta, and Slovakia), allows us to see how much time is spent proportionally by practitioners on direct contact with supervisees or with administrative tasks such as report-writing and completing risk assessments (Rokkan et al. 2015).

The focus of the visual methods pilot was more on the material dimensions of practice, that is, the environments where probation practice takes place (Carr et al. 2015). The reason for this focus was two-fold; firstly, we know that probation practice has a limited repertoire of visual iconography, certainly when compared with the more readily identifiable imagery associated with prisons. Indeed, arguably this lack of readily accessible visual imagery is part of the reason why there has been less focus on probation within penological scholarship, despite the wide-scale growth in the numbers of people being made subject to supervision in the community across many countries (Robinson 2015; Worrall et al. 2017). Secondly, the focus on physical environments was grounded in the view that the material contexts in which the supervision of people subject to probation supervision takes place shape practice and tell us something both about the nature of practice and how probation's subjects are viewed. For instance, the use of particular signage denoting probation offices or overt security measures in meeting areas may tell us something about the enterprise of community supervision in a particular country, or what Shah (2015), in research conducted in the US, describes as its 'linguistic landscape'.[3]

The pilot study using visual methods involved participants from five countries and is reported in Carr et al. (2015). Briefly here, a small number of probation practitioners in each country were asked to take photos of the places in which supervision took place. Participants were also asked to take pictures of anything else that they considered to be relevant. Given the ethical issues involved, participants were directed not to take pictures in which people were identifiable, and this proviso necessarily delimited the research, not least because practice involves supervising people in places! This limitation not-withstanding, the visual data collected illuminated aspects of practice. For example, the authors noted that in many contexts probation practice takes place in visually nondescript buildings with barely visible signage denoting the nature of the enterprise. In one example from Croatia, the probation office was located in a high-rise office block used by several other agencies, while in Northern Ireland, a probation office specifically designated for women was denoted by the sign 'Inspire' in what looked like a shop-front in a city-centre location.

These differences in 'branding' and office locations prompted the research-ers to consider the place of probation within communities and the desirability or otherwise of a more visible presence. On the one hand probation organiza-tions are criticized for not making their work more visible (Maguire and Carr 2013), but on the other hand, what would more visibility mean for those sub-ject to supervision? This question was brought into particularly sharp focus by the branding of 'Community Payback' work, where in England photos taken by one practitioner showed the orange bibs emblazoned with the 'Com-munity Payback' logo that service users had to wear or another photo of the signage on the work-van, advertising 'Offenders are Working Here to Improve Your Community' (see Worrall et al. 2017).

On the surface, one of the advantages of using visual methods, particularly in comparative research, is that issues of language and the question of equiv-alency of meaning, something that dogs comparative research (Nelken 2009), is less to the fore. That said, it is not possible to 'read' visual imagery without reference to the wider cultural frames in which it is produced. Further still, it is possible to misread images based on a lack of knowledge of context or an assumed level of understanding, derived from seeming familiarity. At the end of the day, the authors concluded that visual methods required supplemen-tary explanatory methods, whether that be interviews with participants or accompanying written text (Carr et al. 2015).

Experiencing supervision

An associated body of research that has implications for practice, again ema-nating from the COST Action on Offender Supervision in Europe, has also sought to capture the *experiences* of probation supervision moving beyond interview or survey-based methods. Given that supervision within the com-munity has existed in some countries for over a century, there is a surprising lack of research on how supervision is actually experienced by those who are its subjects. Recent work has used visual (and auditory) methods to explore the contingent character of life for people subject to the disciplinary control of supervision and its associated requirements (McNeill 2018). This has included studies using a photo-elicitation method conducted in England, Germany, the Republic of Ireland, and Scotland (see Fitzgibbon et al. 2017; Fitzgibbon and Healy 2017) and a study specifically exploring women's experiences (Fitzgibbon and Stengel 2017). This work has connected with research that has questioned the benign positioning of supervision in the community, observing also that community supervision involves associated pains (Durnescu 2011; Hayes 2015). Notable within these studies is that fact that community supervision forms part of a tapestry of pervasive wider exclusions and contingent citizenship.

Conclusion

Visual methods have been used to a limited extent to explore aspects of probation practice, including research using video recordings to identify the key characteristics of supervisory encounters and photodocumentation generated by research participants to explore the environments in which supervision takes place. A further emerging body of research has documented subjects' experiences of supervision using visual methods. Part of the reluctance to date to use visual methods may be due to a lack of familiarity with these approaches and/or an understandable caution relating to ethical concerns, such as the need to protect confidentiality and anonymity. However, research in contiguous fields such as social work illustrates the potential for visual methods to generate new insights and literally new ways of seeing. To date, visual research in probation has been relatively small scale and there is clearly potential to develop work in this area, for instance by using visual methods to explore the dialogic nature of supervision and the character and experiences of community sentences from different perspectives.

Notes

1 The review of research was conducted as part of the work of the COST Action on Offender Supervision in Europe (Action IS1106). For more information on the Action and its associated outputs, see www.offendersupervision.eu/about.
2 Trotter et al.'s (2017) study of practitioners' use of challenging skills with young offenders was conducted in Australia and combined observational methods and audio recordings, to allow for cross-coding among researchers. Skeem et al.'s (2007) research of practice in specialist mental health probation programmes in the United States also used audio recordings to assess the dual care and control role of practitioners. Robinson et al. (2011) also used audio recordings to assess the implementation of the STARR (Staff Training Aimed at Reducing Re-Arrest) programme in the United States. For a more recent example of the use of videos to explore aspects of practice see Goldhill (2017).
3 Shah's (2015) study conducted in California, US, explores how the neighbourhood context, and the 'look, feel and location may affect the parolee/parole agent relationship' and ultimately the reintegration process of people returning to the community from prison.

References

Andrews, D. A. and Kiessling, J. J. (1980) Program structure and effective correctional practices: A summary of the CaVIC research. In R. R. Ross and P. Gendreau (Eds.), *Effective Correctional Treatment*. Toronto, ON: Butterworth, pp. 441–463.

Bourgois, P. and Schonberg, J. (2009) *Righteous Dopefiend*. Berkeley: University of California Press.

Bourgon, G., Bonta, J., Rugge, T. and Gutierrez, L. (2014) Technology transfer: The importance of ongoing clinical supervision in translating 'what works' to everyday community supervision. In F. McNeill, P. Raynor and C. Trotter (Eds.), *Offender Supervision: New Directions in Theory, Research and Practice*. London: Routledge, pp. 91–112.

Boxstaens, J., Blay, E., Melendez Pereto, E. and Décarpes, P. (2015) Interpreting performance in offender supervision: The use of observation as a data collection method. *European Journal of Probation*, 7(3), 218–240.

Brown, M. (2014) Visual Criminology and Carceral Studies: Counter-images in the carceral age. *Theoretical Criminology*, 18(2): 176–197.

Carr, N., Bauwens, A., Bosker, J., Donker, A., Robinson, G., Sucic, I. and Worrall, A. (2015) Picturing probation: Exploring the utility of visual methods in comparative research. *European Journal of Probation*, 7(3), 179–200.

Clark, A. (2013) Haunted by images? Ethical moments and anxieties in visual research. *Methodological Innovations Online*, 8(2), 68–81.

Clark, A. and Morriss, L. (2017) The use of visual methodologies in social work research over the last decade: A narrative review and some questions for the future. *Qualitative Social Work*, 16(1), 29–43.

Copes, H., Tchoula, W., Brookman, F. and Ragland, J. (2018) Photo-elicitation interviews with vulnerable populations: Practical and ethical considerations. *Deviant Behavior*, 39(4), 475–494.

Durnescu, I. (2011) Pains of probation: Effective practice and human rights. *Journal of Offender Therapy and Comparative Criminology*, 55, 530–545.

Durnescu, I. (2014) Probation skills between education and professional socialization. *European Journal of Criminology*, 11(4), 429–444.

Durnescu, I., Enengl, C. and Grafl, C. (2013) Experiencing supervision. In F. McNeill and K. Beyens (Eds.), *Offender Supervision in Europe*. Basingstoke: Palgrave Macmillan, pp. 19–50.

Fenge, L. and Jones, K. (2012) Gay and pleasant land? Exploring sexuality, ageing and rurality in a multi-method, performative project. *British Journal of Social Work*, 42(2), 300–317.

Fitzgibbon, W., Graebsch, C. and McNeill, F. (2017) Pervasive punishment: Experiencing supervision. In M. Brown and E. Carrabine (Eds.), *Routledge International Handbook of Visual Criminology*. London: Routledge, pp. 305–319.

Fitzgibbon, W. and Healy, D. (2017) Lives and spaces: Photovoice and offender supervision in Ireland and England. *Criminology and Criminal Justice*. https://doi.org/10.1177/1748895817739665.

Fitzgibbon, W. and Stengel, C. (2017) Women's voices made visible: Photovoice in visual criminology. *Punishment & Society*, 6, 379–393.

Goldhill, R. (2017) Videoing supervision: Messages for probation practice. *Journal of Social Work Practice*, 31(3), 279–292.

Hayes, D. (2015) The impact of supervision on the pains of community penalties in England and Wales: An exploratory study. *European Journal of Probation*, 7(2), 85–102.

Leigh, J. (2015) Crossing the divide between them and us: Using photography to explore the impact organizational space can have on identity and child protection practice. *Qualitative Social Work*, 14(3), 416–435.

Maguire, N. and Carr, N. (2013) Changing shape and shifting boundaries – the media portrayal of probation in Ireland. *European Journal of Probation*, 5(3), 3–23.

McNeill, F. (2018) Mass supervision, misrecognition and the 'Malopticon'. *Punishment & Society*. DOI:10.1177/1462474518755137.

McNeill, F., Raynor, P. and Trotter, C. (2014) *Offender Supervision: New Directions in Theory, Research and Practice*. London: Routledge.

Nelken, D. (2009) Comparative criminal justice. Beyond ethnocentrism and relativism. *European Journal of Criminology*, 6(4), 291–311.

Pauwels, L. (2012) Contemplating the state of visual research: An assessment of obstacles and opportunities. In S. Pink (Ed.), *Advances in Visual Methodology*. London: Sage Publications.

Pauwels, L. (2017) Key methods of visual criminology. An overview of different approaches and their affordances. In M. Brown and E. Carrabine (Eds.), *Routledge International Handbook of Visual Criminology*. London: Routledge, pp. 62–73.

Raynor, P., Uguwidike, P. and Vanstone, M. (2010) Skills and strategies in probation supervision: The Jersey Study. In F. McNeill, P. Raynor and C. Trotter (Eds.), *Offender Supervision: New Directions in Theory, Research and Practice*. Abingdon: Willan, pp. 113–129.

Raynor, P., Ugwudike, P. and Vanstone, M. (2014) The impact of skills in probation work: A reconviction study. *Criminology and Criminal Justice*, 14(2), 235–249.

Robinson, C. R., Van Benschoten, S., Alexander, M. and Lowenkamp, C. T. (2011) A random (Almost) study of staff training aimed at reducing re-arrest (STARR): Reducing recidivism through intentional design. *Federal Probation*, 75, 57–63.

Robinson, G. (2015) The Cinderella complex: Punishment, society and community sanctions. *Punishment & Society*, 18(1), 95–112.

Robinson, G. and Svensson, K. (2013) Practising offender supervision. In F. McNeill and K. Beyens (Eds.), *Offender Supervision in Europe*. Basingstoke: Palgrave Macmillan, pp. 19–50.

Robinson, G. and Svensson, K. (2015) Fish out of water? Introduction to the special issue on innovative methods for comparative research on offender supervision practice. *European Journal of Probation*, 7(3), 171–178.

Rokkan, T., Phillips, J., Lulei, M., Poldena, S. and Kensey, A. (2015) How was your day? Exploring a day in the life of probation workers across Europe using practice diaries. *European Journal of Probation*, 7(3), 201–217.

Rose, G. (2012) *Visual Methodologies: An Introduction to Researching with Visual Materials*. London: Sage Publications.

Shah, R. (2015) Expanding the community: An exploratory analysis of an American parole office's location and its impact on parolees. *British Journal of Criminology*, 55(2), 321–340.

Skeem, J. L., Eno Louden, J., Polaschek, D. and Camp, J. (2007) Assessing relationship quality in mandated community treatment: Blending care with control. *Psychological Assessment*, 19(4), 397–410.

Trotter, C., Evans, P. and Baidawi, S. (2017) The effectiveness of challenging skills in work with young offenders. *International Journal of Offender Therapy and Comparative Criminology*, 61(4), 397–412.

Vanstone, M. and Raynor, P. (2012) *Observing Interview Skills: A Manual for Users of the Jersey Supervision Interview Checklist*. St Helier: Jersey Probation and After-Care Service.

Wilson, S. and Milne, E. J. (2016) Visual activism and social justice: Using visual methods to make young people's complex lives visible across 'public' and 'private' spaces. *Current Sociology*, 64(1), 140–156.

Worrall, A., Carr, N. and Robinson, G. (2017) Opening a window on probation cultures: A photographic imagination. In M. Brown and E. Carrabine (Eds.), *Routledge International Handbook of Visual Criminology*. London: Routledge, pp. 268–279.

87 Evaluating practice

Observation methods

Kimberly R. Kras, Shannon Magnuson, and Kimberly S. Meyer

Introduction

Evaluating evidence-based practices (EBPs) utilized by staff in criminal justice settings is essential for establishing what works in offender reform. Evaluation methods largely include surveys and self-reported data, but the often-forgotten *observation methods* provide significant value for understanding how practices operate day to day. Compared to responding to traditional survey questions (Phillips and Clancy 1972), observation methods provide researchers the opportunity to compare and contrast what staff *say they do* with what *they actually do*. Understanding the conditions under which EBPs are used (or not used) as intended can provide practical insight for organizations about how to adjust, fit, or realign practices/programmes to achieve desired outcomes. However, when conducting evaluations of EBPs, researchers rarely couple traditional evaluation methodologies with true observation methods. Sacrificing such methods comes at the expense of drawing richer and more valuable conclusions about how practices are being (mis)used. This underutilization of observation methods is largely the result of many co-occurring issues, including preoccupation by scholars to principally rely on (and publish) quantitative methods, almost no instruction on qualitative methodologies in graduate programmes to train young scholars (Buckler 2008; Tewksbury et al. 2010), lack of understanding by practitioners on how qualitative methods can complement quantitative findings, and resource and time constraints limiting opportunities to use the method. Regardless of why observation methods are underutilized, their legacy for uncovering *processes* and explaining phenomena should not be dismissed. Moreover, the data observations yield, as part of multimethods projects, necessary context to explain outcome results collected through traditional evaluation methodologies. That is, where traditional evaluations provide answers about what is or is not working, observations frequently account for reasons why.

In this chapter, we contend that evaluation studies cannot be divorced from observation methodology and do so by presenting qualitative traditions, including benefits and limitations. Then, based upon our experiences conducting observation studies in adult and juvenile community corrections and institutional environments, we describe how observations can be used in criminal justice research and evaluation research more broadly. We end with recommendations for conducting observation evaluation studies in community corrections settings.

Observation methods

Observation methods have a long history in social science qualitative research and offer a process for systematically viewing and collecting information about phenomena under study (Denzin and Lincoln 2011). As a distinct qualitative methodology, Creswell and Poth (2017) define observation methods as 'the act of noting a phenomenon in the field setting through the five senses of the observer, often with a note-taking instrument, and recording it for scientific purposes' (p. 166). The field setting can include observations within social, cultural, and individual contexts, with researchers watching and listening to environments, experiences, and interactions to understand how participants interpret events, and how these interpretations impact behaviours. Observation methodologists are interested in three important aspects within a setting: (1) what people say, (2) how people act, and (3) the things/artefacts people use (Spradley 1979). Combined, these data allow researchers to take an interpretivist orientation by focusing on the 'holistic understanding of research participants' views and actions in the context of their lives overall' (Snape and Spence 2003).

Often, the interpretivist orientation occurs via grounded theory. Grounded theory approaches are valuable for evaluation research because they are free from a priori hypotheses, allowing researchers to *ground* all possible patterns and conditions available to explain phenomena in collected data (Charmaz 2006). Grounded theory involves researchers collecting data while simultaneously analyzing it, allowing researchers to develop analytic enquiries they can explore during the next round of data collection (Glaser and Strauss 1967; Charmaz 2006, 2008). This iterative approach is also referred to as the constant comparative method, where each step of the data collection and analysis process presents emergent concepts, which informs subsequent data collection (Glaser 1965). Systematic use of the constant comparative method provides researchers with rigorous analytic strategies required in evaluation research. Observations in concert with grounded theory approaches uncover, unpack, and elucidate social phenomena and social processes in naturalistic and culturally bound environments.

In practice, Snape and Spencer (2003) identify four overarching types of qualitative research: (1) *contextual*, where researchers describe the form or nature of what exists, (2) *explanatory*, which considers the reasons for association between what exists, (3) *generative*, which aids in developing theories about what exists, and (4) *evaluative*, which involves appraising effectiveness of what already exists. While criminology and criminal justice research utilizes all modes of qualitative research, turning to observation methods within evaluation studies more often can provide important contributions to practical and scholarly understanding of how organizations can improve implementation and fidelity of practices to reach intended outcomes.

Programme evaluation takes on two primary tasks – process and outcome evaluations (Rossi et al. 2004). Qualitative methods, especially observation methods, can inform both types of evaluations. In process evaluations, the systematic observation of programme practices can supply researchers and programme staff with much-needed information about whether the programme is being implemented and operating as intended, and explain *how* processes are working (or not working). Researchers can observe and systematically document (often via predetermined observation checklists) how staff actions and programme operations align with intended and theoretically driven programme design. Monitoring the fidelity of practice or programme implementation ensures that intended interventions and evidence-based outcomes do not deteriorate over time (Taxman and Belenko 2011). Similarly, observation strategies and interviewing methods allow researchers to determine programme areas of need, develop evaluation questions, and provide staff with additional outcome measures to demonstrate programme success (Rossi et al. 2004).

In outcome evaluations, the data collected via the process evaluation can explain *why* outcomes appear as they do. Although observation methods do not allow for causal inference, they help support or explain quantitative outcomes. In particular, observation checklists can be used to derive quantitative measurement of theoretical and practical concepts of interest, meaning researchers can assess impacts and evaluate outcomes using statistical methods capable of making causal inferences (Rossi et al. 2004). Observation methods are uniquely suited for this task as they can uncover underlying and new issues emerging outside the evaluation period.

Observation methods for evaluation research in criminal justice

Evaluations are often referred to as quantitatively measuring whether a programme or practice is achieving its desired outcome(s). When desired outcomes, such as fewer rearrests, reconvictions, or returns to custody are not achieved, quantitative measures do not provide clear answers about *why* this is the case. Erroneously, scholars may conclude a programme or practice is 'not working'; however, this conclusion lacks explanatory power to understand the mechanisms behind programme/practice failure. Perhaps the programme/practice lacks the theoretical foundation necessary to be effective; however, it is also possible the programme/practice includes the necessary core components to be effective but implementation issues are mitigating effectiveness as measured through quantitative methods. Implementation concerns explaining failure could include programme characteristics misaligned from internal structures and/or policies, inadequate resources, or insufficient staff training about how to use the programme/practice as intended (Taxman and Belenko 2012; Rossi et al. 2004). Here, as Patton (2002) purported, qualitative or observation evaluative methods can support the objective of accounting for *how* and *why* a practice is or is not being implemented/used. These methods are 'goal free' and 'utilization-focused', meaning they examine the process of how staff actually use programmes/practices to compare them to intended use (Patton 2002).

Examining these processes and mechanisms of use can provide essential information linking organizational structure/protocols, staff training, knowledge, and behaviour to outcomes of interest. For example, while conducting an observation study of community corrections staff in a statewide agency, the agency released a memo explaining it would like to see an increase in the number of monthly urinalysis screenings (UAs) used with clients. During our study, we observed 127 front-line officers and their managers utilizing over 20 programmes/practices, including use of risk screening tools, transferring cases between supervision risk levels and officers and, in particular, conducting UA screenings with clients (Center for Advancing Correctional Excellence 2014). Throughout these observations, staff describe many reasons why they themselves, or staff, generally do not administer additional UAs than what is required. In some instances, staff explain it as a waste of resources since clients already receive multiple monthly UAs via treatment providers. Additionally, staff reported additional testing as an unfair burden to clients who already receive monthly UA testing. Finally, staff explained that UA policy states that staff administering the tests must be certified to do so and must be of the same gender as the client. Staff often described these requirements as major hurdles related to increasing the number of UA tests, as many staff in the office are not the same gender as their clients and are not certified UA technicians. Regardless of the rationale – resources, values, or organizational protocols – these observations provide invaluable context to explain why changes in the number of monthly UAs produced by each office may be unrealistic. Understanding seemingly innocuous micro-decisions and behaviours illuminated patterned behaviours across staff in a statewide agency and provided administrators a deeper understanding of *how* and *why* staff may misuse or poorly implement programmes and practices. In total, observation methods provide agency administrators richer data about the scope of policy/practice misuse throughout the state, the underlying dimensions explaining why, and insight informing comprehensive and effective solutions.

However, using observation methods to understand processes within justice settings does not need to be limited to researchers. It can and *should* be used by agencies and supervisory staff to systematically measure fidelity of practices on their own. For example, as part of a larger eLearning course educating officers about Core Correctional Practices, the Center for Advancing Correctional Excellence (ACE!) at George Mason University partnered with a state Department of Corrections to help them develop a systematic observation protocol to assess fidelity of EBPs staff use routinely (Blasko et al. 2016). In particular, the observation protocol assesses use of the state's risk/need assessment (RNA), case planning practices, and newly trained skills including techniques from motivational interviewing, such as affirmations and reflections. The observation protocol details step by step how each of these practices *should* look and allows observers (typically supervisors or coaches) to rate on a scale of 0 (had an opportunity but did not use) to 3 (excellent use) how the officer performed on a skill during a client interaction. Currently, 12 districts of approximately 150 officers supervising over 6,000 clients use these systematic observations. Following the observation, supervisors then transpose these scores into an online database. Each quarter, supervisors review the observation data (which is now in quantitative form) to understand the skills in which their staff are proficient and which skills require continued coaching. Throughout this process, staff observers can document exchanges between the officer and client that contributed to a successful interaction or those that may need improvement. Often, these extra notes are discussed during feedback sessions between the staff observer and officer following the observation session. As a result, the systematic observations provide autonomy to district staff to improve practices in real time and provide targeted, purposive coaching and mentoring to improve fidelity of practices. Moreover, including an observation component in daily operations allows supervisory and coaching staff to address concerns or commend staff on behaviours that they might otherwise not see via quantitative evaluation procedures. As a result of these observations, the agency can understand the scope of proficiency concerns across the districts and develop larger, regional trainings if necessary.

Best practices for conducting observation methods

Our experience conducting observation research in criminal justice settings is based on studies conducted at the Center for Advancing Correctional Excellence at George Mason University, led by Drs Faye S. Taxman and Danielle Rudes. These studies range from a broad-focused study of how juvenile probation officers and residential counsellors use EBPs (Kras et al. 2015; Rudes et al. 2017, 2011), to more narrowly focused studies of how probation officers use EBPs in adult probation (Kras et al. 2017a; Viglione et al. 2015; Rudes et al. 2017), and how these practices impact organizational functioning (Kras et al. 2017b; Rudes et al. 2018), and how living and working during EBP reform in solitary confinement affects staff and inmates in prisons (Rudes and Magnuson 2018). The necessary protocol for observations in each environment varies; however, below we provide recommendations to design observation protocols in different criminal justice settings and examine the technical and ethical issues inherent in this research.

Developing research foci

Researchers and practitioners can begin developing observation studies by outlining the goals of observations. This may include broad goals such as observing staff throughout their day but can also include targeted foci such as observing staff using a particular practice. Once the goals of observations are more clearly defined, specific foci can be developed. More specific foci may consider:

1 What are staff responsibilities throughout the day?
2 How do staff describe these responsibilities (e.g. do they believe it aligns with agency goals? Do they believe it is part of their job? Do they believe the responsibility is easy/hard?)?
3 How do staff describe how others complete similar tasks?
4 How do staff complete tasks (e.g. what steps do they take, what decisions must they make, and why do they make these decisions)?

During direct observations, observers should not limit themselves to the foci outlined at the beginning of the study. Rather, observers should consider capturing all aspects of the research environment, including the words and actions of people present, experiences, and incidents outside of the designed protocol. This openness is a key feature of grounded theory and exemplifies the qualitative methods mantra 'everything is data'. Further, considering emergent experiences and opportunities during observations allows researchers to more deeply assess the nature of phenomena under study while free from the bias inherent in rigid evaluation schema. These seemingly superfluous interactions may also provide valuable context for office, department, and organizational constraints and/or offer insight into how staff *actually* engage in practices compared to how they *talk* about practices.

For example, in a study of juvenile probation officers' use of EBPs with their clients, we also captured the words and actions of their juvenile probation clients (Kras et al. 2015). In doing so, we were able to understand the effects of officer actions upon their clients' behaviours. Finally, comparing what people say and do – and what they do in comparison to what others say – is paramount, but woefully understudied in process and outcome evaluations. In environments where staff are highly trained in policies or practices, it is important to contrast what is said with what is actually done. Do staff discuss procedures one way but act differently? Does management describe a policy one way, but it is carried out by line staff differently? For example, in one state probation agency, observations revealed that all staff were using a risk assessment instrument; however, virtually no staff (only one) used it correctly. Instead of completing the assessment and using the results for case planning, nearly all officers filed the instrument away and did not refer back to it (Viglione et al. 2015). These and similar questions are applicable in a number of settings, including policing, courts, correctional institutions, and schools; however, across all settings this aspect of evaluation research remains underutilized.

Number of participants and observations

Given the sheer number of participants present in justice settings – from probation officers and clients to judges, prison staff, and prisoners – it can be hard to determine who to observe and how many people to observe. Based upon the goals of the evaluation study, the main subjects of observations will likely be apparent. Yet, the *number* of participants needed to understand how processes are operating within a setting is contingent on the concept of saturation. Saturation requires collecting data until subsequent observations yield no new information (Glaser and Strauss 1967). Across justice settings, it is nearly impossible to establish a set number of participants where saturation will occur. As a result, it is best to begin by observing, listening, and talking to anyone who is willing to participate in the research. In many cases, staff and clients are what Myers (2015) calls 'unbeknownst experts' on life in the system. By this, Myers suggests that anyone within the system can discuss how it operates, and these experts provide a starting point from which to grow the sample. Moreover, triangulating perspectives using observations from multiple viewpoints provides researchers and organizations with rich data regarding the realities of the practices and policies in use and the nature and extent of their effects.

This is ideal; however, limitations in numbers of research staff or access to institutions or other spaces may prevent saturation from being reached. For instance, during our study of solitary confinement in four state prisons led by Danielle Rudes, trips were limited to two days in each facility, and a limited number of research staff were able to attend due to security concerns (Rudes and Magnuson 2018). As a result, researchers collected data continuously throughout a full 24 hours (in researcher shifts) to interview as many inmates as possible and observe staff working during each of the institutions' three discrete shift times, including an overnight shift. Researchers observed staff interactions with inmates and their colleagues, documented the types of tasks completed, and asked staff about barriers and facilitators to their responsibilities. Although researchers observed and documented notes on each of the three shifts similarly, the study's ability to reach saturation in any one of the four institutions is limited by the number of days researchers could spend inside each institution. While the data is limited in the types of conclusions drawn per institution, these observations still provided valuable data that would otherwise not be captured via quantitative methodology. Further, data collected inside of one institution allowed for researchers to ask more poignant questions in the next institution, as expected in the constant comparative method.

Technical issues

Access issues and other barriers exist to conducting observation research. Access to facilities or segments of a study population may limit time spent in agencies or number of participants contacted. Further, as in any study, voluntariness may mean some intended participants may opt out. These issues may restrict use of grounded theory by giving researchers less information to examine and compare. Technical issues inherent in observation research include adapting to and blending in with one's surroundings. If researchers are too obvious as 'outsiders' in the observation environment, staff or the clients they work with (probationers or inmates, most often in our work) may act differently than usual and change the tone or nature of activities observed. For this reason, researchers must strive to blend into their surroundings as much as possible, which requires paying attention to issues such as attire, language, informal norms, and when/where they take notes, to name a few.

Another issue in observation methodology is the appropriateness or feasibility of grounded theory approaches. While grounded theory is the gold standard of qualitative methodology, traditional grounded theory requires that researchers enter the field without preconceived ideas of what they will find and, typically, without research questions (Glaser and Strauss 1967). However, in an era of evaluation research aimed at developing the evidence base for practices, most projects have research questions and objectives they must answer. In light of this dilemma, Charmaz (2006) provides an adaptation of grounded theory, suggesting researchers enter the field *with* pre-conceived research questions, as is typical in evaluation research, but use a grounded theory approach to analyze data. This allows the data to speak for itself while permitting researchers to find answers to their research questions. For example, while conducting observation methods in juvenile residential facilities, we entered the setting with questions about which EBPs staff used and how they used them. During the data analysis phase, we used these questions and foci to deductively analyze the data to provide answers to these questions to the agency. However, we also inductively analyzed the data to allow other themes, grounded in the data, to emerge. For example, we knew that staff had received training regarding trauma and the agency was striving to become more trauma-informed, so we also enquired about whether staff used these practices in their work. These more direct enquiries into a specific area allowed us to learn that staff in these facilities often referenced the need to be sensitive to female juveniles' trauma and facilitated conversations with female youth about their pasts. However, inductive analysis revealed staff did not extend this outlook to male youth, even if they experienced similar child-hood trauma (Meyer et al. 2015). In this example, we entered the field with specific (if general) research questions, but we allowed staff to tell us about topics important to their work, such as trauma. In doing so, we were able to not only answer the broader research questions from this project but also shed light on how staff use a specific practice and how use of that practice differed across staff working with female versus male juveniles.

Ethical issues

Aside from common ethical issues in conducting research in criminal justice settings, observation research has its own specific considerations. First, in a study of staff working in a juvenile detention centre where officers are paired throughout a shift, we encountered concerns from one member of the pair who did not want to participate, while the partner consented. This issue might also occur in policing or other settings where staff work with a regular partner during each shift. In these instances, we observed staff who wanted to participate and minimized interaction with and observation of staff who did not consent. These instances were minimal, but when they did occur, non-consenting staff were not identified in the observation notes, and statements by those staff members were not recorded. The only recording of data from non-consenting staff included their interactions with consenting staff, in which case they were not identified.

Finally, one common occurrence in our observation research is the presence of 'off the record' conversations. Staff often ask whether the conversation is 'off the record' before offering critical information, including their true opinions on policies and practices. Our protocol is to remind staff that we prefer to capture all data points, including real and authentic perceptions, in order to understand the data more holistically. We also remind participants all data are confidential and are always presented in the aggregate so as not to attribute findings to any one person. We also clarify that if they offer details that can only be attributed to them, we collect this information for context but do not include it in any reports. In our experience, this reassurance of the informed consent protocol allays participant concerns and often results in staff providing the unfiltered commentary they originally planned to offer.

Conclusion

Observation methods offer a vital source of information connecting what staff in criminal justice settings say they do versus what they actually do. Garnering this information through survey methods or ad hoc conversations fails to yield rich and in-depth information detailing the processes, dynamics, and mechanisms underlying the practices or behaviours of interest. Evaluation research using observation methods provides for systematic collection of information regarding criminal justice practices while simultaneously gathering data about how implementation occurs and identifying facilitators and barriers to implementation along the way. Observation data collection and constant comparative analysis can inform practitioners and administrators about the key components of practices and policies that align or misalign with work routines, the background and buy-in of staff, and the characteristics of clients directly impacted by policy and practice. Every process and outcome evaluation study in criminal justice should include observation components (or other qualitative methods) to account for the situation-specific and culturally bound nature of the criminal justice environment.

As observation data captures the realities and messiness of what occurs in criminal justice settings, the analytic strategies offer seemingly endless opportunities to understand the complexities of such living and evolving environments. By utilizing observation methods, researchers can facilitate the answering of key research questions, while also uncovering novel phenomena within and about the people, places, and practices that exist in criminal justice organizations. This occurs when researchers establish rapport with individuals working in organizations and developing trusting relationships. These connections help to understand the real processes used as compared to stated procedures. Thus, through relationship building, rigorous data collection, and (adapted) grounded theory analysis strategies, researchers can better frame issues, understand the nuances and complexities of context, and focus on processes that interfere with outcomes.

References

Buckler, K. (2008) The quantitative/qualitative divide revisited: A study of published research, doctoral program curricula, and journal editor perceptions. *Journal of Criminal Justice Education*, 19(3), 383–403.

Blasko, B. L., Souza, K., Via, B., Taxman, F. S., Del Principe, S. and Taxman, F. S. (2016) Performance measures in community corrections: Measuring effective supervision practices with existing agency data. *Federal Probation*, 80, 26.

Center for Advancing Correctional Excellence. (2014) George Mason University. Available at: www.gmuace.org/.

Charmaz, K. (2006) *Constructing Grounded Theory: A Practical Guide Through Qualitative Analysis*. Thousand Oaks, CA: Sage Publications.

Charmaz, K. (2008) Grounded theory as emergent method. In S. N. Hesse-Biber and P. Leavy (Eds.), *Handbook of Emergent Methods*. New York: Guilford Press, pp. 155–172.

Creswell, J. W. and Poth, C. N. (2017) *Qualitative Inquiry and Research Design: Choosing Among Five Approaches*. Los Angeles: Sage Publications.

Denzin, N. K. and Lincoln, Y. S. (Eds.). (2011). *The Sage Handbook of Qualitative Research*. Los Angeles: Sage Publications.

Glaser, B. G. (1965) The constant comparative method of qualitative analysis. *Social Problems*, 12(4), 436–445.

Glaser, B. G. and Strauss, A. L. (1967) *The Discovery of Grounded Theory: Strategies for Qualitative Research*. New York: Aldine De Gruyter.

Kras, K. R., Meyer, K. S. and Rudes, D. S. (2015) *JDRDC Organizational Survey Final Report*. Report Prepared for the County Juvenile and Domestic Relations District Court.

Kras, K. R., Portillo, S. and Taxman, F. S. (2017a) Managing from the middle: Frontline supervisors and perceptions of their organizational power. *Law & Policy*, 39(3), 215–236.

Kras, K. R., Rudes, D. S. and Taxman, F. S. (2017b) Managing up and down: Community corrections middle managers' role conflict and ambiguity during organizational change. *Journal of Crime and Justice*, 40(2), 173–187.

Meyer, K. S., Kras, K. R. and Rudes, D. S. (2015) *Gender & Trauma-Informed Care in Juvenile Corrections*. Report Prepared for Fairfax County Juvenile and Domestic Relations Court Services Unit.

Myers, R. R. (2015) Barriers, blinders, and unbeknownst experts: Overcoming access barriers to conduct qualitative studies of juvenile justice. *The Prison Journal*, 95(1), 66–83.

Patton, M. Q. (2002) Two decades of developments in qualitative inquiry: A personal, experiential perspective. *Qualitative Social Work*, 1(3), 261–283.

Phillips, D. L. and Clancy, K. J. (1972) Some effects of "social desirability" in survey studies. *American Journal of Sociology*, 77(5), 921–940.

Rossi, P. H., Lipsey, M. W. and Freeman, H. W. (2004) *Evaluation: A Systematic Approach*. New York: Sage Publications.

Rudes, D. S., Kras, K. R., Meyer, K. S. and Magnuson, S. (2018) Implementation uptake: Organisational factors affecting evidence-based reform in community corrections in the United States. In P. Ugwudike, P. Raynor and J. Annison (Eds.), *Evidence-Based Skills in Criminal Justice: International Research on Supporting Rehabilitation and Desistance*. London: Policy Press, pp. 79–95.

Rudes, D. S. and Magnuson, S. (2018) *Together Alone: Organizational Change and Perceptions of Punishment, Risk & Health for Those Living and Working in Solitary Confinement*. Report Prepared for the Pennsylvania Department of Corrections.

Rudes, D. S., Viglione, J. and Meyer, K. S. (2017) Risky needs: Risk-entangled needs in probation supervision. In F. S. Taxman (Ed.), *Handbook on Risk and Need Assessment: Theory and Practice*. New York: Routledge, pp. 406–428.

Rudes, D. S., Viglione, J. and Taxman, F. S. (2011) Juvenile probation officers: How the perception of roles affects training experiences for evidence-based practice implementation. *Federal Probation*, 75, 3.

Snape, D. and Spencer, L. (2003) The foundations of qualitative research. In J. Ritchie and J. Lewis (Eds.), *Qualitative Research Practice – A Guide for Social Science Students and Researchers*. London: Sage Publications.

Spradley, J. P. (1979) *The Ethnographic Interview*. Long Grove, IL: Waveland Press.

Taxman, F. S., and Belenko, S. (2011) *Implementing Evidence-based Practices in Community Corrections and Addiction Treatment*. New York: Springer Science & Business Media.

Tewksbury, R., Dabney, D. A. and Copes, H. (2010) The prominence of qualitative research in criminology and criminal justice scholarship. *Journal of Criminal Justice Education*, 21(4), 391–411.

Viglione, J., Rudes, D. S. and Taxman, F. S. (2015) Misalignment in supervision: Implementing Risk/Needs Assessment instruments in probation. *Criminal Justice and Behavior*, 42(3), 263–285.

88 Evaluating women's services

Bridget Kerr

Introduction

One of the few indisputable and simple truths in the field of criminal justice interventions is that women's projects, like any service, want to be effective. Notions of what constitutes *effective* practice, or what *evidence* of effectiveness is meaningful, are highly contested, however, and this presents a dilemma to services and evaluators alike. Happily, progress is being made towards integrating all the available evidence to develop and support practices that reduce reoffending by adhering to the Risk-Need-Responsivity (RNR) principles derived from 'what works' endeavours, whilst attending to specific gender-responsive pathways into (and out of) women's criminalization and supporting women's desistance from offending through their social reintegration. The Swansea Service Evaluation Inventory – Women's Projects (SSEI-W; Kerr et al. 2018) is an instrument that aims to facilitate such an approach.

The SSEI-W was developed as the result of Swansea Service Evaluation Team's (SSET) study piloting a Canadian evaluation tool, the Correctional Program Assessment Inventory-2010 (CPAI-2010; Gendreau et al. 2010) in services in the British Isles, including a women's project in Wales. The CPAI is one of several evaluation instruments that test services' adherence to the principles of effective practice derived from the empirically unrivalled RNR literature. Having been used to evaluate over 700 interventions, the correlation between positive CPAI results and reduced recidivism is now well evidenced (Bonta and Andrews 2017: 249–252). For the SSET study, a primary concern was 'evaluation responsivity', a term coined by Ugwudike (2016: 3) to describe 'the importance of designing research-based evaluation tools that accommodate variations in local service delivery contexts'. The question of whether the CPAI could usefully be developed to address the need for evaluation in the context of women's services in Britain was investigated by analysis of a CPAI evaluation in the women's project alongside feedback on the evaluation process itself from managers and practitioners (Kerr 2018). This chapter outlines the development of the SSEI-W as a response to the strengths and limitations of the CPAI in the women's project.

The SSEI-W evaluation approach

Like its progenitor (the CPAI), the SSEI-W takes a holistic, inclusive approach to evaluation, involving the collection of data through interview, observation, and document review, but addresses 152 items relating to effective, *integrated* practices across eight dimensions. The SSET study found that in the context of women's services it is imperative to look beyond paper processes and hard targets to explore the quality of engagement at every level and with every aspect of a holistic service. Management and practitioners identified a dichotomy of evaluation processes – that of engaging services in meaningful 'reflection' against the subjection of services to superficial 'inspection' (see Figure 88.1) – and saw the CPAI approach as engaging services in a reflective process that is the foundation for change through acceptance of recommendations.

The SSEI-W dimensions

The general structure of the SSEI-W is modelled on the CPAI. The first dimension of the SSEI-W, Dimension A: Description of Service, is descriptive only and contextualizes the evaluation (its corresponding domain in the CPAI is Domain A: Programme Demographics). The remaining domains of the CPAI include items that are scored yes (1) or no (0), according to whether different aspects of practice adhere to RNR principles. In the women's project, the CPAI's narrow focus on gender-neutral RNR practices was found to be inadequate in an integrated context, where desistance, gender-responsive and RNR efforts may be combined in the delivery of holistic services for offenders and nonoffenders alike. The scored dimensions of the SSEI-W, therefore, measure

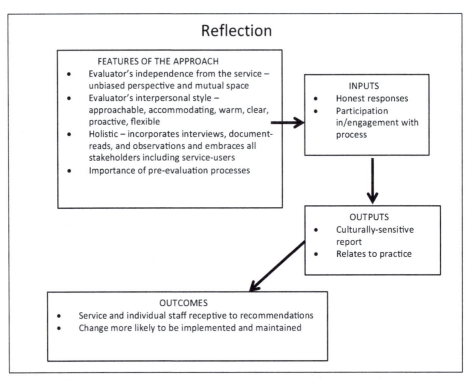

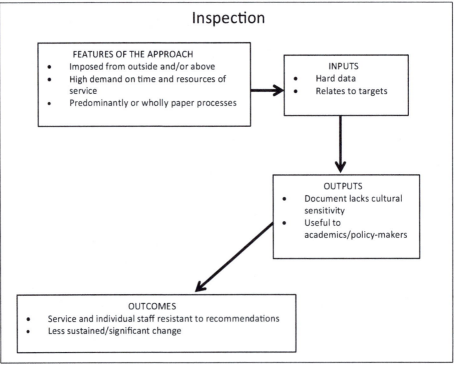

Figure 88.1 Perceptions of evaluation dichotomy, 'reflection' v. 'inspection'

instead adherence to principles derived from RNR, gender-responsive and desistance evidence bases:

A. Description of Service	8 items (none scored)
B. Leadership and Innovation	23 items
C. Quality Assurance	8 items
D. Staff Attributes and Development	13 items
E. Assessment Practices and Impact	13 items
F. Service Characteristics	18 items
G. Collaborative Working	6 items
H. Practice Skills	63 items

Dimension B: Leadership and Innovation

The CPAI evaluation of the women's project found that organizational context, assessed in three domains of the CPAI, was key across almost every other aspect of service and to the usefulness of the evaluation, since the ability to improve practice was linked to effective leadership, ideological commitment, and strategic direction. The SSEI-W responds to this need for evaluation approaches to take account of organizational context.

Dimension B is largely framed around Ellickson and Petersilia's investigations into the correlates of successful implementation in criminal justice which finds, in short, that there must be a close fit between the service and its environment, that all stakeholders must be committed to the service at every level of its operation, and that the service must be resourced and supported at an appropriate level (Ellickson and Petersilia 1983; Petersilia 1990). Additional components of the dimension are derived from further work exploring the processes and organizational settings correlated with success (Gendreau et al. 2001; Harland et al. 1979; Harris and Smith 1996) and evidence from the gender-responsive literature, which indicates that a commitment to prioritize women's issues must be embedded in the organizational structure (Bloom et al. 2003). This combination of evidence is the foundation of items such as:

B1. The service's goals include reducing re-offending, reflect the evidence base for effective work with women (eg, diversion from custody, the provision of social support, family reunification, protection from abusive relationships, recovery from victimisation, etc) and are clearly documented.

(SSEI-W V1.4)

Dimension C: Quality Assurance

Evaluation, as experience, testimony, and research demonstrate, is crucial in the development of effective sustainable services. Put simply by one of the practitioners in the women's project 'if it's not evaluated, then how can you tell that it's working?' In women's services, for which the evidence base is relatively new, incomplete, and evolving, 'documenting the effectiveness of practice addresses the need for empirical research on the outcomes of gender-responsive programmes' (Bloom et al. 2003: 89). Dimension C incorporates the evidence relating to effective quality assurance and evaluation practices, such as the need for the collection of recidivism figures 12 months or more after completion of engagement with the service, since the recidivism of 'treatment groups' is known to be delayed during that first year (Lösel 2001: 80). It is also a key feature of gender-responsive practice to 'go beyond traditional recidivism measures to assess the impact of specific programme attributes on pathways to female criminality' (Bloom et al. 2003: 90). Other items require service-user feedback to be sought, data relating to changes in targeted behaviours and human/social needs to be collated and analyzed, and address the need for standardized data-recording processes across the multiple agencies involved in delivering a holistic service to women, responding to evidence that differences in practice have been impeding researcher access (Jolliffe et al. 2011; Kerr 2018):

> C4. Data relating to measures of interest (eg, whether service-users have experienced domestic abuse, whether service-users are diagnosed as having mental health issues, etc) are recorded in a standardised way, to facilitate external and internal evaluator access.
>
> (SSEI-W V1.4)

Dimension D: Staff Attributes and Development

The second of the SSEI-W dimensions relating to organizational context, Dimension D responds to the need for staff to be selected and trained appropriately. As Covington and Bloom point out, 'programming designed for women can only be as good as its staff' (2007: 28). As above, Dimension D draws on the principles of effective intervention identified by research into exemplary services (Gendreau 1996; Gendreau et al. 2004) and the gender-responsive literature, which indicates, for example, that appropriately selected and trained core practitioners are women; are conversant in, and committed to, the evidence base for work *with* women; and receive specialized training in this respect (Covington and Bloom 2007).

Dimension E: Assessment Practices and Impact

This dimension relates to the fundamental principle that 'gender-responsive screening and assessment tools are utilized, with appropriate treatment matched to the identified needs and assets of each client' (Covington and Bloom 2007: 21). Whilst it is a requirement of the SSEI-W that, in line with the RNR evidence base, service users are categorized as to the level of risk that they present, assessing and responding to the strengths of service users is also key, since:

> Many women already are struggling with a poor sense of self because of the stigma attached to their addictions, their parenting histories, their trauma, or their prison records, for example. It may be non-therapeutic to add another problem to the woman's list of perceived failures.
>   A strength-based (asset) model of treatment shifts the focus from targeting problems to identifying the multiple issues a woman must contend with and the strategies she has adopted to cope.
>   (Covington and Bloom 2007: 20)

Acknowledging the perhaps unnecessary conflict between strengths-based and risk-based approaches, the phrasing of Item E3, for example, aims to appeal to the common ground, since the 'protective factors' of the RNR approach are the 'capabilities' of a strengths perspective:

> E3. Service-users' capabilities/protective factors are assessed as predictors of the reduced likelihood of reoffending or of desistance.
>   (SSEI-W V1.4)

Dimension E also emphasizes the importance of engaging women in assessment and case planning through reciprocal, respectful, and empathic practitioner interactions.

Dimension F: Service Characteristics

The evidence for social learning and cognitive behavioural work with women (e.g. Blanchette and Brown 2006) and the literature regarding behavioural principles and procedures (e.g. Spiegler and Guevremont 2010) provide the basis for Dimension F, which also incorporates key findings from the gender-responsive literature. For example, the service is required to provide a women-only space 'to foster safety and a sense of community' and to 'provide women with practical help with transport and childcare so that they can maintain their involvement' (Gelsthorpe et al. 2007: 54). Dimension F also relates to the provision of services to meet gender-specific needs, such as the integration of services for substance misuse, mental health, and trauma/victimization (Blanchette and Brown 2006; Covington and Bloom 2007).

Desistance theory (e.g. McNeill 2012) has also influenced the development of Dimension F. In addition to being interested in, and aware of, service users' social contexts, the service must also provide opportunities to improve their socio-economic conditions; promote and support healthy relationships with children, families, significant others, and the community; provide and support opportunities for criminalized service users to access services together with non-criminalized women; build long-term community support networks for them; and work with service users *and their support networks* to formulate relapse prevention strategies. To capture integrated work towards the desistance of service users, a woman's social reintegration is incorporated alongside her personal rehabilitation as a measurement of the service's effectiveness:

> F15. Service-users' success in the service is measurable and visible using criteria such as reduction in risk category, engagement with community services, employment, child reunification, managed substance misuse, etc.
>
> (SSEI-W V1.4)

Dimension G: Collaborative Working

The RNR principles of advocacy and brokerage for service users, assessed in Domain H of the CPAI-2010, 'Inter-Agency Communication', are required, or alluded to, in multiple dimensions of the SSEI-W. For instance, Dimension H requires practitioners to make referrals and advocate for service users where appropriate and items referring to the multiplicity of services available to women (in, for example, Dimension D) will, in practice, require practitioners' knowledge of and involvement with a range of providers. Furthermore, the need for holistic delivery of a range of services, exemplified by the 'one-stop shop' approach (Corston 2007), is critical to the development of gender-responsive services, so Dimension G requires 'wraparound services' to be delivered, involving 'a holistically and culturally sensitive plan for each woman that draws on a coordinated range of services within her community' (Covington and Bloom 2007: 14). This enables services to 'take a holistic and practical stance to helping women to address social problems which may be linked to their offending' (Gelsthorpe et al. 2007: 54).

Dimension H: Practice Skills

The final dimension, focused on the assessment of the relationship and structuring skills of practitioners (for which there is a burgeoning international evidence base – see Ugwudike et al. 2018), has been adapted from a pre-existing instrument, the Jersey Supervision Interview Checklist (Raynor et al. 2009). Developed and validated in the British Isles (Raynor et al. 2014), this addresses nine skill sets: interview set-up, non-verbal communication, verbal communication, use of authority, motivational interviewing, pro-social modelling, problem-solving, cognitive restructuring, and overall interview structure. Whilst these skill sets broadly correspond to the Core Correctional Practices itemized in section G of the CPAI-2010 (see Table 88.1), more attention is given to the quality of service-user engagement and each practice principle is broken down into more specific (and more easily observed) items. For example, a total of four CPAI items require that practitioners are 'open warm, and . . . respectful', 'non-blaming, empathic, and genuine', 'flexible, use humour, and are engaging', and 'are enthusiastic and express optimism'. To measure these qualities, the Jersey Checklist incorporates 15 items, including specific instructions relating to the quality of non-verbal communication (e.g. 'open posture/arms legs uncrossed') as well as verbal communication (e.g. 'mostly open questions'). Importantly, caveats regarding the need for flexibility in creating 'genuinely collaborative relationships' and 'making active listening choices' (Nelson-Jones 2011: 51), and for cultural responsiveness in communication, are provided in the Checklist's accompanying manual (Vanstone and Raynor 2012).

The evidence base for these items is supported across the RNR, desistance, and gender-responsive literatures. For example, relationship skills, characterized by empathy, respect, warmth, etc., are a key feature of Core Correctional Practices (Table 88.1), whilst McNeill identifies 'sustained and compassionate support from a trusted source' as the bedrock of desistance processes (2006: 49),

Table 88.1 Core Correctional Practices (CCPs)

Appropriate use of authority	▪ Staff focus their instruction and feedback on the service user's behaviour, without being personal
	▪ Staff are direct and specific
	▪ Staff do not raise their voices
	▪ Staff specify choices and attendant consequences
	▪ Staff are encouraging and respectful
	▪ Staff support words with action
	▪ 'A firm but fair approach'
Appropriate modelling and reinforcement	▪ Staff use a coping model – giving a concrete and vivid demonstration of desired behaviour
	▪ Staff define and model the skill before engaging the service user in progressively difficult practice (i.e. role play)
	▪ Staff are a source of reinforcement rather than punishment
	▪ Reinforcement involves giving or encouraging immediate and detailed description of the benefits of the desired behaviour
	▪ Staff immediately give or encourage detailed description of the undesirability of antisocial behaviours
Skill-building and problem-solving strategies	Staff members help service users to:
	▪ Identify the problem
	▪ Implement a plan
	▪ Clarify goals
	▪ Evaluate options
	▪ Generate alternatives
	▪ Evaluate the plan

(Continued)

Table 88.1 Continued

Relationship factors	Staff are:
	▪ Warm
	▪ Genuine
	▪ Humorous
	▪ Enthusiastic
	▪ Confident
	▪ Empathic
	▪ Respectful
	▪ Flexible
	▪ Committed to helping the service user
	▪ Engaging
	Communication with service users is:
	▪ Directive
	▪ Solution-focused
	▪ Structured
	▪ Non-blaming
	▪ Contingency-based
Motivational interviewing	Staff:
	▪ Develop discrepancy
	▪ Express empathy
	▪ Amplify ambivalence
	▪ Roll with resistance
	▪ Support self-efficacy (Miller and Rollnick 2013)
Cognitive restructuring	Staff:
	▪ Encourage descriptions of problematic situations (e.g. thinking report)
	▪ Draw out descriptions of thoughts and feelings
	▪ Identify thinking deficits
	▪ Guide practice of alternative thinking
	▪ Put in place opportunities to practice less risky thinking (Spiegler and Guevremont 2010; Gendreau et al. 2010)

Note: Items 1–4 are adapted from Andrews and Kiessling (1980) and Dowden and Andrews (2004). The original items also included the use of community resources as a CCP, though Gendreau et al. (2010) redefined this as an individual dimension of effective practice, 'inter-agency communication' (assessed in domain I of the CPAI), and added the elements of motivational interviewing and cognitive restructuring as CCPs in their 2004 summary of key elements

and the gender-responsive literature calls for 'mutual, empathic and empowering' relationships to 'foster growth in women' (Bloom et al. 2003: 55). Egan's skilled helper model describes the importance of non-verbal communication such as facing the service user, maintaining an open posture, being attentive, and appearing relaxed, since 'a respectful, empathic, genuine and caring mind set might well lose its impact if the client does not see these internal attitudes reflected in your external behaviours' (Egan 2002: 70).

The SSEI-W categorization

Like the CPAI, the SSEI-W uses the percentage of items scored 'yes' to categorize services. The *substance* of the CPAI report was perceived by the women's
project to be its qualitative findings and recommendations. However, scoring
and categorization were viewed as valuable in principle, providing a benchmark for interpreting progress, motivating the service, and avoiding complacency. On the other hand, CPAI categories of 'Unsatisfactory', 'Satisfactory',
and 'Very Satisfactory' were rejected as labelling and stigmatizing and a clear
message is that the language of evaluation must be positive and motivational
for the purposes of removing barriers to engagement, enabling dissemination
and facilitating change (see Table 88.2).

A related finding is that meaningful evaluation needs to locate a service
on its continuum of change. In the field of education psychology, Dweck recommends the use of feedback focused on process, strategies, and effort rather
than judgement to develop a 'growth mindset . . . based on the belief that
your basic qualities are things you can cultivate through your efforts' (2017:
7). Such a mindset is characterized by embracing challenge, persistence in the
face of setbacks, and learning from criticism. Dweck advocates the grade of
'Not Yet' (Dweck 2014).

The language of the SSEI-W report subheadings (Table 88.3) is being developed to focus content on the service's progress on its continuum of learning
and change.

Table 88.2 CPAI-2010 and potential SSEI-W categories

Categories of the CPAI-2010 (fixed mindset)		Potential categories of the SSEI-W (growth mindset)	
70%+	Very Satisfactory	70%+	Extremely high level of dedication to effective practices evident
50%–69%	Satisfactory	50%–69%	Dedication to effective practices evident
Below 50%	Unsatisfactory	20%–49%	Working towards effective practices
		0%–19%	Not yet working towards effective practices

Table 88.3 CPAI-2010 and SSEI-W subsections

Subsections of the CPAI-2010 pilot report	Subsections of the SSEI-W report (growth mindset)
Strengths	Progress
Areas for improvement	Opportunities
Recommendations	Potential

Concluding thoughts

The SSEI-W has been developed from the ground up to respond to the culture of women's services in Britain and evidence from the RNR, desistance, and gender-responsive literatures.

Since the evidence base for gender-responsive services is incomplete and in flux, the question of what exactly constitutes effective service has not yet been fully answered and remains open to discovery, interpretation, and debate. For example, the concept of a safe 'women-only' space is yet to be clearly defined in the context of transgender issues (which raise concerns about what constitutes safety for women and trans women alike). The SSEI-W must be used reflexively to respond to practice-level developments as well as the wider literature. The current version was developed to incorporate the best available evidence at the time of writing, but its developers acknowledge that it is not the 'final word' on effective gender-responsive practices.

It is expected that the SSEI-W will nonetheless be an eminently useful addition to the suite of evaluation instruments available in practice and will equip women's projects with the capacity to move forward under the aegis of an unparalleled scientific body of evidence in order to demonstrate their effectiveness and provide genuine, effective alternatives to the imprisonment of women.

References

Andrews, D. A. and Kiessling, J. J. (1980) Program structure and effective correctional practices: A summary of the CaVIC research. In R. R. Ross and P. Gendreau (Eds.), *Effective Correctional Treatment*. Toronto: Butterworth, pp. 441–463.

Blanchette, K. and Brown, S. L. (2006) *The Assessment and Treatment of Women Offenders: An Integrative Perspective*. Chichester: John Wiley & Sons, Ltd.

Bloom, B., Owen, B. and Covington, S. S. (2003) *Gender-Responsive Strategies for Women Offenders: Research, Practice, and Guiding Principles for Women Offenders*. Available at: www.nicic.org.

Bonta, J. and Andrews, D. A. (2017) *The Psychology of Criminal Conduct*, 6th edition. New York: Routledge.

Corston, J. (2007) *The Corston Report: A Report by Baroness Corston of a Review of Women with Particular Vulnerabilities in the Criminal Justice System*. London: Home Office.

Covington, S. S. and Bloom, B. E. (2007) Gender-responsive treatment and services in correctional settings. *Women and Therapy*, 29, 9–33.

Dowden, C. and Andrews, D. A. (2004) The importance of staff practice in delivering effective correctional treatment: A meta-analytic review of core correctional practice. *International Journal of Offender Therapy and Comparative Criminology*, 48, 203–214.

Dweck, C. (2014) *The Power of Believing that You Can Improve*. Presentation at TEDx Norrkoping. Available at: www.ted.com/talks/carol_dweck_the_power_of_believing_that_you_can_improve.

Dweck, C. (2017) *Mindset*. London: Robinson.

Egan, G. (2002) *The Skilled Helper*, 7th edition. Pacific Grove, CA: Brooks Cole.

Ellickson, P. and Petersilia, J. (1983) *Implementing New Ideas in Criminal Justice*. Santa Monica, CA: RAND.

Gelsthorpe, L., Sharpe, G. and Roberts, J. (2007) *Provision for Women Offenders in the Community*. London: Fawcett Society.

Gendreau, P. (1996) The principles of effective interventions with offenders. In A. T. Harland (Ed.), *Choosing Correctional Options That Work: Defining the Demand and Evaluating the Supply*. Thousand Oaks, CA: Sage Publications, pp. 117–130.

Gendreau, P., Andrews, D. A. and Thériault, Y. (2010) *Correctional Program Assessment Inventory – 2010 (CPAI-2010): Scoring Manual and Interview Guide*. Ottawa, ON. Available at: paulgend@bell.net or yvetheri@yahoo.ca.

Gendreau, P., French, S. A. and Gionet, A. (2004) What works (What Doesn't Work): The principles of effective correctional treatment. *Journal of Community Corrections*, 13, 4–30.

Gendreau, P., Goggin, C. and Smith, P. (2001) Implementation guidelines for correctional programs in the "Real World". In G. A. Bernfeld, D. P. Farrington and A. W. Leschied (Eds.), *Offender Rehabilitation in Practice: Implementing and Evaluating Effective Programs*. Chichester: John Wiley & Sons, Ltd, pp. 247–268.

Harland, A., Warren, M. and Brown, E. (1979) *A Guide to Restitution Programming*. Working Paper 17. Albany, NY: Criminal Justice Research Centre.

Harris, P. and Smith, S. (1996) Developing community corrections: An implementation perspective. In A. T. Harland (Ed.), *Choosing Correctional Options That Work: Defining the Demand and Evaluating the Supply*. Thousand Oaks, CA: Sage Publications, pp. 183–222.

Jolliffe, D., Hedderman, C., Palmer, E. and Hollin, C. (2011) *Re-Offending Analysis of Women Offenders Referred to Together Women (TW) and the Scope to Divert from Custody*. London: Ministry of Justice.

Kerr, B. (2018) *Evaluation on Probation: Developing Gender-Responsive and Jurisdictionally Appropriate Evaluation Systems for Offender Services in the British Isles*. Unpublished PhD thesis, Swansea University, Swansea.

Kerr, B., Raynor, P. and Ugwudike, P. (2018) *Swansea Service Evaluation Inventory – Women's Projects (SSEI-W) V1.4*. Swansea: Swansea Service Evaluation Team.

Lösel, F. (2001) Evaluating the effectiveness of correctional programs: Bridging the gap between research and practice. In G. A. Bernfeld, D. P. Farrington and A. W. Leschied (Eds.), *Offender Rehabilitation in Practice: Implementing and Evaluating Effective Programs*. Chichester: John Wiley & Sons, Ltd, pp. 247–268.

McNeill, F. (2006) A desistance paradigm for offender management. *Criminology and Criminal Justice*, 6, 39–62.

McNeill, F. (2012) Four forms of offender rehabilitation: Towards an interdisciplinary perspective. *Legal and Criminological Psychology*, 17, 18–36.

Miller, W. R. and Rollnick, S. (2013) *Motivational Interviewing: Preparing People for Change*, 3rd edition. New York: Guilford Press.

Nelson-Jones, R. (2011) *Basic Counselling Skills: A Helper's Manual*, 3rd edition. London: Sage Publications.

Petersilia, J. (1990) Conditions that permit intensive supervision programs to survive. *Crime and Delinquency*, 36, 126–145.

Raynor, P., Ugwudike, P. and Vanstone, M. (2009) *The Jersey Supervision Interview Checklist Version 7C*. The Jersey Crime and Society Project. Swansea: Centre for Criminal Justice and Criminology.

Raynor, P., Ugwudike, P. and Vanstone, M. (2014) The impact of skills in probation work: A reconviction study. *Criminology and Criminal Justice*, 14(2), 235–249.

Spiegler, M. D. and Guevremont, D. C. (2010) *Contemporary Behaviour Therapy*, 5th edition. Belmont, CA: Wadsworth.

Ugwudike, P. (2016) *Symposium on Innovative Approaches to Evaluating Practices in the Justice System*. Swansea: Swansea Service Evaluation Team, Swansea University. Available at: www.swansea.ac.uk/media/Programme%20NEW.pdf.

Ugwudike, P., Raynor, P. and Annison, J. (Eds.). (2018) *Evidence-Based Skills in Criminal Justice: International Research on Supporting Rehabilitation and Desistance*. Bristol: Policy Press.

Vanstone, M. and Raynor, P. (2012) *Observing Interview Skills: A Manual for Users of the Jersey Supervision Interview Checklist*. The Jersey Crime and Society Project, c/o Jersey Probation and Aftercare Service.

Group programmes with offenders

89

Emma J. Palmer

Introduction

The long-standing response to crime is to punish offenders, something that holds across many countries, cultures, and criminal justice jurisdictions. This punishment can take various forms, from financial penalties through to loss of liberty and more harsh penalties such as torture or death. Although punishment allows retribution to be delivered, there are questions as to how effective it is in reducing crime within a society, whether that is as a deterrent both to the individual and to other members of society. An alternative to punishment is rehabilitation, whereby an attempt is made to bring about change in the offender with the intention of reducing their future criminal behaviour (for a fuller discussion of punishment v. rehabilitation, see McGuire 2018). The rehabilitation of offenders to reduce their future offending often includes some sort of intervention that aims to address the factors that are associated with offending, proposing that if these factors are changed, then so their offending will reduce. Thus, the question becomes: can anything be done to 'change' offenders' behaviour? And if so, does it work?

'What works'

In the early 1970s, a seminal paper was published by Martinson (1974) that argued that 'nothing works' in the rehabilitation of offenders, with a subsequent paper making the point that 'With few and isolated exceptions, the rehabilitative efforts that have been reported so far have had no appreciable effect on recidivism' (Lipton et al. 1975: 25). This stark message was picked up by policymakers and heralded a move away from the idea that it was possible to rehabilitate offenders. However, it was argued by other authors that much of the research that Martinson drew upon was methodologically flawed with little distinction made between research of varying qualities (e.g. Thornton 1987). Gradually the tide turned, with a recognition that it was important to ensure that only the best quality research is used from which to draw conclusions.

There is now a sizeable body of research showing what works in reducing offending. The statistical technique of meta-analysis has been used to review and summarize the overall findings from these studies. Meta-analysis allows for the potential biases and variations in primary research studies, to give a quantifiable measure of treatment impact. There are now over 100 meta-analyses of offender treatment, which consistently report that effective interventions are those that follow the Risk-Need-Responsivity (RNR) principles (Andrews 2001). The *risk principle* states that services should be allocated according to risk; in other words, higher risk offenders should receive more intense services. The *needs principle* states that interventions should address criminogenic needs, i.e. those dynamic risk factors known to be associated with offending. Finally, the *responsivity principle* states that interventions should be designed and delivered to match offenders' learning styles, with specific attention to individual characteristics such as gender, age, or ethnicity. The meta-analyses have also shown that effective interventions are based on a cognitive behavioural approach, structured in nature, and have a high level of programme integrity (Lipsey et al. 2001, 2007; Wilson et al. 2005). Pulling together the findings from meta-analyses, Andrews (1995, 2001) developed the principles of effective practice:

1 Interventions with offenders should be based on a psychological theory of criminal behaviour;
2 This theory should have a personality and social learning theory focus to the risk factors for offending;
3 Strategies for intervention should be based on human service, rather than on principles of retribution, restorative justice, or deterrence;
4 Where possible, interventions should take place in the community in natural settings. However, when it is necessary to use custody, these facilities should be as community-oriented as possible;
5 Offenders' level of risk of reoffending should be assessed and used as the basis for allocation to services;

6   Offenders' dynamic criminogenic needs should be assessed and used as intervention targets;

7   Interventions should be multi-modal in that they should target a range of criminogenic needs to reflect that fact that offending is associated with multiple risk factors;

8   Assessment of risk level and criminogenic needs should be conducted using validated measures;

9   Interventions should have general responsivity, with services matched to offenders' learning styles, motivations, and abilities;

10 Interventions should have specific responsivity and be adapted to take count of the diversity of offenders (e.g. age, gender, ethnicity);

11 Specific responsivity and offenders' strengths/weaknesses should be assessed routinely using standardized tools;

12 Organizational strategies should be used to monitor continuity of services, including relapse prevention work;

13 Organizations should identify areas of practice where staff may use their personal discretion, and these should be clear to all staff;

14 Organizations should develop a service-level policy for the use of the principles of effective service, and this should be clear to all staff;

15 Organizations should set up procedures to monitor the delivery and integrity of interventions, as well as procedures to deal with problems;

16 There should be a focus on development of staff skills required to deliver effective interventions;

17 Managers should have the competencies expected of staff, along with understanding the principles of effective interventions;

18 Programmes should be placed within a wider context at an organizational level.

Based on the meta-analyses results, offender treatment programmes have been developed, many of which are delivered in groups, using structured manuals to deliver the material (Hollin and Palmer 2006).

As well as identifying the characteristics of effective interventions, research also explored *what* needed to be changed to bring about a reduction in reoffending and *how* change could best be brought about. A number of theories have been put forward to explain why people commit crime. While it is not appropriate to consider these in depth here, there is strong evidence for the role of cognition in crime, leading to what has been referred to as the *cognitive model of offender rehabilitation* (Ross and Fabiano 1985a). Essentially, this refers to the role that thinking skills and thinking habits play in behaviour. From the 1980s, research began to show that offenders tended to show distinct patterns of cognitive functioning, such as being more impulsive; having more rigid thinking styles; and having poorer consequential thinking, perspective-taking abilities, and social problem-solving skills (Ross and Fabiano 1985a). While it was not proposed that everyone who displayed these patterns of cognition would commit crime, it was argued that these thinking styles interacted with other risk factors and opportunities to increase the likelihood of committing offences. Other work identified that offenders tend to hold 'cognitive distortions' which focus on the content of people's thoughts, such as having pro-criminal attitudes and beliefs, making it more likely that they will view offending as acceptable and appropriate behaviour. Based on the research outlined above, the vast majority of offender intervention programmes target the criminogenic need factors of cognitive skills, such as impulsivity, social problem-solving, and pro-criminal attitudes and beliefs.

Development of groupwork programmes

The approach of using groupwork programmes to reduce reoffending began during the 1990s. The main way in which these programmes are delivered is in groups of offenders, typically between ten and 15 individuals. While the majority of groupwork programmes are general offending programmes – i.e. suitable for offenders who have committed any offence type – there are others that are offence-specific (e.g. sexual offending or violence). One of the first programmes to be used widely was Reasoning and Rehabilitation (R & R), which was developed in Canada by Ross and Fabiano (1985b). This programme was then taken up by the English and Welsh Prison Service and has informed the basis for a number of programmes over the last 25 years.

Reasoning and Rehabilitation (R & R)

The Reasoning and Rehabilitation (R & R) programme was the first structured groupwork programme that was developed with the aim of reducing reoffending (Ross and Fabiano 1985b). Drawing upon research that showed an association between offending and offenders' thinking styles and social cognition (Antonowicz and Ross 2005), it aimed to bring about changes in these areas to enhance offenders' ability to engage in pro-social behaviours. Specific treatment targets included social-perspective taking, critical reasoning, pro-criminal attitudes and beliefs, and social problem-solving. As a cognitive behavioural intervention, it used techniques such as role play and modelling. R & R was designed to be delivered by a range of staff, including prison and probation officers as well as psychologists. Delivery is supported by video monitoring of sessions and formal feedback provided to programme facilitators in supervision to ensure programme integrity. The R & R programme has now been used in a range of countries, including Canada, the United States, England and Wales, Scotland, Sweden, Denmark, Norway, Australia, and New Zealand. Within England and Wales, it was initially delivered alongside the Enhanced Thinking Skills (ETS) in the Prison Service, and subsequently rolled out to community settings with ETS and the Think First programmes outlined below. However, R & R was discontinued in England and Wales in

2004 with ETS being used in prisons and probation, and Think First in probation only.

Enhanced Thinking Skills (ETS)

Enhanced Thinking Skills (ETS) was developed by the English and Welsh Prison Service (Clark 2000) and drew heavily upon the R & R programme, addressing the same treatment targets using a cognitive behavioural approach. One advantage of ETS over R & R was the shorter length of delivery. Initially implemented in the Prison Service, it was later rolled out into the English and Welsh Probation Service.

Think First

A third groupwork programme developed in England and Wales was Think First (McGuire 2000). As with R & R and ETS, it was originally delivered in the English and Welsh Prison Service, before it began to be used in the community by the Probation Service. Similarly to R & R and ETS, the Think First programme targets thinking styles and patterns using a cognitive behavioural approach; however, it contains an offence-specific approach that requires offenders to consider specific offences that they have committed. It also includes clearly defined pre-group preparation sessions before the main programme to enhance offenders' motivation and engagement, and post-group sessions to assist offenders to develop relapse prevention strategies.

Sex Offender Treatment Programme (SOTP)

The 1990s also saw the development of groupwork programmes to address sexual offending using cognitive behaviour theory, with work in this area led by the English and Welsh Prison Service. From the initial Sex Offender Treatment Programme (SOTP; Grubin and Thornton 1994), a whole suite of programmes were developed, including the Core SOTP, the SOTP Adapted programme for lower intellectually functioning sex offenders, the Extended SOTP that provides a longer and more intensive programme for high-risk and high-need sex offenders, and the Better Lives Booster SOTP for offenders who had successfully completed the main SOTP to allow prisoners to focus on their individual needs in preparation for release. Although initially designed for use in prisons, sex offender treatment programmes were also developed for community settings. These include the Community-Sex Offender Group Programme (C-SOGP), developed in the West Midlands Probation Area in collaboration with the Home Office; the Thames Valley-Sex Offender Group Programme (TV-SOGP), designed by the local health and social services and police along with the Home Office; and the Northumbria-Sex Offender Group Programme (N-SOGP), developed by Northumbria Probation and the Sexual Behaviour Unit at St Nicholas Hospital in Newcastle.

More recently, other programmes have been developed, such as the Healthy Sex Programme (HSP). However, the SOTP suite of programmes has now been withdrawn due to negative findings from a large-scale evaluation.

Thinking Skills Programme (TSP)

In 2009, the Prison Service implemented a new groupwork programme called the Thinking Skills Programme (TSP; Harris and Riddy 2010), which has replaced ETS and is now the only cognitive skills programme delivered in the Prison and Probation Services in England and Wales. While drawing upon ETS, the TSP also takes into account strengths-based approaches such as the Good Lives Model (GLM; Ward and Brown 2004; Ward and Stewart 2003). To do this, it incorporates four individual sessions as well as the 15 groupwork sessions, to emphasize the personal relevance of the programme to individual offenders.

Anger/violence programmes

There are also a number of groupwork programmes developed for violent offending. Some of which also include anger management components (Novaco 1975), although this approach assumes that the violent behaviour was at least partially caused by anger problems, whereas this is not necessarily the case for violent offences (Serin et al. 2009). For example, the Violence Prevention Program (VPP) in Canada is designed for high-risk violent offenders in prison and targets impulsivity, anger control, and aggression-supportive cognitions, and aims to improve offenders' problem-solving skills. New Zealand also has a comprehensive suite of programmes designed to reduce violent reoffending. Since 1988, the Rimutaka Violence Prevention Unit (RVPU) has delivered intensive cognitive behavioural interventions to violent male offenders (Polaschek 2011; Polaschek and Kilgour 2013). The intervention approach taken is a combination of a structured, group-based, cognitive behavioural programme and a democratic therapeutic community approach. In the English and Welsh Prison Service, the Controlling Anger and Learning to Manage It (CALM) programme has been widely used.

Evaluation of the effectiveness of groupwork programmes

Meta-analyses have found that offending behaviour groupwork programmes can impact on reoffending outcomes. As noted earlier in this chapter, these have also highlighted the specific factors which characterize effective programmes. To summarize, programmes that follow the RNR principles are most effective, with structured, cognitive behavioural programmes showing the best outcomes (Lipsey et al. 2001, 2007; Wilson et al. 2005). However, as noted by Hollin and Palmer (2009), it is important to remember that meta-analyses provide an overall summary of research and so it is also necessary to consider evaluations of individual programmes.

General offending behaviour programmes

An early evaluation of R & R in Canada with 1,444 offenders found a significantly lower rate of reconviction for the treatment group, an effect that increased when the 17% of treatment non-completers were removed from the treatment group (Robinson 1995). After R & R and ETS were introduced into the Prison Service in England and Wales, a number of large-scale evaluations were conducted. The first study compared 667 male offenders with a matched no-treatment group, and reported that the treatment group had a significantly lower rate of reconviction than the no-treatment comparison group (Friendship et al. 2002, 2003). Other studies examined change on cognitive skills (the key targets for the programmes), showing that there were changes in the desired direction for the treatment group compared to the no-treatment comparison group (Blud et al. 2003; Wilson et al. 2003).

A few years later another evaluation compared 649 male prisoners who participated in either R & R or ETS with a no-treatment comparison group; however, this time no significant difference was found in two-year reconviction rates between the two groups (Falshaw et al. 2003, 2004). A further study using matched comparison groups was reported by Cann et al. (2003) and examined one- and two-year reconviction. Although there was no significant difference in reconviction between the two groups for both one- and two-year reconviction rates, when the programme non-completers (approximately 9%) were removed from the treatment group, the one-year reconviction rates were significantly lower among the programme completers compared to the comparison group for ETS only. However, this effect had disappeared by the two-year follow-up.

When the R & R, ETS, and Think First programmes were rolled out in the English and Welsh Probation Service, three large-scale evaluation studies were conducted. Using a quasi-experimental design whereby statistical controls were used in the analysis, programme completers were reported to have lower rates of reconviction compared to programme non-completers and a no-treatment comparison group (Hollin et al. 2008; McGuire et al. 2008; Palmer et al. 2007). Another community-based evaluation of R & R in the US was reported by Van Voorhis et al. (2004) and found similar results, with programme completers showing significantly better reconviction and employment outcomes compared to non-completers and the comparison group.

Since the introduction of the TSP in England and Wales, a study by Gobbett and Sellen (2014) compared pre-post psychometric scores for treatment targets for ETS and TSP participants in prison, finding that significant change was found on more measures for the TSP group. However, although a large-scale reconviction outcome study is being conducted for the TSP, no published results are available yet.

Research has suggested that cognitive skills groupwork programmes may be more effective for some groups of offenders than others. One issue that has been explored is level of risk of reoffending. The risk principle proposes that programmes are likely to have a greater impact on medium–high-risk offenders, with little impact expected for low-risk offenders (Andrews 2001). This has been supported by some studies, for example, in the English and Welsh Probation Service. Palmer et al. (2008, 2009) reported that R & R, ETS, and Think First showed no impact on reconviction rates among low-risk offenders. Similarly, studies in the Prison Service in England and Wales have shown a greater impact of ETS on low-medium and high–medium-risk bands, compared to the lowest- and highest-risk prisoners (Friendship et al. 2002). However, more recently Travers et al. (2013) found a treatment effect of ETS on all but the very highest risk offenders. Response to cognitive skills groupwork programmes has also been examined for different offence types in a small number of studies. One of the first evaluations of R & R in Canada by Robinson (1995) reported a significant impact of the programme on sexual, violent (not robbery), and drug offenders, whereas no benefit was found for robbery and non-violent property offenders.

A large-scale evaluation of ETS in the English and Welsh Prison Service also found no impact on robbery and non-violent acquisitive offenders (Travers et al. 2014). Given that offenders in this groups exhibit the treatment needs that ETS and other cognitive skills programmes address, there are clearly other factors that need addressing through treatment. One suggestion by Travers et al. (2014) is that maybe some of these acquisitive offences are driven by problematic drug use and so offenders would usefully benefit more from interventions that address this criminogenic need as well as or instead of cognitive skills programmes.

Sex offender programmes

There have been a number of reviews and meta-analyses of the effectiveness of sex offender programmes. These have shown mixed evidence about the effectiveness of sex offender treatment. For example, an early meta-analysis conducted by Hanson et al. (2002) reviewed 43 studies conducted before 2000. This reported a significant effect of treatment, particularly for those using cognitive behavioural approaches. Similar findings were found by Losel and Schmucker (2005) whose meta-analysis included 69 studies, with cognitive behavioural therapy and behavioural therapy showing positive effects on sexual recidivism, although approaches such as castration, hormone treatment, and more psychotherapeutic approaches showed no impact at all. More recently Beech et al. (2015) reported that systemic and cognitive behavioural therapy showed the biggest treatment gains. However, other meta-analyses have reported less positive results, including Langstrom et al. (2013), who concluded that there is insufficient good quality evaluations to be able to draw firm conclusions as to the effectiveness of sex offender treatment. Within the English and Welsh Prison Service, early evaluations showed positive treatment results (for a review, see Beech and Mann 2002). However, a recent large-scale evaluation concluded that the Core SOTP was not producing reductions in reconviction (and perhaps in some cases, increasing reconvictions) (Mews et al. 2017) and so the SOTP suite of programmes have now been withdrawn.

Violence treatment programmes

There is surprisingly little research on the effectiveness of programmes for violent offenders, although there are a few large-scale meta-analyses and systematic reviews suggesting that it is possible to intervene with adult violent offenders and bring about a reduction in reoffending (Dowden and Andrews 2000; Jolliffe and Farrington 2007; McGuire 2008). The Violence Prevention Program (VPP) in Canada is designed for high-risk violent offenders in prison and targets impulsivity, anger control, and aggression-supportive cognitions and aims to improve offenders' problem-solving skills. An evaluation by Cortoni et al. (2006) reported improved institutional behaviour and better reoffending outcomes for completers compared to the comparison group. In New Zealand, the Rimutaka Violence Prevention Unit (RVPU) has shown some promising results for institutional behaviour and longer-term reconviction outcomes (Polaschek 2011; Polaschek and Kilgour 2013).

Non-completion

The majority of cognitive skills groupwork programmes are designed for offenders to complete all of the material. However, not all offenders who start programmes complete them, with this group referred to as 'non-completers'. This is particularly problematic in community settings – in prison, non-completion rates are typically around 10% (Cann et al. 2003), whereas when R & R, ETS, and Think First were rolled out in the Probation Service in England and Wales, around two-thirds of the 'treatment group' did not complete them (Palmer et al. 2007), although the completion rate has now risen considerably. Another study was able to distinguish between the offenders who were referred to a programme but did not start and those offenders who started but not complete, which reported that around half of the 'treatment group' did not even start (referred to as 'non-starters'). Disentangling completers and non-completers in evaluation research has led to the identification of a 'completion effect', whereby programme completers do significantly better than both no-treatment comparison groups and non-completers – i.e. to get the full benefit of a programme, it is necessary to participate in all of it. The evidence for a completion effect is very robust, being found in a number of jurisdictions and in both prison and community settings (Hollin et al. 2008; McGuire et al. 2008; Palmer et al. 2007; Van Voorhis et al. 2004). Conversely, a 'non-completion effect' has also been identified, whereby non-completion of programmes produces significantly poorer outcomes than those for no-treatment comparison groups. The existence of a completion and non-completion effect has raised a number of questions as to how it can be explained. They main two are (1) are there differences between completers and non-completers? And (2) can these differences explain the discrepancy in the reconviction rates of the two groups?

There are now a number of studies that have reported reliable differences between completers and non-completers. A meta-analysis conducted by Olver et al. (2011) found that non-completers were, on average, younger, had a higher risk of reoffending, had a higher number of previous convictions, were less likely to be employed, and had a more negative attitude towards treatment. Interestingly, these are also predictors of reconviction, which further explains the non-completion effect whereby non-completers have poorer outcomes than both completers and comparison groups. Various explanations have been offered to explain non-completion (see Hollin and Palmer 2009), but identification of the characteristics of non-completers in terms of demographic characteristics and their attitude towards programmes does give us a starting point to work with potential non-completers to enhance their motivation and engagement with programmes.

Responsivity

Less research has been conducted on the RNR principle of responsivity compared to the risk and need principles. One key issue relates to gender. The vast majority of research on offender interventions is on males, raising questions about whether groupwork programmes are appropriate at reducing reoffending for female offenders, or if these programmes need to be adapted or women-specific interventions designed. This point is supported by research in the English and Welsh Probation showing that ETS and TF cognitive behavioural groupwork programmes are not effective with female offenders (Palmer et al. 2015). Recent research has found that women often have gender-specific criminogenic needs or that some areas of criminogenic need might be related to offending in different ways (Brennan et al. 2012; Wright et al. 2012). Therefore, it is perhaps not surprising that groupwork programmes designed for male offenders do not 'work', suggesting that gender-responsive interventions are needed. Similar points can also be made about other responsivity issues, such as ethnic background.

Conclusions

Overall, research provides good evidence that offending behaviour group-work programmes can be effective in reducing reoffending, providing that they follow the RNR principles and that offenders complete them. However, as noted earlier in this chapter, issues relating to non-completing and responsivity issues (such as gender appropriateness) need to be borne in mind when they are developed and implemented.

References

Andrews, D. A. (1995) The psychology of criminal conduct and effective treatment. In J. McGuire (Ed.), *What Works: Reducing Reoffending*. Chichester: John Wiley & Sons, pp. 35–62.

Andrews, D. A. (2001) Principles of effective correctional programs. In L. L. Motiuk and R. C. Serin (Eds.), *Compendium 2000 on Effective Correctional Programming*. Ottawa, ON: Correctional Service, pp. 9–17.

Antonowicz, D. H. and Ross, R. R. (2005) Social problem-solving deficits in offenders. In M. McMurran and J. McGuire (Eds.), *Social Problem-Solving and Offending: Evidence, Evaluation and Evolution*. Chichester: John Wiley & Sons, pp. 91–102.

Beech, A. R., Freemantle, N., Power, C. and Fisher, D. (2015) An examination of potential biases in research designs used to assess the efficacy of sex offender treatment. *The Journal of Aggression, Conflict and Peace Studies*, 7, 204–222.

Beech, A. R. and Mann, R. E. (2002) Recent developments in the assessment and treatment of sexual offenders. In J. McGuire (Ed.), *What Works: Reducing Reoffending*. Chichester: John Wiley & Sons, pp. 259–288.

Blud, L., Travers, R., Nugent, F. and Thornton, D. M. (2003) Accreditation of offending behaviour programmes in HM prison service: "What Works" in practice. *Legal and Criminological Psychology*, 8, 69–81.

Brennan, T., Breitenbach, M., Dieterich, W., Salisbury, E. J. and Van Voorhis, P. (2012) Women's pathways to serious and habitual crime: A person-centered analysis incorporating gender responsive factors. *Criminal Justice and Behavior*, 39, 1481–1508.

Cann, J., Falshaw, L., Nugent, F. and Friendship, C. (2003) *Understanding What Works: Accredited Cognitive Skills Programmes for Adult Men and Young Offenders*. Home Office Research Findings No. 226. London: Home Office.

Clark, D. A. (2000) *Theory Manual for Enhanced Thinking Skills*. Prepared for the Joint Prison Probation Accreditation Panel.

Cortoni, F., Nunes, K. and Latendresse, M. (2006) *An Examination of the Effectiveness of the Violence Prevention Program*. Research Report R-178. Ottawa, ON: Correctional Service.

Dowden, C. and Andrews, D. A. (2000) Effective correctional treatment and violent reoffending: A meta-analysis. *Canadian Journal of Criminology*, 42, 449–467.

Falshaw, L., Friendship, C., Travers, R. and Nugent, F. (2003) *Searching for What Works: An Evaluation of Cognitive Skills Programmes*. Home Office Research Findings No. 206. London: Home Office.

Falshaw, L., Friendship, C., Travers, R. and Nugent, F. (2004) Searching for what works: HM prison service accredited cognitive skills programmes. *British Journal of Forensic Practice*, 6, 3–13.

Friendship, C., Blud, L., Erikson, M. and Travers, R. (2002) *An Evaluation of Cognitive-Behavioural Treatment for Prisoners*. Home Office Research Findings No. 161. London: Home Office.

Friendship, C., Blud, L., Erikson, M., Travers, R. and Thornton, D. M. (2003) Cognitive-behavioural treatment for imprisoned offenders: An evaluation of HM prison service's cognitive skills programmes. *Legal and Criminological Psychology*, 8, 103–114.

Gobbett, M. J. and Sellen, J. L. (2014) An evaluation of HM prison service "Thinking Skills Programme" using psychometric assessments. *International Journal of Offender Therapy and Comparative Criminology*, 58, 454–473.

Grubin, D. and Thornton, D. (1994) A national programme for the assessment and treatment of sex offenders in the English prison system. *Criminal Justice and Behavior*, 21, 55–71.

Hanson, R. K., Gordon, A., Harris, A. J. R., Marques, J. K., Murphy, W., Quinsey, V. L. and Seto, M. C. (2002) First report of the collaborative outcome data project on the effectiveness of psychological treatment for sex offenders. *Sexual Abuse: A Journal of Research and Treatment*, 14, 169–194.

Harris, D. and Riddy, R. (2010) *Theory Manual for the Thinking Skills Programme*. Prepared for the Correctional Services Accreditation Panel. London: Ministry of Justice.

Hollin, C. R., McGuire, J., Hounsome, J. C., Hatcher, R. M., Bilby, C. A. L. and Palmer, E. J. (2008) Cognitive skills offending behavior programs in the community: A reconviction analysis. *Criminal Justice and Behavior*, 35, 269–283.

Hollin, C. R. and Palmer, E. J. (Eds.). (2006) *Offending Behaviour Programmes: Development, Application and Controversies*. Chichester: John Wiley & Sons.

Hollin, C. R. and Palmer, E. J. (2009) Cognitive skills programmes for offenders. *Psychology, Crime and Law*, 15, 147–164.

Jolliffe, D. and Farrington, D. P. (2007) *A Systematic Review of the National and International Evidence on the Effectiveness of Interventions with Violent Offenders*. Ministry of Justice Research Series 16/07. London: Ministry of Justice.

Langstrom, N., Enebrink, R., Lauren, E-M., Lindblom, J., Werko, S. and Hanson, R. K. (2013) Preventing sexual abusers of children from reoffending: Systematic review of medical and psychological interventions. *BMJ: British Medical Journal*, 347, 358.

Lipsey, M. W., Chapman, G. L. and Landenberger, N. A. (2001) Cognitive-behavioral programs for offenders. *Annals of the American Academy of Political and Social Science*, 578, 144–157.

Lipsey, M. W., Landenberger, N. A. and Wilson, S. J. (2007) Effects of cognitive-behavioral programs for criminal offenders. *Campbell Systematic Reviews*, 6.

Lipton, D. S., Martinson, R. and Wilks, J. (1975) *The Effectiveness of Correctional Treatment: A Survey of Treatment Evaluation Studies*. New York: Praeger.

Losel, F. and Schmucker, M. (2005) The effectiveness of treatment for sexual offenders: A comprehensive meta-analysis. *Journal of Experimental Criminology*, 1, 117–146.

Martinson, R. (1974) What works? Questions and answers about prison reform. *The Public Interest*, 10, 22–43.

McGuire, J. (2000) *Theory Manual for Think First*. Prepared for the Joint Prison Probation Accreditation Panel.

McGuire, J. (2008) A review of effective interventions for reducing aggression and violence. *Philosophical Transactions of the Royal Society B*, 363, 2577–2597.

McGuire, J. (2018) Crime and punishment: What works? In G. M. Davies and A. R. Beech (Eds.), *Forensic Psychology: Crime, Justice, Law Interventions*, 3rd edition. Chichester: Wiley-Blackwell, pp. 481–511.

McGuire, J., Bilby, C. A. L., Hatcher, R. M., Hollin, C. R., Hounsome, J. C. and Palmer, E. J. (2008) Evaluation of structured cognitive-behavioral treatment programs in reducing criminal recidivism. *Journal of Experimental Criminology*, 4, 21–40.

Mews, A., Di Bella, L. and Purver, M. (2017) *Impact Evaluation of the Prison-Based Core Sex Offender Treatment Programme*. London: Ministry of Justice.

Novaco, R. W. (1975) *Anger Control: The Development and Evaluation of an Experimental Treatment*. Lexington, MA: D. C. Health.

Olver, M. E., Stockdale, K. C. and Wormith, J. S. (2011) A meta-analysis of predictors of offender treatment attribution and its relationship to recidivism. *Journal of Consulting and Clinical Psychology*, 79, 6–21.

Palmer, E. J., Hatcher, R. M., McGuire, J. and Hollin, C. R. (2015) Cognitive skills programs for female offenders in the community: Effect on reconviction. *Criminal Justice and Behavior*, 42, 345–360.

Palmer, E. J., McGuire, J., Hatcher, R. M., Hounsome, J. C., Bilby, C. A. L. and Hollin, C. R. (2008) The importance of appropriate allocation to offending behaviour programmes. *International Journal of Offender Therapy and Comparative Criminology*, 52, 206–221.

Palmer, E. J., McGuire, J., Hatcher, R. M., Hounsome, J. C., Bilby, C. A. L. and Hollin, C. R. (2009) Allocation to offending behaviour programmes in the English and Welsh probation service. *Criminal Justice and Behavior*, 36, 909–922.

Palmer, E. J., McGuire, J., Hounsome, J. C., Hatcher, R. M., Bilby, C. A. L. and Hollin, C. R. (2007) Offending behaviour programmes in the community: The effects on reconviction of three programmes with adult male offenders. *Legal and Criminological Psychology*, 12, 251–264.

Polaschek, D. L. L. (2011) High-intensity rehabilitation for violent offenders in New Zealand: Reconviction outcomes for high- and medium-risk prisoners. *Journal of Interpersonal Violence*, 26, 644–682.

Polaschek, D. L. L. and Kilgour, T. G. (2013) New Zealand's special treatment units: The development and implementation of intensive treatment for high-risk male prisoners. *Psychology, Crime and Law*, 19, 511–526.

Robinson, D. (1995) *The Impact of Cognitive Skills Training on Post-Release Recidivism Among Canadian Federal Offenders*. Report No. R-41, Research Branch. Ottawa, ON: Correctional Services.

Ross, R. R. and Fabiano, E. A. (1985a) *Time to Think: A Cognitive Model of Delinquency Prevention and Offender Rehabilitation*. Johnson City, TN: Institute of Social Sciences and Arts.

Ross, R. R. and Fabiano, E. A. (1985b) *Reasoning and Rehabilitation: Manual*. Ottawa, ON: AIR Training and Associates.

Serin, R. C., Gobeil, R. and Preston, D. L. (2009) Evaluation of the persistently violent offender treatment program. *International Journal of Offender Therapy and Comparative Criminology*, 53, 57–73.

Thornton, D. M. (1987) Treatment effects on recidivism: A reappraisal of the 'nothing works' doctrine. In B. J. McGurk, D. M. Thornton and M. Williams (Eds.), *Applying Psychology to Imprisonment: Theory and Practice*. London: HMSO, pp. 181–189.

Travers, R., Mann, R. E. and Hollin, C. R. (2014) Who benefits from cognitive skills programs? Differential impact by risk and offense types. *Criminal Justice and Behavior*, 41, 1103–1129.

Travers, R., Wakeling, H. C., Mann, R. E. and Hollin, C. R. (2013) Reconviction following a cognitive skills intervention: An alternative quasi-experimental methodology. *Legal and Criminological Psychology*, 18, 48–65.

Van Voorhis, P., Spruance, L. M., Ritchey, P. N., Listwan, S. J. and Seabrook, R. (2004) The Georgia cognitive skills experiment: A replication of Reasoning and Rehabilitation. *Criminal Justice and Behavior*, 31, 282–305.

Ward, T. and Brown, M. (2004) The Good Lives Model and conceptual issues in offender rehabilitation. *Psychology, Crime and Law*, 10, 243–257.

Ward, T. and Stewart, C. (2003) The treatment of sex offenders: Risk management and good lives. *Professional Psychology: Research and Practice*, 34, 353–360.

Wilson, D. B., Bouffard, L. A. and MacKenzie, D. L. (2005) A quantitative review of structured, group-oriented, cognitive-behavioral programs for offenders. *Criminal Justice and Behavior*, 32, 172–204.

Wilson, S., Attrill, G. and Nugent, F. (2003) Effective interventions for acquisitive offenders: An investigation of cognitive skills programmes. *Legal and Criminological Psychology*, 8, 83–101.

Wright, E. M., Van Voorhis, P., Salisbury, E. J. and Bauman, A. (2012) Gender-responsive lessons learned and policy implications for women in prison. *Criminal Justice and Behavior*, 39, 1612–1632.

Evaluating group programmes

90

A question of design?

Clive R. Hollin

Introduction

There are two main reasons why rehabilitative work with offenders would involve groupwork. First, to give an offender the opportunity to address some problematic issue in their life. Second, to equip the offender with new skills and strategies to reduce further offending. An example of the former lies in the use of social skills training with offenders, once popular with imprisoned young offenders, to improve skills generally (Hollin and Henderson 1981) or to manage a specific personal issue (Hollin and Courtney 1983). However, it is a moot point as to whether an offender with improved social skills will reduce their offending (Hollin and Henderson 1984). The second use of groupwork has the explicit aim of reducing offending, which is the focus here. The goal of reducing reoffending received an impetus with the advent of 'what works' (McGuire 1995) and the growth of offending behaviour programmes (OBPs;

Hollin and Palmer 2006). The various discussion centred on the evaluation of OBPs is of relevance to outcome research generally.

Groupwork in the form of OBPs has been refined for use with offenders of different age, offence type, race, and gender, generating a substantial literature regarding implementation, practice, and evaluation (e.g. Bernfeld et al. 2001; Goggin and Gendreau 2006). Thus, over the past two decades there has been a growth in the use of offending behaviour programmes (OBPs), sometimes within the context of an overarching crime reduction strategy (e.g. Dvoskin et al. 2012).

OBPs provide an example of evidence-based practice and increasing their effectiveness relies upon the generation of high-quality data to inform future developments. While within-programme change, evaluated with relevant measures such as, say, attitudes towards women or anger, is important, judged by traditional significance testing or by clinical significance (McGlinchey et al. 2002), outcome is the bottom line.

Outcome research

Do OBPs lead to reduced offending? In order to give a robust answer to this question, evaluations must adopt the strongest design which is practicable in the given circumstances. The Scientific Methods Scale, widely used in the criminological literature (Farrington et al. 2002), includes a range of designs of varying strength, from a basic correlational design to a fully randomized control trial.

Wilson et al. (2005) suggest that there are three designs of acceptable strength to evaluate the outcome of OPBs. First, a *low-quality quasi-experimental design* comparing a treatment group with no treatment comparison groups. This design has the drawback of uncontrolled differences between the treatment and control groups, potentially introducing a selection bias. Second, *a high-quality quasi-experimental design*, which does not have randomization to treatment and comparison groups but introduces either methodological or statistical control of group differences. Third, an experimental design, in the proper sense, with randomization of allocation to condition; this design, developed principally for drug interventions, is referred to as a Randomised Control Trial (RCT).

Of the three designs, RCTs are seen as the gold standard. However, RCTs can raise practical problems such as difficulties in implementation (Gondolf 2004) and potential ethical and legal problems if treatment is withheld when offenders form a control group. Given these practical issues, is the evidence produced by RCTs significantly different from that from easier-to-implement quasi-experimental studies?

Several studies have compared the relationship between design and outcome. Lipsey (1992) found that randomization to groups had little relationship to outcome. It was the presence or absence of specific non-equivalence between groups, such as age, which were important. Heinsman and Shadish (1996) compared statistically the results of randomized and nonrandomized studies concluding that when '[r]andomized and nonrandomized experiments were equally well designed and executed, they would yield roughly the same effect size' (p. 162). In sympathy with Lipsey, Heinsman and Shadish also point out that with quasi-experimental designs substantial initial differences between groups is ill advised: it follows that control of key variables is important. Babcock et al. (2004) reviewed treatment programmes for domestically violent men. They found no difference in effect size according to type of design. Wilson et al. (2005) found that studies using random allocation and those employing experimental control using statistical methods produced similar findings. Lösel and Schmucker (2005) used the Maryland Scientific Methods Scale to code the methodological quality of sex offender treatment studies. The findings from studies using randomized designs did not differ significantly from those using quasi-experimental designs. Thus, while randomized designs are desirable, they are not essential to produce robust outcome evaluations of group designs (Hollin 2008).

Quasi-experimental designs

A strong quasi-experimental design depends upon a high degree of control of the equivalence of the treatment and control groups. There are two types of strategy which may be used to establish between-group correspondence. The first strategy is to match control and experimental groups on key variables that may be related to outcome. Friendship et al. (2003), for example, matched treatment and comparison groups on several variables, including current offence and probability of reconviction score, which predict reoffending. A drawback with this approach can lie in the practical problem of finding exact matches between groups. The second strategy is to apply statistical control of key variables by, for example, using multivariate statistics to control for variables such as age, risk of reconviction score, and offence type (e.g. Palmer et al. 2007) or with the technique of propensity score analysis (e.g. McGuire et al. 2008).

Real-world evaluation

In practice, assignment to a treatment group does not mean that every member of the group will complete treatment. Although allocated some offenders may never start the programme while others will drop out partway through. Should evaluation take into account the fact that some offenders complete treatment while others do not? Some evaluations borrow from procedures inherent to an RCT using Intention to Treat analysis. In an RCT the formulation of subgroups within the randomized conditions violates randomization and so negates the integrity of the design. Thus, outcome is based on assignment to treatment rather than treatment received. Treatment Received (TR) analysis looks at outcomes according to delivery of the appropriate treatment.

ITT analysis

Intention to Treat analysis (ITT) assesses outcome for all those allocated to treatment, regardless of what happens in the real world. Parker et al. (2014) state that '[e]valuations should use an intention-to-treat (ITT) model' (p. 295). While ITT is instructive about outcome for those allocated to treatment, it is a blunt method by which to gauge the effectiveness of psychological treatment. To argue that ITT, originally devised for bio-medical trials, can be applied to the evaluation of psychological treatment has been labelled as a 'drug metaphor' (Shapiro et al. 1994). It is not difficult to see the severe limitations in Parker et al.'s position. The mistake in a sole reliance on ITT is illustrated by a hypothetical trial of an antibiotic drug to treat infections called, let's say, penicillin. In the trial, 100 infected people are given penicillin tablets: in fact, 60 never take the drug, 25 start but stop before the necessary dosage is complete, and just 15 complete the course, of whom five show a significant improvement at outcome. An ITT analysis would indicate that given its low success rate (just 5% of the sample), penicillin is contra-indicated for treatment of infections.

If substantial numbers of the treatment group do not comply with the treatment regime, then the treatment is seen to fail and there is nothing more to be said. A poor outcome for those who fail to comply with treatment effectively negates learning from positive outcomes for those who fully conform with treatment requirements. The failure to understand outcomes for those within the treatment groups is poor science and leads to stagnation of the evidence base on which effective treatment stands.

ITT can also mask a *negative* effect of treatment. An evaluation of a community treatment programme for female offenders reported by Palmer et al. (2015) used a TR analysis and found no effect of treatment on reoffending. The null finding raises the possibility that there may be a problem in using this particular programme with women offenders. This finding would not have emerged with an ITT, where a null finding could be due to a high rate of noncompliance, and so progress in developing gender-specific treatment would be stalled. Portney and Watkins (2014) point out that there is a risk of overestimating a treatment effect with a TR analysis, but ITT is a highly conservative analysis which can underestimate or even completely miss genuine effects of treatment. The latter outcome is especially likely if the evaluation has a high rate of attrition.

In relying on ITT, Parker et al. have made two choices: first, they have wedded evaluation to a drug metaphor by giving preference to a type of analysis allied to RCTs; second, they prefer not to explore fully what happens in real life.

TR analysis

Treatment Received analysis (TR) is an alternative to ITT which considers the outcome when treatment is delivered as intended. Thus, in the above example, the treatment outcome is the positive gains made by those who complied with the treatment regime, i.e. 5/15 or 33% of the sample. The problem with TR is that subdividing the treatment group may introduce a bias. Thus, for example, those five people with the positive outcome in the fictitious penicillin trial turn out to be vegans, giving the possibility that it is diet, not the drug, that produces an apparent treatment effect.

In practice, ITT and TR provide answers to different questions. ITT is informative about the success of engaging and retaining people in a treatment programme; TR provides details of what happens when treatment is delivered as intended (Sherman 2003). Thus, Gondolf (2004) argues that by considering what happens in the real world of treatment delivery, considering those who complete and those who do not, evidence-based practice can be advanced.

Completers and non-completers

When consideration is given to real-world outcomes, treatment completion becomes an immediate issue. Is it disadvantageous not to complete treatment? Lösel (2001) suggests that evaluations that neglect noncompletion are one sided, given that dropouts have not been considered. This is an important point for practitioners because if noncompletion leads to poor outcome, the completion rates must be improved.

Lipsey (1992) noted that a high level of attrition lowers the treatment effect size. Lösel and Schmucker (2005) found that treatment completers had a better outcome than controls, while dropping out of treatment doubled the odds of reoffending. Wormith and Olver (2002) make the point that '[o]ffender non-completion of treatment is endemic to all correctional intervention' (p. 450). Several evaluations have reported a 'noncompletion effect', whereby if an offender starts a programme but then drops out, there is an adverse effect on reoffending (Cann et al. 2003; Hanson et al. 2002; Hollin et al. 2008; McGuire et al. 2008; Palmer et al. 2007). Three types of explanation for the noncompletion effect have been advanced: first, the research itself is misleading; second, there are pre-intervention differences between completers and noncompleters; third, failure to complete becomes a risk factor for reoffending.

Misleading research

This view adopts an exaggeratedly rigid position regarding the design of treatment outcome studies. It holds any difference in outcome between completers and noncompleters, as found in the quasi-experimental studies, is de facto a consequence of non-randomization to condition. Debidin and Lovbakke (2005) state that reduced rates of recidivism in completers in non-randomized studies '[m]ay be interpreted as selection effects, that is, that the programme simply served to sort those who would do well anyway from those who would not, regardless of the treatment' (p. 47).

Notwithstanding a misplaced faith in the powers of randomized studies (see Hollin 2008), this view essentially holds that offenders who take part in and complete treatment are those who are destined *not* to reoffend and 'do well anyway'. This position raises two questions. First, if completers were going to 'do well anyway' why, nonetheless, is there a substantial rate of reconviction amongst completers? The logical extension of this argument is that with a refined understanding of the characteristics of non-reconvicting completers then these would-do-well-offenders can be turned away from treatment as it is superfluous. Second, is it really the case that for offenders who complete treatment and do not reoffend the treatment programme had absolutely no effect at all? The evidence suggests that treatment content is not irrelevant to outcome. Clarke et al. (2004) found that non-reconvicted completers were clear that they had used their 'improved thinking skills in their everyday lives since leaving prison' (p. 16).

Pre-treatment differences

Wormith and Olver (2002) compared programme completers and noncompleters and found that completers were more likely to have full-time employment prior to imprisonment and had a higher degree of academic attainment; the noncompleters had a higher risk of recidivism. In terms of treatment process, Wormith and Olver report that completion was predicted by attitude towards treatment, rated improvement during treatment, and level of risk of reoffending.

Van Voorhis et al. (2004) randomly assigned parolees to a treatment or control condition: an ITT did not show a significant treatment effect. There was a 60% completion rate and a comparison of *three* groups – completers, non-completers, and comparison – showed a significant treatment effect for the completers in terms of both reduced reoffending and increased employment. A comparison of completers and noncompleters found that the dropouts were younger, and more likely to have a history of violence and to have dropped out of school. Olver et al. (2011) noted that noncompleters tended to be of higher risk of reoffending than completers. In evaluations where between-groups variation in risk are controlled, the noncompletion effect remains evident (e.g. Palmer et al. 2007).

Noncompletion contributes to risk

McMurran and Theodosi (2007) concluded their systematic review: 'It remains entirely possible that noncompletion really does make some offenders more likely to reoffend than if they had not been treated at all' (p. 341). Olver et al. (2011) also suggest that there may be psychological and social consequences for an offender who fails to complete a treatment programme:

> There is the further possibility still that some iatrogenic effect emerges from failure to complete treatment, especially for high risk offenders (e.g., increased antiauthority attitudes, emotional distress, failure to address difficult personal life issues), which may potentiate risk for subsequent recidivism.
>
> (p. 16)

Managing noncompletion

If noncompletion is contra-indicated, then the causal processes require management to ensure efficient use of resources and to enable evaluation (Hatcher et al. 2012). Inappropriate allocation to treatment is a contributing factor to noncompletion. Palmer et al. (2009) considered outcome according to the official risk criterion for taking part in treatment. Thus, some completers were 'Appropriate Risk', some were 'Too Low Risk', and some 'Too High Risk'. The Appropriate group had a significantly higher rate of reconviction than the Too Low group and a significantly lower rate of reconviction than the Too High group. When the outcome is considered for the group as a whole, misallocation by risk is clearly muddying the evaluative waters.

Offender responsivity to treatment content is another factor leading to noncompletion and higher reoffending (Wormith and Olver 2002). McMurran and McCulloch (2007) interviewed noncompleters and, like Wormith and Olver (2002), recorded several reasons for dropping out including release from prison, expulsion from the group, ill health, and opting not to continue. With regard to treatment, some noncompleters said they did not like being in a group; others said that the content was too slow and patronizing, while others felt it was too demanding. This list is lengthened by higher dropout rates among offenders with literacy problems (Briggs et al. 2003), while organizational factors, such as long delays before starting treatment and running up against other criminal justice processes such as parole, can mean that offenders failed to engage with treatment (Clarke et al. 2004). Van Voorhis et al. (2004) recorded an average overall completion rate of 60% in 23 treatment programmes conducted in 16 parole districts. However, the completion rate varied greatly across the districts, from a low of 42% to a high of 80%. These fluctuations in organizational performance leading to high levels of noncompletion have real-world costs, including financial waste, poor service efficiency and hence cost-effectiveness, and a negative effect on staff morale and effectiveness (McMurran et al. 2010; Sturgess et al. 2016).

Conclusion

Evaluation of outcome faces a myriad of issues in attempting to disentangle the cofounding associations between the individual offender, treatment characteristics, organizational factors, completion, noncompletion, and treatment outcome. If this tangle can be unravelled, most probably through triangulation of findings from studies using a range of designs, the evidence base will be significantly increased and so informing the content, implementation, and delivery of offender treatment. In addition, empirical research can lead to methodological (Travers et al. 2014; Travers et al. 2011) and theoretical developments, which may substantially change treatment regimes and refine research methods and designs. There are gains to be made from robust evaluations in terms of reduced crime and hence fewer victims, improvement in the lives of offenders and their families, and financial gains to the taxpayer.

References

Babcock, J. C., Green, C. E. and Robie, C. (2004) Does batterers' treatment work? A meta-analytic review of domestic violence treatment. *Clinical Psychology Review*, 23, 1023–1053.

Bernfeld, G. A., Farrington, D. P. and Leschied, A. W. (Eds.). (2001) *Offender Rehabilitation in Practice: Implementing and Evaluating Effective Programmes*. Chichester: John Wiley & Sons.

Briggs, S., Gray, B. and Stephens, K. (2003) *Offender Literacy and Attrition from the Enhanced Thinking Skills Programme*. West Yorkshire: National Probation Service.

Cann, J., Falshaw, L., Nugent, F. and Friendship, C. (2003) *Understanding What Works: Accredited Cognitive Skills Programmes for Adult Men and Young Offenders*. Home Office Research Findings No. 226. London: Home Office.

Clarke, A., Simmonds, R. and Wydall, S. (2004) *Delivering Cognitive Skills Programmes in Prison: A Qualitative Study*. Home Office Online Report 27/04. London: Home Office.

Debidin, M. and Lovbakke, J. (2005) Offending behaviour programmes in prison and probation. In G. Harper and C. Chitty (Eds.), *The Impact of Corrections on Re-Offending: A Review of 'what works'*, 2nd edition. Home Office Research Study 291. London: Home Office, pp. 31–55.

Dvoskin, J. A., Skeem, J. L., Novaco, R. W. and Douglas, K. S. (Eds.). (2012) *Using Social Science to Reduce Violent Offending*. Oxford: Oxford University Press.

Farrington, D. P., Gottfredson, D. C., Sherman, L. W. and Welsh, B. C. (2002) The Maryland scientific methods scale. In L. W. Sherman, D. P. Farrington, B. C. Welsh and D. L. MacKenzie (Eds.), *Evidence-Based Crime Prevention*. London: Routledge, pp. 13–21.

Friendship, C., Blud, L., Erikson, M., Travers, L. and Thornton, D. M. (2003) Cognitive-behavioural treatment for imprisoned offenders: An evaluation of HM prison service's cognitive skills programmes. *Legal and Criminological Psychology*, 8, 103–114.

Goggin, C. and Gendreau, P. (2006) The implementation and maintenance of high quality services in offender rehabilitation programmes. In C. R. Hollin and E. J. Palmer (Eds.), *Offending Behaviour Programmes: Development, Application, and Controversies*. Chichester: John Wiley & Sons, pp. 209–246.

Gondolf, E. W. (2004) Evaluating batterer counselling programs: A difficult task showing some effects and implications. *Aggression and Violent Behavior*, 9, 605–631.

Hanson, R. K., Gordon, A., Harris, A. J. R., Marques, J. K., Murphy, W., Quinsey, V. L. and Seto, M. C. (2002) First report on the collaborative outcome data project on the effectiveness of psychological treatment for sex offenders. *Sexual Abuse: A Journal of Research and Treatment*, 14, 169–194.

Hatcher, R. M., McGuire, J., Bilby, C. A. L., Palmer, E. J. and Hollin, C. R. (2012) Methodological considerations in the evaluation of offender interventions: The problem of attrition. *International Journal of Offender Therapy and Comparative Criminology*, 56, 447–464.

Heinsman, D. T. and Shadish, W. R. (1996) Assignment methods in experimentation: When do nonrandomized experiments approximate answers from randomized experiments? *Psychological Methods*, 1, 154–169.

Hollin, C. R. (2008) Evaluating offending behaviour programmes: Does only randomisation glister? *Criminology & Criminal Justice*, 8, 89–106.

Hollin, C. R. and Courtney, S. A. (1983) A skills training approach to the reduction of institutional offending. *Personality and Individual Differences*, 4, 257–264.

Hollin, C. R. and Henderson, M. (1981) The effects of social skills training on incarcerated delinquent adolescents. *International Journal of Behavioural Social Work and Abstracts*, 1, 145–155.

Hollin, C. R. and Henderson, M. (1984) Social skills training with young offenders: False expectations and the "failure" of treatment. *Behavioural Psychotherapy*, 12, 331–341.

Hollin, C. R., McGuire, J., Hounsome, J. C., Hatcher, R. M., Bilby, C. A. L. and Palmer, E. J. (2008) Cognitive skills offending behavior programs in the community: A reconviction analysis. *Criminal Justice and Behavior*, 35, 269–283.

Hollin, C. R. and Palmer, E. J. (Eds.). (2006) *Offending Behaviour Programmes: Development, Application, and Controversies*. Chichester: John Wiley & Sons.

Lipsey, M. W. (1992) Juvenile delinquency treatment: A meta-analytic inquiry into the variability of effects. In T. D. Cook, H. Cooper, D. S. Cordray, H. Hartmann, L. V. Hedges, R. J. Light, T. A. Louis and F. Mosteller (Eds.), *Meta-Analysis for Explanation: A Casebook*. New York: Russell Sage Foundation, pp. 83–127.

Lösel, F. (2001) Evaluating the effectiveness of correctional programs: Bridging the gap between research and practice. In G. A. Bernfeld, D. P. Farrington and A. W. Leschied (Eds.), *Offender Rehabilitation in Practice: Implementing and Evaluating Effective Programs*. Chichester: John Wiley & Sons, pp. 67–92.

Lösel, F. and Schmucker, M. (2005) The effectiveness of treatment for sexual offenders: A comprehensive meta-analysis. *Journal of Experimental Criminology*, 1, 117–146.

McGlinchey, J. B., Atkins, D. C. and Jacobson, N. S. (2002) Clinical significance methods: Which one to use and how useful are they? *Behavior Therapy*, 33, 529–550.

McGuire, J. (Ed.). (1995) *What Works: Reducing Reoffending*. Chichester: John Wiley & Sons.

McGuire, J., Bilby, C. A. L., Hatcher, R. M., Hollin, C. R., Hounsome, J. and Palmer, E. J. (2008) Evaluation of structured cognitive-behavioural treatment programmes in reducing criminal recidivism. *Journal of Experimental Criminology*, 4, 21–40.

McMurran, M., Huband, N. and Overton, E. (2010) Non-completion of personality disorder treatments: A systematic review of correlates, consequences, and interventions. *Clinical Psychology Review*, 30, 277–287.

McMurran, M. and McCulloch, A. (2007) Why don't offenders complete treatment? Prisoners' reasons for non-completion of a cognitive skills programme. *Psychology, Crime, & Law*, 13, 345–354.

McMurran, M. and Theodosi, E. (2007) Is treatment non-completion associated with increased reconviction over no treatment? *Psychology, Crime, & Law*, 13, 333–343.

Olver, M. E., Stockdale, K. C. and Wormith, J. S. (2011) A meta-analysis of predictors of offender treatment attrition and its relationship to recidivism. *Journal of Consulting and Clinical Psychology*, 79, 6–21.

Palmer, E. J., Hatcher, R. M., McGuire, J. and Hollin, C. R. (2015) Cognitive skills programs for female offenders in the community: Effect on reconviction. *Criminal Justice & Behavior*, 42, 345–360.

Palmer, E. J., McGuire, J., Hounsome, J. C., Hatcher, R. M., Bilby, C. A. and Hollin, C. R. (2007) Offending behaviour programmes in the community: The effects on reconviction of three programmes with adult male offenders. *Legal and Criminological Psychology*, 12, 251–264.

Palmer, E. J., McGuire, J., Hatcher, R. M., Hounsome, J. C., Bilby, C. A. L. and Hollin, C. R. (2009) Allocation to offending behavior programs in the English and Welsh probation service. *Criminal Justice and Behavior*, 36, 909–922.

Parker, R., Bush, J. and Harris, D. (2014) Important methodological issues in evaluating community-based interventions. *Evaluation Review*, 38, 295–308.

Portney, L. G. and Watkins, M. P. (2014) *Foundations of Clinical Research: Applications to Practice*, 3rd edition. Harlow, Essex: Pearson.

Shapiro, D. A., Harper, H., Startup, M., Reynolds, S., Bird, D. and Suokas, A. (1994) The high water mark of the drug metaphor: A meta-analytic critique of process-outcome research. In R. L. Russell (Ed.), *Reassessing Psychotherapy Research*. New York: Guilford Press, pp. 1–35.

Sherman, L. W. (2003) Misleading evidence and evidence-led policy: Making social science more experimental. *Annals of the American Academy of Political and Social Science*, 589, 6–19.

Sturgess, D., Woodhams, J. and Tonkin, M. (2016) Treatment engagement from the perspective of the offender: Reasons for non-completion and completion of treatment: A systematic review. *International Journal of Offender Therapy and Comparative Criminology*, 60, 1873–1896.

Travers, R., Mann, R. E. and Hollin, C. R. (2014) Who benefits from cognitive skills programs? Differential impact by risk and offense type. *Criminal Justice and Behavior*, 41, 1103–1129.

Travers, R., Wakeling, H. C., Mann, R. E. and Hollin, C. R. (2011) Reconviction following a cognitive skills intervention: An alternative quasi-experimental methodology. *Legal and Criminological Psychology*, 18, 48–65.

Van Voorhis, P., Spruance, L. M., Ritchey, P. N., Listwan, S. J. and Seabrook, R. (2004) The Georgia cognitive skills experiment: A replication of Reasoning and Rehabilitation. *Criminal Justice and Behavior*, 31, 282–305.

Wilson, D. B., Bouffard, L. A. and Mackenzie, D. L. (2005) A quantitative review of structured, group-orientated, cognitive-behavioral programs for offenders. *Criminal Justice and Behavior*, 32, 172–204.

Wormith, J. S. and Olver, M. E. (2002) Offender treatment attrition and its relationship with risk, responsivity, and recidivism. *Criminal Justice and Behavior*, 29, 447–471.

The lost narrative in carceral settings

91

Evaluative practices and methods to improve process and outcomes within institutions

Danielle S. Rudes, Kimberly S. Meyer, and Shannon Magnuson

Introduction

In today's criminal justice organizations and social policy settings, research evaluations are a crucial precursor to understanding and improving both processes and outcomes. Well-designed and rigorous evaluative work allows researchers to peer into the organizational and individual-level systems that frame and support workplace routines. Evaluations help researchers work with and for organizations. First, evaluative research assists criminal justice institutions with solving some of the key challenges they face when implementing or sustaining/maintaining programmes and practices by studying processes they have difficulty studying from within the process itself and because they are often without in-house, trained research assistance. Second, evaluative research also helps researchers understand key organizational challenges and dynamics to inform science and to improve policy/practice recommendations to institutional partners. The most complex and thoughtful evaluations assess strengths and weaknesses in the system, potentially illuminating weak or non-existent fidelity of practices contributing to different-than-expected outcomes. However, even evaluation scholars employing sound methods and painstakingly documenting and analyzing current practices and resources largely focus on several common outcomes (such as recidivism and programme participation) and surface-level processes (such as treatment/service dosage, training types, and materials), while neglecting important interactional and perceptual data that showcase not just *what* is occurring, but *how*. This micro-level data can illuminate key concerns about fidelity of practices, but more specifically, the types of workarounds and pathways staff use when they do not have the resources or knowledge to use practices as intended. Some of this oversight occurs when using quantitatively focused studies without attention to qualitative data. Some occurs due to tight timelines and research staff untrained in collecting/analyzing qualitative data. Some occurs because of the ever-present positivist – sans interpretive – emphasis of criminology and criminal justice studies. Moreover, some occurs due to resource limitations, including financial and time/resource shortages. Whatever the reason for the lack of attention to processual and perceptual data, its absence creates a substantial deficit in evaluative study findings/results affecting both theoretical/conceptual and policy/practice knowledge and implications.

Thus, the crux of the current chapter is to explore how/why processual and perceptual data (at the micro level) improves evaluation research in carceral settings. However, collecting perceptual data that informs practices requires researchers not only garner access to institutions, but also hone their legitimacy within a space typically closed to or wary of researchers. This chapter considers how researchers can gain access and develop questions/data protocols that align with institutional norms within custodial settings. These steps foster a renewed and purposive emphasis on qualitative, perceptual data collection and interpretive analysis for deepening evaluation research and delving beyond *what* is happening to additionally focus on *how and why* it is occurring and what effect, if any, interpersonal/interactional occurrences have on programme/practice outcomes.

Researcher-practitioner partnerships: access to carceral institutions

Access to most institutions – such as schools or hospitals – is often difficult to obtain, but access to correctional institutions (prisons, jails, detention facilities) may be the most challenging to secure. The limited access prison researchers have to these institutions often results from two co-occurring conditions (Wacquant 2002). These include the rise of mass incarceration in the United States (Simon 2000) and the field of criminology's modern preference for quantitative research which can be accomplished via secondary data analysis and without visiting institutions (Myers 2015; Tewksbury et al. 2005). These conditions proffer an environment where institutions feel guarded toward and apprehensive of visitors trying to understand the conditions of confinement/punishment within an overcrowded, and often tightly restricted system. At the same time, it creates a discipline – or collection of scholars – not particularly interested in asking the types of questions that necessitate ground-level access and resisting the distance institutions try to create between themselves and the research community. In a discussion of his experience doing juvenile justice research, Myers (2015) characterizes the barriers he faced as the product of a systematically 'risk-averse system, rather [than] a particularly secretive system' (p. 71). That is not to say that scholars are never interested in these questions and institutions are never willing to provide access, but occurrences where these two conditions collide feel like a major victory to researchers trying to get inside.

While it is possible these co-occurring conditions *precipitated* a decline in ground-level prison research, these conditions maintain an assumptive academic position: researchers are entitled access to institutions. From this position, *institutions* may be perceived as a 'thing' to be studied, but devoid of the reason it is worth studying. Although some research does consider institutions as organizations composed of a unique and historic culture (Liebling and Arnold 2005; Wacquant 2001; Trammell 2009), researchers often forget that institutional autonomy creates more than just culture – it creates a living community. Once evaluators re-orient their task as researching a self-sustaining community – one with its own rules, hierarchy, language, and norms – researchers may be more willing to recognize themselves as intruders and act more sensitively when requesting access to all facets of the institution (selecting different language and reframing requests from the institution). However, recognizing this status is only the first step toward conducting research within these environments.

From this perspective, there are specific ways to gain and maintain access throughout the research process – and potentially beyond – contributing to sharper research questions, richer data, and more clarity within the black box of evaluation research. This includes (1) acknowledging the research(er) burden on the institution as a precursor to working toward collaborative and engaged partnerships and (2) moving conscientiously through the institution's physical space.

Acknowledging the researcher burden to facilitate an engaged partnership

Hosting researchers within a carceral institution involves considerable coordination of both scheduling and operating logistics, including moving staff from traditional work posts to serve as escorts, increasing staff workload due to provision of assistance to researchers throughout the visit, and ensuring the safety of researchers. In a survey of juvenile justice research departments across the US, many agencies reported being more likely to approve research that can yield a benefit for the agency itself (Jeffords 2007). As such, it is imperative researchers work with both the research department (if one exists) and the institutional liaison from initial conception of study ideas to ensure the time and resources used facilitating the study are worth their investment. One way of doing so is by reviewing research questions/objectives with institutional staff and asking for feedback on the questions or incorporating their own questions into the study. This then frames the research as necessary and mutually beneficial and within the bounds of all parties' research interests.

These early conversations with research department/institutional liaisons provide an occasion to describe the study's aims and goals while also gaining insight from institutional staff about their knowledge of or questions about the topic. Although this conversation may present as anecdotal, the stories contribute meaningful insights about how the institution works. This, in turn, facilitates the study and subsequent collection. These initial conversations also proffer a rich opportunity to give back to the institution by potentially generating empirical evidence to support their perceptions, or by producing valuable evidence that provides a new lens from which they may consider how their institution operates.

It is also important to pay attention to the language and jargon used in early conversations. This informs the specific research questions asked of staff and inmates, adds context to findings, and helps researchers navigate the institution once inside. Moreover, understanding the language before entering the institution may help researchers build rapport with study participants and support legitimacy as a prison researcher. For example, in a recent study of solitary confinement units within several state-level adult prisons, our research team learned that the Department of Corrections does not like or use the term 'solitary confinement'. Rather, they prefer the term 'restricted housing'. Knowing this helped our team immensely when navigating the research design and data collection processes. Instead of seeming like unknowing newbies, we spoke their language, did not insult staff/administrators, and fit in better with their protocols.

Further, these conversations should include discussions regarding how the specific study institution operates day to day. This includes the number of staff/inmates working/living inside units of interest, other ancillary staff that contribute to operations/questions of interest, shift times, count times, meal times or meal delivery times, and so on. The logistics of daily operations might influence the design, data collection plans, and perception of researchers as a burden. Having this information during the creation of a research proposal also helps lessen the researcher burden on the institution because the researcher can create protocols consistent with these procedures while staying true to their research goals.

Once a proposal receives approval and the researcher begins scheduling data collection visits, it is imperative researchers remain flexible. Correctional institutions regularly experience audits, lockdowns, and other state/national visitors that may impede data collection. Acknowledging the research/er burden helps facilitate an engaged partnership, and ensures flexibility with a specific institution to allay concerns and help cement the researchers' willingness to begin a real, collaborative relationship. Additionally, working with institutional management to understand daily practice within the institutional environment sometimes means altering or amending data collection activities to match daily institutional routines. This minimizes the disruption for staff and signals empathy and understanding regarding the burden of hosting researchers. For example, during our prison work,[1] we work closely with top administrators and line-level supervisors to design sampling and data collection strategies that do not compromise the goals of the study, but also do not irritate or endanger staff. In one recent project, we hoped to recruit inmates from restricted housing units to participate in a 30- to 45-minute interview by going to their cells, securing their consent, and then asking staff to pull them out for the interview. Once we arrived at the institution, we realized this would not work since staff do not spend the bulk of their time inside the restricted housing pods on each shift. Our initial procedures meant that constant entering and re-entering of the housing pods required staff to leave their usual post to accompany us each time. Instead, upon their recommendations, we completed all recruitment at one time with an escort by going cell to cell and taking a list of inmate names for participation. Then, we randomly chose names from the list for staff to move into safe spaces for us to conduct interviews. This way, staff would only have to accompany us on the pod once and could move inmates, as they had time, throughout the shift. This minor change to our data collection protocol solidified our understanding of institutional needs and led to a stronger relationship with prison staff during our fieldwork. It also created less work for the correctional staff and improved safety and control in the unit overall.

Moving conscientiously through the institution

Researcher-practitioner collaborations encapsulate three important characteristics: (1) mutualism, or a jointly defined research agenda, (2) commitment to continued collaboration to influence practice, and (3) trust among partners (Tseng et al. 2017). 'Trust' broadly means partners follow through on agreements and understand and *anticipate* each other's needs (Tseng et al. 2017). In an institutional setting, facilitating trust includes respecting the institution's main goal to promote a safe and secure environment. As such, researchers should make requests and move through the physical institutional space in ways that align with formal and informal rules of how work occurs inside. Understanding the formal and informal rules helps secure researcher safety, elicit the best data, and promote researcher legitimacy within the space.

Moving conscientiously through the space and anticipating *how* the institution operates begins with the types of materials brought into the institution and the attire worn for data collection. Often, institutions do not allow outside technology (e.g. laptops, cameras, recording devices) and requesting to bring these items into facilities for research creates an unnecessary burden for staff who then have to deny such requests. If possible, limit materials to pens (if allowed) and paper for the research staff. If inmate participants need writing instruments for surveys or other data collection, work with the institution to figure out how this might best be handled. Many institutions issue only approved writing utensils for inmates and will not allow use of others. Many forbid the use of staples in documents given to inmates. Further, researcher clothing considerations include fit and length of shirts, length/type of pant and shoes, and limiting metal in other clothing (e.g. brassieres without underwire, limiting jewellery, belts, and metal in/on shoes) to legitimize the researcher in the space and make entry/exit more efficient.

Once inside the institution, it is imperative to consider the small nuances of functional operations, including waiting for one door to close before requesting another door open, observing the formal way staff address inmates (e.g. Mr Smith v. Dan) and walking a safe distance behind inmates when escorting them to interview spaces. When arriving to units of interest, it is helpful to ask those working in the unit if they have any informal rules or preferences for how to move through their space. This helps staff feel a part of the research process, conveys respect for their place and specific working area, and is an outward display of researchers recognizing their intrusion/burden. These practices also help foster trust within the institution, develop rapport with specific staff, and provide another example of willingness to collaborate, while also keeping researchers and institutional staff safe.

Processual and perceptual data collection and interpretive analysis

Once inside the unit or space of interest, data collection can begin. However, operational time constraints can impede the *quantity* and *quality* of the data collected. Evaluative work in carceral spaces must delve deeper into micro-politics/interactions to capture day-to-day routines, practices, ideologies, and behaviours while paying particular attention to symbols, artefacts, and cultural cues. As such, researchers must adhere to two important principles for data collection: (1) data emerges from the field and (2) everything is data. These principles facilitate collection of deeper, more nuanced data and lead to richer, more interesting and compelling theoretical and policy/practice implications.

Data emerges from the field

The first principle of good qualitative data collection in any environment, but especially in complex environments such as prisons, is that data emerges from the field. While this principle seems obvious in that all data comes from the environment from which it is gathered, the nuanced verbiage *emerges* from the field matters. The data and findings come directly from participants and reflect what participants believe is important. For this reason, it is critical that researchers remain flexible during data collection and allow subjects to share what is important to them and their experiences, perhaps even beyond the research/interview questions. In doing so, researchers develop a narrative that reflects day-to-day operations in the institution, according to the people who live and work there. While research questions and grant objectives will continue to guide projects, the *truth* according to those who live and work inside these institutions comes by asking open-ended questions, listening, and employing probing questions about the immediate responses staff give (even if the responses appear irrelevant or off topic). This allows the field or observed/evaluated participants to share what is important *to them*.

One strategy for eliciting strong and rich narratives includes asking participants to share stories or 'describe a time when' they used a practice or a certain type of event happened. These type of questions allow researchers to understand *conditions under which* something occurs. For instance, when interviewing contact staff (e.g. officers, treatment and other ancillary staff), working across six state-level adult institutions about study themes of prison culture and climate, we asked participants to 'describe a time when you enforced a policy'. We followed by asking staff to 'describe a time when you used your discretion instead of enforcing a policy directly'. This allowed staff to provide narratives of policy adherence while also providing stories about decision-making and discretion. These two types of stories yield rich data about the *types* of decisions staff make and *when and why* they make these decisions. Based upon their stories, we were able to uncover a concentration of policies that staff strictly enforced versus partially enforced or enforced using discretion, as well as develop decision-making themes.

By asking staff to describe their experiences, their responses may answer other identified interview questions while generating new topics/themes not originally considered. Beyond answering the research questions, hearing stories from those who live and work inside institutions helps develop a narrative of what life is like for both shift workers and inmates and illuminates what, *to them*, is important within their working/living experience. Further, it helps prevent casting an early academic lens to questions that might otherwise not reveal/elicit the whole story. For example, in a study of prison restricted housing units focused on mental/physical health and reform adherence, we regularly asked staff about their own mental/physical health concerns while working in these units. During a visit to the control booth, the correctional officer on duty began responding to our questions in what sounded like a canned or rehearsed way. After some time, one researcher asked him to tell us a story by using the open-ended prompt, 'How does that work?' The officer worked into a 15- to 20-minute story about the US Prison Rape Elimination Act (not the focus of our study; PREA is a reform signed in 2003 that tries to eliminate prisoner sexual assault/harassment) and his intense feelings about the Act and the multitude of ways it affected his work life and mental health. This data yielded an unexpected, yet rich, nuanced account of a previous reform that shed light on how/why the institution is handling the current reform. Sticking to the exact research/interview focal questions and/ or not allowing this individual to talk would have prevented researchers from discovering some of the underlying cultural- and individual-level barriers reforms face in this institutional environment.

While using structured interview questions provides consistency between interviews and Institutional Review Boards may require this method, these questions might assume prior knowledge that participants do not have, or lead participants to create answers to questions that are not germane to their working/living experience. For instance, asking staff about recreation time may not make sense or be productive for staff working in a segregation unit where recreation time may be non-existent or exceptionally limited. Starting with questions about their daily routines instead, though, allows researchers to get a sense of what staff *do* know and believe is important. Sometimes that knowledge reflects the aims of the research, but uses different verbiage. In other cases, staff responses may indicate they are unfamiliar with the topic of interest signalling the end of the interview. This strategy can make efficient use of time while avoiding asking questions staff do not know the answers to and causing them to feel uncomfortable. Thus, using stories or more open-ended prompts rather than pre-written questions allows participants to lead with what is important to them and exemplifies the principle of letting data emerge from the field.

Everything is data

The pursuit of an emergent narrative necessitates viewing everything happening in the field as data. This includes disseminated materials, workplace signage, wall colours/covers, sounds, and the types of knick-knacks used to decorate spaces. Just as non-verbal behaviour signals important cues to listeners regarding meaning, these artefacts and symbols tell a deeper story about how/why individuals living or working in this space view their world, their work, and each other. The visualizations provide important insight into individual perceptions within their work environment.

Additionally, while some more positivist scholars might ask questions of qualitative work that pertain to its reliability, validity, and rigour, viewing everything as data allows researchers to triangulate data collection so that different data points (like points on a triangle) provide support for one another, enhancing and improving the legitimacy of the study findings. Specifically, research participants typically – though not always – have an innate desire to provide answers based upon what they perceive the researcher wants to hear (Hewitt 2007). Sometimes this arises from a longing to be helpful. In other cases, it is an attempt to expedite the data collection process. Either way, researchers want to learn about their subjects' experiences and what they value, so subjects volunteering this information work in the researcher's favour toward answering the research and evaluation questions. Subjects' answers to questions then serve as a data point to *what they said* (even if the commentary is what they *perceive* researchers want to hear). Then, if researchers observe what they *do* (i.e. their behaviours) in addition to listening to what they say, it provides a comparison between words and actions. These comparisons may be from individual to self – such as asking if a person's actions are consistent with their words – or across individuals within an institution. Another data point may also include materials they disseminate or reference that may be consistent with or contradictory to what was said as well as how they behaved. For instance, in one study of staff perceptions of trust, culture, and relationships, we observed a variety of cues from staff that elicited their perceptions regarding PREA. While this was not the focus of our research, staff frequently discussed PREA in interviews, in casual conversations, and during our observations of them with inmates and other staff/supervisors. From this triangulation of policy, to verbal description (unsolicited) to physical behaviour (also unsolicited), we pieced together enough data to understand how staff perceived this national reform. In the institutions we studied, staff perceived PREA as partly justified in theory, but also felt, in practice, it was an administrative burden whose message was overshadowed by the cumbersome nature of its implementation into daily work practices (Rudes et al., under review). This finding is tremendously interesting not just for helping understand and improve PREA reforms, but for all reforms within these institutions and others like them. In this regard, the number of data points associated with each participant is more relevant than the number of people studied when collecting evaluative data.

Small (2009) notes the important place of smaller, qualitative studies with sound research design. However, he also notes that the goals and outcomes of such studies should not be evaluated with the same set of tools used to evaluate quantitative projects:

> Generally, the [qualitative] approaches call for logical rather than statistical inference, for case rather than sample-based logic, for saturation rather than representation as the stated aims of research. The approaches produce more logically sensible hypotheses and more transparent types of empirical statements. Regardless of the method, ethnographers facing today's cross-methods discourse and critiques should pursue alternative epistemological assumptions better suited to their unique questions,

rather than retreat toward models designed for statistical descriptive research.

(p. 28)

Small's commentary sheds light on a common, yet inappropriate expectation of qualitative evaluative work – its purpose and value reflect and are measured by the same standards as quantitative work. In evaluative work specifically, qualitative work is not intended to answer the question, 'Does the intervention work?' It is designed to uncover how it does, or does not, work as intended/designed. With this purpose in mind, concerns about sample size and statistical power become less relevant as various data points collected under the lens *everything is data* may provide the necessary data to illuminate the conditions under which an intervention works, and those conditions under which an intervention does not work or at a minimum, is challenged.

Further, methodologically, to allow for comparisons both within individuals and across staff, one option is using Glaser's (1965) constant comparative method. This method requires that analysis begin as soon as the first observations occur. Researchers then review earlier observations before each subsequent field visit and ask questions of their data/method to test whether things observed earlier in the study are consistent across time or person or level within the organization/setting. This method of analysis allows researchers to compare narratives and actions from all parts of the organization (and even the same people on different days) throughout their time in the field and develop a comprehensive understanding that reflects the words *and* actions present in the organization, over time, regardless of the scripted narratives often and first offered.

Illuminating the lost narrative in evaluative studies of carceral institutions

Two major themes guide this chapter on the importance of contextual narratives to improve both process and outcome evaluations in correctional institutional settings. These are not new, but represent a deeper dive into the complexities of qualitative work within evaluation studies, and both themes certainly bear repeating. First, evaluation studies are only as good as the access and relationship between the researcher and the institution. Second, evaluations yield dramatically improved theoretical and practical implications when employing reflective, investigative, and open qualitative methods. While previous scholars note as much (Patton 1997; Sofaer 1999) in their work on qualitative methods in criminal justice and health science evaluations, this prior work largely considers study goal, method matching, study team expertise, and rigour as primary mechanisms for improving the value of qualitative work in programme and practice evaluations. Focusing on how qualitative methods such as interviews and observations play an important explanatory role allows an uncovering of how and why dichotomous independent variables (i.e. got treatment or did not) or dichotomous dependent variables (i.e. improved recidivism or did not) occurred. While the how/why questions *are* the conceptual framework of substantial qualitative studies, the tale of the lost narrative suggests there is more to the story.

First, the narrative begins long before the research study. It is a mutual and collaborative process between the researcher and the researched. When cultivated, curated, and carefully constructed, this relationship positions researchers to ask better questions, improve data collection, face fewer research barriers and ultimately produce research of consequence for both academic audiences and institutional managers and staff. It creates an environment where research aligns with institutional goals and practices, which improves safety, security, and legitimacy. Despite its importance, this relationship is difficult to initiate and sustain. However, once established, this mutually beneficial alignment enhances present and future studies through open communication and shared understandings in a way irreplaceable through alternate means.

Second, data is not just the specific information researchers seek within any particular study. Data is the all-encompassing key that allows researchers to open the 'black box' containing a more holistic understanding of the research environments they study. Data shows us what study participants see, think, feel, experience, and understand. In turn, it reveals what study participants miss, do not understand, misunderstand, and work toward/against when implementing any programme or practice. These are key considerations, not capturable via strictly quantitative methods. Additionally, using only closed and formal interviews misses much of the contextual nuance that can yield answers about *why* the results of evaluation studies are as they are.

Uncovering intra- and inter-organizational context via thoughtful approaches to research is a critical part of any process or outcome evaluation study since poor or less-than-ideal programme/practice effects often come from improper fit, lack of fidelity and poor uptake, acceptability, and feasibility. Additionally, positive programme/practice effects are often undetectable without attention to the nuance of why and how outcomes occur and whether they are replicable and noteworthy. We learn about how and why programmes and practices succeed and fail by actually talking to and observing individuals within their organizational context and asking them to describe their working worlds as they lay couched within the particular practice or programme of study. This data and the subsequently beneficial analysis not only comes from understanding individual-level, micro-interactions between staff, managers, and clients/supervisees, but also from the minutia of day-to-day life visible via tone, verbiage, and emphasis, as well as the meanings behind artefacts and symbols present in workspaces. Even the best surveys and randomized experiments miss this nuance and thus limit their explanatory power in ways that are immeasurable. Despite this frequent research shortcoming, the lost narrative is not actually lost. Rather, it is overlooked, taken for granted, and neglected, leaving lived experiential meaning tucked into hidden spaces researchers cannot not afford to miss. Future pro-gramme and practice development and growth depend on, and in fact must, yield their detection, understanding, and potential.[2]

Six key principles of qualitative methods in carceral evaluation research

1   The narrative (story) begins long before the research study;
2   Access and relationships/partnerships matter greatly;
3   Evaluation greatly improves both theoretically and practically through reflective, thoughtful qualitative methods;
4   Data emerges from the field;
5   Everything is data;
6   Data is not just what the research initially seeks, it is what is found – even without asking – via participant narratives.

Notes

1   Several of our recent studies involve qualitative fieldwork (i.e. interviews and obser-vations) within carceral settings (jail, prison, and juvenile detention). In all of this work, we work closely with institutional partners and within institutional guide-lines to design our sampling and general methodological protocols to align with our research needs, human subjects/ethics concerns, and institutional protocols. The data yield for each of our studies is great, but that outcome largely depends on tre-mendous legwork up front so that data collection met the needs of the researchers and the researched.
2   For more information on observational (qualitative) methods within community corrections (probation/parole), please refer to Chapter 68 in this volume.

References

Glaser, B. G. (1965) The constant comparative method of qualitative analysis. *Social Problems*, 12(4), 436–445.
Hewitt, J. (2007) Ethical components of researcher-researched relationships in qualitative interviewing. *Qualitative Health Research*, 17(8), 1149–1159.
Jeffords, C. R. (2007) Gaining approval from a juvenile correctional agency to conduct external research: The perspective of a gatekeeper. *Youth Violence and Juvenile Justice*, 5(1), 88–99.
Liebling, A. and Arnold, H. (2005) *Prisons and Their Moral Performance: A Study of Values, Quality and Prison Life*. New York: Oxford University Press.
Myers, R. R. (2015) Barriers, blinders, and unbeknownst experts: Overcoming access barriers to conduct qualitative studies of juvenile justice. *The Prison Journal*, 95(1), 66–83.
Patton, M. Q. (1997) *Utilization-Focused Evaluation*, 3rd edition. Beverly Hills, CA: Sage Publications.
Rudes, D. S., Magnuson, S., Portillo, S. and Hattery, A. J. (under review). *Sex Logics: Negotiating the Prison Rape Elimination Act (PREA) Against Its Administrative Burden.*
Simon, J. (2000) The "society of captives" in the era of hyper-incarceration. *Theoretical Criminology*, 4(3), 285–308.

Small, M. L. (2009) 'How many cases do I need?' On science and the logic of case selection in field-based research. *Ethnography*, 10(1), 5–38.

Sofaer, S. (1999) Qualitative methods: What are they and why use them? *Health Services Research*, 34(5), 1101–1118.

Tewksbury, R., DeMichele, M. T. and Miller, M. J. (2005) Methodological orientations of articles appearing in criminal justice's top journals: Who publishes what and where. *Journal of Criminal Justice Education*, 16(2), 265–279.

Trammell, R. (2009) Values, rules, and keeping the peace: How men describe order and the inmate code in California prisons. *Deviant Behavior*, 30(8), 746–771.

Tseng, V., Easton, J. and Supplee, L. (2017) Research-practitioner partnerships: Building two-way streets of engagement. *Social Policy Report*, 30(4), 1–17.

Wacquant, L. (2001) Deadly symbiosis – when ghetto and prison meet and mesh. *Punishment & Society*, 3(1), 95–133.

Wacquant, L. (2002) The curious eclipse of prison ethnography in the age of mass incarceration. *Ethnography*, 3(4), 371–392.

92

Probation research, evidence, and policy

The British experience

Peter Raynor

This chapter is about the development of research on offender rehabilitation and particularly on the impact of probation and similar forms of community sentence. It also describes the often problematic linkages between the evidence provided by research and the policies actually adopted by governments in the development and provision of community sentences. To tell this story, I use the example of Britain and particularly of England and Wales, although (for reasons which will be discussed below) the research often came from other countries. It will become clear, I hope, that there is no simple link between evidence and policy: there are many influences on policy, of which research (and sometimes facts in general) are only one, and are occasionally ignored completely. Similarly there is no simple linear progression in research: many different kinds of research into rehabilitation will be going on at any given time, but particular ideas and approaches achieve impact and influence at particular times and come to dominate the research narrative. These ideas then become the most likely to influence official thinking, but only as one resource in decision-making, alongside other influences such as political ideologies, beliefs about public opinion and the public interest, and money. The vast majority of research in the English-speaking world on probation and on the rehabilitation of people who have committed offences has been carried out in the last 60 years, and the dominant research narratives have swung several times between optimism and pessimism about the impact of probation on reoffending.

In addition, different social science methodologies have tended to dominate research on rehabilitation at different times. I have argued elsewhere (Raynor 2018) that social science, as used in evaluative research, is a three-legged enterprise supported by three sources of knowledge or forms of investigation: understanding, measurement, and comparison. We need understanding, usually acquired by qualitative research methods, to bring into focus the aims of social actors, their beliefs about the processes they are involved in, and the meanings they attach to what they do and to what happens to them. Human action is socially constructed and our social environments are structured by our actions and by those of others (particularly those more powerful than ourselves). Understanding also requires awareness of our own assumptions and our ways of interpreting and shaping experience, because what we learn will be the product of an interaction between our own perceptions and those of our research subjects. This is why qualitative researchers have to try hard to be guided by what they actually find rather than what they expect or hope or prefer to find. However, it is not clear how social science can be *social* without an attempt to understand the meanings of social experience for the people involved. Some notable recent examples of probation research have relied on qualitative methods: for example, research on the occupational culture of probation staff (Mawby and Worrall 2013) and on their beliefs about the quality of probation work and the nature of good practice (Robinson et al. 2014). However, evaluation research in probation needs to go beyond practitioners' beliefs to develop more independent and objective ways to measure the impact of probation practice: What does it change? What difference does it make?

Here we need to depend more on the quantitative procedures of measurement and comparison. Can we actually identify and measure a difference in outcome? Can we reliably estimate whether it is likely to recur? Can we show that the difference is likely to be due to some probation practice or process, not something which would have happened anyway or which occurs simply by chance? These are the scientific procedures which allow us to claim social investigation as a *science*, capable of generating reliable knowledge and building a cumulative knowledge base. Evaluation research, being centrally concerned with whether professional intervention makes a difference, depends on getting these procedures right so that we can learn what works, how it works and in what circumstances, and how we might make it work better. Without understanding, we cannot get far, but without measurement and comparison it is impossible to turn understanding into evidence-based statements about the effectiveness of probation practice. It is, of course, important to measure the right things and make the right comparisons: these need to be logically relevant to testing a hypothesis or answering a research question.

Post-war: optimism in policy, scepticism in research

Probation in Britain (as in America) dates back to the middle of the 19th century, with key legislation passed in 1907. However, its rapid expansion and development, like those of other health and welfare services, belongs to the second half of the 20th century, beginning with the period of social reconstruction following the Second World War. By 1959 the government was able to set out its plans in a white paper 'Penal Practice in a Changing Society' (Home Office 1959), which set out new aspirations for an evidence-based and rehabilitative criminal justice system:

> A fundamental re-examination of penal methods, based on studies of the causes of crime, or rather of the factors which foster or inhibit crime, and supported by a reliable assessment of the results achieved by existing methods, could be a landmark in penal history and illumine the course ahead for a generation.
>
> (p. 7)

The effectiveness of new methods was to be evaluated by the recently established Home Office Research Unit and the methodology for the evaluations was to be pragmatically eclectic, but quantitative where possible ('The Research Unit will apply the basic principles of scientific method and attempt to produce its results in quantitative terms. It will not cling to the methods of any particular discipline or school of thought, but will seek to provide answers to specific questions by whatever means appear most appropriate' [p. 6]).

A significant part of the work of the Home Office Research Unit and of the Cambridge Institute of Criminology (supported largely by Home Office funds) was to focus on probation over the next 17 years.

Other researchers, particularly in the United States, were becoming sceptical about the claims of the young social work profession, with which probation was largely identified at that time (and still should be, though that is another story; see, among others, Raynor and Vanstone 2015). As early as 1943 the sociologist C. Wright Mills argued that attributing social problems to individual malfunctions distracted attention from the need for wider policy reforms (Mills 1943). Even earlier, in 1931, Dr Richard Cabot's presidential address to the American Association of Social Workers called for more evaluation research, resulting eventually in the Cambridge Somerville Youth Study (Powers and Witmer 1951). This substantial and methodologically sophisticated experiment was based on a sample of adolescent boys, of whom half were randomly allocated to supervision by social workers, and their subsequent level of offending was compared to that of the control group of boys who were not allocated to social workers. This design was strong on measurement and comparison, but involved little understanding or control of what the social workers were actually doing. As was widely reported at the time (though not much discussed within British social work), the experimental group did no better than the controls; in fact, they were reported to have offended slightly but not significantly more. (Thirty years later, in a remarkable follow-up study [McCord 1978], it was found that the experimental group had continued to do worse, this time significantly and on a range of indicators including crime, unemployment, alcohol abuse, mental illness, stress-related illness, and earlier death.) The general picture was summed up by Joel Fischer, who undertook a comprehensive review of social work evaluations up to the 1970s and stated his findings like this: 'The bulk of practitioners in an entire profession appear to be practicing in ways which are not helpful or even detrimental to their clients, and, at best, operating without a shred of empirical evidence validating their efforts' (Fischer 1976: 140).

What stands out about the American social work evaluations of that era, when tested against the three-legged model of social science, is that they tended to be relatively well executed with regard to measurement and comparison but they did not really examine, unpack, and understand what social workers were actually doing. 'Casework' was evaluated as if it was one uniform activity, stable, and consistent like a standardized 'treatment'. This was a weakness in the area of understanding, which left open the possibility (recognized by Fischer) that outcomes which showed no overall benefit might be concealing the fact that some practitioners were doing beneficial work, but that their effect was being cancelled out by the poorer work of others so that aggregated effects showed no significant differences from control groups which received no service.

Some similar problems were emerging in research on probation services. For example, an early British study of the results of probation by Radzinowicz (1958), who was a strong advocate of probation, found that reconviction rates looked promising but included no comparison with similar offenders receiving different sentences. When Wilkins (1958) published a similar study but included relevant comparisons, people sentenced to probation had outcomes no better than those receiving other sentences. There are clear parallels in this respect with American social work research. The Home Office Research Unit also carried out, throughout the 1960s and early 1970s, a series of carefully designed and methodologically resourceful descriptive studies of probation aimed largely at developing empirical classifications of probationers and their problems. A very detailed study by Martin Davies (1974) attempted to describe the impact of probation on the social environment of probationers, and argued that only a properly controlled comparative study could show conclusively whether probation was having a positive impact. Such a study was in fact under way, known as IMPACT (Intensive Matched Probation and After-Care Treatment; Folkard et al. 1976): probationers were randomly assigned to normal or 'intensive' caseloads, and subsequent reconviction rates were compared.

The result was a slight but non-significant difference in favour of the control cases: more probation input did not seem to lead to better results. Unfortunately we know little about what the officers were actually doing; understanding of the process is missing, so that measurement and comparison can only give us the results of an input about which all we know is that some people received more of it than others. We cannot tell what methods were in use or how well they were being implemented. As in broader social work research, findings of 'no difference' were the norm at this time. There were occasional exceptions, such as Margaret Shaw's study of pre-release help to prisoners (Shaw 1974), in which those who were randomly allocated to receive more attention from prison welfare officers were reconvicted less, but there was little practical follow-up of this finding until the development of 'resettlement' services some decades later.

The general picture, in the US as well as Britain, seemed to be one of failure, and this was summed up by Robert Martinson in his unauthorized, oversimplified, but highly influential summary (Martinson 1974) of the large research review of the effectiveness of rehabilitation carried out for the New York state government (Lipton et al. 1975). Martinson's conclusion that 'the rehabilitative efforts that have been reported so far have had no appreciable effect on recidivism' (1974: 25), although not a fully accurate summary of the review, was widely reported as meaning 'nothing works'. Although not all criminologists accepted this, it had a political impact, particularly in the Anglophone world, where many politicians were looking for justifications for reductions in public spending. In Britain the director of research in the Home Office summed up as follows:

> Penal 'treatments', as we significantly describe them, do not have any reformative effect. . . . The dilemma is that a considerable investment has been made in various measures and services. . . . Are these services simply to be abandoned on the basis of the accumulated research evidence? Will this challenge evoke a response . . . by the invention of new approaches and new methods?
>
> (Croft 1978: 4)

From 'nothing works' to 'what works?'

After IMPACT, official research on the effectiveness of probation virtually ceased in England and Wales for about 20 years. The 'new approaches and new methods' did gradually appear (Vanstone 2004) but were mostly not systematically evaluated until much later. In the meantime, rehabilitative criminal justice was overshadowed for a while by the 'justice model' of desert-based proportional sentencing (Hood 1974; Von Hirsch 1976) and the work of probation and youth justice was increasingly concentrated on creating opportunities for diversion, or 'alternatives to custody'. If their methods could not reliably change people's behaviour, at least they could use their role in court to influence decisions and to encourage the use of sentences which were seen as less harmful (and usually cheaper). Such approaches attracted support from criminologists (for example, Bottoms and McWilliams 1979) and eventually from the government, which articulated a role for the Probation Service in encouraging the use of non-custodial penalties instead of prison (Home Office 1984). This strategy worked particularly well in juvenile justice (Rutherford 1986). However, too much weight was given during this period to the 'nothing works' research, which was actually quite limited in one main respect. Although often strong on measurement and comparison, it tended to be weak in its understanding of inputs: 'probation' or 'prison' were seen as treatments in their own right, rather than needing to be unpacked to see what different inputs were actually being offered by a range of practitioners, and how well they were being delivered.

Although some research on probation's effectiveness continued outside the government in England and Wales (for example, Raynor 1988; Roberts 1989), the next major steps in research on rehabilitation did not come until research began to benefit from better understanding and control of inputs. Correctional researchers in other countries who had never accepted Martinson's verdict began to carry out meta-analyses looking at the characteristics of different programmes and regimes for offenders to see which were more often associated with positive outcomes. The most influential of these, carried out in Canada (Andrews et al. 1990), combined understanding of inputs with a strong focus on measurement and comparison, and proposed what became the most influential recent approach to rehabilitation, the Risk-Need-Responsivity or RNR model (Bonta and Andrews 2017). Other meta-analyses reached broadly similar conclusions (for example, Lipsey 1992; Lösel 1995; Redondo et al. 2002; McGuire 2002) and a Scottish research review (McIvor 1990) helped to raise awareness of this kind of work in Britain, as did a series of 'what works' conferences (McGuire 1995). The new focus on understanding and describing the service which was actually provided, and the explicit aim of distinguishing between effective and ineffective practice in order to encourage the former, led to a number of innovations and in particular to the development of structured group programmes using cognitive behavioural methods. These aimed to ensure the right inputs from staff by providing detailed manuals and training, and they emphasized programme integrity, that is, delivery as designed.

One of the first programmes of this kind to be tried in probation in Britain, and the first to be thoroughly evaluated, was the Reasoning and Rehabilitation programme developed in Canada (Ross et al. 1988) and introduced in a Welsh probation area (Raynor and Vanstone 1996, 1997; Raynor 1998). Unlike some later, larger evaluations (for example, Hollin et al. 2004), the research on this programme used not only measurement and comparison, with modestly positive findings from a two-year reconviction follow-up, but also used qualitative approaches, interviewing all programme graduates and a number of staff, and documenting the implementation process through participant observation. Some of the lessons learned from this study about, for example, listening to probationers, taking time to do implementation properly, and involving staff through thorough consultation, seemed later to be forgotten: there was a centrally driven rush to roll out programmes on a massive scale to take advantage of the short-term funding available in the government's Crime Reduction Programme from 1999 to 2002 (Maguire 2004; Raynor 2004).

The early results of this huge 'Pathfinder' effort were not as good as had been hoped or expected, with many problems of implementation including poor selection and poor retention of programme participants (Hollin et al. 2004). Thus, the overall message so far seems to be that group programmes, if properly designed, targeted, and delivered, and supported where necessary by appropriate individual supervision, can make a useful contribution to the effectiveness of probation services. The associated research, which produced some positive results and led to many ideas about possible improvements, shows the benefits of a three-legged approach combining measurement and comparison of outcomes with a degree of clarity about inputs, which were defined by the programme designs and manuals at least to the extent of knowing what staff were *meant* to be doing. Many programmes also benefitted from analysis of video recording of programme sessions to check integrity of delivery. For the first time this gave researchers a clearer grasp of what inputs were likely to be producing the measured outputs.

Shifting the focus from programmes to skills

In reality, probation has always depended more on individual supervision than on group programmes, and it continues to do so. The next step in understanding the inputs from practice dates mainly from the early years of the current century. Important precursors were the work of Chris Trotter in Australia in the 1990s (Trotter 1993, 1996) and the recognition of 'Core Correctional Practices' in Canada (Andrews and Kiessling 1980; Dowden and Andrews 2004). Researchers interested in skills carried out a number of studies which, in spite of some differences of method and focus, were all concerned to study the impact of better practice skills. Among the best known of these have been Bonta's STICS study in Canada, which used a random allocation design to compare reconviction rates after supervision by officers who had received additional training in evidence-based practice skills with reconvictions after supervision by officers who had not received the training (Bonta et al. 2011); Trotter's continuing series of studies of the impact of particular practice skills (for example, Trotter 2013; Trotter et al. 2015); Taxman's study of the effects of training in 'proactive community supervision' (Taxman 2008); and the

STARR study (Robinson et al. 2012), which looked at the impact of skills on rearrest rates. The quasi-experimental Jersey Supervision Skills Study (JS3) identified a range of skills used by probation staff in videotaped interviews and found significantly lower reconviction rates among people supervised by more skilled staff (Raynor et al. 2014). The differences in reconviction rates found in these studies are substantial, comparable with or greater than those typically reported in programme evaluations: for example, 21 percentage points in STICS, 14 in STARR, 32 in JS3.

A recent meta-analysis of skills-based research (Chadwick et al. 2015) reports on a number of studies comparing different levels of skill in supervision, which consistently show that more skilled supervision is more effective. In addition, other recent work suggests that successful implementation of initiatives for improvement in skills may depend on good management and appropriate agency culture (Bonta et al. 2013). In England and Wales the SEEDS programme (Skills for Effective Engagement, Development, and Supervision; Rex and Hosking 2014) aimed at a similar effect through staff training, and although the eventual outcomes are unclear, supervision by SEEDS-trained officers has been shown to result in slightly higher levels of compliance (Sorsby et al. 2017). The initiative seems to have been welcomed by staff and managers and SEEDS-based practices are still continuing in some places. Similarly in Jersey the probation staff have themselves devised a process of staff development using the research instruments from the JS3 study to assess and discuss each other's interviews, which they record on video. It appears that this kind of research, combining measurement and comparison with an informed understanding of what practitioners are actually doing, has begun to illuminate a significant part of the probation service's input into supervision and is readily translatable into training initiatives which have the potential to improve practice. There is much more work to be done in this area, and it appears likely that the most productive approaches to future probation research will combine measurement and comparison with a detailed understanding of what practitioners are doing, and why. In the meantime we have come a very long way from 'nothing works', and the three-legged approach to research methods holds plenty of promise for the future, particularly if combined with the insights offered by qualitative research on desistance from offending (Weaver and McNeill 2010; Ward and Maruna 2007).

Evaluating criminal justice in a post-truth world

Evaluation researchers who study probation may also need to pay more attention to the wider policy contexts in which their work is located. This can touch on politically sensitive issues: for example, desistance studies point clearly to difficulty in finding employment as an obstacle to desistance (Bottoms and Shapland 2011), and levels of unemployment reflect wider social structures and, in part, political decisions. More broadly, comparative research on penal systems shows that some societies are consistently more punitive than others (Cavadino and Dignan 2006) and that variations in the use of imprisonment can be linked to social inequality (Wilkinson and Pickett 2009): societies with greater inequality of income tend to make proportionately more use of imprisonment than more equal societies. Britain has been becoming more unequal during recent decades, when the prison population has also been rising. This context has an impact on what penal policy can achieve and on the opportunities for service development, and needs to be taken into account in thinking about the actual and potential effectiveness of services. Social and political context also affect the value attached to evaluative research and the extent of its influence on policy.

Finding evidence is not in itself the whole answer: persuading people that it is in their interests to pay attention to it is another challenge, and the nature of this challenge, and the uses and meanings of evidence, change over time. Before the 1990s the limited research available had little impact on policy and practice in England and Wales (though an early attempt by McGuire and Priestley [1985] to promote evidence-based practice was widely read). The Home Office had largely given up on the search for effectiveness and showed limited interest in research from overseas, or even from Scotland. This changed when probation's search for 'what works' coincided with the dissemination (often by psychologists) of new research on effective practice. The New Labour government elected in 1997 promised evidence-based policymaking and was prepared to invest in the 'Pathfinder' experiments although, as described above, the timescale was too short and the implementation too uneven to deliver the kind of results that probation's leaders hoped for. The peak years for evidence-based development in probation lasted from 1997 to about 2003; by then, politicians who had learned to see evidence as a useful resource began to look for evidence to support preferred policies rather than choosing policies to fit the evidence.

Within criminal justice evidence has been used to support practice developments such as the accreditation of programmes, but major policy changes are based on little or no evidence, or on reports specially commissioned to support them. An early example was the abolition of consent to probation in 1997 (see Raynor 2014); more recent examples are the abolition of probation orders in 2000; the creation of the national Probation Service and marginalization of the judiciary in 2001; the creation of the National Offender Management Service in 2004 following a report by a businessman (Carter 2003); the inclusion of a 'punitive requirement' in every community sentence in 2013, in line with an earlier report by a civil servant (Casey 2008); and finally, in the clearest example of evidence-free policymaking, the decision by Justice Secretary Christopher Grayling to break up and sell off the majority of the Probation Service to private providers in 2014–2015, the creation of Community Rehabilitation Companies, and the attempt to incentivize better performance through 'Payment by Results' (PBR) (Ministry of Justice

2013). Since the privatization, almost all the evidence collected by auditors and independent inspectors (for example, National Audit Office 2016; HM Inspectorate of Probation 2016a, 2016b, 2016c, 2017) shows that it has made community sentences less reliable and less safe, and has done little to create the new resettlement services for short-term prisoners which were part of the rationale for the policy.

Grayling's evidence-free privatization was an early example of what, during 2016, would become known in Britain and the US as 'post-truth' politics. A tendency to shape the evidence to support a pre-existing policy line was not new: for example, it was a feature of Tony Blair's foreign policy leading up to the invasion of Iraq in 2003, and the dangers of this approach were thoroughly exposed by the Chilcot enquiry into the invasion and its aftermath (Chilcot 2016). However, recent developments have gone beyond simply shaping the evidence to managing without it altogether, or to a complete disregard for facts. Recent British political history has been dominated by the 2016 referendum on continued membership of the European Union, in which the successful campaign for a 'leave' vote was based on deliberately misleading propaganda. One senior 'leave' campaigner, Michael Gove (for a short while Grayling's successor as Justice Secretary) claimed that '[t]he British people have had enough of experts' (reported in the *Financial Times*, 3 June 2016). In the US a similar populist rhetoric was a feature of Donald Trump's successful election campaign, and commentators drew parallels with the disastrous populist movements of the 1930s, which used similar appeals to popular prejudice based on widely disseminated and emotive falsehoods. Inconvenient facts are dismissed as 'fake news'. In short, the 21st century so far shows a progression from being *guided* by evidence to using evidence as a *resource to support* policy decisions already made, to *creating* evidence to support policies, and eventually to dispensing with evidence altogether. This emerging style of politics does not provide a promising environment for evaluation research or evidence-based policy in those countries where it is prevalent. However, it is not prevalent everywhere: for example, probation research is flourishing in Europe, and in some of the devolved jurisdictions within the British Isles such as Scotland, Northern Ireland, and the Channel Islands. When post-truth policies fail, factual research on how to make probation more effective will be needed to support the necessary evidence-based reform.

Acknowledgements

This chapter is partly based, with the permission of the editors, on an earlier book chapter: 'The Search for Impact in British Probation: From Programmes to Skills to Implementation', which appears in Ugwudike, P., Raynor, P. and Annison, J,. eds., *Evidence-Based Skills in Criminal Justice: International Research on Supporting Rehabilitation and Desistance*, Bristol: Policy Press, published in

December 2017. Parts of it also formed the basis of a keynote address to the World Congress of Probation in Tokyo, September 2017.

References

Andrews, D. A. and Kiessling, J. (1980) Program structure and effective correctional practices: A summary of the CaVIC research. In R. Ross and P. Gendreau (Eds.), *Effective Correctional Treatment*. Toronto: Butterworth, pp. 441–463.

Andrews, D. A., Zinger, I., Hoge, R. D., Bonta, J., Gendreau, P. and Cullen, F. T. (1990) Does correctional treatment work? A clinically relevant and psychologically informed meta-analysis. *Criminology*, 28(3), 369–404.

Bonta, J. and Andrews, D. A. (2017) *The Psychology of Criminal Conduct*, 6th edition. Abingdon: Routledge.

Bonta, J., Bourgon, G., Rugge, T., Gress, C. and Gutierrez, L. (2013) Taking the leap: From pilot project to wide-scale implementation of the strategic training initiative in community supervision (STICS). *Justice Research and Policy*, 15(1), 17–35.

Bonta, J., Bourgon, G., Rugge, T., Scott, T., Yessine, A. K., Gutierrez, L. and Li, J. (2011) An experimental demonstration of training probation officers in evidence-based community supervision. *Criminal Justice and Behavior*, 38(11), 1127–1148.

Bottoms, A. E. and McWilliams, W. (1979) A non-treatment paradigm for probation practice. *British Journal of Social Work*, 9(2), 159–202.

Bottoms, A. E. and Shapland, J. (2011) Steps Towards Desistance Among Male Young Adult Recidivists. In S. Farrall, M. Hough, S. Maruna and R. Sparks (Eds.), *Escape Routes: Contemporary Perspectives on Life After Punishment*. Abingdon: Routledge, pp. 43–80.

Carter, P. (2003) *Managing Offenders, Reducing Crime: A New Approach*. (Correctional Services Review). London: Home Office.

Casey, L. (2008) *Engaging Communities in Fighting Crime: A Review*. London: Cabinet Office.

Cavadino, M. and Dignan, J. (2006) *Penal Systems: A Comparative Approach*. London: Sage Publications.

Chadwick, N., Dewolf, A. and Serin, R. (2015) Effectively training community supervision officers: A meta-analytic review of the impact on offender outcome. *Criminal Justice and Behavior*, 42(10), 977–989.

Chilcot, J. (Chair.). (2016) *The Report of the Iraq Inquiry*. London: HMSO.

Croft, J. (1978) *Research in Criminal Justice*. Research Study 44. London: HMSO.

Davies, M. (1974) *Social Work in the Environment*. Research Study 21. London: HMSO.

Dowden, C. and Andrews, D. (2004) The importance of staff practice in delivering effective correctional treatment: A meta-analysis. *International Journal of Offender Therapy and Comparative Criminology*, 48(2), 203–214.

Fischer, J. (1976) *The Effectiveness of Social Casework*. Springfield: C. C. Thomas.

Folkard, M. S., Smith, D. E. and Smith, D. D. (1976) *IMPACT Volume II: The Results of the Experiment*. Research Study 36. London: HMSO.

HM Inspectorate of Probation. (2016a) *Transforming Rehabilitation: Early Implementation 5*. Manchester: HMIP.

HM Inspectorate of Probation. (2016b) *An Inspection of Through-the-Gate Resettlement Services for Short-Term Prisoners*. Manchester: HMIP.

HM Inspectorate of Probation. (2016c) *The Effectiveness of Probation Work in the North of London*. Manchester: HMIP.

HM Inspectorate of Probation. (2017) *Annual Report 2017*. Manchester: HMIP.

Hollin, C., Palmer, E., McGuire, J., Hounsome, J., Hatcher, R., Bilby, C. and Clark, C. (2004) *Pathfinder Programmes in the Probation Service: A Retrospective Analysis*. Home Office Online Report 66/04. London: Home Office.

Home Office. (1959) *Penal Practice in a Changing Society*. Cmnd. 645. London: HMSO.

Home Office. (1984) *Probation Service in England and Wales: Statement of National Objectives and Priorities*. London: Home Office.

Hood, R. (1974) *Tolerance and the Tariff*. London: NACRO.

Lipsey, M. (1992) Juvenile Delinquency Treatment: A Meta-Analytic Enquiry into the Variability of Effects. In T. Cook, H. Cooper, D. S. Cordray, H. Hartmann, L. V. Hedges, R. L. Light, T. A. Louis and F. Mosteller (Eds.), *Meta-Analysis for Explanation: A Case-Book*. New York: Russell Sage Foundation, pp. 83–127.

Lipton, D., Martinson, R. and Wilks, J. (1975) *The Effectiveness of Correctional Treatment*. New York: Praeger.

Lösel, F. (1995) The efficacy of correctional treatment: A review and synthesis of meta-evaluations. In J. McGuire (Ed.), *What Works: Reducing Reoffending*. Chichester: Wiley, pp. 79–111.

Maguire, M. (2004) The crime reduction programme in England and Wales: Reflections on the vision and the reality. *Criminal Justice*, 4(3), 213–237.

Martinson, J. (1974) What works? Questions and answers about prison reform. *The Public Interest*, 35, 22–54.

Mawby, R. and Worrall, A. (2013) *Doing Probation Work*. Abingdon: Routledge.

McCord, J. (1978) A thirty-year follow-up of treatment effects. *American Psychologist*, 33(3), 284–289.

McGuire, J. (Ed.). (1995) *What Works: Reducing Reoffending*. Chichester: Wiley.

McGuire, J. (2002) Integrating findings from research reviews. In J. McGuire (Ed.), *Offender Rehabilitation and Treatment*. Chichester: Wiley, pp. 3–38.

McGuire, J. and Priestley, P. (1985) *Offending Behaviour: Skills and Stratagems for Going Straight*. London: Batsford.

McIvor, G. (1990) *Sanctions for Serious or Persistent Offenders*. Stirling: Social Work Research Centre.

Mills, C. W. (1943) The professional ideology of social pathologists. *American Journal of Sociology*, 49(2), 165–180.

Ministry of Justice. (2013) *Transforming Rehabilitation: A Strategy for Reform*. Cm 8619. London: Ministry of Justice.

National Audit Office. (2016) *Transforming Rehabilitation*. London: National Audit Office.

Powers, E. and Witmer, H. (1951) *An Experiment in the Prevention of Delinquency*. New York: Columbia University Press.

Radzinowicz, L. (Ed.) (1958) *The Results of Probation*. A Report of the Cambridge Department of Criminal Science. London: Palgrave Macmillan.

Raynor, P. (1988) *Probation as an Alternative to Custody*. Aldershot: Avebury.

Raynor, P. (1998) Attitudes, social problems and reconvictions in the (STOP) probation experiment. *Howard Journal*, 37(1), 1–15.

Raynor, P. (2004) The probation service 'pathfinders': Finding the path and losing the way? *Criminal Justice*, 4(3), 309–325.

Raynor, P. (2014) Consent to probation in England and Wales: How it was abolished, and why it matters. *European Journal of Probation*, 6(3), 296–307.

Raynor, P. (2018) From 'Nothing Works' to 'Post-Truth': The rise and fall of evidence in British probation. *European Journal of Probation*, 10(1), 59–75.

Raynor, P., Ugwudike, P. and Vanstone, M. (2014) The impact of skills in probation work: A reconviction study. *Criminology and Criminal Justice*, 14(2), 235–249.

Raynor, P. and Vanstone, M. (1996) Reasoning and Rehabilitation in Britain: The results of the straight thinking on probation (STOP) programme. *International Journal of Offender Therapy and Comparative Criminology*, 40(4), 272–284.

Raynor, P. and Vanstone, M. (1997) *Straight Thinking On Probation (STOP): The Mid Glamorgan Experiment*. Probation Studies Unit Report No. 4. Oxford: University of Oxford Centre for Criminological Research.

Raynor, P. and Vanstone, M. (2015) Moving away from social work and half way back again: New research on skills in probation. *British Journal of Social Work*, 46(4), 1131–1147.

Redondo, S., Sanchez-Meca, J. and Garrido, V. (2002) Crime Treatment in Europe: A Review of Outcome Studies. In J. McGuire (Ed.), *Offender Rehabilitation and Treatment*. Chichester: Wiley, pp. 113–141.

Rex, S. and Hosking, N. (2014) Supporting practitioners to engage offenders. In I. Durnescu and F. McNeill (Eds.), *Understanding Penal Practice*. Abingdon: Routledge.

Roberts, C. (1989) *Hereford and Worcester Probation Service Young Offender Project: First Evaluation Report*. Oxford: Department of Social and Administrative Studies.

Robinson, C. R., Lowenkamp, C. T., Holsinger, A. M., VanBenschoten, S., Alexander, M. and Oleson, J. C. (2012) A random study of staff training aimed at reducing re-arrest (STARR): Using core correctional practices in probation interactions. *Journal of Crime and Justice*, 35(2), 167–188.

Robinson, G., Priede, C., Farrall, S., Shapland, J. and McNeill, F. (2014) Understanding quality in probation practice: Frontline perspectives in England and Wales. *Criminology and Criminal Justice*, 14(2), 123–142.

Ross, R. R., Fabiano, E. A. and Ewles, C. D. (1988) Reasoning and Rehabilitation. *International Journal of Offender Therapy and Comparative Criminology*, 32(1), 29–35.

Rutherford, A. (1986) *Growing Out of Crime*. Harmondsworth: Penguin.

Shaw, M. (1974) *Social Work in Prisons*. Research Study 22. London: HMSO.

Sorsby, A., Shapland, J. and Robinson, G. (2017) Using compliance with probation supervision as an interim outcome measure in evaluating a probation initiative. *Criminology and Criminal Justice*, 17(1), 40–61.

Taxman, F. S. (2008) No illusions: Offender and organizational change in Maryland's proactive community supervision efforts. *Criminology and Public Policy*, 7(2), 275–302.

Trotter, C. (1993) *The Supervision of Offenders – What Works? A Study Undertaken in Community Based Corrections, Victoria*. Melbourne: Social Work Department, Monash University and Victoria Department of Justice.

Trotter, C. (1996) The impact of different supervision practices in community corrections. *Australian and New Zealand Journal of Criminology*, 28(2), 29–46.

Trotter, C. (2013) Effective supervision of young offenders. In P. Ugwudike and P. Raynor (Eds.), *What Works in Offender Compliance: International Perspectives and Evidence-Based Practice*. Basingstoke: Palgrave Macmillan, pp. 227–241.

Trotter, C., Evans, P. and Baidawi, S. (2015) The effectiveness of challenging skills in work with young offenders. *International Journal of Offender Therapy and Comparative Criminology*. Online advance access.

Vanstone, M. (2004) *Supervising Offenders in the Community: A History of Probation Theory and Practice*. Aldershot: Ashgate.

von Hirsch, A. (1976) *Doing Justice: The Choice of Punishments*. Report of the Committee for the Study of Incarceration. New York: Hill and Wang.

Ward, T. and Maruna, S. (2007) *Rehabilitation*. Abingdon: Routledge.

Weaver, B. and McNeill, F. (2010) Travelling hopefully: Desistance theory and probation practice. In J. Brayford, F. Cowe and J. Deering (Eds.), *What Else Works? Creative Work with Offenders*. Cullompton: Willan Publishing, pp. 36–60.

Wilkins, L. T. (1958) A small comparative study of the results of probation. *British Journal of Delinquency*, 8(3), 201–209.

Wilkinson, R. and Pickett, K. (2009) *The Spirit Level*. London: Allen Lane.

Index

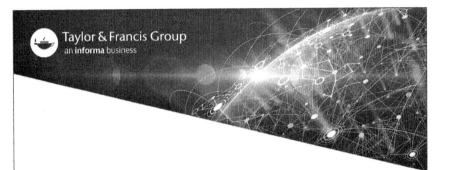